Lecture Notes in Computer Science 4011

Commenced Publication in 1973
Founding and Former Series Editors:
Gerhard Goos, Juris Hartmanis, and Jan van Leeuwen

York Sure   John Domingue (Eds.)

The Semantic Web: Research and Applications

3rd European Semantic Web Conference, ESWC 2006
Budva, Montenegro, June 11-14, 2006
Proceedings

 Springer

Volume Editors

York Sure
University of Karlsruhe
Institute AIFB
Englerstr. 11, 76131 Karlsruhe, Germany
E-mail: sure@aifb.uni-karlsruhe.de

John Domingue
The Open University
Knowledge Media Institute
Milton Keynes MK7 6AA, UK
E-mail: J.B.Domingue@open.ac.uk

Library of Congress Control Number: 2006925964

CR Subject Classification (1998): H.4, H.3, C.2, H.5, I.2, K.4, D.2

LNCS Sublibrary: SL 3 – Information Systems and Application, incl. Internet/Web
and HCI

ISSN   0302-9743
ISBN-10   3-540-34544-2 Springer Berlin Heidelberg New York
ISBN-13   978-3-540-34544-2 Springer Berlin Heidelberg New York

Springer is a part of Springer Science+Business Media

springer.com

© Springer-Verlag Berlin Heidelberg 2006
Printed in Germany

Typesetting: Camera-ready by author, data conversion by Scientific Publishing Services, Chennai, India
Printed on acid-free paper   SPIN: 11762256   06/3142   5 4 3 2 1 0

Preface

This volume contains the main proceedings of the 3rd Annual European Semantic Web Conference (ESWC 2006) held in Budva, Montenegro, June 11-14, 2006. ESWC 2006 showcased the latest results in research and application of Semantic Web technologies – moving us closer to the vision of creating a machine interpretable web.

Following the success of the previous conferences, this year we witnessed a significant increase in submissions. Specifically, we received 181 papers – an increase of 22% over last year. Our review process consisted of three phases. First, each submission was evaluated by at least three members of the Programme Committee. Second, papers and associated reviews were meta reviewed by members of the Senior Programme Committee. In this second phase the meta reviewers led discussions between reviewers and produced an acceptance recommendation. In the last phase, on the basis of the reviews and associated meta review recommendations, the final selections were made jointly by the Programme Chair and the General Chair. Although this process required substantial efforts from the members of the Programme Committees, it ensured that only papers of the highest quality were accepted. The final acceptance of 48 papers for publication and presentation at the conference out of the 181 submissions resulted in an acceptance rate of 26%.

The conference represented research from all over Europe and additionally attracted papers from outside of Europe. Accepted papers came primarily from Germany, Italy, UK, The Netherlands, Spain, Austria, USA, Belgium, China, the Czech Republic, Ireland, and Serbia and Montenegro. The international scientific Programme Committees consisted of members coming from 23 countries spread all over the world including such far away places as Australia and Brazil.

The selected papers cover the following topics:

– Ontology Alignment, Engineering, Evaluation, Evolution and Learning
– Rules and Reasoning
– Searching and Querying
– Semantic Annotation
– Semantic Web Mining and Personalisation
– Semantic Web Services
– Semantic Wiki and Blogging
– Trust and Policies

Each year the popularity of specific research themes as calculated by the number of accepted papers varies. This year the most popular area was Ontology Management incorporating Alignment, Engineering, Evaluation, Evolution and Learning (35%), followed by Rules and Reasoning (13%) and Semantic Annotation (13%). New and upcoming topics in comparison to ESWC 2005, were

Semantic Wiki and Blogging as well as Trust and Policies which together form 10% of the accepted papers.

Invited talks inevitably enrich the scientific programme. Our invited speakers all have the envious amalgamation of a heavyweight research profile combined with the ability to deliver engaging talks. Frank van Harmelen argued in his talk "Where Does It Break? or: Why the Semantic Web Is Not Just 'Research as Usual' " that instead of being (simply) a technological challenge, the Semantic Web forces us to rethink the foundations of many subfields of computer science. Eduard Hovy outlined in his talk "Toward Large-Scale Shallow Semantics for Higher-Quality NLP" how one defines large-scale shallow semantic representation systems and contents adequate for NLP applications, and how one can create the corpus of shallow semantic representation structures that would be required to train machine learning algorithms. Anthony Jameson described in his talk "Usability and the Semantic Web" the difficulties which arise when users with little or no relevant training try to formulate knowledge (e.g., with ontology editors or annotation tools) in a fashion amenable to exploitation by semantic web technologies; or attempt to leverage semantic information while querying or browsing. The abstracts of the invited talks are included in this volume.

Besides the main technical sessions the conference also featured poster and demo sessions (68 submissions), 7 tutorials (out of 11 submitted proposals), 8 workshops (out of 17 submitted proposals), and a special industry-oriented event providing European commerce an opportunity to become even more familiar with semantic web technologies.

A number of European funded project meetings were co-located with ESWC 2006. A doctoral symposium organised by the Knowledge Web Network of Excellence provided a forum for the best young researchers in Europe to present their research. We additionally incorporated a showcase, in conjunction with the poster and demo session, for new European Commission 6th Framework Programme projects, in the area of the Semantic Web, to indicate the directions which European Semantic Web research will take over the next 3-4 years.

ESWC 2006 was sponsored by ESSI (formerly SDK), a group of four European Commission 6th Framework Programme projects known as SEKT, DIP, Knowledge Web and ASG. Collectively these projects aim to improve world-wide research and standardisation in the areas of the Semantic Web and Semantic Web Systems. The conference also received invaluable sponsorship from Onto-Text, iSOCO, LUISA, AKT, and OASIS. Their help was greatly appreciated. We are grateful to Springer for agreeing to publish the proceedings in its Lecture Notes in Computer Science series. We also thank the Zakon Group for providing the open source conference management system OpenConf.

We would like to thank all members of the Programme Committees and the additional reviewers for their tremendous and at the same time very timely efforts in reviewing the submissions. All members of the Organisation Committee were very dedicated to their tasks and deserve our special gratitude. We are thankful to Liliana Cabral (Workshop Chair), Michael Stollberg (Tutorial Chair), Holger Wache (Poster and Demo Chair), Valentina Tamma (Publicity Chair), Oscar

Corcho (Sponsor Chair), Marko Grobelnik and Tina Anžič (Local Organisers), Christen Ensor and Ilona Zaremba (Conference Administration), and Damian Dadswell (Webmaster). Alain Leger spent considerable effort in organising the industry event. Jens Hartmann did an amazing job in ensuring that the online submission and reviewing process was smooth, secure and reliable. We offer many thanks to Tom Heath who co-ordinated the application of Semantic Web technologies to the ESWC, thus making the conference itself a showcase and giving us all a chance to "eat our own dogfood".

We are confident that ESWC 2006 proved to be a highly thrilling event and once again showed the high levels of motivation, dedication, creativity and performance of the Semantic Web community, and we sincerely hope that all attendees found the conference enjoyable and stimulating.

April 2006   York Sure
                                                                John Domingue

Conference Organisation

General Chair	John Domingue (The Open University, UK)
Programme Chair	York Sure (Universität Karlsruhe (TH), Germany)
Workshop Chair	Liliana Cabral (The Open University, UK)
Tutorial Chair	Michael Stollberg (Universität Innsbruck, Austria)
Poster/Demo Chair	Holger Wache (Vrije Univ. Amsterdam, Netherlands)
Industrial Event	Alain Leger (France Telecom, France)
Publicity Chair	Valentina Tamma (Univ. of Liverpool, UK)
Sponsor Chair	Oscar Corcho (University of Manchester, UK)
Local Organisation	Marko Grobelnik (Jožef Stefan Institute, Slovenia)
	Tina Anžič (Jožef Stefan Institute, Slovenia)
Conference Admin.	Christen Ensor (DERI Galway, Ireland)
	Ilona Zaremba (DERI Galway, Ireland)
Webmaster	Damian Dadswell (The Open University, UK)
Online Submissions	Jens Hartmann (Univ. Karlsruhe (TH), Germany)
Semantic Techn. Co-ord.	Tom Heath (The Open University, UK)

Senior Programme Committee

Richard Benjamins (iSOCO, Spain)
Jeremy J. Carroll (Hewlett Packard, UK)
Hamish Cunningham (University of Sheffield, UK)
John Davies (BT, UK)
Jérôme Euzenat (INRIA Rhône-Alpes, France)
Boi Faltings (École Polytechnique Fédérale de Lausanne (EPFL), Switzerland)
Enrico Franconi (Free University of Bozen-Bolzano, Italy)
Carole Goble (University of Manchester, UK)
Nicola Guarino (CNR, Italy)
Frank van Harmelen (Vrije Universiteit Amsterdam, Netherlands)
Ian Horrocks (University of Manchester, UK)
Maurizio Lenzerini (Università di Roma "La Sapienza", Italy)
John Mylopoulos (University of Toronto, Canada)
Dimitris Plexousakis (University of Crete, Greece)
Guus Schreiber (Vrije Universiteit Amsterdam, Netherlands)
Amit Sheth (University of Georgia and Semagix, USA)
Steffen Staab (Universität Koblenz-Landau, Germany)
Rudi Studer (Universität Karlsruhe (TH), Germany)
Katia Sycara (Carnegie Mellon University, USA)

Programme Committee

Andreas Abecker (FZI Karlsruhe, Germany)
Dean Allemang (TopQuadrant Inc., USA)
Jürgen Angele (Ontoprise, Germany)
Anupriya Ankolekar (Universität Karlsruhe (TH), Germany)
Sean Bechhofer (University of Manchester, UK)
Abraham Bernstein (Universität Zürich, Switzerland)
Walter Binder (École Polytechnique Fédérale de Lausanne (EPFL), Switzerland)
Kalina Bontcheva (University of Sheffield, UK)
Paolo Bouquet (Università di Trento, Italy)
Jeen Broekstra (Technical University Eindhoven and Aduna, Netherlands)
Jos de Bruijn (DERI Innsbruck, Austria)
François Bry (Ludwig Maximilians Universität München (LMU), Germany)
Paul Buitelaar (DFKI Saarbrücken, Germany)
Christoph Bussler (Cisco Systems, Inc., USA)
Liliana Cabral (Open University, UK)
Nigel Collier (National Institute of Informatics, Japan)
Oscar Corcho (University of Manchester, UK)
Isabel Cruz (University Illinois at Chicago, USA)
Grit Denker (SRI International, USA)
Jörg Diederich (Universität Hannover and L3S, Germany)
Ying Ding (Universität Innsbruck, Austria)
Martin Dzbor (Open University, UK)
Andreas Eberhart (Hewlett Packard, Germany)
Fabien Gandon (INRIA Sophia-Antipolis, France)
Aldo Gangemi (CNR, Italy)
Mari Georges (ILOG, France)
Fausto Giunchiglia (University of Trento, Italy)
Christine Golbreich (Université de Rennes, France)
Asunción Gómez-Pérez (Universidad Politecnica de Madrid, Spain)
Marko Grobelnik (Jožef Stefan Institute, Slovenia)
Volker Haarslev (Concordia University, Canada)
Axel Hahn (Universität Oldenburg, Germany)
Siegfried Handschuh (DERI Galway, Ireland)
Jeff Heflin (Lehigh University, USA)
Nicola Henze (Universität Hannover, Germany)
Martin Hepp (Universität Innsbruck, Austria)
Pascal Hitzler (Universität Karlsruhe (TH), Germany)
Masahiro Hori (Kansai University, Japan)
Herman ter Horst (Philips Research, Netherlands)
Andreas Hotho (Universität Kassel, Germany)
Jane Hunter (University of Queensland, Australia)
Eero Hyvönen (Helsinki University of Technology (TKK), Finland)
Vangelis Karkaletsis (NCSR Demokritos, Greece)

Vipul Kashyap (Clinical Informatics R&D, Partners Healthcare System, USA)
Atanas Kiryakov (Ontotext Lab, Sirma Group Corp, Bulgaria)
Matthias Klusch (DFKI Saarbrücken, Germany)
Manolis Koubarakis (National and Kapodistrian University of Athens, Greece)
Ruben Lara (Tecnologia, Informacion y Finanzas, Spain)
Alain Leger (France Telecom, France)
Alexander Löser (IBM Research, USA)
Mihhail Matskin (Royal Institute of Technology (KTH) Stockholm, Sweden)
Diana Maynard (University of Sheffield, UK)
Brian McBride (Hewlett Packard, UK)
Vibhu Mittal (Google Research, USA)
Riichiro Mizoguchi (Osaka University, Japan)
Dunja Mladenic (Jožef Stefan Institute, Slovenia)
Ralf Moeller (Technische Universität Hamburg, Germany)
Boris Motik (University of Manchester, UK)
Enrico Motta (The Open University, UK)
Wolfgang Nejdl (Universität Hannover and L3S, Germany)
Leo Obrst (MITRE, USA)
Daniel Olmedilla (Universität Hannover and L3S, Germany)
Jeff Z. Pan (University of Aberdeen, UK)
Elena Paslaru Bontas (Freie Universität (FU) Berlin, Germany)
Terry Payne (University of Southampton, UK)
Paulo Pinheiro da Silva (University of Texas at El Paso, USA)
H. Sofia Pinto (Technical University of Lisbon, Portugal)
Marco Pistore (Università di Trento, Italy)
Aleksander Pivk (Jožef Stefan Institute, Slovenia)
Chris Preist (HP Labs, UK)
Jinghai Rao (Carnegie Mellon University, USA)
Ulrich Reimer (Universität Konstanz and FHS St. Gallen, Switzerland)
Marie-Christine Rousset (Université Grenoble, France)
Stefan Schlobach (Vrije Universiteit Amsterdam, Netherlands)
Daniel Schwabe (PUC-Rio, Brazil)
Michael Sintek (DFKI Kaiserslautern, Germany)
Derek Sleeman (University of Aberdeen, UK)
Kavitha Srinivas (IBM T. J. Watson Research Center, USA)
Ljiljana Stojanovic (FZI Karlsruhe, Germany)
Michael Stollberg (DERI Innsbruck, Austria)
Heiner Stuckenschmidt (Universität Mannheim, Germany)
Gerd Stumme (Universität Kassel, Germany)
Vojtech Svatek (University of Economics, the Czech Republic)
Marko Tadic (University of Zagreb, Croatia)
Hideaki Takeda (National Institute of Informatics, Japan)
Valentina Tamma (University of Liverpool, UK)
Sergio Tessaris (Free University of Bozen-Bolzano, Italy)
Robert Tolksdorf (Freie Universität (FU) Berlin, Germany)

Paolo Traverso (Automated Reasoning Systems Division at ITC/IRST, Italy)
Raphaël Troncy (CWI Amsterdam, Netherlands)
Ubbo Visser (Universität Bremen, Germany)
Holger Wache (Vrije Universiteit Amsterdam, Netherlands)
Krzysztof Węcel (Poznan University of Economics, Poland)
Steve Willmott (Universidad Politécnica de Cataluña, Spain)
Michael Wooldridge (University of Liverpool, UK)

Additional Referees

Gunnar AAstrand
  Grimnes
Sudhir Agarwal
Alessandro Agostini
Paolo Avesani
Sabine Bergler
Petr Berka
Piergiorgio Bertoli
Ian Blacoe
Janez Brank
Steve Cayzer
Xi Deng
Yu Ding
Martin Dvorak
Marc Ehrig
Daniel Elenius
Michael Erdmann
Achille Fokoue
Blaž Fortuna
David Fowler
Marjolein van Gendt
Chiara Ghidini
Rafael González Cabero
Yuanbo Guo
Peter Haase
Conor Hayes
Sven Helmer
Duncan Hull
Sebastian Hübner
Luigi Iannone
Antoine Isaac

Robert Jäschke
Zoi Kaoudi
Alissa Kaplunova
Atila Kaya
Aaron Kershenbaum
Christoph Kiefer
Malte Kiesel
Tim Klinger
Stasinos
  Konstantopoulos
Leila Kosseim
Markus Krötzsch
Reto Krummenacher
Joey Lam
Hangen Langer
Freddy Lecue
Kevin Lee
Peter Ljubic
Mika Maier-Collin
Véronique Malaisé
Annapaola Marconi
David Martin
Iris Miliaraki
Knud Moeller
Meenakshi Nagarajan
Claudia Niederee
Barry Norton
Blaž Novak
Eyal Oren
Hsueh-Ieng Pai
Ignazio Palmisano

Zhengxiang Pan
Joel Plisson
Abir Qasem
Quentin Reul
Marco Ronchetti
Marta Sabou
Leonardo Salayandia
Christoph Schmitz
Thorsten Scholz
Edith Schonberg
Luciano Serafini
Thamar Solorio
Luca Spalazzi
Rodolfo Stecher
Heiko Stoermer
Umberto Straccia
Maria del Carmen
  Suárez-Figueroa
Martin Szomszor
Edward Thomas
Michele Trainotti
Giovanni Tummarello
Daniele Turi
Jiri Vomlel
Peter Vorburger
Yimin Wang
Michael Wessel
Huiyong Xiao
Jianhan Zhu
Floriano Zini

Sponsors

Table of Contents

Rules and Reasoning

Searching and Querying

Semantic Annotation

Semantic Web Mining and Personalisation

Semantic Web Services

Semantic Wiki and Blogging

Trust and Policies

Where Does It Break? or: Why the Semantic Web Is Not Just "Research as Usual"

Frank van Harmelen

Vrije Universiteit Amsterdam
The Netherlands
http://www.cs.vu.nl/~frankh/

Abstract. Work on the Semantic Web is all too often phrased as a technological challenge: how to improve the precision of search engines, how to personalise web-sites, how to integrate weakly-structured data-sources, etc. This suggests that we will be able to realise the Semantic Web by merely applying (and at most refining) the results that are already available from many branches of Computer Science. I will argue in this talk that instead of (just) a technological challenge, the Semantic Web forces us to rethink the foundations of many subfields of Computer Science. This is certainly true for my own field (Knowledge Representation), where the challenge of the Semantic Web continues to break many often silently held and shared assumptions underlying decades of research. With some caution, I claim that this is also true for other fields, such as Machine Learning, Natural Language Processing, Databases, and others. For each of these fields, I will try to identify silently held assumptions which are no longer true on the Semantic Web, prompting a radical rethink of many past results from these fields.

Y. Sure and J. Domingue (Eds.): ESWC 2006, LNCS 4011, p. 1, 2006.
© Springer-Verlag Berlin Heidelberg 2006

Toward Large-Scale Shallow Semantics
for Higher-Quality NLP

Eduard Hovy

Information Sciences Institute
University of Southern California
http://www.isi.edu/natural-language/people/hovy/bio.html

Abstract. Building on the successes of the past decade's work on statistical methods, there are signs that continued quality improvement for QA, summarization, information extraction, and possibly even machine translation require more-elaborate and possibly even (shallow) semantic representations of text meaning. But how can one define a large-scale shallow semantic representation system and contents adequate for NLP applications, and how can one create the corpus of shallow semantic representation structures that would be required to train machine learning algorithms? This talk addresses the components required (including a symbol definition ontology and a corpus of (shallow) meaning representations) and the resources and methods one needs to build them (including existing ontologies, human annotation procedures, and a verification methodology). To illustrate these aspects, several existing and recent projects and applicable resources are described, and a research programme for the near future is outlined. Should NLP be willing to face this challenge, we may in the not-too-distant future find ourselves working with a whole new order of knowledge, namely (shallow) and doing so in increasing collaboration (after a 40-years separation) with specialists from the Knowledge Representation and reasoning community.

Y. Sure and J. Domingue (Eds.): ESWC 2006, LNCS 4011, p. 2, 2006.
© Springer-Verlag Berlin Heidelberg 2006

Usability and the Semantic Web

Anthony Jameson

DFKI – German Research Center for Artificial Intelligence
and International University in Germany
http://dfki.de/~jameson/

Abstract. In addition to its technical implications, the semantic web vision gives rise to some challenges concerning usability and interface design. What difficulties can arise when persons with little or no relevant training try to (a) formulate knowledge (e.g., with ontology editors or annotation tools) in such a way that it can be exploited by semantic web technologies; or (b) leverage semantic information while querying or browsing? What strategies have been applied in an effort to overcome these difficulties, and what are the main open issues that remain? This talk will address these questions, referring to examples and results from a variety of research efforts, including the project SemIPort, which concerns semantic methods and tools for information portals, and Halo 2, in which tools have been developed and evaluated that enable scientists to formalize and query college-level scientific knowledge.

Y. Sure and J. Domingue (Eds.): ESWC 2006, LNCS 4011, p. 3, 2006.

Matching Hierarchical Classifications with Attributes

L. Serafini[2], S. Zanobini[1], S. Sceffer[2], and P. Bouquet[1]

[1] Dept. of Information and Communication Technology, University of Trento, via Sommarive,
14, 38050 Trento, Italy
[2] ITC–IRST, via Sommarive, 15, 38050 Trento, Italy
`simsce@libero.it`, `serafini@itc.it`, `zanobini@dit.unitn.it`

Abstract. Hierarchical Classifications with Attributes are tree-like structures used for organizing/classifying data. Due to the exponential growth and distribution of information across the network, and to the fact that such information is usually clustered by means of this kind of structures, we assist nowadays to an increasing interest in finding techniques to define *mappings* among such structures. In this paper, we propose a new algorithm for discovering mappings across hierarchical classifications, which faces the matching problem as a problem of deducing relations between sets of logical terms representing the meaning of hierarchical classification nodes.

1 Introduction

Hierarchical Classifications with attributes (HCAs) are tree-like structures with the explicit purpose of organizing/classifying some kind of data (such as documents, records in a database, goods, activities, services). Examples are: web directories (see e.g. the Google[TM] Directory or the Yahoo![TM]Directory), content management tools and portals, service registry, marketplaces, PC's file systems. Four very simple examples of such structures are depicted in Figure 1. In particular, consider the leftmost one: it has 4 nodes, labeled with the words IMAGES, TUSCANY, BEACH, MOUNTAIN. The nodes are connected by means of three edges, which are in turn labeled with 'subSet'. Finally, the node IMAGES is associated with an attribute [size = 'large']. As an example, the structure could be used for classifying the pictures taken during a vacation in Tuscany.

Due to the exponential growth and distribution of information across the network, and to the fact that such information is usually clustered by means of this kind of structures, we assist nowadays to an increasing interest in finding techniques to define *mappings* among such structures, namely a set of point-to-point relations between their nodes, in order to maximize the process of information retrieval. A lot of techniques for (semi-)automatically computing mappings have been proposed (see as an example [1, 2, 3, 4, 5]). Such methods associate to each pair of nodes occurring in two different HCAs a real number in [0,1], called *structural similarity*. As an example, consider the HCAs depicted in Figure 1-a: a matching technique could compute a structural similarity n between the two nodes MOUNTAIN.

Despite mappings are defined between HCA *nodes*, they obviously express relations between the *semantics* of HCA nodes. In our example, this means that the meanings of the two nodes MOUNTAIN – which we call *overall semantics* – are n–related. Our claim

Y. Sure and J. Domingue (Eds.): ESWC 2006, LNCS 4011, pp. 4–18, 2006.
© Springer-Verlag Berlin Heidelberg 2006

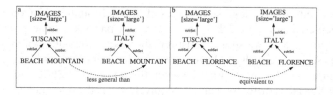

Fig. 1. Two simple pairs of Hierarchical Classifications with Attributes

is that such overall semantics of the nodes, which we can intuitively describe as 'Large size images of Mountains in Tuscany' and 'Large size images of Mountains in Italy' for left and right node respectively, is mainly implicit and it is the result of composing at least two further semantic (in this case, explicit) levels.

The first one, which we call *structural semantics*, is provided by the structure. This semantics says, as an example, that the node TUSCANY is a child of the node IMAGES, that the node ITALY has two children and so on, and that the node IMAGES is associated with an attribute [size = 'large']. It further says that the arcs should be interpreted as 'subSet', as the set of documents that can be classified under the node TUSCANY is a subset of the set of documents that can be classified under the node IMAGES. We want to notice that the relation 'subSet' refers to the documents contained into the nodes and not to the concepts expressed by the labels, as no one would say that the concept 'Italy' is a subset of the concept 'Images'[1]. Anyway, this semantic level is not enough in order to decide for the right interpretation of the node: as an example, both 'large size images of Italy of mountains' (interpretation *A*) and 'large size images of mountains of Italy' (interpretation *B*) have the same probability to be the 'right' interpretation of the node MOUNTAIN of the most left hand HCA of Figure 1.

In order to decide for the right one, we need a further semantic level, which we call *external semantics*. This semantics, provided by the labels, relies on the knowledge associated to English words as 'Images', 'Tuscany', 'Florence' and 'Mountain'. We want to notice that such knowledge is shared by the community of English speakers and that is independent from their occurrence in the HCA. As an example, we know that the 'images' can depict physical objects, that the 'mountains' are physical objects and that 'Tuscany' is a spatial region where mountains occurs. Given this knowledge, we can decide for the interpretation 'large size images of mountains of Italy' (interpretation *B*) as the right one, and discard the other, 'large size images of Italy of mountains' (interpretation *A*), as wrong.

As the mappings express relations between the *overall semantics* of HCA nodes, and, in turn, such semantics strictly depends on these two semantic levels, a trivial consequence is that, in order to determine the 'right' relation holding between two nodes, we need to take into account both structural and external semantics. E.g., consider the two HCAs depicted in Figure 1-a. Intuitively, the relation between the nodes MOUNTAIN is 'less general than', as the documents contained into the leftmost node, intuitively 'large size images of Tuscan Mountains', are a subset of the images contained into the

---

[1] This distinction, in our opinion, is fundamental, as this is why this kind of structures cannot be considered *ontologies*. Indeed, an ontology describes the relations between the concepts, as the Hierarchical Classification describes the relations between sets of documents.

rightmost node, intuitively 'large size images of Italian Mountains'[2]. Consider now the two HCAs depicted in Figure 1-b. These HCAs are pairwise isomorphic to the ones depicted in Figure 1-a, as we simple substitute the label 'mountain' with the label 'Florence'. In this sense, these HCAs have (pairwise) the same structural semantics as the HCAs of Figure 1-a. But the relation between the nodes FLORENCE, corresponding to the nodes MOUNTAIN, is different, namely 'equivalent', as the documents contained into the leftmost node, intuitively 'large size images of Florence in Tuscany' are the same of the documents contained into the rightmost node, intuitively 'large size images of Florence in Italy'. In particular, the different relation is due to a different external semantics: Indeed, in this second case, external semantics provides that 'images' can depict physical objects, that 'Florence' is a physical object, and in particular a city, located both in 'Tuscany' and in 'Italy' (there is only one Florence in Italy and Tuscany).

The paper has the main goal of defining a procedure for matching Hierarchical Classifications with Attributes. In particular, the approach (i) makes explicit the (implicit) overall meaning of each HCA node in a Description Logics term, taking into account both structural and external semantics, and (ii) computes the relation between nodes comparing such DL terms. The paper goes as follows: Section 2 will formally define the matching problem for Hierarchical Classifications with Attributes, Section 3 will describe our approach, Section 4 will provide the algorithm description, and finally Section 5 will show the results of testing the algorithm on real examples.

2   The Problem

First of all, we introduce the notion of Hierarchical Classification with Attributes, whose four very trivial examples are depicted in Figure 1. In this paper we assume labels are English noun phrases. Let $\mathcal{N}$ be the set of such expression[3]. A HCA can be defined as follows:

Definition 1 (Hierarchical Classification with Attributes). *Let* $A = \{\langle a, b \rangle \mid a, b \in \mathcal{N}\}$ *be the set of all the possible pairs of strings in* $\mathcal{N}$ *(the set of attributes), where* $N = \{a \mid a \in \langle a, b \rangle, \langle a, b \rangle \in A\}$ *is the set of* attribute names *and* $V = \{b \mid b \in \langle a, b \rangle, \langle a, b \rangle \in A\}$ *is the set of* attribute values. *A* Hierarchical Classification with Attributes $G = \langle K, E, l_k, l_a \rangle$ *is a 4-tuple, where* K *is a set of nodes,* E *is a set of arcs and* $\langle K, E \rangle$ *is a rooted tree. Furthermore,* $l_k : K \rightarrow \mathcal{N}$ *is a function from nodes to* $\mathcal{N}$ *(the labels of the nodes), and* $l_a : K \rightarrow \{2^A \cup \emptyset\}$ *(the possibly empty set of node attributes).*

A Hierarchical Classification with Attributes can be intuitively described as a rooted tree where each node is associated with a natural language label and a (possibly empty) set of attributes. In this version of the algorithm we use a simplified definition of attribute as pairs name/value.

---

[2] When we say *the documents contained in some node*, we intend the documents *potentially* contained into the node. See [6] for a discussion on that.

[3] Examples of English noun phrases are single common words, as 'images' and 'Tuscany', complex words, as 'United States', expressions containing conjunctions, as 'big and small images'. This set is very difficult (perhaps impossible) to be formalized. In the following, we assume such a set as a primitive element.

Furthermore, let M be the set of all the possible overall meanings that the nodes of an HCA $G = \langle K, E, l_k, l_a \rangle$ can express, and let $\Upsilon : K \rightarrow M$ be a function that associates to each node of the HCA its overall meaning.

The definition of a *mapping*, namely a set of point-to-point relations between pairs of nodes of two distinct HCAs, represents the matching problem standard solution. As we defined a mapping as a set of relations between the overall semantics of the nodes, let $\Re = \{\sqsubseteq, \sqsupseteq, \equiv, \bot\}$ (where $\bot$ means 'disjoint') be the set of symbols expressing relations between meanings. A mapping can be formally defined as follows:

Definition 2 (Mapping). *A mapping $\mathcal{M}$ between two HCAs $G = \langle K, E, l_k, l_a \rangle$ and $G' = \langle K', E', l'_K, l'_a \rangle$ is a set of mapping elements $\langle m, n, R \rangle$ where m is a node in K, n is a node in K' and R is a semantic relation in $\Re$ holding between $\Upsilon(m)$ and $\Upsilon(n)$.*

3   Our Approach

A direct application of Definitions 1 and 2 suggest that a method for computing a mapping expressing relations between node overall semantics should be based, at least, on the following two steps:

Semantic Elicitation: the process for approximating the ideal function Υ;
Semantic Comparison: the process of finding mappings by comparing the Υ values.

As we have to handle machine–readable objects, we need to employ a concrete means to represent the range of the Υ function, i.e. the set of meanings. In this paper, we represent such meanings using Description Logic [7]. Let $S = \langle T, R \rangle$ be a signature for a DL language, where T is a set of primitive concepts and R is a set of primitive roles. Let $L = \langle \mathcal{C}, \mathcal{O} \rangle$ be a DL T–Box, where $\mathcal{C}$ is the set of concepts which can be defined by means of the signature S, and $\mathcal{O}$ a (possibly empty) set of axioms defined over $\mathcal{C}$. L represents the range of the function Υ, namely the set of all the overall meanings possibly expressed by HCA nodes.

In Section 1, we said that the overall meaning of a semantic graph node is the result of the composition of two different levels of semantics: external and internal. [8, 9] claim that the external semantics is given at least by the following knowledge sources:

Lexical knowledge: Such knowledge allows us to determine the (set of) concept(s) denoted by a word. E.g., the word 'Florence' can be used to denote at least two different concepts, namely 'a city in central Italy on the Arno' and 'a town in northeast South Carolina'. Conversely, it can be used to recognize that two different words may refer to the same concept. E.g. the words 'image' and 'picture' can denote the same concept 'a visual representation (of an object or scene or person or abstraction) produced on a surface', i.e. they are synonyms. Formally, let m be the set of words occurring in $\mathcal{N}$ (the set of meaningful expressions). A lexicon $\mathcal{L} : m \rightarrow 2^{T \cup R}$ is a function which associates each word to a set of *primitive concepts* or roles belonging to the signature of a T–Box L. Hereafter, we use Florence#1 to indicate the first concept possibly denoted by the word 'Florence'.

Ontological/World knowledge: This knowledge concerns the relations holding between primitive concepts. For example, the fact that there is a PartOf relation between the concepts Florence#1, as 'a city in central Italy on the Arno', and Italy#1, as 'a republic in southern Europe on the Italian Peninsula', i.e. that 'Florence is part of Italy'. We formally define the ontological knowledge as the set of axioms of a T–Box L (namely $\mathcal{O}$).

On the other hand, the internal semantics is provided by node arrangement into the HCA. E.g., consider the node FLORENCE of the rightmost graph of Figure 1. Since the HCA is a tree, the internal semantics of the node is represented by the fact that the node IMAGES is the root and that the node FLORENCE lies in the path IMAGES/ITALY/ FLORENCE. Furthermore, it says that an attribute [size = 'large'] is associated with the node IMAGES. Finally, it says that the node FLORENCE (possibly) contains a subset of the documents (possibly) contained in the node ITALY, which in turn (possibly) contains a subset of the documents (possibly) contained in the node IMAGES.

During the semantic elicitation step, the two semantic levels will be combined, as shown in Section 4.1, in order to obtain the overall meaning of the nodes. Going on with our example, the intuitive meaning of the node FLORENCE, 'large size images of Florence in Italy', will be approximated with the following DL term:

$$\text{Image\#2} \sqcap \exists \text{size\#1.large\#1} \sqcap \exists \text{about\#1.(Florence\#1} \sqcap \exists \text{PartOf.Italy\#1}) \quad (1)$$

where Image#2 represents the concept 'a visual representation (of an object or scene or person or abstraction) produced on a surface', size#1 the concept 'the physical magnitude of something (how big it is)', Florence#1 the concept 'a city in central Italy on the Arno', and so on.

Finally, the semantic comparison step (Section 4.2) determines the relation holding between two nodes by comparing their meanings (formalized during the semantic elicitation step). For this task, we rely on existent techniques for determining possible entailment between concepts. As an example, imagine that during the semantic elicitation step we determine the following overall semantics for the node FLORENCE of rightmost HCA of Figure 1-b:

$$\text{Image\#2} \sqcap \exists \text{size\#1.large\#1} \sqcap \exists \text{about\#1.(Florence\#1} \sqcap \exists \text{PartOf.Tuscany\#1})(2)$$

During the semantic comparison step, we check if it holds that $\mathcal{O} \models (1) \equiv (2)^4$. From this fact, we can conclude that the relation between the nodes FLORENCE of HCAs of Figure 1 is 'equivalent'.

4 Algorithm Description

In this section, we describe a possible implementation of the two main steps described in the previous section. In this implementation, the lexicon $\mathcal{L}$ is represented by WORD-NET[5]. Both terms T and roles R of the signature S are the synsets of WORDNET. R

---

[4] Of course, this is true only if the ontology provides that Florence#1 $\sqsubseteq$ $\exists$PartOf.Tuscany#1 and Florence#1 $\sqsubseteq$ $\exists$PartOf.Italy#1.

[5] WORDNET [10] is a well-known lexical/ontological repository containing the set of concepts denoted by words (called synsets, i.e. set of synonyms), and a small set of relations (e.g. IsA and PartOf) holding between senses.

contains also two predefined roles: IsA and PartOf. The set of concepts $\mathcal{C}$ is the set of all the allowed expressions built on signature S. The ontology $\mathcal{O}$ is composed both by the IsA and PartOf relations defined in WORDNET and by a further *ad hoc* ontology.

Furthermore, we define *focus* of a node n the part of the structural semantics which we take into account in order to build the overall meaning of n^6. Formally:

Definition 3 (Focus of a node). *The* focus *of a node n of a HCA G is the HCA $F(n) = \langle K', E', l'_k, l'_a \rangle$, such that: (i) K' contains the nodes of the path from the root of G to n; (ii) for each $k \in K'$, K' contains all its attributes too; (iii) all the other elements of $F(n)$ are the restriction of the corresponding component of G on K'.*

Now we can describe the implementation of the two main steps of the algorithm, namely *semantic elicitation* and *semantic comparison*.

4.1 Semantic Elicitation

The semantic elicitation process has the main aim of approximating the meaning of each node of a HCA, namely it is an implementation of the function Υ. If applied to the node FLORENCE of the rightmost HCA of Figure 1-b, it should generate a representation of the intuitive meaning 'large size images of Florence in Italy'. In particular, we apply the following three sub-steps: (i) we build the node *local meaning*, i.e. the meaning of the node taken in isolation (intuitively represented, for nodes IMAGES, ITALY and FLORENCE by 'large size images', 'Italy' and 'Florence'), (ii) we discover possible relations between the local meanings (e.g. a possible relation between the meanings of 'large size images' and 'florence' is that the images are 'about' Florence), and (iii) we combine them, in order to obtain the *global meaning*, namely the meaning of the node in the HCA (intuitively represented by 'large size images about Florence in Italy'). In the following sections we provide a description of them, and an example on how they operate on the node FLORENCE of the rightmost HCA of Figure 1-b.

1. Building the local meaning. In this phase, we consider separately each node of an HCA and, for each of them (with its set of attributes), we generate a DL description in $\mathcal{C}$ which approximates all possible meanings of the node. Imagine that we consider a labeled node with n attributes: The local interpretation of the node is generated starting from the following pattern: label $\sqcap \exists$attName$_1$.filler$_1 \sqcap \ldots \sqcap \exists$attName$_n$.filler$_n$, where label is the label of the node, and attName$_j$ and filler$_j$ are the attribute name and the filler of the jth attribute respectively. In particular, we consider the attribute name as a role and the attribute filler as a range of a DL term. We obtain the space of all the possible interpretations of a node by substituting the words occurring in the pattern (namely the labels of the node, and of the attributes) with each concept possibly denoted by the words themselves w.r.t. lexicon $\mathcal{L}$. Of course, a label, an attribute name or a filler can contain a word not present in the lexicon. In this case, we consider the string itself as a concept. As an example, if we find the word 'frtye' in a label, the resulting concept will

---

[6] Other possible definitions can be provided. In [8] we define focus of a node n the set of nodes occurring in the path from root to n, and their respective children. In the extreme case, we can consider all the nodes of the HCA.

be frtye#1. Obviously no relation of synonymy will be found for this concept, except for concepts denoted by the same string. Furthermore, the current implementation can handle also more complicated cases than single words. In particular, any English noun phrase occurring in the label, in the attribute name or in the filler can be treated. In order to do that, we use a dedicated natural language parser for individuating the syntactic category and the part of speech of the words. The description of such parser is out of the scope of this paper. Details can be found in [11]. Going on our example, as our lexicon provides 7 concepts for the word 'Images', 5 for 'size', 8 for 'large', 1 for 'Italy' and 2 for 'Florence', the space of all the possible interpretations for the nodes IMAGES, ITALY and FLORENCE of rightmost schema of Figure 1-b is the following:

Table 1. Set of all the possible *local interpretations*

$i($IMAGES$)$	$i($ITALY$)$	$i($FLORENCE$)$
Image#1 $\sqcap$ $\exists$size#1.large#1	Italy#1	Florence#1
Image#2 $\sqcap$ $\exists$size#1.large#1		Florence#2
...		
Image#7 $\sqcap$ $\exists$size#5.large#8		

Of course, not all the concepts denoted by words have to be considered in order to compose the node meaning, as some role or concept couldn't be the *right* one w.r.t. *that* node in *that* HCA. E.g., the concept Florence#2 ('a town in northeast South Carolina'), possibly denoted by the word 'Florence', is probably wrong in order to represent the meaning of the node FLORENCE (as the Florence we are talking about seems to be the Florence in Italy). The next phase has the aim of discarding such useless concepts.

First of all, we try to discover semantic relations holding between the concepts associated to nodes, accessing ontology $\mathcal{O}$. In the following, we assume to have a black box function $\mathcal{R} : T \times T \rightarrow R$ which takes as input two concepts and returns the role holding between them[7]. In particular, we search for the relations tieing two different kinds of elements:

Attribute Roles: Consider the node IMAGES, where an attribute occurs. In the previous phase, we build the set of all the possible interpretations for this node ($i($IMAGES$)$). In this step, we access ontology $\mathcal{O}$ for determining if it *explicitly supports* one (or more) of these possible interpretations. As an example, we can discover that $\mathcal{R}($Image#2, large#1$) =$ size#1, namely that the second interpretation of Table 1 is supported by the ontology.

Structural Roles: In this step we search for semantic relations relating concepts belonging to different nodes. In particular, as a focus represents the set of nodes to take into account in order to build the meaning of a node, we search for relations holding between concepts of nodes occurring in the same focus. As an example,

---

[7] The description of this methodology for extracting relations between concepts is out of the scope of this paper. A detailed description can be founded in [11]. As an example of how this procedure works, imagine that the ontology $\mathcal{O}$ contains the following axioms: Image#2 $\sqsubseteq$ $\exists$about#1.Entity#1 and Florence#1 $\sqsubseteq$ Entity#1. Then, $\mathcal{R}($Image#2, Florence#1$) =$ about#1.

consider node FLORENCE. As the node IMAGES occurs in the focus of FLORENCE, we search for a relation holding between the concepts denoted by the word 'Image' and the concepts denoted by the word 'Florence'. In this case we find the following relation: $\mathcal{R}(\text{Image\#2}, \text{Florence\#1}) = \text{about\#1}$.

Table 2 shows the set of relations we find w.r.t. the focus of node FLORENCE. For the relations we use the notation $\langle \text{Image\#2}, \text{large\#1}, \text{size\#1} \rangle$ for indicating the relation $\mathcal{R}(\text{Image\#2}, \text{large\#1}) = \text{size\#1}$ discovered by function $\mathcal{R}$.

Table 2. Set of relations

1	$\langle \text{Image\#2}, \text{large\#1}, \text{size\#1} \rangle$
2	$\langle \text{Image\#2}, \text{Italy\#1}, \text{about\#1} \rangle$
3	$\langle \text{Image\#2}, \text{Florence\#1}, \text{about\#1} \rangle$
4	$\langle \text{Image\#2}, \text{Florence\#2}, \text{about\#1} \rangle$
5	$\langle \text{Florence\#1}, \text{Italy\#1}, \text{PartOf} \rangle$

Then, filtering step is performed by applying the following rules to each concept extracted in the previous phases.

Weak rule: A concept c associated to a word w occurring in a node n can be removed if c it is *not* involved in any relation and exists another concept c' (different from c) associated to w in n which is involved in some relation.

Strong rule: A concept c associated to a word w occurring in a node n can be removed if c it is *not* involved in any IsA or PartOf relation and exists another concept c' (different from c) associated to w in n which is involved in some IsA or PartOf relation.

An example of the application of the first rule is the following. In Table 2 we find that the concept Image\#2 is involved in relations 1–4, while the concepts Image\#1, Image\#3, . . . , Image\#7 are not involved in any relation. From this fact, we can guess that the 'right' concept expressed by the word 'Image' in this node is Image\#2, and the other ones can be discarded. The second rule says something stronger, as a concept can be discarded even if involved in some relation. The idea is that we consider IsA and PartOf relations be strongest than the other ones. As an example, consider the relations 4 and 5. Because of we find a relation PartOf between the concepts Florence\#1 and the concept Italy\#1 (relation 5), we can discard the concept Florence\#2 also if involved in a about\#1 relation (axiom 4). The consequence of this step is to reduce the space of possible interpretations of a node, discarding any interpretation involving discarded concepts. The concepts are considered accessing top-down the hierarchy. Obviously, as these are heuristic rules, mistakes can be performed. Following Table shows the current interpretations for the nodes IMAGES, ITALY and FLORENCE[8].

---

[8] Note that a node can have more than one possible interpretation. When this happens, all the interpretations are kept (ambiguity partially solved). Formally, an interpretation of a node n with more than one possible interpretation is encoded as the disjunction ($\sqcup$) of all the possible interpretations occurring in the $i(n)$ set.

$i(\texttt{IMAGES})$	$i(\texttt{ITALY})$	$i(\texttt{FLORENCE})$
Image#2 ⊓ ∃size#1.large#1	Italy#1	Florence#1

2. Determining the relations between nodes. In this phase, we try to find relations tieing different nodes. To this end, we take into account the subset of the previously extracted relations (see Table 2), and in particular the set of relations holding between concepts belonging to different nodes. Going on our example, we take into account relations 2–5.

As for concepts, not all the relations are the right ones for expressing the node meanings. In order to individuate the 'right' ones, first of all we discard the relations involving discarded concepts, as they refer to no longer existent concepts. The following Table shows the current set of relations.

1	⟨Image#2, large#1, size#1⟩
2	⟨Image#2, Italy#1, about#1⟩
3	⟨Image#2, Florence#1, about#1⟩
5	⟨Florence#1, Italy#1, PartOf⟩

Then we cluster this set in homogeneous triples $\langle \texttt{M}, \texttt{N}, r \rangle$, where M and N are nodes and r is a role in R. In particular, a relation $\langle \texttt{C\#j}, \texttt{D\#k}, \texttt{R\#t} \rangle$ belongs to the triple $\langle \texttt{M}, \texttt{N}, r \rangle$ if C#j is present in $I(\texttt{M})$ (the local interpretation of M), D#k is present in $I(\texttt{N})$ (the local interpretation of N) and R#t $= r$. Let T be such a set of triples: it represents the *relations between nodes*, that we call *edges*. As the meaning of a node n is determined by its focus, in order to build its meaning, we need to take into account the set of edges relating nodes occurring in the focus. Concerning the node FLORENCE, the edges we are interested in are depicted in the following Table:

1	⟨IMAGES, ITALY, about#1⟩
2	⟨IMAGES, FLORENCE, about#1⟩
3	⟨FLORENCE, ITALY, PartOf⟩

Of course, such set can be ambiguous. E.g., may happen that we have two different edges between the same pair of nodes, or that two nodes are mutually in relation, and so on. Formally, let n be a node, F its focus, T_F the set of edges restricted to F and $G = \langle F, T_F \rangle$ the graph obtained by combining the set F of nodes and the set T_F of edges. We define G *not ambiguous* if (i) it is acyclic, (ii) don't exist two edges between the same two nodes and (iii) each node has at most one entering edge. In our example, G results ambiguous: indeed, node ITALY has two entering edges: from IMAGES (edge 1) and from FLORENCE (edge 3)[9]. Let $\Gamma \subseteq 2^G$ be the set of all the possible unambiguous sets of graphs. As the presence of edges 1 and 3 creates the ambiguity, Γ contains the graphs $\langle F, \langle 1, 2 \rangle \rangle$, $\langle F, \langle 2, 3 \rangle \rangle$, $\langle F, \langle 1 \rangle \rangle$, $\langle F, \langle 2 \rangle \rangle$, $\langle F, \emptyset \rangle$. In order to choose the graph

---

[9] Intuitively, it means that the node ITALY, and consequently the concept it denotes, intuitively 'Italy', cannot be considered a modifier of two different concepts, namely 'Florence' (Florence is part of Italy) and 'Images' (images about Italy). Intuitively, we need to decide for the ambiguity between 'images about Italy in Florence' and 'images about Florence in Italy'.

representing the set of 'right' relations between nodes, we apply the two following heuristics rules:

Edges Maximization: Such rule prefers graph(s) with larger set of edges. Intuitively, it selects the set which better connect the nodes in the HCA. In our example, the rule prefers the graphs $\langle F, \langle 1, 2 \rangle \rangle$ and $\langle F, \langle 2, 3 \rangle \rangle$ of Γ;

Path Minimization: Such rule prefers graph(s) minimizing the number of paths representing a node coverage over F. As an example, the rule prefers the graph $\langle F, \langle 2, 3 \rangle \rangle$ of Γ, as can be defined a node coverage using the single path (IMAGES $\xrightarrow{\text{about\#1}}$ FLORENCE $\xrightarrow{\text{PartOf}}$ ITALY)[10].

By applying these rules, we can determine that the graph representing the right set of relations between the nodes occurring in the focus of the node FLORENCE is $\langle F, \langle 2, 3 \rangle \rangle$[11].

3. Composing the meaning. In the last step, local meanings are combined by means of the edges in order to obtain the *global meaning* of a node. Formally, it can be defined as follows:

Definition 4 (Global Meaning). *Let n be a node in a HCA, F the focus of n and $G = \langle F, T \rangle$ a unambiguous graph. Furthermore, let Π the minimal set of paths representing a coverage of G. The global meaning $g(n)$ for the node n is the following DL term:*

$$\bigsqcap_{\pi \in \Pi} I(\pi_0) \sqcap \phi(R^{\pi_0, \pi_1})(I(\pi_1) \sqcap \phi(R^{\pi_1, \pi_2})(I(\pi_2) \sqcap \ldots) \ldots)$$

where $I(\text{Y})$ is the local meaning of the node Y, π_j is the jth elements of the path π (a node of the HCA), R^{π_k, π_j} is the relation between the kth and j^{th} node in π provided by T and $\phi(r)$ is $\emptyset$ if $r = \text{IsA}$, '$\exists r$.' otherwise.

Essentially, we define the global meaning of a node as the conjunction ($\sqcap$) of all the meanings recursively build on the paths of the coverage. In our example, where G contains the single coverage:

$$\text{IMAGES} \xrightarrow{\text{about\#1}} \text{FLORENCE} \xrightarrow{\text{PartOf}} \text{ITALY}$$

the following term (3) represents the *global meaning* for node FLORENCE:

$$\text{Image\#2} \sqcap \exists \text{size\#1.large\#1} \sqcap \exists \text{about\#1.(Florence\#1} \sqcap \exists \text{PartOf.Italy\#1)} \tag{3}$$

4.2 Semantic Comparison

The second macro–step of the algorithm consists in computing the relations holding between nodes comparing their meanings via logical reasoning. In this phase we exploit well–known techniques[12], and in particular we use RACER DL reasoner (see *http://www.sts.tu-harburg.de/~r.f.moeller/racer*).

---

[10] As an example, the other graph, namely $\langle F, \langle 1, 2 \rangle \rangle$, should be represented by the following two paths: IMAGES $\xrightarrow{\text{about\#1}}$ FLORENCE and IMAGES $\xrightarrow{\text{about\#1}}$ ITALY.

[11] When ambiguity arises anyway, we perform a random choice.

[12] Reasoning complexity is directly related to the Description Logic degree we use for encoding the meaning. In this paper we use the $\mathcal{ALC}$ fragment of DL, which guarantees decidability.

Imagine semantic elicitation step has been completed for each node occurring in the two different HCAs $H = \langle K, E, l_k, l_a \rangle$ and $H' = \langle K', E', l'_k, l'_a \rangle$. Then we perform the following reasoning problems for each pair of nodes $k \in K$ and $k' \in K'$ (remember that the function $g()$ returns the DL terms approximating the node meanings):

Entailment problem	Semantic Relation
$\mathcal{O} \models (g(k) \sqcap g(k')) \sqsubseteq \bot$	$\bot$
$\mathcal{O} \models g(k) \equiv g(k')$	$\equiv$
$\mathcal{O} \models g(k) \sqsubseteq g(k')$	$\sqsubseteq$
$\mathcal{O} \models g(k) \sqsupseteq g(k')$	$\sqsupseteq$
otherwise	$*$

Ontological knowledge $\mathcal{O}$ can be used in order to improve reasoning process. In case no relation is founded, we return the generic relation $*$, that we interpret as *possible intersection* or *compatibility*.

E.g, suppose that we want to find the relation holding between the nodes FLORENCE of leftmost and rightmost HCA of Figure 1-b respectively. The semantic elicitation step produces the description (3) for node FLORENCE of the rightmost HCA of Figure 1-b. Now, imagine that we apply the same process to the node FLORENCE of the leftmost HCA of Figure 1-b. We obtain the following DL term:

$$\text{Image\#2} \sqcap \exists\text{size\#1.large\#1} \sqcap \exists\text{about\#1.}(\text{Florence\#1} \sqcap \exists\text{PartOf.Tuscany\#1}) \qquad (4)$$

Moreover, imagine that the ontology $\mathcal{O}$ provides the following axioms[13]: Florence\#1 $\sqsubseteq$ $\exists$PartOf.Italy\#1 (Florence is part of Italy), Florence\#1 $\sqsubseteq$ $\exists$PartOf.Tuscany\#1 (Florence is part of Tuscany) and Tuscany\#1 $\sqsubseteq$ $\exists$PartOf.Italy\#1 (Tuscany is part of Italy). We can easily state that $\mathcal{O} \models (3) \equiv (4)$ holds. So, we can conclude that the *semantic relation* between the nodes FLORENCE of leftmost and rightmost HCAs of Figure 1-b respectively is 'equivalent' ('$\equiv$').

We want to notice that the same process we describe, when applied to the nodes MOUNTAIN of Figure 1-a, gives different results. Indeed, consider the following global meanings associated to the nodes MOUNTAIN of leftmost and rightmost HCA respectively:

$$\text{Image\#2} \sqcap \exists\text{size\#1.large\#1} \sqcap \exists\text{about\#1.}(\text{Mountain\#1} \sqcap \exists\text{located\#1.Tuscany\#1}) \qquad (5)$$

$$\text{Image\#2} \sqcap \exists\text{size\#1.large\#1} \sqcap \exists\text{about\#1.}(\text{Mountain\#1} \sqcap \exists\text{located\#1.Italy\#1}) \qquad (6)$$

As before, imagine that the ontology $\mathcal{O}$ provides the following axioms: Florence\#1 $\sqsubseteq$ $\exists$PartOf.Italy\#1, Florence\#1 $\sqsubseteq$ $\exists$PartOf.Tuscany\#1 Tuscany\#1 $\sqsubseteq$ $\exists$PartOf.Italy\#1 We can state that $\mathcal{O} \models (5) \sqsubseteq (6)$ holds[14]. So, we can conclude that the *semantic relation* between the nodes MOUNTAIN of leftmost and rightmost HCAs of Figure 1-a respectively is 'less general than' ('$\sqsubseteq$').

---

[13] All these axioms are derived from WORDNET.

[14] The conclusion strictly doesn't hold. In the current version of the algorithm, we use the following meta-rule: if A $\sqsubseteq$ $\exists$PartOf.B then A $\sqsubseteq$ B, namely that we treat the 'part of' relation as an 'is a' relation.

5   Testing the Algorithm

The algorithm have been intensively tested on two tasks, driven from the 2nd international ontology alignment competition[15]. The first task consists in trying to align a bibliography ontology against many others ontologies, some related, some others not. The second task consists on aligning subsets of the three biggest web directories available on line, namely Google, Yahoo and Looksmart. We use both as lexical and ontological knowledge WORDNET. No *ad hoc* ontology has been used.

Before introducing the results, we have to formally define the notion of correct result. Let A and B two nodes in two different HCs, and $\langle A, B, R \rangle$ the mapping determined by the algorithm. This is *strongly* correct if in the Golden standard is present a mapping $\langle A', B', R' \rangle$ such that $A = A'$, $B = B'$ and $R = R'$, and is *weakly* correct if $A = A'$, $B = B'$ and $R' \rightarrow R$[16]. As measure of accuracy for the algorithm results, we use the standard *Precision, Recall* and *F-Measure*[17].

Matching The Benchmark. The task consists in aligning a *reference ontology* against 51 other ontologies (hereafter *target ontologies*). The reference ontology is based on one of the first EON Ontology Alignment Contest, and it has been improved by comprising a number of circular relations that were missing from the previous test. The domain of the reference ontology is the Bibliographic references, and represents a subjective view of what must be a bibliographic ontology. It contains 33 named classes. The target ontologies represent a sort of alteration of the reference ontology. In particular, there are 5 categories of alteration: (i) names of entities can be replaced by random strings, synonyms, names with different conventions, strings in another language than English; (ii) comments can be suppressed or translated in another language; (iii) specialization hierarchy can be suppressed, expanded or flattened; (v) classes can be expanded, (namely replaced by several classes) or flattened[18]. On the whole, the target ontologies contains 2,044 named classes. Beside the reference and the target ontologies, a golden standard have been proposed. The algorithm performs all the comparisons in 10 minutes, using a common laptop, namely a *Toshiba A60-122* with the following characteristics: CPU Intel Pentium 4 3.06 GHz, 704 MB RAM, HD 30 GB (4500 RPM), OS Microsoft Windows XP SP2. The following Table reports Average Precision, Recall and F-Measure:

	Precision	Recall	F-Measure
Strong	0.48	0.48	0.47
Weak	0.66	0.64	0.64

---

[15] The testing results can be obtained at http://www.stefanozanobini.net/.

[16] That is the Golden Standard result must imply the algorithm result. As an example, if the relation present in the Golden standard is $\equiv$, than both $\sqsubseteq$ or $\sqsupseteq$ relations are weakly correct, whereas if the relation present in the Golden standard is $\sqsubseteq$, than $\sqsupseteq$ relation is incorrect. Note that both these conditions of correctness are stronger than the standard one, which states that a mapping $\langle A, B, R \rangle$ is correct if in the Golden standard is present a mapping $\langle A', B', R' \rangle$ such that $A = A'$, $B = B'$.

[17] The F-measure is usually defined as $F = 2 * \frac{(Recall \times Precision)}{(Recall + Precision)}$.

[18] See http://oaei.inrialpes.fr/2005/ for a detailed description of the alterations.

Matching Web Directories. The task consists in evaluating the performances of the algorithm on matching real world HCs. The evaluation dataset has been extracted from Google, Yahoo and Looksmart web directories, and consists in 2,265 sub-tasks, where each sub-task is represented by a pair of subsets of the mentioned web directories. Each single subset is represented as an OWL ontology, where classification relations are modeled as OWL *subClassOf* relations. In the following, we call *source* and *target* the first and the second ontology of each sub-task respectively. The set of sources has on the whole 14,845 concepts, while the set of targets has on the whole 20,066 concepts. The algorithm performs all the comparison in 18 minutes, using the same machine as the previous task. As no golden standard has been provided, the algorithm accuracy has been manually verified. Due to time reasons, only a random 3% of the sub-tasks have been verified. The following Table reports Precision, Recall and F-Measure:

	Precision	Recall	F-Measure
Strong	0.65	0.55	0.55
Weak	0.72	0.62	0.61

6   Related Work

The algorithm faces the problem of matching HCs deducing relations between logical terms approximating the meaning of the nodes. Under this respect, to the best of our knowledge, there are no other works to which we can compare ours. Standard graph matching techniques (for a survey, see [12]), essentially rely on finding isomorphisms between graphs or sub-graphs. Of course, as in real world applications graph representations present an high degree of heterogeneity, we can't expect to individuate a perfect match between them. So, methods for computing similarity between pairs of elements have been proposed (see as an example [1, 2, 3, 4, 5]). In particular, such methods compute structural similarity, usually expressed by a real number in [0,1], across all the pairs of nodes occurring in different graphs. Essentially, such structural similarity takes into account only on what we call *structural semantics*, and, essentially, such methods present the drawbacks we show in Section 1.

Recently, approaches which combines graph matching techniques with lexical knowledge have been proposed. The most relevant, in our opinion, are CUPID [13], a completely automatic algorithm for schema matching, and MOMIS [14], a set of semi–automatic tools for information integration of (semi)structured data sources. Both approaches exploit lexical information in order to increase the node similarity. But, as they essentially rely on standard graph matching techniques, taking into account only *structural semantics*, they also partially present the same drawbacks. As an example, in case of equivalent nodes occurring in completely different structures, and completely unrelated nodes that belong to isomorphic structures, the matches fail.

On the other hand, the task of translating some natural language expression into a formal expression is partially shared with the NL community. As an example, [15] proposes a method for building schemas starting from NL statements. The problem is essentially the other way round with respect to the ours, with the main difference that rely essentially on syntactical (grammatical) structure, and not on semantic relations, as we do. [16] proposes a method for interpreting schema elements (with particular emphasis on Web directories). But they essentially analyzes the documents contained on the schemas, as we analyzes the schema.

The problem of individuating the right concept expressed by some word is commonly known as *word sense disambiguation* (see [17] for a survey). We face a similar problem in the filtering step. The heuristics we use are essentially different from the most of that procedures, as they are based on the notion of conceptual distance among concepts (see [18] and [19]), which in turn rely on standard graph matching techniques.

7   Conclusions

In this paper we presented a new approach for matching hierarchical classifications with attributes. The algorithm is essentially an improvement of that one presented in [8], and of its extension in [20]. In particular, we extend the algorithm in order to (i) treat node attributes, (ii) encode the meaning using a more powerful language (Description Logics vs Propositional Logics), and (iii) allow complicate node labels (Noun Phrases expressions vs simple words).

We want to stress that the main algorithm novelty consists in not considering a HC as a (semantically) homogeneous structure. Indeed, its semantic is the result of merging at least two further different semantic levels: *structural semantics* (represented by the backbone of the structure and by the interpretation of the arcs) and *external semantics* (represented by the interpretations of the labels and by the relations between the concepts).

Finally, we want to notice that the approach we describe can be 'easily' extended in order to treat, in principle, any graph-like domain representation.

References

1. Zhang, K., Wang, J.T.L., Shasha, D.: On the editing distance between undirected acyclic graphs and related problems. In Galil, Z., Ukkonen, E., eds.: Proceedings of the 6th Annual Symposium on Combinatorial Pattern Matching. Volume 937., Espoo, Finland, Springer-Verlag, Berlin (1995) 395–407
2. Pelillo, M., Siddiqi, K., Zucker, S.W.: Matching hierarchical structures using association graphs. Lecture Notes in Computer Science **1407** (1998)
3. Milo, T., Zohar, S.: Using schema matching to simplify heterogeneous data translation. In: Proc. 24th Int. Conf. Very Large Data Bases, VLDB. (1998) 122–133
4. Carroll, J., HP: Matching rdf graphs. In: Proc. in the first International Semantic Web Conference - ISWC 2002. (2002) 5–15
5. Euzenat, J., Valtchev, P.: An integrativive proximity measure for ontology alignment. Proceedings of the workshop on Semantic Integration (2003)
6. Benerecetti, M., Bouquet, P., Zanobini, S.: Soundness of schema matching methods. In Proc. of second European Semantic Web Conference (ESWC 2005). Volume 3532 of LNCS., Heraklion, Crete, Greece, Springer (2005) ISBN 3-540-26124-9.
7. Baader, F., Calvanese, D., McGuinness, D., Nardi, D., Patel-Schneider, P., eds.: The Description Logic Handbook. Theory, Implementation and Applications. Cambridge University Press (2003)

8. Bouquet, P., Serafini, L., Zanobini, S.: Semantic coordination: a new approach and an application. In Proc. of The Semantic Web – 2nd international semantic web conference (ISWC 2003). Volume 2870 of LNCS., Sanibel Island, Fla., USA (2003)

9. Bouquet, P., Serafini, L., Zanobini, S.: Coordinating semantic peers. In Proced. of AIMSA-2004, Artificial Intelligence: Methodology, Systems, and Applications. Volume 3192 of LNAI., Varna, Bulgaria (2004)

10. Fellbaum, C., ed.: WordNet: An Electronic Lexical Database. The MIT Press, Cambridge, US (1998)

11. Sceffer, S., Serafini, L., Zanobini, S.: Semantic coordination of hierarchical classifications with attributes. Technical Report 706, DIT, University of Trento (2004) http://eprints.biblio.unitn.it/archive/00000706/.

12. Bunke, H.: Graph matching: Theoretical foundations, algorithms, and applications. In: Proceedings of Vision Interface 2000, Montreal. (2000) 82–88

13. Madhavan, J., Bernstein, P.A., Rahm, E.: Generic schema matching with cupid. In: The VLDB Journal. (2001) 49–58

14. Bergamaschi, S., Castano, S., Vincini, M.: Semantic integration of semistructured and structured data sources. SIGMOD Record **28**(1) (1999) 54–59

15. Woods, W.: Conceptual indexing: A better way to organize knowledge. Technical Report TR-97-61, Sun Microsystems Laboratories (1997)

16. Kavalec, M., Svatek, V.: Information extraction and ontology learning guided by web directory. In: ECAI Workshop on NLP and ML for ontology engineering, Lyon (2002)

17. Ide, N., Veronis, J.: Introduction to the special issue on word sense disambiguation: the state of the art. Comput. Linguist. **24**(1) (1998) 2–40

18. Agirre, E., Rigau, G.: Word sense disambiguation using conceptual density. In: Proceedings of COLING-96, Copenhagen, Danmark (1996) 16–22

19. Resnik, P.: Using information content to evaluate semantic similarity in a taxonomy. In: IJCAI. (1995) 448–453

20. Giunchiglia, F., Shvaiko, P., Yatskevich, M.: S-Match: an algorithm and an implementation of semantic matching. In: Proceedings of ESWS. (2004) 61–75

An Iterative Algorithm for Ontology Mapping Capable of Using Training Data

Andreas Heß

Vrije Universiteit Amsterdam
University College Dublin
andreas@few.vu.nl

Abstract. We present a new iterative algorithm for ontology mapping where we combine standard string distance metrics with a structural similarity measure that is based on a vector representation. After all pairwise similarities between concepts have been calculated we apply well-known graph algorithms to obtain an optimal matching. Our algorithm is also capable of using existing mappings to a third ontology as training data to improve accuracy. We compare the performance of our algorithm with the performance of other alignment algorithms and show that our algorithm can compete well against the current state-of-the-art.

1 Introduction

In this paper, we present an iterative algorithm[1] for ontology mapping that is based on established string distance metrics that have been discussed in literature and on a structural similarity measure that is based on a vector representation of the relations between entities. Furthermore, we show how we can use a given mapping to a third ontology as training data or background knowledge to improve mapping accuracy.

The remainder of this paper is structured as follows: We start with a formal problem formulation in section 2. We continue with a short discussion of related work (section 3). Then, we present our algorithm in detail in section 4. We discuss various parameters and design choices in section 5. Finally, we evaluate the performance of different configurations of our algorithm and show that we can compete well against the current state-of-the-art (see section 6) before we conclude in section 7.

2 Problem Formulation

In various approaches such as [12], the schema mapping problem is cast as a graph matching problem. We follow that notion and treat the entities that we

---

[1] An implementation of our algorithm called dam^2 is available at
http://www.few.vu.nl/~andreas/projects/dam2/

Y. Sure and J. Domingue (Eds.): ESWC 2006, LNCS 4011, pp. 19–33, 2006.
© Springer-Verlag Berlin Heidelberg 2006

are trying to match as nodes in a graph.[2] Therefore, we use the words "node", "vertex" and "entity" synonymously.

We define the mapping problem as identifying pairs of vertices from two edge-labelled directed graphs. Vertices represent entities in the ontology (i.e. classes and properties). The arcs denote relations between these entities, and the labels signify the kind of relation, e.g. "subclass of", "domain" or "range".

Definition 1. *Let $G = (V, A)$ and $G' = (V', A')$ be two directed graphs with V and V' as their set of vertices and A and A' as their set of arcs. We define two partial functions as:*

$$\text{map} : V \rightharpoonup V' \qquad \text{map}' : V' \rightharpoonup V$$

The ontology alignment problem formally consists of finding a number of mappings $v' = \text{map}(v)$ for as many $v \in V, v' \in V'$ as possible. We restrict ourselves to finding mappings for classes and properties only. We define the sets of classes and properties as subsets of V resp. V' and only map classes to classes and properties to properties. Furthermore, we restrict the mapping function to being injective (but not necessarily surjective), i.e. we restrict ourselves to one-to-one-mappings.

We split the problem into two parts: First, we define a similarity function:

Definition 2. *To measure the similarity between vertices from G and G', we define two similarity functions as:*

$$\text{sim} : V \times V' \rightarrow [0, 1] \qquad \text{sim}' : V' \times V \rightarrow [0, 1]$$

We make use of different similarity functions that we denote with indices. We use this similarity function to compute all pairwise similarities between all $v \in V$ and $v' \in V'$. Section 4 describes this step in detail.

The second part of the problem is to convert these pairwise similarities into mappings. We treat the pairwise similarities as a bipartite graph $B = (V + V', E)$ with the entities from V and V' as nodes and a weighted edge where the similarity between two entities $\text{sim}(v, v') > 0$. The problem of obtaining the *map*-relation is then equivalent to the problem of finding a matching in this bipartite graph. We do in general not require that $\text{sim}(v, v') = \text{sim}'(v', v)$. In that case, the edges in the bipartite graph B are directed and the weights are not symmetric. Section 4.5 describes the application of two well-known graph-algorithms to this problem.

3   Related Work

While many approaches have been proposed for schema matching in the past (e.g. Cupid [11]), dedicated algorithms for ontology matching are newer. Among

---

[2] The paper mentioned, [12], but also newer algorithms such as [9] make use of derived graphs or alternative representations such as the pairwise connectivity graph and the similarity propagation graph in [12] or a bipartite graph representation of RDF as in [9]. We do not use such derived graphs in our approach.

these are for example QOM [2] (which is optimised for speed) and OLA [4], which combines a variety of different similarity measures. A very recent development is the Falcon algorithm [9] that has been shown to perform very well.

The level of competition that came along with these different approaches has led to ontology alignment contests. Such contests have taken place at the Information Interpretation and Integration Conference (I^3CON) in 2003, the Third International Workshop on Evaluation of Ontology Based Tools in 2004 [15] and at the Third International Conference on Knowledge Capture (K-CAP 2005) [5]. In section 6, we will compare our own algorithm to those presented at the latter event.

Following [14], we refer to similarity measures that are based on inherent characteristics of an entity as *intrinsic*, where as all structural similarity measures that are based on relations to other entities are referred to as *extrinsic*. Most mapping algorithms adhere to a simple structure: an initial calculation of an intrinsic similarity measure is followed by an iterative calculation of an extrinsic measure before finally the mappings are derived from the pairwise similarities. Ehrig and Staab discuss this structure in greater detail in [2]. Our algorithm adheres to this common structure, too. However, there are two features which make it distinct from other algorithms that we are aware of. The first point where our algorithm differs from others is the way how the extrinsic similarity is computed. In a variety of approaches, extrinsic similarity is basically just the propagated intrinsic similarity of the neighbouring entities. In our approach, we compute extrinsic similarity by using a feature vector. Section 4.2 describes the details.

The second important feature is the way how the similarities are transformed into mappings. While Melnik et al. in [12] propose to compute either a stable marriage or the maximum weighted matching in a bipartite graph to find a good mapping, it seems that most newer ontology mapping algorithms do not do this (e.g. Ehrig and Staab use a simple greedy approach in [2]). In section 4.5 we describe how these two well-known graph algorithms can be used, and an empirical evaluation (see section 6) shows that it increases the performance of the mapping algorithm.

4 The Algorithm

4.1 Computing Intrinsic Similarity

In our implementation, we use distance metrics from the well-known Second-String library[3] as intrinsic similarity measures.

We also experimented with a similarity measure based on WordNet.[4] We used a similarity metric based on Euzenat's implementation in the OWL alignment API [3]. We decided, however, not to use it in the current setup. Preliminary experiments suggested that on many datasets no or only a marginal improvement

---

[3] http://secondstring.sourceforge.net/, see also [1]
[4] http://wordnet.princeton.edu/

can be achieved. This small benefit is, however, contrasted by a much greater computational effort. It may be possible to overcome these limitations by using a more sophisticated algorithm for computing a semantic similarity based on WordNet. This is, however, deferred to future work.

We use URIs, labels, comments and text from individuals and property values as text sources. We conducted experiments with the Jaro-Winkler metric [16] and a version of Levenshtein edit distance [10] that is scaled to the range $[0, 1]$ for comparing labels and local names. We used a soft-token metric with Jaro-Winkler resp. scaled Levenshtein edit distance as the base string distance metric for comparing comments and instance data. To determine the overall intrinsic similarity between two concepts, we use the maximum of these metrics. To avoid overemphasising small similarities, we disregard similarities that are smaller than a threshold of 0.4 and map similarities greater than 0.4 to the full range $[0, 1]$.

4.2   Computing Extrinsic Similarity

The main difference between our approach and existing schema matching algorithms is the way how the extrinsic similarity is computed. In many previous approaches extrinsic or structural similarity is propagated through a graph structure that is determined by the schema or ontology.

In our approach, we use an extrinsic feature vector $\mathbf{de}(v)$ for each entity that captures the relationship between this and other entities and then compute the similarities between these vector representations. The intuition behind using this vector representation is analogous to the assumption that the propagation-based methods make: Two nodes are similar if they are related to similar nodes.

To formally define the extrinsic feature vector, we first have to introduce a function that computes all entities that are connected to an entity v by a relation l. We consider for example subsumption and domain and range of properties as relations.

Definition 3. *We define a function from the set of vertices and the set of labels L to the power set of vertices so that for a given vertex the function finds all vertices adjacent through an arc with a given label:*

$$\text{rel} : V \times L \rightarrow 2^V$$

Let $G = (V, A)$ be a digraph with the set of vertices V and labelled arcs A as a set of ordered triples $(v, w, l) \in V \times V \times L$. Then we define:

$$\text{rel}(v, l) = \{x | v, x \in V \land (v, x, l) \in A\}$$

The definition of $\text{rel}' : V' \times L \rightarrow 2^{V'}$ *is analogous.*

Next, as an intermediate step to our extrinsic feature vector function, we define a *dynamic intrinsic* feature vector function that is basically a vector representation of all similarities between an entity v and all entities $v' \in V'$. "Intrinsic" means that these features are inherent to an entity. "Dynamic" means that their value can change as we get more information about that entity, and can thus make a better prediction about the similarities between this and other entities. Note that the dynamic intrinsic features are typically what we want to compute. In particular, this means that the dynamic intrinsic features are initially unknown.

Definition 4. *We define a dynamic intrinsic feature vector function as a function of an entity:*

$$\mathbf{di} : V \to \mathbb{R}^{|V'|}$$

Analogous to the matrix representation of a graph, we impose an arbitrary total order on V' and denote the first element of V' as v'_0 and the subsequent elements as v'_n for all $n < |V'|$. Then we define $\mathbf{di}$ as follows:

$$\mathbf{di}(v) = [\text{sim}(v, v'_0), \text{sim}(v, v'_1), \ldots, \text{sim}(v, v'_{|V'|-1})]$$

Dynamic extrinsic features are dynamic intrinsic features of related entities:

Definition 5. *We define a dynamic extrinsic feature vector function as a function of an entity.*

$$\mathbf{de} : V \to \mathbb{R}^{|V'|}$$

Assuming a commutative and associative operator $\oplus$ on $\mathbb{R}^d$ and a function rel as per definition 3, we define $\mathbf{de}(v)$ as some combination $\oplus$ of the dynamic intrinsic features $\mathbf{di}(x)$ (see definition 4) of all related entities $x \in \text{rel}(v)$.

$$\mathbf{de}(v) = \bigoplus_{x \in \text{rel}(v)} \mathbf{di}(x)$$

The exact definition of the combination operator $\oplus$ is arbitrary. We use an additive operator in our experiments.

Note that the elements in $\mathbf{de}(v)$ are based on the relations of $v \in V$, but correspond to vertices in V'. In order to compute an extrinsic similarity between v and some v', we have to define an extrinsic feature vector for v' that is based on the relations of $v' \in V'$.

Definition 6. *We define an extrinsic feature vector function as a function of an entity:*

$$\mathbf{de'} : V' \to \mathbb{R}^{|V'|}$$

Based on the total order on V' from definition 4, we define that each element i in $\mathbf{de'}$ is 1, if $v'_i \in \text{rel}(v')$ and 0 otherwise.

Given definitions 5 and 6 we can now easily define an extrinsic similarity $\text{sim}_{\text{ext}}(v, v')$ based on the similarity between the vectors $\mathbf{de}(v)$ and $\mathbf{de'}(v')$. A common similarity measure for two vectors is the dot product, but it is usually better to normalise the similarity measure using the well-known cosine, Dice, Jaccard or overlap coefficients, which are widely used in information retrieval. The similarities based on the extrinsic feature vectors are not symmetric. Since the feature vector is based on the best mapping for each concept, the fact that v maps to v' does not necessarily mean that the best mapping for v' is v, if the overall similarity $\text{sim}(v, v')$ is greater than the similarity of v to all other $x' \in V'$ but less than the similarity $\text{sim}(v', x)$ of v' to some $x \in V$.

Algorithm 1. Iterative Similarity Calculation

---

for $v \in V$ **do**
  $\mathbf{di}_{\text{int}}(v) \leftarrow [\text{sim}_{\text{int}}(v, v'_0), \text{sim}_{\text{int}}(v, v'_1), \dots, \text{sim}_{\text{int}}(v, v'_{|V'|-1})]$
end for
/* Initially, use intrinsic similarity only */
$\mathbf{de}(v) \leftarrow \bigoplus_{x \in \text{rel}(v)} \mathbf{di}_{\text{int}}(x)$
for a fixed number of iterations **do**
  for $v \in V$ **do**
    $\mathbf{di}_{\text{ext}}(v) \leftarrow [\text{sim}_{\text{ext}}(v, v'_0), \text{sim}_{\text{ext}}(v, v'_1), \dots, \text{sim}_{\text{ext}}(v, v'_{|V'|-1})]$
    /* Combine intrinsic and extrinsic similarity */
    $\mathbf{di}(v) \leftarrow \mathbf{di}_{\text{int}}(v) \otimes \mathbf{di}_{\text{ext}}(v)$
  end for
  $\mathbf{de}(v) \leftarrow \bigoplus_{x \in \text{rel}(v)} \mathbf{di}(x)$
end for
return $\forall v \in V : \mathbf{di}(v)$

4.3   Iterative Algorithm

Algorithm 1 formally specifies the iterative method of calculating the overall similarity. We are not restricted to computing $\text{sim}(v, v')$, calculating $\text{sim}(v', v)$ is analogous. Recall that because of the way we the extrinsic similarity is defined they are not necessarily equal.

4.4   Using Training Data

It is quite straightforward to use a previously known mapping to a third ontology to improve mapping accuracy. We assume a third ontology V'' and known mappings of the form (v', v'') with $v' \in V'$ and $v'' \in V''$. We compute the pairwise similarities between all $v \in V$ and both $v'' \in V''$ and $v' \in V'$ as in algorithm 1. Then, for each pair (v', v'') we assume the maximum[5] of $\text{sim}(v, v')$ and $\text{sim}(v, v'')$ as the joint similarity and substitute the similarity values in the mapping algorithm with the joint similarity. Let v'' be the entity that is mapped to v' as by the background knowledge. Then, we substitute the assignments of $\mathbf{di}$ in algorithm 1 with:

$$\mathbf{di}(v) \leftarrow [\max(\text{sim}(v, v'_0), \text{sim}(v, v''_0)), \dots, \max(\text{sim}(v, v'_{|V'|-1}), \text{sim}(v, v''_{|V'|-1}))]$$

Note that this replacement takes places for both the intrinsic and the extrinsic similarity and therefore the subscript has been omitted.

It is of course in principle also possible to use more than one known mapping as training data, but for our experiments we restricted ourselves to cases with a known mapping to just one other ontology. Furthermore, it would be possible to replace the entire similarity function with the output of a machine learning algorithm. In fact, algorithm 1 is very similar to the supervised learning algorithm that we presented in [8] and could be seen as a generalisation thereof.

---

[5] Other ways of defining the joint similarity, for example using the average, are thinkable. Using the maximum is like using a nearest-neighbour classifier.

4.5   Postprocessing Steps

Once we have computed the overall similarities, we have to compute the actual one-to-one mapping. This is the problem of finding a matching in a bipartite graph. A bipartite graph $B = (V + V', E)$ is a graph where the nodes can be split in two groups such that every edge connects two nodes from both partitions. Every similarity that has been calculated in the previous step corresponds to a weighted edge in such a bipartite graph.[6] A matching M in a graph is a set of edges such that no node is incident to more than one edge. In our setting this corresponds to a one-to-one mapping: For every entity in one ontology we want to find one entity in the other ontology. M is called maximum-weighted, if there is no other matching where the sum of all edge weights in the matching is bigger. M is called a stable marriage, if there are no nodes $v \in V$ and $v' \in V'$ such that the edge between v and v' in B is not in M, but has a higher weight than the edges in M that are incident in v and v'.

Gale and Shapley have shown in [6] that for bipartite graphs where the two partitions are of the same size a stable marriage always exists and presented an algorithm for finding such a matching. Because the number of vertices in V and V' is not necessarily equal in our case (if the two ontologies are of different size), a perfect match (in the graph-theoretic sense) is not always possible. It is therefore necessary to modify the termination criterion of the original Gale/Shapley algorithm slightly in a way that is equivalent to adding pseudo nodes and edges with weight zero to the bipartite graph.

Melnik et al. in [12] propose to compute either a stable marriage or the maximum weighted matching to find a good mapping. We compared the two approaches empirically on our data. We used an off-the-shelf implementation of James Munkres' algorithm [13] (also referred to as the Hungarian algorithm) to compute maximum-weighted matchings. As opposed to the Gale/Shapley algorithm, Munkres' algorithm is not suited for graphs with directed edges and asymmetric weights. Due to the way the extrinsic similarity is computed, the edge weights are not necessarily symmetric in our case, but it is of course straightforward to create a graph with undirected edges and symmetric weights simply by addition.

5   Parameters

Our matching algorithm as presented in this paper has various parameters.

In this section, we discuss various options and design choices. The experiments in section 6 show empirically the influence of the parameter settings on the overall performance.

5.1   Structure

Depending on the expressiveness of the underlying ontology language, several relations between classes or properties are defined. We considered super- and

---

[6] Note that this bipartite graph must not be confused with the graph interpretation of the two ontologies! We use a bipartite graph only to determine the final matching once the pairwise similarities have been calculated.

subclass-relations, super- and subproperties, defined properties for a class, domain and range of a property and siblings of classes and properties as possible relations. We performed preliminary experiments on three different combinations of those features: First, we used all available relations. Second, we used all relations except for siblings, and third, we used the subsumption relation only. These experiments have shown that the second setup consistently performed best. In our final evaluation (see next section), we call this configuration "dublin2"[7].

5.2 Number of Iterations

As in our experiments with iterative ensemble classification, we decided to use a fixed number of iterations as termination criterion for reasons of simplicity, and because it is not proven that the algorithm converges. Preliminary empirical experiments suggested that the algorithm is not very sensitive to the exact number of iterations. We set the number of iterations to five, the same as in our earlier work on web service annotation [8].

5.3 Inference

When mapping rich ontologies, it is sometimes possible to exploit knowledge drawn from the ontologies itself to impose constraints on the mappings or to infer mappings. Although we believe that for some mapping tasks exploiting such knowledge could increase the mapping accuracy, such an approach is out of scope of this thesis. We restrict ourselves to using the information obtained through the iterative relational algorithm to compute the final mappings. The set of ontologies we used for evaluating our algorithm does not have a very rich structure, so in comparison with other algorithms that may use such inference, our algorithm has no disadvantage.

5.4 Post-processing

As discussed above, we have to consider at least two ways of creating a mapping from the acquired similarities, if we demand a one-to-one mapping. We can compute either a stable marriage or a maximum weighted matching. In our empirical experiments, we tried both approaches. In the graphs and tables presenting our results we denote configurations that use the Gale/Shapley algorithm (as opposed to a maximum weighted matching) with the letter "g".

We also tried both possible answers to the question when the post-processing step should be applied. We denote the configurations where we applied the post-processing step also in between iterations with the letter "e". In the other experiments, the post-processing step (i.e. applying the Gale/Shapley or Hungarian algorithm) was only performed after the iteration phase of the algorithm has been completed.

---

[7] The OAEI 2005 contest lists our results as "dublin", we keep the name here.

5.5   Intrinsic Similarity

We already discussed the way we compute the intrinsic similarity between two concepts above in section 4.1. However, we could plug an arbitrary string distance metric in our framework. A great variety of string distance metrics – established algorithms as well as ad-hoc measures – is available off-the-shelf in libraries such as the already mentioned SecondString. As mentioned above, we considered the Jaro-Winkler and Levenshtein metrics. Preliminary experiments have shown that with our data, a scaled version of the Levenshtein metric works generally better than Jaro-Winkler. Therefore, we decided to use only the scaled Levenshtein metric in our final experiments. We set the threshold for the soft-token metric to 0.9, i.e. two tokens that have a string similarity greater or equal than 0.9 are considered the same. The suitability of different string distance metrics for several tasks has been extensively discussed in literature, e.g. [1].

5.6   Thresholds

In order to avoid spurious mappings it makes sense to use a minimum similarity threshold. In the ontology mapping scenario, it is not guaranteed that for some concept in one ontology a concept in another ontology actually exists. In these cases, not making a prediction is the correct answer. But also in other cases it is in several scenarios useful not to make a prediction at all rather than making a bad prediction. For example, consider a semi-automated setting where a human annotator has to review suggestions made by the algorithm.

For the precision/recall-graphs, we varied the threshold between 0 and 1 in steps of 0.05. When comparing the different configurations of our algorithm and for comparison with the algorithms from the OAEI 2005 contest we used a zero threshold.

6   Evaluation

We evaluated our algorithm on the benchmark ontologies from the 2005 Ontology Alignment Evaluation Initiative (OAEI 2005, [5]). Most of the benchmark ontologies consist of versions of a base ontology, where different aspects have been changed. For most of the following tests, we concentrate on six interesting ontologies: In two cases (ontologies 205 and 206 from the test suite), all names and labels have been replaced with synonyms or foreign words, and in four cases, independently developed "real-world" ontologies that describe the same domain have been used (301-304).

We tested various configurations of our algorithm and compared the results from these different setups against each other as well as against the published results from the other participants of the contest. The experiments were conducted in order to answer the five basic (groups of) questions:

1. Do we get any benefit from the extrinsic features as opposed to using the intrinsic similarity only?

2. Is it better to compute the maximum weighted matching or is a stable marriage more important? Should we apply this step only after all similarities are computed, or also between iterations?
3. What threshold is optimal?
4. How does our algorithm perform compared to other algorithms in literature? What are the strengths and weaknesses?
5. What is the benefit of using known mappings as training data?

It is important to note that in most of the experiments the difference in performance between the different configurations was quite low, although there are visible trends. However, what the experiments clearly show is that the overall accuracy of ontology mapping is based largely on the initial intrinsic (lexical) mapping. Unfortunately, because it is rarely published what the contributions of the lexical and structural similarities are, it is difficult to compare the strengths and weaknesses to other algorithms. Space restrictions prevent us to present all our results here. For a more detailed discussion, the reader is referred to [7].

6.1 Extrinsic vs. Intrinsic Features

The first question is of course the most crucial one: Is the way how we use the additional relational information, that differs from other methods known in literature, useful? Does it work? To answer this question, we compared the "dublin10" setup with the "dublin2e0" and "dublin20" setup. The "dublin10" setup uses only intrinsic features, "dublin20" and "dublin2e0" use extrinsic features (in five iterations) as well. Both setups compute a maximum-weighted matching, the "dublin2e" configuration also enforces one-to-one mappings in between iterations.

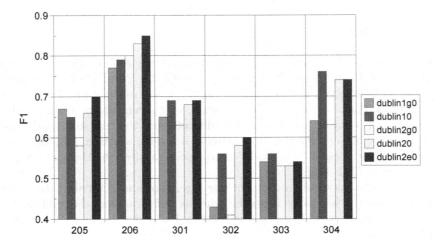

Fig. 1. Comparison of different configurations of our algorithm

The results in figure 1 (note that the scale starts with 0.4 to emphasise the difference between configurations) show that on four ontologies the configuration that uses extrinsic features performs better or equal than the configuration with only the intrinsic features. However, in two of the "real-world" ontologies, using the extrinsic features affects the performance in a negative way. The reason for this is that the ontologies 303 and 304 are structurally different from the base ontology and our algorithm is mislead by this structural difference. In that case, any attempt to make predictions based on the structure must fail. The other four ontologies, especially 205 and 206, are structurally quite similar to the base ontology. Here using the extrinsic features helps.

We conclude from these results that using relational features can improve the performance, but only if the ontologies that are to be matched are not structurally different. This is not only true for our approach. For example, in [9], the authors make the same observation for the Falcon algorithm.

6.2   Stable Marriage vs. Maximum-Weighted Matching

As far as we are aware, most other current algorithms do not explicitly compute stable marriages or maximum-weighted matchings to determine a one-to-one mapping. The Similarity Flooding algorithm [12] is a notable exception. We compared configurations that use a stable marriage with configurations with a maximum-weighted matching. The "dublin2g0" and "dublin1g0" configurations use the Gale/Shapley algorithm to compute a stable marriage while "dublin20" and "dublin10" computes a maximum-weighted matching. Both configurations use no threshold. The "dublin1g0" and "dublin10" configurations do not use extrinsic features. Figure 1 clearly shows that it is better to compute a maximum-weighted matching. This setup outperforms the stable-marriage configuration in almost all cases, sometimes drastically.

In the "dublin2e0" setup, a maximum-weighted matching is applied also in between iterations, where as for "dublin2g0" and "dublin20" the Gale/Shapley resp. the Hungarian algorithm is only applied after the last iteration. This configuration can therefore not directly be compared with "dublin2g0", but in comparison with "dublin20" it becomes clear that enforcing a one-to-one-mapping also in between iterations is better than doing so after the last iteration only.

6.3   Threshold

To find out what value for the threshold is best, we took a closer look at ontologies 205 and 303. Figure 2 shows the relation between the threshold and the precision, recall and F1 measures on ontologies 205 resp. 303. Note that varying the threshold has a quite different effect on the two ontologies. In ontology 205, recall drops faster than precision increases. The maximum F1 is reached at a threshold of 0.05. In ontology 303, precision and recall at threshold 0 are lower than in ontology 205. When raising the threshold, recall drops only slightly while precision increases rather quickly. Maximum F1 is reached at a threshold between 0.7 and 0.85. We have to conclude that the best cut-off value for our

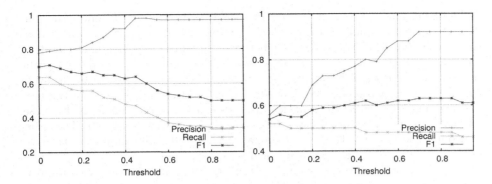

Fig. 2. Relation between threshold and precision, recall and F1 for ontologies 205 (left) and 303 (right)

mapping algorithm depends strongly on the dataset. On the "real world" ontologies 301–304 the threshold is higher, while for the artificial benchmark ontologies the best F1 is reached at a very low threshold.

6.4   Comparison with Other Algorithms

To evaluate our own method, we compared our results against the published results from the 2005 Ontology Alignment Evaluation Initiative ([5]).

The algorithm that performed best in the 2005 contest was the Falcon algorithm [9] by the Southeast University of Nanjin. Falcon uses a bipartite graph representation of an RDF graph to compute structural similarity.

Our own algorithm can, however, compete well with the "FOAM" algorithm developed in Karlsruhe and the "OLA" algorithm. "Edna" is simple algorithm that is based on edit distance of the labels and was included by the organisers of the contest as a baseline. Our algorithm in the "dublin20" setting as submitted to the organisers of the OAEI 2005 performs second best after Falcon. From the 2004 algorithms, the algorithm developed at Stanford has a higher average precision, but a lower average recall than ours. These results are in greater detail presented in [5]. Figure 3 shows the F1 score. To aggregate the results of the individual tests, the organisers of the contest calculated the precision and recall over all mappings of all test.

6.5   Using Training Data

To test the effect of background knowledge on the performance of the alignment, we conducted experiments where we used a given mapping from the target ontology to a third (background) ontology. It is clear that we can expect the biggest improvement in accuracy if the background ontology is very similar to the source ontology. Vice versa, if the source ontology is very dissimilar, we cannot expect an improvement. Our experiments confirmed this intuition. We noticed that in the worst case using background knowledge does not improve the performance

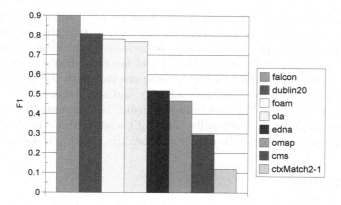

Fig. 3. Overall F1 of the OAEI 2005 alignments

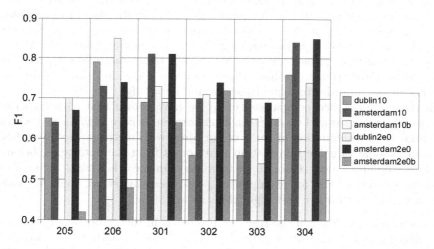

Fig. 4. Performance (F1) of setup with training data compared to normal setup

at all or could even negatively affect the performance slightly. If the right background mapping is selected, however, the performance can be increased by quite a lot. In figure 4, the experiments with training data are denoted as "amsterdam10"[8] for an experiment with intrinsic similarity only and as "amsterdam2e0" for an experiment using extrinsic similarity as well. When testing ontology 205, we used 206 as background ontology and vice versa, for 301 we used 302 as background and vice versa, and for 303 we used 304 and vice versa.

Clearly, the performance on ontologies 205 and 206 are examples for the worst case. The reason for that becomes clear if we look at the performance of the mapping from ontology 205 to 206, i.e. when mapping to the background ontology only instead of the reference ontology 101. For comparison, we include these

---

[8] This part of the research was carried out in Amsterdam, hence this name for the algorithm.

results in the diagram and denote this configuration as "amsterdam10b " resp. "amsterdam2e0b". From these results, we can also see that the improvement of using training data in the 30x ontologies is not only due to the fact that mappings between 301 and 302 resp. 303 and 304 are easy. Rather, the combined approach of using background knowledge outperforms both the simple mapping between the source and the reference ontology and also between the source and the background ontology. We conclude that using known mappings as training data can generally improve the results, but that the algorithm can also be misled, if the background ontology is too different from the source ontology.

7   Conclusion

We have presented a new method for ontology mapping that uses established string distance metrics and an extrinsic feature representation as known from relational learning algorithms. We treat the results of the similarity computation as a bipartite graph and use well-known algorithms from graph theory to compute an optimal one-to-one mapping. With an empirical evaluation, we have shown that our basic ideas work, and that our algorithm can compete with other approaches. Furthermore, we have shown how our algorithm can be used in a supervised way in order to exploit background knowledge.

In the more detailed comparison in [7] we have shown that each algorithm has specific strengths and weaknesses. Therefore, we believe that there is a great potential for a combination of some of our ideas with methods used by others. We ignore some valuable information that comes from the ontologies, because we do not do any logical reasoning or inference. On the other hand, some of the methods proposed here, for example the post-processing steps, could be useful in conjunction with other base algorithms as well.

Acknowledgments. Most of the research presented in this paper was done when the author was at University College Dublin and was supported by grants from Science Foundation Ireland and the US Office of Naval Research. The author would like to thank Nicholas Kushmerick for valuable feedback and support.

References

1. William W. Cohen, Pradeep Ravikumar, and Stephen E. Fienberg. A comparison of string distance metrics for name-matching tasks. In *Proceedings of the IJCAI-03 Workshop on Information Integration on the Web (IIWeb-03)*, pages 73–78, 2003.
2. Marc Ehrig and Steffen Staab. QOM – quick ontology mapping. In *3rd International Semantic Web Conference*, Hiroshima, Japan, 2004.
3. Jérôme Euzenat. An API for ontology alignment. In *3rd International Semantic Web Conference*, Hiroshima, Japan, 2004.
4. Jérôme Euzenat, David Loup, Mohamed Touzani, and Petko Valtchev. Ontology alignment with OLA. In York Sure, Oscar Corcho, Jérôme Euzenat, and Todd Hughes, editors, *Proceedings of the 3rd International Workshop on Evaluation of Ontology based Tools (EON)*, Hiroshima, Japan, 2004.

5. Jérôme Euzenat, Heiner Stuckenschmidt, and Mikalai Yatskevich. Introduction to the ontology alignment evaluation 2005. In *K-CAP 2005 Integrating Ontologies Workshop*, Banff, Alberta, Canada, 2005.
6. David Gale and Lloyd Stowell Shapley. College admissions and the stability of marriage. *American Mathematical Monthly*, 1962.
7. Andreas Heß. *Supervised and Unsupervised Ensemble Learning for the Semantic Web*. PhD thesis, School of Computer Science and Informatics, University College Dublin, Dublin, Ireland, 2005.
8. Andreas Heß and Nicholas Kushmerick. Iterative ensemble classification for relational data: A case study of semantic web services. In *Proceedings of the 15th European Conference on Machine Learning*, Pisa, Italy, 2004.
9. Wei Hu, Ningsheng Jian, Yuzhong Qu, and Qanbing Wang. GMO: A graph matching for ontologies. In *K-CAP 2005 Integrating Ontologies Workshop*, Banff, Alberta, Canada, 2005.
10. Vladimir I. Levenshtein. Binary codes capable of correcting deletions, insertions, and reversals. *Doklady Akademii Nauk SSSR*, 163(4):845–848, 1965. In Russian. English Translation in Soviet Physics Doklady, 10(8) p. 707–710, 1966.
11. Jayant Madhavan, Philip A. Bernstein, and Erhard Rahm. Generic Schema Matching with Cupid. In *Proceedings of the 27th International Conference on Very Large Databases*, pages 129–138, Rome, Italy, 2001.
12. S. Melnik, H. Molina-Garcia, and E. Rahm. Similariy flooding: A versatile graph matching algorithm. In *Int. Conference on Data Engineering (ICDE)*, 2002.
13. James Munkres. Algorithms for the assignment and transportation problems. *SIAP*, 5(1):32–38, 1957.
14. Jennifer Neville and David Jensen. Iterative classification in relational data. In *AAAI Workshop Statistical Relational Learning*, 2000.
15. York Sure, Oscar Corcho, Jérôme Euzenat, and Todd Hughes, editors. *3rd Int. Workshop on Evaluation of Ontology based Tools (EON)*, Hiroshima, Japan, 2004.
16. William E. Winkler and Yves Thibaudeau. An application of the Fellegi-Sunter model of record linkage to the 1990 U.S. decennial census. Technical report, U.S. Bureau of the Census, Washington, D.C., 1991. Statistical Research Report Series RR91/09.

Community-Driven Ontology Matching

Anna V. Zhdanova[1,2] and Pavel Shvaiko[3]

[1] CCSR, University of Surrey, Guildford, UK
[2] DERI, University of Innsbruck, Innsbruck, Austria
a.zhdanova@surrey.ac.uk
[3] DIT, University of Trento, Povo, Trento, Italy
pavel@dit.unitn.it

Abstract. We extend the notion of ontology matching to *community-driven* ontology matching. Primarily, the idea is to enable Web communities to establish and reuse ontology mappings in order to achieve, within those communities, an adequate and timely domain representation, facilitated knowledge exchange, etc. Secondarily, the matching community is provided with the new practice, which is a public alignment reuse. Specifically, we present an approach to construction of a community-driven ontology matching system and discuss its implementation. An analysis of the system usage indicates that our strategy is promising. In particular, the results obtained justify feasibility and usefulness of the community-driven ontology mappings' acquisition and sharing.

1 Introduction

Matching is a plausible solution to the semantic heterogeneity problem in many applications, such as schema/ontology integration, query answering, agent communication, web services discovery, etc. It takes two ontologies, each consisting of a set of discrete entities (e.g., classes, properties) as input and produces as output the relationships (e.g., equivalence, subsumption) holding between these entities [22, 19, 7]. Heterogeneity is typically reduced in two steps: (i) match two ontologies, thereby determining the *alignment* (mappings) and (ii) execute the alignment according to an application needs (e.g., query answering). In this paper, we focus only on the first step, and in particular, on one of the promising directions in matching, which is the *alignment reuse*.

A rationale behind the alignment reuse is that many ontologies to be matched are similar to already matched ontologies, especially if they are describing the same application domain [21, 22]. Eventually, once an alignment has been determined, it can be saved, and further reused as any other data on the Web. Thus, a (large) repository of mappings has a potential to increase the effectiveness of matching systems by providing yet another source of domain specific knowledge. Unlike previous works, e.g., of COMA++ [1], which followed a *private* alignment reuse approach (where access to the system is limited to individual users, who usually do not know each other, hence, they do not communicate with each other); we propose a *public* approach, where any agent, namely Internet user (most importantly communities of users, opposed to individual users) or potentially programs, can match ontologies, save the alignments such that these are available to any other agents' reuse. Thus, enabling the cross-fertilization

Y. Sure and J. Domingue (Eds.): ESWC 2006, LNCS 4011, pp. 34–49, 2006.

between the participating parties and help achieving the goals of these parties cooperatively. We call this approach a *community-driven ontology matching*.

Reuse of mappings created by different users, however, implies resolving, among others, such challenges as the *appropriateness* of mappings when using them in the new applications and *trust* issues. For instance, questions like "What kind of alignment do I need (e.g., partial vs. complete)?", "Can I use this mapping in my application context (e.g., biology, chemistry)?" appear. The answers to such questions substantially depend on who uses the mappings, when, and in which scenarios. In the proposed approach, we address these issues by involving communities in construction and sharing of the (subjective) alignments.

There are two contributions of the paper. The first one includes a community-driven ontology matching approach, its implementation, and usage analysis. Thus, primarily, it enables the Web communities with the facilitated knowledge exchange, a more comprehensive and up-to-date domain representation, and so on. Secondarily, it provides the matching community with the new practice, which is a public alignment reuse. The second contribution includes an analysis of the existing ontology matching systems from the community-driven ontology matching perspective. Thus, it estimates their potential for the reuse in the community-driven matching scenarios.

The rest of the paper is structured as follows. In Section 2, we briefly introduce the ontology matching problem. Community-driven ontology matching is presented in Section 3, while its implementation is addressed in Section 4. Results of the prototype usage are reported in Section 5. Section 6 discusses state of the art matching systems from the community-driven ontology matching perspective. Finally, Section 7 contains some conclusions and outline of the future work.

2 Ontology Matching

Following [10, 22], we define a mapping element (mapping) as a 5-uple: $\langle id, e, e', n, R \rangle$, where id is a unique identifier of the given mapping element; e and e' are the entities (e.g., classes, properties) of the first and the second ontology respectively; n is a *confidence measure* in the [0,1] range holding for the correspondence between the entities e and e'; R is a relation (e.g., *equivalence*, *subsumption*) holding between the entities e and e'. An *alignment* is a set of mapping elements. The matching operation determines the alignment for a pair of input ontologies.

Figure 1 shows two parts of ontologies describing an academic department. For example, according to some matching algorithm based on linguistic and structure analysis, the confidence measure (for the fact that the equivalence relation holds) between

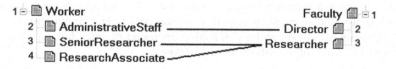

Fig. 1. Two simple ontologies and the alignment

entities with labels Research Associate in ontology on the left, and Researcher in ontology on the right could be 0.68, thereby producing the following mapping element: $\langle id_{4,3}, ResearchAssociate, Researcher, 0.68, = \rangle$. However, the relation between the same pair of entities, according to another matching algorithm which is able to determine that the first entity is *a kind of* the second entity, could be exactly the less general relation (without computing the confidence measure). Thus, in this case, the 5-uple $\langle id_{4,3}, ResearchAssociate, Researcher, n/a, \sqsubseteq \rangle$ is returned to the user.

3 Community-Driven Ontology Matching

In this section, we introduce a community-driven ontology matching problem, provide a motivating scenario for it, and describe the benefits of the approach.

3.1 Problem Statement

By a *community* we mean here a group of individuals that have common interests and (often) maintain their own communication and collaboration environments through, e.g., Semantic Web community portals [6]. Recent research identified a high importance of direct involvement of humans and communities in ontology management: an agent or a human contributor was shown to be an indispensable part of a semantic network [18], and participation of a community in ontology construction was shown as a way to a more complete and up-to-date domain knowledge representation [25].

Being in line with the general ideas of community-driven ontology management, *community-driven ontology matching* extends conventional ontology matching by involving end users, knowledge engineers, and developer communities in the processes of establishing, describing and reusing mappings. More precisely, community-driven ontology matching operation can be defined as follows. It takes as input information from an agent, e.g., a human contributor (such as request, context, personal data), and two ontologies, each consisting of a set of discrete entities (such as classes, properties). Based on the input information, the operation encapsulates, besides conventional ontology matching, some community-driven ontology management operations, such as social network analysis, harvest of additional web data. It determines as output the relations (e.g., equivalence, subsumption) between the entities of the input ontologies, which are particularly tailored to resolve the semantic heterogeneity problem of an agent. All the output relations are represented via *annotated mappings* and are to be propagated to the communities associated with the human contributor.

A specific feature of relations resulting from the community-driven ontology matching is their customization to the user/community and an application requirements. Thus, the community-driven matching process determines *subjective alignments*. Notice that subjective alignments are appropriate for specific tasks in a specific community, but may be inappropriate or even contradicting to practices of other communities.

The community-driven ontology matching operation requires human involvement and utilizes resources of the following (main) types:

Information about Users. This represents information about agents involved in the community-driven ontology matching. For example, their expertise in the domain, experiences with the ontologies being matched, their goals, and so on.

Information about Communities, Groups, Social Networks. This captures relations between agents. For example, which agents belong to the same community, to which agents a particular agent trusts most of all. These links between agents help in recommendation/sharing of an ontology alignment among them, for instance, in choosing a mapping element when multiple alternatives exist.

Tools Facilitating Automatic Ontology Matching. These tools are often based, among others, on linguistic techniques. However, such tools may not be sufficiently helpful when the users have to match ontologies specified in different natural languages, e.g., in English and Arabic. In these cases, one may rely on bi-lingual users and automatic natural language translation systems in addition to tools for automatic ontology matching.

3.2 Motivating Scenario

Suppose a community member wants to be timely informed about the trends happening in his/her communities and potentially interesting trends happening in other communities. Specifically, a biologist wants to be notified about published papers, conferences and other activities associated with the concept *protein* in the biology research community where he/she comes from, as well as in the chemistry research community. Thus, he/she wants to know which papers and activities are considered to be important for both communities.

In order to exemplify community-driven ontology matching, let us consider a simple scenario which involves four researchers from two natural science communities. The researchers are Mark, Michael, Jenny, and Alexander. They are represented by roles held in their communities (i.e., end user, knowledge engineer, developer) and web domains/communities where they interact (e.g., biology, chemistry). These researchers have the following profiles:

name	Mark
interacts	biology, chemistry web applications
role(s)	end user

name	Jenny
interacts	chemistry web application
role(s)	end user, developer

name	Michael
interacts	biology, chemistry web applications
role(s)	end user, knowledge engineer

name	Alexander
interacts	biology, chemistry web applications
role(s)	end user

A community view on ontology matching process is shown in Figure 2. Let us discuss it in detail.

Suppose the following two actions take place:

- Michael creates an alignment m between ontologies coming from biology and chemistry web applications;
- Alexander uses the alignment m.

The result of a tool for community-driven ontology matching is the alignment m, which is recommended to Mark. After the tool recommends a new mapping to Mark, he, as a researcher, can benefit from the extended interoperability between biology and chemistry web applications without applying any effort to rediscover the new

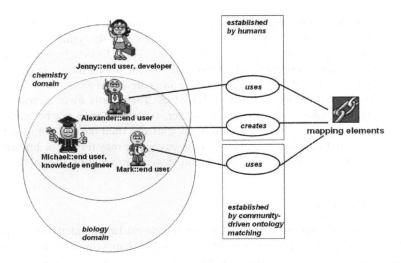

Fig. 2. A community-driven ontology matching process

knowledge (already established by `Michael` and validated by `Alexander`). Whereas, in the proposed scenario, alignment m is not recommended to `Jenny`, because she does not use the `biology` web application.

Process of mapping recommendation to individual users and communities can be varied and qualitatively improved by analysis of individual and community profiles, e.g., reusing information about users' activity and expertise in certain domains, users' collaboration history, users' social networking relations and mutual trust [14].

3.3 Benefits from Employing Community-Driven Ontology Matching

In the given scenario, a biologist will be enabled to match the concepts standing for *protein* in the ontologies of chemists and biologists, and benefit from being easily aware of the community-driven changes. His/her community members can also contribute as well as benefit from mappings created by the scientist. Community-driven ontology matching facilitates mapping discovery and satisfaction from mapping reuse, as, e.g., in the given scenario (i) the mappings used by one of the biologists can be easily found by his/her community via social networking[1], (ii) the mappings established by the biologist will be most likely valid and valuable for his/her community. Therefore, via community-driven ontology matching, Web communities become *self-manageable* with respect to generation of alignments between the ontologies from the participating parties.

Supporting growth of the Semantic Web and *assistance to the ontology matching development community* are the major added values of community-driven ontology matching compared to conventional ontology matching. Let us discuss these points in turn.

Primarily, community-driven ontology matching amounts to scalability and dynamicity characteristics of the Semantic Web. In fact, it extends and preserves advantages given to the communities by the (ordinary) Web.

---

[1] See "knowledgeweb on the people's portal" for an example of identification and representation of a cross-linked research community: http://people.semanticweb.org.

- The ontologies which are constructed, aligned and further evolved by the communities *represent the domain and connection with other domains more comprehensibly* than the ontologies designed and matched by an external knowledge engineer. External knowledge engineers are typically the bottleneck to the ontology comprehensiveness, as they are not capable to capture all the varieties of mapping elements that might take place in a community and associated communities.
- The community-driven ontology matching approach provides a *higher dynamicity and up-to-dateness* to the outside-world changes in time, compared to the conventional ontology matching approach. When ontologies are matched by external knowledge engineers, all the changes need to be captured and introduced by these engineers. With external knowledge experts, the delay in realizing and introducing the changes might take days, weeks or even months. This delay is unacceptable for many dynamic domains, where vocabularies regularly and rapidly change (e.g., business or sport).
- Community-driven ontology matching approach with its subjective alignment *semantically extends the current Web* by following the Web principles of scalable, self-organizable mass of content and structures. In the Web now, anyone is free to publish anything that he/she finds important. End users are to decide whether published Web information and services are exploited or not. In Semantic Web this principle should remain (for it to become large scale). Therefore, we should allow publishing different and even contradicting alignments. Usage of these alignments in proper contexts should be ensured by annotations and services assisting for the choice of a particular alignment for the needs of users and communities.

Secondarily, the community-driven ontology matching naturally assists to creation of a stimulating environment for developers of ontology matching services/systems.

- Ontology matching is an expensive process. In community-driven ontology matching, the expenses are shifted from the ontology/alignment maintainers to the communities employing them. This shift results in *adequate investment distribution* among the ontology entities (e.g., classes and properties) and some particular mapping elements of the alignment. Specifically, the ontology entities or mapping elements of higher importance to the communities gain more support in terms of more associated resources.
- The community-driven ontology matching approach contributes to creation of an environment for an evaluation of automatic matching algorithms. Indeed, as the community-driven ontology matching approach stipulates that the users, depending on their needs, select the most effective or efficient algorithms and systems for ontology matching, *existing ontology matching systems will be improved* permanently in competition for their users.
- Lack of background knowledge, most often domain specific knowledge, is one of the key problems of ontology matching these days [13]. In fact, as recent industry-strength evaluations show [2, 11], most of state of the art systems, for the tasks of matching thousands of entities, perform not with such high values of *recall* (namely ∼30%) as in cases of "toy" examples, where the recall was most often around 80%. To this end, community-driven ontology matching approach provides *yet another*

source of domain specific knowledge, namely a (public) repository of alignments from the past match operations.

Practically, these advantages are gained by introducing an infrastructure that enables the communities to match their ontologies and reuse ontology mappings which are relevant to them. In the rest of the paper we mostly concentrate on technical details supporting the primarily benefits (as identified above). While addressing a technical solution for the secondary benefits is posed as the future work.

4   Implementation

4.1   Architecture

In the context of the World Wide Web, the community-driven ontology matching can be seen as a service, which was created by a community of developers, is used by the community of users, and which fills in a machine processible repository with mappings. The implemented prototype of the community-driven ontology matching service[2] allows semi-automatic ontology matching and saving the approved mapping elements in a publicly available repository, currently, as OWL files. The resulting application runs on a Tomcat server, reusing three major software components: INRIA API [10], OWL API [3] and Jena 2 [5]. A JSP interface to make the application available for the final user and to realize the semi-automatic matching process was implemented.

An architecture of the community-driven ontology matching system is shown in Figure 3. Let us discuss it in detail.

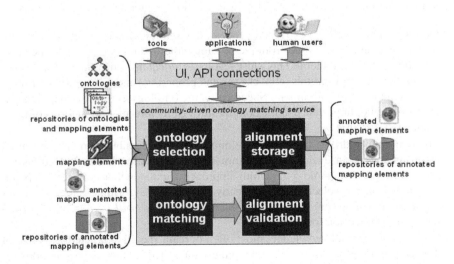

Fig. 3. Architecture of the community-driven ontology matching system

---

[2] The community-driven ontology matching service is available online at http://align.deri.org

The community-driven ontology matching service, depending on the task, may take as input ontologies, ontology repositories, mapping elements, annotated mapping elements and repositories of annotated mapping elements. It may produce as output annotated mapping elements and repositories of annotated mapping elements. The repositories of annotated mapping elements are produced as output instead or in addition to annotated mapping elements depending on the request. The former contains several annotated mapping elements and additional annotations specific to the context or subjectiveness of the identified semantic heterogeneity problem. The output production process is directed by involvement of the communities directly via user interfaces (UI) and indirectly via tools and applications employing community-driven ontology matching services.

Human contributors. These form a crucial part of community-driven ontology matching. The roles of the human contributors are end users, knowledge engineers and developers. The domains for activities of human contributors are any applications which can be represented on the Web (e.g., chemistry, biology).

Tools and Web applications. These provide a platform for alignment reuse in communities. Web applications are usually domain-dependent and gather end communities around a certain topic. They often employ tools. Tools, in turn, are typically created for developer communities. They are domain-independent and may reuse or include mapping repositories (as well as ontologies) to support applications' integration. Tool category also includes various (external) ontology matchers.

Ontologies, mapping elements, repositories of ontologies and mapping elements. In the perspective of Web communities, ontologies are models of a domain shared by a group of individuals who form communities on the basis of this sharing. Mappings link ontology entities, and therefore, provide a basis for interoperation between communities. A repository of ontologies and mapping elements are several ontologies and mapping elements united for a common usage purpose. All the mappings that are validated by a human are stored in an OWL serialization in a publicly available mapping repository. Therefore, usage and experiment with the online version of ontology alignment implementation result in generation of human validated data on matched ontology items[3] that can be reused by Semantic Web applications.

Annotated mapping elements and repositories of annotated mapping elements. In order to select mapping elements which fit best for a desired task, annotated mapping elements are produced by community-driven ontology matching service. Annotation of a mapping element generally contains its usage-related characteristics. Repositories of annotated mapping elements are collections of mapping elements annotated with values corresponding to characteristics specified in Table 1. Depending on specific ontology and alignment selection algorithms, additional mapping characteristics can be considered.

User interfaces and API connections. Community-driven ontology matching is available to all the community members, and visual ontology representations (web-forms, graphics and natural language descriptions) are the ones viewed in the portals user interfaces and commonly shared in human-portal interaction. For the regular Web users (not

---

[3] The mappings acquired from human contributors by the alignment service are available online: http://align.deri.org:8080/people/mappings.owl

Table 1. Characteristics of community-driven ontology mapping repositories

Mapping Characteristics	Sample Values
by what or by whom a mapping element was established	by an automatic ontology matching service http://align.deri.org; manually by a user with an address anna.zhdanova@deri.org
by what or by whom a mapping element was re-established or used	by a community using the Web application http://people.semanticweb.org; by a user community of the Jena tool
how often and when a mapping element was re-established or used	ca. 100 times per day; 2 times per week

necessarily ontology engineers), ontology matching is downsized to provision of natural language descriptions, filling out forms and triggering implicit personalization and ontology instantiation (e.g., resulting from observing actual use of the ontology entities such as calculation of entity popularity measure). Meanwhile, the ontology mappings introduced at the natural language and user-form level have potential to be reused also at the level of machine-to-machine interoperation.

4.2 Functionality

At present, automatic matching of ontologies usually cannot be performed with a due quality. Therefore, we consider semi-automatic matching, where a system suggests mappings between entities of the source ontologies and the user either discards or fol-

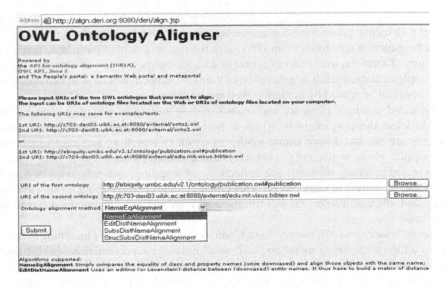

Fig. 4. Ontology and matching method selection

```
Address  http://align.deri.org:8080/deri/saveMappings.jsp
```

OWL Ontology Aligner - Mappings are Saved

Powered by the
the API for ontology alignment (INRIA),
OWL API, Jena 2
and The People's portal: a Semantic Web portal and metaportal

The following mappings are identified:

```
<rdf:RDF
    xmlns:rdf="http://www.w3.org/1999/02/22-rdf-syntax-ns#"
    xmlns:owl="http://www.w3.org/2002/07/owl#" >
  <rdf:Description rdf:about="http://www.example.org/ontology2#journalarticle">
    <rdf:type rdf:resource="http://www.w3.org/2002/07/owl#Class"/>
  </rdf:Description>
  <rdf:Description rdf:about="http://www.example.org/ontology1#journalarticle">
    <rdf:type rdf:resource="http://www.w3.org/2002/07/owl#Class"/>
    <owl:equivalentClass rdf:resource="http://www.example.org/ontology2#journalarticle"/>
  </rdf:Description>
  <rdf:Description rdf:about="http://www.w3.org/2000/01/rdf-schema#subClassOf">
    <rdf:type rdf:resource="http://www.w3.org/2002/07/owl#Class"/>
    <owl:equivalentClass rdf:resource="http://www.w3.org/2000/01/rdf-schema#subClassOf"/>
  </rdf:Description>
</rdf:RDF>
```

Fig. 5. Mapping output

lows these suggestions. With the current implementation, the following functions are offered to the user:

Choose two ontologies to match. User needs to select two ontologies to be matched by inputting URIs of ontologies or specifying files from the local disk (see Figure 4).

Choose a matching algorithm/service. The ontology matching service provides access to a number of different ontology matching algorithms and systems (e.g., edit distance matcher). User selects a desired one and starts the matching process (see Figure 4).

Provide feedback on automatically generated alignment. When the matching process has finished, the system reports the alignment determined. The user can now perform the approve/discard operation of the mapping elements on a per-mapping element basis.

Store the alignment. Once the user has decided that all the necessary mapping elements are in place, he/she will tell the system to store the alignment determined for a later re-use. Thus, the user can save the chosen ontology mappings (in OWL files) in common repository available on the Web for everyone's reuse (see Figure 5).

Reuse the alignment. The user may need to modify manually an existing alignment and reuse the mappings independently from the OWL Ontology Aligner service. For these actions, the user receives confirmed by him/her mappings in an accessible way (see Figure 5).

Extend to annotated mapping repository. In community-driven ontology matching, assigning community-related information to the gained mappings is highly important. Such additional information should convey the details on the context of mapping creation and foreseen usage, i.e., who created the mapping, when, with what instrument, etc. A basic ontology alignment format [10] can be extended with an annotation providing additional community-related information about a mapping as follows:

```
<map> <Cell>
<entity1 rdf:resource='http://www.example.org/ontology1#reviewedarticle'/>
<entity2 rdf:resource='http://www.example.org/ontology2#article'/>
```

```
<measure rdf:datatype='&xsd;float'>0.6363636363636364</measure>
<relation>=</relation>
<dc:creator> <foaf:Person>
<foaf:name>Anna V. Zhdanova</foaf:name>
<rdfs:seeAlso rdf:resource="http://www.ee.surrey.ac.uk/Personal/A.Zhdanova/foaf.rdf"/>
</foaf:Person> </dc:creator> <dc:date>2005-03-30</dc:date>
<dc:contributor rdf:resource="http://align.deri.org"/>
</Cell> </map>
```

As mentioned in §3.1, resulting alignments can formally contradict or subsume each other. Nevertheless, they can be correctly employed in a community-driven Semantic Web environment. The role of alignments' annotations is to ensure a correct interpretation of an alignment in a context of a specific task. Let us consider a simple example. Suppose, one sub-community of biologists may be interested only in journal papers dealing with *protein*. While, another sub-community may be interested in all kinds of papers on the same subject. When a biologist belongs to both of these sub-communities, a reconciliation algorithm is needed in order to decide what kind of information needs to be delivered to the user. Such an algorithm may employ precisions of alignments, biologist's personal data, and other details of the community-driven alignment annotations.

5   Usage Analysis

The community-driven ontology matching service has been available online since November 2004. The usage of the service has been observed for one year. Results of the usage analysis are summarized in Table 2. In particular, the first column lists the characteristics which were analyzed. The second and the third columns represent the statistics, respectively, for the first half of the observation period and for the whole period.

Table 2. Usage analysis results

Characteristics	Observation Period (Nov 04 - Apr 05)	Observation Period (Nov 04 - Oct 05)
Number of the matched entities which were acquired	52 different ontology entities	343 different ontology entities
Number of the mappings which were acquired	29 different mappings	317 different mappings
Number of the ontologies processed /namespaces known via the communities involved	8 different namespaces	20 different namespaces
Identification of who and when used community-driven matching service	anonymous Web users from more than 25 countries	anonymous Web users from more than 40 countries

Table 2 demonstrates (as expected) a relatively infrequent usage of the system just after its launch. For example, during the first half of the exploitation period no new (to the system) ontology namespaces were acquired, namely all 8 namespaces already existed in the ontologies offered to the prototype users as examples. However, during the second half of the observation period, 12 completely new namespaces were acquired. Also, it is worth noticing that the numbers of matched entities and acquired mappings have substantially increased during the second half of the exploitation period.

In general, during the observation time around 750 users accessed the online service. These were mostly researchers and developers. According to the alignments acquired by the prototype, two types of ontologies served most often as input: (i) common knowledge ontologies, with such most frequently used concepts as *Person, Time, Place*, and (ii) domain specific ontologies (e.g., academia), with such most frequently used concepts as *University, Faculty, Publication*. However, ontology entities from more specific domains were acquired as well. Some examples are a museum ontology in Italian and an ontology devoted to electronics of the Dutch origin.

From the experiments with the system, the following two main problems restricting usage of the community-driven ontology matching were identified:

– Still, there exists a relatively small number of OWL ontologies. Moreover, there exists even a smaller number of ontologies which have a meaningful overlap, hence, they are worth being matched. A similar problem (namely, finding real-world OWL ontology matching tasks) has been encountered in the ontology matching contests[4].

– There are no services supporting relatively easy reuse of acquired ontology alignments in predefined scenarios and efficient interaction with the repositories of annotated mappings. We consider these problems to be very important, and therefore, pose addressing them as one of our future work directions.

Thus, the above observations suggest that, on the one hand, the uptake of Semantic Web technology in general, and of community-driven ontology matching in particular, by the Web communities is still slow. However, on the other hand, the usage analysis gives us a preliminary vision of a feasibility of ontology mappings acquisition from the Web communities and their usefulness for those communities.

6 Discussion

There exists a number of semi-automated schema/ontology matching systems, recent surveys on the topic are provided in [21, 22, 19, 7], while state of the art matching approaches can be found in [15, 12, 20, 17, 9, 8][5]. Below, we analyze some state of the art matching systems from the community-driven ontology matching perspective.

PROMPT is an ontology merging and alignment tool with a sophisticated prompt mechanism for possible matching terms [20]. At present, the PROMPT system is supported by its authors. It is an open source system written in Java and can be downloaded from the project web-site[6]. PROMPT handles ontologies expressed in such knowledge representation formalisms as OWL and RDFS. The major obstacle in reusing the PROMPT tool in the community-driven approach comes from the fact that it has being

---

[4] See for details, e.g., http://oaei.inrialpes.fr/2005/ and http://oaei.inrialpes.fr/2004/Contest/

[5] A complete information on the topic can be found at www.OntologyMatching.org

[6] http://protege.stanford.edu/plugins/prompt/prompt.html

developed as the Protégé[7] plug-in. Thus, its source code needs additional modifications in order to be suitably integrated within the community-driven settings.

MAFRA is an ontology mapping framework which aims at matching distributed ontologies and reasoning over the mappings [17]. At present, the MAFRA system is not supported by its authors[8]. The tool is an open source and is implemented in Java. MAFRA handles ontologies expressed in RDFS and DAML+OIL. It has been developed as the KAON[9] plug-in. Thus, as in the PROMPT system case, the reuse in the community-driven approach of the ontology matching component of MAFRA is hindered by its tight integration with KAON and GUI. Finally, up-to-date documentation of the MAFRA code is not available[10].

Alignment API is an implementation of the format for expressing alignments in RDF [10]. At present, Alignment API is supported by its author. It is an open source. It is written (in Java) as an extension of the OWL API [3] and can be downloaded from the project web-site[11]. Alignment API handles ontologies in OWL/RDF. In general, it can be used for various tasks, such as completing partial alignments, thresholding alignments, evaluating results of matching algorithms, and so on. There is a possibility of integrating new matching algorithms, composing matching algorithms, generating transformations in other than OWL knowledge representation formalisms, such as SWRL rules [16] and C-OWL [4]. The API module is easy to understand, install and use. The supporting documentation is also available. Naturally, Alignment API can be easily reused (and was reused as discussed in the paper) in the community-driven ontology matching approach.

COMA++ is a schema/ontology matching tool with an extensible library of matching algorithms, a framework for combining matching results, and a platform for the evaluation of the effectiveness of the different matchers [1]. At present, the COMA++ system is supported by its authors. It is written in Java and can be downloaded from the project web-site[12]. COMA++ handles ontologies expressed in OWL. This system supports the alignment reuse operation, although privately, being limited to the individual users of the system, who usually do not know each other, hence, they do not communicate with each other. In particular, COMA++ supports alignment reuse for entire ontologies and their fragments. Since the system is available only as an executable file, it requires additional efforts to be suitably incorporated within the community-driven ontology matching approach.

FOAM is a framework for ontology matching and alignment which is based on a semi-automatic combination of different heuristics/matchers [9, 8]. At present, the FOAM system is supported by its authors. It is an open source system written in Java and can be downloaded from the project web-site[13]. FOAM handles ontologies in OWL and RDF. The system is easy to install and use. The supporting documentation is also

---

[7] http://protege.stanford.edu/
[8] private communication
[9] http://kaon.semanticweb.org/
[10] http://sourceforge.net/projects/mafra-toolkit/
[11] http://co4.inrialpes.fr/align/align.html
[12] http://dbs.uni-leipzig.de/Research/coma.html
[13] http://www.aifb.uni-karlsruhe.de/WBS/meh/foam/

available. Thus, FOAM can be easily adapted for the settings of the community-driven ontology matching approach.

The above analysis (which has been carried out in more detail with about 15 systems in [24]) shows that though a relatively large number of ontology matching systems were elaborated, only a few of them are available for download and can be potentially reused. Further, we identified that neither of the current ontology matching approaches and tools employs community-related aspects, whenever such aspects have a potential to be beneficial for most of these approaches and tools. PROMPT, Alignment API, and FOAM correspond to our vision of a community-driven ontology matching tool most of all. Due to the above mentioned PROMPT's dependency on Protégé, Alignment API and FOAM (underway) were chosen to serve as a basis for the community-driven ontology matching prototype.

In general, it is worth noting that, for example, engineers of information integration systems would rather use existing matching systems than build their own. However, it is quite difficult to connect existing state of the art matching systems to other systems or embed them into the new environments. They are usually packaged as stand alone systems, designed for communication with a human user. In addition, they are not provided with an interface described in terms of abstract data types and logical functionality. Thus, integration of different matching systems into the new environments is itself a challenging task.

7 Conclusions

We have presented the community-driven ontology matching approach. A prototype supporting the approach was implemented and its usage was analyzed. The results demonstrate feasibility of acquisition and sharing of ontology mappings among the Web communities, thereby supporting, e.g., facilitated knowledge exchange within those communities. Also, by providing a repository of annotated mappings, which is a source of domain specific knowledge, the approach enables other ontology matching systems to produce potentially better results (e.g., a higher recall).

To step forwards, community-driven ontology matching needs more support for detailed alignment annotations and specific employment of information from user profiles, groups, communities, their goals and activities, e.g., in alignment recommendation mechanisms. Also, we are interested in further inclusion into the system of different matching algorithms as well as in the support for ontologies expressed in various (besides OWL) knowledge representation formalisms. Then, establishing protocols for machine to machine annotated alignments exchanges and a better end user interfaces are among the next steps towards a fully-fledged employment of the proposed approach. Finally, we are interested in applying the principles of community-driven ontology matching as a part of community-driven ontology management [23] in practical case studies, going beyond conventional scenarios at Semantic Web portals [6]. In particular, we want to investigate the benefits for human contributors from creating and reusing ontology mappings.

Acknowledgements. This work has been partly supported by the Knowledge Web European network of excellence (IST-2004-507482) and IP SPICE (IST-2006-027617).

References

1. D. Aumüller, H. H. Do, S. Massmann, and E. Rahm. Schema and ontology matching with COMA++. In *Proceedings of SIGMOD, Software Demonstration*, 2005.
2. P. Avesani, F. Giunchiglia, and M. Yatskevich. A large scale taxonomy mapping evaluation. In *Proceedings of ISWC*, pages 67 – 81, 2005.
3. S. Bechhofer, R. Volz, and P. Lord. Cooking the Semantic Web with the OWL API. In *Proceedings of ISWC*, pages 659–675, 2003.
4. P. Bouquet, F. Giunchiglia, F. van Harmelen, L. Serafini, and H. Stuckenschmidt. Contextualizing ontologies. *Journal of Web Semantics*, (26):1–19, 2004.
5. J. Carroll, I. Dickinson, C. Dollin, D. Reynolds, A. Seaborne, and K. Wilkinson. Jena: Implementing the Semantic Web recommendations. In *Proceedings of WWW*, pages 74–83, 2004.
6. O. Corcho, A. Gomez-Perez, A. Lopez-Cima, V. Lopez-Garcia, and M. Suarez-Figueroa. ODESeW. Automatic generation of knowledge portals for intranets and extranets. In *Proceedings of ISWC*, pages 802–817, 2003.
7. A. Doan and A. Halevy. Semantic integration research in the database community: A brief survey. *AI Magazine, Special Issue on Semantic Integration*, 2005.
8. M. Ehrig and S. Staab. QOM: Quick ontology mapping. In *Proceedings of ISWC*, pages 683–697, 2004.
9. M. Ehrig, S. Staab, and Y. Sure. Bootstrapping ontology alignment methods with APFEL. In *Proceedings of ISWC*, pages 186–200, 2005.
10. J. Euzenat. An API for ontology alignment. In *Proceedings of ISWC*, pages 698–712, 2004.
11. J. Euzenat, H. Stuckenschmidt, and M. Yatskevich. Introduction to the ontology alignment evaluation 2005. In *Proceedings of Integrating Ontologies workshop at K-CAP*, 2005.
12. F. Giunchiglia, P. Shvaiko, and M. Yatskevich. Semantic schema matching. In *Proceedings of CoopIS*, pages 347–365, 2005.
13. F. Giunchiglia, P. Shvaiko, and M. Yatskevich. Discovering missing background knowledge in ontology matching. Technical report, DIT-06-005, University of Trento, 2006.
14. J. Golbeck, P. Bonatti, W. Nejdl, D. Olmedilla, and M. Winslett, editors. *Proceedings of the ISWC'04 Workshop on Trust, Security, and Reputation on the Semantic Web*. 2004.
15. W. R. Hage, S. Katrenko, and G. Schreiber. A method to combine linguistic ontology-mapping techniques. In *Proceedings of ISWC*, pages 732–744, 2005.
16. I. Horrocks, P. Patel-Schneider, H. Boley, S. Tabet, B. Grosof, and M. Dean. SWRL: a semantic web rule language combining OWL and RuleML. Technical report, http://www.daml.org/rules/proposal/, 2004.
17. A. Maedche, B. Motik, N. Silva, and R. Volz. MAFRA - A MApping FRAmework for Distributed Ontologies. In *Proceedings of EKAW*, pages 235–250, 2002.
18. P. Mika. Ontologies are us: A unified model of social networks and semantics. In *Proceedings of ISWC*, pages 522–536, 2005.
19. N. Noy. Semantic Integration: A survey of ontology-based approaches. *SIGMOD Record*, 33(4):65–70, 2004.
20. N. Noy and M. Musen. The PROMPT Suite: Interactive tools for ontology merging and mapping. *International Journal of Human-Computer Studies*, (59(6)):983–1024, 2003.
21. E. Rahm and P. Bernstein. A survey of approaches to automatic schema matching. *The VLDB Journal*, (10(4)):334–350, 2001.
22. P. Shvaiko and J. Euzenat. A survey of schema-based matching approaches. *Journal on Data Semantics*, (IV):146–171, 2005.

23. A. V. Zhdanova. The people's portal: Ontology management on community portals. In *Proceedings of the workshop on Friend of a Friend, Social Networking and the Semantic Web (FOAF)*, 2004.

24. A. V. Zhdanova, J. de Bruijn, K. Zimmermann, and F. Scharffe. Ontology alignment solution v2.0. EU IST Esperonto project deliverable (D1.4), 2004.

25. A. V. Zhdanova, R. Krummenacher, J. Henke, and D. Fensel. Community-driven ontology management: DERI case study. In *Proceedings of WI*, pages 73–79, 2005.

Reconciling Concepts and Relations in Heterogeneous Ontologies

Chiara Ghidini and Luciano Serafini

ITC-IRST
Via Sommarive 18
I-38040 Trento, Italy
{ghidini, serafini}@itc.it

Abstract. In the extensive usage of ontologies envisaged by the Semantic Web there is a compelling need for expressing mappings between the components of heterogeneous ontologies. These mappings are of many different forms and involve the different components of ontologies. State of the art languages for ontology mapping enable to express semantic relations between homogeneous components of different ontologies, namely they allow to map concepts into concepts, individuals into individuals, and properties into properties. Many real cases, however, highlight the necessity to establish semantic relations between heterogeneous components. For example to map a concept into a relation or vice versa. To support the interoperability of ontologies we need therefore to enrich mapping languages with constructs for the representation of *heterogeneous mappings*. In this paper, we propose an extension of Distributed Description Logics (DDL) to allow for the representation of mapping between concepts and relations. We provide a semantics of the proposed language and show its main logical properties.

1 Introduction

In the extensive usage of ontologies envisaged by the Semantic Web there is a compelling need for expressing mappings between different and heterogeneous ontologies. These mappings are of many different forms and involve the different components of ontologies.

Most of the formalisms for distributed ontology integration, which are based on the p2p architecture [12], provide a language to express semantic relations between concepts belonging to different ontologies. These classes of languages are usually called *mapping languages* [11, 9]. These formalisms can express that a concept, say MarriedMan, in Ontology 1 is equivalent to the concept Husband in Ontology 2, or that the concept Benedict in Ontology 3 is more specific that the concept Relative in Ontology 4. Few mapping languages allow also to express semantic relations between properties in different ontologies (see [7, 5]). However, to the best of our knowledge, none of the existing approaches support mappings between properties and concepts. Such mappings are necessary to express the semantic relations between two ontologies, when the information represented as a concept in the former is represented as a relation in the

Y. Sure and J. Domingue (Eds.): ESWC 2006, LNCS 4011, pp. 50–64, 2006.

latter, or vice versa. As a practical example consider two ontologies. The first one is the ontology http://www.daml.org/2001/01/gedcom/gedcom which contains the concept Family and the property spouseIn. Family represents the set of families, and spouseIn relates a Human with the family in which he/she is one of the spouses. The second one is the ontology http://ontologyportal.org/translations/SUMO.owl, which contains the relation spouse, which represents the relationship of marriage between two Humans. In integrating these two ontologies one would like to state, for instance, that every family in the first ontology can be mapped into a married couple in the second ontology, or in other words, that that the concept Family can be mapped into the relation spouse.

The goal of this paper is to extend a language for ontology mapping, an to introduce mechanisms for the representation of *heterogeneous mappings* between ontologies. We focus on the mappings between concepts and relations as they provide a challenging example of ontology mismatch, we describe their formal semantics and we study their main properties. We adopt the formal framework of Distributed Description Logics (DDL) [10] because it is a formalism which is explicitly constructed to state expressive relations between heterogeneous languages and domains of interpretation. Summarizing, the claimed contributions of this paper are: (i) an expressive mapping language for heterogeneous ontologies; (ii) a clear semantics for the proposed mapping language, and (iii) an investigation of its basic logical properties.

The paper is structured as follows: in Section 2 we motivate our work with a detailed example. In Section 3 we provide an extension of DDL to represent heterogeneous mappings. In Section 4 we study the main properties of the proposed logic. We end with related work (Section 5) and some final remarks (Section 6).

2   A Motivating Example

Let us consider two ontologies from the web. The first is an extensive ontology describing the domain of Geography developed by a corporation[1], the second is the DAML+OIL representation of the 2001 CIA World Fact Book[2]. We call the first Ontology 1, and the second Ontology 2. Looking at the ontologies in detail we have noticed that both need to represent the notion of geographic coordinates. Figures 1 and 2 report the definition of geographic coordinates from the two ontologies.

While the two ontologies are interested in describing the geographic coordinate system of Earth, they have specific views on how to describe this domain of knowledge. Rather than giving a detailed formalization of the example, we focus on the key elements that are affected by the representation of geographical coordinates in the two ontologies. Ontology 1 does not contain an explicit notion of position on hearth (or geographical coordinate), and expresses positions in terms of Latitude and Longitude (see Figure 1). Ontology 2 takes a different perspective and expresses geographical coordinates as a specific concept LatLon,

---

[1] See http://reliant.teknowledge.com/DAML/Geography.daml
[2] See http://www.daml.org/2001/12/factbook/factbook-ont

```
<rdfs:Class rdf:ID= "Latitude">
  <rdfs:subClassOf
    rdf:resource = "http://reliant.teknowledge.com/DAML/SUMO.owl#Region"/>
  <rdfs:label>latitude</rdfs:label>
  <rdfs:label>parallel</rdfs:label>
  <rdfs:comment>Latitude is the class of Regions,
    associated with areas on the Earth's surface, which are parallels
    measured in PlaneAngleDegrees from the Equator.</rdfs:comment>
</rdfs:Class>

<rdfs:Class rdf:ID= "Longitude">
  <rdfs:subClassOf
    rdf:resource ="http://reliant.teknowledge.com/DAML/SUMO.owl#Region"/>
  <rdfs:label>longitude</rdfs:label>
  <rdfs:label>meridian</rdfs:label>
  <rdfs:comment>Longitude is the class of Regions, associated with areas
    on the Earth's surface, which are meridians measured in PlaneAngleDegrees
    from the PrimeMeridian through GreenwichEnglandUK.</rdfs:comment>
  </rdfs:Class>
```

Fig. 1. Position = Latitude + Longitude

```
<owl:Class rdf:ID="LatLon">
  <rdfs:subClassOf>
    <owl:Restriction>
      <owl:onProperty rdf:resource="#latitude"/>
      <owl:allValuesFrom rdf:resource="&xsd;double"/>
      <factbook:units>degrees</factbook:units>
    </owl:Restriction>
  </rdfs:subClassOf>
  <rdfs:subClassOf>
    <owl:Restriction>
      <owl:onProperty rdf:resource="#longitude"/>
      <owl:allValuesFrom rdf:resource="&xsd;double"/>
      <factbook:units>degrees</factbook:units>
    </owl:Restriction>
  </rdfs:subClassOf>
</owl:Class>
```

Fig. 2. Position = Object with two properties: Latitude and Longitude

which has two properties represented by the roles latitude and longitude which
are numbers of type Double (see Figure 2). A graphical representation of two
different representations of geographical coordinates inspired by the definitions
in Figures 1 and 2 is given in Figure 3. Despite the different choices made by the
ontology designers, there is clear relation between Ontology 1 and Ontology 2,
and in particular between the concepts Latitude and Longitude and the properties
(roles) latitude and longitude, respectively.

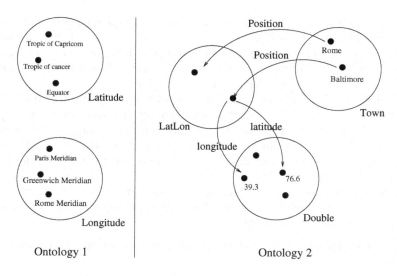

Fig. 3. Representing geographical positions

State of the art formalisms for the representation of distributed ontologies and reasoning, would do very little with this example, except perhaps identifying that Latitude and Longitude in Ontology 1 are related with Double in Ontology 2 (assuming that Latitude and Longitude are represented as doubles also in Ontology 1). But this is an hardly informative mapping, as it does not capture the essential fact that both ontologies are describing the geographic coordinate system of Earth.

3 An Expressive Mapping Language

Description Logic (DL) has been advocated as the suitable formal tool to represent and reason about ontologies. Distributed Description Logic (DDL) [3, 10] is a *natural* generalization of the DL framework designed to formalize multiple ontologies interconnected by semantic mappings. As defined in [3, 10], *Distributed Description Logic* provides a syntactical and semantical framework for formalization of multiple ontologies *pairwise* linked by semantic mappings. In DDL, ontologies correspond to description logic theories (T-boxes), while semantic mappings correspond to collections of *bridge rules* ($\mathfrak{B}$).

In the following we recall the basic definitions of DDL as defined in [10], and we extend the set of bridge rules, introducing new semantic mappings between distributed ontologies.

3.1 Distributed Description Logics: The syntax

Given a non empty set I of indexes, used to identify ontologies, let $\{\mathcal{DL}_i\}_{i \in I}$ be a collection of description logics[3]. For each $i \in I$ let us denote a T-box of

---

[3] We assume familiarity with Description Logic and related reasoning systems, described in [1].

$\mathcal{DL}_i$ as $\mathcal{T}_i$. In this paper, we assume that each $\mathcal{DL}_i$ is description logic weaker or at most equivalent to $\mathcal{SHIQ}$. Thus a T-box will contain all the information necessary to define the terminology of a domain, including not just concept and role definitions, but also general axioms relating descriptions, as well as declarations such as the transitivity of certain roles.

We call $\mathbf{T} = \{\mathcal{T}_i\}_{i \in I}$ a family of T-Boxes indexed by I. Intuitively, $\mathcal{T}_i$ is the description logic formalization of the i-th ontology. To make every description distinct, we will prefix it with the index of ontology it belongs to. For instance, the concept C that occurs in the i-th ontology is denoted as $i : C$. Similarly, $i : C \sqsubseteq D$ denotes the fact that the axiom $C \sqsubseteq D$ is being considered in the i-th ontology.

Semantic mappings between different ontologies are expressed via collections of *bridge rules*. In the following we use A and B as placeholders for concepts and R and S as placeholders for relations.

Definition 1 (Bridge rules). *A bridge rule from i to j is an expression defined as follows:*

$$i : A \xrightarrow{\sqsupseteq} j : B \qquad \text{(concept-onto-concept bridge rule)} \qquad (1)$$

$$i : A \xrightarrow{\sqsubseteq} j : B \qquad \text{(concept-into-concept bridge rule)} \qquad (2)$$

$$i : R \xrightarrow{\sqsupseteq} j : S \qquad \text{(role-onto-role bridge rule)} \qquad (3)$$

$$i : R \xrightarrow{\sqsubseteq} j : S \qquad \text{(role-into-role bridge rule)} \qquad (4)$$

$$i : A \xrightarrow{\sqsupseteq} j : R \qquad \text{(concept-onto-role bridge rule)} \qquad (5)$$

$$i : A \xrightarrow{\sqsubseteq} j : R \qquad \text{(concept-into-role bridge rule)} \qquad (6)$$

$$i : R \xrightarrow{\sqsupseteq} j : A \qquad \text{(role-onto-concept bridge rule)} \qquad (7)$$

$$i : R \xrightarrow{\sqsubseteq} j : A \qquad \text{(role-into-concept bridge rule)} \qquad (8)$$

where A and B are concepts of $\mathcal{DL}_i$ and $\mathcal{DL}_j$ respectively, and R and S are roles of $\mathcal{DL}_i$ and $\mathcal{DL}_j$ respectively. Bridge rules (1)–(4) are called homogeneous bridge rules, and bridge rules (5)–(8) are called heterogeneous bridge rules.

Bridge rules do not represent semantic relations stated from an external *objective* point of view. Indeed, there is no such global view in the web. Instead, bridge rules from i to j express relations between i and j viewed from the *subjective* point of view of the j-th ontology. Let us discuss the different mapping categories.

Homogeneous bridge rules. Bridge rules (1) and (2) have been introduced and studied in [3, 10] with the name of *onto-bridge rule* and *into-bridge rule*, respectively. Intuitively, the concept-into-concept bridge rule $i : A \xrightarrow{\sqsubseteq} j : B$ states that, from the j-th point of view the concept A in i is less general than its local concept B. Similarly, the concept-onto-concept bridge rule $i : A \xrightarrow{\sqsupseteq} j : B$ expresses the fact that, according to j, A in i is more general than B in j. Therefore, bridge rules from i to j provide the possibility of translating into j's ontology (under some approximation) the concepts of a foreign i's ontology. Note, that since bridge rules reflect a subjective point of view, bridge rules from j to i are not necessarily the inverse of the rules from i to j, and in fact bridge rules from i to j do not force the existence of bridge rules in the opposite direction. Thus, the bridge rule

$$i : \mathsf{Article} \xrightarrow{\;\sqsupseteq\;} j : \mathsf{ConferencePaper} \tag{9}$$

expresses the fact that, according to ontology j, the concept Article in ontology i is more general than its local concept ConferencePapers, while the bridge rules

$$i : \mathsf{Article} \xrightarrow{\;\sqsubseteq\;} j : \mathsf{Article} \tag{10}$$

$$i : \mathsf{Article} \xrightarrow{\;\sqsupseteq\;} j : \mathsf{Article} \tag{11}$$

say that, according to ontology j, the concept Article in ontology j is equivalent to its local concept Article. Bridge rules (3) and (4) formalize the analogous intuition for roles. For example, the bridge rule:

$$i : \mathsf{marriedTo} \xrightarrow{\;\sqsubseteq\;} j : \mathsf{partnerOf}$$

says that according to ontology j, the relation marriedTo in ontology i is less general than its own relation partnerOf.

Heterogeneous bridge rules. Bridge rules (5) and (6) define how concepts are mapped into roles. Bridge rule (5) states that from the point of view of j concept A in Ontology i corresponds to its own relation R and A is less general than R. Bridge rule (6), on the contrary, states that A is more general than R. For instance, the bridge rule:

$$1 : \mathsf{Latitude} \xrightarrow{\;\sqsupseteq\;} 2 : \mathsf{latitude}$$

says that according to ontology 2, concept Latitude in ontology 1 is more general than its own relation latitude. That is all latitudes in its own ontology have a corresponding Latitude in ontology 1.

Bridge rules (7) and (8) define how roles are mapped into concepts, and are the counterpart of bridge rules (5) and (6). Bridge rule (7) says that from the point of view of j role A in Ontology i corresponds to its own concept A and R is less general than A. Bridge rule (8), on the contrary, states that R is more general than A. For example, the bridge rule:

$$1 : \mathsf{spouse} \xrightarrow{\;\sqsubseteq\;} 2 : \mathsf{Family}$$

states that every married couple in ontology 1, can be mapped into a family in ontology 2. Similarly the bridge rule. Similarly the bridge rule

$$1 : \mathsf{WorksFor} \xrightarrow{\;\sqsupseteq\;} 2 : \mathsf{WorkingContract}$$

states that every working contract in ontology 2 corresponds to some working relation in ontology 1.

Bridge rules (5)– (8) are important examples of heterogeneous mappings between ontologies, but the list of heterogeneous bridge rules presented in this paper is by no means complete. We have chosen to study the mappings between relations and concepts as they are a clear and interesting example of heterogeneous mapings. To address the problem of ontology mapping and alignment in full, other forms of heterogeneous mappings need to be investigated, among them mappings between individuals and concepts and even more complex mappings involving interconnected parts of different ontologies.

Definition 2 (Distributed T-box). *A distributed T-box (DTB)*

$$\mathfrak{T} = \langle \{\mathcal{T}_i\}_{i \in I}, \mathfrak{B} \rangle$$

consists of a collection $\{\mathcal{T}_i\}_{i \in I}$ *of T-boxes, and a collection* $\mathfrak{B} = \{\mathfrak{B}_{ij}\}_{i \neq j \in I}$ *of bridge rules between them.*

3.2   Distributed Description Logics: The semantics

The semantic of DDL, which is a customization of Local Models Semantics [6, 7], assigns to each ontology $\mathcal{T}_i$ a *local interpretation domain*. The first component of an interpretation of a DTB is a family of interpretations $\{\mathcal{I}_i\}_{i \in I}$, one for each T-box $\mathcal{T}_i$. Each $\mathcal{I}_i$ is called a *local interpretation* and consists of a *possibly empty* domain $\Delta^{\mathcal{I}_i}$ and a valuation function $\cdot^{\mathcal{I}_i}$, which maps every concept to a subset of $\Delta^{\mathcal{I}_i}$, and every role to a subset of $\Delta^{\mathcal{I}_i} \times \Delta^{\mathcal{I}_i}$. The interpretation on the empty domain is denoted with the apex ϵ.

Notice that, in DL, interpretations are defined always on a non empty domain. Therefore $\mathcal{I}^\epsilon$ is not an interpretation in DL. In DDL however we need to provide a semantics for *partially inconsistent* distributed T-boxes, i.e. DTBs in which some of the local T-boxes are inconsistent. $\mathcal{I}^\epsilon$ provides an "impossible interpretation" which can be associated to inconsistent T-boxes. Indeed, $\mathcal{I}^\epsilon$ satisfies every axiom $X \sqsubseteq Y$ (also $\top \sqsubseteq \bot$) since $X^{\mathcal{I}^\epsilon} = \emptyset$ for every concept and role X.

The second component of the DDL semantic are families of domain relations. Domain relations define how the different T-box interact and are necessary to define the satisfiability of bridge rules.

Definition 3 (Domain relation). *A domain relation* r_{ij} *from* $\Delta^{\mathcal{I}_i}$ *to* $\Delta^{\mathcal{I}_j}$ *is a subset of* $\Delta^{\mathcal{I}_i} \times \Delta^{\mathcal{I}_j}$. *We use* $r_{ij}(d)$ *to denote* $\{d' \in \Delta^{\mathcal{I}_j} \mid \langle d, d' \rangle \in r_{ij}\}$; *for any subset D of* $\Delta^{\mathcal{I}_i}$, *we use* $r_{ij}(D)$ *to denote* $\bigcup_{d \in D} r_{ij}(d)$; *for any* $R \subseteq \Delta^{\mathcal{I}_i} \times \Delta^{\mathcal{I}_i}$ *we use* $r_{ij}(R)$ *to denote* $\bigcup_{\langle d, d' \rangle \in R} r_{ij}(d) \times r_{ij}(d')$.

A domain relation r_{ij} represents a possible way of mapping the elements of $\Delta^{\mathcal{I}_i}$ into its domain $\Delta^{\mathcal{I}_j}$, seen from j's perspective. For instance, if $\Delta^{\mathcal{I}_1}$ and $\Delta^{\mathcal{I}_2}$ are the representation of time as Rationals and as Naturals, r_{ij} could be the round off function, or some other approximation relation. This function has to be conservative w.r.t., the order relations defined on Rationals and Naturals.

Domain relation is used to interpret homogeneous bridge rules according with the following definition.

Definition 4 (Satisfiability of homogeneous bridge rules). *The domain relation r_{ij} satisfies a homogeneous bridge rule w.r.t., $\mathcal{I}_i$ and $\mathcal{I}_j$, in symbols $\langle \mathcal{I}_i, r_{ij}, \mathcal{I}_j \rangle \models br$, according with the following definition:*

1. $\langle \mathcal{I}_i, r_{ij}, \mathcal{I}_j \rangle \models i : A \xrightarrow{\sqsubseteq} j : B$, if $r_{ij}(A^{\mathcal{I}_i}) \subseteq B^{\mathcal{I}_j}$
2. $\langle \mathcal{I}_i, r_{ij}, \mathcal{I}_j \rangle \models i : A \xrightarrow{\sqsupseteq} j : B$, if $r_{ij}(A^{\mathcal{I}_i}) \supseteq B^{\mathcal{I}_j}$

where A and B are either two concept expressions or two role expressions.

Domain relations do not provide sufficient information to evaluate the satisfiability of heterogeneous mappings. Intuitively, an heterogeneous bridge rule between a relation R and a concept A connects a pair of objects related by R with an object which is in A. This suggests that, to evaluate heterogeneous bridge rules from roles in i to concepts in j one needs a relation that maps pair of objects in $\Delta^{\mathcal{I}_i}$ into objects of $\Delta^{\mathcal{I}_j}$, and to evaluate a heterogeneous bridge rule from concepts in i to roles in j one needs a relation that maps objects in $\Delta^{\mathcal{I}_i}$ into pairs of objects in $\Delta^{\mathcal{I}_j}$.

Definition 5 (Concept-role and role-concept domain relation). *A concept-role domain relation cr_{ij} from $\Delta^{\mathcal{I}_i}$ to $\Delta^{\mathcal{I}_j}$ is a subset of $\Delta^{\mathcal{I}_i} \times \Delta^{\mathcal{I}_i} \times \Delta^{\mathcal{I}_j}$. A role-concept domain relation rc_{ij} from $\Delta^{\mathcal{I}_i}$ to $\Delta^{\mathcal{I}_j}$ is a subset of $\Delta^{\mathcal{I}_i} \times \Delta^{\mathcal{I}_j} \times \Delta^{\mathcal{I}_j}$.*

We use $cr_{ij}(d)$ to denote $\{\langle d_1, d_2 \rangle \in \Delta^{\mathcal{I}_j} \times \Delta^{\mathcal{I}_j} \mid \langle d, d_1, d_2 \rangle \in cr_{ij}\}$; for any subset D of $\Delta^{\mathcal{I}_i}$, we use $cr_{ij}(D)$ to denote $\bigcup_{d \in D} cr_{ij}(d)$. We use $rc_{ij}(\langle d_1, d_2 \rangle)$ to denote $\{d \in \Delta^{\mathcal{I}_j} \mid \langle d_1, d_2, d \rangle \in rc_{ij}\}$; for any subset R of $\Delta^{\mathcal{I}_i} \times \Delta^{\mathcal{I}_i}$, we use $rc_{ij}(R)$ to denote $\bigcup_{\langle d_1, d_2 \rangle \in R} rc_{ij}(\langle d_1, d_2 \rangle)$.

Domain relation cr_{ij} represents a possible way of mapping elements of $\Delta^{\mathcal{I}_i}$ into pairs of elements in $\Delta^{\mathcal{I}_j}$, seen from j's perspective. For instance, if $\Delta^{\mathcal{I}_1}$ and $\Delta^{\mathcal{I}_2}$ are the representation of geographical coordinates as in Figure 4, cr_{12} could be the function mapping latitude values into the corresponding latitudes. For instance, by setting

$$cr_{12}(\mathsf{TropicOfCancer}^{\mathcal{I}_1}) = \{\langle x, 23.27 \rangle \in \mathsf{latitude}^{\mathcal{I}_2}\}$$

we can represent the fact that the tropic of cancer is associated with pairs of objects $\langle x, y \rangle$ such that y is the latitude of x and y is equal to 23.27 (the latitude of the tropic of cancer). Vice-versa a domain relation rc_{ij} represents a possible way of mapping a pair of $\Delta^{\mathcal{I}_i}$ into the corresponding element in $\Delta^{\mathcal{I}_j}$. For instance, if the pair $\langle \mathsf{John}^{\mathcal{I}_1}, \mathsf{Mary}^{\mathcal{I}_1} \rangle \in \mathsf{spouse}^{\mathcal{I}_1}$, then the fact that

$$rc_{12}(\mathsf{John}^{\mathcal{I}_1}, \mathsf{Mary}^{\mathcal{I}_1}) = \mathsf{family23}^{\mathcal{I}_2}$$

represents the fact that family23 is the family containing the married couple of John and Mary.

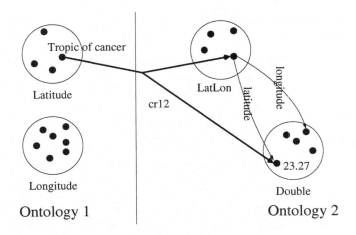

Fig. 4. Concept-role domain relation

Definition 6 (Satisfiability of heterogeneous bridge rules). *The concept-role domain relation cr_{ij} satisfies a concept to role bridge rule w.r.t., $\mathcal{I}_i$ and $\mathcal{I}_j$, in symbols $\langle \mathcal{I}_i, cr_{ij}, \mathcal{I}_j \rangle \models br$, according with the following definition:*

1. $\langle \mathcal{I}_i, cr_{ij}, \mathcal{I}_j \rangle \models i : A \xrightarrow{\sqsubseteq} j : R$, *if* $cr_{ij}(A^{\mathcal{I}_i}) \subseteq R^{\mathcal{I}_j}$
2. $\langle \mathcal{I}_i, cr_{ij}, \mathcal{I}_j \rangle \models i : A \xrightarrow{\sqsupseteq} j : R$, *if* $cr_{ij}(A^{\mathcal{I}_i}) \supseteq R^{\mathcal{I}_j}$

where A is a concept expression of i and R a role expression of j.
The role-concept domain relation rc_{ij} satisfies a role to concept bridge rule w.r.t., $\mathcal{I}_i$ and $\mathcal{I}_j$, in symbols $\langle \mathcal{I}_i, rc_{ij}, \mathcal{I}_j \rangle \models br$, according with the following definition:

1. $\langle \mathcal{I}_i, rc_{ij}, \mathcal{I}_j \rangle \models i : R \xrightarrow{\sqsubseteq} j : A$, *if* $rc_{ij}(R^{\mathcal{I}_i}) \subseteq A^{\mathcal{I}_j}$
2. $\langle \mathcal{I}_i, rc_{ij}, \mathcal{I}_j \rangle \models i : R \xrightarrow{\sqsupseteq} j : A$, *if* $rc_{ij}(R^{\mathcal{I}_i}) \supseteq A^{\mathcal{I}_j}$

where A is a concept expression of j and R a role expression of i.

Definition 7 (Distributed interpretation). A distributed interpretation

$$\mathfrak{I} = \langle \{\mathcal{I}_i\}_{i \in I}, \{r_{ij}\}_{i \neq j \in I}, \{cr_{ij}\}_{i \neq j \in I}, \{rc_{ij}\}_{i \neq j \in I} \rangle$$

of a DTB $\mathfrak{T}$ consists of local interpretations $\mathcal{I}_i$ for each $\mathcal{T}_i$ on local domains $\Delta^{\mathcal{I}_i}$, and families of domain relations r_{ij}, cr_{ij} and rc_{ij} between these local domains.

Definition 8 (Satisfiability of a Distributed T-box). *A distributed interpretation $\mathfrak{I}$ satisfies the elements of a DTB $\mathfrak{T}$ according to the following clauses: for every $i, j \in I$*

1. $\mathfrak{I} \models i : A \sqsubseteq B$, *if* $\mathcal{I}_i \models A \sqsubseteq B$
2. $\mathfrak{I} \models \mathcal{T}_i$, *if* $\mathfrak{I} \models i : A \sqsubseteq B$ *for all* $A \sqsubseteq B$ *in* $\mathcal{T}_i$
3. $\mathfrak{I} \models \mathfrak{B}_{ij}$, *if*

- $\langle \mathcal{I}_i, r_{ij}, \mathcal{I}_j \rangle$ *satisfies all the homogeneous bridge rules in* $\mathfrak{B}_{ij}$,
- $\langle \mathcal{I}_i, cr_{ij}, \mathcal{I}_j \rangle$ *satisfies all the concept-to-role bridge rules in* $\mathfrak{B}_{ij}$,
- $\langle \mathcal{I}_i, rc_{ij}, \mathcal{I}_j \rangle$ *satisfies all the role-to-concept bridge rules in* $\mathfrak{B}_{ij}$

4. $\mathfrak{I} \models \mathfrak{T}$, *if for every* $i, j \in I$, $\mathfrak{I} \models \mathcal{T}_i$ *and* $\mathfrak{I} \models \mathfrak{B}_{ij}$

Definition 9 (Distributed Entailment and Satisfiability). $\mathfrak{T} \models i : C \sqsubseteq D$ *(read as "$\mathfrak{T}$ entails $i : C \sqsubseteq D$") if for every* $\mathfrak{I}$, $\mathfrak{I} \models \mathfrak{T}$ *implies* $\mathfrak{I} \models_d i : C \sqsubseteq D$. $\mathfrak{T}$ *is* satisfiable *if there exists a* $\mathfrak{I}$ *such that* $\mathfrak{I} \models \mathfrak{T}$. *Concept* $i : C$ *is* satisfiable *with respect to* $\mathfrak{T}$ *if there is a* $\mathfrak{I}$ *such that* $\mathfrak{I} \models \mathfrak{T}$ *and* $C^{\mathcal{I}_i} \neq \emptyset$.

4 Characterizing Mappings

In this section we enunciate the most important properties of the extended version of DDL and for each result we provide an example that explains why this property is desirable. We assume familiarity with Description Logics, and in particular with $\mathcal{SHIQ}$. Symbols, $\sqcup$, $\sqcap$, and $^-$ denote the usual union, intersection, and inverse operators of Description Logics. Similarly, $\exists R.C$ is used to denote the existential restriction.

Theorem 1 (General property). *If* $\mathfrak{I} \models i : A \xrightarrow{\sqsupseteq} j : G$, *and* $\mathfrak{I} \models i : B \xrightarrow{\sqsubseteq} j : H$, *then*

$$\mathfrak{I} \models i : A \sqsubseteq B \Longrightarrow \mathfrak{I} \models j : G \sqsubseteq H \tag{12}$$

where the pair A and B and the pair G and H are pairs of homogeneous elements, that is either pairs of concepts or pairs of roles.

Example 1. Let

- $\mathfrak{I} \models i :$ Article $\xrightarrow{\sqsupseteq} j :$ ConferencePaper, and
- $\mathfrak{I} \models i :$ Article $\xrightarrow{\sqsubseteq} j :$ ScientificArticle.

Theorem 1 allows to infer that a conference paper is a Scientific article in O_j, namely $\mathfrak{I} \models j :$ ConferencePaper $\sqsubseteq$ Article, from the fact that $\mathfrak{I} \models i :$ Article $\sqsubseteq$ Article. Similarly, let

- $\mathfrak{I} \models i :$ Couple $\xrightarrow{\sqsupseteq} j :$ partnerOf, and
- $\mathfrak{I} \models i :$ Family $\xrightarrow{\sqsubseteq} j :$ spouseIn $\sqcup$ childIn,

where Couple and Family are concepts and partnerOf, and spouseIn relations. If $\mathfrak{I} \models i :$ Couple $\sqsubseteq$ Family, then $\mathfrak{I} \models j :$ partnerOf $\sqsubseteq$ spouseIn $\sqcup$ childIn.

Theorem 2 (Concept into/onto concept). *If* $\mathfrak{I} \models i : A \xrightarrow{\sqsupseteq} j : G$, *and* $\mathfrak{I} \models i : B_k \xrightarrow{\sqsubseteq} j : H_k$ *for* $1 \leq k \leq n$ *(with* $n \geq 0$*), then:*

$$\mathfrak{I} \models i : A \sqsubseteq \bigsqcup_{k=1}^{n} B_k \Longrightarrow \mathfrak{I} \models j : G \sqsubseteq \bigsqcup_{k=1}^{n} H_k \tag{13}$$

where A, G, B_k and H_k ($1 \leq k \leq n$) are concepts.

Example 2. Let

- $\mathfrak{I} \models i :$ ArchivalPublication $\xrightarrow{\sqsupseteq} j :$ ArchivalPublication,
- $\mathfrak{I} \models i :$ ConferencePaper $\xrightarrow{\sqsubseteq} j :$ Article, and
- $\mathfrak{I} \models i :$ BookChapter $\xrightarrow{\sqsubseteq} j :$ Article.

Theorem 3 guarantees that if $\mathfrak{I} \models i :$ ArchivalPublication $\sqsubseteq$ ConferencePaper $\sqcup$ BookChapter then $\mathfrak{I} \models j :$ ArchivalPublication $\sqsubseteq$ Article.

Theorem 3 (Concept into/onto role). *If* $\mathfrak{I} \models i : A \xrightarrow{\sqsupseteq} j : R$, *and* $\mathfrak{I} \models i : B_k \xrightarrow{\sqsubseteq} j : S_k$ *for* $1 \le k \le n$ *(with* $n \ge 0$), *then:*

$$\mathfrak{I} \models i : A \sqsubseteq \bigsqcup_{k=1}^{n} B_k \Longrightarrow \mathfrak{I} \models j : \exists R.X \sqsubseteq \bigsqcup_{k=1}^{n} \exists S_k.X \tag{14}$$

where A *and* B_k *(*$1 \le k \le n$*) are concepts,* R *and* S_k *(*$1 \le k \le n$*) are roles, and* X *is any arbitrary concept.*

Example 3. Let

- $\mathfrak{I} \models i :$ Parent $\xrightarrow{\sqsupseteq} j :$ hasChild,
- $\mathfrak{I} \models i :$ Mother $\xrightarrow{\sqsubseteq} j :$ motherOf, and
- $\mathfrak{I} \models i :$ Father $\xrightarrow{\sqsubseteq} j :$ fatherOf, and

where Parent, Mother and Father are concepts, while hasChild, motherOf and fatherOf are relations. If $\mathfrak{I} \models i :$ Parent $\sqsubseteq$ Mother $\sqcup$ Father, then $\mathfrak{I} \models j :$ $\exists$hasChild.$X \sqsubseteq \exists$motherOf.$X \sqcup \exists$fatherOf.X, for any concept X.

Theorem 4 (Role into/onto role).

$$\text{If } \mathfrak{I} \models i : R \xrightarrow{\sqsubseteq} j : S, \text{ then } \mathfrak{I} \models i : R^- \xrightarrow{\sqsubseteq} j : S^- \tag{15}$$

$$\text{If } \mathfrak{I} \models i : R \xrightarrow{\sqsupseteq} j : S, \text{ then } \mathfrak{I} \models i : R^- \xrightarrow{\sqsupseteq} j : S^-, \tag{16}$$

Example 4. Let $\mathfrak{I} \models i :$ marriedTo $\xrightarrow{\sqsupseteq} j :$ partnerOf, then $\mathfrak{I} \models i :$ marriedTo$^- \xrightarrow{\sqsupseteq}$ $j :$ partnerOf$^-$. Similarly for the into case.

Corollary 1 (Role into/onto concept). *If* $\mathfrak{I} \models i : R \xrightarrow{\sqsupseteq} j : A$, *and* $\mathfrak{I} \models i : S \xrightarrow{\sqsubseteq} j : B_k$ *for* $1 \le k \le n$ *(with* $n \ge 0$), *then:*

$$\mathfrak{I} \models i : R \sqsubseteq S \Longrightarrow \mathfrak{I} \models j : A \sqsubseteq \bigsqcup_{k=1}^{n} B_k \tag{17}$$

$$\mathfrak{I} \models i : R \sqsubseteq S \Longrightarrow \mathfrak{I} \models j : A \sqsubseteq \bigsqcap_{k=1}^{n} B_k \tag{18}$$

where R, *and* S *are roles and* A *and* B_k *(*$1 \le k \le n$*) are concepts.*

Example 5. Let

- $\Im \models i :$ holdsSeasonalTicketOf $\overset{\sqsupseteq}{\longrightarrow} j :$ SeasonalTicketHolder
- $\Im \models i :$ supporterOf $\overset{\sqsubseteq}{\longrightarrow} j :$ Person, and
- $\Im \models i :$ supporterOf $\overset{\sqsubseteq}{\longrightarrow} j :$ JuventusFan

where holdsSeasonalTicketOf, Person and JuventusFan are concepts, while SeasonalTicketHolder, supporterOf and JuventusFan are relations. If

$$\Im \models i : \text{holdsSeasonalTicketOf} \sqsubseteq \text{supporterOf}$$

then

$$\Im \models i : \text{SeasonalTicketHolder} \sqsubseteq \text{Person} \sqcup \text{JuventusFan}$$

and

$$\Im \models i : \text{SeasonalTicketHolder} \sqsubseteq \text{Person} \sqcap \text{JuventusFan}$$

Corollary 2 (concept into/onto role). *If $\Im \models i : A \overset{\sqsupseteq}{\longrightarrow} j : R$, and $\Im \models i : B \overset{\sqsubseteq}{\longrightarrow} j : S$, then:*

$$\Im \models i : A \sqsubseteq B \Longrightarrow \Im \models j : R^- \sqsubseteq S^- \tag{19}$$

where A, and B are concepts and R and S are roles.

Example 6. Let

- $\Im \models i :$ Mother $\overset{\sqsupseteq}{\longrightarrow} j :$ motherOf
- $\Im \models i :$ Parent $\overset{\sqsubseteq}{\longrightarrow} j :$ hasChild,

where Parent, and Mother are concepts, while hasChild, and motherOf are relations. If $\Im \models i :$ Mother $\sqsubseteq$ Parent, then $\Im \models j :$ motherOf$^-$ $\sqsubseteq$ hasChild$^-$.

Corollary 3 (role into/onto role). *If $\Im \models i : R \overset{\sqsupseteq}{\longrightarrow} j : P$, and $\Im \models i : S \overset{\sqsubseteq}{\longrightarrow} j : Q$, then:*

$$\Im \models i : R \sqsubseteq S^- \Longrightarrow \Im \models j : P \sqsubseteq Q^- \tag{20}$$

where R, S P and Q are roles.

Example 7. Let

- $\Im \models i :$ marriedTo $\overset{\sqsupseteq}{\longrightarrow} j :$ partnerOf, and
- $\Im \models i :$ livingWith $\overset{\sqsupseteq}{\longrightarrow} j :$ friendOf.

If $\Im \models i :$ marriedTo $\sqsubseteq$ leavingWith$^-$, then $\Im \models j :$ partnerOf $\sqsubseteq$ FriendOf$^-$.

Theorem 5 (Role union). *If the DL includes role union $R \sqcup S$, then Theorem 2 can be generalised to all bridge rules, with the only constraint of A and B_k and G and H_k families of homogeneous elements, that is either families of concepts or families of roles.*

5   Related Work

All the mapping languages described in [11] do not support full heterogeneous mappings. In general, however, mapping languages support a limited version of heterogeneous mappings. For instance, in [5], it is possible to express the mapping

$$\forall x.(\exists y.R_1(x,y) \rightarrow C_2(x)) \tag{21}$$

or, similarly, in the original version of DDL one can state the mapping

$$1 : \exists R.\top \xrightarrow{\ \sqsubseteq\ } 2 : C \tag{22}$$

However, the encoding of heterogeneous mappings shown above is not very expressive and its usage can also lead to undesirable consequences. For instance, assume a relation IsMarried exists in ontology 1, and a concept Marriage exists in ontology 2. Assume we want to impose that the relation IsMarried in ontology 1 is equivalent to the concept Marriage in ontology 2, and we only have mappings as in Equation (22). Then, we can only state mappings of the form:

$$1 : \exists \text{IsMarried}.\top \xrightarrow{\ \sqsubseteq\ } 2 : \text{Marriage}$$

$$1 : \exists \text{IsMarried}.\top \xrightarrow{\ \sqsupseteq\ } 2 : \text{Marriage}$$

But these mappings express something rather different from our initial goal as they map single elements of a couple into marriages. Moreover, assume we also have a bridge rule mappings wives in ontology 1 into women in ontology 2 as follows:

$$1 : \text{Wife} \xrightarrow{\ \sqsubseteq\ } 2 : \text{Woman}$$

together with the axiom

$$\text{Wife} \sqsubseteq \exists \text{IsMarried}.\top$$

in ontology 1 stating that a wife is a married entity. From all this we can infer in ontology 2 that a wife is a marriage, i.e.,

$$\text{Wife} \sqsubseteq \text{Marriage}$$

This undesirable conclusion reflects the fact that in mapping the two ontologies, we have identified the participants of a relation, (the married person) with the relation itself (the marriage). To avoid this bad behavior, Omelayenko claims in [8] that mappings between classes and properties are not relevant from an application point of view. We believe that the examples shown in the paper provide a convincing evidence that this is not the case, and that an appropriate formalization of heterogeneous mappings can avoid some of the problems mentioned above.

An effort towards the formalization of heterogeneous mappings between concepts and relations in the area of federated databases is described in [2]. In this work the authors define five types of correspondences between concepts and properties. If A is a concept and R is a relation, they consider the following correspondences:

- A is equivalent to R;
- A is more general to R;
- A is less general to R;
- A and R do overlap;
- A and R do not overlap.

The semantics of the correspondences above can be expressed by the following mappings:

- $\forall x.(A(x) \leftrightarrow \exists y.R(y,x))$;
- $\forall x.(\exists y.R(y,x) \rightarrow A(x))$;
- $\forall x.(A(x) \rightarrow \exists y.R(y,x))$;
- $\exists x.(A(x) \wedge \exists y.R(y,x))$;
- $\forall x.(A(x) \rightarrow \neg\exists y.R(y,x))$.

This semantics is similar to the encoding described in Equation (21). The only difference is that it considers the range of the relation R in place of the domain. Therefore it suffers of problems similar to the ones shown above for Equation (21).

Different forms of mappings (bridge rules) have been studied in other formalisms strictly related to DDL, such as C-OWL [4] and DFOL [7]. Both formalisms do not address the problem of heterogeneous mappings and should therefore be extended in this direction.

6   Concluding Remarks

The language and the semantics presented in this paper constitute a genuine contribution in the direction of the integration of heterogeneous ontologies. The language proposed in this paper makes it possible to directly bind a concept with a relation in a different ontology, and vice-versa. At the semantic level we have introduced a domain relation that maps pairs of object into objects and vice-versa. This also constitute a novelty in the semantics of knowledge integration. We have showed the main formal properties of the mapping language, and we have left the complete characterization of the logic for future work.

References

1. Franz Baader, Diego Calvanese, Deborah L. McGuinness, Daniele Nardi, and Peter F. Patel-Schneider, editors. *The Description Logic Handbook: Theory, Implementation, and Applications*. Cambridge University Press, 2003.
2. J. M. Blanco, A. Illarramendi, and A. Goñi. Building a federated database system: An approach using a knowledge base system. *International Journal of Intelligent and Cooperative Information Systems*, 3(4):415–455, 1994.
3. A. Borgida and L. Serafini. Distributed description logics: Assimilating information from peer sources. *Journal of Data Semantics*, 1:153–184, 2003. LNCS 2800, Springer Verlag.

4. P. Bouquet, F. Giunchiglia, F. van Harmelen, L. Serafini, and H. Stuckenschmidt. C-OWL: Contextualizing ontologies. In *Second International Semantic Web Conference (ISWC-03)*, volume 2870 of *LNCS*, pages 164–179. Springer Verlag, 2003.
5. D. Calvanese, G. De Giacomo, M. Lenzerini, and R. Rosati. Logical foundations of peer-to-peer data integration. In *23rd ACM SIGACT SIGMOD SIGART Sym. on Principles of Database Systems (PODS 2004)*, pages 241–251, 2004.
6. C. Ghidini and F. Giunchiglia. Local models semantics, or contextual reasoning = locality + compatibility. *Artificial Intelligence*, 127(2):221–259, April 2001.
7. C. Ghidini and L. Serafini. Distributed First Order Logics. In *Frontiers Of Combining Systems 2*, Studies in Logic and Computation, pages 121–140. Research Studies Press, 1998.
8. B. Omelayenko. Integrating vocabularies: Discovering and representing vocabulary maps. In *Proceedings of the First International Semantic Web Conference (ISWC-2002)*, volume 2342 of *LNCS*. Springer-Verlag, 2003.
9. L. Serafini, H. Stuckenschmidt, and H. Wache. A formal investigation of mapping language for terminological knowledge. In *19th Joint Conference on Artificial Intelligence (IJCAI-05)*, pages 576–581, 2005.
10. Luciano Serafini, Alex Borgida, and Andrei Tamilin. Aspects of distributed and modular ontology reasoning. In *19th Joint Conference on Artificial Intelligence (IJCAI-05)*, pages 570–575, 2005.
11. H. Stuckenschmidt and M. Uschold. Representation of semantic mappings. In *Semantic Interoperability and Integration*, number 04391 in Dagstuhl Seminar Proceedings. Internationales Begegnungs- und Forschungszentrum (IBFI), Schloss Dagstuhl, Germany, 2005.
12. Ilya Zaihrayeu and Matteo Bonifacio, editors. *Proceedings of the Fist Workshop on Peer-to-Peer Knowledge Management (P2PKM 2004)*, volume 108 of *CEUR Workshop Proceedings*. CEUR-WS.org, 2004.

Empirical Merging of Ontologies — A Proposal of Universal Uncertainty Representation Framework

Vít Nováček[1] and Pavel Smrž[2]

[1] Faculty of Informatics, Masaryk University
Botanická 68a, 602 00 Brno, Czech Republic
xnovacek@fi.muni.cz
[2] Faculty of Information Technology, Brno University of Technology
Božetěchova 2, 612 66 Brno, Czech Republic
smrz@fit.vutbr.cz

Abstract. The significance of uncertainty representation has become obvious in the Semantic Web community recently. This paper presents our research on uncertainty handling in automatically created ontologies. A new framework for uncertain information processing is proposed. The research is related to OLE (Ontology LEarning) — a project aimed at bottom–up generation and merging of domain–specific ontologies. Formal systems that underlie the uncertainty representation are briefly introduced. We discuss the universal internal format of uncertain conceptual structures in OLE then and offer a utilisation example then. The proposed format serves as a basis for empirical improvement of initial knowledge acquisition methods as well as for general explicit inference tasks.

1 Introduction

This paper introduces a novel representation of uncertain knowledge in the domain of automatic ontology acquisition. The framework presented here was designed and developed in the scope of a broader project — OLE — that comprises complex ontological support for Semantic Web applications and knowledge acquisition in general.

The main objective of the ontology acquisition platform OLE is to implement a system that is able to automatically create and update domain specific ontologies for a given domain of the scientific knowledge. We emphasise an empirical approach to the ontology construction by means of bottom-up acquisition of concepts from the domain-relevant resources (documents, web pages, corpus data, etc.). The acquisition process is incrementally boosted by the knowledge already stored in the ontology.

The concepts extracted from a single resource form so called miniontology that is instantly integrated into the current domain ontology. The integration phase is the moment when the need of uncertainty representation arises. Even if

Y. Sure and J. Domingue (Eds.): ESWC 2006, LNCS 4011, pp. 65–79, 2006.

we could obtain precise conceptual constructions from individual resources (e. g. *birds fly*), we will experience infeasible consistency difficulties when trying to establish precise relations between the concepts in broader scope of the whole domain (as illustrated by the popular example: the fact *birds fly* collides with the statements *penguins are birds; penguins do not fly*). Besides the inconsistency handling, there are also important cognitive motivations of the utilisation of uncertainty in our empiric ontologies that led us to the proposal of a novel framework for representing uncertain knowledge. It is called ANUIC (Adaptive Net of Universally Interrelated Concepts).

The rest of the paper is organised as follows. In Section 2 we give a concise description of the ontology acquisition process in the scope of OLE. Section 3 summarises the overall motivation for the designed uncertainty processing mechanisms. This section also overviews important ideas from the cognitive science field that are both inspiring and relevant with respect to the topic. Formal background of uncertain information representation is briefly recalled in Section 4. Sections 5 and 6 define the framework itself and present basic notes on its utilisations. In Section 7, two illustrative examples of uncertain ontology fragment generation and query–processing are given. We conclude the paper and outline future directions of our research in Section 8.

2   Ontology Acquisition Process Within OLE

An ontology acquisition framework is an integral part of the emerging ontology acquisition platform OLE [1, 2]. In the following subsections we give a brief overview of this tool.

As we basically process raw text data (articles, web pages' textual content, natural language corpora etc.), we can dissociate the ontology acquisition in two main phases — *text preprocessing and identification of relevant text's parts* and *creation of ontology from such parts*. These phases are described in subsections 2.1 and 2.2 here, whereas the last subsection 2.3 offers preliminary extraction results.

2.1   Text Preprocessing

OLE processes English plain-text documents and produces the respective ontology for each input resource (miniontology). To increase the efficiency, the input is preprocessed with the aim to pose at least some simple structure on the text and to reduce irrelevant data as well. Especially shallow syntactic structures (that are usually very helpful for some methods of semantic relations' acquisition) are identified in this step. Except of that, a domain dictionary is created and each of the term occurring in the dictionary is annotated by a vector that reflects its average context. This is crucial for other extraction methods, as seen below.

The preprocessing consists of *creating the domain dictionary and annotation of terms by context vectors, splitting of the text into sentences* (while possibly eliminating irrelevant sentences), *text tokenization, POS tagging and lemmatization,* and *chunking*. The steps related to processing of particular resources are based on regular expressions and performed in one pass through the input file. The promising relevance — for example the presence of a lexico-syntactic pattern — is detected and resolved (if possible) at this stage as well.

The tagging and chunking phases of preprocessing depend on task specific utilisation of NLTK natural language toolkit [3] with custom-trained Brill POS tagging algorithm [4] and fast regular expression chunking incorporated. Moreover, the usage of NLTK toolkit (which allows users to train their own POS taggers from annotated data and easily create efficient chunking rules) enables to adapt the whole OLE system even for other languages than English in future.

2.2 Taxonomy Extraction and Ontology Generation

Any extraction algorithm (such as semantic clustering, statistical co-occurrence methods or formal concept analysis) can be integrated into OLE in the form of a plug-in. Such a plug-in is responsible for the concept extraction and precise (or fuzzy) assignment of a class or a property. Then it translates the gained information into an output ontology, or passes it further to other OLE modules (like ontology-merger or reasoner).

The taxonomy (*is-a*) relation is crucial for ontology development. Therefore we have implemented methods for its acquisition first so that we could experiment with practical application of our proposal of novel uncertainty representation framework. In order to build taxonomic skeleton for our ontologies we have implemented a basic pattern-driven *is-a* relation extraction plug-in with relatively high precision but low recall. The pattern-based method gains classes (intensions) and individuals (extensions) that are directly lexicalised in the resources. To increase the overall precision of our system, we have also devised and implemented a novel method that utilises hierarchical clustering of domain terms and consequent autonomous class annotation. This method considers the terms in processed resources as extensions and tries to annotate their groups by appropriate intensional identifiers using the WordNet lexical database [5]. See [2] for detailed description of these methods and their implementation.

The extracted information is stored in the universal format proposed here in Section 5, no matter which extraction technique has been used. The output ontology file can be produced by applying respective translation rules. These rules are implemented as another independent plug-in (likewise the extraction algorithms) responsible for producing the output file in a desired format. Currently, the OWL DL format with our own basic fuzzy extensions is supported, but OLE is able to produce any other format by the same mechanism.

2.3 Preliminary Results of Taxonomy Extraction

Due to problems with evaluation of automatic ontology acquisition (as articulated for example in [6]) we have performed only orientational measures. For the pattern based method, we tested the system with patterns given in Table 1 below[1]. The patterns are presented in common regular expression–like syntax.

Table 1. Patterns for *is-a* relation

Id	The pattern
1	NP such as (NPList | NP)
2	such NP as (NPList | NP)
3[†]	(NPList | NP) (and | or)other NP
4	NP (including | especially) (NPList | NP)
5[‡]	(NPList | NP) (is | was)an? NP
6[†]	(NPList | NP) is the NP
7[†]	(NPList | NP) and similar NP
8[†]	NP like (NPList | NP)

Other patterns can be added easily, but the patterns presented in the table were found to be sufficient for basic evaluation.

For the approximate manual evaluation we randomly chose ten resources from the whole document set (12, 969 automatically downloaded articles from computer science domain in this case). For each miniontology created by OLE system, we computed precision as the ratio of "reasonable" relations compared to all extracted relations. The recall was computed as the ratio of number of extracted terms (nouns) to all terms present in the resource. For all the measures of informal precision (*Pr.*) and recall (*Rec.*), an average value was computed. We present these results in Table 2, provided with respective average original resource size and number of all concepts extracted (in the *M1* row).

Table 2. Selected results of OLE's taxonomy extraction tools

Method	Res. sz. (wrd.)	No. of conc.	No. of rel.	Pr. (%)	Rec. (%)	I (%)
M1 avg.	4093	22.6	14.5	61.16	1.57	3399.17
M2 cl.–cl.	–	47	99	38.38	100	2183.62
M2 cl.–indiv.	–	60	62	51.61	100	5691.05
M2 sum–up	486	107	161	44.99 (avg.)	100 (avg.)	3937.34 (avg.)

In the same table, there are also similar results of clustering–based technique (in the *M2* rows). Due to the strenuousness of manual evaluation of large ontologies we used only a set of 131 concepts (non–unique individuals) from a coherent computer science domain resource. 60 unique individuals and 47 classes were induced. We distinguished between *class–class* and *class–individual* relationships when analysing the precision. The method's approximate recall is 100%, because it processes all the terms within the input data.

---

[1] † — introduced by author, ‡ — modified by author, others adopted according to [7] and [8]; however, the devision of simple patterns is quite easy, therefore similar patterns can be found even in other works.

Precision values for both methods are quite high when we look at the I column in the table. The I values present an improvement in precision over a base–line, which is computed as $\frac{R_R}{N(N-1)}$, where R_R stands for number of reasonable relations and N is the number of concepts in an ontology[2]. Moreover, it is only a "crisp" precision of the extraction phase.

When we incorporate empirical merging of the miniontologies by means of our uncertainty representation framework proposed in Section 5, we can significantly improve the values of precision (among other things) in a certain sense, as shown in Section 7 in more detail.

3   Motivation and Cognitive Observations

The knowledge repositories built by OLE tools must reflect the state of the respective domain empirically according to information contained in the provided resources. Such kind of knowledge is as objective as possible, because it is not influenced by arbitrary considerations about the domain's conceptual structure, but determined by the structure itself.

3.1   Remedy to Emerging Inconsistencies

Nevertheless, the automated empiric approach has an obvious drawback – the threat of inconsistency and possible errors. As we do not generally have an infal-lible "oracle" to tell us how to precisely join or map newly extracted concepts to the ones that are already stored in our ontology, crisp relations between concepts are virtually impossible. We must deal with the inconsistencies somehow.

There are two general kinds of possible inconsistencies in an ontology (virtu-ally any relational inconsistency can be modelled using these[3]):

- *subsumption* inconsistency: given concepts C, D and E, the $C \subseteq D$ and $C \subseteq E$ statements may collide when we represent for example crisp *part-of* relation by the $\subseteq$ symbol (supposing Europe and Asia are disjunct, the '*Turkey is both part of Europe and Asia*' statement is inconsistent);
- *equivalence* inconsistency: given concepts C, D and E, the $C \equiv D$, $C \subset E$ and $D \equiv E$ statements are in conflict (for example when we find out in a text that '*science*', '*knowledge*' and '*erudition*' are synonyms and at the same time we induce that '*knowledge*' is a super–concept of '*erudition*').

Such collisions are hard to be modelled in classic crisp ontology representation frameworks (see [9] or [10]). Implementation of the uncertainty into our knowl-edge representation is a solution for dealing with conflicts in the continuously updated ontology.

---

[2] The $N(N-1)$ is number of all *is-a* relations that can be assigned among all concepts.
[3] As a matter of fact, even the equivalence inconsistency can be modelled by the subsumption one, but we give both of them in order to show clear examples.

3.2 Mental Models Reflection

The second motivation lies in inspiration by the conceptual models that are characteristic for human mind. This topic is closely related to the very definition of *concept* and *meaning*. As stated for example in [11] or [12], people definitely do not represent the meaning of concepts as static crisp structures. The meanings are rather constructed as vague sets of dynamically overlapping referential associations [11], or so called "meaning potentials" with particular instantiation dependent on the context of concept-referring word or sequence of words [13]. These overlapping structures can also be viewed as interconnected in an associative network presented in [14]. We address all these issues in the framework proposal.

In the rest of this section, we will give an informal definition of a concept and its meaning in the perspective of OLE. More precise formulations related to the topic are presented in Section 5. By concept we mean a representation of an entity existing in real world and/or utterable in human language. A concept is determined by its relations to another concepts in the universe then. Such "relational" definition of a concept is partly inspired by poststructuralistic philosophy (see for example [15]). Reference of a concept is then realised by instances of its relational connections. By these instances we mean especially concrete uncertainty measures assigned to each relation a concept is involved into (see Section 5 for details).

Thus we can naturally represent the dynamic conceptual overlap in the meaning of [11], because the assigned relations' measures are continuously updated within new knowledge incorporation process. And by introducing a special relation of *association* we can represent the notion of meaning potentials according to [13]. Using this relation we can associate a concept with a representation of selected co-occurring concepts and impose another useful restriction on the meaning construction (helpful for example when resolving word-sense ambiguities).

4 Uncertainty Formalisations

The uncertain information representation frameworks are determined by three significant courses of contemporary mathematics:

1. extensions of the theory of measure into a more general theory of monotonous measures with respect to the classical measures of information;
2. applications of (conditional) probability theory;
3. extensions of the classical set theory into a more general fuzzy set theory.

Various uncertainty extensions of the information measure theory are mentioned by Klir in [16]. However, in the computer science field there are other probabilistic theories generally accepted, mainly in the scope of:

- Bayesian networks (good overview of the topic is given in [17], specific applications are described in [10] or [9]);

– non-monotonic reasoning and respective probabilistic (or possibilistic) extensions of "classical" (mainly propositional, first order or description) logics (see for example [18] or [19]).

All these more or less probabilistic approaches are no doubt significant for uncertainty representation. However, we dissociate from them in our work for a few important reasons. As we want our ontologies to be built automatically in an empirical manner, it would be very hard to find out appropriate (conditional) probability assignments without any background knowledge (axioms and/or inference rules) at our hand except of the knowledge given by frequencies of particular evidences. Moreover, we would like to assign similar and quite high "belief" measures to certain instances of some relations. Imagine we would like to make our system quite strongly believe that *dog* is very likely a *canine* as well as a *pet*. The strong believe can be intuitively represented for instance as 0.8 value and higher within the $\langle 0, 1 \rangle$ scale. Suppose we induce this belief–measure from data on a probabilistic basis — then we can assign values equal to at most 0.5 to each of the relation instances if we want to have them as similar as possible and reasonably high at the same time. Moreover, the probabilities can limitary decrease to 0 for very large amounts of data with uniform distribution of instances of particular relations.

Coping with these facts would obviously break axioms of usual probability or information measure theory. But with a relatively little effort, we can quite naturally avoid these problems using the notion of fuzzy measure. That is why we prefer using the fuzzy sets and fuzzy logic formalisms to motivate our uncertain knowledge representation proposal.

Fuzzy sets were introduced by Zadeh in 1965 [20]. The theory has been quite developed and widely used in many application domains so far and is quite well known. The most important notion we will use here is a *membership function* that uniquely defines each fuzzy set, assigning a certain degree of respective set's membership to each element in a universal set X. Another crucial term is fuzzy relation (R on $X \times X$) – it is defined as a mapping $R : X \times X \rightarrow \langle 0, 1 \rangle$. Notions of reflexivity, symmetry, transitivity etc. similar to those of classical relations can be adopted even for fuzzy relations. This is very useful for example for explicit reasoning tasks (see [21]) based on set operations. However, this intriguing topic will be discussed more elaborately in another dedicated paper.

5   ANUIC Proposal

ANUIC (Adaptive Net of Universally Interrelated Concepts) forms a backbone of the uncertainty representation in OLE. The formal definition of ANUIC and a few comments on the topic are mentioned in this section.

5.1   Formal Definition

The concepts are stored in a special fuzzy network structure. The network is an oriented multigraph $G = (V, E)$, where V is a set of stored concepts and E is a set of ordered tuples (u, v), where $u \in V, v \in V$. The edges are induced by imprecise concept relations. Multiple edges are allowed as there can exist multiple relations between concepts. A node is a tuple in the form of (c, R, A), where:

- c is a reference word or collocation (a term in general) of the concept. It serves as a master reference index for the node in the network;
- R is a **relational** set of tuples in the form of $(r, c_r, \mu(r))$, where $r \in N$ is an identifier of a relation from a given set N (its members can be usual lexico-semantic relations, such as hyperohyponymy (*is-a*), synonymy, holonymy, meronymy, or domain–specific relations like *used_for*, *appears_in*, *method_of* and so forth). The $c_r \in V$ is again a concept, which is related with the current one by r, and $\mu(r) \in \langle 0, 1 \rangle$ is the fuzzy μ–measure assigned to this observation — see below what exactly this measure represents;
- A is an **associative** set of numeric centroid vectors that are representing the terms occurring near the reference term in average (either throughout the whole domain or specific subdomains); numeric elements of the vectors are gained through mapping of domain terms to integers using a domain dictionary. This supports the meaning potentials remark from Section 3, among other things like induction of vector space on the domain texts (useful for example for concept clustering).

5.2   Conviction Function

Fuzzy appropriateness (μ–measure) of a relation r (for example the *is-a* relation) between concepts (c_1, c_2) is given by a special conviction function (derived from standard sigmoid):

$$\mu(r) = \frac{1}{1 + e^{-s(f_r - \beta)}}$$

where $f_r = \frac{f(r(c1, c2))}{\sum_{c \in V} f(r(c1, c))}$ is the relative frequency of relation instance observations in input data, s is a parameter regulating the "steepness" of the function and β influences the placement of the inflexion point. The domain of the function is real interval $(0, 1\rangle$ (but only rational numbers obviously appear as an input). The range is real interval $(0, 1)$.

This function maps relative frequencies of respective observations in input data to the fuzzy appropriateness measure of the relation. It can model various natural characteristics of human mind like conservativeness, open–mindness (in the meaning of influence of major or minor observations to the overall conviction) and so forth[4].

The function is continuous and thus can be implemented in a very straightforward way. However, it can easily imitate discontinuous jumps in the shape of the curve, which is also very useful. Examples showing shapes of the conviction function are displayed in Figure 1[5]. As we can see on examples, the proposed

---

[4] Thus we can for example fix the meaning of a specific group of concepts and allow meaning variations for another one.

[5] With the relative frequency and μ-measure on the horizontal and vertical axes respectively.

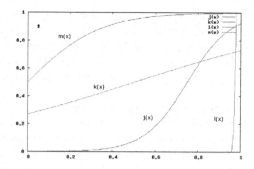

Fig. 1. Examples of various shapes of the conviction function

conviction function allow us to naturally simulate the relative influence the observation frequency has on the relevancy of the observed relation instance. To be more specific, consider the following overview:

- Shape labelled as $m(x)$ presents quite "hesitating" function that assigns relatively high μ-measures (greater than 0.5) even to small frequencies, thus making the system partially believe in almost every evidence, yet preferring the higher frequencies significantly.
- The $j(x)$ function presents a shape assigning relatively low values (in the meaning that they are quite far from 1) even for frequency near or equal to 1. It reflects an "opinion" of the system that even a provisionally sure fact can never be absolutely valid if we consider future observations.
- The shape given by $l(x)$ presents a very "conservative" settings — only very high frequency will get a μ-measure significantly higher than 0, observations with minor frequencies are ignored. The β parameter presents a threshold of these ignored frequencies here.

6   Notes on the μ-measures Interpretation and Processing

In the following subsections we present basic ideas related to utilisations of the principles described in the previous section. We introduce notions of *implicit* and *explicit* reasoning with respect to the automatic empirical ontology acquisition and merging. The notions are also supported by preliminary examples given in Section 7.

6.1   Implicit Reasoning

The implicit reasoning plays mayor role in learning of new knowledge by integration of various examples of empirical evidence for a relation between concepts in an ontology. We induce knowledge by a kind of implicit inference based on comparing the stored information and new sources of evidence in a well–defined manner.

The process of integration of newly coming facts is similar to the process of how people construct their conceptual representations — first they have an almost crisp evidence of a relation between objects (for example that *dogs have four legs*). This opinion is strengthened by further observations of four–legged dogs, but one day they see a cripple dog having only three legs. So they have to add another instance of the "have–number–of–legs" relation, but with much more decreased relevancy (unless they keep seeing other and other different three–legged dogs).

This is analogous to the ontology merging task — when we have a large amount of miniontologies gained from a vast number of domain resources, we can join them simply using their mutual insertion into one complex ANUIC structure. After proper configuration of the conviction function parameters we have qualitatively different representation of the domain — many formerly incorrect relations are mostly marginalised, whereas the empirically more valid relations obtain high μ-measures, signalising strong belief in their appropriateness.

We have found that very good heuristic for configuration of the conviction function parameters presented in Section 5 is dynamic setting of the β inflexion point value. The steepness parameter s can be set arbitrarily (however higher values are generally better for they cause better discrimination). The β for a concept c and relation R is set as:

$$\beta = \frac{1}{|\{\hat{c}|(c, \hat{c}) \in R\}|} \, .$$

Moreover, any relative frequency f higher than 0.5 is modified by weighing the β parameter with $1 - (f - 0.5)$ expression. Only then we obtain for example natural conviction of (almost) 1 when we deal with a single relation instance. Thus we can discriminate very well between the relation instances with significant and insignificant frequencies due to the shape of the conviction function[6]. Concrete example of such an ontology merge is given in Section 7.1.

6.2   Explicit Reasoning

Explicit reasoning conforms to classical definition of reasoning — it stems from explicit inference of new facts based on the facts already stored in an ontology and corresponding rules tailored to our uncertain knowledge representation. It can always be reduced on query–answering. The mechanisms underlying the query processing proposal are rather fuzzy set–based then logic–founded. Thus we can answer also queries difficult or even infeasible when using a classical logical formalism (see Section 7.2 for an example of the query–processing and possible utilisation sketches).

Despite of this, we can always reduce our knowledge repository to the OWL DL format [22]. We can gain a crisp Description Logics approximation by performing an α–reduction using respective α–cuts[7] on fuzzy constructs contained

---

[6] Supposing that the higher the relation frequency is with respect to the average relative frequency for relation edges coming from the c concept, the more is the relation significant and vice versa.

[7] An α–cut of a fuzzy set A is a classical crisp set of objects that have a membership value higher than $\alpha \in \langle 0, 1 \rangle$ with respect to A.

in the ontology and by elimination of possible relations that are restricted in OWL DL. Then we can use widely–adopted Description Logics[8] reasoning on such an approximation in order to learn less–expressive but crisp facts from our knowledge base.

7   Examples of the ANUIC Framework Utilisation

We give an example on practical utilisation of the representation properties of ANUIC for real world data in the first subsection. The second subsection offers an example of how a query could be processed by the ANUIC–based empirical inference engine. We also mention possible related utilisations of the framework within our another project.

7.1   Ontology Merging

We tested the ontology merging on a set of $3,272$ automatically downloaded articles from the computer science domain. The overall size of the resources was $20,405,014$ words. We produced the respective miniontologies by pattern–based OLE module and merged them into one ANUIC structure. Thus we gained a taxonomy with $5,538$ classes, $9,842$ individuals[9] and $61,725$ mutual *is-a* relations. A sample from this ontology is given on Figure 2 — the ovals represent classes, squares individuals and arrows go from sub-concept to its super-concept, labelled by respective μ–measures. For the μ–measures computation we used the dynamic β assignment heuristics described in Section 6.1 and s parameter set to 100, which performed best among various other settings.

It is very hard to formally decide what is the representation's exact improvement when compared to the knowledge stored in the former crisp miniontologies. But we can again give at least an informal statistics — when we consider only the relations with highest μ–measure(s) relevant for a particular concept[10], we can compute an approximate ratio of "reasonable" relations similar to the one presented in Section 2.3. We computed the ratio on a random sample of 50 relations from the whole merged ontology and obtained the value 86 %. We cannot formally compare this ratio even to the informal measures given in Section 2.3, but we clearly see that this truly means a kind of improvement under a certain perspective.

7.2   Query Processing and Possible Utilisations

In the following we show how can a vague but very useful query be processed using ANUIC–based explicit reasoning. Suppose we have the query:

Are the *network* and the *graph* concepts similar?

---

[8] Currently the $\mathcal{SROIQ}$ Description Logic is implemented in OWL DL, version 1.1. proposal, see [23].

[9] We empirically assume that a concept is an individual as long as it has no hyponyms.

[10] Which is by the way a very strong restriction, the range of possible interpretations of the concrete conviction values is much higher.

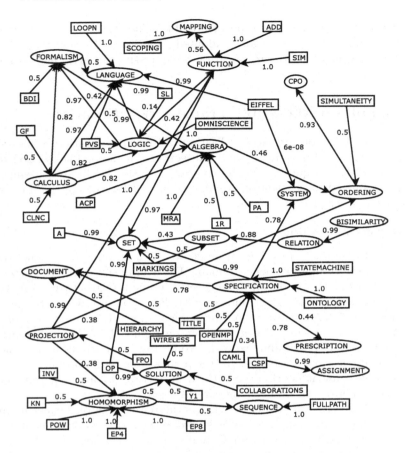

Fig. 2. Sample of the merged ontology

Such a query can hardly be modelled in any classical logic. Nevertheless, it can be very useful — let us give one example for all. The answer to such a query is very significant when we consider different domains. In the computer science domain, for instance, the *network* and *graph* concepts are quite similar (network can be viewed as a kind of graph). On the other hand, in the sociology domain there is no observable similarity between these concepts, albeit the *network* term is widely used (*social network* etc.). Thus we can efficiently use such kind of questions for example in the task of discourse identification.

Now how do we process the above query? Suppose we have the following four kinds of relations stored in our ANUIC structure:

1. *synonymy* (*s* identifier) — usual lexico–semantic relation of meaning similarity; however, this relation does not have to be sufficient when processing vague queries among our empirical knowledge repository;
2. *hyperohyponymy* (*h* identifier) — super/sub–concept lexico–semantic relation;

3. *association* (*a* identifier) — arbitrary co–occurrence relation, its μ–measure shows how often the concepts appear in the vicinity of each other;
4. *antonymy* (*t* identifier) — lexico–semantic relation of meaning dissimilarity.

Let us encode *network* and *graph* concepts as n, g respectively. Let $\mu_r(n, g)$ be the value of μ–measure of relation r between n and g. Then we can express empirical similarity (ψ) as:

$$\psi(n, g) = \gamma_1(\mu_s(n, g) - \mu_t(n, g)) + \gamma_2(\mu_h(n, g) + \mu_h(g, n)) + \gamma_3(\mu_a(n, g) + \mu_a(g, n)),$$

where $\gamma_1, \ldots, \gamma_3$ are real coefficients such that $\gamma_1, \gamma_2, \gamma_3 > 0$ and $\gamma_1 > \gamma_2 > \gamma_3$.

After selecting the γ_i, $i \in \{1, \ldots, 3\}$ coefficients appropriately, we can define a non–decreasing scale of possible similarity values and map their consequent intervals to the respective scale of linguistic fuzzy labels (for example *distinct, almost dissimilar, little similar, moderately similar, very similar, almost same, same*). Thus we can straightforwardly answer the query and/or pass the numeric value for further processing. Supposing we have inserted sufficient amount of data in our knowledge base, answers like this are useful even for rarely occurring concepts and relations. Moreover, the time complexity of the query processing itself is constant — we only need to get the 6 μ–measure values and add them up[11].

The inference engine based on ANUIC format can be directly used in the scope of general knowledge acquisition as well as within more specific Semantic Web tasks. It can be very useful for example for another project we are involved in — PortaGe — that is aimed on automatic generation and personalisation of scientific Semantic Web portals [1]. We can employ the uncertainty representation for example in the automatic extraction of metainformation from the scientific documents, citation analysis, metasearch in digital libraries, analysis of various web pages, meta-data annotation of web resources and source-change analysis. The ontology support would be useful even for general semantics–enhanced search and retrieval tasks among the particular portal's domain.

8   Conclusions and Future Work

We presented the ANUIC framework that deals with uncertain knowledge in ontologies. The framework is motivated by intuitive, yet valuable notion of representation of uncertainty in human mind. The theoretical background of fuzzy sets methodology allows to develop an appropriate calculus and consecutively build novel inference tools to reason among the concepts stored in expressive ANUIC format very efficiently.

Our future work will focus on incorporation of results of another extraction methods (mainly our clustering–based technique) into the ANUIC ontologies in order to increase the recall. A formal development and validation of a specific calculus for ANUIC explicit reasoning is needed then. We will also devise formal evaluation methods and test the framework properly using various data from

---

[11] The lookup for values is performed on efficient hash–like structures.

other distinct domains of available resources. Finally, the mutual correspondence and transformation possibilities between ontologies in ANUIC format and formats like OWL extended by possible fuzzy modifications must be examined. All of the mentioned tasks are no doubt hard, but we demand it will be very challenging to pursue them and refine the ideas behind to gain a sustainable, expressive and efficient universal model of representation of uncertain knowledge.

Acknowledgements

This work has been supported by the Academy of Sciences of the Czech Republic, 'Information Society' national research program, the grant AV 1ET100300419, and partially by the Czech Republic Ministry of Education, Research Plan MSM 6383917201.

References

1. Nováček, V., Smrž, P.: Ontology acquisition for automatic building of scientific portals. In: LNCS. Volume 3831., Springer-Verlag Berlin Heidelberg (2006)
2. Nováček, V.: Ontology learning. Master's thesis, Faculty of Informatics, Masaryk University, Czech Republic (2006) Available at (February 2006): http://nlp.fi.muni.cz/~xnovacek/files/dp.pdf.
3. NLTK: NLTK: Natural Language Toolkit – Technical Reports. (2005) Available at (February 2006): http://nltk.sourceforge.net/tech/index.html.
4. Brill, E.: A report of recent progress in transformation-based error-driven learning. In: Proc. ARPA Human Language Technology Workshop '94, Princeton, NJ (1994)
5. Fellbaum, C., ed.: WordNet: An Electronic Lexical Database. MIT Press (1998)
6. Brewster, C., Alani, H., Dasmahapatra, S., Wilks, Y.: Data driven ontology evaluation. In: Proceedings of LREC 2004. (2004)
7. Hearst, M.A.: Automatic acquisition of hyponyms from large text corpora. In: Proceedings of the 14th conference on Computational linguistics, Morristown, NJ, USA, Association for Computational Linguistics (1992) 539–545
8. Etzioni, O., Cafarella, M., Downey, D., Kok, S., Popescu, A.M., Shaked, T., Soderland, S., Weld, D.S., Yates, A.: Web-scale information extraction in KnowItAll: (preliminary results). In: Proceedings of WWW '04, New York, NY, USA, ACM Press (2004) 100–110
9. Holi, M., Hyvönen, E.: A method for modeling uncertainty in semantic web taxonomies. In: Proceedings of WWW Alt. '04, New York, NY, USA, ACM Press (2004) 296–297
10. Y. Peng, Z. Ding, R.P.: BayesOWL: A probabilistic framework for uncertainty in semantic web. In: Proceedings of Nineteenth International Joint Conference on Artificial Intelligence (IJCAI05). (2005)
11. Hofstadter, D.: Fluid Concepts & Creative Analogies: Computer Models of the Fundamental Mechanisms of Thought. Basic Books, New York (1995)
12. Cuyckens, H., Dirven, R., Taylor, J.R., eds.: Cognitive Approaches to Lexical Semantics. Cognitive linguistics research edn. Volume 23. Mouton de Gruyter, Berlin (2003)

13. Allwood, J.: Meaning potentials and context: Some consequences for the analysis of variation and meaning. In: Cognitive Approaches to Lexical Semantics. Mouton de Gruyter, Berlin (2003) 29–66
14. Ruge, G.: Combining corpus linguistics and human memory models for automatic term association. In Strzalkowski, T., ed.: Natural Language Information Retrieval. Kluwer Academic Publishers (1999) 75–98
15. Derrida, J.: A Derrida Reader: between the Blinds. Harvester Wheatsheaf, New York (1991)
16. Klir, G.J., Wierman, M.J.: Uncertainty-Based Information: Elements of Generalized Information Theory. Physica-Verlag/Springer-Verlag, Heidelberg and New York (1999)
17. Xiang, Y.: Probabilistic Reasoning in Multi-agent Systems: A Graphical Models Approach. Cambridge University Press, Cambridge (2002)
18. Kyburg, H.E., Kyburg, J., Teng, C.M.: Uncertain Inference. Cambridge University Press, Cambridge (2001)
19. Giugno, R., Lukasiewicz, T.: P-$\mathcal{SHOQ}$(D): A probabilistic extension of $\mathcal{SHOQ}$(D) for probabilistic ontologies in the semantic web. In: Proceedings of JELIA '02, London, UK, Springer-Verlag (2002) 86–97
20. Zadeh, L.A.: Fuzzy sets. Journal of Information and Control **8** (1965) 338–353
21. Garmendia, L., Salvador, A.: Computing a transitive opening of a reflexive and symmetric fuzzy relation. In: Proceedings of ECSQARU '05, London, UK, Springer-Verlag (2005) 587–599
22. Bechhofer, S., van Harmelen, F., Hendler, J., Horrocks, I., McGuinness, D.L., Patel-Schneider, P.F., Stein, L.A.: OWL Web Ontology Language Reference. (2004) Available at (February 2006): http://www.w3.org/TR/owl-ref/.
23. Horrocks, I., Kutz, O., Sattler, U.: The even more irresistible $\mathcal{SROIQ}$. Technical report, University of Manchester (2005)

Encoding Classifications into Lightweight Ontologies

Fausto Giunchiglia, Maurizio Marchese, and Ilya Zaihrayeu

Department of Information and Communication Technology
University of Trento, Italy
{fausto, marchese, ilya}@dit.unitn.it

Abstract. Classifications have been used for centuries with the goal of cataloguing and searching large sets of objects. In the early days it was mainly books; lately it has also become Web pages, pictures and any kind of electronic information items. Classifications describe their contents using natural language labels, which has proved very effective in manual classification. However natural language labels show their limitations when one tries to automate the process, as they make it very hard to reason about classifications and their contents. In this paper we introduce the novel notion of *Formal Classification*, as a graph structure where labels are written in a propositional concept language. Formal Classifications turn out to be some form of lightweight ontologies. This, in turn, allows us to reason about them, to associate to each node a normal form formula which univocally describes its contents, and to reduce document classification to reasoning about subsumption.

1   Introduction

In today's information society, as the amount of information grows larger, it becomes essential to develop efficient ways to summarize and navigate information from large, multivariate data sets. The field of classification supports these tasks, as it investigates how sets of "objects" can be summarized into a small number of classes, and it also provides methods to assist the search of such "objects" [8]. In the past centuries, classification has been the domain of librarians and archivists. Lately a lot of interest has focused also on the management of the information present in the web: see for instance the WWW Virtual Library project [1], or directories of search engines like Google, or Yahoo!.

Web directories are often called *lightweight ontologies* [23]. However, they lack at least one important property attributable to the notion of ontology. Namely, that an ontology must be represented in a *formal language*, which can then be used for *automating reasoning* [16]. None of the existing human crafted classifications possesses this property. Because classification hierarchies are written in natural language, it is very hard to automate the classification task, and, as a consequence, standard classification approaches amount to *manually* classifying objects into classes. Examples include DMOZ, a human edited web directory, which *"powers the core directory services for the most popular portals and search*

Y. Sure and J. Domingue (Eds.): ESWC 2006, LNCS 4011, pp. 80–94, 2006.
© Springer-Verlag Berlin Heidelberg 2006

engines on the Web, including AOL Search, Netscape Search, Google, Lycos, DirectHit, and HotBot, and hundreds of others" [22]; and the Dewey Decimal Classification System (DDC) [5]. Although they are based on well-founded classification methodologies, all these classifications have a number of limitations:

– the semantics of a given category is implicitly codified in a natural language label, which may be ambiguous and will therefore be interpreted differently by different classifiers;
– a link, connecting two nodes, may also be ambiguous in the sense that it may be considered to specify the meaning of the child node, of the parent node, or of both. For instance, a link connecting the parent node *"programming"* with its child node *"Java"* may, or may not mean that (a) the parent node means "computer programming" (and not, for example, "events scheduling"); (b) that the child node means "Java, the programming language" (and not "Java, the island"); and (c) that the parent node's meaning excludes the meaning of the child node, i.e., it is "programming and *not* Java";
– as a consequence of the previous two items, the classification task also becomes ambiguous in the sense that different classifiers may classify the same objects differently, based on their *subjective* opinion.

In the present paper we propose an approach to converting classifications into lightweight ontologies, thus eliminating the three ambiguities discussed above. This in turn allows us to automate, through propositional reasoning, the essential task of document classification. Concretely, we propose a three step approach:

– first, we convert a classification into a new structure, which we call *Formal Classification (FC)*, where all the labels are expressed in a propositional Description Logic (DL) language (i.e., a DL language without roles) [3];
– second, we convert a FC into a *Normalized Formal Classification (NFC)*. In NFCs each node's label is a propositional DL formula, which univocally codifies the meaning of the node in the corresponding classification, taking into account both the label of the node and its position within the classification;
– third, we encode document classification in NFCs as a propositional satisfiability (SAT) problem, and solve it using a sound and complete SAT engine.

NFCs are *full-fledged* lightweight ontologies, and have many nice properties. Among them:

– nodes' labels univocally codify the set of documents, which can be classified in these nodes;
– NFCs are *taxonomies* in the sense that, from the root down to the leaves, labels of child nodes are subsumed by the labels of their parent nodes;
– as nodes' labels codify the position of the nodes in the hierarchy, document classification can be done simply by analyzing the set of labels. There is no need to inspect the edge structure of the NFC.

The remainder of the paper is organized as follows. In Section 2 we introduce classifications and discuss how they are used. In Section 3 we motivate a formal approach to dealing with classifications. In Section 4 we introduce the notion of FC as a way to disambiguate labels in classifications. In Section 5 we discuss how we disambiguate links in classifications by introducing the notion of NFC. In Section 6 we show how the essential task of document classification can be fully automated in NFCs by means of propositional reasoning. In Section 7 we discuss related work. Section 8 summarizes the results and concludes the paper.

2   Classifications

Classifications are rooted trees, where each node is assigned a *natural language* label. Classifications are used for the categorization of various kinds of objects, such as books, office documents, web pages, and multimedia files into a set of *categories*. Classifications are also used for searching for objects by browsing the categories and looking inside those, where the objects are likely to be located.

We define the notion of classification as *a rooted tree $C = \langle N, E, L \rangle$ where N is a finite set of nodes, E is a set of edges on N, and L is is a finite set of labels expressed in natural language, such that for any node $n_i \in N$, there is one and only one label $l_i \in L$.*

Labels describe real world entities or individual objects, and the meaning of a label in a classification is the set of documents, that are *about* the entities (or individual objects) described by the label. We call this meaning of labels, the *classification semantics of labels*. Note, that a label can be about a document, e.g., a book; and, in this case, the classification semantics of this label is the set of documents, which are about the book, e.g., book reviews.

There are many methodologies for how to classify objects into classification hierarchies. These methodologies range from the many rigorous rules of DDC [5], "polished" by librarians during more than one hundred years; to less strict, but still powerful rules of classification in a web directory[1]. In all the different cases, a human classifier needs to follow a common pattern, which we summarize in four steps. We discuss the steps below, and we elucidate them on the example of a part of the DMOZ web directory shown in Figure 1.

1. Disambiguating labels. The challenge here is to disambiguate natural language words and labels. For example, the classifier has to understand that in the label of node n_7, the word "*Java*" has at least three senses, which are: an island in Indonesia; a coffee beverage; and an object-oriented programming language;

2. Disambiguating links. At this step the classifier has to interpret links between nodes. Namely, the classifier needs to consider the fact that each non-root node is "viewed" in the *context* of its parent node; and then specify the meanings of the nodes' labels. For instance, the meaning of the label of node n_8, *computers*, is bounded by the meaning of node n_6, *business books publishing*;

3. Understanding classification alternatives. Given an object, the classifier has to understand what classification alternatives for this object are. For instance, the book "*Java Enterprise in a Nutshell, Second Edition*" might potentially be put

---

[1] See, for instance, the DMOZ classification rules at http://dmoz.org/guidelines/.

in all the nodes of the hierarchy shown in Figure 1. The reason for this is that the book is related to both business and technology branches;

4. Making choices. Given the set of classification alternatives, the classifier has to decide, based on a predefined system of rules, where to put the given object. The system of rules may differ from classification to classification, but one rule is commonly followed: the *get-specific* rule. The rule states that any object must be classified in a category (or in several categories), which most *specifically* describes the object. In order to follow this rule, one needs to "dig" deep into the classification schema and find a category, which is located as low as possible in the classification tree, and which is still more general than what the object is about. Note, that there may be more than one such category. For instance, if the get-specific rule was used, then one would classify the above mentioned book into nodes n_7 and n_8, as they most specifically characterize it.

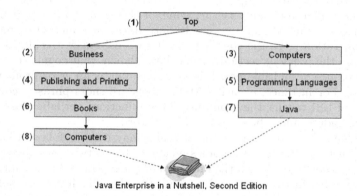

Fig. 1. A part of the DMOZ web directory

Note, that the four steps above are also followed when one is searching for an object by means of classification browsing. The only difference is in that now the categories are searched for where to find the object, and not where to put it.

3   Why Formal Classifications?

Let us exemplify our arguments in favour of a formal approach to classification on the English part of the DMOZ web directory[2]. We report a summary of the statistical analysis we performed on it in Table 1.

Humans have proven to be very effective at performing steps 1 and 2 described in Section 2. However, there are still some challenges to be addressed. The main challenge in step 1 is dealing with the ambiguities introduced by multiple possibilities in meaning. One source of this is in that labels contain many

---

[2] We excluded branches leading to non-English labels, such as "Top/World/" or "Top/Kids_and_Teens/International/".

Table 1. DMOZ statistics

Statistics category	Value
Total English labels	477,786
Tokens per label, avg.	1.81
Total links classified in English labels	3,047,643
Duplicate links, % from the total	10.70%
Nouns and adjectives polysemy, avg.	3.72
"*and*"'s and "*or*"'s per label, avg.	0.23
Total disjunctions per label, avg.	3.79
Root-to-leaf path length, avg.	7.09
Branching factor, avg.	4.00

conjunctions "and"'s and "or"'s, whereas they actually mean inclusive disjunction, i.e., either the first conjunct, or the second, or both. For instance, the phrase "wine and cheese" means either wine, or cheese, or both. Apart from the conjunctions, multiple possibilities are also introduced by punctuation marks denoting enumeration (e.g., the comma), and by words' senses (recall the "Java" example from the previous section). It has been shown, that cognitive reasoning with the presence of multiple possibilities in meaning is an error-prone task for humans [10]. For instance, even if DMOZ labels are short phrases, consisting, on average, of 1.81 tokens, they contain 0.23 conjunctions per label; and average polysemy for nouns and adjectives is 3.72 per word.

The challenge of step 2 is that the classifier may need to follow a long path of nodes in order to figure out a node's meaning. It has two consequences: first, the classifier needs to deal with the growing complexity in ambiguity introduced by each new label in the path; and, second, the classifier has to consider each new label in the context of the labels of the ancestor nodes, and, thus, partly resolve the ambiguity. Note, that the average length of a path from the root to a leaf node in DMOZ is rather high and it constitutes 7.09 nodes.

Steps 3 and 4 are where the real problems for humans begin. Even with classifications of an average size, it is not easy to find all the classification alternatives. With large classifications this task becomes practically unfeasible. For instance, think about possible classification alternatives in DMOZ, which has 477,786 English categories. Thus, at step 3, a human classifier may not be able to enumerate all the possible classification alternatives for an object.

Step 4 requires abundant expertise and profound methodological skills on the side of the classifier. However, even an expert makes subjective decisions, what leads, when a classification is populated by several classifiers, to nonuniform, duplicate, and error-prone classification. If the get-specific rule is used, then the classifier has to parse the classification tree in a top-down fashion, considering at each parent node, which of its child nodes are appropriate for the classification. Note, that even if DMOZ encourages the classification of a Web page in a single category, among 3,047,643 links (classified in English labels), about 10.70% are classified in more than one node[3]. And, about 91.36% of these are classified in

---

[3] We identified duplicate links by exact equivalence of their URLs.

two different nodes. This is not surprising given that DMOZ is populated by more than 70,000 classifiers, and that it has average branching factor of 4.00.

Given all the above described complexity, humans still outperform machines in natural language understanding tasks [20], which are the core of steps 1 and 2. Still, the availability of electronic repositories that encode world knowledge (e.g., [12, 14]), and powerful natural language processing tools (e.g., [17, 12]) allows the machines to perform these steps reasonably well. Moreover, machines can be much more efficient and effective at steps 3 and 4, if the problem is encoded in a formal language, which is what we propose to do in our approach.

4   Disambiguating Labels

Formal Classifications (FCs) are rooted trees, where each node is assigned a *formal language* label. FCs and classifications are related in the sense that a FC is a *formalized* copy of a classification. In other words, a FC has the same structure as the classification, but it encodes the classification's labels in a formal language, capable of encapsulating, at the best possible level of approximation, their classification semantics. In this respect, classifications's labels have at least one nice property. Namely, since labels are meant to describe real world entities, and *not* actions, performed on or by entities, and relations between entities, the labels are mainly constituted of noun phrases; and, therefore, there are very few words which are verbs. This makes it very suitable to use a Description Logic (DL) language as the formal language, as DLs are a precise notation for representing noun phrases [3].

We define the notion of Formal Classification as *a rooted tree* $FC = \langle N, E, L^F \rangle$ *where* N *is a finite set of nodes,* E *is a set of edges on* N, *and* L^F *is a finite set of labels expressed in Propositional Description Logic language* L^C, *such that for any node* $n_i \in N$, *there is one and only one label* $l_i^F \in L^F$.

Converting classifications into FCs automates step 1, as described in Section 2. In our approach we build on the work of Magnini et. al. [13]. We translate a natural language label into an expression in L^C by means of mapping different parts of speech (POSs), their mutual syntactic relation, and punctuation to the classification semantics of labels. We proceed in two steps, as discussed below:

1. Build atomic concepts. Senses of (multi-word) common nouns and adjectives become atomic concepts of L^C, whose interpretation is the set of documents about the entities, which are denoted by the nouns, or which possess the qualities denoted by the adjectives[4]. We enumerate word senses using WordNet [14], and we write [x#i] to denote an atomic concept corresponding to the ith sense of the word x in WordNet. For instance, [programming#2] is an atomic concept, whose interpretation is the set of documents which are about computer programming;

---

[4] Because of their negligibly small presence, we do not consider verbs. We neither consider articles, numerals, pronouns and adverbs. However, their share in the labels of actual classifications is reasonably small. When such words are found, they are just omitted from the label.

and the atomic concept [red#1] denotes the set of documents which are about red entities, e.g., red cats or red hats. Proper nouns become atomic concepts of L^C, whose interpretation is the set of documents about the individual objects, denoted by these nouns. They may be long expressions, denoting names of people, movies, music bands, and so on. Some examples are the movie *"Gone with the Wind"*, and the music band *"The Rolling Stones"*.

2. Build complex concepts. Complex concepts are built from atomic concepts as follows: first, we build formulas for words as the logical disjunction (⊔) of atomic concepts corresponding to the words' senses, and we write [x∗] to denote the disjunction of the senses of word x. For instance, the noun *"Programming"* becomes the concept [programming#1 ⊔ programming#2], whose interpretation is the set of documents which are about event scheduling and/or about computer programming. Second, labels are chunked, i.e., divided into sequences of syntactically correlated parts of words. We then translate syntactic relations of words within chunks to the logical connectives of L^C following a precise pattern. Let us consider few examples.

A set of adjectives followed by a noun group is translated into logical conjunction (⊓) of the formulas corresponding to the adjectives and the nouns. The interpretation of the resulting concept is the set of documents which are about the real world entities denoted by all the nouns, and which possess qualities, denoted by all the adjectives. For instance, the phrase *"long cold winter blizzard"* is translated into the concept [long∗ ⊓ cold∗ ⊓ winter∗ ⊓ blizzard∗]. Prepositions are also translated into the conjunction. The intuition is that prepositions denote some commonality between the objects they relate; and, in terms of the classification semantics, this "commonality" can be approximated to the set of documents which are about the both objects. For instance, the following phrases: *"books of magic"*, *"science in society"*, and *"software for engineering"*, they all denote what the two words, connected by the prepositions, have in common.

Coordinating conjunctions "and" and "or" are translated into the logical disjunction. For instance, *"flights or trains"* and *"animals and plants"* become [flight∗ ⊔ train∗] and [animal∗ ⊔ plant∗] respectively. Punctuation marks such as the period (.), the coma (,) and the semicolon (;) are also translated into logical disjunction. For instance, the phrase *"metro, bus, and trolley"* is converted into the concept [metro∗ ⊔ bus∗ ⊔ trolley∗].

Words and phrases denoting exclusions, such as "excluding", "except", "but not", are translated into the logical negation (¬). For instance, the label *"runners excluding sprinters"* becomes the concept [runner∗ ⊓ ¬sprinter∗]. However, since they are meant to describe what "there is" in the world, and not what "there isn't", labels contain very few such phrases, if at all.

The use of logical connectives, as described above but with the exception of prepositions, allows it to *explicitly* encode the classification semantics of labels. In other words, the interpretation of the resulting formulas explicitly represents the set of documents which are about the natural language labels. The translation of prepositions is an approximation, as they may encode meaning, which only partly can be captured by means of logical conjunction. For example, *"life in war"* and *"life after war"* will collapse into the same logical formula, whereas the classification semantics of the two labels is different. In this respect we are different from [18], where DL roles are used to encode the meaning of labels. The advantage of our approach is in that, while using a simpler subset of DLs, we are able to explicitly capture the semantics of a large portion of the label data in a real classification.

In order to estimate how much of the information encoded into the labels of a real classification can be captured using our approach, we have conducted a grammatical analysis of the DMOZ classification. For doing this, we have used the OpenNLP Tools tokenization and POS-tagging library [17], which reports to achieve more than 96% accuracy on unseen data. In Table 2 we show POS statistics of tokens. Note, that about 77.59% of the tokens (nouns and adjectives) become concepts, and about 14.69% (conjunctions and prepositions) become logical connectives of L^C. WordNet coverage for common nouns and adjectives is quite high, and constitutes 93.12% and 95.01% respectively. Detailed analysis of conjunctions and prepositions shows that about 85.26% of them are conjunctions "and", and about 0.10% are conjunctions "or". In our analysis we found no words or phrases which would result into the logical negation. Only about 4.56% of the tokens are verbs and adverbs in all their forms.

Table 2. DMOZ token statistics

POS	Share
Common nouns	71.22%
Proper nouns	0.18%
Adjectives	6.19%
Conjunctions and prepositions	14.69%
Verbs, adverbs	4.56%
Other POSs	3.16%

Note, that the propositional nature of L^C allows us to *explicitly* encode about 90.13% of label data in DMOZ (i.e., nouns, adjectives, conjunctions "and" and "or"). Still, this is a rough understated estimation, as we did not take into account multi-word nouns. In fact, manual analysis of the longest labels, as well as of the ones with verbs, shows that the majority of these labels represents proper names of movies, games, institutions, music bands, etc.

5   Disambiguating Edges

As discussed in Section 2, the classification semantics of links codifies the fact that child nodes' labels are always considered in the context of their parent nodes. This means that the meaning of a non-root node is the set of documents, which are about its label, and which are *also* about its parent node. We encode the classification semantics of links as a property of nodes in FCs, which we call the *concept at a node*. We write C_i to refer to the concept at node n_i, and we define this notion as:

$$C_i = \begin{cases} l_i^F & \text{if } n_i \text{ is the root of } FC \\ l_i^F \sqcap C_j & \text{if } n_i \text{ is not the root of } FC, \text{ where } n_j \text{ is the parent of } n_i \end{cases} \quad (1)$$

There may be two meaningful relations between the concept of a parent node, and the label of its child node, as represented in Figure 2:

– in case (a) the label of the child node is about the parent node, but it is also about something else. In this case the parent node *specializes* the meaning of the child node by bounding the interpretation of the child node's label with the interpretation of the concept of the parent node. For instance, think about a classification where the root node is labeled "Italy" and its sole child node is labeled "Pictures" (see Figure 2-a). A human can understand that the meaning of the child node is "pictures of Italy" and not "pictures of Germany", for example. In the corresponding FC this knowledge is encoded into the concept at node $C_2 = [\texttt{italy} * \sqcap \texttt{picture}*]$;

– in case (b) the child node represents a *specification* of the parent node, and their relation can be, for instance, an "is-a" or a "part-of" relation. Note, that in this case, differently from case (a), the parent node does not influence the meaning of the child node. Suppose that in the previous example the child node's label is "Liguria" (see Figure 2-b). A human can understand that the meaning of this node is the same as of its label. In the corresponding FC this knowledge is encoded into the concept at node $C_2 = [\texttt{italy} * \sqcap \texttt{liguria}*]$, which can be simplified to $C_2 = [\texttt{liguria\#1}]$, taking into account that both words "Italy" and "Liguria" have only one sense in WordNet, and given that the corresponding axiom $[\texttt{liguria\#1} \sqsubseteq \texttt{italy\#1}]$ is memorized in some background knowledge base.

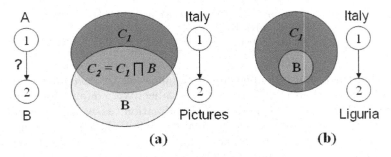

Fig. 2. Edge semantics in FCs

Note, that applying Equation 1 recursively, we can compute the concept at any non-root node n_i as the conjunction of the labels of all the nodes on the path from the root of the FC, n_1, to n_i. This corresponds to how the notion of concept at a node is defined in [7], namely:

$$C_i = l_1^F \sqcap l_2^F \sqcap \ldots \sqcap l_i^F \quad (2)$$

The concept at a node encodes, but only to a certain extent, the path from the root to the node. In fact, there may be more than one way to reconstruct a path from a concept. Atomic concepts in a concept at a node may be "distributed" differently among different number of nodes, which, in turn, may have a different order in the path. The number of nodes may range from one, when the concept at the node is equivalent to the node's label, to the number of clauses in the DNF equivalent of the concept. However, all the possible paths converge to the same semantically equivalent concept. Consider, for instance, node n_8 in the classification shown in Figure 1. All the following paths will converge to the same concept for this node[5]: *"top:publishing_and_printing:business_books:computers"*, *"top:business:publishing_and_printing:computer_books"*.

We use the notion of concept at a node to define a further new structure which we call *Normalized Formal Classification* (NFC). A NFC is *a rooted tree $NFC = \langle N, E, L^N \rangle$ where N is a finite set of nodes, E is a set of edges on N, and L^N is a finite set of labels expressed in L^C, such that for any node $n_i \in N$, there is one and only one label $l_i^N \in L^N$ and $l_i^N \equiv C_i$.*

Note, that the main characteristic of NFCs, that distinguishes them from FCs, is the fact that labels of child nodes are always more specific than the labels of their parent nodes. Particularly, if a taxonomic classification, i.e., a classification with only "is-a" and "part-of" links, is converted into a FC, then the latter is also a NFC. Apart from this, NFCs have a number of important properties relevant to classifications, discussed below:

- the classification semantics of the labels of nodes is the set of documents which *can* be classified in these nodes. We underline the "can" since, as we discuss in the next section, documents which *are* actually classified in the nodes are often a subset of the classification semantics of the labels;
- two nodes, representing in a classification the same real world entities, will have semantically equivalent labels in the NFC. This fact can be exploited for automatic location and/or prevention of adding of such "duplicate" nodes. As an example, consider the different paths that lead to the same concept at a node as described earlier in this section;
- NFCs are full-fledged lightweight ontologies, suitable for the automation of the core classification tasks, such as document classification, as it is discussed in the following section.

6   Document Classification

Before some document d can be classified, it has to be assigned an expression in L^C, which we call the *document concept*, written C^d. The assignment of concepts to documents is done in two steps: first, a set of keywords is retrieved from the document using text mining techniques (see, for example, [19]); the keywords are then converted into a concept using similar techniques to those used in the translation of natural language labels into labels in FCs (see Section 4).

We say that node n_i is a *classification alternative* for the classification of some document d with concept C^d, if $C^d \sqsubseteq l_i^N$. In fact, if this relation holds, then the

---

[5] For sake of presentation we give these examples in natural language.

document is about the classification node, whose semantics is encoded in the label of the NFC. For any given document d and a NFC, we compute the set of classification alternatives for d in the NFC as follows:

$$A(C^d) = \{n_i | C^d \sqsubseteq l_i^N\} \tag{3}$$

By computing Equation 3, we can automate step 3 described in Section 2. The automation of step 4, i.e., making classification choices, depends on what classification algorithm is used. Below we show how it can be automated for some set A of classification alternatives if the get-specific rule (see Section 2) is used:

$$C(A) = \{n_i \in A | \nexists n_j \in A \ (i \neq j), \ such \ that \ l_j^N \sqsubseteq l_i^N\} \tag{4}$$

The set $C(A)$ includes all the nodes in the NFC, whose labels are more general than the document concept, and more specific among all such labels. As labels of child nodes in NFCs are more specific than the labels of their parent nodes, $C(A)$ always consists of nodes which lie as low in the CNF tree as possible, and which are still classification alternatives for the document. Note, that the get-specific rule applies not only to nodes located on the same path from the root, but also to nodes located in different branches. For instance, a document about computer graphics will *not* be classified in the node *"top:computers"* if the more specific node *"top:arts:computers"* exists.

Formula 4 stipulates that the set of documents classified in some node n_i may (and, in most cases will) be a subset of the interpretation of its label l_i^N. In fact, the set of documents which are *actually* classified in n_i excludes those, which belong to the interpretation of labels, which are more specific than l_i^N. We encode this set in the concept D_i which univocally identifies the set of documents classified in node n_i, and, therefore, defines the classification semantics of n_i in the NFC. We compute D_i as follows:

$$D_i = l_i^N \sqcap \neg \bigsqcup (l_j^N | j \neq i, l_j^N \sqsubseteq l_i^N) \tag{5}$$

Computation of Equations 3, 4 and 5 requires verifying whether subsumption holds between two formulas in L^C. As discussed in [6], a problem, expressed in a propositional DL language, can be translated into an equivalent propositional satisfiability problem, and can therefore be solved using sound and complete reasoning procedures of a SAT decider. The translation rules from L^C to a propositional language transform atomic concepts into propositions, less generality into implication (i.e., $[A \sqsubseteq B] \Rightarrow [A \rightarrow B]$), disjunctions and conjunctions into logical or's and and's respectively (e.g., $[A \sqcup B] \Rightarrow [A \vee B]$), and so on. Interested readers are referred to [6] for details. Thus, if we need to check whether a certain relation *rel* holds between two concepts A and B, given some knowledge base $\mathcal{KB}$, which represents our a priori knowledge, we construct a propositional formula according to the pattern shown in Equation 6, and check it for validity:

$$\mathcal{KB} \rightarrow rel(A, B) \tag{6}$$

The intuition is that $\mathcal{KB}$ encodes what we know about concepts A and B, and $rel(A, B)$ holds only if it follows from what we know. In our approach $\mathcal{KB}$ is built as a set of axioms which encode the relations that hold between *atomic* concepts in A and B. As discussed in Section 4, atomic concepts in L^C are mapped to the corresponding natural language words' senses. These senses may be lexically related through the synonymy, antonymy, hypernymy (i.e., the "kind-of" relation, e.g., *car* is a kind of *vehicle*), or holonymy (i.e., the "part-of" relation, e.g., *room* is a part of *building*) relations. These relations can be translated into axioms, which *explicitly* capture the classification semantics of the relation that holds between the two senses. Thus, for instance, the set of documents which are about *cars* is a subset of the set of documents which are about a hypernym of the word "car", *vehicle*. The idea, therefore, is to find the lexical relations using WordNet, and to translate synonymy into logical equivalence, antonymy into disjointness, hypernymy and holonymy into subsumption in L^C.

Let us consider an example. Recall the classification in Figure 1, and suppose that we need to classify the following book: *"Java Enterprise in a Nutshell, Second Edition"*, whose concept is [java#3 ⊓ enterprise#2 ⊓ book#1]. It can be shown, by means of propositional reasoning, that the set of classification alternatives includes all the nodes of the corresponding NFC. For sake of space we provide concrete formulas only for nodes n_7 and n_8, whose labels are $l_7^N = $ [computer * ⊓programming * ⊓language * ⊓java*], and $l_8^N = $ [business * ⊓[publishing * ⊔printing*] ⊓publishing * ⊓books * ⊓computer*]. We can extract the following knowledge from WordNet: the programming language Java is a kind of programming languages, and it is a more specific concept than computer is; books are related to publishing; and enterprise is a more specific concept than business is. We encode this knowledge in the following axioms:

$$a_1 = [\text{java\#3} \sqsubseteq \text{pr\_language\#1}]; \quad a_3 = [\text{book\#1} \sqsubseteq \text{publishing\#1}];$$
$$a_2 = [\text{java\#3} \sqsubseteq \text{computer\#1}]; \quad a_4 = [\text{enterprise\#1} \sqsubseteq \text{business\#2}].$$

We then translate the axioms and the labels into the propositional logic language, and we verify if the condition in Formula 3 holds for the two labels by constructing two formulas, following the pattern of Equation 6, as shown below:

$$(a_2 \wedge a_3 \wedge a_4) \rightarrow (C^d \rightarrow l_8^N); \quad (a_1 \wedge a_2) \rightarrow (C^d \rightarrow l_7^N).$$

Then, we run a SAT solver on the above formulas, which shows that they are tautologies. It means that both nodes n_7 and n_8 are classification alternatives for the classification of the book. Among all the classification alternatives, only these two nodes conform to the get-specific rule, and, therefore, are final classification choices for the classification of the book. The latter can be shown by computing Equation 4 by means of propositional reasoning.

Note, that the edges of the NFC are *not* considered in document classification. In fact, the edges of the NFC become redundant, as their information is implicitly encoded in the labels. As from Section 5, there may be several paths to the same concept. Analogously, given a set of labels, there may be several ways to reconstruct the set of edges of a NFC. However, from the classification point of view, all these NFCs are equivalent, as they classify documents *identically*.

7   Related Work

In our work we adopt the notion of concept at a node as first introduced in [6] and further elaborated in [7]. Moreover, the notion of label of a node in a FC, semantically corresponds to the notion of concept of a label introduced in [7]. In [7] these notions play a key role in the identification of semantic mappings between nodes of two schemas. In this paper, these are the key notions needed to define NFCs.

This work as well as the work in [6, 7] mentioned above is crucially related and depends on the work described in [4, 13]. In particular, in [4], the authors introduce the idea that in classifications, natural language labels can be translated in logical formulas, while, in [13], the authors provide a detailed account of how to perform this translation process. The work in [6, 7] improves on the work in [4, 13] by understanding the crucial role that concepts at nodes have in matching heterogeneous classifications and how this leads to a completely new way to do matching. This paper, for the first time, recognizes the crucial role that the ideas introduced in [4, 6, 7, 13] have in the construction of a new theory of classification, and in introducing the key notion of FC.

A lot of work in information theory, and more precisely on formal concept analysis (see, for instance, [24]) has concentrated on the study of concept hierarchies. NFCs are what in formal concept analysis are called concept hierarchies with no attributes. The work in this paper can be considered as a first step towards providing a computational theory of how to transform the "usual" natural language classifications into concept hierarchies.

The classification algorithm, proposed in this paper, is similar to what in the DL community is called *realization*. Essentially, realization is the task of finding the most specific concept(s) an individual object is an instance of given a hierarchy of concepts [3]. The fundamental difference between the two approaches is in that in DL the concept hierarchy is *not* predefined by the user, but is built bottom-up from atomic concepts by computing the partial ordering of the subsumption relation. In our case, the underlying classification structure is defined solely by the user.

In Information Retrieval, the term *classification* is seen as the *process* of arranging a set of objects (e.g., documents) into *categories* or *classes*. There exist a number of different approaches which try to build classifications *bottom-up*, by analyzing the contents of documents. These approaches can be grouped in two main categories: *supervised classification*, and *unsupervised classification*. In the former case, a small set of training examples needs to be pre-populated into the categories in order to allow the system to automatically classify a larger set of objects (see, for example, [2, 15]). The latter approach uses various machine learning techniques to classify objects, for instance, data clustering [9]. There exist some approaches that apply (mostly) supervised classification techniques to the problem of documents classification into hierarchies [11, 21]. The classifications built following our approach are better and more natural than those built following these approaches. In fact, they are constructed *top-down*, as chosen by the user and not constructed bottom-up, as they come out of the document analysis. Our approach has the potential, in principle, to allow for the automatic classification of (say) the Yahoo! documents into the Yahoo! web directory.

8   Conclusions

In this paper we have introduced the notion of Formal Classification, namely of a classification where labels are written in a propositional concept language. Formal Classifications have many advantages over standard classifications all deriving from the fact that formal language formulas can be reasoned about far more easily than natural language sentences. In this paper we have highlighted how this can be done to perform document classification. However much more can be done. Our future work includes testing the feasibility of our approach with very large sets of documents, such as those classified in the DMOZ directory, as well as the development of a sound and complete query answering algorithm.

Acknowledgements

This work is partially supported by the FP6 project Knowledge Web[6]. We also thank all the members of the KnowDive group, and, especially, Mikalai Yatskevich, for the many useful discussions about earlier versions of this paper.

References

1. The WWW Virtual Library project. see http://vlib.org/.
2. G. Adami, P. Avesani, and D. Sona. Clustering documents in a web directory. *In Proceedings of Workshop on Internet Data management (WIDM-03)*, 2003.
3. Franz Baader, Diego Calvanese, Deborah McGuinness, Daniele Nardi, and Peter Patel-Schneider. *The Description Logic Handbook : Theory, Implementation and Applications*. Cambridge University Press, 2003.
4. P. Bouquet, L. Serafini, and S. Zanobini. Semantic coordination: a new approach and an application. *In Proc. of the 2nd International Semantic Web Conference (ISWO'03). Sanibel Islands, Florida, USA*, October 2003.
5. Lois Mai Chan and J.S. Mitchell. *Dewey Decimal Classification: A Practical Guide*. Forest P.,U.S., December 1996.
6. F. Giunchiglia and P. Shvaiko. Semantic matching. *workshop on Ontologies and Distributed Systems, IJCAI*, 2003.
7. F. Giunchiglia, P. Shvaiko, and M. Yatskevich. S-match: An algorithm and an implementation of semantic matching. *In Proceedings of ESWS'04*, 2004.
8. A.D. Gordon. *Classification*. Monographs on Statistics and Applied Probability. Chapman-Hall/CRC, Second edition, 1999.
9. A. K. Jain, M. N. Murty, and P. J. Flynn. Data clustering: a review. *ACM Computing Surveys*, 31(3):264–323, 1999.
10. Johnson-Laird. *Mental Models*. Harvard University Press, 1983.

---

[6] The Knowledge Web project. See http://knowledgeweb.semanticweb.org/.

11. Daphne Koller and Mehran Sahami. Hierarchically classifying documents using very few words. In Douglas H. Fisher, editor, *Proceedings of ICML-97, 14th International Conference on Machine Learning*, pages 170–178, Nashville, US, 1997. Morgan Kaufmann Publishers, San Francisco, US.
12. Douglas B. Lenat. CYC: A large-scale investment in knowledge infrastructure. *Communications of the ACM*, 38(11):33–38, 1995.
13. Bernardo Magnini, Luciano Serafini, and Manuela Speranza. Making explicit the semantics hidden in schema models. *In: Proceedings of the Workshop on Human Language Technology for the Semantic Web and Web Services, held at ISWC-2003, Sanibel Island, Florida*, October 2003.
14. George Miller. *WordNet: An electronic Lexical Database*. MIT Press, 1998.
15. Kamal Nigam, Andrew K. McCallum, Sebastian Thrun, and Tom M. Mitchell. Text classification from labeled and unlabeled documents using EM. *Machine Learning*, 39(2/3):103–134, 2000.
16. Natalya F. Noy. Semantic integration: a survey of ontology-based approaches. *SIGMOD Rec.*, 33(4):65–70, 2004.
17. The OpenNLP project. See http://opennlp.sourceforge.net/.
18. S. Sceffer, L. Serafini, and S. Zanobini. Semantic coordination of hierarchical classifications with attributes. Technical Report 706, University of Trento, Italy, December 2004.
19. Fabrizio Sebastiani. Machine learning in automated text categorization. *ACM Computing Surveys*, 34(1):1–47, 2002.
20. J. F. Sowa. *Conceptual Structures: Information Processing in Mind and Machine*. Addison-Wesley, 1984.
21. Aixin Sun and Ee-Peng Lim. Hierarchical text classification and evaluation. In *ICDM*, pages 521–528, 2001.
22. DMOZ: the Open Directory Project. See http://dmoz.org/.
23. Michael Uschold and Michael Gruninger. Ontologies and semantics for seamless connectivity. *SIGMOD Rec.*, 33(4):58–64, 2004.
24. Rudolf Wille. Concept lattices and conceptual knowledge systems. *Computers and Mathematics with Applications*, 23:493–515, 1992.

A Method to Convert Thesauri to SKOS

Mark van Assem[1], Véronique Malaisé[1], Alistair Miles[2], and Guus Schreiber[1]

[1] Vrije Universiteit Amsterdam, Department of Computer Science
{mark, vmalaise, guus}@cs.vu.nl
[2] CCLRC Rutherford Appleton Laboratory,
Business and Information Technology Department,
Oxfordshire, OX11 0QX, UK
A.J.Miles@rl.ac.uk

Abstract. Thesauri can be useful resources for indexing and retrieval on the Semantic Web, but often they are not published in RDF/OWL. To convert thesauri to RDF for use in Semantic Web applications and to ensure the quality and utility of the conversion a structured method is required. Moreover, if different thesauri are to be interoperable without complicated mappings, a standard schema for thesauri is required. This paper presents a method for conversion of thesauri to the SKOS RDF/OWL schema, which is a proposal for such a standard under development by W3Cs Semantic Web Best Practices Working Group. We apply the method to three thesauri: IPSV, GTAA and MeSH. With these case studies we evaluate our method and the applicability of SKOS for representing thesauri.

1 Introduction

Thesauri and thesauri-like resources such as MeSH [5] and the Art and Architecture Thesaurus [9] are controlled vocabularies developed by specific communities, often for the purpose of indexing (annotation) and retrieval (search) of resources (images, text documents, web pages, video, etc.). They represent a valuable means for indexing, retrieval and simple kinds of reasoning on the Semantic Web. Most of these resources are represented in databases, as XML files, or some other special-purpose data format. For deployment in Semantic Web applications an RDF/OWL representation is required. Thesauri can be converted to RDF/OWL in different ways. One conversion might define a thesaurus metamodel which represent terms as instances of a class `Term`, while another converts them into literals contained in a property `term`. This can introduce structural differences between the conversions of two thesauri which have the same semantics. Using a common framework for the RDF/OWL representation of thesauri (and thesauri-like resources) either enables, or greatly reduces the cost of (a) sharing thesauri; (b) using different thesauri in conjunction within one application; (c) development of standard software to process them (because there is no need to bridge structural differences with mappings). However, there is a significant amount of variability in features of thesauri, as exemplified by

Y. Sure and J. Domingue (Eds.): ESWC 2006, LNCS 4011, pp. 95–109, 2006.
© Springer-Verlag Berlin Heidelberg 2006

the case studies presented here. The challenge for a common metamodel such as SKOS is to capture the essential features of thesauri and provide enough extensibility to enable specific, locally-important thesaurus features to be represented.

The SKOS Core Guide [6] and the SKOS Core Vocabulary Specification [7] are currently Working Drafts for W3C Working Group Notes. They present the basic metamodel consisting of an RDF/OWL schema, an explanation of the features that the properties and classes of the schema represent. Guidelines and examples for extending SKOS Core are given by a proposed draft appendix to the SKOS Core Guide[1] and another draft proposes additional properties for representing common features in thesauri[2]. Because they are at the proposal stage they have no formal status within W3C process as yet. For the purpose of this paper we take these four documents to represent the SKOS metamodel and guidelines. Together they define (in a non-formal way) what constitutes a "correct" SKOS RDF document. SKOS models a thesaurus (and thesauri-like resources) as a set of `skos:Concept`s with preferred labels and alternative labels (synonyms) attached to them (`skos:prefLabel`, `skos:altLabel`). Instances of the Concept class represent actual thesaurus concepts can be related with `skos:broader`, `skos:narrower` and `skos:related` properties. This is a departure from the structure of many existing thesauri that are based on the influential ISO 2788 standard published in 1986, which has *terms* as the central entities instead of concepts. It defines two types of terms (preferred and non-preferred) and five relations between terms: broader, narrower, related, use and use for. Use and use for are allowed between preferred and non-preferred terms, the others only between preferred terms [2]. More recent standards such as ANSI/NISO Z39-19 acknowledge that terms are "lexical labels" representing concepts, but are still term-based format [1]. Often it is possible to convert a term-based thesaurus into a concept-based one, but sometimes information is lost (examples appear in the paper). The standards (including SKOS) allow polyhierarchies, i.e. a term/concept can have more than one **broader** term/concept.

Careful analysis of a thesaurus may still not result in an error-less, interoperable conversion to SKOS. To help ensure the quality and utility of conversions a structured method is required. This paper addresses a methodological research question: given the SKOS metamodel for thesauri, can a step-wise method be developed that assists in converting thesauri to this metamodel in a correct manner? The method should be able to guide the development of a deterministic program (i.e. does not require human intervention) that generates correct SKOS RDF for a specific thesaurus. We address the research question by first by examining existing thesaurus conversion methods in Section 2. Secondly, we develop our method by refining an applicable existing method in Section 3. Thirdly, we apply our method to three thesauri in Sections 4 through 6. Fourthly, we evaluate our method and the SKOS metamodel in Section 7.

---

[1] http://isegserv.itd.rl.ac.uk/cvs-public/~checkout~/skos/drafts/appextensions.html
[2] http://www.w3.org/2004/02/skos/extensions/spec/

2 Existing Thesaurus Conversion Methods

This section discusses existing methods to convert thesauri. We distinguish conversion methods for specific thesauri, method that convert thesauri to ontologies and methods that convert any thesaurus to RDF/OWL.

A first stream of research presents methods to convert one specific thesaurus from its native format to RDF/OWL, such as for MeSH [11] and the NCI thesaurus [3]. Although the steps and techniques developed for these methods are useful in thesaurus conversion, it is not clear if they can be applied to other thesauri because only features that appear in the specific thesaurus are covered. We do not consider these methods when choosing a method to base ours on.

A second stream of research presents methods with the goal to convert any thesaurus into an *ontology*, such as the work of Soergel et al. [10]. A major difference between thesauri and ontologies is that the latter feature logical is-a hierarchies, while in thesauri the hierarchical relation can represent anything from is-a to part-of. Their method has three steps: (1) define ontology metamodel; (2) define rules to convert a traditional thesaurus into the metamodel, introducing more specific kinds of relationships; and (3) manual correction. The main requirement of the method is to refine the usual thesaurus relationships into more specific kinds of relationships such as "causes", "hasIngredient" and "growsIn". The method does not target a specific output format, although hints are given for conversion to RDFS. It is not clear if the method would convert thesaurus concepts into `rdfs:Classes` with `rdfs:subClassOf` and other relations between them, or rather as instances of a class `Concept` as is in SKOS.

An elaborate 7-step method is defined by Hyvönen [4][3] with the goal of creating a true ontology consisting of an RDFS or OWL class hierarchy. Thesaurus concepts are converted into instances of a metaclass (a subclass of `rdfs:Class`) so that they are simultaneously instances and classes. A main requirement of the method is that conversion refines the traditional BT/NT relationships into `rdf:type`, `rdfs:subClassOf` or `partOf`. Another requirement is to rearrange the class hierarchy to better represent an ontological structure, e.g. to ensure only the real root concepts do not have a parent. Besides refining the relations it retains the original structure by also converting the BT/NT/RT relations into equivalent RDFS properties. It does not currently use SKOS.

A third stream of research presents methods to convert thesauri into RDF/OWL without creating an ontology. Earlier work by Van Assem et al. [12] describes a method to convert thesauri in four steps: (1) preparation; (2) syntactic conversion; (3) semantic conversion; and (4) standardization. In the first step, an analysis is made of the thesaurus and its digital format. This is used in step two to convert to very basic RDF, after which it is converted to more common modeling used in RDF and OWL in step three. In the last step the RDF/OWL metamodel developed for the specific thesaurus is mapped to SKOS. This method is based on two requirements: (a) preservation of the thesaurus' original semantics; and (b) step-wise refinement of the thesaurus' RDF/OWL metamodel.

---

[3] In Finnish, our understanding is based on correspondence with the author.

Work by Miles et al. [8] defines a method to convert thesauri to an earlier version of SKOS in three steps: (1) generate RDF encoding; (2) error checking and validation; and (3) publishing encoding on the web. Three case studies illustrate the method. It is based on two requirements: (a) conversion of a thesaurus to the SKOS model with the goal of supporting thesaurus interoperability (b) preserve all information encoded in the thesaurus. The first step is separated into conversion of thesauri with a "non-standard structure" or "standard structure". Thesauri with "standard structure" are based on the ISO 2788 standard. Such thesauri can be converted into instances of the SKOS schema without loss of information. Thesauri with "non-standard structure" are those who have "structural features that are not described by the standard ISO 2788". The recommendation is to develop an extension of the SKOS schema using `rdfs:subClassOf` and `rdfs:subPropertyOf` to support non-standard features as this solution ensures that both method requirements are met. The method and described cases does not admit of a third category of thesauri, namely those with non-standard structure which cannot be defined as a strict specialization of the SKOS schema (this paper shows examples of these). The second step comprises error checking and validation using the W3C's RDF validator, while the third step is not discussed further.

3   Development of Conversion Method

The development of our method is based on a tentative process with the following components: (a) defining requirements on the method; (b) comparing to existing methods and choosing an applicable one; (c) developing the steps of our method; (d) applying the method; and (e) evaluating the method. This section presents the first three components. We apply the method in Sects. 4 through 6 and evaluate in the discussion. We restrict the scope of our method to monolingual thesauri and do not discuss thesaurus metadata. We also ignore some practical issues such as defining an appropriate namespace for the converted thesaurus.

3.1   Method Goal and Requirements

The general goal of the method is to support interoperability of thesauri encoded in RDF/OWL. The first requirement of the method is to produce conversion programs that convert the digital representations of a specific thesaurus to SKOS. The underlying assumption is that converting to SKOS provides interoperability. A sub-requirement that follows is that the resulting conversion program should produce correct SKOS RDF. The second requirement of the method is that the converted thesaurus is complete (i.e. has all information that is present in the original) as long as this does not violate the previous requirement. For this method we value the goal of interoperability higher than the requirement of being complete.

3.2 Comparison with Existing Methods

Here we compare the goals and requirements to those of existing methods to choose a suitable one to use as a basis for our own. The method by Soergel et al. does not have interoperability of thesauri as a goal. For each thesaurus a new metamodel is developed. Its main requirement is to produce a more refined version of the thesaurus. This is not in opposition to our requirement of completeness, but does introduce more work than necessary to achieve our main goal and may also introduce incorrect interpretations of the thesaurus' relations.

In Hyvönen's method the thesaurus is converted into a rearranged class hierarchy. It does not use a standard metamodel such as SKOS to promote interoperability and it rearranges the thesaurus' original structure. The method by Van Assem et al. also does not have interoperability of thesauri as a goal. The metamodels of different thesauri converted using this method may have structural differences. The method by Miles et al. has the same goal as ours: interoperability of thesauri in RDF/OWL. The stated requirements of using SKOS and of completeness also match. A difference is that it does not acknowledge possible conflicts between these requirements.

3.3 Developing Steps of the Method

The method by Miles et al. has a comparable goal and requirements and therefore we take their method as a starting point and adapt it. We focus here on working out the first step of the method, namely producing a conversion ("encoding") of the thesaurus in correct SKOS RDF. We do not adapt and discuss steps two and three.

The first step in the method by Miles et al. is split in two different processes depending on whether the thesaurus is "standard" or "non-standard". This requires an analysis of the thesaurus, so we include this as a separate activity in our method. Furthermore, the two processes only differ on whether they convert directly to instances of the SKOS schema or into extensions of the SKOS schema (defined with `rdfs:subPropertyOf` and `rdfs:subClassOf`). We decide to merge the two processes, and for each thesaurus feature in the analysis we determine whether to use a class/property from the SKOS schema or define a new subclass/subproperty.

We analyzed which activities need to be performed in the step, starting with its inputs and outputs. The input of the step is the thesaurus digital format, and its documentation (including interviews with experts and applications that

Table 1. Substeps and activities of step 1

Substep	Activity	Output
(A) thesaurus analysis	analyze digital format, analyze documentation	catalogue of data items and constraints, list of thesaurus features
(B) mapping to SKOS	define data item to SKOS schema mapping	tables mapping data items to schema items
(C) conversion program	develop algorithm	conversion program

use the thesaurus such as websites). The output of the step should be a program that transforms the data from the original digital format to SKOS RDF. In some cases the output of the step will also include an extension of the SKOS schema. There are three activities to be performed that link output to input: creating an (algorithm for the) transformation program, defining a mapping between input data items and output SKOS RDF as a basis for the algorithm, analyzing the thesaurus. We split the last activity into two parallel analyses: an analysis of the digital format and of the documentation. Both are helpful to understand which features the thesaurus has and how they are encoded. This results in the substeps and activities summarized in Table 1.

For the thesaurus analysis, we have listed the set of features that appear in common thesauri. We derived this set from studying thesaurus standards [2, 1] and the SKOS documentation listed earlier. There are three sets: one specific to term-based thesauri, one specific to concept-based thesauri and one set that is used in both. *Term-based features* are: term, compound term (combination of two or more terms), "use" relation, "use for" relation, broader term relation between preferred terms, narrower relation between preferred terms, scope note attached to preferred term (indicates scope for which term can be used in indexing), documentation attached to terms such as definitions and historical notes. *Concept-based features* are: concept, compound concept, preferred labels, non-preferred labels, broader concept relation, narrower concept relation, documentation attached to concepts such as definitions and historical notes. General features are: node labels (explained later), facets (a top-level named group of terms or concepts that is not meant for use in indexing itself). SKOS is a concept-based model. Therefore, any feature that cannot be converted into a concept-based or generic feature falls outside the scope of the SKOS schema and thus of SKOS interoperability. Although most term-based features in their most basic form can be converted into concept-based features, there are exceptions.

A sub-activity we would like to highlight here is the identification of unique identifiers in the source to generate the rdf:IDs of skos:Concepts. Some thesauri like MeSH already provide unique identifiers, but others like GTAA do not provide one. A number of options exists: (a) generate completely new identifiers which have no relation to the terms or concepts themselves; or (b) use the name of the preferred term if it is unique (replacing illegal URI characters). The first option has the disadvantage of additional management (a mapping between source terms and identifiers needs to be maintained). The second option has the disadvantage that a concept is not independent of its name. Additional programming is required to ensure that when a term changes name, the corresponding skos:Concept's label is changed, instead of its URI. Currently we have not found a particular reason to prefer one option over the other.

In the next three sections we apply the method to three thesauri. We have chosen IPSV, GTAA and MeSH because they (a) are used in practice; and (b) represent progressively complex thesauri (i.e. non-standard features). The progressive complexity allows us to explore the limitations of our method and of SKOS.

4   Case Study: IPSV

The Integrated Public Sector Vocabulary (IPSV) is a thesaurus developed in the UK for indexing government documents[4]. It is modeled with the ISO2788/BS5723 standards in mind and contains 2732 preferred terms and 4230 non-preferred terms. The IPSV is a result of the merger of three thesauri. The sources and results of the conversion are available on-line[5].

Step A: analyze thesaurus. We used the XML version[6] in our analysis as it is the most complete. IPSV-XML has a DTD which provides the catalogue of data items and their constraints. IPSV-XML is a reasonably standard term-based thesaurus with preferred and non-preferred terms both called <Item>s in the XML data. Columns one and three of Table 2 list the data items and the features (for non-standard features we describe the function instead). IPSV provides unique identifiers for its terms and has a polyhierarchy.

Step B: map data items to SKOS. We have analyzed which data items correspond to which SKOS features or specializations of them (column three of Table 2). Although polyhierarchies are not allowed in ISO 2788, this is allowed in SKOS so this does not hinder a correct conversion. We were not able to find appropriate (specializations of) SKOS properties for the last four data items in the table. The two data items that indicate version information for terms cannot be made subproperties of `skos:altLabel` or `skos:prefLabel` as done for the `AToZ` attribute, because there is no place to store the version number (only literals are allowed for the label properties). A solution would be to attach two new properties to `skos:Concept` that have instances of a class `Term` as range. To these instances we can then attach a property that repeats the term name and then another property with the version number. Although this solution represents the information correctly, it introduces redundancy into the conversion (it repeats the term name with non-SKOS classes and properties). If this is not an issue this solution can be used to remain complete. However, it is a structural work-around because SKOS does not have the ability to attach information on specific `skos:prefLabels` and `skos:altLabels` directly.

Items that are `Obsolete` are removed from the actual thesaurus but are retained to be able to retrieve documents that were indexed with older versions of the thesaurus. The `skos:hiddenLabel` is intended to contain labels that should not be displayed to users but should be available for retrieval purposes, so we create an `ipsv:obsoleteTerm` that is a subproperty of `skos:hiddenLabel`. Shortcuts are attached to terms in the XML, but are actually meant to be able to insert a whole concept within an application, so it is attached to `skos:Concept` as a non-standard feature without a SKOS superproperty.

---

[4] http://www.esd.org.uk/standards/ipsv/index.html
[5] http://thesauri.cs.vu.nl/eswc06/
[6] Also available in other formats, see
   http://www.esd.org.uk/documents/IPSVVersionsAndFormats.pdf

Table 2. Mapping of IPSV Data Items to features and RDFS property/classes. The upper part lists standard features, the middle part specializations and the lower part non-standard features. Omitted closing tags in Data Item column.

Data Item	Feature/function	Property/class
<Item Id="A" ConceptId="B" Preferred="True"> <Name: >X	Preferred Term	skos:Concept with rdf:ID=A, skos:prefLabel=X attached to it
<Item Id="A" ConceptId="B" Type="Synonym"> <Name: >X	Non-Preferred Term	skos:prefLabel=X attached to concept with rdf:ID=B
<Item Type="misspelling"> <Name: >X	common misspelling of a (non)preferred term	skos:hiddenLabel=X
<UseItem>	USE relation	none required
<ScopeNote>X	ScopeNote	skos:scopeNote=X attached to concept created for surrounding <Item>
<BroaderItem Id="X">	Broader Term	skos:broader to Concept with rdf:ID=X
<RelatedItem Concep- tId="X">Y	Related Term	skos:related to Concept with rdf:ID=X
<BroaderItem Id="X" Default="true">	default broader term	ipsv:broaderDefault (subproperty of skos:broader) to Concept with rdf:ID=X
<Item AToZ="true" Preferred="Y">Z	term should be displayed on web-sites	ipsv:displayableAltLabel=Z (subproperty of skos:altLabel) when Y=false, ipsv:displayablePrefLabel=Z (subproperty of skos:prefLabel) when Y=true
<Item Obsolete="true">	obsolete term	ipsv:obsoleteTerm=X (subproperty of skos:hiddenLabel
<Item AddedInVer- sion="X">	X is a real indicating in which IPSV version the term was added	
<Item LastUpdatedIn- Version="X">	X is a real indicating in which IPSV version the term was last changed	
<Shortcut>X	X is a letter; keyboard shortcut for an application	ipsv:shortcut attached to concept created for surrounding <Item>

Step C: create conversion program. We created a SWI-Prolog program that parses the IPSV-XML file and converts it to SKOS RDF using the mappings from step 1b. The program takes an <Item> and applies the matching mappings between data items and SKOS RDF. There is no need for any other information external to the <Item> to generate the triples for that Item. For example, because non-preferred Items also contain the identifier of their preferred Item (in the ConceptId attribute), we can generate the skos:altLabel triple even if the preferred Item that is used to generate the skos:Concept is not yet processed.

Case study summary. The case study took one analyst approximately two weeks to perform and was not very complex as the thesaurus is not complicated and is clearly documented. For a few issues we contacted one of the original developers. We learned that it is not always possible to perform a complete information-preserving conversion as some information on terms was lost.

5   Case Study: GTAA

The GTAA thesaurus is the controlled vocabulary used at The Netherlands Institute for Sound and Vision[7], which archives and indexes most of the public broadcasted TV and radio programs of the Netherlands [8]. GTAA stands for *the Common Thesaurus for Audiovisual Archives*; it is the result of the collaborative work of different institutions concerned with audiovisual documents indexing, including the FilmMuseum of Amsterdam. It contains 159 831 preferred terms, 1900 non-preferred terms, and 88 categories. A sample of the source file, the conversion program and the resulting RDF are available on-line[9].

Step A: analyze thesaurus. We had access to GTAA documentation and data as text files with an ISO-style formatting. This thesaurus is a faceted term-based thesaurus, where only one facet (the Subject facet, used to describe the content of a program) is organized with the ISO 2788 broader term/narrower term hierarchy. The other facets are alphabetical controlled lists, with some scope notes (lists of people's names, geographical location, etc.). The Subject facet contains one non-standard feature called Category. Each term is supplied with at least one Category, providing an alternative way to the normal NT/BT hierarchy for indexers to find them. We list GTAA data items in column one of the upper part of Table 3 and the features they represent in column two.

Step B: map data items to SKOS. Two issues arose in this step. The first one concerns the GTAA BT relationship. In the documentation of the thesaurus, the BT and NT relationships are stated to be each other's inverse. In the data itself, two or more preferred terms can have a NT link with the same narrower term. However, this narrower term has only one BT link to one of the broader terms (instead of multiple BT links). There are two options: either the missing BT links are intended but omitted in the data, or the BT link has a special status, e.g. it is a `defaultBroader` such as in IPSV. After discussion with GTAA experts, and according to the fact that this defaultBroader relationship does not appear in the documentation, we mapped the GTAA BT to `skos:broader` (see column three of Table 3).

Secondly, there are two ways to interpret the CC relationship. Either it is meant to disambiguate different aspects of a term (as in "Chruch-institution" *vs* "Church-building"), or it is a way of grouping terms sharing a specific aspect (as with "Milk_by_animal" and "Cow-milk", "Buffalo-milk", etc.). In the second case, "Milk_by_animal" is called a node label: it is a way of grouping terms, but it should not be used for indexing. These node labels are ususally part of the term hierarchy. The experts indicated that this option was the intended usage of Categories: to provide a grouping of terms under a label that is not used in the indexing process. Nevertheless, they are meant to provide an *alternative*

---

[7] http://www.beeldengeluid.nl/index.jsp
[8] Of the estimated 850,000 hours of audio-visual material that is preserved in the Netherlands, around 700,000 hours is archived by Sound and Vision.
[9] http://thesauri.cs.vu.nl/eswc06/

Table 3. Mapping of GTAA Data Items to features and RDFS property/classes. Upper part lists standard features, the lower part specializations. "Term A" is an actual term in the thesaurus such as "Boat".

Data Item	Feature/function	Property/class
Term A	Preferred Term	`skos:Concept` with `rdf:ID=A`, `skos:prefLabel=A` attached to it
US Term B	Non-Preferred Term	`skos:altLabel=B` attached to concept
CC Category C	Grouping of Preferred Terms by Categories	`skos:member` between a `skos:Collection` (with `rdf:ID=C`) and a `skos:Concept`
BT Term A	Broader Term	`skos:broader`
NT Term A	Narrower Term	`skos:narrower`
RT Term A *or* See also	Related Term	`skos:related`
SN X *or* (X)	ScopeNote	`skos:scopeNote=X` attached to concept created for surrounding Preferred Term
LT	relationship between terms from different facets	`gtaa:hasLinkedTerm` (subproperty of `skos:related`)
DL	relationship between terms within a certain time period	`gtaa:hasDebateLine` (subproperty of `skos:related`)

grouping of the GTAA terms, and thus are not part of the BT/NT hierarchy. Although we mapped the Categories to an existing SKOS construct, namely the `skos:Collection` (see column three of Table 3), this modelling remains a non-standard feature that cannot be processed by SKOS software. The Categories have explicit identifiers, from which we could infer their hierarchy (01 stands for Philosophy, and 01.01 is one of its subdivisions, for instance).

GTAA does not include identifiers for its terms, so we used the preferred term's name as the `rdf:ID` of concepts.

Step C: create conversion program. As our source for the GTAA data was plain text, we created a Perl program to convert it according to the mappings in Table 3. We also had to make some manual corrections for reference errors introduced by thesaurus maintenance. Some relationships were referring to terms of the thesaurus that became obsolete, to terms which changed spelling, or to terms that became non-preferred terms. We corrected the references, or suppressed the relationships when no reference could be found; as these are relatively straightforward decisions no expert involvement was necessary.

Case study summary. The conversion could be made by direct mapping to or by extension of the SKOS schema, except for the Categories. In the conversion process, understanding the GTAA model from textual resources and experts interview, and converting the Categories into a SKOS construct took the longest time. Including programming, the process took about two weeks for one person and a half full time.

6 Case Study: MeSH

The Medical Subject Headings (MeSH) is a large thesaurus-like vocabulary developed by the U.S. National Library of Medicine and used to index millions of biomedical article citations[10]. It contains 22,997 "descriptors", most of which are used to index the subject of articles (two of the trees do not contain subjects but publication types and geographical regions). MeSH is the result of a merger of many different sources. The input data files and results of the conversion are available on-line[11].

Step A: analyze thesaurus. MeSH is available in different formats which contain the same information. We chose the XML version[12] because it is easier to analyze and convert. MeSH-XML has a DTD which provides us with the data catalogue and constraints. MeSH is a concept-based thesaurus without facets. Concepts are called "Descriptors" in MeSH terminology. The MeSH structure is complicated: "Descriptors" contain "Concepts", "Concepts" contain "Terms". Each has a name and a unique identifier, and to each entity documentation is attached such as its date of introduction and historical notes. Descriptors are hierarchically related: each MeSH Descriptor has one or more "TreeNumbers", which implicitly encode its position in a polyhierarchy (e.g. A01.456 is a child of A01). Each Descriptor has a preferred Concept, and each Concept has a preferred Term. MeSH Concepts that appear within one Descriptor can be related to each other with relations "brd", "nrw" and "rel". MeSH has fifteen trees with top-concepts named e.g. "organisms" or "diseases". These appear to be facets, but they are used in idexing articles so we interpret them as normal thesaurus Concepts.

As the MeSH DTD defines almost 90 tags[13] and for each tag different attributes, we only list the exemplary and special data items in column one of Table 4 (the corresponding feature, or function if it is a non-standard feature, is in column two). MeSH Descriptors have a redundant <DescriptorName> and <ConceptName> as these strings are the same as the name of the preferred Concept and Term, respectively.

MeSH has two non-standard features that require special attention. Firstly, so-called Qualifiers are used to indicate specific aspects of Descriptors, such as "pathology" or "abnormalities". They are combined with Descriptors to enable more specific article indexing (e.g. "Abdomen/abnormalities"). Secondly, so-called EntryCombinations relate a non-preferred Descriptor/Qualifier pair to a preferred Descriptor/Qualifier pair (or preferred Descriptor without Qualifier). This is comparable to but slightly different from the ISO 2788 "USE" relation, which can be used to point from a non-preferred non-compound term to a preferred compound term. The difference is that in MeSH the preferred concept is a compound.

Step B: map data items to SKOS. We mapped Descriptor to skos:Concept instances and sub-tags to properties of skos:Concept (see Table 4). Each child Descriptor is linked to its parent(s) - stated implicitly in the <TreeNumber>

---

[10] http://www.ncbi.nlm.nih.gov/entrez/
[11] http://thesauri.cs.vu.nl/eswc06/
[12] http://www.nlm.nih.gov/mesh/filelist.html
[13] An overview of their meaning is given in:
http://www.nlm.nih.gov/mesh/xml_data_elements.html

Table 4. Mapping of representative MeSH Data Items to features and RDFS property/classes. Upper part lists standard features, the middle part specializations and lower part non-standard features. Omitted closing tags in Data Item column.

Data Item	Feature/function	Property/class
`<DescriptorRecord>` `<DescriptorName>` `<String>`X `<DescriptorUI>`Y	Concept	`skos:Concept` with `rdf:ID`=Y and `skos:prefLabel`=X
`<Concept` `PreferredConceptYN="Y">` `<ScopeNote>`X	Scope Note	`skos:scopeNote`=X attached to concept created for surrounding `<DescriptorRecord>`
`<TreeNumber>`X	implicitly indicates Broader Concept	`skos:broader` to concept with `rdf:ID`=X
`<Term` `RecordPreferredTerm="N">` `<String>`B	Non-preferred Label	`skos:altLabel`=B attached to concept with `rdf:ID` found in surrounding Descriptor
`<SeeRelatedDescriptor>` `<DescriptorReferredTo>` `<DescriptorUI>`X `<DescriptorName>`Y	Related Concept	`skos:related` to Concept with `rdf:ID`=X
`<HistoryNote>`X	Historical Note	`mesh:historyNote`=X (subproperty of `skos:historyNote`)
Data Item	**Feature/function**	**Property/Class**
`<EntryCombination>` `<ECIN>` X `<ECOUT>` Y	Compound Concept and special relation (see text). X and Y contain tags with the identifiers of one Descriptor/Qualifier pair in them	`mesh:CompoundConcept` `mesh:Qualifier` `mesh:main` `mesh:qualifier` (subclasses and subproperties of `skos:Concept` and `skos:broader`) `mesh:preferredCombination` (no parent)
`<PublicMeSHNote>`X	Note mixing historical and see also information	`mesh:publicMeSHNote`=X (subproperty of `skos:note`)
`<PreviousIndexing>`X	Historical Note	`skos:historyNote`
`<ConsiderAlso>`X	textual reference to other possible records	`mesh:considerAlso`=X (subproperty of `skos:note`)
`<ActiveMeSHYear>`X	Year in which the Descriptor was part of MeSH	`mesh:activeMeSHYear`=X (subproperty of `skos:editorialNote`)
`<RecordOriginator>`X	Thesaurus where the Descriptor comes from	`mesh:recordOriginator` (suproperty of `skos:note`)
`<DateCreated>`X	Date Descriptor was first created	`mesh:dateCreated`=X (subproperty of `skos:editorialNote`
Data Item	**Feature/function**	**Property/class**
`<ActiveMeSHYear>`	Year in which Descriptor was present in MeSH	`mesh:activeMeSHYear`
`<DescriptorClass>`	Classifies Descriptor into one of four numbered categories, including "topical descriptor" and "publication type"	`mesh:descriptorClass`
`<RunningHead>`	page header used in printed MeSH versions	`mesh:runningHead`
`<LexicalTag>`	lexical category of a `<Term>`	
`<Abbreviation>`	abbreviation of a `<Term>`	

tag(s) - with `skos:broader`. We only map Descriptor names one time, removing the redundancy.

Because the MeSH Concepts and Terms are converted into `skos:prefLabel` and `skos:altLabels`, information about the Concepts and Terms themselves is lost. One example is the Concept's "brd", "nrw" and "rel" relations. These cannot be mapped to the broader/narrower concept feature, because the Descriptor hierarchy is already mapped to that. Two more examples are the Term's <Abbreviation> and <LexicalTag>. Only in cases where it is valid to attach information about a Concept or Term to the Descriptor can this information be preserved by attaching it to the `skos:Concept`, which is not the case for a number of Concept and Term tags. An example where this *is* possible is with a preferred Concept's <ScopeNote>.

To support the use of Descriptor/Qualifier pairs in indexing we introduced classes `mesh:Qualifier` and `mesh:CompoundConcept` as subclass of `skos:Concept`. Qualifiers are a special class of Concepts because they do not have broader/narrower relations themselves. The properties `mesh:main` and `mesh:qualifier` are used to attach a Descriptor (`skos:Concept`) and Qualifier (`mesh:Qualifier`) to the CompoundConcept. By making the properties a subproperty of `skos:broader`, the CompoundConcepts become narrower concepts of their contained concept, so that queries for documents with that concept as subject will also return documents indexed with the CompoundConcept. For the `rdf:ID` of the CompoundConcept the unique Descriptor and Qualifier identifiers are concatenated. We used the same CompoundConcept class to represent <EntryCombination>s which we link with `mesh:preferredCombination`. This last property does not have a SKOS parent. The only candidate `skos:related` has a different semantics: it links preferred concepts that are related in meaning (a symmetric relation), while `mesh:preferredCombination` links a non-preferred concept to a preferred concept (asymmetric relation).

Step C: create conversion program. We created a SWI-Prolog program that parses the MeSH-XML file and converts it to SKOS RDF using the mappings from step B. The program takes a DescriptorRecord tag and converts it into a `skos:Concept`. It also converts the non-standard features of MeSH.

Case study summary. The case study took one analyst approximately two weeks to perform and was relatively complex because of the many non-standard features and ambiguities. We have not yet been able to confirm our decisions with MeSH experts. We learned that some thesauri have complex structures for which no SKOS counterparts can be found (e.g. information on Terms) and that for some features care is required in converting them in such a way that they are still usable for their original purpose (e.g. the CompoundConcepts).

7   Discussion and Evaluation

In this section we first evaluate our method and then discuss the applicability of the SKOS metamodel for representing thesauri. The case studies showed that the method gives appropriate guidance in identifying common features of thesauri. However, we found that two of our three cases had non-standard features which our method cannot anticipate. Further case studies should increase the number of identified non-standard features to be incorporated into the method. For the analysis of the meaning of some features it is necessary to investigate how the feature is used in practice (e.g. GTAA Categories). Conversion of concept-based thesauri should be simpler than term-based thesauri as SKOS is concept-based, but we cannot confirm this as MeSH is not typical of the first category. Although MeSH was not a good choice as a case study in this respect, it did help us in identifying the boundaries of applicability of SKOS (see below). A problematic type of feature are textual notes that mix several kinds of knowledge (e.g. <PublicMeSHNote> contains historical and see also information). Our method does not investigate if it is possible to separate them. We are currently unsure whether such an investigation will result in generic rules that can be incorporated in our method.

The SKOS metamodel itself seems applicable for representing resources which have considerable resemblance to the ISO 2788 standard. From the MeSH case we learned that SKOS does not have a standard class to represent compound concepts, although this is a feature that is defined in ISO 2788. A related ISO feature, the USE relation from non-preferred compound terms to preferred ones has no SKOS counterpart either. Thesauri such as IPSV and MeSH also represent management information about their terms (e.g. date of term creation) which cannot be represented within SKOS itself . One might argue that this information is not relevant to a thesaurus' content. It may represent information on a higher level of abstraction that should not be considered for conversion. However, SKOS does partly supports representing other types of management information e.g. with the skos:changeNote and skos:editorialNote. Besides management information, there is also additional content information on terms that cannot be represented in SKOS, such as the MeSH <LexicalTag>. If it is appropriate to represent additional information on terms, a solution is to introduce into SKOS a new class skos:Term as the range of skos:prefLabel and skos:altLabel. This would enable terms to be entities in themselves to which additional properties can be attached.

Lastly, we note that it is difficult to confirm whether or not a given RDF document is valid SKOS RDF. The draft SKOS Test Set[14] and implementation[15] can simplify this in the future.

Acknowledgements. This work was partly supported by NWO's CHIME and CHOICE projects. The authors wish to thank Stella Dextre Clarke for providing information concerning the IPSV and Eero Hyvönen for correspondence on his method. The authors also thank all participants of *public-esw-thes@w3c.org* who have contributed to the development of SKOS.

References

1. ANSI/NISO. Guidelines for the construction, format, and management of monolingual thesauri. Ansi/niso z39.19-2003, 2003.
2. International Organization for Standardization. Documentation - guidelines for the establishment and development of monolingual thesauri. Iso 2788-1986, 1986.

---

[14] http://isegserv.itd.rl.ac.uk/cvs-public/~checkout~/skos/drafts/integrity.html
[15] http://www.w3.org/2004/02/skos/core/validation

3. J. Goldbeck, G. Fragoso, F. Hartel, J. Hendler, B. Parsia, and J. Oberthaler. The National Cancer Institute's Thesaurus and Ontology. *Journal of Web Semantics*, 1(1), Dec 2003.

4. Eero Hyvönen. Miksi asiasanastot eivät riitä vaan tarvitaan ontologioita? why thesauri are not enough but ontologies are needed? (in finnish). *Tietolinja*, (2), 2005. ISSN 1239-9132, URL: http://www.lib.helsinki.fi/tietolinja/0205/index.html.

5. D. Johnston, S. J. Nelson, J. Schulman, A. G. Savage, and T. P. Powell. Redefining a thesaurus: Term-centric no more. In *Proc. of the 1998 AMIA Annual Symposium.*

6. A. Miles and D. Brickley (editors). SKOS Core Guide. W3C Public Working Draft, World Wide Web Consortium, November 2005. Latest version: http://www.w3.org/TR/swbp-skos-core-guide.

7. A. Miles and D. Brickley (editors). SKOS Core Vocabulary Specification. W3C Public Working Draft, World Wide Web Consortium, November 2005. Latest version: http://www.w3.org/TR/swbp-skos-core-spec/.

8. A. Miles, N. Rogers, and D. Beckett. Migrating Thesauri to the Semantic Web - Guidelines and case studies for generating RDF encodings of existing thesauri. Deliverable 8.8, SWAD-Europe, 2004. URL: http://www.w3.org/2001/sw/Europe/reports/thes/8.8/.

9. T. Peterson. *Introduction to the Art and Architecture Thesaurus.* Oxford University Press, 1994.

10. D. Soergel, B. Lauser, A. Liang, F. Fisseha, J. Keizer, and S. Katz. Reengineering thesauri for new applications: the AGROVOC example. *Journal of Digital Information*, 4(4), 2004.

11. L.F. Soualmia, C. Goldbreich, and S.J. Darmoni. Representing the mesh in owl: Towards a semi-automatic migration. In *Proc. of the 1st Int'l Workshop on Formal Biomedical Knowledge Representation (KR-MED 2004)*, pages 81–87, Whistler, Canada, 2004.

12. M. van Assem, M. R. Menken, G. Schreiber, J. Wielemaker, and B. Wielinga. A method for converting thesauri to rdf/owl. In S. A. McIlraith, D. Plexousakis, and F. van Harmelen, editors, *Proc. of the 3rd Int'l Semantic Web Conf. (ISWC'04)*, number 3298 in Lecture Notes in Computer Science, pages 17–31. Springer-Verlag, 2004.

Ontology Engineering Revisited:
An Iterative Case Study*

Christoph Tempich[2], H.Sofia Pinto[1], and Steffen Staab[3]

[1] Dep. de Engenharia Informática, Instituto Superior Técnico, Lisboa, Portugal
sofia.pinto@dei.ist.utl.pt
[2] Institute AIFB, University of Karlsruhe (TH), 76128 Karlsruhe, Germany
tempich@aifb.uni-karlsruhe.de
[3] ISWeb, University of Koblenz Landau, 56016 Koblenz, Germany
staab@uni-koblenz.de

Abstract. Existing mature ontology engineering approaches are based on some basic assumptions that are often violated in practice, in particular in the Semantic Web. Ontologies often need to be built in a *decentralized* way, ontologies must be given to a community in a way such that individuals have *partial autonomy* over them and ontologies have a life cycle that involves an *iteration* back and forth between construction/modification and use. While recently there have been some initial proposals to consider these issues, they lack the appropriate rigor of mature approaches. i.e. these recent proposals lack the appropriate depth of methodological description, which makes the methodology usable, and they lack a proof of concept by a long-lived case study. In this paper, we revisit mature and new ontology engineering methodologies. We provide an elaborate methodology that takes decentralization, partial autonomy and iteration into account and we demonstrate its proof-of-concept in a real-world cross-organizational case study.

1 Introduction and Motivation

Ontologies are used in order to improve the quality of communication between computers, between humans and computers as well as between humans. An ontology is an agreement supporting such communication and this agreement must be constructed in a comprehensive ontology engineering process. There are several mature methodologies that have been proposed to structure this process and thus to facilitate it (cf. [1, 2, 3]) and their success has been demonstrated in a number of applications.

Nevertheless, these methodologies make some basic assumptions about the ontology engineering process and about the way the resulting ontologies are used. In practice, we observe that these methodologies neglect some important issues:

Decentralization: The methodologies do not take into account that even a medium sized group of stakeholders of an ontology is often quite *distributed* and does not necessarily meet often or easily.

---

* Research reported in this paper has been financed by EU in the IST projects SEKT (IST-2003-506826) and aceMedia (IST-FP6-001765).

Y. Sure and J. Domingue (Eds.): ESWC 2006, LNCS 4011, pp. 110–124, 2006.

Partial Autonomy: Users of an ontology are typically forced to use an ontology as is or to forget about it. A typical situation that we have encountered was that people want to retain a part of the shared ontology and *modify it locally*, i.e. personalize it.

Iteration: The methodologies mention the problem of evolving the ontology, but the cases that support the methodologies are typically cases where the construction phase of the ontology strictly precedes the usage phase of the ontology while we often see the need for interleaving ontology construction and use. Moreover, there is a lack of case studies that support hypothesis about how to iterate in the ontology *evolution* process.

These issues arise naturally for many ontologies and one might claim for all ontologies in the Semantic Web! Recently a number of approaches that touch these issues have been proposed [4, 5, 6] — among them our own, DILIGENT. However, **none** of these approaches *elaborated* their methodological description or *tested* their proposals in a case study with regard to Decentralization, Partial Autonomy and Iteration between the definition and the use of an ontology.

In this paper, we present our approach, DILIGENT. It is based on the process model described in [4]. We add substance to existing proposals by, *(i)*, specifying the internal structure of methodology stages[1] (i.e. their input, output, decision points, actions to be taken in each stage, and available tool support) and, *(ii)*, by providing a comprehensive case study that takes Decentralization, Partial Autonomy as well as Iteration between ontology construction/modification and usage seriously in a real-world case study of 3 months duration, where the ontology was the driving factor of a cross-organizations peer-to-peer knowledge management platform.

In the following, we first revisit ontology engineering methodologies to describe our starting point (Section 2). In Section 3, we survey our way of arriving at the methodology described here. Then we describe the refinements, adaptations and extensions we made to related methodologies in Section 4. Because of space restrictions, this description can only highlight some of our methodological improvements. For the full description we refer the reader to a technical report [7]. We evaluate DILIGENT by comparing it in detail to other methodologies (Section 5) and by validating it through a case study (Section 6) that shows a concrete instantiation of our methodology including two full iterations of the ontology life cycle.

2 Related Work

In the past, there have been OE case studies involving dispersed teams, such as $(KA)^2$ ontology [6] or [8]. However, they usually involved tight control of the ontology, of its development process, and of a small team of ontology engineering experts that could cope with the lack of precise guidelines.

Established methodologies for ontology engineering summarized in [1, 2, 3], focus on the centralized development of static ontologies, i.e. they do not consider iteration between construction/modification and use. **METHONTOLOGY** [1] and the **OTK**

---

[1] To facilitate reading, we introduce here a convention to refer to parts of processes. We call a larger part a 'process stage' or 'stage' and a smaller part, which is also a part of a stage, a 'process action' or 'action'.

methodology [2] are good examples for this approach. They offer guidance for building ontologies either from scratch, reusing other ontologies as they are, or re-engineering them. They divide OE processes into several stages which produce an evaluated ontology for a specific domain. **Holsapple et al.** [9] focus their methodology on the collaborative aspects of ontology engineering but still aim at a static ontology. A knowledge engineer defines an initial ontology which is extended and modified based on the feedback from a panel of domain experts. **HCOME** is a methodology which integrates argumentation and ontology engineering in a distributed setting [5]. It supports the development of ontologies in a decentralized setting and allows for ontology evolution. It introduces three different spaces in which ontologies can be stored: In the *Personal Space* users can create and merge ontologies, control ontology versions, map terms and word senses to concepts and consult the top ontology. The evolving personal ontologies can be shared in the *Shared Space*. The *Shared Space* can be accessed by all participants. In the shared space users can discuss ontological decisions. After some discussion and agreement, the ontology is moved into the *Agreed space*. However, they have neither reported that their methodology had been applied in a case study nor do they provide any detailed description of the defined process stages.

3   Developing the New DILIGENT OE Methodology

In order to arrive at a sound OE methodology we have proceeded in five steps to develop DILIGENT. First, we built on [8] to conceive our initial DILIGENT framework. Second, this framework contained a step for initially constructing a core ontology. With regard to this step, we decided not to develop a new methodology but to adopt the OTK methodology. Third, in order to validate the combined methodology, we analyzed its potential for the past (and ongoing) development process that has led to the biological taxonomy of living species and we conducted a lab experiment case study (cf. [10]). Fourth, we started a real-life case study and reported about its initial state and supporting means in [4]. Fifth, by the sum of these initial methodologies, cases and experiments, we arrived at the new and refined DILIGENT methodology that we present here. The focus of the refinement has been on decentralization, iteration and partial autonomy as well as on guiding users who were not ontology engineering experts. The methodology has been validated by the iterative case study presented in Section 6. Thus, we could repeatedly switch between hypothesis formulation and validation in order to present the result of step five and its validation in the remainder of this paper.

4   The DILIGENT Methodology

In order to give the necessary context for the detailed process description as depicted in Fig. 1 we start by summarizing the overall DILIGENT process model.

4.1   General Process

The **DILIGENT** process [4] supports its participants, in collaboratively building one shared ontology. The process comprises five main activities: (I) **build**, (II) **local adaptation**, (III) **analysis**, (IV) **revision**, (V) **local update**. The process starts by having *domain experts*, *users*, *knowledge engineers* and *ontology engineers* **build**ing an initial ontology. It proposes that the team involved in building the initial ontology should be relatively small, in order to more easily find a small and consensual first version of the shared ontology. At this point, it is not required to arrive at an initial ontology that would cover the complete domain. Once the initial ontology is made available, users can start using it and **locally adapting** it for their own purposes. Typically, due to new business requirements, or user and organization changes, their local ontologies evolve. In their local environment they are free to change the reused shared ontology. However, they are not allowed to directly change the ontology shared by all users.

A board of ontology stakeholders **analyzes** the local ontologies and the users' requests and tries to identify similarities in their ontologies. At this point it is not intended to merge all local ontologies. Rather changes to local ontologies will be analysed by the board in order to decide which changes introduced or requested by the users will be introduced. Therefore, a crucial activity of the board is deciding which changes are going to be introduced in the next version of the shared ontology. A balanced decision that takes into account the different needs of user's evolving requirements has to be found. The board should regularly **revise** the shared ontology, so that the parts of the local ontologies overlapping the domain of the shared ontology do not diverge too far from it. Therefore, the board should have a well-balanced and representative participation of the different kinds of participants involved in the process, which includes *ontology engineers*, *domain experts* and *users*.[2] Once a new version of the shared ontology is released, users can **update** their own **local** ontologies to better use the knowledge represented in the new version. The last four stages of the process are performed in a cyclic manner: when a new common ontology is available a new round starts again.

4.2 DILIGENT Process Stages

In order to facilitate the application of ontology engineering processes in real settings, DILIGENT had to be detailed to provide guidance to its participants. For this purpose, we have analyzed the different process stages in detail. For each stage we have identified (i) major roles, (ii) input, (iii) decisions, (iv) actions, (v) available tools, and (vi) output information. One should stress that this elaboration is rather a recipe or check list than an algorithm or integrated tool set. In different contexts it may have to be adapted or further refined to fit particular needs and settings. Tools may need to be integrated or customized to match requirements of the application context. In Fig. 1 we sketch our results, which are presented in the following. For lack of space we refer the reader to a technical report that includes a more detailed description of all items depicted in Fig. 1 [7]. In this paper we consider 'Local Adaptation', 'Revision', and 'Local Update' at an abstract level, zoom only into the 'Analysis' stage in an exemplary fashion and we omit the 'Build' stage, which is well-covered by existing methodologies [1, 2].

Local Adaptation

Roles: The actors involved in the local adaptation step are users of the ontology. They use the ontology e.g. to retrieve documents which are related to certain topics modelled in the ontology or more structured data like the projects an employee was involved in.

---

[2] These are roles that may overlap.

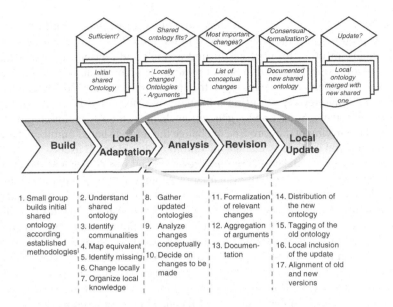

Fig. 1. Process stages (1-5), actions (1-17) and structures

Input: Besides the common shared ontology, in the local adaptation step the information available in the local information space is used. This can be existing databases, ontologies or folder structures and documents.

Decisions: The actors must decide which changes they want to make to their local ontology. Hence, they must decide if and where new concepts are needed and which relations a concept should have. They should provide reasons for their decisions.

Actions: To achieve the desired output the user performs different actions namely (2) *Understand shared ontology*, (3) *Identify communalities between own and shared conceptualization*, (4) *Map equivalent conceptualizations of different actors*, (5) *Identify missing conceptualizations*, (6) *Change conceptualization* and finally (7) *Organize local knowledge according to the conceptualization*.

The last three actions of the process step are performed in a cyclic manner until a new common ontology is available and the entire process step starts again. The single actions performed manually would require a grounded understanding of ontologies and their underlying formal representation. We cannot expect such knowledge from all actors participating in the process. The process should rather be integrated seamlessly in the environment the user works in. Hence we now indicate for each of the actions some available technology to support the actors.

Tool support: Building is supported by existing ontology editors like [11]. In [4] we describe how existing structure on local machines can be utilized to facilitate the creation of ontologies. The tool supports thus actions (3) and (5). We have further integrated ontology mapping to support step (4). (6) is a manual step. (7) is currently a manual step, too, but it could be supported by semi automatic classification.

Output: The output of the process step is a locally changed ontology which better reflects the user's needs. Each change is supported by arguments explaining the reasons for a change. At this point changes are not propagated to the shared ontology. Only in the *analysis step* the board gathers all ontology change requests and their corresponding arguments to be able to evolve the common shared ontology in the *revision step*.

Analysis

In this stage, in the middle of the overall ontology engineering process, the board (cf. the description of DILIGENT in Sec. 2) analyzes incoming requests and observations of changes. The frequency of this analysis is determined based on the frequency and volume of changes to the local ontologies.

Roles: In the analysis stage we can distinguish three roles played by board members: (i) The domain expert decides which changes to the common ontology are relevant for the domain and which are relevant for smaller communities only. (ii) Representatives of the users explain different requirements from the usability perspective. At this stage, work is conducted at a conceptual level. (iii) The ontology engineers analyze the proposed changes from a knowledge representation point of view foreseeing whether the requested changes could later be formalized and implemented.[3]

Input: The analysis stage takes as input the ontology changes proposed and/or made by the participating actors. To be able to understand the change requests, users should provide their reasons for each request. Both manual and automated methods can be used in the previous stages. Besides of arguments by ontology stakeholders, one may here consider rationales generated by automated methods, e.g. ontology learning. The arguments underlying the proposed changes constitute important input for the board to achieve a well balanced decision about which changes to adopt.

Decisions: The board must decide which changes to introduce into the new shared ontology at the conceptual level. Metrics to support this decision are (i) the number of users who introduced a change in proportion to all users who made changes. (ii) The number of queries including certain concepts. (iii) The number of concepts adapted by the users from previous rounds.

Actions: To achieve the desired output the board takes different actions namely (8) *Gather locally updated ontologies and corresponding arguments*, (9) *Analyze the introduced changes* and (10) *Identify changes presumably relevant for a significant share of all actors.*

Tool support: In [4] we present an extension to an ontology editor, which supports actions (8) and (9) and (10). (8) Ontologies can be collected from the users in a peer-to-peer system. Different sorting and grouping mechanisms help the board to analyze the introduced changes systematically. The identification of relevant changes is in the end a community process. Here we support decision making by structured argumentation support as described in [12].

Output: The result is a list of major changes to be introduced that were agreed by the board. All changes which should not be introduced into the shared ontology are filtered. At this stage it is not required to decide on the final modelling of the shared ontology.

---

[3] In the revision stage.

We now detail each one of the proposed actions:[4]

(8) Gather locally updated ontologies and corresponding arguments: Depending on the deployed application the gathering of the locally updated ontologies can be more or less difficult. It is important that the board has access to the local changes from users to be able to analyze them. It might also be interesting not only to analyze the final user ontology, but also its evolution. However, with an increasing number of participants this in-depth analysis might be unfeasible. Since analysis takes place at the conceptual level, reverse engineering is usually an important technique to get the conceptual model from the formalized model [1]. To support users providing their reasons, an argumentation framework that focuses the user on the relevant arguments was developed *cf.* [12].

(9) Analyze introduced changes: The number of change requests may be large and also contradictory. First the board must identify the different areas in which changes took place. Within analysis the board should bear in mind that changes of concepts should be analyzed before changes of relations and these before changes of axioms. Good indicators for changes relevant to the users are (i) overlapping changes and (ii) their frequency. Furthermore, the board should analyze (iii) the queries made to the ontology. This should help to find out which parts of the ontology are more often used. Since actors instantiate the ontology locally, (iv) the number of instances for the different proposed changes can also be used to determine the relevance of certain adaptations.

(10) Identify changes presumably relevant for a significant share of all actors: Having analyzed the changes and having grouped them according to the different parts of the ontology they belong to, the board has to identify the most relevant changes. Based on the provided arguments the board must decide which changes should be introduced. Depending on the quality of the arguments the board itself might argue about different changes. For instance, the board may decide to introduce a new concept that better abstracts several specific concepts introduced by users, and connect it to the several specific ones. Therefore, the final decisions entail some form of evaluation from a domain and a usage point of view. The outcome of this action must be a reduced and structured list of changes that are to be accomplished in the shared ontology.

Revision

Roles: The ontology engineers from the board judge the changes from an ontological perspective more exactly at a formalization level. Some changes may be relevant for the common ontology, but may not be correctly formulated by the users. The domain experts from the board should judge and decide wether new concepts/relations should be introduced into the common ontology even so they were not requested by the users (who may be domain experts or not).

Input: The input for the revision phase is a list of changes at a conceptual level which should be included into the ontology.

Decisions: The main decisions in the revision phase are formal ones. All intended changes identified during the analysis phase should be included into the common ontology. In the revision phase the ontology engineer decides how the requested changes

---

[4] Such a detailed description is available for all actions, but mostly omitted for sake of brevity.

should be formalized. Evaluation of the decisions is performed by comparing the changes on the conceptual level with the final formal decisions. The differences between the original formalization by the users and the final formalization in the shared ontology should be minimal.

Actions: To achieve the desired output the members of the board, mainly its ontology engineers, perform different actions namely (11) *Formalization of the decided changes*, (12) *Aggregation of arguments* and (13) *Documentation*. Judging entails *Evaluation* of proposed changes from a knowledge representation/ontological point of view.

Tool support: For the revision phase we do not envision any special tool support beyond the one provided by classical ontology engineering environments.

Output: The revision phase ends when all changes are formalized and well documented in the common ontology.

Local Update

Roles: The local update phase involves only the users. They perform different actions to include the new common ontology into their local system before they start a new round of local adaptation.

Input: The formalized ontology including the most relevant change request is the input for this step. We also require as an input the documentation of the changes. For a better understanding the user can request a delta to the original version.

Decisions: The user must decide which changes he will introduce locally. This depends on the differences between the own and the new shared conceptualization. The user does not need to update his entire ontology. This stage interferes a lot with the next local adaptation stage. We do not exclude the possibility of conflicts and/or ambiguity between local and shared ontologies, which may entail reduced precision if the ontology is being used in IR applications.[5]

Actions: To achieve the desired output the user takes different actions namely (14) *Distribution of the new ontology to all actors*, (15) *Tagging of the old ontology* to allow for a roll back, (16) *Local inclusion of the updated version* and (17) *Alignment of old and new versions*.

Tool support: The Local update stage is very critical from a usability point of view. Changes cannot be introduced without the user's agreement. Further he should not be bothered too often. In case of equivalent but local conceptualizations it must be possible to change to the common conceptualization. From a technical point of view this stage is supported by tools like KAON *cf.* [13].

Output: The output of the local update phase is an updated local ontology which includes all changes made to the common ontology. However, we do not require the users to perform all changes proposed by the board. The output is not mandatory, since the actors could change the new ontology back to the old one in the local adaptation stage.

---

[5] Ideally one should be able to blacken out the ambiguous parts like in multilevel databases. This has not been transferred to OE yet.

5   Comparison with Related Methodologies

In table 1 we compare DILIGENT to other well known methodologies. We have adapted the categorization of [1] separating *Management of the OE process activities*,[6] *Ontology development oriented activities* and *Ontology support activities*. To the original classification we have added the aspects of **Evolution**, different **Knowledge acquisition** modes and stages during **Documentation**.

Table 1. Summary of ontology engineering methodologies adapted from [1]

Feature			METHONTOLOGY	On-To-Knowledge (OTK)	HCOME	DILIGENT
Management of OE process activities	Scheduling		Proposed	Described	NP	from OTK
	Control		Proposed	Described	NP	from OTK
	Quality assurance		NP	Described	NP	from OTK
Ontology development oriented activities	Pre development processes	Environment study	NP	Proposed	NP	from OTK
		Feasibility study	NP	Described	NP	from OTK
	Development processes	Specification	Descr. in detail	Descr. in detail	Proposed	Described
		Conceptualization	Descr. in detail	Proposed	Proposed	Descr. in detail
		Formalization	Described	Described	Proposed	Descr. in detail
		Implementation	Descr. in detail	Described	Proposed	Described
	Post development processes	Maintenance	Proposed	Proposed	Described	Descr. in detail
		Use	NP	Proposed	Described	Described
		Evolution	NP	NP	Proposed	Descr. in detail
Ontology support activities	Knowledge acquisition		Descr. in detail	Described	NP	Proposed
	■ Distributed know. acquisition		NP	NP	Proposed	Described
	■ Partial autonomy		NP	NP	NP	Described
	Evaluation		Descr. in detail	Proposed	NP	Proposed
	Integration		Proposed	Proposed	NP	Proposed
	Configuration management		Described	Described	NP	from OTK
	Documentation		Descr. in detail	Proposed	Described	from OTK
	■ Results		Descr. in detail	Proposed	Described	from OTK
	■ Decision process		NP	NP	Proposed	Descr. in detail
	Merging and Alignment		NP	NP	Proposed	Proposed

The comparison reveals that DILIGENT is well suited for ontology engineering tasks where distributiveness and change/evolution are of major concern. Further it is the first methodology which formalizes the argumentation taking place in an ontology engineering discussion. Hence, DILIGENT should be used in cases where tracing the engineering decisions is important. This allows future users to understand the different reasons which lead to the conceptualization. We think that these aspects are very important in the context of the semantic web. DILIGENT does not itself support management of OE process activities and Pre development activities, since these are already well supported by other mature methodologies.

6   Case Study Evaluation

The case study described in the following helped us to validate the previously defined methodology and to refine it in a few specific places. To this end, case study evaluation has incorporated the clients and practitioners to help us *understand the diversity* of the process. Before we describe how the DILIGENT ontology engineering process took place in our case study, we describe its organizational setting.

---

[6] Formerly named Ontology Management activities.

6.1   Organizational Setting

A DILIGENT process has been performed in a case study within the domain of tourism service providers of the Balearic Islands. To collaborate on regional issues some organizations set out to collect and share information about *indicators (SDI)* reflecting the impact of growing population and tourist fluxes in the islands, their environment and their infrastructures. For instance, organizations that require *Quality & Hospitality management (QHM)* use the information to better plan, *e.g.*, their marketing campaigns.

Due to the different working areas and goals of the collaborating organizations, it proved impossible to build a centralized ontology satisfying all user requirements. The users emphasized the need for local control over their ontologies. They asked explicitly for a system without a central server, where knowledge sharing was integrated into the normal work, but where different kinds of information, like files, emails, bookmarks and addresses could be shared with others. To this end a generic platform was built that would allow for satisfying the information sharing needs just elaborated using local ontologies, which were linked to a shared ontology. A case study was set up involving both hierarchical and loose organizations. The case study lasted for 3 months.

In this case study most of the tools were being developed at the same time as the process was taking place. Therefore, the administrator had a major role in bridging the gap between our real users and the weaknesses of the tools, for instance by doing the local adaptations for the users since the tools were not error-proof.

6.2   Instantiated DILIGENT Process

We now describe the initial building phase, and the two rounds following the DILI-GENT process focusing on the analysis phase.

Build

$(1)^7$ To build the first version of the shared ontology two domain experts with the help of two knowledge/ontology engineers were involved. In this case, domain experts were also knowledge providers and users.

The OE process started by identifying the main concepts of the ontology through the analysis of competency questions and their answers. The most frequent queries and answers exchanged by users were analyzed. The main objective of the ontology was to categorize documents. The concepts identified were divided into three main modules: "Sustainable Development Indicators (SDI)", "New Technologies (NT)" and "Quality&Hospitality Management (QHM)". From the competency questions the board quickly derived a first ontology with 20 concepts and 7 relations for the "SDI" ontology. For "NT" the board identified 15 concepts and 8 relations and for "QHM" 8 concepts and 5 relations. Between the modules 8 cross module relations were introduced. A part of the result of the initial building stage is visualized in Fig. 2(a).

The first round of our OE process started with the distribution of the three modules of the common ontology to all users. In both rounds, users - during the local adaptation stage - and the board - in the revision stage - could perform ontology change operations. They could *introduce* concepts/relations/instances, *delete* concepts/relations/instances,

---

[7] The numbering here and in the following corresponds to the number of the actions in Fig. 1.

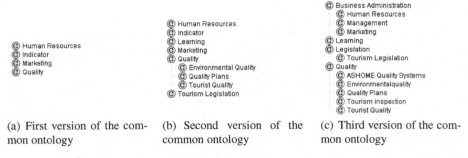

(a) First version of the common ontology

(b) Second version of the common ontology

(c) Third version of the common ontology

Fig. 2. Excerpts from the common ontology evolution

or combine these operations arbitrarily, thus *extend* or *restructure* the ontology. Most frequently the concept hierarchy was changed.

6.3 First Round

The first month of the case study, corresponded to the first round of the DILIGENT process. One organization with seven peers participated. This organization can be classified as a rather loose one.

Local Adaptation

The users in our case study had no OE background. Therefore, they initially regarded the ontology mainly as a classification hierarchy for documents. Consequently they compared their existing folder structures with the common ontology to *(3) identify communalities between their own and the shared conceptualization. (5) Identification of missing conceptualizations* was thus based on mismatches between the common ontology and their local folder structures. Users *(6) changed the common conceptualization* accordingly. This entailed that the *local* documents stored in the folders were *(7) organized according to that conceptualization*. In this organization most of the users were very active and did local adaptations to best serve their own needs.

Analysis

Roles: The board consisted of two ontology engineers and two domain experts/users.

Input: The local adaptations from seven users were collected. Additionally the board had access to the folder structures of those users.

Decisions: All changes introduced were motivated by the users, since they all made sense and were not contradictory on the conceptual level.

Actions:

(8) Gather locally updated ontologies and corresponding arguments: In the first round the board, through the administrator (i) directly accessed the formal local changes on the different peers and (ii) some change requests on the conceptual level. At this stage the board also used (iii) the folder structures as indication for the requirements on the ontology, and it used (iv) the number of documents related to the concepts of the ontology as an indicator for its usage. Additionally, the board received new background knowledge which led to many additions in the "NT" module. The "SDI" module was

© Circulars
  © Learning and Human Resources
  © Legislation
  © Management
© Human Resources
© Learning
© Marketing
© Quality
  © ASHOME Quality System
  © Environmental Quality
  © Quality Plans
  © Tourist Quality
© Tourism Inspection
© Tourism Legislation

(a) Example of a user extension to the first version of the common ontology   (b) Example of a user extension to the second version of the common ontology

Fig. 3. Examples of user extensions to the common ontology

changed based on the formal changes collected electronically. Although the number of changes varied between the different modules the kinds of changes were the same. Therefore, we subsequently focus on the changes introduced to the "QHM" module which are partly visualized in Fig. 2.

(9) Analyze introduced changes: The board analyzed the changes introduced by the users at a conceptual level. They can be categorized as follows:

Elaboration. The elaboration of the ontology was the most often observed action. The board could identify elaborations in three different ways. (i) The users correctly requested either formally or informally to add sub concepts to existing concepts to specialize them. (ii) The users incorrectly added new top level concepts, which were specializations of existing concepts. (iii) Finally they incorrectly refined the wrong concepts. In this way users elaborated the "NT" module with 15 concepts, the "SDI" module with 3 concepts and the "QHM" module also with 3 concepts.

Extension. The board regarded a change as an extension whenever users requested new concepts on the top level. Again, users could not distinguish wether a required concept was an elaboration or an extension. Users extended the "NT" module with 2 concepts and the "QHM" module also with 2 concepts. The "SDI" module was not extended.

Renaming. In two cases the users liked the way the board had conceptualized the domain, but did not agree with the names of the concepts.

Usage. Usage behavior of single concepts in the common ontology was analyzed. This included (i) the number of queries posed to the system containing a specific concept, (ii) the number of documents related to that concept and (iii) the elaboration of a concept. Most of the users did not delete any concepts or ask explicitly to remove concepts. Nevertheless the board concluded, that a concept which was never used should be removed.

(10) Decide on changes to be made: The board decided to introduce all change requests into the common ontology since all were supported by at least two users either through usage or extension/elaborations. Moreover, the domain expert could provide reasonable arguments for the introduction of all changes. Thus, the division of the ontology into 3 modules generated a consensual group of users, already.

Output: The analysis of the local adaptations resulted in 27 changes for the "NT" module, 10 changes for the "QHM" module, and 5 for the "SDI" module.

Revision

After modelling the conceptual changes, the second version of the common ontology contained 54 concepts and 13 relations (figure 2(b)).

Local update

(14) The extensions to the core ontology were distributed to the users. (17) The users were able to align their local ontologies with the new version of the shared and thus the feedback of the users was in general positive.

6.4   Second Round

In the second round the case study was extended to 4 organizations with 21 peers. The users participating in the first round had more experience. One of these organizations was very hierarchical.

Local Adaptation

As in the first round participants (6) changed and (7) used the common ontology according to their needs. Due to the larger number of participants more modifications were introduced. In particular the module "QHM" evolved (*cf.* Fig. 3(b)). In the hierarchical organization not all actors changed the ontology. They delegated the responsability to adapt the ontology to their hierarchical superior according to their organizational needs.

Analysis

Roles: In the second round the board consisted of one domain expert and two ontology engineers. Additionally two users were invited to answer questions to clarify the changes they introduced.

Input: The 21 local ontologies of the users were the input to the second round. Some of the users did not change the common ontology at all. Instead their supervisor was responsible to make all needed modifications for them. In very hierarchical and well defined organizations one single ontology could be adopted by all peers (Fig. 3(b)).

Decisions: In this round the board had to perform reverse engineering on the formal local ontologies from users in order to get conceptual models from them.

Actions:

(8) Gather locally updated ontologies and corresponding arguments: As in the first round the updated ontologies were retrieved electronically. Some of the modification requests were collected interviewing the participants.

(9) Analyze introduced changes: Similar to the first round the modifications did not follow good ontology building practices. With respect to the conceptual modelling decisions the board observed that this time the users modified the ontology on a deeper level than in the first round. Renaming was a bigger issue in this round due to political changes, which required the adoption of new naming conventions. Moreover, generalization took place in two cases. Users introduced concepts which were more abstract than existing ones. The board moved one concept "Indicator" to another module of the ontology, since there the users elaborated it extensively.

In Fig. 3(b) we observe that a user has extended the local version of the common ontology with concepts for Circulars. With help by the domain expert, and taking also into account other local updates, the knowledge engineers inferred on the conceptual level that the module lacked concepts for **Business Administration**. Hence, the board did not only introduce new concepts, but also generalize existing ones 2(c). To exemplify an argumentation thread in favor or against a modelling decision, one may consider the local extension of Circulars performed by one user: **Legislation** was introduced as a subclass of Circulars. The argumentation for a different way of modelling was straightforward, because the board found a Counter Example in the form of a document dealing with Legislation, which was not a Circular. Here, users were requesting an elaboration of Circulars for which the board found a contradicting example. The most convincing arguments were selected and emphasized for documentation purposes. In [12] we present the argumentation framework that allows such argument formalization.

(10) Decide on changes to be made: As in the first round the board included all change requests from users. Again, as in the first round, only few of the concepts in the common ontology were never used.

Output: The board identified 3 changes in the "NT" module, 28 modifications for the "QHM" module and 15 for the "SDI" module.

Revision

The third version of the common ontology contained 95 concepts and 15 relations (Fig. 2(c)).

Local update

(14) As in the first round the new version was distributed to the participants. (16) Updating to the new version is still a problem, since some instances of the ontology might have to be newly annotated to the new concepts of the shared ontology. In our case documents needed a new classification. (17) Partly this problem can be overcome with the help of technology *cf.* [13].

7 Discussion and Conclusions

Decentralization can take different forms. One can have more loose or more hierarchical organizations. We observed and supported both kinds of organizations in this case study. Therefore, the first finding is the fact that this process can be adapted both to hierarchical and to more loose organizations. DILIGENT processes cover both traditional OE processes and more Semantic Web-oriented OE processes, that is with strong decentralization and partial autonomy requirements.

The process helped non OE-expert users to conceptualize, specialize and refine their domain. The agreement met with the formalized ontology was high, as shown by people willing to change their folder structures to better use the improved domain conceptualization. In spite of the technical challenges, user feedback was very positive.

The DILIGENT process proved to be a natural way to have different people from different organizations collaborate and change the shared ontology. The set-up phase for DILIGENT was rather fast, and users could profit from their own proposals (local adaptations) immediately. The result was much closer to the user's own requirements. Moreover, other users profited from them in a longer term. Finally, this case study clearly has shown the need for evolution. Users performed changes and adaptations.

The development of ontologies in centralized settings is well studied and there are established methodologies. However, current experiences from projects suggest that ontology engineering should be subject to continuous improvement rather than a one-time effort and that ontologies promise the most benefits in decentralized rather than centralized systems. To this end we have conceived the DILIGENT methodology. DILIGENT supports domain experts, users, knowledge engineers and ontology engineers in collaboratively building a shared ontology in a distributed setting. Moreover, the methodology guides the participants in a fine grained way through the ontology evolution process, allowing for personalization. We have demonstrated the applicability of our process model in a cross-organizational case study in the realm of tourism industry. Real users were using the ontology to satisfy their information needs for an extended period of time. Two rounds following our methodology were observed and have been described here. To our knowledge, this is the first case study combining all the above mentioned features described in the literature.

References

1. Gómez-Pérez, A., Fernández-López, M., Corcho, O.: Ontological Engineering. Springer (2003)
2. Staab, S., Schnurr, H.P., Studer, R., Sure, Y.: Knowledge processes and ontologies. IEEE Intelligent Systems 16 (2001)
3. Uschold, M., King, M.: Towards a methodology for building ontologies. In: Proc. of IJCAI95 WS, Montreal, Canada (1995)
4. Pinto, H.S., Staab, S., Sure, Y., Tempich, C.: OntoEdit empowering SWAP: a case study in supporting DIstributed, Loosely-controlled and evolvInG Engineering of oNTologies (DILIGENT). In: 1. Euro. Semantic Web Symposium, ESWS 2004, Springer (2004)
5. Kotis, K., Vouros, G.A., Alonso, J.P.: HCOME: tool-supported methodology for collaboratively devising living ontologies. In: SWDB'04: 2. Int. Workshop on Semantic Web and Databases. (2004)
6. Benjamins, V.R., Fensel, D., Decker, S., Gómez-Pérez, A.: (KA)^2: Building ontologies for the internet. International Journal of Human-Computer Studies (IJHCS) 51 (1999) 687–712
7. Sure, Y., Tempich, C., Vrandečić, Z.: D7.1.1. SEKT methodolgoy: Survey and initial framework. SEKT deliverable 7.1.1, Institute AIFB, University of Karlsruhe (2004)
8. Pinto, H.S., Martins, J.: Evolving Ontologies in Distributed and Dynamic Settings. In: Proc. of the 8th Int. Conf. on Princ. of Knowledge Representation & Reasoning (KR2002). (2002)
9. Holsapple, C.W., Joshi, K.D.: A collaborative approach to ontology design. Commun. ACM 45 (2002) 42–47
10. Pinto, H.S., Staab, S., Tempich, C.: DILIGENT: Towards a fine-grained methodology for DIstributed, Loosely-controlled and evolvInG Engineering of oNTologies. In: Proceedings of the 16th European Conference on Artificial Intelligence (ECAI 2004). (2004)
11. Noy, N., Fergerson, R., Musen, M.: The knowledge model of Protégé-2000: Combining interoperability and flexibility. In: Proc. of the 12th Int. Conf. on Knowledge Engineering and Knowledge Management: Methods, Models, and Tools (EKAW 2000), Springer (2000)
12. Tempich, C., Pinto, H.S., Sure, Y., Staab, S.: An argumentation ontology for DIstributed, Loosely-controlled and evolvInG Engineering processes of oNTologies (DILIGENT). In: Second European Semantic Web Conference, ESWC 2005, Springer (2005)
13. Maedche, A., Motik, B., Stojanovic, L.: Managing multiple and distributed ontologies on the semantic web. The VLDB Journal 12 (2003) 286–302

Towards a Complete OWL Ontology Benchmark

Li Ma, Yang Yang, Zhaoming Qiu, Guotong Xie, Yue Pan, and Shengping Liu

IBM China Research Laboratory, Building 19, Zhongguancun Software Park,
ShangDi, Beijing, 100094, P.R. China
{malli, yangyy, qiuzhaom, xieguot, panyue, liusp}@cn.ibm.com

Abstract. Aiming to build a complete benchmark for better evaluation of existing ontology systems, we extend the well-known Lehigh University Benchmark in terms of inference and scalability testing. The extended benchmark, named University Ontology Benchmark (UOBM), includes both OWL Lite and OWL DL ontologies covering a complete set of OWL Lite and DL constructs, respectively. We also add necessary properties to construct effective instance links and improve instance generation methods to make the scalability testing more convincing. Several well-known ontology systems are evaluated on the extended benchmark and detailed discussions on both existing ontology systems and future benchmark development are presented.

1 Introduction

The rapid growth of information volume in World Wide Web and corporate intranets makes it difficult to access and maintain the information required by users. Semantic Web aims to provide easier information access based on the exploitation of machine-understandable metadata. Ontology, a shared, formal, explicit and common understanding of a domain that can be unambiguously communicated between human and applications, is an enabling technology for Semantic Web. W3C has recommended two standards for publishing and sharing ontologies on the World Wide Web: Resource Description Framework (RDF) [3] and Web Ontology Language (OWL) [4,5]. OWL facilitates greater machine interpretability of web content than that supported by RDF and RDF Schema (RDFS) by providing additional vocabulary along with formal semantics. That is, OWL has more powerful expressive capability which is required by real applications and is thus the current research focus. In the past several years, some ontology toolkits, such as Jena [23], KAON2 [22] and Sesame [14], had been developed for ontologies storing, reasoning and querying. A standard and effective benchmark to evaluate existing systems is much needed.

1.1 Related Work

In 1998, Description Logic (DL) community developed a benchmark suite to facilitate comparison of DL systems [18,19]. The suite included concept satisfiability tests, synthetic TBox classification tests, realistic TBox classification tests and synthetic ABox tests. Although DL is the logic foundation of OWL, the developed DL benchmarks are not practical to evaluate ontology systems. DL benchmark suite tested complex

Y. Sure and J. Domingue (Eds.): ESWC 2006, LNCS 4011, pp. 125–139, 2006.

inference, such as satisfiability tests of large concept expressions, and did not cover realistic and scalable ABox reasoning due to poor performance of most systems at that time. This is significantly far away from requirements of Semantic Web and ontology based enterprise applications. Tempich and Volz [16] conducted a statistical analysis on more than 280 ontologies from DAML.ORG library and pointed out that ontologies vary tremendously both in size and their average use of ontological constructs. These ontologies are classified into three categories, taxonomy or terminology style, description logic style and database schema-like style. They suggested that Semantic Web benchmarks have to consist of several types of ontologies.

SWAT research group of Lehigh University [9,10,20] made significant efforts to design and develop Semantic Web benchmarks. Especially in 2004, Guo et al. developed Lehigh University Benchmark (LUBM) [9,10] to facilitate the evaluation of Semantic Web tools. The benchmark is intended to evaluate the performance of ontology systems with respect to extensional queries over a large data set that conforms to a realistic ontology. The LUBM appeared at a right time and was gradually accepted as a standard evaluation platform for OWL ontology systems. More recently, Lehigh Bibtex Benchmark (LBBM) [20] was developed with a learned probabilistic model to generate instance data. According to Tempich and Volz's classification scheme [16], the LUBM is to benchmark systems processing ontologies of description logic style while the LBBM is for systems managing database schema-like ontologies. Different from the LUBM, the LBBM represents more RDF-style data and queries. By participating in a number of enterprise application development projects (e.g., metadata and master data management) with IBM Integrated Ontology Toolkit [12], we learned that RDFS is not expressive enough for enterprise data modeling and OWL is more suitable than RDFS for semantic data management. The primary objective of this paper is to extend the LUBM for better benchmarking OWL ontology systems.

OWL provides three increasingly expressive sublanguages designed for use by specific communities of users [4]: OWL Lite, OWL DL, and OWL Full. Implementing complete and efficient OWL Full reasoning is practically impossible. Currently, OWL Lite and OWL DL are research focuses. As a standard OWL ontology benchmark, the LUBM has two limitations. Firstly, it does not completely cover either OWL Lite or OWL DL inference. For example, inference on cardinality and allValueFrom restrictions cannot be tested by the LUBM. In fact, the inference supported by this benchmark is only a subset of OWL Lite. Some real ontologies are more expressive than the LUBM ontology. Secondly, the generated instance data may form multiple relatively isolated graphs and lack necessary links between them. More precisely, the benchmark generates individuals (such as departments, students and courses) taking university as a basic unit. Individuals from a university do not have relations with individuals from other universities (here, we mean the relations intentionally involved in reasoning.) Therefore, the generated instance is grouped by university. This results in multiple relatively separate university graphs. Apparently, it is less reasonable for scalability tests. Inference on a complete and huge graph is substantially harder than that on multiple isolated and small graphs. In summary, the LUBM is weaker in measuring inference capability as well as less reasonable to generate big data sets for measuring scalability.

1.2 Contributions

In this paper, we extend the Lehigh University Benchmark so that it could better provide both OWL Lite and OWL DL inference tests (except TBox with cyclic class definition. Hereinafter, OWL Lite or OWL DL complete is understood with this exception) on more complicated instance data sets. The main contributions of the paper are as follows.

- The extended Lehigh University Benchmark, named University Ontology Benchmark (UOBM), is OWL DL complete. Two ontologies are generated to include inference of OWL Lite and OWL DL, respectively. Accordingly, queries are constructed to test inference capability of ontology systems.
- The extended benchmark generates instance data sets in a more reasonable way. The necessary links between individuals from different universities make the test data form a connected graph rather than multiple isolated graphs. This will guarantee the effectiveness of scalability testing.
- Several well-known ontology systems are evaluated on the extended benchmark and conclusions are drawn to show the state of arts.

The remainder of the paper is organized as follows. Section 2 analyzes and summarizes the limitations of the LUBM and presents the UOBM, including ontology design, instance generation, query and answer construction. Section 3 reports the experimental results of several well-known ontology systems on the UOBM and provides detailed discussions. Section 4 concludes this paper.

2 Extension of Lehigh University Benchmark

This section provides an overview of the LUBM and analyzes its limitations as a standard evaluation platform. Based on such an analysis, we further propose methods to extend the benchmark in terms of ontology design, instance generation, query and answer construction.

Table 1. OWL Constructs Supported by the LUBM

OWL Lite		OWL DL
RDF Schema Features:	*Property Restrictions:*	*Class Axioms:*
▪ **rdfs:subClassOf**	▪ allValuesFrom	▪ oneOf, dataRange
▪ **rdfs:subPropertyOf**	▪ **someValuesFrom**	▪ disjointWith
▪ **rdfs:domain**		▪ equivalentClass (applied to class expressions)
▪ **rdfs:range**	*Restricted Cardinality:*	▪ rdfs:subClassOf (applied to class expressions)
	▪ minCardinality (only 0 or 1)	
Property Characteristics:	▪ maxCardinality (only 0 or 1)	*Boolean Combinations of Class Expressions:*
▪ **ObjectProperty**	▪ cardinality (only 0 or 1)	▪ unionOf
▪ **DatatypeProperty**		▪ complementOf
▪ **inverseOf**	*(In)Equality:*	▪ intersectionOf
▪ **TransitiveProperty**	▪ equivalentClass	
▪ SymmetricProperty	▪ equivalentProperty	*Arbitrary Cardinality:*
▪ FunctionalProperty	▪ sameAs	▪ minCardinality
▪ InverseFunctional Property	▪ differentFrom	▪ maxCardinality
Class Intersection:	▪ AllDifferent	▪ cardinality
▪ **IntersectionOf**	▪ distinctMembers	*Filler Information:*
		▪ hasValue

2.1 Overview of the LUBM

The LUBM is intended to evaluate the performance of ontology systems with respect to extensional queries over a large data set that conforms to a realistic ontology. It consists of an ontology for university domain, customizable and repeatable synthetic data, a set of test queries, and several performance metrics. The details of the benchmark can be found in [9,10]. As a standard benchmark, the LUBM itself has two limitations. Firstly, it covers only part of inference supported by OWL Lite and OWL DL. Table 1 tabulates all OWL Lite and OWL DL language constructs which are inference-related as well as those supported by the LUBM (in underline).

The above table shows clearly that the LUBM's university ontology only uses a small part of OWL Lite and OWL DL constructs (the used constructs are in underline) and thus covers only part of OWL inference. That is, it cannot exactly and completely evaluate an ontology system in terms of inference capability. In fact, some constructs excluded by LUBM's ontology, such as allValuesFrom, cardinality, oneOf and SymmetricProperty, are very useful for expressive data modeling in practice. For example, using construct hasValue, we can define class "basketBallLover" whose property "like" has a value of "basketBall". We found that the LUBM's ontology is less expressive than some real ontologies. With the increasing uses of ontologies in practical applications, more and more complex ontologies will appear. Obviously, more constructs (hence more inference requirements) should be included for system evaluation.

Another limitation of the LUBM is that the generated instance data may form multiple relatively isolated graphs and lacks necessary links between them for scalability testing. Figure 1(a) shows a simplified example of the LUBM generated instance (the real instance may include more universities and more departments in a university). We can see from this figure that there are two relatively independent university graphs, and two relatively independent department graphs in the same university. Such kind of data is less challenging for scalability testing. As is well known, to evaluate the scalability of a system, we generally observe the system performance changes with the increasing size of the data. Here, the increase of the testing data means that more universities will be generated. Due to the relative independence of the data of different universities, the performance changes of an ontology system on an Relational DBMS (currently, most ontology repositories are on top of RDBMS) with such data sets will be determined to a large extent by the underlying database. This cannot really reveal the inference efficiency of an ontology system, considering the fact that inference on a complete and huge RDF graph is significantly harder than that on multiple isolated and small graphs with comparable number of classes and properties. The underlying reason leading to such a case is that the instance generator of the LUBM creates data using university as a basic unit and does not intentionally construct individuals and relationships across universities. Therefore, we will enhance the instance generator of the LUBM to generate instances in a more practical way. As shown in Figure 1(b), crossing-university and crossing-department relations will be added to form a more complicated graph. For instance, professor can teach course in different departments and universities, and students can have friends from different universities. In the LUBM, it is possible that two persons from different universities graduate from the same university (by property degreeFrom). Here, our intention is to add more links between universities and the links should be involved in reasoning, which is challenging for scalability tests. Compared with the graph in Fig 1(a), the graph in Fig. 1(b) can be used to better characterize the scalability of ontology systems.

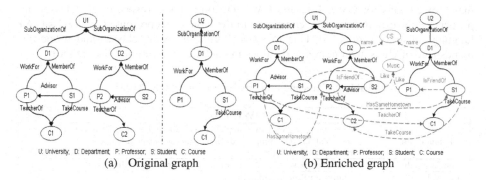

U: University; D: Department; P: Professor; S: Student; C: Course

(a) Original graph   (b) Enriched graph

Fig. 1. Instance Graph Enrichment of the LUBM

2.2 University Ontology Benchmark (UOBM)

Based on our analysis on the LUBM, we can conclude that LUBM is insufficient to evaluate the inference capability and less effective to reflect the scalability of an ontology system. We build University Ontology Benchmark (UOBM) based on the LUBM to solve these two problems. Figure 2 gives an overview of the UOBM. It consists of three major components, ontology selector, instance generator and queries and answers analyzer. These core components are detailed in the following subsections.

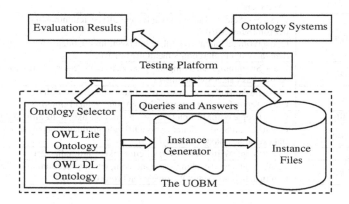

Fig. 2. Overview of the UOBM

2.2.1 Ontology Selector

Different from the original LUBM, the UOBM includes both OWL Lite and OWL DL ontologies. That is, one ontology includes all language constructs of OWL Lite, and another one covers all OWL DL constructs. The user can specify which ontology will be used for evaluation according to specific requirements. As Table 1 shows, a number of OWL constructs are absent in the LUBM. For those absent constructs, we newly define corresponding classes and properties in the UOBM. Table 2 lists our major extensions for OWL Lite and OWL DL ontologies, respectively. Classes and properties corresponding to the constructs in the table are represented in W3C's OWL language abstract syntax [5]. Due to space limitation, some classes and properties, namespace of URIs and enumerated values in oneOf classes are not listed there.

Table 2. Class and Property Extensions of the UOBM

OWL Lite	
allValueFrom	Class(GraduateStudent, complete intersectionOf(restriction(takesCourse, someValueFrom(Thing)), restriction(takesCourse, allValue-From(GraduateCourse))))
minCardinality	Class(PeopleWithHobby, restriction(like, minCardinality(1)))
EquivalentProperty	EquivalentProperty(like, love)
EquivalentClass	EquivalentClass(Person, Humanbeing)
SymmetricProperty	ObjectProperty (isFriendOf, Symmetric, domain(Person), range(Person))
TransitiveProperty	ObjectProperty (hasSameHomeTownWith, Symmetric|Transitive, do-main(Person), range(Person))
FunctionalProperty	ObjectProperty(isTaughtBy, Functional, domain(Course), range(Faculty))
InverseFunctional Property	ObjectProperty(isHeadOf, InverseFunctional, domain(Person), range(Organization))
OWL DL	
disjointWith	DisjointClasses(Man, Woman)
oneOf	Class(Science, oneOf(Physics, Mathematics ....)) Class(Engineer, oneOf(Electical_Engineer, Chemical_Engineer...)) ...
unionOf	Class(Person, unionOf(Man, Woman)) Class(AcademicSubject, unionOf(Science, Engineer, FineArts, Humanitie-sAndSocial))
complementOf	Class(NonScienceStudnet, complementOf(restriction(hasMajor, someVal-ueFrom(Science)))) Class(WomanCollege, complete intersectionOf(College, retriction (hasStu-dent, allValueFrom(complementOf(Man)))))
intersectionOf	Class(SwimmingFan, complete intersectionOf(Person, restriction (isCrazy-About, hasValue(Swimming)))
hasValue	Class(BasketBallLover, restriction(like, value(BasketBall))) Class(TennisFan, restriction(isCrazyAbout, value(Tennis)))...
minCandinality	Class(PeopleWithMultipleHobbies, restriction(like, minCardinality(3)))
maxCandinality	Class(LeisureStudent, intersactionOf(UndergraduateStudent, restric-tion (takesCourse, maxCardinality(2))))
Candinality	Class(PeopleWith2Hobbies, restriction(like, Cardinality(2)))
EquivalentClass	EquivalentClass(TeachingAssistant, complete intersectionOf(Person, restric-tion (teachingAssistantOf, someValueFrom(Course))))

Table 3 shows a comparison between the LUBM and the UOBM in terms of the number of classes, properties and individuals per university. The number of classes and properties used to define ABox are denoted in the bracket. This means that some classes and properties are only used to define class and property hierarchies in TBox and not used to directly restrict individuals. But users can issue queries using such classes and properties constraints. Individuals in TBox are used to define oneOf and hasValue restrictions. We can see from the table that the UOBM can generate much larger and more complex instance graph. More important is that it covers all OWL Lite and OWL DL constructs. An effective evaluation on the benchmark will help researchers to figure out more problems and promote the development of ontology systems. Note that the number of instances shown in Table 3 (e.g., No. of statements per univ.) is assessed based on parameters used in [9] and used in our experiments presented in next section, respectively.

Table 3. Comparison of the LUBM and the UOBM

Benchmark	The LUBM	The UOBM	
		OWL Lite	OWL DL
No. of Classes	43 (22)	51 (41)	69 (59)
No. of Datatype Property	7 (3)	9 (5)	9 (5)
No. of Object Property	25(14)	34(24)	34 (24)
No. of Individuals in TBox	0	18	58
No. of Statements per University	90,000 – 110,000	210,000 – 250,000	220,000 – 260,000
No. of Individuals per University	8,000 – 15,000	10,000 – 20,000	10,000 – 20,000

2.2.2 Instance Generator

Instance generator automatically and randomly creates instances according to user-specified ontology (OWL Lite or OWL DL). Also, the user can specify the size of the generated instance data by setting the number of universities to be constructed. Compared with the LUBM, we extend following properties to link individuals from different departments and universities. As a result, the UOBM will enable the construction of a complicated connected graph instead of multiple relatively-isolated graphs.

- ObjectProperty (isFriendOf, Symmetric, domain(Person), range(Person))
- ObjectProperty(hasSameHomeTownWith, Symmetric|Transitive, domain(Person), range(Person))
- ObjectProperty(takesCourse, domain(Student))
- ObjectProperty (hasMajor, domain(Student), range(AcademicSubject))
- ObjectProperty (like, domain(Person), range(Interest))
  EquivalentProperties(love, like)
- ObjectProperty (isCrazyAbout, super(like), domain(Person), range(Interest))

Instance generator can be configured to generate data sets for specific evaluation. Some important parameters for building a connected graph are listed below.

- Specify ontology, OWL Lite or OWL DL (**parameter for TBox configuration**)
- Specify the probability that a student takes courses of other departments and universities, and the range of the number of courses a student takes.

- Specify the probability that a person has the same hometown with those from other departments and universities. (Affect the ratio of transitive properties as well)
- Specify the probability that a person has friends of other departments and universities, and the range of the number of friends a person has.
- Specify the probability that a university has woman college, and the range of the number of students.
- Specify the probability that a person has some hobbies.

2.2.3 Queries and Answers Analyzer

A set of queries are constructed to evaluate the inference capability and scalability of an ontology system. Queries are designed based on two principles: 1) Queries need search and reasoning across universities so that the scalability of a system can be better characterized. In the original LUBM, some queries are evaluated only on specific universities and departments regardless of the increasing size of the testing data. This results mainly from lacks of links between different universities. 2) Each query supports at least a different type of OWL inference. By this way, if a query cannot be correctly answered, we can easily identify which kind of inference is not well supported. The test queries are listed in appendix with detailed explanations.

Given queries and randomly generated test data, we have to find corresponding correct answers in order to compute completeness and soundness of the inference. The original LUBM does not explicitly provide a method to generate correct results. Our current scheme is to import all statements into an RDBMS such as DB2 or MySQL, and then manually translate each query into SQL queries to retrieve all correct results. It is feasible because we know inference required by every query and can use a DL reasoner for TBox inference and build SQL queries on the inferred TBox for ABox inference and retrieval. Also, we use some tricks for SQL query rewriting, for example, naming convention of instances. The manual translation method has been written into a standalone application in the benchmark. It is convenient to run the application to obtain answer sets.

Using the UOBM, the user can follow a simple approach for performance evaluation of ontology systems. Firstly, the user selects an ontology (OWL Lite or OWL DL) to generate corresponding instances. Then, using the built-in query translation method, the user can obtain correct query results in advance. Finally, based on the selected ontology, generated instances, test queries and correct answers, load time, query response time, inference completeness and soundness of a system can be easily computed. Currently, the UOBM is publicly available at [12].

3 Evaluation of Ontology Systems and Discussions

In this section, we use the UOBM to evaluate several well-known ontology systems and discuss problems deserving further research work based on experimental results. ***This work is not intended to make a complete evaluation for existing OWL ontology systems. From our preliminary experiments, we hope to find some critical problems to promote the development of OWL ontology systems as well as figure out more issues needed to be considered in a complete benchmark.***

3.1 Target Systems and Experiments Setting

In [9], Guo et al. conducted a quantitative evaluation on the LUBM for four knowledge base systems, Sesame's persistent storage and main memory version [14,15], OWLJessKB [13], and DLDB-OWL [8]. They used data loading time, repositories sizes, query response time, query completeness and soundness as evaluation metrics. Experimental results showed that, as a whole, DLDB-OWL outperformed other systems on large-scale data sets. OWLIM [18] is a newly developed high performance repository and is packaged as a Storage and Inference Layer (SAIL) for Sesame. Recently, IBM released its Integrated Ontology Development Toolkit [12], including an ontology repository (named Minerva), EMF based Ontology Definition Metamodel and a workbench for ontology editing. Here, we will evaluate these persistent ontology repositories, DLDB-OWL, OWLIM (version 2.8.2) and Minerva (version 1.1.1).

We will have a brief look at these systems so that we can understand the experimental results better. DLDB-OWL [8] is a repository for processing, storing, and querying large amounts of OWL data. Its major feature is the extension of a relational database system with description logic inference capabilities. It uses the DL reasoner to precompute class subsumption and employs relational views to answer extensional queries based on the implicit hierarchy that is inferred. Minerva [12] completely implements the inference supported by Description Logic Program (DLP), an intersection of Description Logic and Horn Logic Program. Its highlight is a hybrid inference method which uses Racer or Pellet DL reasoner to obtain implicit subsumption among classes and properties and adopts DLP logic rules for instance inference. Minerva designs the schema of the back-end database completely according to the DLP logic rules to support efficient inference. OWLIM is a high-performance semantic repository, wrapped as a Storage and Inference Layer for the Sesame RDF database. OWLIM uses Ontotext's TRREE to perform forward-chaining rule reasoning. The reasoning and query are conducted in-memory. At the same time, a reliable persistence strategy assures data preservation, consistency and integrity.

Our evaluation method is similar to the one used in [9]. Here, 6 test data sets are generated, Lite-1, Lite-5, Lite-10, DL-1, DL-5 and DL-10, where the alphabetic string indicates the type of the ontology and is followed by an integer indicating the number of universities. Each university contains about 20 departments and over 210,000 statements. The most complex and largest data set, DL-10, includes over 2,200,000 statements. Test queries are listed in the appendix of the paper, where 13 queries for OWL Lite tests and 3 more for OWL DL tests. Experiments are conducted on a PC with Pentium IV CPU of 2.66 GHz and 1G memory, running Windows 2000 professional with Sun Java JRE 1.4.2 (JRE 1.5.0 for OWLIM) and Java VM memory of 512M. The following three metrics [9] are used for comparison.

- Load time. The time for loading a data set into memory or persistence storage. It includes reasoning time since some systems do TBox or ABox inference at load time.
- Query response time. The time for issuing a query, obtaining the result set and traversing the results sequentially.
- Completeness and soundness. Completeness measures the recall of a system's answer to a query and soundness measures its precision.

3.2 Evaluation of OWL Ontology Systems

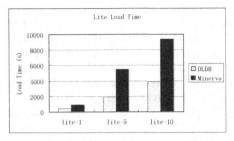 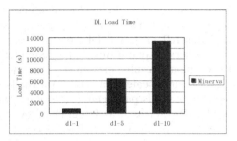

Fig. 3. Load Time Comparison

Figure 3 shows load time of Minerva and DLDB-OWL (hereinafter, DLDB denotes DLDB-OWL). Since OWLIM takes only 29 seconds to load Lite-1, it is too small to plot it in the figure. OWLIM is substantially faster than other two systems as reasoning is done in memory. But, OWLIM cannot complete forward-chaining inference on other data sets due to memory limitation. There are no results for DLDB on DL data sets as an exception was thrown out when loading OWL DL files. DLDB is faster than Minerva to load data sets because it does not conduct ABox materialization at load time. In fact, Minerva's performance on loading and reasoning on OWL data is high, only about 2.5 hours for over 2.2M triples from Lite-10 data set. Its storage schema provides effective support for inference at load time.

OWLIM does inference in memory. Therefore, it can answer queries more quickly than DLDB and Minerva. But its scalability is relatively poor. In most cases, Minerva outperforms DLDB in terms of query response time. The reason is that Minerva does all inference at load time and directly retrieves results using SQL queries at query time, whereas DLDB uses class views which are built based on inferred class hierarchy at load time to retrieve instances at query time. DLDB's view query (a view is equivalent to a query in relational database.) needs to execute union operations in runtime which is more expensive than select operations on pre-built index in most cases. The last three subfigures in Fig. 4 show the scalability of DLDB on Lite data sets and that of Minerva on both Lite and DL data sets, respectively. We observe that for most queries, the query time of DLDB grows dramatically with the increase of the size of the data set. But Minerva scales much better than DLDB. For some queries, such as queries 13 and 15, the query time of Minerva is almost zero and does not change too much since there are few or no results. One may find that Minerva's query time for query 8 increases significantly on DL-10. The reason is that there are a large number of results. Since the query time includes time to traverse results sequentially (the original LUBM uses such a definition as well), it can be affected by the number of results.

Our experiments have confirmed that all three systems are sound, i.e., the precision is 1. Table 4 shows query completeness results. Compared with previous version, OWLIM 2.8.2 can answer all queries correctly. In this new release of OWLIM, more rules are added and inference is made configurable. As is known, OWL-Lite and OWL-DL reasoning cannot be implemented only by rules. That is, OWLIM currently conducts partial OWL DL TBox inference. This is different from DLDB and Minerva

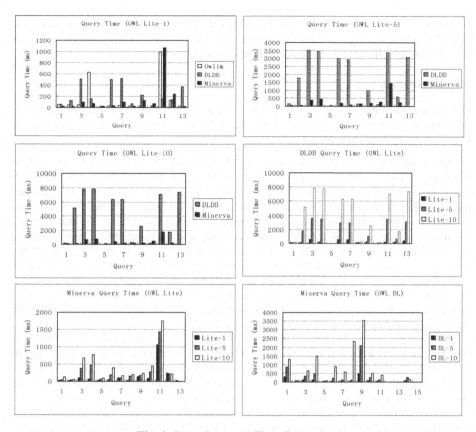

Fig. 4. Query Response Time Comparison

Table 4. Query Completeness Comparison

Query		Q1	Q2	Q3	Q4	Q5	Q6	Q7	Q8	Q9	Q10	Q11	Q12	Q13	Q14	Q15
OWLIM	Lite-1	1	1	1	1	1	1	1	1	1	1	1	1	1	NA	NA
DLDB	Lite-1	1	0.82	1	1	0	0	0	0	0	0.83	0	0.2	0.51	NA	NA
	Lite-5	1	0.81	1	1	0	0	0	0	0	0.59	0	0.12	0.57	NA	NA
	Lite-10	1	0.81	1	1	0	0	0	0	0	0.87	0	0.26	0.53	NA	NA
Minerva	Lite-1	1	1	1	1	1	1	1	1	1	1	1	1	0.67	NA	NA
	Lite-5	1	1	1	1	1	1	1	1	1	1	1	1	0.61	NA	NA
	Lite-10	1	1	1	1	1	1	1	1	1	1	1	1	0.64	NA	NA
	DL-1	1	1	1	1	1	1	1	1	1	1	1	1	0.90	0.96	0
	DL-5	1	1	1	1	1	1	1	1	1	1	1	1	0.88	0.97	0
	DL-10	1	1	1	1	1	1	1	1	1	1	1	1	0.88	0.95	0

which depend on a DL reasoner for TBox inference. Coincidentally, the UOBM does not contain a query that needs subsumption inference not covered by existing OWLIM rules. This indicates that the UOBM should add more complex class definition and corresponding instances and queries. The inference capability of DLDB is relatively weak and it gives 100% complete answers to only 3 queries. Minerva is able to completely and correctly process 12 out of 13 queries. Inference on minCardinality needed by query 13 is not currently supported in Minerva. These three persistence systems use rules for ABox inference. How to support more ABox rules on large-scale data sets which cannot be fit into memory directly deserves more efforts.

3.3 Discussions

From our preliminary experiments, we found some interesting problems about OWL ontology systems as well as some issues needed to be further investigated for a complete OWL ontology benchmark.

Native Storage vs DBMS based approaches. OWLIM can be considered as a native ontology repository since it is directly built on the file system. Compared with DBMS based systems (Minerva and DLDB), it greatly reduced the load time. On the other hand, database systems provide many query optimization features, thereby contributing positively to query response time. For OWLIM-like systems, efforts should be made for functionalities such as transactions processing, query optimization, access control and logging/recovery. A typical example is that in query 4, only an exchange of the order of two triples makes OWLIM's response time about 21 times longer (0.6s vs 13s). This suggests that we should leverage DBMS as much as possible. Of course, we also believe that the underlying database more or less affects the performance of ontology systems. For example, DLDB's performance may change when switching the back-end store from Access to SQL server. We are going to investigate such problems.

TBox inference. Considering the modest size of real ontologies (excluding instances), using mature DL reasoners for TBox inference could be a good choice. In fact, Minerva and DLDB leverages a DL reasoner (such as Pellet, FaCT) to understand complete class subsumption. These illustrated that the combination of DL reasoners for TBox inference and rules for ABox inference is a promising approach.

Query interface. SPARQL language is increasingly used for RDF graph query by both RDF(S) and OWL ontology systems [12,21-23]. But, OWL is different from RDFS. In OWL, it is possible to define new classes by logical expressions. In this sense, SPARQL is not an appropriate query language for OWL, since it imposes a substantial restriction on the users' query choices. We should pay more attentions to OWL query interface, such as OWL-QL in [24].

Instance generation. Currently, the extended benchmark provides users a number of parameters for scalable instance generation. In [20], Wang et al. proposed a learned probabilistic model to generate instance data set based on representative samples. The objective is to help the users find an ontology system which best fit their data environment. It is worthwhile investigating what kind of parameters should be provided so that the generated instances set can best simulate user's data.

Tunable TBox. Currently, we do not find a class which is practically meaningful and needs cyclic definition in university domain. But in other domains, such as life sciences, realistic ontologies do include cyclic class definition. Therefore, to add cyclic class definition which may not have real meaning in university domain could be valuable. Furthermore, real ontologies vary tremendously in their average use of ontological constructs. To automatically create an ontology that is tunable by complexity (not just at the level of OWL DL and OWL Lite, but also in terms of the quantities of constructs that are used) is also valuable for users to use in their tests. This could be future research work for a compete benchmark.

Update Tests. A practical ontology system should deal with frequent update in an efficient manner. At the same time, system consistency should be guaranteed. We are intended to add update tests in the UOBM.

4 Conclusions

This paper presented important extensions to the Lehigh University Benchmark in terms of inference and scalability testing. The extended benchmark can characterize the performance of OWL ontology systems more completely. Furthermore, a preliminary evaluation for several well-known ontology systems was conducted and some conclusions were drawn for future research. Also, some issues worthy to be further investigated for a complete OWL ontology benchmark were discussed and summarized.

Acknowledgements

The authors would like to thank Jeff Heflin, Yuanbo Guo and Zhengxiang Pan of Lehigh University, Atanas Kiryakov and Damyan Ognyanov of OntoText Lab, Kavitha Srinivas, Achille Fokoue, Aaron Kershenbaum and Edith Schonberg of IBM T.J. Watson Research Center for their constructive suggestions and comments.

References

1. T. Berners-Lee, J. Hendler, O. Lassila, The Semantic WEB, Scientific American, 2001.
2. J. Davies, D. Fensel, F. Harmelen, Eds., Towards the Semantic WEB: Ontology-driven Knowledge Management, England: John Wiley & Sons, Ltd., 2002.
3. P. Hayes, Resource Description Framework (RDF): Semantics, W3C Recommendation, http://www.w3.org/ TR/2004/REC-rdf-mt-20040210/#rdf_entail, 2004.
4. Michael K. Smith, Chris Welty, Deborah L. McGuinness, OWL Web Ontology language Guide, http://www.w3.org/TR/owl-guide/, 2004.
5. Peter F. Patel-Schneider, Patrick Hayes, Ian Horrocks, OWL Web Ontology Language Semantics and Abstract Syntax, http://www.w3.org/TR/owl-semantics/, 2004.
6. Michael J. Carey, David J. DeWitt, Jeffrey F. Naughtor, "The 007 Benchmark", Proc. of ACM international conference on Management of data, Volume22, Issue 2, 1993.
7. TPC Database Benchmark, http://www.tpc.org/, 2004.
8. Z. Pan, and J. Heflin, "DLDB: Extending Relational Databases to Support Semantic Web Queries", Proc. of Workshop on Practical and Scaleable Semantic Web Systms, pp. 109-113, 2003.
9. Y. Guo, Z. Pan, and J. Heflin, "An Evaluation of Knowledge Base Systems for Large OWL Datasets", Proc. of Third International Semantic Web Conference, pp. 274-288, 2004.
10. The Lehigh University Benchmark, http://swat.cse.lehigh.edu/projects/LUBMm/index.htm, 2004.
11. Pellet OWL Reasoner, http://www.mindswap.org/2003/pellet/index.shtml, 2004.
12. IBM Integrated Ontology Development Toolkit -- Minerva, http://www.alphaworks.ibm.com/ tech/semanticstk, 2005.

13. Kopena, J.B. and Regli, W.C, "DAMLJessKB: A Tool for Reasoning with the Semantic Web", In Proc. of ISWC2003.
14. Broekstra, J. and Kampman, "A. Sesame: A Generic Architecture for Storing and Querying RDF and RDF Schema", In Proc. of ISWC2002.
15. Sesame, An Open Source RDF Database with Support for RDF Schema Inferencing and Querying, http://www.openrdf.org/, 2002.
16. C. Tempich and R. Volz, "Towards a benchmark for Semantic Web reasoners–an analysis of the DAML ontology library", In Workshop on Evaluation on Ontology-based Tools, ISWC2003.
17. R. Volz, Web Ontology Reasoning with Logic Databases. PhD thesis, AIFB, Karlsruhe, 2004.
18. Q. Elhaik, M.C. Rousset, and B. Ycart, "Generating Random Benchmarks for Description Logics". In Proc. of DL' 98.
19. I. Horrocks, and P. Patel-Schneider, "DL Systems Comparison", In Proc. of DL' 98.
20. S. Wang, Y. Guo, A. Qasem, and J. Heflin, "Rapid Benchmarking for Semantic Web KnowledgeBase Systems", Lehigh University Technical Report LU-CSE-05-026, 2005.
21. OWLIM, OWL Semantic Repository, http://www.ontotext.com/owlim/. 2005.
22. KAON2, http://kaon2.semanticweb.org/.
23. Jena2, http://www.hpl.hp.com/semweb/jena.htm.
24. R. Fikes, P. Hayes, I. Horrocks, "OWL-QL - a language for deductive query answering on the Semantic Web", J. of Web Semantics (2004)

Appendix

Format: [Query No.] Query in form of SPARQL
Description explains the meaning of queries and major inference rules involved.

[Query 1] SELECT DISTINCT ?x
   WHERE   {   ?x   rdf:type   benchmark:UndergraduateStudent   .   ?x   benchmark:takesCourse http://www.Department0.University0.edu/Course0}
   Description: All undergraduate students who take course http://www.Department0.University0.edu/Course0.
   It only needs simple conjunction
[Query 2] SELECT DISTINCT ?x
   WHERE { ?x rdf:type benchmark:Employee }
   Description: Find out all employees
   Domain(worksFor, Employee), <a worksFor b> τ <a rdf:type Employee>
   Domain(worksFor,Employee), researchAssistant β | worksFor.ResearchGroupτresearchAssistantβ Employee
[Query 3] SELECT DISTINCT ?x
   WHERE   {?x   rdf:type   benchmark:Student   .   ?x   benchmark:isMemberOf http://www.Department0.University0.edu }
   Description: Find out all students of http://www.Department0.University0.edu
   Range(takeCourse,Student) , GraduateStudent β ƒ1 takeCourse τ GraduateStudent β Student
[Query 4] SELECT DISTINCT ?x
   WHERE { ?x rdf:type benchmark:Publication . ?x benchmark:publicationAuthor ?y .
   ?y rdf:type benchmark:Faculty . ?y benchmark:isMemberOf http://www.Department0.University0.edu }
   Description: All the publications by faculty of http://www.Department0.University0.edu
   SubClass: Faculty = FullProfessor 7 AssociateProfessor 7…7ClericStaff, Publication=Article 7 …7 Journal
[Query 5] SELECT DISTINCT ?x
   WHERE   {   ?x   rdf:type   benchmark:ResearchGroup   .   ?x   benchmark:subOrganizationOf http://www.University0.edu }
   Description: All research groups of http://www.University0.edu
   Transitive(subOrganizationOf), <a subOrganizationOf b>, <b subOrganizationOf http://www.University0.edu>
      τ <a subOrganizationOf http://www.University0.edu>
[Query 6] SELECT DISTINCT ?x
   WHERE { ?x rdf:type benchmark:Person . http://www.University0.edu benchmark:hasAlumnus ?x }

Description: All alumni of http://www.University0.edu

Inverse(hasAlumni, hasDegreeFrom), <a hasDegreeFrom b> τ <b hasAlumnus a>

[Query 7] SELECT DISTINCT ?x

WHERE   {?x   rdf:type   benchmark:Person   .   ?x   benchmark:hasSameHomeTownWith http://www.Department0.University0.edu/FullProfessor0}

Description: Those who has same home town with http://www.Department0.University0.edu/FullProfessor0

Transitive(hasSameHomeTownWith), Symmetric(hasSameHomeTownWith), <a hasSameHomeTownWIth b>, <c hasSameHomeTownWIth b> τ < a hasSameHomeTownWith c>

[Query 8] SELECT DISTINCT ?x

WHERE   {?x   rdf:type   benchmark:SportsLover   .   http://www.Department0.University0.edu   benchmark:hasMember ?x}

Description: All sports lovers of http://www.Department0.University0.edu

<x like y>, <y rdf:type Sports>, SportLoverβ | like.Sports τ <x rdf:type SportLover>

subProperty(isCrazyAbout, like), SportFanβ | isCrazyAbout.Sportsτ SportFan β SportLover

[Query 9] SELECT DISTINCT ?x

WHERE { ?x rdf:type benchmark:GraduateCourse . ?x benchmark:isTaughtBy ?y .
?y benchmark:isMemberOf ?z . ?z benchmark:subOrganizationOf http://www.University0.edu }

Description: All Graduate Courses of http://www.University0.edu

GraduateStudentη…takesCourse.GraduateCourse, <a rdf:type GraduateStudent>, <a takesCourse b> τ <b rdf:type GraduateCourse>

[Query 10] SELECT DISTINCT ?x

WHERE { ?x benchmark:isFriendOf http://www.Department0.University0.edu/FullProfessor0}

Description: All friends of http://www.Department0.University0.edu/FullProfessor0

Symmetric(isFriendOf), <a isFriendOf b> τ <b isFriendOf a>

[Query 11] SELECT DISTINCT ?x

WHERE { ?x rdf:type benchmark:Person . ?x benchmark:like ?y . ?z rdf:type benchmark:Chair .
?z benchmark:isHeadOf http://www.Department0.University0.edu . ?z benchmark:like ?y}

Description: All people who has same interest with the chair of http://www.Department0.University0.edu

FunctionalProperty(isHeadOf), <a isHeadof b>, <c isHeadOf b) τ <a sameAs c>   // there are some same individuals of chair0

[Query 12] SELECT DISTINCT ?x

WHERE { ?x rdf:type benchmark:Student . ?x benchmark:takesCourse ?y
.?y benchmark:isTaughtBy http://www.Department0.University0.edu/FullProfessor0 }

Description: All students who take course taught by http://www.Department0.University0.edu/FullProfessor0

GraduateStudent η …takesCourse.GraduateCourse 6 ƒ1.takesCourse, Domain(takesCourse, Student) τ Student τ GraduateStudent

[Query 13] SELECT DISTINCT ?x

WHERE { ?x rdf:type benchmark:PeopleWithHobby . ?x   benchmark:isMemberOf http://www.Department0.University0.edu}

Description: All people who has some kind of hobbies in http://www.Department0.University0.edu

Lite Cardinality: PeopleWithHobby(ƒ1like) τ SportLover, <a like b> τ <a rdf:type PeopleWithHobby>

Queries Only for DL

[Query 8]: This query is the same as query 8 in lite, but in context of OWL DL, it will involve more inference rules

Description: Inference rules: SwimmingLoverβ | like.{Swimming}τ SwimmingLover β SportsLover …

[Query 14] SELECT DISTINCT ?x

WHERE { ?x rdf:type benchmark:Woman . ?x rdf:type benchmark:Student . ?x benchmark:isMemberOf ?y .
?y benchmark:subOrganizationOf http://www.University0.edu }

Description: All woman students of http://www.University0.edu

<a,isStudentof b>, <b rdf:type WomanCollege>, WomanCollege β…hasStudent.(—Man), disjoint(Man, Woman), Man7Woman η Person τ <a rdf:type Woman>

[Query 15] SELECT DISTINCT ?x

WHERE   {?x   rdf:type   benchmark:PeopleWithManyHobbies   .   ?x   benchmark:isMemberOf http://www.Department0.University0.edu }

Description: All people who has many hobbies in http://www. Department0.University0.edu

PeopleWithManyHobbiesβƒ3like, <a like b1> … <a like bn>, all different(b1,b2…bn) τ <a rdf:type PeopleWithManyHobbies> // nƒ 3

Modelling Ontology Evaluation and Validation

Aldo Gangemi, Carola Catenacci, Massimiliano Ciaramita, and Jos Lehmann

Laboratory for Applied Ontology, ISTC-CNR, Roma, Italy
{aldo.gangemi, carola.catenacci, m.ciaramita,
jos.lehmann}@istc.cnr.it

Abstract. We present a comprehensive approach to ontology evaluation and validation, which have become a crucial problem for the development of semantic technologies. Existing evaluation methods are integrated into one sigle framework by means of a formal model. This model consists, firstly, of a meta-ontology called O^2, that characterises ontologies as semiotic objects. Based on O^2 and an analysis of existing methodologies, we identify three main types of measures for evaluation: structural measures, that are typical of ontologies represented as graphs; functional measures, that are related to the intended use of an ontology and of its components; and usability-profiling measures, that depend on the level of annotation of the considered ontology. The meta-ontology is then complemented with an ontology of ontology validation called *oQual*, which provides the means to devise the best set of criteria for choosing an ontology over others in the context of a given project. Finally, we provide a small example of how to apply *oQual*-derived criteria to a validation case.

1 Introduction

The need for evaluation methodologies in the field of ontology development and reuse emerged as soon as 1994 (see [21]) and it has grown steadily ever since. Yet, no comprehensive and global approach to this problem has been proposed to date. This situation may become a serious obstacle for the success of semantic technologies, especially in industrial and commercial sectors. A typical example in this sense is the development of the Semantic Web. On the one hand, the idea of conveying semantics through ontologies definitely arouses the interest of large parts of the ICT Industry. Ontologies promise to be crucial components of web-like technologies that are able to cope with high interconnection, constant change and incompleteness. On the other hand, however, the lack of well-understood and shared notions of ontology evaluation and validation significantly slows down the transition of ontologies from esoteric symbolic structures to reliable industrial components.

In this paper we look at existing ontology-evaluation methods from the perspective of their integration into one single framework. To this end, we set up a formal model for ontology evaluation that consists, in the first place, of a meta-ontology – called O^2 – which characterises ontologies as semiotic objects. O^2 is meant to provide a foundation to the elements and features that are targeted by evaluation. Secondly, based on O^2 and an overview of the state of the art (cf. [8]), we provide a provisional catalogue of qualitative and quantitative measures for evaluating ontologies. We

Y. Sure and J. Domingue (Eds.): ESWC 2006, LNCS 4011, pp. 140–154, 2006.
© Springer-Verlag Berlin Heidelberg 2006

identify three main types of measures: <u>structural</u> measures, that are typical of ontologies represented as graphs; <u>functional</u> measures, that are related to the intended use of an ontology and of its components, i.e. their function; <u>usability-profiling</u> measures, that depend on the level of annotation of the considered ontology. Thirdly, the meta-ontology is complemented with an ontology of ontology validation – *oQual* – which allows to pick up ontology elements by means of O^2, provides quality-parameters and, when feasible, their ordering functions. Both O^2 and *oQual* are partly formalized in FOL and are currently maintained as OWL models, plugged into the DOLCE ontology library and its design patterns [25]. In practice, we model ontology evaluation as a diagnostic task based on ontology descriptions. Such descriptions make explicit some knowledge items that are crucial to ontology validation, like e.g.: roles and functions of the elements of the considered ontology; parameters for the descriptions that typically denote the quality of an ontology; and functions that compose those parameters according to a preferential ordering. At the end of the paper, we sketch an analytic examples of the trade-offs needed when composing principles with conflicting parameters, i.e. an application of *oQual*-derived criteria to a validation case. Finally, some conclusions are drawn.

2 O^2: A Semiotic Meta-ontology

The use of meta-ontologies is becoming relevant within the semantic web, because of their easy integration and the shared construction methods with ontologies proper.

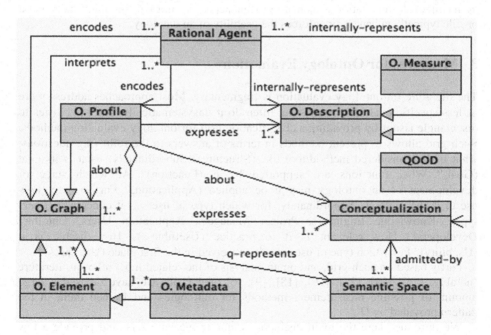

Fig. 1. A UML class diagram depicting the main notions from the O^2 ontology

[12], for instance, have recently proposed an *Ontology Metadata Vocabulary*. Following this tendency, we characterize an ontology as a semiotic object, i.e. an object constituted by an *information object* and an *intended conceptualization* established within a *communication setting*. The basic intuition behind this part of our proposal is that information can be constituted by any pattern that is used to represent another pattern, whereas that representation is interpretable by some rational agent as an explanation, an instruction, a command, etc. This is an idea that goes back at least to Peirce (cf. [17]).

This intuition is formalized by applying an ontology design pattern called *Information↔Description* (see [7]), and originates a new pattern called O^2 (because it is a "meta-ontology"). O^2, in turn, formalizes the following specification: a) an ontology is information of a special kind; b) its patterns are graph-like structures; c) they represent intended conceptualizations, i.e. internal representations (by a rational agent) of *entity types*. For example, it is perfectly possible to define an ontology for subways, but one will hardly consider the graph of the London Underground as an ontology - at most, the latter can be considered as a *model* of an appropriate subway ontology.

In O^2 (Fig.1), an ontology graph has an intended conceptualization and a formal semantic space admitted by the conceptualization. The graph and the conceptualization are 'kept together' by a rational agent who encodes/interprets the graph, while internally representing its intended conceptualization.

An agent can also provide a profile containing metadata that express a "description" of the ontology, e.g. a method to measure the structural or functional properties of an ontology graph, its resulting attributes, its possible quality criteria and values, as well as its lifecycle annotations, such as provenance and informal annotations. A good profile typically enhances or enforces the usability of an ontology.

3 Measures for Ontology Evaluation

The literature on ontology evaluation is fragmentary. Most approaches address more or less specific evaluation issues but often do it unsystematically. Only [11] tries to disentangle issues by providing a classification grid for ontology evaluation methods. Such grid allows to present methods in terms of answers to the following questions: what is the considered method/tool like (Structure)? Subordinately: what is its goal (Goal)? What functions are supported by it (Function)? At which stage of development of an ontology may it be applied (Application)? Furthermore, how useful is the method? Subordinately: for which type of users is it conceived (Users types: Knowledge Engineers, Project Managers, Application Users, Ontology Developers)? How relevant is it to practice (Usefulness)? How usable is it (Usability)? For which type of uses was it conceived in the first place (Use cases)?

Partly based on such grid, and on an analysis of the related most relevant literature (notably, [24], [14], [23], [19], [18], [9], [6], and [16]), we have devised a large amount of possible measurement methods for ontologies and framed them in the pattern provided by O^2.

We introduce here the main distinctions among measure sets, and provide a few examples for some of them. For the full list of identified measures and the detailed state-of-the-art review, see [8].

3.1 Measure Types

As explained above, by ontology we mean a *semiotic object* including graph objects, formal semantic spaces, conceptualizations, and annotation profiles; therefore, we propose to measure ontologies relatively to three main dimensions: structural, functional, and usability-profiling.

The *structural* dimension of ontologies focuses on syntax and formal semantics, i.e. on ontologies represented as *graphs*. In this form, the topological, logical and meta-logical properties of an ontology can be measured by means of a context-free metric.

The *functional* dimension is related to the intended use of a given ontology and of its components, i.e. their function in a context. The focus is on the conceptualization specified by an ontology.

Finally, the *usability-profiling* dimension focuses on the ontology profile (annotations), which typically addresses the communication context of an ontology (i.e. its pragmatics).

Notice that those dimensions follow a partition into *logical types*: structurally, we look at an ontology as an (information) <u>object</u>; functionally, we look at it as a <u>language</u> (information object+intended conceptualization), and from the usability viewpoint, we look at its <u>meta-language</u> (the profile about the semiotic context of an ontology). Therefore, the dimension types correspond to the constituents of the O^2 pattern and heterogeneous measurement methods are needed.

3.2 Measuring the Structural Dimension

In our treatment of the structural dimension, the idea is to define a general function like the following: $M = \langle D, S, mp, c \rangle$, where dimension D is a graph property or concept we want to measure: the intensional counterpart of the metric space; the set of graph elements S is a collection of elements in the graph (which may be seen as the ontology structure); mp is a measurement procedure; and c is a coefficient of measurement error.

The value of M is a real number obtained by applying a measurement procedure mp for a dimension D to a set S of graph elements, modulo a coefficient c (if any), i.e. (with an operational semantics): $mp_{D,c,S} \xrightarrow[yields]{} m \in \Re$

Within the possible sets of graph elements, we have considered the following :

- The set of <u>graph</u> nodes G from a graph g, $G \subseteq S$
- The set of <u>root</u> nodes $ROO \subseteq G$, where the root nodes are those having no outgoing *is-a* arcs in a graph g.
- The set of <u>leaf</u> nodes $LEA \subseteq G$, where the leaf nodes are those having no ingoing *is-a* arcs in a graph g.
- The sets of <u>sibling</u> nodes $SIB_{j \in G}$ connected to a same node j in a graph g through *is-a* arcs.
- The set of <u>paths</u> P where $\forall j \in P \Rightarrow j \subseteq G$, where a path j is any sequence of directly connected nodes in a digraph g starting from a root node $x_{\in ROO}$ and ending at a leaf node $y_{\in LEA}$.

- The set of <u>levels</u> ("generations") L where $\forall j \in L \Rightarrow j \subseteq G$, where a generation j is the set of all sibling node sets having the same distance from (one of) the root node(s) $r_{\in ROO}$ of a digraph g.
- The sets of graph nodes $N_{j \in P}$ from a same path j in a digraph g
- The sets of graph nodes $N_{j \in L}$ from a same level j in a digraph g
- The set MO of <u>modules</u> from a graph g. A *module* is any subgraph sg of g, where the set of graph elements S' from sg is such that $S' \subseteq S$. Two modules sg_1 and sg_2 are *taxonomically disjoint* when only ≥ 0 *is-a* arcs a_i connect sg_1 to sg_2, and each a_i has the same direction.

Several structural measures can be defined, involving:

  a) topological properties such as *depth* (related to the cardinality of paths in a graph), *breadth* (related to the cardinality of paths in a graph), *tangledness* (related to multihierarchical nodes of a graph), and *fan-outness* (related to the 'dispersion' of graph nodes), among others;
  b) logical-adequacy properties such *consistency*, *anonymous classes* and *cycle ratios*, among others;
  c) metalogical-adequacy properties, such as e.g *qualified density* (i.e. presence of meaningful conceptual-relation 'dense' areas, or 'patterns').

For instance, we have defined *depth* (a topological property) as a graph property related to the cardinality of paths in a graph, where the arcs considered are only is-a arcs. This measure only applies to digraphs (directed graphs). E.g., **average depth**, where $N_{j \in P}$ is the cardinality of each path j from the set of paths P in a graph g, and $n_{P \subseteq g}$ is the cardinality of P:
$$m = \frac{1}{n_{P \subseteq g}} \sum_{j}^{P} N_{j \in P}$$

3.3 Measuring the Functional Dimension

The functional dimension is coincident with the main purpose of an ontology, i.e. specifying a given conceptualization, or a set of contextual assumptions about an area of interest. Such specifications, however, are always approximate, since the relationship between an ontology and a conceptualization is always dependent on a rational agent that conceives that conceptualization (the 'cognitive' semantics) and on the semantic space that formally encodes that conceptualization (the 'formal' semantics) (Fig. 1). Hence, an appropriate evaluation strategy should involve a measurement of the degree of how those dependencies are implemented. We call this the *matching problem*.

  The matching problem requires us to find ways of measuring the extent to which an ontology mirrors a given expertise (cf. [20]), competency (cf. [22]), or task: something that is in the experience of a given community and that includes not only a corpus of documents, but also theories, practices and know-how that are not necessarily represented in their entirety in the available documents. This seems to imply that no automatised method will ever suffice and that intellectual judgement will always be needed. However, automatic and semi-automatic techniques can be applied that make evaluation easier, less subjective, more complete and faster [6].

The functional measures provided in [8] are variants of the *precision, coverage,* and *accuracy* measures introduced by [10], which are in turn based on an analogy with the *precision* and *recall* measures widely used in information retrieval (cf. [2]). They include *competence adequacy* (e.g. inter-subjective agreement, task adequacy, task specifity, and topic specificity); *NLP adequacy* (e.g. compliance with lexical distinctions), and *functional modularity* (e.g. ontology stratification, or granularity).

Due to the matching problem, however, the adaptation of precision, recall and accuracy to ontology evaluation is by no means straightforward. Since expertise is by default in the cognitive "black-box" of rational agents, ontology engineers have to elicit it from agents, or they can assume a set of data as a *qualified expression* of expertise and tasks, e.g. texts, pictures, diagrams, database records, terminologies, metadata schemas, etc. Therefore, we distinguish between *black-box* and *glass-box* measurement methods.

Black-box methods require rational agents, because they don't explicitly use knowledge of the internal structure of an expertise (see [8] for a more extensive discussion of these methods).

Glass-box methods require a data set that 'samples' that knowledge, and, on this basis, we can treat the internal structure of those data *as if* it were the internal structure of an expertise.

Based on these assumptions, precision, recall and accuracy of an ontology can be measured against: *a)* experts' judgment, or *b)* a data set assumed as a qualified expression of experts' judgment:

(1) *Agreement (black-box)*: it is measured through the proportion of *agreement* that experts have with respect to ontology elements; when a group of experts is considered, we may also want to measure the *consensus* reached by the group's members.

(2) *User-satisfaction (black-box)*: it can be measured by means of dedicated polls, or by means of provenance, popularity, and trust assessment.

(3) *Task*: what has to be supported by an ontology? (*glass-box*). It deals with measuring an ontology according to its fitness to some goals, preconditions, postconditions, constraints, options, etc. This makes the measurement very reliable at design-time, while it needs a reassessment at reuse-time.

(4) *Topic*: what are the boundaries of the knowledge domain addressed by an ontology? (*glass-box*). It deals with measuring an ontology according to its fitness to an existing knowledge repository. This makes the measurement reliable both at design-time, and at reuse-time, but is based on the availability of data that can be safely assumed as related to the (supposed) topic covered by an ontology. Natural Language Processing (NLP)-based methods fit into this category, and are currently the most reliable method for ontology evaluation, at least for lightweight ontologies.

(5) *Modularity*: what are the building blocks for the design of an ontology? (*glass-box*). It is based on the availability of data about the *design* of an ontology. Therefore, it deals with measuring an ontology according to its fitness to an existing repository of reusable components. This makes the measurement very reliable both at design-time, and at reuse-time. On the other hand, modularity

assessment is only practicable on ontologies that have been designed with an appropriate methodology.

As example of (*glass-box*) NLP-based measurements, consider a case in which the ontology is lexicalized (i.e., it defines, at least to some extent, what instances of classes and relations are called in natural language) and there exists a substantial amount of textual documents that contain information about the content of the ontology. By identifying mentions of ontological elements in a given corpus, it is possible to count the frequency of classes (or relations). The relative frequency of each class *c* (or relation *r*) is the proportion of mentions of ontology instances which are equal to *c*; i.e., $P(c) = count(c)/sum_i count(c_i)$. The relative frequency measures the importance of each class and provides a first simple measure of the ontology quality. For example, in newswire texts the three typical classes of 'person', 'location' and 'organisation' have somewhat similar frequencies, while if the corpus analysis reveals that one of the classes is much more unlikely than the others this means that there is something wrong with the instances of that class. This might indicate that the low frequency class is underrepresented in the ontology, at the lexical level. Recent work has focused also on discovering class attributes and arbitrary relation between classes through automatic or semi-automatic population of ontology objects (see [1], [5], and [4]). In fact, it is possible that new senses of already known instances are discovered, for example because the instance is polysemous/ambiguous (e.g., 'Washington' is both a person and a location).

3.4 Measuring the Usability Profile of Ontologies

Usability-profiling measures focus on the ontology profile, which typically addresses the communication context of an ontology (i.e. its pragmatics). An ontology profile is a set of ontology annotations: the metadata about an ontology and its elements. *Presence, amount, completeness*, and *reliability* are the usability measures ranging on annotations, which have been singled out in our research.

Annotations contain information about structural, functional, or user-oriented properties of an ontology. There are also purely lifecycle-oriented properties, e.g. authorship, price, versioning, organisational deployment, interfacing, etc.

Three basic levels of usability profiling have been singled out: *recognition, efficiency*, and *interfacing*.

The *recognition level* makes objects, actions, and options visible (cf. [13]). Users need an easy access to the instructions for using ontologies in an effective way, and an efficient process to retrieve appropriate meta-information. That is, "give your users the information that they need and allow them to pick what they want". Hence recognition is about having a complete documentation and to be sure to guarantee an effective access.

The *efficiency level* includes organisational, commercial, and developmental annotations. Large organisations tend to be compartmentalized, with each group looking out for its own interests, sometimes to the detriment of the organisation as a whole. Information resource departments often fall into the trap of creating or adopting ontologies that result in increased efficiency and lowered costs for the information resources department, but only at the cost of lowered productivity for the company as a whole. This managing-operating-balance principle translates into some requisites (*parameters*) for the *organisation-oriented design* of ontology libraries (or of distributed ontologies), which provide constraints to one or more of the following entities: *organisation architecture, (complex) application middleware, trading properties, cost, accessibility, development effort.*

The *interfacing level* concerns the process of matching an ontology to a user interface. As far as evaluation is concerned, we are only interested in the case when an ontology includes annotations to interfacing operations. For example, a *contract negotiation* ontology might contain annotations to allow an implementation of e.g. a *visual contract modelling language.* If such annotations exist, it is indeed an advantage for ontologies that are tightly bound to a certain (computational) service. On the other hand, such annotations may result unnecessary in those cases where an interface language exists that maps to the core elements of a core ontology e.g. for contract negotiation.

4   *oQual*: A Model of Ontology Validation

We model ontology validation as a *diagnostic task* over ontology elements, processes, and attributes (Fig. 2). This task involves:

- *Quality-Oriented Ontology Descriptions (qoods),* which are a type of *ontology description* (cf. Fig.1) that provide the *roles* and *tasks* of, respectively, the elements and processes from/on an ontology, and have elementary qoods (called *principles*) as parts. For example, a type of qood is *retrieve*, which formalizes the requirement to be able to answer a certain competency question. In Fig. 2, the *retrieve* type is instantiated as a requirement for the ontology to be able to retrieve the 'family history for a condition related to blood cancer', in an ontology project for 'blood cancer information service'.
- *Value spaces* ("attributes") of ontology elements. For example, the presence of a relation such as: $R(p,f,c,i)$, where Patient(p), Family(f), Condition(c), Indicator(i).
- *Principles* for assessing the ontology fitness, which are modelled as elementary qoods, and are typically parts of a project-oriented qood. For example, 'description of fitness to expertise' is a principle.
- *Parameters* (ranging over the attributes -*value spaces*- of ontologies or ontology elements), defined within a principle. For example, 'relation fitness to competency question' is a parameter for the relation $R(p,f,c,i)$.
- *Parameter dependencies* occurring across principles because of the interdependencies between the value spaces of the measured ontology elements. For example, the 'relation fitness to competency question' parameter is dependent on either 'first-order expressiveness' or 'presence of a relation reification method' parameters ranging on the logical language of the ontology, because the relation $R(p,f,c,i)$ has four arguments and it is not straightforwardly expressible in e.g. OWL(DL).
- *Preferential ordering* functions that compose parameters from different principles. For example, in a 'blood cancer information service' project, the 'relation fitness to competency question' parameter may be composed with the 'computational complexity' parameter.

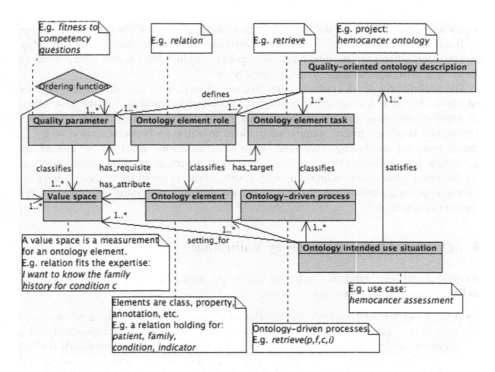

Fig. 2. The *oQual* design pattern applied to a clinical use case. A *qood* based on the *fitness* to competency questions constrains the setting of the intended use for the ontology to be designed in a clinical information project.

- *Trade-offs*, which provide a conflict resolution description when combining principles with conflicting parameters. For example, the two abovementioned parameters might be conflicting when the cost of the expressiveness or of the reification method are too high in terms of computational efficiency. A trade-off in this case describes a guideline to simplify the competency question, or a strategy to implement the relation differently.

The *oQual* formal model is based on the the *Description↔Situation* pattern (cf. [7]) from the DOLCE ontology library ([15]), which is integrated with the *Information↔Description* pattern used for O^2.

Ontology descriptions, roles, parameters, and ordering functions are defined on the results of the measurement types that can be performed on an ontology graph, conceptualization, or profile. The results are represented as regions within value spaces. Quality parameters constrain those regions *within* a particular qood.

5 Applying a *Qood* to a Validation Case

In order to apply *oQual* to an analytic case of trade-off, we need a more detailed presentation of principles and of some of their typical parameters.

5.1 Some Principles and Parameters

Principles are defined here as structured descriptions of the quality of an ontology (*qoods*): they are considered *elementary* qoods because they usually define a limited set of parameters constraining ontology properties in order to support a common *goal*. Principles should also *lack conflicting parameters*.

Here is a list of some qoods emerged in the practice of ontology engineering:

- Cognitive ergonomics
- Transparency (explicitness of organizing principles)
- Computational integrity and efficiency
- Meta-level integrity
- Flexibility (context-boundedness)
- Compliance to expertise
- Compliance to procedures for extension, integration, adaptation, etc.
- Generic accessibility (computational as well as commercial)
- Organizational fitness

The parameters defined by principles can be complex, but at the current state of research, they are usually simple scalars ranging on the measurement value spaces associated with the measures mentioned in Section 3.

Here is a list of parameters defined by the principles introduced above. For an easier understanding, each parameter is presented with the name of the measure on which it ranges, preceded by a + or − sign to indicate the scalar region constrained within the value space:

Cognitive ergonomics. Intuition: this principle prospects an ontology that can be easily understood, manipulated, and exploited by final users. Parameters:

-depth	-breadth
-tangledness	+class/property ratio
+annotations (esp. lexical, glosses, topic)	-anonymous classes
+interfacing	+patterns (dense areas)

Transparency. Intuition: this principle prospects an ontology that can be analyzed in detail, with a rich formalization of conceptual choices and motivations. Parameters:

+modularity	+axiom/class ratio
+patterns	+specific differences
+partitioning	+accuracy
+complexity	+anonymous classes
+modularity design	

Computational integrity and efficiency. Intuition: this principle prospects an ontology that can be successfully/easily processed by a reasoner (inference engine, classifier, etc.). Parameters:

+logical consistency	+disjointness ratio
-tangledness	-restrictions
-cycles	

<u>Meta-level integrity</u>. Intuition: this principle prospects an ontology that respects certain ordering criteria that are assumed as quality indicators. Parameters:

+metalevel consistency   -tangledness

<u>Flexibility</u>. Intuition: this principle prospects an ontology that can be easily adapted to multiple views. Parameters:

+modularity   +partitioning
+context-boundedness

<u>Compliance to expertise</u>. Intuition: this principle prospects an ontology that is compliant to one or more users' knowledge. Parameters:

+precision   +recall
+accuracy

<u>Compliance to procedures for mapping, extension, integration, adaptation</u>. Intuition: this principle prospects an ontology that can be easily understood and manipulated for reuse and adaptation. Parameters:

+accuracy(?)   +recognition annotations (esp. lexical)
+modularity   -tangledness(?)

<u>Organizational fitness</u>. Intuition: this principle prospects an ontology that can be easily deployed within an organization, and that has a good coverage for that context. Parameters:

+recall   +organizational design annotations
+commercial/legal annotations   +user satisfaction
+organizational design annotations

<u>Generic accessibility</u>. Intuition: this principle prospects an ontology that can be easily accessed for effective application. Parameters:

+accuracy (based on task and use cases)   +annotations (esp. policy semantics, application history)
+modularity   -logical complexity

5.2 Preference and Trade-Offs, with an Example in Legal Ontologies

Due to partly mutual independence of principles, the need for a preferential ordering of quality parameters required by different principles often arises, e.g. because of a conflict, or because two parameters from different principles are unsustainable with existing tools or resources. OntoMetric ([14]) is an example of a tool that supports measurement based on a preferential ordering.

A preferential ordering can either define the *prevalence* of a set of parameters from a principle p_1 over another principle p_2, or it can define a composition of the two sets of parameters from p_1 and p_2. A compositions is the result of a *trade-off*. Both prevalence and trade-off descriptions are based on meta-parameters, e.g.: *available resources, available expertise, business relations, tools*, etc.

A simple exemplification of a trade-off for principle composition is the following. *Transparency* and *compliance to expertise* principles usually require *content ontology design patterns* (cf. [7]), involving *hub nodes* (classes with several properties, cf. [16]), then those principles require a *high rate of dense areas* parameter. But dense areas often need the definition of sets of (usually existential) axioms that potentially induce complex (in)direct cycles. Consequently, *high rate of dense areas* depends on a *high complexity* parameter (cf. [3] for the complexity of description logic ports of UML models).

The content design pattern for the *LimitViolation* pattern is an example of such a case (Fig.3). The *LimitViolation* pattern contains the following axioms (restrictions) that constitute a cyclical path, encoded here in OWL abstract syntax (corresponding to the red path in Fig.3):

```
Class(LimitViolation partial restriction(defines
someValuesFrom(ViolationParameter)))

Class(ViolationParameter partial restriction(classifies
someValuesFrom(ValueRegion)))

Class(ValueRegion partial restriction(observedBy
allValuesFrom(LegalControlSystem)))

Class(LegalControlSystem partial restriction(classifiedBy
someValuesFrom(LegalRole)))

Class(LegalRole partial restriction(d-used-by
someValuesFrom(LimitViolation)))

Class(LimitViolation partial restriction(defines
someValuesFrom(ViolationParameter)))

Class(ViolationParameter partial restriction(classifies
someValuesFrom(ValueRegion)))

Class(ValueRegion partial restriction(observedBy
allValuesFrom(LegalControlSystem)))

Class(LegalControlSystem partial restriction(classifiedBy
allValuesFrom(LegalRole)))

Class(LegalRole partial restriction(d-used-by
someValuesFrom(LimitViolation)))
```

If an ontology project using the limit violation axioms is based on a *qood* that aims at both a *transparency* principle, and a *computational efficiency* principle, and we already know (cf. [8]) that computationally efficiency requires a *low rate of cycles parameter*, then we get a conflict of parameters (Fig.4). Therefore, a trade-off may be needed in an ontology project that uses the limit violation axioms. The trade-off can be applied by following two approaches.

The first approach defines a *preference ordering* over the parameters, which in the example leads either to accept the complexity, or to dismiss the pattern. The pattern is in this case essential to the ontology, then, if the *low rate of cycles* is also required because of e.g. available computational resources, we must resort to the second approach: *relaxation of parameters*. The possible methods to relax the parameters should act on either the reasoning algorithm, or the axioms. Since the first cannot be

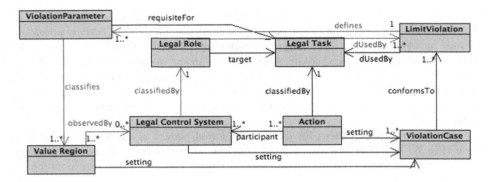

Fig. 3. The *LimitViolation* pattern in UML, showing a potential indirect cycle: a description of limit violation defines violation parameters ranging on some value space (e.g., speed), also assigning (legal) roles and tasks to legally-relevant entities: control systems, vehicles, persons, actions, etc. A violation case conforms to the description if legally-relevant entities and values are classified by parameters, roles, and tasks.

changed easily in most ontology projects, the best practice is to modify the model according to some *tuning practices* e.g. involving generalization over restrictions, which in our example can be done on one of the following axioms by substituting the class in the restriction with its superclass:

```
Class(ValueRegion partial restriction(observedBy
allValuesFrom(ControlSystem)))
```

```
Class(LegalControlSystem partial restriction(classifiedBy
allValuesFrom(Role)))
```

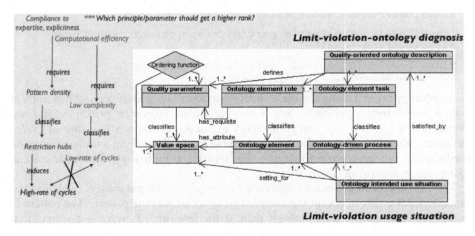

Fig. 4. A *qood* (a diagnosis of an ontology project using the limit violation pattern) that composes two principles requiring conflicting parameters

6 Conclusions and Future Work

O^2 and *oQual* are ontologies that characterise an ontology as a communication object, and allow to make a parametric design of evaluation and validation (diagnostic) tasks. Ontologies are analyzed in their graph and formal elements, functional requirements, and annotation profile. Therefore our approach results in parametric design specifications that address varied measures, ranging from graph properties to logical consistency, precision/recall, intersubjective reliability, etc., which do not suggest *prescriptive* validation of an ontology, but suggest an interactive, distributed validation against well-understood tasks.

Current work is focusing on the empirical assessment of the O^2 and *oQual* ontologies and related methods, by measuring existing ontologies, comparing the quality of distinct ontologies that represent the same domain, creating correlations between user-oriented and structural measures, and creating tools to assist ontology evaluation in large industry- and organization-scale projects (until now, the ontology and the method have been tested on fragments of large ontologies, and only thoroughly in the context of the Italian OntoDev project, featuring a mid-size lightweight ontology repository). Collaboration with the Oyster, Onthology, and KnowledgeZone projects ([26]) are being established in order to harmonize ontology metadata semantics with tools, and to include/extract evaluation annotation in/from current metadata vocabularies.

References

1. Almuhareb A. and Poesio M., (2004), "Attribute-based and value-based clustering: an evaluation", in *Proceedings of the Conference on Empirical Methods in Natural Language Processing*.
2. Baeza-Yates R. and Ribeiro-Neto B., 1999, *Modern Information Retrieval*, Addison Wesley.
3. Berardi D., Calvanese D., De Giacomo G., (2001), "Reasoning on UML Class Diagrams using Description Logic Based Systems", *Proceedings of the KI'2001 Workshop on Applications of Description Logics*.
4. Brewster C., Alani H., Dasmahapatra S. and Wilks Y., (2004), "Data-driven ontology evaluation", in *Proceedings of LREC*.
5. Ciaramita M., Gangemi A., Ratsch E., Saric J., and Rojas I., (2005), "Unsupervised Learning of Semantic Relations between Concepts of a Molecular Biology Ontology", in *Proceedings of the 19th International Joint Conference on Artificial Intelligence*.
6. Daelemans W. and Reinberger M.L., (2004), "Shallow Text Understanding for Ontology Content Evaluation", *IEEE Intelligent Systems*: 1541-1672.
7. Gangemi A., (2005), "Ontology Design Patterns for Semantic Web Content", in Motta E. and Gil Y. (eds.), in *Proceedings of the Fourth International Semantic Web Conference*.
8. Gangemi A., Catenacci C., Ciaramita M., and Lehmann J., (2005), "Ontology evaluation: A review of methods and an integrated model for the quality diagnostic task", *Technical Report*, available at http://www.loa-cnr.it/Publications.html.
9. Gómez-Pérez A., (2003), "Ontology Evaluation", in *Handbook on Ontologies*, S. Staab and R. Studer (eds.), Springer-Verlag, pp. 251–274.

10. Guarino N., (2004), "Towards a Formal Evaluation of Ontology Quality", *IEEE Intelligent Systems*: 1541-1672.
11. Hartmann J., Spyns P., Giboin A., Maynard D., Cuel R., Suárez-Figueroa M.C., and Sure Y., (2004), "Methods for ontology evaluation", *Knowledge Web Deliverable D1.2.3*,
12. Hartmann J., Palma R., Sure Y., Suárez-Figueroa M.C., and Haase P. (2005), "OMV– Ontology Metadata Vocabulary", paper presented at the *Ontology Patterns for the Semantic Web (OPSW) Workshop at ISWC2005*, Galway, Ireland: http://www.research.ibm.com/people/w/welty/OPSW-05/.
13. Kaakinen, J., Hyona, J., and Keenan, J.M., (2002), "Individual differences in perspective effects on on-line text processing", *Discourse Processes*, 33: 159 - 173.
14. Lozano-Tello, A. and Gómez-Pérez A., (2004), "ONTOMETRIC: A method to choose the appropriate ontology", *Journal. of Database Management*, 15(2).
15. Masolo, C., A. Gangemi, N. Guarino, A. Oltramari and L. Schneider, (2004), "WonderWeb Deliverable D18: The WonderWeb Library of Foundational Ontologies", available at http://www.loa-cnr.it/Publications.html.
16. Noy, N., (2004), "Evaluation by Ontology Consumers", *IEEE Intelligent Systems*: 1541-1672.
17. Peirce C.S., (1931-1958), *Collected Papers*, vols. 1-8, C. Hartshorne, P. Weiss and A.W. Burks (eds), Cambridge, MA: Harvard University Press.
18. Porzel R. and Malaka R., (2004), "A Task-based Approach for Ontology Evaluation", in *Proceedings of ECAI04*.
19. Spyns P., (2005), "EvaLexon: Assessing triples mined from texts", *Technical Report 09*, STAR Lab, Brussel.
20. Steels L., (1990), "Components of Expertise", *AI Magazine*, 11, 2: 30-49.
21. Sure Y. (ed.), (2004), "Why Evaluate Ontology Technologies? Because It Works!", *IEEE Intelligent Systems*: 1541-1672.
22. Uschold U. and Gruninger M., (1996), "Ontologies: Principles, Methods, and Applications," *Knowledge Eng. Rev.*, vol. 11, no. 2: 93–155.
23. Welty C. and Guarino N., (2001), "Supporting ontological analysis of taxonomic relationships", *Data and Knowledge Engineering*, vol. 39, no. 1, pp. 51-74.
24. Yao H., Orme A.M., and Etzkorn L., (2005), "Cohesion Metrics for Ontology Design and Application", *Journal of Computer Science*, 1(1): 107-113.
25. http://www.loa-cnr/ontologies/DLP_397.owl, http://dolce.semanticweb.org .
26. http://oyster.ontoware.org; http://www.onthology.org; http://smi-protege.stanford.edu: 8080/KnowledgeZone/.

Benchmark Suites for Improving the RDF(S) Importers and Exporters of Ontology Development Tools

Raúl García-Castro and Asunción Gómez-Pérez

Ontology Engineering Group, Departamento de Inteligencia Artificial,
Facultad de Informática, Universidad Politécnica de Madrid, Spain
{rgarcia, asun}@fi.upm.es

Abstract. Interoperability is the ability of two or more systems to interchange information and to use the information that has been interchanged. Nowadays, interoperability between ontology development tools is low. Therefore, to assess and improve this interoperability, we propose to perform a benchmarking of the interoperability of ontology development tools using RDF(S) as the interchange language. This paper presents, on the one hand, the interoperability benchmarking that is currently in progress in Knowledge Web[1] and, on the other, the benchmark suites defined and used in this benchmarking.

1 Introduction

The number of users of ontology development tools is ever increasing. These users come from academia or from industry, and might have or not deep knowledge on ontology engineering. Each ontology development tool provides a different set of functionalities and the user that develops an ontology prefers one ontology development tool over the others. Hence, users need to interchange ontologies from one ontology development tool to another.

Nowadays, users of ontology development tools do not know whether ontologies can be properly interchanged between two ontology development tools and, if so, which are the consequences of this interchange, such as addition or loss of knowledge. This leads to a slower uptake of ontology development tools by end users, both in the academia and the industrial world. Moreover, the experimentation carried out so far [1] has demonstrated that the degree of ontology interchange between ontology development tools is low.

One of the main goals of the Knowledge Web Network of Excellence is to support the industrial applicability of ontology technology. This involves assessing and improving several types of ontology technology: ontology development tools, alignment tools, annotation tools, querying and reasoning services, and semantic web service technology.

---

[1] http://knowledgeweb.semanticweb.org/

Y. Sure and J. Domingue (Eds.): ESWC 2006, LNCS 4011, pp. 155–169, 2006.

In order *to assess and improve the interoperability of ontology tools, the first task to perform in Knowledge Web is benchmarking the interoperability of ontology development tools by evaluating their RDF(S)*[2] *importers and exporters*, and this is what we present in this paper. Participation in the benchmarking is open to any organization and its current status and its results are publicly available[3]. At the end of the benchmarking process, we will get public results with detailed information about the current interoperability of ontology development tools. This benchmarking will also provide us with mechanisms that can be used to evaluate the RDF(S) importers and exporters of other Semantic Web technology (i.e. mapping tools, annotation tools, etc.).

According to [2], ontology development tools can interoperate in four ways: by mapping ontologies in the source tool to others in the target tool, by translating ontologies to a single pivot language, by translating ontologies to one language in a layered architecture of languages, and by a generalisation of the pivot and the layered approaches that does not require either a fixed pivot language or a fixed layering of languages. This paper only covers the pivot approach, that is, interoperability in terms of interchanging ontologies using a common interchange language. Therefore, the interoperability depends on the correct working of the importers and exporters from and to the different languages.

This paper is structured as follows. Section 2 presents other evaluation initiatives related to this work and the differences found. Section 3 describes briefly the benchmarking methodology being used; Sections 4 and 5 state how this methodology was instantiated to our own case. Section 6 defines how the benchmark suites used in the benchmarking were defined as well as how they are used. Section 7 shows how these benchmark suites have been evaluated according to the desirable properties of benchmark suites. Finally, Section 8 presents the conclusions derived form this work and future lines of work.

2   Related Work

This section introduces the terms benchmark and benchmarking, because they are frequently used in the paper, and explains the benefits of benchmarking over performing tool evaluations. It also presents other related evaluation initiatives and the differences between them and our approach.

2.1   Benchmark and Benchmarking

Benchmarking is a continuous process for improving products, services and processes by systematically evaluating and comparing them to those considered to be the best. This definition, adapted from the business management community [3], is used by some authors in the Software Engineering community [4] while others consider benchmarking as a software evaluation method [5].

---

[2] http://www.w3.org/TR/rdf-schema/
[3] http://knowledgeweb.semanticweb.org/benchmarking_interoperability/

A **benchmark**, by contrast, is a test that measures the performance of a system or subsystem on a well-defined task or set of tasks [6]. However, Sim et al. [7] propose to measure also tools and techniques for comparing their performance.

The reason for benchmarking ontology tools instead of just evaluating them is to obtain several benefits from benchmarking that cannot be obtained from tool evaluations. As Figure 1 illustrates, the evaluation of a tool shows us the weaknesses of the tool or its compliance to quality requirements. If several tools are involved in the evaluation, we also obtain a comparative analysis of these tools and recommendations for users of these tools. When benchmarking several tools, besides all the benefits commented, we gain continuous improvement of the tools, recommendations for developers on the practices used when developing these tools and, from these practices, those that can be considered best practices.

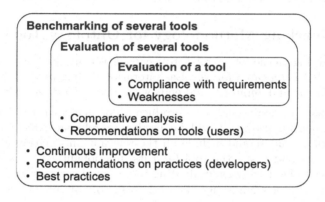

Fig. 1. Benchmarking benefits

2.2 Related Evaluations

In this section, we briefly present two evaluation initiatives related to this work. The first is a benchmark suite for evaluating RDF(S) usage, and the second is a previous evaluation of the interoperability of ontology development tools.

RDF(S) Test Cases. The RDF Test Cases[4] were created by the W3C RDF Core Working Group. These tests check the correct usage of the tools that implement RDF knowledge bases and illustrate the resolution of different issues considered by the Working Group.

The RDF Test Cases could also be used for evaluating RDF(S) importers but, while they provide examples for, and clarification of, the normative definition of the language, our approach aims for an exhaustive evaluation of RDF(S) importers. Another difference is that we distinguish between the benchmarks that depend on the RDF(S) knowledge model and those that depend on the RDF syntax used. Moreover, we only consider valid input ontologies while the RDF Test Cases consider erroneous input ontologies and entailment benchmarks.

---

[4] http://www.w3.org/TR/rdf-testcases/

EON 2003 Interoperability Experiments. The Second International Workshop on Evaluation of Ontology-based Tools (EON 2003) had as main topic the evaluation of the interoperability of ontology-based tools [1]. The main reasons for benchmarking the interoperability of ontology tools two years later are:

- Interoperability is still a great problem in the Semantic Web not solved yet.
- Each experiment presented in the workshop involved only a few tools.
- Some experiments evaluated export functionalities, while others evaluated import functionalities or interoperability.
- No systematic evaluation of the tools was performed since ontology tool developers were just asked to model and interchange a domain ontology. Each experiment used different test strategies, different interchange languages, and different principles for modelling ontologies. Therefore, only specific comments and recommendations were made but not general ones.

3   Benchmarking Methodology for Ontology Tools

The benchmarking methodology for ontology tools is composed of a benchmarking iteration that is repeated forever. Each iteration is composed of three phases (*Plan*, *Experiment* and *Improve*) and ends with a *Recalibration* task:

- **Plan phase.** Its main goal is to produce a document with a detailed proposal for benchmarking. It will be used as a reference document during benchmarking and should include all the relevant information about it: its goal, benefits and costs; the tool (and its functionalities) to be evaluated; the metrics to be used when evaluating these functionalities; and the people involved in the benchmarking. The last tasks of this phase are related to the search for other participant organizations and to the agreement on the benchmarking proposal (both with the organization management and with the other organizations) and on the benchmarking planning.
- **Experiment phase.** In this phase, the organizations must define and execute the evaluation experiments for each of the tools that participate in the benchmarking. The evaluation results must be compiled and analysed, determining the practices that lead to these results and identifying which of them can be considered as best practices.
- **Improve phase.** The first task of this phase is the writing of the benchmarking report, which must include: a summary of the process followed, the results and conclusions of the experimentation, recommendations for improving the tools, and the best practices found during the experimentation. The benchmarking results must be communicated to the participant organizations; afterwards, in several improvement cycles, the tool developers should improve their tools and monitor this improvement.

While the three phases mentioned above are devoted to the improvement of the tools, the goal of the Recalibration task is to improve the benchmarking process itself using the lessons learnt while performing it.

Sections 4 and 5 present how we use this methodology for benchmarking the interoperability of ontology development tools.

4 Plan Phase

Goals Identification. The authors of this paper took the role of benchmarking initiators and prepared the benchmarking, carrying out the first tasks of the benchmarking process.

The goals for benchmarking the interoperability of ontology development tools are related to the benefits pursued through it, and these are:

- To evaluate and improve the interoperability of ontology development tools.
- To obtain recommendations on the interoperability of these tools for users.
- To obtain a deep understanding of the practices used to develop the importers and exporters of these tools.
- To extract from these practices those that can be considered best practices when developing importers and exporters.
- To create consensual processes for evaluating the interoperability of ontology development tools.

Tool and Metrics Identification. The authors of this paper decided to participate in the benchmarking with WebODE [8], since this is the ontology engineering platform being developed by this research group.

Of the different evaluation criteria that can be considered when evaluating ontology development tools, i.e., performance, scalability, interoperability, robustness, etc.; we contemplated only interoperability. An approach for benchmarking the performance and scalability of ontology development tools can be found in [9]. Of the different ways of dealing with interoperability, we have centered our focus on the interoperability of ontology development tools using an interchange language. In our first approach, the language used was RDF(S), in its RDF/XML syntax.

However, we cannot assess interoperability using an interchange language without assessing first the import and export of ontologies to that language. Therefore, the functionalities relevant to the benchmarking are the RDF(S) importers and exporters of the ontology development tools, while the evaluation criteria that will be used for evaluating these tools are:

- The components of the knowledge model of an ontology development tool that can be interchanged with another tool using RDF(S) as interchange language.
- The information added or lost when interchanging these components.

Participant Identification. As WebODE is being developed by the Ontology Engineering Group, it seemed quite straightforward to identify and contact the members of the organization involved with WebODE's RDF(S) importers and exporters and then to select, from this very group, the members of the benchmarking team.

Proposal Writing. The benchmarking proposal, which is now being used as a reference along the benchmarking, did not take the form of a paper document, but of a web page[5], which is publicly available and includes all the relevant information about the benchmarking: motivation, goals, benefits and costs, tools and people involved, planning, related events, and a complete description of the experimentation and the benchmark suites.

Management Involvement. When analysing the benchmarking proposal, the managers of the Ontology Engineering Group agreed on the continuity of the benchmarking and on the allocation of future resources.

Partner Selection. To find other best-in-class organizations willing to participate in the benchmarking, the following actions were taken:

- To research different ontology development tools, both freely available and commercial ones, that could export and import to and from RDF(S) and to contact the organizations that develop them.
- To announce the interoperability benchmarking and to call for participation through the main mailing lists of the Semantic Web area and on those lists specific to ontology development tools.

When writing this paper, five tools are participating in the benchmarking, of these four are ontology development tools: KAON[6], OntoStudio[7], Protégé[8] using its RDF backend, and WebODE[9]; and one is a RDF engine: Corese[10]. In most cases, benchmarking is performed by the developers of the tools.

Planning and Resource Allocation. A plan for the full duration of the benchmarking was not defined since it was decided to plan the benchmarking phase by phase. Then, each of the organizations assigned enough people to perform the benchmarking.

5   Experiment Phase

Experiment Definition. Evaluating the interoperability of ontology development tools using RDF(S) for ontology interchange requires that the importers and exporters from/to RDF(S) of these tools work accurately in order to interchange ontologies correctly. Therefore, the planning for the experimentation included three consecutive stages, shown in Figure 2:

- **Agreement stage.** The quality of the benchmark suites to be used is essential for the results of the benchmarking. Therefore, the first step in the experimentation is to agree on the definition of these benchmark suites, which will be common for all the tools. Section 6 deals with the definition and use of these benchmark suites.

---

[5] http://knowledgeweb.semanticweb.org/benchmarking_interoperability/
[6] http://kaon.semanticweb.org/
[7] http://www.ontoprise.de/content/e3/e43/index_eng.html
[8] http://protege.stanford.edu/
[9] http://webode.dia.fi.upm.es/
[10] http://www-sop.inria.fr/acacia/soft/corese/

- **Evaluation stage 1.** The RDF(S) importers and exporters of the ontology development tools are evaluated with the agreed versions of the benchmark suites.
- **Evaluation stage 2.** Once the RDF(S) importers and exporters have been evaluated, a second stage will cover the evaluation of the ontology interchange between ontology development tools.

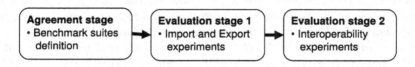

Fig. 2. Experimentation Phases

Experiment Execution. When writing this paper, the benchmarking participants are in the *Evaluation stage 2*, performing the interoperability experiments on the tools after having reached an agreement on the benchmark suites and having performed the import and export experiments. By the beginning of June 2006, the experimentation will be finished, and the results obtained will be available in the benchmarking web page.

Experiment Result Analysis. Once the results of the experimentation on each tool are available, the participants will analyse them as well as the practices that lead to these results. They will also attempt to identify among the practices found whether some of them can be considered best practices.

6   Definition of the Benchmark Suites

This section describes the three benchmark suites used in the benchmarking: the RDF(S) Import Benchmark Suite and the RDF(S) Export Benchmark Suite used in the *Evaluation stage 1*, and the RDF(S) Interoperability Benchmark Suite to be used in the *Evaluation stage 2*.

6.1   RDF(S) Import Benchmark Suite

Our goal when defining the RDF(S) Import Benchmark Suite was to perform an exhaustive evaluation of the RDF(S) import capabilities of the ontology development tools, testing the import of RDF(S) ontologies.

The benchmark suite is composed of benchmarks that import an ontology that models a simple combination of the components of the RDF(S) knowledge model (classes, properties, instances, etc.) [10]. Assessing the import of real, large or complex ontologies can be useless if we do not know if the importer can deal correctly with simple ones. Besides, it is easier to find problems in simple cases than in complex ones. These benchmarks can depend on the RDF(S) knowledge model or on the RDF(S) syntax chosen:

- **Benchmarks that depend on the knowledge model.** These benchmarks check the import of ontologies with different combinations of the RDF(S) knowledge model components. Since the checking of the different syntaxes of the selected RDF serialisation is performed in another group of benchmarks, the syntax selected is one that is easily understood by humans. These benchmarks evaluate the import of single components, all the possible combinations of two components with a property, combinations of more than two components usually appearing together in RDF(S) graphs such as the properties that have both domain and range (*rdf:Property* with *rdfs:domain* and *rdfs:range*); the statements that have subject, predicate and object (*rdf:Statement* with *rdf:subject*, *rdf:predicate* and *rdf:object*); and the definitions of lists (*rdf:List* with *rdf:first*, *rdf:rest* and *rdf:nil*).
- **Benchmarks that depend on the syntax.** These benchmarks check the import of ontologies with the different variants of the RDF/XML syntax, as stated in the RDF/XML Syntax Specification [11] since this is the most commonly used by ontology editors for importing and exporting ontologies.
  - Different syntax of URI references: absolute URI references, URI references relative to a base URI, URI references transformed from *rdf:ID* attribute values, and URI references relative to an *ENTITY* declaration.
  - Language identification attributes (*xml:lang*) in tags.
  - Abbreviations of empty nodes, multiple properties, typed nodes, string literals, blank nodes, containers, collections, and statements.

  In the case of evaluating the import of RDF(S) using other syntax (N3, N-Triples, etc.), only this group of benchmarks should be redefined.

As RDF(S) does not impose any restriction on the combinations of its components, the number of resulting benchmarks is huge (more than 4000) and the benchmark suite has to be pruned, as seen in [12], according to its intended use and to the kind of tools that it is supposed to evaluate: ontology development tools. Therefore, we only considered the RDF(S) components most frequently used for modelling ontologies in these tools: *rdfs:Class*, *rdf:Property*, *rdfs:Literal*, *rdf:type*, *rdfs:domain*, *rdfs:range*, *rdfs:subClassOf*, and *rdfs:subPropertyOf*. The rest of the RDF(S) components have not been dealt with.

Table 1 shows the categories of the benchmark suite, which contains 72 benchmarks, with the number of benchmarks and the components used in each category. A detailed description of such benchmarks can be found in a web page[11].

The definition of each benchmark in the benchmark suite, as Table 2 shows, includes the following fields:

- An identifier for tracking the different benchmarks.
- A description of the benchmark in natural language.
- A graphical representation of the ontology to be imported in the benchmark.
- A file containing the ontology to be imported in the RDF/XML syntax.

---

[11] http://knowledgeweb.semanticweb.org/benchmarking_interoperability/ rdfs_import_benchmark_suite.html

Table 1. Categories of the import benchmarks

Category	No.	Components used
Class	2	*rdfs:Class*
Metaclass	5	*rdfs:Class, rdf:type*
Subclass	5	*rdfs:Class, rdfs:subClassOf*
Class and property	6	*rdfs:Class, rdf:Property, rdfs:Literal*
Property	2	*rdf:Property*
Subproperty	5	*rdf:Property, rdfs:subPropertyOf*
Property with domain and range	21	*rdfs:Class, rdf:Property, rdfs:Literal, rdfs:domain, rdfs:range*
Instance	3	*rdfs:Class, rdf:type*
Instance and property	9	*rdfs:Class, rdf:type, rdf:Property, rdfs:Literal*
Syntax and abbreviation	14	*rdfs:Class, rdf:type, rdf:Property, rdfs:Literal*

Table 2. An example of a benchmark definition

Identifier	I14
Description	Import one class that has the same property with several other classes
Graphical representation	

RDF/XML file	`<rdf:RDF xmlns="http://www.w3.org/2000/01/rdf-schema#"`
	`xmlns:g1="http://www.test.org/graph14#"`
	`xmlns:rdf="http://www.w3.org/1999/02/22-rdf-syntax-ns#"`
	`xmlns:rdfs="http://www.w3.org/2000/01/rdf-schema#">`
	`<Class rdf:about="http://www.test.org/graph14#class1">`
	`  <g1:prop1 rdf:resource="http://www.test.org/graph14#class2"/>`
	`  <g1:prop1 rdf:resource="http://www.test.org/graph14#class3"/>`
	`</Class>`
	`<Class rdf:about="http://www.test.org/graph14#class2"/>`
	`<Class rdf:about="http://www.test.org/graph14#class3"/>`
	`</rdf:RDF>`

The steps for executing each import benchmark are the following:

1. To model into the ontology development tool the expected ontology that results from importing the RDF(S) ontology .
2. To import the file with the RDF(S) ontology into the tool.
3. To compare the imported ontology with the expected ontology and to check whether they are equivalent.

Although these steps can be performed manually, performing them (or part of them) automatically is highly advised when dealing with many benchmarks, especially for comparing the expected and imported ontologies.

The evaluation criteria used for the benchmark suite are:

− **Modelling** (YES/NO). The tool can model the ontology components described in the benchmark.

Table 3. An example of the result of a benchmark execution

Tool	Id	Added	Lost	Model	Execute	Comments
Protégé	I50	class	-	NO	OK	Undefined resources with instances are imported as classes.
WebODE	I50	-	instance	NO	OK	Instances of undefined resources are not imported.

– **Execution** (OK/FAIL). The execution of the benchmark is normally carried out without any problem, and the tool always produces the expected result. When a failed execution occurred, the benchmarking participants were asked to provide information for obtaining the practices used when developing the RDF(S) importers. The information required was the following:
  • The reasons for failing the benchmark execution.
  • If the tool was corrected to pass a benchmark, the changes performed.
– **Information added or lost.** The information added or lost in the ontology interchange when executing the benchmark.

Table 3 shows an example with the results of executing benchmark I50 (Import one instance of a resource, without the resource definition) in two tools. While both tools cannot model an instance of an undefined resource, they produce the expected result, one inserting information and the other losing it.

6.2   RDF(S) Export Benchmark Suite

When defining the RDF(S) Export Benchmark Suite, our goal was to perform an evaluation of the RDF(S) export capabilities of ontology development tools by testing the export of ontologies modelled in these tools.

The benchmark suite for evaluating RDF(S) exporters is composed of benchmarks that export a single ontology with a simple combination of the components of the knowledge models of the tools.

The composition of the RDF(S) Export Benchmark Suite is similar to the composition of the import one. Instead of taking as input the knowledge model of RDF(S), we took as input a common core of the knowledge modelling components that is very frequently used in ontology development tools: classes and class hierarchies, object and datatype properties, instances, and literals.

Table 4 shows the categories of the benchmark suite, that contains 52 benchmarks, with the number of benchmarks and the components used in each category. A detailed description of such benchmarks can be found in a web page[12].

The definition of each benchmark in the benchmark suite, as Table 5 shows, includes the following fields:

– An identifier for tracking the different benchmarks.
– A description of the benchmark in natural language.

---

[12] http://knowledgeweb.semanticweb.org/benchmarking_interoperability/
rdfs_export_benchmark_suite.html

- A graphical representation of the ontology to be exported by the tool.
- The instantiation of the ontology described in the benchmark for each of the participating tools, using the vocabulary and components of these tools.

The steps for executing each export benchmark are the following:

1. To define in RDF(S) the expected ontology resulting from exporting the ontology.
2. To model into the tool the ontology described in the benchmark.
3. To export the ontology modelled using the tool to RDF(S).
4. To compare the exported RDF(S) ontology with the expected RDF(S) ontology to check whether they are equivalent.

As in the case of the import benchmark suite, some automatic mean of performing these steps is highly advisable.

The evaluation criteria used for the export benchmark suite are the same as those from the import benchmark suite, that is, *Modelling*, *Execution* and *Information added or lost*. The only difference with the import criteria is that,

Table 4. Categories of the export benchmarks

Category	No.	Components used
Class	2	*class*
Metaclass	5	*class, instanceOf*
Subclass	5	*class, subClassOf*
Class and object property	4	*class, object property*
Class and datatype property	2	*class, datatype property, literal*
Object property	13	*object property*
Datatype property	9	*datatype property*
Instance	3	*class, instanceOf*
Instance and object property	7	*class, instanceOf, object property*
Instance and datatype property	2	*class, instanceOf, datatype property, literal*

Table 5. An example of a benchmark definition

Identifier	E09
Description	Export one class that is subclass of several classes
Graphical representation	
WebODE's instantiation	Export one concept that is subclass of several concepts
Protégé's instantiation	Export one class that is subclass of several classes
...	...

as there may be a benchmark that defines an ontology that cannot be modelled in a certain tool, that benchmark cannot be executed in the tool, being the *Execution* result *N.E.* (Non Executed). In the import benchmark suite, even if a tool cannot model some components of the ontology, it should be able to import correctly the rest of the components.

6.3   RDF(S) Interoperability Benchmark Suite

Our goal when defining the RDF(S) Interoperability Benchmark Suite was to evaluate the interoperability of ontology development tools by testing the interchange of ontologies from one origin tool to a destination one, and vice versa.

We considered the interchange of a common core of the knowledge modelling components most frequently used for modelling ontologies. These are: classes and class hierarchies, object and datatype properties, instances, and literals. As these components are the same as those in the RDF(S) Export Benchmark Suite, the Interoperability Benchmark Suite is identical to the RDF(S) Export Benchmark Suite and has the same benchmark definitions as presented in Section 6.2.

The interoperability will be checked between each pair of tools. As the RDF(S) exported files of all the tools will be available from the export experiments of the *Experiment stage 1*, participants will not have to export these ontologies again, they will just have to import the exported files into their tools.

The steps for executing each interoperability benchmark are the following:

1. To define in the destination tool the expected ontology resulting from interchanging the ontology.
2. To import the RDF(S) file exported by the origin tool into the destination tool.
3. To compare the interchanged ontology with the expected ontology and to check whether they are equivalent.

The evaluation criteria used for the interoperability benchmark suite are the same as those from the export benchmark suite, that is, *Modelling*, *Execution* and *Information added or lost*.

7   Evaluation of the Benchmark Suites

We have evaluated these benchmark suites according to the main desirable properties of a benchmark suite that many different authors have stated [7, 13, 14, 15]: accessibility, affordability, simplicity, representativity, portability, scalability, robustness, and consensus.

Accessibility. The complete definition of the benchmark suites as well as all the information relevant to the benchmarking are accessible to anyone in a public web page. This page will include, when available, the results obtained when executing the benchmark suites. Thus anyone can execute them and compare their results with the ones available.

Affordability. The costs of using the benchmark suites and analysing their results are mainly human resources. In order to reduce these costs and facilitate the work we provided a clear definition of the benchmark suites and templates to fill in the results.

Simplicity. The benchmark suites are simple and interpretable because we have provided different ways of defining each benchmark, i.e. in natural language, graphically, etc. These benchmark suites and their results are also clearly documented, having a common structure and use.

Representativity. Although the different benchmarks that compose the benchmark suites are not exhaustive or represent real-world ontologies, they represent the different structures of ontologies commonly used when developing these ontologies; and a first evaluation of these simple ontologies is needed before evaluating more complex ones.

Portability. The benchmark suites have been defined at a high level of abstraction, so they are not biased towards a certain tool or tools. Therefore, they can be executed on a wide variety of environments and not just on ontology development tools.

Scalability. The benchmark suites scale to work with tools at different levels of maturity. Also, as their benchmarks are grouped according to the different ontology components that they manage, it is quite easy to increase or decrease the number of benchmarks by considering new components or by taking into account only certain components of interest, respectively.

Robustness. As the results of the benchmark suites depend on the algorithms implemented to perform the import and export of ontologies, they are not influenced by factors irrelevant to the study. Furthermore, running the benchmark suites with the same version of the tools will always produce the same results.

Consensus. The benchmark suites were developed by experts in the domain of ontology translation and interoperability and were assessed and agreed on by the benchmarking partners and by the members of Knowledge Web.

8   Conclusions and Future Work

The interoperability benchmarking described in this paper is now taking place. Although the benchmarking has not reached its *Improve* phase yet, the developers have already improved their tools by correcting the bugs detected while executing the experiments.

Although the benchmarking has not finished yet, we have already learnt some lessons from it. The main one is that benchmarking is a time consuming process both to organize and to participate on it and it is also enduring. Besides, the involvement of tool developers is a primary need, as they are the most appropriate for and capable of analysing and improving the tools.

In addition to the benchmarking participants, other intended users of the work here presented and of its future results are, on the one hand, end users who want to know the current interoperability of ontology development tools before selecting one of these tools and, on the other hand, ontology tool developers who wish to improve the interoperability of their ontology development tools or of any other ontology technology capable of interchanging ontologies by means of their RDF(S) importers and exporters.

The RDF(S) Import Benchmark Suite can be used to evaluate the RDF(S) import capabilities of any tool, while the RDF(S) Export and Interoperability Benchmark Suites can be used to evaluate any kind of interoperability between ontology development tools since these are not dependant on the interchange language.

Once we will have the benchmarking results, we will be able to provide different kind of information about the interoperability of ontology development tools for different groups of people. For example, from an ontology modelled in a certain tool, we can obtain information about the possibility of interchanging that ontology between that tool and any other tool.

The benchmarking web page will also provide mechanisms for updating the interoperability results when the tools are improved, or for inserting the results of a new tool.

Based on the structure and the definition of the benchmark suites, other benchmark suites can be defined to consider the evaluation of interoperability using other languages for interchanging ontologies. We have also started to organise a benchmarking activity[13], similar to this, for benchmarking the interoperability of ontology development tools using OWL[14] as the interchange language.

Acknowledgments

This work is partially supported by a FPI grant from the Spanish Ministry of Education (BES-2005-8024), by the IST project Knowledge Web (IST-2004-507482) and by the CICYT project Infraestructura tecnológica de servicios semánticos para la web semántica (TIN2004-02660). Thanks to all the people participating in the benchmarking: Olivier Corby, York Sure, Moritz Weiten, and Markus Zondler. Thanks to Rosario Plaza for reviewing the grammar of this paper.

References

1. Sure, Y., Corcho, O., eds.: Proceedings of the 2nd International Workshop on Evaluation of Ontology-based Tools (EON2003). Volume 87 of CEUR-WS., Florida, USA (2003)
2. Euzenat, J., Stuckenschmidt, H.: The 'Family of Languages' approach to semantic interoperability. In Omelayenko, B., Klein, M., eds.: Knowledge transformation for the semantic web. IOS press, Amsterdam (NL) (2003) 49–63
3. Spendolini, M.: The Benchmarking Book. AMACOM, New York, NY (1992)

---

[13] http://knowledgeweb.semanticweb.org/benchmarking_interoperability/owl/
[14] http://www.w3.org/TR/owl-features/

 4. Wohlin, C., Aurum, A., Petersson, H., Shull, F., Ciolkowski, M.: Software inspection benchmarking - a qualitative and quantitative comparative opportunity. In: Proceedings of 8th International Software Metrics Symposium. (2002) 118–130
 5. Kitchenham, B.: DESMET: A method for evaluating software engineering methods and tools. Technical Report TR96-09, Department of Computer Science, University of Keele, Staffordshire, UK (1996)
 6. Sill, D.: comp.benchmarks frequently asked questions version 1.0 (1996)
 7. Sim, S., Easterbrook, S., Holt, R.: Using benchmarking to advance research: A challenge to software engineering. In: Proceedings of the 25th International Conference on Software Engineering (ICSE'03), Portland, OR (2003) 74–83
 8. Arpírez, J., Corcho, O., Fernández-López, M., Gómez-Pérez, A.: WebODE in a nutshell. AI Magazine 24 (2003) 37–47
 9. García-Castro, R., Gómez-Pérez, A.: Guidelines for benchmarking the performance of ontology management APIs. In: Proceedings of the 4th International Semantic Web Conference (ISWC2005). Number 3729 in LNCS, Galway, Ireland, Springer-Verlag (2005) 277–292
10. Brickley, D., Guha, R.V. (editors): RDF Vocabulary Description Language 1.0: RDF Schema. W3C Recommendation 10 February 2004 (2004)
11. Beckett, D. (editor): RDF/XML Syntax Specification (Revised). W3C Recommendation 10 February 2004 (2004)
12. García-Castro, R., Gómez-Pérez, A.: A method for performing an exhaustive evaluation of RDF(S) importers. In: Proceedings of the Workshop on Scalable Semantic Web Knowledge Based Systems (SSWS2005). Number 3807 in LNCS, New York, USA, Springer-Verlag (2005) 199–206
13. Bull, J.M., Smith, L.A., Westhead, M.D., Henty, D.S., Davey, R.A.: A methodology for benchmarking java grande applications. In: Proceedings of the ACM 1999 conference on Java Grande. (1999) 81–88
14. Shirazi, B., Welch, L., Ravindran, B., Cavanaugh, C., Yanamula, B., Brucks, R., Huh, E.: Dynbench: A dynamic benchmark suite for distributed real-time systems. In: Proc. of the 11 IPPS/SPDP'99 Workshops, Springer-Verlag (1999) 1335–1349
15. Stefani, F., Macii, D., Moschitta, A., Petri, D.: FFT benchmarking for digital signal processing technologies. In: 17th IMEKO World Congress, Dubrovnik (2003)

Repairing Unsatisfiable Concepts in OWL Ontologies

Aditya Kalyanpur[1], Bijan Parsia[1], Evren Sirin[1], and Bernardo Cuenca-Grau[2,*]

[1] MINDLAB, University of Maryland, College Park, USA[**]
aditya@cs.umd.edu, bparsia@isr.umd.edu, evren@cs.umd.edu
[2] School of Computer Science, University of Manchester, UK
bcg@cs.man.ac.uk

Abstract. In this paper, we investigate the problem of repairing unsat-isfiable concepts in an OWL ontology in detail, keeping in mind the user perspective as much as possible. We focus on various aspects of the repair process – improving the explanation support to help the user understand the cause of error better, exploring various strategies to rank erroneous axioms (with motivating use cases for each strategy), automatically gen-erating repair plans that can be customized easily, and suggesting appro-priate axiom edits where possible to the user. Based on the techniques described, we present a preliminary version of an interactive ontology repair tool and demonstrate its applicability in practice.

1 Introduction

Now that OWL is a W3C Recommendation, one can expect that a much wider community of users and developers will be exposed to the expressive description logic $\mathcal{SHOIN}(\mathcal{D})$ which is the basis of OWL-DL. As semantic descriptions in OWL ontologies become more complicated, ontology debugging becomes an ex-tremely hard task for users, especially for those with little or no experience in description-logic-based knowledge representation. In such cases, ontology debug-ging tools are needed to explain and pinpoint defects in ontological definitions.

A common defect found in OWL Ontologies is unsatisfiable concepts, i.e., concepts which cannot have any individuals. Unsatisfiable concepts are usually a fundamental modeling error, and are also quite easy for a reasoner to detect and for a tool to display. However, determining *why* a concept in an ontology is unsatisfiable can be a considerable challenge even for experts in the formalism and in the domain, even for modestly sized ontologies. The problem worsens significantly as the number and complexity of axioms of the ontology grows.

---

[*] This author is is supported by the EU Project TONES (Thinking ONtologiES) ref: IST-007603.

[**] This work was completed with funding from Fujitsu Laboratories of America Col-lege Park, Lockheed Martin Advanced Technology Laboratory, NTT Corp., Kevric Corp., SAIC, National Science Foundation, National Geospatial-Intelligence Agency, DARPA, US Army Research Laboratory, NIST, and other DoD sources.

Y. Sure and J. Domingue (Eds.): ESWC 2006, LNCS 4011, pp. 170–184, 2006.

In our previous work, we have developed a suite of techniques for debugging unsatisfiable concepts in OWL Ontologies [6]. Our work focused on two key aspects: given a large number of unsatisfiable concepts in an ontology, identifying the *root* and *derived* unsatisfiable concepts from among them; and given a particular unsatisfiable concept in an ontology, extracting and presenting to the user the minimal set of axioms from the ontology responsible for making it unsatisfiable. We have provided an optimized implementation in the reasoner Pellet [14], a UI in the ontology editor Swoop [5], and proposed various enhancements in the display to improve the explanation of the cause of error. We have shown through a user study that these techniques are effective for debugging inconsistency errors in OWL ontologies.

However, while the emphasis was on pinpointing and explaining the errors in OWL ontologies, there was a lack of support for (semi-)automatically repairing or fixing them. Though in most cases, repairing errors is left to the ontology modeler's (/author's) discretion, and understanding the cause of the error certainly helps make resolving it much easier, bug resolution can still be a non-trivial task, requiring an exploration of remedies with a cost/benefit analysis, and tool support here can be quite useful.

In this paper, we present the following main contributions:

- We enhance the information that drives the repair process by modifying our algorithm to capture the part(s) of axiom(s) responsible for an error (section 3.2)
- We propose a technique to generate repair solutions automatically based on strategies used to rank erroneous axioms and a modified Reiter's Hitting Set algorithm (sections 3.3, 3.4). In addition, we consider strategies for rewriting axioms (section 3.5).
- We describe a preliminary implementation of an interactive ontology repair tool and discuss results of a conducted pilot study (section 3.6).

Note that while we focus on repairing unsatisfiable concepts in a consistent OWL Ontology, the underlying problem involves dealing with and rectifying a set of erroneous axioms, and thus the same principles for generating repair solutions are applicable when debugging an inconsistent OWL ontology.

2   Related Work

To our knowledge, the most relevant work is described in [13], where the authors identify minimal conflicting axiom sets responsible for unsatisfiable concepts in an $\mathcal{ALC}$ knowledge base, and then in [11], [12] use Reiter's Hitting Set algorithm to compute repair solutions from the conflict sets.

However, we differ from the work above in two key respects: our axiom-based solution works for a much more expressive description logic $\mathcal{SHOIN}$, and hence OWL-DL, with a finer granularity (identifying erroneous parts of axioms); and we consider ranking axioms for our repair solution and accordingly modify the Reiter's HS algorithm to generate repair plans.

3   Ontology Repair

3.1   Preliminaries

Before proceeding further, we revisit the notion of a MUPS (*Minimal Unsatisfiability Preserving Sub-TBoxes*), which was formally introduced in [13]. Roughly, a MUPS for an atomic concept A is a minimal fragment of the KB in which A is unsatisfiable. Obviously, a concept may have several different MUPS within an ontology. Finding *all* the MUPS of an unsatisfiable concept is a critical task from a debugging point of view, since one needs to remove at least one axiom from each set in its MUPS in order to make the concept satisfiable.

3.2   Continuing Where We Left Off

Improving Axiom-Based Explanation. A key component of our earlier debugging solution was the Axiom Pinpointing service which was used to extract the MUPS of a concept that is unsatisfiable w.r.t. a $\mathcal{SHOIN}$ knowledge base [4]. We have since extended this service to identify *specific parts* of axioms that are responsible for the inconsistency, and we refer to the resultant axiom set as the *precise* MUPS.

We briefly describe the idea behind this extension here (for details of our implementation, see [4]). Since we aim at identifying relevant parts of axioms, we define a function that splits the axioms in a KB K into "smaller" axioms to obtain an equivalent KB K_s that contains as many axioms as possible. This function rewrites the axioms in K in a convenient normal form and split across conjunctions in the normalized version, e.g., rewriting $A \sqsubseteq C \sqcap D$ as $A \sqsubseteq C, A \sqsubseteq D$. In some cases, we are forced to introduce new concept names, only for the purpose of splitting axioms into smaller sizes (which prevents any arbitrary introduction of new concepts); for example, since the axiom $A \sqsubseteq \exists R.(C \sqcap D)$ is not equivalent to $A \sqsubseteq \exists R.C$, $A \sqsubseteq \exists R.D$, we introduce a new concept name, say E, and transform the original axiom into the following set of "smaller" axioms: $A \sqsubseteq \exists R.E$, $E \sqsubseteq C, E \sqsubseteq D, C \sqcap D \sqsubseteq E$. Finally, the problem of finding the *precise* MUPS of an unsatisfiable concept in K reduces to the problem of finding its MUPS in the split version of the KB K_s. Note that to prevent an exponential blowup, we do not split the entire KB beforehand, instead perform a *lazy splitting* of certain specific axioms on the fly (as described in [4]).

```
AI_Dept ≡ owl:Nothing:
1) (AI_Dept ⊑ ((∃hasResearchArea . {AI}) ⊓ (∀offersCourse . AI_Course) ⊓ CS_Department))
2)   ⌞(CS_Department ⊑ (Department ⊓ (∃affiliatedWith . CS_Library)))
3)     ⌞Transitive(affiliatedWith)
4)   ⌞(CS_Library ⊑ (∃affiliatedWith . EE_Library))
5) (EE_Department ⊑ ¬ CS_Department)
6) (EE_Department ≡ (∃affiliatedWith . EE_Library))
```

Fig. 1. Displaying the minimal set of axioms from the ontology (with key entities highlighted and irrelevant parts struck out) responsible for making the concept **AI_Dept** in the **University** ontology unsatisfiable

Given the precise MUPS, any tool used to display it for the purpose of debugging the error can choose a suitable presentation format to highlight the relevant parts. For our debugging tool UI, we chose to strike out irrelevant parts of axioms that do not contribute to the contradiction (see Figure 1). So far, our tests have shown that this form of highlighting makes a significant difference in the presentation and greatly aids repair, since it makes it explicit to the user, the part of the axiom(s) that needs to be altered in order to resolve the bug.

3.3   Strategies for Ranking Axioms

We now discuss a key piece of the repair process: selecting which erroneous axiom(s) to remove from the MUPS in order to fix the unsatisfiable concepts.

For this purpose, an interesting factor to consider is whether the axioms in the MUPS can be *ranked* in order of importance. Repair is then reduced to an optimization problem whose primary goal is to get rid all of the inconsistency errors in the ontology, while ensuring that the highest rank axioms are preserved and the lowest rank axioms removed from the ontology.

A simple criterion to rank axioms is to count the number of times it appears in the MUPS of the various unsatisfiable concepts in an ontology. This idea is similar to the notion of *arity* of the axiom as discussed in [13]. If an axiom appears in n different MUPS (in each set of the MUPS), removing the axiom from the ontology ensures that n concepts turn satisfiable. Thus, higher the frequency, lower the rank assigned to the axiom.

Besides the axiom frequency in the MUPS, we consider the following strategies to rank ontology axioms:

- Impact on ontology when the axiom is removed or altered (need to identify *minimal impact* causing changes)
- Test cases specified manually by the user to rank axioms
- Provenance information about the axiom (author, source reliability, timestamp etc.)
- Relevance to the ontology in terms of its usage

Impact Analysis. The basic notion of revising a knowledge base while preserving as much information as possible has been discussed extensively in belief revision literature [1]. We now apply the same principle to repairing unsatisfiable concepts in an OWL ontology, i.e., we determine the impact of the changes made to the ontology in order to get rid of unsatisfiable concepts, and identify minimal-impact causing changes. Since repairing an unsatisfiable concept involves removing axioms in its MUPS, we consider the impact of axiom removal on the OWL ontology.

A fundamental property of axiom removal based on the monotonicity of OWL-DL is the following: *removing an axiom from the ontology cannot add a new entailment.* Hence, we only need to consider entailments (subsumption, instantiation etc.) that are lost upon axiom removal, and need not consider whether other concepts in the ontology turn unsatisfiable.

For now, we shall only consider subsumption/disjointness (between atomic concepts) and instantiation (of atomic concepts) as the only interesting entailments to check for when an axiom is removed. In the next subsection, we discuss how the user can provide a set of test cases as additional interesting entailments to check for.

As mentioned earlier, our Axiom Pinpointing service computes the minimal set of axioms (justification) responsible for any arbitrary entailment of an OWL-DL ontology . Thus, we can use this service to compute the justification sets for the significant subsumption and instantiation relationships in the ontology. When removing an axiom, we can check if it falls into a particular justification set, and accordingly determine which subsumption and/or instantiation relation(s) would break directly. Axioms to be removed can then be ranked based on the number of entailments they break (higher the rank, lesser the entailments broken).

An important distinction is the entailments resulting from the unsatisfiable concepts in the ontology. Note that when a concept is unsatisfiable, it is equivalent to the bottom concept (or in OWL lingo, `owl:Nothing`), and hence is trivially equivalent to all other unsatisfiable concepts, and is a subclass of all satisfiable concepts in the ontology. In this case, we need to differentiate between the stated or explicit entailments related to unsatisfiable concepts and the trivial ones. Thus, we apply the following strategy: if a given entailment related to an unsatisfiable concept holds in a fragment of the ontology in which the concept is satisfiable, we consider the entailment to be explicit.

There are two techniques to obtain such explicit entailments: the first is a brute-force approach that involves considering all possible (minimal) solutions to fix the unsatisfiable concept in the ontology, and verifying if the entailment still holds in the modified ontology. In order to obtain minimal repair solutions, we can use Reiter's algorithm as seen in the next section. On the other hand, the second approach is much faster (though incomplete) and is based on using the *structural analysis* techniques seen in [6] to detect the explicit relationships involving unsatisfiable concepts without performing large scale ontology changes. For example, we can use the *Ontology Approximation* heuristic to get rid of the contradictions in the ontology while revealing the hidden subsumption entailments.

Having obtained the explicit entailments related to unsatisfiable concepts, we can present them to the user to learn which, if any, of the relationships are (un)desired. This information would then be used in the plan generation phase.

We consider a few examples that highlight the significance of this strategy.

Example 1. In the Tambis OWL ontology[1], the three critical unsatisfiable concepts are: `metal, non-metal, metalloid`. The unsatisfiability arises because each concept is defined to be equivalent to the same complex concept: `chemical ⊓ (=1)atomic-number ⊓ ∃atomic-number.integer`, and also defined to be *disjoint* from each other.

---

[1] Note: All ontologies mentioned in this paper are available online at
http://www.mindswap.org/ontologies/debugging/

In this case, though the disjoint axioms appear in each of the three unsatisfiable concepts MUPS, removing them is not the correct solution, since eliminating the disjointness makes all three concepts metal, non-metal, metalloid equivalent which is probably undesired.

In fact, a better solution is to weaken the equivalence to a subclass relationship in each concept definition, thereby getting rid of the subclasses: chemical ⊓ (=1)atomic-number ⊓ ∃atomic-number.integer ⊑ metal / non-metal / metalloid; and we find that removing these relationships has no impact on other entailments in the ontology.

Example 2. Consider the following *MUPS* of an unsatisfiable concept Ocean-CrustLayer w.r.t. the Sweet-JPL ontology $\mathcal{O}$: { (1) OceanCrustLayer ⊑ CrustLayer, (2) CrustLayer ⊑ Layer, (3) Layer ⊑ Geometric_3D_Object, (4) Geometric_3D_Object ⊑ ∃ hasDimension. {3D}, (5) OceanCrustLayer ⊑ OceanRegion, (6) OceanRegion ⊑ Region, (7) Region ⊑ Geometric_2D_Object, (8) Geometric_2D_Object ⊑ ∃ hasDimension. {2D}, (9) hasDimension is Functional }.

Note that in $\mathcal{O}$, each of the concepts CrustLayer, OceanRegion, Layer, Region, Geometric_3D_Object, Geometric_2D_Object, has numerous individual subclasses.

In this case, removing the functional property assertion on hasDimension from $\mathcal{O}$ eliminates the disjoint relation between concepts Geometric_2D_Object and Geometric_3D_Object, and between all its respective subclasses. Also, removing any of the following axioms $2, 3, 4, 6, 7, 8$ eliminates numerous subsumptions from the original ontology. Thus, using the minimal impact strategy, the only option for repair is removing either 1 or 5, which turns out to be the correct solution, based on the feedback given by the original ontology authors.

User Test Cases. In addition to the standard entailments considered in the previous subsection, the user can specify a set of test cases describing desired entailments. Axioms to be removed can be directly ranked based on the desired entailments they break.

Also, in some cases, the user can specify *undesired* entailments to aid the repair process. For example, a common modeling mistake is when an atomic concept C inadvertently becomes equivalent to the top concept, owl:Thing. Now, any atomic concept disjoint from C becomes unsatisfiable. This phenomenon occurred in the CHEM-A ontology, where the following two axioms caused concept A (anonymized) to become equivalent to owl:Thing: $\{A \equiv \forall R.C, domain(R, A)$ }. Here, specifying the undesired entailment prevented our ontology-effect strategy from considering the impact of removal of the erroneous axiom (in this case, the equivalence, which needed to be changed to a subclass) on this entailment.

Provenance Information Regarding Change. Provenance information about an axiom can act as a useful pointer for determining its importance/rank, i.e., based on factors such as:

- reliability of the source (author, document etc.)
- context/reason for which the axiom was added (specified as an annotation or otherwise)
- time the axiom was specified

OWL has support for adding human-readable annotations to entities in an ontology using `owl:AnnotationProperties` such as *rdfs:label, rdfs:comment*. However, there is no direct provision to annotate assertions or axioms in the ontology, unless one resorts to reification. In general, manually providing provenance information about axioms can be a tedious task, and thus tool support is critical. To address this issue, ontology editors such as Protege [7], KAON [8] and Swoop have the option to maintain an elaborate change log to record provenance information.

In Swoop, we automatically keep track of all changes made to an OWL ontology, storing information such as authorship, date etc of each change. Additionally, we use a *change-ontology* that represents various atomic and complex change operations to serialize the change-log to RDF/XML, which can then be shared among users.

Such information is extremely useful for ranking axioms in a collaborative ontology building context, i.e., if a group of authors are collectively building an ontology, and there exists a precedence level among the authors, i.e., ontology changes made by the supervisor are given higher priority than those made by a subordinate. In this case, for each change made, one can derive the corresponding axioms added to the ontology, and automatically determine the rank of each axiom based on the person making the change.

Syntactic Relevance. There has been research done in the area of ontology ranking [2], where for example, terms in ontologies are ranked based on their structural connectedness in the graph model of the ontology, or their popularity in other ontologies, and the total rank for the ontology is assigned in terms of the individual entity ranks. Since an ontology is a collection of axioms, we can, in theory, explore similar techniques to rank individual axioms. The main difference, of course, lies in the fact that ontologies as a whole can be seen as documents which link to (or import) other ontology documents, whereas the notion of linkage is less strong for individual axioms.

Here, we present a simple strategy that ranks an axiom based on the *usage* of elements in its signature, i.e., for each OWL entity (atomic class, property or individual) in the signature of the axiom, we determine how often the entity has been referenced in other axioms in the ontology, and sum the reference counts for all the entities in the axiom signature to obtain a measure of its syntactic (or structural) relevance.

The significance of this strategy is based on the following intuition: if the entities in the axiom are used (or are referred to) often in the remaining axioms or assertions of the ontology, then the entities are in some sense, core or central to the overall theme of the ontology, and hence changing or removing axioms related to these entities may be undesired. For example, if a certain concept is heavily instantiated, or if a certain property is heavily used in the instance data, then altering the axiom definitions of that concept or property is a change that the user needs to be aware of. Similarly, in large ontologies where certain entities are accidentally underspecified or unused, axioms related to these entities may be given less importance.

The simple strategy presented above can be altered in various ways such as by restricting usage counts to certain axiom types, and/or weighing certain kinds of axioms differently than others (e.g., weighing property attribute assertions such as InverseFunctional higher). This would be motivated by user preferences depending on the ontology modeling philosophy and purpose (e.g., see OntoClean [3]).

3.4   Generating Repair Solutions

So far, we have devised a procedure to find tagged MUPS for an unsatisfiable concept in an OWL-DL ontology and proposed various strategies to rank axioms in the MUPS. The next step is to generate a repair plan (i.e., a set of ontology changes) to resolve the errors in a given set of unsatisfiable concepts, taking into account their respective MUPS and axiom ranks.

Modifying Reiter's Algorithm. For this purpose, we use the Reiter's Hitting Set algorithm [10], which given a diagnosis problem and a collection of conflict sets for that problem, generates minimal hitting sets from the conflict sets. A hitting set for a collection of sets C is a set that touches (or intersects) each set in C. A hitting set is minimal for C, if no proper subset of it is a hitting set for C. This approach was suggested in [12], which generates hitting sets from the MUPS – the idea here is that removing all the axioms in the minimal hitting set removes one axiom from each of the MUPS and thus renders all concepts satisfiable. The same principle applies to our repair solution except that we need to modify the HS algorithm to take into account the axiom ranks.

Given a collection C of conflict sets, Reiter's algorithm introduces the notion of a hitting set tree (HST), which is the smallest edge-labeled and node-labeled tree such that a node n in HST is labeled by a tickmark if C is empty, otherwise its labeled with any set $s \in C$. For each node n, let $H(n)$ be the set of edge labels on the path in HST from the root to n; then the label for n is any set $s \in C$, that satisfies the property $s \cap H(n) \leftarrow \emptyset$, if such a set exists. If n is labeled by a set s, then for each $\sigma \in s$, n has a successor n_σ joined to n by an edge labeled by σ. For any node labeled by a tickmark, the labels of its path from the root $(H(n))$ is a hitting set for C. Also, while generating the HST, if the search along a path exceeds the current optimal solution, the search is terminated earlier, marked by a cross in the label of a node.

Now for our problem, the MUPS of the unsatisfiable concepts correspond to the conflict sets. However, while the normal HST algorithm has the optimality criteria as the minimal path length, we set it as the minimal *path rank* instead, i.e., the sum of the ranks of the axioms in the path $H(n)$ should be minimal. Also, in the standard algorithm, there is no basis for selecting an axiom over

another while building the edges of the HST, whereas we can use the ranks of
the axioms when making a selection to prune down the search space, i.e., at each
stage, we select the lowest ranked axiom while creating a new edge.

Figure 2 shows a HST for a collection $C = \{\{2,5\}, \{3,4,7\}, \{1,6\}, \{4,5,7\},$
$\{1,2,3\}\}$ with the axioms $1 - 7$ ranked as follows: $r(1) = 0.1$, $r(2) = 0.2$, $r(3) =$
0.3, $r(4) = 0.4$, $r(5) = 0.3$, $r(6) = 0.3$, $r(7) = 0.5$, where $r(x)$ is the rank of
axiom x. The ranks are computed based on the factors mentioned earlier, such
as arity, impact analysis etc. each weighed separately if needed using appropriate
weight constants. The superscript for each axiom-number denotes the rank of
the axiom, and P_r is the path rank computed as the sum of the ranks of axioms
in the path from the root to the node. For example, for the leftmost path shown:
$P_r = 0.2 + 0.3 + 0.1 + 0.3 = 0.9$.

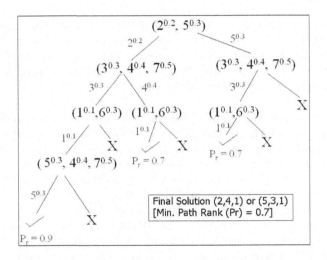

Fig. 2. Modified Reiter's Hitting Set Algorithm: Generating a repair plan based
on ranks of axioms in the MUPS of unsatisfiable concepts

As shown in the figure, by choosing the lowest rank axiom in each set while
constructing the edges of the HST, the algorithm only generates 3 hitting sets,
two of which are minimal, while avoiding numerous path checks (indicated by
the crosses). The repair solution found with the minimal path rank is either
{2,4,1} or {5,3,1}.

However, there is a drawback of using the above procedure to generate repair
plans, i.e., impact analysis is only done at a single axiom level, whereas the
cumulative impact of the axioms in the repair solution is not considered. This
can lead to non-optimal solutions. For example, in the Tambis ontology, where
the three root classes are asserted to be mutually disjoint, removing any one
of the disjoint axioms does not cause as large an impact as removing all the
disjoints together.

In order to resolve this issue, we propose another modification to the algorithm above: each time a hitting-set HS is found, we compute a new path-rank for HS based on the cumulative impact of the axioms in the hitting-set. The algorithm now finds repair plans that minimize these new path-ranks. Note that the early termination condition for paths remains the same since the path rank represents a lower bound, as cumulative impact is always greater than or equal to the sum of individual unique impacts.

Improving and Customizing Repair. The algorithm described above can be used in general to fix any arbitrary set of unsatisfiable concepts, once the MUPS of the concepts and the ranks for axioms in the MUPS is known. Thus, a brute force solution for resolving *all* the errors in an ontology involves determining the MUPS (and ranking axioms in the MUPS) for *each* of the unsatisfiable concepts. This is computationally expensive and moreover, unnecessary, given that strong dependencies between unsatisfiable concepts may exist. Thus, we need to focus on the MUPS of the critical or root contradictions in the ontology.

To achieve this, we make use of a debugging service we have devised in [6] that identifies the *root* unsatisfiable concepts in an ontology, which propagate and cause errors elsewhere in the ontology, leading to *derived* unsatisfiable concepts. Intuitively, a root unsatisfiable concept is one in which a clash or contradiction found in the concept definition does not *depend on the unsatisfiability* of another concept in the ontology; whereas, a derived unsatisfiable concept acquires a contradiction due to its dependence on another unsatisfiable concept. For example, if A is an unsatisfiable concept, then a concept B ($B \sqsubseteq A$) or C ($C \sqsubseteq \exists R.A$) also becomes unsatisfiable due to its dependence on A, and is thus considered as derived.

We have experimented with the root/derived debugging service on numerous OWL ontologies that have a large number of unsatisfiable concepts and found it to be useful in narrowing down the error space quickly, e.g, for the Tambis OWL Ontology, only 3 out of 144 unsatisfiable concepts were discovered as roots in under 5 seconds. From a repair point of view, the key advantage here is that one needs to focus on the MUPS of the root unsatisfiable concepts alone since fixing the roots effectively fixes a large set of directly derived concept bugs.

Also, the service guides the repair process which can be carried out by the user at three different granularity levels:

– *Level 1: Reparing a single unsatisfiable concept at a time*: In this case, it makes sense to deal with the root unsatisfiable concepts first, before resolving errors in any of the derived concepts. This technique allows the user to monitor the entire debugging process closely, exploring different repair alternatives for each concept before fully fixing the ontology. However, since at every step in the repair process, the user is working in a localized context (looking at a single concept only), the debugging of the entire ontology could be prolonged due to new bugs introduced later based on changes made earlier. Thus, the repair process may not be optimal.

– *Level 2: Repairing all root unsatisfiable concepts together*: The user could batch repair all the root unsatisfiable concepts in a single debugging iteration before proceeding to uncover a new set of root/derived unsatisfiable concepts. This technique provides a cross between the tool-automation (done in level 3) and finer manual inspection (allowed in level 1) with respect to bug correction.

– *Level 3: Repairing all unsatisfiable concepts*: The user could directly focus on removing all the unsatisfiable concepts in the ontology in one go. This technique imposes an overhead on the debugging tool which needs to present a plan that accounts for the removal of all the bugs in an optimal manner. The strategy works in a global context, considering bugs and bug-dependencies in the ontology as a whole, and thus may take time for the tool to compute, especially if there are a large number of unsatisfiable concepts in the ontology (e.g. Tambis). However, the repair process is likely to be more efficient compared to level 1 repair.

The number of steps in the repair process depends on the granularity level chosen by the user: for example, using Level 1 above, the no. of steps is atleast the no. of unsatisfiable concepts the user begins with; whereas using Level 3 granularity, the repair reduces to a single big step. To make the process more flexible, the user should be allowed to change the granularity level, as and when desired, during a particular repair session.

3.5 Suggesting Axiom Rewrites

Now, to make our repair solution more flexible, we consider strategies to rewrite erroneous axioms instead of strictly removing them from the ontology[2].

Using Erroneous Axiom Parts. As shown in section 3.2 (see Figure 1), our Axiom Pinpointing service has been extended to identify parts of axioms in the MUPS responsible for making a concept unsatisfiable. Having determined the erroneous part(s) of axioms, we can suggest a suitable rewrite of the axiom that preserves as much as information as possible while eliminating unsatisfiability.

Identifying Common Pitfalls. Common pitfalls in OWL ontology modeling have been enumerated in literature [9]. We have summarized some commonly occurring errors that we have observed (in addition to those mentioned in [9]), highlighting the *meant* axiom and the reason for the mistake in each case.

---

[2] Note that rewriting an axiom involves an axiom removal followed by an addition. Thus, similar to the impact analysis performed for axiom removal, we also need to consider entailments that are introduced when an axiom is added. Currently, we only check if unsatisfiable concepts arise upon axiom addition, and we are working on iterative reasoning techniques (see http://www.mindswap.org/papers/TR-incclass.pdf) to optimally compute other entailments added.

Asserted	Meant	Reason for Misunderstanding
$A \equiv C$	$A \sqsubseteq C$	Difference between Defined and Primitive concepts
$A \sqsubseteq C$ $A \sqsubseteq D$	$A \sqsubseteq C \sqcup D$	Multiple subclass has intersection semantics
domain(P,A) range(P,B)	$A \sqsubseteq \forall P.B$	Global vs. Local property restrictions
domain(P,A) domain(P,B)	domain(P, $A \sqcup B$)	Unclear about multiple domain semantics

A library of error patterns can be easily maintained, extended and shared between ontology authors using appropriate tool support. Once we have identified the axioms in the ontology responsible for an unsatisfiable concept, we can check if any of the axioms has a pattern corresponding to one in the library, and if so, suggest the *meant* axiom to the user as a replacement. We note that in a lot of cases that we have observed, the most common reason for unsatisfiability is the accidental use of equivalence instead of subsumption.

In some cases, an additional heuristic to consider is the label (or ID) of the concept or role, which acts as a pointer to its intended meaning and can be used to detect mismatches in modeling. For example, the unsatisfiable concept OceanCrustLayer seen earlier in the Sweet-JPL OWL ontology was accidentally defined to be a subclass of CrustRegion, instead of CrustLayer.

A combination of the heuristics was used to debug an error in the University ontology. The concept ProfessorInHCIorAI was responsible for the unsatisfiable concepts AI_Student and HCI_Student because there were two separate subclass axioms for ProfessorInHCIorAI, associating it with the student concepts separately, whereas the 'or' in the concept name implied that a disjunction was intended.

3.6   Interactive Repair Tool (Preliminary Evaluation)

We are currently working on an ontology repair plug-in for Swoop. The key design goal is to provide a flexible, interactive framework for repairing unsatisfiable concepts in an ontology by allowing the user to analyze erroneous axioms, weigh axiom ranks as desired, explore different repair solutions by generating plans on the fly, preview change effects before executing the plan and compare different repair alternatives. Moreover, the tool also suggests axiom edits where possible.

Figure 3 is a screenshot of the Swoop repair plugin when used to debug the University OWL ontology. As can be seen, the top segment of the repair frame displays a list of unsatisfiable concepts in the ontology, with the *root* classes marked. The adjacent pane renders the axioms responsible for making the concepts selected in the list unsatisfiable. There are two view modes for this pane – the one shown in Figure 3 displays the erroneous axioms for each unsatisfiable class in separate tables with axioms indented (as described in [6]), and common axioms responsible for causing multiple errors highlighted as shown. The other view (not shown) displays all erroneous axioms globally in a single list.

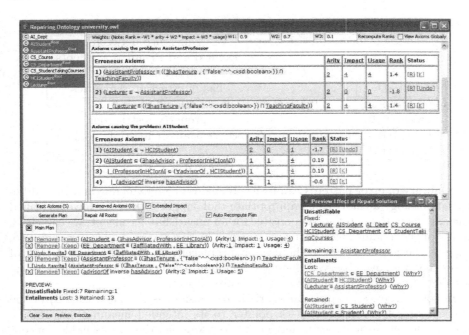

Fig. 3. Interactive Repair in Swoop: Generating a repair plan to remove all root unsatisfiable concepts in the University OWL Ontology. The popup in the lower right corner displays a *preview* of the current repair plan including unsatisfiable concepts that would get fixed and key entailments that would be lost or retained.

The tables display for each axiom, its arity, impact and usage, computed as described earlier. The values for these parameters are hyperlinked, clicking on which pops up a pane which displays more details about the parameter (not shown in the figure). Also, clicking on the table headers re-sorts the results based on the parameter selected. The total rank for each axiom, displayed in the last column of the table, is the weighted sum of the parameter values, with the weights (and thus ranks) being easily reconfigurable by the user. For example, users interested in generating minimal impact plans can assign a higher weight to the impact parameter, while users interested in smaller sized plans can weigh arity higher. The range of the weights is from -1.0 to 1.0.

As discussed earlier, we provide three different granularities for the repair process, i.e., the ability to fix a particular set of unsatisfiable concepts; all the *roots* only; or all the unsatisfiable classes directly in one go. For example, in Figure 3, the user has asked the tool to generate a plan to repair all the roots.

For a repair tool to be effective, it should support the easy customization of the plan to suit the user's needs. In the simple case, the user can either choose to *keep* a particular axiom in the ontology, or forcibly *remove* a particular one. These user-enforced changes are automatically reflected in the plans. In Figure 3, the user has chosen to *keep* the disjoint axioms AIStudent ⊑ ¬HCIStudent, and Lecturer ⊑ ¬AssistantProfessor in the ontology (highlighted in green in the

Table). In the advanced case, the user can choose to keep or remove a particular entailment of the ontology, e.g., a particular subclass relation. The tool then takes these desired and undesired entailments into account when generating a plan.

Finally, axiom rewrites suggested by the tool can be (optionally) included in the plan as well. In the figure, the tool has suggested weakening the two equivalence axioms to subclass relations, which removes the contradictions in the unsatisfiable classes, but preserves the semantics as much as possible. Obviously, the user can directly edit erroneous axioms if desired.

The repair plan can be saved, compared with other plans and executed, after which the ontology changes (which are part of the plan) are logged in Swoop. These changes can be serialized and shared among ontology users (as shown in [5]).

Pilot Study. We conducted a small pilot study involving twelve subjects, who had at least one year's experience with OWL and an understanding of description-logic reasoning that varied greatly (novices to experts). Each subject received a 30 minute orientation including an overview of the semantic errors found in OWL ontologies (using examples of unsatisfiable classes); a brief tutorial of Swoop, demonstrating its key browsing, editing and search features; and a detailed walkthrough of the debugging and repair support in Swoop using a set of toy ontologies.

We selected two OWL Ontologies – University.owl and miniTambis.owl and asked each subject to fix all the unsatisfiable classes in a particular ontology using the debugging techniques seen in [6] (case 1), and in the other ontology using the repair techniques described in this paper (case 2). The subjects were randomly assigned to the two cases, but the overall distribution was equally proportional in that given a particular ontology, an equal number of subjects (six) debugged it with and without using the repair facilities. At the end of the study, our goal was to compare the performance improvement, if any, of using the repair services over the previous debugging services, which were shown to be useful in an earlier study [6].

The results of the study were encouraging. We found that while the quality of the repair solutions in both cases were comparable, the time taken to arrive at a solution in the second case was between 2-8 times less than in first case. More importantly, the subjects felt that in the second case, they understood the different alternatives for repair, and decided on one knowing its overall impact. Three key features appreciated by the subjects were the impact analysis to see lost/retained entailments, the suggested axiom rewrites and the option to modify the plan on the fly by *keeping* or forcibly *removing* axioms.

4   Conclusion

In this paper, we have discussed the problem of repairing unsatisfiable concepts in OWL Ontologies, and provided solutions that tie in nicely with (and extend) our earlier work on explanation and debugging [6]. Thus, we are now in a position to construct an end-to-end framework for interactive debugging and repair of OWL Ontologies, though more extensive testing and evaluation is necessary. Given the nature of the problem, our focus right from the start, has been on the user-experience and in aiding the overall understanding and analysis of the ontology, and the results so far have been in correspondence with our goal.

References

1. Gardenfors P. Makinson D. Alchourron, C. On the logic of theory change: Partial meet contraction and revision functions. 1985. Journal of Symbolic Logic 50 (1985).
2. Li Ding, Rong Pan, Tim Finin, Anupam Joshi, Yun Peng, and Pranam Kolari. Finding and Ranking Knowledge on the Semantic Web. In *Proceedings of the 4th International Semantic Web Conference*, LNCS 3729, pages 156–170. Springer, November 2005.
3. Nicola Guarino and Christopher Welty. Evaluating ontological decisions with ontoclean. *Commun. ACM*, 45(2):61–65, 2002.
4. A. Kalyanpur, B. Parsia, B. Cuenca-Grau, and E. Sirin. Axiom pinpointing: Finding (precise) justifications for arbitrary entailments in $\mathcal{SHOIN}$ (owl-dl). Technical report, UMIACS, 2005-66, 2006. Technical Report.
5. A. Kalyanpur, B. Parsia, E.Sirin, B. Cuenca-Grau, and J. Hendler. Swoop: A web ontology editing browser. *Journal of Web Semantics*, 2005. To Appear.
6. Aditya Kalyanpur, Bijan Parsia, Evren Sirin, and James Hendler. Debugging unsatisfiable classes in owl ontologies. *Journal of Web Semantics, Volume 3 Issue 4*, 2005. (To Appear).
7. N. Noy, M. Sintek, S. Decker, M. Crubezy, R. Fergerson, and M. Musen. Creating semantic web contents with Protégé-2000. *IEEE Intelligent Systems*, 2001.
8. Daniel Oberle, Raphael Volz, Boris Motik, and Steffen Staab. An extensible ontology software environment. In Steffen Staab and Rudi Studer, editors, *Handbook on Ontologies*, International Handbooks on Information Systems, chapter III, pages 311–333. Springer, 2004.
9. Alan Rector, Nick Drummond, Matthew Horridge, Jeremy Rogers, Holger Knublauch, Robert Stevens, Hai Wang, and Chris Wroe. OWL Pizzas: Practical Experience of Teaching OWL-DL: Common Errors & Common Patterns . In *EKAW*, pages 63–81, 2004.
10. R. Reiter. A theory of diagnosis from first principles. 1987. Artificial Intelligence 32:57-95.
11. S. Schlobach. Debugging and semantic clarification by pinpointing. 2005. European Semantic Web Conference ESWC.
12. S. Schlobach. Diagnosing terminologies. In *In Proceedings of AAAI'05*, 2005.
13. S. Schlobach and R. Cornet. Non-standard reasoning services for the debugging of description logic terminologies. In *Proceedings of IJCAI*, 2003.
14. Evren Sirin, Bijan Parsia, Bernardo Cuenca Grau, Aditya Kalyanpur, and Yarden Katz. Pellet: A practical owl-dl reasoner. Technical report, University of Maryland Institute for Advanced Computes Studies (UMIACS), 2005-68, 2005. Available online at http://www.mindswap.org/papers/PelletDemo.pdf.

Winnowing Ontologies Based on Application Use

Harith Alani, Stephen Harris, and Ben O'Neil

Advanced Knowledge Technologies (AKT), School of Electronics and Computer Science,
University of Southampton, Southampton SO17 1BJ, UK
{h.alani, swh, bjon104}@ecs.soton.ac.uk

Abstract. The requirements of specific applications and services are often over estimated when ontologies are reused or built. This sometimes results in many ontologies being too large for their intended purposes. It is not uncommon that when applications and services are deployed over an ontology, only a few parts of the ontology are queried and used. Identifying which parts of an ontology are being used could be helpful to *winnow* the ontology, i.e., simplify or shrink the ontology to smaller, more fit for purpose size. Some approaches to handle this problem have already been suggested in the literature. However, none of that work showed how ontology-based applications can be used in the ontology-resizing process, or how they might be affected by it. This paper presents a study on the use of the AKT Reference Ontology by a number of applications and services, and investigates the possibility of relying on this *usage* information to winnow that ontology.

1 Introduction

Ontologies normally grow to large sizes when the main purpose of building them is to provide an extensive representation of a domain. However, when building or reusing ontologies for the purpose of supporting certain applications, those ontologies are expected to be much smaller in size and be more focused towards meeting the requirements of those applications and services, rather than to provide a generic representation of a domain. A study of the applications submitted to the 2003 Semantic Web (SW, [4]) challenge, showed that most of the ontologies used in those applications were relatively small and simple, but also sufficient for their intended purposes [12].

When designing an ontology, it is highly recommended to keep in mind what the ontology is to be used for to avoid over or under representing the domain [14]. The first step of the methodology proposed by Uschold and Grüninger for building ontologies is to identify its purpose and scope [22]. Grüninger and Fox [8] suggested articulating the requirements for an ontology in the form of a list of *competency questions* that the ontology must be able to answer. This is meant to assure a more fit-for-purpose scoping of the ontology.

However, in spite of such recommendations and methodologies, it is not uncommon to find ontologies that are much larger than actually required by the SW applications and services that the ontologies are meant to support. Most SW users only need to use small portions of existing ontologies to run their applications [15]. Ontology engineers might sometimes prefer to build or reuse extensive and more detailed ontologies for

Y. Sure and J. Domingue (Eds.): ESWC 2006, LNCS 4011, pp. 185–199, 2006.

their applications in preparation for a probable future expansion of requirements, or to allow for an imaginable automatic communication with external agents that perhaps will require a more exhaustive representation of the domain.

Nevertheless, it is logical to expect enduring much higher costs for hosting and running a large and complex ontology than a trimmed-down version of that ontology. This includes costs of maintenance, documentation, change management, visualisation, and scalability. Tools to reduce an ontology to one that better fits certain needs can also greatly aid and encourage reusing existing ontologies [21].

Several approaches and suggestions for semi-automatic trimming or breaking-down of ontologies into smaller sizes have been introduced in the literature. However, to the best of our knowledge, none of the proposed approaches are driven by application needs, or study how applications might be affected by the shrinkage of their supporting ontologies. Manually selecting which parts or classes of an ontology to preserve, which is what most of previous work is based on, can be unreliable. The developer of the ontology or application might not be fully aware of *all* the parts that will be *required* and *used* by the application, and the ones that will never be needed or used. So in the end, the application itself might be the best judge here.

In this paper, we would like to examine how the usage of an ontology by applications can be used to drive the process of reducing the ontology size. To this end, we will study how our project's main ontology is being used by local and external applications and services. The aim of this work is partly to get a better understanding of how and where the ontology is being queried, and more importantly, how this information can be interpreted. We hope that this study will enable us to better scope the ontology and provide some insight into whether such analysis can be used to automatically *winnow* an ontology without affecting its usage. We use the term winnowing to refer to the process of removing any unused parts of an ontology, keeping only the parts that are needed to represent the existing data and run any dependent applications.

2   Related Work

There has been some work in recent years investigating various approaches to trim ontologies for various purposes. These approaches vary in purpose and technique, as described below.

2.1   Ontology Partitioning

Stuckenschmidt and Klein [20] proposed the use of classical clustering algorithms to partition ontologies based on how their class hierarchies are structured. In their approach, each partition will contain classes that are more strongly connected to other classes in this partition rather than to classes in other partitions. The suggested ontology partitioning is therefore based on how the classes are connected in the ontology, regardless of how the ontology is, or can be, used. Nothing in this approach can guarantee that the ontology produced by each cluster is meaningful or usable.

If an application needs to interact with a set of classes that ended up being spread over many of the partitions suggested by the clustering process, then those partitions will have to be remapped or remerged together, thus rendering the whole partitioning process less useful. So even though the approach suggested in [20] is good for a general structure-based scaling down of ontologies, it is not suitable for usage-driven ontology winnowing.

2.2 Ontology Views

Other work suggested generating specific *views* on complex RDFS ontologies using view-querying languages [23, 13]. The aim was to use these views to personalise or simplify ontology structures by creating virtual ones, based on view-selection queries. Another related approach is to limit the *view* of an ontology to only a user-selected class and its neighbourhood [15]. This neighbourhood can be restricted in size by the number of connections it is allowed to span out, which can be set by the user for each property separately.

The above approaches can be useful for quickly limiting how an ontology is viewed or browsed. However, they are not designed, not well suited, for automatic extraction of ontology parts, or for trimming an ontology based on the demands of certain applications and services.

2.3 Ontology Segment Extraction

Bhatt and colleagues [5] developed a distributed architecture for extracting sub-ontologies. In this approach, users were expected to specify which ontology entities to keep, which to remove, and which to leave for the system to decide. This approach suggests using three main rules to minimise ontologies. For a class that is selected to be kept:

– Keep all its superclasses and their inherited relationships.
– Keep all its subclasses and their relationships.
– Keep all attributes with cardinality more than zero.

The experiments reported in [5] were driven by users manually selecting which entities to keep and which ones to throw away. It is not obvious how this approach could apply when the selection process is based on applications actively using the ontology to be winnowed, and if and how such applications might be affected by the process.

Another segmentation work is presented in [16]. They start from a specific class and follow certain paths along the ontology network to create a segment. They have only applied their approach to the GALEN ontology, and only considered segmenting based on a single class selection, rather than with multiple classes as would be the case when based on ontology use. The rules they applied are:

– Keep all superlasses and subclasses of selected class
– Include equivalent classes
– Include properties and classes of any restrictions on included classes.
– Keep all the classes that these properties point to
– Keep superproperties and superclasses of all the included classes from the last 3 steps.

This approach focuses on maintaining the semantics of the ontology, which is why it is more generous in its segmentation that the previous approaches.

2.4   Ontology Use Analysis

Analysing how an ontology is being used is an important step towards better ontology management [18]. In [19], the authors logged ontology usage information in the aim that this might help knowledge engineers to increase the efficiency of search within a given knowledge base (KB). They argued that if an ontology class or property is queried at higher rates then this might indicate a too-broad representation, which could be detailed further in the ontology [19]. On the other hand, if the entity is never queried, then it will be flagged as a good candidate for removal, unless the entity is instantiated in the KB. They also looked at the problem where an entity is frequently queried but not many results are available. They regard this as an indication of a knowledge gap.

Note that the work reported in [18] and [19] only looked at direct user interactions with a KB, rather than at queries steadily coming from external applications. Furthermore, how the ontology is to be changed in line with the information they collected, and how that change will affect further use of the KB, seemed to be out of the scope of their reported work.

Another work that took usage into account is reported in [9]. The aim here was to monitor the use of a simple ontology (the ACM topic hierarchy) by several users, then try to make change recommendations on the items in the hierarchy. The change recommendations were based on how the hierarchy has been queried and modified by the users. However, the ACM ontology which they experimented with is a simple taxonomy, and the user interactions and change recommendations were equally simple.

None of the work reported in this section focussed on processing queries sent by applications and services to their supporting ontologies as an input to software to perform the trimming of these ontologies. In this paper, we investigate applying some variations of the rules proposed in previous work to winnow a locally-developed ontology that have been in use by several applications for over three years.

3   Winnowing the AKT Reference Ontology

Ontology winnowing differs from the approach described in section 2 in that the process of trimming the ontology here is entirely based on *need*. Need is determined by the queries sent to the ontology by any supported applications, and by the underlying data.

In this section we discuss a case study on the usage of a locally maintained ontology; the AKT Reference ontology.

3.1   AKT Reference Ontology

The AKT Reference Ontology (AKTRO[1]) was developed over a period of six months by several partners of the AKT[2] project. This ontology built on a number of smaller ontologies previously developed at various AKT sites. AKTRO currently consists of 175 classes and 142 properties.

AKTRO models the domain of academia. It contains representations for people, conferences, projects, organisations, publications, etc. AKTRO is stored in a triple store;

---

[1] http://www.aktors.org/ontology/

[2] http://www.aktors.org

namely 3Store [11], and is instantiated with information drawn from various databases and information gathering tools (currently stores around 30M triples in the KB). The AKTRO ontology is written in OWL, though 3Store is only capable of RDFS inferencing, and thus AKTRO was stored in 3Store in RDFS.

When the AKTRO was first developed over three years ago, the intention was to create a reference ontology for the whole AKT consortium to avoid the use of several variant ontologies about the same domain within the project. In other words, the aim of that ontology was to provide a reference model, rather than to meet the needs of any specific application or service.

3.2 AKTRO Instantiations

As mentioned above, we maintain a KB with a large number of instantiations made against the AKTRO. Many classes in the ontology have no instances, while others are heavily instantiated. Figure 1 gives some idea on how **sparsely** instantiated the AKTRO is in our repository.

Even though some of these instances might not be required for running some of our applications, they represent an important and resourceful part of the KB and can be considered as a type of ontology use, and hence it was deemed important to make sure that all these instances remain intact.

3.3 Queries to AKTRO

The AKTRO and its KB are used to support a number of on-site and off-site applications, such as OntoCoPI[3], CSAktiveSpace[17], AKT Technologies dynamic web pages[3], Armadillo[7] from Sheffield University, and any other ad hoc works, such as [1], or even queries directly typed by users.

In our case study, we experimented with winnowing AKTRO based on its general use by the above applications and services. Then in a second experiment, we focused the usage analyses of AKTRO on two selected applications only, and extended the winnowing process to take into account query results. The two experiments are described in the following.

4   Experiment 1: Winnowing AKTRO Based on General Use Analysis

Our first winnowing experiment was based on the general use of AKTRO, where all queries from any application or ad hoc query were taken into account [2]. This section details this experiment and its results.

4.1 Query Log

We logged over 193 thousand RDQL queries that have been posed to the AKTRO by various sources. After analysing the logged queries, we found that only 6 classes and 27 properties of our ontology have been explicitly queried (i.e. the URIs of these classes

---

[3] http://www.aktors.org/technologies/

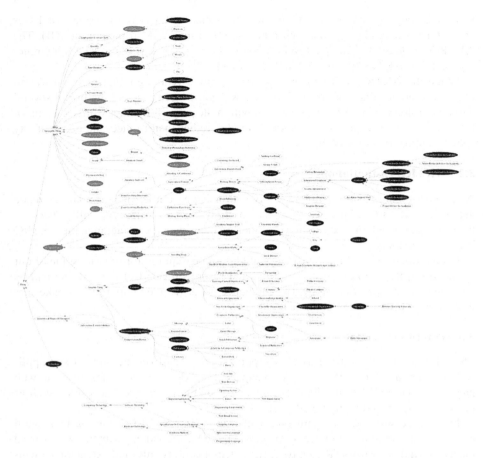

Fig. 1. Space view of the AKT Reference ontology. Classes that are instantiated are shown in black colour. Grey coloured classes are the domains or ranges of instantiated properties.

and properties were given in at least one RDQL query). These classes and properties are given in tables 1 and 2 respectively.

The frequency with which a concept or a property has been queried gives a good indication of whether the query is directly typed in by a person (very low frequency), or rather coming from an application (higher frequencies). However, to make sure that all requests are met, any concept or property that has been queried at least once will be regarded as essential, and included in the winnowed ontology. In the second experiment, only application queries are considered (section 5.3).

Membership of many other classes can be indirectly constrained through properties. For example, if the property *has-project-member* appears in a query, then it is implicitly restricting the bindings for its subject to members of the class of Project and its object to the class of Person, which are the domain and range of this property respectively. This indicates that in addition to instantiations and queries, we also need to find all the

Table 1. Queried classes from the AKT Reference Ontology and the number of times they appeared in the logged queries

Class	Queries	Class	Queries	Class	Queries
Technology	63462	Organization	7554	Research-Area	985
Person	750	Academic	9	Thing	3

Table 2. Queried properties from the AKT Reference Ontology and the number of times they appeared in the logged queries

Property	Queries	Property	Queries
has-title	22478	technology-builds-on	15092
has-key-document	14964	has-author	14809
addresses-generic-area-of-interest	13735	has-appellation	12620
has-email-address	12620	has-web-address	10386
has-date	10210	has-project-leader	9549
has-project-member	9551	owned-by	7602
family-name	7588	full-name	7562
has-relevant-document	7482	works-in-unit	5140
contributes-to	3133	has-telephone-number	2832
has-pretty-name	2034	has-research-interest	1543
sub-area-of	1288	unit-of-organization	960
has-affiliation-to-unit	110	contributes-to-rating	36
has-research-quality	36	given-name	1
has-academic-degree	1		

classes that are domains or ranges of properties that were queried or used by instances (i.e assigned values for some instances).

4.2   Winnowing the Ontology

As stated earlier, our aim is to study how an ontology can be automatically trimmed down based on analysing how the ontology is being used by dependent applications and services. So to complete our experiment, we winnowed the AKT Reference ontology by following these rules:

1. Keep all ontology classes that are directly instantiated with one or more instances. This lead to the inclusion of 54 classes from AKTRO (figure 1).
2. Keep all the ontology properties that are assigned values by at least one instance in the KB. This totalled 69 properties.
3. Keep all classes and properties explicitly mentioned in one or more queries (tables 1 and 2), that are not already found in steps 1 and 2 above. This brought in 1 additional class; *Thing*, and 3 properties; *has-academic-degree, has-key-document*, and *has-relevant-document*.
4. Keep all classes that are domains or ranges of any property found in steps 2 or 3 above. This lead to the inclusion of 13 new classes. Note that some properties have multiple domains and ranges, not all of which are used by our applications. However, for the sake of completeness, all domains and ranges are included.
5. Remove classes and properties not identified in previous steps. Classes and properties will be shifted up the hierarchy if their superclasses are removed.

Remember that AKTO had 175 classes and 142 properties. After applying the rules above, only 68 classes (61.2% reduction), and 72 properties (49.3% reduction) were left. Checking the resulting ontology (lets call it winnAKTRO-1) with a reasoner (Pellet[4]) showed that, in this particular case, the ontology remained consistent.

4.3   Evaluation of winnAKTRO-1

To evaluate the effect of winnowing AKTRO on its supported applications, we compared the results of nearly 1800 carefully selected logged queries using AKTRO against the results when using winnAKTRO-1 [2]. Scripts were used to compare each binding returned for each query from both ontologies to determine whether the results obtained from the two ontologies are an exact match or not.

The comparison revealed that the results of around 3% of the selected queries were different when using winnAKTRO-1 than when using AKTRO. A closer look at the results showed that the failed queries were querying the rdf:type of instances, as in:

```
SELECT ?type
WHERE (<instance-uri>, rdf:type, ?type)
```

This query could be issued by applications that use the type to choose how to render data relating to the instance. For example, an application might ask the above query, then search among the returned types for the Project class, as a way of verifying whether the instance in hand is a project or not. If the Project class is no longer in winnAKTRO-1, then this query will return a different answer than before.

5   Experiment 2: Taking Query Results into Account

The previous winnowing trial showed that, for some RDQL queries, the results were different before and after the winnowing process. This indicates that further steps might be required when winnowing an ontology to avoid such result-mismatches.

We decided to focus this second experiment on two specific applications (CSAktive Space [17] and OntoCoPI [3]) to make sure that the queries in the log can be traced back to their sources. This will also ensure that no arbitrary queries (not required by any application) are logged by mistake. Note that these two applications are the most active users of AKTRO.

In this experiment, we will also take the *results of queries* in the log into account when winnowing the ontology. This will hopefully reduce the results-mismatching problem encountered in experiment 1 (section 4.3).

5.1   Query Log

To make sure we log all possible queries from the two selected applications, the applications were put to extensive use for several hours, and their queries to 3Store were clearly tagged in the log. The result was a query log of just under 13 thousand queries.

---

[4] http://www.mindswap.org/2003/pellet/

Table 3. Properties in AKTRO that are queried explicitly by CSAktive Space and Ontocopi

Properties	Queries	Properties	Queries	Properties	Queries
has-project-leader	1011	has-project-member	1011	has-date	854
has-author	828	works-in-unit	528	address-generic-area-of-interest	506
has-grant-value	253	has-amount	253	has-funding	253
has-telephone-number	157	has-web-address	157	unit-of-organization	123
has-pretty-name	80	has-research-interest	63	sub-area-of	41
contributes-to-rating	22	has-research-quality	22		

After collapsing duplicates, 5 thousand unique queries remained. Number of queries is much less than in previous experiment because of the focus on two applications only.

When analysing the query log it was found that only one class and 17 properties have been explicitly queried. The queried properties and the number of queries that mentioned them is shown in table 3. The queried class was *Person*, and it appeared in 137 queries.

The fact that only one class was explicitly queried supports the observation from the first experiment that applications often rely on properties to filter out the results. OntoCoPI for example often queries the triple store for any individuals connected to a given person instance via specific properties [3]. Such a query will return instances of classes such as Project, Conference, Paper, etc. OntoCoPI then asks for the rdf:type of each returned URI to find their class types.

5.2   Query Results

As mentioned earlier, in this second experiment, the results of the logged queries will also be considered when identifying the class and property URIs to be maintained in the winnowed ontology.

Table 4. Classes in AKTRO that appear in results of queries from CSAktiveSpace and OntoCoPI

Class	Results	Class	Results	Class	Results
Thing	504	Intangible-Thing	424	Publication-Reference	275
Abstract-Information	275	Person	218	Generic-Agent	189
Temporal-Thing	154	Legal-Agent	149	Proceedings-Paper-Reference	135
Affiliated-Person	120	Article-Reference	114	Employee	71
Academic	47	Researcher-In-Academia	29	Working-Person	13
Educational-Employee	13	Technology	9	Book-Section-Reference	7
Book-Reference	6	Researcher	6	PhD-Student	4
Conference-Proceedings-Reference	4	Student	4	Activity	3
Technical-Report-Reference	3	Project	2	Prof	2
Dr	2	Thesis-Reference	1	Professor-In-Academia	1

Table 5. Properties in AKTRO that appear in results of queries from CSAktiveSpace and Onto-CoPI

Properties	Results	Properties	Results	Properties	Results
has-research-interest	781	works-in-unit	724	sub-area-of	305
works-for	168	unit-of-organization	152	has-affiliation-to-unit	128
contributes-to-rating	83	family-name	61	full-name	61
studies-in-unit	54	has-email-address	32	has-appellation	26
has-telephone-number	25	has-fax-number	20	has-affiliation	19
has-postal-address	16	project-involves-organization-unit	11	given-name	9
has-web-address	7	sub-unit-or-organization-unit	6	has-pretty-name	6

When analysing the results of the 13 thousand logged queries, the URIs of 30 classes and 21 properties were found (tables 4 and 5 respectively).

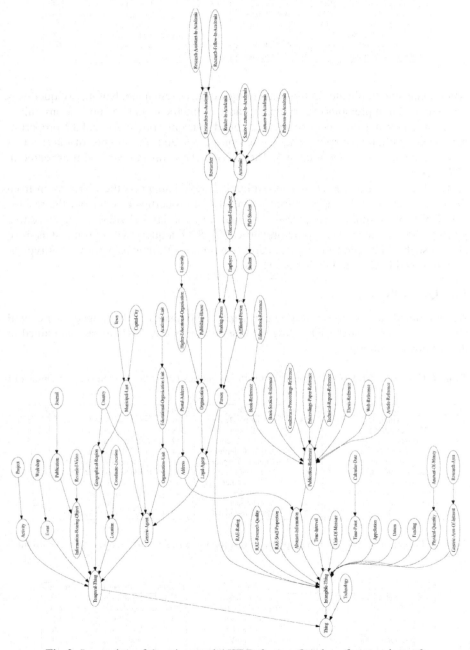

Fig. 2. Space view of the winnowed AKT Reference Ontology for experiment 2

5.3   Winnowing the Ontology

Similarly to section 4.2, the following steps were followed to winnow the ontology:

1. Keep all directly instantiated classes and properties (assigned values for some in-stances). As in experiment 1, 54 classes and 69 properties remained.
2. Keep all classes and properties that were explicitly mentioned in queries. Even though 1 class and 17 properties were explicitly mentioned in the logged queries, they were all instantiated and thus already identified in step 1.
3. Keep all domains and ranges of required properties. 10 new classes were added that were not identified in previous steps.
4. Keep all classes and properties that appear in the results of the logged queries. This includes 30 classes and 21 properties. However, only 7 classes and 0 properties have not been already identified in the previous steps.
5. Remove classes and properties not identified in previous steps. Classes and proper-ties will be shifted up the hierarchy if their superclasses are removed.

Once the rules above were applied to AKTRO and winAKTRO-2 was produced, it had 71 classes, and 69 properties. This is a reduction of 59.5% in classes, and 51.4% in properties when compared to the original ontology (figure 2).

5.4   Evaluation of winnAKTRO-2

The results of all the queries logged in experiment 2 (5K queries) were compared as returned from AKTRO and winnAKTRO-2. The comparison showed a perfect match between the two sets of results, including queries on rdf:type which failed in experiment 1. In other words, the applications used in this experiment have not been affected by the winnowing process, and continued to function as usual. However, the ontology that supports them is now about half of its original size.

6   Discussion

A number of approaches have been suggested in the literature to trim down ontologies to simply make them easier to manage (sec. 2). However, we noticed that none of this work investigated using application queries as a guideline to how an ontology should be winnowed, nor did they study the effect of winnowing an ontology on its current use. Unlike user queries, **application queries tend to be fixed** to some extent at develop-ment time. Therefore, analysing how an application is making use of an ontology can form a good basis for deciding how the ontology is to be winnowed. This, of course, is only possible if the applications are fully developed and their use of the ontology is not expected to change very frequently. However, it is always possible to **revert to the original ontology** if, for example, the requirements of the applications changed, or new applications are developed.

Some ontology-trimming rules have already been proposed (sec. 2). However, we believe that such **rules need to be rechecked and perhaps changed** when applications are involved in the process. For example, some have proposed keeping all subclasses and superclasses of preserved classes ([5, 16]). In our first experiment (sec. 4, this would have meant keeping the entire AKTRO class hierarchy, simply because the top class, *Thing*, was selected for preservation.

In [19], the authors suggested that classes that are queried very often should be broken down to further subclasses. When analysing our query log, we noticed that most queries targeted the more general classes, rather than their subclasses. For example, in experiment 1, there were 750 queries to the class *Person*, but only *one* of its 13 *instantiated* subclasses was queried, 9 times. In experiment 2, none of Person's subclasses were queried, whereas Person appeared in 137 queries. Of course this is somewhat dependent on the applications, and on the type of query filtering used (see below). Nevertheless this observation seems to match the report in [6], which states that people tend to formulate their queries more generally than actually needed. **Query frequency of classes** is therefore not always a reliable indication of whether a class needs further subclassification or not.

Another possible explanation of the high use of certain classes rather than others is, as mentioned earlier, that membership of many classes has been indirectly constrained through properties, rather than explicitly mentioned in queries. For example, the property *has-project-member* appeared in 9551 queries in experiment 1, and in 1011 queries in experiment 2, while the class *Project* (the domain of this property) has not been explicitly queried in either experiment.

One crucial element in our ontology-winnowing approach is of course the **query logs**. That is, the logs of queries sent to the ontology by applications. For the log to be *complete*, one has to make sure that all the applications to winnow the ontology for, have been running long enough to ensure that all their query templates are logged.

In our study, we kept all directly instantiated classes and properties in the winnowed ontology, irrespective of whether they have been queried or not by applications. Stojanovic and colleague [19] believe that unused instances indicates a lack of awareness of their existence. However, we believe that in some cases, non-queried instances are simply not needed by the applications. To minimise the ontology further, one can remove any such classes (if none of their instances are ever queried), along with their instances.

In experiment 1, some queries that involved rdf:type **failed to return the same results** before and after winnowing the ontology (sec. 4.3). This shows that for this query template, and perhaps others, it is important not only to look at the log of queries, but also to **log query answers** when deciding what to keep in the winnowed ontology and what to throw away, or shelf!. This finding agrees with the approach taken in [19], where they analysed query results to acquire information that could potentially be used to tune the ontology. Taking query results into account when winnowing AKTRO in experiment 2 lead to a 100% match of query results to AKTRO and winnAKTRO-2.

However, a point to consider when reserving all classes and properties that appear in query results is how acceptable it is for **certain queries to return different results**. For some queries, it might not be important for the application to receive the exact same answer every time. For example, if the sole aim of a query or a set of queries is to retrieve the ontology structure to display it on the screen, then it might not be a problem if the structure has changed. However, if the aim of the query is, say, to search for all publications of John Smith prior to 2001, then some consistency is expected.

There is no easy way of finding out from the query log which query results have to be preserved (i.e. unchanged before and after winnowing), and which are more flexible. Such knowledge will most likely require some **analysis of the applications** themselves.

When winnowing an ontology, it might be important to maintain its **semantic completeness and consistency**. In our practical oriented approach, the main focus was to preserve only the necessary parts of the ontology to keep the applications running, rather than to hold on to any specific semantics. For example, our winnowing process removed some restrictions in AKTRO because they were not used by any application.

7   Conclusions and Future Work

If the ultimate goal of reusing or building an ontology is to serve specific applications, then it seems sensible to use these application to limit the ontology to smaller and easier to manage sizes. In this paper we described a study we performed on the AKT Reference Ontology which is being used by several applications. We logged large number of queries sent to the ontology from several applications, and applied some rules to winnow the ontology and throw away or shelf any unnecessary parts, regardless of their position in the original ontologies. The winnowed ontology produced in the first experiment turned out to have only 38.8% of the classes, and 50.7% of the properties of the original ontology. Query results were taken into account when producing the second winnowed ontology, which had 59.5% less classes and 51.4% less properties than the original AKTRO.

We have shown through experiments that analysing query syntax to determine which parts of an ontology are being triggered is not enough without also analysing the *results* of those queries. Further developments to this work could include the processing of SPARQL queries, rather than RDQL. This has the advantage that the SPARQL language and protocol are both more tightly defined than RDQL, making the technique easier to apply to other platforms and applications.

We expect our winnowing approach to produce scruffier ontologies, with perhaps less semantic consistency than their originals. Further steps will be needed to maintain consistency while changing the ontology [10]. More of the ontology will need to be preserved if higher semantic consistency is required (e.g. if all constraints must remain in the winnowed ontology). However, this might not be required if the main goal is to simply shrink an ontology with respect to the exact needs of specific applications, without affecting any of their queries. If the applications' needs change, or the knowledge base changes, then the winnowing process should be rerun on the original ontology to produce a new winnowed ontology.

In addition to semantic consistency, we need to pay attention to semantic redundancy that might result from the winnowing process. For example in winnAKTRO-2, *Geographical-Region* is now a subclasses of *Location* as well as of *Temporal-Thing*, and *Location* itself is a subclass of *Temporal-Thing*. A classifier could be used to identify and sort out such cases.

The methodology used in this paper takes into account classes and properties that are explicitly mentioned in queries and/or results, but does not take into account those that are potentially included in the subgraph used by the query engine but not explicitly mentioned. For example, the query:

```
SELECT ?i WHERE (?i rdf:type ?class)
         (?class rdfs:label "WorkingPerson")
```

uses the class WorkingPerson during the query execution without ever mentioning it explicitly, and without it appearing in the results. As it happens no classes or properties are used in only this way by the applications in the study, but it is a possibility that we will investigate in future work. Another related issue is that it some cases (e.g. for clarification or mapping purposes) the ontology is required to contain certain classes or properties without them being instantiated or queried. One possible solution to force our winnowing approach to maintain such entities is for applications to add dummy queries to any classes or properties that they desire to keep in the winnowed ontology.

As mentioned earlier, 3Store only performs RDFS inferencing. AKTRO was stored in RDFS in 3Store. As it happens, none of the restrictions present in the ontology were used in the logged queries, so they were not preserved by the winnowing process. Clearly, for use with an OWL inferencing engine a more sophisticated set of rules would be required to maintain the OWL restrictions.

Acknowledgment

This work is supported under the Advanced Knowledge Technologies (AKT) Inter-disciplinary Research Collaboration (IRC), which is sponsored by the UK Engineering and Physical Sciences Research Council under grant number GR/N15764/01. The AKT IRC comprises the Universities of Aberdeen, Edinburgh, Sheffield, Southampton and the Open University. The views and conclusions contained herein are those of the authors and should not be interpreted as necessarily representing official policies or endorsements, either express or implied, of the EPSRC or any other member of the AKT IRC.

References

1. H. Alani, N. Gibbins, H. Glaser, S. Harris, and N. Shadbolt. Monitoring research collaborations using semantic web technologies. In *Proc. 2nd European Semantic Web Conf. (ESWC)*, pages 664–678, Crete, 2005.
2. H. Alani, S. Harris, and B. O'Neil. Ontology winnowing: A case study on the akt reference ontology. In *Proc. Int. Conf. on Intelligent Agents, Web Technology and Internet Commerce (IAWTIC'2005)*, Vienna, Austria, 2005. IEEE.
3. H. Alani, S. D. K. O'Hara, and N. Shadbolt. Identifying communities of practice through ontology network analysis. *IEEE Intelligent Systems*, 18(2):18–25, 2003.
4. T. Berners-Lee, J. Hendler, and O. Lassila. The semantic web. *Scientific American*, May 2001.
5. M. Bhatt, C. Wouters, A. Flahive, W. Rahayu, and D. Taniar. Semantic completeness in sub-ontology extraction using distributed methods. In *Proc. Int. Conf. on Computational Science and its Applications (ICCSA)*, pages 508–517, Perugia, Italy, 2004. LNCS, Springer Verlag.

6. H. Chen and V. Dhar. Cognitive process as a basis for intelligent retrieval systems design. *Information Processing & Management*, 27(5):405–432, 1991.

7. F. Ciravegna, S. Chapman, A. Dingli, and Y. Wilks. Learning to harvest information for the semantic web. In *Proc. 1st European Semantic Web Symp. (ESWS)*, Crete, Greece, 2004.

8. M. Gruninger and M. S. Fox. Methodology for the design and evaluation of ontologies. In *Proc. Workshop on Basic Ontological Issues in Knowledge Sharing, in IJCAI'95*, Montreal, Canada, 1995.

9. P. Haase, A. Hotho, L. Schmidt-Thieme, and Y. Sure. Collaborative and usage-driven evolution of personal ontologies. In *Proc. Second European Semantic Web Conference (ESWC)*, pages 486–499, Crete, 2005.

10. P. Haase, F. van Harmelen, Z. Huang, H. Stuckenschmidt, and Y. Sure. A framework for handling inconsistency in changing ontologies. In *Proc. 4th Int. Semantic Web Conf. (ISWC)*, Galway, Ireland, 2005.

11. S. Harris and N. Gibbins. 3store: Efficient bulk rdf storage. In *Proc. 1st Int. Workshop on Practical and Scalable Semantic Systems (PSSS'03)*, pages 1–20, FL, USA, 2003.

12. M. Klein and U. Visse. Semantic web challenge 2003. *IEEE Intelligent Systems*, 19(3):31–33, 2004.

13. A. Magkanaraki, V. Tannen, V. Christophides, and D. Plexousakis. Viewing the semantic web through rvl lenses. In *Proc. Second Int. Semantic Web Conf. (ISWC)*, pages 98–112, Sanibel Island, Florida, 2003.

14. N. F. Noy and D. L. McGuinness. Ontology development 101: A guide to creating your first ontology. Technical Report KSL-01-05, Stanford Medical Informatics, March 2001.

15. N. F. Noy and M. A. Musen. Specifying ontology views by traversal. In *3rd Int. Semantic Web Conf. (ISWC'04)*, Hiroshima, Japan, 2004.

16. J. Seidenberg and A. Rector. Web Ontology Segmentation: Analysis, Classification and Use. In *Proceedings 15th International World Wide Web Conference*, Edinburgh, Scotland, 2006.

17. N. Shadbolt, monica schraefel, N. Gibbins, and S. Harris. CS Aktive Space: or how we stopped worrying and learned to love the semantic web. In *2nd Int. Semantic Web Conf*, Florida, 2003.

18. N. Stojanovic, J. Hartmann, and J. Gonzalez. Ontomanager - a system for usage-based ontology management. In *Proc. FGML Workshop. SIG of Germal Information Society*, 2003.

19. N. Stojanovic and L. Stojanovic. Usage-oriented evolution of ontology-based knowledge management systems. In *Int. Conf. on Ontologies, Databases and Applications of Semantics (ODBASE)*, pages 230–242, Irvine, CA, 2002.

20. H. Stuckenschmidt and M. Klein. Structure-based partitioning of large concept hierarchies. In *3rd Int. Semantic Web Conf. (ISWC2004)*, Hiroshima, Japan, 2004.

21. M. Uschold, P. Clark, M. Healy, K. Williamson, and S. Woods. An experiment in ontology reuse. In *Proc. Eleventh Knowledge Acquisition Workshop (KAW)*, Banff, Canada, 1998.

22. M. Uschold and M. Gruninger. Ontologies: principles, methods and applications. *The Knowledge Engineering Review*, 11(2):93–136, 1996.

23. R. Volz, D. Oberle, and R. Studer. Implementing views for light-weight web ontologies. In *Proc. IEEE Database Engineering and Application Symposium (IDEAS)*, Hong Kong, China, 2003.

Resolving Inconsistencies in Evolving Ontologies

Peter Plessers and Olga De Troyer

Vrije Universiteit Brussel, Pleinlaan 2, 1050 Brussels, Belgium
{Peter.Plessers, Olga.DeTroyer}@vub.ac.be

Abstract. Changing a consistent ontology may turn the ontology into an inconsistent state. It is the task of an approach supporting ontology evolution to ensure an ontology evolves from one consistent state into another consistent state. In this paper, we focus on checking consistency of OWL DL ontologies. While existing reasoners allow detecting inconsistencies, determining why the ontology is inconsistent and offering solutions for these inconsistencies is far from trivial. We therefore propose an algorithm to select the axioms from an ontology causing the inconsistency, as well as a set of rules that ontology engineers can use to resolve the detected inconsistency.

1 Introduction

More and more, ontologies are finding their way into a wide variety of software systems. Not only do they serve as the foundation of the Semantic Web [3], ontologies are starting to be applied in content and document management, information integration and knowledge management systems. The use of ontologies enhances systems with extensive reasoning capabilities, improve query possibilities, and ease integration and cooperation between systems.

Until recently, ontologies were mainly *treated* as being static i.e. once the ontology was developed and deployed, the knowledge captured by the ontology was considered to be fixed. Nevertheless, there is a need for ontologies to evolve in course of their lifetime. Reasons for ontology evolution includes changes to the domain represented, modifications of user requirements and corrections of design flaws. As ontologies may be shared by different applications and extended by other ontologies, a manual and ad-hoc handling of such an ontology evolution process is not feasible nor desirable as it is a too laborious, time intensive and complex process [17]. A structured approach is therefore essential to support the ontology engineer in this evolution process.

As ontologies are used to reason about and to infer implicit knowledge from, it is essential for an approach supporting ontology evolution to ensure that ontologies evolve from one consistent state into another consistent state. As changes to an ontology may possibly introduce inconsistencies, a method to detect and resolve inconsistencies in the ontology is required. For OWL DL[1], several reasoners capable of checking for inconsistencies have been developed (e.g., RACER [8], Fact [5], Pellet [9]). These reasoners are based on the description logics tableau algorithm. While such reasoners allow detecting inconsistencies, determining *why* the ontology is inconsistent

---

[1] http://www.w3.org/TR/owl-ref/

Y. Sure and J. Domingue (Eds.): ESWC 2006, LNCS 4011, pp. 200–214, 2006.

and *how* to resolve these inconsistencies is far from trivial. However, pinpointing the concepts that lead to an inconsistent ontology, determining the reasons for the inconsistencies and using these to offer the ontology engineer suggestions how to resolve these inconsistencies *should* be part of an ontology evolution approach.

In literature, three forms of ontology consistency are in general distinguished: Structural Consistency, Logical Consistency and User-defined Consistency [4]. The difference between these three forms is as follows:

- **Structural Consistency:** an ontology is considered structural consistent when the structure of the ontology conforms to the language constructs imposed by the underlying ontology language (e.g., OWL). Structural consistency can be enforced by checking a set of structural conditions defined for the underlying ontology language. Examples of such structural conditions include: 'the complement of a class must be a class', 'a property can only be a subproperty of a property', etc. In case of OWL, the set of structural conditions depends on the variant of OWL used. E.g., the set of structural conditions for OWL Lite will be more restrictive than these for OWL DL.
- **Logical Consistency:** an ontology is considered logical consistent when the ontology conforms to the underlying logical theory of the ontology language. In the case of OWL, this is a variant of description logics. E.g., specifying the range of a property requires the objects of all instantiations of this property to be in this range.
- **User-defined Consistency:** this form of consistency means that users can add their own, additional conditions that must be met in order for the ontology to be considered consistent. E.g., users could require that classes can only be defined as a subclass of at most one other class (i.e. preventing multiple inheritance) in order for the ontology to be considered consistent.

Most research in the field of ontology evolution concerning consistency has been focused on structural consistency. In this paper however, we focus on the problem of logical consistency. We therefore extend our previous work on ontology evolution [10, 11] to support the detection and resolving of logical inconsistencies within OWL DL (and by definition OWL Lite) ontologies. Checking logical consistency can be achieved by running a reasoner on the ontology. To achieve this, most state-of-the-art reasoners have adopted a description logic tableau algorithm as mentioned earlier. Although reasoners can be used to identify unsatisfiable concepts, they provide very little information about which axioms are actually causing the inconsistency. This makes it extremely difficult to offer the ontology engineer solutions to solve the inconsistency.

The contribution of this paper is twofold. First we present an approach that determines the axioms causing a logical inconsistency. We do this by extending the tableau algorithm so that it keeps track of both the transformations performed during the preprocessing step of the algorithm and the axioms (in transformed format) leading to a clash used in the execution of the tableau algorithm itself. Based on this extra information, we have defined an algorithm to determine the axioms causing the inconsistency. The second contribution concerns a set of rules that can be applied by the ontology engineer to actually resolve the inconsistency detected.

The paper is structured as follows. Section 2 describes the process of consistency checking and discusses the principles of a tableau algorithm. Section 3 introduces an algorithm to determine those axioms causing an inconsistency. In section 4, we present the set of rules that can be used by an ontology engineer to resolve the inconsistency detected. Section 5 discusses related work, and finally, Section 6 presents some conclusions.

2   Consistency Checking

The objective of our approach is to verify whether an ontology remains logical consistent after changes have been applied. We differentiate between two possible scenarios based on the common distinction found in literature between TBox (terminological or concept knowledge) and ABox (assertional or instance knowledge):

1. **An axiom was added to the TBox or an existing axiom from the TBox was modified.** To check logical consistency of the ontology, we require two tasks performed sequentially. First, we verify whether the concepts of the TBox itself are still satisfiable (without considering a possible ABox). We refer to this task as the *TBox Consistency Task*. Second, we verify if the ABox remains consistent w.r.t. the modified TBox, called the *ABox Consistency Task*.
2. **An axiom was added to the ABox or an existing axiom from the ABox was modified.** We verify if the ABox remains consistent w.r.t. its TBox (called *ABox Consistency Task*).

Note that we don't take the deletion of an axiom from either the TBox or ABox into account. Because OWL DL is based on a monotonic logic, an ontology can only become inconsistent when new axioms are added or existing ones are changed. An overview of the consistency checking process is shown in Figure 1.

When the user applies changes to the TBox, first the TBox Consistency Task (see ❶) is performed. An inconsistent TBox can be resolved by changing particular axioms of the TBox (see ❷). Note that resolving inconsistencies is an iterative process as

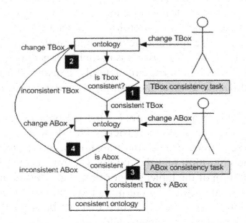

Fig. 1. Overview of consistency checking process.

new changes may introduce new inconsistencies. When the TBox is consistent, the ABox Consistency Task is performed (see ❸). Inconsistencies in the ABox can be resolved either by changing particular axioms of the TBox (see ❷) so that the TBox conforms to the changed ABox, or by changing axioms of the ABox so that the changed ABox forms a valid model for the TBox (see ❹). In Section 3, we present an algorithm to determine which axioms are causing the inconsistency, while in Section 4 we introduce a set of rules that specify which changes can be applied to these axioms to resolve the inconsistency. The checking of TBox and ABox consistency is based on existing OWL reasoners. As the state-of-the-art reasoners are based on a tableau algorithm, we first give a short introduction of the tableau algorithm in the next subsection.

2.1 Tableau Algorithm

We focus in this paper, as already mentioned in the introduction, on the DL variant of OWL. OWL DL conforms to the $\mathcal{SHOIN}(\mathbf{D})$ description logic. The syntax of $\mathcal{SHOIN}(\mathbf{D})$ is summarized in Table 1. We adopt the following convention: A and B are atomic concepts, C and D are complex concepts, R is an abstract role, S is an abstract simple role, T and U are concrete roles, d is a datatype, a, b and c are individuals, and n is a non-negative integer. Based on this syntax, different types of axioms can be formed: concept equivalent axioms $C \equiv D$, concept inclusion axioms $C \sqsubseteq D$, role equivalent axioms $R \equiv S$, role inclusion axioms $R \sqsubseteq S$, transitivity axioms $Trans(R)$, inverse role axioms $R \equiv S^-$, symmetric role axioms $R \equiv R^-$, concept assertions $C(a)$, role assertions $R(a, b)$, individual equalities $a \approx b$ and inequalities $a \not\approx b$. Subsequently, we define an ontology O as a finite set of axioms.

The tableau algorithm allows verifying both the *satisfiability* of a concept C w.r.t. a given TBox i.e. whether C doesn't denote the empty concept, as well as the *consistency* of a given ABox w.r.t. a TBox i.e. whether the assertions in the ABox form a valid model for the axioms defined in the TBox. An ontology O (composed of a TBox $\mathcal{T}$ and ABox $\mathcal{A}$) is considered to be logical consistent if all concepts of the TBox $\mathcal{T}$ are satisfiable and the ABox $\mathcal{A}$ is consistent w.r.t. to this TBox $\mathcal{T}$.

The basic principle of the tableau algorithm used when checking the satisfiability of a concept C is to gradually build a model $\mathcal{I}$ of C, i.e. an interpretation $\mathcal{I}$ in which $C^{\mathcal{I}}$ is not empty. The algorithm tries to build a tree-like model of the concept C by decomposing C using tableau expansion rules. These rules correspond to constructors in the description logic. E.g., $C \sqcap D$ is decomposed into C and D, referring to the fact that if $a \in (C \sqcap D)^{\mathcal{I}}$ then $a \in C^{\mathcal{I}}$ and $a \in D^{\mathcal{I}}$. The tableau algorithm ends when either no more rules are applicable or when a clash occurs. A clash is an obvious contradiction and exists in two forms: $C(a) \Leftrightarrow \neg C(a)$ and $(\leq n\ S) \Leftrightarrow (\geq m\ S)$ where $m > n$. A concept C is considered to be satisfiable when no more rules can be applied and no clashes occurred. The tableau algorithm can be straightforwardly extended to support consistency checking of ABoxes. The same set of expansion rules can be applied to the ABox, requiring that we add inequality assertions $a \not\approx b$ for every pair of distinct individual names.

Important to note is that, although the tableau algorithm allows us to check ontology consistency, the algorithm doesn't provide us any information regarding the axioms causing the inconsistency, neither does it suggest solutions to overcome the inconsistency. In the remainder of this paper we discuss how we can overcome these shortcomings.

Table 1. SHOIN(D) syntax

Syntax	Description	Syntax	Description
$C \sqcap D$	Conjunction	$\leq n\, S$	Atmost restriction
$C \sqcup D$	Disjunction	$\geq n\, S$	Atleast restriction
$\neg C$ or $\neg d$	Negation	$\exists T.d$	Datatype exists
$\exists R.C$	Exists restriction	$\forall T.d$	Datatype value
$\forall R.C$	Value restriction	$\leq n\, T$	Datatype atmost
$\{a, b, c\}$	Individuals	$\geq n\, T$	Datatype atleast

3   Selecting Axioms Causing Inconsistency

In this section we discuss how we extend the tableau algorithm by keeping track of the internal transformations that occur during the preprocessing step and the axioms leading to a clash used in the execution of the algorithm. We therefore introduce *Axiom Transformation Trees* and *Concept Dependency Trees*. Next, we explain how such a Concept Dependency Tree is used to determine the axioms causing the inconsistency. In the last subsection, we explain the overall algorithm and illustrate it with an example.

3.1   Axiom Transformations and Concept Dependencies

To be able to determine the axioms causing an inconsistency, we keep track of both the axiom transformations that occur in the preprocessing step, and the axioms leading to a clash used during algorithm execution. The result of the preprocessing step is a collection of axiom transformations, represented by a set of *Axiom Transformation Trees* (ATT), while the axioms used are represented in a *Concept Dependency Tree* (CDT). We explain the construction of both the ATT and the CDT by means of a simple example. We consider for our example the following TBox $\mathcal{T}$ consisting of the following axioms: $\{PhDStudent \sqsubseteq \neg\forall enrolledIn.\neg Course,\ \exists enrolledIn.Course \sqsubseteq Undergraduate,\ Undergraduate \sqsubseteq \neg PhDStudent,\ PhDStudent\_CS \sqsubseteq PhDStudent\}$.

3.1.1   Axiom Transformation Tree
We give an overview of the different kind of transformations that occur during the preprocessing step of the tableau algorithm:

- **Normalization:** The tableau algorithm expects axioms to be in Negation Normal Form (NNF) i.e. negation occurs only in front of concept names. Axioms can be transformed to NNF using De Morgan's rules and the usual rules for quantifiers. For our example, this means that $PhDStudent \sqsubseteq \neg\forall enrolledIn.\neg Course$ is transformed to $PhDStudent \sqsubseteq \exists enrolledIn.Course$. Other forms of normalization can be treated in a similar way.

- **Internalization:** Another task in the preprocessing step concerns the transformation of axioms to support General Concept Inclusion (GCI) of the form $C \sqsubseteq D$ where C and D are complex concepts. In contrast to subsumption relations between atomic concepts ($A \sqsubseteq B$), which are handled by expansion, this is not possible with GCI. To support GCI, $C \sqsubseteq D$ must first be transformed into $\top \sqsubseteq \neg C \sqcup D$ (meaning that any individual must belong to $\neg C \sqcup D$). In our example, $\exists enrolledIn.Course \sqsubseteq Undergraduate$ is transformed to $\top \sqsubseteq Undergraduate \sqcup \forall enrolledIn.\neg Course$.
- **Absorption:** The problem with GCI axioms is that they are time-expensive to reason with due to the high-degree of non-determinism that they introduce [1]. They may degrade the performance of the tableau algorithm to the extent that it becomes in practice non-terminating. The solution of this problem is to eliminate GCI axioms whenever possible. This is done by a technique called absorption that tries to absorb GCI axioms into primitive axiom definitions.
- **Axiom composition:** different axioms can be composed together into one axiom. E.g., the axioms $C \sqsubseteq A$ and $C \sqsubseteq B$ can be transformed to $C \sqsubseteq A \sqcap B$.

We introduce the notion of an *Axiom Transformation Tree* (ATT) to keep track of the transformations that occur during the preprocessing step i.e. an ATT stores the step-by-step transformation of the original axiom (as defined by the ontology engineer) to their transformed form. When later on the tableau algorithm ends with a clash, the ATTs can be used to retrieve the original axioms by following the inverse transformations from the axioms causing the clash (as found by the tableau algorithm) to the original ones. We define an Axiom Transformation Tree as follows:

Definition (ATT). An Axiom Transformation Tree, notation ATT, is a tree structure starting from one or more axioms ϕ_1, ..., ϕ_n, and ending with a transformed axiom ϕ'. Each branch of the tree represents a transformation and is accordingly labeled as follows:

- $\rightarrow_{NRM}$: transformation into normal form;
- $\rightarrow_{ABS}$: absorption of axioms into primitive axiom definitions;
- $\rightarrow_{GCI}$:   transformation of General Concept Inclusion axioms;
- $\rightarrow_{CMP}$: composition of axioms.

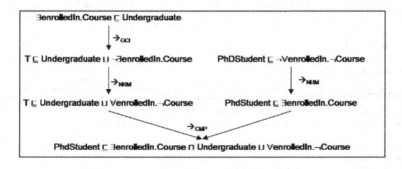

Fig. 2. An ATT for the given example

Figure 2 shows the ATT for the axioms *∃enrolledIn.Course* ⊑ *Undergraduate* and *PhDStudent* ⊑ ¬*∀enrolledIn.¬Course* in our example.

3.1.2 Concept Dependency Tree

The tableau algorithm reasons with the transformed set of axioms resulting from the preprocessing step. In our example this means the following set: {*PhDStudent* ⊑ *∃enrolledIn.Course* ⊓ (*Undergraduate* ⊔ *∀enrolledIn.¬Course*), *Undergraduate* ⊑ ¬*PhDStudent* ⊓ (*Undergraduate* ⊔ *∀enrolledIn.¬Course*), *PhDStudent_CS* ⊑ *PhDStudent* ⊓ (*Undergraduate* ⊔ *∀enrolledIn.¬Course*)}. To test the satisfiability of a concept *C*, the set of tableau rules are applied to expand this concept until either a clash occurs or no more rules are applicable. We now want to store explicitly the different axioms that are used during the tableau reasoning process leading to a clash. We therefore introduce a *Concept Dependency Tree* (CDT):

Definition (CDT). We define a Concept Dependency Tree for a given concept *C*, notation CDT(*C*), as an n-ary tree where $N_1, ..., N_n$ are nodes of the tree and a *child*(N_i,N_j) relation exists to represent an edge between two nodes in the tree. Furthermore, we define *parent* as the inverse relation of *child*, and *child** and *parent** as the transitive counterparts of respectively *child* and *parent*. A node N_i is a tuple of the form ⟨φ, **RA**⟩ where φ is a concept axiom and **RA** is a set of role axioms and assertions.

To construct a CDT, we keep track, for each node added to the tableau, of the path of axioms leading to the addition of that node. When a clash is found between two nodes, the paths of axioms associated with both nodes are used to construct the CDT.

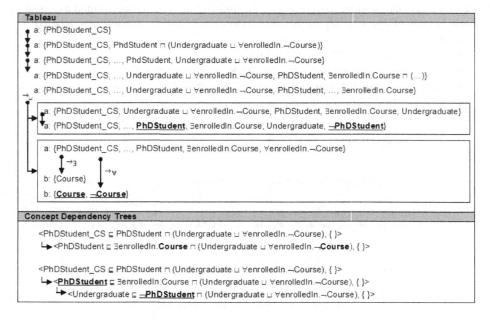

Fig. 3. Example tableau algorithm result and associated CDTs

For each concept axiom ϕ represented in a path, we add a new node N to the CDT (unless such a node already exists) as child of the previous node (if any) so that N = ⟨ϕ, { }⟩. When we encounter a role axiom or assertion ψ, we add it to the **RA** set of the current node N of the CDT so that ψ ∈ **RA** where N = ⟨ϕ, **RA**⟩. Note that cyclic axioms (e.g., $C ⊑ ∀R.C$) don't lead to the construction of an infinite CDT, as reasoners normally include some sort of cycle checking mechanism, such as blocking.

The result of the tableau algorithm testing the satisfiability of the concept *PhDStudent_CS* in our example is shown in Figure 3 at the top, while the CDTs are shown below. The tableau algorithm terminates with a clash between *PhDStudent*(a) ⟺ ¬*PhDStudent*(a) and between *Course*(a) ⟺ ¬*Course*(a). Note that non-deterministic branches in the tableau result in more than one CDT i.e. one for each non-deterministic branch. The CDTs contain the different axioms that lead from the concept examined (in our example *PhDStudent_CS*) to the cause of the inconsistency (the concepts involved in the clash).

3.2 Interpretation of Concept Dependency Trees

We use the CDTs to determine the axioms causing the inconsistency. The interpretation of a CDT differs for the TBox and ABox consistency task. In this section, we will discuss both interpretations.

3.2.1 TBox Consistency Task
The set of axioms of a CDT(C) can be seen as a MUPS (Minimal Unsatisfiability Preserving Sub-TBox) of the unsatisfiable concept C, i.e. the smallest set of axioms responsible for the unsatisfiable concept C [13]. Although removing one of the axioms of the CDT will resolve, by definition of a MUPS, the unsatisfiability of C, we consider it in general bad practice to take all axioms of a CDT into consideration to resolve inconsistencies. We will explain this by means of an example. Assume the following TBox: {$C ⊑ B$, $B ≡ ∃R.D$, $D ⊑ E$, $E ⊑ A ⊓ F$, $F ⊑ ¬A$}. Checking the satisfiability of C will reveal that C is unsatisfiable due to a clash between A(b) ⟺ ¬A(b). The left side of Figure 4 shows the tableau, the right side the associated CDT.

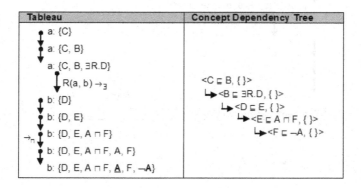

Fig. 4. Example of a CDT in the TBox Consistency Task

Although removing for example the axiom $C \sqsubseteq B$ resolves the unsatisfiability of C, this change fails to address the true cause of the unsatisfiability as the overall TBox remains inconsistent. A concept is considered unsatisfiable if a clash is found in two deterministic branches of the tableau. This implies that the axioms containing the concepts involved in the clash must have a common parent in the CDT. Otherwise, no clash could have occurred between both concepts. Therefore, only the first common parent of these axioms and the axioms along the paths from this first common parent to the clashes are directly involved in the unsatisfiability problem. Changing axioms leading to this common parent (e.g. $C \sqsubseteq B$ or $D \sqsubseteq E$) may resolve the unsatisfiability of the concept under investigation, but doesn't tackle the true cause. We therefore introduce the notion of a *FirstCommonParent* for the CDT, and define it as follows:

Definition (FirstCommonParent). We define ϕ_c as the first common parent for two axioms ϕ_1 and ϕ_2, notation *FirstCommonParent*(ϕ_c, ϕ_1, ϕ_2), iff $\exists N_c \in$ CDT (*parent**(N_c, N_1) $\land$ *parent**(N_c, N_2) $\land$ ¬$\exists N_3$ (*parent**(N_3, N_1) $\land$ *parent**(N_3, N_2) $\land$ *child**(N_3, N_c) $\land$ $N_3 \neq N_c$)) where $N_c = \langle \phi c, \mathbf{RA} \rangle$, $N_1 = \langle \phi_1, \mathbf{RA'} \rangle$ and $N_2 = \langle \phi_2, \mathbf{RA''} \rangle$.

In our example, the axiom $E \sqsubseteq A \sqcap F$ is the first common parent for the axioms containing the concepts involved in the clash. We therefore restrict the set of axioms causing the inconsistency to the following set: $\{ E \sqsubseteq A \sqcap F, F \sqsubseteq \neg A \}$.

3.2.2 ABox Consistency Task

The interpretation of the CDT differs for the ABox consistency task from the TBox consistency task. Consider the example with TBox: $\{ C \sqsubseteq B, B \equiv \forall R.D, E \sqsubseteq A, D \sqsubseteq \neg A \}$ and ABox: $\{ C(a), E(b) \}$. Note that the TBox doesn't contain any unsatisfiable concepts (as we assume that the TBox consistency task was performed previously).

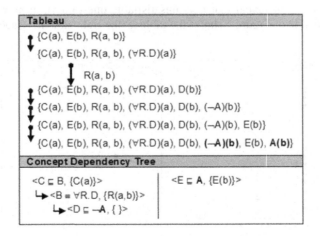

Fig. 5. Example of CDTs in the ABox consistency task

Adding the assertion $R(a, b)$ to the ABox, will result in an inconsistent ABox as a clash occurs between $A(b) \Leftrightarrow \neg A(b)$. At the top of Figure 5 the tableau is shown and at the bottom the CDTs.

Checking the ABox consistency for our example results in two CDTs, one for each individual checked (i.e., a and b). The axioms causing the inconsistency are the axioms resulting from both CDTs, together with axioms of the ABox used during the reasoning process (e.g., $R(a, b)$ as it allowed to trigger the $\rightarrow_\forall$ expansion rule). Note that we only consider axioms present in the original ABox i.e. no individuals added by the tableau algorithm to direct reasoning.

3.3 Axiom Selection

In this section, we give an overview of the overall algorithm to determine the axioms causing an inconsistency based on the interpretations of the CDT given in the previous section. Note that the axioms that will be considered differ for the TBox and ABox consistency task. The algorithm takes as input the clash information, CDTs and ATTs and outputs a set of axioms causing the inconsistency. Before explaining the complete algorithm, we fist need to address the following issues:

- **Mark axioms.** A complete axiom is not necessarily the cause of an inconsistency; instead only parts of the axiom may be the cause. Parts of axioms are causing an inconsistency either because they are the direct cause of the inconsistency, or because they are leading to a concept directly causing the inconsistency. The algorithm therefore marks those parts of the axioms. In order to do so, we introduce the *markAllParents* function that marks all parent nodes of the nodes containing a concept involved in the clash. The pseudo-code of the function is given below:

```
markAllParents(N):
    if not rootNode(N) then
        φ = getConceptAxiom(N);
        C_φ = getLeftPart(φ);
        N_parent = getParentNode(N);
        φ_parent = getConceptAxiom(N_parent);
        mark(def_φ, φ_parent);
        call markAllParents(N_parent)
    end if
```

- **Non-inconsistency-revealing clashes.** Clashes found between transformed axioms by the tableau algorithm, may not always indicate conflicting concepts in the original axioms as defined by the ontology engineer. Figure 3 (see Section 3.1.2) illustrates this. The clash $Course(b) \Leftrightarrow \neg Course(b)$ seems to reveal a contradiction , but when we transform the axioms back to their original form (i.e., *PhDStudent* ⊑ ¬∀*enrolledIn.*__¬*Course*__ and ∃*enrolledIn.*__*Course*__ ⊑ *Undergraduate*) it is clear that they both refer to the same concept ∃*enrolledIn.Course* (although one is in NNF while the other is not). The clash found guided the tableau algorithm, rather than revealing an actual inconsistency.

The structure of the overall algorithm is as follows:

1. For each clash $C(a) \Leftrightarrow D(a)$, lookup the concepts C and D in the leaf nodes of the associated CDTs, and mark these concepts.
2. For each marked node N, mark all parent nodes using the *markAllParents*(N) function.
3. Depending on the task performed (TBox or ABox consistency task) select for each CDT the axioms as described in Section 3.2. This results for each CDT in a set **S** containing the selected axioms.
4. For each set **S**, transform all axioms $\phi \in$ **S** into their original form by applying the inverse transformations of the correct ATT.
5. The union of all sets **S** is the desired set of axioms.

Applying this algorithm to the example introduced in Section 3.1 results in the following set **S**. Underlined concepts are the concepts marked by the algorithm, underlined and bold concepts are the concepts involved in the consistency-revealing clash.
S = {***PhDStudent*** $\sqsubseteq \neg\forall enrolledIn.\neg\underline{Course}$, $\exists enrolledIn.\underline{Course} \sqsubseteq \underline{Undergraduate}$, $\underline{Undergraduate} \sqsubseteq \neg\textbf{\underline{PhDStudent}}$};

4 Resolving Inconsistencies

When an ontology is logical inconsistent this is because the axioms of the ontology are too restrictive as axioms are contradicting each other. To resolve the inconsistency, the restrictions imposed by the axioms should be weakened. In the previous section (see Section 3.3), we have defined an algorithm to determine the set of axioms causing the inconsistency. Changing one of these selected axioms will resolve the detected inconsistency. In the remainder of this section, we present a collection of rules that guides the ontology engineer towards a solution. A rule either calls another rule or applies a change to an axiom. Note that it remains the responsibility of the ontology engineer to decide which axiom he wants to change from the set provided by the approach.

Before we define the different rules, we first introduce the notion of class- and property hierarchy. We call $\mathcal{H}_c$ the class hierarchy of all classes present in the set **S** so that if $(C, D) \in \mathcal{H}_c$ then $C \sqsubseteq D$, and $\mathcal{H}_p$ the property hierarchy of all properties present in the set **S** so that if $(R, S) \in \mathcal{H}_p$ then $R \sqsubseteq S$. Note that these hierarchies don't include classes or properties not included in **S**. Furthermore, we define ψ_t as the top of a hierarchy $\mathcal{H}$ for a concept ψ, notation $top(\psi_t, \psi, \mathcal{H})$, iff $\psi_t \sqsubseteq \psi \wedge \neg\exists\omega \in$ **S**: $\omega \sqsubseteq \psi_t$. Analogous, we define ψ_l as the leaf of a hierarchy $\mathcal{H}$ for a concept ψ, notation $leaf(\psi_l, \psi, \mathcal{H})$, iff $\psi \sqsubseteq \psi_l \wedge \neg\exists\omega \in$ **S**: $\psi_l \sqsubseteq \omega$.

In the remainder of this section, we present a set of rules that guide the ontology engineer to a solution for the detected inconsistency. Note that we don't list the complete set of rules due to space restrictions. First, we define a set of rules that handle the different types of axioms. Secondly, we define the necessary rules to weaken or strengthen the different types of concepts. Note that axioms can always be weakened by removing the axiom. We therefore won't mention this option explicitly in the rules below. The rules for weakening axioms are given below:

- A concept definition $C \equiv D$ can be weakened either by removing the axiom or by weakening C or D (assuming $C \equiv D$ resulted from $C \sqsubseteq D$ in the CDT):

  (4.1) $weaken(C \equiv D) \Longrightarrow strengthen(C)$

  (4.2) $weaken(C \equiv D) \Longrightarrow weaken(D)$

- A concept inclusion axiom $C \sqsubseteq D$ can be weakened by removing the axiom, strengthening C or weakening D. The same rule applies for role inclusion axioms:

  (4.3) $weaken(C \sqsubseteq D) \Longrightarrow strengthen(C)$

  (4.4) $weaken(C \sqsubseteq D) \Longrightarrow weaken(D)$

- A concept assertion $C(a)$ can be weakened by either removing the axiom or by replacing C with a superclass:

  (4.5) $weaken(C(a)) \Longrightarrow change(C(a), D(a))$ where $X \sqsubseteq D$ and $leaf(X, C, \mathcal{H}_c)$

- A role assertion $R(a, b)$ can be weakened by either removing the axiom or by replacing R with a super-property:

  (4.6) $weaken(R(a, b)) \Longrightarrow change(R(a, b), S(a, b))$ where $X \sqsubseteq S$ and $leaf(X, R, \mathcal{H}_p)$

The second part of rules deal with the weakening and strengthening of concepts:

- A conjunction relation $C \sqcap D$ can be weakened (strengthened) by weakening (strengthening) either C or D. The rules for weakening are given below; the rules for strengthening are analogous:

  (4.7) IF $marked(C)$: $weaken(C \sqcap D) \Longrightarrow weaken(C)$

  (4.8) IF $marked(D)$: $weaken(C \sqcap D) \Longrightarrow weaken(D)$

  (4.9) IF $marked(C) \wedge marked(D)$: $weaken(C \sqcap D) \Longrightarrow weaken(C) \vee weaken(D)$

- A disjunction relation $C \sqcup D$ can be weakened (strengthened) by weakening (strengthening) C, D, or both C and D. The rules for weakening are given below; the rules for strengthening are analog:

  (4.10) IF $marked(C)$: $weaken(C \sqcup D) \Longrightarrow weaken(C)$

  (4.11) IF $marked(D)$: $weaken(C \sqcup D) \Longrightarrow weaken(D)$

  (4.12) IF $marked(C) \wedge marked(D)$: $weaken(C \sqcup D) \Longrightarrow weaken(C) \vee weaken(D)$

- An existential quantification $\exists R.C$ can be weakened and strengthened in two manners as it represents both a cardinality restriction ("at least one") and a value restriction. To weaken $\exists R.C$, we either remove $\exists R.C$ if it concerns a cardinality restriction violation, or we weaken C if it concerns a value restriction violation. To strengthen $\exists R.C$, we either add a minimum cardinality restriction if it concerns a cardinality restriction violation, or we strengthen C if it concerns a value restriction violation:

  (4.13) IF $marked(C)$: $weaken(\exists R.C) \Longrightarrow weaken(C)$

  (4.14) IF $marked(R)$: $strengthen(\exists R.C) \Longrightarrow add((\geq 2\ R))$

  (4.15) IF $marked(C)$: $strengthen(\exists R.C) \Longrightarrow strengthen(C)$

- A universal quantification $\forall R.C$ can be weakened (strengthened) by weakening (strengthening) C. The rule for weakening is given below; the rule for strengthening is analogous:

  (4.16) IF $weaken(\forall R.C) \Longrightarrow weaken(C)$

- A maximum cardinality restriction $(\leq n\ R)$ can be weakened either by raising n or by removing the cardinality restriction altogether. To strengthen $(\leq n\ R)$, we can lower n:

(4.17) $weaken((\leq n\ R)) \Longrightarrow changeCardinalityRestriction(R, m)$ where m $\geq$ 1
     if $(\leq n\ R)$ conflicts with $\exists R.C$, or m $\geq \alpha$ if $(\leq n\ R)$ conflicts with $(\geq \alpha\ R)$
(4.18) $weaken((\leq n\ R)) \Longrightarrow remove((\leq n\ R))$
(4.19) $strengthen((\leq n\ R)) \Longrightarrow changeCardinalityRestriction(R, m)$ where m = 0
     if $(\leq n\ R)$ conflicts with $\exists R.C$, or m $\leq \alpha$ if $(\leq n\ R)$ conflicts with $(\geq \alpha\ R)$

- A minimum cardinality restriction $(\geq n\ R)$ can be weakened by either lowering n or by removing the cardinality restriction altogether. To strengthen $(\geq n\ R)$, we can raise n:

(4.20) $weaken((\geq n\ R)) \Longrightarrow changeCardinalityRestriction(R, m)$ where m $\leq \alpha$
     if $(\geq n\ R)$ conflicts with $(\leq \alpha\ R)$
(4.21) $weaken((\geq n\ R)) \Longrightarrow remove((\leq n\ R))$
(4.22) $strengthen((\geq n\ R)) \Longrightarrow changeCardinalityRestriction(R, m)$ where m $\geq \alpha$
     if $(\geq n\ R)$ conflicts with $(\leq \alpha\ R)$

- A negation $\neg C$ is weakened by either removing $\neg C$ or by strengthening C. To strengthen $\neg C$, we need to weaken C:

(4.23) $weaken(\neg C) \Longrightarrow strengthen(C)$
(4.24) $strengthen(\neg C) \Longrightarrow weaken(C)$

- A concept A is weakened either by removing the concept or by replacing it with a superclass of A. To strengthen an atom concept A, we replace it with a subclass of A. When no (appropriate) sub- or superclass exists, we can create one first:

(4.25) $weaken(A) \Longrightarrow change(A, B)$ where $X \sqsubseteq B$ and $leaf(X, A, \mathcal{H}_c)$
(4.26) $strengthen(A) \Longrightarrow change(A, B)$ where $B \sqsubseteq X$ and $top(X, A, \mathcal{H}_c)$

We conclude this section with our example. The selection of axioms consisted of the following axioms: ***PhDStudent*** $\sqsubseteq$ *¬∀enrolledIn.¬Course*, *∃enrolledIn.Course* $\sqsubseteq$ *Undergraduate*, *Undergraduate* $\sqsubseteq$ ***¬PhDStudent***. If, for example, the ontology engineer beliefs that the axiom *∃enrolledIn.Course* $\sqsubseteq$ *Undergraduate* doesn't reflect the real world situation, he could for example change the axiom to *∃enrolledIn.Course* $\sqsubseteq$ *Student*, assuming *Undergraduate* $\sqsubseteq$ *Student*, by following the rules 4.4 and 4.25.

5 Related Work

Change management has been a long-term research interest. Noteworthy in the context of this paper is certainly the work on database schema evolution [13] and maintenance of knowledge-based systems [7]. When considering the problem of ontology evolution, only few approaches have been proposed. [15] defines the process of ontology evolution as the timely adaptation of an ontology to the arisen changes and the consistent propagation of these changes to depending artifacts. In [16], the authors propose a possible ontology evolution framework. They introduce a change representation and discuss the semantics of change for the KAON ontology language. A similar approach has been taken by [6] for the OWL language. The authors of [11][12] propose another approach for the OWL language based on the use of a version log to represent evolution. They define changes in terms of temporal queries on this version log.

On the topic of dealing with consistency maintenance for evolving ontologies, only very little research has been done. [4] presents an approach to localize an inconsistency based on the notion of a minimal inconsistent sub-ontology. The notion of a minimal inconsistent sub-ontology is very similar to the concept of a MUPS introduced by [14]. Although removing one axiom from the minimal inconsistent sub-ontology will resolve an unsatisfiable concept, it can not be guaranteed that this will solve the true cause of the inconsistency (as discussed in this paper). Furthermore, the approach doesn't marking indicating parts of axioms as cause of the inconsistency, but rather treats axioms as a whole.

Some related work has been carried out in explaining inconsistencies in OWL ontologies. The authors of [2] present a Symptom Ontology that aims to serve as a common language for identifying and describing semantic errors and warnings. The Symptom Ontology doesn't identify the cause of the ontology nor does it offer possible solutions to resolve an inconsistency.

Another interesting research area is the field of ontology debugging [10][18]. Their aim is to provide the ontology engineer with a more comprehensive explanation of the inconsistency than is generally provided by 'standard' ontology reasoners. We distinguish two types of approaches: black-box versus glass-box techniques. The first treats the reasoner as a 'black box' and uses standard inferences to locate the source of the inconsistency. The latter modifies the internals of the reasoner to reveal the cause of the problem. While black-box techniques don't add an overhead to the reasoner, more precise results can be obtained using a glass-box technique. Therefore, glass-box techniques are considered a better candidate in the context of ontology evolution. The authors of [9] discuss a glass-box approach which offers the users information about the clash found and selects the axioms causing the inconsistency (similar to a MUPS). The disadvantage of a MUPS is that it doesn't necessarily pinpoints the true cause of the inconsistency. Furthermore, the approach doesn't offer solutions to resolve the detected problem.

6 Conclusion

Ontologies are in general not static, but do evolve over time. An important aspect for evolving ontologies is that they evolve from one consistent state into another consistent state. Checking whether an ontology is consistent can be achieved by means of a reasoner. The problem is that it is in general extremely challenging for an ontology engineer to determine the cause of an inconsistency and possible solutions for the problem based on the output of a reasoner. We therefore presented an algorithm to select the axioms causing the inconsistency. Furthermore, we have presented a set of rules that ontology engineers can use to change the selected axioms to overcome the detected inconsistency.

References

1. Baader, F., Calvanese, D., McGuinness, D., Nardi, D., Patel-Schneider, P.: The description logic handbook: theory, implementation and applications. Cambridge University Press. ISBN 0-521-78176-0 (2003)
2. Baclawski, K., Matheus, C., Kokar, M., Letkowski, J., Kogut, P.: Towards a symptom ontology for semantic web applications. In Proceedings of 3rd International Semantic Web Conference (ISWC 2004), Hiroshima, Japan (2004) 650-667

3. Berners Lee, T., Hendler, J., Lassila, O.: The semantic web: A new form of web content that is meaningful to computers will unleash a revolution of new possibilities. Scientific American (2001) 5(1)
4. Haase, P., Stojanovic, L.: Consistent evolution of OWL ontologies. Asunción Gómez-Pérez, Jérôme Euzenat (Eds.), The Semantic Web: Research and Applications, Second European Semantic Web Conference (ESWC 2005), Lecture Notes in Computer Science 3532 Springer 2005, ISBN 3-540-26124-9, Heraklion, Crete, Greece (2005) 182-197
5. Horrocks, I.: The fact system. In Proceedings of Automated Reasoning with Analytic Tableaux and Related Methods: International Conference Tableaux'98, Springer-Verlag (1998) 307-312
6. Klein, M.: Change Management for Distributed Ontologies. PhD Thesis (2004)
7. Menzies, T.: Knowledge maintenance: the state of the art, The Knowledge Engineering Review (1999) 14(1) 1-46
8. Moller, R., Haarslev, V.: Racer system description. In Proceedings of the International Joint Conference on Automated Reasoning (IJCAR 2001), Siena, Italy (2001)
9. Parsia, B., Sirin, E.: Pellet: An OWL DL reasoner. In Ralf Moller Volker Haaslev (Eds.), Proceedings of the International Workshop on Description Logics (DL2004) (2004)
10. Parsia, B., Sirin, E., Kalyanpur, A.: Debugging OWL ontologies. In Proceedings of the 14th International World Wide Web Conference (WWW2005), Chiba, Japan (2005)
11. Plessers, P., De Troyer, O., Casteleyn, S.: Event-based modeling of evolution for semantic-driven systems. In Proceedings of the 17th Conference on Advanced Information Systems Engineering (CAiSE'05), Publ. Springer-Verlag, Porto, Portugal (2005)
12. Plessers, P., De Troyer, O.: Ontology change detection using a version log, In Proceedings of the 4th International Semantic Web Conference, Eds. Yolanda Gil, Enrico Motta, V.Richard Benjamins, Mark A. Musen, Publ. Springer-Verlag, ISBN 978-3-540-29754-3, Galway, Ireland (2005) 578-592
13. Roddick, J.F.: A survey of schema versioning issues for database systems, Information and Software Technology (1995) 37(7): 383-393.
14. Schlobach, S., Cornet, R.: Non-standard reasoning services for the debugging of description logic terminologies. In Proceedings of IJCAI 2003 (2003)
15. Stojanovic, L., Maedche, A., Motik, B., Stojanovic, N.: Userdriven Ontology Evolution Management. In Proceeding of the 13th European Conference on Knowledge Engineering and Knowledge Management EKAW, Madrid, Spain (2002)
16. Stojanovic, L.: Methods and Tools for Ontology Evolution. Phd Thesis (2004)
17. Tallis, M., Gil, Y.: Designing scripts to guide users in modifying knowledge-based systems. In Proceedings of the 14th National Conference on Artificial Intelligence (AAAI/IAAI 1999), Orlando, Florida, USA (1999) 242-249
18. Wang, H., Horridge, M., Rector, A., Drummond, N., Seidenberg, J.: Debugging OWL-DL ontologies: A heuristic approach. In Proceedings of the 4th International Semantic Web Conference, Eds. Yolanda Gil, Enrico Motta, V.Richard Benjamins, Mark A. Musen, Publ. Springer-Verlag, ISBN 978-3-540-29754-3, Galway, Ireland (2005)

Automatic Extraction of Hierarchical Relations from Text

Ting Wang[1,2], Yaoyong Li[1], Kalina Bontcheva[1],
Hamish Cunningham[1], and Ji Wang[2]

[1] Department of Computer Science, University of Sheffield, Sheffield, S1 4DP, UK
{T.Wang, Y.Li, K.Bontcheva, H.Cunningham}@dcs.shef.ac.uk
[2] Department of Computer, National University of Defense Technology, Changsha,
Hunan, 410073, P.R. China
{tingwang, jiwang}@nudt.edu.cn

Abstract. Automatic extraction of semantic relationships between entity instances in an ontology is useful for attaching richer semantic metadata to documents. In this paper we propose an SVM based approach to hierarchical relation extraction, using features derived automatically from a number of GATE-based open-source language processing tools. In comparison to the previous works, we use several new features including part of speech tag, entity subtype, entity class, entity role, semantic representation of sentence and WordNet synonym set. The impact of the features on the performance is investigated, as is the impact of the relation classification hierarchy. The results show there is a trade-off among these factors for relation extraction and the features containing more information such as semantic ones can improve the performance of the ontological relation extraction task.

1 Introduction

Information Extraction (IE) [4] is a process which takes unseen texts as input and produces fixed-format, unambiguous data as output. It involves processing text to identify selected information, such as particular named entity or relations among them from text documents. Named entities include people, organizations, locations and so on, while relations typically include physical relations (located, near, part-whole, etc.), personal or social relations(business, family, etc.), and membership (employ-staff, member-of-group, etc.).

Until recently, research has focused primarily on use of IE for populating ontologies with concept instances (e.g. [9, 16]). However, in addition to this, many ontology-based applications require methods for automatic discovery of properties and relations between instances. Semantic relations provide richer metadata connecting documents to ontologies and enable more sophisticated semantic search and knowledge access.

One barrier to applying relation extraction in ontology-based applications comes from the difficulty of adapting the system to new domains. In order to overcome this problem, recent research has advocated the use of Machine Learning (ML) techniques for IE. A number of ML approaches have been used for

Y. Sure and J. Domingue (Eds.): ESWC 2006, LNCS 4011, pp. 215–229, 2006.

relation extraction, e.g. Hidden Markov Models (HMM) [7], Conditional Random Fields (CRF) [12], Maximum Entropy Models (MEM) [11]. and Support Vector Machines (SVM) [19]. The experimental results in [19] showed that the SVM outperformed the MEM on the ACE2003 relation extraction data[1].

Zelenko et al [18] proposed extracting relations by computing kernel functions between shallow parse trees. Kernels have been defined over shallow parse representations of text and have been used in conjunction with SVM learning algorithms for extracting person-affiliation and organization-location relations. Culotta et al [5] extended this work to estimate kernel functions between augmented dependency trees.

Zhou et al [19] further introduced diverse lexical, syntactic and semantic knowledge in feature-based relation extraction using SVM. The feature system covers word, entity type, overlap, base phrase chunking, dependency tree and parse tree, together with relation-specific semantic resources, such as country name list, personal relative trigger word list. Their results show that the feature-based approach outperforms tree kernel-based approaches, achieving 55.5% F-measure in relation detection and classification on the ACE2003 training data.

Motivated by the above work, we use the SVM as well and apply a diverse set of Natural Language Processing (NLP) tools to derive features for relation extraction. In particular, several new features are introduced, such as part-of-speech (POS) tags, entity subtype, entity class, entity role, semantic representation of sentences and WordNet synonym set.

In the rest of the paper, we first describe the ACE2004 entity and relation type hierarchy from an ontological perspective (Section 2). Then we give a brief introduction of SVM used as the classifier for relation extraction (Section 3) and explain an extensive set of features used in our experiments (Section 4). Section 5 presents and discusses a series of experiments that investigate the impact of the different features and the classification hierarchy. Finally, we summarise the work and discuss some future directions.

2 The ACE Entity and Relation Hierarchies

Relation extraction from text aims to detect and classify semantic relations between entities according to a predefined entity and relation type system or an ontology. The Automatic Content Extraction (ACE) programme [1] defines this task as Relation Detection and Characterization (RDC). RDC uses the results of named entity recognition, which detects and classifies entities according to a predefined entity type system.

---

[1] SVM has achieved state of the art results in many NLP tasks such as text classification, part of speech tagging and information extraction. This is mainly because, on the one hand, the SVM is an optimal classifier with maximal margin in feature space; on the other hand, NLP tasks typically represent instances by very high dimensional but very sparse feature vectors, resulting in positive and negative examples being distributed into two distinctly different areas of the feature space. As we use a very high dimensional and very sparse feature vector for relation extraction, it can be expected that SVM will have similarly good performance.

In contrast to earlier ACE evaluations, ACE2004 introduced a type and sub-type hierarchy for both entity and relations, an important step towards ontology-based IE. Hence, we evaluate our method on the corpus for learning relation hierarchy

2.1   The ACE2004 Entity Hierarchy

Entities are categorized in a two level hierarchy, consisting of 7 types and 44 subtypes. The entity type includes Person, Organisation, Facility, Location and Geo-political Entity (GPE). Subtype refers to sub-concept of entity concept. For example, The entity type Organisation was divided into the subtypes such as Government, Commercial and Educational. For details see [2].

Each entity has been assigned a class which describes the kind of reference the entity makes to something in the world. The class can be one of four values: Negatively Quantified(NEG), Specific Referential(SPC), Generic Referential(GEN), Under-specified Referential(USP). The occurrence of each entity in the dataset is called an entity mention, which can be one of the following: Names(NAM) , Quantified Nominal Constructions(NOM), Pronouns(PRO), Pre-modifier(PRE).

In addition, GPEs are regarded as composite entities comprising of population, government, physical location, and nation (or province, state, county, city, etc.). Consequently, each GPE mention in the text has a mention role which indicates which of these four aspects is being referred to in the given context: of that mention invokes: Person(PER), Organization(ORG), Location(LOC), and GPE.

2.2   The ACE2004 Relation Hierarchy

In an ontology, the concepts are not only organised in a taxonomy representing IS-A relations, but also linked together by semantic relations such as Part-Whole, Subsidiary, LocatedIn, etc. ACE2004 defines a hierarchy of relations with 7 top types and 22 sub-types, shown in Table 1 [3]. There are 6 symmetric relations (marked with star in table) and the remaining ones are asymmetric relations.

Table 1. ACE2004 relation types and subtypes

Type	Subtype
Physical (PHYS)	Located, Near*, Part-Whole
Personal/Social (PER-SOC)	Business*, Family*, Other*
Employment/Membership/ Subsidiary (EMP-ORG)	Employ-Exec, Employ-Staff, Employ-Undetermined, Member-of-Group, Subsidiary, Partner*, Other*
Agent-Artifact (ART)	User/Owner, Inventor/Manufacturer, Other
PER/ORG Affiliation (OTHER-AFF)	Ethnic, Ideology, Other
GPE Affiliation (GPE-AFF)	Citizen/Resident, Based-In, Other
Discourse (DISC)	(none)

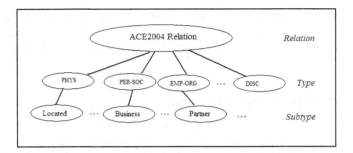

Fig. 1. The hierarchy of the ACE2004 relation types and subtypes

This relation type and subtype hierarchy can also be described as a three levels tree (see Fig 1). In the experiments reported next, we use the ACE2004 corpus to evaluate ontological relation extraction.

3   Using SVM for Relation Extraction

SVM is one of the most successful ML methods, which has achieved the state-of-the-art performances for many classification problems. For example, our experiments in [13] showed that the SVM obtained top results on several IE benchmarking corpora.

As SVM were originally designed for binary classification and relation extraction can be reduced into a multi-class classification problem, we have to extend the SVM for multi-class classification. There exists two approaches to use the SVM for multi-class problem [10]: (i) constructing and combining several SVM binary classifiers via either the one-against-all method or the one-against-one method; (ii) learning a multi-class SVM classifier directly for the multi-class problem. The comparison in [10] shows that one-against-one method is the best in both training time and performance, and suggests that one-against-one method may be more suitable for practical use on large problems than other approaches. Therefore we used the one-against-one method in the experiments (see Section 5.1 for more details).

For a k-class classification task, the one-against-one method constructs $k(k-1)/2$ classifiers where each one is trained on data from two classes, while the one-against-all method learns k classifier each of which is used to separate one class from all others. Although one-against-one method has to train more classifiers than one-against-all does (on k classifiers), each training data is much smaller, resulting into less total training time than the one-against-all method. We used the *Max Wins* voting strategy to predicate the class: apply every classifier to instance $\mathbf{x}$; if one classifier says $\mathbf{x}$ is in the i-th class, then the vote for the i-th class is incremented by one; in the end $\mathbf{x}$ is classified as the class with the largest number of votes.

We built SVM models for detecting the relations, predicting the type and subtype of relations between every pair of entity mentions within the same sentence. As defined in the ACE evaluation, we only model explicit relations rather than implicit ones. For example, the sentence

$$Texas\ has\ many\ cars. \tag{1}$$

explicitly expresses a ART.User/Owner relation between the two entity mentions Texas and many cars. What we need to do is to detect the relation and its type and subtype based on the context information within this sentence. Such context information is usually expressed as a vector consisting of values for some specific attributes, which is called features. Choosing the right features is key to successful application of ML technology.

4   Features for Relation Extraction

Using NLP to derive ML features has been shown to benefit IE results [13]. Features which have been used for relation extractions include word, entity type, mention level, overlap, chunks, syntactic parse trees, and dependency relations [7, 11, 18, 19].

Based on the previous works, we developed a set of features for semantic relation extraction, many of which are adopted from [19]. Moreover, we introduce some new features such as POS tags, entity subtype and class features, entity mention role feature, and several general semantic features. Zhou et al in [19] have designed some relation-specific semantic features, for example, some important trigger words list have been collected from WordNet [15] in order to differentiate the six personal social relation subtypes. However, these lists are too specific to the dataset to be applicable for general purpose relation extraction. Therefore in our method, we introduce instead a set of more general semantic features produced by a semantic analyser and WordNet.

BuChart (which has been renamed to SUPPLE) is a bottom-up parser that constructs syntax trees and logical forms for English sentences [8]. One of its significant characteristics is that it can produce a semantic representation of sentences - called simplified quasilogical form (SQLF). Previously, one of the limitations in applying general semantic information in IE is the relative lack of robustness of semantic analyser. However, BuChart is a general purpose parser that can still produce partial syntactic and semantic results for fragments even when the full sentential parses cannot be determined. This makes it applicable for deriving semantic features for ML-based extraction of semantic relations from large volumes of real text.

WordNet [15] is a widely used linguistic resource which is designed according to psycholinguistic theories of human lexical memory. English nouns, verbs, adjectives and adverbs are organized into synonym sets (called synsets), each representing one underlying lexical concept. In this work, WordNet is used to derive several semantic features based on the synset and hypernym information.

4.1   Using GATE for Feature Extraction

General Architecture for Text Engineering (GATE) [6] is an infrastructure for developing and deploying software components that process human language. It provides or includes from other people a set of NLP tools including tokeniser, gazetteer, POS tagger, chunker, parsers, etc. For the relation extraction task, we make use of a number of GATE components as follows: English Tokeniser, Sentence Splitter, POS Tagger, NP Chunker, VP Chunker, BuChart Parser, MiniPar Parser. To develop more semantic features we also made use of WordNet and derived the synset information as the features.

4.2   Developing Features

In the experiments we tried to use as many NLP features as could be provided by GATE components and which were considered as potentially helpful for modeling the relation extraction task. This is a valid approach due to one advantage of the SVM learning algorithm. Namely, carefully choosing features is crucial for some learning algorithms such as decision trees and rule learning. However, it is no so important for the SVM, because the irrelevant features for one particular binary problem usually distribute evenly over the positive and negative training examples and therefore would have little contribution to the SVM model due to its learning mechanism. Hence, when using SVM, we can put into the feature vector as many features as possible and let the SVM algorithm determine the most useful ones for a given binary classification problem.

In Section 5.3 we will experimentally discuss the contributions of these features to the relation extraction task.

The total feature set consists of 94 features. The rest of the subsection provide an overview of the different types of features we used. Due to space limitations, a complete description is provided in a separate technical report [17].

Word Features. This set consists of 14 features including the word list of the two entity mentions and their heads, the two words before the first mention, the two after the second mention, and the word list between them.

POS Tag Features. Because the word features are often too sparse, we also introduce POS tag features. For example, sentence 1 has been tagged as: *Texas* /NNP *has*/VBZ *many*/JJ *cars*/NNS, where NNP denotes proper name, JJ - adjectives, NNS - plural nouns, etc. Similar to the word features, this set of features includes the POS tag list of the two entity mentions and their heads, the two POS tags before the first mention, the two after the second mention, and the tag list in between.

Entity Features. As already discussed, ACE2004 divides entities into 7 types and all the entity mentions has also been annotated with the entity type , subtype and class, all of which have been used to develop features. For each pair of mentions, the combination of their entity types is taken as the entity type feature. For the example sentence above, there are two entity mentions: *Texas* categorized as GPE, and *many cars* as WEH. In addition, the entity hierarchy is used, because subtypes carry more accurate semantic information for the entity mentions. Therefore, the combination of the entity subtypes of the two entity mentions is provided as the entity subtype feature. The subtypes of the two example mentions are State-or-Province and Land. Finally, each entity has also been annotated with a class which describes the kind of reference for the entity. So the entity class is also used in this paper to predicate semantic relations. The classes for the above two mentions are SPC and USP.

Mention Features. This set of features includes the mention type and role information of both mentions, which is also provided by the ACE2004 annotations. For the example sentence, the mention types for the two mentions in sentence (1) are NAM and NOM, while the mention role for Texas is GPE and there is no role information for the second because only GPE entity can take role information.

Overlap Features. The relative position of the two entity mentions can also be helpful for indicating the relationship between them. For these features, we have considered: the number of words separating them, the number of other entity mentions in between, whether one mention contains the other. As the feature indicating whether one mention contains the other is too general, it has been combined with the entity type and subtype of the two mentions to form more discriminating features.

Chunk Features. GATE integrates two chunk parsers: Noun Phrase (NP) and Verb Phrase (VP) Chunker that segment sentences into noun and verb group chunks. For instance, the example sentence (1) is chunked as: [Texas] has [many cars], in which, Texas and many cars are NPs, while has is the VP between them whose type and voice are FVG (means finite verb phrase) and active. The following information has been used as chunk features: whether the two entity mentions are included in the same NP Chunk or VP Chunk, the type and voice information of the verb group chunk in between if there is any.

Dependency Features. In contrast to Kambhatla [11] and Zhou et al [19], who derive the dependency tree from the syntactic parse tree, we apply MiniPar to directly build the dependency tree. MiniPar is a shallow parser which can determine the dependency relationships between the words of a sentence [14]. Fig 2 shows the dependency tree for the example sentence. From the resulting dependency relationships between words, the dependency features are formed, including: combination of the head words and their dependent words for the two entity mentions involved; the combination of the dependency relation type and the dependent word of the heads of the two mentions; the combination of the entity type and the dependent word for each entity mention's head; the name of the dependency relationship between the heads of the two mentions if there is any; the word on which both the heads of the two mentions depend on if there is any; and the path of dependency relationship labels connecting the heads of the two mentions.

Parse Tree Features. The features on syntactic level are extracted from the parse tree. As we mentioned above, we use BuChart to generate the parse tree and the semantic representation of each sentence. Unlike many full parsers which

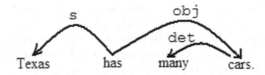

Fig. 2. The dependency tree for the example sentence

would fail if a full sentential parse cannot be found, BuChart can still produce the partial parsing trees and correspondent semantic representations for the fragments. The following list the parse tree in the bracket form for the example sentence,

(s (np (bnp (bnp_core (bnp_head (ne_np (tagged_location_np (list_np "Texas"))))))) (fvp (vp (vpcore (fvpcore (nonmodal_vpcore (nonmodal_vpcore1 (vpcore1 (av (v "has")))))))) (np (bnp (bnp_core (premods (premod (jj "many"))) (bnp_head (n "cars")))))))

Consequently, from the product of the parser, we extract the following features: the lowest and second lowest phrase labels governing each entity mentions involved; the lowest phrase labels governing both entity mentions; the lowest phrase labels governing the heads of both entity mentions; the path of phrase labels connecting both mentions in the parse tree; and that connecting the heads of both mentions.

Semantic Features from SQLF. Using relation- or domain- independent semantic features potentially makes the approach easier to adapt to new domains. BuChart provides semantic analysis to produce SQLF for each phrasal constituent. The logical form is composed of unary predicates that denote entities and events (e.g., chase(e1), run(e2)) and binary predicates for properties (e.g. lsubj(e1,e2)). Constants (e.g., e1, e2) are used to represent entity and event identifiers (see [8] for further details). The (somewhat simplified) semantic analysis of the example sentence in SQLF is

location(e2), name(e2,'Texas'), have(e1), time(e1,present), aspect(e1,simple), voice(e1,active), lobj(e1,e3), car(e3), number(e3,plural), adj(e3,many), lsubj (e1,e2)

From the SQLFs, a set of semantic features is generated, one of which is the path of predicate labels connecting the heads of both mentions in the semantic SQLFs. This path may be too specific to be effective and cause data sparseness problem, so we also take some important predicate labels as separate features, such as the first, second, last and penultimate predicates labels in that path.

Semantic Features from WordNet. To exploit more relation-independent semantic features, we use WordNet together with a simple semantic tagging method to find the sense information for the words in each sentence. Tagging words with their corresponding WordNet synsets (e.g. word sense disambiguation - WSD) is a difficult task, which usually can not achieve accuracy as high as other NLP tasks such as POS tagging. However, WordNet's design ensures that synsets are ordered by importance, so a simple and yet efficient heuristic can be used instead of a WSD module, without major accuracy penalty. The heuristic is to take the first synset from WordNet, which matches the POS tag of the given word. Each synset has been assigned an id (consisting of the POS tag and its offset in the WordNet files) which is used in the features. Similar to the word and POS tag features, the features from WordNet include the synset-id list of the two entity mentions and their heads, the two synset-ids before the first mention, the two after the second mention, and the synset-id list in between. With considerations of the data sparseness problem, we also developed a set of more abstract features by using the hypernym information of each synset, which exactly parallel the synset ones by replacing each synset-id with the id of its hypernym synset.

5   Experiment Results and Analysis

We evaluate our method, especially the contribution of the different features, on the ACE2004 training data. As mentioned above, only explicit relations between pairs of entity mentions within the same sentence are considered. We not only evaluate the performance of the system as a whole, but also investigate in detail several factors which have impact on the performance, such as the features set and the relation classification hierarchy.

5.1   Experimental Settings

The ACE2004 training data consists of 451 annotated files (157,953 words) from broadcast, newswire, English translations of Arabic and Chinese Treebank, and Fisher Telephone Speech collection. Among these files, there are 5,914 relation instances annotated which satisfied the experiment set up described above. The distribution of the instances is listed in Table 2.

Table 2. The distributions of the relation instances in ACE 2004 training data

Type	Subtype	Number	Type	Subtype	Number
PHYS	Located	1029	OTHER	Ethnic	53
	Near	141	-AFF	Ideology	55
	Part-Whole	518		Other	75
PER	Business	197	GPE	Citizen/Resident	368
-SOC	Family	178	-AFF	Based-In	333
	Other	69		Other	87
EMP	Employ-Exec	630	ART	User/Owner	273
-ORG	Employ-Undetermined	129		Inventor/Manufacturer	13
	Employ-Staff	694		Other	7
	Member-of-Group	225	DISC		434
	Subsidiary	300			
	Partner	16			
	Other	90	Total		5,914

Following previous work, in order to focus on the performance of the relation extraction only, we suppose that all named entity mentions have been recognised without mistakes and only evaluate the performance of relation extraction on "true" named entity mentions with "true" chaining (i.e. as annotated by the ACE2004 annotators).

Among the 23 relation subtypes (including DISC which has no subtype), there are 6 symmetric ones. So to model the relation extraction task as multi-class classification, we use two labels to denote each non-symmetric relation and only one label for each symmetric one. Also we assign a label to the class of no-relation, which indicates that there is no relation between the two entity mentions. Consequently, in our experiments, relation extraction is modeled as a 41-class classification task, where each pair of entity mentions is assigned one of these 41 relation classes, based on the features discussed in Section 4. In the following experiments, we use the package LIBSVM[2] for training and testing the SVM classifiers with one-against-one method for multi-class classification which has been described in Section 3.

From Table 2 we can see that the different relation subtypes and types are distributed very unevenly, so we only measure the micro-average of Precision, Recall and F1 measure(which is $2 * Precision * Recall/(Precision + Recall)$), because in such cases macro-average does not reflect the performance reliably.

In each of the following experiments, we performed 5 folds cross validation on the whole data. In every execution, the corpus is spited into a training set (80% of the total files) and a testing set (20% of the total files). All the performance results of Precision, Recall and F1 reported are the means averaged over five runs.

Table 3. The result on different kernel functions

Kernel type	Precision(%)	Recall(%)	F1(%)
Linear	66.41	49.18	56.50
Quadratic	68.96	46.20	55.33
Cubic	71.31	42.39	53.17

5.2   Evaluation on Different Kernels

Since different kernel functions can be used with SVM, in order to select a suitable kernel for relation extraction task, we have implemented experiments to compare three different types of kernels for SVM: the linear, quadratic and cubic kernels. In the comparison, all the features have been used and Table 3 shows the result. The result shows that with all the features the linear kernel is better than both the quadratic and cubic ones. But the t paired test we did using the results from 5-fold cross validation showed that the linear kernel was no significantly better than quadratic kernel at the 95% confidence level (the p-value of the test was 0.088). Since the linear kernel is more simple and efficient than others and obtained better results, in the following experiments we only use the linear kernel with SVM.

---

[2] See http://www.csie.ntu.edu.tw/~cjlin/libsvm/.

5.3   Evaluation on Features

We carried out the experiments to investigate the impact of different features on the performance by adding them incrementally. The features have been added in the order from the shallow to deep to see the effect of different features. Table 4 presents the results from the experiments. It is possible that not only the individual features but also the combinations of features would affect the performance. Hence, more experiments will be done in the future to figure out the effects of the features on relation extraction. It can be seen from the table, the performance improves as more features are used, until the F1 measure reaches 56.78% which is comparable to the reported best results(55.5%) of [19]on the ACE2003 training data. From the new features introduced in this work, the POS tag features and the general semantic features all contribute to the improvement. The improvement of the general semantic features, including semantic features from SQLF and WordNet, is significant at confidence level 95%, as the p-value of the t paired test on the corresponding data is 0.003. The improvement 1.72% (from 55.06% to 56.78%) was even higher than that brought by some syntactic features such as the chunk, dependency and parse tree features which was only 1.54%(from 53.52% to 55.06%) in total. Therefore, the contribution of the semantic features shows that general semantic information is beneficial for relation extraction and should receive further attention.

The entity features lead to the best improvement in performance. It is not surprised because the relation between two entity mentions is closely related to the entity types of the two mentions. Actually we took advantage of the ACE2004 corpus which included not only the entity types but also entity subtype and class. Therefore we used more entity type features than the previous studies using the ACE2003 corpus which only had entity type. Further investigation shows that the two additional features are in fact very helpful: when only using entity type feature the F1 improvement is 10.29%, and when using the other two features additionally, the improvement increase to 13.83%. This result shows that the more accurate information of the entity mentions we have, the better performance can be achieved in relation extraction.

Table 4. The result on different feature sets

Features	Precision(%)	Recall(%)	F1(%)
Word	57.90	23.48	33.38
+POS Tag	57.63	26.91	36.66
+Entity	60.03	44.47	50.49
+Mention	61.03	45.60	52.03
+Overlap	60.51	48.01	53.52
+Chunk	61.46	48.46	54.19
+Dependency	63.07	48.26	54.67
+Parse Tree	63.57	48.58	55.06
+SQLF	63.74	48.92	55.34
+ WordNet	67.53	48.98	56.78

From Table 4, we can also see that the impact of the deep features is not as significant as the shallow ones. Zhou et al [19] show that chunking features are very useful while the dependency tree and parse tree features do not contribute much. Our results even show that features from word, POS tag, entity, mention and overlap can achieve 53.52% F1, while the deeper features (including chunk, dependency tree, parse tree and SQLF) only give less than 2% improvement over simpler processing. As the number of features impacts directly the required size of training data and the efficiency of training and application (more features need more annotated data for training the model and need more computation resources), there is an interesting trade-off in feature selection for relation extraction.

5.4 Experiments on Hierarchical Classification

As already discussed, ACE2004 defined both an entities and relations hierarchy, which provides a data resource for evaluating our method for ontology-based IE. The significant contribution of entity subtype and class features demonstrated above shows that the entity hierarchy information is important for relation extraction. As shown in Fig 1 the relation hierarchy has three levels, so we ran experiments to evaluate our method with these different classification levels: subtype classification – 23 relations at leaf level, type classification – 7 relations at middle level, relation detection – predicating if there is relation between two entity mentions, which can be treated as a binary classification task. The experiments on the three different classification levels have been done separately. In each experiment, the classifier is trained and tested on the corresponding relation labels (e.g. 23, 7, or 1 relations). All these experiments made use of the complete feature set and Table 5 shows the averaged overall results.

Table 5. The result on different classification levels

Level	Precision(%)	Recall(%)	F1(%)
Subtype classification	67.53	48.98	56.78
Type classification	71.41	60.03	65.20
Relation detection	73.87	69.50	71.59

The results show that performance on relation detection level is the highest while that on subtype classification is the lowest. The Precision, Recall and F1 all show the same trend, revealing that it is more difficult to classify on deeper levels of the hierarchy because there are less examples per class and also the classes are getting more similar as the classification level gets deeper. This has been supported by the more detailed results for the relations type EMP-ORG and its subtypes, as shown in Table 6. The performance for the type EMP-ORG when classifying on the type level is the best among all 7 relation types: 77.29% Precision, 75.00% Recall and 76.01% F1 averaged over 5 folds cross validation. However, the performance on the 7 subtypes within EMP-ORG when classifying at subtype level is not only much lower than the result for EMP-ORG overall

Table 6. The result on the subtypes of EMP-ORG

Subtypes	Num	Precision(%)	Recall(%)	F1(%)
Employ-Exec	630	71.37	63.9	67.16
Employ-Undetermined	129	68.76	43.23	51.2
Employ-Staff	694	64.39	60.97	62.25
Member-of-Group	225	62.16	38.55	46.85
Subsidiary	300	83.81	65.29	72.79
Partner	16	0	0	0
Other	90	33.33	5.89	9.9

Table 7. The F1(%) results on different feature sets and classification levels

Features	Relation detection	Type classification	Subtype classification
Word	61.25	41.61	33.38
+POS Tag	60.03	44.13	36.66
+Entity	63.31	57.84	50.49
+Mention	65.57	59.45	52.03
+Overlap	66.84	61.36	53.52
+Chunk	66.61	62.52	54.19
+Dependency	70.01	63.61	54.67
+Parse Tree	70.42	64.05	55.06
+SQLF	70.08	64.24	55.34
+WordNet	71.59	65.20	56.78

but also rather unstable: from zero for Partner to 72.79% for Subsidiary. The two biggest subtypes Employ-Exec and Employ-Staff get only 67.16% and 62.25 % F1 which are much lower than the 76.01% on type level for their parent type EMP-ORG. We consider that the zero result for Partner is mainly due to too few instances. Therefore, the closer distance between the classes at subtype level causes the performance to decrease and become unstable.

We also investigated the influence of different feature sets on the different classification levels (see Table 7). For all of the three classification levels, the improvements are almost stable as more features are introduced and the best performance is achieved with the complete feature set (there is only one exception when add SQLF features in relation detection). But the improvement at various levels is different: as more features are used, the improvement in relation detection is only 10.34% (from 61.25% to 71.59%), while the improvement in type and subtype classification is much more significant: 23.59% (from 41.61% to 65.20%) and 23.40% (from 33.38% to 56.78%). Such difference suggests that features provide more significant effect for classification on deep level. Furthermore, the impact of the SQLF and WordNet synset features on different levels also shows that semantic knowledge will play more important role in extracting fine granularity relations.

6   Conclusions

In this paper we investigated SVM-based classification for relation extraction and explored a diverse set of NLP features. In comparison to previous work, we introduce some new features, including POS tag, entity subtype and class features, entity mention role features and even general semantic features which all contribute to performance improvements. We also investigated the impact of different types of feature and different relation levels.

Further work on using machine learning for relation extraction needs to address several issues. Firstly, although the ACE2004 entity and relation type system provides a hierarchy organization which is somewhat like ontology, it is still very limited for large-scale ontology-based IE. We plan to extend our method and evaluate it on bigger scale ontology. Another interesting future work is to integrate the automatic named entity recognition with relation extraction, which would be more realistic than the experiments described in this paper where relation extraction was based on the gold standard named entities. It would also be interesting to compare the SVM model with other variants of the SVM (such as the SVM with uneven margins) as well as with other ML approaches (such as CRF, MEM and so on) for relation extraction.

Acknowledgements. This research is supported by the EU-funded SEKT project (www.sekt-project.com) , the National Natural Science Foundation of China (60403050) and the National Grand Fundamental Research Program of China under Grant No. 2005CB321802. Thanks to Guodong Zhou for his helpful information about his work.

References

1. ACE. See http://www.nist.gov/speech/tests/ace/
2. Annotation Guidelines for Entity Detection and Tracking (EDT) Version 4.2.6, http://www.ldc.upenn.edu/Projects/ACE/docs/EnglishEDTV4-2-6.PDF. (2004)
3. Annotation Guidelines for Relation Detection and Characterization (RDC) Version 4.3.2, http://www.ldc.upenn.edu/Projects/ACE/docs/EnglishRDCV4-3-2.PDF. (2004)
4. Appelt, D.: An Introduction to Information Extraction. Artificial Intelligence Communications, **12(3)** (1999) 161-172
5. Culotta, A., Sorensen, J.: Dependency tree kernels for relation extraction. Proceedings of 42th Annual Meeting of the Association for Computational Linguistics. 21-26 July Barcelona, Spain (2004)
6. Cunningham, H., Maynard, D., Bontcheva, K., Tablan, V.: GATE: A Framework and Graphical Development Environment for Robust NLP Tools and Applications. Proceedings of the 40th Anniversary Meeting of the Association for Computational Linguistics. Philadelphia, July (2002)
7. Freitag, D., and McCallum A.: Information extraction with HMM structures learned by stochastic optimization. Proceedings of the 7th Conference on Artificial Intelligence (AAAI-00) and of the12th Conference on Innovative Applications of Artificial Intelligence (IAAI-00), 584-589,Menlo Park, CA. AAAI Press (2000)

8. Gaizauskas, R., Hepple, M., Saggion, H., Greenwood, M.A., Humphreys, K.: SUP-PLE: A Practical Parser for Natural Language Engineering Applications. Technical report CS–05–08, Department of Computer Science, University of Sheffield (2005)
9. Handschuh, S., Staab, S., Ciravegna, F.: S-CREAM — Semi-automatic CREAtion of Metadata. Proceedings of the13th International Conference on Knowledge Engineering and Knowledge Management (EKAW02), Siguenza, Spain(2002)
10. Hsu, C.-W., Lin, C.-J.: A comparison of methods for multi-class support vector machines , IEEE Transactions on Neural Networks, 13(2). (2002)415-425
11. Kambhatla, N.: Combining lexical, syntactic and semantic features with Maximum Entropy models for extracting relations. Proceedings of 42th Annual Meeting of the Association for Computational Linguistic. 21-26 July Barcelona, Spain (2004)
12. Lafferty, J., McCallum, A., Pereira. F.: Conditional random fields: Probabilistic models for segmenting and labeling sequence data. In Proc. 18th International Conf. on Machine Learning, Morgan Kaufmann, San Francisco, CA (2001) 282-289
13. Li, Y., Bontcheva, K., Cunningham, H.: SVM Based Learning System For Information Extraction. In Proceedings of Sheffield Machine Learning Workshop, Lecture Notes in Computer Science. Springer Verlag (2005)
14. Lin, D.: Dependency-based Evaluation of MINIPAR. In Workshop on the Evaluation of Parsing Systems, Granada, Spain, May (1998)
15. Miller, A., "WordNet: An On-line Lexical Resource", Special issue of the Journal of Lexicography, vol. 3, no. 4(1990)
16. Motta, E., VargasVera, M., Domingue, J., Lanzoni, M., Stutt, A., Ciravegna, F.: MnM: Ontology Driven Semi-Automatic and Automatic Support for Semantic Markup. Proceedings of the 13th International Conference on Knowledge Engineering and Knowledge Management (EKAW02), Siguenza, Spain(2002)
17. Wang, T., Bontcheva, K., Li, Y., Cunningham, H.: D2.1.2. Ontology-Based Information Extraction. SEKT Deliverable D2.1.2. (2005). http://www.sekt-project.org/rd/deliverables/index_html/
18. Zelenko, D., Aone, C., Richardella, A.: Kernel methods for relation extraction. Journal of Machine Learning Research (2003) 1083-1106
19. Zhou G., Su, J., Zhang, J., Zhang, M.: Combining Various Knowledge in Relation Extraction, Proceedings of the 43th Annual Meeting of the Association for Computational Linguistics (2005)

An Infrastructure for Acquiring High Quality Semantic Metadata

Yuangui Lei, Marta Sabou, Vanessa Lopez, Jianhan Zhu,
Victoria Uren, and Enrico Motta

Knowledge Media Institute (KMi), The Open University, Milton Keynes
{y.lei, r.m.sabou, v.lopez, j.zhu, v.s.uren, e.motta}@open.ac.uk

Abstract. Because metadata that underlies semantic web applications is gathered from distributed and heterogeneous data sources, it is important to ensure its quality (i.e., reduce duplicates, spelling errors, ambiguities). However, current infrastructures that acquire and integrate semantic data have only marginally addressed the issue of metadata quality. In this paper we present our metadata acquisition infrastructure, ASDI, which pays special attention to ensuring that high quality metadata is derived. Central to the architecture of ASDI is a verification engine that relies on several semantic web tools to check the quality of the derived data. We tested our prototype in the context of building a semantic web portal for our lab, KMi. An experimental evaluation comparing the automatically extracted data against manual annotations indicates that the verification engine enhances the quality of the extracted semantic metadata.

1 Introduction

The promise of the semantic web is to automate several information gathering tasks on the web by making web data interpretable to software agents [1]. A condition for realizing this technology is the existence of *high quality* semantic metadata that would provide a machine understandable version of the web. By quality we mean that the semantic metadata should accurately capture the meaning of the data that it describes. For example, it should capture the meaning of each entity as intended in the context of its use (describe "jaguar" as a car or as a animal depending on its context). Further, a single semantic identifier should be attached to each entity even if this entity is referred to in the web page using different variants of its name or its name is misspelled. Also, metadata should be up to date when the described web page changes.

However, as previously debated in the literature [16], the characteristics of the web data hamper the acquisition of quality metadata. Besides its large scale, web data is usually distributed over multiple knowledge sources. These sources are heterogeneous in their level of formality, representation format, content and the quality of knowledge they contain. Integrating data from several of these sources often leads to errors that decrease the quality of the metadata. Also, the

Y. Sure and J. Domingue (Eds.): ESWC 2006, LNCS 4011, pp. 230–244, 2006.
© Springer-Verlag Berlin Heidelberg 2006

data on the web is changing continuously so the derived metadata has to be kept up to date.

Our overview of the most relevant infrastructures that acquire and aggregate semantic web metadata reveals that they offer limited or no support for verifying the quality of the derived metadata. In contrast with these, the system we present here, ASDI, provides several means to ensure the quality of the extracted data. First, it aims to reduce ambiguities by taking into account the context in which an entity is mentioned in order to determine its type. Second, it contains a verification engine that checks the validity of any derived metadata against a repository of trusted domain knowledge and against the information available on the web. Finally, since the whole acquisition process is automatic, it can be automatically run whenever new data becomes available, thus ensuring that the semantic metadata is always up to date.

The rest of the paper is organized as follows. We begin by describing the KMi context in which our prototype was designed and tested (section 2). Based on this description we discuss some of the tasks that an infrastructure needs to perform in order to ensure the quality of the derived semantic metadata. We then investigate how current semantic web infrastructures approach quality control for semantic metadata (section 3). In section 4 we present the ASDI infrastructure and detail its components that play a role in the quality control process. Thereafter, we describe an experimental evaluation of ASDI's validation functionality in section 5. Finally, we conclude our paper with a discussion of our results, the limitations of ASDI and future work in section 6.

2   Building the KMi Semantic Web Portal

We have designed and tested our infrastructure in the context of building a semantic web portal for KMi that would provide an integrated access to various aspects of the academic life of our lab[1]. By relying on semantic web technology the content of the portal is usable both by humans and software agents. While the KMi portal is a particular application, we believe that it provides the generic characteristics of a semantic web application scenario. In this section we briefly describe the particularities of the KMi context that are needed to understand the content of this paper (section 2.1). In the second part of this section, section 2.2, based on our experience with the KMi context, we extract and generalize a set of tasks that should be performed by any integration platform in order to ensure the quality of the extracted metadata.

2.1   The KMi Context

In the case of KMi the data relevant for building the semantic portal is spread in several different data sources such as departmental databases, knowledge bases and HTML pages. Information about people, technologies, projects and research areas is maintained in our departmental databases. Bibliographic data is stored

---

[1] http://semanticweb.kmi.open.ac.uk

in an internal knowledge base. In addition, KMi has an electronic newsletter[2], which now contains an archive of several hundreds of news items, describing events of significance to the KMi members.

Beside its heterogeneous nature, another important feature of the KMi domain data is that it continuously undergoes changes. The departmental databases change to reflect events such as additions of new projects. KMi-related events are reported in the newsletter and added to the news archive. Therefore, the semantic data that underlies the portal has to be often updated.

We decided to use and extend an existing ontology for representing the semantic metadata on which the portal realizes. We use the AKT reference ontology[3], which has been designed to support the AKT-2 demonstrator. We extended this ontology by adding some domain specific concepts, such as *kmi-planet-news-item*, *kmi-research-staff-member*, *kmi-support-staff-member*, etc.

2.2   Tasks for Insuring Metadata Quality

Based on the characteristics of the KMi semantic web portal context, we identify three generic tasks that are related to ensuring semantic metadata quality and which should be supported by any semantic web infrastructure. Note, however, that while this set of tasks is grounded in our practical experience, it is by no means exclusive. The generic tasks are:

A. Extract information from un-structured or semi-structured data sources in an automatic and adaptive manner. Useful knowledge is often distributed in several data sources which can be heterogeneous from the perspective of their level of structure or the used representation language. Methods have to be developed that extract the required data from each data source. It is important to employ *automatic* methods so that the process can be easily repeated periodically in order to keep the knowledge updated. Another important characteristic of the extraction mechanism is that it should be *adaptable* to the content of the sources that are explored. Being able to distinguish the type of an entity depending on its context is a pre-requisite for ensuring the quality of the semantic metadata. For example, we would expect from an adaptive information extraction tool to identify the different meanings that a given term can have on different web sites. For instance, "Magpie" is the name of a project in many web pages related to KMi, and should be identified as such. However, in other web sites it is more likely that it denotes a bird.

B. Ensure that the derived metadata is free of common errors. Since semantic data is typically gathered from different data sources which were authored by different people, it is often the case that it contains several errors, such as different identifiers that refer to the same entity, or instances whose meaning is not clear and needs to be disambiguated. Errors can be caused by data entry mistakes, by information extraction tools, or by the inconsistency and duplication entries of diverse data sources. We envision two major approaches to avoid these errors.

---

[2] http://kmi.open.ac.uk/news
[3] http://kmi.open.ac.uk/projects/akt/ref-onto/

First, one might attempt to tackle these errors before the data has been extracted. In particular, domain specific knowledge can help to avoid some problems, e.g., using lexicons to get rid of some domain specific noisy data. Such knowledge can be either supplied at design time in formats of transformation instructions or be generated automatically and incrementally according to the user's assessment on the performance of the system.

The second way to approach this problem is to clean the semantic data after it has been extracted. This approach requires mechanisms to correctly diagnose the problem at hand and then algorithms to correct each individual problem.

C. Update the semantic metadata as new information becomes available. Since the underlying data sources are likely to change, the whole data acquisition and verification process must be repeated so that the knowledge base is updated in an appropriate fashion.

In our prototype we provide support for all these quality insurance related tasks (as described in section 4). In the following section we overview a set of semantic web applications that rely on data acquisition and integration and describe how they approach the issue of quality control.

3   State of the Art

In this section we describe how existing approaches address semantic metadata quality control. We survey a representative sample of these approaches without performing an exhaustive study of this research direction. In particular, we focus on the approaches which address heterogeneous sources. We therefore leave out the approaches which either support the annotation of textual sources ([17]), the migration of data from structured sources ([2], [14]) and the creation of semantic web data from scratch ([10]).

The On-To-Knowledge project [15] provided one of the first suits of tools to be used for semantics based knowledge management. This tool suite not only supports semantic data acquisition from heterogeneous sources, but also supports ontology sharing, editing, versioning, and visualization. However, it does not provide explicit support to ensure the quality of the acquired semantic data.

The Semantic Content Organization and Retrieval Engine (SCORE) [13] is one of the semantic web based technologies, which has been commercialized. Quality control is addressed by i) enhancement rules which exploit the trusted knowledge to populate empty attribute values and ii) disambiguation mechanisms which make use of domain classification and the underlying trusted knowledge to address ambiguities.

The KIM platform [11] addresses the complete cycle of metadata creation, storage and semantic-based search. It pre-populates its ontology from several publicly available knowledge sources. This populated ontology supports the system to perform named entity recognition (NER) in a wide range of domains. The focus of this work is very much on scaling up and adapting NER to the needs of the semantic web.

The CS AKTive Space [12], the winner of the 2003 semantic web Challenge competition, gathers data automatically on a continuous basis. It relies on Armadillo [4] to achieve the task of automatic data acquisition. Quality control related issues such as the problem of duplicate entities are only weakly addressed (for example, by heuristics based methods or using manual input).

MuseumFinland [6] is the first and largest semantic web based portal that aggregates heterogeneous museum collections. In the MuseumFinland application possible errors are logged by the system for correction by a human user.

The Flink system [9], winner of the 2004 semantic web Challenge competition, is an infrastructure for extracting, aggregating and visualizing online social networks. The data is aggregated in an RDF(S) repository and a set of domain-specific inference rules are used to ensure its quality. In particular, identity reasoning (smushing) is performed to determine if different resources refer to the same individual (i.e., co-relation).

All the approaches mentioned above support acquiring semantic web data from heterogeneous sources in an *automatic* fashion. They typically exploit manually (e.g., On-To-Knowledge, SCORE, MuseumFinland) or semi-automatically (e.g., CS AKTive Space) constructed rules to define how metadata is to be extracted from domain specific structured or semi-structured sources.

Although they do provide comprehensive support for the acquisition activity in their specific problem domain, *the support for quality control is relatively weak*. Even though some co-relation (e.g., in CS AKTive Space and Flink) and disambiguation mechanisms (e.g., in SCORE) have been exploited, quality control has not been fully addressed. For example, the problems of duplicate or erroneous entities have not been addressed in any of the approaches mentioned above. Such problems may significantly de-crease the quality of the acquired semantic data.

4   The ASDI Infrastructure

In this section, we describe the infrastructure that we developed to build the semantic portal at KMi. An important characteristic of ASDI is that, in comparison with the approaches we have described in section 3, it addresses the quality control issue. We first present an overview of the ASDI infrastructure. Then we detail two of the most important layers of the infrastructure that ensure adaptive data extraction and the quality check of this extracted data.

4.1   An Overview

Figure 1 shows the four layered architecture of ASDI, which contains:

A Source Data Layer contains the collection of all available data sources such as semi-structured textual documents (e.g. web pages) or structured data in the form of XML feeds, databases, and knowledge bases.

An Extraction Layer is responsible with the generation of semantic data from the source data layer. It comprises an *automatic and adaptive information extraction tool*, which marks-up textual sources, *a semantic transformation*

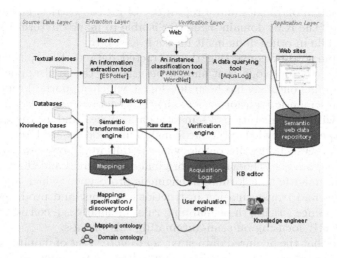

Fig. 1. An overview of the ASDI infrastructure

engine, which converts data from source representations into the specified domain ontology according to the transformation instructions specified in *a mapping ontology*, and a set of *mappings specification/discovery* tools, which support the construction of transformation instructions. The output of this layer consists of i) raw semantic data entries and ii) logs of acquisition operations which describe the provenance of data entries.

A Verification Layer checks the quality of the previously generated semantic data entries. The core component is the *verification engine*, which makes use of a number of semantic web tools to achieve high quality data. While the verification engine is completely automatic, we allow users to inspect the changes made to the semantic data through a *user evaluation engine*. This engine assists users to assess the performance of the system and generates transformation rules according to the feedback given by them. *A KB editor* is also included in this layer to allow users (i.e., knowledge engineers) to inspect the final results and modify them whenever necessary.

An Application Layer sums up all the applications that use the acquired and verified semantic data (stored in the semantic web data repository).

4.2 The Extraction Layer

The role of extraction layer is to acquire data from heterogeneous sources and convert them to semantic web data objects equipped with rich semantic relations.

To address the issue of *adaptive information extraction*, we use ESpotter [18], a named entity recognition (NER) system that provides an adaptive service. ESpotter accepts the URL of a textual document as input and produces a list of the named entities mentioned in that text. The adaptability is realized by means of domain ontologies and a repository of lexicon entries. For example, in the context of the KMi domain, ESpotter is able to mark the term "Magpie" as a project, while in other domains it marks it as a bird.

For the purpose of converting the extracted data to the specified domain ontology (i.e., the ontology that should be used by the final applications), an instance mapping ontology has been developed, which supports i) representation independent semantic transformations, ii) the generation of rich semantic relations along with the generation of semantic data entries, and iii) the specification of domain specific knowledge (i.e. lexicons). This lexicons are later used by the verification process. Using this ontology (see details in [7]) one can define a set of mappings between the schema of the original data sources and the final domain ontology. A semantic transformation engine is prototyped, which accepts structured sources and transformation instructions as input and produces semantic data entries. Since writing these mapping rules manually is a considerable effort, we are currently focusing on semi-automating this process.

To ensure that the acquired data stays *up to date*, a set of monitoring services detect and capture changes made in the underlying data sources and initiate the whole extraction process again. This ensures a sustainable and maintenance-free operation of the overall architecture.

4.3   The Verification Layer

The role of verification layer is to identify problems of the extracted data entries and to resolve them properly. This layer relies on two components. First, an automatic verification engine employs several tools to verify the extracted data. Second, a user evaluation tool allows a knowledge engineer to evaluate and fine-tune the verification process of the engine. We describe both components.

The Verification Engine. The goal of the verification engine is to check that each entity has been extracted correctly by the extraction layer. For example, it checks that each entity has been correctly associated with a concept and in the cases when the type of the entity is dubious it performs disambiguation. This engine also makes sure that a newly derived entity is not a duplicate for an already existing entity. The verification process consists of three increasingly complex steps as depicted in figure 2. These steps employ several semantic web tools and a set of resources to complete their tasks.

Step1: Checking the internal lexicon library. In the first step, *a lexicon library*, which maintains domain specific lexicons, is checked. If no match is found there, the verification process continues.

Step2: Querying the semantic web data repository. The second step uses an ontology-based QA tool, AquaLog [8], to query the already acquired semantic web data (which is assumed to be correct, i.e. trusted) and to solve obvious typos and minor errors in the data. This step contains a disambiguation mechanism, whose role is to de-reference ambiguous entities (e.g., whether the term "star wars" refers to the Lucas' movie or President Reagan's military programme).

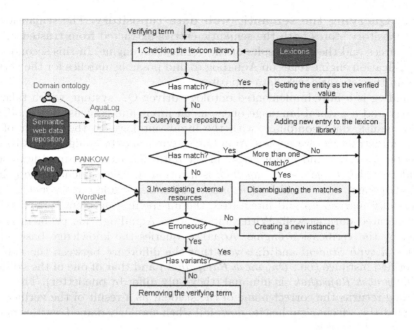

Fig. 2. The overall algorithm of the data verification engine

Step3: Investigating external resources. If the second step fails, the third step relies on investigating external resources such as the web. An instance classification tool is developed, which makes use of PANKOW [3] and WordNet [5], to determine the appropriate classification of the verified entity.

We will now detail all these three steps.

Step1: Checking the lexicon library. The lexicon library maintains domain specific lexicons (e.g., abbreviations) and records the mappings between strings and instance names. One lexicon mapping example in the KMi semantic web portal is that the string "ou" corresponds to the *the-open-university* entity. The verification engine will consider any appearances of this abbreviation as referring to the corresponding entity.

The lexicon library is initialized by lexicons specified through the mapping instruction and expands as the verification process goes on. By using the lexicon library, the verification engine is able to i) exploit domain specific lexicons to avoid domain specific noisy data and ii) avoid repeating the verification of the same entity thus making the process more efficient. However, there is a risk of mis-identifying different entities in different contexts which share the same name. For example, in one context the name *Victoria* may refer to the entity *Victoria-Uren* and in other contexts it may not.

If no match can be found in this step, the engine proceeds to the next step. Otherwise, the verification process ends.

Step2: Querying the semantic web data repository. The semantic web data repository stores both the semantic entries extracted from trusted knowledge sources and the final results of the verification engine. In this second step, the verification engine relies on AquaLog to find possible matches for the verified entity in the semantic web data repository.

AquaLog is a fully implemented ontology-driven QA system, which takes an ontology and a natural language query as an input and returns answers drawn from semantic data compliant with the input ontology. In the context of the ASDI infrastructure, we exploit AquaLog's string matching algorithms to deal with obvious typos and minor errors in the data. For example, in a news story a student called *Dnyanesh Rajapathak* is mentioned. The student name is however misspelled as it should be *Dnyanesh Rajpathak*. While the student name is successfully marked up and integrated, the misspelling problem is carried into the generated data as well. With support from AquaLog, this problem is corrected by the verification engine. AquaLog queries the knowledge base for all entities of type *Student* and discovers that the difference between the name of the verified instance (i.e., *Dnyanesh Rajapathak*) and that of one of the students (i.e, *Dnyanesh Rajpathak*) is minimal (they only differ by one letter). Therefore, AquaLog returns the correct name of the student as a result of the verification. Note that this mechanism has its downfall when similarly named entities denote different real life objects.

If there is a single match, the verification process ends. However, when more matches exist, contextual information is exploited to address the ambiguities.

In the disambiguation step, the verification engine exploits i) other entities appearing in the same news story and ii) the semantic relations contained in the semantic web data repository as the contextual information. To illustrate the mechanism by means of a concrete example, suppose that in the context of the KMi semantic web portal, ESpotter marks *Victoria* as a person entity in a news story. When using AquaLog to find matches for the entity, the verification engine gets two matches: *Victoria-Uren* and *Victoria-Wilson*. To decide which one is the appropriate match, the verification engine looks up other entities referenced in the same story and checks whether they have any relation with any of the matches in the knowledge base. In this example, the *AKT* project is mentioned in the same story, and the match *Victoria-Uren* has a relation (i.e., *has-project-member*) with the project. Hence, the appropriate match is more likely to be *Victoria-Uren* than *Victoria-Wilson*.

Step3: Investigating external resources. When a match cannot be found in the internal resources, the entity can be:

1) **partially correct,** e.g., the entity *IEEE-conference* is classified as an *Organization*,
2) **correct** but new to the system, e.g., the entity *IBM*, is correctly classified as an *Organization*, but the local knowledge sources do not contain this information so it cannot be validated,
3) **miss-classified,** e.g., *sun-microsystems* is classified as a *Person*, and

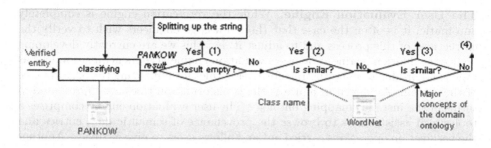

Fig. 3. The algorithm of the instance classification tool

4) **erroneous,** which does not make any sense and should be removed, e.g. the entity *today* classified as a *Person*.

The task of this step is to find out in which category the verified entity falls into. For this purpose, a classification tool is developed, which uses PANKOW and WordNet to support the classification of unknown terms. Figure 3 shows the algorithm of the instance classification tool. We describe each step of this process and provide as an example the process of verifying the *IBM* entity which was classified by ESpotter as an *Organization*.

Step 3.1. The PANKOW service is used to classify the string *IBM*. PANKOW employs an unsupervised, pattern-based approach on web data to categorize the string and produces a set of possible classifications along with ranking values. As shown in figure 3, if PANKOW cannot get any result, the term is treated as erroneous but still can be partially correct. Thus, its variants are investigated one by one until classifications can be drawn. If PANKOW returns any results, the classifications with the highest ranking are picked up. In this example, the term "company" has the highest ranking.

Step 3.2. Next the algorithm uses WordNet to compare the similarity between the type of the verified entity as proposed by the extraction layer (i.e., "organization") and an alternative type for the entity as returned by PANKOW (i.e., "company"). If they are similar (which is the case of the example), it is concluded that the verified entity is classified correctly (its derived type is similar to that which is most frequently used on the web) but it was not added yet into the trusted knowledge base. Thus, a new instance (*IBM* of type *Organization*) needs to be created and added to the repository.

If the two compared terms are not similar, other major concepts of the domain ontology are compared to the web-endorsed type (i.e., "company") in an effort to find a classification for the entity. If one concept is found similar to the web-endorsed type, it is concluded that the verified entity was wrongly classified by the extraction layer. The verification engine then associates the verified entity with the correct concept and places it back to the step 2 (which is to seek matches from the semantic web data repository). Otherwise, it can be safely concluded that the verified entity is erroneous.

The User Evaluation Engine. While the verification engine is completely automatic, it is often the case that the knowledge engineers wish to verify the correctness of this process and to adjust it. For this we are currently developing an user evaluation engine. The user evaluation engine accepts acquisition logs as input and produces semantic transformation rules for improving the performance of the system. As shown in figure 1, the transformation rules are represented in terms of the instance mapping ontology. The user evaluation engine comprises a tool which assists users to browse the provenance of semantic data entries and the verification operations carried out and allows users to give feedback. Another tool generates transformation rules according to user's feedback.

5   Evaluation

The KMi semantic web portal has been running for several months generating and maintaining semantic data from the underlying sources of the KMi web site in an automated way. In this section, we describe an experimental evaluation of the quality control mechanism provided by ASDI. We first describe the evaluation setup and the metrics we use (section 5.1). We then discuss the results of the evaluation (section 5.2).

5.1   Evaluation Setup

We randomly chose 36 news stories from the KMi news archive and then asked several KMi researchers to manually mark them up in terms of *person, organization* and *projects*. Because the annotators have a good knowledge of the KMi domain we consider the result of the annotation as a Gold Standard. We used ASDI to produce semantic data from these news stories and compared the automatically extracted data to the manual annotations. To illustrate the important role of the verification engine, the performance of ESpotter is introduced in the comparison, which shows the quality of the extracted data before and after the verification process.

We assess the results in terms of *recall, precision* and *f-measure*, where recall is the proportion of all possible correct annotations that were found by the system with respect to the ones that can be in principle extracted from the source text, precision is the proportion of the extracted annotations that were found to be correct, and f-measure evaluates the overall performance by treating recall and precision equally.

5.2   Evaluation Results

Table 1 shows the recall rates of ESpotter and ASDI. The manual annotation of the news stories identified 92 people, 74 organizations, and 21 projects. Compared to these manual annotations, ESpotter failed to identify 17 people, 16 organizations, and 5 projects, thus reaching an overall recall of 0.798. ASDI reached a slightly lower recall (0.775) as it missed 21 people, 16 organizations, and 5 projects in comparison with the manual annotation. The major reason for

Table 1. Recall of ESpotter and ASDI

Type	People	Organizations	Projects	Total
Manual annotations	92	74	21	187
ESpotter failures	17	16	5	38
ESpotter Recall	0.815	0.783	0.761	0.798
ASDI failures	21	16	5	42
ASDI Recall	0.771	0.783	0.761	0.775

this lower recall is that the instance classification tool sometimes has problems in providing the appropriate classification. In some cases, PANKOW cannot find enough evidence to produce a satisfactory classification. For example, the classification of the person named "Marco Ramoni" returns an empty result. As a consequence, the verification engine loses one correct entry.

Table 2 shows the precision of ESpotter and ASDI. ESpotter discovered 87 people, 96 organizations, and 19 projects when working on the sample stories. Among them, 11 people and 32 organizations are not correct. This results in an overall precision of 0.787. On the other hand, ASDI obtained 86 person entities, 74 organization entities, and 19 project entities. Among them, 12 person entities and 4 organization entities are wrong. Hence, the overall precision of ASDI is 0.911. Note that the ASDI application improves the precision rate significantly. One major problem of ESpotter is the significant amount of redundant entries. For example, values like "open-university" and "ou" are often treated as the same entity. The verification engine gets rid of this problem by defining lexicons and relying on AquaLog to spot similar entities.

ESpotter derives several inaccurate classifications, which lead to a number of erroneous values, such as considering "IBM global education", or "the 2004 IEEE" *Organization* type entities. These values are successfully corrected during the verification process by looking up their variants. Finally, some erroneous values produced by ESpotter are kept out of the target knowledge base, as they do not make any sense. Examples are "workshop chair", "center", etc.

To give an overall insight in the performance of ASDI versus that of ESpotter we computed the F-measure of these systems by giving equal importance to both Recall and Precision. The values (listed in table 3) show that ASDI performs better than ESpotter. This means that the quality of the extracted data is improved by our verification engine.

Table 2. Precision of ESpotter and ASDI

Type	People	Organizations	Projects	Total
ESpotter discovered	87	96	19	202
ESpotter spurious	11	32	0	43
ESpotter Precision	0.873	0.667	1	0.787
ASDI discovered	86	74	19	179
ASDI spurious	12	4	0	16
ASDI Precision	0.860	0.946	1	0.911

Table 3. F-Measure of ESpotter and ASDI

F-measure	People	Organizations	Projects	Total
ESpotter	0.843	0.72	0.864	0.792
ASDI	0.813	0.856	0.864	0.837

6   Discussion

The core observation that underlies this paper is that, in the case of semantic web applications that rely on acquiring and combining semantic web data from several data sources, it is crucial to ensure that this semantic data has a high quality. By quality here we mean that the semantic data contains no duplicates, no errors and that the semantic descriptions correctly reflect the nature of the described entities. Our survey of a set of semantic web applications that gather data from several sources shows that little or no attention is paid to ensure the quality of the extracted data. In most cases heuristics based algorithms are used to ensure referential integrity. In contrast with these efforts, our semantic web infrastructure, ASDI, focuses on ensuring the quality of the extracted metadata.

Our evaluation of the quality verification module shows that it improved the performance of the bare extraction layer. ASDI outperforms ESpotter by achieving 91% precision and 77% recall. In the context of the KMi portal precision is more important than recall - erroneous results annoy user more than missing information. We plan to improve the recall rate by introducing additional information extraction engines to work in parallel with ESpotter. Such a redundancy is expected to substantially improve recall. Another future work we consider is to evaluate the added value of each component of the verification engine, i.e., determine the improvements brought by each individual component.

An interesting feature of ASDI is that it relies on a set of tools that were developed in the context of the semantic web. These are: the ESpotter adaptive NER system, the PANKOW annotation service and an ontology based question answering tool AquaLog. This is a novelty because many similar tools often adapt existing techniques. For example, the KIM platform adapts off the shelf NER techniques to the needs of the semantic web. By using these tools we show that the semantic web reached a development stage where different tools can be safely combined to produce new, complex functionalities. Another benefit we derived by using these domain independent tools is that our verification engine is highly portable. We are currently making it available as a web service.

Once set up, ASDI can run without any human intervention. This is thanks to the monitors that identify any updates in the underlying data structures and re-initiate the semantic data creation process for the new data.

We are, however, aware of *a number of limitations* associated with ASDI. For example, the manual specification of mappings in the process of setting up the ASDI application makes the approach heavy to launch. We currently address this issue by investing the use of automatic or semi-automatic mapping algorithms. A semi-automatic mapping would allow our tool to be portable across several different application domains.

Another limitation is related to AquaLog's lack of providing a degree of similarity between an entity and its match. For example, when querying for the entity *university-of-London*, AquaLog returns a number of matches which are university entities but it does not specify how similar they are to the entity that is verified. This has caused a number of problems in the KMi portal scenario.

Our general goal for the future is to make our work more generic by providing a formal definition of what semantic data quality is and transforming our prototype into a generic framework for verifying semantic data.

Acknowledgements. This work was funded by the Advanced Knowledge Technologies Interdisciplinary Research Collaboration (IRC), and the Knowledge Sharing and Reuse across Media (X-Media) project. AKT is sponsored by the UK Engineering and Physical Sciences Research Council under grant number GR/N15764/01. X-Media is sponsored by the European Commission as part of the Information Society Technologies (IST) programme under EC Grant IST-FF6-26978.

References

1. T. Berners-Lee, J. Hendler, and O. Lassila. The Semantic Web. *Scientific American*, 284(5):34 – 43, May 2001.
2. C. Bizer. D2R MAP - A Database to RDF Mapping Language. In *Proceedings of the 12th International World Wide Web Conference*, Budapest, 2003.
3. P. Cimiano, S. Handschuh, and S. Staab. Towards the Self-Annotating Web. In S. Feldman, M. Uretsky, M. Najork, and C. Wills, editors, *Proceedings of the 13th International World Wide Web Conference*, pages 462 – 471, 2004.
4. A. Dingli, F. Ciravegna, and Y. Wilks. Automatic Semantic Annotation using Unsupervised Information Extraction and Integration. In *Proceedings of the KCAP-2003 Workshop on Knowledge Markup and Semantic Annotation*, 2003.
5. C. Fellbaum. *WORDNET: An Electronic Lexical Database*. MIT Press, 1998.
6. E. Hyvonen, E. Makela, M. Salminen, A. Valo, K. Viljanen, S. Saarela, M. Junnila, and S. Kettula. MuseumFinland – Finnish Museums on the Semantic Web. *Journal of Web Semantics*, 3(2), 2005.
7. Y. Lei. An Instance Mapping Ontology for the Semantic Web. In *Proceedings of the Third International Conference on Knowledge Capture*, Banff, Canada, 2005.
8. V. Lopez, M. Pasin, and E. Motta. AquaLog: An Ontology-portable Question Answering System for the Semantic Web. In *Proceedings of ESWC*, 2005.
9. P. Mika. Flink: Semantic Web Technology for the Extraction and Analysis of Social Networks. *Journal of Web Semantics*, 3(2), 2005.
10. N.F. Noy, M. Sintek, S. Decker, M. Crubezy, R.W. Fergerson, and M.A. Musen. Creating Semantic Web Contents with Protege-2000. *IEEE Intelligent Systems*, 2(16):60 – 71, 2001.
11. B. Popov, A. Kiryakov, A. Kirilov, D. Manov, D. Ognyanoff, and M. Goranov. KIM - Semantic Annotation Platform. In D. Fensel, K. Sycara, and J. Mylopoulos, editors, *The SemanticWeb - ISWC 2003, Second International Semantic Web Conference, Proceedings*, volume 2870 of *LNCS*. Springer-Verlag, 2003.
12. M.C. Schraefel, N.R. Shadbolt, N. Gibbins, H. Glaser, and S. Harris. CS AKTive Space: Representing Computer Science in the Semantic Web. In *Proceedings of the 13th International World Wide Web Conference*, 2004.

13. A. Sheth, C. Bertram, D. Avant, B. Hammond, K. Kochut, and Y. Warke. Semantic Content Management for Enterprises and the Web. *IEEE Internet Computing*, July/August 2002.

14. L. Stojanovic, N. Stojanovic, and R. Volz. Migrating data-intensive web sites into the semantic web. In *Proceedings of the 17th ACM symposium on applied computing (SAC)*, pages 1100 – 1107. ACM Press, 2002.

15. Y. Sure, H. Akkermans, J. Broekstra, J. Davies, Y. Ding, A. Duke, R. Engels, D. Fensel, I. Horrocks, V. Iosif, A. Kampman, A. Kiryakov, M. Klein, Th. Lau, D. Ognyanov, U. Reimer, K. Simov, R. Studer, J. van der Meer, and F van Harmelen. On-To-Knowledge: Semantic Web Enabled Knowledge Management. In N. Zhong, J. Liu, and Y. Yao, editors, *Web Intelligence*. Springer-Verlag, 2003.

16. F. van Harmelen. How the Semantic Web will change KR: challenges and opportunities for a new research agenda. *The Knowledge Engineering Review*, 17(1):93 – 96, 2002.

17. M. Vargas-Vera, E. Motta, J. Domingue, M. Lanzoni, A. Stutt, and F. Ciravegna. MnM: Ontology Driven Semi-Automatic and Automatic Support for Semantic Markup. In *Proceedings of the 13th International Conference on Knowledge Engineering and Management (EKAW)*, Spain, 2002.

18. J. Zhu, V. Uren, and E. Motta. ESpotter: Adaptive Named Entity Recognition for Web Browsing. In *Proceedings of the Professional Knowledge Management Conference*, 2004.

Extracting Instances of Relations from Web Documents Using Redundancy

Viktor de Boer, Maarten van Someren, and Bob J. Wielinga

Human-Computer Studies Laboratory, Informatics Institute,
Universiteit van Amsterdam
{vdeboer, maarten, wielinga}@science.uva.nl

Abstract. In this document we describe our approach to a specific sub-task of ontology population, the extraction of instances of relations. We present a generic approach with which we are able to extract information from documents on the Web. The method exploits redundancy of information to compensate for loss of precision caused by the use of domain independent extraction methods. In this paper, we present the general approach and describe our implementation for a specific relation instance extraction task in the art domain. For this task, we describe experiments, discuss evaluation measures and present the results.

1 Introduction

The emerging notion of the Semantic Web envisions a next generation of the World Wide Web in which content can be semantically interpreted with the use of ontologies. Following [1], we make a distinction between ontology and knowledge base. An ontology consists of the concepts (classes) and relations that make up a conceptualization of a domain, the knowledge base contains the ontology content, consisting of the instances of the classes and relations in the ontology. The Semantic Web calls for a large number of both ontologies on different domains and knowledge base content.

It has been argued that manual construction of ontologies is time consuming and that (semi-)automatic methods for the construction of ontologies would be of great benefit to the field and there is a lot of research into tackling this problem. For the same reason, to avoid the knowledge acquisition bottleneck, we also would like to extract the ontology content in a (semi)-automatic way from existing sources of information such as the World Wide Web. This task is called ontology population. The content can exist either in the form of actual extracted information stored in some knowledge base for which the ontology acts as the metadata schema, or it can be locally stored web content annotated with concepts from the ontology. Automatic methods for ontology population are needed to avoid the tedious labor of manually annotating documents.

The task of ontology learning can be decomposed into learning domain concepts, discovering the concept hierarchy and learning relations between concepts. We can also decompose ontology population into the extraction of concept instances or instances of relations. In this document, we describe a method for

Y. Sure and J. Domingue (Eds.): ESWC 2006, LNCS 4011, pp. 245–258, 2006.

automatically extracting instances of relations, predefined in an ontology. This task, further defined in the next section, we call *Relation Instantiation*.

A common and generic approach to extracting content is to build the next generation of the web on top of the existing one, that is, to use the World Wide Web as our corpus containing the information we use to extract our content from. For the main part of this document, we will focus on the Web Corpus.

In the next section we will take a closer look at the relation instantiation task and current approaches to it. In Section 3, we briefly look at current approaches to this task.

In Section 4, we will describe the architecture of our method. A case study, evaluation and our results will be discussed in Section 5 and in the last section we will look at related work and further research.

2   Relation Instantiation

In this section, we first describe the relation instantiation task and the assumptions we make, followed by a short description of current approaches to automatic extraction of relation instances.

For our purpose, we define an ontology as a set of labeled classes (the domain concepts) $C_1, ..., C_n$, hierarchically ordered by a subclass relation. Other relations between concepts are also defined ($R : C_i \times C_j$). We speak of a (partly) populated ontology when, besides the ontology, a knowledge base with instances of both concepts and relations from the ontology is also present.

We define the task of relation instantiation from a corpus as follows:

> Given two classes C_i and C_j in a partly populated ontology, with sets of instances I_i and I_j and given a relation $R : C_i \times C_j$, identify for an instance $i \in I_i$ for which $j \in I_j$, the relation $R(i, j)$ is true given the information in the corpus.

Furthermore, in this document we make a number of additional assumptions listed below:

- the relation R is not a one-to-one relation. The instance i is related to multiple elements of I_j.
- we know all elements of I_j.
- we have a method available that recognizes these instances in the documents in our corpus. For a textual corpus such as the Web, this implies that the instances must have a textual representation.
- in individual documents of the corpus, multiple instances of the relation are represented.
- we have a (small) example set of instances of C_i and C for which the relation R holds.

Examples of relation instantiation tasks that meet these assumptions include: extracting the relation between instances of the concept 'Country' and the concept 'City', in a geographical ontology; the extraction of the relation 'appears_in' between films and actors in an ontology about movies or finding the relation 'has_artist' between instances of the class 'Art Style' and instances of the class 'Artist' in an ontology describing the art domain. As a case study for our approach, we chose this last example and we shall discuss this in Section 5.

3   Current Approaches

The current approaches to (semi-)automatic relation instantiation and Ontology Population in general can be divided into two types: Those that use natural language techniques and those that try to exploit the structure of the documents.

The approaches that use natural language adopt techniques such as stemming, tagging and statistical analysis of natural language to do the Information Extraction. Some methods learn natural language patterns to extract the instances. These methods generally perform well on free text but fail to extract information in semi-structured documents containing lists or tables of information.

Secondly, the structure-based extraction methods such as [2] perform well on (semi-)structured documents containing lists or tables with information but they perform poorly on natural language sources. However, most of the content on the Web is highly heterogeneous in structure, even within individual web pages. A generic method for extracting the different kinds of information presented on the World Wide Web should be able to handle different types of documents and more specifically documents that themselves contain variably structured information.

Also, as was argued in [3], the current approaches assume a large number of tagged example instances to be able to learn patterns for extracting new instances. This is a serious limitation for large scale use.

In the next section, we will present our approach to relation instantiation, which is applicable to heterogeneous sources and minimizes the need for tagged example instances.

4   Redundancy Based Relation Instantiation

In this section, we describe our method for relation instantiation. We want the method to be applicable to a wide range of domains and heterogeneous corpora and therefore we use generic methods based on coarse ground features that do not rely on assumptions about the type of documents in the corpus. However, by using these more general methods for the extraction, we will lose in precision since the general methods are not tweaked to perform well on any type of domain or corpus. We need to compensate for this loss.

The Web is extremely large and a lot of knowledge is redundantly available in different forms. Since we choose methods that are applicable to a greater number of sources on the Web than the more specific ones, we have a greater set of documents to extract our information from. We assume that because of the redundancy information on the Web and because we are able to combine information from different sources, we can compensate for this loss of precision.

Our approach to relation instantiation relies on bootstrapping from already known examples of the relation so we also assume that we have a (small) set of instances for which we already know that the given relation holds.

4.1   Outline of the Method

We first now present an outline of the method for the general relation instantiation task described in Section 2. In Section 5, we present how a specific relation instantiation task can be performed using this method. The outline of our method for relation instantiation is shown in Figure 1.

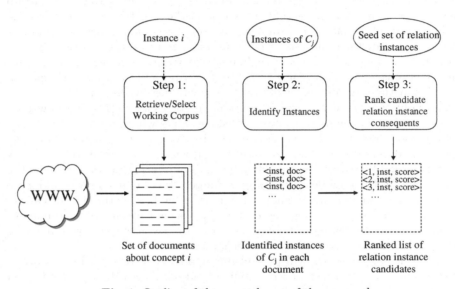

Fig. 1. Outline of the general case of the approach

To extract instances of the relation $R(i,j)$, we first construct a 'working corpus', consisting of a subset of documents from the World Wide Web describing the concept i. These documents are retrieved using a search engine (retrieving the pages that make up the result when searching for the label of the concept). Note that, for reasons of redundancy, we do not require a retrieval module that scores high on 'precision', instead we focus on recall (a high number of pages). The size of the subset is a parameter of the method.

The next step in the approach is the identification of all textual representations of instances of the concept C_j. Since we assume that we know all instances, this step consists of matching the instances to their representations on the corpus documents using a given method.

Once we have identified all instances in the documents as candidates for a new instance of the relation, we integrate the evidence to produce a ranking for these candidates. We do this by calculating a document score DS for each document. This document score represents how likely it is that for each of the instances $j \in I_j$ identified in that document, the relation $R(i, j)$ holds according to the seed set.

After the DS for each document is calculated, for each relation instance candidate an instance score IS is calculated, which is an aggregate of the document scores associated with the candidate. The document and instance scores are defined in section 4.2.

4.2   Document and Instance Scores

We use the seed set to calculate DS and IS. We look for evidence of instances of ontological relations in textual documents and we assume that this relation is represented in the corpus through the occurrence of textual representations of the instances of C_j in documents that are themselves representations of i. If a relatively large number of instances of C_j are already part of our seed set of instances with the relation to i, we can assume that this relation is well represented by this document and that there is evidence that any other instances identified in that document will also be part of this relation. Following this principle we give a document score $DS_{doc,i}$ to each document:

$$DS_{doc,i} = \frac{\mu_{doc}}{\nu_{doc}} \qquad (1)$$

where $\nu_{doc} = |\{j \in I_j, j \text{ in } doc\}|$ and $\mu_{doc,i} = |\{j \in I_j, j \text{ in } doc, R(i, j) \in seedset\}|$

This can be interpreted as the probability that an instance is in the seed set of the relation given that it is an instance of C_j. We use this document score to calculate a score for each of the instances of C_j identified in the corpus that are not in our seed list. The evidence score for each instance is the average of DS_{doc} over the number of used documents: N.

$$IS_j = \frac{\sum^{doc} DS_{doc}}{N} \qquad (2)$$

where $j \in I_j, j \in doc$

We rank all instances of C_j by their instance score. All instances with a score above some threshold are added to the knowledge base as instances of the relation. The threshold is determined empirically.

5   Example: Artists and Art Styles

In this section, we illustrate how the approach works on an example of the relation instantiation task described in Section 2.

5.1   Method Setup

As the domain in which to test our approach, we chose the art domain. We use the method to extract instances of relations between two different existing structured vocabularies widely used in the art domain.

One of the vocabularies is the Art and Architecture Thesaurus [4] (AAT), a thesaurus defining a large number of terms used to describe and classify art. The other is the Unified List of Artist names [5] (ULAN), a list of almost 100.000 names of artists. We took the combination of these two structured vocabularies (in RDF format) and added a relation `aua:has_artist` [1] between the AAT concept `aat:Styles and Periods` and the top-level ULAN concept `ulan:Artist`. This made up our ontology and knowledge base.

In these experiments, the task is to find new instances of the `aua:has_artist` relation between `aat:Styles and Periods` and `ulan:Artist`, with the use of a seed set of instances of this relation. The `aua:has_artist` relation describes which artists represent a specific art style. R is `aua:has_artist`, C_i is `aat: Styles and Periods` and C_j is `ulan:Artist`. This relation satisfies the requirement that it is not a one-to-one relation since a single art style is represented by a number of artists. For each of the experiments, we manually added a number of instances of the `aua:has_artist` relation to the knowledge base.

For each experiment, we first choose for which instance of `aat:Styles and Periods` we will extract new relations. Then, for the working corpus retrieval step, we query the Google[2] search engine using the label string of that instance, for example 'Impressionism', 'Post-Impressionism' or 'Expressionism'. In the experiments described below, we retrieved 200 pages in this way.

Then in step 2, for every document of this corpus, we identify the instances of `ulan:Artist` in that document. The instances (individual artists) are textually represented in the documents in the form of person names. Here we use the Person Name Extraction module of the tOKO toolkit [6]. We then match all person names identified by the module to the instances of `ulan:Artist`, thus filtering out all non-artist person names. One difficulty in this step is disambiguation of names. Because of the large number of artists in the ULAN, unambiguously finding the correct artist with a name proved very difficult. For example, the ULAN lists three different artists named 'Paul Gauguin', thus making it impossible to determine which specific artist is referred to in a document using only the name string.

Rather than resorting to domain-specific heuristic methods such as considering birth dates to improve precision, the method relies on the redundancy of information on the Web to overcome this problem through the occurrence of a full name ('Paul Eugene-Henri Gauguin') in a number of documents. We discard any ambiguous name occurrences and assume that a non-ambiguous name occurrences will appear somewhere in the corpus. This step leaves us with a set of instances of C_j identified in the documents.

In step 3 we determine the document score, DS, for all documents and from that IS for all identified artists, using our seed set. For each of the artists found in the corpus, the scores of the pages it appears on are summarized. We normalize this score and order all artists by this score. In Section 5.3 and 5.4 we present the results of a number of experiments conducted in this way.

---

[1] `aua` denotes our namespace specifically created for these experiments
[2] www.google.com

5.2 Evaluation

Evaluation of Ontology Learning and Population still is an open issue. Since the specific task we tackle resembles Information Retrieval, we would like to calculate standard IR evaluation measures such as precision, recall and the combination: the F-measure. However, this requires us to have a gold standard of all relations in a domain. Although we assume we know all artists, there is no classic gold standard that for an single art style indicates which artists represent that art style. This is due to the fuzziness of the domain. Art web sites, encyclopedias and experts disagree about which individual artists represent a certain art style. Although this fuzziness occurs in many domains, it is very apparent in the Art domain. For our experiments we chose a number of representative web pages on a specific art style and manually identified the artists that were designated as representing that art style. If there was a relative consensus about an artist representing the art style among the pages, we added it to our 'gold standard'. The gold standard we obtained using this method is used to measure recall, precision and F_1-measure values.

5.3 Experiment 1: Expressionism

In our first experiment, we chose 'Expressionism' as the instance of C_i. We manually constructed a gold standard from 12 authoritative web pages. For a total of 30 artists that were considered Expressionists in three or more of these documents we used the relation `aua:has_artist` from Expressionism to those artists as our gold standard. The actual artists that make up our gold standard are shown in Table 1. From these 30 instances of the relation, we randomly selected three instances (italicized in Table 1) as our seed set and followed the approach described above to retrieve the remaining instances of the relation.

Step 1 (the retrieval step) resulted in 200 documents, from this we extracted the person names, matched the names to ULAN artists and calculated the IS score for each artists as described in the previous sections. In Table 2, we show the

Table 1. Our gold standard for 'Expressionism'. The names of the three artists selected for the seed set are italicized.

Paula Modersohn-Becker	Emil Nolde	Edvard Munch
Georges Rouault	George Grosz	Erich Heckel
Kathe Kollwitz	Otto Dix	Lyonel Feininger
Egon Schiele	August Macke	Paul Klee
Ernst Ludwig Kirchner	Max Pechstein	Ernst Barlach
Oskar Kokoschka	Alexei Jawlensky	Francis Bacon
Chaim Soutine	James Ensor	Gabriele Munter
Franz Marc	Karl Schmidt-Rottluff	Heinrich Campendonk
Max Beckmann	Alfred Kubin	Jules Pascin
Wassily Kandinsky	Amedeo Modigliani	Gustav Klimt

Table 2. Part of the resulting ordered list for i = 'Expressionism'. For each identified artist, we have listed whether it appears in the gold standard ('1') or not ('0').

Artist Name	IS	In GS
grosz, george	0.0100	1
emil nolde	0.0097	1
heckel, erich	0.0092	1
marc, franz	0.0060	1
pechstein, max	0.0058	1
max beckman	0.0056	1
kandinsky, wassily	0.0054	1
munch, edvard	0.0042	1
kokoschka, oskar	0.0042	1
schiele egon	0.0041	1
klee, paul	0.0040	1
dix, otto	0.0024	1
alexej von jawlensky	0.0021	1
chaim soutine	0.0020	1
santiago calatrava	0.0016	0
...	...	...

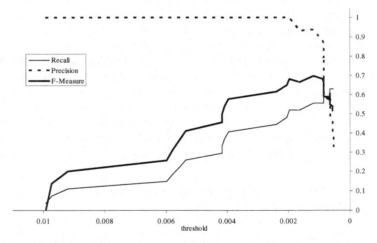

Fig. 2. Recall, precision and F-measure for Experiment 1

top 15 candidates for the instantiation of the relation according to the resulting ranked list.

In Figure 2, we plotted the value for the F-measure against the value for the threshold. The value of F decreases as the value for the threshold decreases. The highest value of F is 0.70 (this occurs at values for recall and precision of respectively 0.56 and 0.94). This highest F-value is obtained with a threshold of 0.0012.

Table 3. Our gold standard for 'Impressionism'. The names of the three artists selected for the seed set are italicized.

Claude Monet	Frederick Bazille	Paul Gauguin
Alfred Sisley	Boudin	Armand Guillaumin
F.C. Frieseke	Gustave Caillebotte	Childe Hassam
Berthe Morisot	Mary Cassat	Edouard Manet
Georges Seurat	Paul Cezanne	Edgar Degas
Camille Pissarro	Camille Corot	Pierre-Auguste Renoir

To test the robustness of the method with respect to the content of the seed set, we performed the same experiments using two different seed sets selected from the gold standard. One seed set consisted of the three most likely artists linked with Expressionist, according to our ordered gold standard. This seed set yielded the same results: a maximum value of F of 0.69 was found (recall = 0.63, precision = 0.77). The other seed set consisted of the three least likely Expressionists, resulting in a lower maximum value of F: 0.58 (recall = 0.63, precision = 0.53).

We also conducted this experiment using different sizes of the seed set (15 seed/15 to be found and 9 seed/21 to be found). These experiments yielded approximately the same maximum values for the F-measure. Before we discuss further findings, we first present the results of a second experiment within the art domain, using a different instance of C_i: Impressionism.

5.4   Experiment 2: Impressionism

From the 11 web pages mentioned in Section 5.2, we identified 18 artists that were added to our gold standard. From these 18 instances of the relation, we again chose three as our seed set and followed the approach described above to retrieve the 15 remaining instances of the relation. Again, the actual artists are shown in Table 3.

We again built a corpus of 200 documents and performed the described steps. In Table 4, we show a part of the resulting ordered list.

Again, we plotted the value of precision, recall and F (Figure 3). In this experiment, F reaches a maximum value of 0.83 (where recall = 0.80 and precision = 0.86) at a threshold value of 0.0084. In this experiment, we also tested for robustness by using different content for the seed set in the same way as in Experiment 1. If the seed set contained the most likely Impressionists according to our ordered Gold Standard, the maximum value of F is 0.72 (recall = 0.60, precision is 0.90). If we start with the least likely Impressionists the maximum value of F is 0.69 (recall = 0.8, precision = 0.6).

5.5   Discussion

In the experiments, we find almost the same maximum value of F under different conditions. In both cases, the first few found artist are always in the gold stan-

Table 4. Part of the resulting ordered list for $i =$'Impressionism'

Artist Name	IS	In GS
edgar degas	0.0699	1
edouard manet	0.0548	1
pierre-auguste renoir	0.0539	1
morisot, berthe	0.0393	1
gogh, vincent van	0.0337	0
cassatt, mary	0.0318	1
cezanne, paul	0.0302	1
georges pierre seurat	0.0230	1
caillebotte, gustave	0.0180	1
bazille, frederic	0.0142	1
guillaumin, armand	0.0132	1
signac paul	0.0131	0
childe hassam	0.0120	1
eugene louis boudin	0.0084	1
sargent, john singer	0.0081	0
...	...	...

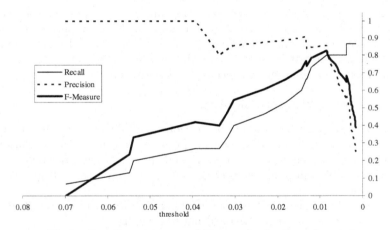

Fig. 3. Recall, precision and F-measure for Experiment 2

dard, after which the precision drops due to the errors made. The values of F are encouraging. There are several reasons that the F-measure does not reach higher values. These can be divided into reasons for lack of precision and for lack of recall.

First of all, one of the reasons for the false positives is due to precision errors of the Person Name Extraction module. For example, in Experiment 2 the misclassified string "d'Orsay" (name of a museum on impressionist art) is first misclassified as a person name and then passes the disambiguation step and is mapped to the ULAN entity "Comte d'Orsay".

Another portion of the error in precision is caused by the strictness of the gold standard that we used. In Experiment 2, Vincent van Gogh is suggested as an Impressionist, he is however, not in our gold standard. However, a number of sources cite him as an Impressionist painter and a less strict gold standard could have included this painter. We assume that this strictness of the gold standard accounts for a lot of the lack of precision.

Errors in recall are also caused by three factors. We find that 2 of the 15 Impressionists and 10 of the 27 Expressionists are not in our ordered list at all. As with precision, errors made by the Person Name Extraction module account for a part of the lack of recall. The module (biased towards English names), has apparent difficulty with non-English names such as 'Ernst Ludwig Kirchner' and 'Claude Monet'. A better Person Name Extractor would yield a higher recall and consequently, a better value for the F-measure.

Another cause for recall errors is the difficulty of the disambiguation of the artist names. From some extracted names, it is even impossible to identify the correct ULAN entity. An example is the string 'Lyonel Feininger'. In the ULAN there are two different artists: one with the name 'Lyonel Feininger' and one with the name 'Andreas Bernard Lyonel Feininger'. Our method cannot determine which one of these entities is found in the text and so the string is discarded.

Of course, a number of artists are not retrieved because they simply do not appear in the same (retrieved) page as one of the artist from a seed list. One way to solve this problem is introduced in the next section.

A problem, not directly related to recall and precision is that from the experiments featured above, it is not possible to a priori determine a standard value for the threshold, with which the value of the F-measure is at a maximum. The optimal threshold value for Experiment 1 is 0.0012, whereas in Experiment 2 it is 0.0043. The lack of a method to determine this threshold value poses a problem when the method is used in different, real life situations. It requires experimentation to find the optimal value for F. In the next section we describe an extension to our method to eliminate the need for a threshold value.

5.6   Bootstrapping

To circumvent the need for a generally applicable value for the threshold for actually adding relation instances, we expanded our method by using bootstrapping. Corpus construction, name extraction and the scoring of documents and instances is done in the same way as in the previous experiments. From the resulting ordered list we take the first artist and add a aua:has_artist relation to our seed list. Then on the next iteration, the document and instance scores are again calculated, using the updated seed list. This bootstrapping eliminates the need for a fixed threshold value and we can examine the effect of the total number of iterations on the performance measures. Recall will also be raised due to the fact that documents that have received a score of zero in a first scoring round can have their document score raised when the newfound instances are added to the seed list. We depict the results in Table 5 and Figure 4.

While we find approximately the same values for the F-measure, we have indeed eliminated the need for a threshold and raised the overall recall (now

Table 5. The first 15 iterative results for $i =$'Expressionism'

Artist Name	Iteration	In GS
grosz, george	1	1
emile nolde	2	1
heckel, erich	3	1
pechstein, max	4	1
max beckman	5	1
vasily kandinsky	6	1
munch, edvard	7	1
kokoschka, oskar	8	1
marc, franz	9	1
klee, paul	10	1
dix otto	11	1
schiele egon	12	1
alexey von jawlensky	13	1
vincent van gogh	14	0
baron ensor	15	1
...	...	...

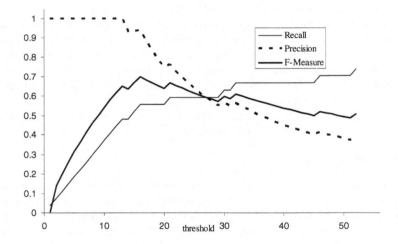

Fig. 4. Recall, precision and F-measure for the Iterative Experiment

only 7 out of 27 Expressionists are never awarded a score higher than 0). We now have the issue of determining when to stop the iteration process. This is the subject of future research.

6   Related Work

Related work has been done in various fields, including Information Extraction, Information Retrieval and Ontology Learning.

The Armadillo system [7] is also designed to extract information from the World Wide Web. The Armadillo method starts out with a reliable seed set, extracted from highly structured and easily minable sources such as lists or databases and uses bootstrapping to train more complex modules to extract information from other sources. Like our method, Armadillo uses redundancy of information on the Web to combine evidence for new instances. One of the differences between Armadillo and our method is that Armadillo does not require a complete list of instances as our method does. The method, however requires specific sources of information as input, depending on the type of information to be extracted using wrappers. Our method requires no extra input defined by the extraction task other than relevant instance extraction modules such as the Person Name Extraction module.

Also, in the method proposed by Cimiano et al. [8], evidence from different techniques is combined to extract information. This method, however attempts to extract taxonomic relations between concepts. Our method can be used to extract instances of non-taxonomic relations as well, as shown by our experiments.

The KnowItAll system [9] aims to automatically extract the 'facts' (instances) from the web autonomously and domain-independently. It uses Machine Learning to learn domain-specific extraction patterns, starting from universal patterns. In combination with techniques that exploit list structures the method is able to extract information from heterogeneous sources.

The Normalized Google Distance [10] is a method that calculates semantic distance between two terms by using a search engine (Google). This method does not use a seed set and could be used to extract instances of relations. However, the method can only determine the distance between two terms (as opposed to our method, which takes ontological instances, that can have multiple terms, as input). The Normalized Google Distance is also unable to distinguish between different types of relations between instances. Using our method, different relations can be examined, due to the use of the seed set. We are currently exploring this in more detail.

7   Conclusions and Further Research

We have argued that for Relation Instantiation, an Information Extraction task, methods that work on heterogeneous sources should become available to extract instances of relations in various domains. We presented a novel approach to this task exploiting the redundancy of information on the Web. We presented an outline for this approach in the form of a framework that is applicable in various domains and described the prerequisites of this approach. A specific instance of a Relation Instantiation problem in the Art domain was presented and we implemented and tested of the method. The recall and precision scores are satisfactory, considering the strict evaluation standards used and suggest further research and testing of the method.

An obvious direction for further research is to test this method in other domains. Examples of domains are geography (eg. which cities are located in a country) and the biomedical domain (which proteins interact with a gene).

Another direction for further research is to expand in such a way that new instances of concept C_j can be added to the ontology, whereas now, only known instances can be part of a instantiated relation.

Also, the notion of exploiting redundancy of information on the web by using generally applicable methods could be expanded in such a way that other subtasks of ontology learning, such as hierarchy construction or concept discovery could be performed.

Acknowledgements

This research was supported by MultimediaN project (www.multimedian.nl) funded through the BSIK programme of the Dutch Government. We would like to thank Anjo Anjewierden and Jan Wielemaker for their extensive programming support.

References

1. Maedche, A., Staab, S.: Ontology learning for the semantic web. IEEE Intelligent Systems **13** (2001) 993
2. Kushmerick, N., Weld, D., Doorenbos, R.: Wrapper induction for information extraction. In: in Proceedings of the Fifteenth International Joint Conference on Artificial Intelligence. (1997) 729737
3. Cimiano, P.: Ontology learning and population. Proceedings Dagstuhl Seminar Machine Learning for the Semantic Web (2005)
4. The Getty Foundation: Aat: The art and architecture thesaurus. http://www.getty.edu/research/tools/vocabulary/aat/ (2000)
5. The Getty Foundation: Ulan: Union list of artist names. http://www.getty.edu/research/tools/vocabulary/ulan/ (2000)
6. Anjewierden, A., Wielinga, B.J., de Hoog, R.: Task and domain ontologies for knowledge mapping in operational processes. Metis Deliverable 4.2/2003, University of Amsterdam. (2004)
7. Ciravegna, F., Chapman, S., Dingli, A., Wilks, Y.: Learning to harvest information for the semantic web. Proceedings of the 2nd European Semantic Web Conference, Heraklion, Greece (2005)
8. Cimiano, P., Schmidt-Thieme, L., Pivk, A., Staab, S.: Learning taxonomic relations from heterogeneous evidence. Proceedings of the ECAI 2004 Ontology Learning and Population Workshop (2004)
9. Etzioni, O., Cafarella, M., Downey, D., Kok, S., Popescu, A., Shaked, T., Soderland, S., Weld, D.S., Yates, A.: Webscale information extraction in knowitall preliminary results. In: in Proceedings of WWW2004. (2004)
10. Cilibrasi, R., Vitanyi, P.: Automatic meaning discovery using google. http://xxx.lanl.gov/abs/cs.CL/0412098 (2004)

Toward Multi-viewpoint Reasoning
with OWL Ontologies

Heiner Stuckenschmidt

Institut für Praktische Informatik
University of Mannheim
A5,6 68159 Mannheim, Germany
heiner@informatik.uni-mannheim.de

Abstract. Despite of their advertisement as task independent representations, the reuse of ontologies in different contexts is difficult. An explanation for this is that when developing an ontology, a choice is made with
respect to what aspects of the world are relevant. In this paper we deal
with the problem of reusing ontologies in a context where only parts of the
originally encoded aspects are relevant. We propose the notion of a viewpoint on an ontology in terms of a subset of the complete representation
vocabulary that is relevant in a certain context. We present an approach of
implementing different viewpoints in terms of an approximate subsumption operator that only cares about a subset of the vocabulary. We discuss the formal properties of subsumption with respect to a subset of the
vocabulary and show how these properties can be used to efficiently compute different viewpoints on the basis of maximal sub-vocabularies that
support subsumption between concept pairs.

1 Introduction

Originally, ontologies where meant as a task-neutral description of a certain
domain of interest that can be reused for different purposes. This idea is also at
the heart of the semantic web vision, where the ontology-based description of
Information is supposed to make it possible to use the information for different
purposes and in different contexts. In practice, however, it has turned out that
the re-use of ontologies for different tasks and purposes causes problems [15].
The reason for this is that ontologies are often not really designed independent
of the task at hand. The development is rather driven by the special needs of
a particular system or task. In general the context of use has an impact on the
way concepts are defined to support certain functionalities. As some aspects of a
domain that are important for one application do not matter for another one and
vice versa, an ontology does not represent the features needed for a particular
application. In this case, there is little hope for direct reuse. Another potential
problem, that we will address in this paper is that an ontology contains too
many aspects of a domain. This can become a problem, because in introduces
unnecessary complexity and can even lead to unwanted conclusions, because
the ontology introduces unwanted distinctions between classes that should be

Y. Sure and J. Domingue (Eds.): ESWC 2006, LNCS 4011, pp. 259–272, 2006.
© Springer-Verlag Berlin Heidelberg 2006

treated in the same way in the current application context. We argue that in order to solve this problem, we have to find ways to enable the representation of different viewpoints on the same ontology, that better reflects the actual needs of the application at hand.

1.1 Related Work

The concept if having different viewpoints on the same model is a well established concept in the area of software engineering [8]. In order to extend this to semantic web systems, the concept of a viewpoint has to be extended to the semantic models used in the system. There has been some work on specifying viewpoints on RDF data, mainly inspired by the concept of views in database systems. The idea is to define rules for extracting an possibly restructuring parts of a basic RDF model to better reflect the needs of a certain user or application. Different techniques have been proposed including the use of named queries [10], the definition of a view in terms of graph traversal operations [11] and the use of integrity constraints for ensuring the consistency of a viewpoint [16]. In this paper, we focus on ontologies represented in description logics, in particular OWL-DL. In the context of description logics, the classical notion of views can only be used in a restricted way as relevant inference problems related to views have been shown to be undecidable [3].

An alternative approach to viewpoints in description logics has been proposed based on the concept of contextual reasoning . Here, each viewpoint is represented in terms of a separate model with a local interpretation [9]. Relations between different viewpoints are represented by context mappings that constrain the local interpretations. Based on these basic principles of contextual reasoning, approaches for representing and linking different viewpoints on the same domain have been developed for description logics [4] and for OWL resulting the C-OWL language [6]. These approaches, however have a slightly different goal as they mainly aim at providing means for integrating different existing models. Our interest is to develop methods that allows us to extract a certain viewpoint from an existing model that best fits the requirements of an application.

An approach that is very similar to this idea is the work of Arara and others [12, 1]. They propose the use of modal description logics for encoding multiple viewpoints in the same ontology by indexing parts of the definitions with the contexts they are supposed to hold in. A drawback of their approach is that they require an extension of the representation language and its semantics to deal with multiple perspectives. In contrast to the contextual approaches mentioned above there currently is no reasoning support for this formalism.

1.2 Contributions and Motivating Example

In this paper, we propose an approach for multi-viewpoint reasoning that do not require an extension to the OWL-DL language. The approach is based on the idea of approximate logical reasoning and uses an approximate subsumption operator that can be tuned to only use a certain part of the definitions in the

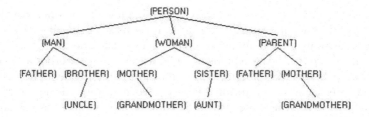

Fig. 1. The Example Ontology

ontology. In particular, we address the problem of efficient computing concept hierarchies that represent a certain viewpoint on a domain in terms of ignoring a certain subset of the vocabulary used in concept expressions.

To clarify this idea we consider the family ontology shown in figure 1. The ontology classifies persons into different concepts according to certain criteria including gender and the presence of children.

The silent assumption underlying this ontology is that all of the criteria used in the definitions are actually relevant for the application. In particular, the assumption is that it is important to distinguish between male and female persons (man vs. woman) and between people with and without children (woman vs. mother).

We can imagine applications that would benefit from an ontology of people, but in which only some of the distinguishing aspects are important. An example would be a system for processing salary information in the German public sector. In such a system it makes sense to distinguish between people with and without children, because the existence of children entitles to special benefits. The distinction between genders in completely irrelevant in this context and even prohibited by laws guaranteeing gender equality. Other applications e.g. related to private pension funds the gender is relevant as there are different regulations with respect to the age in which male and female persons can retire. In this application the existence of children is not important.

The paper is structured as follows. In section 2 first briefly introduce Description Logics as a basis for representing ontologies including some modeling examples from our example ontology and review the notion of approximate deduction in description logics proposed by Cadoli and Schaerf [13]. Section 3 introduces our notion of a viewpoint and its definition in terms of an approximate subsumption operator. In section 4 we discuss some axiomatic properties of the approximate subsumption operators and discuss their use for implementing basic reasoning services relevant for multi-viewpoint reasoning. The paper concludes with a discussion of the approach.

2   The Description Logics $\mathcal{SIN}$

The basic modeling elements in Description Logics are concepts (classes of objects), roles (binary relations between objects) and individuals (named objects).

Based on these modeling elements, Description Logics contain operators for specifying so-called concept expressions that can be used to specify necessary and sufficient conditions for membership in the concept they describe. Basic reasoning tasks associated with these kinds of logics are checking whether an expression is satisfiable (whether it is possible that an object satisfies the membership condition) and deciding subsumption between two concepts (deciding whether a concept expression implies another one). We now look at these issues on a more formal level.

Let C be a set of concept names and R a set of role names. Further let there be a set $R^+ \subseteq R$ of transitive roles (i.e. for each $r \in R^+$ we have $r(x,y) \wedge r(y,z) \Rightarrow r(x,z)$). If now R^- denotes the inverse of a role (i.e. $r(x,y) \Rightarrow r^-(y,x)$) then we define the set of roles as $R \cup \{r^- | r \in R\}$. A role is called a simple role if it is not transitive. The set of concepts (or concept expressions) in $\mathcal{SIN}$ is the smallest set such that:

- $\top$ and $\bot$ are concept expressions
- every concept name A is a concept expression
- if C and D are concept expressions, r is a role, s is a simple role and n is a non-negative integer, then $\neg C$, $C \sqcap D$, $C \sqcup D$, $\forall r.C$, $\exists r.C$, $\geq n\, r$ and $\leq n\, r$ are concept expressions.

A general concept inclusion axioms is an expression $C \sqsubseteq D$ where C and D are concepts, the equivalence axiom $C \equiv D$ is defined as $C \sqsubseteq D \wedge D \sqsubseteq C$ A terminology is a set of general concept inclusion and role inclusion axioms. In the following, we only consider axioms of the form $A \sqsubseteq C$ and $A \equiv C$ where A is an atomic concept name. Further, we assume that all concepts C are in negation normal form (negation only applies to atomic concept names). Note that for every concept can deterministically be transformed into an equivalent concept in negation normal form. Thus this assumption does not impose any restriction on the approach.

This logic covers a significant part of the OWL-DL Language. We exclude the following language elements, because their behavior in connection with the approximation approach presented below needs more investigation:

- Role Hierarchies: It is not clear how to deal with the situation where we want to consider a certain role but not its super-roles.
- Qualified Number restrictions: The use of qualified number restrictions make it hard to predict the effect of restricting reasoning to a sub-vocabulary, because ignoring the type restriction to C in the expression $(\geq n\, r.C)$ makes the overall expression more general whereas ignoring C in $(\leq n\, r.C)$ makes the expression more specific.
- Nominals: The current mechanism for implementing multi-viewpoint reasoning is based on concept and role names and does not cover objects as part of the signature of an ontology.
- General Concept Inclusion Axioms: The presence of general inclusion axioms makes it hard to determine the impact of ignoring parts of the vocabulary on the interpretation of a certain concept.

Examples. In the following we illustrate the use of description logic for defining and reasoning about concepts in our example ontology from figure 1. In particular, we look at the definitions of concepts related to motherhood. In our ontology the concept mother is defined as an intersection of the concepts Woman and Parent stating that each mothers is both, a woman and a parent.

$$\texttt{Mother} \equiv \texttt{Woman} \sqcap \texttt{Parent}$$

These two concepts in turn are defined as special cases of the person concept using the relations `has-gender` and `has-child`. In particular, these relations are used to claim that each woman must have the gender female and that each parent must have a person as a child.

$$\texttt{Woman} \equiv \texttt{Person} \sqcap \exists\texttt{has} - \texttt{gender.Female}$$

$$\texttt{Parent} \equiv \texttt{Person} \sqcap \exists\texttt{has} - \texttt{child.Person}$$

Finally, the concept of a grandmother is defined by chaining the has-child relation to state that every instance of this class is a Woman with a child that has a child itself which is a Person.

$$\texttt{Grandmother} \equiv \texttt{Woman} \sqcap \exists\texttt{has} - \texttt{child.}(\exists\texttt{has} - \texttt{child.Person})$$

Description Logics are equivalent to a fragment of first order logic. Corresponding semantics preserving translation rules from Description logic expressions are given in [2, 5, 14]. Subsumption between concepts ($C \sqsubseteq D$) can be decided based on this semantics. In particular one concept subsumes another if the first order representation of D is implied by the first order representation of C. This way, we can for example find out that `Grandmother` is a subclass of `Mother`.

3   Reasoning with Limited Vocabularies

The idea of reasoning with limited vocabularies has been used in the area of approximate reasoning in order to improve efficiency of propositional inference. Cadoli and Schaerf propose a notion of approximate entailment that allows errors on parts of the vocabulary – in their case propositional letters [13]. We adopt the general idea of allowing errors on parts of the vocabulary and generalize this idea to the case where the vocabulary does not consist of propositional letters, but of concepts and relations. Cadoli and Schaerf also present an extension of their approach to description logics, but in this work the sub-vocabulary does not correspond to concept and role names but rather to the position of a subexpression [7]. As our aim is to provide a mechanism for "switching on and off" certain concept and relation names, we have to find a different way of defining inference with respect to a certain sub-vocabulary.

3.1   Vocabulary-Limited Subsumption

The basic idea of our approach to inference with limited vocabularies is that
terminologies define restrictions on the interpretation of certain concepts. Based
on these restrictions, we can decide whether one concept is subsumed by another
one. In the case of a limited vocabulary, we only want to consider such restrictions
that relate to a certain sub-vocabulary under consideration and ignore other
restriction. If we want to implement this idea, the basic problem is to identify
and eliminate those restrictions that are not related to the sub-vocabulary under
consideration. Here we have to distinguish two kinds of restrictions:

1. the interpretation of a concept can be restricted by claiming that instances
   of this concept belong to a set defined by a Boolean expression over other
   concept names.
2. the interpretation of a concept can be restricted by claiming that instances of
   the concept are related to other object with certain properties via a certain
   relation.

We can deal with the first kind of restriction in the same way as with propositional logic. Therefore we adopt the approach of Cadoli an Schaerf who replace
concepts that are not in the relevant sub-vocabulary as well as their negations
by true. For the case of Description logics this means that we replace concepts
and their negations by $\top$, thus disabling the restriction imposed by them.

The second kind of restrictions can be dealt with by just ignoring those restrictions that are related to a certain relation. This includes the restrictions
on the related objects. More specifically, we can disable these kind of restrictions by replacing subexpressions that contain a relations $r \notin V$ – in particular
subexpressions of the form $(\exists r.C), (\forall r.C), (\geq n\, r)$ and $(\leq n\, r)$ – by $\top$.

Definition 1 (Approximation). *Let* $\mathcal{V} = \mathcal{C} \cup \mathcal{R}$ *be the vocabulary (the set of
all concept and role names) of an ontology. Let further* $V \subseteq \mathcal{V}$ *be a subset of* $\mathcal{V}$
and X *a concept expression in negation normal form, then the approximation of
a concept expression* X *approx*$_V(X)$ *is defined by:*

- *Replacing every concept name* $c \in \mathcal{V} - V$ *that occurs in* X *and its negation
  by* $\top$
- *Replacing every subexpression of* X *that directly contains a slot name* $r \in
  \mathcal{V} - V$ *and its negation by* $\top$

The restriction of terminologies to axioms that only have atomic concept names
on the left hand side allows us to apply the approximation defined above to
complete terminologies in a straightforward way by replacing the right hand
sides of the axioms in a terminology by their approximation. Further, we remove
the definitions of concepts not in V as they are irrelevant. the corresponding
definition of an approximated terminology is the following:

Definition 2 (Approximated Terminology). *Then we define the approximation of a terminology* $\mathcal{T}$ *with respect to sub-vocabulary* V *as*

$$\mathcal{T}_V = \{A \sqsubseteq approx_V(C) | A \in V, (A \sqsubseteq C) \in \mathcal{T}\} \cup$$
$$\{A \equiv approx_V(C) | A \in V, (A \equiv C) \in \mathcal{T}\}$$

The approximated terminology T_V represents the original model while ignoring the influence of the concepts and relations not in V. Consequently, if we can derive a subsumption statement $C \sqsubseteq D$ from this terminology, we can interpret this as subsumption with respect to the sub-vocabulary V.

Definition 3 (Subsumption wrt a sub-vocabulary). *Let T be a terminology with sub-vocabulary $V \subseteq \mathcal{V}$, let further $C, D \in V$ be concept names in V, then we define the notion of subsumption with respect to sub-vocabulary V as:*

$$T \models C \underset{V}{\sqsubseteq} D \Leftrightarrow_{def} T_V \models C \sqsubseteq D$$

In this case, we say that C is subsumed by another concept D with respect to sub-vocabulary V

The definition leaves us with a family of subsumption operators, one for each subset of the vocabulary. Below we illustrate the use of the operator with respect to the motivating example.

Example 1: Gender. We can now apply the notion of subsumption with respect to a sub-vocabulary to our example ontology and exclude certain aspects from the definitions. The first is the case where the target application does not care about the gender of a person. We treat this case by replacing the classical notion of subsumption by subsumption with respect to the vocabulary $\mathcal{V} - \{\texttt{has} - \texttt{gender}\}$. We implement this by replacing subexpressions that directly contain the slot has-gender by $\top$. The result of this operation on the example definitions from above are:

$$\texttt{Woman} \equiv \texttt{Person} \sqcap \top$$

$$\texttt{Parent} \equiv \texttt{Person} \sqcap \exists\texttt{has} - \texttt{child.Person}$$

$$\texttt{Mother} \equiv \top \sqcap \texttt{Parent}$$

$$\texttt{Grandmother} \equiv \texttt{Mother} \sqcap \exists\texttt{has} - \texttt{child.}(\exists\texttt{has} - \texttt{child.Person})$$

As a consequence of this operation, there are a number of changes in the inferable concept hierarchy. In particular, the concept **Mother** becomes equivalent to **Person** with respect to the sub-vocabulary $\mathcal{V} - \{\texttt{has} - \texttt{gender}\}$. The same happens with respect to the concept **Man** which also becomes equivalent to the other two concepts with respect to $\mathcal{V} - \{\texttt{has} - \texttt{gender}\}$. This means that the ontology does not make a distinction between male and female persons any more which is exactly what we wanted to achieve.

Example 2: Children. In the same way, we can implement our second motivating example where we do not want to distinguish between persons with and without children. For this case, we use subsumption with respect to sub-vocabulary $\mathcal{V} - \{\texttt{has} - \texttt{child}\}$. Replacing the corresponding subexpressions in our example by $\top$ leads to the following definitions:

$$\texttt{Woman} \equiv \texttt{Person} \sqcap \exists\texttt{has} - \texttt{gender.Female}$$

$$\text{Parent} \equiv \text{Person} \sqcap \top$$

$$\text{Mother} \equiv \text{Woman} \sqcap \text{Parent}$$

$$\text{Grandmother} \equiv \text{Mother} \sqcap \top$$

In this case, we see that the concept **Parent** becomes equivalent to **Person** with respect to subvocabulary $\mathcal{V} - \{\text{has} - \text{child}\}$. This, in turn makes **Mother** and **Grandmother** equivalent to **Woman**. As we can see, using this weaker notion of subsumption a whole branch of the hierarchy that used to describe different kinds of female parents collapses into a single concept with different names. With respect to our application that does not care about children, this is a wanted effect as we do not want to distinguish between different female persons on the basis of whether they have children or not.

3.2 Defining Viewpoints

As sketched in the motivation, each approximate subsumption operator defines a certain viewpoint on an ontology. In particular, it defines which aspects of a domain are relevant from the current point of view. If we chose the sub-vocabulary such that it does not contain the slot **has-gender** then we state that the corresponding aspect is not of interest for the particular viewpoint implemented by the subsumption operator. This basically means that we actually define a viewpoint in terms of a relevant part of the vocabulary. The corresponding subsumption operator serves as a tool for implementing this viewpoint. Based on this idea we define a viewpoint on an ontology as the set of subsumption relations that hold with respect to a certain sub-vocabulary.

Definition 4 (Viewpoint). *Let $V \subseteq \mathcal{V}$ a sub-vocabulary, then the viewpoint induced by sub-vocabulary V ($\mathcal{P}_V$) is defines as:*

$$\mathcal{P}_V = \{C \sqsubseteq D | C \underset{V}{\sqsubseteq} D\}$$

Example 1: Gender. If we apply the above definition of a viewpoint on our example, we get a modified concept hierarchy, that reflects the corresponding viewpoint on the domain. For the case of the sub-vocabulary $\mathcal{V} - \{\text{has} - \text{gender}\}$ we get the hierarchy shown in figure 2.

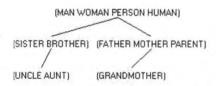

Fig. 2. The Hierarchy if we ignore the gender

If we compare this hierarchy with the original one shown in figure 1, we see that all distinctions that were based on the gender of a person have disappeared from the hierarchy. Now there is a single concept containing men, women, persons and humans a single class containing mothers, fathers and parents as well as a single concept containing brothers and sisters and a single class containing uncles and aunts.

Example: Children. A similar observation can be made when looking at the viewpoint defined by the the sub-vocabulary $\mathcal{V} - \{\texttt{has} - \texttt{child}\}$. The concept hierarchy representing this viewpoint is shown in figure 3.

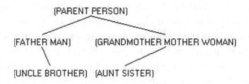

Fig. 3. The Example Ontology if we ignore children

Again, comparing this hierarchy to the original ontology shows that all distinctions that were based on the excluded property have disappeared from the hierarchy. In particular, the root of the hierarchy is now a concept that contains all people and all parents which are now indistinguishable. As in the previous example, this phenomenon occurs across the hierarchy as we now have a single class for women, mothers and grandmothers, a single class for men and fathers as well as a single class for brothers and uncles as well as for sisters and aunts.

4   Multi-perspective Reasoning

The notion of subsumption with respect to a sub-vocabulary comes with new forms of reasoning. We can not longer only ask whether one concept subsumes another, but also whether it does with respect to a certain sub-vocabulary or ask for sub-vocabularies in which a concept subsumes another one. In the following, we first discuss some general properties of the subsumption operator introduced above that defines the relation between subsumption and sub-vocabularies. We then show how we can use the formal properties to efficiently compute viewpoints using sets of maximal vocabularies that ensure subsumption between a pair of concepts.

4.1   Axiomatic Properties of Limited Subsumption

The subsumption with respect to a sub-vocabulary operator has some general properties that we will exploit in the following to define the notion of viewpoint and to discuss the computation of different viewpoints. We briefly present these properties in the following without providing formal proofs, mainly because most of the properties are easy to see from the definition of subsumption with respect to a sub-vocabulary given above.

The first obvious property is the fact that subsumption with respect to the complete vocabulary is exactly the same as classical subsumption. The argument for this is straightforward as in that case, the set of concepts and relations to be removed from concept expressions is empty, so checking limited subsumption is just checking classical subsumption

$$C \sqsubseteq_{\mathcal{V}} D \Leftrightarrow C \sqsubseteq D \tag{1}$$

The properties above describe is an extreme cases of the framework where either the complete vocabulary is considered to be relevant. The interesting cases, however, are those where subsets of the vocabulary are considered. An interesting feature of the approach is that there is a direct correspondence between the relation between different sub-vocabularies and the limited forms of subsumption they define. In particular, the subsumption between two concepts with respect to a sub-vocabulary V_1 implies subsumption between the same concepts with respect to any subset V_2 of V_1.

$$C \sqsubseteq_{V_1} D \Rightarrow C \sqsubseteq_{V_2} D, \text{if } V_2 \subseteq V_1 \tag{2}$$

Another property is concerned with the transitivity of subsumption. It is quite obvious that if C subsumes D and D subsumes E with respect to the same sub-vocabulary, C also subsumes E with respect to this sub-vocabulary. We can generalize this to the case where subsumption relations between the concepts exist with respect to different sub-vocabularies V_1 and V_2.

$$C \sqsubseteq_{V_1} D \wedge D \sqsubseteq_{V_2} E \Rightarrow C \sqsubseteq_{V_1 \cap V_2} E \tag{3}$$

The previous property provides a basis for defining equivalence with respect to a subvocabulary. This basically is the special case of equation 3 where E is the same concept as C. In this case we say that C and D are equivalent with respect to the sub-vocabulary defined as the intersection of the two vocabularies in which one concept subsumes the other. The justification of thus axiom is exactly the same as for equation 3.

$$C \sqsubseteq_{V_1} D \wedge D \sqsubseteq_{V_2} C \Rightarrow C \equiv_{V_1 \cap V_2} D \tag{4}$$

As we will see in the following, these properties are quite useful with respect to defining different viewpoints and to determine important reasoning tasks in the context of multi-viewpoint reasoning.

4.2   Reasoning About Viewpoints

The reasoning tasks we have to consider in the context of multi-viewpoint representations are the same as for standard OWL ontologies. As in OWL, computing subsumption between two concept expressions is one of the basic reasoning tasks many other tasks such as classification and instance retrieval can be reduced to.

What makes reasoning in our framework different from standard reasoning is the fact that we have to deal with many different subsumption operators. In order to reduce the complexity of the task, we can refer to the axiomatic properties shown above and use the implications between subsumption statements to improve reasoning. If we know for example that C is subsumed by D with respect to the complete vocabulary, we do not have to check whether C subsumes D in any sub-vocabulary, as equation 2 tells us that this is always the case.

We can use the same equation to support the computation of a viewpoint. The idea is that in order to compute the viewpoint with respect to a sub-vocabulary V, we do not really have to check whether for each pair of concepts whether subsumption holds with respect to V. It is sufficient if we know that subsumption holds with respect to a larger sub-vocabulary $V' \supseteq V$. It is not directly evident why this helps to reduce reasoning effort as normally computing subsumption with respect to a larger vocabulary is more costly. We can make use of this property, however, if we know the maximal sub-vocabulary V for which $C \sqsubseteq_{V} D$ holds. In this case, we just have to test whether the current sub-vocabulary is a subset of the maximal vocabulary in order to decide conditional subsumption.

Definition 5 (Maximal Subsumption Vocabulary). *Let C and D be concept expressions. A sub-vocabulary $V \subseteq \mathcal{V}$ is called a maximal Subsumption Vocabulary for C and D if*

1. $C \sqsubseteq_{V} D$
2. *there is no $V' \supset V$ such that $C \sqsubseteq_{V'} D$*

Unfortunately, there is not always a unique maximal sub-vocabulary with the required properties. If we look at the following example, we see that C is subsumed by D with respect to $V = \{Q\}$ as $approx_{\{Q\}}(C) = approx_{\{Q\}}(D) = Q$ and that C is subsumed by D with respect to $V = \{R\}$, because in this case we have $approx_{\{R\}}(C) = approx_{\{R\}}(D) = \top \sqcap \exists R.\top$. At the same time, C is not subsumed by D with respect to $V = \{Q, R\}$ as we can easily see.

$$D \equiv Q \sqcap \exists R.Q \tag{5}$$

$$C \equiv Q \sqcap \exists R.(\neg Q) \tag{6}$$

Nevertheless, maximal sub-vocabularies, even though there may be more than one are important with respect to efficient reasoning about viewpoints. In particular, we can store a list of all maximal sub-vocabularies with reach pair of concepts and use equation 2 to test whether a given viewpoint is defined by a sub-vocabulary of one of the maximal ones stored. In this case, we know that C is subsumed by D in the current viewpoint.

This means that computing the set of maximal subsumption vocabularies for each pair of concepts is the primal reasoning task in the context of multi-viewpoint reasoning. In the following we provide a first algorithm for computing maximal subsumption vocabularies as a basis for more advanced reasoning tasks.

Algorithm 1. Maximal Subsumption Vocabulary (MSV)

Require: A set $\mathcal{C}$ of Concept Expressions over Vocabulary $\mathcal{V}$
Require: An ordering $(V_0, V_1, \cdots, V_m)$ on the subsets of $\mathcal{V}$ such that $V_0 = \mathcal{V}$ and
$i < j \Rightarrow |V_i| > |V_j|$
  for all $\{(C, D)|C, D \in \mathcal{C}\}$ **do**
    $MSV(C, D) := \emptyset$
    $Cand(C, D) := (V_0, V_1, \cdots, V_m)$
    for all $V \in Cand(C, D)$ **do**
      if $approx_V(C) \sqsubseteq approx_V(D)$ **then**
        $MSV(C, D) := MSV(C, D) \cup \{V\}$
        $Cand(C, D) := Cand(C, D) - \{V'|V' \subset V\}$
      end if
    end for
  end for

The algorithms computes for every pair C,D of concepts the set $MSV(C, D)$ of maximal Subsumption Vocabularies for C and D. This is done on the basis of a partial ordering of possible sub-vocabularies where the complete vocabulary is the first element in the order and sub-vocabularies are ordered by their cardinality. The algorithm now tests for each vocabulary if C is subsumed by D with respect to this vocabulary starting with the largest one. If this is the case, the vocabulary is added to $MSV(C, D)$ and all subsets of the vocabularies are removed from the order as they do not satisfy the second condition of definition 5. The result is a complete set of maximal subsumption vocabularies for each pair of concepts that can be used for efficiently checking the subsumption with respect to a certain sub-vocabulary. In particular, we can use the result of the algorithm to compute Viewpoints without actually computing subsumption. The corresponding algorithm is given below.

Algorithm 2. Viewpoint

Require: A set $\mathcal{C}$ of Concept Expressions over Vocabulary $\mathcal{V}$
Require: A subvocabulary $V \subseteq \mathcal{V}$
  $\mathcal{P}_V := \emptyset$
  for all $\{(C, D)|C, D \in \mathcal{C}\}$ **do**
    if $\exists V' \in MSV(C, D) : V \subset V'$ **then**
      $\mathcal{P}_V := \mathcal{P}_V \cup \{C \sqsubseteq D\}$
    end if
  end for

The computation can further be optimized by using special index structures that already contain all subsets of $MSV(C, D)$. In this case, a viewpoint can be computed in linear time with respect to the number of concept pairs (quadratic with respect to the number of concepts). This means that based on a centralized generated index structure different applications can efficiently access their personal viewpoint of the model.

5   Discussion

In this paper, we proposed a model for representing and reasoning with multiple viewpoints in description logic ontologies. Our goal was to support the reuse of existing ontologies by applications that consider different aspects of the domain to be relevant. We have shown how we can deal with the case where a new application only considers a subset of the aspects encoded in the ontology relevant using an approximate subsumption operator that only takes a subset of the vocabulary into account.

If we really want to support the reuse of ontologies, we also have to take cases into account, where the aspects relevant to the new application are not a strict subset of the aspects covered by the ontology. In this case, the new aspects have to be integrated into the ontology. Currently this is often not done on the original ontology, because there is a danger of producing unwanted inconsistencies and to destroy existing subsumption relationships. Instead, a new ontology is created and customized to the needs of the new context. We think that the framework for multiple-viewpoints in ontologies can also help in this situation as it makes it possible to extend the original ontology with new aspects while still keeping it intact for its previous applications. The previous applications can just use the viewpoint that corresponds to the vocabulary that existed before the extension.

This possibility to keep one ontology and extend it for different purposes brings us closer to the idea of an ontology as a conceptualization that us actually shared between different applications. The use of viewpoints makes it possible to sign up for a common ontology without being forced to a viewpoint taken by other applications. This increases the chances of reducing the fragmentation of ontology development where a new ontology is created for every new application. The hope is, that the number of ontologies about a certain domain can be reduced to a number of models that represent completely non-compatible views on a domain while applications that have a different but compatible view on the domain use different viewpoints on the same ontology which evolves with every new application that introduces new aspects into the ontology.

From a theoretical point of view, the notion of approximate subsumption is a very interesting one. In this work, we chose a very specific definition and implementation of subsumption with respect to a sub-vocabulary. The definition was directly motivated by the aim to define different viewpoints on the same ontology. In future work we will aim at investigating approximate subsumption based on limited vocabularies in a more general setting. In particular, we will investigate a model-theoretic characterization of approximate subsumption in terms of weaker and stronger approximations (the work presented here is a special form of weaker approximation).

References

1. Ahmed Arara and Djamal Benslimane. Towards formal ontologies requirements with multiple perspectives. In *Proceedings of the 6th International Conference on Flexible Querz Answering Systems*, pages 150–160, 2004.

2. F. Baader, D. Calvanese, D. L. McGuinness, D. Nardi, and P F. Patel-Schneider. *The Description Logic Handbook - Theory, Implementation and Applications.* Cambridge University Press, 2003.
3. Catriel Beeri, Alon Y. Levy, and Marie-Christine Rousset. Rewriting queries using views in description logics. In *Proceedings of The 16th Symposium on Principles of Database Systems*, pages 99–108, 1997.
4. A. Borgida and L. Serafini. Distributed description logics: Assimilating information from peer sources. *Journal of Data Semantics*, 1:153–184, 2003.
5. Alexander Borgida. On the relative expressiveness of description logics and predicate logics. *Artificial Intelligence*, 82(1-2):353–367, 1996.
6. P. Bouquet, F. Giunchiglia, F. van Harmelen, L. Serafini, and H. Stuckenschmidt. C-OWL: Contextualizing ontologies. In *Second International Semantic Web Conference ISWC'03*, volume 2870 of *LNCS*, pages 164–179. Springer, 2003.
7. Marco Cadoli and Marco Schaerf. Approximation in concept description languages. In *Proceedings of the International Conference on Knowledge Representation and Reasoning*, pages 330–341, 1992.
8. A. Finkelstein, J. Kramer, B. Nuseibeh, L. Finkelstein, and M. Goedicke. Viewpoints: a framework for integrating multiple perspectives in system development. *International Journal of Software Engineering and Knowledge Engineering*, 2:31–57, 1992.
9. F. Giunchiglia and C. Ghidini. Local models semantics, or contextual reasoning = locality + compatibility. In *Proceedings of the Sixth International Conference on Principles of Knowledge Representation and Reasoning (KR'98)*, pages 282–289. Morgan Kaufmann, 1998.
10. A. Magkanaraki, V. Tannen, V. Christophides, and D. Plexousakis. Viewing the semantic web through rvl lenses. *Web Semantics: Science, Services and Agents on the World Wide Web*, 1(4):359–375, 2004.
11. N.F. Noy and M.A. Musen. Specifying ontology views by traversal. In *Proceedings of the Third International Conference on the Semantic Web (ISWC-2004)*, 2004.
12. Rami Rifaieh, Ahmed Arara, and Acha-Nabila Benharkat. Muro: A multirepresentation ontology as a foundation of enterprise information systems. In *Proceedings of the 4th International Conference on Computer and Information Technology*, pages 292–301, 2004.
13. M Schaerf and M Cadoli. Tractable reasoning via approximation. *Artificial Intelligence*, 74:249–310, 1995.
14. Dmitry Tsarkov, Alexandre Riazanov, Sean Bechhofer, and Ian Horrocks. Using vampire to reason with owl. In *Proceedings of the International Semantic Web Conference*, pages 471–485, 2004.
15. Andre Valente, Thomas Russ, Robert MacGregor, and William Swartout. Building and (re)using an ontology of air campaign planning. *IEEE Intelligent Systems*, 14(1):27 – 36, 1999.
16. R. Volz, D. Oberle, and R. Studer. Views for light-weight web ontologies. In *Proceedings of the ACM Symposium on Applied Computing SAC 2003*, 2003.

Effective Integration of Declarative Rules with External Evaluations for Semantic-Web Reasoning

Thomas Eiter, Giovambattista Ianni, Roman Schindlauer, and Hans Tompits

Institut für Informationssysteme, Technische Universität Wien
Favoritenstraße 9-11, A-1040 Vienna, Austria
{eiter, ianni, roman, tompits}@kr.tuwien.ac.at

Abstract. Towards providing a suitable tool for building the Rule Layer of the Semantic Web, HEX-programs have been introduced as a special kind of logic programs featuring capabilities for higher-order reasoning, interfacing with external sources of computation, and default negation. Their semantics is based on the notion of answer sets, providing a transparent interoperability with the Ontology Layer of the Semantic Web and full declarativity. In this paper, we identify classes of HEX-programs feasible for implementation yet keeping the desirable advantages of the full language. A general method for combining and evaluating sub-programs belonging to arbitrary classes is introduced, thus enlarging the variety of programs whose execution is practicable. Implementation activity on the current prototype is also reported.

1 Introduction

For the realization of the Semantic Web, the integration of different layers of its conceived architecture is a fundamental issue. In particular, the integration of *rules* and *ontologies* is currently under investigation, and many proposals in this direction have been made. They range from homogeneous approaches, in which rules and ontologies are combined in the same logical language (e.g., in SWRL and DLP [16, 13]), to hybrid approaches in which the predicates of the rules and the ontology are distinguished and suitable interfacing between them is facilitated, like, e.g., [10, 8, 25, 15] (see also [1] for a survey). While the former approaches provide a seamless semantic integration of rules and ontologies, they suffer from problems concerning either limited expressiveness or undecidability, because of the interaction between rules and ontologies. Furthermore, they are not (or only to a limited extent) capable of dealing with ontologies having different formats and semantics (e.g., RDF and OWL) at the same time. This can be handled, in a fully transparent way, by the approaches which keep rules and ontologies separate. Ontologies are treated as external sources of information, which are accessed by rules that also may provide input to the ontologies. In view of the well-defined interfaces, the precise semantic definition of ontologies and their actual structure does not need to be known. This in particular facilitates ontology access as a Web service, where also privacy issues might be involved (e.g., a customer taxonomy in the financial domain).

In previous work [8], HEX-programs were introduced as a generic rule-based language fostering a hybrid integration approach towards implementing the Rule Layer of the Semantic Web ("HEX" stands for *higher-order with external atoms*). They are based on

Y. Sure and J. Domingue (Eds.): ESWC 2006, LNCS 4011, pp. 273–287, 2006.
© Springer-Verlag Berlin Heidelberg 2006

nonmonotonic logic programs, which support constructs such as default negation, under the answer-set semantics, which underlies the generic *answer-set programming* (ASP) paradigm for declarative problem solving. The latter has proven useful in a variety of domains, including planning, diagnosis, information integration, and reasoning about inheritance, and is based on the idea that problems are encoded in terms of programs such that the solutions of the former are given by the models (the "answer sets") of the latter. The availability of default negation allows an adequate handling of conflict resolution, non-determinism, and dealing with incomplete information, among other things.

HEX-programs compensate limitations of ASP by permitting *external atoms* as well as *higher-order atoms*. They emerged as a generalization of *dl-programs* [10], which themselves have been introduced as an extension of standard ASP, by allowing a coupling with description-logic knowledge bases, in the form of *dl-atoms*. In HEX-programs, however, an interfacing with *arbitrary* external computations is realized. That is to say, the truth of an external atom is determined by an external source of computation. For example, the rule $triple(X, Y, Z) \leftarrow \&rdf[url](X, Y, Z)$ imports external RDF theories taking values from the external predicate $\&rdf$. The latter extracts RDF statements from a given set of URLs (encoded in the predicate url) in form of a set of "reified" ternary assertions. As another example, $C(X) \leftarrow triple(X, Y, Z), (X, rdf{:}type, C), not\ filter(C)$ converts triples to facts of a respective type, unless this type is filtered. Here, $C(X)$ is a higher-order atom, where C ranges over predicates constrained by $not\ filter(C)$.

HEX-programs are attractive since they have a fully declarative semantics, and allow for convenient knowledge representation in a modular fashion without bothering about the order of rules or literals in the bodies of rules of a program. However, the presence of external and higher-order atoms raises some technical difficulties for building implemented systems, given the following design goals which should be kept:

Full declarativity. This would mean that the user must be enabled to exploit external calls ignoring the exact moment an evaluation algorithm will invoke an external reasoner. So external calls must be, although parametric, stateless.

Potentially infinite universe of individuals. Current ASP solvers work under the assumption of a given, finite universe of constants. This ensures termination of evaluation algorithms (which are based on grounding), but is a non-practical setting if actual external knowledge must be brought inside the rule layer. Therefore, suitable methods must be devised for bringing finite amounts of new symbols into play while keeping decidability of the formalism.

Expressive external atoms. Interfacing external sources should support (at least) the exchange of predicates, and not only of constants (i.e., individuals). However, the generic notion of an external atom permits that its evaluation depends on the interpretation as a whole. For a practical realization, this quickly gets infeasible. Therefore, restricted yet still expressive classes of external atoms need to be identified.

These problems are nontrivial and require careful attention. Our main contributions are briefly summarized as follows.

We consider meaningful classes of HEX-programs, which emerge from reasonable (syntactic and semantic) conditions, leading to a categorization of HEX-programs. They include a notion of stratification, laid out in Section 3.1, which is more liberal than previous proposals for fragments of the language (e.g., as for HiLog programs [21]), as well as syntactic restrictions in terms of safety conditions for the rules, as discussed in Section 3.2. Furthermore, we consider restricted external predicates with additional semantic annotation which includes types of arguments and properties such as monotonicity, anti-monotonicity, or linearity.

Section 3.3 introduces a method of decomposing HEX-programs into separate modules with distinct features regarding their evaluation algorithm, and Section 3.4 discusses strategies for computing the models of HEX-programs by hierarchically evaluating their decomposed modules.

Finally, we have implemented a prototype of HEX-programs. The current implementation features dl-atoms and RDF-atoms for accessing OWL and RDF ontologies, respectively, but also provides a tool kit for programming customized external predicates. The prototype actually subsumes a prototype for dl-programs [10] we built earlier.

Our results are important towards the effective realization of a fully declarative language which integrates rules and ontologies. While targeted for HEX-programs, our methods and techniques may be applied to other, similar languages and frameworks as well. Indeed, HEX-programs model various formalisms in different domains [8], and special external atoms (inspired by [10]) are important features of other recent declarative rule formalisms for the Semantic Web [25, 15, 24].

2 HEX-Programs

In this section, we briefly recall HEX-programs; for further background, see [8].

Before describing syntax and semantics, we consider an example to give the flavor of the formalism. An interesting application scenario where several features of HEX-programs come into play is *ontology alignment*. Merging knowledge from different sources in the context of the Semantic Web is a crucial task. To avoid inconsistencies which arise in merging, it is important to diagnose the source of such inconsistencies and to propose a "repaired" version of the merged ontology. In general, given an entailment operator $\models$ and two theories T_1 and T_2, we want to find some theory $rep(T_1 \cup T_2)$ which, if possible, is consistent (relative to $\models$). Usually, *rep* is defined according to some customized criterion, so that to save as much knowledge as possible from T_1 and T_2. Also, *rep* can be nondeterministic and admitting more than one possible solution.

HEX-programs allow to define the relation $\models$ according to a range of possibilities; as well, HEX-programs are a useful tool for modeling and customizing the *rep* operator. How HEX coding can achieve these goals is sketched in the following program, P_{ex}:

$$triple(X, Y, Z) \leftarrow url(U), \&rdf[U](X, Y, Z); \tag{1}$$

$$proposition(P) \leftarrow triple(P, rdf:type, rdf:Statement); \tag{2}$$

$$pick(P) \vee drop(P) \leftarrow proposition(P); \tag{3}$$

$$pick(P) \leftarrow axiomatic(P); \tag{4}$$

$$C(rdf:type, X) \leftarrow picked(X, rdf:type, C); \tag{5}$$

$$D(rdf:type, X) \leftarrow picked(C, rdf:subClassOf, D), C(rdf:type, X); \tag{6}$$

$$picked(X, Y, Z) \leftarrow pick(P), triple(P, rdf\!:\!subject, X), \tag{7}$$
$$triple(P, rdf\!:\!predicate, Y), \tag{8}$$
$$triple(P, rdf\!:\!object, Z), \ not\, filter(P); \tag{9}$$
$$\leftarrow \&inconsistent[picked]. \tag{10}$$

P_{ex} illustrates some features of HEX programs, such as:

Importing external theories. Rule (1) makes use of an external predicate $\&RDF$ intended to extract knowledge from a given set of URLs.

Searching in the space of assertions. Rules (2) and (4) choose nondeterministically which propositions have to be included in the merged theory and which not. These rules take advantage of disjunction in order to generate a space of choices.

Translating and manipulating reified assertions. E.g., it is possible to choose how to put RDF triples (possibly including OWL assertions) in an easier manipulatable and readable format, making selected propositions true as with rules (5) and (7).

Defining ontology semantics. The operator $\models$ can be defined in terms of rules and constraints expressed in the language itself, as with rule (6) or constraint (10). The external predicate $\&inconsistent$ takes for input a set of assertions and establishes through an external reasoner whether the underlying theory is inconsistent.

HEX-programs are built on mutually disjoint sets C, X, and G of *constant names*, *variable names*, and *external predicate names*, respectively. Unless stated otherwise, elements from X (resp., C) are denoted with first letter in upper case (resp., lower case); elements from G are prefixed with "$\&$".[1] Constant names serve both as individual and predicate names. Importantly, C may be infinite.

Elements from $C \cup X$ are called *terms*. A *higher-order atom* (or *atom*) is a tuple $(Y_0, Y_1, \ldots, Y_n)$, where $Y_0, \ldots, Y_n$ are terms; $n \geq 0$ is its *arity*. Intuitively, Y_0 is the predicate name; we thus also use the familiar notation $Y_0(Y_1, \ldots, Y_n)$. The atom is *ordinary*, if Y_0 is a constant. For example, $(x, rdf\!:\!type, c)$ and $node(X)$ are ordinary atoms, while $D(a, b)$ is a higher-order atom. An *external atom* is of the form

$$\&g[Y_1, \ldots, Y_n](X_1, \ldots, X_m), \tag{11}$$

where $Y_1, \ldots, Y_n$ and $X_1, \ldots, X_m$ are two lists of terms (called *input list* and *output list*, respectively), and $\&g \in G$ is an external predicate name. We assume that $\&g$ has fixed lengths $in(\&g) = n$ and $out(\&g) = m$, respectively. Intuitively, an external atom provides a way for deciding the truth value of an output tuple depending on the extension of a set of input predicates.

Example 1. The external atom $\&reach[edge, a](X)$ may compute the nodes reachable in the graph $edge$ from the node a. Here, $in(\&reach) = 2$ and $out(\&reach) = 1$.   □

A HEX-*program*, P, is a finite set of rules of form

$$\alpha_1 \lor \cdots \lor \alpha_k \leftarrow \beta_1, \ldots, \beta_n, not\,\beta_{n+1}, \ldots, not\,\beta_m, \tag{12}$$

---

[1] In [8], "#" is used instead of "$\&$"; we make the change to be in accord with the syntax of the prototype system.

where $m, k \geq 0$, $\alpha_1, \ldots, \alpha_k$ are atoms, and $\beta_1, \ldots, \beta_m$ are either atoms or external atoms. For a rule r as in (12), we define $H(r) = \{\alpha_1, \ldots, \alpha_k\}$ and $B(r) = B^+(r) \cup B^-(r)$, where $B^+(r) = \{\beta_1, \ldots, \beta_n\}$ and $B^-(r) = \{\beta_{n+1}, \ldots, \beta_m\}$. If $H(r) = \emptyset$ and $B(r) \neq \emptyset$, then r is a *constraint*, and if $B(r) = \emptyset$ and $H(r) \neq \emptyset$, then r is a *fact*; r is *ordinary*, if it contains only ordinary atoms, and P is ordinary, if all rules in it are ordinary.

The semantics of HEX-programs generalizes the answer-set semantics [12], and is defined using the *FLP-reduct* [11], which is more elegant than the traditional reduct and ensures minimality of answer sets.

The *Herbrand base* of a HEX-program P, denoted HB_P, is the set of all possible ground versions of atoms and external atoms occurring in P obtained by replacing variables with constants from C. The grounding of a rule r, $grnd(r)$, is defined accordingly, and the grounding of program P is $grnd(P) = \bigcup_{r \in P} grnd(r)$.

For example, for $C = \{edge, arc, a, b\}$, ground instances of $E(X, b)$ are, for instance, $edge(a, b)$, $arc(a, b)$, and $arc(arc, b)$; ground instances of $\&reach[edge, N](X)$ are $\&reach[edge, edge](a)$, $\&reach[edge, arc](b)$, and $\&reach[edge, edge](edge)$, etc.

An *interpretation relative to P* is any subset $I \subseteq HB_P$ containing only atoms. We say that I is a *model* of atom $a \in HB_P$, denoted $I \models a$, if $a \in I$. With every external predicate name $\&g \in \mathcal{G}$ we associate an $(n+m+1)$-ary Boolean function $f_{\&g}$ (called *oracle function*) assigning each tuple $(I, y_1 \ldots, y_n, x_1, \ldots, x_m)$ either 0 or 1, where $n = in(\&g)$, $m = out(\&g)$, $I \subseteq HB_P$, and $x_i, y_j \in C$. We say that $I \subseteq HB_P$ is a *model* of a ground external atom $a = \&g[y_1, \ldots, y_n](x_1, \ldots, x_m)$, denoted $I \models a$, iff $f_{\&g}(I, y_1 \ldots, y_n, x_1, \ldots, x_m) = 1$.

Example 2. Associate with $\&reach$ a function $f_{\&reach}$ such that $f_{\&reach}(I, E, A, B) = 1$ iff B is reachable in the graph E from A. Let $I = \{e(b, c), e(c, d)\}$. Then, I is a model of $\&reach[e, b](d)$ since $f_{\&reach}(I, e, b, d) = 1$.   □

Let r be a ground rule. We define (i) $I \models H(r)$ iff there is some $a \in H(r)$ such that $I \models a$, (ii) $I \models B(r)$ iff $I \models a$ for all $a \in B^+(r)$ and $I \not\models a$ for all $a \in B^-(r)$, and (iii) $I \models r$ iff $I \models H(r)$ whenever $I \models B(r)$. We say that I is a *model* of a HEX-program P, denoted $I \models P$, iff $I \models r$ for all $r \in grnd(P)$.

The *FLP-reduct* [11] of P with respect to $I \subseteq HB_P$, denoted fP^I, is the set of all $r \in grnd(P)$ such that $I \models B(r)$. $I \subseteq HB_P$ is an *answer set of P* iff I is a minimal model of fP^I. By $AS(P)$ we denote the set of all answer sets of P.

Example 3. Consider the program P_{ex} from the above, together with the set F of facts $\{url(\text{"http://www.polleres.net/foaf.rdf"}), url(\text{"http://www.gibbi.com/foaf.rdf"})\}$.

Suppose that the two URLs contain the triples $(gibbi, hasHomepage, url)$ and $(gibbi, hasHomepage, url2)$, respectively, and that $\&inconsistent$ is coupled with an external reasoner such that the property $hasHomepage$ is enforced to be single valued. Then, $P_{ex} \cup F$ has two answer sets, one containing the fact $picked(gibbi, hasHomepage, url)$ and the other the fact $picked(gibbi, hasHomepage, url2)$. Note that the policy for picking and/or dropping propositions can be customized by changing the HEX-program at hand.   □

3   Decomposition of HEX-Programs

Although the semantics of HEX-programs is well-defined, some practical issues remain and need further attention:

1. It is impractical to define the semantics of each external predicate by means of a Boolean function. Also, most of the external predicates encountered do not depend on the value of the whole interpretation but only on the extensions of predicates specified in the input. We thus introduce a model in which external predicates are associated with functions whose input arguments are typed.
2. Many external predicates have regular behavior. For instance, their evaluation function may be monotonic with respect to the given input, like for most of the dl-atoms introduced in [10]. These kinds of behaviors need to be formalized so that they can be exploited for efficient evaluation of HEX-programs.
3. It is important to find a notion of mutual predicate dependency and stratification that accommodates the new sorts of introduced constructs, in order to tailor efficient evaluation algorithms.
4. Although the semantics of HEX-programs fosters a possibly infinite Herbrand universe, it is important to bound the number of symbols that have to be actually taken into account, by means of adequate restrictions. In any case, the assumption that oracle functions are decidable is kept, but they may have an infinite input domain and co-domain.

To take the first two points into account, we introduce the following concept:

Definition 1. *Let* &g *be an external predicate,* $f_{\&g}$ *its oracle function, I an interpretation, and* $q \in C$. *Furthermore, we assume that:*

- $in(\&g) = n$ *and* $out(\&g) = m$;
- &g *is associated with a type signature* $(t_1, \ldots, t_n)$, *where each* t_i *is the type associated with position i in the input list of* &g. *A type is either* c *or a nonnegative integer value. If* t_i *is* c, *then we assume the i-th input of* $F_{\&g}$ *is a constant, otherwise we assume that the i-th input of* $F_{\&g}$ *ranges over relations of arity* t_i.
- *For* $a \geq 0$, D_a *is the family of all sets of atoms of arity* a *and* $D_c = C$; *and*
- $\Pi_a(I, q)$ *is the set of all atoms belonging to I having q as predicate name and arity* a, *whereas* $\Pi_c(I, q) = q$.

Then, $F_{\&g} : D_{t_1} \times \cdots \times D_{t_n} \to D_{m-1}$ *is an* extensional evaluation function *iff* $(a_1, \ldots, a_m) \in F_{\&g}(\Pi_{t_1}(I, p_1), \ldots, \Pi_{t_n}(I, p_n))$ *precisely if* $f_{\&g}(I, p_1, \ldots, p_n, a_1, \ldots, a_m) = 1$.

We will call the external predicates associated with an extensional evaluation function and a type signature *typed*. Unless specified otherwise, we will assume in what follows to deal with typed external predicates only.

An evaluation function is a means for introducing an explicit relationship between input and output values of an external atom, and for expressing restrictions on the type of input values. Actual parameters inside external atoms express how, in the context of a given rule, input arguments are given in order to compute the output relation.

Example 4. Associate with predicate &*reach* an evaluation function $F_{\&reach}$ and a type signature $(2,0)$ such that $F_{\&reach}(\Pi_2(I,E),A) = B$, where B is the set of nodes reachable in the graph E from node A in the current interpretation. Let $I = \{e(b,c), e(c,d)\}$. The set of values for X such that I is a model for the atom &*reach*$[e,b](X)$ is $\{c,d\}$ since $F_{\&reach}(\{e(b,c), e(c,d)\}, b) = \{(c), (d)\}$. $\square$

Example 5. The evaluation function of the external predicate &*rdf* is such that the atom &*rdf*$[u](X,Y,Z)$ is bounded to all triples (X,Y,Z) which are in the output of $F_{\&rdf}(\Pi_1(I,u))$, for the current interpretation. The type of u is 1. E.g., if the current interpretation I is $\{u(\text{``http://www.polleres.net/foaf.rdf''}), u(\text{``http://www.gibbi.com/foaf.rdf''})\}$, then $F_{\&rdf}(\Pi_1(I,u))$ will return a set of triples extracted from the two specified URLs. $\square$

Definition 2. *Let* &*g be a typed external predicate and* $F_{\&g}$ *its extensional evaluation function. Let* $\bar{x} = x_1, \ldots, x_n$ *be a ground input list, and let* $\Pi(J,\bar{x}) = \Pi_{t_1}(J,x_1)$, $\ldots, \Pi_{t_n}(J,x_n)$, *for any interpretation J. Then: (i)* &*g is* monotonic, *if* $F_{\&g}(\Pi(I',x)) \subseteq F_{\&g}(\Pi(I'',x))$, *for any* I', I'' *and any* $\bar{x}$, *whenever* $I' \subseteq I''$; *(ii)* &*g is* anti-monotonic, *if* $F_{\&g}(\Pi(I',x)) \subseteq F_{\&g}(\Pi(I'',x))$, *for any* I', I'' *and any* $\bar{x}$, *whenever* $I' \supseteq I''$; *and (iii)* &*g is* linear, *if* $F_{\&g}(\Pi(I' \cup I'',x)) = F_{\&g}(\Pi(I',x)) \cup F_{\&g}(\Pi(I'',x))$ *for any* I', I'' *and any* $\bar{x}$.

Example 6. Intuitively, the &*reach* predicate is monotonic. Indeed, if we add some edge to $G' = \{e(b,c), e(c,d)\}$ so that we have, e.g., $G'' = \{e(b,c), e(c,d), e(c,h)\}$, the set of values for X such that G'' is a model of the atom &*reach*$[e,b](X)$ will grow. In particular, $F_{\&reach}(G',b) = \{\langle c\rangle, \langle d\rangle\}$ and $F_{\&reach}(G'',b) = \{\langle c\rangle, \langle d\rangle, \langle h\rangle\}$. $\square$

Many external predicates of practical interest can be classified as being monotonic. For instance, in most of the cases, dl-atoms as defined in [10] are monotonic.

Example 7. The &*rdf* predicate is linear. Indeed, let $U' = \{u(\text{``http://www.gibbi.com/foaf.rdf''})\}$ and $U'' = \{u(\text{``http://www.polleres.net/foaf.rdf''})\}$. Then, $F_{\&rdf}(U',u) \cup F_{\&rdf}(U'',u) = F_{\&rdf}(U' \cup U'',u))$, i.e., the two requested RDF sources are simply merged by union.[2] $\square$

3.1 Dependency Information Treatment

Taking the dependency between heads and bodies into account is a common tool for devising an operational semantics for ordinary logic programs, e.g., by means of the notions of *stratification* or *local stratification* [18], or through *modular stratification* [20] or *splitting sets* [17]. In HEX-programs, dependency between heads and bodies is not the only possible source of interaction between predicates. In particular we can have:

Dependency between higher order atoms. For instance, $p(A)$ and $C(a)$ are strictly related. Intuitively, since C can unify with the constant symbol p, rules that define $C(a)$ may implicitly define the predicate p. This is not always the case: for instance, rules defining the atom $p(X)$ do not interact with rules defining $a(X)$, as well as $H(a,Y)$ does not interact with $H(b,Y)$.

---

[2] Note that we are assuming a simple &*rdf* predicate where entailment is not performed. HEX-programs offer the possibility to implement RDF semantics either in the language itself or by means of a different external predicate bounded to a suitable reasoner.

Dependency through external atoms. External atoms can take predicate extensions as input: as such, external atoms may depend on their input predicates. This is the only setting where predicate names play a special role.

Disjunctive dependency. Atoms appearing in the same disjunctive head have a tight interaction, since they intuitively are a means for defining a common nondeterministic search space.

Note that the above dependency relations relate *non-ground atoms* to each other rather than predicates. We next formalize the above ideas.

Definition 3. *Let P be a program and a, b atoms occurring in some rule of P. Then:*

1. *a matches with b, symbolically $a \approx_u b$, if there exists a partial substitution θ of variables in a such that either $a\theta = b$ or $a = b\theta$ (e.g., $H(a, Y)$ unifies with $p(a, Y)$; note that this relation is symmetric);*
2. *a positively precedes b, symbolically $a \leq_p b$, if there is some rule $r \in P$ such that $a \in H(r)$ and $b \in B^+(r)$;*
3. *a negatively precedes b, symbolically $a \leq_n b$, if there is some rule $r \in P$ such that $a \in H(r)$ and $b \in B^-(r)$;*
4. *a is disjunctive dependent on b, symbolically $a \approx_d b$, if there is some rule $r \in P$ such that $a, b \in H(r)$ (note that this relation is symmetric);*
5. *a is externally dependent on b, symbolically $a \leq_e b$, if a is an external predicate of form $\&g[\bar{X}](\bar{Y})$, where $\bar{X} = X_1, \ldots, X_n$, and either*
   - *b is of form $p(\bar{Z})$, and, for some i, $X_i = p$, $t_i = $ a, where a is the arity of $p(\bar{Z})$ (e.g., $\&count[item](N)$ is externally dependent on $item(X)$), or*
   - *a is an external predicate of form $\&g[X_1, \ldots, X_n](\bar{Y})$, and there is some variable X_i of type a, and b is an atom of arity a (e.g., $\&DL[p, Q](N)$ is externally dependent on $q(X, Y)$ provided that Q ranges over binary predicates).*

We say that a precedes b, if $a \leq b$, where $\leq = \bigcup_{i \in \{p,n,e\}} \leq_i \cup \bigcup_{i \in \{u,d\}} \approx_i$. Furthermore, a strictly precedes b, symbolically $a < b$, if $a \leq^+ b$ but $b \not\leq^+ a$, where $^+$ is the transitive closure operator.

We can now define several structural properties of HEX-programs.

Definition 4. *Let P be a HEX-program and $\leq$ the relation defined above. We say that P is (i) nonrecursive, if $\leq$ is acyclic; (ii) stratified, if there is no cycle in $\leq$ containing some atom a and b such that $a \leq_n b$; (iii) e-stratified, if there is no cycle in $\leq$ containing some atom a and b such that $a \leq_e b$; and (iv) totally stratified, if it is both stratified and e-stratified.*

For instance, the program P_{ex} from Section 2 is both stratified and e-stratified. Moreover, rules (1) and (2) form a nonrecursive program.

3.2 Dealing with Infinite Domains

Given a HEX-program P, its grounding $grnd(P)$ is infinite in general, and cannot be reduced straightforwardly to a finite portion since, given an external predicate $\&g$, the co-domain of $F_{\&g}$ is unknown and possibly infinite. It is thus important to restrict the usage of external predicates. Such restrictions are intended to bound the number of symbols to be taken into account to a finite totality, whilst external knowledge in terms of new symbols can still be brought into a program.

Definition 5. *Given a rule r, the set of* safe *variables in r is the smallest set X of variables such that (i) X appears in a positive ordinary atom in the body of r, or (ii) X appears in the output list of an external atom $\&g[Y_1, \ldots, Y_n](X_1, \ldots, X_m)$ in the body of r and $Y_1, \ldots, Y_n$ are safe. A rule r is* safe, *if each variable appearing in a negated atom and in any input list is safe, and variables appearing in H(r) are safe.*

For instance, the rule $r : C(X) \leftarrow url(U), \&rdf[U](X, rdf{:}subClassOf, C)$ is safe. Intuitively, this notion captures those rules for which input to external atoms can be determined by means of other atoms in the same rule. Given the extension of the predicate *url*, the number of relevant ground instances of r intuitively is finite and can be determined by repeated calls to $F_{\&rdf}$.

In some cases, safety is not enough for determining finiteness of the set of relevant symbols to be taken in account. This motivates the following stronger notion:

Definition 6. *A rule r is* strongly safe *in P iff each variable in r occurs in some ordinary atom $b \in B^+(r)$ and each atom $a \in H(r)$ strictly precedes b.*

The rule r above is not strongly safe. Indeed, if some external URL invoked by means of $\&rdf$ contains some triple of form $(X, rdf{:}subClassOf, url)$, the extension of the *url* predicate is potentially infinite. The rule

$$r' : instanceOf(C, X) \leftarrow concept(C), obj(X), url(U),$$
$$\&rdf[U](X, rdf{:}subClassOf, C)$$

is strongly safe, if $concept(C)$, $obj(X)$, and $url(U)$ do not precede $instanceOf(C, X)$.

The strong safety condition is, anyway, only needed for rules which are involved in cycles of $\leq$. In other settings, the ordinary safety restriction is enough. This leads to the following notion of a *domain-expansion safe* program. Let $grnd_U(P)$ be the ground program generated from P using only the set U of constants.

Definition 7. *A* HEX-*program P is* domain-expansion safe *iff (i) each rule $r \in P$ is safe, and (ii) each rule $r \in P$ containing some $b \in B(r)$ such that, for each $a \in H(r)$ with $a \not\prec^+ b$, a is strongly safe.*

The following theorem states that we can effectively reduce the grounding of domain-expansion safe programs to a finite portion.

Theorem 1. *For any domain-expansion safe* HEX-*program P, there exists a finite set $D \subseteq C$ such that $grnd_D(P)$ is equivalent to $grnd_C(P)$ (i.e., has the same answer sets).*

Proof (Sketch). The proof proceeds by considering that, although the Herbrand universe of P is in principle infinite, only a finite set D of constants can be taken into account. From D, a finite ground program, $grnd_D(P)$, can be used for computing answer sets.

Provided that P is domain-expansion safe, it can be shown that $grnd_D$ has the same answer sets as $grnd_C(P)$.

A program that incrementally builds D and $grnd_D(P)$ can be sketched as follows: We update a set of *active* ordinary atoms A and a set R of ground rules (both of them initially empty) by means of a function $ins(r, A)$, which is repeatedly invoked over all rules $r \in P$ until A and R reach a fixed point. The function $ins(r, A)$ is such that, given a safe rule r and a set A of atoms, it returns the set of all ground versions of r such that each of its body atom a is either (i) such that $a \in A$ or (ii) if a is external, f_a is true. D is the final value of A, and $R = grnd_A(P)$. It can be shown that the above algorithm converges and $grnd_D(P) \subseteq grnd_C(P)$. The program $grnd_C(P)$ can be split into two modules: $N_1 = grnd_D(P)$ and $N_2 = grnd_C(P) \setminus grnd_D(P)$. It holds that each answer set S of $grnd_C(P)$ is such that $S = S_1 \cup S_2$, where $S_1 \in AS(N_1')$ and $S_2 \in AS(N_2)$. N_1' is a version of N_1 enriched with all the ground facts in $AS(N_2)$. Also, we can show that the only answer set of N_2 is the empty set. From this the proof follows.   □

3.3 Splitting Theorem

The dependency structure of a program P, given by its dependency graph $\leq$, can be employed for detecting modules inside the program itself. Intuitively, a module corresponds to a strongly-connected component[3] of $\leq$ and can be evaluated separately. The introduction of a modular evaluation strategy would allow to use, on the one hand, different evaluation algorithms depending on the nature of the module at hand. For instance, a module without external atoms can be directly evaluated by an efficient ASP solver, whereas a specific algorithm for stratified modules with monotonic external predicates can be devised (see e.g., the evaluation strategy adopted in [7] for dl-programs). On the other hand, such a strategy would enable the evaluation of a broader class of programs, given by the arbitrary composition of modules of different nature.

A way for splitting a program in sub-modules can be given by the notion of a *splitting set* [17]. Intuitively, given a program P, a splitting set S is a set of ground atoms that induce a sub-program $grnd(P') \subset grnd(P)$ whose models $M = \{M_1, \ldots, M_n\}$ can be evaluated separately. Then, an adequate *splitting theorem* shows how to plug in M in a modified version of $P \setminus P'$ so that the overall models can be computed.

The traditional notion of a splitting set and the associated theorem must be adapted in two respects. First, the new notions of dependency have to be accommodated. Second, we need a notion of splitting set built on non-ground programs. Indeed, given P, $grnd(P)$ is in principle infinite. Even if, under reasonable assumptions, we must take only a finite portion of $grnd(P)$ into account, this portion can be exponentially larger than P. This makes the idea of managing sub-modules at the ground level infeasible.

Definition 8. *A* global splitting set *for a* HEX-*program P is a set A of atoms appearing in P such that, whenever $a \in A$ and $a \leq b$, for some atom b appearing in P, then b belongs to A. The* global bottom *of P with respect to A is the set of rules $gb_A(P) = \{r \in P \mid$ for each $a \in H(r)$ there is an element $b \in A$ such that $a \leq_u b\}$.*

---

[3] A *strongly-connected component* (SCC) is a maximal subgraph in which every node is reachable from every other node. Note that we modify this definition and let a single node, which is not part of any SCC, be an SCC by itself.

For example, given the program P

$$triple(X, Y, Z) \leftarrow \&rdf[u](X, Y, Z), \tag{13}$$

$$C(X) \leftarrow triple(X, rdf:subClassOf, C), \tag{14}$$

$$r(X, Y) \leftarrow triple(X, r, C), \tag{15}$$

then, $S = \{triple(X, r, C), triple(X, Y, Z), triple(X, rdf:subClassOf, C), r(X, Y), \&rdf[u](X, Y, Z)\}$ is a splitting set for P. We have $gb_S(P) = \{(13), (15)\}$.

Definition 9. *For an interpretation I and a program Q, the* global residual, $gres(Q, I)$, *is a program obtained from Q as follows:*

1. *add all the atoms in I as facts;*
2. *for each "resolved" external atom $a = \&g[X_1, \ldots, X_n](Y_1, \ldots, Y_m)$ occurring in some rule of Q, replace a with a fresh ordinary atom $d_{\&g}(Y_1, \ldots, Y_m)$ (which we call* additional *atom), and add the fact $d_{\&g}(\bar{c})$ for each tuple $\bar{c} = \langle c_1, \ldots, c_n \rangle$ output by $EVAL(\&g, Q, I)$.*

For space reasons, we omit here the formal notion of a "resolved" external atom and the details of $EVAL(\&g, Q, I)$. Informally, an external atom a is resolved if its actual input list depends only on atoms in I. Thus, the input to $\&g$ is fully determined and its output can be obtained by calling $F_{\&g}$ with suitable parameters. To this end, $EVAL(\&g, Q, I)$ performs one or multiple calls to $F_{\&g}$. The external atom $\&rdf[u](X, Y, Z)$, for instance, has a ground input list. Thus $EVAL(\&g, Q, I)$ amounts to computing $F_{\&g}(\Pi_{p/1}(I, u))$. $EVAL$ is more involved in case of non-ground input terms. Here, some preliminary steps are required.

Intuitively, given a program $P = \{triple(X, Y, Z) \leftarrow \&rdf[url](X, Y, Z)\}$ and the interpretation $I = \{url("http://www.gibbi.com/foaf.rdf")\}$, its residual is

$$gres(P, I) = \{triple(X, Y, Z) \leftarrow d_{rdf}(X, Y, Z), \ldots,$$
$$d_{\&rdf}("me", "http://xmlns.com/foaf/0.1/workplaceHomepage",$$
$$"http://www.mat.unical.it/ianni")\}.$$

We can now formulate a generalization of the Splitting Theorem from [17].

Theorem 2 (Global Splitting Theorem). *Let P be a domain-expansion safe program and let A be a global splitting set for P. Then, $M \setminus D \in AS(P)$ iff $M \in AS(gres(P \setminus gb_A(P), I))$, where $I \in AS(gb_A(P))$, and D is the set of additional atoms in $gres(P \setminus gb_A(P), I)$ with predicate name of form $d_{\&g}$.*

Proof (Sketch). The idea behind the proof is that a splitting set A denotes a portion of P (viz., the bottom $gb_A(P)$) whose answer sets do not depend from the rest of the program. Also, $gb_A(P)$ is the only portion of P necessary in order to compute the extension of atoms appearing in A in any model. That is, for each model $M \in AS(P)$, we have that $M \cap G_A \in AS(gb_A(P))$, where G_A is the set of all ground instances (built from constants in C) of atoms in A. This claim can be exploited in the opposite direction as follows: We first compute $\mathcal{M}' = AS(gb_A(P))$. Then, we simplify P to P_s by removing $gb_A(P)$. The answer sets of $\{gres(P^s, M') \mid M' \in \mathcal{M}'\}$ are answer sets of P provided that additional atoms in D are stripped out. □

The above theorem is a powerful tool for evaluating a HEX-program by splitting it repeatedly in modules, which we consider next.

SPLITTING EVALUATION ALGORITHM
(Input: a HEX-program P; Output: $AS(P)$)

1. Determine the *precedes* relation $\leq$ for P.
2. Partition the set of atoms of P into the set $Comp = \{C_1, \ldots, C_n\}$ of strongly connected components C_i of $\leq$, and define that $C_i \prec C_j$ iff there is some $a \in C_i$ and some $b \in C_j$ such that $a \prec b$.
3. Set $T := Comp$ and $\mathcal{M} := \{\{\}\}$ (the empty model). The set $\mathcal{M}$ will eventually contain $AS(P)$ (which is empty, in case inconsistency is detected).
4. While $T \neq \emptyset$ do:
5.   Pop from T some C such that for no $C' \in T$ we have $C \prec C'$.
6.   Let $\mathcal{M} := \bigcup_{M \in \mathcal{M}} AS(gres(b_C(P), M))$.
7.   If $\mathcal{M} = \emptyset$, then halt (inconsistency, no answer set exists).
8. $P := P \setminus b_C(P)$.

Fig. 1. Splitting algorithm

3.4 Splitting Algorithm

The class of domain-expansion safe HEX-programs encompasses a variety of practical situations. Note that such programs need not be stratified, and may harbor nondeterminism.

We can design a *splitting* evaluation algorithm for HEX-programs P under the following rationale. First of all, P is decomposed into strongly connected components. Then, a partial ordering is created between such components. Given a current set $\mathcal{M}$ of models, for each component C, we evaluate the answer sets of its possible residuals with respect to elements of $\mathcal{M}$. The actual method for computing the answer sets of each residual depends on its structure. The detailed algorithm is depicted in Figure 1.[4]

In fact, we can generalize this algorithm by popping from T a set $E \subseteq T$ of components such that for each $C_i \in E$, $\{C_j \in T \mid C_j \prec C_i\} \subseteq E$ holds (i.e., E is downwards closed under $\prec$ with respect to T). For instance, unstratified components without external atoms may be evaluated at once.

Example 8. Consider program P_{ex} from Section 2. We mimic an iteration of the splitting algorithm. The set $S = \{pick(P), drop(P)\}$ forms a strongly connected component. Assume at the moment of evaluating this component $\mathcal{M}$ contains the single answer set $M = \{proposition(p_1), proposition(p_2), axiomatic(p_2), \ldots\}$. At this stage, P no longer contains rules (1) and (2), so the bottom of S is formed by rules (3) and (4). Then, $gres(b_C(P), M)$ is the following program:

$$proposition(p_1) \leftarrow, \quad proposition(p_2) \leftarrow, \quad \ldots \tag{16}$$

$$axiomatic(p_2) \leftarrow, \tag{17}$$

$$\ldots$$

$$pick(P) \vee drop(P) \leftarrow proposition(P), \tag{18}$$

$$pick(P) \leftarrow axiomatic(P). \tag{19}$$

---

[4] $\mathcal{M}$ may contain exponentially many intermediate models. A variant of the algorithm avoiding this by computing one model at a time is straightforward, but omitted for simplicity.

having two answer set $M_1 = \{\ldots, pick(p_1), pick(p_2), \ldots\}$ and $M_2 = \{\ldots, drop(p_1), pick(p_2), \ldots\}$. Then, P is modified by deleting rules (3) and (4).   □

3.5 Special Algorithms for Components

The above algorithm enables to exploit special evaluation algorithms depending on the specific structure of a given strongly connected component C and its corresponding residual program. In particular:

- recursive positive programs (either e-stratified or not) with monotonic external atoms can be evaluated by an adequate fixed-point algorithm as described in [7];
- programs without external atoms (either stratified or not) can be directly mapped to a corresponding ASP program and evaluated by some ASP solver (e.g., DLV); and
- generic components with generic external atoms can be evaluated by an apposite guess and check strategy (cf. [7]).

3.6 Current Prototype

The experimental prototype for evaluating HEX-programs, dlvhex, mainly follows the algorithm presented in Section 3.4. After transforming the higher-order program into a first-order syntax and decomposing it into its dependency graph, dlvhex uses an external answer-set solver to evaluate each of the components. The functions for computing the external atoms are embedded in so-called *plug-ins*, which are shipped separately and linked dynamically to the main application.

For a more detailed presentation of the implementation, we refer the reader to [9] and http://www.kr.tuwien.ac.at/research/dlvhex.

4 Related Work

A number of works are related to ours in different respects. We group literature into works more tailored to the Semantic Web and others of a more general perspective. The works of Heymans et al. [14, 15] on open and conceptual logic programs fall into the first group. Here, infinite domains are considered, in a way similar to classical logics and/or description logics, but adopting answer-set semantics based on grounding. The syntax of rules is restricted. In [15], call atoms are considered similar to ours, but only restricted to the propositional setting. They also consider preferences, which can be added to our framework in the future.

[10] introduces the notion of a dl-atom, through which a description-logic knowledge base can be interfaced from an answer-set program. The notion of stratification given there is subsumed by the one in this paper, given that stratified dl-programs of [10] can be viewed as an instance of HEX-programs.

Inspired by [10], Antoniou et al. [25] have used dl-atoms for a hybrid combination of defeasible and description logic, and have used in [24] an extension of dl-programs for ontology merging and alignment, which fits our framework. Early work on hybrid combination of logic programs and description logics appeared in [19, 5]. Both works do not consider the issue of bidirectional flow of information to and from external sources and prescribe more restrictive safety conditions. Also similar in spirit is the TRIPLE language [22]. The semantics of TRIPLE considers Horn rules under the well-founded semantics. However, the information flow here is unidirectional.

Ross [21] developed a notion of stratification for HiLog programs, which basically constitute the fragment of HEX-programs without external atoms. Our notion of stratification is more general (as it handles external atoms), and no special range restrictions on predicate variables are prescribed.

The use of external atoms in logic programs under the answer-set semantics dates back to [6], where they have been modeled as generalized quantifiers. In general, this approach (based on the usual reduct by Gelfond and Lifschitz [12]) is different from ours, and no value invention has been considered there. The latter problem has been studied extensively in the database field. For instance, Cabibbo [3] studied decidable fragments of the ILOG language, which featured a special construct for creating new tuple identifiers in relational databases. He developed notions of safety similar to ours (in absence of higher order atoms) and gave conditions such that new values do not propagate in infinite chains.

In a broad sense, value invention, while keeping decidability in ASP, has been considered in [23, 2, 4]. In [23, 2], potentially infinite domains are considered by allowing function symbols, whose usage is restricted. Syrjänen [23] introduced ω-restricted programs, in which, roughly, all unstratified rules according to the dependency graph are put in some special stratum ω at the top level. Then, each function term must be bound by some predicate which belongs to some lower stratum. However, the models of ω-restricted programs have always finite positive part. They are a subclass of Bonatti's finitary programs [2], which have been designed for query answering. The work of Calimeri and Ianni [4] considered ASP with external atoms, but input and output arguments are restricted to constants (individuals), and no higher-order atoms are present. Thus, the framework there is subsumed by ours.

5   Conclusion and Future Work

We have discussed methods and techniques by which an integration of a rule-based formalism that has higher-order features and supports external evaluations, as given by the powerful framework of HEX-programs, can be made effective. In this way, declarative tool support for a wide range of reasoning applications on the Semantic Web at a high level of abstraction can be realized. For example, merging and alignment of ontologies [24], or combining and integrating different information sources on the Web in general, which possibly have different formats and semantics.

The current prototype implementation features atoms for accessing RDF and OWL ontologies, and provides a tool kit for customized external evaluation plug-ins that the user might create for his or her application. Our ongoing work concerns enhancing and further improving the current prototype, as well as extending the classes of effective HEX-programs. Finally, applications in personalized Web information systems are targeted.

Acknowledgement. This work was partially supported by the Austrian Science Funds project P17212 and the European Commission project REWERSE (IST-2003-506779).

References

1. G. Antoniou, C. V. Damásio, B. Grosof, I. Horrocks, M. Kifer, J. Maluszynski, and P. F. Patel-Schneider. Combining Rules and Ontologies. A Survey. Technical Report IST506779/ Linkoeping/I3-D3/D/PU/a1, Linköping University, 2005.
2. P. A. Bonatti. Reasoning with Infinite Stable Models. *Artificial Intelligence*, 156(1):75–111, 2004.
3. L. Cabibbo. The Expressive Power of Stratified Logic Programs with Value Invention. *Information and Computation*, 147(1):22–56, 1998.
4. F. Calimeri and G. Ianni. External Sources of Computation for Answer Set Solvers. In *Proc. LPNMR 2005*, pp. 105–118.
5. F. M. Donini, M. Lenzerini, D. Nardi, and A. Schaerf. AL-log: Integrating Datalog and Description Logics. *J. Intell. Inf. Syst.*, 10(3):227–252, 1998.
6. T. Eiter, G. Gottlob, and H. Veith. Modular Logic Programming and Generalized Quantifiers. In *Proc. LPNMR'97*, pp. 290–309.
7. T. Eiter, G. Ianni, R. Schindlauer, and H. Tompits. Nonmonotonic Description Logic Programs: Implementation and Experiments. In *Proc. LPAR 2004*, pp. 511–527.
8. T. Eiter, G. Ianni, R. Schindlauer, and H. Tompits. A Uniform Integration of Higher-order Reasoning and External Evaluations in Answer Set Programming. In *Proc. IJCAI 2005*.
9. T. Eiter, G. Ianni, R. Schindlauer, and H. Tompits. dlvhex: A System for Integrating Multiple Semantics in an Answer-Set Programming Framework. In *Proc. WLP 2006*, pp. 206–210.
10. T. Eiter, T. Lukasiewicz, R. Schindlauer, and H. Tompits. Combining Answer Set Programming with Description Logics for the Semantic Web. In *Proc. KR 2004*, pp. 141–151.
11. W. Faber, N. Leone, and G. Pfeifer. Recursive Aggregates in Disjunctive Logic Programs: Semantics and Complexity. In *Proc. JELIA 2004*, pp. 200–212.
12. M. Gelfond and V. Lifschitz. Classical Negation in Logic Programs and Disjunctive Databases. *New Generation Computing*, 9:365–385, 1991.
13. B. N. Grosof, I. Horrocks, R. Volz, and S. Decker. Description Logic Programs: Combining Logic Programs with Description Logics. In *Proc. WWW 2003*, pp. 48–57.
14. S. Heymans, D. V. Nieuwenborgh, and D. Vermeir. Nonmonotonic Ontological and Rule-based Reasoning with Extended Conceptual Logic Programs. In *Proc. ESWC 2005*.
15. S. Heymans, D. V. Nieuwenborgh, and D. Vermeir. Preferential Reasoning on a Web of Trust. In *Proc. ISWC 2005*, pp. 368–382.
16. I. Horrocks, P. F. Patel-Schneider, H. Boley, S. Tabet, B. Grosof, and M. Dean. SWRL: A Semantic Web Rule Language Combining OWL and RuleML, 2004. W3C Member Submission.
17. V. Lifschitz and H. Turner. Splitting a Logic Program. In *Proc. ICLP'94*, pp. 23–38.
18. T. Przymusinski. On the Declarative Semantics of Deductive Databases and Logic Programs. In *Foundations of Deductive Databases and Logic Programming.*, pp. 193–216. 1988.
19. R. Rosati. Towards Expressive KR Systems Integrating Datalog and Description Logics: Preliminary Report. In *Proceedings DL'99*, pp. 160–164.
20. K. A. Ross. Modular Stratification and Magic Sets for Datalog Programs with Negation. *J. ACM*, 41(6):1216–1266, 1994.
21. K. A. Ross. On Negation in HiLog. *Journal of Logic Programming*, 18(1):27–53, 1994.
22. M. Sintek and S. Decker. Triple - a Query, Inference, and Transformation Language for the Semantic Web. In *Proc. ISWC 2004*, pp. 364–378.
23. T. Syrjänen. Omega-restricted Logic Programs. In *Proc. LPNMR 2001*, pp. 267–279.
24. K. Wang, G. Antoniou, R. W. Topor, and A. Sattar. Merging and Aligning Ontologies in dl-Programs. In *Proc. RuleML 2005*, pp. 160–171.
25. K. Wang, D. Billington, J. Blee, and G. Antoniou. Combining Description Logic and Defeasible Logic for the Semantic Web. In *Proc. RuleML 2004*, pp. 170–181.

Variable-Strength Conditional Preferences
for Ranking Objects in Ontologies

Thomas Lukasiewicz[1],[*] and Jörg Schellhase[2]

[1] DIS, Università di Roma "La Sapienza"
Via Salaria 113, I-00198 Rome, Italy
`lukasiewicz@dis.uniroma1.it`
[2] Fachgebiet Wirtschaftsinformatik, Universität Kassel
Nora-Platiel-Straße 4, D-34127 Kassel, Germany
`schellhase@wirtschaft.uni-kassel.de`

Abstract. We introduce conditional preference bases as a means for ranking objects in ontologies. Conditional preference bases consist of a description logic knowledge base and a finite set of variable-strength conditional preferences. They are inspired by Goldszmidt and Pearl's approach to default reasoning from conditional knowledge bases in System Z^+. We define a notion of consistency for conditional preference bases, and show how consistent conditional preference bases can be used for ranking objects in ontologies. We also provide algorithms for computing the rankings. To give evidence of the usefulness of this approach in practice, we describe an application in the area of literature search.

1 Introduction

In their seminal works [34, 33], Poole and Smyth deal with the problem of matching instances against models of instances, which are both described at different levels of abstraction and at different levels of detail, using qualitative probability theory. Informally, such problems can be described as follows. Given an instance I and a model of instances M, compute the qualitative probability that the instance I is matching the model M (that is, of I given M). For example, in a geological exploration domain, we may want to determine whether there might be gold in an area. In this case, an instance I may be given by the description of an area, while a model M may be given by a description of areas where gold can be found, and the qualitative probability that I is matching M describes the likelihood that gold may be found in I.

In this paper, we continue this line of research. A serious drawback of the above works [34, 33] on matching instances against models of instances is that they only allow for expressing simple preferences of the form "property α is preferred over property $\neg\alpha$ with strength s" in models of instances. In particular, they do not allow for conditional preferences such as "generally, in the context ϕ, property α is preferred over property $\neg\alpha$ with strength s". In this paper, we try to fill this gap. We present a

---

[*] Alternate address: Institut für Informationssysteme, Technische Universität Wien, Favoritenstraße 9-11, A-1040 Vienna, Austria; e-mail: `lukasiewicz@kr.tuwien.ac.at`.

Y. Sure and J. Domingue (Eds.): ESWC 2006, LNCS 4011, pp. 288–302, 2006.

formalism for ranking objects in description logics that allows for expressing such conditional preferences in models of instances. In a companion paper [30], we present a generalization of this formalism for matchmaking in description logics.

Like Poole and Smyth's work [34, 33], the ranking formalism in this paper is also based on qualitative probabilities. Differently from Poole and Smyth's work [34, 33], however, it requires a technically more involved way of computing qualitative probabilities, since our language for encoding models of instances is more expressive. We especially have to suitably handle *variable-strength conditional preferences*, which are the above statements "generally, in the context ϕ, property α is preferred over property $\neg\alpha$ with strength s" (also called *variable-strength conditional desires* [36]). They bear close similarity to *variable-strength defaults* of form "generally, if ϕ then α with strength s" in default reasoning from conditional knowledge bases (see Section 7).

In this paper, we define a formal semantics for variable-strength conditional preferences, which is based on a generalization of Goldszmidt and Pearl's default entailment in System Z^+ [22]. We focus on the problem of ranking objects against a description of objects. Since we are especially interested in the Semantic Web as the main application context, we assume that objects and descriptions of objects are expressed in the expressive description logics $\mathcal{SHIF}(\mathbf{D})$ and $\mathcal{SHOIN}(\mathbf{D})$, which stand behind the web ontology languages OWL Lite and OWL DL, respectively [23].

The Semantic Web [6, 17] aims at an extension of the current World Wide Web by standards and technologies that help machines to understand the information on the Web so that they can support richer discovery, data integration, navigation, and automation of tasks. The main ideas behind it are to add a machine-readable meaning to Web pages, to use ontologies for a precise definition of shared terms in Web resources, to make use of KR technology for automated reasoning from Web resources, and to apply cooperative agent technology for processing the information of the Web. The Semantic Web consists of several hierarchical layers, where the Ontology layer, in form of the OWL Web Ontology Language [37, 24] (recommended by the W3C), is currently the highest layer of sufficient maturity. OWL consists of three increasingly expressive sublanguages, namely OWL Lite, OWL DL, and OWL Full. OWL Lite and OWL DL are essentially expressive description logics with an RDF syntax [24]. Ontology entailment in OWL Lite (resp., OWL DL) reduces to knowledge base (un)satisfiability in the description logic $\mathcal{SHIF}(\mathbf{D})$ (resp., $\mathcal{SHOIN}(\mathbf{D})$) [23].

The main contributions of this paper can be summarized as follows:

– We introduce conditional preference bases, which consist of a description logic knowledge base and a finite set of conditional preferences. They are syntactically and semantically inspired by Goldszmidt and Pearl's approach to default reasoning from conditional knowledge bases in System Z^+. We define a notion of consistency for conditional preference bases, and show how consistent conditional preference bases can be used for ranking objects in ontologies.
– We also provide algorithms for computing the rankings relative to a conditional preference base. These algorithms are based on a reduction to deciding whether a description logic knowledge base is satisfiable. More precisely, they require a polynomial number of such satisfiability tests, and thus can all be done in polynomial time whenever the satisfiability tests are possible in polynomial time.

– Finally, we describe an application of this approach in literature search. Search query languages of current search engines are very restricted in their expressive power. There are scientific search engines on the web, however, that have valuable metadata about research publications, authors, organizations, and scientific events. We show that conditional preference bases allow for a more powerful query language, which can exploit this metadata better than the current approaches do. In particular, we give some sample queries that (i) explicitly follow different search strategies, (ii) influence the ranking of the query results, (iii) express quality measures, (iv) cluster query results, or (v) restrict queries to different result types.

2   The Description Logics $\mathcal{SHIF}$(D) and $\mathcal{SHOIN}$(D)

In this section, we recall the description logics $\mathcal{SHIF}(\mathbf{D})$ and $\mathcal{SHOIN}(\mathbf{D})$, which stand behind the web ontology languages OWL Lite and OWL DL, respectively [23]. Intuitively, description logics model a domain of interest in terms of concepts and roles, which represent classes of individuals and binary relations between classes of individuals, respectively. Roughly, a description logic knowledge base encodes subset relationships between classes, the membership of individuals to classes, and the membership of pairs of individuals to binary relations between classes.

Syntax. We first describe the syntax of $\mathcal{SHOIN}(\mathbf{D})$. We assume a set of *elementary datatypes* and a set of *data values*. A *datatype* is either an elementary datatype or a set of data values (called *datatype oneOf*). A *datatype theory* $\mathbf{D} = (\Delta^{\mathbf{D}}, \cdot^{\mathbf{D}})$ consists of a *datatype domain* $\Delta^{\mathbf{D}}$ and a mapping $\cdot^{\mathbf{D}}$ that assigns to each elementary datatype a subset of $\Delta^{\mathbf{D}}$ and to each data value an element of $\Delta^{\mathbf{D}}$. The mapping $\cdot^{\mathbf{D}}$ is extended to all datatypes by $\{v_1, \ldots\}^{\mathbf{D}} = \{v_1^{\mathbf{D}}, \ldots\}$. Let $\mathbf{A}$, $\mathbf{R}_A$, $\mathbf{R}_D$, and $\mathbf{I}$ be pairwise disjoint finite nonempty sets of *atomic concepts*, *abstract roles*, *datatype roles*, and *individuals*, respectively. We denote by $\mathbf{R}_A^-$ the set of inverses R^- of all $R \in \mathbf{R}_A$.

A *role* is an element of $\mathbf{R}_A \cup \mathbf{R}_A^- \cup \mathbf{R}_D$. *Concepts* are inductively defined as follows. Every $\phi \in \mathbf{A}$ is a concept, and if $o_1, \ldots, o_n \in \mathbf{I}$, then $\{o_1, \ldots, o_n\}$ is a concept (called *oneOf*). If ϕ, ϕ_1, and ϕ_2 are concepts and if $R \in \mathbf{R}_A \cup \mathbf{R}_A^-$, then also $(\phi_1 \sqcap \phi_2)$, $(\phi_1 \sqcup \phi_2)$, and $\neg\phi$ are concepts (called *conjunction, disjunction*, and *negation*, respectively), as well as $\exists R.\phi$, $\forall R.\phi$, $\geq nR$, and $\leq nR$ (called *exists, value, atleast*, and *atmost restriction*, respectively) for an integer $n \geq 0$. If D is a datatype and $U \in \mathbf{R}_D$, then $\exists U.D$, $\forall U.D$, $\geq nU$, and $\leq nU$ are concepts (called *datatype exists, value, atleast*, and *atmost restriction*, respectively) for an integer $n \geq 0$. We write $\top$ and $\bot$ to abbreviate the concepts $\phi \sqcup \neg\phi$ and $\phi \sqcap \neg\phi$, respectively, and we eliminate parentheses as usual.

An *axiom* has one of the following forms: (1) $\phi \sqsubseteq \psi$ (called *concept inclusion axiom*), where ϕ and ψ are concepts; (2) $R \sqsubseteq S$ (called *role inclusion axiom*), where either $R, S \in \mathbf{R}_A$ or $R, S \in \mathbf{R}_D$; (3) $\mathrm{Trans}(R)$ (called *transitivity axiom*), where $R \in \mathbf{R}_A$; (4) $\phi(a)$ (called *concept membership axiom*), where ϕ is a concept and $a \in \mathbf{I}$; (5) $R(a, b)$ (resp., $U(a, v)$) (called *role membership axiom*), where $R \in \mathbf{R}_A$ (resp., $U \in \mathbf{R}_D$) and $a, b \in \mathbf{I}$ (resp., $a \in \mathbf{I}$ and v is a data value); and (6) $a = b$ (resp., $a \neq b$) (*equality* (resp., *inequality*) *axiom*), where $a, b \in \mathbf{I}$. A *knowledge base KB* is a finite set of axioms. For decidability, number restrictions in *KB* are restricted to simple abstract roles [25].

The syntax of $\mathcal{SHIF}(\mathbf{D})$ is as the above syntax of $\mathcal{SHOIN}(\mathbf{D})$, but without the oneOf constructor and with the atleast and atmost constructors limited to 0 and 1.

Example 2.1. An online store (such as *amazon.com*) may use a description logic knowledge base to classify and characterize its products. For example, suppose that (1) textbooks are books, (2) personal computers and laptops are mutually exclusive electronic products, (3) books and electronic products are mutually exclusive products, (4) any objects on offer are products, (5) every product has at least one related product, (6) only products are related to each other, (7) tb_ai and tb_lp are textbooks, which are related to each other, (8) pc_ibm and pc_hp are personal computers, which are related to each other, and (9) ibm and hp are providers for pc_ibm and pc_hp, respectively. These relationships are expressed by the following description logic knowledge base KB_1:

> $Textbook \sqsubseteq Book$; $PC \sqcup Laptop \sqsubseteq Electronics$; $PC \sqsubseteq \neg Laptop$;
>
> $Book \sqcup Electronics \sqsubseteq Product$; $Book \sqsubseteq \neg Electronics$; $Offer \sqsubseteq Product$;
>
> $Product \sqsubseteq \geq 1\ related$; $\geq 1\ related \sqcup \geq 1\ related^{-} \sqsubseteq Product$;
>
> $Textbook(tb\_ai)$; $Textbook(tb\_lp)$; $PC(pc\_ibm)$; $PC(pc\_hp)$;
>
> $related(tb\_ai, tb\_lp)$; $related(pc\_ibm, pc\_hp)$;
>
> $provides(ibm, pc\_ibm)$; $provides(hp, pc\_hp)$.

Semantics. An *interpretation* $\mathcal{I} = (\Delta^{\mathcal{I}}, \cdot^{\mathcal{I}})$ w.r.t. a datatype theory $\mathbf{D} = (\Delta^{\mathbf{D}}, \cdot^{\mathbf{D}})$ consists of a nonempty (*abstract*) *domain* $\Delta^{\mathcal{I}}$ disjoint from $\Delta^{\mathbf{D}}$, and a mapping $\cdot^{\mathcal{I}}$ that assigns to each atomic concept $\phi \in \mathbf{A}$ a subset of $\Delta^{\mathcal{I}}$, to each individual $o \in \mathbf{I}$ an element of $\Delta^{\mathcal{I}}$, to each abstract role $R \in \mathbf{R}_A$ a subset of $\Delta^{\mathcal{I}} \times \Delta^{\mathcal{I}}$, and to each datatype role $U \in \mathbf{R}_D$ a subset of $\Delta^{\mathcal{I}} \times \Delta^{\mathbf{D}}$. We extend $\cdot^{\mathcal{I}}$ to all concepts and roles, and we define the *satisfaction* of a description logic axiom F in an interpretation $\mathcal{I} = (\Delta, \cdot^{\mathcal{I}})$, denoted $\mathcal{I} \models F$, as usual [23]. The interpretation $\mathcal{I}$ *satisfies* the axiom F, or $\mathcal{I}$ is a *model* of F, iff $\mathcal{I} \models F$. The interpretation $\mathcal{I}$ *satisfies* a knowledge base KB, or $\mathcal{I}$ is a *model* of KB, denoted $\mathcal{I} \models KB$, iff $\mathcal{I} \models F$ for all $F \in KB$. We say that KB is *satisfiable* (resp., *unsatisfiable*) iff KB has a (resp., no) model. An axiom F is a *logical consequence* of KB, denoted $KB \models F$, iff every model of KB satisfies F.

3   Conditional Preference Bases

In this section, we first define the syntax of conditional preferences, which are intuitively statements of form "generally, if ϕ, then α is preferred over $\neg\alpha$ with strength s". We then define the semantics of such statements in terms of object rankings, taking inspiration from default reasoning from conditional knowledge bases in System Z^+.

Syntax. We assume a finite set of *classification concepts* $\mathcal{C}$ (which are the relevant description logic concepts for defining preference relationships). A *conditional preference* is of the form $(\alpha|\phi)[s]$ with concepts $\phi \in \mathcal{C}$ (called its *body*) and $\alpha \in \mathcal{C}$ (called its *head*), and an integer $s \in \{0, \ldots, 100\}$ (called its *strength*). Informally, $(\alpha|\phi)[s]$ expresses that (i) generally, among the objects satisfying ϕ, the ones satisfying α are preferred over those satisfying $\neg\alpha$, and (ii) this preference relationship holds with strength s. Conditional preferences of the form $(\alpha|\top)[s]$ are also abbreviated as $(\alpha)[s]$. A *conditional preference base* is a pair $PB = (T, A, P)$, where T is a description logic knowledge base, A is a finite set of concepts from $\mathcal{C}$, and P is a finite set of conditional preferences. Informally, T contains terminological knowledge, and A contains assertional knowledge about an individual o (that is, A actually represents the set of all $C(o)$ such that $C \in A$), while P contains conditional preferences about the individual o (that is, P actually represents the set of all $(\alpha(o)|\phi(o))[s]$ such that $(\alpha|\phi)[s] \in P$). Observe also that the statements in T and A are *strict* (that is, they must always hold), while the ones in P are *defeasible* (that is, they may have exceptions and thus do not always hold), since P may not always be satisfiable as a whole.

Example 3.1. The assertional knowledge "either a PC or a laptop" and the preference relationships "generally, PC's are preferred over laptops with strength 20", "generally, laptops on offer are preferred over PC's on offer with strength 70", and "generally, inexpensive objects are preferred over expensive ones with strength 90" can be expressed by the conditional preference base $PB = (T, A, P)$, where T is the description logic knowledge base from Example 2.1, $A = \{\top \sqsubseteq PC \sqcup Laptop\}$, and $P = \{(PC)[20], (Laptop|Offer)[70], (Inexpensive)[90]\}$.

Semantics. We now define some basic semantic notions, including objects and object rankings (which are certain functions that map every object to a rank from $\{0, 1, \ldots\} \cup \{\infty\}$), and we then associate with every conditional preference base a set of object rankings as a formal semantics. An *object* o is a set of concepts from $\mathcal{C}$. We denote by $\mathcal{O}_\mathcal{C}$ the set of all objects relative to $\mathcal{C}$. An object o *satisfies* a description logic knowledge base T, denoted $o \models T$, iff $T \cup \{\phi(i) \mid \phi \in o\}$ is satisfiable and entails (resp., does not entail) every concept membership $\phi(i)$ such that $\phi \in o$ (resp., $\phi \notin o$), where i is a new individual. Informally, every object o represents an individual i that is fully specified on $\mathcal{C}$ in the sense that o belongs (resp., does not belong) to every concept $\phi \in o$ (resp., $\phi \notin o$). An object o satisfies a concept $\phi \in \mathcal{C}$, denoted $o \models \phi$, iff $\phi \in o$. An object o satisfies a set of concepts $A \subseteq \mathcal{C}$, denoted $o \models A$, iff o satisfies all $\phi \in A$. A concept ϕ is *satisfiable* iff there exists an object $o \in \mathcal{O}_\mathcal{C}$ that satisfies ϕ. An object o satisfies a conditional preference $(\alpha|\phi)[s]$, denoted $o \models (\alpha|\phi)[s]$, iff $o \models \neg\phi \sqcup \alpha$. We say o satisfies a set of conditional preferences P, denoted $o \models P$, iff o satisfies all $p \in P$. We say o *verifies* $(\alpha|\phi)[s]$ iff $o \models \phi \sqcap \alpha$. We say o *falsifies* $(\alpha|\phi)[s]$, denoted $o \not\models (\alpha|\phi)[s]$, iff $o \models \phi \sqcap \neg\alpha$. A set of conditional preferences P *tolerates* a conditional preference p *under* a description logic knowledge base T and a set of classification concepts $A \subseteq \mathcal{C}$ iff an object o exists that satisfies $T \cup A \cup P$ (that is, o satisfies T, A, and P) and verifies p. We say P is *under T and A in conflict* with p iff P does not tolerate p under T and A.

An *object ranking* κ is a mapping $\kappa \colon \mathcal{O}_\mathcal{C} \to \{0, 1, \ldots\} \cup \{\infty\}$ such that $\kappa(o) = 0$ for at least one object $o \in \mathcal{O}_\mathcal{C}$. It is extended to all concepts ϕ as follows. If ϕ is satisfiable, then $\kappa(\phi) = \min \{\kappa(o) \mid o \in \mathcal{O}_\mathcal{C}, o \models \phi\}$; otherwise, $\kappa(\phi) = \infty$. We say κ is *admissible* with a description logic knowledge base T (resp., a set of concepts A) iff $\kappa(o) = \infty$ for all $o \in \mathcal{O}_\mathcal{C}$ such that $o \not\models T$ (resp., $o \not\models A$). We say κ is *admissible* with a conditional preference $(\alpha|\phi)[s]$ iff either $\kappa(\phi) = \infty$ or $\kappa(\phi \sqcap \alpha) + s < \kappa(\phi \sqcap \neg\alpha)$. We say κ is *admissible* with $PB = (T, A, P)$ iff κ is admissible with T, A, and all $p \in P$.

Consistency. The notion of consistency is inspired by the notion of ε-consistency for conditional knowledge bases [1, 21]. A conditional preference base PB is *consistent* (resp., *inconsistent*) iff an (resp., no) object ranking κ exists that is admissible with PB. Notice that $PB = (T, A, P)$ with $P = \emptyset$ is consistent iff $T \cup A$ is satisfiable. We now summarize some results that carry over from conditional knowledge bases.

The following result shows that the existence of an object ranking that is admissible with $PB = (T, A, P)$, where $P \neq \emptyset$, is equivalent to the existence of a preference ranking on P that is admissible with PB. Here, a *preference ranking* σ on a set of conditional preferences P maps each $p \in P$ to an integer. We say that a preference ranking σ on P is *admissible* with $PB = (T, A, P)$ iff every $P' \subseteq P$ that is under T and A in conflict with some $p \in P$ contains some p' such that $\sigma(p') < \sigma(p)$.

Theorem 3.1. *A conditional preference base $PB = (T, A, P)$ with $P \neq \emptyset$ is consistent iff there exists a preference ranking σ on P that is admissible with PB.*

The next result shows that the consistency of PB is equivalent to the existence of an ordered partition of P with certain properties.

Theorem 3.2. *A conditional preference base $PB = (T, A, P)$ with $P \neq \emptyset$ is consistent iff there exists an ordered partition $(P_0, \ldots, P_k)$ of P such that either (a) every P_i, $0 \leq i \leq k$, is the set of all $p \in \bigcup_{j=i}^{k} P_j$ tolerated under T and A by $\bigcup_{j=i}^{k} P_j$, or (b) for every i, $0 \leq i \leq k$, each $p \in P_i$ is tolerated under T and A by $\bigcup_{j=i}^{k} P_j$.*

We call the unique partition in (a) the *z-partition* of PB.

Example 3.2. The conditional preference base PB of Example 2.1 is consistent. Its z-partition is $(P_0, P_1) = (\{(PC)[20], (Inexpensive)[90]\}, \{(Laptop \mid Offer)[70]\})$.

4   Ranking Objects Under Conditional Preference Bases

In this section, we define object rankings that reflect the conditional preferences encoded in a consistent conditional preference base $PB = (T, A, P)$.

We first rewrite P from a set of defeasible statements to a set of strict statements $P^\star$. Intuitively, this is done by adding exceptions to the bodies of conditional preferences.

Example 4.1. Let the conditional preference base $PB = (T, A, P)$ be given by T and A as in Example 3.1 and $P = \{(PC)[20], (Laptop \mid Offer)[70]\}$. Ignoring the strengths, P encodes that "PCs are preferred over laptops, as long as they are not on offer, because in that case, laptops are preferred over PCs". That is, for technical reasons, laptops on offer always falsify the conditional preference $p = (PC)[20]$. When computing the rank of laptops on offer, we have to avoid such falsifications. We do this by rewriting p and thus PB. The rewritten conditional preference base $PB^\star = (T, A, P^\star)$ is given by $P^\star = \{(PC \mid \neg Offer)[20], (Laptop \mid Offer)[70]\}$. It is obtained from PB by adding the exception $\neg Offer$ to the body of $(PC)[20]$.

A conditional preference base $PB = (T, A, P)$ is *flat* iff its z-partition is given by (P) and thus consists only of one component. Algorithm *flatten* in a companion paper [30] transforms a consistent conditional preference base $PB = (T, A, P)$ into an equivalent flat conditional preference base, denoted $PB^\star = (T, A, P^\star)$.

Table 1. The object rankings κ^{sum} and κ^{lex}

PC	Laptop	Offer	κ^{sum}	κ^{lex}		PC	Laptop	Offer	κ^{sum}	κ^{lex}
o_1 false	false	false	∞	∞	o_5	true	false	false	0	0
o_2 false	false	true	∞	∞	o_6	true	false	true	71	2
o_3 false	true	false	21	1	o_7	true	true	false	∞	∞
o_4 false	true	true	0	0	o_8	true	true	true	∞	∞

We are now ready to define the object rankings κ^{sum} and κ^{lex}. Informally, κ^{sum} associates with every object (as a penalty) the sum of the strengths of all conditional preferences in $P^\star$ that are falsified by o. Roughly, objects with smaller values under κ^{sum} are those that satisfy more conditional preferences with larger strengths. Formally, κ^{sum} is defined as follows for all objects $o \in \mathcal{O}_C$:

$$\kappa^{sum}(o) = \begin{cases} \infty & \text{if } o \not\models T \cup A \\ \sum\limits_{p=(\alpha|\phi)[s] \in P^\star \,:\, o \not\models p} s+1 & \text{otherwise.} \end{cases} \quad (1)$$

The object ranking κ^{lex}, in contrast, is based on a lexicographic order. Roughly, objects with smaller values under κ^{lex} are those that satisfy more conditional preferences with larger strengths, where satisfying one conditional preference of strength s is strictly preferred to satisfying any set of conditional preferences of strength at most $s - 1$. Formally, κ^{lex} is defined as follows for all objects $o \in \mathcal{O}_C$ (where n_j with $j \in \{0, \ldots, 100\}$ is the number of all $p \in P^\star$ of strength j):

$$\kappa^{lex}(o) = \begin{cases} \infty & \text{if } o \not\models T \cup A \\ \sum\limits_{i=0}^{100} |\{p = (\alpha|\phi)[i] \in P^\star \mid o \not\models p\}| \cdot \Pi_{j=0}^{i-1}(n_j + 1) & \text{otherwise.} \end{cases} \quad (2)$$

Example 4.2. The object rankings κ^{sum} and κ^{lex} for *PB* of Example 4.1 are shown in Fig. 1. For example, under both κ^{sum} and κ^{lex}, the object o_4 is strictly preferred over o_3, as desired, since $\kappa^{sum}(o_4) < \kappa^{sum}(o_3)$ and $\kappa^{lex}(o_4) < \kappa^{lex}(o_3)$, respectively.

Summarizing, every object ranking $\kappa \in \{\kappa^{sum}, \kappa^{lex}\}$ of a conditional preference base *PB* represents the preference relationships encoded in *PB*. For every (fully specified) object o, the *rank* of o under *PB* is given by $\kappa(o)$. Every object ranking $\kappa \in \{\kappa^{sum}, \kappa^{lex}\}$ can also be used to compare two objects $o, o' \in \mathcal{O}_C$ as follows. The *distance* between o and o' under *PB* is defined as $|\kappa(o) - \kappa(o')|$. Furthermore, the *(credulous) rank* of a partially specified object (which is simply a concept) ϕ under *PB* is defined as $\min_{o \in \mathcal{O}_C : o \models \phi} \kappa(o)$. Finally, the *(credulous) distance* between two partially specified objects ϕ and ϕ' is defined as $\min_{o,o' \in \mathcal{O}_C : o \models \phi, o' \models \phi'} |\kappa(o) - \kappa(o')|$.

5 Algorithms and Complexity

There are several computational tasks related to conditional preference bases $PB = (T, A, P)$. First, deciding the consistency of *PB* is done by algorithm *consistency* in

---

Algorithm *sum-ranking*

Input: conditional preference base $PB = (T, A, P)$ and set of objects $\mathcal{O} \subseteq \mathcal{O}_{\mathcal{C}}$.
Output: ranking κ^{sum} on $\mathcal{O}$ for PB, if PB is consistent; *nil*, otherwise.

1. **if** PB is inconsistent **then return** *nil*;
2. **for each** $o \in \mathcal{O}$ **do if** $o \models A \cup T$ **then** $\kappa(o) := 0$ **else** $\kappa(o) := \infty$;
3. **if** $P = \emptyset$ **then return** κ;
4. $(T, A, P) := \text{flatten}(T, A, P)$;
5. **for each** $o \in \mathcal{O}$ such that $\kappa(o) \neq \infty$ **do**
6.   **for each** $p = (\alpha|\phi)[s] \in P$ **do if** $o \not\models p$ **then** $\kappa(o) := \kappa(o) + s + 1$;
7. **return** κ.

Fig. 1. Algorithm *sum-ranking*

Algorithm *lex-ranking*

Input: conditional preference base $PB = (T, A, P)$ and set of objects $\mathcal{O} \subseteq \mathcal{O}_{\mathcal{C}}$.
Output: ranking κ^{lex} on $\mathcal{O}$ for PB, if PB is consistent; *nil*, otherwise.

1. **if** PB is inconsistent **then return** *nil*;
2. **for each** $o \in \mathcal{O}$ **do if** $o \models A \cup T$ **then** $\kappa(o) := 0$ **else** $\kappa(o) := \infty$;
3. **if** $P = \emptyset$ **then return** κ;
4. $(T, A, P) := \text{flatten}(T, A, P)$;
5. **for each** $o \in \mathcal{O}$ such that $\kappa(o) \neq \infty$ **do begin**
6. $n := 1$;
7.   **for each** $i := 0$ **to** 100 **do begin**
8. $h := 0$;
9.   **for each** $p = (\alpha|\phi)[i] \in P$ **do if** $o \not\models p$ **then** $h := h + i + 1$
10. $\kappa(o) := \kappa(o) + h \cdot n$;
11. $n := n \cdot (|\{(\alpha|\phi)[s] \in P \mid s = i\}| + 1)$
12.   **end**
13. **end**;
14. **return** κ.

Fig. 2. Algorithm *lex-ranking*

a companion paper [30] (which returns the z-partition of PB, if PB is consistent, and *nil*, otherwise), which generalizes an algorithm for deciding ε-consistency in default reasoning [21]. The extended algorithm is essentially based on $O(|P|^2)$ tests whether a description logic knowledge base is satisfiable. Second, rewriting PB to an equivalent flat conditional preference base PB^* is done by algorithm *flatten* in a companion paper [30], which is similar to a rewriting algorithm in fuzzy default reasoning [16], and which requires $O(|P|^2)$ description logic satisfiability tests. Finally, computing the ranking functions κ^{sum} and κ^{lex} is done by algorithms *sum-* and *lex-ranking* in Figs. 1 and 2, respectively, in a polynomial number of description logic satisfiability tests.

Theorem 5.1. *Given a conditional preference base $PB = (T, A, P)$ and a set of objects $\mathcal{O} \subseteq \mathcal{O}_{\mathcal{C}}$, computing the rankings κ^{sum} and κ^{lex} on $\mathcal{O}$ relative to PB can be done in $O(|P| \cdot (|P| + |\mathcal{C}| \cdot |\mathcal{O}|))$ description logic satisfiability tests.*

Hence, under the assumption that $|P|$ and $|\mathcal{C}|$ are bounded by a constant (which is a reasonable assumption in the application in literature search below), computing the rankings κ^{sum} and κ^{lex} can be done in $O(|\mathcal{O}|)$ description logic satisfiability tests.

Furthermore, if we restrict the class of description logic expressions in PB in such a way that the above satisfiability tests on description logic knowledge bases can be done in polynomial time (for example, such as in DL-Lite [12]), then all the described computational tasks can also be solved in polynomial time.

6   Application: Literature Search

In this section, we describe an application in literature search for the above approach to ranking objects relative to a conditional preference base.

Background. A very important and time consuming task of researchers is finding publications. There exist a lot of possibilities to find relevant research publications over the internet. For instance, there are portals for research publications, portals for ejournals, special purpose search engines for researchers (for example, CiteSeer and Google Scholar), specialized databases, publication databases of institutions, and bibliographic online catalogues. It seems that there is a trend to more diversity and quality regarding online search engines. On the other hand, the "tremendous increase in the quantity and diversity of easily available research publications has exacerbated the problems of information overload for researchers attempting to keep abreast of new relevant research, especially in rapidly advancing fields" [7].

A very powerful instrument for search engines are citation indexes, which can be very well exploited for search processes. Garfield [19] examined the possibilities and advantages of citation indexes. There are a lot of advantages of citation indexes compared to traditional subject indexes. The quality of references tends to be higher than the quality of title words and keywords. Using citation indexes enhances the search productivity (finding the largest possible number of relevant publications) and the search efficiency (minimizing the number of irrelevant publications). Citations are semantically more stable than keywords. Citation indexes can be used in many ways, for example, finding relevant publications through backward and forward navigation, finding out the importance of publications, and identifying research trends [13].

CiteSeer and Google Scholar have recognized the work of Garfield and are using the valuable information of citations. In Google, for example, the ranking algorithm PageRank is based on the linking of web resources [10]. CiteSeer automatically detects scientific publications on the Web and extracts the necessary metadata (citations, citation context, title, etc.), builds the citation index, and performs the full-text indexing [27]. For the ranking of query results, CiteSeer has adopted the ranking algorithm of Google. The CiteSeer database is queried by simple keyword search and returns a list of indexed publications [20]. For each publication, CiteSeer offers a query-sensitive summary, containing the citation context of the publication, links to similar documents and links to author homepages [27]. The user follows citations by browsing the links. For each query result, there are a lot of pieces of information and links that can be used to browse the database. In Google Scholar, one also uses keyword searches that can be restricted, for example, to authors or titles. The search result contains a list of publications that match the query. For each publication, there is a link "cited by" that leads to a list of publications citing the discovered publication.

There are a lot of good search strategies that a researcher can use for the task of finding relevant scientific publications. Bates [4] has identified the following six important information search strategies:

- *Footnote chasing:* Following up footnotes (that is, references) found in publications. This can be done in successive leaps.
- *Citation searching:* Looking for publications that cite certain publications.
- *Journal run:* Identification of a central journal in a research area and then looking up publications in relevant volumes.
- *Area scanning:* Browsing resources that are physically collocated with resources that are regarded as relevant. A good example is a book shelf in a library. In a digital library, one could exploit the classification of resources.
- *Subject searches:* The usage of subject descriptors such as keywords to find relevant publications.
- *Author searching:* To find other publications of an author, which may have a similar topic as a publication one already knows of.

The first two strategies are supported by citation indexes. It would be helpful if the above mentioned search strategies could be explicitly supported by the query languages of search engines. The power of search query languages of scientific search engines should go beyond the classical Boolean keyword searching. It should be enhanced to ask more elaborated queries. The search strategies citation searching, subject searches, and author searching are well supported by CiteSeer and Google Scholar. The search strategy footnote chasing is well supported by CiteSeer, although normally not all citations to a publication are listed. There is no direct support for the search strategy footnote chasing with Google Scholar. The publication has to be found and downloaded. Then the references have to be looked up in the document. CiteSeer and Scholar Google are no help for the search strategy journal run. In order to use the search strategy journal run, one could use Google to find the web site of the journal and then one can browse through the journal's volumes. The search strategy area scanning is not supported by CiteSeer, Google Scholar, and Google.

Actually, to use all the search strategies footnote chasing, citation searching, journal run, subject searches, and author searching, one has to use all the above search engines, and there is no way to exploit the search strategies by the formulation of the search queries. What is also not supported by the mentioned search engines is the possibility to exploit relationships like citations or co-authorship by the formulation of queries. To date, search query languages of most web search engines have little expressive power for formulating semantic queries, cannot be used to explicitly influence the ranking of query results, have no possibilities to formulate ones own quality measures for the query results, have no possibilities to restrict the query results to certain result types (for example, authors, journals, conferences, keywords, and publications), and have no possibilities to influence the clustering of query results. Of course, even most scientists normally do not want to learn a complex query language. Therefore, one has to think about good query assistants that help formulating sophisticated queries. Nevertheless, when the benefit of more sophisticated queries becomes clear, we are convinced that researchers will use such query languages instead of the query assistants.

Literature Search via Conditional Preference Bases. In this section, we show that our approach to conditional preferences bases allows for expressing more sophisticated search queries, and avoids the above mentioned deficiencies. The presented examples also show the expressive power of the formalism proposed in this paper.

The strict terminological knowledge is informally described as follows. We assume the concepts *Publication, JournalPublication, ConfPublication, Person, Publication-medium, Journal, Proceedings, Keyword, Event, Conference,* and *Workshop,* which are related by the concept inclusion axioms *JournalPublication* $\sqsubseteq$ *Publication, ConfPubli-cation* $\sqsubseteq$ *Publication, Conference* $\sqsubseteq$ *Event, Workshop* $\sqsubseteq$ *Event, Journal* $\sqsubseteq$ *Publication-medium,* and *Proceedings* $\sqsubseteq$ *Publicationmedium.* We assume the roles *Author* (relating *Publication* and *Person*), *Coauthor* (on *Person*), *Cite* (on *Publication*), *Publishedin* (relating *Publication* and *Publicationmedium*), *Keywords* (relating *Publication* and *Keyword*), and *hasPublicationmedium* (relating *Event* and *Publicationmedium*). Moreover, the concept *Publication* has the attributes *year, title, publishedat,* and *type.* Finally, we assume the unary function *in_title* of type *string*→ *Publication.*

In the following, some literature search queries are associated with a corresponding conditional preference base $PB = (T, A, P)$, expressed as the conjunction of all the elements in $A \cup P$. For example, consider the following query Q (which supports the search strategy *subject searches*): We are looking for papers with the word "matching" in the title. In case of a conference paper, we prefer papers of international conferences to papers of national conferences. This query is expressed by the following conjunction:

$C = Publication \sqcap in\_title("matching") \sqcap$
$(type("international")|ConfPublication)[70] \sqcap (ConfPublication)[80]$,

which in turn stands for the conditional preference base $PB = (T, A, P)$, where $T = \emptyset$,

$A = \{Publication, in\_title("matching")\}$, and
$P = \{(type("international")|ConfPublication)[70], (ConfPublication)[80]\}$.

Query Q contains two conditional preferences (with the two strengths 70 and 80, respectively, which are directly specified by the user). Intuitively, an object that fulfills query Q has to be a publication with the word "matching" in the title and it should possibly satisfy the two conditional preferences. Publications that satisfy the conditional preferences have a lower rank than publications that falsify them. Query Q therefore divides the publications in the query result into three groups as follows: first international conference publications (lowest rank), second national conference publications (second lowest rank), and third non-conference publications (highest rank).

We now provide several other queries, expressed in the textual and the conjunctive way. The following queries support the search strategy *footnote chasing*:

(1) All references that Ian Horrocks cited in his papers:
    $\exists Cite^-.\exists Author.\{"Ian Horrocks"\}$.
(2) Journal publications that were cited by Ian Horrocks:
    $JournalPublication \sqcap \exists Cite^-.\exists Author.\{"Ian Horrocks"\}$.

The following queries support the search strategy *citation searching*:

(3) All publications that cite the paper "Weaving the Web" of Tim Berners Lee:
$\exists Cite.(title($"Weaving the Web"$) \sqcap \exists Author.\{$"Tim Berners Lee"$\})$.

(4) All publications that cite publications of Ian Horrocks:
$\exists Cite.\exists Author.\{$"Ian Horrocks"$\}$.

(5) All publications that cite papers of ISWC in the year 2000:
$\exists Cite.(ConfPublication \sqcap publishedat($"ISWC"$) \sqcap =_{2000}(year))$.

The following queries support the search strategy *journal run*:

(6) All publications of ISWC after the year 2001:
$ConfPublication \sqcap publishedat($"ISWC"$) \sqcap \geq_{2001}(year)$.

(7) All journals that were cited by Ian Horrocks:
$Journal \sqcap \exists Publishedin^-.(\exists Cite^-.\exists Author.\{$"Ian Horrocks"$\})$.

(8) All conferences with publications that contain the keywords "elearning" and "Semantic Web":
$Conference \sqcap \exists hasPublicationmedium.\exists Publishedin^-$
$(\exists Keywords.\{$"elearning"$\} \sqcap \exists Keywords.\{$"Semantic Web"$\})$.

The following queries support the search strategy *subject searches*:

(9) All publications with "Semantic Web" in the title that were cited at least five times:
$in\_title($"Semantic Web"$) \sqcap \geq_5 Cite^-$.

(10) All publications with "Semantic Web" in the title, that contain at least four literature references that are cited at least ten times:
$in\_title($"Semantic Web"$) \sqcap \geq_4 Cite.(\geq_{10} Cite^-)$.

(11) All publications with the keyword "Semantic Web" and the keywords "OWL" and "DAML+OIL". The ranking is influenced by the strengths of the keywords:
$\exists Keywords.\{$"Semantic Web"$\} \sqcap (\exists Keywords.\{$"OWL"$\})[70] \sqcap$
$(\exists Keywords.\{$"DAML+OIL"$\})[20]$.

The following queries support the search strategy *author searching*:

(12) All publications of Ian Horrocks:
$\exists Author.\{$"Ian Horrocks"$\}$.

(13) All publications of authors who have a joint publication with Tim Berners-Lee:
$\exists Author.\exists Coauthor.\{$"Tim Berners-Lee"$\}$.

(14) All publications that cite publications of coauthors of Tim Berners-Lee and himself, giving a higher rank to publications that cite Tim Berners-Lee:
$(\exists Cite.\exists Author.\exists Coauthor.\{$"Tim Berners-Lee"$\})[30] \sqcap$
$(\exists Cite.\exists Author.\{$"Tim Berners-Lee"$\})[80]$.

Query 14 divides the publications in the query result into three groups as follows: first publications that cite publications that Tim Berners-Lee wrote with colleagues (lowest rank), second publications that cite publications where Tim Berners-Lee was the only author (second lowest rank), and third publications that cite publications of coauthors of Tim Berners-Lee, where Tim Berners-Lee was not an author (highest rank).

Note that queries 9 and 10 include a user-defined quality measure. Query 7 (resp., 8) has the result type journal (resp., conference). Queries 11 and 14 are directly influencing the ranking of the query results, and they are also clustering the query results.

Two important measures for retrieval systems are precision and recall. Let Q be a query, let R be the set of relevant documents to the query Q, let A be the set of documents that a retrieval system returns for Q, and let $Ra = R \cap A$ be the set of relevant documents to Q within A. Then, the notions of *precision* and *recall* are defined by $precision = |Ra| / |A|$ and $recall = |Ra| / |R|$, respectively [3].

Queries 1–7, 12, 13, and 14 are examples where the information need could be specified very precisely, resulting in relative small query results. These are examples that lead to a higher precision and a higher recall. Queries 8–11 contain elements that are based on string comparisons. Although these elements are restricted to titles and keywords, they cannot correctly express the information need. This is a known problem for conventional search engines. Queries 11 and 14 contain conditional preferences. The purpose of the conditional preferences is to influence the clustering and the ranking of the query results. Although there is no effect on precision and recall, this helps the user. Normally users just look at the top results of a result list. The user defined ranking and clustering makes the ranking more transparent to the user and increases the likelihood that the user actually recognizes the most important query results.

7   Related Work

We now give an overview on default reasoning from conditional knowledge bases, and we discuss (less closely) related work on skyline queries and rankings in databases.

The literature contains several different proposals for default reasoning from conditional knowledge bases and extensive work on its desired properties. The core of these properties are the rationality postulates of System P by Kraus et al. [26], which constitute a sound and complete axiom system for several classical model-theoretic entailment relations under uncertainty measures on worlds. They characterize classical model-theoretic entailment under preferential structures, infinitesimal probabilities, possibility measures [15], and world rankings. They also characterize an entailment relation based on conditional objects [14]. A survey of all these relationships is given in [5, 18]. Mainly to solve problems with irrelevant information, the notion of rational closure as a more adventurous notion of entailment was introduced by Lehmann [28]. It is in particular equivalent to entailment in System Z by Pearl [32] (which is generalized to variable-strength defaults in System Z^+ by Goldszmidt and Pearl [22]) and to the least specific possibility entailment by Benferhat et al. [5]. Recently, also generalizations of many of the above approaches to probabilistic and fuzzy default reasoning have been proposed (see especially [29] and [16], respectively).

In the database context, the work [9] proposes an extension of database systems by a *Skyline* operation, which filters out a set of interesting points from a potentially large set of data points. It presents an extension of SQL by Skyline queries along with algorithms for them. The work [2] proposes several approaches to rank database query results, while [11] focuses on top-k query evaluation in web databases, and [31] proposes a decentralized top-k query evaluation algorithm for peer-to-peer networks. In contrast to our approach, none of the above works deals with ranking objects relative to conditional preferences of the form "generally, in the context ϕ, property α is preferred over property $\neg\alpha$ with strength s" in the framework of expressive description logics.

8 Summary and Outlook

We have presented an approach to conditional preference bases, which consist of a description logic knowledge base and a finite set of conditional preferences, and which are given a qualitative probabilistic formal semantics in a generalization of Goldszmidt and Pearl's System Z^+. We have defined the notion of consistency for conditional preference bases and shown how consistent conditional preference bases can be used for ranking objects in ontologies. We have also provided algorithms for these rankings.

We have demonstrated the usefulness of the presented approach in the area of literature search. Search query languages of current search engines are very restricted in their expressive power. There are scientific search engines on the web, however, that have valuable metadata about research publications, authors, organizations, and scientific events. We have shown that conditional preference bases allow for a more powerful query language, which can exploit this metadata better than the current approaches do. In particular, we have given some sample queries that (i) explicitly follow different search strategies, (ii) influence the ranking of the query results, (iii) express quality measures, (iv) cluster query results, or (v) restrict queries to different result types.

An interesting topic of future research is to explore further applications of the presented approach, for example, in personalization tasks and recommender systems.

Acknowledgments. This work has been partially supported by a Heisenberg Professorship of the German Research Foundation (DFG). We thank the reviewers for their constructive comments, which helped to improve this work.

References

1. E. W. Adams. *The Logic of Conditionals*, volume 86 of *Synthese Library*. D. Reidel, Dordrecht, Netherlands, 1975.
2. S. Agrawal, S. Chaudhuri, G. Das, and A. Gionis. Automated ranking of database query results. In *Proceedings CIDR-2003*.
3. R. Baeza-Yates and B. Ribeiro-Neto. *Modern Information Retrieval*. Addison Wesley, 1999.
4. M. Bates. The design of browsing and berrypicking techniques for the on-line search interface. *Online Review*, 13(5):407–431, 1989.
5. S. Benferhat, D. Dubois, and H. Prade. Nonmonotonic reasoning, conditional objects and possibility theory. *Artif. Intell.*, 92(1–2):259–276, 1997.
6. T. Berners-Lee. *Weaving the Web*. Harper, San Francisco, 1999.
7. K. D. Bollacker, S. Lawrence, and C. L. Giles. Discovering relevant scientific literature on the web. *IEEE Intelligent Systems*, 15(2):42–47, 2000.
8. C. Boutilier, R. I. Brafman, C. Domshlak, H. H. Hoos, and D. Poole. CP-nets: A tool for representing and reasoning with conditional ceteris paribus preference statements. *J. Artif. Intell. Res.*, 21:135–191, 2004.
9. S. Börzsönyi, D. Kossmann, and K. Stocker. The Skyline operator. In *Proceedings ICDE-2001*, pp. 421–430.
10. S. Brin and L. Page. The anatomy of a large-scale hypertextual web search engine. In *Proceedings WWW-1998*, pp. 107–117.
11. N. Bruno, L. Gravano, and A. Marian. Evaluating top-k queries over web-accessible databases. In *Proceedings ICDE-2002*, pp. 369–382.

12. D. Calvanese, G. De Giacomo, D. Lembo, M. Lenzerini, and R. Rosati. DL-Lite: Tractable description logics for ontologies. In *Proceedings AAAI-2005*, pp. 602–607.
13. C. Ding, C.-H. Chi, J. Deng, and C.-L. Dong. Citation retrieval in digital libraries. In *Proceedings IEEE SMC-1999*, volume 2, pp. 105–109.
14. D. Dubois and H. Prade. Conditional objects as nonmonotonic consequence relationships. *IEEE Trans. Syst. Man Cybern.*, 24(12):1724–1740, 1994.
15. D. Dubois and H. Prade. Possibilistic logic, preferential models, non-monotonicity and related issues. In *Proceedings IJCAI-1991*, pp. 419–424.
16. F. D. de Saint-Cyr and H. Prade. Handling uncertainty in a non-monotonic setting, with applications to persistence modeling and fuzzy default reasoning. In *Proceedings KR-2006*.
17. D. Fensel, W. Wahlster, H. Lieberman, and J. Hendler, editors. *Spinning the Semantic Web: Bringing the World Wide Web to Its Full Potential*. MIT Press, 2002.
18. D. M. Gabbay and P. Smets, editors. *Handbook on Defeasible Reasoning and Uncertainty Management Systems*. Kluwer Academic, Dordrecht, Netherlands, 1998.
19. E. Garfield. *Citation Indexing — Its Theory and Application in Science, Technology, and Humanities*. John Wiley & Sons, New York, 1979.
20. C. L. Giles, K. D. Bollacker, and S. Lawrence. CiteSeer: An automatic citation indexing system. In *Proceedings ACM Digital Libraries 1998*, pp. 89–98, 1998.
21. M. Goldszmidt and J. Pearl. On the consistency of defeasible databases. *Artif. Intell.*, 52(2):121–149, 1991.
22. M. Goldszmidt and J. Pearl. Qualitative probabilities for default reasoning, belief revision, and causal modeling. *Artif. Intell.*, 84(1–2):57–112, 1996.
23. I. Horrocks and P. F. Patel-Schneider. Reducing OWL entailment to description logic satisfiability. *J. Web Semantics*, 1(4):345–357, 2004.
24. I. Horrocks, P. F. Patel-Schneider, and F. van Harmelen. From $\mathcal{SHIQ}$ and RDF to OWL: The making of a web ontology language. *J. Web Semantics*, 1(1):7–26, 2003.
25. I. Horrocks, U. Sattler, and S. Tobies. Practical reasoning for expressive description logics. In *Proceedings LPAR-1999*, pp. 161–180, *LNCS* 1705, Springer.
26. S. Kraus, D. Lehmann, and M. Magidor. Nonmonotonic reasoning, preferential models and cumulative logics. *Artif. Intell.*, 14(1):167–207, 1990.
27. S. Lawrence, K. D. Bollacker, and C. L. Giles. Indexing and retrieval of scientific literature. In *Proceedings CIKM-1999*, pp. 139-146.
28. D. Lehmann and M. Magidor. What does a conditional knowledge base entail? *Artif. Intell.*, 55(1):1–60, 1992.
29. T. Lukasiewicz. Weak nonmonotonic probabilistic logics. *Artif. Intell.*, 168: 119–161, 2005.
30. T. Lukasiewicz and J. Schellhase. Variable-strength conditional preferences for matchmaking in description logics. In *Proceedings KR-2006*.
31. W. Nejdl, W. Siberski, U. Thaden, and W.-T. Balke. Top-k query evaluation for schema-based peer-to-peer networks. In *Proceedings ISWC-2004*, pp. 137–151.
32. J. Pearl. System Z: A natural ordering of defaults with tractable applications to default reasoning. In *Proceedings TARK-1990*, pp. 121–135.
33. D. Poole and C. Smyth. Type uncertainty in ontologically-grounded qualitative probabilistic matching. In *Proceedings ECSQARU-2005*, pp. 763–774.
34. C. Smyth and D. Poole. Qualitative probabilistic matching with hierarchical descriptions. In *Proceedings KR-2004*, pp. 479–487.
35. M. Stempfhuber. Keep the best — Forget the rest? Towards models for CRISs integrating heterogeneous information. In *Proceedings CRIS-2004*.
36. S.-W. Tan and J. Pearl. Specification and evaluation of preferences under uncertainty. In *Proceedings KR-1994*, pp. 530–539.
37. W3C. OWL web ontology language overview, 2004. W3C Recommendation (10 February 2004). Available at www.w3.org/TR/2004/REC-owl-features-20040210/.

A Metamodel and UML Profile for Rule-Extended OWL DL Ontologies

Saartje Brockmans, Peter Haase, Pascal Hitzler, and Rudi Studer

Institute AIFB, Universität Karlsruhe, Germany
{brockmans, haase, hitzler, studer}@aifb.uni-karlsruhe.de

Abstract. In this paper we present a MOF compliant metamodel and UML profile for the Semantic Web Rule Language (SWRL) that integrates with our previous work on a metamodel and UML profile for OWL DL. Based on this metamodel and profile, UML tools can be used for visual modeling of rule-extended ontologies.

1 Introduction

An ontology defines a common set of concepts and terms that are used to describe and represent a domain of knowledge. The manual creation of ontologies is a labor-intensive, expensive, often difficult, and – without proper tool support – an error-prone task. Visual syntaxes have shown to bring many benefits that simplify conceptual modeling [18]. As for other modeling purposes, visual modeling of ontologies decreases syntactic and semantic errors and increases readability. It makes the modeling and use of ontologies much easier and faster, especially if tools are user-friendly and appropriate modeling languages are applied.

The usefulness of a visual syntax for modeling languages has been shown in practice; visual modeling paradigms such as the Entity Relationship (ER, [4]) model or the Unified Modeling Language (UML, [5]) are used frequently for the purpose of conceptual modeling. Consequently, the necessity of a visual syntax for KR languages has been argued frequently in the past [6, 12]. Particular representation formalisms such as conceptual graphs [19] or Topic Maps [11], for example, are based on well-defined graphical notations.

Description Logic-based ontology languages such as OWL, however, are usually defined in terms of an abstract (text-based) syntax and most care is spent on the formal semantics, neglecting the development of good modeling frameworks. In our previous work [3], we therefore have developed a Meta Object Facility (MOF, [14]) metamodel for the purpose of defining ontologies, called Ontology Definition Metamodel (ODM), with specific focus on the OWL DL language, along with a UML profile for the purpose of visual modeling.

In the meantime, rule extensions for OWL have been heavily discussed [20]. Just recently the W3C has chartered a working group for the definition of a Rule Interchange Format [21]. One of the most prominent proposals for an extension of OWL DL with rules is the Semantic Web Rule Language (SWRL, [9]). SWRL proposes to allow the use of Horn-like rules together with OWL axioms.

Y. Sure and J. Domingue (Eds.): ESWC 2006, LNCS 4011, pp. 303–316, 2006.

A high-level abstract syntax is provided that extends the OWL abstract syntax described in the OWL Semantics and Abstract Syntax document [17]. An extension of the OWL model-theoretic semantics provides a formal meaning for SWRL ontologies.

The definition of a visual notation for SWRL rules is currently missing. Therefore, this paper defines a metamodel and UML profile for SWRL that extends and complements our previous metamodel and UML profile for OWL DL. Our goal is to achieve an intuitive notation, both for users of UML and description logics as well as for rule-based systems. Naturally, the proposed metamodel has a one-to-one mapping to the abstract syntax of SWRL and OWL DL and thereby to their formal semantics.

The paper is organized as follows: Section 2 introduces the Meta Object Facility (MOF) and our previous work on an OWL DL metamodel along with its UML profile. Section 3 presents our extensions of the ODM towards SWRL rules. Section 4 introduces a UML Profile for the modeling of rules and explains the major design choices made in order to make the notation readable and intuitive both for users with UML background and for users with a background in OWL and rule-based systems. In Section 5 we discuss related work. We conclude in Section 6 by summarizing our work and discussing future research.

2   An Ontology Definition Metamodel of OWL Within the MOF Framework

This section introduces the essential ideas of the Meta Object Facility (MOF) and shows how the Ontology Definition Metamodel (ODM) and the UML Ontology Profile (UOP) fit into this more general picture. The need for a dedicated visual ontology modeling language stems from the observation that an ontology cannot be sufficiently represented in UML [8]. The two representations share a set of core functionalities such as the ability to define classes, class relationships, and relationship cardinalities. But despite this overlap, there are many features which can only be expressed in OWL, and others which can only be expressed in UML. Examples for this disjointness are transitive and symmetric properties in OWL or methods in UML. For a full account of the conceptual differences we refer the reader to [10].

UML methodology, tools and technology, however, seem to be a feasible approach for supporting the development and maintenance of ontologies. The general idea of using MOF-based metamodels and UML profiles for this purpose is depicted in Figure 1 and explained in the following:

1. The ODM and the UOP are grounded in MOF, in that they are defined in terms of the MOF meta-metamodel, as explained in Section 2.1.
2. The UML profile defines a visual notation for OWL DL ontologies, based on the above mentioned metamodel. Furthermore, mappings in both directions between the metamodel and this profile are established.
3. Specific OWL DL ontologies instantiate the Ontology Definition Metamodel. The constructs of the OWL DL language have a direct correspondence with

those of the ODM. Analogously, specific UML models instantiate the UML Ontology Profile. The translation between the UML models and OWL ontologies is based on the above mappings between the ODM and the UOP.

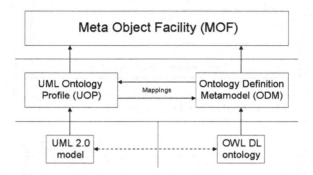

Fig. 1. An ontology to UML mapping allows existing tools to operate on compatible aspects of ontologies

2.1 Meta Object Facility

The Meta Object Facility (MOF) is an extensible model driven integration framework for defining, manipulating and integrating metadata and data in a platform independent manner. The goal is to provide a framework that supports any kind of metadata and that allows new kinds to be added as required. MOF plays a crucial role in the four-layer metadata architecture of the Object Management Group (OMG) shown in Figure 2. The bottom layer of this architecture encompasses the raw information to be described. For example, Figure 2 contains information about a wine called ElyseZinfandel and about the Napa region, where this wine grows. The model layer contains the definition of the required structures, e.g. in the example it contains the classes used for grouping information. Consequently, the classes wine and region are defined. If these are combined, they describe the model for the given domain. The metamodel defines the terms in which the model is expressed. In our example, we would state that models are expressed with classes and properties by instantiating the respective meta classes. Finally, the MOF constitutes the top layer, also called the meta-metamodel layer. Note that the top MOF layer is hard wired in the sense that it is fixed, while the other layers are flexible and allow to express various metamodels such as the UML metamodel or the ODM.

2.2 Ontology Definition Metamodel

The Ontology Definition Metamodel (ODM, [3]) defines a metamodel for ontologies. This metamodel is built on the MOF framework, which we explained in Section 2.1. We defined an Ontology Definition Metamodel for OWL DL using a notation which is accessible for users of UML as well as for OWL DL ontology engineers. A metamodel for a language that allows the definition of ontologies

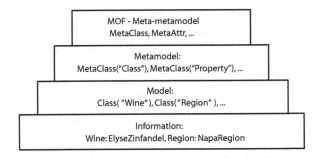

Fig. 2. OMG Four Layer Metadata Architecture

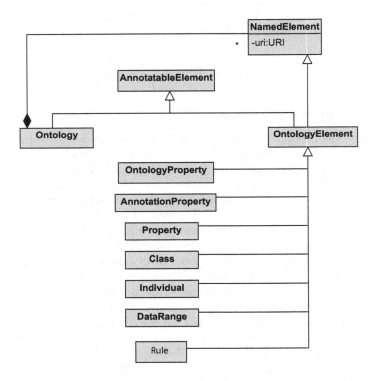

Fig. 3. Main Elements of the Ontology Definition Metamodel

naturally follows from the modeling primitives offered by the ontology language. The proposed metamodel has a one-to-one mapping to the abstract syntax of OWL DL and thereby to the formal semantics of OWL. It primarily uses basic well-known concepts from UML2, which is the second and newest version of UML. Additionally, we augmented the metamodel with constraints specifying invariants that have to be fulfilled by all models that instantiate the metamodel. These constraints are expressed in the Object Constraint Language [23], a declar-

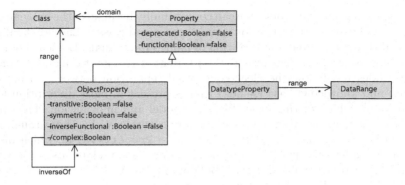

Fig. 4. Properties

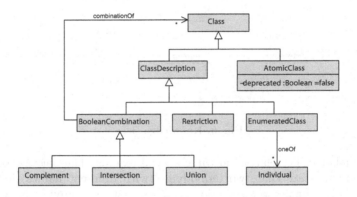

Fig. 5. Classes

ative language that provides constraint and object query expressions on object models that cannot otherwise be expressed by diagrammatic notation.

Figure 3 shows the main elements of the ODM. Every element of an ontology is a `NamedElement` and hence a member of an `Ontology`.

Properties, as shown in Figure 4, represent named binary associations in the modeled knowledge domain. OWL distinguishes two kinds of properties, so-called object properties and datatype properties. A common generalization of them is given by the abstract metaclass `Property`. Properties can be functional and their domain is always a class. Object properties may additionally be inverse functional, transitive, symmetric, or inverse to another property. Their range is a class, while the range of datatype properties are datatypes.

Users can relate properties by using two types of axioms: property subsumption (`subPropertyOf`) specifies that the extension of a property is a subset of the related property, while property equivalence (`equivalentProperty`) defines extensional equivalence.

Class descriptions are depicted in Figure 5. In contrast to UML, OWL DL does not only allow to define simple named classes. Instead, classes can be formed using a number of class constructors. One can conceptually distinguish the boolean combination of classes, class restrictions, and enumerated classes. `EnumeratedClass` is defined through a direct enumeration of named individuals. Boolean combinations of classes are provided through `Complement`, `Intersection` and `Union`.

OWL does not follow the clear conceptual separation between terminology (T-Box) and knowledge base (A-box) that is present in most description logics and in MOF, which distinguishes between model and information. The knowledge base elements (cf. Figure 6) are part of an ontology. An `Individual` is an instantiation of a `Class` and is the subject of a `PropertyValue`, which instantiates a `Property`. Naturally, an `ObjectPropertyValue` relates its subject with another `Individual` whilst a `DatatypePropertyValue` relates its subject with a `DataValue`, which is an instance of a `DataType`.

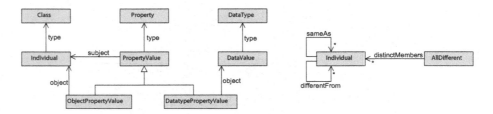

Fig. 6. Knowledge Base

Individuals can be related via three special axioms: The `sameAs` association allows users to state that two individuals (with different names) are equivalent. The `differentFrom` association specifies that two individuals are not the same. `AllDifferent` is a simpler notation for the pairwise difference of several individuals.

For a full specification of the OWL DL metamodel, we refer to [3].

2.3 UML Ontology Profile

The UML ontology profile (UOP) describes a visual UML syntax for modeling ontologies. We provide a UML profile that is faithful to both UML2 and OWL DL, with a maximal reuse of UML2 features and OWL DL features. Since the UML profile mechanism supports a restricted form of metamodeling, our proposal contains a set of extensions and constraints to UML2. This tailors UML2 such that models instantiating the ODM can be defined. Our UML profile has a basic mapping, from OWL class to UML class, from OWL property to binary UML association, from OWL individual to UML object, and from OWL property filler to UML object association. Extensions to UML2 consist of custom UML stereotypes, which usually carry the name of the corresponding OWL DL language element, and dependencies. Figure 7 (left) shows an example of two classes `Wine` and `WineGrape`, visually depicted as UML classes, which are connected via the object property `madeFromGrape`, depicted as a UML association. Some extensions to UML2 are used in the example in Figure 7 (right),

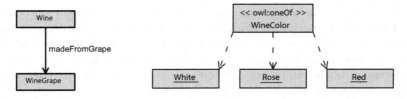

Fig. 7. A fragment of the UML profile: The ObjectProperty and oneOf constructs

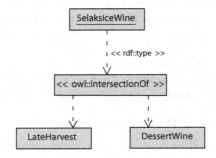

Fig. 8. A fragment of the UML profile: An individual of a complex class description

which shows that an enumerated class is connected to the enumerated individuals by dependencies. A stereotype denotes the enumerated class, whereas the UML notation for objects is used for individuals. Another example, depicted in Figure 8, shows an individual `SelaksIceWine` of the intersection between the classes `LateHarvest` and `DessertWine`.

3   A Metamodel for SWRL Rules

We propose a metamodel for SWRL rules as a consistent extension of the metamodel for OWL DL ontologies which we described in the previous section of this paper. Figure 9 shows the metamodel for SWRL rules. We discuss the metamodel step by step along the SWRL specifications. Interested readers may refer to the specifications [9] for a full account of SWRL. For a complete reference of the formal correspondence between the metamodel and SWRL itself and the OCL constraints for the rule metamodel, we refer the reader to [2].

3.1   Rules

SWRL defines rules as part of an ontology. The SWRL metamodel defines `Rule` as a subclass of `OntologyElement`. `OntologyElement` is defined in the OWL DL metamodel (Figure 3) as an element of an `Ontology`, via the composition link between `NamedElement` and `Ontology`. As can also be seen in Figure 3, the class `OntologyElement` is a subclass of the class `AnnotatableElement`, which defines that rules can be annotated. As annotations are modeled in the ODM, a URI reference can be assigned to a rule for identification.

A rule consists of an antecedent and a consequent, also referred to as body and head of the rule, respectively. Both the antecedent and the consequent consist of a set of atoms which can possibly be empty, as depicted by the multiplicity in Figure 9. Informally, a rule says that *if* all atoms of the antecedent hold, *then* the consequent holds. An empty antecedent is treated as trivially true, whereas an empty consequent is treated as trivially false.

The same antecedent or consequent can be used in several rules, as indicated in the metamodel by the multiplicity on the association between **Rule** on the one hand and **Antecedent** or **Consequent** on the other hand. Similarly, the multiplicities of the association between **Antecedent** and **Atom** and of the association between **Consequent** and **Atom** define that an antecedent and a consequent can hold zero or more atoms. The multiplicity in the other direction defines that the same atom can appear in several antecedents or consequents. According to the SWRL specifications, every **Variable** that occurs in the **Consequent** of a rule must occur in the **Antecedent** of that rule, a condition referred to as "safety".

3.2   Atoms, Terms and Predicate Symbols

The atoms of the antecedent and the consequent consist of predicate symbols and terms. According to SWRL, they can have different forms:

- $C(x)$, where C is an OWL description and x an individual variable or an OWL individual, or C is an OWL data range and x either a data variable or an OWL data value;
- $P(x, y)$, where P is an OWL individual valued property and x and y are both either an individual variable or an OWL individual, or P is an OWL data valued property, x is either an individual variable or an OWL individual and y is either a data variable or an OWL data value;

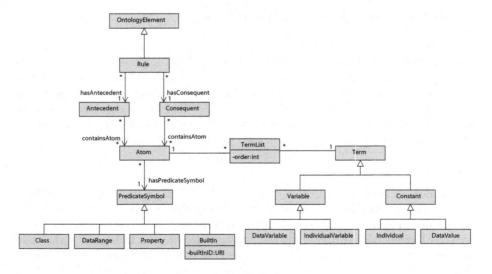

Fig. 9. The Rule Definition Metamodel

- sameAs(x, y), where x and y are both either an OWL individual or an individual variable;
- differentFrom(x, y), where x and y are both either an OWL individual or an individual variable;
- builtIn($r, x, ...$), where r is a built-in predicate and x is a data variable or OWL data value. A builtIn atom could possibly have more than one variable or OWL data value.

The first of these, OWL description, data range and property, were already provided in the ODM, namely as metaclasses `Class`, `DataRange` and `Property`, respectively. As can be seen in Figure 9, the predicates `Class`, `DataRange`, `Property` and `BuiltIn` are all defined as subclasses of the class `PredicateSymbol`, which is associated to `Atom`. The remaining two atom types, `sameAs` and `differentFrom`, are represented as specific instances of `PredicateSymbol`.

To define the order of the atom terms, we put a class `TermOrder` in between `Atom` and `Term`. This UML association class connects atoms with terms and defines the term order via the attribute `order`.

4   A UML Profile for Rules

UML provides an extension mechanism, the UML profile mechanism, to tailor the language to specific application areas. The definition of such a UML extension is based on the standard UML metamodel. In this section, we propose a UML profile for modeling SWRL rules which is consistent with the design considerations taken for the basic UML Ontology Profile. For a complete reference of the relationship between the UML profile and the metamodel introduced in Section 3, we refer the reader to [2]. Figure 10 shows an example of a rule, which defines that when a vintager does not like the wine made in his winery, he is a bad vintager. We introduce the profile in an order based on the SWRL metamodel introduced in Section 3.

4.1   Rules

As can be seen in Figure 10, a rule is depicted by two boxes connected via a dependency with the stereotype `rule`. All atoms of the antecedent are contained

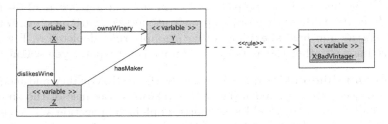

Fig. 10. BadVintager(x) $\leftarrow$ ownsWinery(x, y) $\land$ dislikesWine(x, z) $\land$ hasMaker(z, y)

in the box at the origin of the dependency, whereas the box at the end contains the consequent. This way, antecedent and consequent can easily be distinguished, and it also allows to distinguish between the rule atoms and the OWL DL facts which are depicted in similar ways. The left box of our example contains the three variable definitions and the three properties that are defined between these variables. The consequent-box on the right contains the definition of the variable X from which it is known which class it belongs to. We explain the specific design considerations of these concepts in the following subsections.

4.2   Terms

Although the existing UOP already comprises a visual syntax for individuals and data values, namely by applying the UML object notation, it does not include a notation for variables since OWL DL ontologies do not contain variables. We decided to depict variables in the UML object notation as well, since a variable can be seen as a partially unknown class instance. We provide a stereotype `variable` to distinguish a variable. Figure 11 shows a simple example for a variable, an individual and a data value.

Fig. 11. Terms

4.3   Predicate Symbols in Atoms

Class description and data range. A visual notation for individuals as instances of class descriptions is already provided in the UOP for OWL DL. An atom with a class description and a variable as its term, is illustrated similarly. An appropriate stereotype is added. An example of this can be seen in the consequent in Figure 10. A visual construct for a data range definition using individuals is contained in the UOP for OWL DL as well, namely represented in the same way as class individuals. Data range constructs containing variables are also depicted in a similar fashion.

Properties. Object properties are depicted as directed associations between the two involved elements. A datatype property is pictured as an attribute. These notations were provided for properties of individuals by the UOP for OWL DL, and we follow them to depict properties of variables. The antecedent of the rule in Figure 10 contains three such object properties between variables, `ownsWinery`, `dislikesWine` and `hasMaker`. The other example rule, depicted in Figure 13, contains amongst other things twice the datavalued property `yearValue`.

sameAs and differentFrom. According to the UOP, equality and inequality between objects are depicted using object relations. Because of the similarity between individuals and variables, as shortly explained in Section 4.2, we propose to use the same visual notation for `sameAs` and `differentFrom` relations between two variables or between a variable and an object.

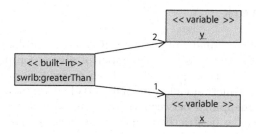

Fig. 12. Built-in predicates

Built-in predicates. For the visual representation of built-in relations, we use usual associations to all participating variables and data values, similar to the `owl:AllDifferent` concept provided in the basic UOP. To denote the built-in relation, we provide the stereotype `built-in` together with the specific built-in ID. The names of the associations denote the order of the arguments, by numbers. Figure 12 shows an example of a built-in relation `swrlb:greaterThan`, which is defined to check whether the first involved argument is greater than the second one. For the six most basic built-ins, `swrlb:equal`, `swrlb:notEqual`, `swrlb:lessThan`, `swrlb:lessThanOrEqual`, `swrlb:greaterThan` and `swrlb:greaterThanOrEqual`, we provide an alternative notation. Instead of depicting the stereotype and the name of the built-in, an appropriate icon can be used. Figure 13 depicts a rule example using this alternative notation for built-in predicates. This rule states that if the year value of a wine (y) is greater than the year value of another wine (x), then the second wine (x) is older than the first one (y). Next to the built-in predicate, Figure 13 shows six variables with the properties `hasVintageYear`, `yearValue` and `olderThan`.

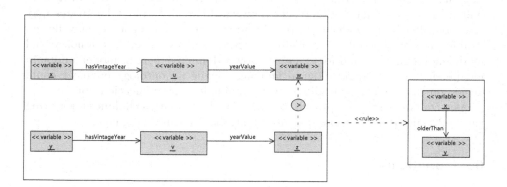

Fig. 13. $\text{olderThan}(x,y)$ ← $\text{hasVintageYear}(x,u)$ ∧ $\text{hasVintageYear}(y,v)$ ∧ $\text{yearValue}(u,w)$ ∧ $\text{yearValue}(v,z)$ ∧ $\text{swrlb:greaterThan}(z,w)$

5   Related Work

As a response to the original call of the OMG for an Ontology Definition Meta-model [16], the OMG has received a number of diverse proposals (see [3] for a comparison). The various proposals have been merged into one submission [10] that covered several metamodels for RDF, OWL, Common Logic, and Topic Maps, as well as mappings between them. Our proposed metamodel departs from this approach as it strictly focuses on OWL DL and is tailored to its specific features, with the advantage that it has a direct mapping between the metamodel and OWL DL. Also, none of the other OMG proposals so far has considered rule extensions. To the best of our knowledge, our work presents the first MOF-based metamodel and UML profile for an ontology rule language.

DL-safe rules [13] are a decidable subset of SWRL. As every DL-safe rule is also a SWRL rule, DL-safe rules are covered by our metamodel. Using additional constraints it can be checked whether a rule is DL-safe. It should be noted that SWRL is not the only rule language which has been proposed for ontologies. Other prominent alternatives for rule languages are mentioned in the W3C Rule Interchange Format Working Group charter [21], namely the Web Rule Language WRL [1] and the rules fragment of the Semantic Web Service Language SWSL [7]. These languages differ in their semantics and consequently also in the way in which they model implicit knowledge for expressive reasoning support. From this perspective, it could be desirable to define different metamodels, each of which is tailored to a specific rules language.

From the perspective of conceptual modeling, however, different rule languages appear to be very similar to each other. This opens up the possibility to reuse the SWRL metamodel defined in this paper by augmenting it with some features to allow for the modeling of language primitives which are not present in SWRL. As a result, one would end up with a common metamodel for different rules languages. An advantage of the latter approach would be a gain in flexibility. Intricate semantic differences between different ontology languages may often be difficult to understand for the practitioner, and hence it may be desirable to provide simplified modeling support in many cases. A common visual modeling language would for example allow a domain expert to model a domain independent of a concrete logical language, while an ontology engineer could decide on the language paradigm most suitable for the application domain.

As a complementary approach to using visual modeling techniques for writing rules, [22] discusses a proposal to use (controlled) natural language.

6   Conclusion

We have presented a MOF metamodel for the Semantic Web Rule Language SWRL. This metamodel tightly integrates with our previous metamodel for OWL DL. The validity of instances of this metamodel is ensured through OCL constraints. We also provided a UML profile for this metamodel. It employs the extensibility features of UML2 to allow a visual notation for the modeling of rule-extended ontologies which is particularly adequate for users familiar with UML. We plan to provide an implementation as a next step.

Future work may also include the modeling of other logics-based rule languages. The outcome of the W3C working group to establish a Rule Interchange Format is currently open. It is likely that several rule languages will need to co-exist, which will require techniques for rule language interoperability. Here, the model driven approaches of MOF might provide useful techniques to achieve such interoperability, for example based on the Query View and Transformation (QVT, [15]) framework, which allows the definition and automated execution of mappings between MOF-based metamodels.

Acknowledgements

Research for this paper has been partially funded by the EU under the projects SEKT (IST-2003-506826) and NeOn (IST-2005-027595), by the German Federal Ministry of Education and Research (BMBF) under the SmartWeb project (01 IMD01 A) and by the German Research Foundation (DFG) under the Graduate School IME – Universität Karlsruhe (TH).

References

1. J. Angele, H. Boley, J. de Bruijn, D. Fensel, P. Hitzler, M. Kifer, R. Krummenacher, H. Lausen, A. Polleres, and R. Studer. *Web Rule Language (WRL)*. World Wide Web Consortium, September 2005. W3C Member Submission, http://www.w3.org/Submission/WRL/.
2. S. Brockmans and P. Haase. A Metamodel and UML Profile for Rule-extended OWL DL Ontologies –A Complete Reference. Technical report, Universität Karlsruhe, March 2006. http://www.aifb.uni-karlsruhe.de/WBS/sbr/publications/owl-metamodeling.pdf.
3. S. Brockmans, R. Volz, A. Eberhart, and P. Loeffler. Visual Modeling of OWL DL Ontologies using UML. In F. van Harmelen, S. A. McIlraith, and D. Plexousakis, editors, *The Semantic Web – ISWC 2004*, pages 198–213. Springer-Verlag, 2004.
4. P. P. Chen. The entity-relationship model – toward a unified view of data. *ACM Transactions on Database Systems*, 1(1):9–36, 1976.
5. M. Fowler. *UML Distilled*. Addison-Wesley, third edition, 2004.
6. B. R. Gaines. An Interactive Visual Language for Term Subsumption Languages. In J. Mylopoulos and R. Reiter, editors, *Proc. of 12th Int. Joint Conf. on Art. Int.*, pages 817–823, Sydney, Australia, August 1991. Morgan Kaufmann.
7. B. Grosof, M. Kifer, and D. L. Martin. Rules in the Semantic Web Services Language (SWSL): An overview for standardization directions. In *Proceedings of the W3C Workshop on Rule Languages for Interoperability, 27-28 April 2005, Washington, DC, USA*, 2005.
8. L. Hart, P. Emery, B. Colomb, K. Raymond, S. Taraporewalla, D. Chang, Y. Ye, and M. D. Elisa Kendall. OWL full and UML 2.0 compared, March 2004. http://www.itee.uq.edu.au/$\sim$colomb/Papers/UML-OWLont04.03.01.pdf.

9. I. Horrocks, P. F. Patel-Schneider, H. Boley, S. Tabet, B. Grosof, and M. Dean. *SWRL: A Semantic Web Rule Language Combining OWL and RuleML*. World Wide Web Consortium, May 2004. W3C Member Submission, `http://www.w3.org/Submission/2004/SUBM-SWRL-20040521/`.

10. IBM, Sandpiper Software. *Ontology Definition Metamodel, Fourth Revised Submission to OMG*, November 2005.

11. ISO/IEC. Topic Maps: Information Technology – Document Description and Markup Languages. ISO/IEC 13250, `http://www.y12.doe.gov/sgml/sc34/document/0129.pdf`, December 1999.

12. R. Kremer. Visual Languages for Knowledge Representation. In *Proc. of 11th Workshop on Knowledge Acquisition, Modeling and Management (KAW'98)*, Voyager Inn, Banff, Alberta, Canada, April 1998. Morgan Kaufmann.

13. B. Motik, U. Sattler, and R. Studer. Query answering for OWL-DL with rules. In F. van Harmelen, S. McIlraith, and D. Plexousakis, editors, *International Semantic Web Conference*, Lecture Notes in Computer Science, pages 549–563, Hiroshima, Japan, 2004. Springer.

14. Object Management Group. Meta Object Facility (MOF) Specification. Technical report, Object Management Group (OMG), April 2002. `http://www.omg.org/docs/formal/02-04-03.pdf`.

15. Object Management Group. MOF 2.0 Query / Views / Transformations – Request for Proposal. `http://www.omg.org/docs/ad/02-04-10.pdf`, 2002.

16. Object Management Group. Ontology Definition Metamodel – Request For Proposal, March 2003. `http://www.omg.org/docs/ontology/03-03-01.rtf`.

17. P. F. Patel-Schneider, P. Hayes, and I. Horrocks. *OWL Web Ontology Language Semantics and Abstract Syntax*. World Wide Web Consortium, 10. Februar 2004. Recommendation. http://www.w3.org/TR/2004/REC-owl-semantics-20040210/.

18. W. Schnotz. Wissenserwerb mit Texten, Bildern und Diagrammen. In L. J. Issing and P. Klimsa, editors, *Information und Lernen mit Multimedia und Internet*, pages 65–81. Belz, PVU, Weinheim, third, completely revised edition, 2002.

19. J. F. Sowa. Conceptual graphs summary. In P. Eklund, T. Nagle, J. Nagle, and L. Gerholz, editors, *Conceptual Structures: Current Research and Practice*, pages 3–52. Ellis Horwood, New York, 1992.

20. *Accepted Papers of the W3C Workshop on Rule Languages for Interoperability, 27-28 April 2005, Washington, DC, USA*, 2005. http://www.w3.org/2004/12/rules-ws/accepted.

21. W3C. Rule interchange format working group charter. `http://www.w3.org/2005/rules/wg/charter`, 2005.

22. A. Walker. Understandability and semantic interoperability of diverse rules systems. `http://www.w3.org/2004/12/rules-ws/paper/19`, April 2005. Position Paper for the W3C Workshop on Rule Languages for Interoperability.

23. J. Warmer and A. Kleppe. *Object Constraint Language 2.0*. MITP Verlag, 2004.

Visual Ontology Cleaning: Cognitive Principles and Applicability*

Joaquín Borrego-Díaz and Antonia M. Chávez-González

Departamento de Ciencias de la Computación e Inteligencia Artificial.
E.T.S. Ingeniería Informática-Universidad de Sevilla.
Avda. Reina Mercedes s.n. 41012-Sevilla, Spain
{jborrego, tchavez}@us.es

Abstract. In this paper we connect two research areas, the Qualitative Spatial Reasoning and visual reasoning on ontologies. We discuss the logical limitations of the mereotopological approach to the visual ontology cleaning, from the point of view of its formal support. The analysis is based on three different spatial interpretations wich are based in turn on three different spatial interpretations of the concepts of an ontology.

1 Introduction

It is commonly accepted that for achieving a satisfactory sharing of knowledge in the envisioned Semantic Web (SW), it will be necessary to build ontologies. They play a key role in the reasoning services for Knowledge Bases (KB) in the SW [17]. Practical management of ontologies, such as extension, refinement and versioning technologies will be essential tasks.

From the point of view of the Knowledge Representation (KR) paradigm, ontology revision comes from the fact that the discourse domain may not be faithfully represented by an ontology (a well known working principle in KR). In many cases, end-users need to interact and transform the ontology. Even if the ontology designer thinks that the ontology is final, the end-user may think the opposite, or simply that the ontology is incorrect. In fact, it should be feasible to achieve the agreement designer-user. This agreement is essential for the assimilation of SW technologies into non-academic community portals, for example.

Unfortunately, several reasons obstruct the agreement. The first one is that end users do not know the logical formalisms behind ontology web languages. Therefore, the user can not know hidden principles on which ontologies are built. It does not help to increase the understanding of technologies involved in SW tools. Anyway, this fact might not be important if he uses amenable technologies for representing/repairing the anomalies founded in its own ontology project. Visual encodings are very interesting for such pourposes.

End-user preferences on visual representation are well known in other related fields such as Formal Concept Analysis or Data Engineering. The spatial

---

* Supported by project TIN2004-03884 of Spanish Ministry of Education and Science, cofinanced by FEDER founds.

metaphor is a powerful tool in human information processing. The user will feel encouraged to repair the anomaly, although there exist some obstacles: on the one hand, visual reparation may not be corresponded by a logical reparation of the ontology source. This occurs if there is no a formal semantics for supporting the change; on the other hand, repairs can be logically complex. Domain experts often underestimate the amount of time required to produce an ontology, and consequently they build an ontology based on a large scope. The resulting conceptual ontologies are consequently a mix of both domain and task ontology concepts which are hard to manage [22].

Paraphrasing [23], visual cleaning of ontologies is important for future end-users of ontology debugging systems due mainly to three reasons:

1. It allows the user to summarize ontology contents.
2. User's information is often fuzzily defined. Visualization can be used to help the user to get a nice representation.
3. Finally, visualization can therefore help the user to interact with the information space.

There is not a generally accepted representation mechanism that translates every possible changes in the visual representation into the specification of the ontology. In fact, this is an interesting problem in the design of visual reasoning tools. Current end-user tools are mostly based on facilitating the understanding of the ontology (see e.g. [14], [21]) facilitating very limited graphical changes to the user. In order to augment such features, we need formally sound mappings between (visual) representations and Knowledge Bases (KBs) (expressed, for example, in Description Logics). Note that such mappings have to translate logical notions for supporting the logical impact of arrangements on the spatial representation (for example, when new concepts are inserted). These issues are critical and we need to solve them in order to integrate solutions in systems for visual representation of information [14]. This goal is far away of being achieved for classical Information Visualization (IV) tools. IV is the use of computer-supported, interactive and visual representations of abstract data to amplify cognition [9]. The goal of Visual Ontology Cleaning (VOC) should be to reason spatially for visually debugging and repairing of ontologies . Therefore, it should have aditional features, different from classical user analysis, querying and navigation/browsing.

A second limitation concerns to the scalability of debugging problem. It is hard to manage visual representations of large ontologies, although a broad spectrum of tools has been designed [14]. It is sometimes sufficent to locate which small portion of the ontology supports the anomaly. This task can be facilitated by Automated Reasoning Systems (ARS). ARS are useful both for debugging ontologies [1] [2][27] (although several foundational problems exist [4]), and for the computer-assisted evolution of robust ontologies [6] [7]. If an ARS find a proof of an anomalous result, it can recover an *argument* from the proof. An argument is a pair formed by a consistent portion of the KB and the entailed result (an *ontological argument*). In this case, it seems natural to consider the repairing of the self argument to cut such inference [3]. The argument is often a very small portion of the ontology, and therefore it is easily represented. Despite its modest size, it provides more useful information about the anomaly than the full ontology. Furthermore, the reparation is model-based. That is, the user keep in mind the intended model that ontology represents, and this model induces the changes. Therefore, argument repairing is a relatively easy task. Thus, for the pourposes of this paper, we might consider the ontological argument as the anomalous ontology.

In this paper we investigate some KR issues behind the sound mereotopological representation of the conceptualization induced by small ontologies (namely the mentioned ontological arguments) [3]. The intended aim of such representation is the understanding and repairing of ontologies. Specifically, those considered as anomalous (although consistent) due to errors in the concept structure. In this paper the spatial representation and algorithmic repairing are described; we do not describe here the (future) implementation. The advantage of this approach is that visual reparation stage hides formal semantics that supports the change, facilitating in this way its use by non experts.

The structure of the paper is as follows. The next section introduces a well-known mereotopological approach to qualitative spatial reasoning. Section 4 is devoted to study whether the Mereotopological reasoning can be interpreted as an abstract metaontology. It is proved, using logical types (sect. 3) that such interpretation does not support the work with instances inaccurately classified. In sections 5,6 we suggest new approachs based on the representation of frontiers and vague regions, respectively. The paper concludes with some closing remarks about the presented framework.

2   Mereotopology and First Cognitive Principle

The thesis that supports this paper is the following principle

> **Main Cognitive Principle (MCP):** If we aim to use spatial reasoning for cleaning ontologies, we have to provide a theory on spatial entities for translating the impact of spatial arrangements into revisions of the ontology source.

In order to satisfy the MCP, a theory on Qualitative Spatial Reasoning (QSR) has to be selected. In this way, the following sub-principle is choosen:

> **First Cognitive Principle (CP1):** The concepts of a conceptualization associate to a clear ontology can be topologically represented by means of regular non-empty regions.

That is, there is a model of the ontology whose universe is the bidimensional or tridimensional space, and that model interprets concept symbols as regions. It is evident that the represented knowledge will depend of topological relations. The starting-up of CP1 needs of a robust theory to reason with spatial regions.

$$DC(x,y) \leftrightarrow \neg C(x,y) \qquad\qquad (x \text{ is disconnected from } y)$$
$$P(x,y) \leftrightarrow \forall z[C(z,x) \rightarrow C(z,y)] \qquad (x \text{ is part of } y)$$
$$PP(x,y) \leftrightarrow P(x,y) \wedge \neg P(y,x) \qquad (x \text{ is proper part of } y)$$
$$EQ(x,y) \leftrightarrow P(x,y) \wedge P(y,x) \qquad (x \text{ is identical with } y)$$
$$O(x,y) \leftrightarrow \exists z[P(z,x) \wedge P(z,y)] \qquad (x \text{ overlaps } y)$$
$$DR(x,y) \leftrightarrow \neg O(x,y) \qquad\qquad (x \text{ is discrete from } y)$$
$$PO(x,y) \leftrightarrow O(x,y) \wedge \neg P(x,y) \wedge \neg P(y,x) \qquad (x \text{ partially overlaps } y)$$
$$EC(x,y) \leftrightarrow C(x,y) \wedge \neg O(x,y) \qquad (x \text{ is externally connected to } y)$$
$$TPP(x,y) \leftrightarrow PP(x,y) \wedge \exists z[EC(z,x) \wedge EC(z,y)] \qquad (x \text{ is a tangential prop. part of } y)$$
$$NTPP(x,y) \leftrightarrow PP(x,y) \wedge \neg \exists z[EC(z,x) \wedge EC(z,y)] \qquad (x \text{ is a non-tang. prop. part of } y)$$

Fig. 1. Axioms of RCC

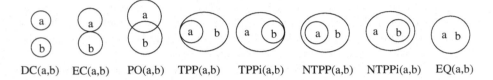

DC(a,b)   EC(a,b)   PO(a,b)   TPP(a,b)   TPPi(a,b)   NTPP(a,b)   NTPPi(a,b)   EQ(a,b)

Fig. 2. The relations of RCC8

Aditionally, the theory must facilitate the knowledge interchange between the ontology and spatial models.

The selected theory is the well known *Region Connection Calculus* (RCC) [13]. RCC is a mereotopological approach to QSR; it describes topological features of spatial relationships. It has been used in several subfields of AI, for example, in GIS and spatial databases [24] [16].

In RCC, the *spatial entities* are non-empty regular sets. The ground relation is the *connection*, $C(x,y)$, with intended meaning: *"the topological closures of* x *and* y *intersect"*. The basic axioms of RCC are

$$\forall x[C(x,x)] \quad \forall x,y[C(x,y) \rightarrow C(y,x)]$$

and a set of definitions on the main spatial relations (fig. 1), jointly with another set of auxiliary axioms (see [13]).

The set of binary relations formed by the eight jointly exhaustive and pairwise disjoint (JEPD) relations given in figure 2 is denoted by RCC8. If this set is thought as a calculus for Constraint Satisfaction Problems (CSP), every set of basic relations is considered. This calculus has been deeply studied by J. Renz and B. Nebel in [26]. Other interesting calculus is RCC5, based on the set $\{DR, PO, PP, PPi, EQ\}$. Roughly speaking, the main difference between RCC5 and RCC8 is that the latter one allows one to represent knowledge that depends on topological frontiers, while the former one does not allow. The cognitive impact of this distinction on the spatial representation of a concept has to be discussed (as we will do, in fact). Nevertheless, it has been empirically constated that RCC8 is more adequate than RCC5 as a tool for representing topological relations discriminated by humans [19].

3   Background: 1-Types in Ontologies

For analyzing the first spatial interpretation showed in thi paper types are required. The use of types is a classic tool in Model Theory (see e.g. [11]). We succintly describe here their main features. Given a consistent ontology Σ, a 1-*type* is a (maximal) set of formulas $\{\varphi_k(x)\}_k$ finitely satisfiable. That is, such that for any $F \subseteq \mathbb{N}$ (F finite), the theory

$$\Sigma + \{\exists x \bigwedge_{k \in F} \varphi_k(x)\}$$

is consistent. The ontology Σ *realizes* the type if that theory is consistent when $F = \mathbb{N}$. Equivalently, Σ realizes the type if the theory $\Sigma + \{\varphi_k(a) \; : \; k \in \mathbb{N}\}$ is consistent, being a a new constant symbol.

For a correct definition of types it has to consider First Order Logic (FOL) formulas. Types contain formulas that can not be translated into DL. Nevertheless, general FOL formulas are not needed in the proof of Theorem 1 below. Only the constructors *negation* and *intersection* are needed.

The set $S(\Sigma) = \{p \; : \; p \text{ is a type of } \Sigma\}$ is the *space of types* for Σ. For a concept C, let $S_\Sigma(\mathsf{C}) := \{p \in S(\Sigma) : \mathsf{C} \in p\}$ be the set of types containing C. It will be denoted by $[\mathsf{C}]$ if Σ has been previously fixed. It is easy to see that

$$[\mathsf{C}] \cap [\mathsf{D}] = [\mathsf{C} \wedge \mathsf{D}] \text{ and } [\neg\mathsf{C}] = S(\Sigma) \smallsetminus [\mathsf{C}]$$

Given a model $I \models \Sigma$ and a an element of its universe, the *type of a in I* is $[a] = tp_I(a) = \{\varphi(x) : I \models \varphi(a)\}$. Fixed I, it will be denoted $[a]$.

4   RCC as a Meta-ontology (I): Strong Interpretation

The use of RCC to visually represent the concepts turns RCC8 into an ontology on conceptual relations. The idea can be translated in different ways.

The straightforward approach consists in interpreting the concepts as regions in some model of the theory. Thus, in the *strong interpretation*, the intended meaning of $\mathsf{C}(\mathbf{x}, \mathbf{y})$ is: *there exist a common element in the concepts* $\mathbf{x}, \mathbf{y}$ *in some model I of the ontology.*

Definition 1. (Strong Interpretation of RCC as a metaontology) *Two concepts* $\mathsf{C}_1, \mathsf{C}_2$ *of an ontology* Σ *are* Σ-**connected** *(denoted by* $\mathsf{C}_\Sigma(\mathsf{C}_1, \mathsf{C}_2)$*) if*

$$\Sigma \not\models \mathsf{C}_1 \sqcap \mathsf{C}_2 \equiv \bot$$

The remaining RCC relations can be interpreted by means of its corresponding definition (depicted in fig. 1). Note that the strong interpretation works on abstract spatial encodings of Σ. That is, it does not work on a concrete spatial interpretation of concepts. The following result states a logical limitation of the strong interpretation of RCC as meta-ontology.

Theorem 1. *The strong interpretation does not discriminate RCC8 as ontological relations between concepts. Concretely, it has the following characterizations:*

1. $C_{\Sigma}(C_1, C_2) \iff S_{\Sigma}(C_1) \cap S_{\Sigma}(C_2) \neq \emptyset$
2. $DC_{\Sigma}(C_1, C_2) \iff S_{\Sigma}(C_1) \cap S_{\Sigma}(C_2) = \emptyset$
3. $P_{\Sigma}(C_1, C_2) \iff S_{\Sigma}(C_1) \subseteq S_{\Sigma}(C_2)$
4. $PP_{\Sigma}(C_1, C_2) \iff S_{\Sigma}(C_1) \subsetneq S_{\Sigma}(C_2)$
5. $EQ_{\Sigma}(C_1, C_2) \iff \Sigma \models C_1 \equiv C_2.$
6. $O_{\Sigma}(C_1, C_2) \iff C_{\Sigma}(C_1, C_2)$
7. $PO_{\Sigma}(C_1, C_2) \iff \begin{cases} S_{\Sigma}(C_1) \cap S_{\Sigma}(C_2) \neq \emptyset \wedge\ S_{\Sigma}(C_1) \nsubseteq S_{\Sigma}(C_2) \wedge \\ \wedge\ S_{\Sigma}(C_2) \nsubseteq S_{\Sigma}(C_1) \end{cases}$
8. $DR_{\Sigma}(C_1, C_2) \iff DC_{\Sigma}(C_1, C_2)$
9. *If* C_1, C_2 *and* $R \in \{EC, TPP, NTPP, TPPi, NTPPi\}$, *then* $\neg R_{\Sigma}(C_1, C_2)$.

Proof. Let us only show three cases (the complete proof appears in [10]).

(1) By definition, $C_{\Sigma}(C_1, C_2)$ means $\Sigma \nvDash C_1 \sqcap C_2 \equiv \bot$. Let I be a model whith $C_1^I \cap C_2^I \neq \emptyset$. By interpreting a new constant a as an element of the intersection, it certifies that $\Sigma \cup \{(C_1 \sqcap C_2)(a)\}$ is consistent. In fact,

$$[a] \in [C_1 \sqcap C_2]$$

therefore, $[C_1 \sqcap C_2] \neq \emptyset$. Hence it holds $S_{\Sigma}(C_1) \cap S_{\Sigma}(C_2) \neq \emptyset$. The converse is trivial: if $p \in S_{\Sigma}(C_1) \cap S_{\Sigma}(C_2)$, any element realizing this type in a model I is an element of $C_1^I \cap C_2^I$. Thus, $C_{\Sigma}(C_1, C_1)$.

(3) Assume proved (1) and (2). By definition of P, $P_{\Sigma}(C_1, C_2)$ means

$$\forall C_3\ (S_{\Sigma}(C_3) \cap S_{\Sigma}(C_1) \neq \emptyset \to S_{\Sigma}(C_3) \cap S_{\Sigma}(C_2) \neq \emptyset) \tag{†}$$

We proceed to show that this condition is equivalent to $S_{\Sigma}(C_1) \subseteq S_{\Sigma}(C_2)$ (thus, (3) will be proved):

It suffices to show that the condition is necessary.

Let us consider $p \in S_{\Sigma}(C_1)$ (that is, $C_1 \in p$). Suppose, contrary to our claim, that $p \notin S_{\Sigma}(C_2)$. Hence $C_2 \notin p$. Since p is maximal, $\neg C_2 \in p$. Therefore, $C_1 \in p$ and $\neg C_2 \in p$, thus

$$p \in S_{\Sigma}(C_1) \cap S_{\Sigma}(C_1 \sqcap \neg C_2)$$

Then it follows that $S_{\Sigma}(C_1) \cap S_{\Sigma}(C_1 \sqcap \neg C_2) \neq \emptyset$. Consequently, by (†)

$$S_{\Sigma}(C_2) \cap S_{\Sigma}(C_1 \sqcap \neg C_2) \neq \emptyset$$

From this, we obtain $p' \in [C_1 \sqcap \neg C_2]$ and $p' \in [C_2]$. This is impossible because $\{C_1 \sqcap \neg C_2, C_2\}$ can not be contained in a type (it is inconsistent).

(5) Suppose proved from (1) to (4). By definition, $EQ_{\Sigma}(C_1, C_2)$ is

$$P_{\Sigma}(C_1, C_2) \wedge P_{\Sigma}(C_2, C_1)$$

By (3), this is equivalent to $S_{\Sigma}(C_1) \subseteq S_{\Sigma}(C_2)$ and $S_{\Sigma}(C_2) \subseteq S_{\Sigma}(C_1)$. Therefore $S_{\Sigma}(C_1) = S_{\Sigma}(C_2)$.

Finally, the last condition is equivalent to $\Sigma \models C_1 \equiv C_2$. It is trivial to see that it is sufficient. Let us see that it is necessary:

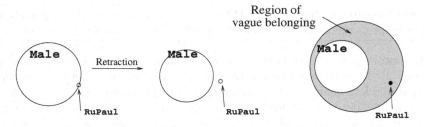

Fig. 3. Two kinds of representation of a problematic instance in the frontier (left, right) and solving by retraction the first one (middle) (right)

Let $I \models \Sigma$ and a some realization of C_1 in I, $I \models \mathsf{C}_1(a)$. Thus,

$$[a] = \{\phi : I \models \phi(a)\} \in S_{\Sigma}(\mathsf{C}_1)$$

So $[a] \in S_{\Sigma}(\mathsf{C}_2)$. Therefore, $I \models \forall x(\mathsf{C}_1(x) \rightarrow \mathsf{C}_2(x))$. In DLs, $I \models \mathsf{C}_1 \sqsubseteq \mathsf{C}_2$. Similarly, $I \models \mathsf{C}_2 \sqsubseteq \mathsf{C}_1$ holds. Thus, $\Sigma \models C_1 \equiv C_2$.

It sould be pointed out that the above interpretation might be not usable in practice. The connection between concepts is based on entailment. Therefore, it can have high algorithmic complexity when we deal with expressive description logics (the consistency of concepts and, hence, satisfiability, is EXPTIME-hard in $\mathcal{ALC}$, cf. [8]). Strong connection reduces to subsumption (hence to a satisfiability problem):

$$C_{\Sigma}(\mathsf{C}_1, \mathsf{C}_2) \text{ if and only if } \Sigma \not\models \mathsf{C}_1 \sqsubseteq \neg\mathsf{C}_2$$

Theorem 1 says that, thinking RCC as a metaontology, this theory can not represent *frontier-sensitive* knowledge. Nevertheless, sometimes it seems cognitively natural to consider the frontier of a concept as formed by elements in which the user has not confidence on its correct classification in the concept. This can occur when the user works with a *notion*, a rough idea of the concept that attempts to specify. The notion becomes in a *concept* when its behavior is constrained by new axioms that relate it with the former concepts. By allocating the problematic instances near of the frontier it will be easy to discard them by a simple topological movement (a retraction, see fig. 3).

5   RCC as Meta-ontology (II): Weak Interpretation

As it has been commented, strong interpretation can be not advisable due to its computational complexity for ontological arguments of larger size. Other limitation is that our cognitive capability is reduced to RCC5. In this section a new interpretation is introduced. This is based on the following idea: if it were possible to represent RCC8-relations in visual encodings, the topological frontiers of the regions could be endowed of cognitive features. The following principle is useful for both the *weak interpretation* defined bellow and the *vague interpretation* defined in the next section (see figure 3).

> **Second Cognitive Principle (CP2):** The frontier of a spatial interpretation of a concept C represents the individuals with doubtful membership to C.

The ontology RCC has been used as formal support for CP2 in ontology cleaning [3]. The idea is based on the translation of relations between concepts into spatial relationships among spatial representations of these concepts. It is, at the same time, based on studies about the relation between logical consistency of Constraint Satisfaction Problems in RCC and spatial consistency [25]. The main step of the cited cleaning cycle consists in a translation of logical information on conceptual relations of the ontology into a CSP on spatial relations. Solving this CSP, a spatial encoding of conceptual relations is obtained. This approach is useful to repair arguments suffering anomalies due to the conceptualization. It works with *spatial interpretations*.

Definition 2. *A **spatial interpretation** I of Σ is a interpretation in the language of Σ, such that $I : concepts(\Sigma) \cup indiv(\Sigma) \rightarrow \Omega$, where Ω is a T_3 connected topological space such that $I \models \Sigma$ and for each $C \in concepts(\Sigma), I(C)$ is an open regular set in Ω and for each $a \in indiv(\Sigma), I(a)$ is a point.*
A spatial model *of Σ is a spatial interpretation which is a model of Σ.*

The following theorem guarantees that the weak interpretation is useful for analysing knowledge bases in DL, since it preserves the consistency.

Theorem 2. *[10] The CSP associate to Σ is spatially consistent if Σ is consistent.*

Moreover, it is possible to obtain a spatial model on the plane formed by polygonal regions [25].

Once formalized the notion of spatial model, spatial arrangements can be formally justified and classified [10]. In figure 4 we present a simple example of visual repairing (of the ontology of Figure 7, left) following a cleaning cycle presented in [3] (see fig. 6). Note that, although one can think that the ontology source is correct, it is assumed that the end-user thinks it is anomalous (he thinks that it is an ontological argument that deficently classifies to *Rupaul*). The cycle is based on the following stages:

1. First, it builds a constraint satisfaction problem (CSP) on the spatial relational calculus RCC8 (or RCC5). The problem is solved obtaining a consistent scenario, represented in 2D. Facts of the Abox are added as points.
2. The user is requested to make *reticular* or *topological* arrangements on the graphical representation. Reticular arrangements represent refinements of relationships between concepts, and topological arrangements imply substitution of a relationship by another one, disjoint with the former one but *cognitively near* of that. The user must lastly think that she/he has a fair RCC8(5) representation. This gives a table of spatial constraints on notions of the provisional ontology.
3. A translation from RCC into DL is applied. In the resulting ontology, some relationships have changed and new concepts may have been induced.

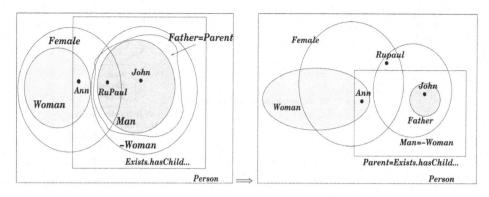

Fig. 4. Spatial representation of an anomalous argument (left) and the solution proposed (right)

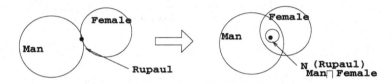

Fig. 5. New Notion induced. The user has to interpret/discard it, because it transforms $DR_\Sigma(Man, Female)$ into $PO_\Sigma(Man, Female)$

4. Finally, the user interprets (or discards) the new objects (individuals or concepts) that the translation may induce (see Fig. 5).

The result of the process is a new ontology modified according to the preferences of the user. The impact of this arrangement on the ontology is shown in fig. 7 (right). Furthermore, in complex or huge ontologies, it is convenient to use, for cleaning tasks, other relaxed spatial interpretations. Since the ontology we are representing is regarded as defective, it is possible to make a spatial characterization less detailed than the offered one by the CSP [3].

There is a natural relationship between strong and weak interpretations.

Theorem 3. *[10] The following conditions are equivalent:*

1. $C_\Sigma(C_1, C_2)$
2. *There is a spatial interpretation I of Σ such that $I \models C(C_1, C_2)$.*

6 RCC as Meta-ontology (III): Vague Interpretation

Strong and weak interpretation work with precise regions. In both cases, the interpretation of C is a subset. The *vague interpretation* deals with the spatial interpretation of the concepts by *vague* regions. A vague region can be represented by means of two regular regions although there are other options such as egg-yolk [12], topological spaces with pulsation [10], rough sets, etc.

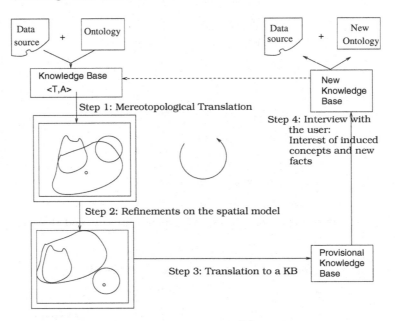

Fig. 6. Visual Ontology Cleaning Cycle [3]

In order to work wiht vague regions, a robust extension of RCC ([6, 7, 10]) is needed. The extension needs of the re-interpretation of the ontology. In figure 8 we present one of the seven possible robust extensions of the ontology RCC given in [6]. The interpretation is based on *pulsation*. A pulsation in a topological space $\Omega = (\mathcal{X}, \mathcal{T})$ is a map that associates to each regular set X a set $\sigma(X)$ such that its closure contains the closure of X; $\overline{X} \subseteq \overline{\sigma(X)}$. In Fig. 8, the topological interpretation of the new relation $I(a, b)$ is $PP(a, b) \wedge EQ(\sigma(a), \sigma(b))$ (see Fig. 8, right). The reasoning of vague regions is based on the following principle:

Third Cognitive Principle (CP3): Given a spatial interpretation I, the region $\sigma(I(C)) \setminus I(C)$ represents the set of individuals with doubtful membership to C

In order to apply this principle for visual encoding, it considers the concept and its *approximate definition* in the ontology.

From now on, it is assumed that Σ is an unfoldable DL-ontology, that is, the left-hand sides of the axioms (defined concepts) are atomic and the right hand sides contain no direct or undirect references to defined concepts.

Definition 3. *Let Σ be a DL ontology. The approximate definition according to Σ is a map σ that associates to any $\mathsf{C} \in concepts(\Sigma)$ a DL-formula as follows:*

$$\sigma(\mathsf{C}) = \begin{cases} \mathsf{C}, & \text{if } \mathsf{C} \text{ is a defined concept} \\ \sqcap\{\mathsf{D} : \mathsf{C} \sqsubseteq \mathsf{D} \in \Sigma\}, & \text{if } \mathsf{C} \text{ is a primitive concept} \\ \top, & \text{if } \mathsf{C} \text{ is an atomic concept} \end{cases}$$

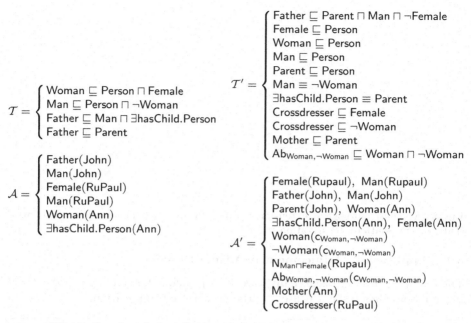

Fig. 7. Ontology before (left) and after the spatial repairing (right)

Two concepts $C_1, C_2 \in concepts(\Sigma)$, will be said Σ-**connected** under σ, which will be denoted by $C_\Sigma^\sigma(C_1, C_2)$, if $C_\Sigma(\sigma(C_1), \sigma(C_2))$. The formula $\sigma(C_1)$ will be named the associate **notion** to C_1 in Σ.

The notion is defined for any concept. Nevertheless, in practice, this definition is not used intensively for atomic concepts (in the analysis of anomalies). It is that because the undefinition of the notions of an atomic concept can be deliberated: they are primitive concepts of the ontology (abstract concepts in many cases). Thus, it is not advisable to force to the user to refine them. The spatial idea of Σ-connection under σ is obviously that of the topological connection of the pulsation of sets. Now, $\sigma(C)$ represents a DL formula associate to a concept C. Notice that the new connection is related with the previous one:

$$C_\Sigma^\sigma(C_1, C_2) \iff \Sigma \not\models \sigma(C_1) \sqcap \sigma(C_2) \equiv \bot$$

Therefore, given two concepts C_1, C_2 in the ontology Σ and $R \in RCC8$,

$$R_\Sigma^\sigma(C_1, C_2) \iff R_\Sigma(\sigma(C_1), \sigma(C_2))$$

However, there is no cognitive reason to consider frontiers in vague regions, because the undefinition is represented by $\sigma(I(C)) \setminus I(C)$. Thus, RCC5 is more adequate in this case [12]. Starting with C_Σ^σ, it is possible both to classify *all* the relative positions between concepts/notions and, in due course, to repair them by using spatial reasoning preserving consistency [10].

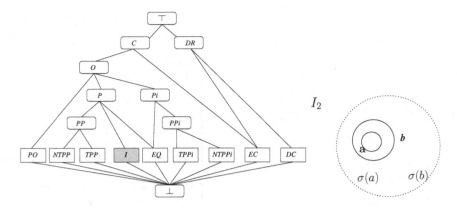

Fig. 8. A *robust* ontological extension of RCC by insertion of an uncertain relation (left) and its spatial interpretation (right)

6.1   Application: Advicement of Visual Repairs

The following principle is actually a working principle for refining specifications. Its soundness has to be accepted by the user in that application.

Fourth Cognitive Principle (CP4): If the RCC5-relation between spatial concepts does not agree with that of their corresponding notions, it may be necessary to adjust the spatial representation in order to ensure the agreement

---

To illustrate how CP4 can be applied in a simple case, let us consider

$$\Sigma = \begin{cases} \text{Omnivorous} \sqsubseteq \text{Carnivorous} \sqcap \text{Herbivorous} \\ \text{Carnivorous} \sqsubseteq \text{Animal}, \quad \text{Herbivorous} \sqsubseteq \text{Animal} \\ \text{Omnivorous}(\text{Bear}) \end{cases}$$

We deduce that $PO_\Sigma(\text{Carnivorous, Herbivorous}) \wedge EQ_\Sigma^\sigma(\text{Carnivorous, Herbivorous})$.

A simple way to solve this conflict, under the consideration of the user, relies on adding two constants b_1, b_2 to accurate the partial overlapping of notions (in the notion of a concept but not in the other one). In such a way, $PO_\Sigma(\mathsf{C}_1, \mathsf{C}_2)$ and $PO_\Sigma^\sigma(\mathsf{C}_1, \mathsf{C}_2)$ holds. After this step, the new knowledge base is:

$$\Sigma' = \begin{cases} \text{Omnivorous} \sqsubseteq \text{Carnivorous} \sqcap \text{Herbivorous} \\ \text{Carnivorous} \sqsubseteq \text{Animal} \sqcap \neg\{b_2\}, \quad \text{Herbivorous} \sqsubseteq \text{Animal} \sqcap \neg\{b_1\} \\ \text{Herbivorous}(b_2), \quad \text{Carnivorous}(b_1), \quad \text{Omnivorous}(\text{Bear}) \end{cases}$$

Therefore, $PO_{\Sigma'}^\sigma(\text{Carnivorous, Herbivorous}) \wedge PO_{\Sigma'}^\sigma(\text{Carnivorous, Herbivorous})$.

Graphically, the spatial adjustment consists in inserting two skolem constants in the spatial encodings of the notions (see Fig. 9, left). The interpretation of new constants b_1, b_2 (actually they are Skolem constants) is requested to the user. There are other more complex cases that imply more complex ontological revisions (figure 9 shows two examples based on individual insertion).

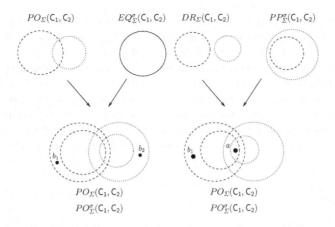

Fig. 9. Two examples of spatial arrangements based on CP4

6.2   Auxiliary Principles

Once CP4 is applied, an optional principle is useful for nonmonotonic reasoning on the visual encoding:

Fifth Cognitive Principle (CP5): Once CP4 is satisfied and the visual repairing is done, analyse whether is sound the following transformation on the final ontology: $C \sqsubseteq \sigma(C) \in \Sigma \mapsto C \equiv \sigma(C)$

CP5 is a completation-based principle that would allow to find a *definitional ontology*. That is, it can allow to transform the ontology source into an ontology which satisfies most of definitional principles given in [5]. However, the logical categoricity is weakened by some sort of spatial categoricity.

7   Closing Remarks

There exist a great number of methods for visual representation of ontologies, supporting a variety of tasks such as data analysis and queries ([14], [15]). However these works are mostly focused on visual representation and they lack both inference mechanisms and formal semantics. Unlike such visual encodings, RCC8 (RCC5) representations outlined here operate beyond just primarily mapping the ontology information/conceptualization structure. RCC8-based spatial encoding provides formal semantics where spatial arrangements mean ontology revision. Moreover, the encoding stablishes a correspondence between the conceptualization implicit in the Ontology and a realm well known to the user. We described several spatial encodings based on different mereotopological interpretations of the ontologies. The spatial encoding are a sort of concept map [18] (because it identifies the interrelationships among concepts) enhanced with sound reasoning on the representation. Furthermore, we exploit logical features of RCC to analyse the impact of revision on the self ontology.

It is worth pointing out that it would be possible for that anomaly to come from other reasons different from the conceptualization. Future will be focused on mereotopological encodings of roles, in order to assist the user in the repair of anomalous arguments caused by roles. This phase is essential prior to the full implementation of a VOC-system. Finally, note that the visual encoding can be unmamnageable for medium size ontologies. Our reparation method is argumentative (that is, it does not use representations of the whole ontology). However, if we want a whole representation, it would be interesting to adapt the spatial semantics to work with other visual encodings as the hyperbolic plane [20].

References

1. J. A. Alonso-Jiménez, J. Borrego-Díaz, A. M. Chávez-González and J.D. Navarro-Marín, A Methodology for the Computer-Aided Cleaning of Complex Knowledge Databases. *Proc. 28th Conf. of IEEE Industrial Electronics Soc. IECON 2002, pp. 1806-1812, 2003.*
2. J. Alonso-Jiménez, J. Borrego-Díaz, A. M. Chávez-González, M. A. Gutiérrez-Naranjo and J. D. Navarro-Marín, Towards a Practical Argumentative Reasoning with Qualitative Spatial Databases, *16th Int. Conf. on Industrial & Eng. Appl. of Artificial Intelligence and Expert Systems IEA/AIE 2003*, LNAI 2718, Springer, 2003, pp. 789-798.
3. J.A. Alonso-Jiménez, J. Borrego-Díaz, A. M. Chávez-González, Ontology Cleaning by Mereotopological Reasoning. *DEXA Workshop on Web Semantics WEBS 2004*, pp. 132-137 (2004).
4. J. A. Alonso-Jiménez, J. Borrego-Díaz, A. M. Chávez-González and F. J. Martín-Mateos, Foundational Challenges in Automated Data and Ontology Cleaning in the Semantic Web, *IEEE Intelligent Systems*, 21(1):42-52 (2006).
5. B. Bennett, The Role of Definitions in Construction and Analysis of Formal Ontologies, *Logical Formalization of Commonsense Reasoning (2003 AAAI Spring Symposium)*, 27-35, AAAI Press, 2003.
6. J. Borrego-Díaz and A. M. Chávez-González, Extension of Ontologies Assisted by Automated Reasoning Systems, *10th Int. Conf. on Computer Aided Systems Theory, EUROCAST 2005*, LNCS 3643, pp. 247-253, Springer, 2005.
7. J. Borrego-Díaz and A. M. Chávez-González, Controlling Ontology Extension by Uncertain Concepts Through Cognitive Entropy, *Proc. of ISWC'05 Workshop on Uncertainty Reasoning for the Semantic Web*, pp. 56-66 (2005).
8. Calvanese, K., de Giacomo,G., Lenzerini, M., Nardi, D. Reasoning in Expressive Description Logics. In Alan Robinson y Andrei Voronkov (eds.) *Handbook of Automated Reasoning*, pp. 1581-1634 Elsevier Science Pub. (2001).
9. S. Card, J. Mckinlay and B. Shneiderman (eds.) *Readings in Information Visualization: Using Vision to Think*, Morgan Kauffman, 1999.
10. A. M. Chávez-González, *Automated Mereotopological Reasoning for Ontology Debugging* (spanish), Ph.D. Thesis, University of Seville, 2005.
11. C.C. Chang, H.J. Keisler, *Model Theory*, North Holland, 1977.
12. A.G. Cohn and N.M. Gotts, The 'Egg-Yolk' Representation of Regions with Indeterminate Boundaries in P. Burrough and A. M. Frank (eds), *Proc. GISDATA Specialist Meeting on Geographical Objects with Undetermined Boundaries*, GIS-DATA Series, vol. 3, Taylor and Francis, pp. 171-187 (1996).

13. A. G. Cohn, B. Bennett, J. M. Gooday and N. M. Gotts. Representing and Reasoning with Qualitative Spatial Relations about Regions. chapter 4 in O. Stock (ed.), *Spatial and Temporal Reasoning*, Kluwer, Dordrecth, 1997.

14. C. Fluit, M. Sabou, F. Harmelen. Ontology-based Information Visualization, in V. Geroimenko, C. Chen (eds.), *Visualizing the Semantic Web*. Springer (2003).

15. C. Fluit, M. Sabou, F. Harmelen. Supporting User Tasks Through Visualization of Light-weight Ontologies, in S. Staab and R. Studer (eds.), *Handbook on Ontologies in Information Systems*, Springer-Verlag (2003).

16. M. Grohe and L. Segoufin, On first-order topological queries, *ACM Trans. Comput. Log.* 3(3) (2002) pp. 336-358.

17. I. Horrocks, D.L. McGuinnes, C. A. Welty. Digital Libraries and Web-Based Information Systems. In F. Baader et al. (ed.) *The Description Logic Handbook*, pp. 436-459. Cambridge University Press (2003).

18. B. Gaines, M. Shaw, Concept Maps as Hypermedia Components, *Int. Journal of Human-Computer Studies* 43(3):323-361 (1995).

19. M. Knauff, R. Rauh and J. Renz, A Cognitive Assessment of Topological Spatial Relations: Results from an Empirical Investigation, *Proc. 3rd Int. Conf. on Spatial Inf. Theory (COSIT'97)*, LNCS 1329, 193-206, Springer-Verlag, Berlin (1997).

20. J. Lamping, R. Rao, and P. Pirolli. A focus + context technique based on hyperbolic geometry for visualizing large hierarchies, *ACM Conference on Human Factors in Computing Systems (CHI'95)* (1995).

21. Y. Mao, Z. Wu, H. Chen, X. Zheng, An Interactive Visual Model for Web Ontologies, *Proc. Knowl. Eng. Systems KES 2005*, LNAI 3862, pp. 866-872 (2005).

22. H. Mizen, C. Dolbear and G. Hart, Ontology Ontogeny: Understanding How an Ontology is Created and Developed, *Proc. First International Conference on Geospatial Semantics (GeoS 2005)*, LNCS 3799, pp. 15,29, 2005.

23. F. Murtagh, T. Taskaya, P. Contreras, J. Mothe and K. Englmeier, Interactive Visual Interfaces: A Survey, *Artificial Intelligence Review* 19:263-283, 2003.

24. C. Papadimitriou, D. Suciu and V. Vianu, Topological Queries in Spatial Databases, *J. Computer System Sci.* 58 (1):29-53 (1999).

25. J. Renz. A Canonical Model of the Region Connection Calculus. *Proc. 6th Int. Conf. on Principles of Knowl. Rep. and Reasoning (KR'98)* (1998).

26. J. Renz, B. Nebel. On the Complexity of Qualitative Spatial Reasoning: A Maximal Tractable Fragment of the Region Connection Calculus, *Artificial Intelligence* 108(1-2): 69-123 (1999).

27. D. Tsarkov, A. Riazanov, S. Bechhofer, and I. Horrocks, Using Vampire to Reason with OWL. *2004 Int. Semantic Web Conference (ISWC 2004)*, LNCS 3298 Springer, 2004, pp. 471-485.

Rules with Contextually Scoped Negation

Axel Polleres[1,2], Cristina Feier[1], and Andreas Harth[1]

[1] Digital Enterprise Research Institute Innsbruck, Austria and Galway, Ireland
[2] Universidad Rey Juan Carlos, Madrid, Spain
axel@polleres.net, {cristina.feier, andreas.harth}@deri.org

Abstract. Knowledge representation formalisms used on the Semantic Web adhere to a strict open world assumption. Therefore, nonmonotonic reasoning techniques are often viewed with scepticism. Especially negation as failure, which intuitively adopts a closed world view, is often claimed to be unsuitable for the Web where knowledge is notoriously incomplete. Nonetheless, it was suggested in the ongoing discussions around rules extensions for languages like RDF(S) or OWL to allow at least restricted forms of negation as failure, as long as negation has an explicitly defined, finite scope. Yet clear definitions of such "scoped negation" as well as formal semantics thereof are missing. We propose logic programs with *contexts* and *scoped negation* and discuss two possible semantics with desirable properties. We also argue that this class of logic programs can be viewed as a rule extension to a subset of RDF(S).

1   Introduction

The current Web is a huge network linking between different sources of data and knowledge, formatted for human users. Such linked knowledge bases become particularly interesting when it comes to discussions about the next generation of the Web, the Semantic Web. Technologies like RDF(S) [5] and OWL [16] shall allow us to describe meta-data and the structure of such meta-data in an unambiguous way using standardized vocabularies, also called ontologies. These ontologies let you infer additional knowledge about the meta-data published on the Web. Meta-data descriptions and ontologies are to be distributed over the Web just like current Web pages as machine-readable knowledge bases accessible via URIs. Different approaches exist for combining such meta-data from different sources. A common approach is to import and/or simply reuse the vocabulary of one ontology in the definition of another, for instance using common namespaces or OWL's import mechanism. A more fine-grained approach is in the form of so-called mappings or bridge rules [4] that connect entities from different knowledge bases. Eventually, standardized rule languages, which allow for the definition of such mappings or other combinations of meta-data in general are the natural next evolution step on W3C's agenda.   Still, there are many unresolved issues around the proper integration of ontology language recommendations such as RDFS and OWL with existing rule languages. For instance, nonmonotonic features of such rule languages are viewed with partial scepticism[1]. In particular,

---

[1] cf. http://lists.w3.org/Archives/Public/public-sws-ig/2004Jan/0040.html

Y. Sure and J. Domingue (Eds.): ESWC 2006, LNCS 4011, pp. 332–347, 2006.

it is argued that the use of negation as failure is invalid in an open environment such as the Web where knowledge is notoriously incomplete. Still, two of the proposals for rule languages on the Web, namely WRL [1] and SWSL Rules [2], include negation as failure as a language feature, however leaving critical questions about the suitability of negation as failure in a Web context open. Recently, the term "scoped negation" emerged in discussions around this topic, to describe a restricted form of negation as failure over a closed *scope*. "Scoped negation as failure" is also explicitly mentioned as one of the extensions to be investigated by W3C's recently established Rule Interchange Format (RIF) working group[2]. However, clear definitions of what "scope" and "scoped negation" actually mean and what the formal semantics for this form of negation should be are missing.

Contributions. In this paper we present a logic programming framework for the combination of interlinked rule bases on the Web and show how scoped negation as failure fits in such a framework. A peculiarity of our rule language is that it allows "open" as well as "closed" rules: On the one hand, universally valid, open rules shall be allowed which apply to any available statement on the Web. This is in accordance with RDF and OWL which also allow that several sources define statements and axioms affecting the same resource.[3] On the other hand, we also define closed rules which are only evaluated with respect to a particular context, that is a (finite and known set of) web-accessible rule base(s).

We ensure in our language that negation as failure is always "scoped", i.e. that the search for failure in a rule body is not depending on any "open" rules. This way we circumvent the undesirable non-monotonic effects of negation as failure in open environments such as the Web. Thereby we achieve a weak form of monotonicity, called *"context-monotonicity"* which intuitively means that negation as failure behaves monotonically with respect to the set of web-accessible rule-bases that an agent is aware of. In order to achieve context-monotonicity we propose two alternative semantics for sets of rule bases with scoped negation, namely (a) contextually bounded semantics and (b) contextually closed semantics. Both semantics are defined in terms of translations to normal logic programs. Remarkably, these translations make no commitment to a particular semantics used for negation as failure upfront, be it well-founded or stable, and allow for direct implementations on top of many existing rule engines which adopt either of these semantics.

We further demonstrate that our language can be viewed as a rule extension of (a subset of) RDFS.

Paper Overview. The remainder of this paper is organized as follows: In section 2 we illustrate by means of simple examples what we understand by context, "open" and "closed" rules, and queries. We formally introduce the syntax for logic programs with contexts and scoped literals in section 3.1. We then define a formal requirement for a proper semantics for such programs called context-monotonicity. The two alternative semantics fulfilling this requirement

---

[2] cf. http://www.w3.org/2005/rules/wg/charter.

[3] Actually, a strong argument why semantics of these languages assume an open world.

are presented in sections 3.2 and 3.3. We relate our approach to RDF(S) in section 4 and slightly extend our notion of scope to unions of contexts in section 5. Finally, we discuss some related works and draw conclusions in sections 6 and 7.

2   Context, Open Rules and Scoped Negation

In the following, we will give an informal description of our notion of context, logic programs with open vs. closed rules and introduce our understanding of scoped negation as failure for such programs. We will base these explanations on simple examples. The underlying formal definitions are given in section 3.1.

Context. For tracking provenance of a single fact or rule, we associate a *context* with each statement. We define a context as the URI of a Web-accessible data source (i.e. the location where a set of rules and facts is accessible). That means the context *<URI>* is associated with all the rules and facts retrieved when you type *URI* in your browser.

Rules and Queries. In the context of our rule language, we assume a Web of logic programs, published at different URIs. In order to illustrate this, we assume programs describing movies, directors and ratings as shown in Figure 1. The notation we use is the usual syntax known from e.g. PROLOG systems.

```
http://www.moviereviews.com/          http://www.b-movies.com/
rated(m1,bad).                        rated(m1,classic).
rated(X,bad) :- directedBy(X,"Ed Wood").   (*) rated(m3,classic).
http://www.polleres.net/
rated(m2,bad). movie(m2).
http://www.imdb.com/
sciFiMovie(m1). hasTitle(m1,"Plan 9 from Outer Space"). directedBy(m1,"Ed Wood").
sciFiMovie(m2). hasTitle(m2,"Matrix Revolutions"). directedBy(m2,"Andy Wachowski").
directedBy(m2,"Larry Wachowski").
sciFiMovie(m3). hasTitle(m3,"Bride of the Monster"). directedBy(m3,"Ed Wood").
movie(X) :- sciFiMovie(X).
```

Fig. 1. Four Programs describing rules and data about movies, directors and ratings

A typical feature which we adopt from RDF is that different sources (contexts) are allowed to talk about the same resource. This shall allow to draw additional conclusions from combining contexts. For instance, in our example, three contexts http://www.imdb.com/, http://www.moviereviews.com/ and http://www.b-movies.com/ talk about the same movie m1. A semantic search engine might gather arbitrary programs like the ones shown in Figure 1 on the Web from different contexts and allow us to ask queries about particular movies. Queries can be formalized as rules, e.g.

$$\text{"Give me movies which are rated as bad"} \tag{1}$$

can be expressed by the following simple rule:

```
answer(X) :- movie(X), rated(X,bad).
```

We call a rule like this "open" since it is not restricted to a particular context, but in principle all movies and ratings at all possible contexts on the Web are of interest.

Assume that the search engine, which has to evaluate this query is aware of the contexts `http://www.imdb.com/`, `http://www.moviereviews.com/`, `http://www.b-movies.com/`, where we would expect `m1` and `m3` as answers. The easiest and straightforward way to evaluate such a query then would be to retrieve these three programs, build the union of all rules and facts and and then evaluate the resulting logic program with one of the standard techniques. Note that `rated(m3,bad)` is inferred by another "open" rule from the combination of two contexts.

Usually, in such a Web search scenario we would accept incompleteness of the given answers, since we cannot expect that our fictitious search engine has complete knowledge about the whole Web. For instance, the search engine might not be aware of the personal movie reviews of one of the authors published at `http://www.polleres.net/`, see Figure 1 and would thus not return `m2` as an answer for query (1). But at least we can be sure that all answers are sound, as long as programs consist of positive rules only.

Scoped Literals. Recall the "open" rule (*) in `http://www.moviereviews.com/` saying that everything directed by Ed Wood is bad. If we want to determine the provenance of a certain atom (i.e., "to which context does a particular fact belong to") this is easy for facts such as `rated(m1,bad)`. However, we have certain difficulties to determine the provenance of atoms inferred by (open) rules via information from other contexts. For instance, does the inferred atom `rated(m3,bad)` "belong" to context `http://www.moviereviews.com/` or context `http://www.imdb.com/` (which was needed to satisfy the body of the rule)? In this paper, we will adopt the view that all facts inferred by rules belong to the context of the rule that triggered the new fact.[4]

Now that we have given an informal definition of provenance of atoms inferred from distributed logic programs, we can ask queries about facts restricted to a certain context, like for instance:

$$\text{"Give me movies which are rated as bad by } \texttt{http://www.moviereviews.com/"} \quad (2)$$

We will use the following notation for such a query/rule in this paper:

`answer(X) :- movie(X), rated(X,bad)@http://www.moviereviews.com/.`

where we call the atom `rated(bad)@http://www.moviereviews.com/` a *scoped* literal. By making the context explicit, we do no longer need to bother about information concerning ratings from other sources such as the ones from `http://www.polleres.net/`.

However, we still have not solved the problem about incomplete information here since the atom `rated(bad)@http://www.moviereviews.com/` again

---

[4] Note that an atom can belong to several contexts. We remark that there are more involved proposals for handling provenance of data on the Semantic Web, see e.g. [7].

depends on an open rule; i.e., as soon as the search engine would become aware of an additional source saying that a particular other movie was directed by Ed Wood it could again infer additional information from the rule (*) in Figure 1. This problem could be solved by making rule (*) more explicit. If we know that IMDB has complete knowledge about all movies by Ed Wood we could replace the rule (*) by its closed off version, adding a scope just as we did for query (2):

```
rated(X,bad)  :- directedBy(X,"Ed Wood")@http://www.imdb.com.        (**)
```

Now, under the assumption that `http://www.imdb.com` stores all `directedBy(·)` atoms as explicit facts not depending on any other (open) rules, we can indeed be sure to get *complete* information about the ratings for query (2).

The example shows that one has to be aware that scoped literals do not solve the problem of incompleteness per se; completeness is only achievable if none of rules which the scoped literal depends on contains open literals. As it turns out, this issue becomes more severe in combination with negation as failure.

Scoped Negation as Failure. Let us now focus on negative queries such as:

$$\text{"Give me movies which are not ranked as bad"} \qquad (3)$$

Such queries can be expressed in a rule language with negation as failure (**not**):

```
answer(X)  :- movie(X), not rated(X,bad).
```

However, here we end up in a dilemma due to the inherent non-monotonicity of negation as failure: Unless we have complete information about *any* rating ever published, we can never be sure to find correct answers to such a query.

What we aim at in this paper is a more cautious form of negation, i.e. *scoped negation as failure*, which allows us to ask negative queries with explicit scope, such as:

$$\text{"Give me movies which are not ranked as bad by } \texttt{moviereviews.com} \text{"} \qquad (4)$$

Now, if the ratings on `moviereviews.com` solely depend on facts and "closed" rules such as (**), we can safely return correct answer. We will give a formal definition of this condition, which we call *contextual boundedness*, in section 3.1. For instance, contextual boundedness is violated by the combination of queries such as (4) and open rules such as (*).

Contextually bounded use of scoped negation as failure intuitively guarantees that even if we become aware of new contexts with additional information, we do not need to retract any query answers. We will call this desirable property *context-monotonicity* in the following.

3   Programs with Context and Scoped Negation

In this section, we provide the formal basis for the rule and query language informally introduced in section 2. We will allow to express contextually scoped queries and rules in a way that guarantees sound answers despite of incomplete knowledge and the inherent non-monotonicity of negation as failure. We propose two approaches to achieve this, either (a) we syntactically guarantee contextually bounded use of negation, or (b) we close off open rules referenced by scoped literals. We will define semantics for both these options by means of appropriate transformations to normal logic programs which then can be evaluated using one of the standard semantics for negation as failure.

3.1 Definitions

Definition 1 (Scoped Atoms, Literals). *If $t_1, \ldots, t_n$ are constants or variables and c is a constant then $c(t_1, \ldots, t_n)$ is an atom. A scoped atom is of the form $a@u$ where u is a URI and a is an atom.*[5] *A literal is either*

- *a (possibly scoped) atom – positive literal*
- *or a negated scoped atom of the form not $t@u$ – negative literal,*

*i.e. all negative literals **must** be scoped.*

Note that we do not make a distinction between constant symbols and predicate symbols, since the usage is clear from the syntax. Neither do the constants and URIs necessarily need to be disjoint.

Definition 2 (Program). *A program P is a set of rules of the form*

$$h : - l_1, \ldots, l_n.$$

Where h is an unscoped atom, and $l_1, \ldots l_n$ are literals and all variables occurring in h or in some negative body literal do also appear in a positive body literal. Each program P has a URI p and we make the assumption that each program can be accessed via its URI. The URI p is also called context *of P.*

The informal semantic meaning of scoped literals is that literals referenced via an external context represent links to other programs accessible over the Web.

Definition 3 (Link, Closure). *Let P, Q be programs with names p and q, respectively. We say that program P links to a program Q if P contains a scoped body literal (not) $a@q$ (direct link) or P contains a rule with a scoped body literal (not) $a@r$ such that the program R dereferenced by r links to Q. Given a set of Programs $\mathcal{P}$ we denote by the closure $Cl(\mathcal{P})$ the set of all programs in $\mathcal{P}$ plus all programs which are linked to programs in $\mathcal{P}$.*

Definition 4 (Contextual Boundedness). *A rule is contextually bounded iff each negative body literal not $a@p$ is contextually bounded.*

A scoped literal (not) $a@p$ is called contextually bounded, iff each rule r in the program dereferenced by name p with head h where h is unifiable with a is strongly contextually bounded.

---

[5] Note that we do not allow variables or parameterized contexts such as for example in TRIPLE[8] or FLORA-2 [13].

A rule is strongly contextually bounded *iff it has either an empty body or each body literal is scoped and contextually bounded.*

A program is (strongly) contextually bounded if each of its rules is (strongly) contextually bounded.

Intuitively, contextual boundedness means that a literal is (recursively) only depending on scoped literals. From our above definition, we see that we can separate each program into its "open" and "closed" parts:

Definition 5. *Let P be a program, then we denote by $\lfloor P \rfloor$ the program only consisting of the strongly contextually bounded rules in P and by $\lceil P \rceil$ the program consisting only of not strongly contextually bounded rules in P.*

Intuitively, $\lfloor P \rfloor$ denotes a set of rules which is based only on a set of rules closed over explicitly given contexts, whereas $\lceil P \rceil$ defines all "open" rules in P. This means that $\lfloor P \rfloor$ is "self-contained", i.e., independent of the contexts which the agent (in our example the search engine) is aware of, whereas $\lceil P \rceil$ is not.

Next, let us define queries before we describe an intuitive requirement which we would expect from the proper semantics for respective query answers:

Definition 6 (Query, Query Answer). *We denote by $Cn_S(\mathcal{P})$ the set of consequences from a set of programs $\mathcal{P}$ wrt. semantics S. A query q is a special context consisting of a single rule:*

$$\texttt{answer}(x_1, \ldots, x_n) \; :\!- \; l_1, \; \ldots, \; l_k.$$

where $x_1, \ldots x_n$ are all variables and **answer** *is a special predicate symbol not allowed in other contexts. We define a query answer wrt. an agent A as a tuple of constants $(c_1, \ldots c_n)$, such that* **answer**$(c_1, \ldots, c_n) \in Cn_S(\mathcal{P}_A \cup q)$, *where $\mathcal{P}_A$ denotes the set of contexts which A is aware of.*

Context-Monotonicity. Let us consider we ask a query q to a search engine A. Here, the set $\mathcal{P}_A$ is unknown to the user and only known to A. Although A might gather tremendous amounts of URIs, i.e. programs, in an open environment such as the Web, one can never be sure that A has complete knowledge. We would expect the following intuitive requirement fulfilled by our semantics:

Whatever query you ask to an agent A, the results should return a maximum set of answers which are entailed by the semantics with respect to the contexts known to A. Additionally, the semantics we choose should guarantee, that in case that A becomes aware of additional knowledge (i.e. programs), none of the previous answers need to be retracted. Thus, we require that our semantics is monotonic with respect to the addition of contexts i.e.

$$\mathcal{P} \subseteq \mathcal{R} \Rightarrow Cn_S(\mathcal{P}) \subseteq Cn_S(\mathcal{R})$$

where $\mathcal{P}, \mathcal{R}$ are sets of contexts. We will further refer to this requirement as *context-monotonicity*. Note that context-monotonicity can be viewed as soundness of query answers: Although completeness can never be achieved, due to openness of the environment, at least we want to be sure that our semantics only returns sound answers.[6] The claim for context-monotonicity may be viewed as contradictory to the inherent non-monotonicity of negation as failure. However, the intention here is as follows: Negation as failure is allowed, as long as it is restricted to an explicit scope. This view corresponds to the usual use of negation in a database sense where a closed world assumption is made rather than meaning negation "by default". I.e., we allow a closed world view as long as it is explicit where to close off.

3.2   Contextually Bounded Semantics

In the following, we define the semantics of programs under the assumption that all programs are contextually bounded, i.e. that no program negatively references to a contextually unbounded atom. The semantics is defined in terms of a simple rewriting in two variants, based on the stable and well-founded semantics for logic programs, respectively. As it turns out, context-monotonicity is guaranteed for both variants.

For a contextually bounded program p we define a rewriting $tr_{CB}(p)$ by replacing each rule h :- $l_1, \ldots, l_n$. with the rule $h@p$:- $l_1, \ldots, l_n$.

Definition 7 (Contextually Bounded Consequences). *Let* $\mathcal{P} = \{p_1, \ldots, p_k\}$ *be a set of programs. Then we define* $Cn_{CB}(\mathcal{P})$ *as follows:*
Let $\mathcal{P}_{CB} = \bigcup_{p \in Cl(\mathcal{P})} tr_{CB}(p) \cup p_1 \cup \ldots \cup p_k$, *then*

- $Cn_{CB}^{sms}(\mathcal{P}) = \bigcap \mathcal{M}(\mathcal{P}_{CB})$ *where* $\mathcal{M}(\Pi)$ *denotes the set of all stable models[11] of a program* Π, *i.e. we define* $Cn_{CB}^{sms}(\mathcal{P})$ *by the cautious consequences of* $\mathcal{P}_{CB}$ *under the stable model semantics.*
- $Cn_{CB}^{wfs}(\mathcal{P}) = M(\mathcal{P}_{CB})$ *where* $M(\Pi)$ *denotes the well-founded model [10] of program* Π.

We now investigate the two semantic variants wrt. context-monotonicity:

Proposition 1. *Context-monotonicity holds for* Cn_{CB}^{sms} *under the assumption that all programs are contextually bounded for any set of programs* $\mathcal{P}$.

Proof. (sketch) Let us assume that context-monotonicity does not hold, i.e. there exist programs p, r such that $Cn_{CB}(p) \nsubseteq Cn_{CB}(\{p, r\})$. From this, we conclude that there exists some atom a in $\mathcal{M}(p_{CB})$ which is not in $M(p_{CB} \cup r_{CB})$. By the working of the stable model semantics we know that this can only be the case if a depends negatively on some literal in r_{CB}. However, due to the fact that each negation is scoped and the contextual boundedness assumption, this would imply that there exists some rule of the form $b@r_i : -body$ in r_{CB} which is satisfied in all stable models of $p_{CB} \cup r_{CB}$ but not in p_{CB} and which stems from a strongly contextually bounded rule $b : -body$ in program r_i. However, since then r_i would necessarily be in $Cl(p)$ and thus $b@r_i : -body$ in p_{CB} we get a contradiction, because therefore also $body$ solely depends on rules in p_{CB}.

---

[6] Obviously, this only holds under the somewhat idealized assumption that in the "Web of programs" only trustworthy knowledge providers publish their knowledge.

By similar arguments we can show:

Proposition 2. *Context-monotonicity holds for Cn_{CB}^{wfs} under the assumption that all programs are contextually bounded.*

A simple counterexample shows that context-monotonicity no longer holds when the requirement for contextual boundedness is dropped:

```
p:                          r:
a :- not b@p.  b :- c.      c.
```
Here, the rewriting $\{p\}_{CB}$ yields:

```
a :- not b@p.     b :- c.
a@p :- not b@p.  b@p :- c.
```

which obviously has a $\in Cn_{CB}^{sms,wfs}(p)$, whereas $\{p, r\}_{CB}$ would extend the above program by the facts c. and c@r. such that a $\notin Cn_{CB}^{sms,wfs}(\{p, r\})$.

The restriction to contextually bounded programs is justified in an open environment only under the assumption that existing programs once published under a certain URI do not change and all previously published programs always remain accessible. Under this assumption, publishing new programs always needs to be preceded by a check for contextual boundedness. Note that the condition of contextual boundedness was defined with this assumption in mind: Publishing/adding new programs should not ever break context-monotonicity. However, obviously contextual boundedness is not stable against changes of single programs as the following example shows:

```
p:                          r:
a.                          b :- not a@p.
```

Here, p is obviously contextually bounded. Upon publication of r contextual boundedness could be checked and granted with respect to p. However, if one later on changes p by adding the single "open" rule a :- c. contextual boundedness of r would be broken. Unfortunately, such violations can not be checked upon change of a program, since in an open and decoupled environment p would not be aware of which other programs link to it.

Thus, in the next section we try to define an alternative rewriting which is more restrictive in the sense that it allows to infer less consequences under both the stable or well-founded semantics, but is more resistant against program changes, since it is independent of contextual boundedness.

3.3   Contextually Closed Semantics

Let p be an arbitrary program, then we define the program $tr_{CC}(p)$ by rewriting each rule $h : -l_1, \ldots, l_n$. in p to $h@p : -l'_1, \ldots, l'_n$. where

$$l'_i = \begin{cases} l_i & \text{in case } l_i \text{ is scoped} \\ l_i@p & \text{otherwise} \end{cases}$$

Intuitively, under this semantics the semantics of scoped literals changes to "(*not*) $a@p$ is true if and only if a can(not) be derived from p *alone*".

Definition 8 (Contextually Closed Consequences). *Let $\mathcal{P} = \{p_1, \ldots, p_k\}$ be a set of programs. Then we define $Cn_{CC}(\mathcal{P})$ as follows:*
Let $\mathcal{P}_{CC} = \bigcup_{p \in Cl(\mathcal{P})} tr_{CC}(p) \cup p_1 \cup \ldots \cup p_k$, then

- $Cn_{CC}^{sms}(\mathcal{P}) = \bigcap \mathcal{M}(\mathcal{P}_{CC})$ where $\mathcal{M}(\Pi)$ is the set of all stable models of Π.
- $Cn_{CC}^{wfs}(\mathcal{P}) = M(\mathcal{P}_{CC})$ where $M(\Pi)$ is the well-founded model of Π.

Context-monotonicity is trivially fulfilled under this translation both in the stable and well-founded variants, since negation is automatically "closed off" to the linked contexts only. Note that, in case all programs are contextually bounded the semantics still does not coincide, but contextually closed semantics is indeed more restrictive than contextually bounded semantics:

Proposition 3. *For any set of contextually bounded programs* $\mathcal{P}$

$$Cn_{CC}^{sms,wfs}(\mathcal{P}) \subseteq Cn_{CB}^{sms,wfs}(\mathcal{P})$$

Proof. (sketch) We want to show that: $Cn_{CC}^{sms}(\mathcal{P}) \subseteq Cn_{CB}^{sms}(\mathcal{P})$ and $Cn_{CC}^{wfs}(\mathcal{P}) \subseteq Cn_{CB}^{wfs}(\mathcal{P})$, respectively.

Note that by construction for each rule $h : -l_1, \ldots, l_n$. in $\lfloor Cl(\mathcal{P}) \rfloor$ stemming from program p there is a rule $h@p : -l_1, \ldots, l_n$. in $\mathcal{P}_{CB} \cap \mathcal{P}_{CC}$. We denote this set of rules by *floor*. Note that $Lit(floor)$ is a splitting set [15] for both $\mathcal{P}_{CB}$ and $\mathcal{P}_{CC}$ and thus the stable models for both $\mathcal{P}_{CB}$ and $\mathcal{P}_{CC}$ coincide on *floor*.

We can argue similarly for the well-founded semantics that the well-founded models of $\mathcal{P}_{CB}$ and $\mathcal{P}_{CC}$ coincide on *floor*, since both $\langle floor, \mathcal{P}_{CC} \setminus floor \rangle$ and $\langle floor, \mathcal{P}_{CB} \setminus floor \rangle$ are stratified pairs [18].

Moreover, $\mathcal{P}_{CB} \setminus floor$ and $\mathcal{P}_{CC} \setminus floor$ are (due to contextual boundedness) both positive logic programs modulo stratified input negation for literals from *floor*.[7] That means that both $\mathcal{P}_{CB} \setminus floor$ and $\mathcal{P}_{CC} \setminus floor$ extend the stable models (or the well-founded model[8]) of *floor*. Moreover, for each stable model (or the well-founded model) m of *floor* and each rule $h@p : -l'_1, \ldots l'_n$. which is satisfied in $\mathcal{P}_{CC} \setminus floor \cup m$ there is a corresponding rule $h@p : -l_1, \ldots l_n$. which is satisfied in $\mathcal{P}_{CB} \setminus floor \cup m$. Finally, each of the remaining rules $h : -l_1, \ldots l_n$. with an unscoped head in $\mathcal{P}_{CC} \setminus floor \cup m$ is also present in $\mathcal{P}_{CB} \setminus floor \cup m$. This proves that proving that the consequences of $\mathcal{P}_{CB}$ are a superset of the consequences of $\mathcal{P}_{CC}$ for both the well-founded and the stable semantics.

Indeed, there are consequences under contextually bounded semantics which are invalid under contextually closed semantics, for instance:

```
p:                r:
a :- b@r. c.      b :- c.
```

Here, the query $a?\{p\}$ is true with respect to contextually bounded semantics but not with respect to contextually closed semantics.

This reflects the intuition that contextually closed semantics draws inferences more cautiously and allow less interferences between programs, but does in trade not run into problems with contextually unbounded programs.

---

[7] By "input negation" we mean that given the stable models (or well-founded model) of *floor* as "input fats" for $\mathcal{P}_{CB} \setminus floor$ and $\mathcal{P}_{CC} \setminus floor$ only these input facts can occur negatively in rule bodies.

[8] Since both well-founded semantics and stable model semantics coincide on stratified programs, we do not need to treat them separately for the remainder of the proof.

4 RDF(S) Plus Rules

In the Semantic Web, RDF is currently gaining more and more momentum. Thus, it is worthwhile to apply our context-aware rule language with scoped negation on arbitrary knowledge bases, consisting of RDF, RDFS and Logic Programming style rules with scoped negation distributed over the Web at different URIs. In this section we introduce a straightforward LP-compliant notion of a subset of RDF and investigate how it interacts with the semantics we have defined so far. To this end we will define a subset of the RDFS semantics in terms of open rules. As it turns out, we will need to slightly extend our definition of scoped literals to make it work. Based on this conclusion we will finally present a variant of contextually closed semantics in section 5.

We use a simplified syntax of RDF(S) here in terms of logic programming to show that the major part of RDFS can be understood as a set of facts and rules in a logic program. As implicit from [12] and partly shown in [8], large parts of RDF(S) can be embedded in logic programming. To this end, we use logic programs which express each statement $\langle S, P, O \rangle$ by a single atom triple(S,P,O). Almost all of the RDFS semantics itself can be expressed by the following program

```
http://www.example.org/rdfs-semantics :
 triple(P,rdf:type,rdf:Property)  :- triple(S,P,O).
 triple(S,rdf:type,rdfs:Resource)  :- triple(S,P,O).
 triple(O,rdf:type,rdfs:Resource)  :- triple(S,P,O).
 triple(S,rdf:type,C)  :- triple(S,P,O), triple(P,rdfs:domain,C).
 triple(O,rdf:type,C)  :- triple(S,P,O), triple(P,rdfs:range,C).
 triple(C,rdfs:subClassOf,rdfs:Resource):- triple(C,rdf:type,rdfs:Class).
 triple(C1,rdfs:subClassOf,C3)  :- triple(C1,rdfs:subClassOf,C2),
                                    triple(C2,rdfs:subClassOf,C3).
 triple(S,rdf:type,C2)          :- triple(S,rdf:type,C1),
                                    triple(C1,rdfs:subClassOf,C2).
 triple(C,rdf:type,rdfs:Class)  :- triple(S,rdf:type,C).
 triple(C,rdfs:subClassOf,C)    :- triple(C,rdf:type,rdfs:Class).
 triple(P1,rdfs:subPropertyOf,P3) :- triple(P1,rdfs:subPropertyOf,P2),
                                    triple(P2,rdfs:subPropertyOf,P3).
 triple(S,P2,O)                 :- triple(S,P1,O),
                                    triple(P1,rdfs:subPropertyOf,P2).
 triple(P,rdfs:subPropertyOf,P)  :- triple(P,rdf:type,rdf:Property).
```

plus the respective axiomatic triples in RDF/RDFS, cf. [12, Sections 3.1 and 4.1]. For simplicity, we ignore XML literals, data types, containers and blank nodes here. Additional issues related with these features of RDF are out of the scope of this paper. We can now simply view the above program as a new context with the URI http://www.example.org/rdfs-semantics .

In order to illustrate the interplay of our semantics with this RDFS formulation, we revisit the examples from section 2 in terms of RDF, see Figure 2.

Our intention is to embed the RDFS semantics as a set of open rules in our framework. For this, we assume that an agent which answers a query is always aware of the RDFS context. However, as we will see, this is not enough.

http://www.moviereviews.com/ triple(ex:m1,ex:rate,ex:bad).	http://www.polleres.net/ triple(ex:m2,ex:rate,ex:bad). triple(ex:m2,rdf:type,movie).

```
http://www.imdb.com/
triple(ex:m1,rdf:type,ex:sciFiMovie). triple(ex:m1,ex:title,"Plan 9 from Outer Space").
triple(ex:m1,ex:directedBy,"Ed Wood").
triple(ex:m2,rdf:type,ex:sciFiMovie). triple(ex:m2,ex:title,"Matrix Revolutions").
triple(ex:m2,ex:directedBy,"Andy Wachowski"). triple(ex:m2,ex:directedBy,"Larry
Wachowski").
triple(ex:m3,rdf:type,ex:sciFiMovie). triple(ex:m3,ex:title,"Bride of the Monster").
triple(ex:m3,ex:directedBy,"Ed Wood").
triple(ex:sciFiMovie,rdf:subClassOf,ex:movie).
```

Fig. 2. RDF versions of some of the programs from Figure 1

Note that negative literals that depend on RDFS inferences, immediately cause violations of contextual boundedness. Let us consider the query

$$\text{"Give me all movies } not \text{ listed at http://www.imdb.com/"} \tag{5}$$

asked to a search engine aware of contexts http://www.example.org/rdfs-semantics, http://www.imdb.com/, http://www.moviereviews.com/, and http://www.polleres.net/, cf. (2). The straightforward formulation of this query

```
answer(X) :- triple(X,rdf:type,ex:movie),
             not triple(X,rdf:type,ex:movie)@http://www.imdb.com/.
```

violates contextual boundedness because of the dependency between the negative literal from the query and the following RDFS rule:

```
triple(S,rdf:type,C2):- triple(S,rdf:type,C1),
                        triple(C1,rdfs:subClassOf,C2).
```

Now let us see how the same query is evaluated wrt. the contextually-closed semantics. We expect the answer to this query to be empty. However, the above-mentioned RDFS rule which should allow one to derive that ex:m1 and ex:m2 are movies listed by http://www.imdb.com/, will never be applied because of the working of tr_{CC}, and the final answer will be ex:m2.

We extend our syntax by allowing unions of contexts in literal scopes to deal with this problem, which allows us to reformulate the query above as follows:

$$\text{"Give me all movies not listed at http://www.imdb.com/, } under\ additional \\ consideration\ of \text{ http://www.example.org/rdfs-semantics"} \tag{6}$$

which could be written as

```
answer(X) :- triple(X,rdf:type,ex:movie),
    not triple(X,rdf:type,ex:movie)@
    {http://www.example.org/rdfs-semantics, http://www.imdb.com/}.
```

We need to extend tr_{CC} to handle unions of contexts in scoped literals, as we will show in the next section. Note that we do not cover unions of contexts as an extension of tr_{CB} due to the inherent violation of contextual boundedness.

5   Contextually Closed Semantics with Context Sets

The basic intuition behind extending contextually closed semantics with unions of contexts in scoped literals is as follows: A literal scoped over a union of contexts shall be evaluated with respect to and closed over the union of the respective programs. Thus, we adapt the definition of tr_{CC} as follows:

Let $\mathcal{P}$ be an arbitrary set of programs, then $tr_{CC}(\mathcal{P})$ is defined by rewriting each rule $h : -l_1, \ldots, l_n.$ in any of the programs in $\mathcal{P}$ to $h@\mathcal{P} : -l'_1, \ldots, l'_n.$ where

$$l'_i = \begin{cases} l@\mathcal{R} & \text{in case } l_i = l@\mathcal{R} \text{ is a scoped literal with possibly set scope } \mathcal{R} \\ l_i@\mathcal{P} & \text{otherwise} \end{cases}$$

plus recursively adding $tr_{CC}(\mathcal{R})$ for any scoped body literal $l@\mathcal{R}$.

Note that this more general definition is equivalent to the original definition of tr_{CC} despite it per se includes the relevant part of the closure already. That means, we can also simplify the definition of $\mathcal{P}_{CC}$ in Definition 8 as follows:

$$\mathcal{P}_{CC} = \bigcup_{p \in (\mathcal{P})} (tr_{CC}(p) \cup p)$$

The remainder of Definition 8 can stay as is for this generalization. As we can easily verify, query (6) would be correctly answered under this semantics.

6   Related Works

FLORA-2 [13] is a query answering system based on the logic programming fragment of F-Logic [14], a frame-based syntactic variant of first-order logic popular for ontology reasoning. FLORA-2's module mechanism allows a form of scoped negation as failure using the well-founded semantics. Negative queries can be posed to a certain module. However, variables can be used in the place of the module identifier, in which case the scope of the query (negation) is the union of all the modules registered with the system at that point in time. This rather unrestricted way for defining scoped negation does not fulfill our monotonicity criterion with respect to the addition of new modules in the general case. Anyway, FLORA-2 is a system and per se does not define the semantics of programs and queries defined on the Web, nor are any assumptions made that modules need to coincide with contexts (i.e. URIs) in our sense. Implementations of our transformations on top of FLORA-2 are possible.

N3 [3] is a language for representing RDF rules on the Web. It has a form of scoped negation as failure and without an explicit notion of context. In N3 negation appears in the form of an infix operator `log:notIncludes`[9] that links two (possibly complex) formulas and that succeeds whenever the first formula does not include the second one. However, a formula is not necessarily closed in our sense and can have infinite size in N3 due to the presence of blank nodes

---

[9] `http://www.w3.org/2000/10/swap/doc/Reach`

(existentials) in the head of the rules.[10] This leads to a possibly infinite search space for negation as failure, which is undesirable and contradictive with the requirement of context-monotonicity.

TRIPLE [8] is another logic programming engine particularly tailored for RDF reasoning and querying with the support of scoping over possibly parameterized contexts, allowing union, intersection and set difference over contexts. The authors outline that nonmonotonic negation interpreted under the well-founded semantics can be supported. Since variables are allowed in parameterized contexts, similar considerations apply as for FLORA-2.

C-OWL [4] is a proposed extension of OWL by contexts and bridge rules. An interesting feature of this language is that its semantics makes use of so-called *local model semantics* where for each context there exists a local set of models and a local domain of interpretation. These kinds of semantics are opposed to the *global model semantics* where there exists a global model and a global domain of interpretation. Global model semantics have the disadvantage that local inconsistency propagates to the whole, which is not desirable on the Web. Our semantics follows a global model nature: When building on top of stable semantics local inconsistency propagates to the whole model. Note that the well-founded variants of our semantics do not involve inconsistency, and thus local inconsistencies cannot arise. Investigation of the relations and possible integrations with C-OWL are on our agenda.

Finally, we point out that the idea behind scoped negation as failure is orthogonal to the so-called local closed world assumption [9]. Instead of stating "local complete knowledge" as is done in local closed world assumption, we merely impose to explicitly close off any use of negation over a context, not making any statement about whether the knowledge of this context is indeed complete.

7 Conclusion

In this paper we discussed logic programs under contextually scoped negation and provided two possible semantics based on simple translations to normal logic programs. The rationale behind was keeping these translations lightweight in order to facilitate direct implementations with existing engines based on either the stable or well-founded semantics, while preserving context-monotonicity. Although our framework is general we emphasized the fruitful application of our approach in the context of rules on top of RDF and RDFS.

This work is a first step towards a proper definition for scoped negation for the upcoming RIF working group in W3C. Open issues like for instance the treatment of full RDF including blank nodes, data types, etc. require further investigation. Also, the transformations to normal logic programs provided in this paper still possibly contain redundant rules and might be subject to optimizations for actual implementations. As for future extensions, it seems to be useful to extend our definition of scope not only to unions but also intersections or

---

[10] http://lists.w3.org/Archives/Public/public-cwm-bugs/2005Jul/0000.html

set difference of contexts. More refined concepts of context such as e.g. so-called named RDF graphs [6] could also serve as a basis for further investigations.

We set the basis for a rule based query language. It is well-known that query languages like SQL naturally translate into queries expressed by logic programs. However, without negation as failure (for modeling set difference) such a query language is incomplete. Scoped negation is a natural and lightweight candidate to extend RDF query languages such as for instance SPARQL [17] and N3 [3] in this direction.

Acknowledgments. The authors thank Jos de Bruijn, Rubén Lara, and Michael Kifer for fruitful discussions and the anonymous reviewers for their useful feedback. This work is partially supported by the EC projects DIP, KnowledgeWeb, Infrawebs, SEKT, and ASG; by the FIT-IT projects RW^2 and TSC; by SFI grant SFI/02/CE1/I13; by the CICyT project TIC-2003-9001-C02.

References

1. J. Angele et al. Web rule language (WRL). W3C Member Submission, http://www.w3.org/Submission/WRL/, June 2005.
2. S. Battle, et al. Semantic Web services Framework (SWSF). W3C Member Submission, http://www.w3.org/Submission/SWSF/, May 2005.
3. T. Berners-Lee, D. Connolly, E. Prud'homeaux, and Y. Scharf. Experience with N3 rules. In *W3C Workshop on Rule Languages for Interoperability*, Washington, D.C., USA, Apr. 2005.
4. P. Bouquet, F. Giunchiglia, F. van Harmelen, L. Serafini, and H. Stuckenschmidt. C-OWL: Contextualizing ontologies. In *Second International Semantic Web Conference - ISWC 2003*, Sanibel Island, FL, USA, 2003.
5. D. Brickley, R. V. Guha (eds.), and B. McBride (series ed.). RDF Vocabulary Description Language 1.0. Feb. 2004. W3C Recommendation, http://www.w3.org/TR/2004/REC-rdf-schema-20040210/.
6. J. Carroll, C. Bizer, P. Hayes, and P. Stickler. Named graphs. *Journal of Web Semantics*, 3(4), 2005.
7. Paulo Pinheiro da Silva, Deborah L. McGuinness, and Rob McCool. Knowledge provenance infrastructure. *IEEE Data Engineering Bulletin*, 26(4), 2003.
8. S. Decker, M. Sintek, and W. Nejdl. The model-theoretic semantics of TRIPLE. Technical report, 2002.
9. O. Etzioni, K. Golden, and D. Weld. Tractable closed world reasoning with updates. In *KR'94: Principles of Knowledge Representation and Reasoning*, Bonn, Germany, 1994.
10. A. Van Gelder, K. Ross, and J.S. Schlipf. Unfounded sets and well-founded semantics for general logic programs. In *7th ACM Symposium on Principles of Database Systems*, Austin, Texas, 1988.
11. M. Gelfond and V. Lifschitz. The stable model semantics for logic programming. In *5th Int'l Conf. on Logic Programming*, Cambridge, Massachusetts, 1988.
12. P. Hayes. RDF semantics. W3C Recommendation, http://www.w3.org/TR/rdf-mt/, Feb. 2004.
13. M. Kifer. Nonmonotonic reasoning in FLORA-2. In *8th Int'l Conf. on Logic Programming and Nonmonotonic Reasoning (LPNMR'05)*, Diamante, Italy, 2005.

14. M. Kifer, G. Lausen, and J. Wu. Logical foundations of object-oriented and frame-based languages. *JACM*, 42(4), 1995.

15. V. Lifschitz and H. Turner. Splitting a logic program. In Pascal Van Hentenryck, editor, *11th Int'l Conf. on Logic Programming (ICLP'94)*, Santa Margherita Ligure, Italy, June 1994.

16. D.L. McGuinness and F. van Harmelen. OWL Web ontology language overview. W3C Recommendation,
    `http://www.w3.org/TR/2004/REC-owl-features-20040210/`, Feb. 2004.

17. E. Prud'hommeaux and A. Seaborne (eds.). SPARQL Query Language for RDF, July 2005. W3C Working Draft.

18. J.S. Schlipf. Formalizing a Logic for Logic Programming. AMAI,5(2-4), 1992.

Beagle++: Semantically Enhanced Searching and Ranking on the Desktop

Paul-Alexandru Chirita, Stefania Costache, Wolfgang Nejdl, and Raluca Paiu

L3S Research Center / University of Hanover
Deutscher Pavillon, Expo Plaza 1
30539 Hanover, Germany
{chirita, ghita, nejdl, paiu}@l3s.de

Abstract. Existing desktop search applications, trying to keep up with the rapidly increasing storage capacities of our hard disks, offer an incomplete solution for information retrieval. In this paper we describe our Beagle++ desktop search prototype, which enhances conventional full-text search with semantics and ranking modules. This prototype extracts and stores activity-based metadata explicitly as RDF annotations. Our main contributions are extensions we integrate into the Beagle desktop search infrastructure to exploit this additional contextual information for searching and ranking the resources on the desktop. Contextual information plus ranking brings desktop search much closer to the performance of web search engines. Initially disconnected sets of resources on the desktop are connected by our contextual metadata, PageRank derived algorithms allow us to rank these resources appropriately. First experiments investigating precision and recall quality of our search prototype show encouraging improvements over standard search.

1 Introduction

The capacity of our hard-disk drives has increased tremendously over the past decade, and so has the number of files we usually store on our computer. It is no wonder that sometimes we cannot find a document any more, even when we know we saved it somewhere. Ironically, in quite a few of these cases, the document we are looking for can be found faster on the World Wide Web than on our personal computer.

Web search has become more efficient than PC search due to the boom of web search engines and to powerful ranking algorithms like the PageRank algorithm introduced by Google [12]. The recent arrival of desktop search applications, which index all data on a PC, promises to increase search efficiency on the desktop. However, even with these tools, searching through our (relatively small set of) personal documents is currently inferior to searching the (rather vast set of) documents on the web. This happens because these desktop search applications cannot rely on PageRank-like ranking mechanisms, and they also fall short of utilizing desktop specific characteristics, especially context information.

Y. Sure and J. Domingue (Eds.): ESWC 2006, LNCS 4011, pp. 348–362, 2006.

We therefore have to enhance simple indexing of data on our desktop by more sophisticated ranking techniques, otherwise the user has no other choice but to look at the entire result sets for her queries – usually a tedious task. The main problem with ranking on the desktop comes from the lack of links between documents, the foundation of current ranking algorithms (in addition to TF/IDF numbers). A semantic desktop offers the missing ingredients: By gathering semantic information from user activities, from the contexts the user works in[1], we build the necessary links between documents.

We begin this paper by presenting related work in Section 2, continuing with our proposed desktop system architecture described in detail in Section 3. In this paper we enhance and contextualize desktop search based on both resource specific and semantic metadata collected from different available contexts and activities performed on a personal computer. We describe the semantics of these different contexts by appropriate ontologies in Section 3.3, and then propose a ranking algorithm for desktop documents in Section 3.4. For this latter aspect, we focus on recent advances of PageRank-based ranking, showing how local (i.e., context-based) and global ranking measures can be integrated in such an environment. We are implementing our prototype on top of the open source Beagle project [10], which aims to provide basic desktop search in Linux. Section 4 gives a detailed description of our prototype, and shows how we extended Beagle with additional modules for annotating and ranking resources. In Section 5 we investigate the quality of our algorithms in a typical desktop search scenario, and illustrate how our extended Beagle++ search infrastructure improves the retrieval of search results in terms of number (recall) and order (precision) of results, using context and ranking based on this information.

2   Previous Work

The difficulty of accessing information on our computers has prompted several first releases of desktop search applications recently. The most prominent examples include Google desktop search [11] (proprietary, for Windows) and the Beagle open source project for Linux [10]. Yet they include *no* metadata whatsoever in their system, but just a regular text-based index. Nor does their competitor MSN Desktop Search [14]. Finally, Apple Inc. promises to integrate an advanced desktop search application (named *Spotlight Search* [2]) into their upcoming operating system, Mac OS Tiger. Even though they also intend to add semantics into their tool, only explicit information is used, such as file size, creator, or metadata embedded into specific files (images taken with digital cameras for example include many additional characteristics, such as exposure information). While this is indeed an improvement over regular search, it still misses contextual information often resulting or inferable from explicit user actions or additional background knowledge, as discussed in the next sections.

---

[1] Studies have shown that people tend to associate things to certain contexts [17], and this information should be utilized during search. So far, however, neither has this information been collected, nor have there been attempts to use it.

Swoogle [7] is a search and retrieval system for finding semantic web documents on the web. The ranking scheme used in Swoogle uses weights for the different types of relations between Semantic Web Documents (SWD) to model their probability to be explored. However, this mainly serves for ranking between ontologies or instances of ontologies. In our approach we have instances of a fixed ontology and the weights for the links model the user's preferences.

Facilitating search for information the user has already seen before is also the main goal of the *Stuff I've Seen (SIS)* system, presented in [8]. Based on the fact that the user has already seen the information, contextual cues such as time, author, thumbnails and previews can be used to search for and present information. [8] mainly focuses on experiments investigating the general usefulness of this approach though, without presenting more technical details.

The importance of semantically capturing users' interests is analyzed in [1]. The purpose of their research is to develop a ranking technique for the large number of possible semantic associations between the entities of interest for a specific query. They define an ontology for describing the user interest and use this information to compute weights for the links among the semantic entities. In our system, the user's interest is a consequence of her activities, this information is encapsulated in the properties of the entities defined, and the weights for the links are manually defined.

An interesting technique for ranking the results for a query on the semantic web takes into consideration the inferencing processes that led to each result [16]. In this approach, the relevance of the returned results for a query is computed based upon the specificity of the relations (links) used when extracting information from the knowledge base. The calculation of the relevance is however a problem-sensitive decision, and therefore task oriented strategies should be developed for this computation.

3   An Architecture for Searching the Semantic Desktop

3.1   Overview

This chapter will present our 3-layer architecture for generating and exploiting the metadata enhancing desktop resources. At the bottom level, we have the physical resources currently available on the PC desktop. Even though they can all eventually be reduced to files, it is important to differentiate between them based on content and usage context. Thus, we distinguish structured documents, emails, offline web pages, general files[2] and file hierarchies. Furthermore, while all of them do provide a basis for desktop search, they also miss a lot of contextual information, such as the author of an email or the browsing path followed on a specific web site. We generate and store this additional search input using RDF metadata, which is placed on the second conceptual layer of our architecture. Finally, the uppermost layer implements a ranking mechanism over all resources on the lower levels. An importance score is computed for each desktop item,

---

[2] Text files or files whose textual content can be retrieved.

supporting an enhanced ordering of results within desktop search applications. The architecture is depicted in Figure 1. In the next subsections we describe each of its layers following a bottom-up approach.

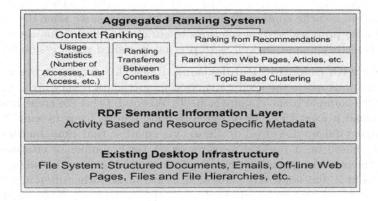

Fig. 1. Desktop Ranking System Architecture

3.2   Current Desktop Infrastructure and Its Limitations

Motivation and Overview. Today the number of files on our desktops can easily reach 10,000, 100,000 or more. This large amount of data can no longer be ordered with manual operations such as defining explicit file and directory names. Automatic solutions are needed, preferably taking into account the activity contexts under which each resource was stored/used. In our prototype we focus on three main working contexts of email exchanges, file procedures (i.e., create, modify, etc.), and web surfing. Furthermore, we investigate an additional extended context related to research and scientific publications. In the following paragraphs, we discuss how the resources associated to these contexts are currently encountered, and which (valuable) information is lost during their utilization. Subsequent sections present solutions to represent this information and exploit it for desktop search applications.

Email Context. One of the most flourishing communication medium is surely email communication. International scientific collaboration has become almost unthinkable without electronic mail: Outcomes of brainstorming sessions, intermediate versions of reports, or articles represent just a few of the items exchanged within this environment. Similarly, Internet purchasing or reservations are usually confirmed via email. Considering the continuous increase of email exchanges, enhanced solutions are necessary to sort our correspondence. More, when storing emails, a lot of contextual information is lost. Most significant here is the semantic connection between the attachments of an email, its sender and subject information, as well as the valuable comments inside its body. This information should be explicitly represented as RDF metadata, to enable both enhanced search capabilities for our inbox, as well as the exploitation of the semantic links between desktop files (e.g., PDF articles stored from attachments), the person that sent them to us and the comments he added in the email body.

Files and File Hierarchy Context and Web Cache Context. Similar to the discussion above, various semantic relationships exist in other contexts such as file and web cache context. Due to space limitations, we refer the reader to [5], where we proposed several solutions to enrich the information associated to file and directory names, as well as to previously visited resources on the Web.

Working with Scientific Publications. Research activities represent one of the occupations where the need for contextual metadata is very high. The most illustrative example is the document itself: Where did this file come from? Did we download it from CiteSeer or did somebody send it to us by email? Which other papers did we download or discuss via email at that time, and how good are they (based on a ranking measure or on their number of citations)? We might remember the general topic of a paper and the person with whom we discussed about it, but not its title. These situations arise rather often in a research environment and have to be adressed by an appropriate search infrastructure.

3.3   RDF Semantic Information Layer

Motivation and Overview. People organize their lives according to preferences often based on their activities. Consequently, desktop resources are also organized according to performed activities and personal profiles. Since, as described above, most the information related to these activities is lost on our current desktops, the goal of the RDF semantic information layer is to record and represent this data and to store it in RDF annotations associated to each

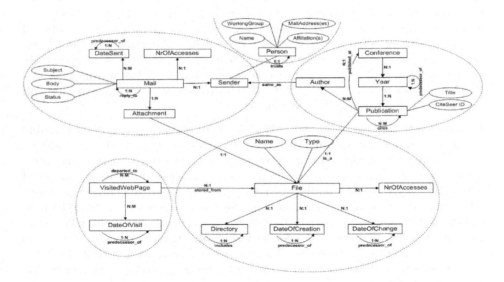

Fig. 2. Contextual Ontology for the Semantic Desktop

resource. Figure 2 depicts an overview image of the ontology that defines appropriate annotation metadata for the context we are focusing on in this paper. The following paragraphs will describe these metadata in more detail.

Email Metadata. Basic properties for the email context refer to the date when an email was sent or accessed, as well as its subject and body text. The status of an email can be described as seen/unseen or read/unread. A property "reply to" represents email thread information, the "has attachment" property describes a 1:n relation between an email and its attachments. The "sender" property gives information about the email sender, which can be associated to a social networking trust scheme, thus providing valuable input for assessing the quality of the email according to the reputation of its sender.

File and Web Cache Specific Metadata. For these, we again refer the reader to our previous work [5] which describes the ontologies associated to these activity contexts. An overview can be found in the lower half of Figure 2.

Scientific Publications Metadata. The Publication class represents a specific type of file, with additional information associated to it. The most common fields are "author", "conference", "year", and "title", which comprise the regular information describing a scientific article. Additionally, we store the paper's CiteSeer ID if we have it. The publication context is connected to the email context, if we communicate with an author or if we save a publication from an email attachment. Of course, since each publication is stored as a file, it is also connected to the file context, and thus to the file specific information associated to it (e.g., path, number of accesses, etc.).

3.4   Aggregated Ranking System

Motivation and Overview. As the amount of desktop items has been increasing significantly over the past years, desktop search applications will return more and more hits to our queries. Contextual metadata, which provide additional information about each resource, result in even more search results. A measure of importance is therefore necessary, which enables us to rank these results. The following paragraphs describe such a ranking mechanism, based on the Google PageRank algorithm [12].

Basic Ranking. Given the fact that rank computation on the desktop would not be possible without the contextual information, which provides semantic links among resources, annotation ontologies should describe all aspects and relationships among resources influencing the ranking. The identity of the authors for example influences our opinion of documents, and thus "author" should be represented explicitly as a class in our publication ontology.

Second, we have to specify how these aspects influence importance. Object-Rank [4] has introduced the notion of authority transfer schema graphs, which extend schemas similar to the ontologies previously described, by adding weights and edges in order to express how importance propagates among the entities and resources inside the ontology. These weights and edges represent authority transfer annotations, which extend our context ontologies with the information we need to compute ranks for all instances of the classes defined in the context ontologies.

Figure 3 depicts our context ontology plus appropriate authority transfer annotations. For example, authority of an email is split among the sender of the email, its attachment, the number of times that email was accessed, the date when it was sent and the email to which it was replied. If an email is important, the sender might be an important person, the attachment an important one and/or the number of times the email was accessed is very high. Additionally, the date when the email was sent and the previous email in the thread hierarchy also become important. As suggested in [4], every edge from the schema graph is split into two edges, one for each direction. This is motivated by the observation that authority potentially flows in both directions and not only in the direction that appears in the schema: if we know that a particular person is important, we also want to have all emails we receive from this person ranked higher. The final ObjectRank value for each resource is calculated based on the PageRank formula (presented in Section 4.3).

Using External Sources. For the computation of authority transfer, we can also include additional external ranking sources to connect global ranking computation and personalized ranking of resources on our desktop. These external ranking sources are used to provide the seed values for the calculation of the

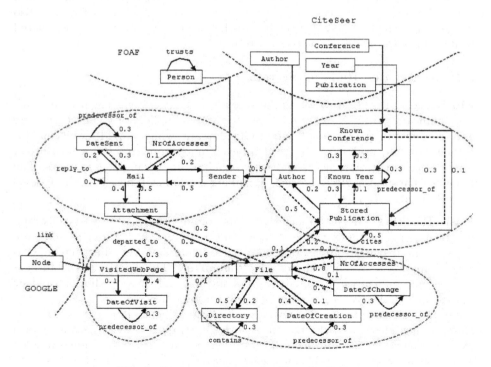

Fig. 3. Contextual Authority Transfer Schema

personal ranking. Our prototype ontology includes three global ranking services, one returning Google ranks, the second one ranks computed from the CiteSeer database and the last one from the social network described with FOAF.

The ObjectRank value for each resource is calculated based on the PageRank formula and the seed values for this computation integrate information from external ranking systems and personalized information. We use the following external ranking systems as the most relevant for our purpose:

- *Ranking for articles.* Co-citation analysis is used to compute a primary rank for the article [15]. Because of the sparse article graph on each desktop this rank should be retrieved from a server that stores the articles (in our case all metadata from CiteSeer and DBLP).
- *Recommendations.* We may receive documents from other peers together with their recommendations. These recommendations are weighted by a local estimate of the sender's expertise in the topic [9, 6].

Personalization. Different authority transfer weights express different preferences of the user, translating into personalized ranking. The important requirement for doing this successfully is that we include in a users ontology all concepts, which influence her ranking function. For example, if we consider a publication important because it was written by an author important to us, we have to represent that in our context ontology. Another example are digital photographies, whose importance is usually heavily influenced by the event or the location where they were taken. In this case both event and location have to be included as classes in our context ontology. The user activities that influence the ranking computation have also to be taken into account, which translates to assigning different weights to different contexts.

4   Beagle^{++} Prototype

Our current prototype is built on top of the open source Beagle desktop search infrastructure, which we extended with additional modules: metadata generators, which handle the creation of contextual information around the resources on the desktop, and a ranking module, which computes the ratings of resources so that search results are shown in the order of their importance. The advantage of our system over existing desktop search applications consists in both the ability of identifying resources based on an extended set of attributes – more results, and of presenting the results according to their ranking – to enable the user to quickly locate the most relevant resource.

4.1   Current Beagle Architecture

The main characteristic of our extended desktop search architecture is metadata generation and indexing on-the-fly, triggered by modification events generated upon occurrence of file system changes. This relies on notification functionalities provided by the kernel. Events are generated whenever a new file is copied to hard disk or stored by the web browser, when a file is deleted or modified, when a new email is read, etc. Much of this basic notification functionality is provided on Linux by an inotify-enabled Linux kernel, which is used by Beagle.

Our Beagle++ prototype keeps all the basic structure of Beagle and adds additional modules that are responsible for generating and using the contextual annotations enriching the resources on our desktop. The main components of the extended Beagle prototype are Beagled++ and Best++, as seen in Figure 4, "++" being used to denote our extensions. Beagled++ is the main module that deals with indexing of resources on the desktop and also retrieving the results from user queries. Best++ is responsible for the graphical interface, and communicates with Beagled++ through sockets. When starting Beagle, the query driver is started and waits for queries. The Best++ interface is initialized, too, and is responsible for transmitting queries to Beagled++ and visualization of answers.

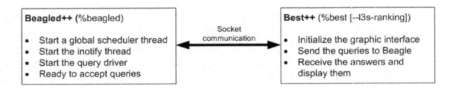

Fig. 4. Extended Beagle Desktop Search

4.2   Extending Beagle with Metadata Generators

Depending on the type and context of the file / event, metadata generation is performed by appropriate metadata generators, as described in Figure 5. These applications build upon an appropriate RDFS ontology as shown in [5], describing the RDF metadata to be used for that specific context. Generated metadata are either extracted directly (e.g. email sender, subject, body) or are generated using appropriate association rules plus possibly some additional background knowledge. All of these metadata are exported in RDF format, and added to a metadata index, which is used by the search application together with the usual full-text index [13].

The architecture of our prototype environment includes four prototype metadata generators according to the types of contexts described in the previous sections. We added a new subclass of the LuceneQueryable class, MetadataQueryable, and, from this one, derived four additional subclasses, dealing with the generation of metadata for the appropriate contexts (Files, Web Cache, Emails and Publications). The annotations we create include the corresponding elements depicted in the ontology graph Figure 2. They are described in detail in [5]. A new one is the publication metadata generator, described in the next paragraph.

Publication Metadata Generator. For the experiments described in this paper, we have implemented a metadata generator module which deals with publications. For each identified paper, it extracts the title and tries to match

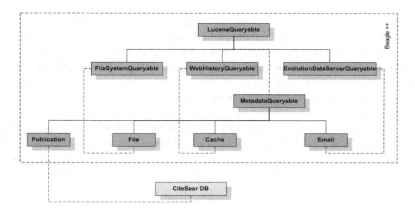

Fig. 5. Beagle Extensions for Metadata Support

it with an entry into the CiteSeer publications database. If it finds an entry, the application builds up an RDF annotation file, containing information from the database about the title of the paper, the authors, publication year, conference, papers which cite this one and other CiteSeer references to publications. All annotation files corresponding to papers are merged in order to construct the RDF graph of publications existing on one's desktop.

4.3   Extending Beagle with a Ranking Module

Each user has his own contextual network / context metadata graph and for each node in this network the appropriate ranking as computed by the algorithm described in section 3.4. The computation of rankings is based on the link structure of the resources as specified by the defined ontologies and the corresponding metadata. We base our rank computation on the PageRank formula

$$r = d \cdot A \cdot r + (1 - d) \cdot e \tag{1}$$

applying the random surfer model and including all nodes in the base set. The random jump to an arbitrary resource from the data graph is modeled by the vector e. [6] shows how, by appropriately modifying the e vector, we can take the different trust values for the different peers sending information into account. A is the adjacency matrix which connects all available instances of the existing context ontology on one's desktop. The weights of the links between the instances correspond to the weights specified in the authority transfer annotation ontology divide by the number of the links of the same type. When instantiating the authority transfer annotation ontology for the resources existing on the users desktop, the corresponding matrix A will have elements which can be either 0, if there is no edge between the corresponding entities in the data graph, or they have the value of the weight assigned to the edge determined by these entities, in the authority transfer annotation ontology, divided by the number of outgoing links of the same type.

The original Beagle desktop search engine uses the facilities provided by Lucene.NET for ranking the results, which means that Beagle's hits are scored only based on TF/IDF measures. Such a ranking scheme gives good results in the case of documents explicitly containing the keywords in the query. Still, as discussed above, TF/IDF alone is not sufficient, as it does not exploit any additional hints about importance of information.

We have therefore implemented a new ranking scheme in Beagle^{++}, which profits from the advantages offered by TF/IDF, but takes into account Object-Rank scores as described in this paper. For all resources existing on the desktop this scheme computes the ranks with our ObjectRank-based algorithm presented above, and the resulting ranks are then combined with the TF/IDF scores provided by Lucene.NET using the following formula:

$$R'(a) = R(a) * TF \times IDF(a), \tag{2}$$

where:

a - represents the resource

$R(a)$ - is the computed ObjectRank

$TFxIDF(a)$ - is the TF/IDF score for resource a

This formula guaranties that the hits will have a high score if they both have a high ObjectRank and a TF/IDF score.

The user is able to chose one of the two available ranking schemas: the one provided by Beagle, based on TF/IDF measures, or the one we developed, based on ObjectRank plus TF/IDF. The first scheme is implicit. For the second one, users have to specify an additional parameter when starting the Best client: *%best –l3s-ranking*.

5   Experiments

5.1   Experimental Setup

We did a first evaluation of our algorithms by conducting a small scale user study. Colleagues of ours provided a set of their locally indexed publications, some of which they received as attachments to emails (thus containing rich contextual metadata associated to them from the specific email fields). Then, each subject defined her *own* queries, related to their activities, and performed search over the above mentioned reduced images of their desktops. In total, 30 queries were issued. The average query length was 2.17 keywords, which is slightly more than the average of 1.7 keywords reported in other larger scale studies (see for example [8]). Generally, the more specific the test queries are, the more difficult it is to improve over basic textual information retrieval measures such as TFxIDF. Thus, having an average query length a bit higher than usual can only increase the quality of our conclusions.

For comparison purposes, we sent each of these queries to three systems: (1) the original Beagle system (with output selected and sorted using solely TFxIDF), (2) an intermediate version of Beagle^{++} enhanced only with activity based metadata (using the same TFxIDF measure for ordering its output, but giving more importance to metadata results than to regular desktop items), and (3) the current Beagle++, containing enhancements for both metadata support and desktop ranking. For every query and every system, each user rated the top 5 output results using grades from 0 to 1, as follows: 0 for an irrelevant result, 0.5 for a relevant one, and 1 for highly relevant one.

5.2   Methodology

Even when semantic information (e.g., RDF annotations, etc.) is integrated as part of a search system, the traditional measures from information retrieval theory can and should still be applied when evaluating system performance. We therefore used the ratings of our subjects to compute average precision and recall values at each output rank [3]. In general, precision measures the ability of an (information retrieval) system to return *only* relevant results. It is defined as:

$$\text{Precision} = \frac{\text{Number of } Relevant \text{ Returned Results}}{\text{Number of Returned Results}} \quad (3)$$

Recall is its complement: It measures the ability of a system to return *all* relevant documents, and is computed using the formula below:

$$\text{Recall} = \frac{\text{Number of Relevant Returned Results}}{\text{Total Number of Relevant Results Available in the Entire System}} \quad (4)$$

Both measures can be calculated at any rank r, i.e., considering only the top r results output by the application. For example, even if the system has returned 2000 hits for some user query, when calculating precision at the top-3 results, we consider only these three as returned results. This is necessary for large scale environments, such the World Wide Web, and more recently, the PC desktop, because it impossible to check the relevance of all output results – even in the desktop environment, it is not uncommon to obtain several hundreds of search results to a given query. Restricting the calculation of precision and recall to various ranks is also useful in order to investigate the quality of the system at different levels. Usually, in a healthy information retrieval system, as the rank level is increased, recall is also increasing (the denominator remains the same, while the numerator has the possibility to increase), whereas precision is decreasing (because most of the relevant results should be at the very top of the list).

Another important aspect is calculating the total number of available relevant results. For search engines, including desktop ones, an approximation must be used, as the datasets they cope with are too large. In this paper, we consider this amount to be equal to the total number of (unique) relevant results returned by the three systems we investigated. For every query, each system returned 5 results, 15 in total. Thus, the minimum possible total number of relevant results is 0 and the maximum is 15. Similarly, the maximum number of relevant results a system can return is 5 (since it only outputs 5 results), indicating that the recall will not necessarily be 1 when restricting the computation to rank 5. This version of recall is called *relative recall* [3].

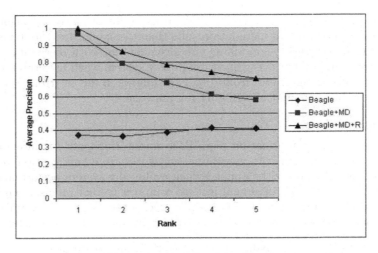

Fig. 6. Average Precision Results

5.3   Results and Discussion

As the main purpose of our experimental analysis was to produce a first estimate
of each system's performance, we averaged the precision values at each rank from
one to five for all 30 queries submitted by our experts. The results we obtained
are depicted in Figure 6. We first notice that the current Beagle Desktop Search
is rather poor, containing more qualitative results towards rank 4 to 5, rather
than at the top of the result list. This is in fact explainable, since Beagle only uses
TFxIDF to rank its results, thus missing any kind of global importance measure
for the desktop resources. On the contrary, our first prototype, consisting of

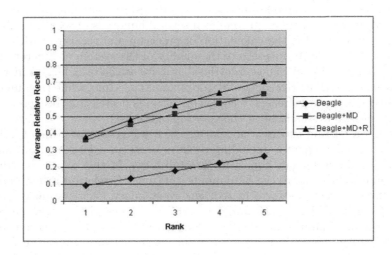

Fig. 7. Average Relative Recall Results

Beagle enhanced with RDF metadata annotations, already performs very well. An important reason for this high improvement is that metadata are mostly generated for those resources with high importance to the user, whereas the other automatically installed files (e.g., help files) are not associated with metadata, and thus ranked lower. When we have metadata describing a desktop item, more text is inherently available to search for, and thus this item is also easier to find. Finally, the precision values are even higher for our second prototype, which adds our desktop ranking algorithm to the metadata-extended version of Beagle. Clearly, ranking pushes our resources of interest more towards the top of the list, yielding even higher desktop search output quality.

In the second part of the evaluation, we drew similar conclusions with respect to the average recall values (depicted in Figure 7): The recall of Beagle is very low, whereas that of our prototypes is almost three times better (owing to the additional information available as metadata, especially comments to the paper included in the emails). The difference between our prototypes is relatively small, which is correct, since recall analyzes the amount of good results returned, and both our systems yield relevant results. We thus conclude that enhancing Beagle with RDF metadata annotations significantly increases its recall (as metadata usually represents additional, highly relevant text associated to each desktop file), whereas adding desktop ranking further contributes with a visible improvement in terms of precision.

6   Conclusions and Future Work

We presented two main contributions that enhance traditional desktop search, focusing on how regular text-based desktop search can be enhanced with semantics / contextual information and ranking exploiting that information. Searching for resources then will not only retrieve explicit results but also items inferred from the users' existing network of resources and contextual information. Maintaining the provenance of information can help the search engine take into account the recommendations from other users and thus provide more retrieved results. The ranking module, by exploiting contextual information, improves retrieval precision and presentation of search results, providing more functionality to desktop search.

There are quite a few interesting additional contexts, that are worth investigating in the future: metadata embedded in multimedia files, the relations between objects embedded within each other (a presentation including pictures, tables, charts, etc.), or chat history. A further interesting question we want to investigate in the future is how to learn contextual authority transfer weights from user feedback on ranked search results. Additionally we are experimenting with extended INEX datasets[3] to evaluate the performance of our system on larger data sets.

---

[3] http://inex.is.informatik.uni-duisburg.de/2005/

Acknowledgements

This work was supported by the Nepomuk project funded by the European Commission under the 6th Framework Programme (IST Contract No. 027705).

References

1. B. Aleman-Meza, C. Halaschek, I. B. Arpinar, and A. Sheth. Context-aware semantic association ranking. In *Semantic Web and Databases Workshop*, 2003.
2. Apple spotlight search. http://developer.apple.com/macosx/tiger/spotlight.html.
3. R. A. Baeza-Yates and B. A. Ribeiro-Neto. *Modern Information Retrieval*. ACM Press / Addison-Wesley, 1999.
4. A. Balmin, V. Hristidis, and Y. Papakonstantinou. Objectrank: Authority-based keyword search in databases. In *VLDB*, Toronto, Sept. 2004.
5. P. A. Chirita, R. Gavriloaie, S. Ghita, W. Nejdl, and R. Paiu. Activity based metadata for semantic desktop search. In *Proc. of the 2nd European Semantic Web Conference*, Heraklion, Greece, May 2005.
6. A. Damian, W. Nejdl, and R. Paiu. Peer-sensitive objectrank: Valuing contextual information in social networks. In *Proc. of the International Conference on Web Information Systems Engineering*, November 2005.
7. L. Ding, T. Finin, A. Joshi, R. Pan, R. S. Cost, Y. Peng, P. Reddivari, V. C. Doshi, and J. Sachs. Swoogle: A search and metadata engine for the semantic web. In *Proc. of the 13th ACM Conf. on Information and Knowledge Management*, 2004.
8. S. Dumais, E. Cutrell, J. Cadiz, G. Jancke, R. Sarin, and D. C. Robbins. Stuff i've seen: A system for personal information retrieval and re-use. In *SIGIR*, 2003.
9. S. Ghita, W. Nejdl, and R. Paiu. Semantically rich recommendations in social networks for sharing, exchanging and ranking semantic context. In *Proc. of the 4th International Semantic Web Conference*, 2005.
10. Gnome beagle desktop search. http://www.gnome.org/projects/beagle/.
11. Google desktop search application. http://desktop.google.com/.
12. Google search engine. http://www.google.com.
13. T. Iofciu, C. Kohlschütter, W. Nejdl, and R. Paiu. Keywords and rdf fragments: Integrating metadata and full-text search in beagle++. In *Proc. of the Semantic Desktop Workshop held at the 4th International Semantic Web Conference*, 2005.
14. Msn desktop search application. http://beta.toolbar.msn.com/.
15. A. Sidiropoulos and Y. Manolopoulos. A new perspective to automatically rank scientific conferences using digital libraries. In *Information Processing and Management 41 (2005) 289qZ12*, 2005.
16. N. Stojanovic, R. Studer, and L. Stojanovic. An approach for the ranking of query results in the semantic web. In *ISWC*, 2003.
17. J. Teevan, C. Alvarado, M. Ackerman, and D. Karger. The perfect search engine is not enough: A study of orienteering behavior in directed search. In *Proc. of CHI*, 2004.

RDFBroker: A Signature-Based High-Performance RDF Store

Michael Sintek and Malte Kiesel

DFKI GmbH, Kaiserslautern, Germany
{sintek, kiesel}@dfki.uni-kl.de
http://www.dfki.uni-kl.de/~{sintek, kiesel}

Abstract. Many approaches for RDF stores exist, most of them using very straight-forward techniques to store triples in or mapping RDF Schema classes to database tables. In this paper we propose an RDF store that uses a natural mapping of RDF resources to database tables that does not rely on RDF Schema, but constructs a schema based on the occurring signatures, where a signature is the set of properties used on a resource. This technique can therefore be used for arbitrary RDF data, i.e., RDF Schema or any other schema/ontology language on top of RDF is not required. Our approach can be used for both in-memory and on-disk relational database-based RDF store implementations.

A first prototype has been implemented and already shows a significant performance increase compared to other freely available (in-memory) RDF stores.

1 Introduction

RDF has been developed to facilitate semantic (meta-)data exchange between actors on the (Semantic) Web [1]. Its primary design rationale was simplicity; therefore, a lowest common denominator of knowledge representation formalisms suited for this task has been chosen: triples, or statements of the form *subject, predicate, object*. But exactly for the same reason, being a lowest common denominator of knowledge representation formalisms, it is suited neither for internal use in general applications[1] nor for efficient handling in established databases which are optimized to handle tables or n-tuples, not ternary statements/binary predicates. Also, naive handling of triples leads to inefficient memory usage since data is implicitly duplicated.[2]

We therefore propose (and implemented a first prototype of) an RDF store that on the one hand allows *efficient import and export of RDF data*, but on the other hand allows *adequate and efficient access from applications* (i.e., from the applications that serve as actors on the Semantic Web, e.g., web services). Unlike

---

[1] Applications' data structures are typically object-oriented and not statement-oriented.

[2] A resource with four properties needs four statements, each having the resource's URI as object.

Y. Sure and J. Domingue (Eds.): ESWC 2006, LNCS 4011, pp. 363–377, 2006.

other similar approaches which restrict themselves to supporting exactly one (application-adequate) schema formulated in a schema language such as RDFS or OWL, we believe that we should stay *schema independent*, for two simple reasons: there is no "one-size-fits-all" schema/ontology language, and because of the distributed and chaotic nature of the Semantic Web, an application might not have full access to the schema, the schema might be incomplete or even non-existent, or the data is, at least at intermediate stages, simply not schema-compliant.

Our approach is based on the notion of *signatures*, where a signature of a resource is the set of properties used on that very resource (at a specific point of time in an application). This approach allows Semantic Web data to be represented as normal (database) relations (with signatures being the database column headings), which are much more application-adequate and, at the same time, much more efficient wrt. space and time than naive approaches that directly store triples. Especially queries that access multiple properties of a resource simultaneously (which, in our experience, form the vast majority of queries) benefit from this approach.

We furthermore *benefit from database technology* that has been optimized for performing queries on normal database tables, i.e., tables that group structurally similar objects, which in our case are resources with the same properties. Standard database technology is not very efficient (esp. wrt. queries) when you simply map triples to one large table (plus some tables for compressing namespaces etc.), since then data usually accessed together is arbitrarily distributed over the database, resulting in many (non-consecutive) parts ("pages") from hard disk being accessed for one query.

Apart from the obvious benefits of our approach when using on-disk databases, the approach also shows considerable *performance improvements* when storing RDF data in memory, esp. for queries accessing multiple properties for a single resource.

A first (in-memory) prototype, the *RDFBroker*, has been realized as part of the OpenDFKI open-source initiative.[3]

In the following, we will first explain the major concepts of RDFBroker (section 2), give some details on the implementation (section 3), show first results of evaluating our approach (section 4), list some related work (section 5), and finally conclude the paper and describe plans for future work (section 6).

2   RDFBroker Concepts

RDFBroker mainly relies on the concept of signatures and signature tables which are organized in a lattice-like structure. On these tables, normal operations known from relational algebra are applied. In the following, we will formally define these basic concepts.

---

[3] http://rdfbroker.opendfki.de/

2.1   Signatures

Definition 1. *The* signature $\Sigma_G(s)$ *of a resource s wrt. an RDF graph*[4] *G is the set of properties that are used on s in G:*

$$\Sigma_G(s) = \{p \mid \exists o : \langle s, p, o \rangle \in G\}$$

When it is understood from the context (or irrelevant) which graph is being referred to, we just write $\Sigma(s)$.

Definition 2. *The* signature set Σ_G *for an RDF graph G is the set of all signatures occurring in it, i.e.,*

$$\Sigma_G = \{\Sigma_G(s) \mid \exists p, o : \langle s, p, o \rangle \in G\}$$

Definition 3. *A* signature $\Sigma(s_1)$ subsumes *a signature* $\Sigma(s_2)$ *iff*

$$\Sigma(s_1) \subseteq \Sigma(s_2)$$

Definition 4. *The* signature subsumption graph $\mathcal{G}_G$ *for an RDF graph G is the directed acyclic graph with vertices* Σ_G *and edges according to the subsumes relation between signatures, i.e.,* $\mathcal{G}_G = (\Sigma_G, \subseteq)$.

The simplified signature subsumption graph $\mathcal{G}'_G$ *for an RDF graph G is the graph that results from the signature subsumption graph by deleting all edges that can be reconstructed from the transitivity and reflexivity of* $\subseteq$.

Note that the (simplified) signature subsumption graph has, in general, more than one "root." Adding $\emptyset$ and $\bigcup_s \Sigma_G(s)$ (for all subjects s in G) turns it into a lattice. We will see later (Sect. 3.1) that adding $\emptyset$ is used for implementing the basic operators on RDF graphs.

Example 1. Let's consider the simple RDF graph depicted in Fig. 1.

The signatures for the four subjects Person, $p1, p2, p3$ that occur in P are:

$$\Sigma_P(\text{Person}) = \{\text{rdf} : \text{type}\}$$
$$\Sigma_P(p1) = \{\text{rdf} : \text{type}, \text{rdfs} : \text{label}, \text{firstName}, \text{lastName}\}$$
$$\Sigma_P(p2) = \{\text{rdf} : \text{type}, \text{firstName}, \text{lastName}, \text{email}, \text{homepage}\}$$
$$\Sigma_P(p3) = \{\text{rdf} : \text{type}, \text{firstName}, \text{lastName}\}$$

We therefore have the following signature set:

$$\Sigma_P = \left\{ \begin{array}{l} \{\text{rdf} : \text{type}\}, \{\text{rdf} : \text{type}, \text{rdfs} : \text{label}, \text{firstName}, \text{lastName}\}, \\ \{\text{rdf} : \text{type}, \text{firstName}, \text{lastName}, \text{email}, \text{homepage}\}, \\ \{\text{rdf} : \text{type}, \text{firstName}, \text{lastName}\} \end{array} \right\}$$

The simplified signature subsumption graph $\mathcal{G}_P$ is shown in Fig. 2.

---

[4] For simplicity, an RDF graph G is a set of subject-predicate-object triples $\langle s, p, o \rangle$. Special aspects of RDF like BNodes, reification, containers, and datatypes are not handled in this paper.

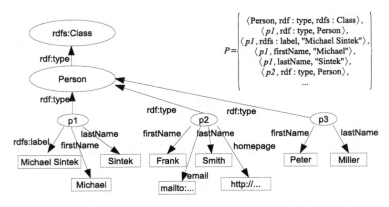

Fig. 1. A Sample RDF Graph: Persons

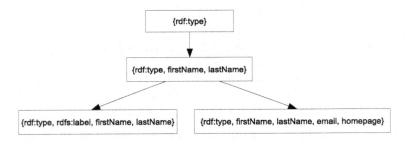

Fig. 2. Sample Simplified Signature Subsumption Graph

2.2   Signature Tables

The basis of our approach is the storage of an RDF graph entirely in tables that correspond to the signatures occurring in the graph. These tables are defined in the following.

Definition 5. *The signature table* $\mathcal{T}_G(\{p_1,\ldots,p_n\})$ *for a signature* $\{p_1,\ldots,p_n\} \in \Sigma_G$ *for an RDF graph* G *is a two dimensional table with headings* (rdf:about, $p_1,\ldots,p_n$) *(where the* p_i *are canonically ordered) and entries as follows: for each subject* s *in* G *with* $\Sigma_G(s) = \{p_1,\ldots,p_n\}$, *there is exactly one row in the table, where the rdf:about column contains* s *and column* p_i *contains the set of values for this property on* s, *i.e.,* $\{v \mid \langle s,p_i,v\rangle \in G\}$.

Definition 6. *The signature table set* $\mathcal{T}_G$ *for an RDF graph* G *is defined as* $\mathcal{T}_G = \{\mathcal{T}_G(s) \mid s \in \Sigma_G\}$.

The signature table set for Ex. 1 ($\mathcal{T}_P$) looks like this:

rdf:about	rdf:type
Person	rdfs:Class

rdf:about	rdf:type	firstName	lastName
p3	Person	"Peter"	"Miller"

rdf:about	rdf:type	rdfs:label	firstName	lastName
$p1$	Person	"Michael Sintek"	"Michael"	"Sintek"

rdf:about	rdf:type	firstName	lastName	email	homepage
$p2$	Person	"Frank"	"Smith"	mailto:...	http://...

2.3 Algebraic Database Operations

Now that we have mapped an RDF graph to a set of tables,[5] we can lay the foundation for queries (and rules) by defining the algebraic operations used in (relational) databases. We define two sets of database operators, those directly operating on RDF graphs and those operating on the resulting tables.

On RDF graphs, we define only two operators, namely the projection $\dot{\pi}$ and a combined projection and selection $[\dot{\pi}\dot{\sigma}]$. On the resulting tables, we allow the usual set of algebraic operators known from relational databases, i.e., $\pi, \sigma, \times, \bowtie$, $\cup, \cap, -, \ldots$.

Definition 7. *The projection $\dot{\pi}$ on an RDF graph G for a property tuple $(p_1, \ldots, p_n)$ is defined as follows:*

$$\dot{\pi}_{(p_1,\ldots,p_n)}(G) = \bigcup \pi_{(p_1,\ldots,p_n)}(t)$$
$$\text{for all } t = \mathcal{T}_G(s) \text{ with } s \in \Sigma_G \text{ and } \{p_1, \ldots, p_n\} \subseteq s$$

where π is the normal database projection operator slightly modified to work on non-normalized tables (since the entries are set-valued).

It would be sufficient to have only the projection operator $\dot{\pi}$ defined on RDF graphs, as we allow the full range of database operators to be applied to the resulting tables. Since all relational algebra expressions can be reformulated such that some projections occur first, we do not need any of the other operators to directly work on RDF graphs.

But this would mean that we have to copy all tuples from signature tables as the first step, which would not be very wise for efficiency reasons. Therefore, we also define a combined selection and projection operator, $[\dot{\pi}\dot{\sigma}]$.[6]

Definition 8. *The projection-selection $[\dot{\pi}\dot{\sigma}]$ on an RDF graph G for a property tuple $p = (p_1, \ldots, p_n)$ and a condition C is defined as follows:*

$$[\dot{\pi}\dot{\sigma}]_p^C(G) = \pi_p \bigcup (\sigma_C \circ \pi_{p'})(t)$$
$$\text{for all } t = \mathcal{T}_G(s) \text{ with } s \in \Sigma_G \text{ and } p' \subseteq s$$
$$\text{and } p' = \{p_1, \ldots, p_n\} \cup \text{properties}(C)$$

where π and σ are the normal database selection operators (modified as π above), and properties(C) *is the set of properties that occur in C.*

---

[5] or, in the case of multiple RDF graphs, to several sets of tables, allowing access to named graphs which are nicely supported by our approach

[6] Note that we do not define an operator $\dot{\sigma}$ on RDF graphs since signature tables that would naturally be involved in a single selection are of varying arity.

The essential parts of these two definitions are the subsumption restrictions ($\{p_1, \ldots, p_n\} \subseteq s$ and $p' \subseteq s$, resp.), i.e., in both cases we only consider the signature tables with signatures that are subsumed by the properties occurring in the operators.

2.4 RDF Schema Semantics

Although RDFBroker is designed to work efficiently on RDF graphs without RDFS (or any other schema), we believe that is very important to provide an efficient implementation of the RDFS semantics as RDFS is used as ontology language in most applications dealing with mass data and therefore being a target for our system.

In the following, we define the (simplified)[7] RDFS semantics G^{RDFS} of an RDF graph mainly with the help of the (conjointly computed) transitive closures of rdfs:subClassOf and rdfs:subPropertyOf, the class propagation for rdf:type, and the value propagation for rdfs:subPropertyOf,[8] which follows directly from the RDF/S model theory [2]. Note that the naive approach to compute the transitive closures and propagations separately (or in any fixed order) is not correct (e.g., this would not catch the case where one defines a subproperty of rdfs:subClassOf (or even rdfs:subPropertyOf itself)).

Definition 9. *The (simplified) RDFS immediate consequence operator[9] T_{RDFS} for an RDF graph G is defined as follows:*[10]

$$
\begin{aligned}
T_{\mathrm{RDFS}}(G) = G \cup{} & \{\langle p, \mathrm{sPO}, q\rangle \mid \{\langle p, \mathrm{sPO}, r\rangle, \langle r, \mathrm{sPO}, q\rangle\} \subseteq G\} \\
\cup{} & \{\langle p, \mathrm{sCO}, q\rangle \mid \{\langle p, \mathrm{sCO}, r\rangle, \langle r, \mathrm{sCO}, q\rangle\} \subseteq G\} \\
\cup{} & \{\langle s, \mathrm{type}, c\rangle \mid \{\langle c', \mathrm{sCO}, c\rangle, \langle s, \mathrm{type}, c'\rangle\} \subseteq G\} \\
\cup{} & \{\langle s, p, o\rangle \quad \mid \{\langle p', \mathrm{sPO}, p\rangle, \langle s, p', o\rangle\} \subseteq G\}
\end{aligned}
$$

Theorem 1. *The (simplified) RDF Schema semantics of an RDF graph G is the fixpoint of T_{RDFS}:*

$$
G^{\mathrm{RDFS}} = \bigcup_{n \in \mathbb{N}_0} T_{\mathrm{RDFS}}^n(G \cup AP)
$$

where AP are the axiomatic triples $\langle \mathit{rdf{:}type}, \mathit{rdfs{:}domain}, \mathit{rdfs{:}Resource}\rangle, \ldots$ as defined in the RDF/S model theory.

We will show in Sect. 3.4 that T_{RDFS} can be directly used to implement G^{RDFS}.

---

[7] We explicitly ignore here some details of the RDFS semantics, namely rdfs:domain and rdfs:range, as their correct handling is sometimes counterintuitive when coming from a database or logic programming perspective.

[8] $\{\langle p, \mathrm{rdfs{:}subPropertyOf}, q\rangle, \langle s, p, o\rangle\} \subseteq G^{\mathrm{RDFS}} \to \langle s, q, o\rangle \in G^{\mathrm{RDFS}}$

[9] which is similar to the normal immediate consequence operator T_P

[10] with sPO = rdfs:subProperyOf, sCO = rdfs:subClassOf, and type = rdf:type

2.5 Sample Queries

In the following, we give some sample queries for the RDF graph P from Exa. 1.

Example 2. 'Return first name and last name for all persons.'

$$r = [\dot{\pi}\dot{\sigma}]^{\text{rdf:type=Person}}_{(\text{firstName,lastName})}(P)$$

Example 3. 'Find first name, email address, and homepage for the person with last name "Smith"':

$$r = [\dot{\pi}\dot{\sigma}]^{\text{rdf:type=Person}\wedge\text{lastName="Smith"}}_{(\text{firstName,email,homepage})}(P)$$

The current implementation does not support complex selection conditions, we therefore have to evaluate the query in several steps:[11]

$$r = \pi_{(\bar{1},\bar{3},\bar{4})}(\sigma_{\bar{2}=\text{"Smith"}}([\dot{\pi}\dot{\sigma}]^{\text{rdf:type=Person}}_{(\text{firstName,lastName,email,homepage})}(P)))$$

3 Implementation

The in-memory variant of RDFBroker is currently being implemented with JDK 1.5. It uses Sesame's RIO parser, which could easily be replaced by any streaming parser generating "add statement" events.

Most of the concepts of Sect. 2 have directly corresponding implementations plus appropriate index structures (e.g., there is an index for each column in a signature table, currently realized as a hash table).

Our approach benefits heavily from well-known database optimization techniques. E.g., queries are reformulated such that selections and joins on multiple columns access small tables and columns which hold many different values (and are therefore discriminating) first, thus reducing the size of intermediate results as fast as possible.

In the following, we describe some aspects of the implementation in detail (some of which have not yet been realized in our first prototype, like updates and the RDFS semantics).

3.1 The Operators $\dot{\pi}$ and $[\dot{\pi}\dot{\sigma}]$

The efficient implementation of $\dot{\pi}$ and $[\dot{\pi}\dot{\sigma}]$, which form the basis of all queries, is obviously vital for our RDF store. The implementation of these operators requires the lookup of the signature tables $\mathcal{T}_G(s)$ for all signatures s where the properties occurring in the operator subsume s, as defined in Def. 7 and Def. 8.

The signature table lookup is performed by first looking up the matching signatures in the simplified signature subsumption graph and then retrieving the associated signature tables.

The signature lookup for properties $p = \{p_1, \ldots, p_n\}$ is performed by the following (informally described) algorithm, which is also exempflified in Fig. 3:

---

[11] Column numbers for relational operators are marked with a bar on top: $\bar{1}, \bar{2}, \bar{3}, \ldots$.

(a) add $\emptyset$ as an artificial root to the simplified signature subsumption graph $\mathcal{G}'_G$ (making it a "meet-semilattice"[12])

(b) starting at $\emptyset$, find all minimal signatures s which are subsumed by p, i.e., for which $p \subseteq s$ holds

(c) add all signatures which are subsumed by these minimal signatures (simply by collecting all signatures reachable from the minimal ones using a depth-first walk)

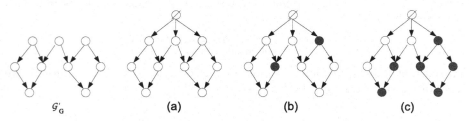

$\mathcal{G}'_G$ **(a)**   **(b)**   **(c)**

Fig. 3. Algorithm: Lookup of Signatures

3.2 Merging of Signature Tables

An important source for optimization are the signature tables and their organization in the subsumption graph. First tests with the system revealed that sometimes many small tables are generated which are responsible for overhead, which we wish to avoid. The obvious solution for this is pruning the subsumption tree by merging small adjacent signatures tables (i.e., which share many properties) or merging small tables with subsumed big ones. A sketch for a greedy algorithm (which tries to minimize the number of NULL values to be added and the number of merge operations) is as follows:

(a) pick the smallest signature table and mark it to be merged

(b) pick the smallest signature table adjacent to a signature table marked to be merged (and sharing substantially many properties) and mark it also

(c) repeat (b) until the size of all marked signature tables exceeds some threshold; if the threshold cannot be exceeded, mark the directly subsumed table with the smallest signature to be merged

(d) merge all marked signature tables

(e) repeat (a) – (d) until no single signature table exists that is smaller than some threshold

Fig. 4 shows the result of applying this algorithm on some sample signature subsumption graph.

The resulting signature subsumption graphs are often very similar to user defined schemas, which is what we expect since co-occurrence of properties is the basis for (manually) defining classes in an schema/ontology. We therefore expect our approach to perform similar to mapping an RDF Schema to an (object-) relational database directly.

---

[12] i.e., an partially ordered set where for any two elements there exists an infimum (greatest lower bound) but not necessarily a supremum in the set

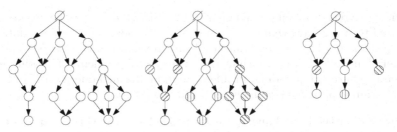

Fig. 4. Algorithm: Merging of Signatures

3.3   Updates

Updates (i.e., inserts, deletes, and value updates) can easily be realized on top of our RDF store, but some operations come with performance penalties when they change the signature of a subject resource, which then has to migrate from one signature table to another. To improve this, special methods will be used to allow mass updates to be handled efficiently. In the case of mass inserts, e.g., either a whole RDF graph is added all at once, thus allowing first the property values per subject to be collected (as it is done for parsing already), or applications use methods like `add(Resource, Map<URI,Value>)` to explicitly add many property values for one subject at once.

Since the merging of signature tables results in allowing NULL values in merged tables, this reduces the likelihood that database rows have to migrate from one table to another.

3.4   RDF Schema

In general, two main approaches exist to implement the RDFS semantics: compute the triples resulting from the RDFS semantics in advance and materialize them, or compute them on demand. Since our main goal currently is high-performance for queries, we decided to take the first approach.

Materializing the RDF Schema semantics G^{RDFS} of an RDF graph G can directly be based on Theorem 1, analogously to the realization of logic programming with the well-known immediate consequence operator T_P (for a deductive database / logic program P) [3]. For this, the semi-naive bottom-up evaluation is used, i.e., the T_{RDFS} operator is not evaluated on the full data set from all previous rounds in the fixpoint computation, but restricted in the sense that certain parts of T_{RDFS} are checked only against the data newly produced in the previous round. Furthermore, the materialization of the propagation for rdf:type is not necessary and can be handled by query rewriting, which will drastically reduce the number of additionally created data.

3.5   Natural Data Handling and Querying

One of our promises is that our RDF store is application-adequate. Therefore, we allow queries and data handling using traditional programming languages (in our prototype implementation, Java) in a very natural way.

Queries. Higher-level query languages like SPARQL have the disadvantage compared to using Java that they do not nicely cooperate with Java data: e.g., query parameters have to be translated into textual representations matching the query language syntax, which involves the typical problems of quoting special characters, character encoding, problems with malformed queries at runtime, no support from typical development environments,[13] etc.

Example 4. For the Exa. 3 query, the Java code looks like this (C_equals creates an equality selection condition and projection/selection indices are 0-based):

```
p.projectAndSelect(
        p.properties(FIRSTNAME, LASTNAME, EMAIL, HOMEPAGE),
        p.C_equals(p.RDF_TYPE, PERSON))
    .select(p.C_equals(1, p.literal("Smith")))
    .project(0,2,3);
```

Comparing Java-based queries (using algebraic operators) with standard declarative query languages is difficult. Both approaches have benefits and drawbacks: Java-based queries allow simple debugging since intermediate results are available. Manual optimization is easily possible without having to know much about the query engine's internals. On the other hand, declarative query languages are easier to read (since inherently they describe only the *goal* of the query in a simpler syntax), and automatic optimization can be done to some degree.

Data Handling. Normal RDF store APIs provide only triple-based methods for manipulating the RDF data which is uncomfortable for most applications as the typical view on an application's data is an object-oriented view. With additional tools such as RDF2Java [4] or RDFReactor [5] that introduce an abstraction layer this problem can be solved from the programmer's point of view. However, these approaches still map to triples internally. Using RDFBroker and its object/resource-centric data representation, it is possible to provide a natural data interface without mapping between data representations.

4   Evaluation

For our first in-memory prototype, we evaluated the (RDFBroker-specific) distribution of signature tables and load times, memory consumption, and query execution times by comparing them to the behavior of other freely available RDF stores, using several queries on a large database and measuring database load times on three different databases.

We used RDF data from TAP[14] which comes with RDF files of sizes up to about 300 MB. In particular, for evaluating load times

---

[13] Standard IDEs feature autocompletion which helps a lot in coding but does not work with queries which are just strings to the IDE.

[14] http://sp11.stanford.edu/

tuples per table	tuples	tables
1–10	8941	4137
11–100	15375	506
101–1000	13730	62
1001–10000	0	0
10001–100000	117288	2
100001–1000000	130939	1

Fig. 5. Signature Table Distribution

	1.7MB DB		24MB DB		298MB DB	
	load time	memory	load time	memory	load time	memory
RDFBroker	500ms	66MB	7,500ms	102MB	102,000ms	945MB
Jena	800ms	36MB	11,000ms	70MB	151,000ms	822MB
Sesame	300ms	28MB	4,500ms	83MB	74,000ms	408MB

Fig. 6. Load Times and Memory Consumption of RDFBroker, Sesame, and Jena

we used `swirl-SiteArchitectureEmporis.rdf` (1.7MB and 17,086 triples), `swirl-SitePlacesWorldAirportCodes.rdf` (24MB and 245,578 triples), and `swirl-SiteMoviesIMDB.rdf` (298MB and 3,587,064 triples). For testing query performance, we used `swirl-SiteMoviesIMDB.rdf` exclusively. The RDF store implementations we compared are Sesame [6], Jena [7], and of course RDFBroker.[15] The evaluation environment was an Athlon 64 3000+ (3530 bogomips) with 2GB RAM running Linux 2.6.12.3 i686 and Sun Java 1.5.0-2. The evaluation software can be found on the RDFBroker project website.

Signature Table Distribution. With `swirl-SiteMoviesIMDB.rdf` (298MB, 3,587,064 triples, 286,273 resources in subject position, 4,708 signature tables), we got the distribution of signature tables shown in Fig. 5, i.e., there are 4,137 tables of size 1–10 tuples that hold a total of 8941 tuples, ..., and there is exactly one table that holds 130,939 tuples. This is exactly what we expect for mass data: most of the data is in very few tables (in this case, three tables hold 87% of all tuples).

Load Times and memory consumption for the three RDF files are shown in Fig. 6. Since RDFBroker currently uses Sesame's "Rio" parser, its load times are similar to Sesame's performance. The creation of signature tables and exhaustive indices explains the higher values.

Queries. We measured the execution times and memory consumption (see Fig. 7) for several queries, ranging from simple "retrieval" of property values over path expressions to joins that are not representable as path expressions. In Appendix A, we list the SeRQL queries for evaluating Sesame for completeness.

---

[15] For all implementations we enabled RDF validation on load and disabled inferencing.

	Query 1		Query 2		Query 3		Query 4	
	time	memory	time	memory	time	memory	time	memory
RDFBroker	70ms	4MB	1200ms	63MB	260ms	4MB	160ms	10MB
Jena	4300ms	82MB	8700ms	26MB	70ms	3MB	-	-
Sesame	1400ms	24MB	2200ms	46MB	50ms	2MB	-	-

Fig. 7. Query Times and Memory Consumption of RDFBroker, Sesame, and Jena

Query 1: 'return some interesting properties of all movies': This operates heavily on the queried instances' properties. As to be expected, RDFBroker performs very fine in this case since the signature tables nicely match the query's structure.

$$[\dot{\pi}\dot{\sigma}]^{\text{rdf:type=imdb:Movie}}_{\text{(rdf:about,rdfs:label,imdb:PropertyCountry,PropertySound\_Mix...)}}$$

Query 2: 'find names for persons casted in movies': This is a join query that in many high-level RDF query languages is expressed as a path expression. Since this is a very common query, most systems come up with optimized algorithms for it. Still, RDFBroker's performance was the best.

$$[\dot{\pi}\dot{\sigma}]^{\text{rdf:type=imdb:Movie}}_{\text{(rdf:about,rdfs:label,imdb:creditedCast)}} \bowtie_{\bar{3}=\bar{1}} [\dot{\pi}\dot{\sigma}]^{\text{rdf:type=imdb:Person}}_{\text{(rdf:about,rdfs:label)}}$$

Query 3: 'find persons playing in movies three cast hops separated from Kevin Bacon': This query is related to the Bacon Number.[16] Since it is a path expression using only one property, RDFBroker is not optimized for this kind of query, and has to walk over thousands of tables multiple times.[17]

Query 4: 'find movies with same title and return some useful properties on them, like release year, cast, genre, ...':

$$[\dot{\pi}\dot{\sigma}]^{\text{rdf:type=imdb:Movie}}_{\text{(rdf:about,rdfs:label,imdb:creditedCast,...)}} \bowtie_{\bar{2}=\bar{2},\bar{1}\neq\bar{1}} [\dot{\pi}\dot{\sigma}]^{\text{rdf:type=imdb:Movie}}_{\text{(rdf:about,rdfs:label,...)}}$$

RDFBroker evaluated this query in less than 200ms, while Sesame and Jena were not able to finish it (we stopped after 30 minutes). Probably joins that are not path expressions are not handled "properly" in the sense that they are evaluated by first computing the complete cartesian product.

Conclusion. For standard queries, the RDFBroker approach performs very well. The prototype's memory consumption is higher than that of other RDF stores. Both characteristics are most likely due to the fact that currently all database columns get indexed which leads to high performance but counteracts the potential benefit of small memory footprint that is inherent of the approach. We will address this in future RDFBroker versions, as well as implementing table merging to reduce the overhead of walking over thousands of tables for queries accessing only few properties.

---

[16] http://en.wikipedia.org/wiki/Bacon_number

[17] We expect this kind of query to perform much better in RDFBroker when we use table merging.

5   Related Work

Since most RDF frameworks such as Sesame [6] or Jena [7] allow using RDBMSs as storage backends, quite a lot of previous work on this area is available. An overview of different RDF frameworks can be found in [8]; an overview of different approaches of mapping RDF to standard DBs can be found in [9] and [10].

There are several RDF frameworks that rely on native storage such as YARS [11], Redland [12], or BRAHMS [13]. Often, these implementations perform superior with special types of queries. BRAHMS, for example, is very fast when searching semantic associations—semantic association paths leading from one resource to another resource.

In [10], several RDBMS mapping characteristics are presented along with a generic performance comparison of the approaches described. The approaches outlined use one or more tables with at most three columns, one table representing either triples, properties, or RDFS class instances. The drawback of this compared to our approach is that properties of one resource get scattered over multiple tables and/or rows—an advantage is that no support for sets in table cells is needed.

The definition of the mapping characteristics in the same paper are a bit too narrow and cannot be applied to our approach easily—while, for example, no schema is needed for our approach, it is not *schema-oblivious* in terms of the cited paper since we do not use only one table for storing triples.

In [14], an approach to derive table layout from the data or using machine learning-based query analysis approaches is described. This leads to high initial costs and requires a large amount of data for initial training. Our approach is much more lightweight especially concerning initial setup. However, we do not support query analysis at all.

For performance comparison and test data generation several tools have been described, mostly using using a Zipfian distribution when generating class instances. See [10] and Store-Gen [14] for a further description of synthetic data generators.

6   Conclusions and Future Work

In this paper, we introduced RDFBroker, an RDF store using signatures as the basis for storing arbitrary RDF data. Since signatures and their organization in a lattice-like structure approximate user-defined schemas/ontologies (and thus also make RDF data accessible from applications in a more natural way), RDFBroker performs similar to hand-coded (object-) relational databases. Comparison of our first prototype with other RDF stores showed that even for the in-memory case queries can be evaluated more efficiently than with standard techniques using triples as the basis for storage organization.

Our approach can handle, on standard hardware, already fairly large knowledge bases (RDF files with several hundred MBs) in main memory. For mass data, we will make use of on-disk databases (which requires support of multiple-valued attributes), which lets us expect even higher differences in performance compared to existing RDF stores which store RDF data in on-disk databases.

We also intend to support query and esp. rule language standards like SPARQL and the result of the W3C Rule Interchange Format Working Group that has just been founded, where we will profit from well-investigated deductive database technologies (like magic set transformation). We furthermore plan to provide a natural programming API for manipulation of the RDF data stored in RDFBroker, where the interface classes can be build as known from our RDF2Java [4] tool. Our future plans also include using a P2P network (or grid) to improve performance by using in-memory (instead of on-disk) stores in peers and using the signature subsumption graph for distributing the data, routing queries, and developing appropriate peer leave/join algorithms.

Acknowledgments. This work has been supported in part by the SmartWeb project, which is funded by the German Ministry of Education and Research under grant 01 IMD01 A, and by the NEWS project, which is funded by the IST Programme of the European Union under grant FP6-001906.

References

1. Berners-Lee, T., Hendler, J., Lassila, O.: The semantic web. Scientific American (2001) 34–43
2. Hayes, P.: RDF semantics (2004) W3C Recommendation. http://www.w3.org/TR/rdf-mt/.
3. Lloyd, J.W.: Foundations of logic programming. Springer-Verlag New York, Inc., New York, NY, USA (1984)
4. Sintek, M., Schwarz, S., Kiesel, M.: RDF2Java (2005) http://rdf2java.opendfki.de/.
5. Völkel, M., Sure, Y.: RDFReactor - from ontologies to programmatic data access. Poster and Demo at ISWC2005 (2005)
6. Broekstra, J., Kampman, A., van Harmelen, F.: Sesame: An architecture for storing and querying rdf data and schema information. In Fensel, D., Hendler, J.A., Lieberman, H., Wahlster, W., eds.: Spinning the Semantic Web, MIT Press (2003) 197–222
7. Wilkinson, K., Sayers, C., Kuno, H.A., Reynolds, D.: Efficient RDF storage and retrieval in Jena2. In Cruz, I.F., Kashyap, V., Decker, S., Eckstein, R., eds.: SWDB. (2003) 131–150
8. SWAD: SWAD-europe deliverable 10.1: Scalability and storage: Survey of free software / open source RDF storage systems (2002) http://www.w3.org/2001/sw/Europe/reports/rdf_scalable_storage_report/.
9. SWAD: SWAD-europe deliverable 10.2: Mapping semantic web data with RDBMSes (2003) http://www.w3.org/2001/sw/Europe/reports/scalable_rdbms_mapping_report.
10. Theoharis, Y., Christophides, V., Karvounarakis, G.: Benchmarking database representations of RDF/S stores. In Gil, Y., Motta, E., Benjamins, V.R., Musen, M.A., eds.: International Semantic Web Conference. Volume 3729 of Lecture Notes in Computer Science., Springer (2005) 685–701

11. Harth, A., Decker, S.: Optimized index structures for querying RDF from the web. In: 3rd Latin American Web Congress, Buenos Aires - Argentina, Oct. 31 - Nov. 2 2005. (2005)
12. Beckett, D.: The design and implementation of the redland RDF application framework. Computer Networks **39**(5) (2002) 577–588
13. Janik, M., Kochut, K.: BRAHMS: A workbench RDF store and high performance memory system for semantic association discovery. In: 4th International Semantic Web Conference. (2005)
14. Ding, L., Wilkinson, K., Sayers, C., Kuno, H.A.: Application-specific schema design for storing large RDF datasets. In Volz, R., Decker, S., Cruz, I.F., eds.: PSSS. Volume 89 of CEUR Workshop Proceedings., CEUR-WS.org (2003)

Appendix A. SeRQL Queries Used in the Evaluation

Query 1: 'return some interesting properties of all movies'

```
SELECT MovieLabel, Year, Runtime, Color, Language, Country, Sound
   FROM {MovieURI} rdf:type {imdb:Movie}; rdfs:label {MovieLabel};
                  imdb:PropertyCountry {Country}; ...
   USING NAMESPACE imdb = <http://data.imdb.com/data/>
```

Query 2: 'find names for persons casted in movies'

```
SELECT Movie, Title, Cast, PersonName
   FROM {Movie} rdf:type {imdb:Movie}; rdfs:label {Title};
               imdb:creditedCast {Cast} rdfs:label {PersonName}
   USING NAMESPACE imdb = <http://data.imdb.com/data/>
```

Query 3: 'find persons playing in movies three cast hops separated from Kevin Bacon'

```
SELECT DISTINCT PersonName
  FROM {StartPerson} imdb:PropertyActor_filmography {Movie1}
    imdb:creditedCast {Cast1} imdb:PropertyActor_filmography {Movie2}
      imdb:creditedCast {Cast2} imdb:PropertyActor_filmography {Movie3}
        imdb:creditedCast {Cast3} rdfs:label {PersonName}
  WHERE StartPerson = imdb:PersonKevin_Bacon_8_July_1958
  USING NAMESPACE imdb = <http://data.imdb.com/data/>
```

Towards Distributed Information Retrieval in the Semantic Web: Query Reformulation Using the oMAP Framework*

Umberto Straccia[1] and Raphaël Troncy[2]

[1] ISTI-CNR, Via G. Moruzzi 1, 56124 Pisa, Italy
straccia@isti.cnr.it
[2] CWI Amsterdam, P.O. Box 94079, 1090 GB Amsterdam, The Netherlands
raphael.troncy@cwi.nl

Abstract. This paper introduces a general methodology for performing distributed search in the Semantic Web. We propose to define this task as a three steps process, namely *resource selection, query reformulation/ontology alignment* and *rank aggregation/data fusion*. For the second problem, we have implemented *oMAP*, a formal framework for automatically aligning OWL ontologies. In oMAP, different components are combined for finding suitable mapping candidates (together with their weights), and the set of rules with maximum matching probability is selected. Among these components, traditional terminological-based classifiers, machine learning-based classifiers and a new classifier using the structure and the semantics of the OWL ontologies are proposed. oMAP has been evaluated on international test sets.

1 Introduction

Information Retrieval (IR) studies the problem of finding a (ranked) set of documents that are relevant for a specific information need of a user. One of the premises of the Semantic Web is that it provides the means to use metadata that help determining which documents are relevant. In a Semantic Web-based version of IR, not only the sheer amount of data, but also the differences among the local metadata vocabularies, call for a distributed approach. In this paper, we propose a three-step framework for distributed, Semantic Web-enabled Information Retrieval. The first step is *resource selection*, because on the Semantic Web it is unlikely that for any given query the full Web has to be queried. The second step, *query reformulation and ontology alignment* deals with the differences in the vocabularies used by the user and the selected information resources. The third and last step, *aggregation and data fusion* integrates the ranked results from the individual resources into a single ranked result list. In this paper, we focus on the second step for which we describe an efficient model that is compared with other approaches using the independent OAEI[1] benchmarks.

---

* This work was carried out during the tenure of an ERCIM fellowship.
[1] http://oaei.inrialpes.fr.

Y. Sure and J. Domingue (Eds.): ESWC 2006, LNCS 4011, pp. 378–392, 2006.
© Springer-Verlag Berlin Heidelberg 2006

The paper is organized as follows. We briefly present in the next section our main problem: distributed search over the Semantic Web. Then, we introduce in Section 3 *oMAP*, a framework whose goal is to automatically align all the entities defined in two OWL ontologies. These mappings are then used for the query reformulation process. The mappings are obtained by combining the prediction of different classifiers. We describe the set of classifiers used: terminological, machine learning-based and we present a new one, based on the structure and the semantics of the OWL axioms. We have evaluated oMAP on an independent test set provided by an international ontology alignment contest and we show our results with respect to the other competitors in Section 4. Finally, we provide some related work and give our conclusions and future work in Section 5.

2   Motivating Problem

In Information Retrieval the task of Distributed IR (DIR) [3] is the task, given an information need, of accessing (and retrieving from) in an effective way distributed information resources [2]. DIR has been proposed to overcome the difficulties of centralized approaches. For instance, information resources become more and more "proprietary" and not crawl-able. That is, more and more the content information resources (e.g. Web repositories, Digital Libraries) cannot be crawled anymore and, thus, indexed by a centralized Web retrieval engine. Documents may be accessed by issuing a specific query to the information resource only and remain mostly hidden to Web search engines. DIR is an effective solution to this problem as it aims at, given an information request, to discover the relevant information resources and to query them directly. So, in DIR we do not require to crawl and index documents, but just to select relevant resources and submitting appropriately a query to them. In the following, we show how DIR can be reformulated in the context of the Semantic Web.

2.1   Towards Distributed Search in the Semantic Web

In order to effectively cope with very large amounts of knowledge, the task of distributed search in the Semantic Web may be defined in terms of three different sub-tasks. Let us assume that an agent A has to satisfy an information need Q_A expressed in a query language $\mathcal{Q}_A$, whose basic terms belong to an ontology O_A, defined using the ontology language $\mathcal{O}_A$. Let us assume also that there are a large number of ontology-based Web resources $\mathscr{S} = \{\mathcal{S}_1, \ldots, \mathcal{S}_n\}$ accessible to A, where each Web resource $\mathcal{S}_i$ provides access to its Web pages by having its own ontology O_i, ontology language $\mathcal{O}_i$ and query language $\mathcal{Q}_i$ (see Figure 1).

Then, the agent should perform the following three steps to satisfy its information need:

1. **Resource selection:** The agent has to *select* a subset of some *relevant* resources $\mathscr{S}' \subseteq \mathscr{S}$, since it is not reasonable to assume that it will access and query all the resources;

---

[2] The techniques of DIR are also applied in so-called *Metasearch engines* [27]

Query Q

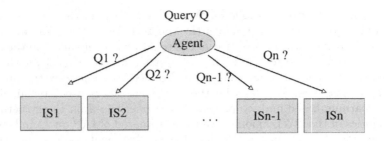

Fig. 1. Distributed Information Retrieval

2. **Query reformulation:** For every selected resource $\mathcal{S}_i \in \mathscr{S}'$ the agent has to *re-formulate* its information need Q_A into the query language $\mathcal{L}_i$ provided by the resource;
3. **Data fusion and rank aggregation:** The results from the selected resources have to finally be merged together.

That is, an agent must know *where* to search, *how* to query, and *how* to combine the information and ranked lists provided back from querying different and heterogeneous resources. As information resources continue to proliferate, these problems become major obstacles to information access. This is an ineffective manual task for which accurate automated tools are desired.

As noted previously, the problem of DIR has already been addressed in the context of textual IR. Our approach to DIR in the Semantic Web is incremental and tries to follow the way IR addressed the issue. The tasks of automated resource selection and the one of query reformulation seem to be the more problematic ones, while the data fusion and rank aggregation issue may be solved apparently by applying directly existing techniques [19]. Therefore, the latter will not be discussed further in this paper.

In IR, both the automated resource selection and the query-reformulation tasks are fully automatic and do not require human intervention. In order to make resource selection effective and automatic, in DIR, an agent has to compute an approximation of the content of each information resource. Based on this approximation, the agent is then able to select resources and perform query reformulation effectively. The approximation is computed by relying on the so-called *query-based resource sampling methodology* (see, e.g. [4]). This method consists of computing automatically an approximation of the content of a resource, relying on a sampling technique. Roughly, it consists of a series of quasi-random queries submitted to the information resource. In the context of textual IR, it has been shown that the retrieval of a few documents is a sufficient representation of the content of information resource [4]. In automated resource selection, this approximation is then used to decide whether a resource may contain relevant information with respect to the agents' information need [3]. For ontology-based information resources such an approximation may contain the ontology the information resource relies on and some annotated documents (called instances) retrieved using quasi-random queries.

For the query reformation task, the agent relies on so-called transformation rules, which dictates how to translate concepts and terms of the agent's vocabulary into the vocabulary of the information resource. Once the set of rules is given, the query transformation is relatively easy. What is difficult is to learn these rules automatically. In the context of the Semantic Web, these rules are essentially rules which map an entity (concept or property) in the agent's ontology into one or several entities of the information resource's ontology. Therefore, the major difficulty is in learning these *ontology mappings* automatically. Again, to do this, we may rely on the approximation computed so far through query-based sampling. The ontology of the agent, the ontology of the information resource and some annotated documents will allow the agent to learn these mappings automatically. This task is called *Ontology Alignment* in the Semantic Web. Furthermore, from a DIR perspective, these mappings are often established only to a degree of probability to which the mapping is true. [16] also shows that this degree cannot be neglected during the DIR process without loosing in retrieval effectiveness.

In summary, while numerous works deal with one of the three sub-tasks described above for distributed textual IR, to the best of our knowledge, very few works address the issue of distributed search in the context of the Semantic Web, where documents are well-structured and annotated semantically using terms belonging to a (formal) ontology. In this paper we tackle the second task, namely the problem of query reformulation in general and automatically learning mapping rules in particular, in the context of OWL-annotated resources. The first task (resource selection) will be addressed in future work.

2.2   Query Reformulation

In the context of database schema matching, [16] proposes to rely on *Probabilistic Datalog* (pDatalog for short) [12] to express mapping rules and use it for query reformulation. We show that we can use it in our context as well. pDatalog, for which an effective implementation exists, is an extension to Datalog, a variant of predicate logic based on function-free Horn clauses. Queries and mapping rules are probabilistic rules (see examples below). The mapping rules we consider are of the form

$$\alpha_{i,j}\ T_j(x) \leftarrow S_i(x)$$

stating that the source entity S_i may be aligned to the target entity T_j with the probability $\alpha_{j,i}$. For instance, by relying on Figure 2, we may establish the mappings:

$$
\begin{aligned}
&0.78\ \texttt{Creator}(d,x) \leftarrow \texttt{Author}(d,x) \\
&0.22\ \texttt{Creator}(d,x) \leftarrow \texttt{Editor}(d,x) \\
&0.90\ \texttt{Journal}(y) \quad\ \leftarrow \texttt{Periodical}(y)\ .
\end{aligned}
\tag{1}
$$

The first rule establishes that the probability that the creator x of document d is the also the author of d is 78%, while in the remaining 22% the creator is the editor. The third rule is similar. So, for instance, for the agent's ontology ("Ontology2") and the resource's ontology ("Ontology1"), if the agent's information need is "find a periodical paper whose author is Straccia and the document is about IR", then this request can be represented by the agent by means of the pDatalog rule [3]

1.00 $\mathrm{Query}(d) \leftarrow \mathrm{Periodical}(d), \mathrm{Author}(d, \text{``Straccia''}), \mathrm{KeyWordSearch}(d, \text{``IR''})$

The reformulation of the query with respect to the information resource based on "Ontology1", using the mapping rules, gives us the query:

0.702 $\mathrm{Query}(d) \leftarrow \mathrm{Journal}(d), \mathrm{Creator}(d, \text{``Straccia''}), \mathrm{KeyWordSearch}(d, \text{``IR''})$

(where $0.702 = 0.78 \cdot 0.9$), i.e. find all journal papers created by Straccia and about IR. This is exactly the query to be submitted to the information resource based on "Ontology1". Once the query is submitted to the information resource, for instance using PIRE [16], the degree of relevance of a retrieved document is multiplied with the degree of the corresponding rule. The documents are ranked then according to this final score. Note that without the weight of the rules, we would erroneously give the same preference to documents authored or edited by Straccia, i.e. the weights give more importance to documents matching "author" than those matching "editor" As the example above shows and as already stated previously, once the weighted mappings are established the query reformulation is rather easy. In the following, we will describe how to establish the mappings automatically.

3   oMAP: An Implemented Framework for Automatically Aligning OWL Ontologies

oMAP [23] is a framework whose goal is to automatically align two OWL ontologies, finding the best mappings (together with their weights) between the entities defined in these ontologies. Our approach is inspired by the data exchange problem [11] and borrows from others, like GLUE [6], the idea of using several specialized components for finding the best set of mappings.

We draw in section 3.1 the general picture of our approach. Then, we detail several classifiers used to predict the *weight* of a possible mapping between two entities. These classifiers are terminological (section 3.2) or machine learning-based (section 3.3). Finally, we propose a classifier working on the structure and the formal semantics of the OWL constructs, thus using the meaning of the entities defined in the ontology (section 3.4).

3.1   Overall Strategy

Our goal is to automatically determine "similarity" relationships between classes and properties of two ontologies. For instance, given the ontologies in Figure 2, we would like to determine that an instance of the class Conference is likely an instance of the class Congress, that the property creator should subsume the property author, or that the class Journal is disjoint from the class Directions.

---

[3] The predicate $\mathrm{KeyWordSearch}(d, x)$ performs a key word search of key x in document d and gives back the probability that document d is about x.

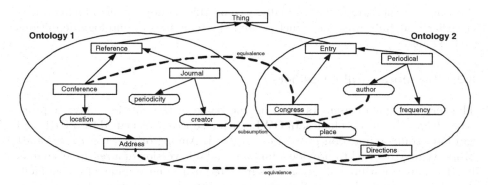

Fig. 2. Excerpt of two bibliographic ontologies and their mappings

Theoretically, an ontology *mapping* is a triple $\mathcal{M} = (\mathbf{S}, \mathbf{T}, \Sigma)$, where $\mathbf{S}$ and $\mathbf{T}$ are respectively the source and target ontologies, and Σ is a finite set of *mapping constraints* of the form:

$$\alpha_{i,j}\ T_j \leftarrow S_i$$

where S_i and T_j are respectively the source and target entities. The intended meaning of this rule is that the entity S_i of the source ontology is mapped onto the entity T_j of the target ontology, and the confident measure associated with this mapping is $\alpha_{i,j}$. Note that a source entity may be mapped onto several target entities and conversely. But, we do not require that we have a mapping for every target entity.

Aligning two ontologies in *oMap* consists of three steps:

1. We form a possible Σ, and estimate its quality based on the quality measures for its mapping rules;
2. For each mapping rule $T_j \leftarrow S_i$, we estimate its quality $\alpha_{i,j}$, which also depends on the Σ it belongs to, i.e. $\alpha_{i,j} = w(S_i, T_j, \Sigma)$;
3. As we cannot compute all possible Σ (there are exponentially many) and then choose the best one, we rather build iteratively our final set of mappings Σ using heuristics.

Similar to GLUE [6], we estimate the weight $w(S_i, T_j, \Sigma)$ of a mapping $T_j \leftarrow S_i$ by using different classifiers $CL_1, \ldots, CL_n$. Each classifier CL_k computes a weight $w(S_i, T_j, CL_k)$, which is the classifier's approximation of the rule $T_j \leftarrow S_i$. For each target entity T_j, CL_k provides a rank of the plausible source entities S_{i_k}. Then we rely on a priority list on the classifiers, $CL_1 \prec CL_2 \prec \ldots \prec CL_n$ and proceed as follows: for a given target entity T_j, select the top-ranked mapping of CL_1 if the weight is non-zero. Otherwise, select the top-ranked mapping provided by CL_2 if non-zero, and so on.

In the following we present several classifiers that are currently used in our framework. It is worth noting that some of the classifiers consider the terminological part of the ontologies only, while others are based on their instances (i.e.

the values of the individuals). Finally, we end this section by introducing a new classifier that fully uses the structure and the semantics of ontology definitions and axioms.

3.2   Terminological Classifiers

The terminological classifiers work on the name of the entities (class or property) defined in the ontologies. In OWL, each resource is identified by a URI, and can have some annotation properties attached. Among others, the `rdfs:label` property may be used to provide a human-readable version of a resource's name. Furthermore, multilingual labels are supported using the language tagging facility of RDF literals. In the following, we consider that the name of an entity is given by the value of the `rdfs:label` property or by the URI fragment if this property is not specified.

Same entity names. This binary classifier CL_{SN} returns a weight of 1 if and only if the two classes (or properties) have the same name, and 0 otherwise:

$$w(S_i, T_j, CL_{SN}) = \begin{cases} 1 & \text{if } S_i, T_j \text{ have same name,} \\ 0 & \text{otherwise} \end{cases}$$

Same entity name stems. This binary classifier CL_{SS} returns a weight of 1 if and only if the two classes (or properties) have the same *stem*[4] (for the English text, we use the Porter stemming algorithm [18]), and 0 otherwise:

$$w(S_i, T_j, CL_{SS}) = \begin{cases} 1 & \text{if } S_i, T_j \text{ have same } stem, \\ 0 & \text{otherwise} \end{cases}$$

String distance name. This classifier CL_{ED} computes some similarity measures between the entity names (once downcased) such that the Levenshtein distance [15] (or edit distance), which is given by the smallest number of insertions, deletions, and substitutions required to transform one string into the other. The prediction is then computed as:

$$w(S_i, T_j, CL_{ED_1}) = 1 - \frac{dist_{Levenshtein}(S_i, T_j)}{\max(length(S_i), length(T_j))}$$

Another possible variant is:

$$w(S_i, T_j, CL_{ED_2}) = 1/\exp\left(\frac{dist_{Levenshtein}(S_i, T_j)}{|length(S_i) + length(T_j)|}\right)$$

We can then threshold this measure and consider only the mappings $T_j \leftarrow S_i$ such that $w(S_i, T_j, CL_{ED}) \geq 0.9$.

---

[4] The root of the terms without its prefixes and suffixes.

Iterative substring matching. This classifier CL_{IS} proposed by [22] also considers the commonalities and differences between the two strings but in a more stable and discriminating way. The prediction is computed as:

$$w(S_i, T_j, CL_{IS}) = Comm(S_i, T_j) - Diff(S_i, T_j) + winkler(S_i, T_j)$$

where

- $Comm(S_i, T_j) = \frac{2 \times \sum_i length(maxComSubString_i)}{length(S_i) + length(T_j)}$,
- $Diff(S_i, T_j) = \frac{uLen_{S_i} \times uLen_{T_j}}{p + (1-p) \times (uLen_{S_i} + uLen_{T_j} - uLen_{S_i} \times uLen_{T_j})}$ with $p^5 \in [0, \infty)$, and $uLen_{S_i}$, $uLen_{T_j}$ represents the length of the unmatched substring from the initial strings S_i and T_j scaled with the string length, respectively,
- $winkler(S_i, T_j)$ stands for the improvement of the result using the method introduced by Winkler in [26].

WordNet distance name. This classifier CL_{WN} computes another similarity measure between the entity names using the WordNet®[6] relational dictionary. The prediction is obtained by[7]:

$$w(S_i, T_j, CL_{WN}) = \begin{cases} 1 & \text{if } S_i, T_j \text{ are synonyms,} \\ \max\left(sim, \frac{2*lcs}{length(S_i) + length(T_j)}\right) & \text{otherwise} \end{cases}$$

where

- lcs is the longest common substring between S_i and T_j (also named "substring similarity" in [9]),
- $sim = \frac{|synonym(S_i)| \cap |synonym(T_j)|}{|synonym(S_i)| \cup |synonym(T_j)|}$ where $|synonym(S_i)|$ is the cardinality of the set of all synonyms of S_i.

3.3   Machine Learning-Based Classifiers

An ontology often contains some individuals. It is then possible to use machine learning-based classifiers to predict the weight of a mapping between two entities. In the following, we define, for each instance of an OWL ontology, u as a set of strings obtained by gathering: (*i*) the label for the named individuals, (*ii*) the data value for the datatype properties and (*iii*) the type for the anonymous individuals and the range of the object properties.

For example, using the abstract syntax of [14], let us consider the following individuals :

---

[5] The parameter p can be adjusted, but the experiments reported in [22] show that the value 0.6 tends to give the best results.

[6] WordNet: http://wordnet.princeton.edu/.

[7] Of course, many other WordNet based classifiers exist (or new ones can be developed). Anyway, they can easily be added to oMAP. Their effectiveness will be evaluated in future work.

Individual (x_1 type (`Conference`)
    value (`label` "`3rd European Semantic Web Conference`")
    value (`location` x_2))
Individual (x_2 type (`Address`)
    value (`city` "`Budva`") value (`country` "`Montenegro`"))

Then, the text gathered u_1 for the named individual x_1 will be ("`3rd European Semantic Web Conference`", "`Address`") while u_2 for the anonymous individual x_2 will be ("`Address`", "`Budva`", "`Montenegro`").

We describe in the following typical and well-known classifiers that we used in oMAP: the kNN classifier and the Naive Bayes [20].

kNN classifier. The algorithm of the k-nearest neighbors is based on the calculus of the distances between an unknown form and all the forms of a reference base. It is particularly popular for text classification [20]. In our CL_{kNN} classifier, each class (or property) S_i acts as a category, and training sets are formed from the instances x (which have u as value) of S_i:

$$Train = \bigcup_{i=1}^{s} \{(S_i, x, u) : (x, u) \in S_i\}$$

For every instance $y \in T_j$ and its value v, the k-nearest neighbors TOP_k have to be found by ranking the values $(S_i, x, u) \in Train$ according to their similarity $RSV^8(u, v)$. The prediction weights are then computed by summing up the similarity values for all x which are built from S_i, and by averaging these weights $\tilde{w}(y, v, S_i)$ over all instances $y \in T_j$:

$$w(S_i, T_j, CL_{kNN}) = \frac{1}{|T_j|} \cdot \sum_{(y,v) \in T_j} \tilde{w}(y, v, S_i) \ ,$$

$$\tilde{w}(y, v, S_i) = \sum_{(S_l, x, u) \in TOP_k, S_i = S_l} RSV(u, v) \ ,$$

$$RSV(u, v) = \sum_{m \in u \cap v} Pr(m|u) \cdot Pr(m|v) \ ,$$

$$Pr(m|u) = \frac{tf(m, u)}{\sum_{m' \in u} tf(m', u)} \ ,$$

$$Pr(m|v) = \frac{tf(w, v)}{\sum_{m' \in v} tf(m', v)}$$

Here, $tf(m, u)$ (*resp.* $tf(m, v)$) denotes the number of times the word m appears in the string u (seen as a bag of words).

Naive Bayes text classifier. The classifier CL_{NB} uses a Naive Bayes text classifier [20] for text content. Like the previous one, each class (or property) S_i acts as a category, and training sets are formed from the instances x (which have u as value) of S_i:

---

[8] The *Retrieval Status Value* is the similarity among two vectors of word, i.e. the sum is the scalar product among the two vectors u and v, i.e. the cosine of the angle among the two vectors.

$$Train = \bigcup_{i=1}^{s} \{(S_i, x, u) : (x, u) \in S_i\}$$

For example, the triple $(\texttt{Conference}, x_1, u_1)$ will be considered, where x_1 and u_1 are defined above.

For each $(y, v) \in T_j$, the probability $Pr(S_i|v)$ that the value v should be mapped onto S_i is computed. In a second step, these probabilities are combined by:

$$w(S_i, T_j, CL_{NB}) = \sum_{(y,v) \in T_j} Pr(S_i|v) \cdot Pr(v)$$

Again, we consider the values as bags of words. With $Pr(S_i)$ we denote the probability that a randomly chosen value in $\bigcup_k S_k$ is a value in S_i. If we assume independence of the words in a value, then we obtain:

$$Pr(S_i|v) = Pr(v|S_i) \cdot \frac{Pr(S_i)}{Pr(v)} = \frac{Pr(S_i)}{Pr(v)} \cdot \prod_{m \in v} Pr(m|S_i)$$

Together, the final formula is:

$$w(S_i, T_j, CL_{NB}) = Pr(S_i) \cdot \sum_{(y,v) \in T_j} \prod_{m \in v} Pr(m|S_i)$$

If a word does not appear in the content for any individual in S_i ($Pr(m|S_i) = 0$), we assume a small value to avoid a product of zero.

3.4   A Structural Classifier

Besides these well-known algorithm in information retrieval and text classification, we introduce a new classifier, CL_{Sem}, which is able to use the semantics of the OWL definitions while being guided by their syntax. In other words, this classifier computes similarities between OWL entities by comparing their syntactical definitions. It is used in the framework *a posteriori*. Indeed, we rely on the classifier preference relation $CL_{SN} \prec CL_{SS} \prec CL_{ED_1} \prec CL_{ED_2} \prec CL_{IS} \prec CL_{NB} \prec CL_{kNN}$. According to this preference relation, a set Σ' of mappings is determined. This set is given as input to the structural classifier. Then the structural classifier tries out all alternative ways to extend Σ' by adding some $T_j \leftarrow S_i$ if no mapping related to T_j is present in Σ'. Any extension of Σ' is denoted below by Σ ($\Sigma' \subseteq \Sigma$).

In the following, we note with $w'(S_i, T_j, \Sigma)$ the weight of the mapping $T_j \leftarrow S_i$ estimated by the classifiers of the previous sections, where S_i (*resp.* T_j) is a concept or property name of the source (*resp.* target) ontology. Note that in case the structural classifier is used alone, we set: $w'(S_i, T_j, \Sigma) = 1$. The formal recursive definition of CL_{Sem} is then given by:

1. If S_i and T_j are property names:

$$w(S_i, T_j, \Sigma) = \begin{cases} 0 & \text{if } T_j \leftarrow S_i \notin \Sigma \\ w'(S_i, T_j, \Sigma) & \text{otherwise} \end{cases}$$

2. If S_i and T_j are concept names: let assume that their definitions are $S_i \sqsubseteq C_1 \ldots and \ldots C_m$ and $T_j \sqsubseteq D_1 \ldots and \ldots D_n$, and we note $\mathcal{D} = \mathcal{D}(S_i) \times \mathcal{D}(T_j)^9$, then:

$$w(S_i, T_j, \Sigma) = \begin{cases} 0 & \text{if } T_j \leftarrow S_i \notin \Sigma \\ w'(S_i, T_j, \Sigma) & \text{if } |\mathcal{D}| = 0 \text{ and } T_j \leftarrow S_i \in \Sigma \\ \frac{1}{(|Set|+1)} \cdot \left(w'(S_i, T_j, \Sigma) + \max_{Set} \left(\sum_{(C_i, D_j) \in Set} w(C_i, D_j, \Sigma) \right) \right) & \text{otherwise} \end{cases}$$

3. Let $C_S = (Q R.C)$ and $D_T = (Q' R'.D)$, where Q, Q' are quantifiers $\forall$ or $\exists$ or cardinality restrictions, R, R' are property names and C, D are concept expressions, then:

$$w(C_S, D_T, \Sigma) = w_Q(Q, Q') \cdot w(R, R', \Sigma) \cdot w(C, D, \Sigma)$$

4. Let $C_S = (op\ C_1 \ldots C_m)$ and $D_T = (op'\ D_1 \ldots D_m)$, where the concept constructors op, op' in the concepts C_S, D_T are in prefix notation, op, op' are the concept constructors among $\sqcap, \sqcup, \neg$ and $n, m \geq 1$, then:

$$w(C_S, D_T, \Sigma) = w_{op}(op, op') \cdot \frac{\max_{Set} \left(\sum_{(C_i, D_j) \in Set} w(C_i, D_j, \Sigma) \right)}{\min(m, n)}$$

where:

- $Set \subseteq \{C_1 \ldots C_m\} \times \{D_1 \ldots D_n\}$ and $|Set| = \min(m, n)$,
- $(C, D) \in Set, (C', D') \in Set \Rightarrow C \neq C', D \neq D'$.

We give in the Table 1 the values for w_Q and w_{op} we used.

Table 1. Possible values for w_{op} and w_Q weights

w_{op} is given by:

	$\sqcap$	$\sqcup$	$\neg$
$\sqcap$	1	1/4	0
$\sqcup$		1	0
$\neg$			1

w_Q is given by:

	$\exists$	$\forall$
$\exists$	1	1/4
$\forall$		1

	$\leq n$	$\geq n$
$\leq m$	1	1/3
$\geq m$		1

4   Evaluation

The problem of aligning ontologies has already produced some interesting works. However, it is difficult to compare theoretically the various approaches proposed since they base on different techniques. Hence, it is necessary to compare them on common tests. This is the goal of the Ontology Alignment Evaluation Initiative (OAEI[10]) since two years, who set up contests and benchmark tests for assessing

---

[9] $\mathcal{D}(S_i)$ represents the set of direct (immediate) parent concepts of S_i.
[10] http://oaei.inrialpes.fr

the strengths and weakness of the available tools. We have thoroughly evaluated *oMAP* with the data of the OAEI 2005 campaign [24]. We present below the updated results of our new approach with respect to the other competitors of this contest for two different scenarios: systematic benchmark tests based on bibliography data (section 4.1), and the alignment of three large web directories (Google, Looksmart and Yahoo) which fits perfectly with our web distributed search scenario (section 4.2).

oMAP is freely available at: http://homepages.cwi.nl/~troncy/oMAP and all these results can be reproduced.

4.1   Aligning Bibliographic Data: The OAEI Benchmarks

The *benchmarks tests* are systematic benchmarks series produced for identifying the areas in which each alignment algorithm is strong and weak. Taking back the tests of the 2004 contest [25] and extending them, there are based on one particular ontology dedicated to the very narrow domain of bibliography and a number of alternative ontologies of the same domain for which alignments are provided. The overall score of *oMAP* for this task is quite good (see Table 2, the results of the other competitors are based on [1]).

Table 2. Overall results for the OAEI benchmark tests, oMAP is given in the last column

algo	edna		Falcon		FOAM		ctxMatch		Dublin20		CMS		OLA		oMAP	
Test	Prec.	Rec.	Prec.	Rec.	Prec.	Rec.	Prec.	Rec.	Prec.	Rec.	Prec.	Rec.	Prec.	Rec.	Prec.	Rec.
1xx	0.96	1.00	1.00	1.00	0.98	0.65	0.87	0.34	1.00	0.99	0.74	0.20	1.00	1.00	**1.00**	**1.00**
2xx	0.41	0.56	0.90	0.89	0.89	0.69	0.72	0.19	0.94	0.71	0.81	0.18	0.80	0.73	**0.80**	**0.63**
3xx	0.47	0.82	0.93	0.83	0.92	0.69	0.37	0.06	0.67	0.60	0.93	0.18	0.50	0.48	**0.93**	**0.65**
H-mean	0.45	0.61	0.91	0.89	0.90	0.69	0.72	0.20	0.92	0.72	0.81	0.18	0.80	0.74	**0.85**	**0.68**

However, *oMAP* has poor performance for the tests 25x and 26x where all labels are replaced with random strings. Actually, the terminological and machine-learning based classifiers give wrong input to our structural classifier. This classifier is then not able to counterbalance this effect and give also wrong alignments. It is the typical case where the other classifiers should be turn off and the structural classifier should work alone. In this specific case, the computing time increases but the performances are much better.

4.2   Aligning Web Categories

The *directory real world case* consists of aligning web sites directory using the large dataset developing in [2]. These tests are blind in the sense that the expected alignments are not known in advance. As explained in [1], only recall results are available. The results for web directory matching task are presented on the Table 3 (the results of the other competitors are based on [1]). The web directories matching task is a very hard one, since the best systems found

Table 3. Overall results for the web categories alignment, oMAP is given in the last column

Falcon	FOAM	ctxMatch	Dublin20	CMS	OLA	oMAP
31.17%	11.88%	9.36%	26.53%	14.08%	31.96%	**34.43**

about 30% of mappings form the dataset (i.e. have Recall about 30%). *oMAP* gives already good results but a complete analysis of them should provide some improvements in a very near future.

5   Related Work and Conclusion

In this paper, we have proposed a three-step framework for distributed, Semantic Web-enabled Information Retrieval. For the second step, namely *query reformulation and ontology alignment*, we have described *oMAP*, an efficient tool for automatically aligning OWL ontologies, whereas the first step, namely *resource selection*, will be addressed in future work. *oMAP* uses different classifiers to estimate the quality of a mapping. Novel are the use of machine learning-based classifiers and a classifier which uses the structure of the OWL constructs and thus the semantics of the entities defined in the ontologies. We have implemented the whole framework and evaluated it on the OAEI benchmark tests with respect to the other competitors.

The alignment problem for ontologies, as well as the matching problem for schemas, has been addressed by many researchers so far and are strictly related. Some of the techniques applied in schema matching can be applied to ontology alignment as well, taking additionally into account the formal semantics carried out by the taxonomies of concepts and properties and the axioms of the ontology. Among the works related to ontology alignment, FOAM [7, 8] propose to combine different similarity measures from pre-existing hand-established mapping rules. Besides the validity of these rules could be generally put into question, this method suffers from not being fully automatic. [17] has developed an interesting approach: from anchor-pairs of concepts that seem to be close (discovered automatically or proposed manually), their *hors-context* similarity are computed analyzing the paths in the taxonomy that link the pairs of concepts. This method has been implemented into the ANCHOR-PROMPT tool which has, until now, one of the best performance. [10] have adapted works on similarity calculus for object-based knowledge representation languages to the Semantic Web languages. A global similarity measure taking into account all the features of the OWL-Lite language has been proposed, capable to treat both the circular definitions and the collections. For a complete state of the art on the numerous ontology alignment approaches proposed, see [5, 21].

Our future work will concentrate on the major issue left out so far, namely automated resource selection. To this end, we plan to extend methods for query-based sampling and automated resource selection from the textual IR resources to ontology-based information resources. Furthermore, the *oMAP* framework could still be improved. The combination of a rule-based language with an expressive ontology language like OWL has attracted the attention of many researchers [13] and is considered now as an important requirement. Taking into account this additional semantics of the ontologies appear thus necessary. Additional classifiers using more terminological resources can be included in the framework, while the effectiveness of the machine learning part could be improved using other measures like the KL-distance. While to fit new classifiers into our model is straightforward theoretically, practically finding out the most appropriate one or a combination of them is quite more difficult. In the future, more variants should be developed and evaluated to improve the overall quality of *oMAP*.

Acknowledgments

The authors wish to thank in particular Jacco van Ossenbruggen and Lynda Hardman for insightful discussions and helpful comments.

References

1. B. Ashpole, M. Ehrig, J. Euzenat, and H. Stuckenschmidt, editors. *K-CAP 2005 Workshop on Integrating Ontologies (IntOnt'05)*, Banff, Canada, 2005.
2. P. Avesani, F. Giunchiglia, and M. Yatskevich. A Large Scale Taxonomy Mapping Evaluation. In *4th International Semantic Web Conference (ISWC'05)*, pages 67–81, Galway, Ireland, 2005.
3. J. Callan. Distributed Information Retrieval. In W.B. Croft, editor, *Advances in Information Retrieval*, pages 127–150. Kluwer Academic, 2000.
4. J. Callan and M. Connell. Query-Based Sampling of Text Databases. *ACM Transactions on Information Systems*, 19(2):97–130, 2001.
5. KW Consortium. State of the Art on Ontology Alignment. Deliverable Knowledge Web 2.2.3, FP6-507482, 2004.
6. A. Doan, J. Madhavan, R. Dhamankar, P. Domingos, and A. Halevy. Learning to Match Ontologies on the Semantic Web. *The VLDB Journal*, 12(4):303–319, 2003.
7. M. Ehrig and S. Staab. QOM - quick ontology mapping. In *3rd International Semantic Web Conference (ISWC'04)*, pages 683–697, Hiroshima, Japon, 2004.
8. M. Ehrig, S. Staab, and Y. Sure. Bootstrapping Ontology Alignment Methods with APFEL. In *4th International Semantic Web Conference (ISWC'05)*, pages 186–200, Galway, Ireland, 2005.
9. J. Euzenat. An API for ontology alignment. In *3rd International Semantic Web Conference (ISWC'04)*, pages 698–712, Hiroshima, Japon, 2004.
10. J. Euzenat and P. Valtchev. Similarity-based ontology alignment in OWL-Lite. In *15th European Conference on Artificial Intelligence (ECAI'04)*, pages 333–337, Valence, Spain, 2004.
11. R. Fagin, P.G. Kolaitis, R.J. Miler, and L. Popa. Data Exchange: Semantics and Query Answering. In *9th International Conference on Database Theory (ICDT'03)*, pages 207–224, Sienne, Italie, 2003.
12. N. Fuhr. Probabilistic Datalog: Implementing Logical Information Retrieval for Advanced Applications. *Journal of the American Society for Information Science*, 51(2):95–110, 2000.

13. I. Horrocks and P.F. Patel-Schneider. A proposal for an OWL rules language. In *13th International World Wide Web Conference (WWW'04)*, pages 723–731, 2004.

14. I. Horrocks, P.F. Patel-Schneider, and F. van Harmelen. From SHIQ and RDF to OWL: The making of a web ontology language. *Journal of Web Semantics*, 1(1):7–26, 2003.

15. V.I. Levenshtein. Binary codes capable of correcting deletions, insertions, and reversals (Russian). *Doklady Akademii Nauk SSSR*, 163(4):845–848, 1965. English translation in Soviet Physics Doklady, **10**(8):707–710, 1966.

16. H. Nottelmann and U. Straccia. sPLMap: A probabilistic approach to schema matching. In *27th European Conference on Information Retrieval (ECIR'05)*, pages 81–95, Santiago de Compostela, Spain, 2005.

17. N.F. Noy and M.A. Musen. Anchor-PROMPT: Using non-local context for semantic matching. In *Workshop on Ontologies and Information Sharing at IJCAI'01*, Seattle, Washington, USA, 2001.

18. M.F. Porter. An algorithm for suffix stripping. *Program*, 14(3):130–137, 1980.

19. M.E. Renda and U. Straccia. Web Metasearch: Rank vs. Score Based Rank Aggregation Methods. In *18th Annual ACM Symposium on Applied Computing (SAC'03)*, pages 841–846, Melbourne, Florida, USA, 2003.

20. F. Sebastiani. Machine learning in automated text categorization. *ACM Comuting Surveys*, 34(1):1–47, 2002.

21. P. Shvaiko and J. Euzenat. A Survey of Shema-based Matching Approaches. *Journal on Data Semantics (JoDS)*, 2005.

22. G. Stoilos, G. Stamou, and S. Kollias. A String Metric for Ontology Alignment. In *4th International Semantic Web Conference (ISWC'05)*, pages 624–637, Galway, Ireland, 2005.

23. U. Straccia and R. Troncy. oMAP: Combining Classifiers for Aligning Automatically OWL Ontologies. In *6th International Conference on Web Information Systems Engineering (WISE'05)*, pages 133–147, New York City, New York, USA, November, 20-22 2005.

24. U. Straccia and R. Troncy. oMAP: Results of the Ontology Alignment Contest. In *Workshop on Integrating Ontologies*, pages 92–96, Banff, Canada, 2005.

25. Y. Sure, O. Corcho, J. Euzenat, and T. Hughes, editors. *3rd International Workshop on Evaluation of Ontology-based Tools (EON'04)*, Hiroshima, Japon, 2004.

26. W. Winkler. The state record linkage and current research problems. Technical report, Statistics of Income Division, Internal Revenue Service Publication, 1999.

27. C. Yu, W. Meng, King-Lup, W. Wu, and N. Rishe. Efficient and Effective Metasearch for a Large Number of Text Databases. In *8th International Conference on Information and Knowledge Management (CIKM'99)*, pages 217–224, Kansas City, Missouri, USA, 1999.

PowerAqua: Fishing the Semantic Web

Vanessa Lopez, Enrico Motta, and Victoria Uren

Knowledge Media Institute & Centre for Research in Computing, The Open University.
Walton Hall, Milton Keynes,MK7 6AA, United Kingdom
{v.lopez, e.motta, v.s.uren}@open.ac.uk

Abstract. The Semantic Web (SW) offers an opportunity to develop novel, sophisticated forms of question answering (QA). Specifically, the availability of
distributed semantic markup on a large scale opens the way to QA systems
which can make use of such semantic information to provide precise, formally
derived answers to questions. At the same time the distributed, heterogeneous,
large-scale nature of the semantic information introduces significant challenges.
In this paper we describe the design of a QA system, PowerAqua, designed to
exploit semantic markup on the web to provide answers to questions posed in
natural language. PowerAqua does not assume that the user has any prior information about the semantic resources. The system takes as input a natural
language query, translates it into a set of logical queries, which are then answered by consulting and aggregating information derived from multiple heterogeneous semantic sources.

1 Introduction

The development of a semantic layer on top of web contents and services, the *Semantic Web* [1], has been recognized as the next step in the evolution of the World Wide
Web as a distributed knowledge resource. The Semantic Web brings to the web the
idea of having data formally defined and linked in a way that they can be used for
effective information discovery, integration, reuse across various applications, and for
service automation.

Ontologies play a crucial role on the SW: they provide the conceptual infrastructure supporting semantic interoperability, addressing data heterogeneity [2] and opening up opportunities for automated information processing [3]. However, because of
the SW's distributed nature, data will inevitably be associated with different ontologies and therefore ontologies themselves will introduce heterogeneity. Different ontologies may describe similar domains, but using different terminologies, while others
may have overlapping domains: i.e. given two ontologies, the same entity can be
given different names or simply be defined in different ways.

Our goal is to design and develop a Question Answering (QA) system, able to exploit the availability of distributed, ontology-based semantic markup on the web to
answer questions posed in natural language (NL). A user must be able to pose NL
queries without being aware of which information sources exist, the details associated

Y. Sure and J. Domingue (Eds.): ESWC 2006, LNCS 4011, pp. 393–410, 2006.
© Springer-Verlag Berlin Heidelberg 2006

with interacting with each source, or the particular vocabulary used by the sources. We call this system *PowerAqua*.

PowerAqua follows from an earlier system, AquaLog [4], and addresses its main limitation, as discussed in the next section.

2   The AquaLog Question Answering System

AquaLog [4] is a fully implemented ontology-driven QA system, which takes an ontology and a NL query as an input and returns answers drawn from semantic markup compliant with the input ontology. In contrast with much existing work on ontology-driven QA, which tends to focus on the use of ontologies to support query expansion in information retrieval [5], AquaLog exploits the availability of semantic statements to provide precise answers to complex queries expressed in NL.

An important feature of AquaLog is its ability to make use of generic lexical resources, such as WordNet, as well as the structure of the input ontology, to make sense of the terms and relations expressed in the input query. Naturally, these terms and relations normally match the terminology and concepts familiar to the user rather than those used in the ontology.

Another important feature of AquaLog is that it is *portable with respect to ontologies*. In other words, the time required to configure AquaLog for a particular ontology is negligible. The reason for this is that the architecture of the system and the reasoning methods are completely domain-independent, relying on an understanding of general-purpose knowledge representation languages, such as OWL[1], and the use of generic lexical resources, such as WordNet. AquaLog also includes a learning mechanism, which ensures that, for a given ontology and community of users, its performance improves over time, as the users can easily correct mistakes and allow AquaLog to learn novel associations between the relations used by users, which are expressed in natural language, and the ontology structure.

AquaLog uses a sequential process model (see Figure 1), in which NL input is first translated into a set of intermediate representations – these are called *query triples*, by the Linguistic Component. The Linguistic Component uses the GATE infrastructure and resources [6] to obtain a set of syntactic annotations associated with the input query. The set of annotations is extended by the use of *JAPE* grammars to identify terms, relations, question indicators (who, what, etc.), features (voice and tense) and to classify the query into a category. Knowing the category of the query and having the GATE annotations for the query, it becomes straight-forward for the Linguistic Component to automatically create the Query-Triples. Then, these query triples are further processed and interpreted by the Relation Similarity Service Component, which uses the available lexical resources and the structure and vocabulary of the ontology to map them to ontology-compliant semantic markup or triples.

However AquaLog suffers from a key limitation: at any time it can only be used for one particular ontology. This of course works well in many scenarios, e.g. in company

---

[1] A plug-in mechanism and a generic API ensure that different Knowledge Representation languages can be used.

intranets where a shared organizational ontology is used to describe resources. However, if we consider the SW *in the large,* this assumption no longer holds. As already
pointed out, the semantic web is heterogeneous in nature and it is not possible to determine in advance which ontologies will be relevant to a particular query. Moreover, it
is often the case that queries can only be solved by composing heterogeneous information derived from multiple information sources that are autonomously created and
maintained. Hence, to perform effective QA on the semantic web, we need a system
which is able to locate and aggregate information, without any pre-formulated assumption about the ontological structure of the relevant information.

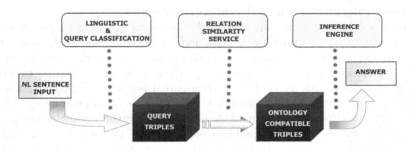

Fig. 1. The AquaLog Data Model

3 QA for the Semantic Web: Multiple-Ontology Scenario

In the previous sections we have sketched our vision for a QA system suitable for the
semantic web, PowerAqua, and we have also explained why AquaLog does not quite
fit the bill. In this section we address the problem in more detail and we examine the
specific issues which need to be tackled in order to develop PowerAqua. It should be
noted that here we only focus on the issues which are specific to PowerAqua and are
not tackled already by AquaLog. For instance, we will not be looking at the problem
of translating from NL into triples: the AquaLog solution, which is based on GATE,
can be simply reused for PowerAqua.

Resource discovery and information focusing
PowerAqua aims to support QA on the open, heterogeneous Semantic Web. In principle, any markup associated with any ontology can be potentially relevant. Hence, in
contrast with AquaLog, which simply needs to retrieve all semantic resources which
are based on a given ontology, PowerAqua has to automatically identify the relevant
semantic markup from a large and heterogeneous semantic web[2]. In this paper we do

---

[2] Here we do not need to worry about the precise mechanism used to index and locate an ontology and the relevant semantic markup. Various solutions are in principle possible depending
on the SW evolution, here we can simply assume that the semantic web will provide the appropriate indexing mechanisms, much like the cluster architecture used by Google provides
indexing mechanisms for the web as a whole.

not address the problem of scalability or efficiency in determining the relevance of the ontologies, in respect to a query. Currently, there are ontology search engines, such as Swoogle [7] and different RDF ontology storage technologies suitable for processing SW information [8], e.g. 3store and Sesame servers.

Mapping user terminology into ontology terminology
A key design criterion for both AquaLog and PowerAqua is that the user is free to use his / her own terminology when posing a query. So, while this is an issue also for AquaLog, a critical problem for PowerAqua, not applicable to AquaLog, is that of different vocabularies used by different ontologies to describe similar information across domains [9].

Integrating information from different semantic sources
Queries posed by end-users may need to be answered not by a single knowledge source but by consulting multiple sources, and therefore, combining the relevant *information* from different repositories. On other occasions more than one source contains a satisfactory answer to the same query. Thus, if there is a complete translation into one or more ontologies or if the current partial translation, in conjunction with previously generated partial translations, is equivalent to the original query, the data must be retrieved from the relevant ontologies and appropriately combined to give the final answer. Interestingly, the problem of integrating information from multiple sources in the first instance can be reduced to the problem of identifying multiple occurrences of individuals in the sources in question.

4 Methodology: Query-Driven Semantic Mapping Algorithm Step by Step

The algorithm presented here covers the design of the whole PowerAqua system. However the AquaLog components reusable for PowerAqua have already been described in detail in [4], so here they will be described only briefly. In this paper, we focus primarily on the issues of mapping user terminology into ontology terminology in a semantic web multi-ontology scenario, and the information integration problem.

To help the reader make sense of the algorithm shown in Figure 2, we will use the query "What is the capital of Spain?" as a running example throughout. This query is particularly useful to present the issues introduced in section 3, especially when describing the different ways in which the PowerAqua algorithm interprets the above query and the query "Was *Capital*[3] written in Spain?".

4.1 Step 1: Linguistic and Query Classification Analysis

The Linguistic Component's task is to map the NL input query into Query-Triples. The role of the Query-Triples is simply to provide an easy way to manipulate the input. AquaLog linguistic component [4] is appropriate for the linguistic analysis thanks to its ontology portable and independent nature, and therefore, it is reused for PowerAqua.

---

[3] Book written by Karl Marx (1867).

4.1.1 Running Example

The example query "What is the capital of Spain?" is classified as a *wh-query*[4] that represents a binary relationship where there is not any information about the type of the *query term (focus)*, and generates the linguistic triple: <?, capital, Spain>. However, the relation "is the capital of" contains the noun "capital", therefore, we need to take into account that the triple may be restructured as a triple with an implicit relation between the term "capital" and "Spain".

The second example query "Was Capital written in Spain?" is translated into a basic affirmative/negative query that generates the triple: <capital, written, Spain>.

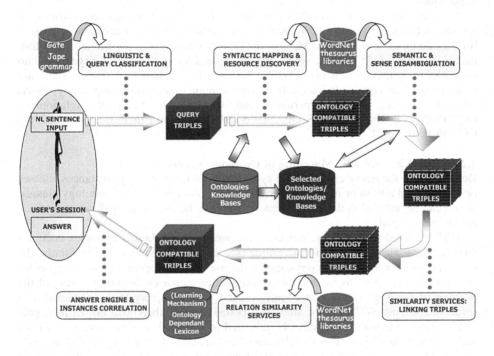

Fig. 2. Algorithm step by step

4.2 Step 2: Syntactic Term Mapping and Resource Discovery

The initial selection of candidate ontologies, which may have the potential to answer the query, is entirely done by syntax driven techniques (SDT). Note that we use the same terminology as [10] referring to syntactic matching when the matching between two nodes is computed using the labels of the nodes. SDT looks

---

[4] The set of "wh-queries" are the ones starting with: what, when, where, are there any, does anybody, how many, and also imperative commands like list, give, tell, name, show. "wh-queries" like "who" can be interchanged into "which person/organization", "where" into "which location" and so on.

for similarities between labels by means of string-based metrics[5], taking into account abbreviations, acronyms and domain and lexical knowledge.

4.2.1 Phase a: Extending the Query Vocabulary with Lexical and Domain Knowledge

To maximize recall, with respect to other ontology search systems that only looks for classes or instances that have labels matching a search term either exactly or partially [11], each term in the query, or noun in the relation if any (relations may be formed by a noun plus verbs and prepositions) is extended with its synonyms, hypernyms and hyponyms.

The current version of WordNet provides *a priori* lexical and domain knowledge. As Ide and Veronis state [12], WordNet is the most used lexical resource at present for disambiguation in English. Most of the research methods in the literature are limited to WordNet [13]. Nouns, verbs, adjectives, and adverbs are each organized into networks of synonyms sets (*synsets*). Each synset has a gloss to define it. There are nine types of semantic relations defined on the noun subnetwork: hyponymy (IS-A) relation, and its inverse hypernymy; six meronymic (PART-OF) relations – COMPONENT-OF, MEMBER-OF, SUBSTANCE-OF and their inverses; and the COMPLEMENT-OF relation.

4.2.2 Phase b: Syntactic Matching of Ontology Terms

Depending on the query category, the system will look for ontology instances, classes or both to map a term or its lexical variations. The system looks for ontology classes, which can be handled in the client memory, through the use of string distance metrics, also used in AquaLog.

SDT are used in AquaLog, however, the weakness of these techniques becomes more evident when applied to PowerAqua (see example in section 4.2.4). Firstly, the discovery of user terms in the ontology by the use of SDT becomes increasingly computationally expensive as the number of ontologies increases. Secondly, many of the discovered ontology terms syntactically related with the query terms, obtained as a result of applying SDT, may be similarly spelled words (labels) that do not have precisely matched meanings. As already indicated in section 3, in this paper we will not address the issues to do with the efficiency and scalability of the algorithm in determining the relevance of the ontology and terms by use of SDT, but we will focus on the issue of disambiguating among the possible interpretations of a query.

4.2.3 Phase c: Complete Coverage of the Triple by Candidate Ontologies

A criterion for filtering candidate ontologies is to select the ones that present potential candidates mappings for all the terms within a triple, if any. In other words, if ontology 1 presents a possible complete translation of a query triple, while ontology 2 only presents a partial translation of the same triple, the later will be discarded. Similarly, the coverage of an ontology given the search terms is used as a measure in the ontology ranking approach on AKTiveRank [11].

Consider the query "Which wine is appropriate with chicken?". The term "wine" has a syntactic mapping with the term "wine" belonging to an ontology of colors, and

---

[5] http://secondstring.sourceforge.net/

with the term "wines" related to an ontology of food and wines. Similarly, the term "chicken" maps to an ontology of farming and to the same food and wine ontology. Since the food and wine ontology presents a complete potential translation for the triple we retain it, and we discard both the farming and color ontologies, which only present partial translations.

However, we may find the case in which none of the available ontologies contains a whole translation of the triple. Consider the query "Which researchers play football?", where we can find an ontology about researchers and an ontology about footballers. In this case, the linguistic triple <researchers, play, football> should be restructured and translated into two triples solved by different ontologies: <?, is-a, researcher> and <?, is-a, footballer>.

In some cases, it may happen that no candidate terms are found due to the vocabulary used in some ontologies, e.g. labels with multiple words. In this case, if there is a possible mapping for one of the two query terms on the triple, we can identify a set of possible candidate terms that can complete the triple through the ontology relationships valid for this mapped term.

4.2.4 Running Example

Through WordNet we get the synonyms, hypernyms and hyponyms presented in Table 1.

Table 1. Lexical related Words obtained in WordNet

Capital (glosses)	Synonyms	Hypernyms	Hyponyms
#1: assets available for use in the production of further assets	working capital	assets	stock, venture capital, risk capital, operating capital
#2: wealth in the form of money or property	-	assets	endowment, endowment fund, means, substance, principal, corpus, sum
#3: a seat of government	-	seat	Camelot, national / provincial / state capital
#4: one of the large alphabetic characters used as the first letter	capital letter, uppercase, majuscule	character, grapheme, graphic symbol	small capital, small cap
#5: a book written by Karl Marx	Das Kapital, Capital	book (*instance-of*)	-
#6: the upper part of a column that supports the entablature	capital, chapiter, cap	top	-

As said in 4.1.1, the relation in the query example "What is the capital of Spain?" is the noun "capital", and therefore it can be understood as a) an ontology relation or as a b) query term that should be mapped into an ontology class. After running phases b and c, the system obtains the following ontologies:

- Ontology 1: Geographical information. Contains the terms "capital-city" as a candidate mapping for "capital" and "Spain" as an instance of "country". There is a direct relation that connects "capital-city" and "country".
- Ontology 2: Financial ontology. Contains the terms "capital" and "Spain" as an instance of "country". The classes "capital" and "country" are related through the concept "company".
- Ontology 3: Country statistics. Contains the term "Spain".

- Ontology 4: flights information. Contains the term "Logrono" (a Spanish city), where "Logrono" is a WordNet hyponym of the only synset of "Spain".

In Ontology 1 and 2, the query triple "capital" is understood as an ontology class, and therefore, the resultant triple will be an unknown relation between "capital-city / capital" and "Spain". For the ontology 3 and 4 "capital" is understood as an ontology relation, therefore the ontologies contains only a mapping for the term "Spain", as relations are not addressed until the step in section 4.4.

At this stage we have selected the candidate ontology terms that potentially will be part of the equivalent ontology semantic query by a simple lexical analysis of the labels (SDT). In the next phase the system performs sense disambiguation using the ontology semantics and WordNet to analyze the meaning and discard non-related ontology terms mapped in this phase.

Also, it is worth mentioning that in the question "Was Capital written in Spain?", where the triple is *<capital, written, Spain>*, the system should only obtain the following ontology:

- Ontology 5: Bibliographic information. Contains the terms "Das-Kapital" as an instance of "book", also "Spain" as an instance of a "country" (e.g. where a book is published, at this stage we do not know if "published" is the same as "written").

This is because the category of the query (affirmative-negative) is telling us that the term "capital" should be mapped into the instance "Das-Kapital", while in "What is the capital of Spain?" "capital" should be mapped into a class, and thanks to WordNet we know that "book" is related to "capital" by an "instance-of" kind of relationship not by an "hypernym".

4.3   Step 3: Semantic Mapping from User Terminology into Ontology Terminology

The mapping between user and ontology terms becomes increasingly complicated as the number of ontologies increases. SDT (string metrics, lexicon, synonyms) used to select the candidate terms and ontologies are obviously not enough to identify relevant terms in the heterogeneous scenario introduced by multiple ontologies. A semantic mapping component that considers the content of an information item and its intended meaning is needed because:

- Calling the user to disambiguate between possible ontology candidate terms is not feasible because of the broad space of syntactically obtained distributed terms[6]: spelled words (labels) may have not precisely matched meanings. Relationships between word senses, not words, are needed. If we know the possible *senses* for the user's query we can filter the candidate results without the user's feedback.
- To answer a query the system may need to combine partial answers from more than one ontology, or two ontologies may provide compatible answers, e.g. answers which can be merged, to the same query. Semantic interoperability between

---

[6] Interactivity should be the last resort for the *Similarity Services* (section 4.4) where, after a deep analysis of the ontology, domain knowledge does not further help to automatically perform disambiguation.

two concepts is only possible if they are semantically equivalent, or in other words, instance information from different ontology classes can be correlated / integrated only if the ontology classes are semantically equivalent. We make the assumption that two ontology classes may be semantically equivalent, and denote compatible information, if the WordNet *senses* associated with the labels of the classes, in the context of their position in the ontology taxonomy, share some similarity. Otherwise they are just classes that share lexically-related labels but they refer to different domains and therefore their information is not compatible.

In this step the semantic equivalence of the candidate ontology terms obtained in step 2 is studied. As a consequence, ontology terms that are syntactically related to the terms in the query, but are not semantically equivalent, are discarded as potential mappings. The semantic equivalence, and therefore the word sense disambiguation (WSD), is measured through the notion of *similarity*. Many reasonable similarity measures and strategies exist in the literature for WSD (see [12] for a state of the art). Hence, to maximize our system applicability we propose a sense-based similarity matcher algorithm in section 4.3.1. This algorithm applied to PowerAqua is described in the steps 4.3.2 and 4.3.3.

4.3.1 Semantic Equivalence Between Two Terms: Sense-Based Similarity Algorithm

To study similarity between terms the meaning of each term should be made explicit by an interpretation of its label and position in the ontology taxonomy (see 4.3.3). Note that similarity is a more specialized notion than association or relatedness. Similar entities are semantically related by virtue of their similarity (bank-trust company). Dissimilar entities may also be semantically related by lexical relationships such as meronym (*car-wheel)* and antonymy (*hot-cold)*, or just by any kind of functional relationship or frequent association (*pencil-paper, penguin-Antarctica*) [13]. Taking the example in [14] doctors are minimally similar to medicines and hospitals, since these things are all instances of "something having concrete existence, living or nonliving" (although they may be highly associated), but they are much more similar to lawyers, since both are kinds of professional people, and even more similar to nurses, since both are professional people within the health professions.

In *Hierarchy distance based matchers* [15] the relatedness between words is measured by the distance between two concepts/senses in a given input hierarchy. In particular, similarity between words is measured by looking at the shortest path between two given concepts/senses in the WordNet "IS-A" taxonomy of concepts.

Two words are similar if any of the following holds:

1. They have a synset in common (e.g. "human" and "person")
2. A word is a hypernym/hyponym in the taxonomy of the other word.
3. If there exists an allowable "is-a" path connecting a synset associated with each word –in the WordNet taxonomy-.
4. Additionally, if any of the previous cases is true and the definition (gloss) of one of the synsets of the word (or its direct hypernyms/hyponyms) includes the other word as one of its synonyms, we said that they are strongly similar.

For evaluating points 2 and 3 we make use of two WordNet indexes: the *depth* and the *common parent index (C.P.I)*. At the top of WordNet hierarchy are 11 abstract concepts or *unique beginners* (e.g. "entity"), the maximum depth in the noun hierarchy is 16 nodes. The shorter the path between two terms [14] the more similar they are, e.g. depth=1 represents case 3 ("is-a" path). However, a widely acknowledged problem is that the approach typically "relies on the notion that links in the taxonomy represent uniform distances", but typically this is not true and there is a wide variability in the "distance" covered by a single taxonomic link [13]. Resnik [14] established that one criterion of similarity between two concepts is the extent to which they share information in common, which, in an IS-A taxonomy, can be determined by inspecting the relative position of the most-specific concept that subsumes them both. With the use of the C.P.I we can immediately identify this lowest super-ordinate concept (lso) between two terms, or the most specific common subsumer. The number of links (depth) is still important to distinguish between any two pairs of concepts having the same lso. Apart from point 1 of the algorithm, in which the words have a synset in common, the most immediate case occurs in point 2 (C.P.I = 1, Depth = 1), e.g. while comparing "poultry" and "chicken" we notice that "poultry#2" is the common subsumer (hypernym) of "chicken#1".

4.3.2 Phase a: Filtering Non-semantically Equivalent Candidate Ontology Terms with Respect to a Query by the Use of Similarity

SDT (string algorithms, synonyms) were used in the previous phases to select the first set of candidate terms and ontologies to map a query. Because of the use of SDT, the ontology mapped term and the query term do not necessarily share the same meaning. However, they must share some similarity in common; otherwise the candidate ontology term is discarded.

For instance, for a query like "What investigators work in the akt project?" the system, using string algorithms over WordNet synonyms, discovers the following terms as possible candidate mappings for "investigators": "researcher", "KMi-researchers", "research-worker", "research-area". Using the WordNet "IS-A" taxonomy we must find at least one synset in common with the mapped ontology term and the query term or a short/relevant path in the IS-A WordNet taxonomy that relates them together. Otherwise it is discarded as a solution.

Here, "researcher" and "investigator" have a synset in common, namely "research-worker, researcher, investigator – a scientist who devotes himself to doing research". We get the same for "research-worker" and "KMi-researchers" (nominal compound which lemma is "researcher"). However "research-area" will be discarded (even if they may be highly associated) because not only do they not share any sense in common but also there is not a relevant "IS-A" path that connects "researcher" with "research-area"; "researcher" is connected to the root through the path "scientist/man of science" and "person", while "research-area" is connected through "investigation" which is connected to "work".

4.3.3 Phase b: Analysis of the Semantic Interoperability Between Candidate Ontology Terms by Means of Similarity Measures

Different ontology mappings for the same query term may represent different meanings of the query term, and therefore they are not necessarily semantically equivalent. Two classes are semantically interoperable or two instances are semantically equivalent if they are similar, following the algorithm in 4.3.1, for any of its possible

WordNet *synsets*. The meaning of an ontology term is determined not only by its label but by its position in the ontology taxonomy (ancestors and descendants) and by the meaning of the rest of the concepts in the same taxonomy path (the context where the class or instance occurs).

The algorithm used to obtain the set of possible WordNet synsets valid for an ontology term as part of an ontology taxonomy is inspired by the algorithm described in [16] to make explicit the semantics hidden in schema models: Let L be a generic label for a concept and L1 either an ancestor label or a descendant label of L and let s* and s1* be respectively the sets of WordNet senses of a word in L and a word in L1. If one of the senses belonging to s* is either a synonym, hypernym, holonym, hyponym or a meronym of one of the senses belonging to s1*, these two senses are retained and all the other senses are discarded. As an example, imagine *Apple* (which can denote either a fruit or a tree) and *Food* as its ancestor; since there exits a hyponymy relation between *apple#1* (denoting a fruit) and *food#1*, we retain *apple#1* and discard *apple#2* (denoting a tree). Note this phase works better when the ontology term is a class instead of an instance, as WordNet may not have the correct sense for a proper name. This phase is further described in the running example.

4.3.4 Running Example

Going back to the example "What is the capital of Spain?" the mappings for "capital" for the geographical and financial ontologies are "capital-city" and "capital" respectively. After execution of *phase a* both interpretations remain, as the lemma for both terms is the same as the query term "capital" and therefore, in principle, they have all the synsets in common. In *phase b* the system will study whether both interpretations are semantically equivalent by obtaining the *sense* of the mapped term in the context of the ontology it belongs to.

For instance, we run the algorithm of similarity presented in 4.3.1 to obtain the *synset* of the term "capital" in the geographical ontology. We obtain the results presented in table 2 when trying to find an allowable path between all the senses of the candidate ontology word "capital" and all the senses of its ancestor "city" (please note that blank means that either there is not an allowable path or the depth is too long to be considered as relevant).

Analyzing the results of table 2 we can quickly filter *capital#c, capital#f, city#1, city#2* and discard the others. A deeper study will show that *capital#c* is more likely than *capital#f* because there are only 2 common subsumers in the latter (entity and location), both of them representing abstracts top elements of the WordNet taxonomy, while in the former we have 3 common subsumers. We can not study the descendants of "capital" in the ontology because none exist. The study of the next direct ascendant of "city" ("geographical-unit") does not offer additional information (the fine-grainedness of WordNet sense distinctions, e.g. in this case city#1 and city#2, is a frequently cited problem). Moreover, the hypernym of *capital#c* is *"seat#5"*, defined as "seat –centre of authority (*city* from which authority is exercised)". The word "city" is used as part of its definition. Therefore *capital#c* is strongly related to *"city"*.

After *phase b* it is clear that in the financial ontology "capital" is referred to senses #1 and #2, while in geographical ontology "capital" is referred to sense *#3*.

Table 2. Similarity between "capital" and its ontology ancestor "city" using WordNet "IS-A" taxonomy

	City#1 (large and densely populated urban area.., metropolis)	City#2 (an incorporated administrative district ..)	City#3 (people living in large municipality)
Capital#a (assests ..)			
Capital#b (wealth ..)			
Capital#c (seat of government)	**Depth** = 8, **Iso** = region **Num_so** (common subsumers) = 3 (region, location, entity)	**Depth** = 7, **Iso** = region **Num_so** = 3 (entity, location, region)	
Capital#d (capital letter)			
Capital#e (book by Karl Marx)			
Capital#f (upper part column)	**Depth** = 8, **Iso** = location **Num_so** = 2 (entity, location)	**Depth** = 7, **Iso** = location **Num_so** = 2 (entity, location)	

Therefore both terms in different ontologies are not semantically equivalent and their information cannot be correlated (even if they share the same label) which means that the system must select one of them using ontology semantics or query relatedness in the following steps.

4.3.5 Selection of Candidate Ontology Terms Using the Notion of Relatedness

After the execution of previous steps, we have narrowed down to two the valid mappings for the linguistic triple: *?(capital, Spain)*, one in the geographical ontology and the other one in the financial ontology. We also know that there is not semantic interoperability or equivalence between the class "capital" represented in both ontologies, therefore only one mapping will be valid to create the final ontology compliant triple.

The next step (section 4.4) is the study of the ontology taxonomy and relationships to analyze the *relatedness* between ontology terms to choose a correct mapping for the query. However, it is worth mentioning that we also consider the study of the sense of term "capital" in the user's query by using the idea of relatedness found in the computational linguistics literature. Most approaches assume that words that appear together in a sentence can be disambiguated by assigning to them the senses that are most closely related to their neighboring words [17]. For instance, in "What is the capital of Spain?", for a human user it is obvious that *capital#c*, should be adopted when considering only Spain as the neighborhood term. Pendersen and his colleagues [17] have made available a Perl implementation of six WordNet measures evaluated in [13] plus their own sense disambiguation algorithm based on glosses [17] to assign a meaning to every content word in a text. Basically, these measures look for a path connecting a synset associated with each word, e.g. in Hirst and St-Onge measure the intuition behind is "the longer the path and the more changes of direction (upward for hypernym and meronym; downward for hyponym and holonym and horizontal for antonymy) the lower the weight". In [17] *extended semantic gloss matchers* measure semantic relatedness between concepts (and its ancestors/descendants according to the *is-a* WordNet hierarchy) that is based on the number of shared words in their definitions (glosses).

SDT based on text is not mature enough because there are useful computational methods in the literature only for *quantifying semantic distances for non-ad hoc relationships.* However, *r*elatedness includes not just the WordNet relationships but also *associative* and *ad hoc* relationships. These can include just about any kind of functional relation or frequent association in the world (i,e bed-sleep), sometimes constructed in the context, and cannot always be determined purely from *a priori* lexical resources such as WordNet.

We believe that in our PowerAqua scenario we can take advantage of the relatedness expressed in the ontology semantics to filter the correct candidate ontology triples equivalent to the user query triples, without the need to apply techniques for text relatedness. This is explained in section 4.4.

4.4 Relation Similarity Services and Linking Triples

Essentially, the relation similarity service (RSS) tries to make sense of the input query and express it in the form of ontology relationships between ontology terms. The RSS is invoked after all the linguistic terminology is mapped into ontology terms (classes or instances). The RSS is responsible of creating the ontology compliant triples by a) linking the mapped ontology terms to create triples and b) linking the triples between themselves. For the step a) to create the triples, a pair of ontology terms is linked by relationships within the same ontology to which the terms belong. For step b) while different triples may belong or not to different ontologies they have to be also linked by at least one common term.

AquaLog mechanisms for step a) and b) can be reused. Briefly, for step a) AquaLog looks for a set of possible ontology relationships between two terms by looking at the structure in the ontology. This set is further disambiguated by the use of distance metrics, or as the vocabulary of the user may have a number of discrepancies with the vocabulary of the ontology it also uses WordNet and a learning mechanism. For step b) sentences that are structurally ambiguous, in the way they are linked, can be disambiguated using domain knowledge or in the last instance by calling the user to choose between alternative readings.

There is not a single strategy here; basically it depends on the query category and ontology structure. A typical situation is when the structure of triples in the ontology do not match the way the information was represented in the query triples. We explore this situation with the following example: consider the query "which KMi researchers working in the Semantic Web have publications in the ESWC conference?" and the subset of ontologies in figure 3. The resultant semantically equivalent mappings or ontology-compliant-triples are presented in table 3. Note that the first query triple *<KMi researchers, working, Semantic Web>* has a translation in both ontologies, while the second query triple *<KMi researchers, have publications, eswc conference>* can only be resolved by the second ontology.

The number of query triples is fixed *a priori* for each query category, however the final number of ontology triples is not obvious at the first stage and it is dependent on the ontology semantics. Therefore, triples must be created at run-time to generate an equivalent representation according to the ontologies. Linguistic terms can be mapped into ontology classes (i.e., "Kmi-researchers"), instances ("Semantic-web-area", "ISWC conference), or even a new triple (like the nominal compound "KMi researchers" into the triple <academics, Belongs-to, KMi>).

Different situations can be found by the similarity services when looking for a proper relation mapping. For instance, the simple case is when a linguistic relation is mapped into a ontology relation like "working" into "has-interest-on" in the case of the first triple. In other cases, to map a relation a new triple must be created, for instance, the relation "have publications" is mapped in the ontology B though the mediating concept "papers", and a new triple is created to represent the indirect relationship (*<academics, wrote, papers> <papers, accepted-in, european semantic web conference>*). Other mapping situations can be found in [4].

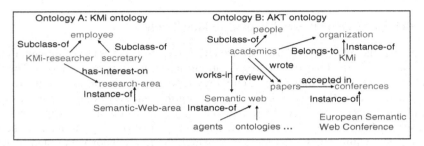

Fig. 3. Ontology scenario example

Table 3. Triples representation

Query-triples (linguistic triples)	Onto-triples (ontology compatible triples)	
<kmi researchers, working, semantic web>	*Ontology 1:* [kmi-researchers, has-interest-on, semantic-web-area]	*Ontology 2:* [academics, belongs-to, kmi] [academics, works-in, semantic-web]
<kmi researchers, have publications, eswc conference>	*Ontology 2:* [academics, wrote, papers] [papers, accepted-in, european semantic web conference]	

4.4.1 Running Example

As said before, through the use of WordNet and the ontology we have narrowed down to two valid non-equivalent mappings for the linguistic triple: *<capital, ?, Spain>*, one in the geographical ontology and the other one in the financial ontology. A deeper analysis of the ontology relationships will find a direct relation that connects any country, e.g. Spain, with its capital for the geographical ontology. However, in the financial ontology there is not a direct relation between countries and capital. There is a mediating concept that represents a company, that has a series of capital goods and it is based in a country. This is a strong indication that the geographical ontology is more related to our query and should be selected.

For the linguistic triple <?, capital, Spain> where capital is considered a relation, a relationship analysis will uncover the relation "is-capital-of" between "country" and "city" in ontology 3 (country statistics), while in the ontology 4 (flight information) there are not any relations similar to "is-capital-of". Therefore ontology 3 is selected.

Note that both triple representations are valid representations of the query and semantically equivalent to each other (they refer to "city" as the ascendant of "capital" in one ontology or as the type of the relation "is-capital-of" in the other ontology). In the next phases of the algorithm, an answer can be generated by correlating both results, e.g. identifying the common instance "Madrid" as an answer, or by selecting one representation.

4.5 Generating an Answer

A key issue when generating an answer is to identify if semantically equivalent concepts in the ontology triples have overlapping information and, in such a case, perform the fusion of instances. For example, in the *KMi semantic web portal ontology*, the instance "Nigel Shadbolt" from the class "researcher" has some basic information, but an instance about the same person has also been defined in the *AKT web portal ontology* under the class "AKT-researcher".

4.5.1 Phase a: Operational Combination of Triples

AquaLog provides two mechanisms (depending on the triple categories) for operationally integrating the triples information to generate an answer. These mechanisms are: (1) and/or link: e.g., in "who has an interest in ontologies or in knowledge reuse?", the result will be a fusion of the instances of people who have an interest in ontologies and the people who are interested in knowledge reuse; (2) conditional link, in which we can differentiate between: a) conditional link to a term: e.g. in "which KMi academics work in the akt project sponsored by eprsc?" the second triple *<akt project, sponsored, eprsc>* must be resolved and the instance representing the "akt project sponsored by eprsc" identified to get the list of academics required for the first triple *<KMi academics, work, akt project>*; and b) conditional link to a triple: e.g. in "What are the homepages of the researchers working on the semantic web?" the second triple *<researchers, working, semantic web>* must be resolved and the list of researchers obtained prior to generating an answer for the first triple *<?, homepage, researchers>*.

4.5.2 Information Correlation: Identify Common Instances

It is common to get semantically equivalent triples from different ontologies, as a translation of one query triple. The challenge is to identify the instances in common between the two equivalent terms in each triple. For example, the query "Who are the academics working on the Semantic Web?" might have a complete translation in the ontology X about researchers in KMi, ontology Y about academics in the University of Trento and ontology Z about the AKT consortium. Ontologies X and Y have no instances in common. However, ontologies X and Z contain overlapping information, as many of the academics in KMi belong to the AKT project. Common instances must be identified to give a complete non-redundant answer.

Furthermore, for queries represented by partial translations from different ontologies the identification of common instances is also a key issue. For instance, the query "What are the citations for the publications of Enrico Motta?" is solved by an ontology about citations and an ontology about academics in which the instance "Enrico Motta" is related to his publications. The publications from the academics ontology must be identified in the citations ontology.

Identifying whether two instances from semantically equivalent concepts are the same is not an easy task. Instances may not have the same name, and information about the same instance can have different purposes, e.g. the description of a car for sale or for an environmental study. We can use the OWL mechanism which identifies the attributes that provide sufficient evidence that two instances are the same. However, further mechanisms need to be adopted, e.g., use of joint probability approaches similar to GLUE[3] over the instance full name (from the taxonomy root) and its textual content (word frequency over attributes and values)

5   Related Work

The AquaLog linguistic component, reused for PowerAqua, in combination with the SW scenario provides a new twist on the old issues associated to asking natural language queries to databases (NLDB). See [4] for comparisons between AquaLog and previous work in NLDB and open-domain NL QA systems. Here, we look at the solutions proposed in the literature to address semantic heterogeneity in information systems.

The Semantic Knowledge Articulation Tool (SKAT) [18] uses a first order logic notation to specify declarative matching rules between ontology terms. SKAT initially attempts to match nodes in the two graphs based on their labels and their structural similarity. The idea of presenting a conceptually unified view of the information space to the user, the *world-view*, is studied in [19]. The user can pose declarative queries in terms of the objects and the relations in the *world-view*. Given a query to the *world-view*, the query processor in the global information system poses subqueries to the external sources that contain the information relevant to answer a query. In order to do that, the semantic of the contents of the external sites is related to the *world-view* through the use of a description language. These solutions have an intrinsic limitation to be applied to the open-world domain introduced by the SW scenario, where the distributed sources are constantly growing. And therefore, it is not possible to apply any closed-domain solution for environments with well-defined boundaries, like corporate intranets, in which the problem can be addressed by the specification of shared models like mapping rules, global ontologies/vocabularies, and definitions of conversion libraries or functions between semantic data/values, among others. The manual effort needed to maintain any kind of centralized/global shared approach for semantic mapping (i.e. to implement the previous solution) in the SW is not only very costly, in terms of maintaining the mappings for such a highly dynamic environment that evolves quickly, but also has the added difficulty of "negotiating" a shared model that suits the needs of all the parties involved [20].

In Query Processing in Global Information Systems [9] user queries are rewritten by using inter-ontology relationships to obtain semantic translations across ontologies. There are two restrictions: firstly the user must subscribe to the terminology and model captured by a chosen ontology. Secondly, the solution to the vocabulary problem is obtained through the declarative representation of synonym relationships relating ontology terms. The disadvantages are: 1) synonym relationship mappings must be maintained between terms in the user ontology and the underlying repositories. 2) Every time there is a change in the structure of underlying repositories the mappings of the component ontology must be change. 3) Such synonym relationships should be defined when a new ontology is added to the system (its centralized nature may affect the efficiency of the system). The advantage is that different partial answers can be easily correlated since all of them are expressed in the language of the user ontology.

CUPID [21] analyzes the factors that affect effectiveness of algorithms for automatic semantic reconciliations; however, this is a complementary goal to ours: our system matches terms and relations in an user's query with distributed ontologies while they match data repositories and ontologies. In GLUE [3] the probability of matching two concepts is studied by analyzing the available ontologies using a relaxation labeling methods; however, this approach is not very adaptable because it analyzes all the ontology concepts. Finally, In our QA-driven scenario there is no need for obtaining mappings for each pair of concepts belonging to different ontologies, in which the level of effort is at least linear in the number of matches to be performed [22] (see algorithms for the Match operator [22]). In our run-time scenario only relevant concepts to the user's query are analyzed (on-demand driven approach).

6 Summary

We have presented the design of PowerAqua, a novel QA system which provides answers drawn from multiple, heterogeneous and distributed ontologies on the Web. PowerAqua evolved from AquaLog, an implemented ontology-based QA system limited to one ontology at a time. The issues derived from opening the system with respect to the SW have been addressed here. A prototype based on the algorithm presented here will be implemented in the following months.

Acknowledgements

This work was partially supported by the AKT project sponsored by UK EPSRC and by the EU OpenKnowledge project (FP6-027253). Thanks to Yuangui Lei and Marta Sabou for useful input.

References

1. The Semantic Web. Berners-Lee, T., Hendler, J. and Lassila, O. *Scientific American, 284(5):* 33-43 (2001)
2. Semantic Integration of Heterogeneous Information Sources Using a Knowledge-Based System. Adams T., Dullea J., Clark P., Sripada S. and Barrett T. *In Proc. of the 5th International Conference on Computer Science and Informatics,* (2000).
3. Learning to Map between Ontologies on the Semantic Web. Doan A., Madhavan J., Domingos P., and Halevy A. *In Proc. of the World-Wide Web Conference* (2002).
4. AquaLog: An Ontology-portable Question Answering System for the Semantic Web. Lopez V., Pasin M. and Motta E. *In Proc. of the 2nd European Semantic Web Conference* (2005)
5. Question Answering on the SW. Mc Guinness,D. *IEEE Intelligent Systems,19(1)82-85* (2004)

6. Cunningham, H., Maynard, D., Bontcheva, K., Tablan, V.: GATE: A Framework and Graphical Development Environment for Robust NLP Tools and Applications. *In Proc. of the 40th Anniversary Meeting of the Association for Computational Linguistics (ACL'02).* Philadelphia (2002).

7. Swoogle: A semantic web search and metadata engine. X L. Ding et al. *In Proc. 13th ACM Conf. on Information And Knowledge Management* (2004)

8. An Evaluation of Knowledge Base Systems for Large OWL Datasets. Guo, Y., Pan, Z., Heflin, J. *International Semantic Web Conference* 274-288 (2004)

9. OBSERVER: An approach for Query Processing in Global Information Systems based on Interoperation across Pre-existing Ontologies. Mena E., Kashyap V., Sheth A. and Illarramendi A. *Distributed and Parallel Databases* 8(2): 223-271 (2000)

10. S-Match: an algorithm and an implementation of semantic matching. Giunchiglia F., Shvaiko P and Yatskevich M. *In Proc. of the 1t European Semantic Web Symposium* (2004).

11. Ontology Ranking based on the Analysis of Concept Structures. Alani, H. and Brewster, C. *In Proc, of the 3th International Conference on Knowledge Capture* (2005).

12. Word Sense Disambiguation: The State of the Art. Ide N. and Veronis J. *Computational Linguistics*, 24(1):1-40. (1998).

13. Evaluating WordNet-based measures of semantic distance. Budanitsky, A. and Hirst, G. *Computational Linguistics* (2006).

14. Disambiguating noun grouping with respect to WordNet senses. Resnik P. *In Proc. of the 3rd Workshop on very Large Corpora.* MIT (1995).

15. Element Level Semantic Matching. Giunchiglia F. and Yatskevich M. *Meaning Coordination and Negotiation Workshop, ISWC* (2004).

16. Making Explicit the Semantics Hidden in Schema Models. Magnini B., Serafín L., and Speranza M. *In Proc. of the Workshop on Human Language Technology for the Semantic Web and Web Services*, held at *ISWC-2003*, Sanibel Island, Florida, (2003).

17. Extended Gloss Overlaps as a Measure of Semantic Relatedness. Banerjee S., and Pedersen T. *International Joint Conference on Artificial Intelligence* (2003).

18. Semi-automatic Integration of Knowledge Sources. Mitra P., Wiederhold G., Jannink J. *In Proc. of the 2nd International Conf.erence on Information Fusion.* (1999).

19. Data Model and Query Evaluation in Global Information Systems. Levy A., Y., Srivastava D. and Kirk T. *Journal of Intelligence Information Systems.* 5(2): 121-143 (1995).

20. Semantic coordination: a new approach and an application. Bouquet P., Serafini L. and Zanobini S. *International Semantic Web Conference* 130-145 (2003).

21. Generic schema matching with cupid. Madhavan, J., Bernstein, P.A. and Rahm, E. *The Very Large Databases Journal*: 49-58 (2001)

22. A survey of approaches to automatic schema matching. Rahm E. and Bernstein P. A. *The VLDB Journal — The International Journal on Very Large Data Bases* 10(4): 334-350, (2001).

Information Retrieval in Folksonomies: Search and Ranking

Andreas Hotho[1], Robert Jäschke[1,2], Christoph Schmitz[1], and Gerd Stumme[1,2]

[1] Knowledge & Data Engineering Group, Department of Mathematics and Computer Science,
University of Kassel, Wilhelmshöher Allee 73, D–34121 Kassel, Germany
http://www.kde.cs.uni-kassel.de
[2] Research Center L3S, Expo Plaza 1, D–30539 Hannover, Germany
http://www.l3s.de

Abstract. Social bookmark tools are rapidly emerging on the Web. In such systems users are setting up lightweight conceptual structures called folksonomies. The reason for their immediate success is the fact that no specific skills are needed for participating. At the moment, however, the information retrieval support is limited. We present a formal model and a new search algorithm for folksonomies, called *FolkRank*, that exploits the structure of the folksonomy. The proposed algorithm is also applied to find communities within the folksonomy and is used to structure search results. All findings are demonstrated on a large scale dataset.

1 Introduction

Complementing the Semantic Web effort, a new breed of so-called "Web 2.0" applications is currently emerging on the Web. These include user-centric publishing and knowledge management platforms like Wikis, Blogs, and social resource sharing tools.

These tools, such as Flickr[1] or del.icio.us,[2] have acquired large numbers of users within less than two years.[3] The reason for their immediate success is the fact that no specific skills are needed for participating, and that these tools yield immediate benefit for each individual user (e.g. organizing ones bookmarks in a browser-independent, persistent fashion) without too much overhead. Large numbers of users have created huge amounts of information within a very short period of time. The frequent use of these systems shows clearly that web- and folksonomy-based approaches are able to overcome the knowledge acquisition bottleneck, which was a serious handicap for many knowledge-based systems in the past.

Social resource sharing systems all use the same kind of lightweight knowledge representation, called *folksonomy*. The word 'folksonomy' is a blend of the words 'taxonomy' and 'folk', and stands for conceptual structures created by the people. Folksonomies are thus a bottom-up complement to more formalized Semantic Web technologies, as they rely on *emergent semantics* [11, 12] which result from the converging

---

[1] http://www.flickr.com/
[2] http://del.icio.us
[3] From discussions on the del.icio.us mailing list, one can approximate the number of users on del.icio.us to be more than three hundred thousand.

Y. Sure and J. Domingue (Eds.): ESWC 2006, LNCS 4011, pp. 411–426, 2006.
© Springer-Verlag Berlin Heidelberg 2006

use of the same vocabulary. The main difference to 'classical' ontology engineering approaches is their aim to respect to the largest possible extent the request of non-expert users not to be bothered with any formal modeling overhead. Intelligent techniques may well be inside the system, but should be hidden from the user.

A first step to searching folksonomy based systems – complementing the browsing interface usually provided as of today – is to employ standard techniques used in information retrieval or, more recently, in web search engines. Since users are used to web search engines, they likely will accept a similar interface for search in folksonomy-based systems. The research question is how to provide suitable ranking mechanisms, similar to those based on the web graph structure, but now exploiting the structure of folksonomies instead. To this end, we propose a formal model for folksonomies, and present a new algorithm, called *FolkRank*, that takes into account the folksonomy structure for ranking search requests in folksonomy based systems. The algorithm will be used for two purposes: determining an overall ranking, and specific topic-related rankings.

This paper is organized as follows. Section 2 reviews recent developments in the area of social bookmark systems, and presents a formal model. Section 3 recalls the basics of the PageRank algorithm, describes our adaptation to folksonomies, and discusses experimental results. These results indicate the need for a more sophisticated algorithm for topic-specific search. Such an algorithm, FolkRank, is presented in Section 4. This section includes also an empirical evaluation, as well as a discussion of its use for generating personal recommendations in folksonomies. Section 5 concludes the paper with a discussion of further research topics on the intersection between folksonomies and ontologies.

2   Social Resource Sharing and Folksonomies

Social resource sharing systems are web-based systems that allow users to upload their resources, and to label them with arbitrary words, so-called *tags*. The systems can be distinguished according to what kind of resources are supported. Flickr, for instance, allows the sharing of photos, del.icio.us the sharing of bookmarks, CiteULike[4] and Connotea[5] the sharing of bibliographic references, and 43Things[6] even the sharing of goals in private life. Our own system, *BibSonomy*,[7] allows to share simultaneously bookmarks and bibtex entries (see Fig. 1).

In their core, these systems are all very similar. Once a user is logged in, he can add a resource to the system, and assign arbitrary tags to it. The collection of all his assignments is his *personomy*, the collection of all personomies constitutes the *folksonomy*. The user can explore his personomy, as well as the personomies of the other users, in all dimensions: for a given user one can see all resources he had uploaded, together with the tags he had assigned to them (see Fig. 1); when clicking on a resource one

---

[4] http://www.citeulike.org/
[5] http://www.connotea.org/
[6] http://www.43things.com/
[7] http://www.bibsonomy.org

Fig. 1. Bibsonomy displays bookmarks and BibTeX based bibliographic references simultaneously

sees which other users have uploaded this resource and how they tagged it; and when clicking on a tag one sees who assigned it to which resources.

The systems allow for additional functionality. For instance, one can copy a resource from another user, and label it with one's own tags. Overall, these systems provide a very intuitive navigation through the data. However, the resources that are displayed are usually ordered by date, i. e., the resources entered last show up at the top. A more sophisticated notion of 'relevance' – which could be used for ranking – is still missing.

2.1   State of the Art

There are currently virtually no scientific publications about folksonomy-based web collaboration systems. The main discussion on folksonomies and related topics is currently taking place on mailing lists only, e.g. [3]. Among the rare exceptions are [5] and [8] who provide good overviews of social bookmarking tools with special emphasis on folksonomies, and [9] who discusses strengths and limitations of folksonomies. In [10], Mika defines a model of semantic-social networks for extracting lightweight ontologies from del.icio.us. Besides calculating measures like the clustering coefficient, (local) betweenness centrality or the network constraint on the extracted one-mode network, Mika uses co-occurence techniques for clustering the folksonomy.

There are several systems working on top of del.icio.us to explore the underlying folksonomy. CollaborativeRank[8] provides ranked search results on top of del.icio.us bookmarks. The ranking takes into account how early someone bookmarked an URL and how many people followed him or her. Other systems show popular sites (Populicious[9]) or focus on graphical representations (Cloudalicio[10], Grafolicious[11]) of statistics about del.icio.us.

---

[8] http://collabrank.org/

[9] http://populicio.us/

[10] http://cloudalicio.us/

[11] http://www.neuroticweb.com/recursos/del.icio.us-graphs/

Confoto,[12] the winner of the 2005 Semantic Web Challenge, is a service to annotate and browse conference photos and offers besides rich semantics also tagging facilities for annotation. Due to the representation of this rich metadata in RDF it has limitations in both size and performance.

Ranking techniques have also been applied in traditional ontology engineering. The tool Ontocopi [1] performs what is called Ontology Network Analysis for initially populating an organizational memory. Several network analysis methods are applied to an already populated ontology to extract important objects. In particular, a PageRank-like [2] algorithm is used to find communities of practice within sets of individuals represented in the ontology. The algorithm used in Ontocopi to find nodes related to an individual removes the respective individual from the graph and measures the difference of the resulting Perron eigenvectors of the adjacency matrices as the influence of that individual. This approach differs insofar from our proposed method, as it tracks which nodes benefit from the removal of the invidual, instead of actually preferring the individual and measuring which related nodes are more influenced than others.

2.2   A Formal Model for Folksonomies

A folksonomy describes the users, resources, and tags, and the user-based assignment of tags to resources. We present here a formal definition of folksonomies, which is also underlying our BibSonomy system.

Definition 1. *A folksonomy is a tuple* $\mathbb{F} := (U, T, R, Y, \prec)$ *where*

- *U, T, and R are finite sets, whose elements are called* users, tags *and* resources, *resp.,*
- *Y is a ternary relation between them, i. e.,* $Y \subseteq U \times T \times R$, *called tag assignments (TAS for short), and*
- $\prec$ *is a user-specific subtag/supertag-relation, i. e.,* $\prec \subseteq U \times T \times T$, *called* subtag/supertag relation.

The personomy $\mathbb{P}_u$ *of a given user* $u \in U$ *is the restriction of* $\mathbb{F}$ *to u, i. e.,* $\mathbb{P}_u := (T_u, R_u, I_u, \prec_u)$ *with* $I_u := \{(t, r) \in T \times R \mid (u, t, r) \in Y\}$, $T_u := \pi_1(I_u)$, $R_u := \pi_2(I_u)$, *and* $\prec_u := \{(t_1, t_2) \in T \times T \mid (u, t_1, t_2) \in \prec\}$, *where* π_i *denotes the projection on the ith dimension.*

Users are typically described by their user ID, and tags may be arbitrary strings. What is considered as a resource depends on the type of system. For instance, in del.icio.us, the resources are URLs, and in flickr, the resources are pictures. From an implementation point of view, resources are internally represented by some ID.

In this paper, we do not make use of the subtag/supertag relation for sake of simplicity. I. e., $\prec = \emptyset$, and we will simply note a folksonomy as a quadruple $\mathbb{F} := (U, T, R, Y)$. This structure is known in Formal Concept Analysis [14, 4] as a *triadic context* [7, 13]. An equivalent view on folksonomy data is that of a tripartite (undirected) hypergraph $G = (V, E)$, where $V = U \dot\cup T \dot\cup R$ is the set of nodes, and $E = \{\{u, t, r\} \mid (u, t, r) \in Y\}$ is the set of hyperedges.

---

[12] http://www.confoto.org/

2.3   Del.ico.us — A Folksonomy-Based Social Bookmark System

In order to evaluate our retrieval technique detailed in the next section, we have analyzed the popular social bookmarking sytem del.icio.us, which is a server-based system with a simple-to-use interface that allows users to organize and share bookmarks on the internet. It is able to store in addition to the URL a description, an extended description, and tags (i. e., arbitrary labels). We chose del.icio.us rather than our own system, BibSonomy, as the latter went online only after the time of writing of this article.

For our experiments, we collected data from the del.ico.us system in the following way. Initially we used `wget` starting from the top page of del.icio.us to obtain nearly 6900 users and 700 tags as a starting set. Out of this dataset we extracted all users and resources (i. e., del.icio.us' MD5-hashed urls). From July 27 to 30, 2005, we downloaded in a recursive manner user pages to get new resources, and resource pages to get new users. Furthermore we monitored the del.icio.us start page to gather additional users and resources. This way we collected a list of several thousand usernames which we used for accessing the first 10000 resources each user had tagged. From the collected data we finally took the user files to extract resources, tags, dates, descriptions, extended descriptions, and the corresponding username.

We obtained a core folksonomy with $|U| = 75,242$ users, $|T| = 533,191$ tags and $|R| = 3,158,297$ resources, related by in total $|Y| = 17,362,212$ TAS.[13] After inserting this dataset into a MySQL database, we were able to perform our evaluations, as described in the following sections.

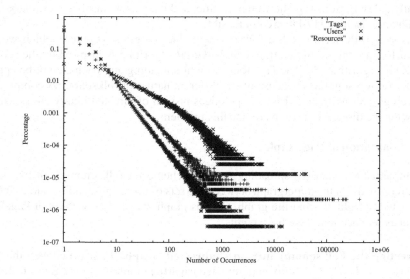

Fig. 2. Number of TAS occurrences for tags, users, resources in del.icio.us

---

[13] 4,313 users additionally organised 113,562 of the tags with 6,527 so-called *bundles*. The bundles will not be discussed in this paper; they can be interpreted as one level of the $\prec$ relation.

As expected, the tagging behavior in del.icio.us shows a power law distribution, see Figure 2. This figure presents the percentage of tags, users, and resources, respectively, which occur in a given number of TAS. For instance, the rightmost '+' indicates that a fraction of $2.19 \cdot 10^{-6}$ of all tags (i. e. one tag) occurs 415950 times – in this case it is the empty tag. The next '+' shows that one tag ("web") occurs 238891 times, and so on. One observes that while the tags follow a power law distribution very strictly, the plot for users and resources levels off for small numbers of occurrences. Based on this observation, we estimate to have crawled most of the tags, while many users and resources are still missing from the dataset. A probable reason is that many users only try posting a single resource, often without entering any tags (the empty tag is the most frequent one in the dataset), before they decide not to use the system anymore. These users and resources are very unlikely to be connected with others at all (and they only appear for a short period on the del.icio.us start page), so that they are not included in our crawl.

3   Ranking in Folksonomies Using Adapted PageRank

Current folksonomy tools such as del.icio.us provide only very limited search support in addition to their browsing interface. Searching can be performed over the text of tags and resource descriptions, but no ranking is done apart from ordering the hits in reverse chronological order. Using traditional information retrieval, folksonomy contents can be searched textually. However, as the documents consist of short text snippets only (usually a description, e. g. the web page title, and the tags themselves), ordinary ranking schemes such as TF/IDF are not feasible.

As shown in Section 2.2, a folksonomy induces a graph structure which we will exploit for ranking in this section. Our *FolkRank* algorithm is inspired by the seminal PageRank algorithm [2]. The PageRank weight-spreading approach cannot be applied directly on folksonomies because of the different nature of folksonomies compared to the web graph (undirected triadic hyperedges instead of directed binary edges). In the following we discuss how to overcome this problem.

3.1   Adaptation of PageRank

We implement the weight-spreading ranking scheme on folksonomies in two steps. First, we transform the hypergraph between the sets of users, tags, and resources into an undirected, weighted, tripartite graph. On this graph, we apply a version of PageRank that takes into account the edge weights.

Converting the Folksonomy into an Undirected Graph.   First we convert the folksonomy $\mathbb{F} = (U, T, R, Y)$ into an *un*directed tripartite graph $\mathbb{G}_\mathbb{F} = (V, E)$ as follows.

1. The set V of nodes of the graph consists of the disjoint union of the sets of tags, users and resources: $V = U \dot\cup T \dot\cup R$. (The tripartite structure of the graph can be exploited later for an efficient storage of the – sparse – adjacency matrix and the implementation of the weight-spreading iteration in the FolkRank algorithm.)

2. All co-occurrences of tags and users, users and resources, tags and resources become undirected, weighted edges between the respective nodes: $E = \{\{u, t\}, \{t, r\}, \{u, r\} \mid (u, t, r) \in Y\}$, with each edge $\{u, t\}$ being weighted with $|\{r \in R : (u, t, r) \in Y\}|$, each edge $\{t, r\}$ with $|\{u \in U : (u, t, r) \in Y\}|$, and each edge $\{u, r\}$ with $|\{t \in T : (u, t, r) \in Y\}|$.

Folksonomy-Adapted Pagerank. The original formulation of PageRank [2] reflects the idea that a page is important if there many pages linking to it, and if those pages are important themselves. The distribution of weights can thus be described as the fixed point of a weight passing scheme on the web graph. This idea was extended in a similar fashion to bipartite subgraphs of the web in HITS [6] and to n-ary directed graphs in [15]). We employ the same underlying principle for our ranking scheme in folksonomies. The basic notion is that a resource which is tagged with important tags by important users becomes important itself. The same holds, symmetrically, for tags and users. Thus we have a graph of vertices which are mutually reinforcing each other by spreading their weights.

Like PageRank, we employ the random surfer model, a notion of importance for web pages that is based on the idea that an idealized random web surfer normally follows hyperlinks, but from time to time randomly jumps to a new webpage without following a link. This results in the following definition of the rank of the vertices of the graph the entries in the fixed point $\vec{w}$ of the weight spreading computation $\vec{w} \leftarrow dA\vec{w} + (1 - d)\vec{p}$, where $\vec{w}$ is a weight vector with one entry for each web page, A is the row-stochastic[14] version of the adjacency matrix of the graph $G_{\mathbb{F}}$ defined above, $\vec{p}$ is the random surfer component, and $d \in [0, 1]$ is determining the influence of $\vec{p}$. In the original PageRank, $\vec{p}$ is used to outweigh the loss of weight on web pages without outgoing links. Usually, one will choose $\vec{p} = \mathbf{1}$, i.e., the vector composed by 1's. In order to compute personalized PageRanks, however, $\vec{p}$ can be used to express user preferences by giving a higher weight to the components which represent the user's preferred web pages.

We employ a similar motivation for our ranking scheme in folksonomies. The basic notion is that a resource which is tagged with important tags by important users becomes important itself. The same holds, symmetrically, for tags and users, thus we have a tripartite graph in which the vertices are mutually reinforcing each other by spreading their weights. Formally, we spread the weight as follows:

$$\vec{w} \quad \leftarrow \quad \alpha\vec{w} + \beta A\vec{w} + \gamma\vec{p} \tag{1}$$

where A is the row-stochastic version of the adjacency matrix of $\mathbb{G}_{\mathbb{F}}$, $\vec{p}$ is a preference vector, $\alpha, \beta, \gamma \in [0, 1]$ are constants with $\alpha + \beta + \gamma = 1$. The constant α is intended to regulate the speed of convergence, while the proportion between β and γ controls the influence of the preference vector.

We call the iteration according to Equation 1 – until convergence is achieved – the *Adapted PageRank* algorithm. Note that, if $||\vec{w}||_1 = ||\vec{p}||_1$ holds,[15] the sum of the weights in the system will remain constant. The influence of different settings of the parameters α, β, and γ is discussed below.

---

[14] i.e., each row of the matrix is normalized to 1 in the 1-norm.

[15] ...and if there are no rank sinks – but this holds trivially in our graph $G_{\mathbb{F}}$.

As the graph G_F is undirected, part of the weight that went through an edge at moment t will flow back at $t + 1$. The results are thus rather similar (but not identical) to a ranking that is simply based on edge degrees, as we will see now. The reason for applying the more expensive PageRank approach nonetheless is that its random surfer vector allows for topic-specific ranking, as we will discuss in the next section.

3.2 Results for Adapted PageRank

We have evaluated the Adapted PageRank on the del.ico.us dataset described in Section 2.3. As there exists no 'gold standard ranking' on these data, we evaluate our results empirically.

First, we studied the speed of convergence. We let $\vec{p} := 1$ (the vector having 1 in all components), and varied the parameter settings. In all settings, we discovered that

Table 1. Folksonomy Adapted PageRank applied without preferences (called *baseline*)

Tag	ad. PageRank	User	ad. PageRank
system:unfiled	0,0078404	shankar	0,0007389
web	0,0044031	notmuch	0,0007379
blog	0,0042003	fritz	0,0006796
design	0,0041828	ubi.quito.us	0,0006171
software	0,0038904	weev	0,0005044
music	0,0037273	kof2002	0,0004885
programming	0,0037100	ukquake	0,0004844
css	0,0030766	gearhead	0,0004820
reference	0,0026019	angusf	0,0004797
linux	0,0024779	johncollins	0,0004668
tools	0,0024147	mshook	0,0004556
news	0,0023611	frizzlebiscuit	0,0004543
art	0,0023358	rafaspol	0,0004535
blogs	0,0021035	xiombarg	0,0004520
politics	0,0019371	tidesonar02	0,0004355
java	0,0018757	cyrusnews	0,0003829
javascript	0,0017610	bldurling	0,0003727
mac	0,0017252	onpause_tv_anytime	0,0003600
games	0,0015801	cataracte	0,0003462
photography	0,0015469	triple_entendre	0,0003419
fun	0,0015296	kayodeok	0,0003407

URL	ad. PageRank
http://slashdot.org/	0,0002613
http://pchere.blogspot.com/2005/02/absolutely-delicious-complete-tool.html	0,0002320
http://script.aculo.us/	0,0001770
http://www.adaptivepath.com/publications/essays/archives/000385.php	0,0001654
http://johnvey.com/features/deliciousdirector/	0,0001593
http://en.wikipedia.org/wiki/Main_Page	0,0001407
http://www.flickr.com/	0,0001376
http://www.goodfonts.org/	0,0001349
http://www.43folders.com/	0,0001160
http://www.csszengarden.com/	0,0001149
http://wellstyled.com/tools/colorscheme2/index-en.html	0,0001108
http://pro.html.it/esempio/nifty/	0,0001070
http://www.alistapart.com/	0,0001059
http://postsecret.blogspot.com/	0,0001058
http://www.beelerspace.com/index.php?p=890	0,0001035
http://www.techsupportalert.com/best_46_free_utilities.htm	0,0001034
http://www.alvit.de/web-dev/	0,0001020
http://www.technorati.com/	0,0001015
http://www.lifehacker.com/	0,0001009
http://www.lucazappa.com/brilliantMaker/buttonImage.php	0,0000992
http://www.engadget.com/	0,0000984

$\alpha \neq 0$ slows down the convergence rate. For instance, for $\alpha = 0.35, \beta = 0.65, \gamma = 0$, 411 iterations were needed, while $\alpha = 0, \beta = 1, \gamma = 0$ returned the same result in only 320 iterations. It turns out that using γ as a damping factor by spreading equal weight to each node in each iteration speeds up the convergence considerably by a factory of approximately 10 (e. g., 39 iterations for $\alpha = 0, \beta = 0.85, \gamma = 0.15$).

Table 1 shows the result of the adapted PageRank algorithm for the 20 most important tags, users and resources computed with the parameters $\alpha = 0.35, \beta = 0.65, \gamma = 0$ (which equals the result for $\alpha = 0, \beta = 1, \gamma = 0$). Tags get the highest ranks, followed by the users, and the resources. Therefore, we present their rankings in separate lists.

As we can see from the tag table, the most important tag is "system:unfiled" which is used to indicate that a user did not assign any tag to a resource. It is followed by "web", "blog", "design" etc. This corresponds more or less to the rank of the tags given by the overall tag count in the dataset. The reason is that the graph $G_{\mathbb{F}}$ is undirected. We face thus the problem that, in the Adapted PageRank algorithm, weights that flow in one direction of an edge will basically 'swash back' along the same edge in the next iteration. Therefore the resulting is very similar (although not equal!) to a ranking based on counting edge degrees.

The resource ranking shows that Web 2.0 web sites like Slashdot, Wikipedia, Flickr, and a del.icio.us related blog appear in top positions. This is not surprising, as early users of del.ico.us are likely to be interested in Web 2.0 in general. This ranking correlates also strongly with a ranking based on edge counts.

The results for the top users are of more interest as different kinds of users appear. As all top users have more than 6000 bookmarks; "notmuch" has a large amount of tags, while the tag count of "fritz" is considerably smaller.

To see how good the topic-specific ranking by Adapted PageRank works, we combined it with term frequency, a standard information retrieval weighting scheme. To this end, we downloaded all 3 million web pages referred to by a URL in our dataset. From these, we considered all plain text and html web pages, which left 2.834.801 documents. We converted all web pages into ASCII and computed an inverted index. To search for a term as in a search engine, we retrieved all pages containing the search term and ranked them by $tf(t) \cdot \vec{w}[v]$ where $tf(t)$ is the term frequency of search term t in page v, and $\vec{w}[v]$ is the Adapted PageRank weight of v.

Although this is a rather straightforward combination of two successful retrieval techniques, our experiments with different topic-specific queries indicate that this adaptation of PageRank does not work very well. For instance, for the search term "football", the del.icio.us homepage showed up as the first result. Indeed, most of the highly ranked pages have nothing to do with football.

Other search terms provided similar results. Apparently, the overall structure of the – undirected – graph overrules the influence of the preference vector. In the next section, we discuss how to overcome this problem.

4   FolkRank – Topic-Specific Ranking in Folksonomies

In order to reasonably focus the ranking around the topics defined in the preference vector, we have developed a differential approach, which compares the resulting rankings with and without preference vector. This resulted in our new *FolkRank* algorithm.

4.1   The FolkRank Algorithm

The FolkRank algorithm computes a topic-specific ranking in a folksonomy as follows:

1. The preference vector $\vec{p}$ is used to determine the topic. It may have any distribution of weights, as long as $||\vec{w}||_1 = ||\vec{p}||_1$ holds. Typically a single entry or a small set of entries is set to a high value, and the remaining weight is equally distributed over the other entries. Since the structure of folksonomies is symmetric, we can define a topic by assigning a high value to either one or more tags and/or one or more users and/or one or more resources.
2. Let $\vec{w_0}$ be the fixed point from Equation (1) with $\beta = 1$.
3. Let $\vec{w_1}$ be the fixed point from Equation (1) with $\beta < 1$.
4. $\vec{w} := \vec{w_1} - \vec{w_0}$ is the final weight vector.

Thus, we compute the winners and losers of the mutual reinforcement of resources when a user preference is given, compared to the baseline without a preference vector. We call the resulting weight $\vec{w}[x]$ of an element x of the folksonomy the *FolkRank* of x.

Whereas the Adapted PageRank provides one global ranking, independent of any preferences, FolkRank provides one topic-specific ranking for each given preference vector. Note that a topic can be defined in the preference vector not only by assigning higher weights to specific tags, but also to specific resources and users. These three dimensions can even be combined in a mixed vector. Similarly, the ranking is not restricted to resources, it may as well be applied to tags and to users. We will show below that indeed the rankings on all three dimensions provide interesting insights.

4.2   Comparing FolkRank with Adapted PageRank

To analyse the proposed FolkRank algorithm, we generated rankings for several topics, and compared them with the ones obtained from Adapted PageRank. We will here discuss two sets of search results, one for the tag "boomerang", and one for the URL http.//www.semanticweb.org. Our other experiments all provided similar results.

The leftmost part of Table 2 contains the ranked list of tags according to their weights from the Adapted PageRank by using the parameters $\alpha = 0.2, \beta = 0.5, \gamma = 0.3$, and 5 as a weight for the tag "boomerang" in the preference vector $\vec{p}$, while the other elements were given a weight of 0. As expected, the tag "boomerang" holds the first position while tags like "shop" or "wood" which are related are also under the Top 20. The tags "software", "java", "programming" or "web", however, are on positions 4 to 7, but have nothing to do with "boomerang". The only reason for their showing up is that they are frequently used in del.icio.us (cf. Table 1). The second column from the left in Table 2 contains the results of our FolkRank algorithm, again for the tag "boomerang". Intuitively, this ranking is better, as the globally frequent words disappear and related words like "wood" and "construction" are ranked higher.

A closer look reveals that this ranking still contains some unexpected tags; "kassel" or "rdf" are for instance not obviously related to "boomerang". An analysis of the user ranking (not displayed) explains this fact. The top-ranked user is "schm4704", and he has indeed many bookmarks about boomerangs. A FolkRank run with preference

Table 2. Ranking results for the tag "boomerang" (two left at top: Adapted PageRank and FolkRank for tags, middle: FolkRank for URLs) and for the user "schm4704" (two right at top: Adapted PageRank and FolkRank for tags, bottom: FolkRank for URLs)

Tag	ad. PRank	Tag	FolkRank	Tag	ad. PRank	Tag	FolkRank
boomerang	0,4036883	boomerang	0,4036867	boomerang	0,0093549	boomerang	0,0093533
shop	0,0069058	shop	0,0066477	lang:ade	0,0068111	lang:de	0,0068028
lang:de	0,0050943	lang:de	0,0050860	shop	0,0052600	shop	0,0050019
software	0,0016797	wood	0,0012236	java	0,0052050	java	0,0033293
java	0,0016389	kassel	0,0011964	web	0,0049360	kassel	0,0032223
programming	0,0016296	construction	0,0010828	programming	0,0037894	network	0,0028990
web	0,0016043	plans	0,0010085	software	0,0035000	rdf	0,0028758
reference	0,0014713	injuries	0,0008078	network	0,0032882	wood	0,0028447
system:unfiled	0,0014199	pitching	0,0007982	kassel	0,0032228	delicious	0,0026345
wood	0,0012378	rdf	0,0006619	reference	0,0030699	semantic	0,0024736
kassel	0,0011969	semantic	0,0006533	rdf	0,0030645	database	0,0023571
linux	0,0011442	material	0,0006279	delicious	0,0030492	guitar	0,0018619
construction	0,0011023	trifly	0,0005691	system:unfiled	0,0029393	computing	0,0018404
plans	0,0010226	network	0,0005568	linux	0,0029393	cinema	0,0017537
network	0,0009460	webring	0,0005552	wood	0,0028589	lessons	0,0017273
rdf	0,0008506	sna	0,0005073	database	0,0026931	social	0,0016950
css	0,0008266	socialnetworkanalysis	0,0004822	semantic	0,0025460	documentation	0,0016182
design	0,0008248	cinema	0,0004726	css	0,0024577	scientific	0,0014686
delicious	0,0008097	erie	0,0004525	social	0,0021969	filesystem	0,0014212
injuries	0,0008087	riparian	0,0004467	webdesign	0,0020650	userspace	0,0013490
pitching	0,0007999	erosion	0,0004425	computing	0,0020143	library	0,0012398

Url	FolkRank
http://www.flight-toys.com/boomerangs.htm	0,0047322
http://www.flight-toys.com/	0,0047322
http://www.bumerangclub.de/	0,0045785
http://www.bumerangfibel.de/	0,0045781
http://www.kutek.net/trifly_mods.php	0,0032643
http://www.rediboom.de/	0,0032126
http://www.bws-buhmann.de/	0,0032126
http://www.akspiele.de/	0,0031813
http://www.medco-athletics.com/education/elbow_shoulder_injuries/	0,0031606
http://www.sportsprolo.com/sports%20prolotherapy%20newsletter%20pitching%20injuries.htm	0,0031606
http://www.boomerangpassion.com/english.php	0,0031005
http://www.kuhara.de/bumerangschule/	0,0030935
http://www.bumerangs.de/	0,0030935
http://s.webring.com/hub?ring=boomerang	0,0030895
http://www.kutek.net/boomplans/plans.php	0,0030873
http://www.geocities.com/cmorris32839/jonas_article/	0,0030871
http://www.theboomerangman.com/	0,0030868
http://www.boomerangs.com/index.html	0,0030867
http://www.lmifox.com/us/boom/index-uk.htm	0,0030867
http://www.sports-boomerangs.com/	0,0030867
http://www.rangsboomerangs.com/	0,0030867

Url	FolkRank
http://jena.sourceforge.net/	0,0019369
http://www.openrdf.org/doc/users/ch06.html	0,0017312
http://dsd.lbl.gov/ hoschek/colt/api/overview-summary.html	0,0016777
http://librdf.org/	0,0014402
http://www.hpl.hp.com/semweb/jena2.htm	0,0014326
http://jakarta.apache.org/commons/collections/	0,0014203
http://www.aktors.org/technologies/ontocopi/	0,0012839
http://eventseer.idi.ntnu.no/	0,0012734
http://tangra.si.umich.edu/ radev/	0,0012685
http://www.cs.umass.edu/ mccallum/	0,0012091
http://www.w3.org/TR/rdf-sparql-query/	0,0011945
http://ourworld.compuserve.com/homepages/graeme_birchall/HTM_COOK.HTM	0,0011930
http://www.emory.edu/EDUCATION/mfp/Kuhn.html	0,0011880
http://www.hpl.hp.com/semweb/rdql.htm	0,0011860
http://jena.sourceforge.net/javadoc/index.html	0,0011860
http://www.geocities.com/mailsoftware42/db/	0,0011838
http://www.quirksmode.org/	0,0011327
http://www.kde.cs.uni-kassel.de/lehre/ss2005/googlespam	0,0011110
http://www.powerpage.org/cgi-bin/WebObjects/powerpage.woa/wa/story?newsID=14732	0,0010402
http://www.vaughns-1-pagers.com/internet/google-ranking-factors.htm	0,0010329
http://www.cl.cam.ac.uk/Research/SRG/netos/xen/	0,0010326

weight 5 for user "schm4704" shows his different interests, see the rightmost column in Table 2. His main interest apparently is in boomerangs, but other topics show up as well. In particular, he has a strong relationship to the tags "kassel" and "rdf". When a community in del.ico.us is small (such as the boomerang community), already a single user can thus provide a strong bridge to other communities, a phenomenon that is equally observed in small social communities.

A comparison of the FolkRank ranking for user "schm4704" with the Adapted PageRank result for him (2nd ranking from left) confirms the initial finding from above, that the Adapted PageRank ranking contains many globally frequent tags, while the FolkRank ranking provides more personal tags. While the differential nature of the FolkRank algorithm usually pushes down the globally frequent tags such as "web", though, this happens in a differentiated manner: FolkRank will keep them in the top positions, *if* they are indeed relevant to the user under consideration. This can be seen for example for the tags "web" and "java". While the tag "web" appears in schm4704's tag list – but not very often, "java" is a very important tag for that user. This is reflected in the FolkRank ranking: "java" remains in the Top 5, while "web" is pushed down in the ranking.

The ranking of the resources for the tag "boomerang" given in the middle of Table 2 also provides interesting insights. As shown in the table, many boomerang related web pages show up (their topical relatedness was confirmed by a boomerang aficionado). Comparing the Top 20 web pages of "boomerang" with the Top 20 pages given by the "schm4704" ranking, there is no "boomerang" web page in the latter. This can be explained by analysing the tag distribution of this user. While "boomerang" is the most frequent tag for this user, in del.icio.us, "boomerang" appears rather infrequently. The first boomerang web page in the "schm4704" ranking is the 21st URL (i. e., just outside the listed TOP 20). Thus, while the tag "boomerang" itself dominates the tags of this user, in the whole, the semantic web related tags and resources prevail. This demonstrates that while the user "schm4704" and the tag "boomerang" are strongly correlated, we can still get an overview of the respective related items which shows several topics of interest for the user.

Let us consider a second example. Table 3 gives the results for the web page http://www.semanticweb.org/. The two tables on the left show the tags and users for the adapted PageRank, resp., and the two ones on the right the FolkRank results. Again, we see that the differential ranking of FolkRank makes the right decisions: in the Adaptive PageRank, globally frequent tags such as "web", "css", "xml", "programming" get high ranks. Of these, only two turn up to be of genuine interest to the members of the Semantic Web community: "web" and "xml" remain at high positions, while "css" and "programming" disappear altogether from the list of the 20 highest ranked tags. Also, several variations of tags which are used to label Semantic Web related pages appear (or get ranked higher): "semantic web" (two tags, space-separated), "semantic_web", "semweb", "sem-web". These co-occurrences of similar tags could be exploited further to consolidate the emergent semantics of a field of interest. While the discovery in this case may also be done in a simple syntactic analysis, the graph based approach allows also for detecting inter-community and inter-language relations.

Table 3. Ranking for the resource http://www.semanticweb.org (Left two tables: Adapted PageRank for tags and users; right two tables: FolkRank for tags and users. Bottom: FolkRank for resources).

Tag	ad. PRank	User	ad. PageRank	Tag	FolkRank	User	FolkRank
semanticweb	0,0208605	up4	0,0091995	semanticweb	0,0207820	up4	0,0091828
web	0,0162033	awenger	0,0086261	semantic	0,0121305	awenger	0,0084958
semantic	0,0122028	j.deville	0,0074021	web	0,0118002	j.deville	0,0073525
system:unfiled	0,0088625	chaizzilla	0,0062570	semantic_web	0,0071933	chaizzilla	0,0062227
semantic_web	0,0072150	elektron	0,0059457	rdf	0,0044461	elektron	0,0059403
rdf	0,0046348	captsolo	0,0055671	semweb	0,0039308	captsolo	0,0055369
semweb	0,0039897	stevag	0,0049923	resources	0,0034209	dissipative	0,0049619
resources	0,0037884	dissipative	0,0049647	community	0,0033208	stevag	0,0049590
community	0,0037256	krudd	0,0047574	portal	0,0022745	krudd	0,0047005
xml	0,0031494	williamteo	0,0037204	xml	0,0022074	williamteo	0,0037181
research	0,0026720	stevecassidy	0,0035887	research	0,0020378	stevecassidy	0,0035840
programming	0,0025717	pmika	0,0035359	imported-bo...	0,0018920	pmika	0,0035358
css	0,0025290	millette	0,0033028	en	0,0018536	millette	0,0032103
portal	0,0024118	myren	0,0028117	.idate2005-04-11	0,0017555	myren	0,0027965
.imported	0,0020495	morningboat	0,0025913	newfurl	0,0017153	morningboat	0,0025875
imported-bo...	0,0019610	philip.fennell	0,0025338	tosort	0,0014486	philip.fennell	0,0025145
en	0,0018900	mote	0,0025212	cs	0,0014002	webb.	0,0024671
science	0,0018166	dnaboy76	0,0024813	academe	0,0013822	dnaboy76	0,0024659
.idate2005-04-11	0,0017779	webb.	0,0024709	rfid	0,0013456	mote	0,0024214
newfurl	0,0017578	nymetbarton	0,0023790	sem-web	0,0013316	alphajuliet	0,0023668
internet	0,0016122	alphajuliet	0,0023781	w3c	0,0012994	nymetbarton	0,0023666

URL	FolkRank
http://www.semanticweb.org/	0,3761957
http://flink.semanticweb.org/	0,0005566
http://simile.mit.edu/piggy-bank/	0,0003828
http://www.w3.org/2001/sw/	0,0003216
http://infomesh.net/2001/swintro/	0,0002162
http://del.icio.us/register	0,0001745
http://mspace.ecs.soton.ac.uk/	0,0001712
http://www.adaptivepath.com/publications/essays/archives/000385.php	0,0001637
http://www.ontoweb.org/	0,0001617
http://www.aaai.org/AITopics/html/ontol.html	0,0001613
http://simile.mit.edu/	0,0001395
http://itip.evcc.jp/itipwiki/	0,0001256
http://www.google.be/	0,0001224
http://www.letterjames.de/index.html	0,0001224
http://www.daml.org/	0,0001216
http://shirky.com/writings/ontology_overrated.html	0,0001195
http://jena.sourceforge.net/	0,0001167
http://www.alistapart.com/	0,0001102
http://www.federalconcierge.com/WritingBusinessCases.html	0,0001060
http://pchere.blogspot.com/2005/02/absolutely-delicious-complete-tool.html	0,0001059
http://www.shirky.com/writings/semantic_syllogism.html	0,0001052

The user IDs can not be checked for topical relatedness immediately, since they are not related to the users' full names – although a former winner of the Semantic Web Challenge and the best paper award at a Semantic Web Conference seems to be among them. The web pages that appear in the top list, on the other hand, include many well-known resources from the Semantic Web area. An interesting resource on the list is PiggyBank, which has been presented in November 2005 at the ISWC conference. Considering that the dataset was crawled in July 2005, when PiggyBank was not that well known, the prominent position of PiggyBank in del.icio.us at such an early time is an interesting result. This indicates the sensibility of social bookmarking systems for upcoming topics.

These two examples – as well as the other experiments we performed – show that FolkRank provides good results when querying the folksonomy for topically related elements. Overall, our experiments indicate that topically related items can be retrieved with FolkRank for any given set of highlighted tags, users and/or resources.

Our results also show that the current size of folksonomies is still prone to being skewed by a relatively small number of perturbations – a single user, at the moment, can influence the emergent understanding of a certain topic in the case that a sufficient number of different points of view for such a topic has not been collected yet. With the growth of folksonomy-based data collections on the web, the influence of single users will fade in favor of a common understanding provided by huge numbers of users.

As detailed above, our ranking is based on tags only, without regarding any inherent features of the resources at hand. This allows to apply FolkRank to search for pictures (e. g., in flickr) and other multimedia content, as well as for all other items that are difficult to search in a content-based fashion. The same holds for intranet applications, where in spite of centralized knowledge management efforts, documents often remain unused because they are not hyperlinked and difficult to find. Full text retrieval may be used to find documents, but traditional IR methods for ranking without hyperlink information have difficulties finding the most relevant documents from large corpora.

4.3   Generating Recommendations

The original PageRank paper [2] already pointed out the possibility of using the random surfer vector $\vec{p}$ as a personalization mechanism for PageRank computations. The results of Section 4 show that, given a user, one can find set of tags and resources of interest to him. Likewise, FolkRank yields a set of related users and resources for a given tag. Following these observations, FolkRank can be used to generate recommendations within a folksonomy system. These recommendations can be presented to the user at different points in the usage of a folksonomy system:

- Documents that are of potential interest to a user can be suggested to him. This kind of recommendation pushes potentially useful content to the user and increases the chance that a user finds useful resources that he did not even know existed by "serendipitous" browsing.
- When using a certain tag, other related tags can be suggested. This can be used, for instance, to speed up the consolidation of different terminologies and thus facilitate the emergence of a common vocabulary.
- While folksonomy tools already use simple techniques for tag recommendations, FolkRank additionally considers the tagging behavior of other users.
- Other users that work on related topics can be made explicit, improving thus the knowledge transfer within organizations and fostering the formation of communities.

5   Conclusion and Outlook

In this paper, we have argued that enhanced search facilities are vital for emergent semantics within folksonomy-based systems. We presented a formal model for folksonomies, the *FolkRank* ranking algorithm that takes into account the structure of folksonomies, and evaluation results on a large-scale dataset.

The FolkRank ranking scheme has been used in this paper to generate personalized rankings of the items in a folksonomy, and to recommend users, tags and resources. We have seen that the top folksonomy elements which are retrieved by FolkRank tend to fall into a coherent topic area, e.g. "Semantic Web". This leads naturally to the idea of extracting *communities of interest* from the folksonomy, which are represented by their top tags and the most influential persons and resources. If these communities are made explicit, interested users can find them and participate, and community members can more easily get to know each other and learn of others' resources.

Another future research issue is to combine different search and ranking paradigms. In this paper, we went a first step by focusing on the new structure of folksonomies. In the future, we will incorporate additionally the full text that is contained in the web pages addressed by the URLs, the link structure of these web pages, and the usage behavior as stored in the log file of the tagging system. The next version will also exploit the tag hierarchy.

Currently, spam is not a serious problem for social bookmarking systems. With the increasing attention they currently receive, however, we anticipate that 'spam posts' will show up sooner or later. As for mail spam and link farms in the web, solutions will be needed to filter out spam. We expect that a blend of graph structure analysis together with content analysis will give the best results.

When folksonomy-based systems grow larger, user support has to go beyond enhanced retrieval facilities. Therefore, the internal structure has to become better organized. An obvious approach for this are semantic web technologies. The key question remains though how to exploit its benefits without bothering untrained users with its rigidity. We believe that this will become a fruitful research area for the Semantic Web community for the next years.

Acknowledgement. Part of this research was funded by the EU in the Nepomuk project (FP6-027705).

References

1. Harith Alani, Srinandan Dasmahapatra, Kieron O'Hara, and Nigel Shadbolt. Identifying Communities of Practice through Ontology Network Analysis. *IEEE Intelligent Systems*, 18(2):18–25, March/April 2003.
2. Sergey Brin and Lawrence Page. The Anatomy of a Large-Scale Hypertextual Web Search Engine. *Computer Networks and ISDN Systems*, 30(1-7):107–117, April 1998.
3. Connotea Mailing List. https://lists.sourceforge.net/lists/listinfo/connotea-discuss.
4. B. Ganter and R. Wille. *Formal Concept Analysis: Mathematical foundations*. Springer, 1999.
5. Tony Hammond, Timo Hannay, Ben Lund, and Joanna Scott. Social Bookmarking Tools (I): A General Review. *D-Lib Magazine*, 11(4), April 2005.
6. Jon M. Kleinberg. Authoritative sources in a hyperlinked environment. *Journal of the ACM*, 46(5):604–632, 1999.

7. F. Lehmann and R. Wille. A triadic approach to formal concept analysis. In G. Ellis, R. Levinson, W. Rich, and J. F. Sowa, editors, *Conceptual Structures: Applications, Implementation and Theory*, volume 954 of *Lecture Notes in Computer Science*. Springer, 1995.

8. Ben Lund, Tony Hammond, Martin Flack, and Timo Hannay. Social Bookmarking Tools (II): A Case Study - Connotea. *D-Lib Magazine*, 11(4), April 2005.

9. Adam Mathes. Folksonomies – Cooperative Classification and Communication Through Shared Metadata, December 2004. http://www.adammathes.com/academic/computer-mediated-communication/folksonomies.html.

10. Peter Mika. Ontologies Are Us: A Unified Model of Social Networks and Semantics. In Yolanda Gil, Enrico Motta, V. Richard Benjamins, and Mark A. Musen, editors, *ISWC 2005*, volume 3729 of *LNCS*, pages 522–536, Berlin Heidelberg, November 2005. Springer-Verlag.

11. S. Staab, S. Santini, F. Nack, L. Steels, and A. Maedche. Emergent semantics. *Intelligent Systems, IEEE [see also IEEE Expert]*, 17(1):78–86, 2002.

12. L. Steels. The origins of ontologies and communication conventions in multi-agent systems. *Autonomous Agents and Multi-Agent Systems*, 1(2):169–194, October 1998.

13. Gerd Stumme. A finite state model for on-line analytical processing in triadic contexts. In Bernhard Ganter and Robert Godin, editors, *ICFCA*, volume 3403 of *Lecture Notes in Computer Science*, pages 315–328. Springer, 2005.

14. R. Wille. Restructuring lattice theory: An approach based on hierarchies of concepts. In I. Rival, editor, *Ordered Sets*, pages 445–470. Reidel, Dordrecht-Boston, 1982.

15. W. Xi, B. Zhang, Y. Lu, Z. Chen, S. Yan, H. Zeng, W. Ma, and E. Fox. Link fusion: A unified link analysis framework for multi-type interrelated data objects. In *Proc. 13th International World Wide Web Conference*, New York, 2004.

DEMO - Design Environment for Metadata Ontologies

Jens Hartmann[1], Elena Paslaru Bontas[2], Raúl Palma[3], and Asunción Gómez-Pérez[3]

[1] Institute AIFB, University of Karlsruhe, Germany
hartmann@aifb.uni-karlsruhe.de
http://www.aifb.uni-karlsruhe.de/WBS/
[2] Networked Information Systems,
Institute of Computer Science, Free University of Berlin, Germany
paslaru@inf.fu-berlin.de
[3] Ontology Engineering Group, Laboratorio de Inteligencia Artificial
Facultad de Informática, Universidad Politécnica de Madrid, Spain
rpalma@delicias.dia.fi.upm.es

Abstract. Efficient knowledge sharing and reuse—a pre-requisite for the realization of the Semantic Web vision—is currently impeded by the lack of standards for documenting and annotating ontologies with metadata information. We argue that the availability of metadata is a fundamental dimension of ontology reusability. Metadata information provides a basis for ontology developers to evaluate and adapt existing Semantic Web ontologies in new application settings, and fosters the development of support tools such as ontology repositories. However, in order for the metadata information to represent real added value to ontology users, it is equally important to achieve a common agreement on the terms used to describe ontologies, and to provide an appropriate technology infrastructure in form of tools being able to create, manage and distribute this information. In this paper we present DEMO, a framework for the development and deployment of ontology metadata. Besides OMV , the proposed core vocabulary for ontology metadata, the framework comprises an inventory of methods to collaboratively extend OMV in accordance to the requirements of an emerging community of industrial and academia users, and tools for metadata management.

1 Introduction

As the Semantic Web grows, increasing numbers of private and public sector communities are developing ontologies which represent their domain(s) of interest. As ontologies are also intended to act as commonly agreed domain conceptualizations[7] it is expected that reuse will play a crucial role in the widespread dissemination of ontology-driven technologies. First, reusability is an intrinsic property of ontologies, originally defined as means for *"knowledge sharing and reuse"*[13]. Sharing and reusing existing ontologies increases their quality—as they are continuously accessed, used and revised by many people—and the quality of the applications using them—since these applications become (more) interoperable and are provided with a deeper, machine-processable understanding of the underlying domain. Second, analogously to other engineering disciplines, reusing existing ontologies—if performed in an efficient way—reduces the costs

Y. Sure and J. Domingue (Eds.): ESWC 2006, LNCS 4011, pp. 427–441, 2006.

related to ontology development, since it avoids the re-implementation of the components, which are already available on the Web and can be directly or after some additional customization integrated to a target ontology. Finally, access to available ontologies across the Web is a fundamental requirement for the dissemination of Semantic Web Services, which are envisioned to automatically use these sources in order to describe their capabilities and for interprocess communication.

While finding a solution to the problematic trade-off between usability in a specific application setting and wide-scale reusability is often considered an art more than a science, poor reusability can be significantly alleviated by resorting to several design principles, which have proved their relevance across various computer science disciplines confronted with this issue: *modularity* and *decomposition* along abstraction and functionality levels, the deployment of *standardized* tools and technologies, as well as careful *documentation* of the development process and up-to-date *component repositories*. Current research achievements in the Semantic Web field provide a feasible basis for many of these principles to be put into practice. The usage of standardized ontology representation languages in conjunction with the ubiquitous URI-based access on Semantic Web resources and the emergence of ontology management methods and tools definitely constitute a solid inventory for building more reusable ontologies. However their wide-scale reusability is still impeded by the lack of standards for documenting and annotating ontologies with metadata information, which is in the same time a pre-requisite for the realization of fully-fledged ontology repositories on the Web. At present, Semantic Web ontologies are poorly documented (at most), while additional clarifying information is spread across the Web in various forms, thus not being optimally available to potential ontology users. Further on, current repositories restrict to a minimal set of search and navigation services, usually offering a simple Web interface to the ontological resources. Their limited retrieval functionality is significantly influenced by the absence of metadata information about the administrated ontologies.

A first step towards the alleviation of this situation is the development of a feasible metadata schema for the systematic description of ontologies. Represented in a machine-processable form this schema would provide a basis for a more effective access and exchange of ontologies across the Web. However, in order for it to represent real added value to ontology users, it is equally important to achieve a common agreement on the terms used to describe ontologies, and to provide appropriate tools being able to create, manage and distribute metadata information.

Our contribution consists of the **DEMO** (**D**esign **E**nvironment for **M**etadata **O**ntologies), framework for the development and deployment of an ontology metadata vocabulary. The main part of the framework is the **OMV** model (**O**ntology **M**etadata **V**ocabulary), which is intended to capture reuse-relevant information about ontologies (i.e. ontology metadata) in a machine-understandable form. Further on, the framework is concerned with methodologies, methods and tools to support the dissemination of OMV towards a *representative* metadata vocabulary, which reflects the needs of an expending community of ontology users w.r.t. ontology reuse. In particular, DEMO focuses on the evolution and extension of OMV ; we introduce a technical, methodological and organizational setting to allow interested parties to effectively contribute to this initiative and foresee extensions of the core model for more specific reuse activities (such as the evaluation of ontologies, their engineering process etc).

The remainder of this paper is organized as follows: we introduce DEMO, its goals, contents and realization in Section 2. The main components of the framework are described in Sections 3 to 5. Section 3 addresses the development process of the current OMV metadata model. Further on, it accounts for the procedure currently applied to operationalize the evaluation and refinement of the OMV core on the basis of large scale agreement discussions with partners of the EU Network of Excellence KnowledgeWeb.[1] The contents of the metadata schema is detailed in Section 4, while extension modules, which focus on a particular topic or activity of the reuse process, are discussed in Section 5. Our approach is compared against related work in the area of ontology reuse and metadata in Section 6. We conclude with a brief description of the limitations of the current approach and sketch the planned future work (Section 7).

2   DEMO - A Design Environment for Metadata Ontologies

Developing and maintaining an ontology metadata vocabulary is a long-term, resource-intensive process for every involved participant, as it requires a well-defined operational structure and appropriate technological support. The current state of the OMV model is the result of an intensive collaboration among many Semantic Web experts affiliated to academia or industry. Our experiences in the development of the OMV so far (see Section 3), consolidated by general engineering guidelines recommended by the majority of ontology engineering methodologies currently available, indicated the need of an environment which provides support to systematically realize and promote ontology metadata vocabularies for the Semantic Web.

DEMO (Design Environment for Metadata Ontologies) aims at providing this kind of support at *organizational, methodological* and *technological* level. The mission of the framework can be categorized as follows:

- Provision of an *organizational infrastructure* for the development and maintenance of a commonly agreed metadata vocabulary for ontologies. In particular this includes the facilitation of equitable participation mechanisms for the organizations involved in the DEMO activities.
- Identification and application of suitable methodologies and technologies to support the complete life cycle of the OMV Core.
- Development and maintenance of the OMV Core.
- Promotion of OMV extensions relying on the OMV Core.
- Provision of an appropriate technical infrastructure for the enumerated activities.

DEMO aims to establish and ensure an efficient engineering process and application of the proposed ontology metadata vocabulary. For usability and extendability reasons, DEMO distinguishes between the OMV Core and OMV extensions. The former provides information about the core metadata vocabulary which should be sufficient for an efficient reuse and access of ontologies in the Semantic Web (see Section 3). For

---

[1] http://knowledgeweb.semanticweb.org/

specific applications or differentiated aspects of ontologies, e.g. detailed evolution information of an ontology, it foresees the development and usage of OMV extension modules. This flexible mechanism allows on the one hand all participants to engineer a base vocabulary (i.e. the OMV Core) and on the other hand, to provide more detailed information by developing domain, task or application-specific vocabularies (i.e. OMV Extensions).

The framework is divided into several functional components in accordance to the aforementioned objectives:

- The **Engineering Component** is responsible for the development and maintenance of the OMV Core.
- The **Evolution Component** is authorized to perform changes on the OMV Core according to the requirements of the OMV users.
- The **Extensions Component** coordinates the realization of extension modules.
- The **Applications Component** is responsible for the propagation of the OMV results to new application scenarios, demonstrating the usability of the metadata standards in these applications and contributing to their evaluation in real-world settings.

From an organizational perspective, DEMO activities are driven and supervised by the **Management Board (MB)**, consisting of representatives from the **OMV Consortium**, which includes all active OMV contributors. A central organization objective of DEMO is to keep the barrier low for participants to join the OMV Consortium and to get involved in the development and recommendation process. Complementary to this distinction, DEMO foresees several **Working Groups (WG)** corresponding to the aforementioned components (WG Engineering, WG Evolution, WGs Extensions, WGs Applications), which are further organized in working group board and members.

DEMO provides the technical means required for metadata management and maintenance for the Semantic Web in form of the semantic engineering platform OntoWare[2] which provides a scalable, collaborative software and ontology engineering environment for the collaborating partners.

3   The Development of the OMV Core Ontology

The OMV core ontology was realized in accordance to the present research achievements in Ontology Engineering, a field in which several elaborated methodologies have already proved their applicability in real-world situations (refer to [3] for a description of and a comparison among the most relevant ones). The development process is performed in five stages, which are described in the remaining of this section.

3.1   Requirements Analysis

In this step we elaborated an inventory of requirements for the metadata model as a result of a systematic survey of the state of the art in the area of ontology reuse. Besides analytical activities, we conducted extensive literature research, which focused

---

[2] c.f. http://ontoware.org

on theoretical methods [16, 4, 12], but also on case studies on reusing existing ontologies [22, 18, 15], in order to identify the real-world needs of the community w.r.t. a descriptive metadata format for ontologies. Further on, the requirements analysis phase was complemented by a comparative study of existing (ontology-independent) metadata models and of tools such as ontology repositories and libraries (implicitly) making use of metadata-like information. An overview of the results of this study is given in Section 6. The main requirements identified in this process step are the following:

Accessibility: Metadata should be accessible and processable for both humans and machines. While the human-driven aspects are ensured by the usage of natural language concept names, the machine-readability requirement can be implemented by the usage of Web-compatible representation languages (such as XML or Semantic Web languages, see below).

Usability: This requirement states for the necessity of building a metadata model which 1). reflects the needs of the majority of ontology users, as reported by current case studies in ontology reuse, but in the same time 2). allows proprietary extensions and refinements in particular application scenarios. The realization of the latter is further discussed in Section 5. From a content perspective, usability can be maximized by taking into account multiple metadata types, which correspond to specific viewpoints on the ontological resources and are applied in various application tasks. Despite the broad understanding of the metadata concept and the use cases associated to each definition, several key aspects of metadata information have already established across computer science fields [14]:

- **Structural metadata** relates to statistical measures on the graph structure underlying an ontology. In particular we mention the number of specific ontological primitives (e.g. number of classes, instances). The availability of structural metadata influences the usability of an ontology in a concrete application scenario, as size and structure parameters constraint the type of tools and methods which are applied to aid the reuse process.

- **Descriptive metadata** relates to the domain modelled in the ontology in form of keywords, topic classifications, textual descriptions of the ontology contents etc. This type of metadata plays a crucial role in the selection of appropriate reuse candidates, a process which includes requirements w.r.t. the domain of the ontologies to be re-used.

- **Administrative metadata** provides information to help manage ontologies, such as when and how it was created, rights management, file format and other technical information.

Interoperability: Similarly to the ontology it describes, metadata information should be available in a form which facilitates metadata exchange among applications. While the syntactical aspects of interoperability are covered by the usage of standard representation languages (see "Accesibility"), the semantical interoperability among machines handling ontology metadata information can be ensured by means of a formal and explicit representation of the meaning of the metadata entities, i.e. by conceptualizing the metadata vocabulary itself as an ontology.

Separation between Knowledge and Implementation Levels: In accordance to the recommendations of current ontology engineering methodologies it should be clearly distinguished between the conceptual model of an ontology and particular implementations (in various languages, syntaxes, versions etc.). The realization of this criterion is illustrated in Section 4.

3.2 Categorisation

On the basis of the aforementioned analysis we designed the core structure of the metadata model in terms of classes and properties/attributes of these classes. In order to increase the usability of the model w.r.t. its extendability we assigned the metadata entities to three usage categories (in the style of XML Schema):

- **Required**: These metadata facts are mandatory. Missing elements lead to incomplete metadata descriptions of ontologies and are handled accordingly by metadata management tools.
- **Optional**: The specification of optional metadata elements, though not mandatory, increases the reusability of the corresponding ontology.
- **Extensional**: This class of metadata elements is not represented in detail in the core model, but can be further elaborated in extension modules (see Section 5).

Further on, every metadata entity was labelled in accordance to a predefined naming schema and carefully documented.

3.3 Implementation

Due to the high accessibility and interoperability requirements, as well as the nature of the metadata, which is intended to describe Semantic Web ontologies, the conceptual model designed in the previous step was implemented in the OWL language. An implementation as XML-Schema or DTD was estimated to restrict the functionality of the ontology management tools using the metadata information (mainly in terms of retrieval capabilities) and to impede metadata exchange at semantical level. Further on, a language such as RDFS does not provide a means to distinguish between required and optional metadata properties. The implementation was performed manually by means of a common ontology editor.

3.4 Evaluation

The evaluation of the first draft of the metadata model was conducted in two parallel phases: on one hand, the content of the model was subject to human-driven evaluation w.r.t. the inventory of the included metadata elements, their meaning and labelling. On the other hand the usability of the proposed OMV was tested in several application settings.

The content-based evaluation was performed by conducting interviews with a group of experts in the area of Ontology Engineering. Considering that the people best placed to give a comprehensive assessment of the ontology metadata vocabulary are currently researchers being directly involved in theoretical or practical issues of Ontology Engineering, we organized an expert group of four academics affiliated in this community and in the EU Network of Excellence KnowledgeWeb which evaluated the model against a pre-defined set of criteria[5]:

- **Consistency**: this criterion refers to the existence of explicit or implicit contradictions in the represented ontological content.
- **Completeness**: according to [5], an ontology is complete if it (explicitly or implicitly) covers the intended domain.
- **Conciseness**: complementary to the previous feature, conciseness states for the redundancy-free representation of the application domain of an ontology and for the avoidance of useless definitions.
- **Expandability/Sensitiveness**: the criterion refers to the possibility of adding new definitions to the ontology without altering the existent content.

The aforementioned evaluation framework was extended with two dimensions: **readability**, which accounts for the usage of intuitive labels to denominate the OMV entities, and **understandability**, which mainly relates to the quality of the documentation of the metadata model.

The evaluation resulted in changes on both conceptual and implementation levels of the OMV ontology. In the following we summarize the key aspects of the evaluation process:

- **Consistency**: according to human judgement and to the automatic consistency checking no inconsistencies were found.
- **Completeness**: during the evaluation the participants identified several aspects which were missing in the initial draft of OMV . For instance, information about the representation language of an ontology (syntax, representation paradigm etc.) were found to be insufficiently covered by OMV . As a result we introduced concepts such as `RepresentationParadigm` and `OntologyRepresentationLanguage` to account for these aspects. Further on, a classification of tasks ontologies are typically designed for was included in form of a root concept `OntologyTask` and more specialized sub-concepts such as `SemanticSearch` or `SemanticAnnotation`.
- **Conciseness**: parallel to extending the ontology, the experts expressed their concerns w.r.t. a series of concepts which were too specific for a core metadata vocabulary. Most of these concepts related to particular aspects of the engineering process in which the corresponding ontology was originally created and of the evaluation of the ontology (the concepts `OntologyReviews`, `OntologyReviewer` etc.). These aspects were removed from the OMV core and transferred to the OMV extensions (see Section 5).
- **Readability**: the naming of particular metadata entities was one of the most challenging parts of the evaluation process. The experts proposed alternative names for several fundamental OMV concepts, such as those representing the conceptual model and the implementation of an ontology, respectively (see below). Finally an agreement was achieved with the result that the original names of these two metadata entities were changed to `Conceptualization` and `Implementation`, respectively. Further on, the experts indicated the poor readability of abbreviated concept labels, which were modified accordingly.
- **Understandability**: the experts evaluated the OMV model favorably. They were able to easily understand its scope, content and limitations and expressed their confidence in its usability.

In summary, the results of the expert-driven evaluation significantly contributed to the quality of the OMV ontology, confirming our expectations towards the realization of a standardized metadata schema for Semantic Web ontologies. However, the evaluation process has already pointed out the main challenge of our approach, which is related to the achievement of a common agreement in a large community of ontology users w.r.t. their requirements and perceptions about ontology metadata. This issue is addressed in the next section.

3.5 Evolution

As aforementioned the real added value of the proposed metadata vocabulary is fundamentally determined by the representativeness of its content and its dissemination across the Semantic Web community. For this purpose one of the foci of the DEMO environment is the provision of an organizational and methodological setting, which allows the OMV consortium to participate at the metadata development initiative.

For the realization of this goal we take advantage of the results already available in the Ontology Engineering community w.r.t collaboratively building ontologies in distributed environments. Based on the long-standing tradition of argumentation and conflict mediation research in Knowledge Management, Agent-based Computing or Linguistics, approaches such as [17, 11, 19] provide a deep analysis of the challenges of such engineering settings and means to operationalize it at process and technology level. They describe the organizational setting of evolving multi-site ontology development processes and propose an inventory of tools which can be used to optimize the achievement of commonly accepted agreements w.r.t. ontology modelling decisions.

For the collaborative refinement of the current OMV Core we decided to apply the DILIGENT methodology[17], because, compared to alternative approaches, it provides a more fine-grained description of the underlying process model, whose validity has been tested in several case study.

The organizational structure of the OMV consortium is fully compatible with the recommendations of the aforementioned methodology. The working group responsible for the OMV evolution (WG Evolution, see Section 2) is divided into a working group board and its members. As foreseen by the DILIGENT methodology[17],[3] a first version of the shared ontology (in our case the OMV Core ontology described in this paper) was already distributed to the members of the working group, which will submit their change requests accompanied by the arguments justifying them in regular time spans to the working group board. The board analyzes the requests on the basis of their arguments, decides upon the changes and releases a new version of the OMV Core, which is analyzed by the rest of the participants. The tools supporting the evolution activity are provided by the OntoWare platform.

The evolution process aiming at realizing a representative metadata vocabulary for Semantic Web ontologies is still in its infancy. However, we are confident that, given the positive feedback received during the development of the current OMV version and the willingness of many academia and industrial institutions to get involved in this process, the proposed OMV will evolve towards a high-quality metadata standard.

---

[3] Due to space considerations, we restrict to a minimal description of the process model in this paper.

In the following we turn to a more detailed description of the current OMV core ontology, while OMV extensions are addressed in Section 5.

4   The Ontology Metadata Vocabulary - OMV Core

As the result of the requirements distilled from comprehensive literature and case study research we designed a first version of the OMV core ontology, which is subject of a recently initiated evolution process (see Section 3). The main components of the ontology, manually implemented in OWL, are presented in the remaining of this section.

4.1   Conceptualization vs. Implementation

OMV distinguishes between the **ontology conceptualization** and an **ontology implementation** as concrete realization of an ontology in a particular representation language. This separation is based on the observation that any ontology is based on a language-independent conceptual model. The conceptualization represents the view of the engineering team upon the application domain, which then is implemented using an ontology editor and stored in a specific format. The same conceptualization might result in several implementations, with various classes, properties and axioms, depending on the concrete representation paradigm, language and syntax. Therefore we define:

- **Ontology Conceptualization:** An *Ontology Conceptualization (OC)* represents the abstract or core idea of an ontology. It describes the core properties of an ontology, independent from any implementation details.
- **Ontology Implementation:** An *Ontology Implementation (OI)* represents a specific implementation of a conceptualization. Therefore, it describes implementation-specific properties of an ontology.

The distinction between OC and OI leads to an efficient mechanism, for tracking multiple ontology versions, as well as for different representations of one knowledge model in different languages. Technically, the two are modelled as separate classes connected by means of the relation `realizes`. This means that there may be many possible ontology implementations for one conceptualization, but one ontology implementation can only `implement` one conceptual model.

An instance of the OI class should not be able to exist without a corresponding conceptualization. However, for practical reasons, we allow the existence of the two independently of each other. We cannot assume that every existing ontology will be annotated by its original author who might have created the underlying conceptualization.

An excerpt of the main classes and properties of the OMV core ontology are illustrated in figure 1. The ontology is available for download in several ontology formats.[4]

It should be noticed that there exist several properties defined at the classes OC and OI which are denominated with similar names, but have a different semantics. Consider, for instance, an ontology engineer developing an ontology in OWL using the RDF/XML syntax and annotating it with OMV . The values of the properties of the corresponding OC and OI individuals definitely overlap to some extent (e.g., both would have the

---

[4] OMV representations are available at `http://ontoware.org/projects/omv/`

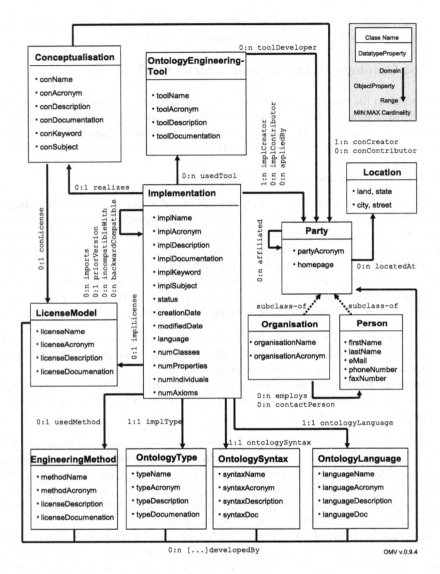

Fig. 1. OMV Overview

same `party` as `creator`, but they do not necessarily have the same number of ontological primitives). However, a new implementation of the ontology in, for instance, F-Logic would result in new values for these properties (e.g. not only a new creator or creation date, but eventually a different number of classes, properties, since the ways the same conceptual model is implemented using two different knowledge representation paradigms might vary).

4.2   Basic Classes of OMV

The OMV focuses on the two main classes OC and OI for representing core information about ontologies. However, additional classes are required to adequately represent ontology-related information, especially in the context of the Semantic Web (Figure 1).

Common ontology engineering assumes that ontologies are created and owned by Person(s) or Organizations. We group these two classes under the generic class Party by a subclass-of relation. A Party can have several locations by referring to a Location and can *create* or *contribute* to a OntologyConceptuali zation or OntologyImplementation, respectively. Tools such as ontology editors can be referred to by the class OntologyEngineeringTool, which itself can be developedBy a Party. The different existing syntactical representations and ontology languages are representable by OntologySyntax, OntologyLanguage and RepresentationParadigm. OMV further contains the class Ontology EngineeringMethodology which makes explicit the methodology (or methodologies) used during the engineering process. Ontologies might be categorized according to various dimensions[6]. Those types are modelled as sub-classes of Ontology Type. For commercial settings it might be relevant to propose usage licenses which can be realized by the class LicenseModel relating to each OntologyConceptuali sation or OntologyImplementation.

Exemplary, the SWRC ontology project is applying OMV to annotate their Semantic Web Research Community Ontology [21]. The core idea of the SWRC ontology is to model entities of research communities and their relationships. This conceptualization of SWRC (core idea) originated several different implementations of SWRC. As a first result, OMV increases the transparency within the engineering process and supports the dissemination due facilitating reuse and discovery of SWRC[5].

5   The Development of OMV Extensions

The OMV Core is intended to represent a commonly agreed metadata for the Semantic Web. In contrast to that, we are aware that for specific domains, tasks or communities extensions in any direction might be required. These extensions should be compatible to the OMV Core, but in the same time fulfill the requirements of a domain, task or community-driven setting. In order to ensure the compatibility to the commonly agreed core, one of the goals of DEMO is the elaboration of a procedure to supervise and promote the creation of new OMV extension modules.

An OMV extension can be originated by members of the **OMV Working Group Extensions**. The group provides deliverables documenting their work for the public. Initially, it creates a charter, nominates a responsible chair and sets up a technical infrastructure, for example a Web site and mailing-list. Such a charter describes the initial motivation and explains specific requirements for a planned OMV extension. The character of an OMV extension is a metadata ontology itself which imports the OMV core ontology. There are no restricting modelling guidelines to be met. However DEMO provides a basic inventory of design decisions and guidelines, which are recommended to

---

[5] The ontology and metadata example are available at http://swrc.ontoware.org/.

be applied for the extension modules[8]. The engineering team of an extension ontology might resort to the same engineering methodologies and tools as those applied for the OMV Core (see Section 3).

The first DEMO working group on OMV extensions has already been initiated. It aims at the realization of an OMV extension module on the topic Ontology Evaluation. Its results are intended to be applied in the EU Network of Excellence KnowledgeWeb as a support tool for the OOA (Ontology Outreach Advisory) initiative, whose goal is to provide consultancy, promote and outreach high-quality ontological content in key industrial sectors of the Semantic Web such as eHealth or eRecruitment.[6] From a ontology engineering perspective, the working group elaborated a first draft of a metadata schema relying on the OMV Core, which describes various aspects of the ontology evaluation field: typical methods applied to evaluate an ontology from multiple points of view (e.g. consistency checking, validation, requirements-based evaluation, ontological evaluation) and in particular application scenarios (e.g. NLP-based evaluation methods), roles involved in the evaluation process (e.g. reviewer), tools (e.g. reasoners, validators). As in the case of the OMV Core, the evaluation module is currently subject of revisions within the members of the working group.

6 Related Work

Metadata and metadata standards have a long-tradition in a variety of computer sciences areas, such as digital libraries or data management and maintenance systems. We will briefly mention related metadata standards, including in particular those ones relevant for the Semantic Web. The **Dublin Core (DC)** metadata standard is a simple yet effective element set for describing a wide range of networked resources[7]. It includes two levels: Simple (with fifteen elements) and Qualified, including an additional element as well as a group of element refinements (or qualifiers) that adapt the semantics of the elements for resource discovery purposes. The **Reference Ontology**[1] is a domain ontology that gathers, describes and has links to existing ontologies. However its focus is to characterize ontologies from the user point of view, and provides only a list of property-value pairs for describing ontologies. The Semantic Web search engine **SWOOGLE**[2] makes use of an implicitly defined metadata schema, which covers information which can be extracted automatically from ontology implementations. Our approach includes and extends this metadata vocabulary. Ideally, future versions of SWOOGLE would also take into account the additional vocabulary defined in OMV . Further on, the issue of creating a metadata standard for ontologies is addressed by various ontology repositories initiatives. However, the majority of these repositories rely on a restricted, implicitly declared vocabulary, whose meaning is not machine-understandable. The **DAML ontology library** provides a catalog of DAML ontologies that can be browsed by different properties[8]. The **FIPA ontology service**[20] defines an agent wrapper of open knowledge base connectivity. The **SchemaWeb Directory**

---

[6] http://knowledgeweb.semanticweb.org/
[7] c.f. http://dublincore.org/
[8] c.f. http://www.daml.org/ontologies/

is a repository for RDF schemas expressed in RDFS, OWL and DAML+OIL[9]. Finally we mention the ontology metadata example presented in [10] emerged within the EU Network of Excellence **Knowledge Web**. The metadata consists only of attribute-value pairs, and does not consider the distinction between conceptualizations and implementations. However, the work presented there provided a preliminary basis for the OMV ontology introduced in this paper.

7   Conclusions and Future Work

In this paper we present DEMO, a framework for the development and deployment for ontology metadata. Besides OMV , the proposed core vocabulary for ontology metadata, the framework comprises an inventory of methods to collaboratively extend OMV in accordance to the requirements of a emerging community of industrial and academia users, to develop extension modules for particular applications, user communities or aspects of the reuse process, as well as tools for metadata management.

The proposed OMV Core captures information that is similar to other metadata standards, such as Dublin Core. However, it goes beyond this general-purpose level and provides a vocabulary for capturing information about **ontologies**, represented in a well-defined machine and human interpretable language. The differences between arbitrary information sources and ontologies make the usage of metadata standards such as Dublin Core inappropriate. When talking about ontologies, there is a distinction between the conceptual representation of an application domain (the ontology at knowledge level) and its various implementations (in particular representation languages). As these two parts are characterized by different properties, the metadata about ontologies should be able to differentiate between the semantic conceptualization and its particular realization as a concrete ontology document. Besides, aspects related to application scenario, scope, purpose, or evaluation results are essential coordinates for a successful ontology reuse and should be captured by the ontology metadata schema. On the other hand, besides structural and technical information on ontologies—which can be captured automatically—there is a strong demand for representing descriptive metadata, like authorship information, categorizations or underlying methodologies. The enumerated factors indicate the need for a ontology-specific metadata vocabulary, which, though remaining compatible to information represented in generic metadata standards like Dublin Core, is customized to the particular requirements of ontology sharing and reuse.

Within the DEMO environment we initiated an activity aiming at achieving a broad scale agreement on the OMV contents and representation, which was received favorably by both academia and industry institutions and will continue in the future. As a first result of DEMO activities, the *WG Applications* developed the P2P metadata sharing tool Oyster[10] and the metadata portal ONTHOLOGY[11]. Both systems compose an interlocked metadata management framework and contribute to the development and dissemination activities [9].

---

[9] c.f. http://www.schemaweb.info
[10] c.f. http://oyster.ontoware.org/
[11] c.f. http://www.onthology.org/

While the basis technical infrastructure for the DEMO activities is provided by the OntoWare platform, we are experimenting with methods and heuristics to operationalize the metadata generation process and to check the quality of the existing metadata information. These tasks, though not trivial, can be automatized to a considerable extent due to the ontology-based representation of the OMV .

Acknowledgments. This proposal is based on a huge number of discussions and many helpful arguments by persons from academia and industry. Especially we would like to thank our colleagues York Sure (AIFB), M. Carmen Suárez-Figueroa (UPM), Peter Haase (AIFB), Denny Vrandecic(AIFB) and Rudi Studer (AIFB). Furthermore, we thank our partners from the EU project Knowledge Web for their present and future collaboration.

References

1. J. Arpirez, A. Gomez-Porez, A. Lozano-Tello, and H. Pinto. Reference Ontology and (ONTO)2 Agent: The Ontology Yellow Pages. *Knowledge and Information Systems*, 2:387–412, 2000.
2. L. Ding et al. Swoogle: A search and metadata engine for the semantic web. In *Proc. of the 13th ACM Conf. on Information and Knowledge Management*, pages 58–61, 2004.
3. M. Fernandez-Lopez and A. Gomez-Perez. Overview and analysis of methodologies for building ontologies. *Knowledge Engineering Review*, 17(2):129–156, 2002.
4. A. Gangemi, D. M. Pisanelli, and G. Steve. An overview of the ONIONS project: Applying ontologies to the integration of medical terminologies. *Data Knowledge Engineering*, 31(2):183–220, 1999.
5. A. Gomez-Perez. Evaluation of ontologies. *Int. Journal of Intelligent Systems*, 16(3), 2001.
6. A. Gómez-Pérez, M. Fernández-López, and O. Corcho. *Ontological Engineering*. Springer, 2003.
7. T. R. Gruber. Toward principles for the design of ontologies used for knowledge sharing. *Int. J. Hum.-Comput. Stud.*, 43(5-6):907–928, 1995.
8. J. Hartmann and R. Palma. OMV - Ontology Metadata Vocabulary for the Semantic Web, 2005. Technical Report V. 1.0, available at http://omv.ontoware.org/.
9. J. Hartmann, Y. Sure, R. Palma, P. Haase, M.C. Suarez-Figueroa, R. Studer, and A. Gomez-Perez. Ontology metadata vocabulary and applications. In Robert Meersman, editor, *International Conference on Ontologies, Databases and Applications of Semantics. In Workshop on Web Semantics (SWWS)*, OCT 2005.
10. KnowledgeWeb European Project. Identification of standards on metadata for ontologies (Deliverable D1.3.2 KnoweldgeWeb FP6-507482), 2004.
11. K. Kotis, G. A. Vouros, and J. Padilla Alonso. HCOME: tool-supported methodology for collaboratively devising living ontologies. In *SWDB'04: 2. Int. Workshop on Semantic Web and Databases*, 2004.
12. A. Lozano-Tello and A. Gomez-Perez. ONTOMETRIC: A Method to Choose the Appropriate Ontology. *Journal of Database Management*, 15(2), 2004.
13. R. Neches, R. E. Fikes, T. Finin, T. R. Gruber, T. Senator, and W. R. Swartout. Enabling technology for knowledge sharing. *AI Magazine*, 12(3):35–56, 1991.
14. National Information Stadards Organization. Understanding metadata. NISO Press, 2004.
15. E. Paslaru Bontas, M. Mochol, and R. Tolksdorf. Case Studies on Ontology Reuse. In *Proceedings of the IKNOW05 International Conference on Knowledge Management*, 2005.

16. H. S. Pinto and J. P. Martins. A methodology for ontology integration. In *Proc. of the International Conf. on Knowledge Capture K-CAP01*, 2001.

17. H. S. Pinto, S. Staab, and C. Tempich. Diligent: Towards a fine-grained methodology for distributed, loosely-controlled and evolving engineering of ontologies. In *Proc. of the ECAI04*, pages 393–397, 2004.

18. T. Russ, A. Valente, R. MacGregor, and W. Swartout. Practical Experiences in Trading Off Ontology Usability and Reusability. In *Proc. of the Knowledge Acquisition Workshop (KAW99)*, 1999.

19. S. Buckingham Shum, E. Motta, and J. Domingue. Augmenting design deliberation with compendium: The case of collaborative ontology design. In *Proc. of the HypACoM02 Workshop: Facilitating Hypertext-Augmented Collaborative Modeling*, 2002.

20. H. Suguri et al. Implementation of FIPA Ontology Service. In *Proc. of the Workshop on Ontologies in Agent Systems, 5th Int. Conf. on Autonomous Agents Montreal, Canada*, 2001.

21. Y. Sure, S. Bloehdorn, P. Haase, J. Hartmann, and D. Oberle. The SWRC ontology - Semantic Web for Research Communities. In Carlos Bento, Amilcar Cardoso, and Gael Dias, editors, *Proceedings of the 12th Portuguese Conference on Artificial Intelligence - Progress in Artificial Intelligence (EPIA 2005)*, volume 3803 of *LNCS*, pages 218 – 231, Covilha, Portugal, DEC 2005. Springer.

22. M. Uschold, M. Healy, K. Williamson, P. Clark, and S. Woods. Ontology Reuse and Application. In *Proc. of the Int. Conf. on Formal Ontology and Information Systems FOIS98*, 1998.

An Environment for Semi-automatic Annotation of Ontological Knowledge with Linguistic Content

Maria Teresa Pazienza and Armando Stellato

AI Research Group, Dept. of Computer Science, Systems and Production
University of Rome, Tor Vergata
Via del Politecnico 1, 00133 Rome, Italy
{pazienza, stellato}@info.uniroma2.it

Abstract. Both the multilingual aspects which characterize the (Semantic) Web and the demand for more easy-to-share forms of knowledge representation, being equally accessible by humans and machines, push the need for a more "linguistically aware" approach to ontology development. Ontologies should thus express knowledge by associating formal content with explicative linguistic expressions, possibly in different languages. By adopting such an approach, the intended meaning of concepts and roles becomes more clearly expressed for humans, thus facilitating (among others) reuse of existing knowledge, while automatic content mediation between autonomous information sources gets far more chances than otherwise. In past work we introduced OntoLing [7], a Protégé plug-in offering a modular and scalable framework for performing manual annotation of ontological data with information from different, heterogeneous linguistic resources. We present now an improved version of OntoLing, which supports the user with automatic suggestions for enriching ontologies with linguistic content. Different specific linguistic enrichment problems are discussed and we show how they have been tackled considering both algorithmic aspects and profiling of user interaction inside the OntoLing framework.

1 Introduction

The multilingual aspects which characterize the (Semantic) Web and the demand for more easy-to-share forms of knowledge representation, being equally accessible by humans and machines, depict a scenario where formal semantics must coexist side-by-side with natural language, all together contributing to the shareability of the content they describe. The role of different cultures and languages is fundamental in a real World *aWare* Web and, though English is widely accepted as a "lingua franca" all over the world, much effort must be spent to preserve other idioms as they express different cultures. As a consequence, multilinguality has been cited as one of the six challenges for the Semantic Web [2].

These premises suggest that semantic web ontologies, delegated to express machine-readable information on the Web, should be enriched to both cover formally expressed conceptual knowledge and expose its content in a linguistically motivated fashion.

Y. Sure and J. Domingue (Eds.): ESWC 2006, LNCS 4011, pp. 442–456, 2006.

Even more could be done: revisiting ontology development process under this perspective, would in fact guarantee this scenario to become a suitable framework upon which even machine oriented task, like mediation and discovery, would benefit of this greater expressivity.

Following this intent, in [7,8] we defined OntoLing, a Protégé [5,6] plug-in offering a modular and scalable framework for supporting manual annotation of ontological data with information from different, heterogeneous linguistic resources.

We present now an improved version of OntoLing, which prompts the user with automatic suggestions for enriching ontologies with linguistic content. We explain how and why different kinds of linguistic enrichment processes should be performed and focus our attention on one of these tasks, showing how its automatization has been obtained, considering both algorithmic aspects and profiling of user interaction in the context of OntoLing framework.

2   Linguistic Enrichment of Ontologies: Different Possible Tasks

We introduced the expression "Linguistic Enrichment of Ontologies" to identify a series of different processes sharing the common objective of improving the linguistic expressivity of an ontology, through the exploitation of existing Linguistic Resources (LRs, from now on). The nature of this "linguistic expressivity" strongly depends on the LRs used for linguistic enrichment and on the specific goals the enrichment process will achieve. In the following sections we describe three different enrichment tasks, together with possible scenarios in which these tasks may be applied.

2.1   Using a LR's Semantic Structure as a Controlled Vocabulary: Semantic Enrichment of Ontologies

In this class of Linguistic Enrichment tasks, the semantic structure of a given LR (provided it has one), is used as a controlled vocabulary for the ontology and related application. What is required is just identification of *pointers* from ontological data to semantic elements of the linguistic resource. Access to pure linguistic information is then guaranteed by the links between the semantic and linguistic structure of the LR.

As a first example, consider an NLP ontology-based application, dedicated to whatsoever kind of text analysis task (e.g. Information Extraction), and which is strongly coupled with a semantic lexicon for extracting linguistic information from the text. The semantic pointers are needed to easily move from extracted, neutral, "linguistic information", which is processed in terms of lexical concepts, to "events" which are represented by the ontology.

As a further example, consider a scenario where distributed information sources must be aligned by mediators relying on a common form of knowledge. This committed knowledge is represented by so called "upper ontologies", or "upper models" which contain a first stratification of general concepts. Examples in literature [1] report of adoption, instead of an ontology, of the semantic structure of an existing linguistic resource [4] as a interlingua for guaranteeing communication between autonomous distributed agents.

2.2 Explicit Linguistic Enrichment

When no semantic commitment has been established between autonomously developed information sources, no further solution exists for reaching semantic interoperability than relying on the very last form of *shared* knowledge representation: natural language. It is the form used by humans to pass from their own conceptualization of the world, to any form of shareable communication, being it spoken, written, or even related to formal representations of knowledge (also a good programming style ask for variables and functions being expressed through *evocative* labels). Indeed, stating direct links between ontological content (which is often scarcely modeled, upon a linguistic point of view) and linguistic expressions, may represent the only viable solution to increase the shareability of the represented knowledge.

Moreover, the improved range of expressions for denoting a concept and the (possible) presence of natural language descriptions for ontological data, facilitate reuse of existing knowledge, which is made more comprehensible also for humans.

2.3 Producing Multilingual Ontologies

Exploitation of existing bilingual resources may help in the development of multilingual ontologies, in which different multilingual expressions coexist and share the same ontological knowledge. The multilingual enrichment process, mainly if considered upon already enriched ontologies, may beneficiate of a greater linguistic expressivity of the source data and thus exploit different techniques for obtaining proper translations for ontology concepts and roles.

3 Techniques for Semantic/Linguistic Enrichment of Ontologies

While OntoLing's underlying model for accessing LRs is thought for supporting all of the above tasks, in this work we focus on techniques and solutions for automatizing the first task which has been presented: semantic enrichment of ontologies. This represents in fact a first necessary step through which all of the other tasks may be accomplished.

3.1 The Linguistic Enrichment Environment: Adopted Terminology

For sake of clarity, we will adopt from now on a terminology inherited from two well known standards for ontological and linguistic resources: OWL and WordNet model.

OWL [3] has recently been accepted as a W3C recommendation for the representation of ontologies on the Web, so we have adopted its ontological model for our framework and will use its nomenclature for distinguishing ontological objects into *classes*, *properties* (*object properties* and *datatype properties*) and *individuals*. Frame based models for knowledge representation can equally be considered inside this framework, with *slots* taking the role of properties and *instances* acting as individuals of the OWL model. We adopt in fact the term *frame* to address any ontological object whose type needs not to be specified.

WordNet [4] is an on-line lexical reference system whose design is inspired by current psycholinguistic theories of human lexical memory. English nouns, verbs, adjectives and adverbs are organized into synonym sets (synsets), each representing one underlying lexical concept. Several wordnets have been developed for other languages [11, 9], which have thus favored a large diffusion of the model which inspired the original English version. As only those LRs which expose (cfr. [7, 8]) a semantic structure (like WordNet) may be elected for the semantic enrichment task, we decided to adopt notation borrowed from the WordNet Model to address linguistic elements from LRs. We thus use terms like *synset* (or *lexical concept*, or *semantic element*), *sense* and *synonym*, under the meaning they assume in WordNet-like lexical databases.

We prefer in general to avoid use of term *concept* in any formal statement, as it is adopted in different communities with different meanings: a synset is a *lexical concept* in WordNet, while an OWL class implements a *concept* in Description Logics theory, furthermore, other ontology traditions use "concept" to mean every generic ontology construct, thus including properties and instances other than classes.

3.2 The Semantic Enrichment Task

Objective of semantic enrichment task is to identify *pointers* from ontological objects (*frames*) to semantic entities (e.g. *synsets*, for WordNet) of a linguistic resource.

Before detailing our semantic enrichment process, we describe a few empirical results we collected during our research. These results took the form of morphosyntactic and semantic evidences recognized over several pairs of ontologies and linguistic resources, which could be used to guide the enrichment process.

All the reported examples refer to semantic enrichment of a DAML ontology[1] about baseball, downloaded from the DAML library of ontologies[2], using WordNet as a source for linguistic knowledge.

3.3 Taxonomy-Alignment Evidences

In case the semantic structure of a given LR has been organized as a taxonomy of broader/narrower linguistic concepts, similarities between this taxonomy and that of the ontology may provide useful evidences for an enrichment task. The IS-A relation of ontologies has however well defined semantics, while taxonomical links of LRs may often confuse different informal and/or ambiguous relationships (specialization, part-of, relatedness etc...); nonetheless, an analysis of these similarities typically leads to interesting and reliable results. The intuition behind this strategy is that *if* a semantic pointer links a frame-synset pair $<F,S>$, *then* other frame-synset pairs (where the frame is more specific/more generic that F and the synset is narrower/broader than S), have a good probability of being linked through a semantic pointer. We call this phenomenon the "sense-alignment square".

In Fig. 1 below, the semantic pointer between F_H and S_H already exists and represents an evidence for assessing a new semantic pointer over the pair $<F_L, S_L>$.

An example of this configuration is represented by the class labeled as *Hit* in the baseball ontology: this class has been eligible for 14 potential senses in WordNet. Of these 14 senses one is represented by the synset noun.124696, whose gloss states:

[1] http://www.daml.org/2001/08/baseball/baseball-ont for the original DAML version.
[2] http://www.daml.org/ontologies/

a successful stroke in an athletic contest (especially in baseball); "he came all the way around on Williams"hit"

This synset is more general than another WordNet synset, noun.39042, which is described by the following gloss:

a base hit on which the batter stops safely at second base; "he hit a double to deep centerfield"

and which has among its synonyms the word "double". Finally, closing the alignment-square, *Double* is another class of the ontology, which is a subclass of *Hit*. Thanks to this evidence, both *Hit*-noun.124696 and *Double*-noun.39042 pairs result as good candidates for being linked through a semantic pointer.

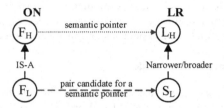

Fig. 1. The sense-alignment square

3.4 Evidences Resulting upon Analysis of Glosses from the Linguistic Resource

Glosses offer natural language descriptions of concepts. Though their content is generally intended as an easy reference for human readability, it represents indeed a useful mean for discovering relations which have no explicit semantic counterpart in the resource they come from.

From the glosses reported in the previous example, we could learn that a "double" is a kind of "base hit" (though the meaning of "hit" is not formally specified by the gloss), even if the resource lacked of a taxonomical structure, thus binding the two lexical concepts together in a broader/narrower relation.

A further example is represented by the class *Division* (again in the DAML baseball ontology). WordNet offers 12 different senses for the term "division". The gloss of the correct synset, noun.7741947, states:

a league ranked by quality; "he played baseball in class D for two years"; "Princeton is in the NCAA Division 1-AA".

Again, we could learn that a "division" is a "league", and *League* is one of the classes of the ontology. This case is however different from the previous one: in fact in the ontology tree, *Division* has not been conceived as a type of *League*. Nonetheless, a further analysis of ontological context reveals that *Division* appears in the restricted range of a property of class *League*. The co-occurrence of these two terms in the gloss, together with the presence of the range restriction binding the two classes labelled by the terms, suggests noun.7741947 as a potential candidate for *Division*.

There are however cases where a supposed interesting relation is not formally expressed in the ontology. An example is given by the class *Out*: we report here the gloss of its correct matching synset:

(baseball) a failure by a batter or runner to reach a base safely in baseball; "you only get 3 outs per inning".

we observe that "base" is a term appearing in the above gloss and that, at the same time, *Base* is a class in the ontology. Unfortunately, *Base* is not bound by any onto-logical relation to *Out*. Should this combination be discarded as a mere fortuity? May be not: the baseball ontology for example, with its 104 frames (considering classes and properties), may in fact be considered as a very domain-specific representation, where the sole presence of few concepts is enough to consider them semantically re-lated in some way.

A final consideration: it may happen that glosses describing synsets which are can-didate for enrichment of different ontology frames, contain common references to concepts of which no trace is present in the ontology. Oddly enough, the ontology about baseball which we used for our examples, contains no specific lexical nor con-ceptual reference to "baseball" itself! On the other hand, many WordNet definitions contain the word baseball in their glosses, so that, in those cases, it is quite easy for a human to immediately choose the right sense from the given set of candidates, just af-ter a glimpse at the list of glosses. An automatic process should be able to discover even these "hidden" correlations and weight their effectiveness appropriately.

4   The Feature Model

To take into account all previous considerations, and to maintain a scalable approach towards new possible strategies and LR configurations, we adopted a probabilistic model based on a feature space which is produced upon the observed evidences.

We have thus defined a *Plausibility Matrix* M_P as a two-dimensional matrix on a $O{\times}L$ space, where O is the cardinality of the ontological objects and L is the cardinal-ity of the semantic data in the linguistic resource. Each element $M_P(i,j)$ of the matrix represents the plausibility that the ontological object i be matched with the lexical concept j. Analogously, an *Evidence Matrix* M_E contains in each element $M_E(i,j)$ the set of evidences which contribute to the computation of element $M_P(i,j)$ in the Plausi-bility Matrix.

The Discovery Phase. The linguistic dimension in the two matrices is far broader than the ontological one. An efficient enrichment process should thus consider a first discovery phase in which lexical anchors between the ontology and the LR are thrown to define possible candidates for linguistic enrichment. Each anchor represents a po-tential pointer from the ontology to the LR, and is discovered thanks to lexical simi-larity measures (use of string matching distances, possibly made smarter through knowledge of morphosyntactic properties of the natural language under analysis). In this phase it is important to drop as many anchors as possible, as they will represent the whole search space which is screened during the linguistic enrichment process. The trade-off is therefore lightly biased towards recall rather than precision, as the lat-ter, in this case, is only important for reducing the computational cost of the process. The result of the discovery phase is thus a subspace L^A represented by all synsets in L which have been anchored as potential targets for semantic pointers.

The Semantic Enrichment Function. Once an L^A space has been extracted, we can then define the linguistic enrichment function f^{se} :

$$f^{se} : O \times L^A \mapsto [0..1] \tag{1}$$

This function maps pairs of elements from the ontology and the (restricted) linguistic resources into a confidence interval [0..1] representing the plausibility for assessing the presence of a semantic pointer between them.

The whole function f^{se} is realized through two main phases: by first the analysis of the linguistic and semantic similarities of the ontology and of the LR will lead the production of the *Evidence Matrix* M_E; the *Plausibility Matrix* M_P, based on the previously captured evidences, is then evaluated upon M_E.

There may exist mutual dependencies between contributions of features for different frame-synset pairs. For this reason, f^{se} is actually an iterative process $f^{se} = f^{se}(t)$; in particular, computation of the plausibility matrix takes this general form:

$$M_P(t) = f\left(M_E, M_P(t-1), M_P(0)\right) \tag{2}$$

To adopt a smarter notation for addressing plausibilities of single frame-synset pairs, we define:

$$p(F, S, t) \stackrel{def}{=} M_P(F, S) \text{ with } M_P = M_P(t) \tag{3}$$

Finally, we define a *candidate pair* <F,S> as a pair of elements $F \in O$ and $S \in L^C$, where $p(F,S,0) \neq 0$.

5 Instantiating f^{se}

The formulas in equations (1,2) are declarative forms representing classes of functions for realizing a semantic enrichment process, which are compatible with our model. In this section we present our realization of the semantic enrichment function, according to the two defined phases.

5.1 Computing Plausibilities

In our experiments, we specified this function according to the following desiderata:

1. *prizing* candidate pairs characterized by positive evidences
2. *punishing* candidate pairs characterized by negative evidences
3. evaluate quantitative factors associated to different kind of evidences (representing the *strength*, or *presence*, of the evidence)
4. take into account inherent polysemy of every label associated to ontology concepts

The following equation has thus been conceived for computing elements of the Plausibility Matrix:

$$p(t) = \frac{p_0 + \left(1 - \prod_{i=1}^{n}\left(1 - \rho(v_i, t)\right)\right) \cdot (1 - p_0)}{1 + \left(1 - \prod_{i=1}^{m}\left(1 - \rho(v_i, t)\right)\right) \cdot \left(\frac{1}{p_0} - 1\right)} \tag{4}$$

$p(t)$ is actually a smarter notation (to avoid abuse of indices in the formula) for $p(F, S, t)$, while $p_0 = p(0)$. p_0 value depends on τ_{high} and τ_{low}, two parameters representing the threshold over (resp. under) which a frame-synset pair must automatically be accepted (rejected), and on the ambiguity (number of senses for word) of the term denoting F, according to the following formula:

$$p_0 \doteq \frac{\tau_{high} - \tau_{low}}{a} + \tau_{low} \tag{5}$$

For each evidence v_i, a weighted feature is then computed through the function $\rho(v_i, t)$, whose value depends on the type of evidence v_i and on the instantiation of its associated parameters. In the following section details are provided about the structure of the different features v_i.

5.2 Extracting Evidences

Following the experiences we summarized in section 3, we formalized methods for extracting interesting evidences and for mapping their content into features for our f^{se} function.

First of all, we define the search space over ontological relations which is investigated for every class of evidences:

Def. A *conceptual sphere* of a frame F over a set of relations R is a collection of frames linked to F through a relation $r \in R$. If r is a transitive relation, its closure may be limited to n allowed *hops*, depending on ontology's size; n is called the *range* of the sphere wrt the r dimension.

The conceptual sphere (sometimes called *context* in literature) for the Taxonomy-Alignment evidences has obviously been defined over the sole IS-A relationship, and its allowed range depends on the dimension of the ontology.

For gloss-based evidences we restricted the IS-A relation to cover only super concepts of the frame to be enriched; moreover, we considered both domain and range specifications of properties, and range restrictions of properties for specific classes. Computation of the sphere also depends on the nature of the ontological object under analysis. In figure 3 the algorithm for computing the conceptual sphere for classes, properties and individuals has been shown.

Taxonomy-alignment evidences: These kind of evidences assume the following form:

$$v \doteq \langle \, frame, synset, \text{sgn} \, \rangle$$

where frame-synset is a *candidate pair* whose alignment influences the plausibility of the candidate pair which is being evaluated. The associated weighted features are computed through this formula:

$$\rho(v_i,t) \doteq \sigma_{TA} \cdot \text{sgn} \cdot p(frame, synset, t-1)$$

where σ_{SA} is a coefficient related to this type of evidences and p(*frame*, *synset*, *t*-1) is the plausibility of the <*frame*, *synset*> pair at time *t*-1. sgn is 1 if *v* is a positive evidence, -1 if it is a negative one. Negative features for this kind of evidence are represented by configurations like that in fig. 2 below:

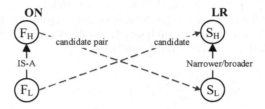

Fig. 2. negative evidence for sense-alignment

Here, <F_H,S_L> and <F_L,S_H> represent mutual negative influences, so that the plausibility of each pair is decreasing that of the other.

Gloss-mentioned Related Concepts: The strategy for extracting these evidences is based on the intuition that the glosses of the candidate synsets which best define a given frame *F*, may contain linguistic references to other concepts contained in the *conceptual sphere* of *F*.

The extraction of this kind of evidences is described by the following algorithm:

```
for each Frame rc ∈ ConceptualSphere do
    MtchLvl ← match(rc, gloss),
    if MtchLvl ≠ 0
    Evidences ← Evidences ∪ evd(GR, rc, MtchLvl)
    end if
end for
```

where *Evidences* is the set of evidences related to a given <*F,S*> pair, *Conceptual-Sphere* is the conceptual sphere built around *F* and *gloss* is the gloss of *S*. GR is a tag denoting membership of the extracted evidences to this class of features. *MtchLvl* is a degree of lexical similarity between the term from the gloss and the label of the matching concept: this value is obtained on the basis of raw string matching distances and comparative morphological analysis of the two terms.

Gloss-mentioned Generic concepts: Sometimes glosses of a candidate synset may disclose useful correlations between ontology concepts, which are unfortunately not captured by existing ontological relationships. In most cases nothing could be done and this phenomenon should simply be treated as a lack of information: the concepts can be recognized, upon human common sense, as potentially related (and they actually represent an evidence for a correct semantic pointer!), but they are not connected by any sort of relationship in the ontology (see related example in section 3.4)

Should the ontology be of modest size, offering a specification of a conceptualization of a very limited domain, it is nonetheless possible to consider each concept as somewhat related to the others. Under this hypothesis, given a $<F, S>$ pair and a gloss *gloss* for synset S, this strategy considers as an evidence every occurrence of a term inside *gloss* which is also a label for a frame, even if no apparent relation with F exists.

> **for each** *term t* $\in$ *gloss* **do**
> $F\ rc \leftarrow$ find(Ontology, *t*, *MtchLvl*),
>   **if** *rc* $\neq$ null
>   *Evidences* $\leftarrow$ *Evidences* $\cup$ evd(GG, *rc*, *MtchLvl*)
>   **end if**
> **end for**

Both these two gloss-based features are defined by the following expression:

$$v \doteq \langle MatchingLevel \rangle$$

and their contribution to f^{se} is:

$$\rho(v_i, t) \doteq \sigma_{GR/GG} \cdot MatchingLevel$$

```
computeConceptualSphere(Frame frm, int DepthRange) SET OF Frame
input frm: the class, property or individual which has been selected for linguistic enrichment
        DepthRange: the number of allowed hops along the IS-A relation for retrieving super concepts of frm
output     ConceptualSphere: the conceptual sphere surrounding frm
begin
FrameType type ← getOntoType(frm)
SET OF Frame ConceptualSphere ← {}
if (type = class  or type = property)
    ConceptualSphere ← ConceptualSphere ∪ getSuperConcepts(frm, DepthRange)
else  //frm is an instance
    Classes ← getClasses(frm)
    for each class ∈ Classes do
        ConceptualSphere ← ConceptualSphere ∪ {class} ∪ getSuperConcepts(class, DepthRange)
    end for
end if
if (type = class)
    for each property p, class c | frm.hasRestriction(p,c) or c.harRestriction(p,frm)
        ConceptualSphere ← ConceptualSphere ∪ { c } ∪ { p }
if (type = instance)
    for each property p ∈ ( frm.getOwnRelationalProperties() ) do
        ConceptualSphere ← ConceptualSphere ∪ { p } ∪ frm.getOwnPropertyValues(p)
end if
if (type = property)
    for each class c ∈ ( domain(frm) ∪ range(frm) ) do
        ConceptualSphere ← ConceptualSphere ∪ {class}
end if
return ConceptualSphere
end
```

Fig. 3. Algorithm for realizing the conceptual sphere for gloss-based evidences

Gloss-overlap between candidate synsets: A user manually doing linguistic enrichment knows the domain covered by the ontology and therefore would prefer senses whose glosses report domain related terms (see last example in section 3.4).

Analogously, this strategy checks for possible term overlaps between glosses of synsets which appear as candidates for enriching concepts appearing each in the conceptual sphere of the other. Of course, overlapping terms must be properly filtered, to remove co-occurrences of articles, particles and very common words.

Instead of adopting large stop-lists, which may reveal to be incomplete, we exploit the whole set of glosses of the same resource which is used for linguistic enrichment, as a large corpus for statistically determining the distribution of terms. Thresholds may then be established for filtering very common terms which bear no informative evidence. Formally:

```
for each Frame rf_i ∈ ConceptualSphere do
    for each synset s_ij ∈ candidateSynsets(rf_i) do
        let rfgloss[i,j] ← s_j.getGloss()
    end for
    for each term t, t ∈ gloss and t ∈ rfgloss[i,j]
        let freq = LR.getGlossFrequency(t)
        if !filter(freq)
            Evidences ← Evidences ∪ evd(GO, rf_i, s_i, freq)
        end if
    end for
end for
```

As for taxonomy-alignment, even this third gloss-based strategy produces mutual influences among features: the collected evidences are in fact dependent upon the plausibility of candidate $<rc, s_i>$ pairs. Their structure is in fact:

$$v \doteq \langle MatchingLevel, frame, synset \rangle$$

and ρ assumes is computed this way:

$$\rho(v_i, t) \doteq \sigma_{GO} \cdot MatchingLevel \cdot p(frame, synset, t-1)$$

MatchingLevel is in this case also dependant on the frequency of the observed overlapping term.

6   Supporting Linguistic Enrichment of Ontologies in OntoLing

In line with OntoLing's highly modular architecture, we defined abstract layers for supporting automatic linguistic enrichment of ontologies at different levels. The schema in figure 4 extends OntoLing architecture [7] with new interfaces for:

- accessing a generic module for linguistic enrichment
- invoking standard methods for storing/caching information necessary for the enrichment task, from both the ontology the linguistic resource

We have provided a first realization of the enrichment interface through the implementation of the previously discussed techniques for semantic enrichment of ontologies. The storage and caching API have been realized according to diverse technologies and solutions, each of them thought for matching specific requirements. Mainly, these solutions can be split into two main categories:

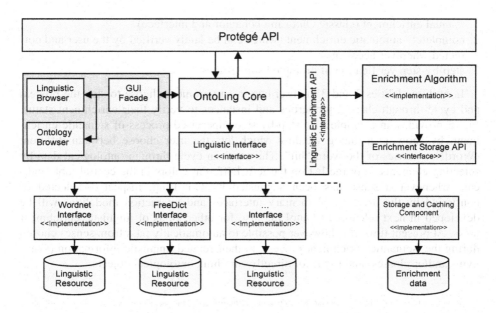

Fig. 4. OntoLing Architecture

- disk storage/caching of data
- in-memory storage

The first class has been thought to provide a scalable environment where even thousands of ontological objects, linguistic elements and relations between them can be easily handled. We provided one implementation for this category, based on use of database technologies. Different drivers may be loaded at run time for accessing available and preferred DBMSs. A dedicated driver for a popular java embedded DBMS [12] has been bundled into the application, to make OntoLing immediately operative without need of any external technology.

Aim of the second class of solutions is to maximize performances by storing data directly in memory, thus providing fast access to ontological and linguistic information during the enrichment process. This approach is ideal whenever size of the ontology and complexity of the linguistic resource do not require massive memory usage. Currently, two implementations are available to realize this solution:

- A prolog DB, which represents linguistic and ontological objects (and the relations between them) into sets of prolog facts
- An specific driver for an in-memory DBMS, sharing the same SQL implementation of already described DBMS solution.

Finally, a new interface has been produced for interacting with the user, which can initially choose between three different modalities:

1. manual enrichment (classic OntoLing behavior and interface)
2. completely automatic enrichment (which can be lately verified by the user and corrected wherever necessary)
3. step-by-step verification of prompted suggestions

In both modalities 2 and 3 the user can in any moment choose to stop the process and cycle through classes, properties and instances to verify their enrichment status. Fig. 5 provides an example of a step-by-step supervised process of semantic enrichment, by showing a dialog window which lets the user choose between different (WordNet) senses of the word "hit". The user can cycle through ontological data by selecting elements from the list on the left. Different colors in the central table indicate whenever a sense has been suggested by OntoLing, inspected, selected or confirmed by the user. Supplementary interfaces and interaction modalities will be developed in next releases of OntoLing also for other kinds of linguistic enrichment tasks. At present time, it is however possible to automatically pass from senses chosen during the semantic enrichment process, to their related linguistic information (synonyms and/or glosses) and use it for directly enriching ontological objects.

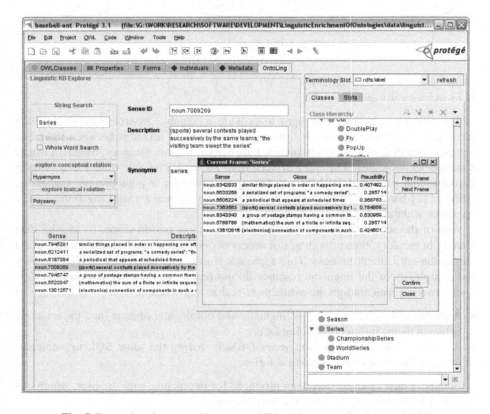

Fig. 5. Prompting the user with suggested WordNet senses for the word "hit"

7   Automatic Semantic Enrichment: Experimental Results and Final Remarks

To evaluate our enrichment process, we ran two experiments on enriching two public domain ontologies with synsets from WordNet. In reporting performances, standard Precision & Recall metrics have been adopted, instead of simple Hit Percentages, because for any given Frame, the system may propose a suggestion (right or wrong) or not. We also reported F-measure [10] which combines recall and precision in a single efficiency measure (it is the harmonic mean of precision and recall):

$$F = 2*(recall*precision)/(recall+precision)$$

The first experiment has been performed on the baseball ontology chosen for our examples. The ontology, is composed of 78 classes, 26 properties and 13 individuals. Of these objects, 60 classes and 21 properties were considered for semantic enrichment (we performed the experiment limiting to the ontology schema, so we provide statistics only for classes and properties) during the discovery phase. The number of non ambiguous concepts (including both classes and properties) is 20 (~ 24,7% of the whole concept set) while the average ambiguity, (measured as the average polysemy of considered terms, wrt WordNet synset structure), is ~ 9,16. Two annotators were initially hired to realize two documents (one per annotator) reporting the most evocative synset for each concept. The documents have then been compared and a final decision has been taken where discrepancies were found, to produce the oracle used in the experiments. The observed inter-annotator agreement on the two original documents has been however of 98.76% (one re-discussed decision out of the whole set).

Recall has been measured towards the number of concepts which can be enriched with the considered LR. The terms offered by any linguistic resource represent in fact the whole search space, and each evaluation of a linguistic enrichment process has only sense if considered wrt a specific LR. Fine tuning of evidence-typed σ-parameters has been performed over a collection of several small ontologies and/or portions of them, before running the experiment, whose results are reported in table 1.

The second experiment has been run on an ontology related to the university academic domain[3], developed in the context of the EU funded project MOSES (IST-2001-37244). This ontology has been built, in OWL language, over a preexisting DAML ontology[4] from the official DAML repository and finalized for representing the Italian university domain. As a consequence, while the original language in which concepts were expressed was English, many of the concepts added for describing the Italian academic institutions had only Italian labels. Though we plan for the future to define a two step enrichment process which is able to rely on multiple linguistic resources (for different languages) even for dealing with this kind of situations, we evaluated our algorithms over those parts of the ontology which were eligible for monolingual enrichment. More than half of the classes (100 out of 192) emerged during the discovery phase, while only a very small part of the properties (9 out of 100) have been discovered: this is probably due to the large amount of properties added during the customization to the Italian

---

[3] http://www.mondeca.com/owl/moses/ita.owl
[4] http://www.cs.umd.edu/projects/plus/DAML/onts/univ1.0.daml

Table 1. Evaluation of linguistic enrichment over two publicly available ontologies

Ontology	Precision	Recall	F-Measure
Baseball Ontology	80%	39,5%	52,89%
Moses Italian	81,48%	42,72%	56,05%

domain. We report in table 1 evaluation of the algorithm for both the experiments. Detailed analysis of the test data on the first experiment revealed that, though only 40% of the original corpus (ontology) has been correctly annotated with WordNet synsets, another 50% contains the right choice in a high ranked position (second or third suggestion, or even first but under the established plausibility threshold).

A similar observation holds for precision, where the 20% wrong hits gave only few plausibility points over the correct ones. This reveals to be in line with the intended nature of the task, which is to be seen as part of a computer-aided, linguistically motivated approach to ontology development, more than a mere disambiguation problem.

References

1. Beneventano D., Bergamaschi S., Guerra, F., Vincini, M: Building an integrated Ontology within SEWASIE system. In proceedings of the First International Workshop on Semantic Web and Databases (SWDB), Co-located with VLDB 2003 Berlin, Germany, September 7-8, 2003
2. V. R. Benjamins, J. Contreras, O. Corcho and A. Gómez-Pérez. Six Challenges for the Semantic Web. *SIGSEMIS Bulletin*, April 2004.
3. M. Dean and G. Schreiber, editors: OWL Web Ontology Language Guide. 2004. W3C Recommendation (10 February 2004).
4. C. Fellbaum: WordNet - An electronic lexical database. MIT Press, (1998).
5. J. Gennari, M. Musen, R. Fergerson, W. Grosso, M. Crubézy, H. Eriksson, N. Noy, and S. Tu. The evolution of Protégé-2000: An environment for knowledge-based systems development. *International Journal of Human-Computer Studies*, 58(1):89–123, 2003.
6. H. Knublauch, R. W. Fergerson, N. F. Noy, M. A. Musen. The Protégé OWL Plugin: An Open Development Environment for Semantic Web Applications *Third International Semantic Web Conference - ISWC 2004*, Hiroshima, Japan. 2004
7. M. T. Pazienza, A. Stellato: The Protégé OntoLing Plugin: Linguistic Enrichment of Ontologies in the Semantic Web. In *Poster Proceedings of the 4th International Semantic Web Conference (ISWC-2005)* Galway, Ireland, November, 2005
8. M.T. Pazienza, A. Stellato: Linguistically motivated Ontology Mapping for the Semantic Web. *Semantic Web Applications and Perspectives 2nd Italian Semantic Web Workshop (SWAP 2005)*, December 2005
9. S. Stamou, K. Oflazer, K. Pala, D. Christoudoulakis, D. Cristea, D. Tufiş, S. Koeva, G. Totkov, D. Dutoit, M. Grigoriadou (2002). *BALKANET: A Multilingual Semantic Network for the Balkan Languages*. Proceedings of the International Wordnet Conference, January 21-25, Mysore, India, 12-14.
10. C. J. Van Rijsbergen, *Information Retrieval*. 2nd edition, London, Butterworths, 1979
11. P. Vossen. *EuroWordNet: A Multilingual Database with Lexical Semantic Networks*, Kluwer Academic Publishers, Dordrecht, 1998
12. http://www.daffodildb.com/

Turning the Mouse into a Semantic Device: The *seMouse* Experience*

Jon Iturrioz, Sergio F. Anzuola, and Oscar Díaz

The Onekin Group
Department of Languages and Computer Systems
University of Basque Country
Pᵒ Manuel de Lardizabal, 1
20.018 San Sebastián (Spain)
{jon.iturrioz, jibfeans, oscar.diaz}@ehu.es

Abstract. The desktop is not foreign to the semantic way that is percolating broad areas of computing. This work reports on the experiences on turning the mouse into a semantic device. The mouse is configured with an ontology, and from then on, this ontology is used to annotate the distinct desktop resources. The ontology plays the role of a clipboard which can be transparently accessed by the file editors to either export (i.e. annotation) or import (i.e. authoring) meta-data. Traditional desktop operations are now re-interpreted and framed by this ontology: copy&paste becomes annotation&authoring, and folder digging becomes property traversal. Being editor-independent, the mouse accounts for portability and maintainability to face the myriad of formats and editors which characterizes current desktops. This paper reports on the functionality, implementation, and user evaluation of this "semantic mouse".

Keywords: Semantic Annotation, Knowledge Management, Metadata and Ontologies.

1 Introduction

Hard-disk drives enjoy an increasing storage capacity that, however, has not come along with a similar improvement on mechanisms that harness this storage power. It is at least dubious whether current desktops have scaled to handle a number of files that doubles or triples the ones a layman held a few years ago. Scalability not only includes fault-tolerance or performance stability, but also the availability of tools that permit the end user to harness this power. The lack of appropriate tools for locating, navigating, relating or sharing bulky file sets are preventing PC users from taking full benefit of their storage power.

Current efforts on enhancing operating systems with automatic meta-data extraction support (e.g. Spotlight for MAC[1] or WinFS for Windows[2]) strive to overcome this

---

* This paper is an extension of a demostration poster presented at the First Semantic Desktop Workshop.

[1] http://www.apple.com/macosx/features/spotlight/

[2] http://msdn.microsoft.com/library/default.asp?url=/library/en-us/dnwinfs/html/winfs03112004.asp

Y. Sure and J. Domingue (Eds.): ESWC 2006, LNCS 4011, pp. 457–471, 2006.

shortcoming. However, these proposals are format-oriented. That is, the extension of the file (e.g. *.doc .ppt .html*) determines the meta-data to be extracted. If all files belong to the same extension, identical meta-data is extracted from all of them. The extractor does not consider the semantics of the content, but the format of the container. This falls short in a desktop setting where the meta-data to be extracted is highly dependent on the user's mental model. The ontology should not be format-centric but user-centric. But this can be cumbersome if appropriate tooling is missing.

Distinct works strive to provide sophisticated new environment or enhancing current tools for achieving the semantic desktop[17, 18, 2]. However, most often this implies for the user to move to a new editor when annotating (like in *SMORE* [12]), or to learn a new "ontological interface" when files from different formats are edited (like in *SemanticWord [19]*). This can pose important usability issues that refrain the adoption of the semantic desktop.

Based on this observation, this work rather than providing separate tools for annotation & authoring, enhances a popular tool for traditional copy&paste operations: the mouse. This will certainly facilitate user adoption.

To this end, the *semantic mouse* (*seMouse*) is introduced. By clicking on its middle button, *seMouse* exports/imports properties from the *ontology,* regardless of the editor you are working with. It does not matter whether you are working with *Word, Excel, PowerPoint, Adobe Acrobat, Netscape*, etc, the "semantic" button is available for annotation/authoring.

The rest of the paper is organized as follows. Section 2 addresses related work. Section 3 introduces *seMouse* through five scenarios, namely, file classification, annotation, authoring, semantic navigation and ontology editing. As previously mentioned, usability is one of the main objectives of our tool, so an evaluation is addressed in section 4. The architecture of the implementation is introduced in section 5. Finally, conclusions are given.

2   Framing the Work

This work aligns with current efforts for desktops to become semantic-aware[9, 3, 17]. The endeavors target different goals, namely, semantic infrastructure (e.g. *Gnowsis* [17]), resource organization (e.g. *Fenfire* [4], *Haystack* [13]), annotation/authoring of resources (e.g. *SemanticWord [19]*).

For the purpose of this paper, approaches to inlaying semantics into desktops can be classified in accordance with the coupling between editing concerns (e.g. spelling, grammar checking, layout) and "ontological" concerns (e.g. authoring, annotation). Some approaches to annotation detach the process of annotation from that of authoring (e.g. *Ont-O-Mat* [6]). Others, like *SMORE* [12], do both (i.e. authoring and annotation) but using *ad-hoc* editors.

By contrast, *SemanticWord [19]* integrates semantic capabilities into *MS Word* editor so that the text of the document can be analyzed and annotated as it is being typed, appearing to the author as a service analogous to *Word's* spelling and grammar checking. Moreover, the *MS Word* GUI is augmented with toolbars that support the annotation process. The use of a popular editor certainly facilitates the introduction of these

Table 1. Tool comparison table

Feature	Ont-O-Mat	Semantic Word	OntoOffice	SMORE	seMouse
coupling	Proprietary editor	Word plug-in	MS Office plug-in	Proprietary editor	Windows plug-in
file-format support	HTML	MS Word documents	MS Office Documents	HTML, mail format	Any type
attachment availability	Yes	Yes	No	No	No
GUI device for semantic interactions	Drag & drop	Toolbars and cascading menus	MS SmartTags	Right mouse button and forms	Center mouse button and pop-up menus
Annotation subject	Text	Text	File	Text	File
Automatic metadata extraction	Yes, using *Amilcare*	Yes, using *AeroDAML*	No	No	No

techniques into the desktop. Unfortunately, this only works for *Word*. Other editors would require similar enhancements.

Table 1 compares distinct approaches along the following dimensions:

- **coupling**, which denotes how semantic tooling (i.e. annotation, authoring) is coupled with either the resource format, the editor or the operating system. The editor alternative admits two additional options depending on whether the editor has been developed *ad hoc* for annotation purposes, or it is realized as a plug-in for an existing editor. According to this criterion, *seMouse* is the less coupled solution.
- **file-format support**, which indicates the type of formats the tool can handle. This is somehow related with the previous criterion in the sense that the lesser the coupling, the broader the file types handled by the tool. By working at the operating-system level, *seMouse* can be integrated with any editor available for *Windows*.
- **attachment availability**, which refers to the possibility of attaching the metadata to the file itself. Most formats permit to do so. This is an interesting option in case a file needs to be shared with other users or environments. However, the vocabulary and attaching mechanism used commonly depends on the format/editor used. For instance, Adobe is promoting the *Extensible Metadata Platform* (XMP) initiative[3] whereas *OpenOffice*[4] has a different set of metadata which also overlaps (but does not totally coincide) with *Dublin Core*[5]. To complicate things further, how metadata is attached to the document can also vary. As a result of this heterogeneity and proprietary formats, extracting the embedded metadata results in a high programming and maintenance effort as it has been particularized for each format.
- **GUI device for semantic interactions**, which refers to the GUI device used for annotation/authoring. Loose-coupling approaches complicate a seamless integration (if any) with the GUI of the chosen editor. For semantic-lite tooling, this can pose no problem as the mouse can give enough support. This is the option taken by

---

[3] http://www.adobe.com/products/xmp/main.html
[4] http://www.openoffice.org
[5] http://dublincore.org

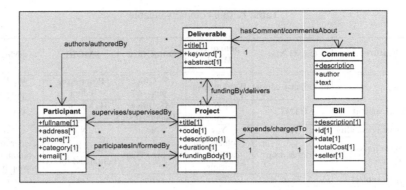

Fig. 1. A sample ontology

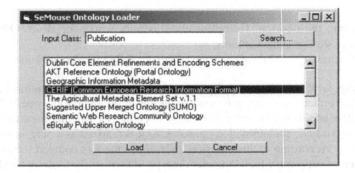

Fig. 2. SeMouse window to load the ontology

seMouse. However, more sophisticated tooling can make the mouse fall short, and require a tighter integration with the editor's GUI. *SemanticWord* is a nice example.
– **annotation subject**, which indicates the granularity of the element being annotated. Alternatives include the file as a whole, or regions of text within a file.
– **automatic metadata extraction,** where the availability of mechanisms for automatic annotation is indicated.

This work strives to introduce ontological concerns as seamless as possible into current desktops. Hence, our preferences align with those of *SemanticWord.* However, the myriad of formats which can be found in current desktop (e.g *.doc, .xml, .gif, .java, .pdf* to mention a few), and the corresponding editors, vindicate the use of an editor-independent solution. Our bet is to use the mouse to attain this aim.

Rather than using the extensibility technology provided by each editor (e.g. *ActiveX* controls in the case of *Word*), we move down to the operating system so that the solution can be available to no matter which editor. The result is *seMouse* (Semantic *MOUSE*), an annotation/authoring tool that achieves editor-independence by working at the operating-system level. By clicking on its middle button, data can be exported/imported from the *ontology* regardless of the editor you are working with.

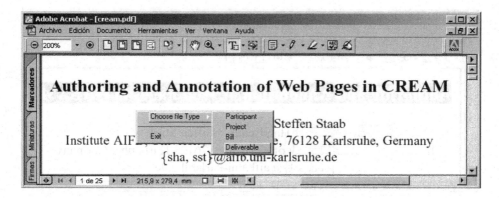

Fig. 3. Scenario 1: file classification

In this way, the user does not have to move to a new editor when annotating (like in *SMORE*), nor has to learn a new "ontological interface" when files from different formats are edited (like in *SemanticWord*).

The downside is usability. Enhancing current editors with "ontological concerns" certainly leads to more appealing and sophisticated interfaces. *SemanticWord* is a case in point. However, this advantage dilutes in a multi-editor scenario, where the *seMouse* approach ensures the same annotation/authoring tool no matter which editor is being used.

Another comparison of semantic annotation tools can be found in [14].

3   *seMouse* at Work

seMouse is an annotation/authoring extension of the mouse device that achieves editor-independence by working at the operating-system level. This section introduces *seMouse* with the help of an example.

Consider the heterogeneous documents that goes with a research project. This includes the project proposal (e.g. one Word file), bills payed with the project funding (e.g. twenty *Excel* files), papers as deliverables of the project (e.g. twenty files in both *.pdf* and *.doc* formats), participants (whose desktop counterpart can be either the home-page, an *.html* resource, or a *.pdf* resource) and comments (being realized as either emails or .doc resources).

Regardless of their format and folder location, it is likely that a high degree of content reuse as well as frequent contextual navigations within this "file space" happens. Being in a participant -an html file-, you frequently need to locate her project proposals -Word files-, or being in a project proposal, the associated papers -PDF files- are commonly accessed. This contextual navigation indicates the existence of a mental model. This mental model is made explicit through an ontology. This ontology serves then to configure *seMouse*. From then on, the mouse can be used to annotate & author file documents.

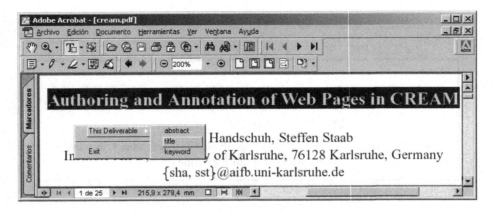

Fig. 4. Scenario 2: annotation. Some text is selected. Being a *deliverable* file, the menu displays properties of this class. The text will become the value of the chosen property.

As an example consider the ontology depicted in figure 1. It includes four classes which are characterized by a set of value-based properties (e.g. *title, keyword, abstract*). Associations are defined between these classes (e.g. a project is *supervisedBy* a participant).

However the tool is open to load any ontology stored in web ontology repositories[6] using the window shown in the figure 2 . The user introduces the name of a required class, and the system using the web services offered by the ontology repositories, shows in a scrollable listbox all the ontologies that contains the input class. The user must select the appropriate ontology clicking on the load button, and the ontology is uploaded on the semantic desktop.

Once seMouse is configured with the ontology, interactions with the underlying ontology are achieved via mouse clicks. Specifically, pressing the middle button on the mouse causes an interaction with the ontology manager (part of the seMouse installation). This interaction is context-schema sensitive, i.e. the button accomplishes distinct operations depending on the place the pointer sits on. Next paragraphs introduce five scenarios of the use of the semantic mouse.

Scenario 1: file classification (see figure 3). First of all, files need to be identified as instances of any of the ontology's classes. This is achieved by opening a file, and pressing the middle button. A menu pops up for the user to indicate to which class this file is a resource.

Scenario 2.1: property annotation (see figure 4). Annotation&authoring becomes the counterpart of copy&paste in traditional desktops, with the difference that now these operations are conducted along the ontology net. What is being exported(i.e. copy) is no longer a string but a class property of the ontology.

If a file has already been categorized, the annotation process may begin. If some text is selected, the mouse is used to export this text as part of the value of a property as it is shown in figure 4. Of course, the set of properties will depend on the class of

---

[6] schemaweb.info or swoogle.umbc.edu.

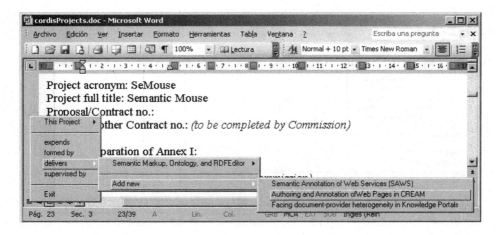

Fig. 5. Scenario 2: annotation. No text is selected. The menu shows associations of the file class.

the resource. In the example, *title, keyword* and *abstract* correspond to properties of the *deliverable* class.

Scenario 2.2: association annotation (see figure 5). Once a file has been categorized, if no text is selected, the middle button is used to establish associations with other files. This situation is exemplified in figure 5. In this case, the CORDIS project template [7] for EEC projects has been used. This Word document has been classified as *Project* class instance, and when the middle button is pressed, a menu pops up for the user to link the current resource with other target resources. The menu is customized for the current resource, that is, the associations are restricted to those available for the current resource, whereas the target of all the associations are also limited to those files of the appropriated class. In the example, if the user selects the *delivers* association, the association can only be established with *Deliverable* files, since this is the destination class of the *delivers* association. The upper part of the *delivers* menu shows all the associations already annotated.

Scenario 3: authoring (see figure 6). Associations being set during annotation can now be exploited. For instance, the *project* resource can import the title of its associated *deliverable* resources. In the example, the article *"Authoring and Annotation of Web Pages in CREAM"* appears as a *deliverable* of the current file. By selecting this article, the menu is extended right wise to show up its properties. The user can select one of these properties, and its value is inserted at the cursor place.

Scenario 4: semantic navigation (see figures 7 and 8). File location in current desktops frequently implies folder digging. By contrast, semantic navigation strives to exploit the associative behavior of the human memory. A resource can be located from the resources it is related to. That is, the ontology provides the context to facilitate resource location.

---

[7] http://dbs.cordis.lu/cordis-cgi/autoftp?FTP=/documents_r5/natdir0000035/
   s_2064005_20050316_104351_2064en.wd9.doc&ORFN=2064en.wd9.doc

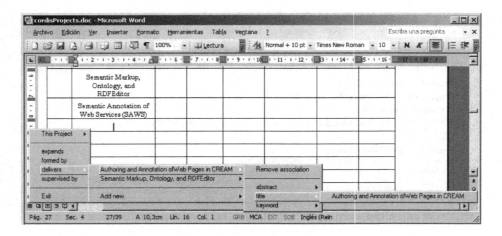

Fig. 6. Scenario 3: authoring. The *title* of a *deliverable* is imported into a *project* resource.

Once a file has been selected, semantically-related files can be located by pressing the middle button, regardless of the folders where these files are physically located, providing a resource-centric navigation. This facilitates location of neighbor resources, but it may be cumbersome whenever browsing is required. In this case, a graph-based RDF visualizer can be a better option (see [5] for an overview of RDF visualizers).

In this work, the *Welkin*[8] editor has been extended for our purposes. Figure 8 depicts the graph for our sample problem. Some of the nodes stand for resources (i.e. documents). *Welkin* has been extended so that clicking on one of these nodes makes the corresponding resource to be edited. In this way, *Welkin* becomes a "resource explorer".

If the user does not want to use external applications, another available way to navigate through the associations of the resource is shown in the figure 7. The user clicks the middle button on a resource, and selecting one of its associations, all the resources related with chosen association are displayed in a search window.

Scenario 5: ontology editing. Back to the desktop, the ontology can be edited by pressing the middle button of the mouse with no file selected. In this case, the associated action calls an ontology editor like Protégé [8].

Nevertheless, some authors argue that current tools for ontology creation are too difficult for ordinary users [15, 14]. The authors empirically found that *"the effort to select a class before typing in an annotation discouraged use of the tool"* (Protégé in this case)*"*. This observation is pertinent in the context of this work as we care for usability.

So far, *seMouse* is a tool for authoring and annotation, and we take the ontology for granted. However, the semantic desktop should provide for seamless ontology creation as well. In [15] the authors discuss an extreme approach to authoring whereby users immediately created metadata without defining the ontology first: *"it is our belief*

---

[8] http://simile.mit.edu/welkin/index.html

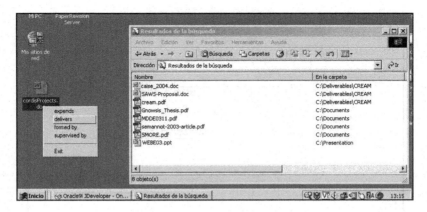

Fig. 7. Scenario 4: semantic navigation. The user can navigate along the associations: from a *project* resource to its deliverables.

that ontologies can be created later in a bottom-up fashion, as the by-product of creating and using data, rather than a straightjacket that inhibits the evolution of domain vocabularies".

We plan to extend *seMouse* for ontology creation. Rather than creating classes and properties out of the blue, *seMouse* will facilitate dynamic definition of classes and properties, as resources are being annotated and investigate on how much meta-data can be automatically inferred from the type and context of the resource.

4   Evaluating *seMouse* Usability

We adopt ISO's broad definition of usability [1] as consisting of three distinct aspects:

– *Effectiveness*, which is the accuracy and completeness with which users achieve certain goals. Indicators of effectiveness include quality of solution and error rates. In this study, we use quality of solution as the primary indicator of effectiveness, i.e. a measure of the outcome of the user's interaction with the system.
– *Efficiency*, which is the relation between (1) the accuracy and completeness with which users achieve certain goals and (2) the resources expended in achieving them. Indicators of efficiency include task completion time and learning time. In this study, we use task completion time as the primary indicator of efficiency.
– *Satisfaction*, which is the users' comfort with and positive attitudes toward the use of the system. Users' satisfaction can be measured by attitude rating scales such as SUMI [10]. In this study, we use preference as the primary indicator of satisfaction.

Subjects. The experiment was conducted among 6 PhD students. They have a good background on computing but they have never been exposed to semantic issues. Hence, a ten-minute talk was given introducing the purpose and functionality of *seMouse*.

Given material. Two documents were prepared. First, a UML diagram of the figure 1 describing the ontology and second, a document describing the set of 16 files of distinct

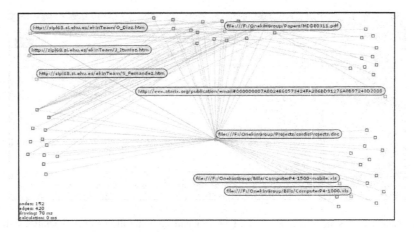

Fig. 8. Graphical representation of our sample domain using Welkin

types (PDF, DOC, PPT and HTML) and of different semantic concepts (Projects, Deliverables and Participants). Table 2 indicates for each file its class and its associations corresponding to a fictitious project. Students were familiar with the UML notation so they quickly caught the main classes and associations of the ontology.

Tasks. In the experiment each subject has to complete the task of creating a knowledge folder. This includes:

1. file classification. Each file should be classified according to its class (scenario 1). The 16 files correspond to 2 *projects*, 10 *deliverables*, and 4 *participants*.
2. annotation. The key property of each resource (i.e. *title, fullname,* etc) is annotated and the associations between the resources are now established (scenario 2).
3. authoring. Once a *project* document is open, take advantage of the relationships to fill in the *tables of participants* and *deliverables* as shown in scenario 3.

4.1 Results

Effectiveness. All the students complete their tasks without any additional help. This makes us think that the GUI is intuitive enough. It should be noted that the number of resources to be annotated, sixteen, was rather small, although there are not yet experiences on the average size of resources handled by a layman on his daily tasks. If the number of resources is too large, the solution is not within the scope of desktop tooling but content management frameworks. Nevertheless, the notion of knowledge folder also helps to split the resource bulk into meaningful clusters so that *seMouse* does not have to cope with too numerous resources.

Efficiency. The classification and "key attribute" annotation took on average, 30". On the other hand, the students spent 10" on average to establish an association between

Table 2. Resources and their associations to be established by the participants during the test

	Key attribute	File type	Class	Relation
1	Semantic Web	.doc	Project	delivers:[3][4][5][6] [7][8][9][10] formedBy:[13][14][15]
2	Personal Information Management	.doc	Project	delivers:[3][4][5][6] [11][12] formedBy:[13][14][16]
3	Authoring and Annotation of Web Pages in CREAM	.pdf	Deliverable	fundingBy:[1][2]
4	Incremental Formalization of Document Annotations	.pdf	Deliverable	fundingBy:[1][2]
5	Trends in Database Development: XML, .NET, WinFS	.ppt	Deliverable	fundingBy:[1][2]
6	Semantic Annotation of Web Services (SAWS)	.doc	Deliverable	fundingBy:[1][2]
7	Semantic (Web) Technology in Action: Ontology Driven Information Systems for Search, Integration and Analysis	.doc	Deliverable	fundingBy:[1]
8	OWL: An Ontology Language for the Semantic Web	.ppt	Deliverable	fundingBy:[1]
9	The Semantic Desktop: an architecture to leverage document processing with metadata	.pdf	Deliverable	fundingBy:[1]
10	Towards the Self Annotating Web	.pdf	Deliverable	fundingBy:[1]
11	Mining the Semantic Web	.doc	Deliverable	fundingBy:[2]
12	Semantic Word Processing for Content Authors	.pdf	Deliverable	fundingBy:[2]
13	Steffen Staab	.html	Participant	participatesIn:[1][2]
14	Siegfried Handschuh	.html	Participant	participatesIn:[1][2]
15	Yolanda Gil	.html	Participant	participatesIn:[1]
16	Tim Berners-Lee	.html	Participant	participatesIn: [2]

Table 3. Questionnaire to assess *seMouse* usability

Questions about the method	Strongly Agree	Agree	Neutral	Disagree	Strongly Disagree	User Results
1. The annotation of documents enhances the navigation and localization of resources	❑	❑	❑	❑	❑	4.5
2. The time consumed in annotating a document, pays off	❑	❑	❑	❑	❑	4.5
General questions about SeMouse	Strongly Agree	Agree	Neutral	Disagree	Strongly Disagree	
3. The seMouse interface is well structured	❑	❑	❑	❑	❑	3
4. I understand the enabled operations at each time	❑	❑	❑	❑	❑	3.25
5. Overloading the mouse with the semantic operations is intuitive	❑	❑	❑	❑	❑	3.7
Questions about SeMouse functionality	Strongly Agree	Agree	Neutral	Disagree	Strongly Disagree	
6. The annotation of documents (class and properties) is intuitive	❑	❑	❑	❑	❑	4.7
7. The process of associating documents is intuitive	❑	❑	❑	❑	❑	3.85
8. The authoring of information is intuitive	❑	❑	❑	❑	❑	3.5

two resources. The last task, authoring, i.e. obtaining the *participants'* name and *deliverables'* title took on average, 15" per resource.

Satisfaction. To measure this property a questionnaire was provided to the subjects. Table 3 summarizes the result of the test along the Likert scale: Strongly agree (5), Agree (4), Neutral (3), Disagree (2), Strongly disagree (1). All the students agree on the usefulness of semantic annotation for improving location and navigation in the resource space. As for *seMouse*, questions 3 and 4 show that the students were neutral about its GUI. More interesting is the deviations on the opinion about overloading the mouse with semantic operations: 2 strongly agree, 2 agree and 2 disagree. Although they all appreciate the format-independence provided by *seMouse*, some of them were not accustomed to use the middle button that they found counter-intuitive. This situation can however improve as the users get more practice on using this gadget. Finally, classification and annotation was found intuitive to be achieved through *seMouse*. Association establishment was found more complicated.

5   The *seMouse* Architecture

The DOGMA initiative [11] is promoting a formal-ontology engineering framework that basically consists of a three-layer architecture, namely, the layer of the heterogeneous data sources, the ontology layer, and the consumers' layer. Mappings between these layers are established with the help of wrappers that lift these data sources onto a common ontology model and of integration modules (mediators in the dynamic case) that reconcile the varying semantics of the different data sources.

Basically, we follow this architecture where both sources and consumers are restricted to be resource handlers (either readers or editors); the ontology model is OWL; and the flow between resource handlers and the ontology is achieved through the mouse. The issue of semantic heterogeneity is not addressed in this work.

The *seMouse* architecture comprises three components (see figure 9), namely, the **OntologyManager** component, which is realized using *Joseki* [9], the **SemanticDesktop** component, which is supported as a specialization of *WindowsXP,* and the **ResourceHandler** whose interfaces are supported by editors or readers of documents (see figure 9).

The *IOntologyManager* interface comprises methods to add/remove/update OWL triples as well as to query and check the existence of a given resource. All these methods find their realizations in the *Joseki* implementation where *OWL* triples are stored in the *Jena DBMS* [10].

The *resourceHandler* component holds two interfaces, *IReader* and *IEditor,* which permit to extract or paste data from/to a file, respectively. Readers such as Acrobat Reader only support *IReader*, whereas editors such as Word support both *IReader* and *IEditor.* Implementation wise, these interfaces are supported through the *WndProc* function of *Windows.* Whenever anything happens to a window, the operating system will call this function informing what has occurred. The *message* parameter contains the message sent. The resource handler can then trap any message. In this case, however, only two messages need to be caught: copy and paste.

The *ISemanticDesktop* interface describes those operations that mediate between the resource handlers and the ontology manager. Its functionality resembles a kind of clipboard, exporting and importing metadata among files (operations *getText( )* and *setText( )*). Interactions with the semantic desktop are accomplished by pressing the middle button of the mouse (e.g. the *sendMessage(WM_MBUTTONDOWN)* operation).

---

[9] http://www.joseki.org
[10] http://www.hpl.hp.com/semweb/jena.htm

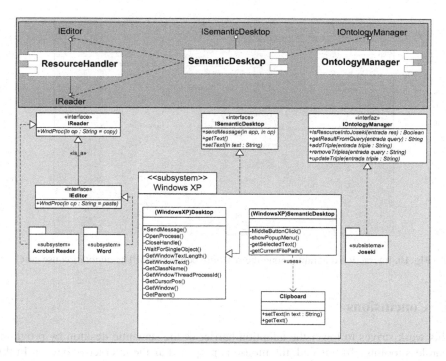

Fig. 9. The *seMouse* architecture

Figure 10 depicts the interaction diagram among the *seMouse* components. The *semanticDesktop* component has been unfolded to show its implementation classes, namely, *messageDispatcher, hook*[11], *clipboard* and the *semanticDesktop* class itself.

Figure 10 considers an annotation scenario. A file is opened and some text is selected. By pressing the middle button of the mouse, a two step annotation process is initiated. First (1.1), the mouse device sends a middle-button click message to the *messageDispatcher*. When the *dispatcher* detects that there is a hook associated to this message, the *hook* is called (1.2); finally (1.3), the *hook* invokes the *semanticDesktop* which causes a menu to be popped up. In the second interaction (2.1), the user, through the mouse device, selects the annotation operation to apply to the selected text (2.2). The *semanticDesktop* sends a copy message to the *resourceHandler* through the *messageDispatcher*, and (2.3) the application copies the selected text into the clipboard. Finally (2.4), the text is retrieved by the *semanticDesktop* from the clipboard which, in turn, builds up the OWL triple.

---

[11] A Window *hook* is *"a point in the system message-handling mechanism where an application can install a subroutine to monitor the message traffic in the system and process certain types of messages before they reach the target window procedure"* [16]. So, hooks are basically event handlers that catch the message sent to the window. Through hooks, these messages can be modified or even discarded before they even reach the target window. In this implementation we caught just one message: *WM_MBUTTONDOWN* which is sent if the middle button on the mouse has been pressed. This has been attained using the *Cool Mouse* utility [7].

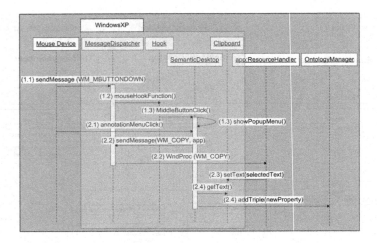

Fig. 10. Interaction diagram among the *seMouse* components. The *annotation* use case.

6   Conclusions

This work strives to lower the adoption barrier of the semantic desktop by providing seamless tooling. To this end, the mouse is proposed as the interactive device. In this way, traditional desktop operations are now re-interpreted and framed by the ontology: copy&paste becomes annotation&authoring, and folder digging becomes property traversal. Moreover, through the mouse, the user can classify, annotate, author, and locate a file as a resource of the underlying ontology. Being editor-independent, the mouse accounts for portability and maintainability to face the myriad of formats and editors which characterizes current desktops.

Similar to other areas of computing, a balance is needed between generality (e.g. format-independence, editor-independence, etc), and functionality (i.e. the semantic tooling available). *seMouse* illustrates a semantic-lite approach where a compact set of functions are available to no matter which editor within *Windows*.

Acknowledgments. This work is partially supported by the Spanish Science and Technology Ministry (MCYT) under contract TIC2002-01442. Sergio F. Anzuola enjoys a doctoral grant from the University of the Basque Country.

References

1. ISO 9241-11. Ergonomic requirements for office work with visual displays terminals(VDTs) - Part 11: Guidance on usability. Technical report, ISO, 1998.
2. Adam Cheyer, Jack Park, and Richard Giuli. IRIS: Integrate. Relate. Infer. Share. In *1st Workshop on The Semantic Desktop*, November 2005.
3. Stefan Decker and Martin Frank. The Social Semantic Desktop. Technical report, Digital Enterprise Research Institute (DERI), May 2004.

4. Benja Fallenstei. Fentwine: A navigational rdf browser and editor. In *Proceedings of 1st Workshop on Friend of a Friend, Social Networking and the Semantic Web*, August 2004.
5. John Gilbert and Mark H. Butler. Review of existing tools for working with schemas, metadata, and thesauri. Technical report, Hewlett Packard Laboratories, October 2003.
6. Siegfried Handschuh and Steffen Staab. Authoring and Annotation of Web Pages in CREAM. In *The Eleventh International World Wide Web Conference WWW2002*, pages 462–473, 2002.
7. Shelltoys Inc. Cool Mouse - Mouse Wheel and Middle Mouse Button Utility, 2004. http://www.shelltoys.com/mouse_software/index.html.
8. Stanford Medical Informatics. The Protégé; ontology editor and knowledge acquisition system, 2004. http://protege.stanford.edu/.
9. Jon Iturrioz, Oscar Díaz, Sergio F. Anzuola, and Iker Azpeitia. The Semantic Desktop: an architecture to leverage document processing with metadata. In *Proceedings of the VLDB Workshop on Multimedia and Data Document Engineering (MDDE'03)*, September 2003.
10. Kirakowski J. and Corbett M. SUMI: The software usability measurement inventory. *British Journal of Educational Technology*, 24(3):210–212, 1993.
11. Mustafa Jarrar and Robert Meersman. Formal Ontology Engineering in the DOGMA Approach. In *On the Move to Meaningful Internet Systems, 2002 - DOA/CoopIS/ODBASE 2002 Confederated International Conferences DOA, CoopIS and ODBASE 2002*, pages 1238–1254. Springer-Verlag, 2002.
12. Aditya Kalyanpur, James Hendler, Bijan Parsia, and Jennifer Golbeck. SMORE - Semantic Markup, Ontology, and RDF Editor. http://www.mindswap.org/papers/SMORE.pdf, 2004.
13. David R. Karger and Dennis Quan. Haystack: A User Interface for Creating, Browsing, and Organizing Arbitrary Semistructured Information. In *CHI 2004 Conference on Human Factors in Computing Systems*, April 2004.
14. Brian Kettler, James Starz, William Miller, and Peter Haglich. A Template-based Markup Tool for Semantic Web Content. In *4th International Semantic Web Conference 2005,ISWC2005*, November 2005.
15. Robert MacGregor, Sameer Maggon, and Baoshi Yan. MetaDesk: A Semantic Web Desktop Manager. In *Knowledge Markup and Semantic Annotation Workshop, ISWC 2004*, November 2004.
16. Steve McMahon. Win32 Hooks in VB - The vbAccelerator Hook Library, 2003. http://www.vbaccelerator.com/home/VB/Code/Libraries/Hooks/vbAccelerator_Hook_Library/article.asp.
17. The Gnowsis Project. Leo sauermann, 2005. http://www.gnowsis.com.
18. The Haystack Project. Haystack team, 2005. http:/haystack.lcs.mit.edu.
19. Marcelo Tallis. Semantic Word Processing for Content Authors. In *Workshop Notes of Knowledge Markup and Semantic Annotation Workshop (SEMANNOT 2003). Second International Conference on Knowledge Capture (K-CAP 2003)*, October 2003.

Managing Information Quality in e-Science Using Semantic Web Technology

Alun Preece[1], Binling Jin[1], Edoardo Pignotti[1], Paolo Missier[2], Suzanne Embury[2], David Stead[3], and Al Brown[3]

[1] University of Aberdeen, Computing Science, Aberdeen, UK
[2] University of Manchester, School of Computer Science, Manchester, UK
[3] University of Aberdeen, Molecular and Cell Biology, Aberdeen, UK
info@qurator.org
http://www.qurator.org

Abstract. We outline a framework for managing information quality (IQ) in e-Science, using ontologies, semantic annotation of resources, and data bindings. Scientists define the quality characteristics that are of importance in their particular domain by extending an OWL DL IQ ontology, which classifies and organises these domain-specific quality characteristics within an overall quality management framework. RDF is used to annotate data resources, with reference to IQ indicators defined in the ontology. Data bindings — again defined in RDF — are used to represent mappings between data elements (e.g. defined in XML Schemas) and the IQ ontology. As a practical illustration of our approach, we present a case study from the domain of proteomics.

1 Introduction

Information is viewed as a fundamental resource in the discovery of new scientific knowledge. Scientists expect to make use of information produced by other labs and projects in validating and interpreting their own results. A key element of e-Science is the development of a stable environment for the conduct of information-intensive forms of science. Problems arise due to variations in the quality of the information being shared [3]. Data sets that are incomplete, inconsistent, or inaccurate can still be useful when scientists are aware of these deficiencies.

The Qurator project[1][6] is developing techniques for managing information quality (IQ) using Semantic Web technology. In contrast to previous IQ research, which has tended to focus on the identification of generic, domain-independent quality characteristics (such as accuracy, currency and completeness) [13], we allow scientists to define the quality characteristics that are of importance in their particular domain. For example, one group of scientists may record "accuracy" in terms of some calculated experimental error, while others might define it as a function of the type of equipment that captured the data.

In order to support this form of domain-specific IQ, we identify three key requirements, each of which can be met using Semantic Web technologies:

---

[1] Funded by the EPSRC Programme Fundamental Computer Science for e-Science: GR/S67593 & GR/S67609 — *Describing the Quality of Curated e-Science Information Resources.*

Y. Sure and J. Domingue (Eds.): ESWC 2006, LNCS 4011, pp. 472–486, 2006.

- Scientists must be able to *use* the domain-specific IQ descriptions, by giving them precise, meaningful definitions, and creating executable metrics based on them. They must also be able to *reuse* definitions created by others, by browsing and querying an organised collection of definitions. To meet this requirement, we propose an extensible *IQ ontology* containing basic domain-independent IQ terms, upon which definitions of domain-specific concepts can be built. By defining the ontology in OWL DL, new descriptors can be classified automatically within the overall IQ framework, allowing user-scientists to locate useful definitions.
- IQ descriptions for specific resources need to be computed and associated with those resources. IQ descriptions of a resource are essentially quality metadata, and can be used to derive higher-order IQ metrics or rankings over sets of resources. As metadata about resources, IQ descriptions can be captured as *semantic annotations* expressed in RDF and related to concepts in the IQ ontology. Annotations are generated by data checking services, sometimes using secondary data sources (e.g. reference datasets), and it is necessary to retain provenance information about how the annotations themselves were derived. This can be done by attaching provenance information to the RDF annotation instances.
- Resources include data and services; both of these kinds of resource are modelled by concepts in the IQ ontology, so that the ontology can express which kinds of IQ descriptor make sense for which kinds of resource. The relationship between actual types of resource (for example a particular data model expressed as an XML Schema, or as a relational database schema) and the abstract models of those resources in the IQ ontology needs to be stated explicitly in order to determine, for a given resource, which checking services are applicable. We refer to these relationships — between the "ontology space" and the "data/service space" — as *bindings*, which can be captured using an RDF schema.

We claim several novel aspects here. To the best of our knowledge, our IQ ontology is the first systematic attempt to capture domain-specific and domain-independent quality descriptors in a semantic model. Moreover, we argue that the use of OWL DL supports the necessary extensibility of the core ontology with domain-specific quality definitions. The annotation and binding RDF schemas are both intended to be generic, reusable components; we were unable to find any previous solution that met our requirements for these.

To provide a concrete illustration of how the elements of our framework can be used in practice, Section 2 introduces a case study in the domain of biology, specifically proteomics. Section 3 gives an overview of the Qurator framework, and the following sections present each of the three components in detail: Section 4 introduces the IQ ontolology, Section 5 describes the binding schema, and Section 6 presents the annotation model. In Section 7 we show how the various components have been implemented within a desktop tool used by biologists to manage their data and metadata.

2   Case Study: Protein Identification

Proteomics is the study of the set of proteins that are expressed under particular conditions within organisms, tissues or cells. Proteins play a vital role in most, if not all, cellular activities — understanding their regulation and function is therefore of fundamental importance to biologists. One experimental approach that is widely used to gain information about the large-scale expression of proteins involves extracting the soluble proteins from a biological sample, then separating them by a technique known as 2-dimensional gel electrophoresis (2DE). This results in a characteristic distribution of protein spots within a rectangular gel (Figure 1). Many hundreds of proteins can be separated from a single sample in this way and the relative amounts of each determined.

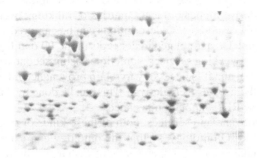

Fig. 1. Sample gel produced by the 2DE technique; the dark areas are protein spots

The identification of proteins in such experiments is routinely obtained by peptide mass fingerprinting (PMF). In this technique, the protein within the gel spot is first digested with an enzyme that cleaves the protein sequence at certain predictable sites. The fragments of protein that result (called peptides) are extracted and their masses are measured in a mass spectrometer. The experimental list of peptide masses (the "fingerprint") is then compared against theoretical peptide mass lists, derived by simulating the process of digestion on sequences extracted from a protein database (e.g. NCBInr[2]). Since, for various reasons, it is unlikely that an exact match will be found, the protein identification search engines (e.g. Mascot[3]), that perform this task typically return a list of potential protein matches, ranked in order of search score. Different search engines calculate these scores in different ways, so their results are not directly comparable. It may therefore be difficult for the experimenter and subsequent users of the data to decide whether a particular protein identification is acceptable or not.

There is a debate in progress that seeks to define what information is required when reporting the results of protein identifications by mass spectrometry. For peptide mass fingerprinting, it has been suggested that this should include the number of peptides matched to the identified protein, the number that were not matched in the mass spectrum, and the sequence coverage observed [1].

It would be useful for biologists seeking to interpret the results of proteomic experiments to have a tool that can apply certain quality preferences to a list of protein

---

[2] ftp://ftp.ncbi.nlm.nih.gov/blast/db/blastdb.html

[3] http://www.matrixscience.com/

matches, for the purposes of accepting or questioning a protein identification result. Such functionality would be particularly useful to scientists wishing to compare protein identification results generated by other labs with those produced within their own. There are two readily accessible indicators that can be used to rank protein identification data and which are independent of the particular search engine used:

- *Hit ratio*: the number of peptide masses matched, divided by the number of peptide masses submitted to the search. This indicator effectively combines the number of matched peptides and the number of unmatched peptides mentioned above. Ideally, most of the peaks in the spectrum should be accountable for by the protein identified, but because of the presence of other components and unpredicted modifications to the matched peptides the hit ratio is unlikely to reach unity.
- *Mass coverage*: the number of amino acids contained within the set of matched peptides, expressed as a fraction of the total number of amino acids making up the sequence of the identified protein and multiplied by the total mass (in kDa) of the protein. Mass coverage is considered superior to the sequence coverage, because peptide mass fingerprints of equal quality give low (percent) sequence coverage for large proteins and high (percent) coverage for small proteins.

These two indicators can be combined in a logical expression that allows us to classify protein matches as acceptable or unacceptable. A software tool could then allow the user-scientist to set threshold values (that is, acceptance criteria) for each metric independently and to see the effect in real time of altering any or all of the threshold values on the acceptability of the data set. This is an example of the kind of quality-aware data analysis that Qurator aims to support.

3   Overview of the Qurator IQ Framework

Before we present the details of the three main components of the Qurator framework — IQ ontology, bindings, annotations — this section gives an overview of how these elements fit together. Figure 2 sets out the key relationships between the various individuals and classes. At the top we have the elements of the IQ ontology, which includes definitions of domain-independent IQ concepts such as Accuracy[4] and also classes of domain-specific indicator such as Hit Ratio and Mass Coverage from the proteomics domain. The IQ ontology also models the various kinds of abstract data entities to which we might wish to apply IQ indicators, such as a Protein Hit obtained from a PMF database search. The ontology then captures the fact that the Hit Ratio indicator applies to a Protein Hit. Finally, the ontology defines the various kinds of data checking function available, as described in detail in Section 4.

At the bottom of Figure 2 we have instances of specific resources (r), for example a particular protein hit derived from a database search. These are often represented in XML; in the proteomics case the PEDRo data model [12] is widely used for this purpose, by means of the PEDRo XML Schema[5].

---

[4] Throughout this paper, sans-serif font is used for ontology and schema terms from the Qurator framework.

[5] http://pedro.man.ac.uk/files/PEDRoSchema.xsd

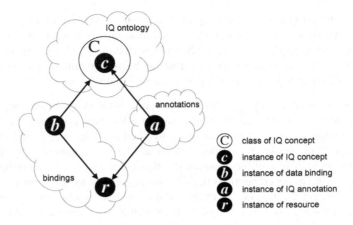

Fig. 2. Overview of the elements of the Qurator IQ framework

Bindings and annotations both relate resources to elements of the IQ ontology. An instance of a binding (*b*) relates a resource instance (*r*) to the corresponding class in the ontology (C); e.g. a specific PEDRo protein hit list to the model class Protein Hit. One of the main uses of bindings is to determine which parts of the IQ conceptualisation are relevant to a particular concrete data model. So, for example, the binding from a PEDRo protein hit structure to the ontology Protein Hit class also lets us identify relevant indicators (such as Hit Ratio) and associated checking functions. For details, see Section 5.

An instance of an annotation (*a*) relates a specific resource instance (*r*) to the instance of a quality concept (*c*). For example, an instance of Hit Ratio with a specific value (e.g. 0.45) might be associated with an individual concrete PEDRo protein hit via an annotation. The IQ instance is said to annotate the associated resource. Further details of annotations are given in Section 6. The difference between bindings and annotations is that the former relate data schema elements (or service types) to the corresponding ontology classes, while the latter relate individual items of data to individual pieces of quality evidence. In other words, bindings define which IQ concepts relate to which kinds of data or service, while annotations associate individual computed IQ descriptors with specific pieces of data.

4   A Semantic Model for Information Quality

As explained in Section 1, a scientist's goal with respect to quality is to determine the suitability of a data set for a given purpose. In our case study, scientists want to assess whether a set of protein identification (PI) experiment results can be safely used as input to a new *in silico* experiment. The scientists' exercise is one of knowledge elicitation: the tacit knowledge regarding quality properties of interest needs to be made explicit and formalized. As we will see, this is also a novel opportunity for scientists to test hypotheses regarding their understanding of quality within a domain. One such hypothesis, described in the next section, is that a small number of measurable quantities associated with the output of protein identification algorithms can be used to discriminate effectively between acceptable and unacceptable matches.

We now present a semantic model that supports such a knowledge elicitation process, by providing a vocabulary and semantic structure for expressing information quality. The model allows scientists to share and reuse their understanding of quality, as well as to perform semi-automated quality assessments on data sets of interest to them.

4.1 Basic Ontology Structure

A number of different existing quality properties can potentially describe suitability, such as *Currency*, *Completeness* or *Accuracy*, definitions of which have been proposed in the existing information quality literature (e.g. [3, 8, 13]). Some of these definitions are given in abstract terms: accuracy for example is defined as the "distance" between a value v and a second value v' that is considered correct, with further distinctions being made based on how the distance is measured [10]. Our model is based on the assumption that scientists should not be concerned with such definitions, and that they should instead be able to state their quality requirements in operational terms, by describing *decision procedures* that determine the suitability of the data.

Nevertheless, our goals of knowledge sharing and reuse mandate the use of a common vocabulary for quality. Our approach is therefore to let users express operational properties of quality in their own terms, while at the same time providing a semantic structure that includes suitable axiomatizations of the definitions found in the literature. We argue, and demonstrate on the practical example presented in this section, that the knowledge representation framework can then be used to establish a relationship between user-provided operational definitions and the axiomatizations.

In practice, let us suppose that our scientists are interested in the "credibility" of published PI experimental results, defined in terms of likelihood of false positives — that is, that a claim of a given protein being present in a sample is false. The biologists involved in this research are proposing decision procedures for computing the likelihood of false positives, based on a small set of measurable quantities, namely the Hit Ratio and the Mass Coverage, which are combined using a logical expression to produce an overall quality score.

In general, the task of defining decision procedures amounts to identifying a collection of measurable indicators, and demonstrating, usually in an experimental way, that they indeed allow a distinction to be made between acceptable and unacceptable data. In some cases, decision models can be semi-automatically generated from sets of examples, with the help of machine learning techniques [14]. In other cases, ad hoc methods have been developed for statistical quality control of experimental data [5, 7].

In the ontology, we model these concepts by introducing Quality Assertions (QA for short); these are decision procedures that are based upon some Quality Evidence (QE), which consists either of measurable attributes called Quality Indicators, or recursively, of functions of those indicators, Quality Metrics. Three main sources of indicators are common in practice:

- *Provenance* metadata, which provides a description of the processes that were involved in producing the data [4, 15].

- *Quality functions* that explicitly measure some quality property, for instance the completeness of a data set relative to a second, reference data set; these functions are typically available from toolkits for data quality assessment with reference to specific issues [2].
- Metadata that is produced as part of the data processing; for example, the Hit Ratio and Mass Coverage indicators are defined as the output of the matching algorithm used for protein identification.

Focusing primarily on the second and third category, we model the indicator-bearing environment as a collection of Data Analysis Tools that may incorporate multiple Data Test Functions, and which are applied to some Data Entity. Indicators are either parameters to or output of these analysis tools. Thus, Hit Ratio and Mass Coverage are part of the output of a test function called PIMatch, used in the PMFMatchAnalysisTool. To continue with our example, a quality metric called PMF Match Ranking associates a "credibility score" to each data in the set, using a function of our two indicators. This score can be used either to classify data as acceptable/non acceptable according to a user-defined threshold, or to rank the data set. Here we will assume that our decision procedure is a classification function called PI-Topk, that provides a simple binary classification of the data set according to the credibility score and to a user-defined threshold.

A QA is applied to collections of data items, which are individuals of the Data Entity class, using the values for the indicators associated to those items. Our example of Data Entity is a protein hit generated by the mass spectrometer, as explained in Section 2, which is used as input to our PMFMatchAnalysisTool.

The following is a summary of the classes and relationships introduced above, using informal notation for the sake of readability; user-defined axioms for the proteomics case study are in bold:[6]

1. Quality-Assertion is based on Quality-Evidence;
2. Quality-Indicator is-a Quality-Evidence;
3. Quality-Metric is-a Quality-Evidence;
4. Quality-Metric is based on Quality-Indicator;
5. Quality-Evidence is output of Data-test-function;
6. Data-analysis-tool is based on Data-test-function;
7. **MassCoverage is-a Quality-Evidence;**
8. **HitRatio is-a Quality-Evidence;**
9. **PIMatch is-a Data-test-function;**
10. **PMFMatchAnalysisTool is-a Data-analysis-tool;**
11. **PMFMatchAnalysisTool is based on PIMatch;**
12. **PIMatch requires input ProteinHit;**
13. **HitRatio is output of PIMatch;**
14. **MassCoverage is output of PIMatch;**
15. **PMF-Match-Ranking is a Quality-Metric;**
16. **PMF-Match-Ranking is based on MassCoverage;**
17. **PMF-Match-Ranking is based on HitRatio;**
18. **PI-Topk is based on PMF-Match-Ranking.**

---

[6] The full IQ ontology is available from the "Downloads" section at http://www.qurator.org.

4.2   Classification of User-Defined Quality Properties Through Reasoning

As mentioned, one goal of this model is to provide a shared collection for top-level, abstract information quality concepts like "accuracy", and to enforce their consistent use. Specifically, we claim that it should be possible to let scientists add only concepts that are familiar to them to the ontology, like those described earlier, while at the same time providing useful entailments that enrich the shared top-level concepts.

In this section, we report on early experiments that support this claim. The main idea is to encourage users to annotate their domain-specific concepts with simple and concrete quality features, to the extent that they are familiar with them, and to use reasoning over OWL DL to entail additional quality properties, or to determine inconsistencies.

Building on the structure described so far, we begin by adding a top-level Quality Property class, with a number of subclasses for Consistency, Timeliness, Currency, and more. Our collection for these concepts currently includes about 20 classes, organized into a three-level hierarchy. Also, we add a root class for Quality Characterization, whose subclasses include Confidence-QC, Reputation-QC, Specificity-QC, and more. These are examples of the "concrete" properties that scientists can more easily associate to specific indicators, or indicator-bearing functions or tools. Thus, we expect users to be able to assert that the PIMatch function has a Confidence-QC, because its purpose, from the quality perspective, is to provide information on the confidence in the experiment result. Note that the ontology model allows a single piece of evidence, or function, to have multiple quality characterizations. The only user assertion for the example is:

PIMatchReport has quality characterization Confidence-QC.

We then introduce OWL DL axioms that describe classes of evidence that have the same quality characterization; given that users may quality-characterize either indicators, metrics, functions, or tools, a sample definition is as follows:

> Confidence evidence includes all and only the quality metrics or indicators whose quality characterization includes Confidence-QC, union all indicators that are output of functions, or of tools that use functions, whose quality characterization includes Confidence-QC.

Here is the OWL DL definition for this class:

ConfidenceEvidence ≡
    (QtyMetric ⊓ (∃ metric-based-on-indicator ConfidenceEvidence) ⊔
    (QtyIndicator ⊓ ∃ is-output-of (∃hasQC ConfidenceQC)) ⊔
    (QtyIndicator ⊓ ∃ is-parameter-of (∃hasQC ConfidenceQC)) ⊔
    (QtyIndicator ⊓ ∃ hasQC ConfidenceQC)

Using the user-defined assertion above, the definitions in the previous section, and this class definition, an OWL DL reasoner[7] entails the following:
    PIMatchReport ⊑ ConfidenceEvidence,
    HitRatio ⊑ ConfidenceEvidence,
    MassCoverage ⊑ ConfidenceEvidence,

---

[7] RacerPro has been used for these experiments, http://www.racer-systems.com/

PMFMatchRanking ⊑ ConfidenceEvidence.

We now define the Accuracy class in terms of the underlying quality characterization, expressing the following:

> Any quality property that is based on a decision procedure that makes use of Confidence or Specificity evidence, can be classfied as Accuracy.

Formally:

Accuracy ≡
   (∃ QtyProperty-from-QtyPreference (∃ pref-based-on-evidence
   (ConfidenceEvidence ⊔ SpecificityEvidence)))

This last definition allows the ontology to be extended in a consistent way using standard reasoning. Firstly, given a user-defined but yet unclassified quality property, let us call it PI-Acceptability, that is based on the PI-Topk procedure, the reasoner entails that the property is a subclass of Accuracy. Conversely, users may classify PI-Acceptability within the IQ top-level taxonomy; in this case, the reasoner verifies the consistency of this classification.

The experiment shows that it is possible, using suitable DL assertions, to (i) provide axiomatic definitions of traditional quality properties, in terms of an underlying quality characterization vocabulary, and (ii) to use those axioms to propagate, or test the consistency of, user-defined and domain specific quality assertions. As explained in the introduction, the motivation here is to facilitate the use and reuse of definitions in the ontology: consistency checking supports extension of the ontology, and the classification of domain-specific descriptors under generic concepts (such as "accuracy") is intended to assist users in locating useful concepts.

5   Bindings

As we have shown, the IQ ontology includes semantic models of data resources and the quality analysis services which can be applied to them. The actual data resources have a native definition and presentations; quality test functions applicable on the data might have multiple implementations in different programming languages. For example, a `ProteinHit`[8] XML element, defined in the PEDRo XML schema, may be an input parameter of a HitRatioCalculator function, implemented as a Web service. We designed a generic data model to capture the mapping relationships between data or service resources and their semantic definition. The basic structure of the binding model is presented in Figure 3. There are four core concepts in the Binding model:

Resource refers to any resource that can be located on the Web. We distinguish two sub types of resource: DataResource and ServiceResource. The former refers to any resource which stores information (e.g. an XML file or database table); the latter type represents any service, application or procedure which performs action on a DataResource (e.g. a Web service). We define three categories of DataResource:

---

[8] Throughout the remainder of this paper, `typewriter` font is used for data elements from XML schemas, and XML syntax fragments.

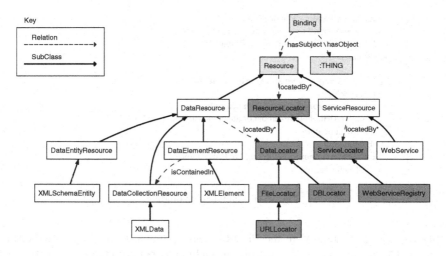

Fig. 3. Overview of the Qurator binding model

- DataEntityResource represents elements defined in a data schema/structure, for example the `ProteinHit` element defined in the *PEDRo.xsd* schema, or a column defined in a DB table.
- DataElementResource represents a data element inside a collection, for example an XML element specified by an XPath, or a database tuple.
- DataCollectionResource represents a collection of data elements, for example an XML document, a database table, or a text file.

A Binding relates a Resource to a semantic concept in some ontology (for example, in the IQ ontology from the previous section). This relationship is defined by two properties on the binding:

- hasSubject identifies the subject of the binding, which is always a locatable Resource (data or service).
- hasObject identifies the object of the binding, which can be any semantic concept in any ontology (represented in our ontology diagram with the most general concept :THING — for example, this could be any class in our IQ Ontology).

ResourceLocator identifies a global locator for a specific resource. Since the resource is categorised into DataResource and ServiceResource, the ResourceLocator has two types: DataLocator and ServiceLocator. Due to various ways to access the data resources, the data locator can have different types. For example, for a data document, we can use a URL to retrieve it; while for a DB table, a DB connector API could be used (such as JDBC). Similarly, ServiceLocator has different types; for example, the locator of a quality annotation web service can be referred to a WSDL description and the endpoint of the service is presented in this WSDL description.

Figure 4 shows an example binding between a data resource and an IQ ontology class; here, the entity `&q;` refers to the Qurator IQ Ontology and the prefix `b:` identifies terms from the binding model. The data resource `#XMLSchemaEntity1` represents the

```
<b:Binding rdf:about="#binding0">
  <b:hasSubject rdf:resource="#xmlSchemaEntity1"/>
  <b:hasObject  rdf:resource="&q;ProteinHit"/>
</b:Binding>

<b:XMLSchemaEntity rdf:about="#xmlSchemaEntity1">
  <b:locatedBy>
    <b:URLLocator rdf:about="#urlLocator2">
      <b:hasURL>http://example.org/schema/PEDRo.xsd</b:hasURL>
    </b:URLLocator>
  </b:locatedBy>
  <b:hasEntityName>ProteinHit</b:hasEntityName>
</b:XMLSchemaEntity>
```

Fig. 4. An example data binding

entity `ProteinHit` defined in the PEDRo XML Schema, located by a URLLocator instance. The instance `#binding0` represents a binding between the `ProteinHit` data entity and the concept ProteinHit in the IQ Ontology.

Bindings are bi-directional: the binding from resource to concept is used to identify which IQ indicators and associated checking functions are applicable to a particular concrete (e.g. XML) data model; the binding from concept to resource is used to locate concrete data and service implementations (e.g. Web services) to run a data check. Examples of this usage are given in Section 7. Bindings are defined as RDF resources to allow metadata to be associated with the bindings themselves, such as provenance information.

Our binding model was influenced by the XML-to-RDF mappings in WEESA [9]. The key difference, however, is that we are not aiming to map data from the XML "data space" to the RDF "semantic space" or vice versa. In our framework, concrete data and service instances are associated with corresponding ontological concepts by means of the bindings, but there is no translation or transformation of one to the other.

6   Annotation Model

An important aspect of the Qurator approach is to share and reuse quality annotation information on data resources among user-scientists. In order to achieve this we provide a data model which formalises annotation information with semantic support. The structure of our annotation model is shown in Figure 5. The concepts shaded in the figure are defined externally to the annotation model: prefixes b and q identify the binding model and the IQ ontology respectively.

The property hasAnnotation represents the relationship that a b:Resource is annotated with quality information recorded in an AnnotationResult. AnnotationResult defines a class of resource that records the output and related information from one run of some quality annotation service. These annotation results are a group of instances of one particular q:QtyEvidence class; the property referenceTo records the name of the relevant class, and the property hasAnnotationElement records individual annotation result elements, each of which contains an individual q:QtyEvidence instance.

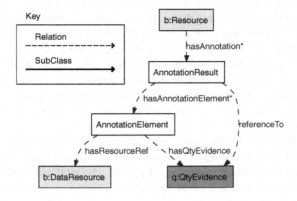

Fig. 5. Structure of Annotation Model

```
<a:AnnotationResult rdf:about="#hitRatio1">
 <a:referenceTo rdf:resource="&q;HitRatio" />
 <a:hasAnnotationElement rdf:resource="#aElement1" />
 <a:hasAnnotationElement rdf:resource="#aElement2" />
 ...
</a:AnnotationResult>
```

(a) An **AnnotationResult**

```
<a:AnnotationElement rdf:about="#aElement1">
 <a:hasResourceRef rdf:resource="#proteinHit1" />
 <a:hasQtyEvidence>
  <q:HitRatio rdf:about="#qtyEvidence1">
   <q:hasValue> 0.45 </q:hasValue>
  </q:HitRatio>
 </a:hasQtyEvidence>
</a:AnnotationElement>

<b:XMLElement rdf:about="#proteinHit1">
 <b:isContainedIn rdf:about="#xmlData1" />
 <b:locatedBy>
  <b:XMLElementLocator>
   <b:hasXPath>/.../Spot[2]/PeakList[1]/ProteinHit[1]</b:hasXPath>
  </b:XMLElementLocator>
 </b:locatedBy>
</b:XMLElement>
```

(b) An **AnnotationElement**

```
<b:Binding>
 <b:hasSubject rdf:resource="#poteinHit1" />
 <b:hasObject rdf:resource="&q;ProteinHit" />
</b:Binding>
```

(c) A **Binding** to an XML element

Fig. 6. Examples of the annotation model in use

An AnnotationElement relates one individual instance of q:QtyEvidence to one individual annotated resource, using the properties hasQtyEvidence and hasResourceRef respectively. It is worth noting that the annotated data elements here are individual ProteinHit XML elements, not a protein identification experiment as a whole.

Figure 6 shows an instance of Annotation which refers to the quality evidence class q:HitRatio and has several annotation elements. Figure 6(b) shows one of the AnnotationElements, which indicates that the XML element identified by the XPath to DB Search[1]/ProteinHit[1] is annotated by an instance of q:HitRatio with the value 0.45.

Figure 6(c) shows a b:Binding which binds the annotated protein hit ProteinHit[1] to the class ProteinHit in the IQ ontology. Although space prevents us from showing this, the various annotated elements are all part of a b:DataCollectionResource, which in practice would normally be located by a LSID.[9]

The main difference between our annotation model and that of other frameworks, for example [my]Grid [11], is the way in which annotations are related to both ontology concepts and data resources. The (abstract) conceptual space and the (concrete) data space are kept separate, with annotations — like the bindings in Section 5 — associating elements in the two spaces. The main advantage of this approach is flexibility: an annotation can be easily attached to any kind of resource, and easily associated with any IQ ontology concept. We also support the attachment of provenance information to instances of AnnotationResult, including the identify of the particular checking function used to generate the annotations, and the data selections used as input. Details of this provenance information are omitted for space reasons; however, we are exploring the use of existing provenance architectures for capturing some of these data [4, 15].

7   Protein Identification IQ Service

The Pedro[10] data entry tool is commonly used in proteomics — and several other e-Science domains — to enter and manage XML-based data. To make our approach convenient to user-scientists we have therefore embedded elements of the Qurator framework in the Pedro desktop software. Figure 7 shows a screenshot of the augmented Pedro tool. The top-left area of the screen is the XML document tree and the right-hand panel is the data entry area. When the user starts-up the tool, they are prompted to select the data model on which they will work, for example the PEDRo model for proteomics data. Choice of the data model then drives the content of the top-left and right-hand panels in the standard Pedro environment: users may enter and edit data, and export it to various formats.

Our augmented version of Pedro introduces the lower-left panel, which contains a tree view of the portions of the IQ ontology relevant to the loaded data model. These elements are obtained by querying the ontology dynamically. For the PEDRo data model, they include domain-specific elements such as ProteinHit and HitRatio as well as associated generic concepts such as ConfidenceEvidence. This panel allows users to discover

---

[9] http://lsid.sourceforge.net/
[10] http://pedrodownload.man.ac.uk/

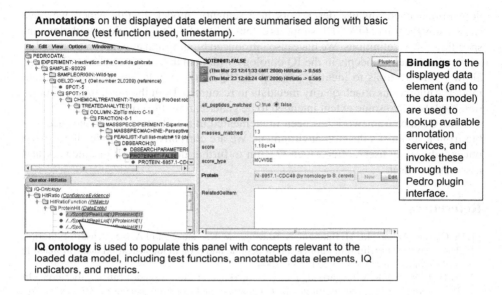

Fig. 7. Augmented "quality-aware" version of the Pedro data entry tool

available indicators for the data model at hand, and follow hyperlinks to explore the ontology.

The augmented tool also uses Pedro's plugin model to invoke any available test functions for the model at hand. If the user clicks on the *Plugins* button at the top-right of Figure 7 they are offered two services, to annotate the data with respect to the HitRatio and MassCoverage indicators which are important to biologists (see Section 2). The choice of available service is determined dynamically, using available bindings obtained from an online *binding repository*. Invoking these services results in annotations being added to an online *annotation repository*. (The augmented Pedro desktop tool is configured to act as a client to these two repositories.) By querying the annotation repository, Pedro can retrieve any annotations associated with the displayed data elements shown in the right-hand panel.

It is worth emphasising that the augmented Pedro tool is intended to be a natural and convenient way for user-scientists to access the facilities of the Qurator framework; however, there is nothing in the framework specific to its use in the Pedro tool. In fact, we also have Web interfaces to the various data-checking services, and are developing interfaces that allow them to be invoked as part of e-Science workflows.

8   Conclusion

The Qurator project offers a framework for managing information quality in an e-Science context, allowing user-scientists to specify their IQ requirements against a formal ontology, so that the definitions are machine-manipulable. To the best of our knowledge, this ontology is the first systematic attempt to capture generic and domain-dependent quality descriptors in a semantic model. In this paper, we have shown how the use of OWL DL supports extensibility of the core ontology with domain-specific quality definitions. We have also introduced binding and annotation models that serve to associate concepts in the IQ ontology with data and service entities. Bindings allow IQ-aware tools to identify parts of the IQ ontology relevant to a specific data model. Annotations attach quality metadata to resources. Both the binding and annotation models are to some extent intended to be generic, reusable components.

The Qurator framework has been implemented in a collection of services accessible from a scientist's desktop environment. We are currently gathering feedback from our collaborating users, after which we aim to further develop the IQ framework and associated toolset.

References

1. S. Carr, R. Aebersold, M. Baldwin, A. Burlingame, K. Clauser, and A. Nesvizhskii. Editorial: The need for guidelines in publication of peptide and protein identification data. *Molecular and Cellular Proteomics*, 3:531–533, 2004.
2. M.G. Elfeky, A.K. Elmagarmid, and V.S. Verykios. Tailor: a record linkage tool box. In *Proceedings of the 18th International Conference on Data Engineering (ICDE 2002)*, San Jose, CA, Feb. 2002. IEEE Computer Society.
3. L. English. *Improving Data Warehouse and Business Information Quality*. Wiley, 1999.
4. P. Groth, M. Luck, and L. Moreau. Formalising a protocol for recording provenance in Grids. In *Proc 3th UK e-Science All Hands Meeting*, pages 147–154, 2004.
5. J. Listgarten and A. Emili. Statistical and computational methods for comparative proteomic profiling using liquid chromatography-tandem mass spectrometry. *Molecular & Cellular Proteomics*, 4(4):419–434, 2005.
6. P. Missier, S. Embury, M. Greenwood, A. Preece, and B. Jin. An ontology-based approach to handling information quality in e-science. In *Proc 4th e-Science All Hands Meeting*, 2005.
7. A.I. Nesvizhskii and R. Aebersold. Analysis, statistical validation and dissemination of large-scale proteomics datasets generated by tandem ms. *Drug Discovery Today*, 9(4):173–181, 2004.
8. T.C. Redman. *Data quality for the information age*. Artech House, 1996.
9. G. Reif, H. Gall, and M. Jazayeri. WEESA - web engineering for semantic web applications. In *Proceedings of the 14th International World Wide Web Conference*, 2005.
10. M. Scannapieco, P. Missier, and C. Batini. Data quality at a glance. *Databanken-Spektrum*, 14:6–14, 2005.
11. N. Sharman, N. Alpdemir, J. Ferris, M. Greenwood, P. Li, and C. Wroe. The myGrid information model. In *Proc 3rd e-Science All Hands Meeting*, 2004.
12. C. F. Taylor et al. A systematic approach to modeling, capturing, and disseminating proteomics experimental data. *Nature Biotechnology*, 21(3):247–254, March 2003.
13. R. Wang and D. Strong. Beyond accuracy: what data quality means to data consumers. *Journal of Management Information Systems*, 12(4):5–34, 1996.
14. I. H. Witten and E. Frank. *Data Mining: Practical Machine Learning Tools and Techniques, 2nd Edition*. Morgan Kaufmann, 2005. ISBN 0-12-088407-0.
15. J. Zhao, C. Wroe, C. Goble, R. Stevens, D. Quan, and M. Greenwood. Using semantic web technologies for representing e-science provenance. In *Third International Semantic Web Conference (ISWC2004)*, number 3298 in LNCS, pages 92–106, Hiroshima, Japan, November 2004. Springer-Verlag.

Annotated RDF*

Octavian Udrea, Diego Reforgiato Recupero, and V.S. Subrahmanian

University of Maryland, College Park MD 20742, USA
{udrea, diegoref, vs}@cs.umd.edu

Abstract. There are numerous extensions of RDF that support temporal reasoning, reasoning about pedigree, reasoning about uncertainty, and so on. In this paper, we present *Annotated RDF* (or aRDF for short) in which RDF triples are annotated by members of a partially ordered set (with bottom element) that can be selected in any way desired by the user. We present a formal declarative semantics (model theory) for annotated RDF and develop algorithms to check consistency of aRDF theories and to answer queries to aRDF theories. We show that annotated RDF captures versions of all the forms of reasoning mentioned above within a single unified framework. We develop a prototype aRDF implementation and show that our algorithms work very fast indeed - in fact, in just a matter of seconds for theories with over 100,000 nodes.

1 Introduction

Since the adoption of "Resource Description Framework" (RDF) as a web recommendation by the W3C, there has been growing interest in using RDF for knowledge representation [1, 2, 3, 4]. Extensions to RDF have included temporal extensions [5], fuzzy extensions [6, 7], provenance management methods [2], and others.

In this paper, we propose an extension of RDF called *Annotated RDF* (or aRDF for short) that builds upon *annotated logic* [8, 9] which has been subsequently used, extended and improved [10] for a wide range of knowledge representation tasks. In aRDF, you can start with any partially ordered set that you like as long as it has has a bottom element[1]. $\mathcal{A}$ could capture fuzzy or possibilistic values [2, 7] or timestamps [5] or - as we shall show - pedigree information or temporal-fuzzy information, and so on. We present a syntax for aRDF in Section 2 - in essence, an aRDF triple consists of an ordinary RDF triple together with an annotation (member of $\mathcal{A}$). We then present a declarative (model-theoretic) semantics for aRDF, together with notions of consistency and entailment in Section 3 — unlike ordinary RDF, an aRDF theory can be inconsistent and hence we provide a consistency check algorithm, together with

---

* Work supported in part by ARO grant DAAD190310202, AFOSR grant FA95500510298, the Joint Institute for Knowledge Discovery, and by a DARPA subcontract from the Univ. of California Berkeley.

[1] Suppose $(\mathcal{A}, \preceq)$ is a partially ordered set. $\perp \in \mathcal{A}$ is the "bottom element" of $\mathcal{A}$ iff $\perp \preceq x$ for all $x \in \mathcal{A}$.

Y. Sure and J. Domingue (Eds.): ESWC 2006, LNCS 4011, pp. 487–501, 2006.
© Springer-Verlag Berlin Heidelberg 2006

a result that whenever the partial order is a lattice, consistency is guaranteed. In Section 4, we present algorithms to answer three types of atomic queries, each with one unknown, together with an algorithm to answer conjunctive queries. We then present our prototype implementation and experiments in Section 5 — our experiments show that our framework is very efficient to implement in practice.

2   aRDF Syntax

We assume the existence of a partially ordered finite set $(\mathcal{A}, \preceq)$ where elements of $\mathcal{A}$ are called *annotations* and $\preceq$ is a partial ordering on $\mathcal{A}$. We further assume $\mathcal{A}$ has a bottom element. For example, we could have any of the following scenarios:

1. $\mathcal{A}_{fuzzy}$ may be the set of all real numbers in the closed interval $[0, 1]$ with the usual "less than or equals" ordering on it.
2. $\mathcal{A}_{time} = \mathbf{N}$ could be the set of all non-negative integers (denoting time points) with the usual "less than or equals" ordering on it.
3. $\mathcal{A}_{time-int} = \{[x, y] \mid x, y \in \mathbf{N}$ could be the set of all time intervals. The interval $[x, y]$ as usual denotes the set of all $t \in \mathbf{N}$ such that $x \leq t \leq y$. The inclusion ordering $\subseteq$ is a partial ordering on this set.
4. $\mathcal{A}_{pedigree}$ could be an enumerated set of sources with a partial ordering on them. If $s_1, s_2 \in \mathcal{A}_{pedigree}$, then we could think of $s_1 \preceq s_2$ to mean that s_2 has "better" pedigree than s_1.
5. $\mathcal{A}_{set-pedigree}$ could be the power set of $\mathcal{A}_{pedigree}$ with the Egli-Milner ordering which says that $S_1 \preceq S_2$ iff $(\forall s_1 \in S_1)(\exists s_2 \in S_2)s_1 \sqsubseteq s_2 \wedge (\forall s_2 \in S_2)(\exists s_2 \in S_1)s_1 \sqsubseteq s_2$. Note here that $\sqsubseteq$ is the ordering on $\mathcal{A}_{pedigree}$.
6. $\mathcal{A}_{fuztime}$ could be the set of all pairs (x, y) such that $x \in [0, 1]$ is a fuzzy value and y is a time point. The $\preceq$ ordering on $\mathcal{A}_{fuztime}$ can be defined as $(x, y) \preceq (x', y')$ iff $x \leq x'$ and $y \leq y'$.

These are just a few examples of partial orders. All the partial orders above except $\mathcal{A}_{pedigree}$ and $\mathcal{A}_{set-pedigree}$ are complete lattices[2]. Note that one can construct arbitrary combinations of partial orders by taking the Cartesian Product of two known partial orders and taking the pointwise ordering on the Cartesian Product as shown in the definition of $\mathcal{A}_{fuztime}$.

Suppose now that $(\mathcal{A}, \preceq)$ is an arbitrary but fixed partially ordered set. As in the case of RDF, we also assume the existence of some arbitrary but fixed set $\mathcal{R}$ of resource names, a set $\mathcal{P}$ of property names, and a set $dom(p)$ of values associated with any property name p.

An *annotated RDF-ontology* (aRDF-ontology for short)[3] is a finite set of triples $(r, p : a, v)$ where r is a *resource* name, p is a *property* name, $a \in \mathcal{A}$ and v is a

---

[2] A partially ordered set $(X, \leq)$ is a complete lattice iff (i) every subset of X has a unique greatest lower bound and (ii) every *directed* subset of X has a unique least upper bound. A set $Y \subseteq X$ is directed iff for all $y_1, y_2 \in Y$, there is an $x \in X$ such that $y_1 \leq x$ and $y_2 \leq x$.

[3] We will often abuse the term ontology to refer to both the intensional part (the schema) and the extensional part (the instance).

value (which could also be a resource name). In particular, this representation also supports RDF Schema triples such as[4]: (i) $(A, rdfs : subClassOf, B)$ indicates a subclass relationship between classes (which are also resources); (ii) $(X, rdf : type, C)$ indicates that a resource X is an instance of some class C; (iii) $(p, rdfs : subPropertyOf, q)$ denotes a sub-property relation between $p, q \in \mathcal{P}$[5]. We denote by $rdfs : subPropertyOf^*$ the reflexive, transitive closure of $rdfs : subPropertyOf$.[6] Once $\mathcal{R}, \mathcal{P}$ and $dom(\cdot)$ are fixed, we use the notation $Univ$ to denote the set of all triples (r, p, v) where $s \in \mathcal{R}, p \in \mathcal{P}$ and $v \in dom(p)$. Throughout the rest of this paper, we will assume that $\mathcal{R}, \mathcal{P}, \mathcal{A}, \preceq, dom(\cdot)$ are all arbitrary, but fixed.

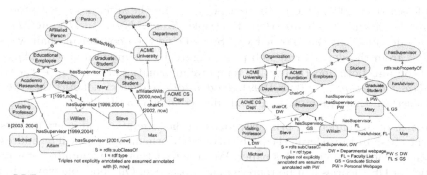

(a) aRDF graph annotated with $\mathcal{A}_{time-int}$ (b) aRDF graph annotated with $\mathcal{A}_{pedigree}$

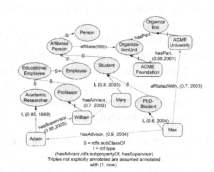

(c) aRDF graph annotated with $\mathcal{A}_{fuztime}$

Fig. 1. Three example aRDF ontology graphs

Definition 1. *(aRDF Ontology graph). Suppose $\mathcal{O}$ is an aRDF-ontology. An* aRDF ontology graph *for O is a labeled graph (V, E, λ) where*

---

[4] $rdfs : range$ and $rdfs : domain$ are also possible, as well as any other RDFS constructs. The paper focuses primarily on aRDF instances, therefore $rdfs : subPropertyOf$ schema constructs are particularly important.

[5] Note we did not require that $\mathcal{P} \cap \mathcal{R} = \emptyset$.

[6] We do not address reification and containers in RDF due to space constraints.

(1) $V = \mathcal{R} \cup \bigcup_{p \in \mathcal{P}} dom(p)$ *is the set of nodes.*

(2) $E = \{(r, r') \mid$ *there exists a property p such that* $(r, p : a, r') \in O\}$ *is the set of edges.*

(3) $\lambda(r, r') = \{p : a \mid (r, p : a, r') \in O\}$ *is the edge labeling function.*

It is easy to see that there is a one-to-one correspondence between aRDF-ontologies and aRDF-ontology graphs. Hence, we will often abuse notation and interchangeably talk about both aRDF ontologies and aRDF ontology graphs.

Example 1. Figure 1 shows three examples[7] of aRDF ontology graphs. Figure 1(a) is annotated with elements of $\mathcal{A}_{time-int}$. Therefore, the triple $(William, rdf : type : [1991, now], Professor)$ denotes the fact that William has been a Professor since 1991. Figure 1(b) uses $\mathcal{A}_{pedigree}$ for the annotation, with the partial order given in the figure. Here, the triple $(Steve, chairOf : DW, ACME\ CS\ Dept)$ denotes that the knowledge of Steve being the department chair was obtained from the department web page. Figure 1(c) is annotated with $\mathcal{A}_{fuztime}$ and contains both uncertainty and temporal information. For instance, the triple $(Adam, rdf : type : (0.85, 1999), AcademicResearcher)$ denotes that we are 85% certain that Adam was an academic researcher until 1999.

The rest of the paper will primarily focus on the semantics and query processing at the aRDF instance level; the problem of aRDF schema queries will be addressed in an extended version of this paper. We note that there are a number of ways in which aRDF theories can be represented in practice. One possible way is to use quadruples[8]; another possibility is the use of reification. Since aRDF semantics and query processing are the focus of this paper, we omit a lengthy discussion on representation issues.

As in the case of OWL, we differentiate between *transitive* and *non-transitive* properties. The RDFS semantics already specifies transitivity for rdfs:subClassOf and rdfs:subPropertyOf relations. The reader may view the specification of transitive properties as a poor man's inference capability for RDF instance data. We assume that all properties in $\mathcal{P}$ are marked transitive or non-transitive. For instance, in Figure 1(b) we consider *hasSupervisor* to be a transitive property[9].

Definition 2 (p-Path). *Let O be an aRDF ontology graph, p a transitive property in O and suppose $r, r' \in O$ are two nodes. There is a p-path between r and r' if there exist $t_1 = (r, p_1 : a_1, r_1), \ldots, t_i = (r_{i-1}, p_i : a_i, r_i), \ldots, t_k = (r_{k-1}, p_k : a_k, r') \in O$ such that $\forall\ i \in [1, k]$ $(p_i, rdfs : subPropertyOf^*, p)$. We will denote a p-path Q by the set of triples $\{t_1, \ldots, t_k\}$ that form the path; we also say $A_Q = \{a_1, \ldots, a_k\}$ is the annotation of the p-path Q.*

Example 2. Consider the aRDF ontology graph shown in Figure 1(c) and suppose the *hasSupervisor* property is transitive. The triples $(Max, hasAdvisor :$

---

[7] In all examples, classes are represented with circular node and instances with rectangular nodes.

[8] A quadruple-based approach is currently discussed for representing contexts/data provenance in RDF — see http://www.w3.org/2001/12/attributions/.

[9] Although this is not generally the case, we assume this for the sake of the example.

$(0.9, 2004), Adam)$ and $(Adam, hasSupervisor : (0.95, 2003), William)$ form a
$hasSupervisor$-path. Similarly, in Figure 1(b), assuming $hasSupervisor$ and
$hasAdvisor$ are transitive properties, the triples $(Max, hasAdvisor : DW,$
$William)$ and $(William, hasSupervisor : GS, Steve)$ form a $hasSupervisor$-
path, since $(hasAdvisor, rdfs : subPropertyOf, hasSupervisor)$.

3   aRDF Semantics

In this section, we provide a declarative semantics for aRDF ontologies and study
consistency of such ontologies.

Definition 3. *An aRDF-interpretation I is a mapping from $Univ$ to $\mathcal{A}$.*

Definition 4. *An aRDF-interpretation I satisfies $(r, p : a, v)$ iff $a \preceq I(r, p, v)$.
I satisfies an aRDF-ontology O iff:*

(S1) I satisfies every $(r, p : a, v) \in O$.
*(S2) For all transitive properties $p \in \mathcal{P}$ and for all p-paths $Q = \{t_1, \ldots, t_k\}$ in
      O, where $t_i = (r_i, p_i : a_i, r_{i+1})$, and for all $a \in \mathcal{A}$ such that $a \preceq a_i$ for all
      $1 \leq i \leq k$, it is the case that $a \preceq I(r_1, p, r_{k+1})$.*

O is consistent *iff there is at least one aRDF-interpretation that satisfies it. O
entails $(r, p : a, v)$ iff every aRDF-interpretation that satisfies O also satisfies
$(r, p : a, v)$.*

The definition of satisfaction and the complex definition of case (S2) above are
best illustrated with an example.

Example 3. Let O be the aRDF ontology graph in Figure 1(c), where $\mathcal{A} =
\mathcal{A}_{fuztime}$. Suppose the $hasSupervisor$ property is transitive. Let $I_0(t) = (1, now)$
$\forall t \in Univ$. I_0 satisfies O and hence O is consistent. Furthermore, $O \models$ *(Mary,
hasAdvisor: (0.7,2001), William)* because for any satisfying interpretation, *(0.7,
2001)* $\preceq$ *(0.7, 2003)* $\preceq$ *I(Mary, hasSupervisor, William)*.

The intuition behind item (S2) of Definition 4 is related to the notion of entailment. For instance, in Figure 1(c) — with $hasSupervisor$ transitive —, from
the triples $(Max, hasAdvisor : (0.9, 2004), Adam)$ and $(Adam, hasSupervisor :
(0.95, 2003), William)$, we can infer that with 90% probability, William was
Max' supervisor until 2003, since $\forall (p, t) \in \mathcal{A}_{fuztime}$ s.t. $(p, t) \preceq (0.9, 2004)$ and
$(p, t) \preceq (0.95, 2003)$ (i.e. $\forall (p, t) \preceq (0.9, 2003)$), $(p, t) \preceq$ *I(Max, hasSupervisor,
William)*.

It is immediately clear from Definition 4 that unlike RDF ontologies which are
always consistent, aRDF ontologies can be inconsistent. Consider the aRDF ontology graph in Figure 1(b) and assume the $hasSupervisor$ property is transitive.
We can identify the following sources of inconsistency:

1. The triples $(Mary, hasSupervisor : PW, William)$ and $(Mary, hasSuper-
   visor : FL, William)$[10] indicate that for any interpretation I, we cannot have

---

[10] The presence of such triples is reasonable since it indicates the same information was
obtained from different sources for which we cannot compare the pedigree according
to the partial order given.

that $PW \preceq I(Mary, hasSupervisor, William)$ and $FL \preceq I(Mary, hasSupervisor, William)$, which contradicts item (S1) from Definition 4.

2. The presence of the different $hasSupervisor$-paths $\{$ $(Max, hasAdvisor:FL, William), (William, hasSupervisor:GS, Steve)\}$ and $\{(Max, hasSupervisor : DW, Steve)\}$ means that for any interpretation I, we cannot have that $FL \preceq I(Max, hasSupervisor, Steve)$ and $DW \preceq I(Max, hasSupervisor, Steve)$, thus contradicting item (S2) from Definition 4.

We now state a necessary and sufficient condition for checking consistency of an aRDF ontology.

Theorem 1. *Let O be an aRDF ontology. O is consistent iff:*

(C1) $\forall p \in \mathcal{P}$ *and* $\forall\ r, r' \in \mathcal{R}$ *such that* $\exists$ *distinct* $a_1, \dots a_k \in \mathcal{A}$ *and* $\forall i \in [1, k]\ \exists (r, p : a_i, r') \in O$, *then* $\exists\ a \in \mathcal{A}\ s.t.\ \forall i \in [1, k]\ a_i \preceq a$ *AND*

(C2) $\forall p \in \mathcal{P}$ *transitive,* $\forall r, r' \in \mathcal{R}$, *let* $\{Q^1, \dots, Q^k\}$ *be the set of different p-paths between r and r' and let $\{A_{Q^1}, \dots, A_{Q^k}\}$ be the annotations for these p-paths. Let $B_{Q^i} = \{a \in \mathcal{A} | a \preceq a'\ \forall a' \in A_{Q^i}\}$. Then $\exists\ a \in \mathcal{A}\ s.t.$ $\forall b \in \bigcup_{i \in [1,k]} B_{Q^i}, b \preceq a$[11].*

The following result states that if we require $\mathcal{A}$ to be a partial order with a top element[12], then we are guaranteed consistency.

Corollary 1. *Let $\mathcal{A}$ be a partial order with a top element. Then any aRDF ontology O annotated w.r.t. $\mathcal{A}$ is consistent.*

The justification is immediate, since the interpretation that maps every triple in $Univ$ to the top element satisfies any aRDF ontology.

Theorem 1 provides an immediate algorithm for checking the consistency of aRDF ontologies. We present this algorithm in Figure 2.

Example 4. Let O the aRDF ontology graph in Figure 1(b). When we run our consistency check algorithm and execution reaches line 4 with $(r, p, r')=(Mary, hasSupervisor, William)$, $A = \{PW, FL\}$ from line 2. Since $\nexists\ a \in \mathcal{A}$ s.t. $PW, FL \preceq a$, the algorithm will determine that the ontology is inconsistent.

Now consider the same aRDF ontology without the triple $(Mary, hasSupervisor : PW, William)$. In this case, the algorithm will proceed to the loop starting on line 6. However, for the iteration for which $p = hasSupervisor$ on line 6 and $(r, r') = (Max, Steve)$ on line 9, the set P' will contain the two possible $hasSupervisor$-paths from Max to $Steve$ detailed in Example 3. Then on line 12, $A = \{\{DW\}, \{FL, GS\}\}$ and on line 13 $B = \{DW, FL\}$ and since $\nexists\ a \in \mathcal{A}$ s.t. $DW, FL \preceq a$, the algorithm will return *False* on line 14.

The following result states the correctness of our consistency check algorithm.

Proposition 1 (Consistency check correctness). *The aRDFconsistency on input $(O, \mathcal{A}, \preceq)$ returns True iff O is consistent.*

---

[11] Note that (C2) implies (C1) when p is transitive, since paths of length 1 are possible.

[12] An element $\top \in \mathcal{A}$ is a "top" element if $x \preceq \top$ for all $x \in \mathcal{A}$.

Algorithm aRDFconsistency$(O, \mathcal{A}, \preceq)$
Input: aRDF ontology O and annotation $(\mathcal{A}, \preceq)$.
Output: *True* if O is consistent, *False* otherwise.
Notation: For a property p we write $SP(p) = \{q \in \mathcal{P} | (q, rdfs : subPropertyOf^*, p)\}$. We denote by $O|_p$ the restriction of the aRDF graph O to triples labeled with properties in $SP(p)$. $N(O)$ denotes the set of nodes in the aRDF ontology graph O.

1. **for** $(r, p, r') \in \{(r, p, r') | \exists \, a \in \mathcal{A} \ s.t. \ (r, p : a, r') \in O\}$ **do**
2. $A \leftarrow \{a \in \mathcal{A} | (r, p : a, r') \in O\}$;
3.   **if** $|A| > 1$ **then**
4.   **if** $\nexists \, a \in \mathcal{A} \ s.t. \ \forall a' \in A, a' \preceq a$ **return** *False*;
5. **end**
6. **for** $p \in \mathcal{P}$ transitive **do**
7. $O' \leftarrow O|_p$;
8. $P \leftarrow \{paths \ Q \subseteq O' | \nexists Q' \subseteq O' \wedge Q' \supset Q\}$;
9.   **for** $(r, r') \in N(O') \times N(O')$ **do**
10. $P' \leftarrow \{Q \in P | r, r' \text{ are the first and last node respectively in } Q\}$;
11.   **if** $|P'| > 0$ **then**
12. $A \leftarrow \{A_Q | Q \in P'\}$;
13. $B \leftarrow \{b \in \mathcal{A} | \exists A_Q \in A \ s.t. \ \forall \, a \in A_Q, b \preceq a\}$;
14.   **if** $\nexists \, a \in \mathcal{A} \ s.t. \ \forall b \in B, b \preceq a$ **then return** *False*;
15.   **end**
16.   **end**
17. **end**
18. **return** *True*;

Fig. 2. Consistency checking algorithm for aRDF ontologies

The consistency check algorithm runs in polynomial time as shown below.

Proposition 2 (Consistency check complexity). *Let O be an aRDF ontology graph and let $n = |N(O)|$, let $e = |O|$ and let $p = |\mathcal{P}|$. Let $(\mathcal{A}, \preceq)$ be a partial order and let $a = |\mathcal{A}|$*[13]*. Then aRDFconsistency$(O, \mathcal{A}, \preceq)$ is $\mathcal{O}(p \cdot (n^3 \cdot e + n \cdot a^2))$.*

The result follows from the loop on lines 6—17. For any transitive property, we first compute the set of all maximal paths in $O|_p$ (line 8). Since we have to keep the paths in memory (and not only their cost), this operation can be performed in at most $n^3 \cdot e$ steps in a modified version of Floyd's algorithm that records the paths explored. The loop on line 9 iterates through all the maximal paths found — there can be at most $2n$ of them. For each such path we compute the set A (line 12), which takes at most e steps, since any maximal path is of length less than or equal to e. The size of each A set is bounded by a and the number of maximal paths for the entire graph is at most $O(n)$, meaning line 13 will be run at most $\mathcal{O}(n \cdot a^2)$ times. Line 14 is run at most $\mathcal{O}(n \cdot a^2)$ times as well, since $|B|$ is bounded by a.

4   aRDF Query Processing

In this section, we consider aRDF-queries. We assume the existence of sets of variables ranging over resources, properties, values and $\mathcal{A}$. A term over one of these sets is either a member of that set or a variable ranging over that set. An *aRDF query* is a triple $(R, P : A, V)$ where R, P, A, V are all terms over

---

[13] We assume without loss of generality that $a < e$, since we can use at most one annotation for each edge.

resources, properties, annotations and values respectively. An aRDF query of the above form is atomic if at most one term in it is a variable.

Example 5. Consider the aRDF ontology graph in Figure 1(c). The following are aRDF atomic queries:

- What was the relationship between Max and William until 2002 with 80% probability? $(Max, ?p : (0.8, 2002), William)$.
- Who was Mary's supervisor until 2002 with 70% probability? *(Mary, has-Supervisor:(0.7,2002), ?v)*.
- Who was affiliated with ACME University until 2002 with 65% probability? *(?r, affiliatedWith:(0.65,2002),ACME University)*.

Definition 5 (Semi-unifiable aRDF triples). *Two aRDF triples $(r, p : a, v)$, $(r', p' : a', v')$ are θ semi-unifiable iff there exists a substitution θ such that $r\theta = r'\theta$ and $p\theta = p'\theta$ and $v\theta = v'\theta$.*

As usual, $r\theta$ denotes the application of θ to r.

Definition 6 (Query answer). *Let O be a consistent aRDF ontology and let $q = (r_q, p_q : a_q, v_q)$ be a query on O. Let $A_O(q) = \{(r, p : a, v) \mid (r_q, p_q : a_q, v_q)$ is semi-unifiable with q and $O \models (r, p : a, v) \wedge ((a$ is a variable$) \vee (a_q \preceq a))\}$. The answer to q is defined as $Ans_O(q) = \{(r, p : a, v) \in A_O(q) \mid \not\exists S \subseteq Ans_O(q) - \{(r, p : a, v)\}$ s.t. $S \models (r, p : a, v)\}$.*

$A_O(q)$ consists of all ground (i.e. variable-free) instances of q that are entailed by O. However, $A_O(q)$ may contain redundant triples - for example, using our $time - int$ partial ordering, if $(r, p : [1, 100], v)$ is in $A_O(q)$, then there is no point including redundant triples such as $(r, p : [1, 10], v)$ in it. $Ans_O(q)$ eliminates all such redundant triples from $A_O(q)$.

Example 6. Consider the queries in Example 5. The answers are:

- $Ans_O(q) = \{(Max, hasSupervisor : (0.9, 2003), William)\}$. Note that the answer does not include for instance $(Max, hasSupervisor : (0.9, 2001), William)$ since the latter triple is already entailed by a triple in the answer.
- $Ans_O(q) = \{Mary, hasAdvisor : (0.7, 2003), William)\}$.
- $Ans_O(q) = \{Max, affiliatedWith : (0.7, 2003), ACME University)\}$.

The following result specifies a condition that must hold when O entails a ground aRDF triple.

Theorem 2. *Let O be a consistent aRDF ontology and let $(r, p : a, v)$ be an aRDF triple. $O \models (r, p : a, v)$ iff one of the following conditions holds:*

(E1) $\exists (r, p : a_1, v), \ldots, (r, p : a_k, v) \in O$ and let A be the set of values a' such that $a_i \preceq a' \ \forall i \in [1, k]$ ($|A| \geq 1$ since O is consistent). Then $\forall a' \in A$, $a \preceq a'$.

(E2) $\exists$ *p-paths* $Q^1, \ldots, Q^k$ *between* r *and* v. *Let* $B_{Q^i} = \{b \in \mathcal{A} | b \preceq a' \ \forall a' \in A_{Q^i}\}$. *Let* A *be the set of values* a' *such that* $\forall \ b \in \bigcup_{i \in [1,k]} B_{Q^i}, b \preceq a'$ *($|A| \geq 1$ since O is consistent). Then $\forall \ a' \in A$, $a \preceq a'$.*

Given an ontology O, we can infer new triples from O using the following two operators, f_1, f_2:

1. $f_1(O) = \{(r, p : a, v) | \exists \ (r, p : a_1, v), (r, p' : a_2, v) \in O \ s.t. \ (p', rdfs : subPropertyOf^*, p) \wedge a$ is a minimal upper bound[14] of $a_1, a_2\}$.
2. $f_2(O) = \{(r, p : a, v) | \exists (r, p' : a_1, r'), (r', p'' : a_2, v) \in O \ s.t. \ (p', rdfs : subPropertyOf^*, p) \wedge (p'', rdfs : subPropertyOf^*, p) \wedge (\forall \ a' \in \mathcal{A}, (a' \preceq a_1 \wedge a' \preceq a_2) \Rightarrow (a' \preceq a)) \wedge (a$ minimal with these properties w.r.t. $\preceq)\}$.

Let $\mu(O) = f_1(O) \cup f_2(O)$.

Proposition 3 (Closure of O). μ *is a monotonic operator, i.e.* $O_1 \subseteq O_2$ *implies* $\mu(O_1) \subseteq \mu(O_2)$. *Hence, by the Tarski-Knaster theorem, it has a least fixpoint denoted by* lfp(O) *called the* closure *of* O.

Example 7. Let O be the aRDF ontology in Figure 1(c). Then lfp(O) contains all triples in O and the triple *(Max, hasSupervisor: (0.9,2003), William)*.

The following result is a necessary and sufficient condition for entailment by an aRDF ontology.

Proposition 4. *Let O be an* aRDF *ontology.* $O \models (r, p : a, v)$ *iff* $(r, p : a, v) \in$ lfp(O) *or* $\exists (r', p' : a', v') \in$ lfp(O) *s.t.* $\{(r', p' : a', v')\} \models (r, p : a, v)$.

Proposition 5. *Let O be a consistent* aRDF *ontology and q a query on O. Then* $Ans_q(O) \subseteq$ lfp(O).

The above proposition gives us a very simple algorithm for answering queries.

1. Consider query $q = (r, p : a, v)$ on aRDF ontology O. Compute lfp(O).
2. $A \leftarrow \{(r', p' : a', v') \in$ lfp(O)$|(r', p' : a', v')$ semi $-$ unifiable with $q \wedge ((a$ is a variable$) \vee (a \preceq a'))\}$.
3. Eliminate from A triples $(r, p : a, v)$ entailed by subsets of $A - \{(r, p : a, v)\}$.

However, we can do much better by avoiding the costly computation of lfp(O).

4.1   Answering Atomic Queries

Although the closure of an aRDF ontology gives a simple method of computing the answer to queries, its computation is potentially expensive. We show more efficient algorithms for answering atomic queries. The algorithm for queries of type $q = (r, p : a, ?v)$ is given in Figure 3; computing the answers to atomic queries of type $q = (?r, p : a, v)$ is very similar and omitted for reasons of space.

---

[14] a is an minimal upper bound of a_1, a_2 iff $a_1 \preceq a$ and $a_2 \preceq a$ and there is no other a' such that $a' \preceq a$ and $a_1, a_2 \preceq a'$.

Algorithm atomicAnswerV$(O, \mathcal{A}, \preceq, q)$
Input: Consistent aRDF ontology O, annotation $(\mathcal{A}, \preceq)$ and query $q = (r, p : a, ?v)$.
Output: $Ans_O(q)$.
Notation: For a property p we write $SP(p) = \{q \in \mathcal{P} | (q, rdfs : subPropertyOf^*, p)\}$. We denote by $O|_p$ the restriction of the aRDF graph O to triples labeled with properties in $SP(p)$.

```
1.  O ← O|_p;
2.  Ans ← ∅;
3.  if p is non-transitive then
4.      for (r, p', v') ∈ {(r, p' : a', v') ∈ O} do
5.          A ← {a' ∈ A|(r, p' : a', v') ∈ O};
6.          B ← {b ∈ A|∀a ∈ A, a ⪯ b};
7.          C ← {c ∈ B| ∄c' ∈ B, c' ≠ c s.t. c' ⪯ c};
8.          Ans ← Ans ∪ {(r, p' : c, v')|c ∈ C ∧ a ⪯ c};
9.      end
10. else if p transitive then
11.     for all v' s.t. ∃ Q¹, …, Qᵏ p-paths from r to v' do
12.         B ← {b ∈ A|∃i ∈ [1, k] s.t. ∀ a' ∈ A_{Qⁱ}, b ⪯ a'};
13.         C ← {c ∈ A|∀b ∈ B, b ⪯ c};
14.         D ← {d ∈ C| ∄ d' ∈ C, d' ≠ d s.t. d' ⪯ d};
15.         Ans ← Ans ∪ {(r, p : d, v')|d ∈ D ∧ a ⪯ d};
16.     end
17. end
18. return Ans;
```

Fig. 3. Answering atomic aRDF queries $(r, p : a, ?v)$

Example 8. Consider the aRDF ontology graph in Figure 1(c) and the query $(Max, hasSupervisor : (0.8, 2002), ?v)$. Since $hasSupervisor$ is transitive, the algorithm will go on the second branch, starting at line 10. The loop on line 11 iterates through all the values reachable through $hasSupervisor$-paths from Max, which are exactly $\{Adam, William\}$. Let us consider the second iteration, where $v' = William$. There is only one $hasSupervisor$-path between Max and $William$, containing triples $(Max, hasAdvisor : (0.9, 2004), Adam)$ and $(Adam, hasSupervisor : (0.95, 2003), William)$. Then $A_{Q^1} = \{(0.9, 2004), (0.95, 2003)\}$. Therefore B is exactly the set of pairs (p, t) s.t. $(p, t) \preceq (0.9, 2003)$. C will be the set of pairs (p, t) greater than $(0.9, 2003)$ and thus $D = \{(0.9, 2003)\}$. Therefore, the triple $(Max, hasSupervisor : (0.9, 2003), William)$ will be added to Ans.

The following theorem states that $atomicAnswerV$ is correct.

Proposition 6. $atomicAnswerV(O, \mathcal{A}, \preceq, q)$ *returns* $Ans_O(q)$.

The following result says that $atomicAnswerV$ runs in polynomial time.

Proposition 7. *Let O be an aRDF ontology graph and let n be the number of vertices in the ontology graph O, let $e = |O|$ and let $p = |\mathcal{P}|$. Let $(\mathcal{A}, \preceq)$ be a partial order and let $a = |\mathcal{A}|$. Then $atomicAnswerV(O, \mathcal{A}, \preceq, q)$ is $\mathcal{O}(n^2 \cdot e + n \cdot e \cdot a^2)$.*

The complexity result is given by the loop on lines 11—16. We start by determining all values reachable by p-paths from r and the corresponding paths, which can be done in $\mathcal{O}(n^2 \cdot e)$ since v is fixed. Since there are at most $\mathcal{O}(n)$ paths originating from r, each with at most $O(e)$ edges and the size of the annotation for each path is bounded by a, line 12 will be run at most $\mathcal{O}(n \cdot e \cdot a^2)$ times. Since the sizes of B, C, D are all bounded by a, the same result holds for lines 13—15.

Algorithm atomicAnswerP(O,$\mathcal{A}$, $\preceq$, q)
Input: Consistent aRDF ontology O, annotation $(\mathcal{A}, \preceq)$ and query $q = (r, ?p : a, v)$.
Output: $Ans_O(q)$.

1. $Ans \leftarrow \emptyset$;
2. **for** all p' such that $\exists\, Q^1, \ldots, Q^k$ p'-paths from r to v **do**
3. $B \leftarrow \{b \in \mathcal{A} | \exists i \in [1, k]\ s.t.\ \forall\, a' \in A_{Q^i}, b \preceq a'\}$;
4. $C \leftarrow \{c \in \mathcal{A} | \forall b \in B, b \preceq c\}$;
5. $D \leftarrow \{d \in C |\ \not\exists\, d' \in C, d' \neq d\ s.t.\ d' \preceq d\}$;
6. $Ans \leftarrow Ans \cup \{(r, p' : d, v) | d \in D \wedge a \preceq d\}$;
7. **end**
8. **return** $\{(r', p' : a', v') \in Ans |\ \not\exists\, S \subseteq Ans - \{(r', p' : a', v')\}\ s.t.\ S \models (r', p' : a', v')\}$;

Fig. 4. Answering atomic aRDF queries $(r, ?p : a, v)$

An even tighter complexity bound holds when the annotation is a complete lattice. In this case, after computing the set A on line 11, we can simply compute the least upper bound of the elements in A and thus obtain set C (on line 13). For complete lattices such as $\mathcal{A}_{time-int}$, this can be done in at most a linear number of steps in $|A|$. Thus, the overall complexity of the algorithm becomes $\mathcal{O}(n^2 \cdot e + n \cdot e \cdot a)$.

Algorithm $atomicAnswerP$ given in Figure 4 computes the answer to atomic queries with an unknown property. The main difference from $atomicAnswerV$ is that the graph we need to explore is the one containing all paths between r and v, instead of the one containing all p-paths starting at r. Depending on the shape of the aRDF ontology (e.g., breadth vs. depth), either search space may be larger, but the worst case complexity is identical. Algorithm $atomicAnswerA$ given in Figure 5 computes the answer to atomic queries with unknown annotation. For $atomicAnswerA$, r, p, v are all known therefore the step in which we compute all paths (line 11) can be performed in at most $\mathcal{O}(n \cdot e)$ steps. Therefore, $atomicAnswerA$ is $\mathcal{O}(n \cdot e \cdot a^2)$. Correctness results for both $atomicAnswerV$ and $atomicAnswerA$ similar to Proposition 6 are immediate.

Algorithm atomicAnswerA(O,$\mathcal{A}$, $\preceq$, q)
Input: Consistent aRDF ontology O, annotation $(\mathcal{A}, \preceq)$ and query $q = (r, p : ?a, v)$.
Output: $Ans_O(q)$.
Notation: For a property p we write $SP(p) = \{q \in \mathcal{P} | (q, rdfs : subPropertyOf^*, p)\}$. We denote by $O|_p$ the restriction of the aRDF graph O to triples labeled with properties in $SP(p)$.

1. $O \leftarrow O|_p$;
2. $Ans \leftarrow \emptyset$;
3. **if** p is non-transitive **then**
4.   **for** $(r, p', v) \in \{(r, p' : a', v) \in O | p' \in SP(p)\}$ **do**
5. $A \leftarrow \{a' \in \mathcal{A} | (r, p' : a', v) \in O\}$;
6. $B \leftarrow \{b \in \mathcal{A} | \forall a \in A, a \preceq b\}$;
7. $C \leftarrow \{c \in B |\ \not\exists c' \in B, c' \neq c\ s.t.\ c' \preceq c\}$;
8. $Ans \leftarrow Ans \cup \{(r, p' : c, v) | c \in C\}$;
9.   **end**
10. **else if** p transitive **then**
11. $\{Q^1, \ldots, Q^k\} \leftarrow \{p\text{-paths from } r \text{ to } v\}$;
12. $B \leftarrow \{b \in \mathcal{A} | \exists i \in [1, k]\ s.t.\ \forall\, a' \in A_{Q^i}, b \preceq a'\}$;
13. $C \leftarrow \{c \in \mathcal{A} | \forall b \in B, b \preceq c\}$;
14. $D \leftarrow \{d \in C |\ \not\exists\, d' \in C, d' \neq d\ s.t.\ d' \preceq d\}$;
15. $Ans \leftarrow Ans \cup \{(r, p : d, v) | d \in D\}$;
16. **end**
17. **return** Ans;

Fig. 5. Answering atomic aRDF queries $(r, p : ?a, v)$

The methods of computing query answers for atomic queries can be extended with minimal changes to the case of queries with multiple variables[15]; for reasons of space, we omit such algorithms.

4.2 Conjunctive Queries

Let O be a consistent aRDF ontology. We define conjunctive queries as a set $Q = \{q_1, \ldots, q_m\}$ of atomic queries, where $q_i = (r_i, p_i : a_i, v_i)$. The answer can be defined similarly to that of atomic queries as $Ans_O(Q) = \{S \subseteq O | \exists \theta \; s.t. \; \forall i \in [1, m], \exists (r, p : a, v) \in S \; s.t.((r, p : a, v) \; \theta \; semi-unifiable \; with \; q_i) \wedge ((a_i \; variable) \vee (a_i \preceq a)) \wedge (\not\exists S' \in Ans_O(Q) \; s.t. \; S' \models S)\}$. The algorithm for computing answers to conjunctive queries given in Figure 6 is based on the observation that a conjunctive query is apartially instantiated aRDF graph; thus, inexact graph matching algorithms [11] between the graph corresponding to Q and subgraphs of lfp(O) give potential answer sets.

Algorithm conjunctAnswer(O,$\mathcal{A}$, $\preceq$, Q)
Input: Consistent aRDF ontology O, annotation $(\mathcal{A}, \preceq)$ and query $Q = \{q_i = (r_i, p_i : a_i, v_i) | i \in [1, m]\}$.
Output: $Ans_O(q)$.
Notation: For a property p we write $SP(p) = \{q \in \mathcal{P} | (q, rdfs : subPropertyOf^*, p)\}$. We denote by $O|_p$ the restriction of the aRDF graph O to triples labeled with properties in $SP(p)$. $N(O)$ denotes the set of nodes in the aRDF ontology graph O.

1. **if** Q contains no variable property queries **then**
2. $O \leftarrow O|_{\bigcup_i SP(p_i)}$;
3. $Ans \leftarrow \emptyset$;
4. **do**
5. $O \leftarrow O'$;
6.   **for** all paths R in O on some property p between some r, r' **do**
7. $B \leftarrow \{b \in \mathcal{A} | \forall \; a \in A_R, b \preceq a\}$;
8. $C \leftarrow \{c \in \mathcal{A} | \forall \; b \in B, b \preceq c\}$;
9. $D \leftarrow \{d \in C | \not\exists \; d' \in C, d' \neq d, d' \preceq d\}$;
10. $O' \leftarrow O \cup \{(r, p : d, r') | d \in D\}$;
11.   **end**
12.   **for** $(r, p, r') \in \{(r, p, r') | \exists \; a \neq a' \in \mathcal{A} \; s.t. \; (r, p : a, r'), (r, p : a', r') \in O\}$ **do**
13. $A \leftarrow \{a \in \mathcal{A} | (r, p : a, r') \in O\}$;
14. $B \leftarrow \{b \in \mathcal{A} | \forall a \in A, a \preceq b\}$;
15. $C \leftarrow \{c \in B | \not\exists c' \in B, c' \neq c \; s.t. \; c' \preceq c\}$;
16. $O' \leftarrow O \cup \{(r, p : c, r') | c \in C \wedge a \preceq c\}$;
17.   **end**
18. **while** $O = O'$;
19. $G_Q \leftarrow$ the graph corresponding to Q;
20. **for** all matchings between G_Q and O **do**
21. $ok \leftarrow true$;
22.   **for** $i \in [1, m]$ **do**
23. $(r, p : a, v) \leftarrow$ the triple in O matched to q_i;
24.   **if** $\neg(a_i \; variable) \wedge \neg(a_i \preceq q)$ **then**
25. $ok \leftarrow false$;
26.   **break**;
27.   **end**
28.   **end**
29.   **if** ok **then**
30. $Ans \leftarrow Ans \cup \{$ set of triples matched to $G_Q\}$;
31. **end**
32. **return** Ans;

Fig. 6. Answering conjunctive aRDF queries

---

[15] However, the complexity of these algorithms remains polynomial.

Algorithm *conjunctAnswer* starts by computing the closure lfp(O) in the loop on lines 4—18. Elements corresponding to f_1 in Definition 3 are computed on lines 12—16, whereas elements corresponding to f_2 are computed on lines 6—11. After lfp(O) is computed, inexact graph matchings [11] are used to determine potential answers to the conjunctive query (line 20). Each triple in the potential answer is checked against the annotation (if constant) of the respective query (22—28). If all triples have "better" annotations than the corresponding query triples, the answer is stored (line 30). The complexity of *conjunctAnswer* is at worst case exponential since the computation of lfp(O) increases the size of the aRDF ontology polynomially and may be performed a number of times polynomial in the size of the ontology.

5   Experimental Results

Our experimental prototype of the aRDF query system was implemented in approximately 1100 lines of Java code; the experiments were performed on an Intel Pentium 4 Mobile processor machine at 2.30 GHz and 512MB DDR SDRAM, running Debian Linux 1.3.3.4-9. The experiments were run using synthetically generated aRDF datasets ranging from 10,000 to 100,000 aRDF triples, using an uniform distribution for the random generator. The following parameters were constant throughout the generation process: (i) $|\mathcal{P}| = 100$, (ii) 10 transitive properties, (iii) $|\mathcal{A}| = 20$, (iv) 10 subproperty relations.

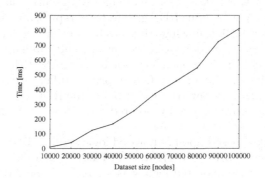

Fig. 7. aRDFconsistency running time

The first set of experiments shown in Figure 7 show the time needed for consistency checking. We see that aRDFconsistency takes under 1 second for graphs of 100,000 nodes. Figure 8(a) describes the query running time for the three algorithms detailed where queries were randomly generated. The main points that determine the behavior observed in Figure 8(a) and 8(b) are: (i) in line 11 of *answerV* we look for p-paths originating at a known r; (ii) line (2) of *answerP* we look for any transitive property paths between a known r and v; (iii) line (11) of *answerA* determines p-paths between a known r and v. It is

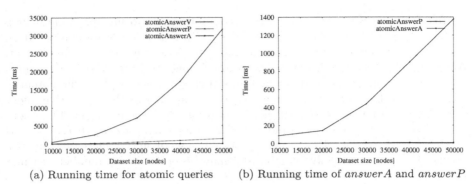

(a) Running time for atomic queries   (b) Running time of *answerA* and *answerP*

Fig. 8. Query running time

easy to see why (iii) is the fastest, since r, v, p are all known. We can also see that for the experimental setting described, (i) takes more time than (ii); this is due to the relatively small number of properties in the graphs[16].

6   Related Work

There has been considerable work on extending RDF with new features such as time intervals (statements saying something is true at all time points in an interval [5]), uncertainty [6, 7](though these are just one page position papers) and provenance [2] which describes a model for representing named RDF graphs, thus allowing statements about RDF graphs to be represented in RDF. [5] gives a model for temporal RDF, allowing triples to be specified as true for a finite time interval. [12] defines a model for representing multi-dimensional RDF, where information can be context dependent; for instance the title of a book may be represented in different languages. Our approach differs from all of the above: (i) we define a general framework for extending the RDF data model with annotations from an arbitrary partially ordered set; (ii) we give efficient algorithms for querying annotated RDF ontologies.

Our framework is based upon annotated logic [8, 9] — however, by examining RDF triples, we can provide far greater efficiency than annotated logic was able to provide. Moreover, annotated logic was unable to handle the kinds of queries shown where properties and the annotations desired were unknown.

To the best of our knowledge, this is the first paper that has attempted to provide a single framework - where by swapping a new partial order (with bottom) for another - we can get different types of reasoning capabilities in RDF. We have shown that annotated RDF is capable of supporting diverse forms of reasoning as well as combinations of reasoning (e.g. via `fuztime`), has a rich declarative semantics, and provides an efficient computational engine for application building.

---

[16] A phenomenon normally encountered in real-world RDF graphs, as we can see from most ontologies at `www.daml.org`.

References

1. Kahan, J., Koivunen, M.R.: Annotea: an open rdf infrastructure for shared web annotations. In: WWW '01: Proceedings of the 10th international conference on World Wide Web, New York, NY, USA, ACM Press (2001) 623–632
2. Carroll, J.J., Bizer, C., Hayes, P., Stickler, P.: Named graphs, provenance and trust. In: WWW '05: Proceedings of the 14th international conference on World Wide Web, New York, NY, USA, ACM Press (2005) 613–622
3. Karvounarakis, G., Alexaki, S., Christophides, V., Plexousakis, D., Scholl, M.: Rql: a declarative query language for rdf. In: WWW '02: Proceedings of the 11th international conference on World Wide Web, New York, NY, USA, ACM Press (2002) 592–603
4. Gutierrez, C., Hurtado, C., Mendelzon, A.O.: Foundations of semantic web databases. In: PODS '04: Proceedings of the twenty-third ACM SIGMOD-SIGACT-SIGART symposium on Principles of database systems, New York, NY, USA, ACM Press (2004) 95–106
5. Gutiérrez, C., Hurtado, C.A., Vaisman, A.A.: Temporal rdf. In: ESWC. (2005) 93–107
6. D. Dubois, M., Prade, H.: Possibilistic uncertainty and fuzzy features in description logic: a preliminary discussion. In: Proc. Workshop on Fuzzy Logic and the Semantic Web (ed. E. Sanchez). (2005) 5–7
7. Straccia, U.: Towards a fuzzy description logic for the semantic web. In: Proc. Workshop on Fuzzy Logic and the Semantic Web (ed. E. Sanchez). (2005) 3–3
8. Kifer, M., Subrahmanian, V.S.: Theory of generalized annotated logic programming and its applications. J. Log. Program. **12** (1992) 335–367
9. Leach, S.M., Lu, J.J.: Query processing in annotated logic programming: Theory and implementation. J. Intell. Inf. Syst. **6** (1996) 33–58
10. Fitting, M.: Bilattices and the semantics of logic programming. J. Log. Program. **11** (1991) 91–116
11. Hlaoui, A., Wang, S.: A new algorithm for inexact graph matching. In: ICPR (4). (2002) 180–183
12. Gergatsoulis, M., Lilis, P.: Multidimensional rdf. In: Proc. 2005 Intl. Conf. on Ontologies, Databases, and Semantics (ODBASE). Volume 3761., Springer (2005) 1188–1205

A Multilingual/Multimedia Lexicon Model for Ontologies

Paul Buitelaar[1], Michael Sintek[2], and Malte Kiesel[2]

[1] DFKI GmbH, Language Technology, Stuhlsatzenhausweg 3,
66123 Saarbruecken, Germany
paulb@dfki.de
[2] DFKI GmbH, Knowledge Management, Erwin-Schrödinger-Straße,
67608 Kaiserslautern, Germany
{sintek, kiesel}@dfki.de

Abstract. Ontology development is mostly directed at the representation of domain knowledge and much less at the representation of textual or image-based symbols for this knowledge, i.e., the multilingual and multimedia lexicon. To allow for automatic multilingual and multimedia knowledge markup, a richer representation of text and image features is needed. At present, such information is mostly missing or represented only in a very impoverished way. In this paper we propose an RDF/S-based lexicon model, which in itself is an ontology that allows for the integrated representation of domain knowledge and corresponding multilingual and multimedia features.

1 Introduction

Ontologies define the semantics for a *set of objects* in the world using a *set of classes*, each of which may be identified by a particular *symbol* (either linguistic, as image, or otherwise). In this way, ontologies cover all three sides of the "semiotic triangle" that includes *object, referent,* and *symbol,* i.e., an *object* in the world is defined by its *referent* and represented by a *symbol* (Ogden and Richards, 1923 – based on Peirce, de Saussure and others).

Currently, ontology development and the Semantic Web effort in general have been mostly directed at the *referent* side of the triangle, and much less at the *symbol* side. To allow for automatic multilingual and multimedia knowledge markup a richer representation is needed of the linguistic and image-based symbols for the object classes that are defined by the ontology. At present, such information is mostly missing or represented only in a very impoverished way, leaving the semantic information in an ontology without a grounding to the human cognitive and linguistic domain. For instance, according to the collection of ontologies available through OntoSelect[1] (see Buitelaar et al., 2004), currently only about 9% of ontologies represent multilingual terms for classes and/or properties.

Linguistic symbols, i.e., simple words or more complex terms, are represented in a lexicon that provides the meaning of these words or terms, besides a more or less

---

[1] http://olp.dfki.de/OntoSelect/

Y. Sure and J. Domingue (Eds.): ESWC 2006, LNCS 4011, pp. 502–513, 2006.

extensive representation of their linguistic features, e.g., if the word is a noun or a verb, if it is atomic or can be split into multiple words, etc. Similarly, a lexicon of images can be defined that represent which prototypical image, or more precisely, which set of image features corresponds to which ontology class. Here, we will discuss a multilingual/multimedia lexicon model that will allow for the representation of linguistic and image symbols for ontology classes and properties.

2 Ontologies and Multilingual/Multimedia Features

An ontology describes a knowledge model of a particular domain of discourse at a particular point of time and is shared between two or more actors in the domain. As the ontology defines the agreed semantics of the domain, all relevant content will be marked-up with knowledge according to the ontology. The definition of the ontology in turn depends primarily[2] on the content that has already been interpreted. Accordingly, content production and interpretation will drive the adaptation of the ontology infrastructure, and ontology adaptation will drive content interpretation and production.

In order to arrive at such a continuous 'hermeneutic cycle' of content and knowledge production and interpretation, a rich representation of domain knowledge and content features is needed. Here we propose an integrated approach that organizes content and knowledge in several layers:

- *content layer* (outermost layer)
  This layer consists of multilingual (text documents) and multimedia data (images, video and/or mixed image and text documents).
- *features layer* (1st inner layer)
  This layer consists of extracted features for the data in the content layer. For multilingual data, this ranges from comparatively informal feature vectors gathered by use of statistical methods to formalized descriptions of the content of text documents, typically extracted by use of natural language processing and information extraction methods. For multimedia data, this will be mostly limited to informal features as used in color histograms and similar.
- *feature association layer* (2nd inner layer)
  This layer consists of ontology-based representations of the multilingual and multimedia features also occurring in the features layer. While in the *features layer* features are associated with multilingual and multimedia data, in the *feature association layer* the features are associated with ontology classes and relations.
- *ontology layer* (central layer)
  This layer consists of ontology classes and relations, with which the data in the content layer is to be interpreted (i.e., annotated) by use of the extracted and represented features in the *features layer* and the *feature association layer*.

---

[2] Aside from more generic knowledge of the physical world, time, space, etc. that will be inherited from an upper-level ontology.

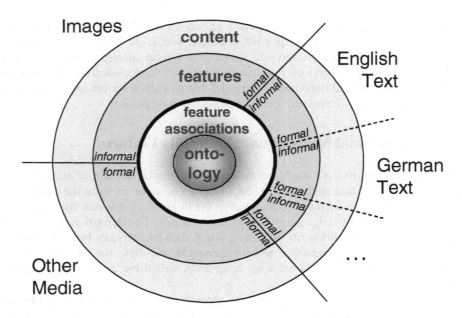

Fig. 1. Interacting Layers in Feature Extraction and Representation

3   Towards an Ontology-Based Representation of Multilingual and Multimedia Features

In the following, we describe how to represent multilingual and multimedia features in ontologies and how to link them to ontology concepts.

3.1   Representation of Multilingual and Multimedia Features

Multilingual features consist of a list of term variants - for each language covered by the ontology - with lexical and context information for each term:

- *language-ID*: ISO-based unique identifier for the language of each term
- *part-of-speech*: (possibly ISO-based) representation of the part of speech of the head of the term
- *morphological decomposition*: representation of the morphological structure (segments, head, modifiers) of a term
- *syntactic decomposition*: representation of the syntactic structure (segments, head, modifiers) of a term
- *statistical and/or grammatical context model*: representation of the linguistic context of a term in the form of N-grams, grammar rules or otherwise

Multimedia features will be represented by MPEG-7 descriptors (see also Petridis et al., 2004) for properties such as:

- *color*: color space, structure, layout; dominant color, scalable color
- *texture*: homogeneous texture, texture browsing, edge histogram
- *shape*: contour-based, region-based, 3-D, multiple-views

3.2 Annotating Ontology Classes with Multilingual and Multimedia Features

To represent terminology in different languages as well as multimedia features, we created an RDF/S-based domain knowledge representation introducing meta-class ClassWithFeats and meta-property PropertyWithFeats, as shown in Figure 2. Using meta-classes and meta-properties allows us to connect content features to classes and properties directly. In ontology tools such as Protégé (Noy et al., 2001), using ClassWithFeats as meta-class for a domain class results in additional widgets getting displayed along with the standard class widgets such as Name and Documentation. In these new widgets, the features of the corresponding class or property can be entered, populating the feat:lingFeat and feat:imgFeat properties for each class.

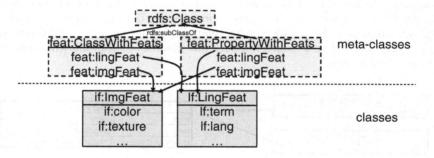

Fig. 2. ClassWithFeats and PropertyWithFeats

For instances, we attached the feat:lingFeat property to the root class of the domain ontology. This way every instance of the knowledge base can get annotated with linguistic information, e.g., allowing representation of language-dependent names. The same can be done with the feat:imgFeat property.

The integrated ontology-based feature representation we propose is based on ongoing work in the context of the SmartWeb[3] project on mobile Semantic Web access for intelligent information services in the soccer domain. The proposed feature representation is currently used in the SmartWeb ontology on sports events and related issues (see also section 5).

Figure 3 shows the ontology with example (domain) classes and associated linguistic and image features: the ontology contains the class o:FootballPlayer with subclasses o:Defender and o:Midfielder. All these classes are instances of the meta-class feat:ClassWithFeats which allows them to use the feature-association properties feat:lingFeat and feat:imgFeat.

---

[3] http://www.smartweb-project.de/

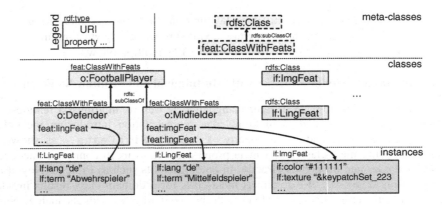

Fig. 3. Ontology and Examples (simplified) – *Defender, Midfielder*

Figure 4 depicts the part of our ontology in detail that deals with the representation of linguistic features, which is mainly the morphosyntactic decomposition of phrases and word forms down to stems, roots, morphemes, affixes etc. Apart from having linguistic properties like gender, number, part of speech, case, etc., word forms have the property `semantics` which is a back link into the ontology allowing semantics to be assigned to them.

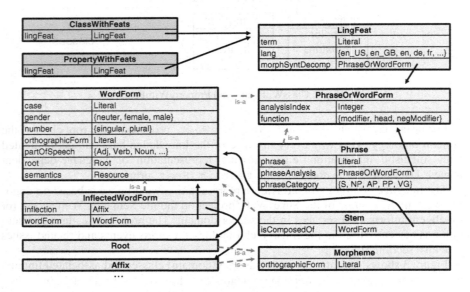

Fig. 4. Linguistic Features in Detail

Figure 5 shows a sample application of this part of the ontology, the decomposition of the German term "Fußballspielers" (= "of the football player"): `inst1` indicates that is an inflected word form (where the inflection is for forming the genitive) with stem "Fußballspieler" (inst2, "footballplayer"), which can be decomposed into two stems, "Fußball" (inst3 , "football") and "Spieler" (inst8 , "player"); this is recursively continued for "Fußball" which is composed of the stems "Fuß" and "Ball" (inst5 and inst7, "foot" and "ball").

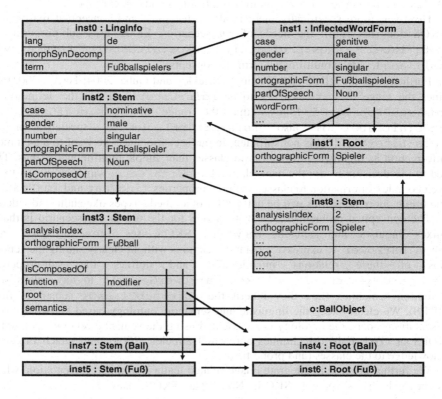

Fig. 5. Morphosyntatic Decomposition of "Fußballspielers"

4 Comparison with Related Work

The multilingual/multimedia lexicon model we propose has some overlap with related proposals, of which we discuss the most prominent ones here:

- SKOS: Simple Knowledge Organization System
- OntoWordNet
- LMF: Lexical Markup Framework

Of these, SKOS originates out of the W3C working group on "Best Practices for the Semantic Web"[4], whereas LMF is a working draft of the ISO working group on Language Resources Management TC37/SC4[5] (Francopoulo, 2006).

---

[4] http://www.w3.org/2001/sw/BestPractices/
[5] http://www.tc37sc4.org

4.1 SKOS - Simple Knowledge Organization System

Although there is some overlap with SKOS[6] (Miles and Brickley, 2005a, 2005b), the proposed representation is richer as it will include not only multilingual terms for classes (and properties) but also multimedia features and context models.

However, more specifically there is also a technical and conceptual reason why SKOS does not fulfill the needs of our scenario[7]: SKOS uses sub-properties of `rdfs:label` (`skos:prefLabel`, `skos:altLabel`) together with `xml:lang` to attach multilingual terms to concepts.

Furthermore, the RDFS specification[8] (Brickley and Guha, 2004; Hayes, 2004) defines the range of `rdfs:label` to be `rdfs:Literal`. From the definition of `rds:subPropertyOf` follows that the range of `skos:prefLabel` and `skos:altLabel` is also `rdfs:Literal` (or a specialization of `rdfs:Literal`). This is not sufficient in our scenario since we want to attach more information as linguistic information to classes than simple multilingual strings. This led to our decision to use the meta-class `ClassWithFeats`, which allows us to attach complex information to classes with the properties `lingFeat` and `imgFeat` (in the future, more properties will be defined for other media types like audio and video).

The conceptual problem we see with SKOS for the use in our scenario is that it mixes linguistic and semantic knowledge. SKOS uses `skos:broader` and `skos:narrower` to express "semantic" relations without clearly stating the semantics of these relations intentionally, and defines the sub-properties `skos:broaderGeneric` and `skos:narrowerGeneric` to have class subsumption semantics (i.e., they inherit the `rdfs:subClassOf` semantics from RDFS). We clearly keep the linguistic and semantic, ontology-based knowledge representations apart: the ontology is represented using the semantic relations defined in RDFS or OWL-Full[9] (McGuinnes and van Harmelen, 2004), and attach linguistic knowledge to the classes (and properties).

We further propose to integrate image-related features in this representation, which is beyond the scope of SKOS. Note that SKOS uses `foaf:depiction`, `skos:prefSymbol`, and `skos:altSymbol` to attach images to concepts, but not complex feature descriptions.

4.2 Wordnets and OntoWordNet

Our approach in effect integrates a domain-specific multilingual wordnet into the ontology, although also the wordnet model does not distinguish clearly between linguistic and semantic information - see e.g. (Miller et al., 1995) on WordNet and (Vossen, 1998) on EuroWordNet.

---

[6] http://www.w3.org/TR/swbp-skos-core-guide/
[7] In fact, our argumentation applies to all approaches based on `rdfs:label` and `xml:lang` to attach multilingual labels to classes and relations.
[8] http://www.w3.org/TR/rdf-schema/
[9] OWL Lite and OLW DL do not support meta-classes and meta-properties (see http://www.w3.org/TR/owl-features/)

Alternative lexicon models that are more similar to our approach include (Bateman et al., 1995; Alexa et al., 2002), but these concentrate on the definition of a top ontology for lexicons instead of text/image features for domain ontology classes and properties as in our case. This is also the main difference with the proposed OntoWordNet model (Gangemi et al., 2003), which aims at merging the foundational ontology DOLCE (Gangemi et al., 2002) with WordNet to provide the latter with a formal semantics.

4.3 LMF – Lexical Markup Framework

Closest to our goals is the LMF or Lexical Markup Framework by the ISO working group on Language Resources Management TC37/SC4. "The goals of LMF are to provide a common model for the creation and use of very large scale lexical resources, to manage the exchange of data between and among these resources, and to enable the merging of large numbers of different individual electronic resources to form large global electronic resources. ... The ultimate goal of LMF is to create a modular structure that will enable true content interoperability across all aspects of lexical resources."

The main difference with LMF and the lexicon model proposed here is the strict division of linguistic and semantic knowledge. In LMF these are integrated in the same model by way of a lexical semantics slot, whereas in our model all lexical semantics is to be found in the domain ontology - that is outside of the lexicon model per se. On top of this, our model allows also for the representation of non-linguistic, i.e. multimedia features.

Nevertheless, the aims and structure of LMF and our model are sufficiently similar to investigate ways of merging the two proposals. We envision this as a potential enrichment on both sides, as our model has a more principled approach to knowledge representation that builds directly on current standards in this area (i.e. RDFS), whereas the LMF model has a strong background in the representation of linguistic knowledge.

5 Applications

The integrated LingInfo approach allows for cross-lingual, cross-media feature extraction, representation and employment as follows:

- *text2image - cross-lingual acquisition of German content features by use of represented English content features*
  i.e., if we know which terms express a class in English then we can build a classifier for the classification of images that occur in the context of English terms for this class
- *image2text - cross-media acquisition of German content features by use of represented multimedia features*
  i.e., if we know which images represent instances for a specific class then we can extract German terms for this class from surrounding German text
- *text2text - cross-media acquisition of multimedia content features by use of represented English content features*

i.e., if we know which terms express a class in English and the context features (i.e. words) for these terms and possible translations into German then we can build a cross-lingual classifier for recognition of unseen German terms for this class

- *text2class, image2class - data-driven adaptation of domain knowledge representation for a class by use of represented English terminology*
  i.e., if we know which terms express a class in English and the context words for these terms then we can detect a change in the semantic model for this class by monitoring any change in the context words - similar with image feature models

5.1 Application of LingInfo in SmartWeb

LingInfo is developed and used within the SmartWeb project, which aims at the development of a complex multi-modal question answering and dialog system that derives answers from unstructured resources such as the Web, from automatically acquired knowledge bases and from web services.

A central component is SWIntO, the SmartWeb Integrated Ontology (Oberle et al. in prep.), which consists of three layers: the upper model DOLCE (Gangemi et al., 2002), the domain-independent model SUMO (Niles and Pease, 2001) the SportEvents ontology, focused mainly on soccer, and further task ontologies. The SportEvents ontology contains about 400 direct classes, all of which are provided with linguistic information as described above.

Enriching the ontology with linguistic information is an incremental process, by which some information can be derived semi-automatically from annotated corpora. In this way, lexicons (and grammars) of available tools are in effect tuned to the soccer domain and become fully integrated with the SmartWeb ontology. Alternatively, if such resources cannot be integrated into LingInfo (e.g. due to copyright problems), pointers may be used to refer to external resources.

Multimedia information is not yet being added to the ontology on a larger scale, but also here a semi-automatic approach will be explored that exploits automatically annotated image collections - where the annotation is performed on the basis of the textual context of the images (Buitelaar et al. 2006).

5.2 LingInfo in Information Extraction from Text

In the SmartWeb project, the LingInfo model is interfaced with the information extraction (IE) system SProUT (Drozdzynski et al., 2004). Based on the information encoded in LingInfo, we automatically extract gazetteer entries for named entities, with back-references to the ontology. For terms associated with concepts, we recompile the relevant parts of the ontology, including LingInfo, into a type hierarchy used in the IE system. Thus, LingInfo information can be used to consistently identify and mark up (inflected) occurrences of domain-relevant terms. The following example may illustrate this. It displays an excerpt of the SWIntO ontology that has been compiled into a type hierarchy defined in TDL[10], the representation language used by SProUT:

---

[10] Type Description Language – see (Krieger and Schäfer 1994) for details.

```
PlayerAction :< SportMatchAction.

SingleFootballPlayerAction :< PlayerAction.

FootballTeamAction :< PlayerAction.

GoalKeeperAction :< SingleFootballPlayerAction.

AnyPlayerAction :< SingleFootballPlayerAction.
```

Properties associated with these concepts are translated to TDL *attributes* of the corresponding *types*, e.g. the property inMatch of the SWIntO class Sport-MatchAction translates to the TDL attribute INMATCH that is inherited by all subtypes of the TDL type SportMatchAction. The SWIntO property CommittedBy that is defined for the SWIntO class SingleFootballPlayerAction translates to a corresponding TDL attribute COMMITTEDBY of the TDL type SingleFootballPlayerAction, and is again inherited by all its subtypes:

```
SportMatchAction := swinto_out & [INMATCH Football].

SingleFootballPlayerAction := swinto_out & [COMMITTEDBY
FootballPlayer].
```

Multilingual (e.g. German) terms that are encoded as LingInfo instances are compiled into TDL lexical types:

```
"Teamaktion" :< FootballTeamAction.

"Spieleraktion" :< PlayerAction.

"Torwartaktion" :< GoalkeeperAction.

"Gesperrt" :< Banned.
```

SProUT extraction patterns can thus be triggered by lexical types, and define output structures that correspond directly to the classes and properties of the SWIntO ontology. For instance, the extraction rule below matches an extraction pattern for the SWIntO (SportEvents) class BanEvent with attributes CommittedBy and In-Match that is triggered for instance by the German LingInfo term "gesperrt". Example sentences from the SmartWeb development corpus[11] to which this rule applies are as follows:

"... ist Petrow für die Partie gegen Schweden gesperrt." ("... has Petrow been banned for the match against Sweden")

"... ist David Trezeguet von der FIFA für zwei Spiele gesperrt worden." ("... has David Tezeguet been banned by FIFA for two matches")

---

[11] See also http://www.dfki.de/sw-lt/olp2_dataset/

```
banned_player :>

@seek(player) & [IMPERSONATEDBY #player, INMATCHTEAM #team1]

(@seek(weekday_only) & [DOFW #dofw])? (token{0,2}
 @seek(soccer_institutions))?  token{0,3}
 @seek(game_teams) & [INTOURNAMENT #tour, TEAM2 #team2] morph & [STEM banned, SURFACE #event])

-> playeraction &
    [SPORTACTIONTYPE #event,
     COMMITTEDBY footballplayer &
          [IMPERSONATEDBY #player],
     INMATCH match &
          [INTOURNAMENT #tour, MATCHTYPE #match, TEAM1 #team1, TEAM2 #team2]].
```

Fig. 6. SProUT Extraction Rule for the SWIntO Class `BanEvent`

6   Conclusions and Future Work

In this paper we proposed a model for the representation of multilingual and multimedia content features in ontologies, which will allow for more efficient automatic processing of textual and image data in knowledge markup, ontology learning and other applications such as dialog processing, summarization, machine translation, etc.

The model we propose clearly separates domain knowledge on sets of objects from linguistic- and image-related knowledge on terms and images used for referring to such objects. In this way, our proposal extends traditional knowledge representation models used in ontology definition as well as current models used in defining computational lexicons (i.e. Wordnets) and thesauri (i.e. SKOS).

In future work we also intend to expand the model towards the representation of multilingual and multimedia content features for instances. In this way, the knowledge base for a given ontology will be able to represent the linguistic and/or image context for extracted facts.

Acknowledgements

This research has been supported in part by the SmartWeb project, which is funded by the German Ministry of Education and Research under grant 01 IMD01 A.

References

M. Alexa, B. Kreissig, M. Liepert, K. Reichenberger, L. Rostek, K. Rautmann, W. Scholze-Stubenrecht, S. Stoye *The Duden Ontology: an Integrated Representation of Lexical and Ontological Information* In: Proc. of the OntoLex Workshop at LREC, Spain, May 2002.

J. A. Bateman, R. Henschel and F. Rinaldi *Generalized Upper Model 2.0: documentation* Report of GMD/Institut für Integrierte Publikations- und Informationssysteme, Darmstadt, Germany, 1995.

D. Brickley, R.V. Guha (eds.) RDF Vocabulary Description Language 1.0: RDF Schema. World Wide Web Consortium, 2004.

P. Buitelaar, Th. Eigner, Th. Declerck *OntoSelect: A Dynamic Ontology Library with Support for Ontology Selection* In: Proc. of the Demo Session at the International Semantic Web Conference, Hiroshima, Japan, Nov. 2004.

P. Buitelaar, P. Cimiano, S. Racioppa and M. Siegel *Ontology-based Information Extraction with SOBA* In: Proc. of the International Conference on Language Resources and Evaluation (LREC), 2006.

W. Drozdzynski, H.-U. Krieger, J. Piskorski, U. Schäfer, F. Xu *Shallow Processing with Unification and Typed Feature Structures - Foundations and Applications.* In Künstliche Intelligenz, 1/2004.

G. Francopoulo, M. George, N. Calzolari, M. Monachini, N. Bel, M. Pet, C. Soria *Lexical Markup Framework (LMF)* In: Proc. of the International Conference on Language Resources and Evaluation (LREC), 2006.

A. Gangemi, Guarino, N., Masolo, C., Oltramari, A. and L. Schneider. 2002. *Sweetening Ontologies with DOLCE.* In Proceedings of the 13th International Conference on Knowledge Engineering and Knowledge Management (EKAW), Siguenza, Spain, pp. 166-181.

A. Gangemi, Navigli R, Velardi P *The OntoWordNet Project: extension and axiomatization of conceptual relations in WordNet.* Meersman R, et al. (eds.), Proceedings of ODBASE03 Conference, Springer, 2003.

P. Hayes (ed.) *RDF Semantics.* World Wide Web Consortium, 2004.

H.-U. Krieger and U. Schafer *TDL---a type description language for constraint-based grammars* In Proceedings of the 15th International Conference on Computational Linguistics (COLING), pp. 893-899, 1994.

D.L. McGuinness, F. van Harmelen (eds.) *OWL Web Ontology Language Overview.* W3C Recommendation 10 February 2004.

A. Miles, D. Brickley (ed.) *SKOS Core Vocabulary Specification.* W3C Working Draft 10 May 2005a.

A. Miles, D. Brickley (eds.) *SKOS Core Guide.* W3C Working Draft 10 May 2005b.

G. A. Miller *WORDNET: A Lexical Database for English.* Communications of ACM (11): 39-41, 1995.

I. Niles and Pease, A. *Towards a standard upper ontology.* In: FOIS '01: Proceedings of the international conference on Formal Ontology in Information Systems, ACM Press (2001)

N. F. Noy, M. Sintek, S. Decker, M. Crubezy, R. W. Fergerson, & M. A. Musen. *Creating Semantic Web Contents with Protege-2000.* IEEE Intelligent Systems 16(2):60-71, 2001.

D. Oberle, A. Ankolekar, P. Hitzler, P. Cimiano, C. Schmidt, M. Weiten, B. Loos, R. Porzel, H.-P. Zorn, M. Micelli, M. Sintek, M. Kiesel, B. Mougouie, S. Vembu, S. Baumann, M. Romanelli, P. Buitelaar, R. Engel, D. Sonntag, N. Reithinger, F. Burkhardt, J. Zhou *DOLCE ergo SUMO: On Foundational and Domain Models in SWIntO (SmartWeb Integrated Ontology),* in preparation.

Ch. K. Ogden and I. A. Richards *The meaning of meaning - A study of the influence of language upon thought and of the science of symbolism.* London: Kegan Paul, Trench, Trubner & Co., 1923.

K. Petridis, I. Kompatsiaris, M. G. Strintzis, S. Bloehdorn, S. Handschuh, S. Staab and N. Simou *Knowledge Representation for Semantic Multimedia Content Analysis and Reasoning* In: Proc. of the European Workshop on the Integration of Knowledge, Semantics and Digital Media Technology, Royal Statistical Society, London, 25-26 Nov. 2004.

Vossen P. (ed). EuroWordNet: A Multilingual Database with Lexical Semantic Networks. Kluwer Academic Publishers, Dordrecht, 1998

Semantic Network Analysis of Ontologies

Bettina Hoser[1], Andreas Hotho[2], Robert Jäschke[2,3],
Christoph Schmitz[2], and Gerd Stumme[2,3]

[1] Chair of Informationservices and Electronic Markets, School of Economics and Business
Engineering, Universität Karlsruhe (TH), Zirkel 2, D–76128 Karlsruhe, Germany
[2] Knowledge & Data Engineering Group, Department of Mathematics and Computer Science,
University of Kassel, Wilhelmshöher Allee 73, D–34121 Kassel, Germany
[3] Research Center L3S, Expo Plaza 1, D–30539 Hannover, Germany

Abstract. A key argument for modeling knowledge in ontologies is the easy re-use and re-engineering of the knowledge. However, current ontology engineering tools provide only basic functionalities for analyzing ontologies. Since ontologies can be considered as graphs, graph analysis techniques are a suitable answer for this need. Graph analysis has been performed by sociologists for over 60 years, and resulted in the vivid research area of Social Network Analysis (SNA). While social network structures currently receive high attention in the Semantic Web community, there are only very few SNA applications, and virtually none for analyzing the structure of ontologies.

We illustrate the benefits of applying SNA to ontologies and the Semantic Web, and discuss which research topics arise on the edge between the two areas. In particular, we discuss how different notions of centrality describe the core content and structure of an ontology. From the rather simple notion of degree centrality over betweenness centrality to the more complex eigenvector centrality, we illustrate the insights these measures provide on two ontologies, which are different in purpose, scope, and size.

1   Introduction

A key argument for modeling knowledge in ontologies is the easy re-use and re-engineering of the knowledge. However, beside consistency checking, current ontology engineering tools provide only basic functionalities for analyzing ontologies. Since ontologies can be considered as (labeled, directed) graphs, graph analysis techniques are a promising tool. Sociologists have performed graph analysis since for over 60 years. In the late 1970ies, Social Network Analysis (SNA) emerged as a research area out of this work. Its aim is to analyze the structures of social communities. Typical applications include the analysis of relationships like friendship, communication patterns (e. g., phone call graphs), and the distribution of attendants over several events. While social structures are currently a steeply rising topic within the Semantic Web community (e. g., friend-of-a-friend networks,[1] social tagging systems like del.icio.us.org or www.bibsonomy.org, or semantics-based P2P networks [21]), Social Network *Analysis* has only been applied marginally up to now on ontologies and the Semantic Web.

---

[1] http://www.foaf-project.org/

Y. Sure and J. Domingue (Eds.): ESWC 2006, LNCS 4011, pp. 514–529, 2006.
© Springer-Verlag Berlin Heidelberg 2006

In this paper, we will discuss the use of SNA for analyzing ontologies and the Semantic Web. While the SNA community has already discovered the internet and the Web as fruitful application domains for their techniques a while ago (e. g., analysing the link structure of the internet [16], and email traffic [17, 22, 25]), SNA applications for the Semantic Web are only emerging slowly. We advocate here a systematic development of *Semantic Network Analyis (SemNA)*, as the adoption of SNA to ontologies and the Semantic Web. In this paper, we show that the application of both basic and advanced SNA techniques to ontologies provide a powerful tool for analyzing the structure of the ontology. We adapt SNA tools to ontology analysis, and discuss the findings. In particular, we discuss how different notions of centrality describe the core content and structure of an ontology. From the rather simple notion of degree centrality over betweenness centrality to the more complex eigenvector centrality based on Hermitian matrices, we illustrate the insights these measures provide on two ontologies, which are different in purpose, scope, and size. The results may be used for selecting the right ontology for a specific application, as well as for re-engineering ontologies.

SemNA is a sub-area of Semantic Web Mining [4]. that addresses the mining of the Semantic Web. To this end, we consider ontologies as (both vertex- and edge-)labeled, directed graphs. As we will discuss below, the existence of different types of nodes and edges (which are reflected in the labels) is a problem for standard SNA approaches. We will discuss solutions for this problem. In this paper, we present two selected applications, and discuss the use of different SNA techniques for analyzing ontologies. The examples will illustrate the deep insights we were able to gain from the two ontologies.

Testcases: SWRC and SUMO ontologies. The SWRC ontology[2] provides a vocabulary about publications, authors, academic staff and the like. It consists of 54 concepts and 70 relations. Figure 1 shows a graphical representation of the ontology. Rectangles represent concepts, relations are shown as rounded boxes.

We selected the SWRC ontology as our first example, as it is a handy size, and as we know its structure rather well, since some of the authors have contributed to its construction. We are thus able to validate the resulting SNA findings (which were computed independently by the non-ontology author) with our insight in the history of the SWRC ontology. The promising results (which were also surprising for the authors) motivated us to consider a larger ontology, the SUMO ontology, where we only knew about its general purpose, but no details about its structure nor its content.

The aim of the Suggested Upper Merged Ontology (SUMO)[3] is to express the most basic and universal concepts for creating a framework for merging ontologies of different domains. With its 630 concepts and 236 relations, SUMO is significantly larger than the SWRC ontology. This information is about all we knew about SUMO when performing our analysis. We are thus in exactly the situation of an ontology engineer who wants to gain deeper insights to a previously unknown ontology.

Organization of the paper. This paper is organized as follows. In the next section, we will provide a brief overview over the history and main lines of research in Social Network Analysis. In Section 3, we will apply a representative selection of SNA

---

[2] http://ontobroker.semanticweb.org/ontologies/swrc-onto-2001-12-11.oxml
[3] http://www.ontologyportal.org/

techniques to a representative set of ontologies with different structures. In particular, we will analyse the most central parts of the ontology, and will study the eigenvector system assigned to the ontology. Section 4 addresses further applications of SNA for the Semantic Web. In the conclusion, we summarize our experiences, and will discuss the research issues that arise when applying SNA to ontologies and the Semantic Web.

2   Social Network Analysis

Already as early as the 1930's Moreno [19] started to describe social relationships within groups using so called *sociograms*. A sociogram is a graph where the members of an observed population are represented as nodes and the relationships among members as edges. The step from modelling relationships between entities of a graph to a structural analysis of these graphs started by using the results from graph theory as early as the 1960's. Pioneers in this field are Harary, Norman and Cartwright [7]. To use the tools of graph theory to analyze and thus describe structures of social networks and to interpret these results in the context of anthropological and sociological contexts was the major achievement of these researchers. The notion of *Social Network Analysis (SNA)* was used to subsume all tools for methodological as well as functional analysis of such group structures.

The two aspects of SNA, the functional aspect and the structural aspect, each highlight a different perspective of research. The functional view focuses on how the function of a network is determined by the structure of a given network. Thus the question of flow between nodes is very prominent. The structural view on the other hand is more interested in the question of structure per se and what statements about a given network can be made based on the analysis of structure alone. Both aspects can be viewed separately, but for some objects of interest, such as organizations, a combined approach may be more appropriate. Since the use of SNA tools in the semantic web environment is just starting out, we will focus in this paper on the structuralist view on SNA, in particular on different notions of centrality. The concept of centrality has many different branches. Just to name a few: in/out degree centrality, betweenness centrality, information centrality, eigenvector centrality. For a good overview see [9].

Wasserman and Faust [26, p.205-219] describe to a great extent the history of rank prestige index, which is an eigenvector centrality based concept. This index is based on the idea, that the rank of a group member depends on the rank of the members he or she is connected to. Stated in mathematical terms this yields the eigenvalue equation (for an eigenvalue equal to 1). The components of the principal eigenvector are the rank prestige indices of each group member. This concept is implemented in the hub-and-authority algorithms of Kleinberg [15] and also in the PageRank algorithm proposed by Page and Brin [6].

There have been different approaches to the analysis of unbalanced graphs. All concepts work very well on undirected and unweighted graphs. But if none of these restrictions apply for a given graph, difficulties arise. Freeman [10] proposed to use the possibility to split any asymmetric square matrix into its symmetric and skew-symmetric part, perform a singular value decomposition of the skew-symmetric matrix, and showed, that the result could be interpreted as a ranking of dominance. Tyler et al. [25] could identify subgroups in unbalanced email networks by analyzing betweenness centrality in the form of inter-community edges with a large betweenness value. These edges are then removed until the graph decomposes into separate communities, thus re-organizing the graph structure.

Barnett and Rice [2] showed that the transformation of asymmetrical data into matrices that avoid negative eigenvalues may result in the loss of information. This is one of the reasons why we will transform the adjacency matrix into a Hermitian matrix in Subsection 3.3.

Beside considering the direction of links as discussed, the notion of a graph can be refined in several ways. One-mode graphs consider just one type of nodes (e. g., participants of an email network), while two-mode graphs distinguish between two types of nodes (but still have only one type of edges), forming thus a bipartite graph (e. g., persons and events they are visiting). More general, n-mode graphs distinguish n types of nodes. The edges may also be typed. Extending the definition of [26], we call a *n-mode multigraph with k edge types* a graph where the nodes may be labeled with n different types and the edges with k different labels. This reflects exactly the structure of an (RDFS-based) ontology. Since the interpretation of such complex graphs is more difficult, one often tries to preprocess the data in order to obtain a 1- or 2-mode graph with only one relation, i. e., with one type of edges. Of course the chosen preprocessing transformation has to be taken into account when interpreting the results.

To analyze networks more easily, several software tools have been developed. These packages include, but are not limited to UCINet,[4] Pajek,[5] and Visone.[6] There are also packages for R[7] and also some implementations in Java.[8] For a good overview on SNA and its history refer to Wasserman and Faust [26] and Freeman [11].

3   Network Analysis of Ontologies

Ontologies can be considered as n-mode multi-graphs with k edge types. As argued above, n-mode multi-graphs with k edge types are hard to analyze when n is larger than 2 or 3, and k is larger than 1. Therefore we follow the usual approach of projecting them first to a 1- or 2-mode 1-plex network. In the sequel of this section, we will first illustrate the benefit of some basic SNA approaches, before performing a more sophisticated analysis, based on the analysis of the eigenvectors of the adjacency matrix. To show the diversity of results that can be expected from such an analysis, we will apply the basic techniques to two different ontologies: the SWRC and the SUMO ontology, which differ in purpose, scope, and size.

3.1   Preprocessing the Ontologies

As SNA works on graphs, we first transform the ontology into a suitable graph. As in all knowledge discovery (KDD) applications (and probably more so than in the average

---

[4] http://www.analytictech.com/ucinet.htm

[5] http://vlado.fmf.uni-lj.si/pub/networks/pajek/

[6] http://www.visone.info/

[7] http://www.stat.ucl.ac.be/ISdidactique/Rhelp/library/sna/html/00Index.html

[8] http://jung.sourceforge.net/index.html

KDD scenario), the interpretation of the final results is highly sensitive to the decisions made during preprocessing.

A standard approach (which we use also) of turning n-mode networks with k edge types into a (directed or undirected) graph is to collect all types of nodes into just one set of nodes, and to ignore the edge types.[9] We will keep the typing information, though, and refer to it during the analysis.

As a first step, we set up a directed graph for the input ontology in the following way: Technical artifacts were pruned from the ontology. In the KAON ontology API,[10] which we used, these comprise the artificial root concept present in all ontologies, and entities for lexical information such as labels and word stems. Each concept and each property became a node in the graph. Between two concepts C_1 and C_2, a directed edge (C_1, C_2) was added if C_1 is a direct subconcept of C_2. For each property node, edges are added from the each domain concept to the property node, and from the property node to each range concept (unless the property is scalar-valued or untyped), as well as from the property to each superproperty.

The adjacency matrix A of this graph has one row and one column for each node. If there is an edge from the ith to the jth node, then $a_{ij} := 1$, else $a_{ij} := 0$. This matrix is the subject of our subsequent analysis. For the SWRC ontology, A has thus 54+70 rows and 54+70 columns, with entries 0 and 1. The matrix for the SUMO ontology is structured in the same way, with $630 + 236 = 866$ rows and columns in total.

3.2 Basic Methods of Network Analysis

The intuitive approach to analyze a network, represented as a graph $G := (V, E)$ with nodes (or vertices) $v \in V$ and edges $e \in E$, is to start with the number of connections each node has. A node that has many connections is presumed to be important, while a node without connections is presumed to be irrelevant. This concept is called *degree centrality*. In the adjacency matrix A the degree centrality c_k of a vertex in an undirected graph can be calculated as the row or column sum $c_k = \sum_l^n a_{kl}$ of A. If the connection between two nodes has no directional preference this is just called *degree*. If the relationship has an inherent direction, like in 'person A called person B' then the degree is categorized into *in-* (column sums) and *outdegree* (row sums) depending on whether the connection ends at a node or starts at a given node.

The *betweenness centrality* is the (normalized) number of shortest paths between any two nodes that pass through the given node. The betweenness centrality provides often a high degree of information, as it describes the location of a node in the graph in a global sense, while in- and outdegree consider the direct neighbor nodes only.

Based on the degree centrality we can define the *density* d of a network. Let the network describe a non-directional relationship between nodes, then the density is defined as the number of existing connections divided by the number $N := \frac{|V|(|V|-1)}{2}$ of all possible edges as $d = \frac{\sum_{kl} a_{kl}}{N}$. Thus a completely connected network has a density

---

[9] A more frequent way for handling different edge types is to perform a sequence of analyses, one for each edge type. For ontologies, however, this approach is not suitable, as most edge types (beside 'is_a' and eventually 'part_of') appear only once.

[10] http://kaon.semanticweb.org/

of 1. In the directed case one has to keep in mind that at most two connections are possible between two nodes. Thus the density d_d becomes $d_d = \frac{\sum_{kl} a_{kl}}{|V|(|V|-1)}$. This concept is not useful anymore when multiple connections are allowed or when the connections become valued or weighted, because no total number of possible connections can be given in that case.

Another measure of how well a graph is connected is its *diameter*. For all pairs A, B of nodes, we calculate the shortest path from A to B, and take then the maximum over their lengths. The well-known *small-world phenomenon* states that social networks have a small diameter. Diameter and density are used for comparing networks.

Global comparison of SWRC and SUMO. To analyze the given ontologies, we calculated for each of them the diameter and the density of the network. The results are shown in Table 1. These indices were generated using Pajek.

Table 1. Size, diameter, and density of SWRC and SUMO

	# concepts	# relations	diameter	density
SWRC	54	70	16	0.015
SUMO	630	236	27	0.0024

Compared to typical social networks, the density of the SWRC ontology (0.015) is very sparse. SUMO has an even sparser density with 0.0024. The fact that the difference between both ontologies is approx. one magnitude, which is in the same ratio as their difference in size, indicates that the concepts in both ontologies have a similar number of properties attached in average. It might be interesting to analyze more ontologies to check whether this is some kind of constant stemming from ontology engineering principles. We assume that ontologies are scale-free networks because of their construction.

For studying both ontologies in more details, we computed as next step for all their nodes indegree, outdegree and betweenness centrality.

The SWRC ontology in detail. Table 2 shows the indegrees, outdegrees and betweenness centralities of the nodes in the graph extracted from the SWRC ontology. While the degrees could still be read from Fig. 1, the betweenness centrality has to be listed.

Considering the degrees only, one observes that the BibTeX part of the ontology was modeled with the highest level of detail: BibTeX-related concepts such as 'Book' and 'InCollections' have high outdegrees (i. e. a large number of properties) but no indegree, while the related properties such as 'author', 'month', and 'address' have large indegree.

Properties which apply to all kinds of publications, such as 'title' and 'year', have a low degree, as they are attached to 'Publication' only and are inherited by its subclasses. This is a result of the way we set up the adjacency matrix. An alternative way of setting up the matrix is to model explicitly also the inherited attributes. This is an example for the fact that the modeling step has to be taken into account for the interpretation of the SNA results.

The betweenness centrality gives us a more global description of the roles of nodes in the graph. For SWRC, it returns first of all 'Organization' and 'Project', followed in short distance by Academic Staff' and 'Research Topic'. These are thus the concepts

Table 2. Degree and betweenness centrality of concepts (# 1–54) and relations (# 55–124)

#	Label	d_o	d_i	b_c	#	Label	d_o	d_i	b_c	#	Label	d_o	d_i	b_c
1	Academic Staff	10	4	0.102	43	Research Topic	3	1	0.079	85	homepage	0	1	0.
2	Administrative Staff	1	0	0.	44	SoftwareComponent	2	0	0.	86	howpublished	0	2	0.
3	Article	7	0	0.	45	Software Project	2	0	0.	87	institution	0	0	0.
4	Assistant Professor	1	0	0.	46	Student	2	3	0.027	88	Is About	1	1	0.078
5	Associate Professor	1	0	0.	47	Technical Report	3	1	0.014	89	IsWorkedOnBy	1	1	0.069
6	Association	1	0	0.	48	TechnicalStaff	1	0	0.	90	Isbn	0	1	0.
7	Book	13	0	0.	49	Thesis	6	2	0.01	91	Journal	0	1	0.
8	Booklet	5	0	0.	50	Topic	1	1	0.	92	Keywords	0	1	0.
9	Conference	2	0	0.	51	Undergraduate	1	0	0.	93	Location	0	2	0.
10	Department	2	0	0.	52	University	3	2	0.041	94	member	0	2	0.
11	Development Project	1	1	0.004	53	Unpublished	3	0	0.	95	member Of PC	1	1	0.01
12	Employee	2	4	0.025	54	Workshop	2	0	0.	96	month	0	11	0.
13	Enterprise	1	0	0.	55	Abstract	0	1	0.	97	name	0	6	0.
14	Event	6	9	0.019	56	address	0	9	0.	98	Note	0	1	0.
15	Exhibition	1	0	0.	57	Affiliation	1	1	0.019	99	number	0	6	0.
16	Faculty Member	1	3	0.013	58	AtEvent	1	1	0.	100	organization	0	4	0.
17	Full Professor	1	0	0.	59	author	0	10	0.	101	organizer Or Chair Of	1	1	0.01
18	Graduate	1	1	0.016	60	booktitle	0	2	0.	102	Pages	0	4	0.
19	In Book	13	0	0.	61	carried Out By	1	1	0.009	103	participant	1	1	0.001
20	In Collection	14	0	0.	62	carriesOut	1	1	0.033	104	phone	0	1	0.
21	In Proceedings	12	0	0.	63	Chapter	0	2	0.	105	Photo	0	1	0.
22	Institute	3	0	0.	64	cooperate With	0	2	0.	106	Price	0	1	0.
23	Lecture	2	0	0.	65	Date	0	2	0.	107	product	1	1	0.001
24	Lecturer	1	0	0.	66	Dealt With In	1	1	0.004	108	projectInfo	1	1	0.009
25	Manager	1	0	0.	67	Describes Project	1	1	0.004	109	publication	0	2	0.
26	Manual	6	0	0.	68	Developed By	1	1	0.017	110	Publisher	0	5	0.
27	Master Thesis	1	0	0.	69	develops	1	1	0.006	111	publishes	1	1	0.01
28	Meeting	4	1	0.001	70	edition	0	4	0.	112	School	1	1	0.012
29	Misc	3	0	0.	71	editor	0	6	0.	113	series	0	8	0.
30	Organization	8	10	0.134	72	Email	0	1	0.	114	source	0	1	0.
31	Person	7	5	0.024	73	employs	1	1	0.013	115	has student	1	1	0.002
32	PhDStudent	4	1	0.024	74	Event Title	0	1	0.	116	Studies At	1	1	0.024
33	Ph DThesis	1	0	0.	75	fax	0	1	0.	117	Supervises	1	1	0.023
34	Proceedings	9	0	0.	76	financedBy	1	1	0.009	118	supervisor	1	1	0.006
35	Product	2	3	0.017	77	Finances	1	1	0.033	119	TechnicalReport	1	1	0.017
36	Project	7	7	0.12	78	Given By	1	1	0.	120	Title	0	2	0.
37	Project Meeting	1	0	0.	79	Has Part Event	1	1	0.	121	Type	0	3	0.
38	Project Report	2	0	0.	80	Has Parts	0	3	0.	122	Volume	0	6	0.
39	Publication	5	14	0.022	81	hasPrice	0	1	0.	123	Works AtProject	0	2	0.
40	Report	2	2	0.005	82	head	0	2	0.	124	Year	0	1	0.
41	Research Group	3	1	0.01	83	Head Of	1	1	0.011		Mean (Degree)	1.82	1.82	–
42	Research Project	1	1	0.004	84	head Of Group	1	1	0.008		Std (Degree)	2.84	2.55	–

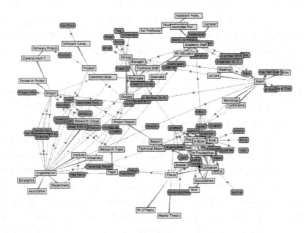

Fig. 1. The SWRC Ontology

that play a 'bridging role' in SWRC; they are used for describing (chains of) other objects (these are the incoming edges), and they are described by (chains of) other objects (the outgoing edges). From a database perspective, these are typical candidates for joins in a query.

Table 3. Highest out- and indegrees of SUMO concepts

	Outdegree	Indegree		Outdegree	Indegree
Process	20	10	BinaryObject	3	102
Object	15	21	AsymmetricRelation	2	71
RealNumber	13	15	UnaryFunction	3	54

The SUMO ontology in detail. We also computed the list of in, out and between degrees of the concepts and relations of the SUMO ontology. Due to space restrictions, we omit this list. The means of in- and outdegree (which are obviously equal, as each outgoing edge has to go in somewhere) are at 2.07. The standard deviation is 1.67 for the outdegrees, and 5.8 for the indegrees. The large difference of the standard deviations indicates a heterogeneity in the way of modeling.

When looking at the concepts and relations with out- and indegrees differing largely from the mean, this heterogeneity can be explained. The highest indegree has the concept 'BinaryPredicate' ($d_i = 102$), and the highest outdegree has the concept 'Process' ($d_o = 20$). The former shows that this technical notions is important for the designers of the ontology. However, this concept is conceptually not part of the domain of interest of the ontology, but rather a meta-construct. If the KR language permitted different arity relations, this would be modeled with language constructs and not by reification. The latter, on the other hand, indicates that 'Process', which is indeed a concept of the domain of interest, is modelled in a high level of detail by providing many properties that a process can have. As in the SWRC ontology, the betweenness centrality emphasizes more on the conceptual part of the ontology: the top node according to this measure is 'Object', followed by 'Formula', 'Entity', 'Physical', 'List', 'Process'. These are the central nodes of the SUMO ontology.

3.3 Eigensystem Analysis

Compared to the centrality measures described so far, the eigensystem of the adjacency matrix provides an overall view of the network, while still allowing a very detailed structure analysis of its parts.

Eigenvector centrality measurements have become a standard procedure in the analysis of group structures. Mostly symmetric (dichotomized) data has been used. Bonacich and Lloyd [5] present an introduction of the use of eigenvector-like measurements of centrality for asymmetric data. The analysis of directed, weighted, asymmetric relationships within a social network poses some difficulties. In this paper we will use a method based on the status (rank prestige) index method [26, p.205-219], that was adapted by the first author to complex adjacency matrices. We sketch the principal approach here (the technical details are presented in [13] and [14]) and adapt it to the analysis of ontologies.

In the following, we consider an ontology as a network which can be modeled as a directed, weighted graph $G = (V, E)$ with V denoting the set of nodes or members and E denoting the set of edges, links or communications between different members. Self references (loops) are excluded.

We use the following construction rules for a complex adjacency matrix H of the initial graph G: First, we construct a square complex adjacency matrix C with n nodes from the possibly weighted real valued adjacency matrix A of graph G by $C = A + iA^t$

with $a_{kl} = m + ip$ where m is the number of outbound edges (or equivalently the weight of the outbound edge) from node k to node l, p is the number of inbound edges (or equivalently the weight of the inbound edge) from node l to node k, and i is representing the imaginary unit ($i^2 = -1$). As can be seen, $c_{kl} = i\overline{c_{lk}}$ holds. Then we rotate C by multiplying it with $e^{-i\frac{\pi}{4}}$ in order to obtain a Hermitian matrix H, i.e., $H := C \cdot e^{-i\frac{\pi}{4}}$. For the proof see [14].

The fact that the resulting matrix is Hermitian has the advantage that it has full rank and thus a complete orthogonal eigenbasis can be found. The consequence is that H can be represented by a Fourier sum as the sum of all orthogonal projectors $P_k = \mathbf{x_k x_k^*}$, weighted by the corresponding eigenvalue λ_k: $H = \sum_{k=1}^{n} \lambda_k P_k$. Since all eigenvalues are real, they can be sorted by absolute value. In addition the eigenvalue can be used to calculate the covered data variance. These characteristics can be used to analyze a network structure at different levels of relevance as will be shown later in this paper.

Under this similarity transformation the coordinate independent characteristics of the original directional patterns are kept, no information is lost. For instance, more outbound than inbound links lead to a negative sign of the imaginary part of h_{kl}, while more inbound than outbound links lead to a positive sign of the imaginary part of h_{kl}. Now one can analyze the eigensystem of the matrix H in order to gain insights into the structure of the underlying ontology.

Eigensystem analysis of the SWRC ontology. We start by using the adjacency matrix A for the SWRC ontology from subsection 3.2, and construct the matrix H as described above. This matrix is the subject of further examination.

Let us first have a look at the distribution of the eigenvalues of H as shown in Fig. 2. The diagram suggests a symmetry in the spectrum. This indicates that major components of the network are star like in structure. As the concept hierarchy of SWRC is a tree, this hierarchy has a snowflake structure if considered as graph. Hence our observation that stars are predominant indicates that the concept hiararchy has a more important influence on the overall structure of the SWRC ontology than the non-hierarchical relationships.

Fig. 3 displays the cumulative covered variance of the ontology. One can see that the first two eigenvalues cover already 29 % of the variance of the system, that it has a clear

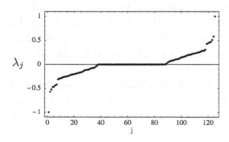

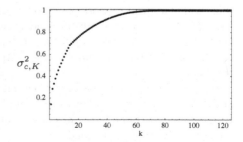

Fig. 2. Eigenspectrum of the ontology sorted by value

Fig. 3. Cumulative covered variance $\sigma_{c,K}^2$ of the SWRC ontology by eigenvalues λ_k

distance to the following eigenvalue, and that the first 14 eigenvalues cover approx. 70 % of the overall variance. The remaining eigenvalues contribute marginally only.

In Fig. 4 we now take a more detailed look at the eigenvectors and their components. The lefthand side gives the eigenvalues of each eigenvector, the righthand side gives covered data variance, each eigenvector is represented horizontally with the components numbered 1 through 125 on the bottom, and each eigenvector component is represented as a colored (or gray scaled) field.

The eigenvector components are complex valued, indicating in the phase of the complex number the direction of the connection with respect to the central node, and in the absolute value the relevance of the node in this eigenvector. The color representation lends itself naturally. The absolute value of the component is given by the brightness of the colored field. In gray scales an absolute value of 0 or near 0 is black, while an absolute value close to 1 is bright or has a saturated color. The phase of the complex number is represented by color where a phase of 0 is given as red and counter clockwise $\frac{\pi}{4}$ is yellow, $\frac{\pi}{2}$ is yellow-green, $\frac{3}{4}\pi$ green, $-\pi$ cyan, $-\frac{3}{4}\pi$ blue, $-\frac{\pi}{2}$ blue-magenta, $-\frac{\pi}{4}$ magenta and coming back to red. Thus for example the field with the coordinates 1.0, 39 is bright red which indicates an eigenvalue with high absolute value and phase 0.

By checking for the largest eigenvector component in each of the eigenvectors (colored red) corresponding to these eigenvalues we can see which concept/relation of the ontology is most central: In the first eigenvector (i. e., the lowest row in Fig. 4, with eigenvalue $+1$), the brightest color is in column 39, which is the concept 'Publication'. The fact that the same column shows in the eigenvector for the negative of the eigenvalue (i. e., in the second row from below, with eigenvalue -1) the same phase (as it is red as well) indicates that the concept 'Publication' is the center of a star like structure. The concept 'Organization' (= column 29) follows (at some distance) with the third and fourth eigenvector. This confirms that publications were in the key focus of the developers of SWRC – a finding we were already pointed to when analysing the in- and outdegrees in the previous subsection. In fact, this fits with the history of the development of the SWRC ontology, which started by transforming the BibTeX format into an ontology.

When looking further down the eigenvalues, we observe that of the three concepts 'Academic Staff', 'Employee' and 'Person', 'Academic Staff' already becomes relevant in the fifth eigenvector, while 'Person' becomes relevant as late as the 11th eigenvector. 'Employee' does not feature as a central concept in any eigenvector. This observation raises the question if the concepts 'Employee' and 'Person' are really needed by the applications the SWRC ontology is targeted to, or if they eventually have just been added because 'one is usually doing so' when designing an ontology.

In Fig. 4, we observe also that the concept 'Academic Staff' *interlaces* with 'Organisation', 'Project' and 'Person'. This behavior is visible by observing that while 'Academic Staff' is colored red in the fifth eigenvector (eigenvalue -0.52), it changes color already in the next line and goes back to red again in line 10 and again in line 14. The three other concepts are colored red in the remaining eigenvectors in between. The absolute values of the eigenvalues do not come in strict pairs of equal absolute value but different sign, thus the three star like structures can not be clearly separated into blocks. The pattern of connection of AcademicStaff to the rest of the network is not

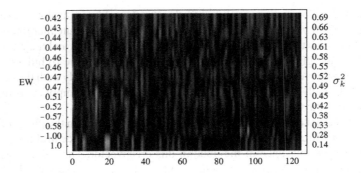

Fig. 4. The 14 strongest eigenvectors of the ontology

Fig. 5. Back rotated partial sum of first two eigenprojectors

easily explained. The pattern of AceademicStaff is distrubed by other structures that have approximately the same amount of connections, thus seperating the eigenvalues.

When considering the eigenvectors of the 36th to 44th eigenvalue (which are out of Fig.4 due to space restrictions), we observe that the concepts 'Assistant Professor', 'Associate Professor', and 'Full Professor' (columns 4, 5, and 17) behave identically with respect to 'Faculty Member' (column 16). As these three concepts are also very similar from an ontology engineering point of view, we take this as a hint that, in a re-engineering step, they should be unified to a single concept, with an additional attribute like 'status'.

Finally, we take a look at the partial sums as described earlier. In Fig. 5 we see the partial sum of the Fourier sum of the first two eigenprojectors weighted by

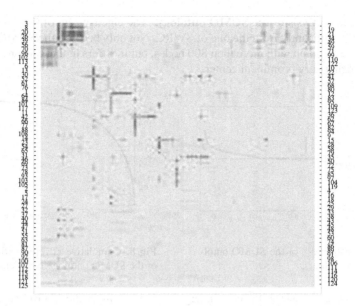

Fig. 6. Back rotated partial sum of first 14 eigenprojectors

their eigenvalues and rotated back ($\sum_{k=1}^{2} \lambda_k P_k$). This figure was generated by using an adapted k-means cluster algorithm based on the eigensystem. To define the initial cluster centers we use the eigenvector components with the highest absolute value of those eigenvectors that have a negative eigenvalue. We further restrict the selection to all those eigenvectors where the eigenvalues add up to explain data variance to a pre-defined level of 70%. Thus we do not need to set the number of clusters ex ante. An approximated block matrix is generated when we then sort the eigenvectors and re-arrange the eigenvector components accordingly before calculating the eigenprojector. Since the matrices are hermitian, the blocks are symmetric but different in color. The color-coding is the same as in Fig. 4. What is clearly visible is the BibTeX structure as a block in the upper left hand corner. It shows a very strong outbound connection from concepts like 'Book', 'InBook', etc. to Publication', 'address' and 'edition' for example.

If we now take the partial sum of the first 14 eigenprojectors we bring more detail to the picture. In Fig. 6 we see in addition to the BibTeX block five right angles in the matrix plot. These five structures belong to the concepts of 'Organisation', 'Academic Staff', 'Project', 'Event' and 'Person'. As this matrix can be read as a 'partial adjacency matrix', such right angles are the structure one expects for stars in the graph: one central node pointing from/to several nodes around it. Different to the BibTeX block that is visible in the upper left hand corner, these concepts play thus a central role in their surroundings. The color of the horizontal part of the angle indicates the direction: for 'Organization', it is green, hence this concept has many inbound edges – its subcon-cepts. The red color for 'Acadamic Staff' comes from its many outbound properties. 'Project', 'Event' and 'Person' have both incoming and outcoming edges/properties.

Eigensystem analysis of the SUMO ontology. The eigensystem of the SUMO ontology differs significantly from the one of SWRC. Not only because the SUMO ontology is modeled as a graph with more then 800 nodes, but if differs in that this ontology does not have such a very prominent center.

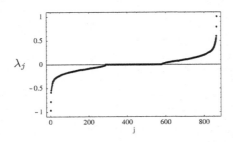

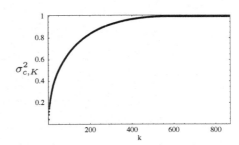

Fig. 7. Eigenspectrum of the SUMO ontology sorted by value

Fig. 8. Cumulative covered variance $\sigma^2_{c,K}$ of the SUMO ontology by eigenvalues λ_k

The spectrum of SUMO (given in Fig. 7) shows – as in the SWRC case – a very strong symmetry, thus suggesting star like structures which come again from the concept hierarchy where several subconcepts all point to their common superconcept. Different to SWRC, the cumulative covered variance (Fig. 8) shows a rather slow incline. While the first two eigenvalues of the SWRC ontology covered already 29% of the data variance, the first two eigenvalues of SUMO cover only about 10 %. The incline then goes without any obvious steps. This suggests that many concepts need to be taken into account to explain the complete ontology. Otherwise said, the degree of detail in SUMO seems to be more balanced than in SWRC.

Due to space restrictions, we cannot display the equivalents of Figs. 4 to 6 for SUMO here. We only present the major insights of our analysis verbally. The concept 'Binary Predicate' contributes most to the interpretation of the first two eigenvectors. 'Asymmetric Relation' seems to follow the same pattern in connecting to other nodes. Thus it is the second strongest concept in the first two eigenvectors. The fact that these two concepts also have a high absolute value in the following six eigenvectors further indicates that these two concepts also contribute to a high extent to the interpretation of these patterns. This might tells us that, in SUMO, these two concepts play a predominant role.

The third and fourth eigenvectors are most strongly influenced by the concepts 'Unary Function', 'Total Valued Relation' and 'Unit of Measure'. These three concepts have similar incoming connections from many concepts which are all of the form '...Fn'. This can be taken as a hint that these bundles of relations could be unified if there were a suitable construct in the KR formalism.

Concluding this section, we summarize that the out-/indegree analysis (and in particular the different differences of the standard deviations for out- and indegree) showed us that SUMO is more heterogenous in its way of modeling (due to the lack of a construct for higher-arity relations in the KR language) than SWRC, but that it is – according to the eigensystem analyis – more homogenous in the distribution of the coverage of different sub-domains of interest.

4 Other Applications of SNA in the Semantic Web Context

There are interesting first results from emerging SNA applications in the Semantic Web context. Mike [18] defines a model of semantic-social networks for extracting light-weight ontologies from folksonomies. Besides calculating such measures as the clustering coefficient, (local) betweenness centrality or the network constraint on the extracted one-mode network, Mika uses co-occurence techniques for clustering the concept network. Stuckenschmidt [23] uses network analysis to partition an ontology into a disjoint and covering set of concepts. After creating a dependency graph of the ontology and computing the strength of the dependencies the line island method [3] is used to determine strongly related concepts. These are then used to form a partition of the ontology graph. The tool Ontocopi described in [1] performs what is called Ontology Network Analysis for initially populating an organizational memory. Several network analysis methods are applied to an already populated ontology to extract important objects. In particular, a PageRank-like [6] algorithm is used to find communities of practice of individuals represented in the ontology.

Another field of interest regarding SemNA are Friend Of A Friend (FOAF)[11] networks which are studied for instance in [20] and [8]. Both articles focus on analysing the structure of the social network yielded by a large collection of FOAF documents.

5 Conclusion

In this paper, we have shown that Social Network Analysis provides a promising set of tools for analyzing ontologies and Semantic Web applications, providing deep insights into the structure of ontologies and knowledge bases. In particular, we have seen that the analysis of a given ontology can be done very thoroughly at different levels of granularity.

While the degree based measures from SNA already give an insight into the importance of certain concepts and properties of the ontology, the eigenvector analysis provides a detailed analysis of the importance of entities and the structure of the ontology. Little used "dummy" concepts, as well as candidates for concept fusion can be detected, and the topical clusters within the ontology and their structure can be shown using the eigenprojectors. The analysis is also useful for selecting the right ontology for reuse from a set of candidate ontologies. The eigenvalue analysis provides deep insights into the structure and focus of each ontology and supports the selection of the most suitable result.

As the two research areas Semantic Web and Semantic Network Analysis met only recently, open issues are still abundant, and provide a rich domain of research for the coming years:

- As seen above, SNA deals well with one- to n-mode networks with one relation. However, ontologies typically consist of more than one or two concepts, and of more than just one kind of relation. A systematic analysis of preprocessing steps which transform an ontology into a one- or two-mode network, as well as the interpretation of the results, is thus needed.

---

[11] http://www.foaf-project.org/

- One step further in this direction is the interesting and far from trivial research question how to expand existing SNA approaches to n-mode multigraph data sets.
- The interpretation of the standard eigenvector analysis needs currently some experience. Future work includes the use of cluster algorithms for rearranging the dimensions of the vector space such that similar dimensions are visualized together.
- (Description) Logics based ontologies describe relations (such as the subsumption hierarchy) implicitly only. It has to be studied whether these relations have to be computed explicitly before SNA techniques can be applied in a meaningful way.
- The next step after analyzing the ontologies is to turn the outcome into support for search, navigation, browsing, and restructuring ontologies and knowledge bases. Seeing the large field of SNA techniques, though, we expect a lot more techniques and tools to come up within the next years.
- Another direction of research is the comparison with philosophical aspects of ontology engineering. The OntoClean [12] method provides a framework for the evaluation of ontological decisions bsaed on philosophical notions e.g. of Identity or Polysemy. Correlations between the structural and philosophical properties of ontologies will have to be researched.

References

1. Harith Alani, Srinandan Dasmahapatra, Kieron O'Hara, and Nigel Shadbolt. Identifying Communities of Practice through Ontology Network Analysis. *IEEE Intelligent Systems*, 18(2):18–25, March/April 2003.
2. George A. Barnett and Ronald E. Rice. Longitudinal non-euclidean networks: Applying galileo. *Social Networks*, 7:287–322, 1985.
3. Vladimir Batagelj. Analysis of large networks - Islands. Presented at Dagstuhl seminar 03361: Algorithmic Aspects of Large and Complex Networks, August/September 2003.
4. B. Berendt, A. Hotho, and G. Stumme. Towards semantic web mining. In *Proc Int. Semantic Web Conference*, Sardinia, Italy, 2002.
5. P. Bonacich and P. Lloyd. Eigenvector-like measurement of centrality for asymmetric relations. *Social Networks*, 23:191 – 201, 2001.
6. Sergey Brin and Lawrence Page. The Anatomy of a Large-Scale Hypertextual Web Search Engine. *Computer Networks and ISDN Systems*, 30(1-7):107–117, April 1998.
7. Frank Harary ; Robert Z. Norman ; Dorwin Cartwright. *Structural models : an introduction to the theory of directed graphs*. Wiley, New York, 1965.
8. Li Ding, Lina Zhou, Timothy W. Finin, and Anupam Joshi. How the Semantic Web is Being Used: An Analysis of FOAF Documents. In *HICSS*. IEEE Computer Society, 2005.
9. M.G. Everett and S.P. Borgatti. The centrality of groups and classes. *Journal of Mathematical Sociology*, 23(3):181–201, 1999.
10. Linton C. Freeman. Uncovering organizational hierarchies. *Computational & Mathematical Organization Theory*, 3(1):5 – 18, 1997.
11. Linton C. Freeman. *The Development of Social Network Analysis: A Study in the Sociology of Science*. BookSurge Publishing, 2004.
12. Nicola Guarino and Christopher A. Welty. Evaluating ontological decisions with OntoClean. *Commun. ACM*, 45(2):61–65, 2002.
13. Bettina Hoser. *Analysis of Asymmetric Communication Patterns in Computer Mediated Communication Environments*. PhD thesis, Universität Karlsruhe, 2005.

14. Bettina Hoser and Andreas Geyer-Schulz. Eigenspectralanalysis of Hermitian Adjacency Matrices for the Analysis of Group Substructures. *Journal of Mathematical Sociology*, 29(4):265–294, 2005.

15. Jon M. Kleinberg. Authoritative sources in a hyperlinked environment. In *Ninth Annual ACM-SIAM Symposium*, pages 668 – 677, Jan 1998.

16. Jon M. Kleinberg. Authoritative sources in a hyperlinked environment. *JACM*, 46(5):604–632, sep 1999.

17. Barry Wellman Laura Garton. Social impacts of electronic mail in organizations: A review of research literature. *Communication Yearbook*, 18:434–453, 1995.

18. Peter Mika. Ontologies Are Us: A Unified Model of Social Networks and Semantics. In Yolanda Gil, Enrico Motta, V. Richard Benjamins, and Mark A. Musen, editors, *ISWC 2005*, volume 3729 of *LNCS*, pages 522–536, Berlin Heidelberg, November 2005. Springer-Verlag.

19. J.L. Moreno. *Who shall survive? : a new approach to the problem of Human Interrelations*, volume 58 of *Nervous and mental disease monograph series*. Nervous and Mental Disease Publ., Washington, 1934.

20. John C. Paolillo, Sarah Mercure, and Elijah Wright. The Social Semantics of LiveJournal FOAF: Structure and Change from 2004 to 2005. In Stumme et al. [24].

21. Christoph Schmitz. Self-organization of a small world by topic. In *Proc. 1st International Workshop on Peer-to-Peer Knowledge Management*, Boston, MA, August 2004.

22. Michael F. Schwartz and David C. M. Wood. Discovering Shared Interests Using Graph Analysis. *Communications of the ACM*, 36(8):78 – 89, Aug 1993.

23. Heiner Stuckenschmidt. Network Analysis as a Basis for Ontology Partitioning. In Stumme et al. [24].

24. Gerd Stumme, Bettina Hoser, Christoph Schmitz, and Harith Alani, editors. *Proc. ISWC 2005 Workshop on Semantic Network Analysis*, Galway, Ireland, November 2005.

25. J. R. Tyler, D. M. Wilkinson, and B. A. Huberman. Email as spectroscopy: Automated discovery of community structure within organizations. *cond-mat/0303264*, 2003.

26. Stanley Wasserman and Katherine Faust. *Social Network Analysis: Methods and Applications*, volume 8 of *Structural Analysis in the Social Sciences*. Cambridge University Press, Cambridge, 1 edition, 1999.

Content Aggregation on Knowledge Bases Using Graph Clustering

Christoph Schmitz, Andreas Hotho, Robert Jäschke, and Gerd Stumme

Knowledge and Data Engineering Group, Universität Kassel
{lastname}@cs.uni-kassel.de
http://www.kde.cs.uni-kassel.de

Abstract. Recently, research projects such as PADLR and SWAP have developed tools like Edutella or Bibster, which are targeted at establishing peer-to-peer knowledge management (P2PKM) systems. In such a system, it is necessary to obtain provide brief semantic descriptions of peers, so that routing algorithms or matchmaking processes can make decisions about which communities peers should belong to, or to which peers a given query should be forwarded.

This paper provides a graph clustering technique on knowledge bases for that purpose. Using this clustering, we can show that our strategy requires up to 58% fewer queries than the baselines to yield full recall in a bibliographic P2PKM scenario.

1 Introduction: Ontology-Based P2PKM

Recently, a lot of effort has been spent on building peer-to-peer systems using semantic web technology [22, 5, 2, 15], based on a notion of peer-to-peer based, personal knowledge management (P2PKM for short). In such a scenario, users will model their knowledge in personal knowledge bases, which can then be shared with other users via a peer-to-peer network.

Many use cases for P2PKM have been implemented recently. In the PADLR and ELENA projects[1], a P2P infrastructure is established for the exchange of learning material; Bibster[2] is a tool for sharing BibTeX entries between researchers; the SCAM tool[3] for knowledge repositories connects to a P2P network. In these systems, each peer builds a knowledge base on top of a common ontology such as LOM and ACM CCS.

One crucial point in such a P2P network is that query messages need to be *routed* to peers which will be able to answer the query without flooding the network with unnecessary traffic. Several proposals have been made recently as to how the network can self-organize into a topology consisting of communities around common topics of interest, a structure which is beneficial for routing, and how messages can be routed in this topology [20, 21, 8, 23]. All of these are based on the idea of routing indices [3]. In a routing index, peers store an aggregated

---

[1] http://www.l3s.de/english/projects/projects_overview.html
[2] http://bibster.semanticweb.org
[3] http://scam.sourceforge.net/

Y. Sure and J. Domingue (Eds.): ESWC 2006, LNCS 4011, pp. 530–544, 2006.

view of their neighbors' contents, enabling them to make content-based routing decisions.

One missing link towards these self-organized network topologies is the extraction of expertises – semantic self-descriptions – of peers from the peers' knowledge bases. In this paper, a method of extracting these expertises using a clustering technique on the knowledge base is proposed and evaluated.

The remainder of this paper is structured as follows: After a brief review of an ontology-based P2P knowledge management scenario and related work, we will introduce technical preliminaries in Section 2. In Section 3 the automatic generation of self-descriptions of peers' knowledge bases through the use of graph clustering will be shown. Section 4 presents evaluation results for a bibliographic P2PKM scenario. Section 5 concludes and discusses future work.

1.1 Related Work

To the best of our knowledge, the exact problem discussed in this paper has not been treated before. There are, however, related areas which touch similar topics.

Knowledge-rich approaches from the text summarization area [10, 9] use algorithms on knowledge representation formalism to extract salient topics from texts in order to generate summaries. We compare our approach to the one in [10] in Section 4.

In semantic P2P overlays, peers need some means of obtaining a notion of other peers' contents for routing tables and other purposes. [13] and others rely on observing the past behavior of peers – queries sent and answered – to guess what kind of information peers contain, including some fallback strategies to overcome the bootstrapping problem. In [8], peers publish their expertise containing *all* topics they have information about without any aggregation, which will be a resource consumption problem for larger knowledge bases and networks.

Keyword-based P2P information retrieval systems can make use of the bag-of-words or vector-space models for IR. [19] proposes the use of Bloom filters to maintain compact representations of contents for routing purposes. These techniques, however, do not provide a semantically aggregated view of the contents, but rather a bitwise superposition of keywords which loses semantic relationships between related keywords.

Much work has been done on graph clustering (e. g. [16]) in a variety of areas. Most of these algorithms, though, do not readily yield representatives such as the centroids from the k-modes algorithm used in Section 3, and/or may not be naturally adapted to the shared-part/personal-part consideration used in Section 2.3.

2 Basics and Definitions

2.1 P2P Network Model

As in [20], the following assumptions are made about about peers in a P2PKM network:

- Each peer stores a set of *content items*. On these content items, there exists a *similarity function* called *sim*. We assume $sim(i,j) \in [0,1]$ for all items i, j, and the corresponding *distance function* $d := 1 - sim$ shall be a metric. For the purpose of this paper, we assume *content items* to be entities from a knowledge base (cf. Section 2.2), and the metric to be defined in terms of the ontology as described in Section 2.4.
- Each peer provides a self-description of what its knowledge base contains, in the following referred to as *expertise*. Expertises need to be much smaller than the knowledge bases they describe, as they are transmitted over the network and used in other peers' routing indices. A method of obtaining these expertises is outlined in Section 3. Formally, an expertise consists of a set $\{(c_i, w_i) | i = 1 \ldots k\}$ of pairs mapping content items c_i to real-valued weights w_i.
- There is a relation *knows* on the set of peers. Each peer knows a certain set of other peers, i. e., it knows their expertises and network address (e. g. IP address, JXTA ID, ...). This corresponds to the routing index as proposed in [3]. In order to account for the limited amount of memory and processing power, the size of the routing index at each peer is limited.
- Peers query for content items on other peers by sending query messages to some or all of their neighbors; these queries are forwarded by peers according to some *query routing strategy*, which uses the *sim* function mentioned above to decide which neighbors to forward messages to.

2.2 Ontology Model

For the purpose of this paper, we use the view on ontologies proposed by the KAON framework [6]. Following the simplified nomenclature of [6], an *ontology* consists of *concepts* with a subclassOf partial order, and relations between concepts. A *knowledge base* consists of an ontology and *instances* of concepts and relations. Concepts and instances are both called *entities* (for details cf. [6]).

Another important feature of KAON is the inclusion mechanism for knowledge bases, enabling the implementation of the shared and personal parts of knowledge bases as introduced in the next section.

2.3 Shared and Personal Parts of the Knowledge Bases

Based on the use cases mentioned in Section 1, all peers $P_i, i = 1 \ldots n$, in the system are assumed to *share* a certain part O of their ontologies: in the case of e-learning, this could be the Learning Object Metadata (LOM)[4] standard plus a classification scheme; when exchanging bibliographic metadata as in Bibster, this would be an ontology reflecting BibTeX and a classification scheme such as ACM CCS[5], etc.

Additionally, the knowledge base KB_i of each peer P_i contains *personal* knowledge PK_i which is modeled by the user of the peer and is not known a-priori

---

[4] http://ltsc.ieee.org/wg12
[5] http://www.acm.org/class

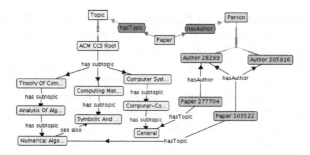

Fig. 1. Example Knowledge Base

to other peers. Querying this knowledge efficiently and sharing it among peers is the main task of the P2PKM system. Formally, we can say that for all i, $KB_i = O \cup PK_i$.

In Figure 1, the ontology used in the evaluation in Section 4 is shown. In this case, the shared part O comprises the concepts Person, Paper, Topic, and their relations, as well as the topics of the ACM CCS. The personal knowledge PK_i of each peer contains instantiations of papers and persons and their relationships to each other and the topics for the papers of each individual author in DBLP with papers in the ACM digital library (cf. 4.1 for details).

For the purpose of this paper, an agreement on a shared ontology O is assumed. The problem of ontologies emerging in a distributed KM setting [1], of ontology alignment, mapping, and merging [4], are beyond the scope of this work.

2.4 Ontology-Based Metrics

An ontology of the kind we use is a labeled, directed graph: the set of nodes comprises the entities, and the relations between entities make up the set of edges. An edge between entities in this graph expresses relatedness in some sense: the instance `paper37` may have an instanceOf edge to the concept `Paper`, `Paper` and `Topic` would be connected by an edge due to the `hasTopic` relation, etc.

On this kind of semantic structure, [17] has proposed to use the distance in the graph-theoretic sense (length of shortest path) as a semantic distance measure.

Metric Used in the Evaluation. We follow this suggestion and apply it to the abovementioned graph as follows:

- To each edge, a length is assigned; taxonomic edges (instanceOf, subclassOf) get length 1, while non-taxonomic edges are assigned length 2. This reflects the fact that `subclassOf(PhDStudent, Person)` is a closer link between these concepts than, say, `rides(Person, Bicycle)`.
- Edge lengths are divided by the average distance of the incident nodes from the root concept. This reflects the intuition that top-level concepts such as `Person` and `Project` would be considered less similar than, e.g., `Graduate Student` and `Undergraduate` farther from the root.

Similarity, Relatedness, and Semantic Distances – Why Edge Counting? The notions of semantic similarity (things having similar features) and relatedness (things being associated with each other) have long been explored in various disciplines such as linguistics and cognitive sciences. Discussions about these phenomena and their respective properties have lasted for decades (cf. [24, 7]). While most of this discussion is outside the scope of this paper, some key points [7] are worth mentioning: Thematic relatedness and similarity are distinct phenomena, but both can get mixed up or influence each other.

In the context of this paper, where the goal is to provide self-descriptions of knowledge in a P2PKM system, some more influences on the choice of the semantic distance should be noted:

- The ontologies to be used in P2PKM will be engineered specifically for KM purposes. Thus, regarding a relation between two concepts as an indication that these two have something to do with each other reflects the intention of a knowledge engineer to express relatedness.
- In a P2PKM system, domain specific ontologies will be used. These represent a conceptualization of a small part of the world which is relevant for the given domain, so that stray associations such as *lamp – round glowing object – moon – . . .*, which might occur in a "world ontology", will be avoided.
- Modeling idiosyncrasies of certain tools and formalisms such as described in the next section need to be anticipated. This can be done by allowing for flexible weighting and filtering strategies.

Various constraints are present on other kinds of metrics which have led to the use of an edge-counting metric for the purpose of this paper. Approaches such as [18] or [24] assume the presence of full text or linguistic background knowledge; others such as [14] only use concepts and an instanceOf relationship, neglecting instances and non-taxonomic relationships altogether. To yield maximum flexibility and to use as much of the modeled content as possible, an edge counting approach was chosen for this paper.

Keeping this discussion in mind, one needs to be aware of what kinds of similarity and/or relatedness should be expressed in modeling the ontology and parameterizing the metric.

Pitfalls on Real-World Ontologies. While the edge-counting metric seems straightforward, applying it to real-world ontologies turned out to be non-trivial:

Noise and Technical Artifacts. Often not all of the content of a knowledge base is used to model a certain domain as such; e. g., in KAON, lexical information is represented as first-class entities in the knowledge base. This yields entities which are not relevant for the semantic distance computation. There is also a root class which every entity is an instance of, which would render our approach to calculating distances useless.

Modeling Idiosyncrasies. Engineering an ontology implies design decisions, e. g. whether to model something as an instance or as a concept [25]. These decisions carry implications for the weighting of edges, e. g. when taxonomic relationships are expressed by a relation which is not one of `instanceOf`, `subclassOf`.

To overcome these problems, we have implemented extensive entity filtering and weighting customization strategies which are applied prior to the metric computation itself.

Choice of Parameters. One obvious question is where the parameters, weighting schemes and filtering rules necessary for this kind of metric should come from. These can be agreed upon just like the ontology to be used itself. When stakeholders deside that there should be a "see also" relation between topics, they could also agree on its importance or non-importance for retrieval tasks (cf. the discussion about the value of non-taxonomic relations in [17]).

Secondly, this kind of semantic metric will not primarily be used to reflect human judgment of similarity or relatedness directly, but to structure a network topology. For this type of use, optimal parameters can be determined in simulation experiments or might be learned over the lifetime of the system.

2.5   *k*-Modes Clustering

In Section 3, we will use an extension of k-modes clustering [11] to obtain aggregations of knowledge bases. The basic version of k-modes clustering for partitioning a set S of items into k clusters $S_1, \ldots, S_k$ such that $S = \bigcup_i S_i$ works as follows:

1. Given k, choose k elements $C_i, i = 1 \ldots k$ of S as *centroids*
2. Assign each $s \in S$ to the cluster S_i with $i = \arg \min_j d(C_j, s)$
3. For $i = 1 \ldots k$, recompute C_i such that $\sum_{s \in S_i} d(C_i, s)$ is minimized.
4. Repeat steps 2 and 3 until centroids converge.

This algorithms yields (locally) optimal centroids which minimize the average distance of each centroid to its cluster members. A variation we will use is *bisection k-modes clustering*, which produces k clusters by starting from an initial cluster containing all elements, and then recursively splitting the cluster with the largest variance with 2-modes until k clusters have been reached.

As the algorithm is randomized, it may happen that a cluster cannot be split although k clusters have not been reached. In that case, we retry a fixed number of times before accepting the clustering.

3   Graph Clustering for Content Aggregation

As mentioned in the motivation, a peer needs to provide an expertise in order to be found as an information provider in a P2PKM network. From the discussion above, the following requirements for an expertise can be derived:

- The expertise should provide an aggregated account of what is contained in the knowledge base of the peer, meaning that using the similarity function, a routing algorithm can make good a-priori guesses of what can or cannot be found in the knowledge base. More specifically, the personal part PK_i should be reflected in the expertise.
- The expertise should be much smaller than the knowledge base itself, preferably contain only a few entities, because it will be used in routing indices and in computations needed for routing decisions.

With these requirements in mind, we propose the use of a clustering algorithm to obtain an expertise for each peer.

3.1 Clustering the Knowledge Base

We use a version of bi-section k-modes clustering for the extraction of such an expertise. As mentioned before, k-modes clustering yields centroids which are locally optimal elements of a set regarding the average distance to their cluster members.

Using the semantic metric, these centroids fulfill the abovementioned requirements for an expertise: We can compute a *small* number of centroids, which are – on the average – *semantically close* to every member of their respective clusters, thus providing a good *aggregation* of the knowledge base.

In order to apply this algorithm in our scenario, however, some changes need to be made:

- The set S to be clustered has to consist only of the *personal parts* PK_i of the knowledge bases. Otherwise, the structure of the shared part (which may be comparatively large) will shadow the interesting structures of the personal part.
- The *centroids* C_i will not be chosen from the whole knowledge base, but only from the shared part O of the ontology. Otherwise, other peers could not interpret the expertise of a peer.

The expertise for each knowledge base is obtained by clustering the knowledge base as described, obtaining a set $\{C_i \mid i = 1 \ldots k\} \subseteq O$ of entities from the ontology as centroids for a given k. The expertise then consists of the pairs $\{(C_i, |S_i|) | i = 1 \ldots k\}$ of centroids and cluster sizes. Because we restricted the choice of centroids to be from O, we get expertises that other peers can interpret from clustering the elements of KB_i.

3.2 Determining the Number of Centroids

One problem of the k-modes algorithm is that one needs to set the value of k beforehand. As the appropriate number of topics for a given knowledge base may not be known a-priori, we use the *silhouette coefficient* [12], which is an indicator for the quality of the clustering. In short, it determines how well clusters are separated in terms of the distances of each item to the nearest and the second nearest centroid: if each item is close to its own centroid and far away from the others, the silhouette coefficient will be large, indicating a good clustering.

4   Experimental Evaluation

In the following sections, we will try to verify three hypotheses:

1. Extracting a good expertise from a knowledge base is harder for large knowledge bases.
2. With larger expertises, the retrieval results improve.
3. The clustering strategy extracts expertises which are useful for retrieval.

The intuition is as follows: Extracting a good expertise from a large knowledge base is harder than from a small one, as the interests of a person interested in many areas will be more difficult to summarize than those of someone who has only few fields of interest. With larger expertises, the retrieval results improve, because if we spend more space (and processing time) for describing someone's interests, we can make better guesses about what his knowledge base contains. As the clustering strategy tries to return the centroids which are as close as possible to all cluster members, we assume that it gives a good approximation of what a knowledge base contains.

4.1   Setup

To evaluate the usefulness of the expertise extraction approach from the previous sections, we consider a P2PKM scenario with a self-organized semantic topology as described in [20, 8, 23]: the expertises of peers are stored in routing tables, where similarity computations between queries and expertises in the routing indices are used to make greedy routing decisions when forwarding queries.

If the routing strategy of this network works as intended, the peers which published an expertise closest to a given query will be queried first. In the following experiment, the quality of the expertises is evaluated in isolation based on that observation: An expertise was extracted for each peer. All of the shared entities of the ontology were used in turn as queries. For each query, the authors were sorted in descending similarity of the closest entity of the expertise to the query. Ties were resolved by ordering in decreasing weight order.

The evaluation is based on the bibliographic use case mentioned in Section 1: there are scientists in the P2P network sharing bibliographic information about their publications. An ontology according to Figure 1 is used. Only the top level concepts (Person, Topic, Paper) and the ACM classification hierarchy are shared among the peers. Each user models a knowledge base on his peer representing his own papers.

We instantiated such a set of knowledge bases using the following data:

- For 39067 papers from DBLP which are present in the ACM Digital Library, the topics were obtained from the ACM website. There are 1474 topics in the ACM Computing Classification System. Details on the construction of the data set and the conversion scripts can be found on http://www.kde.cs.uni-kassel.de/schmitz/acmdata.

- To yield non-trivial knowledge bases, only those authors who wrote papers on at least 10 topics were considered. This left 317 authors. A discussion of this pruning step can be found in Section 4.3.

For each of the summarization strategies described below, we show the number of authors which had to be queried in order to yield a given level of recall. This is an indicator for how well the expertises capture the content of the authors' knowledge bases: the better the expertises, the fewer authors one needs to ask in order to reach a certain level of recall.

This is a variation of the usual precision-against-recall evaluation from information retrieval. Instead of precision – how many of the retrieved documents are relevant? – the relative number of the queried authors which are able to provide papers on a given topic is measured.

4.2   Expertise Extraction Strategies

In comparison with the clustering technique from Section 3, the following strategies were evaluated. The expertise size was fixed to be 5 except where noted otherwise.

Counting (#5): The occurrences of topics in each author's knowledge base were counted. The top 5 topics and counts were used as the author's expertise.

Counting Parents (#P5): As above, but each topic did not count for itself, but for its parent topic.

Random (R5): Use 5 random topics and their counts.

Wavefront (WFL7/WFL9): Compute a wavefront of so-called *fuser concepts* [10]. A fuser concept is a concept many descendants of which are instantiated in the knowledge base. The intuition is that if many of the descendants of a concept occur, it will be a good summary of that part of the knowledge base. If only few children occur, a better summarization would be found deeper in the taxonomy.

There are two parameters in this computation: a threshold value between 0 and 1 for the *branch ratio* (the lower the branch ratio, the more salient the topic), and a minimal depth for the fuser concepts. There are some problems in comparing this strategy with the other strategies named here:

- It is not possible to control the number of fuser concepts returned with the parameters the strategy offers.
- Leaves can never be fuser concepts, which is a problem in a relatively flat hierarchy such as ACM CCS, where many papers are classified with leaf concepts.
- All choices of parameters yielded very few fuser concepts.

The expertise consisted of the fuser concepts as returned by the wavefront computation with the inverse of the branch ratio as weights. If the number of fuser concepts was less than 5, the expertise was filled up with the leaf concepts occurring most frequently. We examined thresholds of 0.7 (WFL7) and 0.9 (WFL9) with minimal depth 1.

Clustering (C5/C37): The expertise consisted of centroids and cluster sizes determined by a bisection-k-modes clustering as described in Section 3. C5 used a fixed k of 5, while C37 selected the best $k \in \{3, \dots, 7\}$ using the silhouette coefficient. 20 retries were used in the bi-section k-means computation.

4.3   Results

In this section, results are presented for the different strategies. The values presented are averaged over all queries (i. e. all ACM topics), and, in the cases with randomized algorithms (C5, C37, R5), over 20 runs.

Note that all strategies except C37 returned expertises of size 5, while in C37, the average expertise size was slightly larger at 5.09. Table 3 shows the distribution of expertise sizes for C37.q

Pruning of the Evaluation Set. In order to yield interesting knowledge bases to extract expertises from, we pruned the ACM/DBLP data set as described in Section 4.1. Thus, only the knowledge bases of authors which have written papers on at least 10 topics were considered.

Table 1. Full vs. pruned data: Fraction of authors (%) queried to yield given recall, C5 strategy

Recall	full data	pruned data
10%	0.01	4.09
30%	0.04	4.93
50%	0.07	6.43
70%	0.16	12.53
90%	0.55	18.73
100%	3.45	22.88

Table 1 presents a comparison of the full and the pruned dataset for the C5 strategy. It can be seen that the full data require querying only a fraction of the authors which is one or two orders of magnitude *smaller* than the pruned data. This indicates that the first hypothesis holds; the pruning step yields the "hard" instances of the problem.

Influence of the Expertise Size. Intuitively, a larger expertise can contain more information about the knowledge base than a smaller one. In the extreme case, one could use the whole knowledge base as the expertise.

To test the second hypothesis, Figure 2 and Table 2, show the influence of the expertise size on retrieval performance for the C5 clustering strategy.

While the small number of data points for each recall level do not lend themselves to a detailed quantitative analysis, it is clear that the expertise size has the expected influence in the clustering technique: the larger the expertise is, the

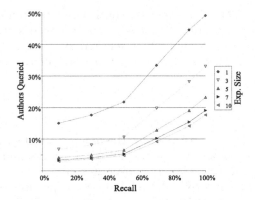

Fig. 2. Influence of Expertise Size (C5 Strategy)

Table 2. Percentage of Authors Queries against Expertise Size (C5 Strategy)

Recall	\multicolumn{5}{c}{Expertise Size}
	1	3	5	7	10
10%	15.06	6.80	4.09	3.38	3.03
30%	17.66	8.16	4.93	4.12	3.69
50%	21.79	10.59	6.43	5.35	4.82
70%	33.37	19.79	12.53	10.21	9.18
90%	44.57	28.20	18.73	15.44	14.15
100%	49.07	33.04	22.88	19.10	17.67

Table 3. Distribution of Expertise Sizes for C37

Exp. Size	Percentage of Authors
3	20%
4	15%
5	21%
6	23%
7	21%
Avg.: 5.09	

more detail it can provide about the knowledge base, and the better the retrieval performance is.

Note that the resources a peer would be willing to spend on storing routing tables and making routing decisions are limited, so that a trade-off between resources set aside for routing and the resulting performance must be made, especially as network and knowledge base sizes grow larger.

Influence of the Summarization Strategy. Finally, we evaluate the performance of the clustering strategies against the other strategies mentioned above.

Table 4 and Figure 3 show that the k-modes clustering compares favorably against the other strategies: fewer authors need to be asked in order to find a

Table 4. Percentage of Authors Queried against Recall; σ: Standard Deviation

Recall	WFL7	WFL9	C5 (σ)	C37 (σ)	#5	#P5	R5 (σ)
			Authors Queried				
10%	6.11	6.37	4.09 (.28)	**3.10** (.18)	10.69	9.25	6.96 (.48)
30%	7.16	7.43	4.93 (.28)	**3.80** (.19)	12.15	10.72	8.26 (.52)
50%	9.61	9.86	6.43 (.32)	**5.01** (.21)	15.33	13.67	11.33 (.61)
70%	19.06	19.67	12.53 (.52)	**9.65** (.33)	27.43	23.38	24.04 (.82)
90%	28.97	29.78	18.73 (.64)	**14.78** (.47)	39.45	33.91	35.16 (.93)
100%	34.35	35.37	22.88 (.75)	**18.42** (.48)	44.15	39.27	39.65 (.83)

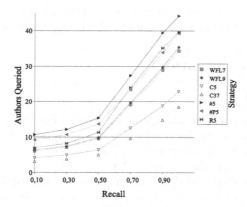

Fig. 3. Percentage of Authors Queried against Recall

given proportion of the available papers on a certain topic. This is an indication that the clustering technique will yield expertises which can usefully be applied in a P2PKM system with a forwarding query routing strategy based on routing indices. For example, to yield 100% recall, 58% fewer (18.42% vs. 44.15%) peers would have to be queried when using C37 instead of the #5 strategy. With C37 and a routing strategy that contacted best peers first, $100\% - 18.42\% \approx 81\%$ of the peers could be spared from being queried while still getting full recall.

The standard deviations σ of the randomized strategies given in Table 4 show that while the actual results of the C5, C37, and R5 runs may vary, the quality of the results for querying is stable.

To get an impression about why the clustering strategies work better than the others, consider one author whose papers are labelled with the following topics[6]: B.5, B.6, B.6, B.6.1.a, B.6.1.a, B.6.3.b, B.7, B.7.1.c, B.8, B.8, C.0.d, C.3.e, C.5.3.f, D.3.2, G.1, I.5.4.g, J.

The different strategies delivered the results shown in Table 5. It can be seen that the clustering strategies find the best balance between spreading the expertise over all occuring topics, and on the other hand generalizing so that

---

[6] Note that the fourth level topics do not have names of their own originally; we attached artificial IDs to distinguish them

Table 5. Sample Results for Different Strategies

#P5	#5	R5	WFL7	WFL9	C5	C37
B. (6)	B.6.1.a (2)	B.6.1.a (2)	C. (3)	C. (3)	B. (11)	B.6 (10)
B.6.1 (2)	B.6 (2)	B.6.3.b (1)	B.6.1.a (2)	B.6.1.a (2)	C. (3)	C. (3)
B.6.3 (1)	B.8 (2)	D.3.2 (1)	B. (2)	B. (2)	I.5.4.g (1)	J. (1)
C.0 (1)	B.6.3.b (1)	C.5.3.f (1)	B.6 (1.5)	B.6 (1.5)	D.3.2 (1)	G.1 (1)
B.7.1 (1)	B.5 (1)	B.7 (1)	B.6.3.b (1)	B.6.3.b (1)	G.1 (1)	D.3.2 (1)
						I.5.4.g (1)

many occuring topics are subsumed under one expertise entry. This happens due to the way the clustering strategy spreads the clusters over the ontology graph, maxminizing the coherence within clusters. Most other strategies, e. g. , did not consider any of the topics outside the B and C parts of ACM CCS.

5   Summary and Outlook

5.1   Conclusion

In this paper, an algorithm which can be used to extract semantic summaries – called *expertises* – from knowledge bases is proposed. A motivation for the necessity of this kind of summary is given, namely, that such summaries are needed for routing tables in semantic P2P networks.

We demonstrate that the clustering method outperforms other strategies in terms of queries needed to get a given recall on a set of knowledge bases from a bibliographic scenario. We also show qualitatively that larger knowledge bases are harder to summarize, and that larger expertises are an advantage in determining which peers to query.

5.2   Outlook and Work in Progress

Evaluation in Context. This paper provides evidence that the clustering procedure extracts suitable expertises for a P2PKM setting. The next step will be combining the clustering with self-organization techniques for P2PKM networks as described in [20]. Note that usually the value of aggregations or summaries is measured by evaluating it against human judgment. In our case, however, the aggregations will be evaluated with regard to their contribution to improving the performance of the P2P network.

Scalability Issues. Computing the metric as described above is very expensive, as it needs to compute all-pairs-shortest-paths. For large ontologies having tens or hundreds of thousands of nodes, this is prohibitively expensive. In the current evaluation, the shortest paths needed are computed on the fly, but for a real-world P2PKM implementation, some faster solution needs to be found. The obvious idea of pre-computing the metric does not mitigate the problem very much, because maintaining the shortest path lengths requires $O(n^2)$ storage.

On possible direction of investigation is to look at the actual usage of the metric in a P2PKM system. If the community structure of the network leads to a locality in the use of the metric, caching and/or dynamic programming strategies for the metric computation may be feasible.

Test Data and Evaluation Methodology. Other than in Information Retrieval, for example, there are neither widespread testing datasets nor standard evaluation methods available for Semantic Web and especially P2PKM applications. In order to compare and evaluate future research in these areas, standardized data sets and measures need to be established.

Acknowledgement. Part of this research was funded by the EU in the Nepomuk project (FP6-027705).

References

1. K. Aberer, P. Cudré-Mauroux, M. Hauswirth. The Chatty Web: Emergent Semantics Through Gossiping. In *Proc. 12th International World Wide Web Conference.* Budapest, Hungary, May 2003.
2. M. Bonifacio, R. Cuel, G. Mameli, et al. A peer-to-peer architecture for distributed knowledge management. In *Proc. 3rd International Symposium on Multi-Agent Systems, Large Complex Systems, and E-Businesses MALCEB'2002.* Erfurt, Germany, October 2002.
3. A. Crespo, H. Garcia-Molina. Routing indices for peer-to-peer systems. In *Proc. International Conference on Distributed Computing Systems (ICDCS).* Vienna, Austria, July 2002. ISSN 0734-2071.
4. J. de Bruijn, F. Martin-Recuerda, D. Manov, et al. State-of-the-art survey on ontology merging and aligning (SEKT project deliverable 4.2.1). `http://sw.deri.org/~jos/sekt-d4.2.1-mediation-survey-final.pdf`, 2004.
5. M. Ehrig, P. Haase, F. van Harmelen, et al. The SWAP data and metadata model for semantics-based peer-to-peer systems. In M. Schillo, M. Klusch, J. P. Müller, et al. (eds.), *Proc. MATES-2003. First German Conference on Multiagent Technologies,* vol. 2831 of *LNAI,* pp. 144–155. Springer, Erfurt, Germany, SEP 2003. ISSN 0734-2071.
6. M. Ehrig, S. Handschuh, A. Hotho, et al. KAON - towards a large scale Semantic Web. In K. Bauknecht, A. M. Tjoa, G. Quirchmayr (eds.), *Proc. E-Commerce and Web Technologies, Third International Conference, EC-Web 2002,* no. 2455 in LNCS. Springer, Aix-en-Provence
7. D. Gentner, S. K. Brem. Is snow really like a shovel? Distinguishing similarity from thematic relatedness. In M. Hahn, S. C. Stoness (eds.), *Proc. Twenty-First Annual Meeting of the Cognitive Science Society.* Mahwah, NJ, 1999. ISBN 3-540-40317-5.
8. P. Haase, R. Siebes. Peer selection in peer-to-peer networks with semantic topologies. In *Proc. 13th International World Wide Web Conference.* New York City, NY, USA, May 2004.
9. U. Hahn, U. Reimer. Knowledge-based text summarization: Salience and generalization operators for knowledge base abstraction. In I. Mani, M. T. Maybury (eds.), *Advances in Automatic Text Summarization.* MIT Press, 1999.
10. E. Hovy, C.-Y. Lin. Automated text summarization in SUMMARIST. In I. Mani, M. T. Maybury (eds.), *Advances in Automatic Text Summarization.* MIT Press, 1999.

11. Z. Huang. Extensions to the k-means algorithm for clustering large data sets with categorical values. *Data Min. Knowl. Discov.*, 2(3):283–304, 1998. ISSN 1384-5810. doi: http://dx.doi.org/10.1023/A:1009769707641.

12. L. Kaufman, P. J. Rousseeuw. *Finding Groups in Data: An Introduction to Cluster Analysis*. John Wiley, 1990. ISBN 1-58133-109-7.

13. A. Löser, C. Tempich, B. Quilitz, et al. Searching dynamic communities with personal indexes. In Y. Gil, E. Motta, V. R. Benjamins, et al. (eds.), *Proc. 4th International Semantic Web Conference, ISWC 2005*. Galway, Ireland, Nov. 2005.

14. A. Maedche, S. Staab. Measuring similarity between ontologies. In *Proc. Of the European Conference on Knowledge Acquisition and Management - EKAW-2002. Madrid, Spain, October 1-4, 2002*, vol. 2473 of *LNCS/LNAI*. Springer, 2002. ISBN 1-58133-109-7.

15. W. Nejdl, B. Wolf, C. Qu, et al. Edutella: A p2p networking infrastructure based on rdf. In *Proc. 11th International World Wide Web Conference (WWW 2002)*. Honolulu, Hawaii, May 2002.

16. A. Pothen. Graph partitioning algorithms with applications to scientific computing. In D. E. Keyes, A. Sameh, V. Venkatakrishnan (eds.), *Parallel Numerical Algorithms*, pp. 323–368. Kluwer, 1997.

17. R. Rada, H. Mili, E. Bicknell, et al. Development and application of a metric on semantic nets. *IEEE Transactions on Systems, Man and Cybernetics*, 19(1):17–30, January/February 1989.

18. P. Resnik. Using information content to evaluate semantic similarity in a taxonomy. In *Proc. Fourteenth International Joint Conference on Artificial Intelligence, IJCAI 95*. Montreal, Canada, August 1995.

19. P. Reynolds, A. Vahdat. Efficient peer-to-peer keyword searching. In M. Endler, D. C. Schmidt (eds.), *Middleware*, vol. 2672 of *Lecture Notes in Computer Science*. Springer, 2003. ISBN 3-540-40317-5.

20. C. Schmitz. Self-organization of a small world by topic. In *Proc. 1st International Workshop on Peer-to-Peer Knowledge Management*. Boston, MA, August 2004.

21. C. Schmitz, S. Staab, C. Tempich. Socialisation in peer-to-peer knowledge management. In *Proc. International Conference on Knowledge Management (I-Know 2004)*. Graz, Austria, June 2004.

22. J. Tane, C. Schmitz, G. Stumme. Semantic resource management for the web: An elearning application. In *Proc. 13th International World Wide Web Conference*. New York, May 2004.

23. C. Tempich, S. Staab, A. Wranik. Remindin': Semantic query routing in peer-to-peer networks based on social metaphors. In W3C (ed.), *Proceedings of the 13th International World Wide Web Conference (WWW 2004)*, pp. 640–649. ACM, New York, USA, MAY 2004.

24. A. Tversky. Features of similarity. *Psychological Review*, 84(4):327–352, 1977.

25. C. A. Welty, D. A. Ferrucci. What's in an instance? Tech. Rep. #94-18, RPI Computer Science Dept., 1994.

Dynamic Assembly of Personalized Learning Content on the Semantic Web

Jelena Jovanović[1], Dragan Gašević[2], and Vladan Devedžić[1]

[1] FON, School of Business Administration, University of Belgrade, Serbia and Montenegro
{jeljov, devedzic}@fon.bg.ac.yu
[2] School of Interactive arts and Technology, Simon Fraser University Surrey Canada
dgasevic@sfu.ca

Abstract. This paper presents an ontology-based approach for automatic decomposition of learning objects (LOs) into reusable content units, and dynamic reassembly of such units into personalized learning content. To test our approach we developed TANGRAM, an integrated learning environment for the domain of Intelligent Information Systems. Relying on a number of ontologies, TANGRAM allows decomposition of LOs into smaller content units, which can be later assembled into new LOs personalized to the user's domain knowledge, preferences, and learning styles. The focus of the presentation is on the ontologies themselves, in the context of user modeling and personalization. Furthermore, the paper presents the algorithm we apply to dynamically assemble content units into personalized learning content. We also discuss our experiences with dynamic content generation and point out directions for future work.

1 Introduction

Reusing learning objects (LOs) across educational applications is a great idea, but not easily achievable in practice. A recent study by Brooks et al. [1] has shown that current e-learning standards and specifications (such as the IEEE LOM standard) are rather restrictive in terms of the variety of metadata they capture and imprecise in expressing the structure of such metadata. Moreover, few of the metadata fields proposed by such specifications are actually used in learning object repositories (LORs) to annotate the LOs, which reduces the possibility for agents to retrieve the LOs. As a result, nearly all LO-based courses are created directly by instructional designers, who explicitly hand craft the LOs for the purpose. Furthermore, Robert and Gingras [12] conducted an experiment showing that teachers mostly reuse their own material, and only some LOs created by other teachers. The reusability of other people's LOs largely depends on the teacher's instructional practices and teaching style, as well as on the type of content of those LOs (presentations, diagrams, tests, etc.). The practice of handcrafting new LOs from existing ones shows that authors very often copy-and-paste parts of existing LOs into newly created LOs. In other words, rather than reusing entire LOs for their courses, they manually reuse their parts.

This creates the idea of reusable content units at a granularity finer than LO as a whole. We have developed an ontology-based approach for automatic decomposition

Y. Sure and J. Domingue (Eds.): ESWC 2006, LNCS 4011, pp. 545–559, 2006.

of LOs into reusable fragments, and dynamic reassembly of such fragments into personalized learning content.

1.1 Problem Statement

The objectives of this paper are:

- to explain the rationale for using ontologies to enable on-the-fly assembly of personalized learning content out of reusable content units;
- to present an example of how such an ontology-based approach is implemented in a specific learning environment, called TANGRAM;
- to discuss practical implementation details and experience with dynamic generation of personalized learning content.

The focus of the presentation is on the ontologies themselves, in the context of user modeling and personalization. The principles we discuss are implementation-independent. On the other hand, their implementation in TANGRAM helped us reveal important practical details we were not aware of initially.

The rest of the paper is structured to follow the order of the objectives stated above.

2 The Rationale

The approach that we propose can be summarized as follows: reuse existing content units to dynamically generate new learning content tailored to satisfy the needs of a specific student. To overcome the problem of interoperability between disparate domains, we based our approach on Semantic Web technologies, ontologies in particular.

The starting point in our approach is the classification of ontologies in the domain of eLearning suggested in [13]. This classification differentiates between the following types of ontologies: 1) content (domain) ontologies that formally describe the subject matter (topics) of learning content; 2) structural ontologies that formalize the content structure; and 3) context ontologies that specify the pedagogical/instructional role of the content. In our approach, a LO is represented in a structural ontology compliant format, whereas concepts of a domain ontology are used to semantically describe the LO's content. In addition, the concepts from a context ontology are used to mark up LOs with their pedagogical/instructional roles. The proposed approach also assumes annotation of each component of a LO, thus making individual components reusable.

Explicitly defined structure of a LO facilitates adaptation of the LO, as it enables direct access to each of its components and their tailoring to the specific features of a student. Besides, being able to directly access components of a LO, we are empowered to dynamically, on-the-fly create new, personalized learning content.

To be reusable, a domain ontology must not contain any information related to topics sequencing and navigation. On the other hand, it does make sense to formally represent an optimal learning path through the domain. Accordingly, we use a special ontology for that purpose. Finally, a user model ontology is used to enable formal representation of users' data and exchange of these data with other learning applications.

3 Ontologies for Dynamic Assembly of Personalized Content

To test the feasibility of the proposed approach to dynamic assembly of personalized learning content, we have developed TANGRAM – an integrated learning environment for the domain of Intelligent Information Systems (IIS). TANGRAM is implemented as a Web application built on top of a repository of educational content and intended to be useful to both content authors and students interested in the domain of IIS. Fig. 1 illustrates TANGRAM's architecture and depicts the ontologies it uses. These ontologies are concisely described in the following subsections[1]. Additionally, to annotate content units in TANGRAM, we defined a profile of the IEEE LOM RDF Binding specification[2]. The profile defines a subset of the IEEE LOM elements that we found necessary to support the intended functionalities of the system [9].

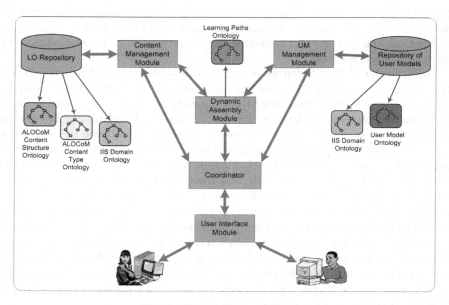

Fig. 1. TANGRAM's architecture

3.1 ALOCoM-Based Ontologies

In our previous collaborative research efforts with the ARIADNE research group from K.U. Leuven, Belgium, we developed ALOCoM ontology as a content structure ontology based on the Abstract Learning Object Content Model (ALOCoM) [14]. The ontology defines concepts and relationships that enable formal definition of the structure of a LO. To learn more about this ontology, interested readers should refer to [10]. However, our latest research led to a major revision of the ALOCoM ontology and its division into: ALOCoM Content Structure ontology (ALOCoMCS) and ALOCoM Content Type ontology (ALOCoMCT).

---

[1] All ontologies can be downloaded from: http://iis.fon.bg.ac.yu/TANGRAM/ ontologies.html
[2] http://kmr.nada.kth.se/el/ims/md-lomrdf.html

Being based on the common model, these two ontologies share the same root concepts: Content Unit (CU), Content Fragment (CF), Content Object (CO) and Learning Object (LO). CU is an abstract concept aimed at representing content of any level of granularity. CFs are CUs in their most basic form, like text, audio and video. These elements can be regarded as raw digital resources that cannot be further decomposed. A CO is an aggregation of CFs and/or other COs. Navigational elements enable sequencing of CFs in a CO. LOs aggregate COs around a learning objective. However, in our ALOCoM-based ontologies, these basic types of CUs are considered from completely different perspectives – ALOCoMCS is about content structuring, whereas ALOCoMCT focuses on potential instructional/pedagogical roles of CUs.

3.2 Domain Ontology

The SKOS Core ontology[3] is used as the basis of the IIS course domain ontology[4]. Being specifically developed to describe taxonomies and classification schemes, the SKOS Core ontology has an excellent variety of properties to describe relationships between topics in a course.

Each concept of the IIS domain is represented as an instance of the *skos:Concept* class, whereas the conceptual scheme of the domain is represented as an instance of the *skos:ConceptScheme* class. The SKOS' property *skos:inScheme* is used to associate all defined instances of the *skos:Concept* class to the conceptual scheme of the IIS domain. Likewise, each identified domain concept is assigned one or more aliases (i.e., alternative terms typically used in literature when referring to a concept) using the SKOS properties *skos:prefLabel*, *skos:altLabel*, and *skos:hiddenLabel*. SKOS semantic properties, i.e. properties derived from the *skos:semanticRelation* property, enabled us to structure the IIS domain in a generalization hierarchy (via the *skos:broader* and its inverse *skos:narrower* properties), as well as to define semantic relations between concepts belonging to different branches of the hierarchy (via the *skos:related* property). We used the *skos:hasTopConcept* property to relate the most general domain concepts (such as intelligent agents, Semantic Web, etc.) to the IIS concept scheme, thus formally stating that these concepts form the top level of the created concepts hierarchy. Fig. 2 shows an excerpt of the ontology that defines 'XML Schema' as a domain concept.

```
<skos:Concept rdf:ID="xml_schema">
    <skos:broader rdf:resource="#xmltech"/>
    <skos:prefLabel rdf:datatype="http://www.w3.org/2001/XMLSchema#string">XML Schema
    </skos:prefLabel>
    <skos:hiddenLabel rdf:datatype="http://www.w3.org/2001/XMLSchema#string">xsd
    </skos:hiddenLabel>
    <skos:inScheme rdf:resource="#iis-concept-scheme"/>
</skos:Concept>
```

Fig. 2. excerpt from the SKOS-based IIS domain ontology

---

[3] http://www.w3.org/2004/02/skos/core/
[4] Actually, we used SKOS Core OWL binding available at:
http://ai.usask.ca/mums/schemas/2005/01/27/skos-core-dl.owl

One should note that the domain ontology does not contain any information regarding topics sequencing, in terms of the order in which the topics should be presented to the learners. That kind of information is stored separately in the Learning Paths ontology.

3.3 Learning Paths Ontology

The Learning Paths (LP) ontology defines learning trajectories through the topics defined in the domain ontology. We defined this ontology as an extension of the SKOS Core ontology that introduces three new properties: *lp:requiresKnowledgeOf*, *lp:isPrerequisiteFor*, and *lp:hasKnowledgePonder*. The first two are semantic properties defining prerequisite relationships between domain topics, whereas the third one defines difficulty level of a topic on the scale from 0 to 1.

The properties *lp:requiresKnowledgeOf* and *lp:isPrerequisteFor* are defined as sub-properties of the *skos:semanticRelation* property of the SKOS Core ontology. These properties are defined as mutually inverse and transitive. One should note that unlike the Dublin Core properties *dc:requires* and *dc:isRequiredBy*[5] that establish dependency of prerequisite type among physical LOs, the properties we introduced are intended to describe similar relations on the level of domain concepts.

As Fig. 3 suggests, the LP ontology relates instances of the domain ontology through an additional set of relationships reflecting a specific instructional approach to teaching/learning IIS. The main benefit of decoupling the domain model in this way is to enable reuse of the domain ontology – even if the applied instructional approach changes, the domain ontology remains intact.

```
<skos:Concept rdf:about="http://tangram/iis-domain.owl#xml_schema">
  <lp:isPrerequisiteFor rdf:resource="http://tangram/iis-domain.owl#xslt"/>
  <lp:requiresKnowledgeOf rdf:resource="http://tangram/iis-domain.owl#xml">
  <lp:requiresKnowledgeOf rdf:resource="http://tangram/iis-domain.owl#xpath">
  <lp:hasKnowledgePonder rdf:datatype="http://www.w3.org/2001/XMLSchema#float">0.4
  </lp:hasKnowledgePonder>
</skos:Concept>
```

Fig. 3. An excerpt from the Learning Paths ontology for the domain of IIS

3.4 User Model Ontology

We developed a User Model (UM) ontology to help us formally represent relevant information about TANGRAM users (content authors and students). The ontology focuses exclusively on the user information that proved to be essential for TANGRAM's functionalities. To enable interoperability with other learning applications and exchange of users' data, we based the ontology on official specifications for user modeling: IEEE PAPI Learner[6] and IMS LIP[7]. Furthermore, since we did not want to end up with another specific interpretation of the official specifications, potentially incompatible with existing learning applications, we explored existing solutions, like the ones presented in [4] and [11]. The result is a modular UM ontology that:

---

[5] http://dublincore.org/documents/dcmi-terms/

[6] http://edutool.com/papi

[7] http://www.imsglobal.org/profiles

- uses some parts of the UM ontology developed for the ELENA project and described in [4]; specifically, we use the elements aimed for representing students' performance (as proposed by the IEEE PAPI Learner specification) and their preferences (as specified in the IMS LIP);
- introduces new constructs for representing users' data that the official specifications do not declare and the existing ontologies either do not include at all, or do not represent in a manner compliant to the needs of TANGRAM.

In the center of Fig. 4[8] one can notice class *um:User* that formally describes the concept of a TANGRAM user. Each user, i.e. instance of this class, is related to a set of his/her personal data via the *um:hasPersonalInfo* property. Personal data are formally represented with the *um:PersonalInfo* class and its datatype properties: *um:username* and *um:password* properties that keep values of secure login data, as well as *um:name* property representing the user's name. Each user can be a member of one or more organizations (*um:Organization*). Specifically, the user can be a member of a university (*um:University*), a research centre (*um:ResearchCentre*) and/or a research group (*um:ResearchGroup*). Additionally, for each user the system needs data about his/her role/position in the formal organization (s)he belongs to. Therefore,

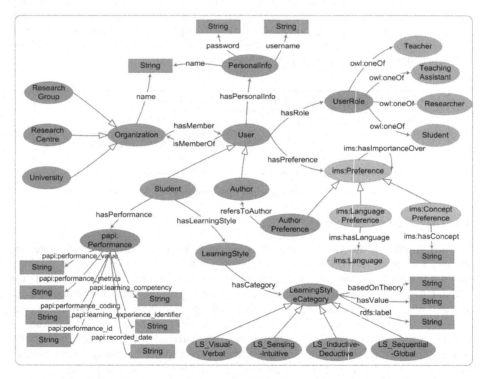

Fig. 4. Graphical representation of the TANGRAM's User Model Ontology

---

[8] Classes and properties that do not have namespace prefix in Fig. 4 belong to the um: http://tangram/user-model/complete.owl namespace.

we introduced property *um:hasRole* that relates an instance of the *um:User* class with an appropriate instance of the *um:UserRole* class. The latter class formalizes the concept of a role/position a user typically has in an educational environment and is specified as an enumeration (via *owl:oneOf* construct) of the following instances: *um:Teacher*, *um:TeachingAssistant*, *um:Researcher*, *um:Student*. Of course, this enumeration can be extended to encompass additional roles if needed. Further, each user can have certain preferences (*um:hasPreference*) regarding language (*ims:-LanguagePreference*) and/or domain topics (*ims:ConceptPreference*). Representation of users' preferences is taken from the user model ontology developed for the ELENA project [4] and is fully compliant with the IMS LIP specification (hence *ims* prefix). Class *ims:Preference*, formally representing a user's preference, can have *ims:hasImportanceOver* property that defines priority (i.e. importance) of a preference for a specific user. Furthermore, the ontology introduces *um:AuthorPreference* class as a subclass of *ims:Preference* in order to represent users' preferences regarding authors of learning content. The property *um:refersToAuthor* associates this specific type of a user's preference with his/her favorite author of learning content (one or more of them).

The remaining classes and properties of the TANGRAM UM ontology are exclusively aimed at formal representation of students' data. Each student (*um:Student*) is assigned a set of performance-related data (via *um:hasPerformance* property) represented in the form of the *papi:Performance* class and the following set of properties[9]:

1. the *papi:learning _competency* property refers to a concept of the domain ontology that formally describes the subject matter of the acquired knowledge in the best way (i.e. contains URI of that concept);
2. the *papi:learning_experience_identifier* property identifies a CU that was a part of the learning material used for learning. In TANGRAM, each instance of the *papi:Performance* class has a number of properties of this type – one for each CU used to assemble the learning content for the student;
3. the *papi:performance_coding* and *papi:performance_metrics* properties define respectively the coding system and the metrics used to evaluate a student's performance level (i.e., the level of the acquired knowledge);
4. the *papi:performance_value* property keeps information about the real value/level of the acquired knowledge measured in terms of the specified metrics and coding system;
5. the *papi:recorded_date* property is aimed at representing date and time when the performance was recorded, i.e. when the learning process took place.

Additionally, for each student the system keeps data about his/her learning style. Representation of learning styles in the UM ontology is based on the Felder & Silverman model of learning styles [6]. This model recognizes 5 categories of learning styles: 1) Visual-Verbal, 2) Sensing-Intuitive, 3) Sequential-Global, 4) Inductive-Deductive and 5) Active-Reflective. The learning style of a student is formally represented by the *um:LearningStyle* class in the UM ontology. This class is associated (via the *um:hasCategory* property) with the *um:LearningStyleCategory* class that formally stands for one specific aspect (category) of the learning style. Specifically, TANGRAM implements the learning categories defined in the Felder & Silverman

---

[9] The prefix *papi:* is used to denote that the Performance class and its properties are defined according to the PAPI Learner Specification.

model and introduces one subclass of the *um:LearningStyleCategory* class to represent each of those categories (e.g. *um:LS_Visual-Verbal*)[10]. To make the ontology more general and easily extensible, we assigned the property *um:basedOnTheory* to the *um:LearningStyleCategory* class, thus enabling the introduction of learning style categories defined by other authors. The class *um:LearningStyleCategory* is also attached the *um:hasValue* property aimed at representing the position of a specific student on the continuum defined by the opposite poles of a learning style category. The range of this property is restricted to double values between -1 and 1 (inclusively). The boundary values (-1 and 1) represent the two extreme poles of each learning style category. For example, assigning the value of -1 to the *um:hasValue* property of the *um:LS_Visual-Verbal* class means that the learner is highly visual. On the opposite, *um:hasValue* property with the value of 1 identifies a highly verbal learner.

4   Personalized Learning in TANGRAM

TANGRAM provides adaptation of learning content to the specific needs of individual students. Currently, it is focused on enabling personalized learning experience to students interested in the domain of IIS. Two basic functionalities of the system from the students' perspective are:

- Provision of learning content adapted to the student's current level of knowledge of the domain concept of interest, his/her learning style, and other personal preferences.
- Quick access to a particular type of content about a topic of interest, e.g. access to *examples* of RDF documents or *definitions* of the Semantic Web (both topics belong to the domain of IIS).

In this section we focus on the former functionality and explain in details how it is implemented in TANGRAM.

4.1   Initialization of the User Model

A student must register with the system during the first session. Through the registration procedure the system acquires information about the student sufficient to create an initial version of his/her model. The student is required to fill in a simplified version of the Felder&Silverman questionnaire for determining the student's learning style[11]. The acquired data enables the system to create personalized learning content for the student.

As for initial determination of the student's knowledge about the IIS domain, the system relies on the student's self-assessment. During the registration procedure, the student is asked to estimate his/her level of knowledge of the main sub-domains of the IIS domain (e.g. Intelligent Agents, Semantic Web). In particular, the student is presented with the following set of options: 'Never heard of the topic', 'Have a basic idea', 'Familiar with', 'Know well' and 'Demand advanced topics', and has to choose

---

[10] We did not consider Active-Reflective learning style category, as it emphasizes social aspects of a learning process that TANGRAM currently is not able to support.

[11] The questionnaire is known as "Index of Learning Styles", and is available at http://www. engr.ncsu.edu/learningstyles/ilsweb.html

the one that reflects his\her knowledge best. Internally, TANGRAM converts the student's selection for each sub-domain into its numerical counterpart (0, 0.2, 0.4, 0.6 or 0.8, respectively). These numerical values are later compared to the values of the *lp:hasKnowledgePonder* property assigned to the domain concepts in the LP ontology, to let the system determine the student's initial position in the IIS domain space and provide him/her with proper guidance and support.

4.2 Dynamic Assembly of Personalized Learning Content

A learning session starts after the user (registered and authenticated as a student) selects a sub-domain of IIS to learn about. The system performs a sort of comparative analysis of data stored in the student's model and in the LP ontology. Specifically, the LP ontology is queried for the set of domain concepts that are essential for successful comprehension of the topics from the chosen sub-domain. More precisely, the query targets the concepts related via *lp:requiresKnowledgeOf* property to the topics encompassed by the chosen sub-domain. Subsequently, the student model is queried for data about the student's level of knowledge about the selected sub-domain and the identified set of prerequisite concepts. Information resulting from this analysis is used to provide adaptive guidance and direct the student towards the most appropriate topics for him/her at that moment. To achieve this, we make use of link annotation and hiding techniques [2]. Specifically, hierarchical organization of concepts of the selected sub-domain is visualized as an annotated tree of links (shown in the upper left corner of Fig. 5). We use the following link annotations:

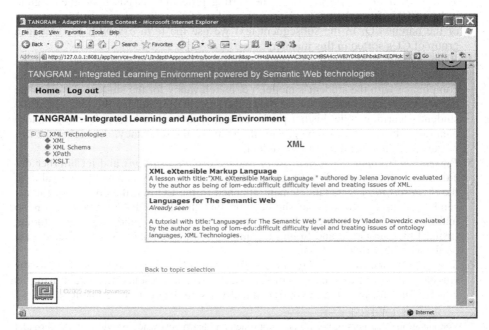

Fig. 5. Screen shot of a page presenting a ranked list of generated assemblies (i.e. their descriptions)

1. blue bullet preceding a link to a domain concept denotes that the student knows the topic that the link points to,
2. green bullet denotes a recommended domain concept, i.e. a concept that the student has not learned yet, but has knowledge about all prerequisite topics,
3. red bullet is used to annotate a domain topic that the student is still not ready for as (s)he is ignorant of the prerequisite topics.

Link hiding technique is used to prevent the student from accessing topics that are too advanced for him/her. In other words, links annotated with red bullets are made inactive.

After the student selects one concept from the topics tree, the system initiates the process of dynamic assembly of learning content on the selected topic. The process is based on the following algorithm:

1. *Query the LOR for content units covering the selected domain topic.* The query is based on the *dc:subject* metadata element of the CUs from the repository. If the repository does not contain CUs on the selected topic, the further steps of the algorithm depend on the student's learning style, i.e. on its Sequential-Global dimension, to be more precise[12]. If the student belongs to the category of global learners, the algorithm proceeds normally. Otherwise, the system informs the student that the learning content on the selected topic is currently unavailable and suggests other suitable topics.
2. *Classify the retrieved content units into groups according to the same parent LO criterion.* In other words, CUs originating from the same slide presentation are put in the same group.
3. *Sort components in each group.* The sorting procedure is based on the original order of CUs from the group, i.e. on the value of the *alocomcs:ordering* property of the parent LO. In the subsequent text we use the term *assembly* to refer to a group of CUs sorted in this manner.
4. *Rank assemblies according to their compliance with the student model.* Each assembly is assigned a double value (relevancy) between 0 and 1 that reflects its compliance with the student's model, i.e. its relevancy for the student. To calculate the relevancy of an assembly we query the student's model for the data about the student's learning style, his/her preferred author as well as his/her learning history data (already seen CUs). The greater the value of the relevancy, the higher the importance of the assembly for the student.
5. *Present the student the sorted list of assemblies' descriptions* and let him/her decide which one to take (Fig. 5). Description of an assembly is actually the value of the *dc:description* metadata element attached to the LO that the content of the assembly originates from. One should note that the TANGRAM does not aim to make a choice for a student. Instead, the system provides guidance to the student (using link annotation and hiding techniques), and eventually lets him/her decide on the assembly to learn from.
6. *Show the student the learning content from the selected assembly.* As soon as the student selects one assembly from the list, the system presents its content using its generic form for presentation of dynamically assembled learning content.

---

[12] Whereas global learners prefer holistic approach and learn best when provided with a broader context of the topic of interest, sequential learners tend to be confused/disoriented if the topics are not presented in a linear fashion [6].

7. *Update the student model.* Specifically, the system creates an instance of the *papi:Performance* class in the student model and assigns values to its properties (see Section 3.4 for details). For example, the *papi:performance_value* property is assigned a value that reflects the level of mastery of the domain topic. If it was a topic recommended by the system, the property is assigned the maximum value (1). However, if the assembly covered an advanced topic, due to the lack of more appropriate learning content, this property is set to 0.35. This approach was inspired by the work of De Bra et al [3] and is based on the assumption that the student, due to the lack of the necessary prerequisite knowledge was not able to fully understand the presented content.

5 Discussion

In this section we discuss our experiences with the process of dynamic content assembly, emphasizing its most challenging aspects. Actually, we draw attention to the deficiencies of the presented algorithm and explain their origins.

Current implementation of the algorithm explained above uses exclusively slides (instances of *alocomc:Slide* class) for dynamic generation of personalized learning content. All our attempts to base the assembly process on CUs of lower granularity levels (*alocomcs:Paragraph, alocomcs:List, alocomcs:ListItem,...*) ended unsuccessfully: we did not manage to automatically generate coherent learning content out of those components. Additionally, one might argue that an assembly is nothing more than a slide presentation from which someone has taken out slides that do not deal with the relevant domain topic(s). However, it should be noted that our original idea was completely different. We intended to build new learning materials by combining CUs from diverse LOs. Nonetheless, this objective turned out as too ambitious: proper sequencing of small size components, as well as meaningful arrangement of their content, authoring styles, terminology and other relevant features proved to be an insurmountable task.

We recognized the lack of precise semantic descriptions of a CU's content as the major obstacle for using small-size CUs in the process of automatic content assembly. To make these statements clearer, let us consider a small example. Fig. 6 presents two slides from different slide presentations, authored by different authors, but covering the same domain concept – the concept of the XML Schema. Additionally, both slides have the same instructional role – they provide examples of some specific features of XML Schema. Let us assume that a student requested a learning content on XML Schema and the system has started executing algorithm presented in Section 4.1. Obviously, the slides from Fig. 6 will be in the set of the CUs retrieved from the LO repository in the first step of the algorithm. To create a coherent learning content out of the collected CUs, the system has to determine how to properly sequence those CUs. Proper sequencing assumes: 1) sequential introduction of complexity – simple concepts should always be introduced before complex topics, 2) respect of the student's learning style, particularly, in the context of our example, some students prefer to be first presented with definitions and then provided with examples of a domain

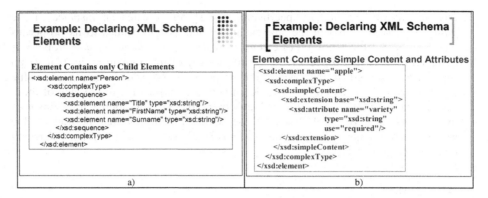

Fig. 6 Sample slides annotated with the XML Schema domain ontology concept

topic, whereas others are inclined towards the opposite approach. Semantic annotations of CUs are the primary source of information for resolving the problem of proper sequencing. In particular, the most relevant are: *dc:subject* metadata element pointing to a concept from the domain ontology and *alocom-meta:type* element pointing to the formal representation of the instructional role of a CU (i.e. concept from the ALOCoMCT ontology). Since the domain ontology only has 'XML Schema' concept to represent any content related to this very broad topic, it is clear that both slides from Fig. 6 will have the same value for the *dc:subject* metadata. Additionally, both slides have the same instructional role (*alocomct:Example*). In such a situation, the dynamic assembly subsystem can only guess the right order of the CUs. On the other hand, for people familiar with XML Schema concepts it is easy to deduce that slide (b) should precede slide (a), as comprehension of the example from slide (b) is a prerequisite for understanding the example on slide (a). However, the system does not know this, as its sole source of knowledge is the IIS domain ontology that does not contain detailed knowledge about the XML Schema concept.

To resolve this problem we need a more precise formal description of the IIS domain. In other words, the employed domain ontology needs to be significantly enlarged: each leaf class of the current ontology should be substituted with a set of concepts and relationships that describe the domain topic more precisely. Accordingly, we intend to organize the domain ontology in modules, including the core part (the IIS domain ontology in its current state) and a number of extensions, one for each complex concept of the current ontology. The OWL ontology language, we used to encode the IIS ontology,provides support for such a modular approach. Additionally, each extension of the domain ontology needs to be accompanied by a corresponding extension of the LP ontology defining an optimal learning path through the concepts of the extension. Finally, TANGRAM's subsystem for automatic semantic annotation of CUs needs to be improved if we want to fully exploit the potentials that semantically rich domain ontology offers. Although the initial evaluations of this subsystem proved to be rather satisfactory, our intention is to further improve it with more advanced text mining and information extraction techniques.

6 Related Work

Farell et al. have developed the Dynamic Assembly Engine (DAE), aimed at automatic assembly of LOs into simple, short, focused, Web-based custom courses [5]. The process is based upon the learner's request and consists of searching a LOR for relevant LOs and sequencing the retrieved LOs into a coherent learning path. Being partially inspired by the work of Farrell et al., our approach to dynamic content assembly exhibits some common traits with theirs'. Nonetheless, as TANGRAM is based on a content structure ontology (ALOCoMCS ontology), it enables reuse of CUs of different granularity levels. In other words, TANGRAM allows one to reuse not only LOs (as DAE does), but also smaller CUs (COs and CFs). Furthermore, unlike our system, DAE does not keep the users data relevant for content adaptation (e.g. learning style, preferences, knowledge of the domain topics). Instead the adaptation is based exclusively on the user's request, i.e. keyword query, desired level of detail, and the amount of time available for learning. Like TANGRAM, DAE uses its own profile of the IEEE LOM metadata schema. However, while TANGRAM's profile is used to annotate both LOs and their components (i.e. reusable CUs of divers granularity levels), in DAE the developed profile is used exclusively for annotating LOs. Another similarity of the two systems lies in their usage of a domain ontology for semantic annotation of LOs. Furthermore, the two systems use similar taxonomies to annotate LOs with instructional roles.

OntAWare provides an environment comprising a set of software tools that support learning content authoring, management and delivery [8]. It enables semi-automatic generation of LOs out of appropriate domain ontologies. Actually, LOs are produced by the application of graph transformations to these ontologies. However, since ontologies are aimed primarily for machine (not human) consumption, they typically contain terse and often scarce, human-readable descriptions of concepts and their relationships. Therefore, content generated solely from a domain ontology can be used as a skeleton for a LO, rather than as a LO per se. Further, adaptation of learning content is of a limited scope and is based solely on a student's browsing history – a track of domain concepts presented to the student during his/her single session with the system. Students' personal traits are not considered at all. Additionally, the algorithm for dynamic composition of LOs is hard-coded, making it difficult to change the instructional approach to content authoring. Learning Paths ontology makes such a change in TANGRAM much easier.

Henze [7] has developed a framework for creating and maintaining Personal Readers that provide personalized contextual information on the currently considered LO, like recommendations about additional readings, more general/detailed information, exercises, quizzes, etc. The driving principle of this framework is to expose different personalization functionalities as services which are coordinated by a mediator service. Each personalization service performs a specific kind of a LO personalization, based on the LO's metadata, user's characteristics and an appropriate domain ontology. At the current state, Personal Reader employs a very simple user model that keeps track of the learning resources the user has visited. LO's metadata must be fully IEEE LOM compliant, if it is to be processed by the system. Concepts of the domain ontology are used to enhance LOs annotations with semantic metadata. The flexibility offered by such a service-oriented architecture, made us rethink the current design of our system and made it service oriented.

7 Conclusion

The paper presents an approach to dynamic assembly of personalized learning content using the Semantic Web technologies. The peculiarity of our approach is that we reuse existing content units of different granularity levels to dynamically generate new learning content compliant to the specific needs of each individual student. To evaluate the feasibility of the proposed approach we developed TANGRAM, a web-based learning environment for the domain of Intelligent Information Systems. TANGRAM enables on-the-fly assembly of new learning content compliant to the student's knowledge of the subject domain, his/her preferences and learning style. Furthermore, TANGRAM allows quick access to a particular type of content about a domain topic of interest. Although TANGRAM supports exclusively the domain of IIS, it can be easily repurposed for other domains if appropriate domain ontology and its related learning path ontology are provided.

While working on TANGRAM's implementation we became aware of same important practical details concerning dynamic assembly of CUs originating from different sources (i.e. LOs) - for example, the problem of ordering of CUs dealing with the same domain concept. In our future research we address this issue by defining a richer domain ontology, as well as by further improving TANGRAM's subsystem for automatic semantic annotation of CUs. We also plan to extend our solution to enable repurposing content of other types of LOs beside slide presentations.

References

1. Brooks, C., McCalla, G., and Winter, M., "Flexible Learning Object Metadata", In Proc. of the Int'l Workshop on Applications of Semantic Web Technologies for E-Learning, Amsterdam, The Netherlands, 2005.
2. Brusilovsky, P, "Methods and Techniques of Adaptive Hypermedia," Adaptive Hypertext and Hypermedia, Kluwer Academic Publishers, the Netherlands, 1998, pp. 1-43.
3. De Bra, P., Aroyo, L., and Cristea, A., Adaptive Web-based Educational Hypermedia, Book chapter in: Web Dynamics, Adaptive to Change in Content, Size, Topology and Use, (Eds.) Mark Levene, Alexandra Poulovassilis, pp. 387-410, Springer, 2004
4. Dolog, P., and Nejdl, W., "Challenges and Benefits of the Semantic Web for User Modeling," In Proc. of AH2003 Workshop at 12th Int'l WWW Conf., Budapest, Hungary, May 2003.
5. Farrell, R., Liburd, S. D., and Thomas, J. C., "Dynamic Assembly of Learning Objects," In Proc. of the 13th Int'l WWW Conf., New York, USA, 2004, pp. 162-169.
6. Felder, R., and Silverman, L., "Learning and Teaching Styles In Engineering Education," Journal of Engineering Education, Vol.78, No.7, pp. 674–681, 1988.
7. Henze, N., "Personal Readers: Personalized Learning Object Readers for the Semantic Web," Proc. of the 12th Int'l Conf. on Artificial Intelligence in Education, Amsterdam, The Netherlands, 2005.

8. Holohan, E., Melia, M., McMullen, D., and Pahl, C., "Adaptive E-Learning Content Generation based on Semantic Web Technology", In Proc. Int'l Workshop on Applications of Semantic Web Technologies for E-Learning, Amsterdam, The Netherlands, 2005

9. Jovanović, J., Gašević, D., and Devedžić, V., "TANGRAM: An Ontology-based Learning Environment for Intelligent Information Systems," Proc. of the 10th World ELearn Conf, Vancouver, Canada, 2005, pp. 2966-2971.

10. Jovanović, J., Gašević, D., Verbert, K., and Duval, E., "Ontology of learning object content structure," *Proc. of the 12th Int'l Conf. on Artificial Intelligence in Education*, Amsterdam, The Netherlands, 2005, pp.322-329.

11. Keenoy, K., Levene, M., & Peterson, D., (2003.) "Personalisation and Trails in Self e-Learning Networks", SeLeNe Working Package 4 Deliverable 4.2. [Online]. Available at: http://www.dcs.bbk.ac.uk/selene/reports/Del4.2-2.1.pdf.

12. Robert, J.-M., and Gingras, G., "Experimental study on the reuse of learning objects and teaching practices", Proc. Int'l Conf. on Education and Technology, Calgary, Canada, 2005.

13. Stojanović, Lj. et al. (2001). "eLearning in the Semantic Web," Proc. of the WWW2001 Int'l Conf., Orlando, USA.

14. Verbert, K., Klerkx, J., Meire, M., Najjar, J., and Duval, E., "Towards a Global Component Architecture for Learning Objects: an Ontology Based Approach," *Proc. of OTM 2004 Workshop on Ontologies, Semantics and E-learning*, Agia Napa, Cyprus, 2004.

Interactive Ontology-Based User Knowledge Acquisition: A Case Study

Lora Aroyo[1], Ronald Denaux[1], Vania Dimitrova[2], and Michael Pye[2]

[1] Eindhoven University of Technology, Faculty of Mathematics and Computer Science,
P.O.Box 513, 5600 MB Eindhoven, The Netherlands
[2] School of Computing, University of Leeds, LS2 9NA, Leeds - UK
l.m.aroyo@tue.nl, vania@comp.leeds.ac.uk

Abstract. On the Semantic Web personalization technologies are needed to deal with user diversity. Our research aims at maximising the automation of acquisition of user knowledge, thus providing an effective solution for multi-faceted user modeling. This paper presents an approach to eliciting a user's conceptualization by engaging in an ontology-driven dialog. This is implemented as an OWL-based domain-independent diagnostic agent. We show the deployment of the agent in a use case for personalized management of learning content, which has been evaluated in three studies with users. Currently, the system is being deployed in a cultural heritage domain for personalized recommendation of museum resources.

1 Introduction

The rapid expansion of semantics-enriched services on the Web results in an exponential growth of the users of these services. They differ in their capabilities, expectations, goals, requirements, preferences and usage context. The one-size-fits-all approach to developing Web applications is becoming inappropriate. To fulfill the Semantic Web vision of improving the way computers and people work together, *context-aware* and *user-adaptive* technologies that take into account the *users' perspective* are needed [1]. User-adaptive systems automatically tailor their behavior to the needs of individual users. They can recommend items or documents that relate to the user's interests, provide links to relevant resources according to the user's goal, or offer explanation when needed. With the addition of explicit semantics, user-adaptive systems become context-aware.

A critical aspect in the realization of personalization is the acquisition of knowledge about the users. Traditionally it is represented in a *user model* [2]. The depth of the represented understanding about the users can vary from simple user profiles that focus mainly on users' preferences to sophisticated models that capture users' conceptualizations [3]. In the *open world* context the latter capture individual users' viewpoints, spanning from knowledge engineers to naive users. They also define the semantics of the user knowledge representation, thus facilitating the effective integration of the users within semantics-aware systems. This enables knowledge-enhanced reasoning to align the perspectives of

Y. Sure and J. Domingue (Eds.): ESWC 2006, LNCS 4011, pp. 560–574, 2006.

users and system designers, where various mismatches in meaning can be discovered and taken into account for more effective adaptation. The acquisition and maintenance of user conceptual models requires robust methods that integrate seamlessly in semantics-enhanced Web-based systems. An example of such an approach is proposed in here and is illustrated in an e-learning case study.

Why did we chose an e-learning use case? E-learning is a key application domain where the empowering role of semantics-enhanced technologies is being acknowledged. The Web is becoming the most popular educational medium nowadays, at schools, universities, and for professional training [4]. A prominent new stream of research on Educational Semantic Web [5] is being established. Recent successes in this field include semantics-based annotation and sharing of educational resources [6, 7, 8], as well as supporting the construction and sharing of knowledge among communities of learners and teachers [9, 10]. Although there are initial attempts to develop semantic-aware personalization technologies for Web-based educational systems [11, 12], this research is still in an embryonic stage. On the other hand, adaptive learning systems are well advanced in the addressing of the user' needs [13]. As pointed by Wolpers and Nejdl, future research in the Educational Semantic Web should include, among others, capturing the perspectives of different users based on observations from a variety of sources, and representing these perspectives in interoperable learner models [4]. The approach presented in this paper is a contribution in this direction. Furthermore, the proposed approach is domain-independent, and is currently being instantiated in museum and digital library domains.

The paper describes an ontology-based dialog agent, called OWL-OLM, that elicits and maintains a model of the user's conceptualization. The architecture of OWL-OLM is presented in Section 2, and the main components are described in the follow-up sections: domain ontology and a user model (Section 3) and dialog maintenance (Section 4). We illustrate the deployment of OWL-OLM within an RDF/OWL-based system for personalized management of learning content, called OntoAIMS Resource Browser (Section 6). It uses a multi-faceted user model built by collecting, interpreting and validating user data from diverse sources, such as user preferences, diagnostic dialog and monitoring the user interaction with the system [14]. The evaluation of OntoAIMS Resource Browser is outlined in Section 7. Finally, we discuss related and future work.

2   Architecture of OWL-OLM

OWL-OLM uses the STyLE-OLM framework for interactive ontology-based user modeling [15] and extends it to work with an OWL-based domain ontology and a user model. The architecture of OWL-OLM is presented in Figure 1.

The *Dialog Agent* is the main OWL-OLM component which maintains the user-knowledge acquisition dialog. The user-agent interaction is geared towards achieving the goal of the user, according to which the agent defines its *dialog goals*. For example, in a learning situation the user may want to be recommended what to read next on a certain topic. The goal of the dialog agent in this case would be to asses the current state of the user's knowledge according to the requirements for the particular course task. In a museum case, the user may want to be recommended which painting to view next in the context of the user's current preferences. To do so, dialog subgoals are defined (e.g. to probe the user's knowledge of concepts related to the task or the preferences set). In addition, the user may want to clarify some part of the domain, so he asks questions. Dialog subgoals will be then to answer the user's questions and help him clarify the particular domain aspects.

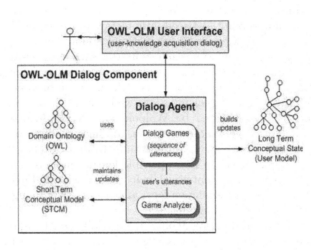

Fig. 1. The architecture of OWL-OLM

A *Domain Ontology* built in OWL is used to maintain the dialog and to update the user's *Short-Term Conceptual State*. The latter is also represented in OWL and provides a model of the user's conceptualization gathered throughout the dialog. Section 3 gives details.

The dialog agent maintains a *dialog episode goal*, which is divided into *subgoals* that trigger *Dialog Games* - sequences of utterances to achieve a specific sub-goal, see Section 4.1.

The agent uses also a *Game Analyzer* that analyzes each user's utterance to decide the agent's response and to update the user's short-term conceptual state, see Section 4.2. When a dialog episode finishes, the short-term conceptual state is used to update the user's *Long-Term Conceptual State*, referred to as the *User Model*. The belief revision algorithm used in [15] is employed.

The user interacts with the system by using a graphical *user interface*, issustrated in Figure 2. The interface uses JGraph[1] to present, create, and modify graphical utterances. The main components of OWL-OLM are described next.

3   Domain Ontology and a User's Conceptual Model

OWL-OLM is built as a user modeling component to be integrated in Semantic Web applications. OWL-OLM follows a general dialog framework that is domain independent and produces OWL-based user model. The only restriction imposed is that a URI of a domain ontology has to be provided, and that this ontology has to be defined in OWL. For the current instantiation, example from which

---

[1] http://www.jgraph.com/

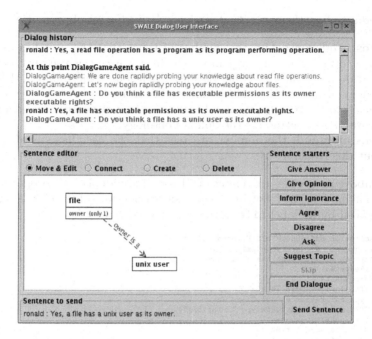

Fig. 2. Example of OWL-OLM interface - utterance **(2)** from the dialog in Section 5

was given in Section 5, we use basic Linux ontology[2] which includes concepts from an introductory Linux course taught at the University of Leeds, UK. The ontology was built by a domain expert from Eindhoven University of Technology by using Protégé [16], and is used in a Linux course, see Section 6.

OWL-OLM uses Jena 2.1 [17] extensively for input and output of OWL ontologies and models, creating and changing OWL resources and resolving domain ontology queries (in the Dialog Agent). The OWL generic reasoner from Jena is employed to make inferences from the domain ontology.

As shown in the OWL-OLM architecture (Figure 1), the dialog agent extracts a user's *Short Term Conceptual State*, used to tune the user's *Long Term Conceptual State*. The main idea of a conceptual state is that it gives a partial model of a user's conceptualization which is linked to one or more existing ontologies. A user's conceptual state is defined in OWL-OLM as a triple of URIs pointing to a *Conceptual model*, a *Domain ontology* and a *User*. The *conceptual model* is specified in OWL resembling an ontology specification, i.e. it defines classes, individuals, and properties, and uses OWL properties to define relationships. It makes links to resources defined in the domain ontology, when possible (a resource can represent a concept or a relationship between concepts [18]).

---

[2] SWALE project, `http://wwwis.win.tue.nl:8080/~swale/blo`

To indicate how the conceptual model is derived, a set of properties [3] is used:

- **times_used_correctly**: the number of times that the user has used a resource correctly, i.e. the way in which the resource was used was supported by the domain ontology either because the resource was found in the domain ontology or because it could be inferred from it.
- **times_used_wrongly**: the number of times that the user has used a resource in a way that contradicts the domain ontology.
- **times_affirmed**: the number of times that the user has stated he knows about this resource.

The above properties are related to classes, individuals, and properties in the conceptual model. The following excerpt shows the state of the class **Filesystem _node** (called by its label **file** in the example in Section 5).

```
<rdf:Description rdf:about="blo:Filesystem_node">
    <rdfs:comment rdf:datatype="xmls:string">
        Any set of data that has a pathname on the
        filesystem.
    </rdfs:comment>
    <rdfs:label>file</rdfs:label>
    <rdf:type rdf:resource="owl:Class"/>
    <aimsUM:times_used rdf:datatype="xmls:long">
        12</aimsUM:times_used>
    <aimsUM:times_used_correctly
        rdf:datatype="xmls:long">
        10</aimsUM:times_used_correctly>
    <aimsUM:times_used_wrongly
        rdf:datatype="xmls:long">
        2</aimsUM:times_used_wronlgy>
    <aimsUM:times_affirmed rdf:datatype="xmls:long">
        3</aimsUM:times_affirmed>
    <aimsUM:times_denied rdf:datatype="xmls:long">
        1</aimsUM:times_denied>
</rdf:Description>
```

This example shows that the user has used the class **Filesystem_node** a total of 12 times; 10 times supported by the domain ontology and twice not supported. He has stated 3 times that he knows the concept **Filesystem_node** and once that he does not. Classes, individuals, object properties, and datatype properties are annotated in the same way.

We also need to capture the relations between concepts that the user builds. In order to associate the properties described above with these relations we use *reified statements* [18]. For instance, in utterance **(15)** in the example given in Section 5 the user states that class **Move_file_operation** is a subclass of **Command**. We can create a reified statement referring to this relationship and add the **aimsUM:times_used_wrongly** property to this statement, as shown below:

```
<rdf:Description rdf:nodeID="A273">
    <rdf:type
        rdf:resource="rdf:Statement"/>
    <rdf:subject
        rdf:resource="blo:Move_file_operation"/>
    <rdf:predicate
```

---

[3] An RDF specification of those properties, http://wwwis.win.tue.nl/~swale/aimsUM

```
   rdf:resource="rdfs:subClassOf"/>
  <rdf:object rdf:resource="blo:Command"/>
  <aimsUM:times_used
    rdf:datatype="xmls:long">1
  </aimsUM:times_used>
  <aimsUM:times_used_wrongly
    rdf:datatype="xmls:long">1
  </aimsUM:times_used_wrongly>
 </rdf:Description>
```

The above denotes that the user has used the `rdfs:subClassOf` relationship between `Move_file_operation` and `Command`. This is more detailed than only associating properties with the individual classes, as in the first excerpt.

4 Dialog Maintenance

4.1 Dialog Games

The dialog in OWL-OLM is organized as a series of dialog games that represent the dialog episodes. A dialog game $\mathcal{DG}$ in OWL-OLM is defined as:

$$\mathcal{DG} = (\mathcal{C}, \mathcal{P}, \mathcal{R}, \mathcal{U}, \mathcal{S})$$

where: $\mathcal{C}$ is a set of domain concepts and relations targeted in the game used to maintain a *global focus* [19]; $\mathcal{P}$ is a set of *preconditions* which define conditions of the state of the system (e.g. a history of previous utterances or a user's current conceptual state) which are needed to trigger the game; $\mathcal{R}$ is a set of *postconditions* that define conditions of the state of the system (e.g. changes in the user's conceptual state) which become valid when the game ends; $\mathcal{U}$ is a set of *rules* to generate dialog utterances; $\mathcal{S}$ defines the *scope* that is a set of concepts used to maintain a dialog focus space [19]. The definition follows the formalization in [15] which is derived from a linguistic dialog games model [20].

The building blocks of every dialog are *utterances*: sentences interchanged between the dialog agent and the user. Each utterance consists of three parts: an originator, intention, and OWL statement. *Originator* is the producer of the utterance, which can be the dialog agent or the user.

OWL statement is the domain-related proposition of an utterance. An OWL statement is a small OWL model that defines a set of concepts and relations. The OWL model is restricted to only *one semantic relation*, as it represents the domain-related semantics of a single utterance. OWL statements are used to (a) extract a section of an OWL ontology and only focus on this section; (b) generate text templates to render the semantics enclosed by the OWL statement, for the interface with the user; and (c) exchange very focused information about the exact relationship between a small number of classes, individuals and ontology properties, which is critical for diagnosing users and identifying mismatches between the user's conceptual model and the domain ontology, as shown later. Table 1 illustrates some OWL statements.

Intention states the dialog purpose of the utterance, i.e. the intention of the originator of the utterance. Sample intention operators used in OWL-OLM are

Table 1. Some types of OWL statements used in OWL-OLM

Name	Basic RDF triple(s)	Comment
Empty	none	Used in combination with intentions which do not require an OWL statement
SingleClass	c rdf:type owl:Class	Defines a single class c.
SingleObjectProperty	p rdf:type owl:ObjectProperty	Defines a single object property p without a domain or range
InstanceOf	i rdf:type c	Declares that i is an individual of class c
SubClass	c_1 rdfs:subClassOf c_2	States that class c_1 is a subclass of class c_2
ObjectProperty	p rdf:domain c p rdf:range r	Defines that class c has an object property p
QueryInstance	i rdf:type c i rdf:type swaleQ:QuestionResource	Declares that i is an individual of class c and that i is a question
QueryClassOfInd	i rdf:type c c rdf:type swaleQ:QuestionResource	i is an individual of c and c is a question
QueryDtPropDomain	p rdf:domain c c rdf:type swaleQ:QuestionResource	Class c has a datatype property p and c is a question

[4] (1) **Give Answer**, where the originator is answering a previous utterance which was a question with the semantics enclosed in the OWL statement; (2) **Agree**, where the originator states that he agrees with the semantics enclosed in the OWL statement; (3) **Ask**, where the originator asks whether the semantics described in the OWL statement is true.

To achieve effective dialogs, which feel natural and efficient to the user, several problems have been tackled. Firstly, a *dialog focus* is maintained, so that the interaction is structured and organized. In terms of utterances, this means that consecutive utterances should have a concept in common whenever possible. For this, a scope of relevant concepts is maintained. Secondly, the *dialog continuity* is ensured to provide a logical exchange of utterances. This means that each utterance has to be a logical response to the previous one. Cue phrases are used when a game is opened, closed, or re-initiated, to show the logical flow and to communicate the dialog goal, as in the example in Section 5. Thirdly, to *avoid repetition of utterances* a history of the dialog is maintained to exclude already said utterances. Finally, *mixed initiative* is maintained to allow both participants in the dialog to introduce a new topic and ask clarification questions.

4.2   Game Analyzer

We will now explain how OWL-OLM analyzes the utterances received from the user and how the results of this analysis are used to decide the next move of the Dialog Agent and to update the user's conceptual state. The following features are analyzed:

- The *scope* and intention of two consecutive utterances are compared. If the scopes do not match, the agent has to decide whether to follow the user and change the dialog focus or to stay in the current scope;
- The *incoming utterance* is analyzed to determine whether it asks a question to the system, which triggers a question answering game;

---

[4] See screen shots for more examples.

- The *OWL statement* of the incoming utterance is compared to the domain ontology to determine whether the semantic relation described by the OWL statement is supported by the domain ontology;
- If an OWL statement is not supported by the domain ontology, the agent checks for a *recognizable mismatch* between the statement and the ontology.

During the analysis, the default OWL reasoner of Jena [17] is used to infer relationships that follow from the domain ontology. The reasoner is used to determine whether the OWL statement of an utterance is supported by the domain ontology. This is the case if and only if every RDF triple in the statement can be inferred from the domain ontology.

4.3 Mismatches

When the user submits an utterance that cannot be verified by the domain ontology, this is considered as a mismatch. We define a *mismatch* as any RDF triple in the utterance's OWL statement which cannot be found in the existing domain ontology. In this way we can determine the type of mismatch by using the basic building blocks in OWL. The semantics of a mismatch is that a resource or relationship in the OWL statement is not supported by the domain ontology. Table 2 shows some of the types of mismatches which can be detected.

Table 2. Mismatches detected in OWL-OLM

Type	Comment
Unknown	None of the other types apply
OntClass	A class cannot be found
Individual	An individual cannot be found
ObProp	An object property cannot be found
DtProp	A datatype property cannot be found
SubClass	A subclass relationship cannot be found
InstanceOf	The link between an individual and its class cannot be found
ObProp-Rel	The domain ontology (DO) doesn't suggest that two resources are related by this object property
DtProp-Rel	The DO doesn't suggest that two resources are related by this datatype property
Domain	The DO doesn't suggest that a resource is the domain of a property
Range	The DO doesn't support that a resource is the range of a property
ObProp-Val	The DO doesn't support that a resource has this value for this object property

By classifying the types of mismatches OntoAIMS Resource Browser is able to define dialog games to clarify each of the recognized mismatches. For instance, an example of clarification dialog is given in Section 5: utterance **(19)** prompts a mismatch of a type *SubClass*, which is recognized by OWL-OLM and a clarification dialog game (see utterances **(14)** - **(19)**) is initiated.

4.4 Answering Questions

Two different types of questions are catered for: those which can be answered with an yes or no (*yes/no questions*) and those where the answer contains an element missing in the question (*open questions*). The latter are based on OWL statements that have special resource type - a *question resource*. A **question**

resource is any resource in an OWL model which is marked as being the same as the resource `swale_:Question_Resource`[5]. This means we can mark any resource R in an OWL statement as being a question resource by adding the following RDF triple to the OWL model: (`R rdfs:sameAs swale_:Question_Resource`)

Questions are answered by transforming them to queries and feeding these to any OWL query answering mechanism. OWL-OLM uses Jena [17] to find triples in the domain ontology which match the query. A user's question may interrupt the current dialog game and initiate a new game where the Dialog Agent tries to answer the question as best as it can and to probe for relevant knowledge.

5 An Illustrative Example

We illustrate here the application of OWL-OLM for the acquisition of user knowledge with an example from the OntoAIMS Resources Browser (see Section 6). OntoAIMS employs OWL-OLM to extract a conceptual model of the learner and uses this model to recommend an appropriate to his knowledge state learning task or learning resources. The User in this example is a student who follows an introductory Web-based course on "Linux Operating System". The OWL-OLM Dialog Agent utilizes an existing domain ontology [21] to explore aspects of the User's conceptualization of the topic "Files and operations on files". The interaction is conducted in a graphical way (see fig. 2) but due to space limit is presented here only in the text form generated in the dialog history of OWL-OLM.

Opening a Probing Dialog Game

> **(1) DialogAgent**: I'll try to suggest a suitable task for you. I will first ask you some questions related to "Files and operations on files".
> **(2) DialogAgent**: Do you think a `file` has a `unix user` as its `owner`?
> **(3) User**: Yes, a `file` has a `unix user` as its `owner`.
> **(4) DialogAgent**: Do you think a `file` has a `path` as its `full name`?
> **(5) User**: I don't know whether a `file` has a `path` as its `full name`.

The agent opens the *dialog episode* and informs what the *goal* is. It then initiates a *probing dialog game* to elicit the part of the user's conceptualization related to the current task. It begins with the concept `file`, which is the main concept in this topic, and checks whether the user knows concepts linked to `file` – utterances **(2)** - **(5)**. Figure 2 shows the OWL-OLM interface for utterance **(2)**. The OWL statement of a dialog utterance is rendered in a graphical form, while the intention is rendered as a sentence opener. To construct his reply, utterance **(3)**, the user edits the diagram with the OWL statement by using basic graphical commands. Also, when he double clicks on an object, he can edit its class/individual name, add/delete properties, or create links with other objects. To state intention, the user uses a sentence opener, see the buttons group to the right in Figure 2. The textual form of the composed dialog utterance is shown in the bottom. To send his utterance, the user clicks on the **Send sentence** button. The utterance is added to the the dialog history, shown at the top.

---

[5] `http://wwwis.win.tue.nl/~swale/swale_question`

User Question - A New Game Is Initiated

(6) **User:** Can you tell me more about what can be the `group readable right` of a `file`?

(7) **DialogAgent:** As far as I know, a `file` has a `readable permission` as its `group readable right`.

(8) **User:** [*Skip*]

(9) **DialogAgent:** Let us return to discussing `files`.

(10) **DialogAgent:** We will continue with discussing about. `moving files`.

(11) **DialogAgent:** Do you know what `moving file` is?

(12) **User:** I think that `moving file` is a `command`.

The user interrupts the dialog by asking a question (**6**). The agent suspends the current dialog game and initiates a new game to *answer the user's question*. It sends a query to the domain ontology and then composes the answer. The agent then waits to see whether the user has more questions. Since the user's questions have been answered, the agent returns to the dialog game that probes what the user knows about `file`. When finished the agent closes the game that probes for `files`. It then opens a dialog game that probes for another main concept – `moving files` – and starts with probing for the parent. The user answer in utterance (**12**) indicates a *mismatch* (see Section 4.3). According to the domain ontology used by the agent, `moving a file` is a `file operation` not a `command`. The agent again suspends the probing game and starts a *clarification game*.

Mismatch Is Recognized - A Clarification Game Is Initiated

(13) **DialogAgent:** Why do you think `moving file` is a `command`.

(14) **DialogAgent:** Do you think `moving a file` is also a `file operation`?

(15) **User:** Yes, I think that `moving a file` is a `file operation`.

(16) **DialogAgent:** Do you think a `command` has a `version`?

(17) **User:** Yes, a `command` has a `version`.

(18) **DialogAgent:** You think that `moving file` is a `file operation`, as well as a `command`.

(19) **User:** I don't think that `moving file` is a `command`.

The agent first checks for an alignment between the user's conceptualization and the domain ontology (utterance (**14**)), and then checks for inherited properties from the `subClass` link between `moving file` and `file operation`. If the answer is positive, the agent checks for an inherited property from the `subClass` link the user makes between `moving file` and `command`. Because the user does not confirm the property, the agent checks the property for `command` to highlight the inheritance link the user makes between `moving files` and `command`. At the end, the agent checks again the mismatch, which is now corrected by the user.

6   Use of OWL-OLM for Adaptive Content Management

In this section we demonstrate how OWL-OLM was utilized to enable personalization in a semantic-aware e-learning system, called OntoAIMS Resource

Browser. OntoAIMS Resource Browser[6] is an ontology-based version of the AIMS Resource Broswer *adaptive information management system* [22] providing an information searching and browsing environment that enables users to identify the most appropriate course task to work on and to find and learn the relevant terminology and resources necessary for performing this particular task.

OntoAIMS Resource Browser uses ontologies to represent the aspects of the application semantics, to allow a strict separation of domain-dependent data, application-related data and resources, and to further enable reusability and sharing of data on the Semantic Web. A *Domain Ontology* represents the domain terms and their relationships. The content is annotated and stored in a *Resource model*, linked to the terms of the domain ontology. The course aspects are modeled as a hierarchy of course tasks in a *Course Task Model*. Each task specifies domain terms and learning objects as part of the task prerequisites, input and output. Adaptive mechanisms are employed for sequencing the course tasks and thus providing the most efficient way for the users to navigate through the structure, terminology and learning material of the course. In OntoAIMS Resource Browser, the learners use a graphical environment for browsing through a graphical representation of the domain conceptual space, and to browse through a collection of semantically annotated resources ranked by the system according to their relevance to the task and the user query, see Figure 3.

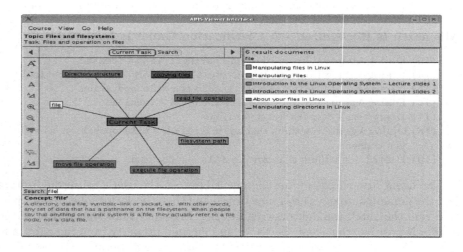

Fig. 3. OntoAIMS resource browser

A key role in the ranking and recommending of tasks and resources in OntoAIMS is played by the *User Model*. OntoAIMS aims at covering an extensive range of user's aspects, e.g. goals, conceptual state, preferences, personal characteristics, etc. thus allowing an unobtrusive way to collect various user data.

---

[6] Accessible at: http://swale.comp.leeds.ac.uk:8080/staims/viewer.html, username *visitor*, password *visitor*.

Dialogs similar to the example shown in Section 5 are conducted by the OWL-OLM agent within OntoAIMS to (a) validate the analysis of the user data, (b) elicit a user's conceptual state, and (c) build and maintain a dynamic user model as a basis for a personalized information management process.

7   Evaluation Studies with Users

Three user studies were conducted with the current instantiation of OntoAIMS Resource Browser in a domain of Linux. Initially, *six users*, postgraduate students and staff from the universities of Leeds and Eindhoven, took part in video recorded and monitored think aloud walk through sessions, as well as in detailed usability questionnaires. An improved version of the system was used in a second study with *ten first year Computing students* at Leeds. It followed a two-week introductory course on Linux. The users were asked to study resources on Linux recommended by the system. Detailed description of the OntoAIMS Resource Browser evaluation is given in [23]. A final version was presented as an Interactive Event at the AIED'05 conference and was tested with *ten international experts in Learning Management Systems*.

In general, the users appreciated the help and guidance provided by OntoAIMS resource browser and regarded the system as useful. The dialogs to discover the level of user's knowledge lasted about 5-10 minutes, which saved significant time for these users (who otherwise would have been offered reading on topics they were familiar with). Less knowledgeable users became aware of aspects of the domain they did not know (which were addressed in the OWL-OLM dialog), and liked that the system recommended basic Linux reading. OWL-OLM was regarded as a key tool seamlessly integrated in the whole environment, and was seen both as *complying with the overall goal* and *unobtrusive*. The dialog was seen as coherent by the users. The evaluation revealed also pitfalls, to be addressed in the next OWL-OLM versions, with respect to mismatches dialogs, smooth switch between the dialog and OntoAIMS Resource Browser, awareness how the conceptual model is used for adaptation, and several interface issues. The purpose of these first three studies were to test the usability and effectiveness of the dialog as a user model elicitation mechanism. With the current extension of the system and its deployment in other application domains, we plan to perform studies to test the advantages of the user modeling approach with respect to the recall and precision of resource and task recommendations.

8   Related Work and Discussion

Different perspectives of enabling personalization on the Semantic Web are being addressed recently. Our work on OntoAIMS Resource Browser is situated within the field of User-adaptive Web-based Information Systems [24] that capitalize on adaptation techniques to provide individual users with the *right* service at the *right* time and in the *right* way. The OWL-OLM approach is similar to the interactive sessions used in HUMOS [25]. While HUMOS uses a very simple probing dialog to elicit initial, fairly basic profile of the user, OWL-OLM considers more in-depth interactions that extract enhanced user models. By using Semantic Web technologies, enriched semantics for the user data can be achieved to allow for more efficient reasoning and, thus, more accurate user modeling results. Stojanovic [26] in his comprehensive query refinement approach proofs also the need and the benefit of an interactive 'step-by-step' query refinement process, which considers the user's perspective on the domain conceptualization in the retrieval process. The approach capitalizes on the improvement of the user and context modeling versus the improvement of the information retrieval process. In addition to this, our work shows how such interactive approach can be realized and visualized with an OWL domain ontology. An example of an NLP-based interactive knowledge acquisition interface is given by Chklovski and Gil [27]. As in OWL-OLM it shows the need for a clarification dialog with the user to correctly specify domain knowledge from multiple perspectives. Moreover, the authors prove the efficiency of using semantic rich structures to "collect semantically interpretable knowledge while interacting in natural language", as exemplified in OWL-OLM as well.

A strong argument is being formed recently to stress the importance of sharable and reusable user models, as well as personalization methods on the Semantic Web[1]. Both OWL-OLM and OntoAIMS Resource Browser contribute to an on-going work in this area [28, 11]. The work we present on eliciting a user's conceptualization based on an existing domain ontology relates to the research on aligning and reconciling ontologies, reviewed in [29, 30]. However, there is a crucial difference between the *user-expert* alignment considered in OWL-OLM and the alignment of two (or more) expert ontologies considered in existing, widely used tools, such as PROMPT [31]. Results from their empirical studies on aligning expert user's ontologies as well as the existing, robust ontology aligning algorithms (e.g. using word concordances and synonyms) can be very useful to extend the OWL-OLM mismatch patterns. Most of the methodologies applied for building shared ontologies have a dialog part at some stage to enable experts to clarify aspects of their conceptualizations. This confirms that approaches like OWL-OLM are viable for capturing a user's conceptualization. Finally, the user modeling dialog in OWL-OLM is similar to negotiation between agents who share knowledge and clarify meaning, e.g. [32].

9   Conclusion and Future Work

plus We presented OWL-OLM - a novel framework for eliciting a user's conceptualization based on an ontology-driven dialog. We focused on the formal specification and the architectural design of the diagnostic dialog by illustrating the following aspects: (a) maintaining dialog coherence, (b) answering different questions and (c) identifying mismatches. OWL-OLM makes extensive use of Jena for OWL-based reasoning to maintain the dialogue and update the user model. We demonstrated the utilization of OWL-OLM in OntoAIMS Resource Browser - an RDF/OWL-based software architecture for adaptive learning content management. User studies showed that the user model extracted by OWL-OLM could be used to improve personalization in OntoAIMS Resource Browser. Other applications explored are *digital libraries* and *museums*, where effective help can only be provided if a user's view on the subject domain is considered. Possible other applications include *online banking*, where a probing dialog can be used to quickly identify what conceptual models the users have of key terms, or *online catalogues*, where the search is driven by some taxonomy which may often differ from the user's perception of the domain. In overall, the novel aspects demonstrated in this paper are: (a) ontological approach for integration of methods for eliciting and utilizing user models; (b) improved adaptation functionality resulted from that integration, validated in studies with real users; (c) support of interoperability and reusability on the educational Semantic Web.

Future work will focus on the development of a good classification of user's mismatches and patterns for clarification dialog based on systematic studies of empirical and computational approaches for ontology aligning and reconciliation. In-depth studies are needed to design effective knowledge elicitation tools suited not for ontology engineers, but for users with a wide range of experiences. Finally, it appears useful to provide also a text form for communication and to allow the users to choose a preferred interaction medium.

Acknowledgments. The research was partly supported by the UK-Netherlands Partnership in Science program and the EU Network of Excellence PROLEARN.

References

1. Henze, N.: Personalization functionality for the semantic web: Identification and description of techniques. Technical report, REWERSE EU NoE (2004)
2. Kobsa, A.: User modeling in dialog systems: Potentials and hazards. Artificial Intelligence and Society **1** (1990) 214–240
3. Jameson, A.: User-adaptive systems. Technical report, UM03 Tutorial (2003)
4. Wolpers, M., Nejdl, W.: European e-learning: Important research issues and application scenarios. In: ED-Media'04 Conference, Lugano, Switzerland (2004) 21–25
5. Anderson, T., Whitelock, D.: The Educational Semantic Web: Visioning and Practicing the Future of Education. Volume 1. (2004)
6. L. Stojanovic, S.S., Studer, R.: elearning based on the semantic web. In: World Conference on the WWW and Internet (WebNet'01), Florida, USA (2001) 23–27
7. Aroyo, L., Dicheva, D.: The new challenges for e-learning: The educational semantic web. Journal of Educational Technology and Society **7** (2004) 59–69
8. Duval, E.: Learning technology standardization: making sense of it all. International Journal on Computer Science and Information Systems **1** (2004) 33–43
9. Simon, B., Dolog, P., Miklós, Z., Olmedilla, D., Sintek, M.: Conceptualising smart spaces for learning. Journal of Interactive Media in Education (2004(9))
10. Stutt, A., Motta, E.: Semantic learning webs. Journal of Interactive Media in Education: Special Issue on the Educational Semantic Web **10** (2004)
11. Dolog, P.: Identifying relevant fragments of learner profile on the semantic web. In: SW-EL'04 at International Semantic Web Conference, Hiroshima, Japan (2004)

12. N. Henze, P., Nejdl, W.: Reasoning and ontologies for personalized e-learning. Journal of Educational Technology & Society **7** (2004)
13. Berners-Lee, T., Hendler, J., Lassila, O.: The defining characteristics of intelligent tutoring systems research: Itss care, precisely. International Journal of Artificial Intelligence in Education **10** (1999)
14. Denaux, R., Aroyo, L., Dimitrova, V.: An approach for ontology-based elicitation of user models for the semantic web. In: WWW05(poster). (2004)
15. Dimitrova, V.: Style-olm: Interactive open learner modelling. Int. Journal of Artificial Intelligence in Education **13** (2003) 35–78
16. Noy, N., Sintek, M., Crubezy, M., Fergerson, R., Musen, M.: Creating semantic web contents with protege-2000. IEEE Intelligent Systems 16(2) (2001) 60–71
17. Carroll, J., et al.: Jena: Implementing the semantic web recommendations. In: WWW'04. (2004) 74–83
18. Miller, E., Manola, F.: Rdf primer. http://www.w3c.org/TR/ (2004)
19. Lecoeuche, R., Mellish, C., Barry, C., Robertson, D.: User-system dialogues and the notion of focus. The Knowledge Engineering Review **13** (1998)
20. Levin, J., Moore, J.: Dialogue games: Meta-communication structures for natural language interaction. Cognitive Science (1978)
21. Denaux, R., Dimitrova, V., Aroyo, L.: Interactive ontology-based user modeling for personalized learning content management. In: AH 2004: Workshop Proceedings Part II. (2004) 338–347
22. Aroyo, L., Dicheva, D.: Aims: Learning and teaching support for www-based education. Int. Journal for Continuing Engineering Education and Life-long Learning (IJCEELL) **11** (2001) 152–164
23. Denaux, R., Dimitrova, V., Aroyo, L.: Integrating open user modeling and learning content management for the semantic web. In: International Conference on User Modeling, UM05. (2004)
24. Brusilovsky, P., Tasso, C.: Special issue on user modelling for web information retrieval. User Modeling and User Adapted Interaction **14** (2004)
25. Micarelli, A., Sciarrone, F.: Anatomy and empirical evaluation of an adaptive web-based information filtering system. User Modeling and User-Adapted Interaction **14** (2004) 159–200
26. Stojanovic, N.: On the role of a user's knowledge gap in an information retrieval process. In: Proceedings of K-CAP'05, ACM Press (2005) 83–90
27. Chklovski, T., Gil, Y.: Improving the design of intelligent acquisition interfaces for collecting world knowledge from web contributors. In: Proceedings of K-CAP'05, ACM Press (2005) 35–42
28. Bra, P.D., Aroyo, L., Chepegin, V.: The next big thing: Adaptive web-based systems. Journal of Digital Information, 5(1) (2004)
29. Klein, M.: Combining and relating ontologies: an analysis of problems and solutions. In Gomez-Perez, A., Gruninger, M., Stuckenschmidt, H., Uschold, M., eds.: Workshop on Ontologies and Information Sharing, IJCAI'01, Seattle, USA (2001)
30. Ehrig, M., Sure, Y.: Ontology mapping – an integrated approach. In: Proceedings of the 1st European Semantic Web Symposium. (2004)
31. Noy, N.F., Musen, M.A.: PROMPT: Algorithm and tool for automated ontology merging and alignment. In: IJCAI–01 Workshop on Ontologies and Information Sharing. (2000) 63–70
32. C.Bailin, S., Truszkowski, W.: Ontology negotiation between intelligent information agents. The Knowledge Engineering Review **17** (2002) 7–19

Matching Semantic Service Descriptions with Local Closed-World Reasoning

Stephan Grimm[1], Boris Motik[1], and Chris Preist[2]

[1] FZI Research Center for Information Technologies at the University of Karlsruhe
Karlsruhe, Germany
{grimm, motik}@fzi.de
[2] HP Laboratories
Bristol, UK
chris.preist@hp.com

Abstract. Semantic Web Services were developed with the goal of automating the integration of business processes on the Web. The main idea is to express the functionality of the services explicitly, using semantic annotations. Such annotations can, for example, be used for service discovery—the task of locating a service capable of fulfilling a business request. In this paper, we present a framework for annotating Web Services using description logics (DLs), a family of knowledge representation formalisms widely used in the Semantic Web. We show how to realise service discovery by matching semantic service descriptions, applying DL inferencing. Building on our previous work, we identify problems that occur in the matchmaking process due to the open-world assumption when handling incomplete service descriptions. We propose to use autoepistemic extensions to DLs (ADLs) to overcome these problems. ADLs allow for non-monotonic reasoning and for querying DL knowledge bases under local closed-world assumption. We investigate the use of epistemic operators of ADLs in service descriptions, and show how they affect DL inferences in the context of semantic matchmaking.

1 Introduction

Semantic Web Services have been recently proposed as a technology for the automated integration of business processes. The key idea is to represent the functionality of a Web Service explicitly, using so-called *semantic annotations*. These are useful for numerous purposes, such as, for example, *service discovery*—the process of locating Web Services capable of fulfilling a business request.

In the Semantic Web, annotation is a piece of machine-interpretable meta data based on ontological vocabularies formulated by means of an ontology language. The Web Ontology Language (OWL) [20] is a W3C recommendation language for building ontologies in the Semantic Web. As part of the Web Service Modelling Ontology initiative (WSMO), the Web Service Modelling Language (WSML) [4] was recently proposed as an ontology language specifically tuned to annotating Web Services. Certain variants of both languages, namely OWL-DL and WSML-DL, are based on description logics (DL), a family of knowledge representation

Y. Sure and J. Domingue (Eds.): ESWC 2006, LNCS 4011, pp. 575–589, 2006.
© Springer-Verlag Berlin Heidelberg 2006

formalisms with a clearly defined semantics and well-understood computational properties [3].

Several approaches to service discovery based on description logics have already been proposed in [26, 18, 17]. Along these lines, in this paper we extend our work from [10] and present a DL-based approach for modelling semantics of Web Services. We build on establishing a clear correspondence between the DL modelling primitives and the modeller's intention. In this way, we explain the intuition behind the DL constructs in the service context and thus give guidelines for their application.

Furthermore, we identify problems that occur when DL inferencing is applied to matching semantic service annotations. Namely, DLs are monotonic logics with open-world semantics: the inability to prove a fact does not imply its contrary 'by default'. This often requires a modeller to *overspecify* a situation and to include information that humans take for granted by common-sense. Sometimes, it is not even possible to completely specify semantic service annotations without making some default assumptions. Our analysis shows that the lack of common-sense information in the domain model or in service annotations leads to false matches, thus significantly degrading the quality of the discovery platform.

To address these deficiencies in a systematic way, we propose to base service discovery on a non-monotonic logical formalism that allows for local closed-world reasoning by referring to facts which are *explicitly known*. This compensates for imprecision in domain ontologies and service annotations.

Numerous non-monotonic formalisms have already been developed, such as default logic, circumscription or various extensions of logic programming with negation-as-failure [2]. However, we base our service discovery framework on an autoepistemic extension to description logic (ADL) from [5], namely the logic $\mathcal{ALCK}$. ADLs are proper extensions of description logics, so the same principles can be applied to obtain autoepistemic extensions of OWL-DL or WSML-DL. Moreover, the reasoning algorithm from [5] extends the well-known tableau algorithm implemented in DL reasoning systems, such as RACER [11], FaCT [13] or Pellet [25]. Therefore, we believe that ADLs are a good fit with the existing technological Semantic Web infrastructure. To verify the practicability of our approach for matching semantic descriptions, we have implemented a simple ADL reasoner, as a testing environment to verify our examples for service discovery.

2   The Service Discovery Problem

We introduce the problem of service discovery by means of an example taken from the travelling domain. Let us assume that a company needs to frequently book business trips for its employees. To stay competitive, for any single booking this company wants to contact several travel agencies and pick the one providing the best offer. In such a business transaction, the company plays the role of the *requester* and the travel agencies play the role of *providers* of a travelling service.

In order to allow this process to be automated, the electronically available travel agencies provide access to their booking services via Web Service interfaces. Furthermore, both the requester company and the travel agencies need to specify the functionality of the services they request or provide in a declarative way, using semantic annotations.

In [21] the notion of a *concrete service* has been introduced, which represents a particular business transaction. An example of a concrete service, offered by some travel agency A, is 'selling a flight ticket from Frankfurt to London at a particular date and time for 50 Euro'. However, A also provides other concrete services, which vary depending on the cities, date or price. The set of all concrete services is approximated as an *abstract service* [21]. For example, A might advertise "selling flight tickets between cities in Europe". Similarly, another travel agency B advertises an abstract service for 'selling flight tickets from Europe to the US', which includes concrete services such as 'selling a flight ticket from Frankfurt to New York'.

In the same way, the business needs of the requester company correspond to concrete services, such as 'selling a ticket from Frankfurt to London for November 5th'. Similar to the agencies, the company summarises all intended concrete services in an abstract service, such as 'selling a ticket from Germany to the UK'.

We introduce the notion of *capability description* as a formal specification, used by requesters and providers, to represent an abstract service. In their capability descriptions the requester company and the travel agencies intend to capture the set of all concrete services they are willing to accept. Here, capability descriptions are expressed informally, however, in Section 4 we show how to express them in a formal language to make them machine-processable. Our capability descriptions are similar in functionality to WSMO Web Service capabilities [16] or OWL-S service profiles [1]. However, they are different in that they base on an abstract ontological description of service functionality rather than on a state transition model with pre- and postconditions.

In [21], the process of selecting a service to fulfil a request is split into two consecutive phases. The *service discovery* phase is concerned with the identification of abstract services relevant for the request. This is done by matching the capability description of the requester to the capability descriptions of providers, to determine whether they are compatible. In Section 4 we show how description logic inferences can be used for this purpose. In this sense, service discovery is based on the capability descriptions of requesters and providers, and does not involve information that is obtained by invoking any Web Service.

The service discovery phase is followed by the *service definition* phase, where the set of potential providers is further narrowed, and the concrete service to be performed is specified in detail. As discussed in [14], this process often includes negotiation and requires information which is not captured in the capability descriptions for abstract services (such as preferences or additional business constraints that are not publicly available). In this paper we focus on the service discovery phase, and leave the service definition phase to our future work.

3   Description Logics and Their Autoepistemic Extension

In this section we describe an autoepistemic extension to the description logic (DL) formalism that we will use throughout the paper. We start with an intuitive view on the basic DL $\mathcal{ALC}$ and its autoepistemic extension $\mathcal{ALCK}$. Then we revisit the formal syntax and semantics of $\mathcal{ALCK}$ and introduce epistemic queries and the satisfiability of an $\mathcal{ALCK}$ concept w.r.t. an $\mathcal{ALC}$ knowledge base.

Description Logics

DLs [3] are a family of knowledge representation formalisms that provide the formal underpinning of certain ontology languages for the Semantic Web, such as WSML-DL [4] or OWL-DL [20]. The basic syntax elements of DLs are *concepts*, such as *City* or *Airplane*, *roles*, such as *transportationMeans* or *from*, and *individuals*, such as *Frankfurt* or *Airbus380*. Primitive concepts can be combined into complex concepts using concept constructors. In this paper, we consider the basic DL $\mathcal{ALC}$, which provides the propositional connectives and restricted existential and universal role quantification. For example, a complex concept *Journey* $\sqcap$ $\exists$ *from* . *UKCity* $\sqcap$ $\forall$ *transpMeans* . $\neg$ *Airplane* intuitively represents a journey from somewhere in the UK by a transportation means different from an airplane.

A DL knowledge base consists of axioms and is split into a TBox and an ABox. *Concept inclusion axioms* in the TBox state subset relationship between concepts; for example, *Airplane* $\sqsubseteq$ *Vehicle* states that airplanes are kinds of vehicles. *Assertion axioms* in the ABox describe the state of the world; for example, *UKCity*(*London*) states that London is a city in the UK, and *train*(*Berlin*, *Hamburg*) states that Berlin is connected by train to Hamburg.

Autoepistemic Description Logics

Autoepistemic logic is a formalism concerned with the notion of 'knowledge' and allows introspection of knowledge bases—that is, asking what a knowledge base *knows*. In [5], the basic DL $\mathcal{ALC}$ has been extended by the autoepistemic knowledge operator **K**, yielding the autoepistemic description logic $\mathcal{ALCK}$. The **K**-operator can be applied as a constructor to both concepts and roles, and can intuitively be paraphrased as 'known to be'.

To understand the intuition behind the **K**-operator, consider the knowledge base *KB* = { *City*(*Frankfurt*), *train*(*Frankfurt*, *Paris*)}, and the concept *D* = *City* $\sqcap$ $\exists$ *train* . $\neg$ *GermanCity*, which can be paraphrased as 'cities which are connected by train to some city outside Germany'. Since *KB* does not say whether *Paris* is a German city or not, *Frankfurt* is not in the extension of *D*. On the contrary, consider the autoepistemic concept *D'* = *City* $\sqcap$ $\exists$ **K** *train* . $\neg$ **K** *GermanCity*, which can be intuitively paraphrased as 'cities which are *known* to be connected by train to something which is not *known* to be a German city'. Based on the facts in *KB*, we cannot derive that *Paris* is a German city. Therefore, *Paris* is *not known* to be a German city, and thus *Frankfurt* is in the extension of *D'*.

These autoepistemic extensions allow for local closed-world reasoning [7] and a logical reconstruction of non-monotonic features of frame-based knowledge representation systems, such as concept and role closure, defaults, integrity constraints and procedural rules [23]. In Section 5 we apply local closed-world reasoning to the matching of service capability descriptions.

The Language $\mathcal{ALCK}$

We now formally introduce the syntax and semantics of $\mathcal{ALCK}$ [5]. The following rules define the syntax of this language, where C, D denote concepts, A denotes a primitive concept, r denotes a role and p denotes a primitive role:

$$
\begin{aligned}
C, D &\longrightarrow \quad A \mid \top \mid \bot \mid C \sqcap D \mid C \sqcup D \mid \neg C \mid \forall r.C \mid \exists r.C \mid \mathbf{K}C \\
r &\longrightarrow \quad p \mid \mathbf{K}p
\end{aligned}
$$

An *epistemic interpretation* is a pair $(\mathcal{I}, \mathcal{W})$ where $\mathcal{I} = (\Delta^{\mathcal{I}}, \cdot^{\mathcal{I}})$ is a *first-order interpretation* with interpretation domain $\Delta^{\mathcal{I}}$ and interpretation function $\cdot^{\mathcal{I}}$, and $\mathcal{W}$ is a set of first-order interpretations, seen as possible worlds. The following equations define how the syntax elements of $\mathcal{ALCK}$ are epistemically interpreted.

$$
\begin{aligned}
\top^{\mathcal{I},\mathcal{W}} &= \Delta^{\mathcal{I}} & , \quad \bot^{\mathcal{I},\mathcal{W}} &= \emptyset \\
A^{\mathcal{I},\mathcal{W}} &= A^{\mathcal{I}} \subseteq \Delta^{\mathcal{I}} \;, & p^{\mathcal{I},\mathcal{W}} &= p^{\mathcal{I}} \subseteq \Delta^{\mathcal{I}} \times \Delta^{\mathcal{I}} \\
(C \sqcap D)^{\mathcal{I},\mathcal{W}} &= C^{\mathcal{I},\mathcal{W}} \cap D^{\mathcal{I},\mathcal{W}} \\
(C \sqcup D)^{\mathcal{I},\mathcal{W}} &= C^{\mathcal{I},\mathcal{W}} \cup D^{\mathcal{I},\mathcal{W}} \\
(\neg C)^{\mathcal{I},\mathcal{W}} &= \Delta^{\mathcal{I}} \setminus C^{\mathcal{I},\mathcal{W}} \\
(\forall r.C)^{\mathcal{I},\mathcal{W}} &= \{a \in \Delta^{\mathcal{I}} \mid \forall b.(a,b) \in r^{\mathcal{I},\mathcal{W}} \to b \in C^{\mathcal{I},\mathcal{W}}\} \\
(\exists r.C)^{\mathcal{I},\mathcal{W}} &= \{a \in \Delta^{\mathcal{I}} \mid \exists b.(a,b) \in r^{\mathcal{I},\mathcal{W}} \wedge b \in C^{\mathcal{I},\mathcal{W}}\} \\
(\mathbf{K}C)^{\mathcal{I},\mathcal{W}} &= \bigcap_{\mathcal{J} \in \mathcal{W}} C^{\mathcal{J},\mathcal{W}} \\
(\mathbf{K}r)^{\mathcal{I},\mathcal{W}} &= \bigcap_{\mathcal{J} \in \mathcal{W}} p^{\mathcal{J},\mathcal{W}}
\end{aligned}
$$

Primitive concepts are interpreted as subsets of $\Delta^{\mathcal{I}}$, and primitive roles are interpreted as subsets of $\Delta^{\mathcal{I}} \times \Delta^{\mathcal{I}}$. The boolean connectives and existential and universal role quantification are interpreted in terms of set operations on $\Delta^{\mathcal{I}}$, as in $\mathcal{ALC}$ [3]. An epistemic concept $\mathbf{K}C$ is interpreted as the set of all individuals which belong to the concept C in all first-order interpretations in $\mathcal{W}$, i.e. in all possible worlds. Thus, applying $\mathbf{K}$ to concept C produces the set of objects that are members of C in all possible worlds; in other words, these objects are definitely *known to be* members of C. Similarly, an epistemic role $\mathbf{K}p$ is interpreted as the pairs of individuals that belong to the role p in all possible worlds.

An epistemic interpretation satisfies an inclusion axiom $C \sqsubseteq D$ if $C^{\mathcal{I},\mathcal{W}} \subseteq D^{\mathcal{I},\mathcal{W}}$, and it satisfies an assertion axiom $C(a)$ or $r(a,b)$ if $a^{\mathcal{I}} \in C^{\mathcal{I},\mathcal{W}}$ or $(a^{\mathcal{I}}, b^{\mathcal{I}}) \in r^{\mathcal{I},\mathcal{W}}$, respectively. An *epistemic model* for an $\mathcal{ALCK}$ knowledge base KB is a maximal non-empty set $\mathcal{W}$ of first-order interpretations such that, for each $\mathcal{I} \in \mathcal{W}$, the epistemic interpretation $(\mathcal{I}, \mathcal{W})$ satisfies all axioms in KB. The maximality condition for $\mathcal{W}$ ensures that there is no other first-order interpretation $\mathcal{I} \notin \mathcal{W}$ which also satisfies all the axioms in KB. In this way, the $\mathbf{K}$-operator allows to refer to definitely known facts by intersecting *all* possible worlds of KB.

Epistemic Queries and Concept Satisfiability

In this paper we assume that KB does not contain occurrences of the **K**-operator; that is, KB is an $\mathcal{ALC}$ knowledge base. Then, KB has at most one epistemic model $\mathcal{M}(KB)$, comprising all its first-order models. An *epistemic query* [5] over an $\mathcal{ALC}$ knowledge base KB is an $\mathcal{ALCK}$ concept assertion of the form $C(a)$. We say that KB entails $C(a)$, written $KB \models C(a)$, if, for every first-order interpretation $I \in \mathcal{M}(KB)$, the epistemic interpretation $(\mathcal{I}, \mathcal{M}(KB))$ satisfies $C(a)$.

A tableaux calculus for answering epistemic queries has been presented in [5]. However, in Section 5 we require checking satisfiability of epistemic concepts with respect to a knowledge base KB, which we define next. This inference can be performed by a straightforward extension of the calculus from [5].

Definition 1 (Concept Satisfiability). *For a satisfiable $\mathcal{ALC}$ knowledge base KB, an $\mathcal{ALCK}$ concept C is satisfiable w.r.t. KB if there is a first-order interpretation $I \in \mathcal{M}(KB)$ such that $C^{(I, \mathcal{M}(KB))} \neq \emptyset$.*

4   Modelling Service Capabilities in Description Logics

We now show how to use description logics to model capability descriptions for services. In particular, we focus on mapping the notions introduced in Section 2 into the description logic framework, based on our previous work in [10]. Furthermore, we identify incomplete capability descriptions as a key problem for service discovery.

4.1   From Concrete Services to Capability Descriptions

We map a concrete service, representing a specific business transaction, to the relational structure in a first-order interpretation $\mathcal{I}$. Such an interpretation can be understood as a directed labelled graph, which represents various properties of services. For example, the bottom left part of Figure 1 shows a relational structure which corresponds to a concrete service for travelling between Frankfurt and London on an Airbus 380.

We express a capability description using a DL concept. Under a first-order interpretation, such a concept is mapped to a set of individuals. Thus, concepts provide a natural way of modelling sets of concrete services. For example, at the top of Figure 1 we show a capability description S, which describes 'travelling between EU cities'. In $\mathcal{I}$, this concept is interpreted as a set $S^{\mathcal{I}}$ of individuals, representing the concrete services accepted by S. Since the service description does not specify the actual cities, $S^{\mathcal{I}}$ contains concrete services for different pairs of cities, such as Frankfurt and London, or Berlin and Hamburg.

Capability descriptions usually refer to commonly used domain ontologies. These ontologies define the background knowledge in a certain domain of interest in form of DL axioms. For example, in the travelling domain, they define terms such as 'City', 'Journey' or 'Airplane'.

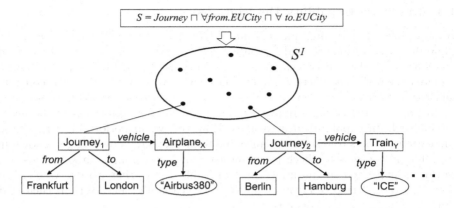

Fig. 1. A Capability Description Specifying Several Concrete Services

4.2 Variance and Incompleteness in Capability Descriptions

Recall from Section 2 that the main purpose of a capability description is to describe a set of concrete services which vary on several parameters. Hence, we say that capability descriptions introduce *variance due to intended diversity* [10], which manifests itself by allowing the capability description to specify several concrete services, each having different parameter values. The fact that the capability description S allows concrete services for travelling between Frankfurt and London, and Hamburg and Berlin, is an example of variance due to intended diversity. Using DL concept expressions as a description technique allows us to express this variance in a compact form, without listing all possible pairs of cities explicitly.

Moreover, we also identify *variance due to incomplete knowledge* [10], which is caused by the fact that capability descriptions do not completely specify all parameters. For example, a travel agency might not explicitly specify the types of payment it is willing to accept. This detail may be off-loaded from the service discovery to the service definition phase. However, this does not mean that a concrete service would not have any payment information; it simply means that the type of payment has not been specified. Each concrete service will still contain a certain type of payment. Variance due to incomplete knowledge is captured by assuming different *possible worlds*. In each of these possible worlds unspecified information is resolved in a particular way. In DL, variance due to incomplete knowledge is reflected by the fact that a knowledge base can have several different first-order interpretations, each corresponding to a particular possible world. Notice that this actually coheres to open-world semantics in description logics.

In Section 5 we show how epistemic operators can be incorporated into capability descriptions in order to close off parts of the domain model and to control and reduce variance due to incomplete knowledge by ruling out some of the possible worlds.

4.3   Matching Capability Descriptions

We now define a matching function $match(KB, S_r, S_p)$, which returns *true* if the capability descriptions S_r and S_p match, *false* otherwise. The basic idea behind matching is to check if two capability descriptions, issued by a requester and a provider, respectively, specify any common concrete service [26]. Such concrete services might then be taken as a basis to enter into the service definition phase.

Technically, matching is reduced to checking the non-emptiness of the intersection of both capability descriptions. However, when performing this check, there are two ways to resolve variance due to incomplete knowledge, as shown in [10]. The first one is to check if the intersection is non-empty in *some* possible world, as presented in the upper part of Table 1. In other words, we check if there is a way to resolve incompleteness in the capability descriptions such that they specify a common concrete service.

Another possibility is to check if the intersection of concept extensions is non-empty in *each* possible world, as shown in the lower part of Table 1. This is a stronger check: regardless of how we resolve incompleteness in capability descriptions, we need a concrete service that is common to both descriptions.

Related approaches to service discovery use similar matching techniques. 'Satisfiability of concept conjunction' was first proposed in [8, 26] and [24], and was subsequently considered in [19, 18, 17, 14, 10]. Furthermore, many of these works use 'entailment of concept subsumption', which checks if one of the sets of accepted concrete services is a subset of the other in each possible world. However, as discussed in [10], this inference has not shown to be beneficial for our notion

Table 1. Using DL Inferences for Matching Service Capabilities

Inference:	*Satisfiability of Concept Conjunction*
Function:	$match_{int}(KB, S_r, S_p)$
Formula:	$S_r \sqcap S_p$ is satisfiable w.r.t. KB
Situation:	
Intuition:	Is there a way to resolve unspecified details such that S_r and S_p specify some common concrete service?
Inference:	*Entailment of Concept Non-Disjointness*
Function:	$match_{ndj}(KB, S_r, S_p)$
Formula:	$KB \cup \{S_r \sqcap S_p \sqsubseteq \bot\}$ is unsatisfiable
Situation:	
Intuition:	Do S_r and S_p specify some common concrete service, regardless of how unspecified details are resolved?

of compatibility between two descriptions S_r and S_p: we treat concrete services as alternative specifications of service parameters, and thus, having a single concrete service in the extension of the sets is already sufficient for our capability descriptions to be compatible. Subsumption and equivalence matching applied to pairs (S_r, S_p) of descriptions has been used for establishing a ranking among service providers in [19, 17, 14]. However, in our setting the partial subsumption check between two provider descriptions S_{pA} and S_{pB}, defined in [10], provides a more fine-grained ranking based on the options the requester has later on in the service definition phase. In this work, we do not consider ranking but focus on the characteristics of the matching inferences in a local closed-world setting.

In [15], and also partly in [14], the authors consider a different description approach based on specifying services in terms of state transitions. They base matching on transaction logic, a formalism capable of explicitly representing changes in the world. In this way, they do not only consider the discovery phase, but also address partly the service definition phase.

4.4   Problems in Matching Capability Descriptions

Both ways of matching, $match_{int}$ and $match_{ndj}$, cause problems in certain cases [10], which we illustrate next on our running example. Let us assume that the requester company asks for a flight from a city in the UK, and that two providers A and B offer flights from cities in the EU and the US, respectively.

Example 1 (Problems with Matching Service Descriptions).

$$KB = \{ \ UKCity \sqsubseteq EUCity, \ Flight \sqsubseteq \exists from . \top \ \}$$

$$\begin{aligned} S_r &= Flight \ \sqcap \ \forall from . UKCity \\ S_{pA} &= Flight \ \sqcap \ \forall from . EUCity \\ S_{pB} &= Flight \ \sqcap \ \forall from . USCity \end{aligned}$$

First, consider matching capability description S_r against S_{pA}. Since the requester asks for a flight from a UK city, and A offers flights from an EU city, we intuitively expect the two descriptions to match. However, by applying the DL inferences, we get that $match_{int}(KB, S_r, S_{pA}) = true$, but $match_{ndj}(KB, S_r, S_{pA}) = false$. In the second case, the unintuitive result is due to the fact that we never specified that A actually offers any services. Hence, there is a way to resolve this incompleteness in the specification by choosing a possible world in which the extension of S_{pA} is empty. Therefore, matching fails, since it is not the case that the intersection of S_r and S_{pA} is non-empty in each possible world.

Second, consider matching capability description S_r against S_{pB}. Since the requester asks for flights from UK cities, but B offers flights from US cities, we would expect matching to fail. However, by applying the DL inferences, we get that $match_{int}(KB, S_r, S_{pB}) = true$, but $match_{ndj}(KB, S_r, S_{pB}) = false$. In the first case, the unintuitive result is due to the fact that we never said that UK and US cities are disjoint. Therefore, matching succeeds, since there is a possible world in which some city is in the extension of both $UKCity$ and $USCity$.

Both of these problems principally arise from the existence of unwanted possible worlds. To reduce the number of unintuitive matches, it would be desirable to reduce the variance due to incomplete knowledge, and to rule out those possible worlds which are 'obviously' wrong.

In the first case, this could be achieved by adding the assertion $Flight(a)$, for some new individual a, to the knowledge base before matching is performed, ruling out possible worlds in which $Flight$ is empty.

In the second case, the false positive match with $match_{int}$ could be 'repaired' by adding the disjointness axiom $EUCity \sqcap USCity \sqsubseteq \bot$ to the knowledge base, eliminating possible worlds in which a city can be in both the EU and the US.

In any case, we would have to include additional facts, such as disjointness constraints, which in practice often has the drawback of overloading the specification with 'obvious' information. In general, domain ontologies in the Semantic Web cannot be expected to contain such additional information, since they are reusable domain vocabularies and different ontologies might have been developed for different purposes.

As we shall see in the following section, non-monotonic features and local closed-world reasoning allow us to address this important problem of *overspecification* by dealing with incompleteness in an alternative way. A pure closed-world system, on the other hand, would not equally support the desired variance. Since in [10] we identified other problems with successfully using $match_{ndj}$ when several restrictions on roles are combined, we will focus on $match_{int}$, which has already been applied in an industrial logistics scenario in [22] on service descriptions in OWL-DL.

5   Epistemic Operators in Capability Descriptions

The autoepistemic extension to DL provides a means to exclude unwanted first-order interpretations in a controlled way. In this section, we show how the problems described in Section 4.4 can be overcome by realising local closed-world reasoning using the **K**-operator in capability descriptions.

5.1   Locally Closing Worlds in Capability Descriptions

Description logics employ the *open-world* semantics, under which, if a fact is not derivable from the knowledge base, its contrary cannot be assumed 'by default'. This is considered appropriate for the Semantic Web, due to its open nature. However, in a controlled scenario such as service discovery, it is sometimes beneficial to assume that all relevant facts about a subset of the domain are known; this is known in the literature as *local closed-world assumption* [7, 12]. The local closed-world assumption can be applied to DL knowledge bases in form of *concept closure* and *role closure* [23], which enable us to assume that all individuals of a concept, or all pairs of individuals of a role are known.

Concept Closure
The **K**-operator can be used to restrict the extension of a concept to those individuals that belong to this concept in each possible world, which is denoted by

concept closure. Recall from the definition of the semantics of $\mathcal{ALCK}$ in Section 3 that an expression $\mathbf{K}C$ is interpreted as the intersection of extensions over all first-order interpretations. Intuitively, this can be paraphrased by 'the set of individuals that are *known* to belong to C'. The following example extends Example 1 by applying the pattern of concept closure to city concepts.

Example 2 (concept closure).

$$KB = \{ \; UKCity \sqsubseteq EUCity, \; Flight \sqsubseteq \exists \, from . \top, \; UKCity(London) \; \}$$

$$S_r = Flight \; \sqcap \; \forall \, from . \mathbf{K} \, UKCity$$
$$S_{p_A} = Flight \; \sqcap \; \forall \, from . \mathbf{K} \, EUCity$$
$$S_{p_B} = Flight \; \sqcap \; \forall \, from . \mathbf{K} \, USCity$$

The $\mathcal{ALC}$ knowledge base *KB* states that every UK city is also an EU city, that any flight must specify the property *from* and that the individual *London* is an explicitly asserted UK city. The $\mathcal{ALCK}$ concepts S_r, S_{p_A} and S_{p_B} are the service capability descriptions issued by a requester and providers A and B. The requester requires a flight from somewhere in the UK, whereas the providers advertise flights from EU and US locations, respectively. In contrast to Example 1, in this example all parties use the pattern of concept closure to restrict the property *from* to only those individuals that are known to be cities in the UK, the US or Europe, respectively.

We use the extended notion of concept satisfiability from Definition 1 in Section 3 to check satisfiability of the $\mathcal{ALCK}$ concept $S_r \sqcap S_p$ w.r.t. the $\mathcal{ALC}$ knowledge base *KB* in *match*$_{int}$. As we show next, the application of *match*$_{int}$ in Example 2 yields the intuitively desired matching behaviour.

First, consider matching the capability description S_r against S_{p_A} using *match*$_{int}$. The satisfiability of $S_r \sqcap S_{p_A}$ requires the existence of an individual which is both known to be a *UKCity* and known to be a *EUCity*. The individual *London* is explicitly stated to be a *UKCity* in *KB*, so it is known to be a *UKCity*. This individual is also known to be a *EUCity* because of the inclusion axiom in *KB*. Hence, $S_r \sqcap S_{p_A}$ is satisfiable w.r.t. *KB* and thus *match*$_{int}(KB, S_r, S_{p_A}) = true$. Notice that without the explicitly introduced individual *London*[1] this satisfiability would not hold because there would be no individual which meets the above mentioned conditions in each possible world.

Second, consider matching the capability description S_r against S_{p_B} using *match*$_{int}$. The satisfiability of $S_r \sqcap S_{p_B}$ requires the existence of an individual which is both known to be a *UKCity* and known to be a *USCity*. However, there is no such individual and therefore *match*$_{int}(KB, S_r, S_{p_B}) = false$. Of course there are first-order interpretations in which *UKCity* and *USCity* have common individuals, namely, some in which *London* is both a *UKCity* and a *USCity*, but for such individuals this is not the case in each possible world.

---

[1] The individual *London* here can be seen as a representative for all explicitly modelled cities in some domain ontology with a geographic context.

Role Closure

The **K**-operator can also be used to restrict the extension of a role to those pairs of individuals that are connected by this role in each possible world, which is denoted as *role closure*. Recall from the definition of the semantics of $\mathcal{ALCK}$ in Section 3 that an expression $\mathbf{K}r$ is interpreted as the intersection of role extensions over all first-order interpretations. Intuitively, this can be paraphrased by 'all pairs of individuals that are *known* to be connected by r'. The following example applies the pattern of role closure to a role *train* that denotes the connection of two cities via the continental train network.

Example 3 (role closure).

$$KB = \{ \ GermanCity \sqsubseteq EUCity, \ UKCity \sqsubseteq EUCity, \ Flight \sqsubseteq \exists from.\top,$$
$$UKCity(London) \ , \ GermanCity(Berlin) \ , \ GermanCity(Hamburg) \ ,$$
$$train(Berlin, Hamburg) \ , \ train(Hamburg, Berlin) \qquad \qquad \}$$

$$S_r = Flight \ \sqcap \ \forall from.(\mathbf{K}\,EUCity \sqcap \exists \mathbf{K}\,train.\top)$$
$$S_{p_A} = Flight \ \sqcap \ \forall from.\mathbf{K}\,GermanCity$$
$$S_{p_B} = Flight \ \sqcap \ \forall from.\mathbf{K}\,UKCity$$

The $\mathcal{ALC}$ knowledge base KB states that both German cities and UK cities are cities in the EU and that the individuals *London, Berlin* and *Hamburg* are explicitly stated to be such cities. Furthermore, KB states that the individuals *Berlin* and *Hamburg* are connected via the train network. In the $\mathcal{ALCK}$ concept S_r the requester requires a flight from a known EU city which is known to be connected to the train network. This is achieved by applying concept closure to the concept *EUCity* and role closure to the role *train*. The providers advertise travelling from locations in Germany and in the UK, respectively. Also Example 3 shows the intuitively expected matching behaviour.

First, consider matching the capability description S_r against S_{p_A} using $match_{int}$. There are two known German cities, *Berlin* and *Hamburg*, which are both known to have connection to the train network. Furthermore, they both are also known to be EU cities due to the inclusion axiom. Therefore, $match_{int}(KB, S_r, S_{p_A}) = true$ and provider A matches the request.

Second, consider matching the capability description S_r against S_{p_B} using $match_{int}$. The only known UK city is *London* but it is not known to be connected to the train network. Therefore, $match_{int}(KB, S_r, S_{p_B}) = false$ and provider B fails to match the request, although *London* is known to be a EU city. Due to the local closure of worlds, only the known train connections explicitly modelled in the domain knowledge are taken into account.

Without the **K**-operator applied to the role *train* in S_r, provider B would also match the request because, due to the open-world assumption, *London* would have train connection in some possible world. Alternatively to the usage of **K**, one would have to complete the specification by listing all the cities which have no connection to the continental train network, by axioms like $\forall train.\bot(London)$.

5.2 Benefits of Locally Closing Worlds

By using the **K**-operator in capability descriptions to locally close off worlds, we have excluded unwanted first-order interpretations (that is, possible worlds), reducing variance due to incomplete knowledge. In this way, we have avoided over-specifying the domain, but have succeeded in removing false positive matches.

In Example 2, there is no need to explicitly state disjointness between non-related city concepts, since by the use of **K** we restrict their extensions to known cities only, for which EU and US do not overlap. In general, adding disjointness constraints is no real solution to the problem, since not all imaginable cities can be covered in the specification. A requester or provider might introduce a new city concept which is not explicitly related to the existing city concepts in any ontology. Intuitively, we would not want this unrelated city concept to match against any other. Hence, we avoid such additional constraints by locally closing off city concepts, assuming full knowledge about this part of the world.

In Example 3, we avoid to list all the cities that are *not* connected to the train network in addition to those that are. Here the use of **K** allows us to handle a partial and incomplete description of the state of the world by closing off the role *train*, assuming full knowledge about all train connections between cities.

Since the use of **K** makes matching dependent on the state of the world, it should only be applied to concepts or roles for which there is some ABox information present. For example, when requesting a flight carried out by a Star Alliance partner, **K** would most likely be applied as follows: $S = Flight \sqcap \forall\, carriedOutBy.$**K**$StarAlliancePartner$. For the discovery system, assertions of air carriers to the Star Alliance, such as $StarAlliancePartner(Lufthansa)$, is static ABox information present in some domain ontology. In combination with other such information about the state of the world, like $GermanCarrier(Lufthansa)$, this request would match a provider that offers flights carried out by German carriers. Thus, **K** can safely be applied to $StarAlliancePartner$ in S, preventing the specification from being overloaded with information about which airlines are no such partners. On the contrary, in settings similar to those from our Examples, no information about concrete flights and their carriers occurs in the domain knowledge. Domain ontologies rather speak of flights in more general terms, using TBox information such as $Flight \sqsubseteq \neg ShipCruise$ to distinguish them from other forms of travelling. Therefore, **K** is not applied to $Flight$ or to $carriedOutBy$ in S. The discovery system benefits from leaving this part of the world open, not requiring travel agencies to list all the concrete flights they offer.

5.3 An Implementation of the Matchmaking Framework

We have verified these examples with our prototypical implementation of a reasoner for $\mathcal{ALCK}$ according to the calculus presented in [5]. Based on this calculus, we implemented a decision procedure for satisfiability of $\mathcal{ALCK}$ concepts w.r.t $\mathcal{ALC}$ knowledge bases as well as for epistemic query answering. It can be used as a testing environment for small examples[2].

---

[2] The implementation is available at http://www.fzi.de/downloads/wim/KToy.zip

6 Summary and Outlook

In this paper, we have described a DL-based framework for discovery of services in the Semantic Web. We have presented an intuitive way to map the business needs of requesters and providers to the formal DL constructs. Thus, we have provided a basis for modelling guidelines which meet well the modeller's intuition. We have identified problems of DL-based matching related to open world semantics. We have shown how an autoepistemic extension to DL can be used to overcome those problems. In particular, we have shown how the application of epistemic operators in service capability descriptions can be used to realise local closed-world reasoning in a controlled way, preventing overspecification of capability descriptions and domain ontologies. We also implemented a testing environment for reasoning with $\mathcal{ALCK}$ concepts together with $\mathcal{ALC}$ knowledge bases, in order to verify our examples.

We plan to investigate the extension of $\mathcal{ALCK}$ with features of expressive description logics, such as number restrictions, nominals or inverse roles, which proofed to be useful in the context of describing service semantics [17, 10]. We also intend to investigate reasoning with arbitrary $\mathcal{ALCK}$ knowledge bases and to explore the formalism presented in [6, 23], which introduces an additional epistemic operator **A**, capturing the notion of 'assumption'. This formalism allows for the whole range of non-monotonic features, such as default rules and integrity constraints, which we have applied in a Semantic Web context in [9]. We intend to incorporate these features into our discovery framework to further improve the matching of capability descriptions. Moreover, we plan to systematise the use of epistemic operators in service capability descriptions to obtain intuitive modelling constructs that abstract from the underlying logical formalism.

References

1. The OWL Service Coalition. OWL-S 1.1 release. Available at http://www.daml. org/services/owl-s/1.1/, November 2004.
2. Grigoris Antoniou. *Nonmonotonic Reasoning*. MIT Press, 1997.
3. F. Baader, D. Calvanese, D. McGuinness, D. Nardi, and P. Patel-Schneider, editors. *The Description Logic Handbook*. Cambridge University Press, January 2003.
4. J. de Bruijn, H. Lausen, A. Polleres, and D. Fensel. The Web Service Modeling Language WSML: An Overview. In *Proceedings of the 3rd European Semantic Web Conference (ESWC)*, 2006.
5. F. M. Donini, M. Lenzerini, D. Nardi, W. Nutt, and A. Schaerf. An Epistemic Operator for Description Logics. *Artificial Intelligence*, 100(1-2):225–274, 1998.
6. F. M. Donini, D. Nardi, and R. Rosati. Description Logics of Minimal Knowledge and Negation as Failure. *ACM Transactions on Computational Logic*, 3(2):177–225, 2002.
7. O. Etzioni, K. Golden, and D. Weld. Tractable Closed World Reasoning with Updates. In *Proceedings of the 4th International Conference on Knowledge Representation and Reasoning (KR1994)*, pages 178–189. Morgan Kaufmann, 1994.
8. J. Gonzlez-Castillo, D. Trastour, and C. Bartolini. Description Logics for Matchmaking of Services. In *Proc. of the KI-2001 Workshop on Appl. of DL*, 2001.

9. S. Grimm and B. Motik. Closed-World Reasoning in the Semantic Web through Epistemic Operators. In *CEUR Proceedings of the OWL Experiences and Directions Workshop*, Galway, Ireland, 2005.
10. S. Grimm, B. Motik, and C. Preist. Variance in e-Business Service Discovery. In *Proceedings of the 1st Int. Workshop SWS'2004 at ISWC 2004*, November 2004.
11. V. Haarslev and R. Möller. Description of the RACER System and its Applications. In *International Workshop on Description Logics*, 2001.
12. J. Heflin and H. Munoz-Avila. LCW-based Agent Planning for the Semantic Web. In *Proc. of AAAI Workshop on Ontologies and the Semantic Web(WS-02-11)*, 2002.
13. I. Horrocks. Using an Expressive Description Logic: FaCT or Fiction? In *Proceedings of the 6th International Conference on Knowledege Representation and Reasoning (KR1998)*, pages 636–645. Morgan Kaufmann, 1998.
14. U. Keller, R. Lara, H. Lausen, A. Polleres, and D. Fensel. Automatic Location of Services. In *Proc. of the 2nd European Semantic Web Conference(ESWC)*, 2005.
15. M. Kifer, R. Lara, A. Polleres, C. Zhao, U. Keller, H. Lausen, and D. Fensel. A Logical Framework for Web Service Discovery. In *Proceedings of the 1st International Workshop SWS'2004 at ISWC 2004*, November 2004.
16. H. Lausen, D. Roman, and U. Keller. Web service Modeling Ontology - Standard (WSMO-Standard). Working draft. Technical report, Digital Enterprise Research Institute (DERI), March 2004. http://www.wsmo.org/2004/d2/v0.2/.
17. L. Li and I. Horrocks. A Software Framework For Matchmaking Based on Semantic Web Technology. In *Proceedings of the 12th World Wide Web Conference*, 2003.
18. T. Di Noia, E. Di Sciascio, F.M. Donini, and M. Mogiello. A System for Principled Matchmaking in an Electronic Marketplace. *Journal of E-Commerce vol.9*, 2004.
19. M. Paolucci, T. Kawamura, T. Payne, and K. Sycara. Semantic Matching of Web Service Capabilities. In *Proceedings of the 1st International Semantic Web Conference (ISWC)*, pages 333–347, 2002.
20. P. F. Patel-Schneider, P. Hayes, I. Horrocks, and F. van Harmelen. OWL Web Ontology Language; Semantics and Abstract Syntax, W3C Candidate Recommendation. http://www.w3.org/TR/owl-semantics/, November 2002.
21. C. Preist. A Conceptual Architecture for Semantic Web Services. In *Proceedings of the 3rd International Semantic Web Conference (ISWC)*, 2004.
22. C. Preist, J. Esplugas-Cuadrado, S. Battle, S. Grimm, and S. Williams. Automated B2B Integration of a Logistics Supply Chain Using Semantic Web Services Technology. In *Proc. of the 4th Int. Semantic Web Conference (ISWC)*, 2005.
23. R. Rosati. Autoepistemic Description Logics. *AI Communications, IOS Press*, 11(3–4):219–221, 1998.
24. E. Di Scasio, F. M. Dononi, M. Mongiello, and G. Piscitelli. A Knowledge Based System for Person-to-Person E-Commerce. In *Proc. of the KI-2001 Workshop on Applications of Description Logics*, 2001.
25. E. Sirin, B. Parsia, B. Cuenca Grau, A. Kalyanpur, and Y. Katz. Pellet: A Practical OWL-DL Reasoner. Technical report, University of Maryland Institute for Advanced Computer Studies (UMIACS), 2005. http://mindswap.org/papers/PelletDemo.pdf.
26. D. Trastour, C. Bartolini, and C. Preist. Semantic Web Support for the Business-to-Business E-Commerce Lifecycle. In *Proceedings of the Eleventh International Conference on World Wide Web*, pages 89–98, 2002.

The Web Service Modeling Language WSML: An Overview

Jos de Bruijn[1], Holger Lausen[1], Axel Polleres[1,2], and Dieter Fensel[1]

[1] Digital Enterprise Research Institute (DERI) Galway, Ireland and Innsbruck, Austria
{jos.debruijn, holger.lausen, dieter.fensel}@deri.org
[2] Universidad Rey Juan Carlos, Madrid, Spain
axel@polleres.net

Abstract. The Web Service Modeling Language (WSML) is a language for the specification of different aspects of Semantic Web Services. It provides a formal language for the Web Service Modeling Ontology WSMO which is based on well-known logical formalisms, specifying one coherent language framework for the semantic description of Web Services, starting from the intersection of Datalog and the Description Logic $\mathcal{SHIQ}$. This core language is extended in the directions of Description Logics and Logic Programming in a principled manner with strict layering. WSML distinguishes between conceptual and logical modeling in order to support users who are not familiar with formal logic, while not restricting the expressive power of the language for the expert user. IRIs play a central role in WSML as identifiers. Furthermore, WSML defines XML and RDF serializations for inter-operation over the Semantic Web.

1 Introduction

Web Services[1] are pieces of functionality which are accessible over the Web. Current technologies such as WSDL allow to describe the functionality offered by a Web Service on a syntactical level only. For automation of tasks, such as Web Service discovery, composition and execution, semantic descriptions of Web Services are required. Since Semantic Web technology enables this formal description of Web content, the combination of Semantic Web with Web Service is the natural next step to be taken.

This combination is often referred to as Semantic Web Services [16]. In this context, the Web Service Modeling Ontology WSMO [17] provides a conceptual model for the description of various aspects of Services towards such Semantic Web Services (SWS). In particular, WSMO distinguishes four top-level elements:

Ontologies. Ontologies provide formal and explicit specifications of the vocabularies used by the other modeling elements. Such formal specifications enable automated processing of WSMO descriptions and provide background knowledge for Goal and Web Service descriptions.

Goals. Goals describe the functionality and interaction style from the requester perspective.

---

[1] Throughout this paper we use the terms "Service" and "Web Service" interchangeably.

Y. Sure and J. Domingue (Eds.): ESWC 2006, LNCS 4011, pp. 590–604, 2006.

Web Service descriptions. Web Service descriptions specify the functionality and the means of interaction provided by the Web Service.

Mediators. Mediators connect different WSMO elements and resolve heterogeneity in data representation, interaction style and business processes.

The Web Service Modeling Language WSML takes into account all aspects of Web Service description identified by WSMO. WSML comprises different formalisms in order to investigate their applicability to the description of SWS. Since our goal is to investigate the applicability of different formalisms to the description of SWS, it would be too restrictive to base our effort on existing language recommendations such as OWL [6]. A concrete goal in our development of WSML is to investigate the usage of different formalisms, most notably Description Logics and Logic Programming, in the context of Ontologies and Web services.

We see three main areas which benefit from the use of formal methods in service descriptions: *Ontology description, Declarative functional description of Goals and Web services*, and *Description of dynamics*. In its current version WSML defines a syntax and semantics for ontology descriptions. The underlying formalisms which were mentioned earlier are used to give a formal meaning to ontology descriptions in WSML. For the functional description of Goals and Web services, WSML offers a syntactical framework, with Hoare-style semantics in mind. However, WSML does not yet formally specify the exact semantics of the functional descriptions of services. The description of the dynamic behavior of Web services (choreography and orchestration) in the context of WSML is currently under investigation, but has not been integrated in WSML at this point. Thus, in this paper we primarily focus on ontology description in WSML, where it turns out that WSML already includes many potentially useful features lacking in previous approaches.

We give an overview of WSML and its language layering in Section 2. The normative human-readable syntax of WSML is described in Section 3, followed by key features of WSML which are described in Section 4. Section 5 describes related approaches for the description of Semantic Web Services and Ontologies. We draw conclusions and outline future work in Section 6.

2 WSML Layering

Figure 1(a) shows the different variants of WSML and the relationships between them. These variants differ in logical expressiveness and in the underlying language paradigms and allow users to make the trade-off between provided expressiveness and the implied complexity for ontology modeling on a per-application basis.

WSML-Core is based on by the intersection of the Description Logic $\mathcal{SHIQ}$ and Horn Logic, based on Description Logic Programs [8]. It has the least expressive power of all the WSML variants. The main features of the language are concepts, attributes, binary relations and instances, as well as concept and relation hierarchies and support for datatypes.

WSML-DL captures the Description Logic $\mathcal{SHIQ}(\mathbf{D})$, which is a major part of the (DL species of) OWL [6].

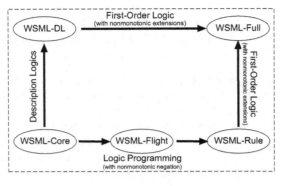
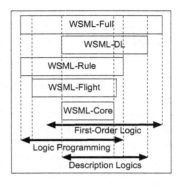

(a) Language variants   (b) Layering

Fig. 1. WSML Variants and Layering

WSML-Flight is an extension of WSML-Core which provides a powerful rule language. It adds features such as meta-modeling, constraints and nonmonotonic negation. WSML-Flight is based on a logic programming variant of F-Logic [12] and is
   semantically equivalent to Datalog with inequality and (locally) stratified negation.
   WSML-Flight is a direct syntactic extension of WSML-Core and it is a semantic
   extension in the sense that the WSML-Core subset of WSML-Flight agrees with
   WSML-Core on ground entailments (cf. [11]).
WSML-Rule extends WSML-Flight with further features from Logic Programming,
   namely the use of function symbols, unsafe rules and unstratified negation under
   the Well-Founded semantics.
WSML-Full unifies WSML-DL and WSML-Rule under a First-Order umbrella with
   extensions to support the nonmonotonic negation of WSML-Rule. The semantics
   of WSML-Full is currently an open research issue.

As shown in Figure 1(b), WSML has two alternative layerings, namely, WSML-Core
$\Rightarrow$ WSML-DL $\Rightarrow$ WSML-Full and WSML-Core $\Rightarrow$ WSML-Flight $\Rightarrow$ WSML-Rule
$\Rightarrow$ WSML-Full. For both layerings, WSML-Core and WSML-Full mark the least and
most expressive layers. The two layerings are to a certain extent disjoint in the sense
that inter-operation in WSML between the Description Logic variant (WSML-DL) on
the one hand and the Logic Programming variants (WSML-Flight and WSML-Rule)
on the other, is only possible through a common core (WSML-Core) or through a very
expressive superset (WSML-Full).

3   General WSML Syntax

In this section we introduce the general WSML syntax which encompasses all features
supported by the different language variants. We describe the restrictions imposed on
this general syntax by the different variants. These restrictions follow from the logical
language underlying the specific language variant, as described in the previous section.

WSML makes a clear distinction between the modeling of the different conceptual elements on the one hand and the specification of complex logical definitions on the other. To this end, the WSML syntax is split into two parts: the conceptual syntax and logical expression syntax. The conceptual syntax was developed from the user perspective, and is independent from the particular underlying logic; it shields the user from the peculiarities of the underlying logic. Having such a conceptual syntax allows for easy adoption of the language, since it allows for an intuitive understanding of the language for people not familiar with logical languages. In case the full power of the underlying logic is required, the logical expression syntax can be used. There are several entry points for logical expressions in the conceptual syntax, namely, axioms in ontologies and capability descriptions in Goals and Web Services.

We will first describe the use of Web identifiers and concrete data values in Section 3.1. The different kinds of WSML definitions and a general explanation of the conceptual syntax are given in Section 3.2. The logical expression syntax is described in Section 3.3. Finally, we briefly outline the XML and RDF serializations in Section 3.4.

3.1 Identifiers in WSML

WSML has three kinds of identifiers, namely, IRIs, sQNames, which are abbreviated IRIs, and data values.

An *IRI* (Internationalized Resource Identifier)[2] uniquely identifies a resource in a Web-compliant way. The IRI proposed standard is the successor of the popular URI standard and has already been adopted in various W3C recommendations. IRIs are delimited using an underscore and a double quote '_"' and a double quote '"', for example: _"http://www.wsmo.org/wsml/wsml-syntax#".

In order to enhance legibility, an IRI can be abbreviated to an sQName, which is short for 'serialized QName', and is of the following form: *prefix#localname*. The prefix and local part may be omitted, in which case the name falls in the default namespace. Our concept of an 'sQName' corresponds with the use of QNames in RDF and is slightly different from QNames in XML, where a QNames is not merely an abbreviation for an IRI, but a tuple <namespaceURI, localname>.

Data values in WSML are either strings, integers, decimals or structured data values, reflecting the XML Schema datatypes. WSML defines constructs which reflect the structure of data values. For example, the date "March 15th, 2005" is represented as: _date(2005,3,15). In logical expressions, constructed data values can be used in the same way as constructed terms, with the difference that constructed terms may not be nested inside constructed data values.

3.2 Conceptual Syntax

The WSML conceptual syntax allows for the modeling of Ontologies, Web Services, Goals and Mediators. It is shared between all variants, with the exception of some restrictions which apply on the modeling of ontologies in WSML-Core and WSML-DL.

Ontologies. An ontology in WSML consists of the elements **concept, relation, instance, relationInstance** and **axiom**. Additionally, an ontology may have

---

[2] IETF RFC 3987: http://www.ietf.org/rfc/rfc3987.txt

non-functional properties and may import other ontologies. We start the description of WSML ontologies with an example which demonstrates the elements of an ontology in Listing 1, and detail the elements below.

```
wsmlVariant _"http://www.wsmo.org/wsml/wsml−syntax/wsml−flight"
namespace { _"http://example.org/bookOntology#",
        dc _"http://purl.org/dc/elements/1.1/"}
ontology _"http://example.org/bookOntology"
    nonFunctionalProperties
        dc#title  hasValue "Example Book ontology"
        dc#description hasValue "Example ontology about books and shopping carts"
    endNonFunctionalProperties
    concept book
        title  ofType _string
        hasAuthor ofType author
    concept author subConceptOf person
        authorOf inverseOf(hasAuthor) ofType book
    concept cart
        nonFunctionalProperties
            dc#description hasValue "A shopping cart has exactly one id
                and zero or more items, which are books."
        endNonFunctionalProperties
        id ofType (1) _string
        items ofType book
    instance crimeAndPunishment memberOf book
        title  hasValue "Crime and Punishment"
        hasAuthor hasValue dostoyevsky

    relation authorship(impliesType author, impliesType document)
        nonFunctionalProperties
            dc#relation hasValue authorshipFromAuthor
        endNonFunctionalProperties

    axiom authorshipFromAuthor
        definedBy
            authorship(?x,?y) :− ?x[authorOf hasValue ?y] memberOf author.
```

Listing 1. An Example WSML Ontology

Concepts. The notion of concepts (sometimes also called 'classes') plays a central role in ontologies. Concepts form the basic terminology of the domain of discourse. A concept may have instances and may have a number of attributes associated with it. The non-functional properties, as well as the attribute definitions, are grouped together in one frame, as can be seen from the example concept book in Listing 1.

Attribute definitions can take two forms, namely *constraining* (using **ofType**) and *inferring* (using **impliesType**) attribute definitions[3]. Constraining attribute definitions define a typing constraint on the values for this attribute, similar to integrity constraints in Databases; inferring attribute definitions imply that the type of the values for the attribute is inferred from the attribute definition, similar to range restrictions on properties in RDFS [3] and OWL [6]. Each attribute definition may have a number of features associated with it, namely, transitivity, symmetry, reflexivity, and the inverse of an attribute, as well as minimal and maximal cardinality constraints.

Constraining attribute definitions, as well as cardinality constraints, require closed-world reasoning and are thus not allowed in WSML-Core and WSML-DL. As opposed

---

[3] The distinction between inferring and constraining attribute definitions is explained in more detail in [5, Section 2].

to features of roles in Description Logics, attribute features such as transitivity, symmetry, reflexivity and inverse attributes are local to a concept in WSML. Thus, none of these features may be used in WSML-Core and WSML-DL. For a motivation on the use of constraining attributes, see [5].

Relations. Relations in WSML can have an arbitrary arity, may be organized in a hierarchy using **subRelationOf** and the parameters may be typed using parameter type definitions of the form (**ofType** *type*) and (**impliesType** *type*), where *type* is a concept identifier. The usage of **ofType** and **impliesType** correspond with the usage in attribute definitions. Namely, parameter definitions with the **ofType** keyword are used to check the type of parameter values, whereas parameter definitions with the **impliesType** keyword are used to infer concept membership of parameter values.

The allowed arity of the relation may be constrained by the underlying logic of the WSML language variant. WSML-Core and WSML-DL allow only binary relations and, similar to attribute definitions, they allow only parameter typing using the keyword **impliesType**.

Instances. A concept may have a number of instances associated with it. Instances explicitly specified in an ontology are those which are shared as part of the ontology. However, most instance data exists outside the ontology in private databases. WSML does not prescribe how to connect such a database to an ontology, since different organizations will use the same ontology to query different databases and such corporate databases are typically not shared.

An instance may be member of zero or more concepts and may have a number of attribute values associated with it, see for example the instance crimeAndPunishment in Listing 1. Note that the specification of concept membership is optional and the attributes used in the instance specification do not necessarily have to occur in the associated concept definition. Consequently, WSML instances can be used to represent semi-structured data, since without concept membership and constraints on the use of attributes, instances form a directed labelled graph. Because of this possibility to capture semi-structured data, most RDF graphs can be represented as WSML instance data, and vice versa.

Axioms. Axioms provide a means to add arbitrary logical expressions to an ontology. Such logical expressions can be used to refine concept or relation definitions in the ontology, but also to add arbitrary axiomatic domain knowledge or express constraints. The axiom authorshipFromAuthor in Listing 1 states that the relation authorship exists between any author and any book of which he is an author; consequently, ⟨dostoyesksy, crimeAndPunishment⟩ is in the relation authorship. Logical expressions are explained in more detail in Section 3.3.

Web Services. A Web Service has a capability and a number of interfaces. The capability describes the Web Service functionality by expressing conditions over its pre- and post-states[4] using logical expressions; interfaces describe how to interact with

---

[4] Pre-state (post-state, respectively) refers to the state before (after, respectively) the execution of the Web Service.

the service. Additionally, WSML allows to specify non-functional properties of a Web Service. Listing 2 describes a simple Web Service for adding items to a shopping cart.

```
webService _"http://example.org/bookService"
  nonFunctionalProperties
    dc#title  hasValue "Example book buying service"
    dc#description  hasValue "A simple example web service for adding items to a shopping cart"
  endNonFunctionalProperties

  importsOntology _"http://example.org/bookOntology"
  capability
    sharedVariables {?cartId, ?item}
    precondition
      definedBy
        ?cartId  memberOf _string and ?item  memberOf book.
    postcondition
      definedBy
        forall ?cart (?cart[id  hasValue ?cartId] memberOf cart implies
          ?cart[items hasValue ?item]).
```

Listing 2. A WSML Web Service description

Capabilities. Preconditions and assumptions describe the state before the execution of a Web Service. While preconditions describe conditions over the information space, i.e., conditions over the input; assumptions describe condition over the state of world which can not necessarily be directly checked. Postconditions describe the relation between the input and the output, e.g., a credit card limit with respect to its values before the service execution. In this sense, they describe the information state after execution of the service. Effects describe changes in the real world caused by the service, e.g., the physical shipment of some good. The **sharedVariables** construct is used to identify variables which are shared between the pre- and postconditions and the assumptions and effects. Shared variables can be used to refer to the same input and output values in the conditions of the capability. Listing 2 describes a simple Web Service for adding items to a shopping cart: given a shopping cart identifier and a number of items, the items are added to the shopping cart with this identifier.

Interfaces. Interfaces describe how to interact with a service from the requester point-of-view (**choreography**) and how the service interacts with other services and goals it needs to fulfill in order to fulfill its capability (**orchestration**), which is the provider point of view. Choreography and orchestration descriptions are external to WSML; WSML allows to reference any choreography or orchestration identified by an IRI.

Goals. Goals are symmetric to Web Services in the sense that Goals describe desired functionality and Web Services describe offered functionality. Therefore, a Goal description consists of the same modeling elements as a Web Service description, namely, non-functional properties, a capability and a number of interfaces.

Mediators. Mediators connect different Goals, Web Services and Ontologies, and enable inter-operation by reconciling differences in representation formats, encoding styles, business protocols, etc. Connections between Mediators and other WSML elements can be established in two different ways:

1. Each WSML element allows for the specification of a number of used mediators through the **usesMediator** keyword.
2. Each mediator has (depending on the type of mediator) one or more sources and one target. Both source and target are optional in order to allow for generic mediators.

A mediator achieves its mediation functionality either through a Web Service, which provides the mediation service, or a Goal, which can be used to dynamically discover the appropriate (mediation) Web Service.

3.3 Logical Expression Syntax

We will first explain the general logical expression syntax, which encompasses all WSML variants, and then describe the restrictions on this general syntax for each of the variants. The general logical expression syntax for WSML has a First-Order Logic style, in the sense that it has constants, function symbols, variables, predicates and the usual logical connectives. Furthermore, WSML has F-Logic [12] based extensions in order to model concepts, attributes, attribute definitions, and subconcept and concept membership relationships. Finally, WSML has a number of connectives to facilitate the Logic Programming based variants, namely default negation (negation-as-failure), LP-implication (which differs from classical implication) and database-style integrity constraints.

Variables in WSML start with a question mark, followed by an arbitrary number of alphanumeric characters, e.g., ?x, ?name, ?123. Free variables in WSML (i.e., variables which are not explicitly quantified), are implicitly universally quantified outside of the formula (i.e., the logical expression in which the variable occurs is the scope of quantification), unless indicated otherwise, through the **sharedVariables** construct (see the previous Section).

Terms are either identifiers, variables, or constructed terms. An atom is, as usual, a predicate symbol with a number of terms as arguments. Besides the usual atoms, WSML has a special kind of atoms, called *molecules*, which are used to capture information about concepts, instances, attributes and attribute values. The are two types of molecules, analogous to F-Logic:

– An *isa* molecule is a concept membership molecule of the form A **memberOf** B or a subconcept molecule of the form A **subConceptOf** B with A and B arbitrary terms
– An *object* molecule is an attribute value expressions of the form $A[B$ **hasValue** $C]$, a constraining attribute signature expression of the form $A[B$ **ofType** $C]$, or an inferring attribute signature expression of the form $A[B$ **ofType** $C]$, with A,B,C arbitrary terms

WSML has the usual first-order connectives: the unary negation operator **neg**, and the binary operators for conjunction **and**, disjunction **or**, right implication **implies**, left implication **impliedBy**, and dual implication **equivalent**. Variables may be universally quantified using **forall** or existentially quantified using **exists**. First-order formulae are obtained by combining atoms using the mentioned connectives in the usual way. The following are examples of First-Order formulae in WSML:

// every person has a father
forall ?x (?x **memberOf** Person **implies exists** ?y (?x[father **hasValue** ?y])).
// john is member of a class which has some attribute called 'name'
exists ?x,?y (john **memberOf** ?x and ?x[name **ofType** ?y]).

Apart from First-Order formulae, WSML allows the use of the negation-as-failure symbol **naf** on atoms, the special Logic Programming implication symbol **:-** and the integrity constraint symbol **!-**. A logic programming rule consists of a *head* and a *body*, separated by the **:-** symbol. An integrity constraint consists of the symbol **!-** followed by a rule body. Negation-as-failure **naf** is only allowed to occur in the body of a Logic Programming rule or an integrity constraint. The further use of logical connectives in Logic Programming rules is restricted. The following logical connectives are allowed in the head of a rule: **and**, **implies**, **impliedBy**, and **equivalent**. The following connectives are allowed in the body of a rule (or constraint): **and**, **or**, and **naf**. The following are examples of LP rules and database constraints:

// every person has a father
?x[father **hasValue** f(?y)] :− ?x **memberOf** Person.
// Man and Woman are disjoint
!− ?x **memberOf** Man and ?x **memberOf** Woman.
// in case a person is not involved in a marriage, the person is a bachelor
?x **memberOf** Bachelor :− ?x **memberOf** Person and naf Marriage(?x,?y,?z).

Particularities of the WSML Variants. Each of the WSML variants defines a number of restrictions on the logical expression syntax. For example, LP rules and constraints are not allowed in WSML-Core and WSML-DL. Table 1 presents a number of language features and indicates in which variant the feature can occur.

Table 1. WSML Variants and Feature Matrix

Feature	Core	DL	Flight	Rule	Full
Classical Negation (**neg**)	-	X	-	-	X
Existential Quantification	-	X	-	-	X
(Head) Disjunction	-	X	-	-	X
n-ary relations	-	-	X	X	X
Meta Modeling	-	-	X	X	X
Default Negation (**naf**)	-	-	X	X	X
LP implication	-	-	X	X	X
Integrity Constraints	-	-	X	X	X
Function Symbols	-	-	-	X	X
Unsafe Rules	-	-	-	X	X

- *WSML-Core* allows only first-order formulae which can be translated to the DLP subset of $\mathcal{SHIQ}(\mathbf{D})$ [8]. This subset is very close to the 2-variable fragment of First-Order Logic, restricted to Horn logic. Although WSML-Core might appear in the Table 1 featureless, it captures most of the conceptual model of WSML, but has only limited expressiveness within the logical expressions.
- *WSML-DL* allows first-order formulae which can be translated to $\mathcal{SHIQ}(\mathbf{D})$. This subset is very close to the 2-variable fragment of First-Order Logic. Thus, WSML

DL allows classical negation, and disjunction and existential quantification in the heads of implications.

- *WSML-Flight* extends the set of formulae allowed in WSML-Core by allowing variables in place of instance, concept and attribute identifiers and by allowing relations of arbitrary arity. In fact, any such formula is allowed in the head of a WSML-Flight rule. The body of a WSML-Flight rule allows conjunction, disjunction and default negation. The head and body are separated by the LP implication symbol.

  WSML-Flight additionally allows meta-modeling (e.g., classes-as-instances) and reasoning over the signature, because variables are allowed to occur in place of concept and attribute names.

- *WSML-Rule* extends WSML-Flight by allowing function symbols and unsafe rules, i.e., variables which occur in the head or in a negative body literal do not need to occur in a positive body literal.

- *WSML-Full* The logical syntax of WSML-Full is equivalent to the general logical expression syntax of WSML and allows the full expressiveness of all other WSML variants.

The separation between conceptual and logical modeling allows for an easy adoption by non-experts, since the conceptual syntax does not require expert knowledge in logical modeling, whereas complex logical expressions require more familiarity and training with the language. Thus, WSML allows the modeling of different aspects related to Web services on a conceptual level, while still offering the full expressive power of the logic underlying the chosen WSML variant. Part of the conceptual syntax for ontologies has an equivalent in the logical syntax. This correspondence is used to define the semantics of the conceptual syntax. Notice that, since only parts of the conceptual syntax are mapped to the logical syntax, only a part of the conceptual syntax has a semantics in the logical language for ontologies. For example, non-functional properties are not translated (hence, the name 'non-functional'). The translation between the conceptual and logical syntax is sketched in Table 2.

Table 2. Translating conceptual to logical syntax

Conceptual	Logical
concept A subConcepOf B	A **subConceptOf** B.
concept A B **ofType** (0 1) C	A[B **ofType** C]. !− ?x **memberOf** A and ?x[B **hasValue** ?y, B **hasValue** ?z] and ?y != ?z.
concept A B **ofType** C	A[B **ofType** C].
relation A/n **subRelationOf** B	$A(x_1,...,x_n)$ **implies** $B(x_1,...,x_n)$
instance A **memberOf** B C **hasValue** D	A **memberOf** B. A[C **hasValue** D].

3.4 WSML Web Syntaxes

The WSML XML syntax is similar to the human-readable syntax, both in keywords and in structure. We have defined the XML syntax through a translation from the human-readable syntax [4] and have additionally specified an XML Schema for WSML[5]. Note that all WSML elements fall in the WSML namespace http://www.wsmo. org/wsml/wsml-syntax#.

WSML provides a serialization in RDF of all its conceptual modeling elements which can be found in [4]. The WSML RDF syntax reuses the RDF and RDF Schema vocabulary to allow existing RDF(S)-based tools to achieve the highest possible degree of inter-operation. As a result, WSML can be seen as an extension of RDF(S).

4   Key Features of WSML

There are a number of features which make WSML unique from other language pro-posals for the Semantic Web and Semantic Web Services. These key features are mainly due to the two pillars of WSML, namely (1) a *language independent conceptual model* for Ontologies, Web Services, Goals and Mediators, based on WSMO [17] and (2) *reuse* of several well-known logical language paradigms in *one* syntactical framework. More specifically, we see the following as the key features of WSML:

One syntactic framework for a set of layered languages. We believe different Se-mantic Web and Semantic Web Service applications need languages of different expressiveness and that no single language paradigm will be sufficient for all use cases. With WSML we investigate the use of Description Logics and Logic Pro-gramming for Semantic Web Services.

Normative, human readable syntax. It has been argued that tools will hide language syntax from the user; however, as has been seen, for example, with the adoption of SQL, an expressive but understandable syntax is crucial for successful adoption of a language. Developers and early adopters of the language will have to deal with the concrete syntax. If it is easy to read and understand it will allow for easier adoption of the language.

Separation of conceptual and logical modeling On the one hand, the conceptual syn-tax of WSML has been designed in such a way that it is independent of the under-lying logical language and no or only limited knowledge of logical languages is required for the basic modeling of Ontologies, Web Services, Goals, and Media-tors. On the other hand, the logical expression syntax allows expert users to refine definitions on the conceptual syntax using the full expressive power of the underly-ing logic, which depends on the particular language variant chosen by the user.

Semantics based on well known formalisms. WSML captures well known logical formalisms such as Datalog and Description Logics in a unifying syntactical frame-work, while maintaining the established computational properties of the original formalisms through proper syntactic layering. The variants allow the reuse of tools already developed for these formalisms. Notably, WSML allows to reuse efficient querying engines developed for Datalog and efficient subsumption reasoners devel-oped in the area of Description Logics. Inter-operation between the paradigms is achieved through a common subset, WSML-Core, based on DLP [8].

---

[5] http://www.wsmo.org/TR/d16/d16.1/v0.21/xml-syntax/wsml-xml-syntax.xsd

WWW Language. WSML has a number of features which integrate it seamlessly in the Web. WSML adopts the IRI standard, the successor of URI, for the identification of resources, following the Web architecture. Furthermore, WSML adopts the namespace mechanism of XML and datatypes in WSML are compatible with datatypes in XML Schema [2] and datatype functions and operators are based on the functions and operators of XQuery [15]. Finally, WSML defines an XML syntax and an RDF syntax for exchange over the Web. When using the RDF syntax, WSML can be seen as an extension of RDFS.

Frame-Based syntax. minus .1em Frame Logic [12] allows the use of frames in logical expressions. This allows the user to work directly on the level of concepts, attributes, instances and attribute values, instead of at the level of predicates. Furthermore, variables are allowed in place of concept and attribute identifiers, which enables meta-modeling and reasoning over the signature in the rule-based WSML language variants.

5 Related Work

In this section we review existing work in the areas of Semantic Web and Semantic Web Services languages and compare it to WSML.

RDFS. RDFS [3] is a simple ontology modeling languages based on triples. It allows to express classes, properties, class hierarchies, property hierarchies, and domain- and range restrictions. Several proposals for more expressive Semantic Web and Semantic Web Service descriptions extend RDFS, however there are difficulties in semantically layering an ontology language on top of RDFS:

1. RDFS allows the use of the language vocabulary as subjects and objects in the language itself.
2. RDFS allows the use of the same identifier to occur at the same time in place of a class, individual, and property identifier.

We believe that the number of use cases for the first feature, namely the use of language constructs in the language itself, is limited. However, the use of the same identifier as class, individual and property identifier (also called meta-modeling) is deemed useful in many cases. WSML does not allow the use of the language constructs in arbitrary places in an ontology, but does allow meta-modeling in its Flight, Rule and Full variants.

WSML is an extension of a significant part of RDFS; it does not allow the use of language constructs in the language itself and does not allow full treatment of blank nodes, because this would require reasoning with existential information, which is not allowed in the rule-based WSML variants. WSML provides a significant extension of RDFS through the possibility of specifying local attributes, range and cardinality constraints for attributes and attribute features such as symmetry, transitivity and reflexivity. Furthermore, WSML (in its rule-based variants) provides an expressive rule language which can be used for the manipulation of RDF data.

OWL. The Web Ontology Language OWL [6] is a language for modeling ontologies based on the Description Logic paradigm. OWL consists of three species, namely OWL

Lite, OWL DL and OWL Full, which are intended to be layered according to increasing expressiveness. OWL Lite is a notational variant of the Description Logic $\mathcal{SHIF}(\mathbf{D})$; OWL DL is a notational variant of the Description logic $\mathcal{SHOIN}(\mathbf{D})$. The most expressive species of OWL, OWL Full, layers on top of both RDFS and OWL DL. We compare OWL with the ontology description component of WSML, since OWL does not offer means to describe Web Services, Goals and Mediators.

WSML-Core is a semantic subset of OWL Lite. WSML-DL is semantically equivalent to OWL DL. However, there is a major difference between ontology modeling in WSML and ontology modeling in OWL. WSML uses an epistemology which abstracts from the underlying logical language, whereas OWL directly uses Description Logics epistemology; WSML separates between conceptual modeling for the non-expert users and logical modeling for the expert user. Arguably, these properties could make WSML easier to use as an ontology language. This is, however, merely a conjecture and would required extensive user testing to verify its correctness.

WSML-Flight and WSML-Rule are based on the Logic Programming paradigm, rather than the Description Logic paradigm. Thus, their expressiveness is quite different from OWL. On the one hand, WSML-Flight/Rule allow chaining over predicates and non-monotonic negation, but do not allow classical negation and full disjunction and existential quantification. We conjecture that both the Description Logics and Logic Programming paradigms are useful on the Semantic Web (cf. [11]). With WSML we capture both paradigms in one coherent framework. Interaction between the paradigms is achieved through a common subset, WSML-Core.

OWL-S. OWL-S [1] is an OWL ontology for the modeling of Semantic Web Services. It has been recognized that the expressiveness of OWL alone is not enough for the specification of Web Services (e.g. [13]). To overcome this limitation OWL-S allows the use of more expressive languages such as SWRL [9], KIF and DRS. However, the relation between the inputs and output described using OWL and the formulae in these languages is sometimes not entirely clear.

Comparing the language suggestions for WSML and OWL-S it turns out that while OWL-S aims at combining different notations and semantics with OWL for the description of service conditions and effects, WSML takes a more cautious approach: WSML does not distinguish between languages used for inputs/output and other description elements of the Web Service, but provides one uniform language for capability descriptions. Additionally, the languages suggested for OWL-S are all based on classical logic, whereas WSML also offers the possibility to use (nonmonotonic) Logic Programming.

Finally, WSML is based on the conceptual model of WSMO, which differs significantly from the OWL-S conceptual model for Web Service modeling. For a detailed comparison, see [14].

6   Conclusions and Future Work

In this paper we have presented the Web Service Modeling Language WSML, a language for the specification of different aspects related to Semantic Web Services, based on the Web Service Modeling Ontology WSMO [17]. WSML brings together different logical language paradigms and unifies them in one syntactical framework, enabling the reuse of proven reasoning techniques and tools. Unlike other proposals for Semantic Web and Semantic Web Service languages, WSML has a normative human readable syntax that makes a separation between conceptual and logical syntax, thereby enabling conceptual modeling from the user point-of-view according to a language-independent meta-model (WSMO), while not restricting the expressiveness of the language for the expert user. With the use of IRIs (the successor of URI) and the use of XML and RDF, WSML is a language based on the principles of the Semantic Web and allows seamless integration with other Semantic Web languages and applications.

The definition of an inter-operability layer between the Description Logic and Rules paradigms, in the form of WSML-Core, enables the use and extension of the same core ontology for a number of different reasoning tasks supported by a number of different reasoners, most notably subsumption reasoning using Description Logic reasoners and query answering using Logic Programming reasoners.

Future work for WSML consists of the application of the language to various use cases and the improvement of WSML tools, such as editors and reasoners[6]. From the language development point of view, the semantics of WSML-Full has not yet been defined; we are currently looking into several nonmonotonic logics, such as Autoepistemic and Default Logic. There are approaches which combine expressive Description Logics with nonmonotonic logic programming without requiring the expressiveness of WSML-Full (e.g.). Incorporating such approaches in WSML is a matter of ongoing investigation. We are working on defining the operational semantics for the Web Service capability. Such operational semantics is necessary for the automation of several Web Service related tasks, such as discovery [10]. It might turn out, however, that different tasks need different operational semantics. Finally, the Web Service choreography and orchestration are currently place-holders in WSML; work is ongoing to fill these place-holders.

Acknowledgments

We would like to thank all members of the WSML working group, especially Eyal Oren and Rubén Lara, for their comments and input to this document. We thank the anonymous reviewers for useful feedback.

This work was funded by the European Commission under the projects ASG, DIP, KnowledgeWeb, and SEKT; by Science Foundation Ireland under Grant No. SFI/02/CE1/I13; and by the FIT-IT (Forschung, Innovation, Technologie - Informationstechnologie) under the project RW^2.

References

1. D. Martin, M. Burstein, J. Hobbs, O. Lassila, D. McDemott, S. McIlraith, S. Narayanana, M. Paolucci, B. Parsia, T. Payne, E. Sirin, N. Srinivasan and K. Sycara. *OWL-S: Semantic markup for web services.* Member Submission 22, W3C, November 2004. http://www.w3.org/Submission/2004/SUBM-OWL-S-20041122/ .

---

[6] An overview of currently available tools can be found at: http://tools.deri.org/wsml/

2. P. V. Biron and A. Malhotra, editors. *XML Schema Part 2: Datatypes*. 2004. `http://www.w3.org/TR/xmlschema-2/`.

3. D. Brickley and R. V. Guha.   RDF vocabulary description language 1.0: RDF schema. Recommendation 10 February 2004, W3C, 2004. `http://www.w3.org/TR/rdf-schema/`.

4. J. de Bruijn, editor. *The Web Service Modeling Language WSML*. 2005. WSMO Final Draft D16.v0.21. `http://www.wsmo.org/TR/d16/d16.1/v0.21/`.

5. J. de Bruijn, A. Polleres, R. Lara, and D. Fensel. OWL DL vs. OWL Flight: Conceptual modeling and reasoning on the semantic web. In *Proc. WWW2005*, Chiba, Japan. 2005.

6. M. Dean and G. Schreiber, editors. *OWL Web Ontology Language Reference*. 2004. W3C Recommendation 10 February 2004.

7. T. Eiter, T. Lukasiewicz, R. Schindlauer, and H. Tompits. Combining answer set programming with description logics for the semantic web. In *Proc. KR2004*, 2004.

8. B. N. Grosof, I. Horrocks, R. Volz, and S. Decker. Description logic programs: Combining logic programs with description logic. In *Proc. WWW2003*, Budapest, Hungary, 2003.

9. I. Horrocks, P. F. Patel-Schneider, H. Boley, S. Tabet, B. Grosof, and M. Dean. SWRL: A semantic web rule language combining OWL and RuleML. Member submission 21 may 2004, W3C, 2004. `http://www.w3.org/Submission/SWRL/`.

10. U. Keller, R. Lara, H. Lausen, A. Polleres, and D. Fensel. Automatic location of services. In *Proc. ESWC2005*. 2005.

11. M. Kifer, J. de Bruijn, H. Boley, and D. Fensel. A realistic architecture for the semantic web. In *Proc. RuleML-2005*, Ireland, Galway. 2005.

12. M. Kifer, G. Lausen, and J. Wu. Logical foundations of object-oriented and frame-based languages. *JACM*, 42(4):741–843, 1995.

13. R. Lara, H. Lausen, S. Arroyo, J. de Bruijn, and D. Fensel. Semantic web services: description requirements and current technologies. In *Semantic Web Services for Enterprise Application Integration and e-Commerce workshop (SWSEE03), in conjunction with ICEC 2003*, Pittsburgh, PA, USA.

14. R. Lara, A. Polleres, H. Lausen, D. Roman, J. de Bruijn, and D. Fensel.   A conceptual comparison between WSMO and OWL-S.   Final draft D4.1v0.1, WSMO, 2004. `http://www.wsmo.org/TR/d4/d4.1/v0.1/`.

15. A. Malhotra, J. Melon, and N. Walsh.   Xquery 1.0 and xpath 2.0 functions and operators.   Candidate Recommendation, W3C, 2005.   `http://www.w3.org/TR/xpath-functions/`.

16. S. McIlraith, T. C. Son, and H. Zeng. Semantic web services. *IEEE Intelligent Systems, Special Issue on the Semantic Web*, 16(2):46–53, 2001.

17. D. Roman, U. Keller, H. Lausen, R. L. Jos de Bruijn, M. Stollberg, A. Polleres, C. Feier, C. Bussler, and D. Fensel. Web service modeling ontology. *Applied Ontology*, 1(1):77–106, 2005.

18. R. Rosati. $\mathcal{DL} + log$: Tight integration of description logics and disjunctive datalog. In *Proc. KR2006*, 2006.

On the Semantics of Functional Descriptions of Web Services

Uwe Keller, Holger Lausen, and Michael Stollberg

Digital Enterprise Research Institute (DERI)
University of Innsbruck, Austria
{firstname.lastname}@deri.org

Abstract. Functional descriptions are a central pillar of Semantic Web services. Disregarding details on how to invoke and consume the service, they shall provide a black box description for determining the usability of a Web service for some request or usage scenario with respect to the provided functionality. The creation of sophisticated semantic matchmaking techniques as well as exposition of their correctness requires clear and unambiguous semantics of functional descriptions. As existing description frameworks like OWL-S and WSMO lack in this respect, this paper presents so-called *Abstract State Spaces* as a rich and language independent model of Web services and the world they act in. This allows giving a precise mathematical definition of the concept of Web Service and the semantics of functional descriptions. Finally, we demonstrate the benefit of applying such a model by means of a concrete use case: the *semantic analysis* of functional descriptions which allows to detect certain (un)desired semantic properties of functional descriptions. As a side effect, semantic analysis based on our formal model allows us to gain a formal understanding and insight in matching of functional descriptions during Web service discovery.

1 Introduction

Enabling automated detection of Web services that adequately serve a given request or usage scenario is a main objective of Semantic Web service technology. Therefore, the functional description of a Web service specifies the provided functionality. Disregarding detailed information on how to invoke and consume the Web service the purpose of functional descriptions is to provide a black box description of *normal runs* of a Web service, i.e. without regard to technical or communication related errors that might occur during service usage.

In the most prominent overall description frameworks for Semantic Web services, functional descriptions are essentially *state-based* and use at least *prestate and poststate constraints* to characterize intended executions of a Web service. In OWL-S [13], *Service Profiles* encompass the functional description that is described by the in- and output, and by preconditions and results. Their counterpart in WSMO [11] are *capabilities* that are defined by preconditions, assumptions, postconditions, and effects. However, both models lack of clear and unambiguous semantics for functional descriptions [9]. This is essential for developing appropriate semantic matchmaking mechanisms for discovery, or for proving the correctness of functional descriptions - in general for any sort of symbolic computation based on functional descriptions in these frameworks.

Y. Sure and J. Domingue (Eds.): ESWC 2006, LNCS 4011, pp. 605–619, 2006.
© Springer-Verlag Berlin Heidelberg 2006

With respect to this necessity, we present a rigorous formal model of Web services and the world they act as the basis for clear semantic definitions of functional descriptions. Addressing the most fine-grained perspective on Web services and their functional descriptions as identified in previous work [7, 8] (namely, the level of rich semantic descriptions) we aim at applicability of the presented model in *any* setting where *state-based functional descriptions* are used, e.g. in frameworks like OWL-S and WSMO. Since both do *not* restrict themselves to a *particular* language for describing states (i.e. preconditions and postconditions), a formal definition that is usable for these frameworks must be modular and independent of the language chosen for describing state-conditions.

The contribution of this paper is as follows:

- we present so-called *Abstract State Spaces* as a sufficiently rich, flexible, and language independent model for describing Web services and the world they act in (Sec. 2)
- based on the model we describe what a functional description actually is and properly specify their formal semantics (Sec. 2)
- we give concise, formal definitions of all concepts involved in our model (Sec. 3)
- we demonstrate the applicability of the introduced model by a specific use case: the semantic analysis of functional descriptions (Sec. 4). In particular, we clearly define desirable properties of functional descriptions like realizability and semantic refinement and show how to determine these properties algorithmically based on existing tools in a provably correct way. Hereby, we can reconstruct generalized versions of results on matching between component specifications that are well-known in the software component community [18], but (based on our formal model) get some additional insights the relation between the *semantic notion* of refinement and the *syntactic criterion* for checking semantic matches, that have can not be discussed in [18] (see [10] for a deeper discusson).

The Bigger Picture. The model presented in this paper can be considered as a small first step towards a mathematical model for *service-oriented architectures*. Based on a more emcompassing and rich mathematical model, we will be able to give semantics to formal descriptions of such *architectures* and (similarly to what we discussed for the simple case of capabilities here) to reason about such descriptions in a well-understood and verifiably correct way by extension and refinement of the presented basic model. We expect that the presented model provides a suitable and flexible foundation for such non-standard extensions.

Overview of the Solution. As a part of rich model description frameworks like OWL-S and WSMO, functional descriptions of Web services $\mathcal{D}$ are *syntactic expressions* in some specification language $\mathcal{F}$ that is constructed from some (non-logical) signature $\Sigma^{\mathcal{F}}$. Each expression $\mathcal{D} \in \mathcal{F}$ captures specific requirements on Web services W and can be used to constrain the set of all Web services to some subset that is interesting in a particular context. Hence, the set of Web services W that satisfy the functional description $\mathcal{D}$ (denoted by $W \models_{\mathcal{F}} \mathcal{D}$) can be considered as actual meaning of $\mathcal{D}$. This way, we can define a natural *model-theoretic semantics* for functional descriptions by defining a satisfaction relation $\models_{\mathcal{F}}$ between Web services and functional descriptions. In comparison to most common logics, our semantic structures (i.e interpretations that are used to assign expressions $\mathcal{D}$ a truth value) are simply a bit more complex. In fact, they can be seen as generalizations of so-called Kripke structures [1, 17].

In general, various simpler syntactic elements are combined withing a functional description $\mathcal{D} \in \mathcal{F}$. State-based frameworks as the ones mentioned above use at least preconditions and postconditions. Whereas $\mathcal{D}$ refers to Web services, these conditions refer to simpler semantic entities, namely *states*, and thus in a sense to a "static" world. Such state conditions ϕ are expressions in (static) language $\mathcal{L}$ over some signature $\Sigma^{\mathcal{L}}$. Single states s determine how the world is perceived an external observer of the world and thus the truth value of these conditions. Formally, we have a satisfaction relation $\models_{\mathcal{L}}$ between states s and state expressions ϕ, where $s \models_{\mathcal{L}} \phi$ denotes that ϕ holds in state s. In essence, we can observe that on a syntactic level a language $\mathcal{L}$ for capturing static aspects of the world is *extended* to a language $\mathcal{F}$ that captures dynamic aspects of the world.

In order to define a similar extension on a semantic level, we *extend* the definition of the satisfaction $\models_{\mathcal{L}}$ (in $\mathcal{L}$) to a definition of satisfaction $\models_{\mathcal{F}}$ (in $\mathcal{F}$). This way, our definition is highly modular, language-independent to a maximum extent and focuses on the description of dynamics (i.e. possible *state transitions*) as the central aspect that the functional description language $\mathcal{F}$ adds on top of state description language $\mathcal{L}$. It can be applied to various languages $\mathcal{L}$ in the very same way as it only requires a model-theoretic semantics for the static language $\mathcal{L}$ (which almost all commonly used logics provide). Furthermore, our model-theoretic approach coincides to the common understanding of functional descriptions to be *declarative* descriptions *what* is provided rather than *how* the functionality is achieved.

2   Towards a Model of Web Services

The following introduces *Abstract State Spaces* as a flexible approach for defining a rigorous, formal model of Web services, the world they act in, and the meaning of functional descriptions. While introducing the model informally in the following, mathematically concise definitions are given in Section 3.

A changing world. We consider the world as an entity that changes over time. Entities that act in the world (which can be anything from a human user to some computer program) can affect how the world is perceived by themselves or other entities at some specific moment. At each point in time, the world is in one particular state that determines how the world is perceived by the entities acting therein. We need to consider some language for describing the properties of the world in a state. In the following we assume an *arbitrary* (but fixed) signature Σ (that usually is based on domain ontologies), and some language $\mathcal{L}(\Sigma)$ derived from the signature.

We use classical First-order Logic for illustration purposes in the following, however we stress that we are by no means bound to this specific language, i.e. other languages such as WSML or OWL can easily be used instead in our framework. Consider a signature $\Sigma \supseteq \{isAccount(\cdot), balance(\cdot), \geq, 0, 1, 2, \ldots\}$ that allows to talk about bank accounts and their balance. Then, $\mathcal{L}(\Sigma)$ allows comparing the respective values, for instance by expressions like $\forall ?x.(isAccount(?x) \Rightarrow balance(?x) \geq 0)$ stating that the balance of any account needs to be non-negative. In the context of dynamics and properties of the world that change, it is useful to distinguish between symbols in Σ that are supposed to have always the same, fixed meaning (e.g. $\geq, 0$) and thus can not be affected by any entity that acts in the world, and symbols that can be affected and thus can change their meaning during the execution a Web Service (e.g. $isAccount(\cdot)$, $balance(\cdot)$). We refer to the former class of symbols by *static symbols* (denoted by Σ_S) and the latter by *dynamic symbols* (denoted by Σ_D).

Abstract State Spaces. We consider an abstract state space $\mathcal{S}$ to represent all possible states s of the world. Each state $s \in \mathcal{S}$ completely determines how the world is perceived by each entity acting in $\mathcal{S}$. Each statement $\phi \in \mathcal{L}(\Sigma)$ of an entity about the (current state of) the world is either true or false. Thus, a state $s \in \mathcal{S}$ in fact *defines* an interpretation $\mathcal{I}$ (of some signature Σ). However, not all Σ-Interpretations $\mathcal{I}$ represent senseful observations since $\mathcal{I}$ might not respect some "laws" that the world $\mathcal{S}$ underlies, e.g. that the balance of any bank account is not allowed to be negative. In the following, we assume that these laws are captured by a background ontology $\Omega \subseteq \mathcal{L}(\Sigma)$ and denote the set of Σ-Interpretations that respect Ω (i.e. the models of Ω) by $Mod_\Sigma(\Omega)$. Considering our example signature from above and a background ontology Ω with $\{\forall ?x.(isAccount(?x) \Rightarrow balance(?x) \geq 0), isAccount(acc_1), isAccount(acc_2)\} \subseteq \Omega$, the following interpretation denotes a state $\mathcal{I} : balance(acc_1) = 10$. In contrast, the interpretation $\mathcal{I} : balance(acc_2) = -40$ does not denote a state in $\mathcal{S}$ (wrt. Ω).

Changing the World. By means of well-defined change operations, entities can affect the world and modify their current state. Such operations denote state transitions in $\mathcal{S}$. In our setting, these change operations are single concrete *executions* of Web services W. Following [8, 7], a change operation is represented by a *service* S that is accessed via a Web service W. S is achieved by executing W with some given input data $i_1, \ldots, i_n$ that specify (for a service provider) *what* kind of particular *service* S accessible via W is requested by the client, i.e. $S \approx W(i_1, \ldots, i_n)$.

Given input data $i_1, \ldots, i_n$, the execution of a Web service W essentially causes a state transition τ in $\mathcal{S}$, transforming the current state of the world $s \in \mathcal{S}$ into a new state $s' \in \mathcal{S}$. However, a transition τ will in general not be an *atomic transition* $\tau = (s, s') \in \mathcal{S} \times \mathcal{S}$ but a sequence $\tau = (s_0, \ldots, s_n) \in \mathcal{S}^+$, where $s_0 = s$, $s_n = s'$ and $n \geq 1$. In every intermediate state s_i in τ some effect can already be perceived by an enitity. This is especially relevant for Web services that allow accessing long lasting activities that involve multiple conversation steps between the requester and the Web service W. If we consider e.g. some international bank transfer having as concrete input data the information to transfer \$20 from acc_2 to acc_1 the web service execution might involve the following intermediate state between s_{pre} and s_{post} :

$$s_{pre} : balance(acc_1) = 10 \wedge balance(acc_2) = 100$$
$$s_1 : balance(acc_1) = 10 \wedge balance(acc_2) = 80$$
$$s_{post} : balance(acc_1) = 30 \wedge balance(acc_2) = 80$$

Outputs as Changes of an Information Space. During the execution $W(i_1, \ldots, i_n)$ of a Web service W, W can send some information as output to the requester. We consider these outputs as updates of the so-called *information space* of the requester of a service S. More precisely, we consider the *information space* of some service requester as a set $IS \subseteq U$ of objects from some universe U. Every object $o \in IS$ has been received by the requester from W during the execution $W(i_1, \ldots, i_n)$. During the execution the information space itself evolves: starting with the empty set when the Web service is invoked the execution leads to a monotonic sequence of information spaces $\emptyset = IS_0 \subseteq IS_1 \subseteq \ldots \subseteq IS_k$. Within our bank transfer example, during some financial transaction $tid891$ we might first receive a message acknowledgment $msgid23$ and then a confirmation that the transaction has been approved and initialized:

$$IS_1 = \{ack(20051202, msgid23, tid891)\}$$
$$IS_2 = \{ack(20051202, msgid23, tid891), confirm(acc_1, acc_2, 20, tid891)\}$$

Observations in Abstract States. Our aim is to describe *all* the effects of Web service executions for a requester. Obviously, a requester can observe in every state $s \in S$ world-related properties represented by statements ϕ in $\mathcal{L}(\Sigma)$ that hold in s. However, additionally there might be other aspects that an observer of the world can perceive in an abstract state s. In our model, this includes at least the information space $IS \subseteq U$ described above. Thus, an abstract state $s \in S$ in a sense „corresponds" to *all observations* (relevant for the uses of our formal model) that can be made in s. For our purpose here, this means all pairs of Σ-interpretations $\mathcal{I} \in Mod_\Sigma(\Omega)$ and (possible) information spaces $IS \subseteq U$. Consequently, we represent the observations related to a state s by an observation function $\omega : S \to Mod_\Sigma(\Omega) \times \mathcal{P}(U)$ that assigns every state $s \in S$ a pair $(\mathcal{I}, IS)$ of a Σ-interpretation $\mathcal{I}$ (respecting the domain laws Ω) and an information space IS. We denote the first component of $\omega(s)$ by $\omega_{rw}(s)$ (*real-world properties*: how an entity perceives the world) and the second component by $\omega_{is}(s)$ (*information space*: how the invoker perceives the information space). However, we require the observation function ω to be a (fixed) total function as is can *not* be arbitrary. This means that the observations $\omega(s)$ of any entity are well-defined in *every* abstract state s. Moreover, any perception representable in terms of $\mathcal{L}(\Sigma)$ and U that is consistent with the domain model Ω should actually corresponds to some abstract state $s \in S$ by means of ω, so that ω is surjective[1]. By considering abstract states as *abstract* objects without a predefined or fixed structure, and the separated assignement of a formal structure representing the actual observations that can be made in a state (by means of ω), we are able to address extensions of our model that might be needed in future extensions in a clean and modular way (e.g. when formally describing conversations between a group of agents in the world). Moreover, we can easily include representation of contextual aspects [3] in our model (e.g. that a state s is observed differently by various agents).

Web Service Executions. Given some input $i_1, \ldots, i_n$, the Web service execution $W(i_1, \ldots, i_n) = (s_0, \ldots, s_m)$ starting in state s_0 induces a sequence of observations $(\omega(s_0), \ldots, \omega(s_m))$ which can be made by the service requester during the execution. However, not all such sequences τ of abstract states actually do represent a meaningful state-transition caused by execution of W. For τ to faithfully represent some $W(i_1, ..., i_n)$ we need to require at least that for any two adjacent states s, s' in

---

[1] However, since we assume a fixed signature Σ and thus a limited language for describing observations about the world, we do not assume that ω is injective, i.e. there could be distinct states s, s' of the world which can *not* be distinguished by the (limited) language $\mathcal{L}(\Sigma)$, i.e. $\omega_{rw}(s) = \omega_{rw}(s')$.

$W(i_1, \ldots, i_n)$ some change can be observed by the invoker, and that objects which are in the information space (i.e. have been received by the invoker) at some point in time during the execution can not disappear until the execution is completed. As discussed later, in general we need to require some further constraints on a sequence τ such that we can interpret τ as a possible run $W(i_1, \ldots, i_n)$ of a Web service W. We call s_0 the pre-state of the execution, s_m the post-state of the execution, and all other states in $W(i_1, \ldots, i_n)$ intermediate states.

Web Services. A Web service W then can be seen as a set of executions $W(i_1, \ldots, i_n)$ that can be delivered by the Web service in any given state of the world to a requester when being equipped with any kind of valid input data $i_1, \ldots, i_n$. However, in order to keep track of the input data that caused a specific execution, we need to represent a Web service in terms of a slightly richer structure than a set, namely a mapping between the provided input values $i_1, \ldots, i_n$ and the resulting execution $W(i_1, \ldots, i_n)$. Figure 1 illustrates the proposed model.

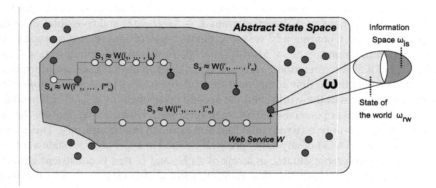

Fig. 1. An abstract Model of the World and Web services therein

Functional Description of Web Services. Combining state-related descriptions with a functional description (or capability) essentially creates a constraint on possible Web Service executions. Executions of a Web service W whose capability has been described in terms of a capability description $\mathcal{D}$ (where $\mathcal{D}$ contains a prestate-constraint ϕ^{pre} and a post-state constraint ϕ^{post}) can no longer be arbitrary possible executions τ in an abstract state space $\mathcal{S}$, but whenever the prestate s_0 of τ respects ϕ^{pre} then the final state s_m of τ must respect ϕ^{post}. Otherwise, τ is not considered to represent an actual execution of a Web service W with capability $\mathcal{D}$.

3   Abstract State Spaces and Web Services

We will now give a series of definitions which capture the preceding semi-formal discussion in a rigorous way.

In the following, let Σ be some signature, $\mathcal{L}(\Sigma)$ be some logic over signature Σ and $\Omega \subseteq \mathcal{L}(\Sigma)$ be some background theory capturing relevant domain knowledge. Let $\Im(\Sigma)$ denote the set of Σ-interpretations in $\mathcal{L}(\Sigma)$ and $\Im(\Sigma, \mathcal{U})$ denote the set of Σ-interpretations such that for all $\mathcal{I} \in \Im(\Sigma)$ the universe considered in $\mathcal{I}$ (denoted by $universe(\mathcal{I})$) is a subset of $\mathcal{U}$. For a set U we use $\mathcal{P}(U)$ to denote the powerset of U. Let $Mod_\Sigma(\Omega, \mathcal{U})$ denote the Σ-Interpretations $\mathcal{I} \in \Im(\Sigma, \mathcal{U})$ which satisfy the domain model Ω (i.e. $\mathcal{I} \models_{\mathcal{L}(\Sigma)} \Omega$). We denote the meaning of a symbol $\alpha \in \Sigma$ that is assigned by an interpretation $\mathcal{I}$ by $meaning_\mathcal{I}(\alpha)$.

Given a signature $\Sigma_0 = \Sigma_D \cup \Sigma_S$ that is partitioned into a set Σ_D of dynamic symbols and a set Σ_S of static symbols, we extend Σ_0 to a signature Σ by adding a (new) symbol α_{pre} for each $\alpha \in \Sigma_D$. The set of these pre-variants of symbols is denoted by Σ_D^{pre}. Furthermore, add a new symbol out to Σ_0. The intention is as follows: Σ_S contains symbols that are interpreted always in the same way (static symbols), Σ_D contains symbols whose interpretation can change during the execution of a Web service (dynamic symbols), and Σ_D^{pre} contains symbols that are interpreted during the execution of a Web service as they have been right before starting the execution. Finally, out denotes the objects in the information space. The symbols that have been added to Σ_0 can be used when formulating post-state constraints to describe changes between pre-states and post-states in a precise way.

Definition 1 (Abstract State Space). *An **abstract state space** $\mathcal{A} = (\mathcal{S}, \mathcal{U}, \Sigma, \Omega, \omega)$ is a 5-tuple such that (i) $\mathcal{S}$ is a non-empty set of **abstract states**, (ii) $\mathcal{U}$ is some non-empty set of objects called the **universe** of $\mathcal{A}$ (iii) $\Omega \subseteq \mathcal{L}(\Sigma)$ is consistent (iv) $\omega : \mathcal{S} \to Mod_\Sigma(\Omega, \mathcal{U}) \times \mathcal{P}(\mathcal{U})$ is a total surjective function that assigns to every abstract state s a pair of a Σ-interpretation $\omega_{rw}(s)$ satisfying Ω and an information space $\omega_{is}(s)$ and (v) for all $s, s' \in \mathcal{S}$ and $\alpha \in \Sigma_S : meaning_{\omega_{rw}(s)}(\alpha) = meaning_{\omega_{rw}(s')}(\alpha)$.* $\square$

In $\mathcal{A}$, Ω can be considered as a domain ontology representing (consistent) background knowledge about the world. It is used in any sort of descriptions, like preconditions etc. Clause (v) captures the nature of static symbols. In the following, $\mathcal{A}$ always denotes an abstract state space $\mathcal{A} = (\mathcal{S}, \mathcal{U}, \Sigma, \Omega, \omega)$.

For interacting with a Web service W, a client can use a technical interface. When abstracting from the technical details, every such interface basically provides a set of values as input data. The required input data represent the abstract interface used for interaction with the Web service from a capability point of view.

Definition 2 (Web Service Capability Interface, Input Binding). *A **Web service capability interface** IF of a Web service W is a finite sequences of names $(i_1, \dots, i_n)$ of all required input values of a W. An **input binding** β for a Web service capability interface IF in $\mathcal{A}$ is a total function $\beta : \{i_1, \dots, i_n\} \to \mathcal{U}$. The set of all input bindings for IF in $\mathcal{A}$ is denoted by $In_\mathcal{A}(IF)$.* $\square$

An input binding essentially represents the input that is provided by the invoker of a Web service W during the *entire* execution of W.

Definition 3 (Web Service Execution). *A (possible) **Web service execution** in $\mathcal{A}$ is finite sequences $\tau = (s_0, \dots, s_m) \in \mathcal{S}^+$ of abstract states such that for all $0 \le j < m$*

and $0 \leq i, k \leq m$ *(i)* $\omega(s_j) \neq \omega(s_{j+1})$, *(ii)* $\emptyset = \omega_{is}(s_0) \subseteq \omega_{is}(s_1) \subseteq \ldots \subseteq \omega_{is}(s_m)$, *(iii)* $universe(\omega_{rw}(s_i)) = universe(\omega_{rw}(s_k))$, *(iv)* $\omega_{is}(s_i) \subseteq universe(\omega_{rw}(s_i))$, *(v) for all* $\alpha \in \Sigma_D$: $meaning_{\omega_{rw}(s_0)}(\alpha) = meaning_{\omega_{rw}(s_i)}(\alpha_{pre})$ *and (vi)* $meaning_{\omega_{rw}(s_i)}(out) = \omega_{is}(s_i)$. *We denote the set of all possible Web service executions in* $\mathcal{A}$ *by* $Exec(\mathcal{A})$.   □

This definition gives detailed conditions under which a sequence τ can be considered as a Web service execution. Clause (iii) requires that within an execution the universes which are related to abstract states s_j are the same[2]. In other words, universes (which are used to interpret state-based expression) that are related by an execution are not arbitrary, but specifically related to each other. In particular, (iii) ensures that within a functional description $\mathcal{D}$ postconditions can talk about *every object* that the precondition can refer to as well. Hence, precise comparisons between various states of an execution becomes possible. Clause (iv) requires that for every abstract state that involved in the execution its information space is part of the universe of the abstract state. This allows to relate and compare information space objects with real-world objects in state-based expressions. Finally, clauses (v) and (vi) ensure that in all intermediate and final states, the pre-versions α_{pre} of dynamic symbols α are interpreted as α in the prestate s_0 of the execution and that the symbol *out* represent the respective information space.

Definition 4 (Web Service, Web Service Implementation). *A **Web service implementation** W of some Web service capability interface $IF = (i_1, \ldots, i_n)$ in $\mathcal{A}$ is a total function ι : $In_{\mathcal{A}}(IF) \times \mathcal{S} \to Exec(\mathcal{A})$ that defines for all accepted input bindings in $In_{\mathcal{A}}(IF)$ and abstract states $s \in \mathcal{S}$ the respective Web service execution of W in $Exec(\mathcal{A})$. Formally, we require for ι that $\iota(\beta, s) = (s_0, \ldots, s_m)$ implies $s_0 = s$ for all $s \in \mathcal{S}, \beta \in In_{\mathcal{A}}(IF)$. A **Web service** $W = (IF, \iota)$ is a pair of a Web service capability interface IF and a corresponding Web service implementation ι of IF.*   □

One can consider the mapping ι as a marking of execution sequences in $\mathcal{A}$ by the input data that triggers the execution. Since we define a Web service implementation in terms of a function which maps to single Web service executions, we consider *deterministic* Web services, i.e the execution is fully determined by the input binding β and the intial state s_0 only. Any sort of uncertainty about what is going to happen when executing W (e.g. unexpected failures due to the environment the Web service is embedded in) is not considered in our model. In being a total function on $In_{\mathcal{A}}(IF) \times \mathcal{S}$, the definition reflects the fact that ι represents an (abstract) *implementation*, i.e. (unlike for specifications) every possible effect in every situation is *fully determined* by ι.

Based on this formal machinery, we can now formalize the meaning of functional descriptions $\mathcal{D} \in \mathcal{F}$ that are based on a state-description language $\mathcal{L}(\Sigma)$. In the following, we write $\mathcal{I}, \beta \models_{\mathcal{L}(\Sigma)} \phi$ to express that formula $\phi \in \mathcal{L}(\Sigma)$ is satisfied under Σ-interpretation $\mathcal{I}$ and variable assignment β. We assume that a functional description $\mathcal{D} = (\phi^{pre}, \phi^{post}, IF_{\mathcal{D}})$ consists of a precondition $\phi^{pre} \in \mathcal{L}(\Sigma_0)$, and a postcondition

---

[2] In order to model dynamic universes (e.g. object creation and deletion) one needs to model object existence in the state-description language $\mathcal{L}$ itself, for instance by a dynamic unary relation `existing`.

$\phi^{post} \in \mathcal{L}(\Sigma)$. $IF_{\mathcal{D}} \subseteq FreeVars(\phi^{pre}, \phi^{post})$ denotes the set of (free) variable names in $\mathcal{D}$ which represent inputs for the Web service under consideration. The logical expressions ϕ^{pre} and ϕ^{post} usually refer to some background ontology $\Omega \subseteq \mathcal{L}(\Sigma)$.

Definition 5 (Extension of an Input Binding, Renaming). *Let β be an input binding for some Web service capability interface $IF = (i_1, \ldots, i_n)$, V be a set of symbol names and $U \subseteq \mathcal{U}$. A total function $\beta' : \{i_1, \ldots, i_n\} \cup V \to U$ is called a V-**extension** of β in U if $\beta'(i_j) = \beta(i_j)$ for all $1 \le j \le n$.*

*Let π be some function and β an input binding for IF. Then we denote by $rename_{\pi}(\beta)$ the input binding β' for IF' that is derived from β by replacing all pairs $(n, v) \in \beta$ with $n \in dom(\pi)$ by $(\pi(n), v)$. We call $rename_{\pi}(\beta)$ **renaming of β by π**.* □

An extension of an input binding β is used in the next definition to ensure that every variable that occurs free in a precondition or postcondition can be assigned a concrete value. Otherwise, no truth-value can be determined for these statements. The renaming represents on a technical level the effect of renaming input names in a Web service interface by the corresponding names in the interface used in the Web service description.

Definition 6 (Capability Satisfaction, Capability Model). *Let $W = (IF, \iota)$ be a Web service in $\mathcal{A}$ and $\mathcal{D} = (\phi^{pre}, \phi^{post}, IF_{\mathcal{D}})$ be a functional description of a Web service. Let FV denote the set of free variables in ϕ^{pre} and ϕ^{post} and U denote $universe(\omega_{rw}(s_0))$. W **satisfies capability** $\mathcal{D}$ in $\mathcal{A}$ if and only if (i) there exists a subset $IF' \subseteq IF_{\mathcal{D}}$ of the inputs of $\mathcal{D}$ and a bijection $\pi : IF \to IF'$ between IF and IF' such that (ii) for all input bindings $\beta \in In_{\mathcal{A}}(IF)$ and abstract states $s \in \mathcal{S}$: for all FV-extensions β' of $rename_{\pi}(\beta)$ in U: if $\iota(\beta, s) = (s_0, \ldots, s_m)$ for some $m \ge 0$ and $\omega_{rw}(s_0), \beta' \models_{\mathcal{L}(\Sigma)} \phi^{pre}$ then $\omega_{rw}(s_m), \beta' \models_{\mathcal{L}(\Sigma)} \phi^{post}$*

*In this case we write $W \models_{\mathcal{F}} \mathcal{D}$ and call the Web service W a **capability model** (or simply model) of $\mathcal{D}$ in $\mathcal{A}$.* □

Clause (i) essentially requires (interface) compatibility between the Web service and the inputs refered to in Web service description. Note, that we do not require syntactic equality between these names, but only equivalence up to some renaming π. Moreover, it is perfectly fine for models of $\mathcal{D}$ to only use a proper subset IF' of the inputs $IF_{\mathcal{D}}$ mentioned in capability $\mathcal{D}$. Clause (ii) defines the meaning of preconditions and postcondition. Please note, that free variables in these expressions are implicitly universally quantified by our definition.

4 Applying the Formal Model for Semantic Analysis

For demonstrating the suitability of the proposed model, this section shows its beneficial application for semantic analysis of functional descriptions Based on our model-theoretic framework, we can carry over several semantic standard notions from mathematical logic [2, 4] that refer to formal descriptions and are based on the *model* notion to our particular context in a meaningful way. For a deeper and extended discussion of the topic, we refer the interested reader to [10].

Realizability. We define *realizability* of a description $\mathcal{D}$ as the corresponding notion to satisfiability in a logic $\mathcal{L}$: A functional description $\mathcal{D}$ is **realizable in an abstract state space** $\mathcal{A}$ iff. there is a Web service W in $\mathcal{A}$ that satisfies $\mathcal{D}$, i.e. $W \models_{\mathcal{F}} \mathcal{D}$.

Consider the following functional description $\mathcal{D} = (\phi^{pre}, \phi^{post}, IF_\mathcal{D})$ describing Web services for account withdraws: $IF_\mathcal{D} = \{?acc, ?amt\}$

$$\phi^{pre} : ?amt \geq 0 \qquad \phi^{post} : balance(?acc) = balance_{pre}(?acc) - ?amt$$

At a first glance, the given description seems to be implementable within some Web service W that satisfies $\mathcal{D}$. However, taking a closer look at the respective domain ontology it becomes obvious that this actually is not the case. The ontology defines that a balance might not be negative, but the precondition does not prevent the balance being less then the withdraw. Let's assume that there is a Web service W realizing $\mathcal{D}$. When considering an input binding β with $\beta(?amt) > balance_{pre}(?acc)$, then the precondition is satisfied and thus the postcondition should hold in the final state of the respective execution, i.e. $\omega_{rw}(s_m), \beta \models \forall ?acc.balance(?acc) < 0$. However, this is inconsistent with the domain ontology since $\Omega \models balance(?acc) \geq 0$ and thus s_m can not exist in $\mathcal{A}$. This is a contradiction and shows that no Web service W with $W \models_\mathcal{F} \mathcal{D}$ can exist. To fix the description such that it becomes realizable, we need to extend the precondition to $\phi^{pre} : 0 \leq ?amt \wedge ?amt \leq balance(?acc)$.

The example illustrates the usefulness of the notion of realizability. It provides a tool for detecting functional descriptions that contain flaws that might not be obvious to the modelers. Moreover, we as we will see soon, we can often rephrase the problem of realizability of a description $\mathcal{D} \in \mathcal{F}$ to a well-understood problem in $\mathcal{L}$ for which algorithms already exist. We first turn to an important other notion of which realizability turns out to be a special case (in conformance as with the original notions in mathematical logic).

Functional Refinement. The notion of logical entailment is usually defined as follows: An formula ϕ logically entails a formula ψ iff every interpretation $\mathcal{I}$ which is a models of ϕ (i.e. $\mathcal{I} \models_\mathcal{L} \phi$) is also a model of ψ. Substituting interpretations by Web services, formulae by functional descriptions and the satisfaction $\models_\mathcal{L}$ by capability satisfaction $\models_\mathcal{F}$ we derive a criteria that captures *fuctional refinement*: Let $\mathcal{D}_1, \mathcal{D}_2 \in \mathcal{F}$ be functional descriptions. $\mathcal{D}_1$ **is a functional refinement of** $\mathcal{D}_2$ in $\mathcal{A}$ (denoted by $\mathcal{D}_1 \sqsubseteq \mathcal{D}_2$) iff. for each Web service W in $\mathcal{A}$, $W \models_\mathcal{F} \mathcal{D}_1$ implies $W \models_\mathcal{F} \mathcal{D}_2$. Intuitively speaking, $\mathcal{D}_1 \sqsubseteq \mathcal{D}_2$ means that $\mathcal{D}_1$ is more specific than $\mathcal{D}_2$: Every Web service (no matter which one) that provides $\mathcal{D}_1$ can also provide $\mathcal{D}_2$. In other words, $\mathcal{D}_1$ must describe some piece of functionality that always fits the requirements $\mathcal{D}_2$ as well. However, Web services that provide $\mathcal{D}_2$ do not have to satisfy $\mathcal{D}_1$ and therefore, a Web service that provides $\mathcal{D}_1$ can do something more specific than required by $\mathcal{D}_2$.

For illustration, consider some Web service description $\mathcal{D}_1 = (\phi_1^{pre}, \phi_1^{post}, IF_1)$ with $IF_1 = \{?prs, ?acc\}$ that advertises the ability to provide access credentials for a particular web site ($http://theSolution.com$). A domain ontology specifies that if some web site has some content and someone can access the web site, then he (is able to) know about the content. Furthermore, $http://theSolution.com$ is a web site providing the ultimate answer to life (the universe and everything) and some constant $accessFee$ has a value less then 42.[3]

---

[3] Note that we do not expect such knowledge in one central domain ontology, but a number of knowledge bases (generic, provider- and requester-specific). For simplicity we assume Ω being already aggregated.

ϕ_1^{pre} :$account(?p, ?acc) \land balance(?acc) \geq accessFee$

ϕ_1^{post} :$balance(?acc) = balance_{pre}(?acc) - accessFee$

   $\land$ **out**$(password(?prs, http{:}//theSolution.com))$

   $\land isValid(password(?prs, http{:}//theSolution.com))$

$\Omega \models \forall ?ws, ?co, ?prs. content(?ws, ?co) \land access(?prs, ?ws) \Rightarrow knows(?prs, ?co)$

   $content(http{:}//theSolution.com, answer2Life), accessFee \leq 42$

   $\forall ?prs, ?ws. isValid(password(?prs, ?ws)) \Rightarrow access(?prs, ?ws))$

Using our formal definition we now can examine another definition $\mathcal{D}_2 = (\phi_2^{pre}, \phi_2^{post}, IF_2)$ with $IF_2 = \{?prs, ?acc\}$ and check if it is a functional refinement of the previous description.

ϕ_2^{pre} : $account(?prs, ?acc) \land balance(?acc) \geq 100$ ϕ_2^{post} :$knows(?prs, answer2Life)$

This notion can beneficially be applied within functionality-based matchmaking. For instance, let's assume that a Person me is seeking for the ultimate answer to life ($knows(me, answer2Life)$); me has an account $acc123$ with a current balance of 174 USD. Given this information (and our domain ontology Ω) and considering the specific input binding $\beta(?prs) = me, \beta(?acc) = acc123$, we can infer that any Web service W that is advertised to provide capability $\mathcal{D}_2$ can serve for me's purpose as the precondition ϕ_2^{pre} is satisfied for the input β. In consequence, for the specific input β the service delivers what is described the postcondition ϕ_2^{post}; therefrom, we can infer $knows(me, answer2Life)$. However, since $\mathcal{D}_1 \sqsubseteq \mathcal{D}_2$ we know as well, that any Web service W' that is advertised to provide capability $\mathcal{D}_1$ is perfectly suitable for me and his endeavor as well. The notion of functional refinement can then be used to pre-index some set of Web service description, such that for a given request it is not necessary to consider all available description but only a subset identified by the pre-indexing.

Our framework allows to proof the following theorem (see [10]), which is especially useful for reducing the problem of determining functional refinement (and eventually all other semantic analysis notions we discuss in this section) to a well-defined proof obligation in the language $\mathcal{L}$ underlying $\mathcal{F}$.

Theorem 1 (Reduction of Functional Refinement from $\mathcal{F}$ to $\mathcal{L}$). *Let* $\mathcal{D}_1 = (\phi_1^{pre}, \phi_1^{post}, IF_1)$ *and* $\mathcal{D}_2 = (\phi_2^{pre}, \phi_2^{post}, IF_2)$ *be functional descriptions in* $\mathcal{F}$ *with the same interfaces, i.e.* $IF_1 = IF_2$. *Let* $[\phi]_{\Sigma_D^{pre} \to \Sigma_D}$ *denote the formula* ϕ' *which can be derived from* ϕ *by replacing any dynamic symbol* $\alpha \in \Sigma_D$ *by its corresponding pre-variant* $\alpha_{pre} \in \Sigma_D^{pre}$. *Then* $\mathcal{D}_1 \sqsubseteq_{\mathcal{F}} \mathcal{D}_2$ *if* $\Omega \cup [\Omega]_{\Sigma_D^{pre} \to \Sigma_D} \models_{\mathcal{L}} ([\phi_2^{pre}]_{\Sigma_D^{pre} \to \Sigma_D} \land [\phi_1^{pre}]_{\Sigma_D^{pre} \to \Sigma_D} \land \phi_1^{post} \Rightarrow \phi_2^{post})$ $\square$

This gives us the following: If there is an algorithm or an implemented system that allows us to determine logical entailment in $\mathcal{L}$, then we can use the very same system or algorithm to determine functional refinement for descriptions of the capability language $\mathcal{F}$, i.e. in principle no new calculus for dealing with $\mathcal{F}$ is needed (at least for the purpose semantic analysis). However, the algorithm which can be derived from Theorem 1 is no longer a heuristic, but *provably correct*. For further discussion, variants and generailzations of the theorem, we refer to [10].

To be able to formulate the next corollary (which is an immediate consequence of the definition of realizability and functional refinement), we use $\perp^{IF}$ to denote a description $D \in \mathcal{F}$ that is trivially unrealizable, i.e. $D = (true, false, IF)$.

Corollary 1 (Realizability vs. Refinement). *A functional description* $\mathcal{D} = (\phi^{pre}, \phi^{post}, IF)$ *is not realizable iff* $\mathcal{D} \sqsubseteq \perp^{IF}$ ☐

The corollary simply states that any description which is more specific than the trivially unrealizable functional description must be unrealizable as well. In the light of Theorem 1, it shows that we can reduce realizability of $\mathcal{D}$ to a well-defined proof obligation in $\mathcal{L}$ as well. Hence we can deal with realizability algorithmically based on existing tools.

Omnipotence. For any functional description $\mathcal{D}$ we can consider the dual notion of being not realizable at all, i.e. having every Web service W in $\mathcal{A}$ as a model. This notion corresponds to the classical notion of validity and obviously represents another form of ill-defined or unacceptable type of description. It matches all possible Web services, no matter what they actually do. Service providers could use such (non-trivially) omnipotent descriptions to advertise their Web services in some registry to get maximal visibility. A trivially omnipotent functional description in $\mathcal{F}$ is $\top^{IF} = (true, true, IF)$.

As an immediate consequence we can derive the following corollary which shows that we can reduce omnipotence of $\mathcal{D}$ to a well-defined proof obligation in $\mathcal{L}$ as well and thus deal with it algorithmically based on existing tools:

Corollary 2 (Omnipotence vs. Refinement). *A functional description* $\mathcal{D} = (\phi^{pre}, \phi^{post}, IF)$ *is omnipotent iff* $\top^{IF} \sqsubseteq \mathcal{D}$ ☐

The corollary simply states that any description which is more general than the trivially omnipotent functional description must be omnipotent as well.

Summary. Semantic analysis can be seen as both, (i) a concrete example of symbolic computation with functional descriptions that we can formally ground in our formal model, and (ii) as a problem that is interesting in itself. Using our model, we are able to rigorously define various useful notions that enable us to analyze and relate functional descriptions semantically. We have shown that we can reduce the various relevant notions to well-defined proof obligations in the underlying language $\mathcal{L}$ without making severe restrictions or assumptions on that language. Using our framework, we are able to proof the correctness of the reduction. Given the a wealth of different languages that co-exist on the Semantic Web (and the ones that might still be invented), our uniform treatment provides a universal approach to the semantics of functional description independent of the language used.

5   Related Work

By defining the semantics of functional description we provide a basis for applications like semantic Web service repositories and discovery engines (as illustrated in the use case for our formalism and the corresponding examples). Work in this area has previously leveraged a different (less detailed) formal view on the concept of a Web Service:

Web services there have been formally considered as *sets of objects* (input, outputs). On a description (language) these sets allow for a natural representation by means of concepts in Description Logics. Matching then has been reduced to standard reasoning tasks in the language [15, 12], however the dynamics associated with a detailed (state-based) perspective on Web services, can not be represented in such a setting. Until recently, it seemed to be a common practice in the Semantic Web Community when considering semantic descriptions of Web service, to strictly focus on languages (e.g. description logics) rather than an adequate (language-independent) mathematical model of the objects of invest igation that underlies such descriptions. The latter question is conceptually interesting and compatible with various concrete representation languages such as Description Logics, First-order Logics, etc. as we have demonstrated in this paper.

In the area of software specification, functional descriptions of are a well studied phenomena. Hoare [5] introduced the approach describing a component by its pre- and post-conditions. Numerous systems have been developed since then [14, 6, 16] that follow the same line of description. They have significant commonalities with our framework, such as constructs for identifying inputs and outputs as well as means to reference symbols in pre-state formulae from the post-state. However our framework is different in two dimensions: (1) we do not fix the underlying language and therefore address the current situation in the Semantic Web with various different languages used in various formalisms, and (2) we explicitly take the existence of background knowledge (represented by some Ontology Ω) and the notion of side effect in the real world modelled into account. In particular, Theorem 1 in Section 4, represents a generalization of a well-known criterion proposed in the software component community for specification matching [18]. The *Guarded Plugin Match* defined by

$$match_{guarded-pm}(\mathcal{D}_1, \mathcal{D}_2) = (\phi_2^{pre} \Rightarrow \phi_1^{pre}) \wedge (\phi_1^{pre} \wedge \phi_1^{post} \Rightarrow \phi_2^{post})$$

is the equivalent to the necessary condition presented in Theorem 1. However, [18] covers a much simpler scenario, where specifications do not contain *dynamic* functions. Futhermore, our criterion explicitly deals with a background ontology Ω on which the functional descriptions $\mathcal{D}_1, \mathcal{D}_2$ are based. In contrast to our work (i.e. Theorem 1), [18] gives no formal investigation of how the criterion called *Guarded Plugin Match* actually relates to the *semantic notion* of functional refinement, which is to be detected by means of a well-defined proof obligation.

6   Conclusions and Future Work

We have defined Abstract State Spaces as a formal model for appropriately describing how Web services act in the world and change it. The main features of the proposed model are: (i) language independence to a maximum extent, and (ii) modular and flexible definitions that can easily be extended to fit the needs for specific applications.

Language independence, in particular, means that our approach is applicable to a variety of static description language (capturing properties of single states). Thus, it is especially suitable for application in frameworks like OWL-S and WSMO that describe the functionality provided by Web services in a state-based manner. On basis of our model, we have rigorously defined the semantics of functional descriptions. We demonstrated the applicability and benefit of our model in terms of a concrete use case, namely the semantic analysis of functional descriptions. Therein, we have illustrated how to capture several interesting and naturally arising properties of functional descriptions, in particular *functional refinement* and *realizability*. We have given mathematically concise definitions and exemplified how to device a provably correct algorithm for semantic analysis based on existing algorithms and systems. The use case followed throughout the explications supports our thesis: the correctness of any sort of symbolic computation based on functional descriptions of Web services can be analyzed and exposed in our framework.

While this paper presents the basic model, we plan to apply it to frameworks like WSMO and OWL-S that strive for genericity and independence of specific static languages for state descriptions. In particular, we plan to develop a matching mechanism following the defined notion of functional refinement in order to provide a component with clear defined functionality for functional Web service discovery. Furthermore, we consider several extensions of the model, namely integrating *execution invariants* as properties that are guaranteed not to change during execution of a Web service (see [10] for details), the distinction between complete and incomplete functional description (i.e. some sort of closed-world modelling), as well as integrating behavioral descriptions like choreography and orchestration interfaces that are concerned with the intermediate states in order to consume, respectively achieve the functionality of a Web service.

The model presented in this paper can be considered as a first small first step towards an adequate mathematical model for service-oriented architectures. For this, one needs to consider and represent a lot more aspects of the world and its states e.g. multiple agents interacting in a distributed setting and communicating with each other in a concurrent fashion and integrate respective elements in the mathematical model. We expect that the presented model provides a flexible and extensible foundation for such non-standard extensions. Based on a concise and rich model, we will be able to give semantics to formal descriptions of such *architectures* and (similarly to what we discussed for the simple case of capabilities here) to reason about such descriptions in a well-understood and verifiably correct way by extension and refinement of the presented basic model.

Acknowledgements. This material is based upon works supported by the EU within the Knowledge Web Network of Excellence (FP6-507482), the DIP project (FP6-507483), and by the Austrian Federal Ministry for Transport, Innovation, and Technology under the project $\mathbf{RW}^2$ (FFG 809250). The authors would like to thank the members of the WSMO working group (www.wsmo.org) for fruitful input and discussion to the presented work.

References

1. P. Blackburn, M. de Rijke, and Y. Venema. *Modal Logic*. Cambridge University Press, 2001.
2. H. B. Enderton. *A Mathematical Introduction to Logic*. Academic Press, second edition edition, 2000.

3. G. F. and B. P. Introduction to Contextual Reasoning. An Artificial Intelligence Perspective. Technical report, ITC-IRST, Technical Report #9705-19, May 1997.

4. M. Fitting. *First-Order Logic and Automated Theorem Proving.* Springer-Verlag, second edition edition, 1996.

5. C. A. R. Hoare. An axiomatic basis for computer programming. *Commun. ACM*, 12(10):576–580, 1969.

6. C. B. Jones. *Systematic Software Development using VDM.* Prentice-Hall, Upper Saddle River, NJ 07458, USA, 1990.

7. U. Keller, R. Lara, H. Lausen, A. Polleres, and D. Fensel. Automatic Location of Services. In *Proceedings of 2nd European Semantic Web Conference (ESWC)*, pages 1–16, 2005.

8. U. Keller and R. Lara (eds.). WSMO Web Service Discovery. Deliverable D5.1v0.1 Nov 12 2004, WSML Working Group. online: http://www.wsmo.org/TR/.

9. R. Lara, D. Roman, A. Polleres, and D. Fensel. A Conceptual Comparison of WSMO and OWL-S. In *Proc. of the 2nd European Conference on Web Services*, 2004.

10. H. Lausen. Functional Description of Web Services. Deliverable D28.1v0.1 Jan 13 2006, WSML Working Group, 2006. online: http://www.wsmo.org/TR/.

11. H. Lausen, A. Polleres, and D. Roman (eds.). Web Service Modeling Ontology (WSMO). W3C Member Submission 3 June 2005, 2005. online: http://www.w3.org/Submission/WSMO/.

12. L. Li and I. Horrocks. A Software Framework for Matchmaking Based on Semantic Web Technology. In *WWW'03*, Budapest, Hungary, May 2003.

13. D. Martin (ed.). OWL-S: Semantic Markup for Web Services. W3C Member Submission 22 November 2004, 2004. online: http://www.w3.org/Submission/OWL-S.

14. B. Meyer. *Eiffel: the Language.* Prentice Hall PTR, 1992.

15. M. Paolucci, T. Kawamura, T. Payne, and K. Sycara. Semantic Matching of Web Service Capabilities. In *ISWC*, pages 333–347. Springer Verlag, 2002.

16. J. Spivey. *The Z Notation, A Reference Manual.* Prentice-Hall International, second edition edition, 1992.

17. J. van Benthem. *Handbook of logic in artificial intelligence and logic programming: epistemic and temporal reasoning*, volume 4, chapter Temporal logic, pages 241–350. Oxford University Press, Oxford, UK, 1995.

18. A. M. Zaremski and J. M. Wing. Specification matching of software components. *ACM Transactions on Software Engineering and Methodology*, 6(4):333–369, 1997.

A Minimalist Approach to Semantic Annotations for Web Processes Compositions*

Marco Pistore[1], Luca Spalazzi[2], and Paolo Traverso[3]

[1] Università di Trento - Via Sommarive 14 - 38050 Povo - Trento - Italy
pistore@dit.unitn.it
[2] Università Politecnica delle Marche - Via Brecce Bianche - 60131 Ancona - Italy
spalazzi@diiga.univpm.it
[3] ITC-irst - Via Sommarive 18 - 38050 Povo - Trento - Italy
traverso@irst.itc.it

Abstract. In this paper we propose a new approach to the automated composition of distributed processes described as semantic web services. Current approaches, such as those based on OWL-S and WSMO, in spite of their expressive power, are hard to use in practice. Indeed, they require comprehensive and usually large ontological descriptions of the processes, and rather complex (and often inefficient) reasoning mechanisms. In our approach, we reduce to the minimum the usage of ontological descriptions of processes, so that we can perform a limited, but efficient and useful, semantic reasoning for composing web services. The key idea is to keep separate the procedural and the ontological descriptions, and to link them through semantic annotations. We define the formal framework, and propose a technique that can exploit simple reasoning mechanisms at the ontological level, integrated with effective reasoning mechanisms devised for procedural descriptions of web services.

1 Introduction

The importance of describing web services at the *process-level* is widely recognized, a witness being the standard languages for describing business processes, like BPEL [1], and the most popular standards for semantic web services, like OWL-S [4] and WSMO [22]. In a process-level description, a web service is not simply represented as an "atomic" component that can be executed in a single step. Instead, the interface of the service describes its behavior, i.e., a flow of interactions with other services structured according to different control constructs, e.g., sequentially, conditionally, and iteratively. Behavioral descriptions of web services can be published in standard languages, e.g., as *abstract* BPEL *specifications*, OWL-S *process models*, and WSMO *interfaces*. They constitute a key element for several application domains where web services are proposed as the basis for interoperability and integration of (business) processes that are distributed over the network. This is the case, for instance, of several e-Government, e-Banking, and e-Commerce applications.

---

* This work is partially funded by the European project FP6-507482 "Knowledge Web" , by the MIUR-FIRB project RBNE0195K5, "Knowledge Level Automated Software Engineering", and by the MIUR-PRIN 2004 project "Advanced Artificial Intelligence Systems for Web Services".

Y. Sure and J. Domingue (Eds.): ESWC 2006, LNCS 4011, pp. 620–634, 2006.

Recent research is focusing on the key problem of the automated composition of web services described at the process level [10, 7, 3, 20, 15, 13, 14]. However, the research is still at an early stage. From one side, some approaches do not deal with semantic web services, and cannot thus exploit the ability to do reasoning about what services do. This is the case of techniques for composing BPEL processes [15, 13] and of theoretical frameworks for the composition of services represented as finite state automata [7, 3]. From the other side, the approaches that have been proposed so far to exploit semantic descriptions (see, e.g., [10, 20, 14, 22]) are based on the idea that processes should be described by means of comprehensive ontologies. They have the practical disadvantage to require long descriptions that are time- and effort- consuming, and that are very hard to propose in practice for industrial applications. Such semantic descriptions of web services are based on expressive languages such as OWL [9] or WSMO [22], and require complex reasoning mechanisms. Indeed, for instance, the OWL family of languages are based on the description logics $\mathcal{SHIQ}$ and $\mathcal{SHIOQ}$, that have reasoning services that are EXPTime and NEXPTime, respectively [19].

In this paper, we propose a practical approach to the composition of semantic web services. We aim at automated composition techniques that exploit a limited, but still useful, amount of semantic reasoning. The key idea is to keep separate the procedural and the ontological descriptions, and to use semantic annotations to link them. First, the behavior of a web service is defined in languages that have been designed to describe processes. Then, the semantics of data exchanged and of the operations performed by the processes is described in a separate ontological language. Finally, the two descriptions are linked by semantic annotations of the behavioral descriptions that map to the ontological concepts. Annotations are necessary to give semantics to the exchanged data (e.g., which relations exist between the data given in input to the service and the data received as answers from the service), as well as to define the effects and outcomes of the service executions (e.g., to identify the successful executions of the service and distinguish them from the failures, and to describe the effects associated to the successful executions).

We apply this idea to the case of processes described in BPEL. More precisely, we give semantics to abstract BPEL processes in terms of state transition systems, in such a way that variables that are used in messages exchanged among BPEL processes constitute the state variables of the associated state transition systems. The meaning of these variables is defined by an annotation function that maps them to an ontological language, which, in this paper, is based on the $\mathcal{ALN}$ description logic and a generalized acyclic TBox [2]. Given this formal framework, we can express composition requirements as *semantic goals*, i.e., expressions in a language whose terms refer to ontological descriptions. We define formally the automated composition problem with semantic goals and propose an automated composition technique that translates semantic goals into *ground goals*, i.e., goals that refer to the state variables of the process. We can thus exploit efficient automated composition algorithms that have been devised for non-annotated BPEL compositions [15, 13].

The paper is structured as follows. In Section 2, we describe a reference example that is used all along the paper. In Section 3 we formally define semantic annotations for state transition systems that describe BPEL processes, and the language for describing semantic goals. In Section 4, we formally define the composition problem, while in Section 5 we describe the automated composition technique. We conclude with a description of some related work.

2   Overview of the Approach: An Example

We aim at the automated synthesis of a new composite service that interacts with a set of existing component web services in order to satisfy a given composition requirement. More precisely, we assume that we have already identified the services that will be combined into the composite service[1], and that we are now facing the problem of defining the executable process that can interact with these existing services in order to achieve the composition requirement.

Example 1. Our running example consists in the composition of existing transport and accommodation services in order to provide a Virtual Travel Agency (VTA) service. The VTA is responsible for defining a suitable vacation package, according to the requests of the user. The selection of the service providers may depend on the constraints given by the end user and by domain knowledge: for instance, if the destination of the trip is Paris and the duration is one week, we know that the trip can be done by flight or by train (but not, e.g., by ship), and that suitable accommodations are in hotel and in guest houses (but not in apartments). We can hence assume that we have selected four suitable services (FlightReservation, TrainReservation, HotelReservation, Guesthouse-Reservation).

According to our approach each web service exploited in the composition defines:

– an ontology defining the relevant terminology,
– an interface process defining the interactions necessary to execute the service, and
– an annotation of the choreography that defines (partial) correspondences between the ontology and the process.

In the following, we assume that the ontologies provided by the different services have been mapped into a global common ontology that defines all the relevant concepts of the composition scenario. We will also assume that the interface processes are annotated according to this global ontology.

Example 2. The common ontology for the VTA composition scenario discussed in Example 1 is depicted in Figure 1 using the standard description logic notation. This ontology contains a part that is general for the VTA domain (Date, Client, Location, Trip, Accommodation), and that can be seen as part of the domain knowledge. It also contains other concepts that are specific of the actual web services that we are going to exploit in the composition (Flight, Train, Hotel, GuestHouse), and that can be obtained by mapping the local ontology of each web service into the common ontology.

---

[1] This step is of course very complex. We will not further discuss these steps in the paper, since our focus is different. We assume that any of the techniques for service discovery and selection discussed in the literature are applied to these steps.

$$Date \doteq \forall year.Number \sqcap \forall month.Number \sqcap \forall day.Number$$
$$Client \doteq \forall name.String \sqcap \forall gender.Gender$$
$$Gender \sqsubseteq \top$$
$$Status \sqsubseteq \top$$
$$Location \doteq \forall name.String$$
$$Trip \doteq \forall id.String \sqcap (\leq 1id) \sqcap (\geq 1id) \sqcap \forall date.Date \sqcap \forall start.Location \sqcap$$
$$\forall destination.Location \sqcap \forall pax.Client \sqcap \forall status.Status$$
$$Accomodation \doteq \forall id.String \sqcap (\leq 1id) \sqcap (\geq 1id) \sqcap \forall date.Date \sqcap$$
$$\forall location.Location \sqcap \forall pax.Client \sqcap \forall status.Status$$
$$Flight \sqsubseteq Trip \sqcap \forall seatNumber.String$$
$$Train \sqsubseteq Trip \sqcap \forall seatNumber.String$$
$$Hotel \sqsubseteq Accommodation \sqcap \forall roomNumber.String$$
$$GuestHouse \sqsubseteq Accommodation \sqcap \forall roomNumber.String$$

Fig. 1. The terminology of the running example

male : Gender,   female : Gender,
available : Status,   notAvailable : Status,   booked : Status,   cancelled : Status

Fig. 2. The common part of each ABox in the running example

*Notice that, in the definition of Trip and Accommodation, we have the role **status** whose values are restricted to be of the concept Status. This role captures what is the current status of the client request. Indeed, when a trip (accommodation) is available, the status assumes the value **available**; when a trip (accommodation) is not available, the status assumes the value **notAvailable**; and finally, when a trip (accommodation) has been booked (cancelled), the status assumes the value **booked** (**cancelled**). The possible values (instances) for the concept Status are listed in the ABox in Figure 2.*

In our approach, the interface processes defining the interaction behaviors of the component services are defined in abstract BPEL. BPEL [1] provides an operational description of the (stateful) behavior of web services on top of the service interfaces defined in their WSDL specifications. An abstract BPEL description identifies the partners of a service, its internal variables, and the operations that are triggered upon the invocation of the service by some of the partners. Operations include assigning variables, invoking other services and receiving responses, forking parallel threads of execution, and non-deterministically picking one amongst different courses of actions. Standard imperative constructs such as if-then-else, case choices, and loops, are also supported.

Example 3. In Figure 3 we report (the relevant parts of) the abstract BPEL specification of the FlightReservation service in the scenario discussed in Example 1.[2]

---

[2] The specification contains some annotations in boldface: they are not part of the BPEL language, and we will explain their meaning later on in this section.

```
<process name="FlightReservation">
    <variables>
        <variable name="req" messageType="flightRequest"/>
            <!-- "req" contains parts "/req/start", "/req/des", and "/req/date" -->
        <variable name="pax" messageType="paxInformation"/>
            <!-- "pax" contains part "/offer/client" -->
        <variable name="offer" messageType="flightOffer"/>
            <!-- "offer" part "/offer/fl" -->
    </variables>
    <sequence name="main">
        <receive operation="request" variable="req"
            semann="/req/start : Location, /req/dest : Location, /req/date : Date"/>
        <switch name="checkAvailability">
            <case name="isNotAvailable">
                <invoke operation="not_avail" semann="/offer/fl : Flight, /offer/fl.status = notAvailable"/>
            </case>
            <otherwise name="isAvailable">
                <assign name="prepareOffer">
                    <copy><from opaque="yes" semann="/offer/fl : Flight, /offer/fl.start = /req/start,
                        /offer/fl.destination = /req/dest, /offer/fl.date = /req/date"/>
                    <to variable="offer" part="fl"/></copy>
                </assign>
                <invoke operation="offer" inputVariable="offer" />
                <pick name="waitAcknowledge">
                    <onMessage operation="ack" variable="pax"
                        semann="/pax/client : Client, /offer/fl.pax = /client/pax, /offer/fl.status = booked"/>
                    <onMessage operation="nack" semann="/offer/flight.status = cancelled"/>
                </pick>
            </otherwise>
        </switch>
    </sequence>
</process>
```

Fig. 3. The annotated BPEL process of the *FlightReservation* service

The process starts with a declaration of the variables that are used in input/output messages: req *is the input variable that specifies the start and destination locations and the date of the flight;* pax *specifies the details on the client booking the flight;* offer *is the flight offered to the client, including flight identifier and seat number. The* messageType *declaration specifies the structure of a variable used for sending/receiving messages. Such structure is detailed in the* WSDL *specification associated to the* BPEL *code, which we omit for lack of space.*

The rest of the abstract BPEL *specification describes the interaction flow. The FlightReservation service is activated by a request from a client (*receive *instruction corresponding to operation* request*). The information on desired flight submitted by the client is stored in variable* req*. Depending on its internal availability (*switch *instruction named* checkAvailability*), the flight provider can either send an answer refusing the request (*invoke *instruction corresponding to operation* not_avail*), or prepare and send the information regarding a specific flight. In the latter case, the flight and seat number are determined and assigned to variable* offer *within the* assign *statement named* prepareOffer*. The way in which the information is obtained is not disclosed and published by the abstract* BPEL*: the sources of the data, assigned to the variables by the* copy *constructs, are "*opaque*". The opaqueness mechanism allows for presenting the external world with an abstract view of the business logic, which hides the portions that the designer does not intend to disclose, and which is robust to changes with respect to the actual way in which the internal business logic is defined (e.g., calls to* *specific data bases of the flight reservation company). Once the offer has been sent to the client (invoke instruction corresponding to operation offer), the FlightReservation service suspends (instruction pick), waiting for the customer either to acknowledge the acceptance of the flight offer (onMessage specification corresponding to operation ack; we remark that this message carries the information on the client booking the flight), or to refuse the offer (onMessage specification corresponding to operation nack). Only in the former case the interaction with the service is successful, and the flight has been booked.*

Notice that the process described in Figure 3 is only one of the possible interfaces. Different flight providers could adopt different approaches, e.g., requiring that the information on the client is given at the beginning of the process rather than during the acknowledgement, or providing to the user a second choice if the first flight offer is refused.

A BPEL specification provides a very detailed description of the interactions that need to be carried out with a web service in order to exploit it. However, this is still not sufficient to allow for the purpose of automatically composing such web service with other services. Indeed, it is necessary to describe also the "semantic" aspects of such interactions. We do this by extending the BPEL specification with "semantic annotations" (the **semann** attributes in Figure 3).

In our example, it is necessary first of all to associate concepts in the ontology to the (parts of the) input and output messages exchanged by the process. This is the role, for instance of the semantic annotations "/req/start : Location, /req/dest : Location, /req/date : Date" of the receive activity for operation request, at the beginning of the BPEL process. Moreover, it is necessary to express "semantic" relations among the input and output data values exchanged during the interaction with the web service, e.g., between the start and destination locations and dates requested by the client and the flight returned by the reservation service. This is done in annotation "/offer/fl.start = /req/start, /offer/fl.destination = /req/dest, /offer/fl.date = /req/date" of the opaque assignment. A further usage of semantic annotations is to define the outcome of an interaction with a web service. In our example it is clear that a flight has been booked only if a flight is available, the reservation service sends an offer, and the user acknowledges the acceptance of the offer. To express this in the BPEL specification, we add annotation "/offer/status = booked" to the activity corresponding to the reception of the acknowledgement.

The semantic annotations are necessary to compensate the specificities of the interface at hand, and to put it in relation with the common ontology. We remark, however, that the semantic annotations that have to be added to this purpose are very limited if compared to processes defined in languages such as OWL-S or WSMO. As we will see, they are sufficient for the automated composition task we are interested in.

3   BPEL Processes as Annotated STSs

We encode BPEL processes (extended with semantic annotations) as *annotated state transition systems* which describe dynamic systems that can be in one of their possible states (some of which are marked as *initial states*) and can evolve to new states as a result of performing some *actions*. We distinguish actions in *input actions, output actions*, and τ. *Input actions* represent the reception of messages, *output actions* represent messages sent to external services, and τ is a special action, called *internal action*, that represents internal evolutions that are not visible to external services. In other words, τ represents the fact that the state of the system can evolve without producing any output, and without consuming any inputs. A *transition relation* describes how the state can evolve on the basis of inputs, outputs, or of the internal action τ. Concerning the *states*, we associate to each state a set of *concept assertions* and *role assertions*. This configures a state as the assertional component (or ABox) of a knowledge representation system based on a given description logic where the ontology plays the role of the terminological component (or TBox). Therefore, *concept assertions* are formulas of the form $a : C$ (or $C(a)$) and state that a given individual a belongs to (the interpretation) of the concept C. *Role assertions* are formulas of the form $a.R = b$ (or $R(a, b)$) and state that a given individual b is a value of the role R for a. As a consequence, each action can be viewed as a transition from a state consisting in an ABox to a different state consisting in a different ABox.

Definition 1 (State transition system [16]). *A state transition system Σ is a tuple $\langle S, S^0, \mathcal{I}, \mathcal{O}, \mathcal{R} \rangle$ where:*

- *S is the finite set of states;*
- *$S^0 \subseteq S$ is the set of initial states;*
- *$\mathcal{I}$ is the finite set of input actions;*
- *$\mathcal{O}$ is the finite set of output actions;*
- *$\mathcal{R} \subseteq S \times (\mathcal{I} \cup \mathcal{O} \cup \{\tau\}) \times S$ is the transition relation.*

Definition 2 (Annotated state transition system). *An annotated state transition system is a tuple $\langle \Sigma, \mathcal{T}, \Lambda \rangle$ where:*

- *Σ is the state transition system,*
- *$\langle \mathcal{T}, \Lambda \rangle$ is the annotation,*
- *$\mathcal{T}$ is the terminology (TBox) of the annotation,*
- *$\Lambda : S \rightarrow 2^{\mathcal{A}_{\mathcal{T}}}$ is the annotation function, where $\mathcal{A}_{\mathcal{T}}$ is the set of all the concept assertions and role assertions defined over $\mathcal{T}$.*

Example 4. Figure 4 shows a textual description of the annotated STS corresponding to the annotated BPEL code of Figure 3. The set of states S (the section STATE in Figure 4) models the steps of the process and the evolution of the concept and the role assertions. pc is a variable that ranges over the set of states S and thus holds the current execution step of the service (e.g., pc = checkAvailability when it is ready to check whether the flight is available). The set of initial states S^0 is represented by the section INIT in Figure 4.

The concepts used in the annotated STS are listed in the section CONCEPT of Figure 4. They must be defined in the terminology $\mathcal{T}$.

According to the formal model, we distinguish among three different kinds of actions (see the sections INPUT and OUTPUT of Figure 4). The input actions $\mathcal{I}$ model all the incoming requests to the process and the information they bring (e.g., request is used for the receiving of the flight reservation request). The output actions $\mathcal{O}$ represent outgoing

```
PROCESS FlightReservation;
STATE  pc : { START, receive_request, checkAvailability, isNotAvailable, isAvailable, invoke_not_available,
            prepareOffer, invoke_offer, waitAcknowledge, END_NA, END_ACK, END_NACK };
INIT  pc = {START};
CONCEPT Flight; Location; Date; Client; Status;
INPUT request(Location, Location, Date); ack(Client); nack();
OUTPUT flightOffer(Flight); not_avail();
TRANS
    pc = START  -[TAU]->  pc = receive_request;
    pc = receive_request  -[INPUT request(req_start,req_dest,req_dat)]->  pc = checkAvailability
    pc = checkAvailability  -[TAU]->  pc = isNotAvailable;
    pc = checkAvailability  -[TAU]->  pc = isAvailable;
    pc = isNotAvailable  -[TAU]->  pc = invoke_not_available;
    pc = invoke_not_available  -[OUTPUT not_avail()]->  pc = END_NA;
    pc = isAvailable  -[TAU]->  pc = prepareOffer;
    pc = prepareOffer  -[TAU]->  pc = invoke_offer,
    pc = invoke_offer  -[OUTPUT offer(offer_fl)]->  pc = waitAcknowledge;
    pc = waitAcknowledge  -[INPUT ack(pax_client)]->  pc = END_ACK;
    pc = waitAcknowledge  -[INPUT nack()]->  pc = END_NACK;
ANNOTATION FUNCTION
    LAMBDA( checkAvailability) = { req_start : Location, req_dest : Location, req_date : Date };
    LAMBDA( END_NA) = { offer_fl : Flight, offer_fl.status = notAvailable } ∪ LAMBDA( checkAvailability);
    LAMBDA( invoke_offer) = { offer_fl : Flight, offer_fl.date = req_date, offer_fl.start = req_start,
            offer_fl.destination = req_dest } ∪ LAMBDA( checkAvailability);
    LAMBDA( END_ACK) = { pax_client : Client, offer_fl.pax = pax_client, offer_fl.status = booked}
            ∪ LAMBDA( invoke_offer);
    LAMBDA( END_NACK) = {offer_fl.status = cancelled} ∪ LAMBDA( invoke_offer);
```

Fig. 4. The annotated STS corresponding to the **FlightReservation** process

messages (e.g., flightOffer is used to bid a flight). The action τ is used to model internal evolutions of the process, such as assignments and decision making.

The evolution of the process is modelled through a set of possible transitions (the section TRANS in Figure 4). Each transition defines its applicability conditions on the source state, its firing action, and the destination state. For instance, pc = checkAvailability -[TAU]-> pc = isNotAvailable states that an action τ can be executed in state checkAvailability and leads to the state isNotAvailable; this transition models the decision of the reservation service that no flight is available.

The annotation function Λ (see the section ANNOTATION FUNCTION in Figure 4) models how the assertions vary depending on the states. For instance, LAMBDA(END_NACK) = {req_start : Location, req_dest : Location, req_date : Date, offer_fl : Flight, offer_fl.start = req_start, offer_fl.destination = req_dest, offer_fl.date = req_date, offer_fl.status = cancelled} represents the fact that state END_NACK contains, among others, the concept assertions fl : Flight (i.e., fl is an individual that belongs to the concept Flight) and the role assertions offer_fl.start = req_start and offer_fl.status = cancelled (the roles start and destination of the individual fl are filled with the individuals req_start and cancelled).

We remark that each TRANS clause and each LAMBDA clause of Figure 4 corresponds to different elements in the transition relation $\mathcal{R}$ and in the annotation function Λ, respectively. For example, the transition and the LAMBDA clause described above generate different elements of $\mathcal{R}$ and Λ depending on which individuals req_date, req_start, req_dest we have in the destination state. Concerning cancel, it has been defined in Figure 2 and, thus, it denotes the same individual in all the states (i.e., all the ABoxes).

The definition of the state transition system provided in Figure 4 is parametric w.r.t. the individuals that can be associated to concepts Flight, Location, Date, Client. In order to obtain a concrete state transition system (a set of concrete ABoxes) and to apply the automated synthesis techniques described in this paper, finite set of individuals have to be assigned concepts Flight, Location, Date, Client. A possible approach to assign these individuals consists in defining appropriate concept assertions in the common part of the ABoxes (e.g., the part of ABoxes depicted in Figure 2). Another, better technique is to use knowledge level techniques such as the ones in [13] to avoid an explicit enumeration of the individuals of Flight, Location, Date, Client.

We have formally defined a translation that associates an annotated state transition system to each component service, starting from its annotated BPEL specification. In Figure 4 we have reported the translation for the specific case of the flight booking service, with minor changes (e.g., in the order of the clauses and in some automatically generated names) to improve the readability. We omit the formal definition of the translation, which can be found at http://www.astroproject.org/.

According to the above definitions, when we have to check if a given assertion p is true in a given state $s \in S$ we have to apply instance checking denoted as $\langle T, \Lambda(s) \rangle \models p$. On the other hand, ABoxes play no active role when checking subsumption [17], therefore subsumption can be checked without considering what is the current state (i.e., the current ABox). For example, when we have to check $\langle T, \Lambda(s) \rangle \models C \sqsubseteq D$, we only need to check $\langle T, \emptyset \rangle \models C \sqsubseteq D$. Furthermore, let us assume to use $\mathcal{ALN}$ as description logic and a generalized acyclic TBox as T [2]. This language is expressive enough to describe non-trivial examples as the VTA domain. The computational complexity of subsumption w.r.t. an acyclic terminology is NP-complete, while the computational complexity of instance checking is P [6], which makes the reasoning problems tractable, and, e.g., less complex than those of OWL-S.

4   Web Process Composition Problem

According to our approach, the inputs of the composition problem are (1) a global ontology $\langle T, \mathcal{A} \rangle$, (2) a set of annotated BPEL processes, or, equivalently, of annotated STSs $\langle \Sigma_i, T, \Lambda_i \rangle$, defining the component services, and (3) a composition requirement ρ, that formalizes these desired properties of the composite service to be synthesized. Inputs (1) and (2) have been already described. We now focus on the definition of the composition requirement.

*Example 5. We want the VTA to **define and book a vacation package** according to the request of a client. This means we want the VTA to reach the situation where a trip has been booked from the start location to the destination specified by the user, and for the dates specified by the user; moreover, an accommodation has been booked for the same destination and dates. However, this goal of the VTA may be impossible to achieve. It might be impossible to book the trip or the accommodation for the given destination or, in more realistic descriptions of the VTA, the package defined by the VTA may be too expensive. We cannot avoid these situations, and we therefore cannot ask the composite service to guarantee that a vacation package is always defined and* *booked. Nevertheless, we would like the VTA to* **try** *(do whatever is possible) to satisfy it. Moreover, in the case the "**define and book a vacation package**" requirement is not satisfied, we do not want to book the trip only or the accommodation only. That is, either trip and accommodation are both booked, or none of them has to be booked. Let us call this requirement "**no booking is pending**". Our global composition requirement would therefore be something like:*

> **try to define and book a vacation package;**
> **upon failure, guarantee that no booking is pending.**

We remark that, when composing web services, it is often the case that composition requirements have the structure described in the previous example, i.e., they define a "primary condition" to be achieved whenever possible, and a "recovery condition" that has to be achieved in all the cases the main condition fails.[3]

Besides the principal and the recovery conditions, a composition requirement also defines two sets of concept assertions. The first one, that we call *input concept assertions*, can be seen as input parameters for the composition requirements, such as desired trip destination and dates, which can be assumed to exist in the ABox of the global ontology. The second set, called *output concept assertions*, describes the elements that have to be defined by the web service composition, in our case the trip and the accommodation.

We now give the formal definition of composition requirement.

Definition 3 (Composition requirement). *Let $\mathcal{T}$ be the terminology for the composition problem. A composition requirement is a tuple $\rho = \langle i, o, p, r \rangle$, where:*

- *i is a set of input concept assertions for $\mathcal{T}$;*
- *o is a set of output concept assertions for $\mathcal{T}$;*
- *p is a goal condition on $\langle \mathcal{T}, i \cup o \rangle$ specifying the primary condition;*
- *r is a goal condition on $\langle \mathcal{T}, i \cup o \rangle$ specifying the recovery condition.*

Goal conditions p and r are expressions in the following grammar:

$$p ::= a : C \mid a.R = b \mid p \ OR \ p \mid p \ \& \ p \mid NOT \ p$$

where $a : C$ is a concept assertion and $a.R = b$ is a role assertion defined w.r.t. $\mathcal{T}$.

Example 6. The composition requirement of the VTA scenario is based on the following input concept assertions: **start : Location** *(the starting location for the travel),* **dest : Location** *(the destination of the travel),* **date : Date** *(the dates of the travel), and* **client : Client** *(the client who is booking the travel). The output concept assertions are:* **tr : Trip** *(the trip returned by the VTA) and* **ac : Accommodation** *(the accommodation returned by the VTA).*

As discussed in Example 5, the principal goal requires to book a suitable trip and a suitable accommodation:

---

[3] In [15, 16] we consider a more general language for specifying composition requirements. Composition requirements consisting of a main and of a recovery condition are enough for the purposes of the paper.

tr.date = date & tr.start = start & tr.destination = dest & tr.pax = client
& ac.date = date & ac.location = dest & ac.pax = client &
& tr.status = booked & ac.status = booked

The recovery condition of the composition requirement specifies that neither the trip not the accommodation has to be booked, and can be represented as follows:

tr.status $\neq$ booked & ac.status $\neq$ booked

In the composition requirements, the semantic annotations introduced in the BPEL processes play a fundamental role for defining conditions on the outcomes of web service executions. For instance, the semantic annotations defining correspondences between the input and output messages of the flight reservation service make it clear which values have to be passed to that service in order to book the flight. Moreover, the value assigned to offer_fl.status in the final activities of the different branches of the process make it possible to distinguish successful executions (with the flight booked) from failures (due to non-available flights or to a reservation cancellation).

Now that we have defined all the inputs of the composition, we are ready to provide a formal definition of composition problem. In the following, we re-use the definitions already proposed in [15, 16], adapted to the case of annotated STSs.

The first step in the definition of composition problem consists in merging the annotated STSs $\Gamma_i = \langle \Sigma_i, \mathcal{T}, \Lambda_i \rangle$ corresponding to the different component services into a single STS $\Gamma_{\parallel} = \langle \Sigma_{\parallel}, \mathcal{T}, \Lambda_{\parallel} \rangle$ defining the combined behavior of the component services. More precisely, $\Sigma_{\parallel} = \Sigma_1 \parallel \Sigma_2 \parallel \cdots \parallel \Sigma_n$ is the STS defining the *parallel product* of the Σ_i, where each component evolves independently from the others, that is, each transition of $\Sigma_{\parallel}$ corresponds to a transition of one of the components (see [15, 16] for a formal definition). Moreover, $\Lambda_{\parallel}$ associates to each state of $\Sigma_{\parallel}$ all the annotations of the corresponding states of $\Sigma_1, \Sigma_2, \ldots, \Sigma_n$.

The automated synthesis of the composite service consists in generating a new state transition system Σ_c that, once connected to $\Sigma_{\parallel}$, satisfies the composition requirement. We now define formally the state transition system describing the behaviors of Σ when connected to Σ_c.

Definition 4 (Controlled system [16]). *Let* $\Sigma = \langle \mathcal{S}, \mathcal{S}^0, \mathcal{I}, \mathcal{O}, \mathcal{R} \rangle$ *and* $\Sigma_c = \langle \mathcal{S}_c, \mathcal{S}_c^0, \mathcal{I}_c, \mathcal{O}_c, \mathcal{R}_c \rangle$ *be two state transition systems such that* $\mathcal{I} = \mathcal{O}_c$ *and* $\mathcal{O} = \mathcal{I}_c$. *The state transition system* $\Sigma_c \triangleright \Sigma$, *describing the behaviors of system* Σ *when controlled by* Σ_c, *is defined as follows:*

$$\Sigma_c \triangleright \Sigma = \langle \mathcal{S}_c \times \mathcal{S}, \mathcal{S}_c^0 \times \mathcal{S}^0, \mathcal{I}, \mathcal{O}, \mathcal{R}_c \triangleright \mathcal{R} \rangle$$

where:

- $\langle (s_c, s), \tau, (s_c', s) \rangle \in (\mathcal{R}_c \triangleright \mathcal{R})$ *if* $\langle s_c, \tau, s_c' \rangle \in \mathcal{R}_c$;
- $\langle (s_c, s), \tau, (s_c, s') \rangle \in (\mathcal{R}_c \triangleright \mathcal{R})$ *if* $\langle s, \tau, s' \rangle \in \mathcal{R}$;
- $\langle (s_c, s), a, (s_c', s') \rangle \in (\mathcal{R}_c \triangleright \mathcal{R})$, *with* $a \neq \tau$, *if* $\langle s_c, a, s_c' \rangle \in \mathcal{R}_c$ *and* $\langle s, a, s' \rangle \in \mathcal{R}$.

This definition can be easily extended to the case of an annotated STS. Indeed, the composite service Σ_c has no annotations, and hence the annotations of a state of $\Sigma_c \triangleright \Gamma$ are those of the corresponding state in Γ.

In a web service composition problem, we need to generate a Σ_c that guarantees the satisfaction of a composition requirement ρ. This is formalized by requiring that the controlled system $\Sigma_c \triangleright \Gamma_{\|}$ must satisfy ρ, written $\Sigma_c \triangleright \Gamma_{\|} \models \rho$.

Definition 5 (goal satisfaction). *Let* $\Gamma = \Sigma_c \triangleright \Gamma_{\|}$, *and let* $\rho = \langle i, o, p, r \rangle$ *be a composition requirement.*

- *We say that* Γ *strongly satisfies* ρ, *written* $\Gamma \models_s \rho$ *if all final states* s *of* Γ *are such that* $\langle \mathcal{T}, \Lambda(s) \cup i \cup o \rangle \models p$.
- *We say that* Γ *weakly satisfies* ρ, *written* $\Gamma \models_w \rho$ *if all final states* s *of* Γ *are such that* $\langle \mathcal{T}, \Lambda(s) \cup i \cup o \rangle \models p$ *or* $\langle \mathcal{T}, \Lambda(s) \cup i \cup o \rangle \models r$.
- *We say that* Γ *satisfies* ρ, *written* $\Gamma \models \rho$ *if:*
  - $\Gamma \models_s \rho$, *or*
  - $\Gamma \models_w \rho$, *and there is no* $\Gamma' = \Sigma_c' \triangleright \Gamma$ *such that* $\Gamma' \models_s \rho$.

According to this definition, a controlled system satisfies a composition goal if: either (1) all the states reached at the end of the computation satisfy the principal condition (in this case we say that the goal is satisfied in a strong way), or (2) all the states reached at the end of the computation satisfy either the principal or the recovery condition (in this case we say that the goal is satisfied in a weak way) and no strong satisfying controller can be defined (i.e., a weak satisfaction is the best we can achieve).

Definition 6 (Composition problem [16]). *Let* $\Gamma_1, \ldots, \Gamma_n$ *be a set of annotated state transition systems on the same terminology* $\mathcal{T}$, *and let* ρ *be a composition requirement. The composition problem for* $\Gamma_1, \ldots, \Gamma_n$ *and* ρ *is the problem of finding a state transition system* Σ_c *such that*[4]

$$\Sigma_c \triangleright (\Gamma_1 \| \ldots \| \Gamma_n) \models \rho.$$

5 Automated Synthesis of the Process Composition

In [15, 16], an algorithm is described that automatically generates the composite service Σ_c starting from the component services $\Sigma_1, \ldots, \Sigma_n$ and the composition requirement ρ. Moreover, the algorithm has been implemented within the ASTRO toolset (see http://www.astroproject.org/) and applied to different domains, showing that it is able to compose complex services in a very small amount of time, much smaller than the time required for a manual implementation of the composite process.

However, in [15, 16] the component STSs did not exploit semantic annotations, and the composition requirement was based on propositional logic instead of description logic and ontologies. Our goal is to extend the approach of [15, 16] to the case of process composition with semantic annotations. There are different ways to achieve this.

---

[4] The definition of composition problem in [15, 16] takes into account a further requirement for the composite process, that is, it should be deadlock free. Intuitively, this means that the system should never reach a state where both the component services and the composite services are blocked waiting for inputs. For simplicity, we omitted this property from the definition reported in this paper.

Here, we adopt a very simple approach, consisting in transforming the constraints in the composition requirement into propositional formulas through a *grounding* process. Once this has been done, the semantic annotations of the component STSs can be interpreted as "syntactic" annotations, that are not subject to subsumption, and the algorithm of [15, 16] can be reused. We now describe in detail the grounding process.

The aim of the composition process is to define in a suitable way the output individuals of the composition goal, so that the principal or recovery conditions are satisfied. The grounding process consists in looking in the ontology for all the concepts that are subsumed by the concepts of the output concept assertions in the goal, and to reformulate the conditions in the goal using the union of all these concepts for the output individuals, as shown in the following example.

Example 7. The goal in Example 6 defines two output concept assertions, tr: Trip and ac: Accommodation. In the terminology of Figure 1, there are two concepts subsumed by Trip, namely Flight and Train, and two concepts subsumed by Accommodation, namely Hotel and GuestHouse. Taking this into account, the principal goal can be grounded as follows:

> tr: (Trip ⊔ Flight ⊔ Train) & tr.status = booked
> & tr.date = date & tr.start = start & tr.destination = dest & tr.pax = client
> & ac: (Accommodation ⊔ Hotel ⊔ GuestHouse) & ac.status = booked
> & ac.date = date & ac.location = dest & ac.pax = client

Similarly, the recovery condition can be grounded as:

> tr: (Trip ⊔ Flight ⊔ Train) & tr.status ≠ booked
> & ac: (Accommodation ⊔ Hotel ⊔ GuestHouse) & ac.status ≠ booked

The following result shows the correctness of re-using the existing algorithms of [15, 16] on the ground requirement.

Theorem 1 (Soundness and completeness w.r.t. composition). *Let ρ be a composition requirement and ρ_g be the corresponding grounded requirement w.r.t. terminology $\mathcal{T}$. Then*

$$\Sigma_c \vartriangleright (\Gamma_1 \parallel \ldots \parallel \Gamma_n) \models \rho \qquad \text{iff} \qquad \Sigma_c \vartriangleright (\Sigma_1 \parallel \ldots \parallel \Sigma_n) \models_g \rho_g$$

where $\models_g$ is satisfiability with goal conditions interpreted as propositional formulas.

6 Related Work and Conclusions

In this paper we propose a practical approach to the composition of semantic web services. We keep separated the procedural and the ontological description of services, and link them through semantic annotations. We then integrate reasoning mechanisms at the ontological and at the process level.

This approach is novel with respect to existing literature. Form the one side, several works propose approaches to process-level composition that do not address explicitly the need for (reasoning about) semantic descriptions of web services [7, 3, 15, 13]. From the other side, most of the work on automated composition of semantic web services has focused so far on the problem of composition at the functional level, i.e., composition of atomic services that can be executed in a single request-response step (see, e.g. [11, 5]).

The work on WSDL-S and METEOR-S [18, 12, 21] provides semantic annotations for WSDL. It is close in spirit to ours, but does not deal with semantically annotated (BPEL) process-level descriptions of web services. The work in [8] is also close in spirit to our general objective to bridge the gap between the semantic web framework and languages proposed by industrial coalitions. However, [8] focuses on a different problem, i.e., that of extending BPEL with semantic web technology to facilitate web service interoperation, while the problem of automated composition is not addressed.

Recently, an increasing amount of work is dealing with the problem of composing semantic web services taking into account their behavioral descriptions [10, 23, 20, 14, 22]. In this context, the research community is following two related but different main approaches: OWL-S [4] and WSMO [22]. Approaches based on OWL-S [10, 23, 20, 14] are different from the one proposed in this paper, since, in OWL-S, even processes are described as ontologies, and therefore there is no way to separate reasoning about processes and reasoning about ontologies. The approach undertaken in WSMO is closer in spirit to ours: processes are represented as Abstract State Machines, a well known and general formalism to represent dynamic behaviors. The idea underlying WSMO is that the variables of Abstract State Machines are all defined with terms of the WSMO ontological language. Our processes work instead on their own state variables, some of which can be mapped to a separated ontological language, allowing for a minimalist and practical approach to semantic annotations and for effective reasoning to compose services automatically. Indeed, the aim of the work on WSMO is to propose a general language and representation mechanism for semantic web services, while we focus on the problem of providing effective techniques for composing automatically semantic web services.

It would be interesting to investigate how our approach can be applied to WSMO Abstract State Machines rather than BPEL processes, and how the idea of minimalist semantic annotations can be extended to work with WSMO orchestration languages and mechanisms, such that we could exploit our automated composition techniques effectively in this framework. In this context, we plan also to integrate our proposal for automated composition with techniques for web service discovery, a problem that we do not address in this paper.

References

1. T. Andrews, F. Curbera, H. Dolakia, J. Goland, J. Klein, F. Leymann, K. Liu, D. Roller, D. Smith, S. Thatte, I. Trickovic, and S. Weeravarana. Business Process Execution Language for Web Services (version 1.1), 2003.
2. F. Baader and W. Nutt. Basic Description Logics. In F. Baader, D. Calvanese, D. McGuinness, D. Nardi, and P. Patel-Schneider, editors, *The Description Logic Handbook*, pages 43–95. Cambridge University Press, 2003.
3. D. Berardi, D. Calvanese, G. De Giacomo, M. Lenzerini, and M. Mecella. Automatic composition of E-Services that export their behaviour. In *Proc. ICSOC'03*, 2003.
4. The OWL Services Coalition. OWL-S: Semantic Markup for Web Services, 2003.

5. I. Constantinescu, B. Faltings, and W. Binder. Typed Based Service Composition. In *Proc. WWW'04*, 2004.

6. F. M. Donini. Complexity of Reasoning. In F. Baader, D. Calvanese, D. McGuinness, D. Nardi, and P. Patel-Schneider, editors, *The Description Logic Handbook*, pages 96–136. Cambridge University Press, 2003.

7. R. Hull, M. Benedikt, V. Christophides, and J. Su. E-Services: A Look Behind the Curtain. In *Proc. PODS'03*, 2003.

8. D. Mandell and S. McIlraith. Adapting BPEL4WS for the Semantic Web: The Bottom-Up Approach to Web Service Interoperation. In *Proc. of ISWC'03*, 2003.

9. D. L. McGuinness and F. van Harmelen. OWL Web Ontology Language Overview. W3C Recommendation, 2004.

10. S. Narayanan and S. McIlraith. Simulation, Verification and Automated Composition of Web Services. In *Proc. WWW'02*, 2002.

11. M. Paolucci, K. Sycara, and T. Kawamura. Delivering Semantic Web Services. In *Proc. WWW'03*, 2002.

12. A. Patil, S. Oundhakar, A. Sheth, and K. Verma. METEOR-S Web Service Annotation Framework. In *Proc. WWW'04*, 2004.

13. M. Pistore, A. Marconi, P. Bertoli, and P. Traverso. Automated Composition of Web Services by Planning at the Knowledge Level. In *Proc. IJCAI'05*, 2005.

14. M. Pistore, P. Roberti, and P. Traverso. Process-level compositions of executable web services: on-the-fly versus once-for-all compositions. In *Proc. ESWC'05*, 2005.

15. M. Pistore, P. Traverso, and P. Bertoli. Automated Composition of Web Services by Planning in Asynchronous Domains. In *Proc. ICAPS'05*, 2005.

16. M. Pistore, P. Traverso, P. Bertoli, and A. Marconi. Automated Synthesis of Composite BPEL4WS Web Services. In *Proc. ICWS'05*, 2005.

17. A. Schaerf. *Query Answering in Concept-Based Knowledge Representation Systems: Algorithms, Complexity, and Semantic Issues*. Dottorato di Ricerca in Informatica, Università degli Studi di Roma "La Sapienza", Italia, 1994.

18. A. Sheth, K. Verna, J. Miller, and P. Rajasekaran. Enhacing Web Service Descriptions using WSDL-S. In *EclipseCon*, 2005.

19. S. Tobies. *Complexity Results and Practical Algorithms for Logics in Knowledge Representation*. PhD thesis, RWTH Aachen, 2001.

20. P. Traverso and M. Pistore. Automated Composition of Semantic Web Services into Executable Processes. In *Proc. ISWC'04*, 2004.

21. K. Verma, A. Mocan, M. Zarembra, A. Sheth, and J. A. Miller. Linking Semantic Web Service Efforts: Integrationg WSMX and METEOR-S. In *Proc. SDWP'05*, 2005.

22. SDK WSMO working group. The Web Service Modeling Framework - http://www.wsmo.org/.

23. D. Wu, B. Parsia, E. Sirin, J. Hendler, and D. Nau. Automating DAML-S Web Services Composition using SHOP2. In *Proc. ISWC'03*, 2003.

Protocol Mediation for Adaptation in Semantic Web Services

Stuart K.Williams[1], Steven A. Battle[1], and Javier Esplugas Cuadrado[2]

[1] Hewlett-Packard Laboratories, Filton Road,
Stoke Gifford, Bristol, BS34 8QZ, UK
{skw, steve.battle}@hp.com
[2] Hewlett-Packard Espanola SL, Jose Echegaray n°8,
La Rozas, Spain. 28230
javier.esplugas.cuadrado@hp.com

Abstract. Protocol mediation enables interaction between communicating parties where there is a shared conceptual model of the intent and purpose of the communication, and where the mechanics of communication interaction vary. The communicating partners are using different protocols to achieve the same or similar ends. We present a description driven approach to protocol mediation which provides a more malleable approach to the integration of web services than the current rigid 'plug-and-socket' approach offered by description technologies such as WSDL. It enables the substitution of one service provider with another even though they use different interaction protocols. Our approach is centred on the identification of common domain specific protocol independent communicative acts; the description of abstract protocols which constrain the sequencing of communicative acts; and the description of concrete protocols that describe the mechanisms by which the client of a web service interface can utter and perceive communicative acts.[1]

1 Introduction

Web service technology places powerful tools in the hands of developers enabling independent invention and re-invention of web service interfaces. Businesses will develop and deploy web service interfaces to visible aspects of their business process. Many of these interfaces encapsulate similar if not identical concepts. However the factoring of otherwise similar interfaces will vary. The mechanics of interaction protocols will differ. Yet conceptually they encapsulate similar if not identical interaction metaphors. Consider the familiar catalogue, cart, checkout metaphor of a typical eCommerce web site. The human user is guided through the process by their recognition of the metaphor, their intuition about the process they are engaged in and the continuous guidance provided by the user interface decoration (labels on buttons, explanatory text etc.). The human user is unconstrained about which of many available on-line stores they trade with. Our aim is to provide a similar level of flexibility for automated web service clients in the selection and use of service providers.

---

[1] This work was conducted as part of the EU funded Semantic Web enable Web Services project (SWWS EU IST-2002-37134).

Y. Sure and J. Domingue (Eds.): ESWC 2006, LNCS 4011, pp. 635–649, 2006.

By analogy, WSDL [1] supports description of the syntactic operation of individual user interface controls; BPEL [2] describes the service provider processes which respond to control invocations; WS-CHOR [3] describes a global view of the sequencing constraints on externally visible messages exchanged between multiple parties in web service interactions. However, in the current web service stack there is no machine readable account of what a particular web service interaction or sequence of web service interactions actually accomplish.

In this paper we describe a framework for providing rich service descriptions that enable web service clients to adapt their interaction behaviour to the constraints of a particular provider's web service interface. This removes cost and time from the process of integrating new service providers and enables consumers of web services greater freedom and flexibility to dynamically choose service providers. For service providers it also means access to a broader customer base and results in a service oriented economy where service consumer/provider relationships are formed on the basis of business fundamentals without requiring an exact fit between the client and provider sides of a particular web service interface.

In section 2 we introduce the topic of protocol mediation more fully. In section 3 we introduce a case study scenario drawn from the IST EU Semantic Web enabled Web Services project (SWWS EU IST-2002-37134) which we use as a running example through the remainder of the paper. Section 4 gives a detailed presentation of the protocol mediation framework developed in the SWWS project. Section 5 describes our interface description language. Section 6 discusses related work. Finally section 7 presents our conclusions and ideas for further work.

2 Protocol Mediation

Bridging or gatewaying between compatible protocols has been studied since the 1980's [11, 13, 14] continuing through a period of considerable work in the field of Open Systems Interconnection (OSI) [8, 12] and the Internet. Our work on protocol mediation draws inspiration from that work. We make particular use of the concepts of abstract service definition [8, 12] and gateways/half-gateways. Much of the previous work was focussed on mediating between protocols established by standard-isation processes. In contrast, our work on protocol mediation is focussed on the dynamic instantiation of description driven mediation behaviour. Our work is moti-vated by the existence of similarly intentioned, independently created, and evolving protocols which are an inevitable consequence with the successful adoption of Web Service technologies.

Figure 1 illustrates protocol mediation the form of a protocol gateway made up of two half gateways and a relaying function. Two processes, X and Y, wish to communicate with one another at a business level. Each process adopts some role with respect to the interaction. For example, process Y may act on behalf of the provider of some (business) service, while process X may act on behalf of a consumer of that service. Unfortunately, process X and process Y communicate using two different protocols, P1 and P2, each of which has capabilities C1 and C2 respectively, expressed in the abstract as the protocol layer services of P1 and P2.

Clearly if effective communication is to occur between processes X and Y, some mediation must occur.

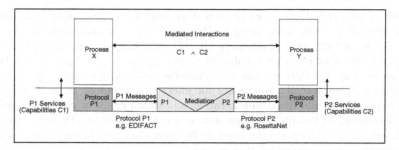

Fig. 1. Protocol Mediation – A conceptual model

It should be equally clear that it is only possible to mediate in the intersection of the capabilities of the two protocols. If the mediated channel becomes too impoverished to support the required interaction, some other approach becomes necessary and either process X or Y or both needs to have their behaviour changed to address the missing capability in some other way. This is known as "process mediation" and is not the subject of this paper.

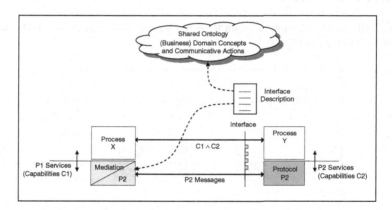

Fig. 2. Description Driven Adaptation

It is possible to associate the mediation element more strongly with one party or the other. One can slide the mediation element toward, say, process X. At some point, the presence of P1 in the system becomes somewhat vestigial and the mediation component becomes logically absorbed within the infrastructure supporting process X. Figure 2 illustrates this diagrammatic manipulation. Process X continues to make use of P1's protocol layer services and capabilities (restricted to those that lie at the intersection with protocol P2's capabilities). However, only protocol P2 messages are exchanged externally. The P2 protocol provider and process Y are unchanged. Figure 2 also introduces the notion of there being an exposed interface at process Y which is described with a rich behavioural description which is consumed by a mediation component.

Our behavioural descriptions rely on abstracting the communicative actions [5, 6] of a protocol from the underlying mechanisms of that communication. This echoes the practice of the OSI community [8, 12] of specifying the service abstraction separately from its message vocabulary, encoding and rules of procedure. However we make our descriptions machine readable and interpretable by a mediation component. Conceptually we regard an interaction protocol as animating domain concept instances and the communicative acts which result in changes in their state are themselves part of the ontological structure of the domain. Thus, the ontology of the interface description is what needs to be shared between partners rather than prior agreement on a specific interaction protocol.

The description driven adapter of Figure 2 may be thought of as a 'half-gateway' and it should be possible to use two such structures and descriptions of the interfaces that they each face to create a description driven 'full-gateway' or mediator structure as shown in Figure 1. It should be apparent that rather than relaying protocol messages between protocol P1 and protocol P2, such a mediator relays the common communicative actions of protocols P1 and P2.

3   Logistics Scenario

Figure 3 illustrates the supply chain logistics scenario used as a case study in SWWS to motivate our work [9, 10].

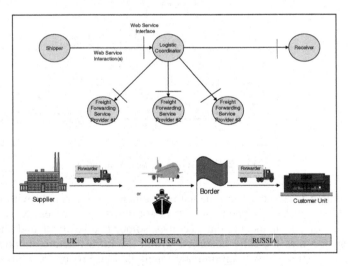

Fig. 3. Multi-leg Shipment Logistics Scenario

The diagram illustrates four different logical roles: Shipper, Logistic Coordinator, Freight Forwarding Services Provider and the Receiver. The scenario requires replacement of Freight Forwarder #2. The replacement provider uses RosettaNet [15] for interacting with the logistics coordinator whereas the replaced provider uses

EDIFACT [16]. This choice of message sets is compounded by local variations in the way that different businesses use the message formats.

Our goal is to provide a rich description of the interaction protocol use across a freight forwarding service provider's web service interface. Our intent is that the user of an interface has a rich enough description of the syntax and semantics of the interface to enable it to adapt its behaviour to the constraints of that interface.

4   The SWWS Protocol Mediation Framework

Under the assumption that we are not at liberty to redesign, alter or replace an existing interaction protocol, our approach is to provide a sufficiently rich machine readable description of the protocol. A mediation component within the client system can then adapt its interaction behaviour to meet the interface constraints of the service provider in much the same way as a human user of an eCommerce web site adapts their interaction behaviour on the basis of the controls and surrounding UI narrative presented to them.

Thus, classic web service clients can use classic integration techniques organized around programmers retrieving WSDL [1] descriptions from UDDI registries in order to write integration code whilst a semantic web service client containing a protocol mediation component retrieves a rich description of the interface and adapts its behaviour to suit.

The following sections introduce the components of our framework: communicative acts [5] and primitives which model the significant domain specific communications between interacting parties; abstract protocols which describe the conversational structure of the exchange of primitives used to model communicative acts and which are used operationally to restrict primitive sequencing; concrete protocols which elaborate the concrete interaction behaviours required to initiate and perceive communicative acts across a particular concrete interface; and message filters which are used to bind inbound messages or web service invocations either to concrete behaviours within existing active conversation instances or to factories that create new conversation instances. Interactions between a service provider or consumer agent and the communication infrastructure are modelled as primitive events accompanied by knowledge bases containing relevant domain instances.

4.1   Roles and Communicative Acts

Our first step is to identify the communicative acts [5, 6] associated with our domain and the roles involved in communication which have some correspondence with the concept of illocutionary particles and roles articulated in the ISLANDER framework [7]. We regard roles and communicative acts as part of the ontology which structures concepts within the domain. In our logistics scenario we identify the following 6 communicative acts that occur between a Logistics Coordinator (LC) and a freight forwarding service provider (FF) about a particular shipment journey leg:

Although only short names are used here, in practice, within a web ontology, the names of all concepts (and communicative acts) are made global through the use of URI [21].

Table 1. Communicative acts involved in a Logistics Journey Leg

Communicative Act	Direction	Communicative intent
informReadyForCollection	LC to FF	Inform the FF that the shipment is available for collection.
requestShipmentStatus	LC to FF	Request an update of the shipment status from the FF.
informShipmentStatus	FF to LC	Inform the LP of the shipment status
informReadyToDeliver	FF to LC	Inform the LP that the FF is ready to deliver the shipment.
informShipmentDelivered	FF to LC	Inform the LP (and provide proof) that the FF has infact delivered the shipment.
requestPayment	FF to LC	Request payment for delivering the shipment from the LP.

The utterance and perception of communicative acts by the logistics coordinator and freight forwarding services provider are significant events in the interaction between partners as the physical movement of the corresponding shipment progresses. We model these events as the service primitives of a communication protocol in the style adopted by the OSI Basic Reference Model [8].

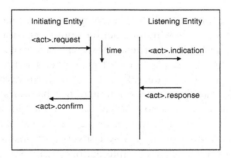

Fig. 4. Sequencing of Abstract Protocol Service Primitives

The occurrence of a communicative act is modelled as the occurrence of 4 primitives illustrated in Figure 4. Two primitive events are experienced at the initiating party which utters the communicative act and, in the absence of failure, two primitive events are experienced at a listening party which perceives the communicative act. The four primitives of the communicative act, <act>, model:

- the initiation of the act by the initiating agent, <act>.request;
- the perception of the communicative act by a listening/responding agent, <act>.indication;
- acknowledgement by the listening/responding agent that the act has been perceived, <act>.response;
- and reporting the outcome of the communicative act to the initiating agent, <act>.confirm.

The `.response` and `.confirm` primitives effectively model a technical acknowledgement that the communication has reached its intended recipient. Any substantive response motivated by the communicative act itself is modelled as a subsequent communication in the opposite direction. Communicative acts therefore achieve a single domain level communication, but may correspond to an exchange of one or more lower level messages or web service operations.

At the initiator, the outcome of a communicative act falls into one of three broad categories:

- Success: The communication is known (by the initiator) to have reached the intended recipient.
- Exception: The communication is known (by the initiator) to have failed to reach the intended recipient.
- Indeterminate: The outcome of the communicative act is unknown (to the initiator).

This provides the basic framework for modelling communication between agents. Each communicative act may carry information (a message) from initiating agent to responding agent and return status information about the outcome of the communication. An important facet of our model is that the occurrence of a `.request` pri-mitive at the initiator is always followed by an occurrence of a `.confirm` primitive, even if the latter reports that the outcome of the communication is indeterminate or failure.

4.2 Abstract Protocol

The next step in our process is to observe that the sequencing of communicative acts is constrained. In our example scenario, the dialog about a given shipment commences with the utterance of an `informReadyForCollection` and ends either with an `informShipmentDelivered` or a `requestPayment`. The structure of these conversational constraints can be captured in the form a monitoring process which (impractically) takes a global view of the system, the occurrence of a communicative act only being possible when it is admissible by the monitoring process. The behaviour of the monitoring process may be expressed in a number of formalisms, such as the ad-hoc notation in figure 5 or more formally using process algebra's such as CCS [18] or UML style Harel State Charts[17] as in figure 6.

```
seq( informReadyForCollection,
     par( repeat( seq( requestShipmentStatus,
                       informShipmentStatus ) ),
          seq( informReadyToDeliver,
               par( requestPayment,
                    informShipmentDelivered )
          )
     )
)
```

Fig. 5. Simplifed ad-hoc expression of the Abstract Protocol for Journey Leg monitoring and execution

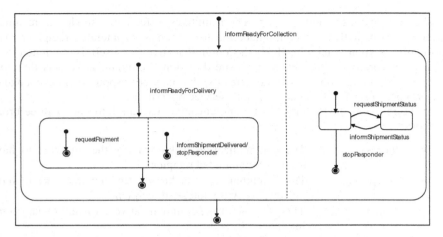

Fig. 6. UML/Harel State Chart expression the Abstract Protocol for Journey Leg monitoring and execution

Note that as specified here these behavioural expressions treat a communicative act as an atomic occurrence, however, as stated earlier we have modelled each as a sequence of four primitives, two of which are experienced by each party to the communication. The basic patterns above can be specialized to the consumer and provider roles with appropriate re-labelling of events. In addition, since the primary motivation for treating a communicative act as four discrete events is to enable explicit consideration of errors handling, different behaviours may be added to cater for the different kinds of outcome listed above: success, exception and indeterminate.

Our concept of an abstract protocol corresponds closely with the ISLANDER [7] concept of a scene and its accompanying dialogical framework.

4.3 Concrete Protocol

In the previous section we considered the role based sequencing constraints on the occurrence of abstract primitives crossing the boundary between a service provider agent or a service consumer agent and the underlying entities that realise concrete interaction behaviours, see figure 7. We now consider the interface specific concrete protocol description which binds the occurrence of these primitives to concrete protocol behaviours. Descriptions are divided into initiating and responding behaviours.

Initiating behaviours are associated with the occurrence of a .request primitive and ultimately giving rise to the corresponding .confirm primitive. Responding behaviours perceive the occurrence of a communicative act generally through the arrival of a message or an inbound invocation of a web service operation which gives rise to a .indication primitive. A responding behaviour may remain active beyond the occurrence of the corresponding .response primitive in order to absorb duplicated inbound messages or to repeat apparently lost outbound messages in accordance with the requirements of the concrete protocol.

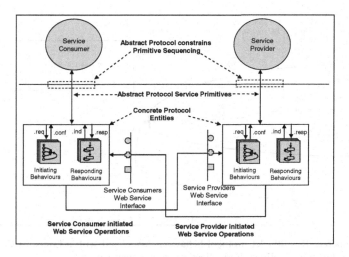

Fig. 7. Abstract and Concrete Protocols

Both initiating and responding behaviours may involve both the sending and receiving of one or more messages or the inbound and outbound invocation of one or more web service operations. For example, in RosettaNet, lost business action messages may be retransmitted a prescribed number of times at prescribed intervals, typically 3 times at 30 minute intervals. This behaviour is embedded in the concrete protocol and is not exposed to the service consumer/provider except in as much as it may give rise to failed or indeterminate outcomes.

The abstract protocol acts as a guard which ensures that abstract service primitives cannot occur except when they are admissible. The concrete protocol descriptions provide an expression of how to initiate and perceive the communicative acts initiated and perceived. These behaviours can also be described as processes using any of the formalisms noted earlier. However the actions associated with state transitions need to be capable of performing simple computations and manipulations on message content. We use a simple event, guard, and action model to described concrete behaviours as simple state machine processes. Figure 8, below, illustrates the concrete RosettaNet protocol behaviour required of a freight forwarding service initiating the informReadyForCollection communicative act. Similarly, figure 9 illustrates the corresponding behaviour required of the freight forwarding services provider in order to perceive the occurrence of the same communicative act. One of the important complex operations that we hide here is the extraction of domain instance information from inbound messages and the generation outbound message content from the instances of the domain ontology. This is the problem of data mediation, and our approach to this is described elsewhere [19]. The operation of these concrete behaviours coordinates the lifting and lowering of domain knowledge between message structure and ontology instances.

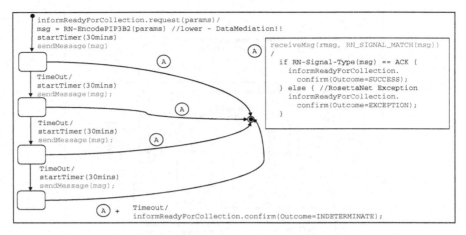

Fig. 8. Concrete RossettaNet protocol behaviour associated with a Logistics Coordinator initiating uttering an informReadyForCollection communicative act

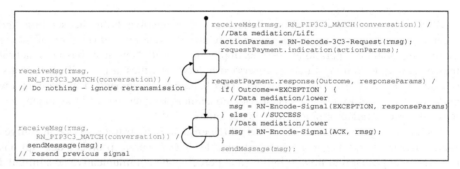

Fig. 9. Concrete RosettaNet protocol behaviour associated with a Freight Forwarder perceiving the occurrence of an informReadyForCollection communicative act

The message driven transitions shown in figures 8 and 9 involve the installation of message filters specified by the second parameter in the `receiveMsg` statements. When a message driven transition is followed the triggering message, which matches the corresponding filter is made available for computation via the variable nominated in the first parameter. A given state may have a number of message driven transitions to the same or to different successor states. Conceptually, on entry to a state with message driven transitions, the relevant filter expressions are installed to associate inbound messages with a given instance of a state transition. On transition, conceptually, all those filters are removed and on entry to a new state any filters relevant to that state are installed. In this way, messages are directed towards appropriate transitions. If multiple transitions are possible from a state, then the choice of which transition is actually taken is non-deterministic, however the message is only assigned to the nominated variable and thereby consumed if the particular message driven transition is actually taken.

5 Rich Service Description

The previous section introduced all the important elements of a rich service interface description.

- A domain ontology which structures the concepts associated with domain.
- A catalogue of roles adopted by the participants of domain interactions and the communicative acts which each role utters or perceives.
- On a per role basis, an expression of the abstract protocol which governs of the sequencing of the occurrence of the primitives modelling communicative acts.
- On a per provider per role basis, an expression of the concrete protocol associated with the utterance and perception of communicative.
- Associated with each concrete protocol description is an expression of the data mediation transformations that extract domain instance information from inbound messages and draw on domain instances in the formulation of outbound messages.

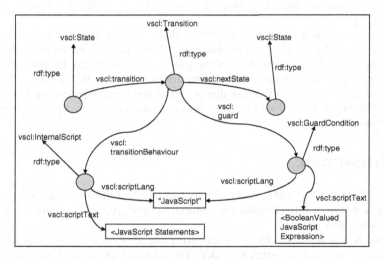

Fig. 10. A state transition in VSCL

During the course of the SWWS project we devised a "Very Simple Choreography Language" (VSCL) which embodies these elements. Abstract protocols are described as a collection of roles and each role is described in terms of the communicative acts which it initiates or perceives. The occurrence of primitives is constrained by a monitoring process. On per interface basis a concrete protocol is described in terms of the required concrete behaviour a peer role must adopt which is scoped by reference to the corresponding abstract protocol and role. Each primitive that a given role experiences is bound to the concrete behaviour required to either initiate or perceive the associated communicative act. Both the monitoring behaviours of abstract protocols and the concrete behaviours of concrete protocols are described as processes which are expressed as finite state machines in the manner described previously.

The abstract syntax of VSCL is expressed as an OWL [4] ontology [22]. A common part abstract and concrete VSCL descriptions is the description of finite state machine processes. VSCL descriptions are written in RDF [23] using properties drawn from the VSCL ontology [22]. Figure 10 illustrates how a transition between two states is encoded in VSCL.

With respect to the example scenario presented in section 3 the VSCL description of the abstract journey leg protocol is available at [24] while the corresponding concrete protocol description provided by a freight forwarding services provider that uses the RosettaNet [15] protocol is available at [25].

The transition behaviours available in VSCL include: message driven, primitive driven, event driven and time driven transitions; sending receiving and replying to messages; raising events and primitives; forking concurrent processes (figures 5 and 6 illustrate the use of concurrency). In order to augment process behaviours with variables for storage and procedures which can perform computation over those variable we provide the ability to include scripted behaviours. In our prototype implementation we used the Mozilla open source embeddable Javascript engine, Rhino [26].

For protocol mediation, it is important that a description of a service provider's interface describes the roles and associated behaviours required of a user of that interface. The role and behaviour of the interface provider may be made explicit, but that is not strictly necessary. The assumption we make is that a service provider is economically motivated to ensure that potential service consumers are able to use the service provided. Hence, we place the onus is on the service provider to provide a rich description.

6 Related Work

OWL-S [4], WSMO [28] are two activities in the field of semantic web service description. We briefly consider the connection between these activities and the ideas discussed in this paper.

OWL-S is a natural vehicle for capturing the abstract protocols that describe the interfaces with each logistics provider. The protocol of figure 5 may be translated straightforwardly into an OWL-S composite process using sequential, iterative and concurrent process compositions. The leaves of this abstract process are described here as communicative acts, so can we identify OWL-S processes with such acts. Communicative acts certainly address the *actions* performed by agents, except that the communication is an intrinsic component of the action. This suggests that they really fit into a service-oriented, rather than a message-oriented, model. OWL-S processes are also designed to represent the actions of agents so we seem to have a good match. However, with the standard OWL-S to WSDL grounding, mapping each atomic process onto a WSDL operation can lead us astray. The problem is that there is nothing to stop a service provider mapping a pair of communicative acts onto a single operation, and hence a single atomic process. For example, it is reasonable to ground the requestShipmentStatus and informShipmentStatus in the separate request and response messages of a single WSDL operation. The knock-on effect is that we have to model this with a single atomic-process. This decision bubbles up through the design of the interface forcing the designer to conflate two otherwise distinct acts all the way up the model. On the plus side, the current grounding is not mandated as the only possible grounding. Indeed, the concrete protocol described by the VSCL of section 5 may be thought of as a description-driven grounding that allows us to map these conceptually distinct acts to (different parts of) the same WSDL operation.

The work of the SWWS and WSMO projects are both motivated by the Web Services Modelling Framework (WSMF) [29] and there has been an on-going exchange of ideas between both projects. Our work is focussed in the mediation of interaction protocols and is most closely related to WSMO Orchestration and Choreography [30]. WSMO uses Abstract State Machines (ASM) as a formalism for describing both choreography and orchestrations. WSMO choreography is most closely aligned with our notion of an abstract protocol, whilst WSMO orchestration is most closely aligned with our notion of concrete protocols. Our work on SWWS has taken the 'easier' path abstracting communicative intent as communicative acts to which a semantic account could be given. WSMO takes the more challenging path of goal driven interaction intended to bring about desired change in the partial state of a world model.

7 Conclusions

Current practice in Web Service integration relies of a rigid plug and socket fit between the provider and consumer of a web service interface. We have demonstrated an approach that provides for description driven adaptation. Our approach relies on the provision of a rich description of the behaviour required of the user of a web service interface. Whilst this places a significant additional burden on the provider of the web service interface, it provides for massive leverage, since it vastly reduces the integration work required of a consumer of that interface. In effect we have provided a more malleable approach to the description of web service interfaces that enables interoperability and substitution were there is significant conceptual overlap between alternate interfaces.

Our approach relies on there being a shared understanding of the semantics of domain specific communicative acts and requires understanding of the semantics of individual web service operations on the part of the provider of the enriched interface description. This obviates the need for a machine readable semantic description of each web service operation, however, this results in concrete protocol descriptions that are somewhat imperative with respect to the behaviours associated with state transitions. Nevertheless, at both the abstract and concrete level, the structure of the concurrent state machines used to specify behavioural constraints is exposed and potentially available for more formal analysis with respect to the desired safety and liveliness properties of the combine abstract/concrete behaviour.

A prototype mediation component which implements the framework described in this paper has been was developed as part of the SWWS project and used as part of the logistics case study demonstrator described in [10].

Acknowledgements

The authors gratefully acknowledge the support of the EU who partially funded this work under SWWS consortium under agreement IST-2002-37134. In addition we extend particular thanks to Silvestre Losada, Oscar Corcho and Jorge Pérez Bolaño of Intelligent Software Components S.A. (ISOCO) [32] for their work implementing protocol mediation component discussed in this paper. Finally we would like to thank our colleague Chris Preist for his feedback on early drafts of this paper.

References

1. Christensen, E., Cubera, F., Meredith,G., and Weerawarana, S.: "Web Services Description Language (WSDL) 1.1", W3C Note (15 March 2001), <http://www.w3.org/ TR/ 2001/ NOTE-wsdl-20010315>
2. Andrews, T., Curbera, F., Dholakia, H., Goland, Y., Klein, J., Leymann, F., Liu, K., Roller, D., Smith, D., Thatte, S., Trickovic, I., and Weerawarana, S.: "Business Process Execution Language for Web Services – Version 1.1" BEA Systems, IBM, Microsoft, SAP AG and Sibel Systems Whitepaper (5 May 2003), <ftp://www6.software.ibm.com/ software/developer/library/ws-bpel.pdf>
3. Kavantzas, N., Burdett, D., Ritzinger, G., Fletcher, T., and Lafon, Y.: "Web Services Choreography Description Language Version 1.0", W3C Working Draft (17 December 2004), <http://www.w3.org/TR/2004/WD-ws-cdl-10-20041217/>
4. Martin, D. et. al: "OWL-S: Semantic Markup for Web Services", W3C Member submission (November 2004) <http://www.w3.org/Submission/2004/SUBM-OWL-S-20041122/>
5. Searle, J.R, "Speech Acts – An essay in the philosophy of language", Cambridge University Press, 1969
6. "FIPA Communicative Act Library Specification", FIPA, 2002. <http://www.fipa.org/ specs/fipa00037/SC00037J.pdf>
7. Esteva, M., Sierra, C.: "ISLANDER 1.0 language definition", Technicl Report of the Institut d'Investigació en Intel.ligència Artificial, IIIA-TR-02-02, 2002 <http://www.iiia. csic.es/~marc/islander-report.pdf>
8. ISO 7498/CCITT X.200, "Open Systems Interconnect Basic Reference Model", 1994 International Standards Organisation.
9. Esplugas-Cuadrado, J., Preist, C., Williams, S., "Integration of B2B Logistics Using Semantic Web Services", Lecture Notes in Computer Science, Volume 3192, Aug 2004
10. Chris Preist, Javier Esplugas-Cuadrado, Steven A. Battle, Stephan Grimm, Stuart K.Williams, Automated Business-to-Business Integration of a Logistics Supply Chain Using Semantic Web Services Technology, Lecture Notes in Computer Science, Volume 3729, Oct 2005, Page 987
11. Bochmann, G.V., "Higher-level protocols are not necessary end-to-end", ACM SIGCOMM Comput. Commun. Rev., Vol 13, No 2, April 1983.
12. Tomas, J.G., Pavon, J., and Pereda, O., "OSI service specification: SAP and CEP modelling", ACM SIGCOMM Comput. Commun. Rev., Vol 17, No 1-2, Jan-Apr 1987
13. Calvert ,L., and Lam, S. S., "Deriving a protocol converter: a top-down method", ACM SIGCOMM Comput. Commun. Rev., Vol 19, No 4, Sept. 1989.

14. Tao, Z. , Bochmann, G.V., Dssouli, R., "A formal method for synthesizing optimized protocol converters and its application to mobile data networks", Mobile Networks and Applications, Vol.2 No.3, p.259-269, Dec. 1997
15. "RosettaNet Implementation Framework: Core Specification Version 2.00.01", March 2002, <http://www.rosettanet.org>
16. ISO 9735, "Electronic data interchange for administration, commerce and transport (EDIFACT) -- Application level syntax rules", 2002, International Standards Organisation
17. Harel, D. "Statecharts: A Visual Formalism for Complex Systems", Science of Computer Programming, Vol , No 3 p. 231-274 June 1987
18. Milner, R., "Communications and Concurrency", Prentice-Hall, ISBN 0-13-115007-3, 1989.
19. Battle, S. "Round Tripping between XML and RDF", Poster ISWC 2004, <http:// iswc2004.semanticweb.org/posters/PID-BRRGVFRE-1090254811.pdf>
20. Berners-Lee, T., Fielding, R., Masinter, L., "Uniform Resource Identifier (URI): Generic Syntax.", RFC 3986, IETF, January 2005. <http://www.ietf.org/rfc/rfc3986.txt>
21. Dean, M., Schreiber, G. (eds), "OWL Web Ontology Language Reference" W3C Recommendation, 10 Feb 2004. < http://www.w3.org/TR/2004/REC-owl-ref-20040210/>
22. VSCL Ontology <http://swws.semanticweb.org/ontologies/protocolMediation/vscl>
23. Beckett, D. (ed), "RDF/XML Syntax Specification (Revised)", W3C Recommendation,10 February 2004, < http://www.w3.org/TR/2004/REC-rdf-syntax-grammar-20040210/>
24. Sample VSCL Abstract Protocol Description <http://swws.semanticweb.org/ wp8/ logistics>
25. Sample VSCL Concrete Protocol Description<http://swws.semanticweb.org/ontologies/ choreo/rn.owl>
26. Mozilla Rhino: JavaScript for Java <http://www.mozilla.org/rhino>
27. Waldo, J., Wyant, G., Wollrath, A. and Kendal, S., "A Note on Distrubuted Computing", Sun Microsystems Laboratories, Inc TR-94-29, Nov. 1994, <http://research.sun.com/ techrep/1994/smli_tr-94-29.pdf>
28. Feier, C. (ed), "WSMO Primer", DERI Working Draft, Apr 2005, <http://www.wsmo.org/ TR/d3/d3.1/v0.2/>
29. Fensel, D., Bussler, C., "The Web Service Modeling Framework WSMF." In: Electronic Commerce Research and Applications, Vol. 1, Issue 2, Elsevier Science B.V., Summer 2002. <http://www.wsmo.org/papers/publications/wsmf.paper.pdf>
30. Roman, D., Scicluna, J., Feier, C. (eds), "Ontology Based Choreography and Orchestration of WSMO Services", DERI International, March 2005, <http:// www. wsmo.org/ TR/d14/v0.2/>
31. BEA, IBM, "BPELJ: BPEL for Java" Joint Whitepaper, March 2004, <ftp://www6. software.ibm.com/software/developer/library/ws-bpelj.pdf>
32. Intelligent Software Components <http://www.isoco.com>

Ideas and Improvements for Semantic Wikis

Jochen Fischer, Zeno Gantner, Steffen Rendle,
Manuel Stritt, and Lars Schmidt-Thieme

Department of Computer Science, University of Freiburg
Georges-Köhler-Allee 51, D-79110 Freiburg, Germany
{jocfisch, ganter ,stritt, lst}@informatik.uni-freiburg.de,
steffen@rendle.de

Abstract. We present an architecture for combining wikis containing hypertext with ontologies containing formal, structured information. A web-based ontology editor that supports collaborative work through versioning, transactions and management of simultaneous modifications is used for ontology evolution. In wiki pages, ontology information can be used to render dynamic content and answer user queries. Furthermore, query templates are introduced that simplify the use of queries for inexperienced users. The architecture allows easy integration with existing ontology frameworks and wiki engines. The usefulness of the approach is demonstrated by a prototypical implementation as well as a small case study.

1   Introduction

A wiki, short for WikiWikiWeb [1], is a website that allows collaborative creation and editing of hypertext content, usually expressed in a simple markup language. *COW, Combining Ontologies with Wikis*[1], is a novel approach to build a *semantic wiki*, by bringing together two different concepts: easy content evolution with the help of wikis, and formal knowledge representation using ontologies. We use the KAON tool suite [2] as back-end for an ontology editor and a query processor; a simple text wiki engine complements the system's functionality. Our approach is different from other semantic wikis in two aspects: The ontology data is edited and stored outside the text wiki, and we implemented so-called query templates, which can be particularly useful for inexperienced users (figure 1).

Although there are already some approaches to using wiki-like systems (see section 2) in the context of ontologies [3] and the Semantic Web [4], still a lot remains to be explored in this field. Requiring detailed knowledge about languages like RDF or OWL would contradict an important aspect of the wiki idea: simplicity and ease of use. It would be comparable to forcing the use of full HTML in text wikis, instead of a more user-friendly and minimalistic syntax.

---

[1] http://www.informatik.uni-freiburg.de/cgnm/software/cow/, available under the terms of the GNU General Public License.

Y. Sure and J. Domingue (Eds.): ESWC 2006, LNCS 4011, pp. 650–663, 2006.

This paper is structured as follows. In the beginning, we give an overview on semantic wikis developed so far. Then we present COW's architecture, and how ontology editing works in the application, with special focus on problems that may occur during simultaneous editing. Next, we introduce COW's query functionality. Finally, we show how these features could be used in a concrete application, a small biographical lexicon.

2   Related Work

Platypus Wiki [5] is a wiki engine that allows entering RDF and OWL statements in addition to natural language text. Unlike our system, it treats the statements in the ontology language as text, instead of providing information on a conceptual level. It also lacks ontology querying, which COW offers both interactively and integrated in the text wiki.

Rhizome[2] [6] is a wiki-like content management system built on top of the RDF application server Raccoon. Metadata is described by the RxML language. RxPath is used for querying the RDF model. Again, the drawbacks are the rather complicated RxML, the difficulty of querying, and the lack of support for collaborative work.

MediaWiki[3], the software behind Wikipedia, enables the user to categorize articles, or, more generally, wiki pages. Categories themselves can also be included in other categories. While this is useful for grouping articles, the associations encoded directly and indirectly using the category feature are not exploited e.g. for improving search results. Beyond categorization and links, there is no possibility of adding formal, well-defined information to the content. COW allows building ontologies that are more complex than a taxonomy of categories. There is an approach to extend MediaWiki with so-called "semantic links", which encode relations between page subjects [7].

WikSAR [8] and SemWiki[4] are wiki engines which allow entering semantic content in the normal text. Both systems offer query mechanisms, however they lack query templates. Again semantic information has to be represented in a formal language and is stored as part of normal wiki pages.

Similar to other wikis COW adopts the web-based user interface from semantic wikis like Platypus or Rhizome. Hence the system can be accessed by any web browser. In contrast to other semantic wikis like WikSAR, a frame-based view for ontology editing is implemented, similarly to Protégé [9] or WebODE [10]. The ontology data itself is not stored in a text wiki, but in a separate database, where it is kept consistent. Several existing text wikis can be adapted to work with the software. To make use of the ontology data, COW uses the KAON query language and extends it by query templates, which will be described later in this article.

---

[2] http://rhizome.liminalzone.org/
[3] http://www.mediawiki.org/
[4] http://www.dello.net/semwiki/

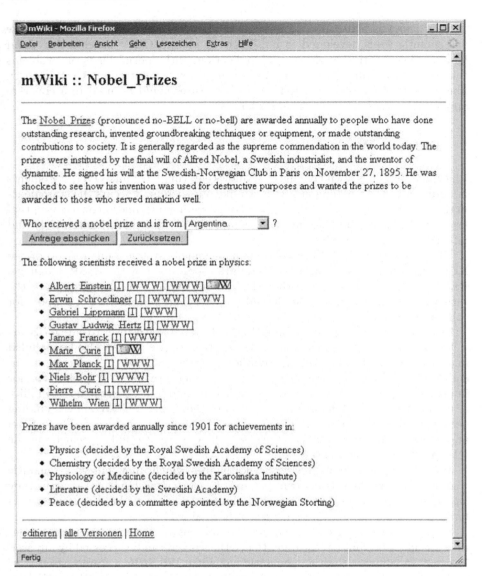

Fig. 1. COW renders normal text (top and bottom of the page), query templates (the question with the pull-down menu), and dynamic content (list in the center)

3   Architecture

COW has a multi-tier architecture (fig. 2) consisting of the following parts: persistence layer, ontology layer, abstraction layer, and an HTML-based user interface.

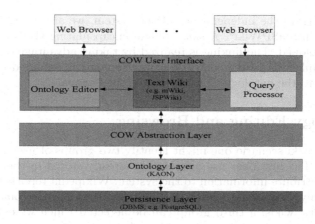

Fig. 2. COW Architecture

All end-user interaction with COW is done with a standard web browser using only plain HTML. Neither Java applets nor JavaScript are used. Thus we support one of the wiki principles, namely low client-side requirements.

Abstraction and Ontology Layer

An abstraction layer for language refinement and version management separates the wiki and ontology editor components from a general purpose ontology framework. This layer provides a lightweight, string-based interface to communicate with the front-end, stores the ontology permanently in a database, and is able to handle queries.

COW uses the ontology framework KAON [2] to implement the interface of the abstraction layer. A useful feature of KAON is the evolution log, a list stored in a meta-ontology where all ontology changes are logged. This log enables us to restore any previous version of the ontology. The framework does not allow inconsistent states of the ontology. After applying a change, either the ontology is consistent or an exception will be thrown (and caught). In combination with the locking mechanism, which will be described later, this ensures effective collaborative editing of the ontology. Internally COW uses the ontology language RDF plus extensions like transitive and inverse properties. To support the reusing ontology information we provide a dynamic page which exports the complete ontology in OWL.

Integration into Existing Wiki Engines

Although we implemented a minimalistic wiki engine, we designed the other components of the system to be as independent as possible from the used wiki engine. Little work is necessary to combine the ontology editor and the query engine with the text wiki.

To demonstrate the independence of the system, we also integrated COW's functionality into JSPWiki[5]. A small plugin encapsulating the query functionality was developed. The linking is realized by taking advantage of the concept of interwiki links[6]: E.g., the code [Concept:Person] is rendered to an HTML link pointing to the ontology view of the concept Person.

4   Ontology Editing and Browsing

In a classical wiki scenario one might identify two groups of users: readers and contributors. The first ones use information already stored in the system. The later ones contribute information to the system. Wikipedia reports that at least 99% of its daily visitors are readers and only less than 1% are contributors[7].

For semantic wikis, a third group can be detected which we call "experts": People with sufficient understanding of knowledge representation mechanisms to contribute to the semantic data of the web site, especially the ontology structure. Note that these three groups are not disjoint: Both text contributors and experts usually also act as readers, although they should not be regarded as typical members of the group.

For the success of a semantic wiki it is crucial that the system is capable of serving the needs of all three groups. Because the group of readers is the vast majority the overall success of a system depends mostly on them. That is why the systems should be designed to be easy and intuitive for these readers. Secondly it is important that inexperienced contributors can work on the system, so that the content can grow fast.

We think that today's semantic wikis address mostly the group of experts. By separating the ontology storage from the wiki text, we avoid confusion among the contributors who are not experts.

In order to allow inexperienced users to help populating the ontology, COW has a slot-based graphical ontology editor. This way instances may be created without much expertise. It is important to note that no user has to learn a formal language like RDF or OWL.

We created a simple web-based ontology editor component, because, at the time of COW's initial development, there was no such system available. Today, we might consider using pOWL [11].

5   Ontology Locking, Transactions, and Versioning

For collaborative work on ontologies, our system supports ontology versioning, transactions and locking of editing sessions. The objective of these features is to

---

[5] http://www.jspwiki.org/

[6] See http://c2.com/cgi/wiki?InterWiki for an explanation.

[7] Estimimation based on last available visitor statistics of October 2004. There are 917,000 daily visitors and there are only about 11,000 contributors that have ever edited more than 5 pages. http://en.wikipedia.org/wikistats/DE/-TablesWikipediaZZ.htm

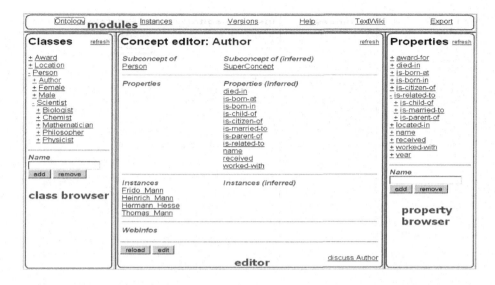

Fig. 3. Screenshot of the editor with the ontology browser as active module

keep the ontology consistent and to provide an natural and simple workflow to the user.

Locking Strategy for Editing Ontology Elements

A central problem of simultaneous editing of ontologies is how to synchronize different editing sessions. In text wikis, every page is the atomic element for editing operations. When a user starts to edit a page, the wiki system locks this page for other editing operations until the user applies his changes or after a certain time threshold expires. Other wiki engines use a "first come, first served" strategy for check-ins. Locking mechanisms for ontology systems are more complicated because of dependencies between several entities. For example if user A edits instance I of concept C and user B adds a slot with domain C, the editing session of user B depends on A's changes. Therefore, locking of single entities is not sufficient. On the other hand, locking the ontology as a whole obviously is an obstacle for concurrent editing, especially for large ontologies that many people want to work on simultaneously. Furthermore, as locking should be applied only if necessary, and in wikis users sometimes start the edit mode, but do not apply any changes, any locking mechanism which is applied at check-out time is unnecessary restrictive.

COW's checks are performed when the user commits changes. These checks guarantee that the result of the check-in is comprehensible for the user. The changes to an entity are refused by the system if the editor view of this entity has changed in the meantime. With this strategy users always know the exact effects of their editing operations. All dependencies causing a change of the edit

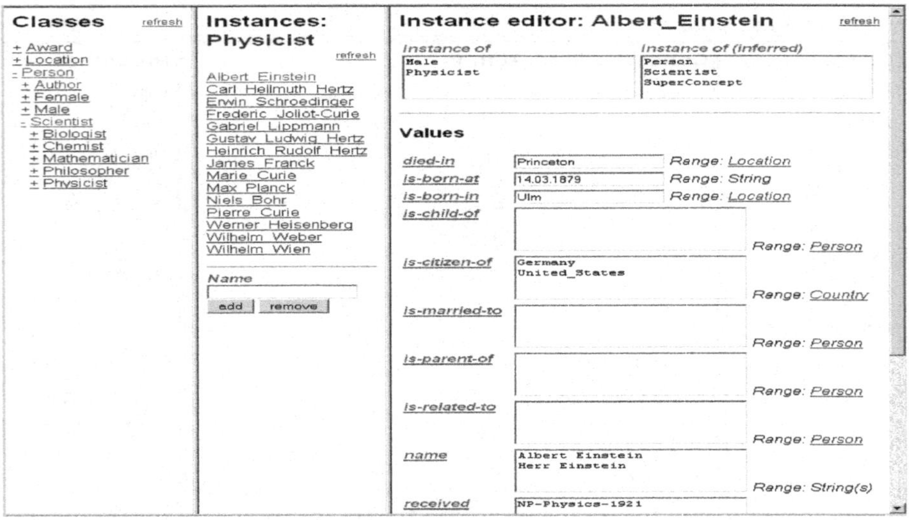

Classes	refresh	Instances: Physicist	Instance editor: Albert_Einstein	refresh

Classes refresh
+ Award
+ Location
- Person
  + Author
  + Female
  + Male
  - Scientist
    + Biologist
    + Chemist
    + Mathematician
    + Philosopher
    + Physicist

Instances: Physicist refresh
Albert Einstein
Carl Hellmuth Hertz
Erwin Schroedinger
Frederic Joliot-Curie
Gabriel Lippmann
Gustav Ludwig Hertz
Heinrich Rudolf Hertz
James Franck
Marie Curie
Max Planck
Niels Bohr
Pierre Curie
Werner Heisenberg
Wilhelm Weber
Wilhelm Wien

Name
[   ]
add   remove

Instance editor: Albert_Einstein   refresh

Instance of
Male
Physicist

Instance of (inferred)
Person
Scientist
SuperConcept

Values

died-in   Princeton   Range: Location
is-born-at   14.03.1879   Range: String
is-born-in   Ulm   Range: Location
is-child-of
                                          Range: Person
is-citizen-of   Germany
                   United_States
                                          Range: Country
is-married-to
                                          Range: Person
is-parent-of
                                          Range: Person
is-related-to
                                          Range: Person
name   Albert Einstein
                   Herr Einstein
                                          Range: String(s)
received   NP-Physics-1921

Fig. 4. Screenshot of the instance editor with instance **Albert Einstein** in edit mode

view are considered, even inferred ones. Fig. 5 shows how our locking mechanism works.

We have tested our strategy in our case study, where we have built and populated the ontology simultaneously. The system had to refuse editing operations quite rarely even though our ontology changed often. Generally, our locking mechanism stayed in the background and did not disturb working collaboratively.

Transactions for Ontology Modification

In RDF-based knowledge representation, the smallest unit of information is an RDF triple. As triples of an editing session depend on each other, changes on the knowledge base should be performed according to the ACID principles[8]. Thus we offer a transaction mode for ontologies, which guarantees that either all changes are applied or none.

Ontology Versioning

The most important design issue with respect to ontology versioning is the granularity of the versioning method. Versioning every entity – concepts, instances, properties – on its own would imply that previous versions of each entity could be restored independently from the rest of the ontology. Unfortunately, this would be very complicated because of dependencies between ontology entities. Even if it were possible to find a strategy that can manage different versions of entities

---

[8] Atomicity, consistency, isolation, and durability are the key properties of transactions in database management systems. See [12].

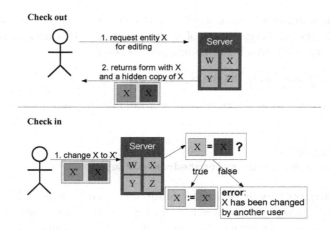

Fig. 5. Demonstration of the locking mechanism. Saving X is accepted if and only if the editing view, including possible inferred values, of X has not been changed.

and handles the dependencies in a way that ensures a consistent ontology [13], it would be everything but comprehensible to the user.

Our approach versions the whole ontology. If users want to restore old versions, they have to set the complete ontology to the old state. With regard to simplicity, we think that this is an effective way that is traceable by the users. Of course a roll-back to an older version of the complete ontology might imply a lot of changes. It's out of the focus of this paper to implement state-of-the-art ontology-versioning, which is still an active topic of research. For example, a more elabotative approach could version independent domains in an ontology seperately, which might be an interesting feature for future work.

6 Querying Ontologies Inside the Wiki

An application for browsing and editing both a text collection and an ontology requires the possibility to search the text as well as query the content of the ontology. In COW, the users specify queries, either using a dedicated page, or by directly embedding them into wiki pages. The query results, usually instances, provide both hyperlinks to the article pages and to the ontology browser.

Normal queries are statements in the KAON query language, which will be described briefly below. Additionally, we developed *query templates* that can be added to wiki pages. These templates are queries with free variable parameters, which have to be filled by the user executing the query. Note that this is realized by passing queries to the underlying ontology framework. Other query languages could be supported by using another ontology framework or by adding components supporting the language.

KAON offers a comfortable language for querying ontologies. In analogy to SQL, which is a closed language over relations, the language is closed over conceptual descriptions.

The simplest queries are questions about facts that are directly stored in an ontology, like the property values of a given instance. If a user wants to know when Albert Einstein was born, he has just to enter

```
<#day-of-birth> IN:1 !#Albert_Einstein!
```

Besides this, the system can also answer queries by using its inference mechanism:

```
[#Physicist] AND
    SOME(<#is-born-in>.<#located-in>=!#Europe!)
```

#Albert_Einstein will be in the result set, even though it is not directly stored in the ontology that he was born in Europe. It is not even stored that his home town, Ulm, is located in Europe, but KAON's reasoning engine derived this from the information that Ulm is located in Germany, Germany is located in Europe, and the <#located-in> property is transitive. As the <#located-in> property is not reflexive, the query will not yield persons for whom it is only stated that they were born in Europe. Thus to get correct results, one has to enhance the query a little bit further:

```
[#Physicist] AND (SOME(<#is-born-in>.<#located-in>=!#Europe!)
                  OR SOME(<#is-born-in>=!#Europe!))
```

While KAON's query language is fairly simple and offers lots of useful constructs, it still has disadvantages for its use in a system that wants to be user-friendly for non-experts which it will never overcome: It is a formal language with strict syntax and semantics, and there might be subtle differences between the user's conceptual model and the actual ontology which will have a undesirable or at least unexpected impact on the query results.

Because we do not see a viable alternative to a formal query language, we decided to use such a language in COW, to empower at least the users having the necessary expert knowledge to use the query feature.

As the queries are stored on the wiki pages, other users can look them up and use them as examples or boilerplates for constructing their own queries. By and by, a collection of useful queries might be accumulated in the wiki.

Query Templates

One way to facilitate the reuse of queries is *query templates*, queries with place-holders waiting to be filled by the user with instances or literal values. Expert users may create typical questions on important concepts of the ontology, e.g. persons and awards in our case study, which then can be used by all users who want to get information from the system. As a wiki also serves as a communication platform for its user community, people also might approach others for getting certain queries implemented. This can make a semantic wiki a more useful tool than a normal collaborative editor for ontologies.

A *query template* is a triple (q, t, s), where

- q is a query containing placeholder variables enclosed in dollar signs ("$"),
  each variable may occur several times in the query;
- t is a string containing a natural language phrase - usually a question -
  representing the query, each variable in q occurs exactly once in t together
  with a type statement;
- s is a set of tuples containing the mappings from all non-string variables to
  the queries that yield the set of (property) instances that will be presented
  to the user as values to be selected for the variables.

A placeholder variable has the form `$NAME$`, a variable with a type statement
has the form `$NAME:type$`, where `type` can be `instance`, `concept`, `property`,
or `literal`. For example:

```
q='SOME (<#worked-with>=$PERSON$)'
t='Who worked with $PERSON:instance$'
s={('PERSON','[#Person]')}
```

In the wiki, this query template will be displayed as the question formulated
above. All the variables are replaced by pull-down menus or input fields inside the
question. After filling out or selecting all the items, the user will be redirected
to a page where the results of the query are presented. We think that other
semantic wikis can profit from the concept of query templates as well, because
such templates can be implemented on top of any query language.

Queries to the ontology are not limited to question answering. Because the
query results are rendered into the wiki pages, they can also serve as a means
of dynamically displaying content. Changes in the ontology are then directly
reflected on the wiki pages. Possible examples include received awards and lists
of works in biographical articles, and index pages, e.g. "all chemists" or "all
Nobel prize winners".

So wiki pages can consist of a combination of normal text and ontology data
rendered to text. With respect to our defined user groups the following scenario is possible: A contributor creates a new wiki page describing the life of
Albert Einstein. In this description he writes about the scientists Albert Einstein worked with. When an expert contributor sees this, he might replace the
text formulated in natural language with a semantic query (template). For example he could create a query that yields all scientists who worked with Albert
Einstein and further extend the query by a parameter 'country' so that users
can query the ontology for all scientists who worked with Albert Einstein and
live in a specific country (fig. 8). Such dynamic content depends on the ontology,
but it is accessible transparently for all kinds of users. Even a reader with no
knowledge about ontologies is able to read the natural language text and select
a parameter in a drop down box to get specific information. Fig. 6 shows how a
dynamic page is created and fig. 7 shows how a reader sees it.

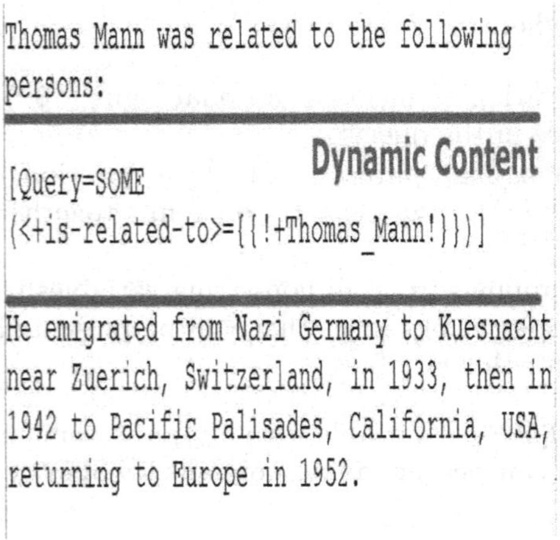

Thomas Mann was related to the following persons:

Dynamic Content

[Query=SOME
(<+is-related-to>={{!+Thomas_Mann!}})]

He emigrated from Nazi Germany to Kuesnacht near Zuerich, Switzerland, in 1933, then in 1942 to Pacific Palisades, California, USA, returning to Europe in 1952.

Fig. 6. Queries can be used as dynamic content

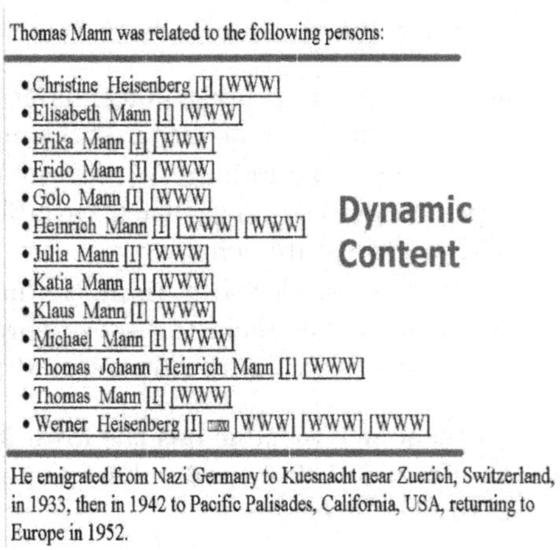

Thomas Mann was related to the following persons:

- Christine Heisenberg [I] [WWW]
- Elisabeth Mann [I] [WWW]
- Erika Mann [I] [WWW]
- Frido Mann [I] [WWW]
- Golo Mann [I] [WWW]
- Heinrich Mann [I] [WWW] [WWW]
- Julia Mann [I] [WWW]
- Katia Mann [I] [WWW]
- Klaus Mann [I] [WWW]
- Michael Mann [I] [WWW]
- Thomas Johann Heinrich Mann [I] [WWW]
- Thomas Mann [I] [WWW]
- Werner Heisenberg [I] ▭ [WWW] [WWW] [WWW]

Dynamic Content

He emigrated from Nazi Germany to Kuesnacht near Zuerich, Switzerland, in 1933, then in 1942 to Pacific Palisades, California, USA, returning to Europe in 1952.

Fig. 7. COW renders dynamic content

7 Case Study: A Biographical Lexicon

We created a small biographical lexicon, containing Nobel Prize winners, their families and coworkers. The natural language content has been taken from the Wikipedia. Important information of the content of biographies like day and place of birth, citizenship and so on have been formalized in the ontology. We created three main classes: Award, Person and Location each with several subclasses. The ontology is populated with 37 instances of Person, 12 of Award and 52 of Location.

The combination of an ordinary wiki together with an ontology leads to an impressive boost of information retrieval. To get a feeling for this extension, we will examine a small example. The user wants to add a new instance called Albert Einstein. Einstein worked together with Max Planck, so he adds the instance Albert_Einstein and fills its worked-with property slot with the existing instance Max_Planck. As the the property worked-with is symmetric, COW is able to infer that also Max Planck worked together with Albert Einstein. This fact is also shown the instance view of Max_Planck.

The benefit is that we get additional information through the ontology view of Max_Planck without editing the instance manually. The ontology not only provides additional information, it also can be used for queries. Queries can directly be implemented into the articles, which allows the representation of dynamic content. If you want to add a list of coworkers in the biography of Albert Einstein, a query can be inserted which updates the list on each page view, using the ontology data. The walk-through shown in fig. 8 summarizes how COW can be used for this kind of application and how users can profit from semantic information.

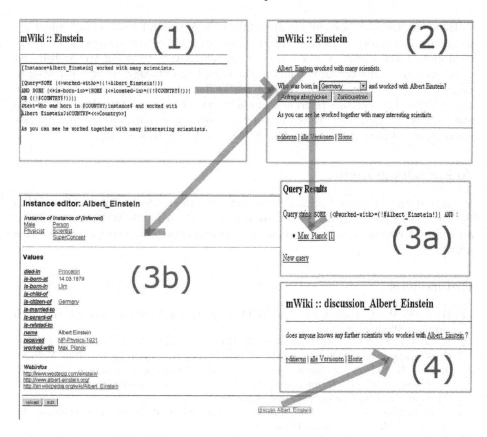

Fig. 8. Query templates are embedded into normal wiki text (1). COW renders this query as a question with forms to be filled out by the user (2). The user has the possibility to execute the query and view the result (3a) or to click on an instance to see further information (3b). Talk pages allow discussions about any entity (4)

8 Conclusion

We presented an architecture for extending wikis for unstructured information to also maintain formalized structured information by *Combining Ontologies with Wikis* (COW). COW has all features of a common wiki and additionally allows the collaborative evolution of an ontology. In contrast to existing semantic wiki systems, it offers an easy-to-use ontology editor and does not confront normal users with ontology data inside the page source code. The editor's smart locking mechanism enables multiple users to work on the knowledge base without unnecessary conflicts; transactions guarantee the ontology to remain consistent. By querying the ontology, dynamic content as part of wiki pages can be created and users can issue queries. Queries can be formulated by means of a formal query language as well as using simple query templates.

In our future work, we will extend COW by input templates, a complementary mechanism to query templates. Input templates will allow inexperienced users to populate the ontology via forms as an alternative to using the web-based ontology editor. Instead of versioning the complete ontology, we will investigate more fine-grained version control policies. Other extensions could be automatic renaming of the entities referenced in a query or a query template when the ontology is changed, the use of ontology engines other than KAON, and queries in emerging standard languages like SPARQL [14] or RDQL [15].

Acknowledgements

We would like to thank Ljiljana Stojanovic and Boris Motik (formerly at AIFB Karlsruhe) for patiently answering our questions regarding KAON, and the three anonymous reviewers whose comments and suggestions helped to improve this article.

References

1. B. Leuf, W. Cunningham. The Wiki Way: Quick Collaboration on the Web Addison-Wesley Longmann, 2001.
2. E. Bozsak, M. Ehrig, S. Handschuh, A. Hotho, A. Maedche, B. Motik, D. Oberle, C. Schmitz, S. Staab, L. Stojanovic, N. Stojanovic, R. Studer, G. Stumme, Y. Sure, J. Tane, R. Volz, V. Zacharias. KAON - Towards a large scale Semantic Web. In *E-Commerce and Web Technologies, Third International Conference, EC-Web 2002*, Aix-en-Provence, France, September 2002.
3. T. R. Gruber. A Translation Approach to Portable Ontologies. In *Knowledge Acquisition* Volume 5 Issue 2, 1993.
4. T. Berners-Lee, J. Hendler, O. Lassila. The Semantic Web. In *Scientific American*, May 2001.
5. R. Tazzoli, P. Castagna, S. Campanini. Towards a Semantic Wiki Wiki Web. Poster Track, *3rd International Semantic Web Conference (ISWC2004)*, Hiroshima, Japan, November 2004.
6. A. Souzis. Building a Semantic Wiki. In *IEEE Intelligent Systems, vol. 20, no. 5*, September/October 2005.
7. M. Völkel, M. Krötzsch, D. Vrandecic, H. Haller, R. Studer. Semantic Wikipedia. In *Proceedings of the 15th International Conference on World Wide Web (WWW 2006)*, Edinburgh, Scotland, May 2006.
8. D. Aumueller, S. Auer. Towards a Semantic Wiki Experience – Desktop Integration and Interactivity in WikSAR. In *Proceedings of the 1st Workshop on The Semantic Desktop. 4th International Semantic Web Conference*, Galway, Ireland, November 2005.
9. N. Noy, M. Sintek, S. Decker, M. Crubézy, R. Fergerson, M. Musen. Creating Semantic Web Contents with Protégé-2000. In *IEEE Intelligent Systems*, Volume 16 Issue 2.
10. O. Corcho, M. Fernández-López, A. Gómez-Pérez, O. Vicente. WebODE: An Integrated Workbench for Ontology Representation, Reasoning and Exchange. *13th International Conference on Knowledge Engineering an Knowledge Management (EKAW'02)*, October 2002.

11. S. Auer. pOWL – A Web Based Platform for Collaborative Semantic Web Development. In *Proc. of 1st Workshop Workshop Scripting for the Semantic Web (SFSW'05)*, Hersonissos, Greece, 2005.

12. C. J. Date, An Introduction to Database Systems, Seventh Edition, 2000.

13. B. Parsia, E. Sirin, A. Kalyanpur. Debugging OWL Ontologies. In *Proceedings of the 14th International World Wide Web Conference*, Chiba, Japan, 2005.

14. E. Prud'hommeaux, A. Seaborne (editors). SPARQL Query Language for RDF. *W3C Working Draft*, February 2006.

15. A. Seaborne. RDQL – A Query Language for RDF. *W3C Member Submission*, January 2004.

WikiFactory: An Ontology-Based Application for Creating Domain-Oriented Wikis

Angelo Di Iorio, Valentina Presutti, and Fabio Vitali

University of Bologna, Mura Anteo Zamboni 7, 40127 Italy

Abstract. Wikis play a leading role among the web publishing environments, being collaborative tools used for fast and easy writing and sharing of content. Although powerful and widely used, wikis do not support users in the aided generation of content specific for a given domain but they still require manual, time-consuming and error-prone interventions. On the other hand, semantic portals support users in browsing, searching and managing content related to a given domain, by exploiting ontologies. In this paper we propose a specific application of web ontologies, applied to the wikis: exploiting an ontological description of a domain in order to deploy a customized wiki for that specific domain. We describe the design of an ontology-based framework, named WikiFactory, that aids users to automatically generate a complex and complete wiki website related to a specific area of interest with few efforts. In order to show the applicability of our framework, we present a specific case study that describes the main WikiFactory capabilities in constructing the wiki website for a Computer Science Department in a University.

1 Introduction

Wikis are collaborative tools used for fast and easy writing and sharing of content on the Web. They provide a simple, quick, informal way to create web sites, web applications, shared environment for discussion and document collections, tools for distributed cooperative writing, and so on. The success of grassroot, yet authoritative, information sources based on wiki technologies (examples include sites such as Wikipedia [25], Portland Pattern Repository [6] or World66 [28]) is greatly due to the informal, unimposing, encouraging relaxed attitude towards open contributions that is the true mark of wiki applications.

Wikis are, at heart, a collection of text documents that are displayed as HTML pages through a simple server-side collection of scripts. Interfaces for editing and creating new content, as well as text conventions for expressing some text styles and hypertext links, allow some complexity in the final result. Yet wikis remain fundamentally generic tools, and what they are good for, substantially, is creating large and flat collections of web pages linked to each other. It is very hard (or, rather, it is very easy but completely manual) to create structures, especially repeating structures, and preorganizing content and pages for large scale, structured, systematic expression of organized content.

Thus, while it might be very fascinating that users are allowed to create fairly sophisticated content and sites without special applications, and without

Y. Sure and J. Domingue (Eds.): ESWC 2006, LNCS 4011, pp. 664–678, 2006.

any knowledge of HTML, CSS, HTTP, and any other basic web technologies, it could be frustrating to discover that all wikis will require that not only the actual content pages, but navigation lists, intermediate pages, recurring substructures, etc., need to be specified manually and repeated manually as many times as required by the complexity of the content to be put on line. For instance, a university faculty that decides to put on-line a wiki to describe its course offering, might find appealing that the wiki allows easy editing of each course page to each individual professor, but also discouraging that it has to create one by one all individual pages for courses, classes, professors, rooms, events, exams, and so on.

Each domain suggests a basic and natural structure of subsites, navigation patterns, organization of home and intermediate pages, automatic inter-site links, down to the content template of each individual page. Current generation wiki clones do not provide tools for the aided generation of domain-oriented wikis. Furthermore, since a wiki is a live entity continuously generated and updated and modified, the need for aided generation of substructures exists throughout the useful life of the wiki itself.

The creation of domain-oriented publishing environments can be supported by the emerging Semantic Web technologies. The Semantic Web is an extension of the current Web where information is given in a machine understandable form [3] by means of a fundamental "'tool'": the ontology. Web ontologies are collections of semantic classes and relations that provide us with a powerful way to express assertions and constraints about the world, and consequently about every specific domain of knowledge. Some technologies have been introduced to manage such web ontologies: Web Ontology Language (OWL) [26], that is the standard language for the definition of Web ontologies, and Resource Description Framework (RDF) [27], that is the base model of the Semantic Web.

In this paper we propose a specific application of web ontologies, applied to the wikis: exploiting an ontological description of a domain in order to deliver a customized wiki for that specific domain. We have designed a framework, named WikiFactory, that automatically builds a domain-based wiki, taking in input the description of the world where that wiki will be used. The most relevant advantage of such approach is clear: simplifying the creation of the wiki pages, avoiding users to manually set their internal structures and links. Moreover, these pages are natively decorated with metadata, directly extracted from the input ontology. As semantic portals do, the domain-oriented wikis simplify the creation, searching and management of content in a specific domain of interest.

Actually, WikiFactory has another relevant goal, that is the delivery of a reliable, available and scalable wiki. Another limitation with current generation wikis, in fact, is that they work in a best effort way with no expectation of these requirements. Organizations who need strong guarantees in terms of high availability of the services, or guaranteed support for a large number of users at the same time, or for robustness of the service in face of hardware or network failures, would surely decide that no wiki can provide these guarantees, and therefore turn to different kinds of software. Thus, besides being domain-oriented, wikis produced by WikiFactory are Qos-enabled, that is able to guarantee a given quality of service. We term these kind of wikis B-Wiki.

In this paper we only focus the attention on the ontological aspects of WikiFactory, by investigating some issues related to the use of ontologies for the creation of specialized wikis. Issues and solutions about QoS requirements and the deployment of the complete B-Wiki will not be discussed here. The rest of the paper is structured as follows. Section 2 discusses some related works. Section 3 describes the proposed WikiFactory framework with its principal components. Section 4 presents a case study that shows the applicability of the framework. Section 5 presents some concluding remarks and future works.

2   Related Works

All wiki applications (the so-called WikiClones, to stress that they are derived from the original and true WikiWikiWeb application [24]) share the same basic philosophy of open editing and a common approach to simple text-based syntax for editing and content writing, but distinguish from each other for the additional services and application modules they offer to their users. These features cover the most varied areas: PurpleWiki [11] provides a full control on content fragments, JotSpot[9] integrate collaborative tools, SnipSnap[10] allows users to in-line organigrams and UML diagrams and a lot of other examples can be cited.

Particularly interesting are those projects that aim at integrating wikis with Semantic Web technologies, known as "'SemanticWikiWikiWebs [23]"'. Pytypus[19] is a collaborative semantic engine that uses RDF as a base technology: wiki pages are annoted with RDF and stored in a semantic database, in order to be easily searched by agents. Platypus Wiki [17] offers a simple user interface to create wiki pages with metadata based on W3C standards such as RDF [27] and OWL [26]. Rhizome [2] allows users to create content with explicit semantics, with little effort. Instead of the common wiki syntax, Rhyzome uses a specialized plain-text format, called ZML: users can annotate documents and express statements on resources without using RDF, but simply editing ZML pages and following simple rules (server-side, a specialized engine transforms this content in RDF statements and manages a rich network of metadata). Similarly, RDFWiki [16] provides users a simple text-based interface to edit content but stores all data as RDF. Users can express predicates on objects, and all wiki content can be exported as N-Triples. Similarly PeriPeri[4] allows users to decorate the wiki pages, adding metadata to the top of a page like an email header. With WikSar[7], authors can also embed on pages commands to gather content from all the available data in the repository. SemperWiki[12] aims at integrating such searching and indexing funcionalities with a usable interface and a personal space for each user.

Other projects deal with the automatic extraction of information and reasoning about wikis. In [14] authors propose an implementation to make content of Wikipedia understandable and processable by machines. They suggest the introduction of typed links among pages as a simple way to achieve this goal, without loosing the soundness and usability of Wikipedia. WikiSense [13] aims at applying data-mining techniques to MediaWiki (the wiki-clone which Wikipedia relies on) in order to automatically extract the underlying web of concepts and relations.

Even if not directly connected with wikis, many projects by the Semantic Portals Community share issues and solutions with our work and are worth to be mentioned and compared each other. For instance, OntoWebber [29] is an integrated system that exploits ontologies to create different models and views of data, and present them on the web. The declarative model behind OntoWebber supports users throughout the whole life-cycle of a web-site and allows them to easily instantiate web pages from heterogeneous data sources.

Similarly SCWP [21] uses ontologies to generate and manage community web portals and to make heterogeneous information easily sharable among heterogeneous sub-systems. The same research group produced KA2 [20], a flexible ontology that can be used for different domains and handled by different semantic tools. Based on an artificial intelligence approach, SEAL [1] exploits ontologies to strengthen searching, import, conversion and managing of data within web portals too. Particularly interesting is the approach proposed in EnerSearch [22], whose sub-goal is hiding the complexity of ontologies and providing users a simplified interface to search and insert data.

WikiFactory adopts a similar approach but designed and implemented for wikis: hiding the complexity within the system and simplifying the internal data model, it simplifies the automatic generation and management of content, and consequently indexing and searching.

3   Using Ontologies to Build a Domain-Oriented Wiki with WikiFactory

Building a domain-oriented publishing environment (for instance, a wiki) from an ontological description is not a simple and straightforward process. Two separate worlds, in fact, need to be merged into the output: on the one hand, we have the *domain*, a set of actors, properties and actions strictly related to the reality we are describing and apparently unrelated to the world of the wikis; on the other hand, we have the *wikis*, general tools for writing and sharing content on the web, that can be used for any domain. In order to present how WikiFactory works we will explain, firstly, what makes a domain-oriented wiki different from a generic one (and so, we will outline the features of an ontological description of such wiki) and then, how WikiFactory actually transforms such ontology into the final output.

3.1   Describing a Domain-Oriented Wiki

At first glance, a "'domain-oriented"' wiki can be defined as a wiki whose pages hold data and information useful in that domain. For instance, in a wiki customized for a university we expect that any home-page of a lecturer holds his name, his title, office hours, a list of the courses he teaches and so on, while an enrollment page contains some instructions and a form. In a wiki of a football team we expect that there's a page about the league match calendar (formatted as a set of tables, one for each match-day), a page about the history (consisting of different paragraphs), a page with the short-list of the team, and so on.

A domain-oriented wiki is also characterized by a set of pages, linked each other according to some patterns. We expect, for instance, that any wiki about a football team has a home-page linked with a page about the short-list of a team, a page about the history of the club, and a page for any player, and so on. In a wiki for the University, we expect that, for any course, there is a home-page, a page with a list of exams (linked to another page for the exams enrollment) and so on. At this level, the wiki is not only composed by some disconnected pages (whose internal structures and data are described by the ontology), but contains well-defined sub-areas, composed of a proper set of linked pages.

The data mentioned so far cover only the first installation of a wiki. Although this automatic deployment saves users' time and resources, another issues still remains unsolved: updating wikis once they live on web servers. Today users have to manually perform these tasks: whenever a university that uses a wiki plans to provide a new course, for instance, an user manually adds to the wiki a home-page for that course, creates specific pages for the exams and manually links all these resources. It should be useful to use a wiki that automatically creates (or proposes to create) some pages, whenever other pages are manually created by the authors: in the example of a university course, we expect that all the pages related to a course are automatically added to the wiki, whenever an user creates a course home-page.

3.2   Deploying a Domain-Oriented Wiki

In the previous section we have identified three main aspects that a domain-oriented ontology for wikis can describe: static pages, clusters of pages and run-time behaviour. The main goal of WikiFactory is just translating these data into the actual wiki pages and scripts, following the same schema: (i) producing pages for each element of the domain, composed by a set of internal and structured components, (ii) producing clusters of pages organized according to a given pattern and (iii) adding to the wiki some scripts that generate clusters of pages or provide services at run-time.

Before going on discussing about the ontology within WikiFactory and its internal processing, it is worth giving an overview of the whole framework. The WikiFactory framework consists of four principal components, namely the *Ontology creation supporting tool*, the *Repository*, the *WikiFactory Application*, and the *QoS Manager* as depicted in Fig 1.

The framework uses two ontologies: the domain specific ontology, which describes the domain, and the WikiFactory ontology, which describes the generic wiki elements and contructs. These two input objects are elaborated by a designer with an ontology creation tool (e.g., Protege [18]), in order to produce an extension of the domain ontology, which describes services and structures of a

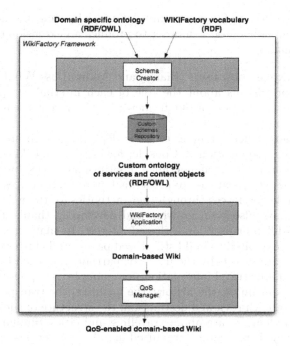

Fig. 1. The Wiki Factory Framework

wiki useful for that domain. Note that a manual intervention by the designer is required in order to translate the generic constructs of the WikiFactory ontology into specialized constructs for a given domain.

After having derived the domain-oriented wiki ontology, the designer simply saves it into the Repository. Any ontology extension stored in the database (one for each supported domain) can be processed by the WikiFactory Application. WikiFactory application is the core of the whole framework, in charge of translating ontologies into wikis: more details about this component will be provided in 4.2. The output of WikiFactory Application is then passed to the QoS Manager in order that produces and instantiates the final wiki (or rather, B-Wiki). As we said, discussing about the QoS Manager is out of the scope of this paper: here we only describe all the components involved in the deployment of a domain-oriented wiki, by focusing on their internal architecture and interaction.

We have identified two different users (i.e., roles) who use the WikiFactory for different purposes. Note that we do not want to define a methodology associated to the use of WikiFactory, but we believe that the description of these roles can be useful to explain how the framework actually works. The identified roles are:

- the final user, we name Bianca, i.e., an inexperienced user who adds content to the domain-oriented wiki and uses the final wiki every day for carrying out her tasks;

- an expert ontology designer, we name Andrea, who analyzes the requirements of the domain expert users in order to produce an extension of the ontology for that domain;

In order to explain how users (Bianca and Andrea) use WikiFactory, to provide readers more details about the role of each internal component, and to show a concrete application of our framework, we present a case study in the next section.

Actually, many other examples of wikis deployable from an ontological description could be also mentioned. Consider for instance, a wiki supporting Public Administration tasks: given a detailed description of roles, bureaucratic steps and forms, WikiFactory can create predefined areas and services, which in turn support and guide employees through their activities on the wiki itself.

Most wikis have also been growing and developing thanks to spontaneous contribution of different users on a shared interest. In that case, an ontological approach can be exploited to build structured pages (and clusters of them), that can be authored afterwards by the users, or partially authored by an automatic process. A wiki about travel information, for example, is supposed to have some pages about the amenities, the history, the facilities, the transportation system and whatever, for each reviewed destination: the structure of such a wiki can be derived from ontological data about travelling and cities. Similarly, a wiki for a community of wine lovers can be organized in different sections and subsections, according to the ontological classification of the reviewed wines, but thousands of similar examples can be cited.

4   A Case Study: Computer Science Department

The environment of our case study is the Computer Science Department (CSD) of a university, say the University of Bologna, that manages such common university activities as teaching, research projects and locations management, and bureaucracy. The CSD can use a wiki to make content and services accessible through the Web, and to support its internal workflows. This wiki is not a generic wiki but it has internal structures, content and services specific for the University domain, that can be described by an ontology. According to our approach, the CSD domain is described by an OWL ontology named CSD-Ontology. Fig. 2 shows the use case diagram drawn by Andrea for the CSD. Notice that, these use cases do not cover all the services the CSD needs and provides the users with; however, for the purpose of our discussion we can omit some of them.

Andrea has identified three possible actors in the CSD domain: Faculty, Students, and Administrative clerks. A Faculty member uses the wiki in order to reserve classrooms and/or laboratories for lessons and exams, to take a book from the library and order new books, to upload training aids, and so on. A student can use the wiki to browse and download training aids, to enroll for an exam, and to take a book from the library. The Administrative clerk uses the wiki in order to manage funds (for example a financial plan for a specific

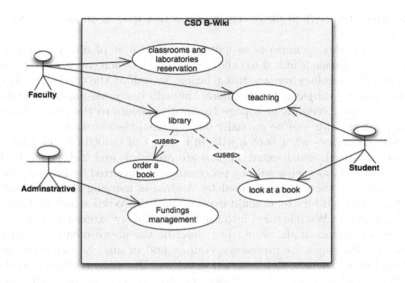

Fig. 2. The CSD Use case

research project). Let us show how such a wiki can be produced and deployed by WikiFactory.

4.1 Creating Ontologies

Any content and service mentioned so far, is delivered or implemented by a specific service of the CSD wiki. To this end, Andrea has to describe the CSD-Ontology extension for these custom wiki-services. Consider, for instance, the concepts depicted by the fragment of the CSD-Ontology shown in Fig. 3: a Professor holds a Course that is related to a specific Topic, that is, a Professor

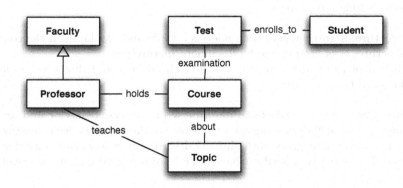

Fig. 3. The CSD-Ontology (a fragment)

teaches that Topic. A Student enrolls for a Test that is an examination for a Course.

A wiki for this scenario is supposed to have, first of all, a page for each Professor. That page is linked to other pages, one for each course thaught by the Professor (the ontology reports this relation, as well as the connection between a course and its subject). Furthermore, the wiki has some pages for managing each course, as a syllabus or a page to enroll students to the exam. Note that also this information can be partially derived from the ontology.

Andrea describes what such a wiki will consist of (which are the pages, how they are organized, which extra services are provided) and, subsequently, Wiki-Factory instantiates such a wiki by processing data inserted by Bianca (the final user). Basically, the task performed by Andrea is merging the CSD-Ontology concepts (provided him by domain experts) and the WikiFactory Ontology (already included in WikiFactory) into the CSD-Ontology extension. The ontology produced for the example, would just describe the above mentioned structure of a wiki, with pages for professors, courses and exams. As expected such an ontology follows the schema discussed in 3.1 and describes (i) the internal components of each page, (ii) the clusters of inter-connected pages and (iii) the dynamic behaviour of the wiki, when installed.

The following list briefly summarized a subset of the WikiFactory ontology concepts. Specifically the list gives an idea of the ontology and covers the concepts we need in order to describe the CSD scenario. First of all we need constructs to describe single pages:

- Topic Component: an element that composes a topic or topic template such as TextBlock, List or Table;
- Template: a set of topic components, organized according to a given structure;
- Topic: represents a page of the wiki; it consists of topic components and may or may not be associated to a template;

In order to describe clusters of pages, we need constructs to express relations and groups linked resources:

- Structure: a graph where each node is a topic and can be itself the root of a structure. It is used to model document hierarchies;
- Link: a piece of text associated to a URL address and that gives users the access to that resource;

Finally we need constructs to describe wiki services, behavior and actions. Although we are still discussing about this side of the ontology, we probably need only a construct that gives an high-level description of a service, linked with a resource that actually describes the service from a procedural perspective:

- Service: is a task performed by the wiki. The service has a reference to a resource that describes it in terms of a process.

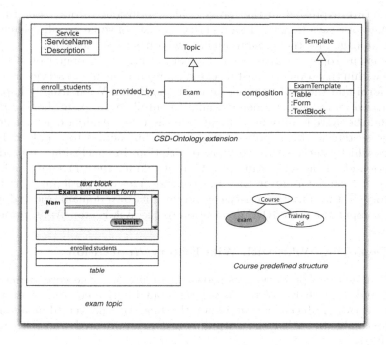

Fig. 4. The exam wiki topic

By referring to the above described fragment of the CSD-Ontology, Andrea derives the description of:

- the structure of a course: that is a predefined graph of topics (i.e., wiki pages) useful to manage content and resources related to a course (e.g. training aid, program and test enrollment);
- each topic in the structure;
- the exam enrollment service for the students.

Fig. 4 depicts the Course structure and the Exam topic definition. The structure Course represents a predefined graph of Topics related to the concept of course (when a Faculty uses the wiki he simply has to ask a new course area, and the related wiki pages are automatically created). The course structure consists of three topics: Course (the root of the structure), Exam, Training Aid. Andrea can also define constraints on the topics: for instance, he can state that the Exam topic can only exist in the context of the course structure (this means that the Exam topic cannot exist autonomously).

Moreover, Andrea can describe what each Topic consists of. For example, Exam is a topic that contains a text area, a form element, and a table element. The key aspect is that a relatively small set of Topic Component exists, that can be assembled to produce any final Topic. As we discuss in the following subsection, WikiFactory is able to produce a wiki, where any kind of page keeps the structure expressed in the ontological description. In our case study, the CSD-Ontology says that the Exam entity consists of some specific elements, so any Exam page into the domain-oriented wiki has these elements.

The exam Topic is also associated to some services, i.e. operations to be performed within this topic. For instance, the exam enrollment is a service associated to the form and the table composing the topic Exam. What usually happens is summarized as follows: a student wants to enroll to an exam, he/she fills the form and the system automatically update the table. Andrea does not describe how the system works to provide this service, but he has to simply indicate a resource which contains this workflow description. In conclusion, he produces a description of all the interesting pages into a wiki for the University and all the services that can be useful in the same context. This description is stored in the repository, so that any University can produce its own domain-oriented wiki by giving in input the same RDF description to the WikiFactoryApplication.

4.2   Deploying Wikis with Wiki Factory Application

The WikiFactory Application, as shown in Figure 5, is the core engine of the system and is in charge of producing the domain-oriented wiki. Note that at this stage the produced output is not the final B-Wiki yet (domain-oriented and Qos-enabled); rather the output is a domain-oriented wiki with no QoS capabilities.

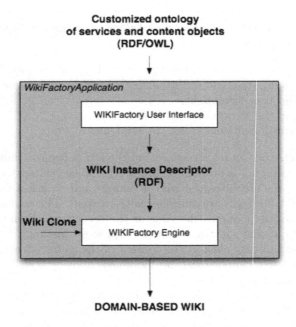

Fig. 5. The Wiki Factory Application

The actor involved in using the WikiFactory Application is Bianca, who wants to configure a wiki: from her perspective, the WikiFactory Application is a configuration tool that is being used in order to select the services the wiki will provide users and the topics it will consist of. Bianca, without having any skill about ontologies and the functioning of the wiki application, selects which wiki topics and services will be included in the final wiki installation. The internal process within the WikiFactory Application is completely transparent to Bianca, who has to simply fill in checkboxes, options and forms by means of a graphical interface.

She is first asked to select the domain, and then to choose the data to be included in the domain-oriented wiki. For instance, she indicates the name of lectures of the Department (and insert data for each of them) and the course they teach. Since the WikiFactory Application knows (from the ontology provided by Andrea) that any course has an exam, the final wiki will automatically have a page for each teacher, subsequently a page for each of his courses, and finally a page to handle the corresponding exam. Furthermore Bianca can select other services useful for the community such as forum, bullettin-boards, calendars.

What Bianca perceives as a simple task of selecting services, structures and topics and filling them with relevant data, is actually supported by a complex process within the WikiFactory Application. This aspect is worth being remarked: our framework is designed to minimize the effort required to the users, by hiding the complexity of the internal system components. The interface used by Bianca is not only usable but, most of all, it is customized for a specific domain: she does not have to learn a different formalism to express content and relations; neither has she to handle ontologies and wikis. Indeed, the WikiFactory Application, by taking in input the ontological description provided by Andrea, will dynamically present her a simple and transparent interface.

Note that our approach does not damage the easy-to-use approach of wikis, rather it does strenghten its power. The final output of WikiFactory, in fact, remains a wiki where users can keep on accessing and taking advantages from such systems (actually, being the application completely independent from the platform where content will be deployed, users can keep on using their preferred softwares too). What really changes is the process of authoring repeatable fragments, pages and clusters of pages which becomes simpler and faster, since some manual, error-prone and time-consuming actions are replaced by a simple selection of features and insertion of data.

In order to be processed within the system, the data inserted by Bianca have to be transformed into something closer to the wiki concepts (she does not describe them in terms of wiki objects, but as information). An intermediary output of the whole process is a Wiki Instance Descriptor. The Wiki Instance Descriptor is a description of what Bianca has selected and filled with data. There is a difference between a Wiki Instance Descriptor produced by Bianca and the extended ontology produced by Andrea: while the latter describes all the elements and services available in a given domain, the first describes only content and services selected by the Department of Computer Science. Another user like Bianca working in a different department inserts data of different teachers and exams and probably selects different services. The RDF description stored in the Repository specifies what a wiki for the University can contain, while the Wiki Instance Descriptor says what the wiki of the Department of Computer Science actually contains.

In other words, the Wiki Instance Descriptor gives a high-level description of the outgoing wiki. The final step performed by the WikiFactory Application, in particular by a sub-component we termed WikiFactory Engine, is to map such a description into a specific wiki-clone. WikiFactory Application, in fact, does not produce a new wiki-clone, but customizes some of the existing wiki-clones in order to provide the same functionalities. The goal is not to produce another brother of TWiki [15] or Purple [11] UseMod [8], but to use (if necessary, by extending) each of them. In our case study, after having inserted data, Bianca is asked to select a specific wiki-clone on which the outcoming domain-oriented wiki will be installed.

The solution we propose relies on a strong assumption: it is possible to identify a set of basic wiki services and content elements available in any wiki-clone that compose the final pages. Any wiki-page, in fact, can be segmented into a number of objects like paragraphs, tables, lists and so on, although any clone uses its own syntax and constructs pages can be easily generated from an high-level description. Also the services can be combined in order to obtain more complex services and features. By having an abstract definition of each basic service and by knowing how they can be combined into a more complex one, the WikiFactory Engine actually transforms a Wiki Instance Descriptor into a wiki instance. We are investigating rules and patterns to decompose wiki services and a language to be used.

5   Concluding Remarks and Future Works

Wikis are a new and exciting technology whose applications are wide and extremely innovative. On the other hand, before organizations can reliably start using them for large scale applications, wikis need to improve on the limitations that the current implementations suffer from.

We have identified two key issues in wikis: on the one hand, support for automatic generation and maintenance of domain-oriented content and structures, and on the other hand specification of quality of service parameters that are honored by wiki applications to provide guarantees of scalability and availability of the provided services and content. In this paper we have investigated the automatic deployment of a domain-oriented wiki taking in input ontological description of the domain. The development of web applications according to ontologies, with examples taken from the description of a university department, has been already described in [5]. Moving off such analysis, we have designed a modular framework based on Semantic Web technologies that aims at creating a semantic wiki, minimizing users' effort.

Preliminary implementations of many of the described modules exist and have been tested independently but we are currently investigating on the integrability of these intermediate results.

WikiFactory is a lively ongoing project, whose content and results have only been sketched in this paper. More detailed and up-to-date results can be always found in its web site, justifiably enough a wiki itself, at the address http://swe.web.cs.unibo.it/WikiFactory/.

Acknowledgements

We wish to thank our colleagues Giorgia Lodi and Andrea Ceccanti who work on the Quality of Service aspects of WikiFactory and help us with interesting and fruitful discussions about the whole project. We also wish to thank the Prof. Fabio Panzieri of University of Bologna and our colleague Jaksa Vuckovic for their precious comments and suggestions on earlier versions of this paper.

References

1. Maedche A., Staab S., Stojanovic N., Studer R., and Sure Y. A Framework for Developing SEmantic portALs. In *18th British National Conference on Databases*, Oxford, UK, July 2001. LNCS Springer Verlag.
2. Souzis A. Rhizome position paper. In *Proceedings of the 1st Workshop on Friend of a Friend, Social Networking and the Semantic Web*, September 2004.
3. Berners-Lee T., Hendler J., and Lassila O. The Semantic Web. *The scientific american*, 2001.
4. Chris Purcell. Periperi. http://www.srcf.ucam.org/ cjp39/Peri/PeriPeri.
5. P. Ciancarini and V. Presutti. Towards Ontology Driven Software Design. In M. Wirsing, S. Balsamo, and A. Knapp, editors, *Proc. 8th "Monterey Workshop": Radical Innovations of Software and Systems Engineering in the Future*, pages 158–168, Venice, Italy, October 2002.
6. Portland community. Portland Pattern Repository's Wiki. http://www.c2.com/cgi/wiki?WelcomeVisitors.
7. Aumueller David. Semantic authoring and retrieval within a Wiki. In *Demos and Posters of the 2nd European Semantic Web Conference (ESWC 2005)*, Heraklion, Greece, May 2005.
8. Herman. Moin Moin Wiki. http://twistedmatrix.com/users/jh.twistd/moin/moin.cgi/.
9. JotSpot Inc. Jotspot beta: the application wiki. http://www.jotspot.com/.
10. Jugel Matthias L. and Schmidt Stephan J. Snipsnap: the easy weblog and wiki software. http://www.snipsnap.org/space/.
11. Kim E. E. Purplewiki. http://purplewiki.blueoxen.net/cgi-bin/wiki.pl.
12. Daniel Kinzler. SemperWiki: a semantic personal Wiki. In *The Semantic Desktop - Next Generation Personal Information Management and Collaboration Infrastructure at the International Semantic Web Conference*, Galway, Ireland, November 2005.
13. Daniel Kinzler. WikiSense Mining the Wiki. In *Proceedings of Wikimania 2005*, Frankfurt, Germany, August 2005.

14. Krotzch Markus, Denny Vrandecic, and Max Volkel. Wikipedia and the Semantic Web The Missing Links. In *Proceedings of Wikimania 2005*, Frankfurt, Germany, August 2005.
15. Thoeny P. TWiki: Enterprise Collaboration Platform. http://twiki.org.
16. Palmer Sean B. Rdfwiki. http://infomesh.net/2001/rdfwiki/.
17. Platypus Wiki. The Semantic Wiki Wiki Web. http://platypuswiki.sourceforge.net/.
18. The Protégé Ontology Editor and Knowledge Acquisition System. http://protege.stanford.edu.
19. Pytypus Home Page. http://www.pytypus.org/.
20. Benjamins V. R., Fensel D., Decker S., and Perez A.G. KA2: Building Ontologies for the Internet: a Mid Term Report. *International Journal of Human-Computer Studies*, (51):687–712, March 1999.
21. Staab S., Angele J., Decker S., Erdmann M., Hotho A., Maedche A., Schnurr H., Studer R., and Sure Y. Semantic Community Web Portals. In *Proceedings of the 9th International World Wide Web Conference*, pages 1–6, Amsterdam, May 2000. ACM.
22. Staab S. and Studer R. Ontology-based Content Management in a Virtual Organization. *Handbook on Ontologies*, pages 687–712, 2003.
23. Semantic Wiki Wiki Web. http://c2.com/cgi/wiki?SemanticWikiWikiWeb.
24. Wiki Wiki Web. Cunningham and Cunningham Inc. http://c2.com.
25. Wikipedia. Wikipedia Home Page. http://www.wikipedia.org.
26. World Wide Web Consortium. OWL Web Ontology Languagefamily of specifications. http://www.w3.org/2004/OWL/, 2004.
27. World Wide Web Consortium. RDF Resourcs Description Framework family of specifications. http://www.w3.org/RDF/, 2004.
28. World66. World66 home. http://www.world66.com/.
29. Jin Y., Xu S., and Decker S. Ontowebber: Model-driven ontology-based web site management. In *Proceedings of SWWS'01, The first Semantic Web Working Symposium*, California, USA, July 30 - August 1 2001.

Using Semantics to Enhance the Blogging Experience

Knud Möller, Uldis Bojārs, and John G. Breslin

Digital Enterprise Research Institute, National University of Ireland, Galway
{knud.moeller, uldis.bojars, john.breslin}@deri.org

Abstract. Blogging, as a subset of the web as a whole, can benefit greatly from the addition of semantic metadata. The result — which we will call *Semantic Blogging* — provides improved capabilities with respect to search, connectivity and browsing compared to current blogging technology. Moreover, Semantic Blogging will allow new ways of convenient data exchange between the actors within the blogosphere — blog authors and blog users alike. This paper identifies *structural* and *content-related* metadata as the kinds of semantic metadata which are relevant in the domain of blogging. We present in detail the nature of these two kinds of metadata, and discuss an implementation for creating such metadata in a convenient and unobtrusive way for the user, how to publish it on the web, and how to best make use of it from the point of view of a blog consumer.

1 Introduction

Blogs (or weblogs) [19] are online journals or diaries, created by people to express personal or professional views on their world or on observed items that may be of interest to others. Blogs are updated habitually by their creators and are usually presented in reverse chronological order. There are several popular blogging software publishing tools available at present including Movable Type, WordPress, Blogger and LiveJournal.

Howevever, these blogging tools lack the means to add any formal semantics to the blog posts, apart from fixed category topics or free-text keyword tags. Therefore blogs, and the posts that they contain, lack sufficient semantic information regarding the topics that they are talking about or how the current topic under discussion relates to previous blog discussion threads. By augmenting blog posts with machine interpretable metadata, novel ways of both querying and navigating blog information become possible. Metadata about a blog or blog post can be classified as belonging to one of two domains, which we call i) *structure* and ii) *content*. Augmenting a blog with structural and content metadata, as well as the new possibilities which arise from that, is called *Semantic Blogging* [5].

Structure generally speaking refers to the form of a blog. *Structural metadata* identifies and describes things such as the individual parts of a blog (i.e. posts, comments, ...) and their relations, as well as relations between blogs or posts from separate blogs (or any other kind of structured publishing platform).

Y. Sure and J. Domingue (Eds.): ESWC 2006, LNCS 4011, pp. 679–696, 2006.

680   K. Möller, U. Bojārs, and J.G. Breslin

Complementing structural metadata is *content metadata*, which describes the topic of a blog post — what the post is *about* — e.g. a person, an event, a publication or a webpage. The specific form of content metadata depends on the nature of the topic described. If the topic is a person the blog post talks about, then the metadata for this topic would be that person's name, contact details, etc. If it is an upcoming meeting, then the metadata would be the start and end time, location, etc.

1.1   Example Scenario

Consider the following blogging scenario, as it would probably take place using current web and blogging technology:

Person *A* works in a research group at a university. One day *A*'s supervisor Prof. Gyro Gearloose tells him that he will give a presentation later that week. *A* writes the following post in his blog: *"On friday, 15h there will be a presentation on martian numismatics by Gyro in Room 205. He also wrote an interesting paper on the subject recently, in case you want to read up on it."* He adds links to an official page announcing the event and to Prof. Gearloose's paper.

B comes across *A*'s post on the web. She thinks it's interesting and mentions it in her own blog: *"I read about this really interesting presentation on martian numismatics! I wonder how this relates to cytherian heraldics, so I will definitely go."*

C, being an avid reader of *B*'s blog, decides he also wants to go to this presentation. However, *B* didn't mention any details about the event, and even neglected to provide a link back to *A*'s original post. To get the information he wants, *C* now has to search for "martian numismatics" on the web. With some luck, he finds *A*'s post. He manually enters the details for the presentation into his calendaring application, so that he will be alerted ahead of the event. Also, because he is currently writing his PhD thesis on martian numismatics, *C* downloads the paper and adds the bibliographic details to a database of papers he keeps on his computer. After some searching on the web he finds out that "Gyro" actually refers to Prof. Gyro Gearloose, finds his homepage and enters the professors contact details into his electronic addressbook, in case he has some more questions on the topic.

While, in this scenario, all three participants eventually get where they want, it is a long road and requires a lot of searching and manual copying of data, especially for *C*. In the ideal world, where the Web has become the Semantic Web and Blogging has become Semantic Blogging, the scenario would look slightly different: Aided by a semantic blogging system, *A* would attach formal semantic metadata about the presentation (where, when, what, who, ...), Prof. Gearloose (e.g. his contact details) and his paper (bibliographic details) to his blog post. When *B* writes about *A*'s post, she would add structural metadata, indicating that this is a reply to some other post, as well as where to find this post. Finally, *C* would easily get from *B*'s post to *A*'s post, by navigating the follow-up structure which is made accessible through structural metadata. From there, he would simply import the semantic metadata into his own desktop applications, without having to search for and copy them manually. Spinning the story further, C might even have been able to get the metadata directly from B's post (because it is a reply to the original post). Furthermore, another person, let's call her D, who is a fan of Prof. Gearloose, would have been able to find A's post directly, by performing a conceptual search for upcoming presentations by Prof. Gearloose, making use of the semantic metadata that is now available within the blogosphere.

1.2   Problems and Solution Formulation

As illustrated by the previous example, the current blogging experience suffers from the fact that there is little or no semantic metadata available in blogs. The topic of a blog post is never made explicit in a machine-interpretable way (with the exception of flat category or tagging systems).

The RSS family (e.g. RDF Site Summary (RSS1.0)[1]) and similar newsfeed technologies are the most popular method for syndicating blog posts or obtaining metadata about a blog's internal structure. Syndication allows the copying of one blog's content into another blog (or into a news reader or aggregator). However, these technologies are limited to basic concepts such as title, description and date as well as a fixed number of the most recently-published blog posts.

In the Semantic Web, meaning can be derived from blogs in a number of ways if advanced blog features are modelled in an ontology and blog data instances are then provided using this ontology. By utilising the existing SIOC[2] (Semantically-Interlinked Online Communities) ontology [2], which was designed to describe a variety of online discussion methods including blogs, we can export more metadata from a server about the internal structure of blog posts. By deriving as much metadata from the underlying blog data stores as possible, connections between concepts can be maintained in a machine-interpretable format for future re-use. Posts on a blog can be linked to their comments, by defining reply connections in either or both directions. The posts can also be linked to the user account that created them, and links between related posts within the blog can be made.

Interlinking within the blogosphere is currently mainly composed of untyped links between posts and users, as well as trackbacks (a manually created link from one blog post to another, external blog post) and blog rolls (lists of other blogs which a blog author wants to point out). However, trackbacks and blog rolls are limited in that there is no information available on why such a link was created: if the posts are on a related topic; if the original poster is a friend of the referencing poster; if the referencing user agrees or disagrees with the original post; etc.

By using SIOC to materialize the internal structure and also connections between blogs in the global blogosphere, we can harness data across blogs and blogging platforms in new ways. Similar blogs may be linked together, either through explicit links or implicitly through the posts and comments that they

---

[1] http://purl.org/rss/1.0/spec
[2] http://rdfs.org/sioc/

contain and the users that created them. Posts may have related posts on other sites, and using SIOC, bidirectional trackback links can be created from the original post to the follow-up. A set of posts can also be formed if they share the same topic resource, or if the topic resources are mapped to each other. Posts and comments by the same user or group of users can be tracked across different blogs. Threaded discussions can be merged or split across blog sites by identifying remote child or parent posts. Most importantly, SIOC is not limited to blog discussions: blog posts or comments can also be related to similar forum threads, Usenet newsgroup postings or mailing list messages if they have been made available using the SIOC ontology.

1.3   Paper Overview

This paper will detail how we can overcome some of the limitations outlined in Sect. 1.1 and how the blogging experience can be augmented using Semantic Web technologies. We will detail in Sect. 2 how both a blog's content and structure can be described using a number of ontologies. Section 3 will describe the creation steps for this content and structure metadata from a client's desktop and blogging platform's web server respectively. The publishing methods for the content-related and structural metadata are detailed in Sect. 4, and Sect. 5 will then show how the metadata can be utilised and consumed by Semantic Web applications such as an RDF browser or enhanced blog reader. Section 6 will be a review of related work in this area, and finally in Sect. 7 we will outline how our work can be further enhanced through custom semantic browsing and querying applications.

2   Metadata

Metadata in the blogosphere formally describes a blog and its individual posts. These descriptions are essentially typed assertions about relations between the blog, its posts, authors, other web-resources — or just about anything that can be specified using some unique identifier (specifically, a Uniform Resource Identifier (URI)). The two following sections will in turn look at *structural* and *content-related* metadata.

As regards the choice of metadata format, we suggest the use of the Resource Description Format (RDF) as the model for making blog metadata explicit. RDF's graph model makes it much better suited to represent complex objects and relations than the simpler tree structure of XML. Furthermore, since RDF does not impose any specific schema on a given graph and uses URIs as its sole identification scheme, it allows us to integrate data from various sources and conforming to various ontologies or vocabularies. This is especially important with respect to content-related metadata, which can originate from arbitrary sources and be expressed using arbitrary vocabularies. Also, both structural and content-related metadata may well come from different sources and eventually need to be integrated, in order to form a complete graph of blog metadata.

2.1   Structure

As mentioned in the solution formulation, we have chosen SIOC as the ontology for making instances of blog and post structure available. This ontology is described using RDF Schema (RDFS), and instance data is made available in RDF.

Blog Concepts in SIOC. The classes in the SIOC ontology of relevance to blogs are `Site`, `Forum`, `Post`, `User` and `Usergroup`, and the main properties linking these classes are shown in Fig. 1.

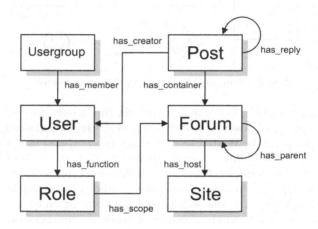

Fig. 1. Main Terms in the SIOC Ontology

`Site` is the location of an online community or set of communities, and in the context of blogs, it will house one or many blogs. This concept is useful since we can assign a user as the administrator of a site, having moderator control over all blogs hosted at that site.

`Forum` can be thought of as a channel or discussion area on which posts are made. In the context of blogs, it is a single blog channel. A forum is linked to the site that hosts it. Blog owners can moderate other user's replies to their own blog posts. Blogs may also have a set of subscribed users who are notified when new posts are made.

`Post` is an article or message posted by a user to a blog. A series of posts may be threaded if they share a common subject and are connected by reply (within a site) or trackback (between sites) relationships.

`User` is an online account belonging to a person who is a member of a community site, such as a blogging area. They are connected to blog posts that they create or edit, to blogs that they can post to or have subscribed to, to blog sites that they administer, and to other users that they know. Users can be organised in a `Usergroup` to control post access to blog areas.

Making Post Connections. One of the main use cases for SIOC import involves connecting related post entries between blogs and community sites. Adding SIOC data to posts would open up the connection possibilities as depicted in Fig. 2. Some of these will now be described.

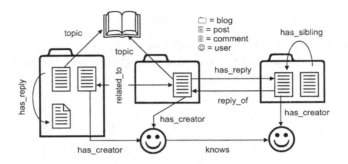

Fig. 2. Structural Relations in the Blogosphere

One of the limitations of trackbacks is that the link is only created in one direction, i.e. from an original post to a referencing post. Using the `related_to` property of SIOC, two posts can be related to each other (and others) in both directions. Apart from an explicit linking of posts, there are other methods of linking blog posts using SIOC, for example, if they share a common topic, creator or container.

A recent development in online discussion methods is an article or post that appears in multiple blogs, or has been copied from one forum to another relevant forum. In SIOC, we can treat these copies of posts as siblings of each other if we think of the posts as non-identical twins that share most characteristics but differ in some manner. For example, a post is created on one blog and categorised with the topic "TV", but has been copied to another blog with multiple topics such as "Sci-Fi" or "Art". We can avoid duplication of common data in the creation of siblings by linking to the new sibling, the instance of which only contains the changed properties (in the example, the properties `has_container` and `topic` would change). A number of blog engines support blogging in multiple languages. This leads to multi-language blogs, where the same post can have translations in two or more languages. Related posts across multiple blogs and community sites may also be in different languages. The `has_sibling` property in SIOC can be used for linking these multiple versions or related posts together, with a locale property (with values such as `en` or `fr_CA`) illustrating what language the respective sibling posts are in.

The SIOC ontology allows us to annotate blog posts with topic metadata, allowing the matching of documents on specific topics with each other. While it may be more difficult to require a user to assign a topic to a post at creation time, it is more likely that a forum will have an associated topic or set of topics that can be propagated to the posts it contains. In order to define a topic or category hierarchy, we propose to use the SKOS framework [1] and create mappings between these concepts and a common category system.

2.2   Content

Content-relatad metadata describes anything a blog-author wishes to converse about — people, events, books, music, etc. In other words, content metadata covers a very broad domain, especially when compared to the rather specific domain of structural metadata. The exact nature of the metadata will therefore vary significantly between posts: metadata about people might contain their names, homepage or contact-details, a paper might be described in terms of its publisher, title, etc., and an event will have properties such as a start and end time, an organizer, etc. Thus, while it is feasible to define a specific set of concepts and properties to express the whole domain of blog *structure*, it is difficult and problematic to define and establish an ontology to cover all possible blog *content*. Therefore, we propose the use of small, vertical ontologies or vocabularies to describe blog content. Each of these ontologies only covers a certain kind of content, such as people, publications or events. Ideally, one will use ontologies which are already established and widely used — searching, finding and interlinking blog content will then be much easier. In the following paragraphs we will present a number of such small ontologies. All of them are open, well tested and widely used in their respective domain.

FOAF and vCard. The Friend of a Friend (FOAF) Project [3] is developing and maintining an RDFS ontology to describe people, mainly from the point of view of an addressbook context — a person's name, address, phone number, homepage, etc. The name of the ontology stems from the fact that FOAF also has a means to express whom a person knows, who their friends are. This is achieved by relating one `foaf:Person` instance to another via the `foaf:knows` property. In this way a huge, decentralized network of people — or friends of friends of friends — is established. In a lot of aspects, FOAF is very close to the vCard [7] vocabulary, which covers a similiar domain. While vCard doesn't have the networking capabilities of FOAF, it allows for more detail with respect to specifying addresses. Both ontologies are often used together. vCard is not usually expressed in RDF, but a W3C note exists for representing vCard Objects in RDF/XML[3].

BibTeX. BibTeX [16] is a format for expressing bibliographic metadata, mainly for scientific publications. It is very well integrated in, but otherwise independent from the LaTeX system for typesetting. Publications are classified according to types such as *Proceedings*, *Book* or *Article*, and further specified using attributes such as *author*, *title* or *year*, depending on the type of the publication. Like vCard, BibTeX has its own non-RDF representation format, but several implementations in RDF-based ontologies like Semantic Web for Research Communities (SWRC)[4].

---

[3] `http://www.w3.org/TR/vcard-rdf`
[4] `http://ontoware.org/projects/swrc/`

iCalendar. iCalendar [8] is an open format for the specification and exchange of event metadata, or, more specifically, calendaring and scheduling data. The iCalendar format has recently gained some attention in the public through Apple's *iCal* calendaring application — hoewever, even though iCal is built on top of the iCalendar format, the two are completely independent of each other. Similar to the vCard and BibTeX formats, iCalendar precedes the definition of RDF and has its own representation format. However, a W3C workspace[5] exists that is committed to providing an RDF implementation of iCalendar, as well as a number of tools to provide automatic conversion.

3   Creation Stage

In the previous section we have described the kind of metadata that would be beneficial to find, search for and interlink information from blogs and other resources on the web. In this section, we are going to discuss how such metadata are created. A general requirement for any system that involves the use of metadata is, that the generation of metadata must involve as little work for the user as possible. If Semantic Blogging meant that a blog author had to manually type some RDF/XML code each time they wanted to blog about anything, it would never be adopted beyond a small group of technologically minded people. Even the use of forms to enter metadata would still be far too labour-intensive for Semantic Blogging to achieve any significant impact. Instead, as discussed in Jim Hendler's fundamental article [10], metadata should be generated automatically or semi-automatically while the user performs ordinary tasks they would perform anyway, or even completely without the involvement of the user.

Due to the different nature of structural and content metadata, different strategies have to be applied, as will be discussed in the rest of this section. The strategies we intend to adopt for both kinds of metadata are rooted in previous work done by the authors of this paper.

3.1   Structure

Blogs are usually small scale systems consisting of one or more contributors and a community of readers, but their power lies in the large amount of blog data that is available for harvesting. Most blog engines already have RSS export functionality. Since the majority of these blog engines are based on open source software, it is straightforward to modify existing export functions to generate SIOC metadata conforming to the SIOC ontology. In order to retrieve full structural metadata we need to use more of the information available to the blog engine. We have created a plugin for the WordPress blog engine that uses the functions provided by this engine to access its database and export a full set of structural metadata using the SIOC ontology.

The WordPress SIOC plugin[6] exports information about the main blog data entities — including data about the weblog itself, users creating content, posts

---

[5] http://www.w3.org/2002/12/cal/
[6] http://rdfs.org/sioc/wordpress/

and comments that these users have created, topics of these posts and other internal and external structural metadata.

SIOC metadata for blog posts consists of a `sioc:Post` resource and its properties. A URI used to identify the blog post is generated by the blog engine (and is identical to its physical URL). In Table 1 we provide details of the various mappings between entities in WordPress and SIOC metadata, while the central properties used to express the structure of a blog post are described in Table 2.

Table 1. Mappings of WordPress Concepts to SIOC

Weblog info ->	`sioc:Site`, `sioc:Forum`, `sioc:Usergroup`
Author ->	`sioc:User`
Posts ->	`sioc:Post`
Comments ->	`sioc:Post` linked to by `sioc:reply`

Table 2. Properties of `sioc:Post`

`sioc:has_creator`	links a post to a user that created it
`sioc:title`	contains title of the post
`sioc:created_at`	creation date and time
`sioc:content`	contents of the post
`sioc:topic`	indicates topics or content of the post
`sioc:has_reply`	links a post to its replies and comments

Additionally, the SIOC properties `related_to` and `links_to` are used to make the connections between posts explicit. Information about resources the post links to is extracted from the post's body and expressed using the `links_to` property (this might be as simple as collecting hyperlinks within the post). The `related_to` property is used to store and reuse links to related articles that are inferred by consumers of SIOC data.

Finally, the WordPress SIOC plugin also creates `rdfs:seeAlso` links, which point consumers of RDF data to additional machine-interpretable metadata (e.g. created by a tool like semiBlog [14]).

3.2 Content

As discussed in Sec. 2.2, metadata which describes the content of a post can span over a wide range of domains: metadata about people, events, publications, music, etc. Our previous work on the *semiBlog* blog authoring environment has shown how reusing existing desktop data can be a successful strategy for generating content-related semantic metadata for such a variety of domains. One of the central assumptions is that bloggers will often already have metadata about the topics of their blog available on their desktop[7]. A blog author who blogs about a person will probably already have an entry for that person in

---

[7] We use the term *desktop* as a metaphor for the entire working environment within a user's computer.

their electronic addressbook, someone who blogs about an upcoming event will have this event in their calendaring application, a researcher blogging about an interesting paper might have a BibTEX-entry of this paper available. While a blog author composes a new blog post, the data that already exists in some form on their desktop will be automatically transformed into an RDF graph using an appropriate ontology or vocabulary. E.g., an addressbook entry would be transformed into FOAF, while an event from a calendaring application would be transformed into iCalendar-RDF. The resulting metadata is then attached, turning an ordinary blog post into a semantic blog post.

Reusing metadata from a blog author's desktop in an easy and unobtrusive way requires convenient access to this data. This can best be ensured if the blog authoring environment is implemented as a desktop application. The authoring environment can then e.g. make use of public APIs of the various applications that provide data (electronic addressbook, calendaring application, bibliographic database, etc.), access the system-wide pasteboard for easy drag-and-drop of complex data from these applications or make use of the index of a metadata-enabled file system. For completeness sake, we should note that a desktop-based implementation has disadvantages such as requiring a manual install, possibly being tied to one desktop or even operating system, etc.

In the case of semiBlog, application developers can develop plugins for various data sources. Each plugin can accept data from a specific source and knows how to transform it from its proprietary, application-specific source format into a set of RDF triples. This is illustrated in Fig. 3.

A user can write his blog in semiBlog as they would in any other, non-semantic authoring environment: the application allows to create new posts, write and format text and add pictures. The blog author can then annotate his entry by dragging objects from other applications onto the post in semiBlog. The relevant

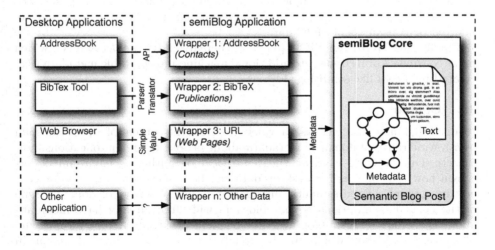

Fig. 3. Creating content metadata from desktop applications

plugins convert the incoming data and produce equivalent RDF graphs. Finally, these will be merged into one bigger graph, which contains the content-related metadata for the complete post.

Naming the Metadata. An interesting general problem arises in the creation stage of content-related metadata: when generating metadata from desktop objects, semiBlog is essentially creating RDF resources which represent the topics of a blog post. E.g., when the post discusses a person A, semiBlog will create a resource which represents A. Each such resource can be assigned a URI to make it uniquely identifiable. URIs ensure that data from various sources can be integrated, since resources with the same URI will be considered identical. The problem, however, is that semiBlog cannot know which URI to choose for each resource it creates — it is not obvious what the URI of any given thing in the world is. We have identified three general naming strategies:

- *Random URI* - Generating a random URI by using a Universally Unique IDentifier (UUID) generator algorithm, e.g. [13]. This is the easiest solution and also the one currently employed by semiBlog. However, it breaks the idea that resources which represent the same real world object have the same URI, since different semiBlog instances would create different URIs. Explicit `owl:sameAs` statements could still identify equality, however, this equality would first have to be inferred in some way. A solution might be rules or heuristics such as the inverse functional property `mbox` used in FOAF, which determines that instances of `foaf:Person` which have the same values for `foaf:mbox` are considered equal.
- *Desktop URI* - Internally semiBlog uses URIs to identify objects on the desktop, from which the semantic metadata will be generated. However, these URIs identify information items, and not the real-world entities which are described by these, and are therefore not used externally.
- *URI authority* - Instead of deciding itself, semiBlog could gather as much information as possible about the resource in question, and forward it to some external service. This service can then determine the URI on the basis of the given information. However, since such a service doesn't exist at the moment, this approach is also not an option.

Even though approaches such as the 'tag' URI scheme[8], which is "designed to be unique across space and time while being tractable to humans", may prove useful for naming resources, they don't fully solve the problem we are facing: an application such as semiBlog would still not be able to figure out which tag URI to use for a given desktop object.

4   Publishing Stage

Publishing is the stage where semantic metadata is made available to the world, e.g. to a human reader who is accessing the blog through a browser, or an

---

[8] http://www.faqs.org/rfcs/rfc4151.html

automatic agent which is looking for RDF on the web. The following sections will first briefly describe how content-related metadata generated by semiBlog is prepared and sent to an arbitrary blogging platform. Then we will illustrate how the WordPress SIOC plugin can be used to automatically integrate this data with the structural metadata it produced on a WordPress[9] installation.

4.1 Preparing Content Metadata

The general strategy for publishing content-related semantic metadata produced with the semiBlog application is very simple: a link is created for each object with which the blog author annotated his post. The link points to some location on the web where the RDF metadata about this object can be found. All links are then added to the bottom of the HTML code of the post and typed as mime-type `application/rdf+xml`, so that they can be recognized and picked up by specialized crawlers (e.g. by the WordPress SIOC plugin, see Sec. 4.2). One major advantage of our approach is that a blog user is not restricted in his choice of a blogging engine, since it is irrelevant whether or not it accepts upload of RDF or any method for publishing metadata at all. In fact, the blogging platform won't even know it just received a semantic blog post — as far as it is concerned, it only received some HTML code. What is necessary, however, is that semiBlog has access to *some* service that can accept and publish RDF (such as an RDF repository like YARS [9]), which it would then link to. An example of a post with added metadata within the WordPress blogging platform can be seen in the screenshot in Fig. 4.

Fig. 4. Screenshot of a blog post with links to attached metadata

Different blogging platforms require different methods of programmatic access for inserting new posts or change existing ones. Some wide-spread methods

---

[9] `http://wordpress.org/`

are XML Remote Procedure Call (XML-RPC)[10] based APIs like the MetaWeblog API[11] and the MovableType API[12], or Blogger's Atom API[13]. semiBlog acknowledges this situation by offering plugin interfaces for publishing blog content (three different interfaces for text, metadata and media content). Application developers can implement these interfaces for any access method they would like to use.

4.2   Integration with Structural Metadata

In the following paragraphs we will show step by step how a blog post enriched with content-related metadata is transferred to a WordPress installation, where it is automatically integrated with the structural metadata produced by the WordPress SIOC plugin.

1. After producing the metadata, semiBlog uploads it to an external service which can receive and publish RDF. This service will provide semiBlog with a URL where this specific piece of metadata is available. Depending on the nature of this service, these URLs could point to files which contain RDF code, or could be complex queries which will return a view on an RDF repository such as YARS.
2. semiBlog adds links to these URLs to the blog post and transfers it to the WordPress installation, using the MetaWeblogAPI through XML-RPC.
3. When activated (by requesting data from a specific PHP script), the SIOC plugin in the WordPress engine will derive SIOC metadata about the desired post from the blog engine (its database and internal logic).
4. As a part of this process, the plugin will extract the URLs of the content metadata from the post's body and link to them using `rdfs:seeAlso` statements. Using `rdfs:seeAlso` is common practice to indicate additional information to a given resource, and allows consumers of the SIOC data to include the metadata provided by semiBlog.
5. The result is a combined graph of structural and content metadata, as illustrated in Fig. 5.

Thus the SIOC plugin integrates all metadata about a blog post and acts as a bridge between the data generated by semiBlog and users of RDF data that would not examine a blog post's body looking for additional *content metadata*. This allows semiBlog to be generic and work with any blog engine, while at the same time it provides an extended functionality if the blog is hosted on a blog engine that has a SIOC export capability.

---

[10] http://www.xmlrpc.com/
[11] http://www.xmlrpc.com/metaWeblogApi
[12] http://www.sixapart.com/movabletype
[13] http://code.blogger.com/archives/atom-docs.html

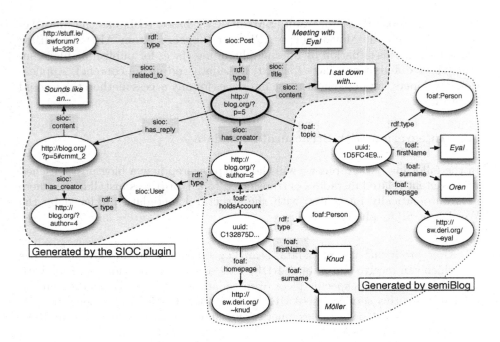

Fig. 5. A combined SIOC and semiBlog graph

5   Consuming Stage

Once semantic metadata has been attached to a blog and made available, there
are a number of ways to consume and make use of this data. We will outline
some scenarios in this section.

5.1   The Semantic Web as a Clipboard

We have suggested that content-related metadata can be generated by accessing
existing desktop data and transforming it into RDF. This can be made to work
both ways, as it has been shown in [15]. Using a metadata-aware blog reader,
a user can detect metadata attached to a blog post, and import it into his own
desktop applications in the way the author had exported it before. This kind
of data exchange through a blog could also be described as using the web as
a clipboard, and would be very useful as a communication channel within any
kind of organizational context.

5.2   Crawling and Browsing the Metadata

Having annotated blog entries with semantic metadata enables the collection,
querying and browsing of this information and the blog entries it describes. First
we collect metadata, and mirror it in an RDF store, where it will be indexed and

probably be enriched with data from other sources. This data can then be used by semantic applications built on top the RDF store. Cf. [2] for a closer look at this scenario.

Crawling. The SIOC plugin provides an auto-discovery link, which functions as a starting point for RDF crawlers and applications by indicating where to find RDF data about the blog or a particular post:

```
<link rel="meta" type="application/rdf+xml" title="SIOC"
      href="http://blog.org/wp-sioc.php"/>
```

The metadata is then collected by an RDF crawler that recursively traverses `rdfs:seeAlso` and similar links and submits the data into the RDF store. The following steps illustrate in more detail how the crawler works in our case:

1. Use auto-discovery hints to find the URL where the SIOC plugin has published RDF data.
2. Collect RDF data provided directly by the SIOC plugin.
3. Recursively traverse `rdfs:seeAlso` links to crawl RDF data provided by semiBlog or other sources.
4. Submits data into an RDF data store (e.g. YARS).

Query and Browsing. The metadata in the RDF store can then be queried directly using a RDF query language such as N3QL[14] or SPARQL[15], and be displayed in browser applications that are capable of rendering the raw metadata in a form better suited for human users. We have created the prototype of a node browser, which displays the content and structural metadata stored in the RDF store, showing the links between blog posts and the things they are describing and allowing to navigate these connections by exploiting the RDF graph model. The browser is still under development, but available for testing online[16].

6   Related Work

So-called folksonomies or community-based tagging systems such as Technorati[17] or del.icio.us[18] provide a simple yet effective way of adding content-related metadata to blogs (and web pages in general). However, this flat and string-based metadata clearly lacks the expressive power of an RDF based solution.

A number of recent papers have specifically investigated the topic of Semantic Blogging from different angles. [11] discuss a semantic blogging prototype built on top of the Semantic Web browser Haystack [17]. The authors interpret blog entries mainly as annotations of other blog entries and web resources in general,

---

[14] http://www.w3.org/DesignIssues/N3QL.html
[15] http://www.w3.org/TR/rdf-sparql-query/
[16] http://rdfs.org/sioc/browser
[17] http://www.technorati.com/
[18] http://del.icio.us

and devise a platform to realise this in terms of the Semantic Web. The paper also underlines the inherent semantic structure of blogs and their entries as such, and presents a way of formalizing these semantics. [4] puts a strong emphasis on the use of semantic technologies to enhance the possibilities of blog consumption, by allowing viewing, navigation and querying with respect to semantics. The paper describes a prototype for both creation and browsing of semantic blogs. While the prototype only deals with bibliographic metadata as annotations to blog entries, the authors point out that the same technologies can be used for any kind of metadata. [18] describes a platform called Semblog. Metadata such as FOAF descriptions of blog authors are linked to their blogs through the blog's RSS1.0 feed. In this way, the blog as a whole is annotated with metadata about its author. On a more fine-grained level individual blog entries are classified by linking them to personalised ontology. To implement their platform, the authors provide both a Perl CGI-based tool called RNA and a standalone Windows-based tool called Glucose.

7   Future Work

When creating a new post, it would be useful if, as well as being able to copy and paste content from a blog post, the formal content metadata could also be transferred. Equally, post references could be dragged and dropped into a new or edited post (for example, to create a trackback or related to link between posts) to create typed links between posts. This is along the lines of the RDF clipboard idea by Tim Berners-Lee[19].

Leveraging the full potential of SIOC requires the provision of custom programs and user interfaces specially tailored towards browsing SIOC data. In the consuming stage, we discussed how the Node Browser application can be used to navigate and search for aggregated information from both a blog's content and structure - similarly other RDF browsers such as BrownSauce [20] could be used. However, it would be useful to have a more graphical method for browsing not only this information, but also to allow one to navigate from a post to its related posts or "distributed conversations" across different blog sites. This could be a "SIOC explorer" application that would allow users to browse SIOC-enabled sites transparently without the need for data warehousing, simply by traversing rdfs:seeAlso and other links in RDF. A similar open source application already exists: Foafscape[21] is a browser for navigating FOAF-related RDF data to display hyperlinked graphs of Friend of a Friend data.

Another aspect of future work is in relation to the argumentative nature of blog discussions, in a similar way that [graphical] issue-based information systems ([g]IBIS) [6], [12] examined the argumentative nature of design and planning discussions. At first glance, a user is unable to tell if a blog post and resulting

---

[19] http://www.w3.org/2001/sw/Europe/reports/xml_sw_prototype_math_logic/#Part1

[20] http://brownsauce.sourceforge.net/

[21] http://foafscape.berlios.de/

discussion is overall supporting or opposing the topic(s) being discussed. For example, a person is researching medicine X for which they have a prescription, but they only want blog discussions on the negative aspects of X (already knowing the advantages). It would be desirable to provide details of an argumentative structure so that the associated meaning of the proposition/counter-proposition synthesis could be instantly recognised when browsing blog discussion topics. Some reply types such as agree or disagree have been ontologised by the W3C[22], but these may be augmented with some level or scale of agreement.

8   Conclusions

This paper detailed a means for enhancing a user's blogging experience by leveraging the fusion of two kinds of metadata related to blog posts: content-related and structural. We described ways of creating such metadata in a convenient and unobtrusive way for the user, by dragging and dropping object annotations from a user's desktop and by instantiating structural metadata that is automatically created during the blogging process. We detailed how such metadata can be published on the web through a popular blogging platform, and finally we described how metadata can be reused in posts or utilised for cross-site browsing by a blog consumer.

Acknowledgements

This material is based upon works supported by the Science Foundation Ireland under Grant No. SFI/02/CE1/I131.

References

1. A.J.Miles, N.Rogers, and D.Beckett.   SKOS Core RDF Vocabulary, 2004. http://www.w3.org/2004/02/skos/core/.
2. J. G. Breslin, A. Harth, U. Bojārs, and S. Decker. Towards Semantically-Interlinked Online Communities. In *The 2nd European Semantic Web Conference (ESWC '05), Heraklion, Greece, Proceedings, LNCS 3532*, pages 500–514, May 2005.
3. D. Brickley and L. Miller. FOAF Vocabulary Specification. http://xmlns.com/foaf/0.1.
4. S. Cayzer. Semantic Blogging and Decentralized Knowledge Management. *Communications of the ACM*, 47(12):47–52, December 2004.
5. S. Cayzer. Semantic Blogging: Spreading the Semantic Web Meme. In *XML Europe 2004, Amsterdam, Netherlands, Proceedings*, April 2004.
6. J. Conklin and M. Begeman. gIBIS - A Hypertext Tool for Exploratory Policy Discussion. In *The Conference on Computer-Supported Cooperative Work, Proceedings*, pages 140–152, 1988.
7. F. Dawson and T. Howes. vCard MIME Directory Profile, 1998.   RFC 2426: http://www.ietf.org/rfc/rfc2426.txt.

---

[22] http://www.w3.org/2001/12/replyType

8. F. Dawson and D. Stenerson. Internet Calendaring and Scheduling Core Object Specification (iCalendar), 1998. RFC 2445: http://www.ietf.org/rfc/rfc2445.txt.
9. A. Harth and S. Decker. Optimized Index Structures for Querying RDF from the Web. In *3rd Latin American Web Congress, Buenos Aires, Argentina, Proceedings*, pages 71–80, October 31 to November 2 2005.
10. J. Hendler. Agents and the Semantic Web. *IEEE Intelligent Systems*, 16(2):30–37, March/April 2001.
11. D. R. Karger and D. Quan. What Would It Mean to Blog on the Semantic Web? In S. A. McIlraith, D. Plexousakis, and F. van Harmelen, editors, *Third International Semantic Web Conference (ISWC2004), Hiroshima, Japan, Proceedings*, pages 214–228. Springer, November 2004.
12. W. Kunz and H. W. J. Rittel. Issues as Elements of Information Systems. Technical Report WP-131, University of California, Berkeley, 1970.
13. P. Leach, M. Mealling, and R. Salz. A Universally Unique IDentifier (UUID) URN Namespace, 2005. RFC 4122: http://www.ietf.org/rfc/rfc4122.txt.
14. K. Möller, J. G. Breslin, and S. Decker. semiBlog - Semantic Publishing of Desktop Data. In *14th Conference on Information Systems Development (ISD2005), Proceedings*, Karlstad, Sweden, August 2005.
15. K. Möller and S. Decker. Harvesting Desktop Data for Semantic Blogging. In *1st Workshop on the Semantic Desktop at ISWC2005, Galway, Ireland, Proceedings*, pages 79–91, November 2005.
16. O. Patashnik. BibTexIng, February 8 1988. BibTeX Documentation.
17. D. Quan, D. Huynh, and D. R. Karger. Haystack: a Platform for Authoring End User Semantic Web Applications. In *Second International Semantic Web Conference (ISWC2003), Proceedings*, 2003.
18. H. Takeda and I. Ohmukai. Semblog Project. In *Activities on Semantic Web Technologies in Japan, A WWW2005 Workshop*, 2005.
19. J. Walker. Weblog. In D. Herman, M. Jahn, and M.-L. Ryan, editors, *Routledge Encyclopedia of Narrative Theory*, page 45. Routledge, London and New York, 2005.

WSTO: A Classification-Based Ontology for Managing Trust in Semantic Web Services

Stefania Galizia

Knowledge Media Institute & Centre for Research in Computing
The Open University, Milton Keynes, UK
S.Galizia@open.ac.uk

Abstract. The aim of this paper is to provide a general ontology that allows the specification of trust requirements in the Semantic Web Services environment. Both client and Web Service can semantically describe their trust policies in two directions: first, each can expose their own guarantees to the environment, such as, security certification, execution parameters etc.; secondly, each can declare their trust preferences about other communication partners, by selecting (or creating) '*trust match criteria*'. A reasoning module can evaluate trust promises and chosen criteria, in order to select a set of Web Services that fit with all trust requirements. We see the trust-based selection problem of Semantic Web Services as a classification task. The class of selected Semantic Web Services (SWSs) will represent the set of all SWSs that fit both client and Web Service exposed trust requirements. We strongly believe that trust perception changes in different contexts, and strictly depends on the goal that the requester would like to achieve. For this reason, in our ontology we emphasize first class entities "goal", "Web Service" *and* "user", and the relations occurring among them. Our approach implies a centralized trust-based broker, *i.e.* an agent able to reason on trust requirements and to mediate between goal and Web Service semantic descriptions. We adopt IRS-III as our prototypical trust-based broker.

1 Introduction

With the widespread proliferation of Web Services, trustworthiness will become a determining factor of any given service's success. Conversely, trust-based automatic discovery and selection will become a significant requirement from a requester's point of view.

In the literature, the notion of "trust" is defined in different ways according to the application domain. We draw on two major approaches: trust based on *ability* and trust based on *reliability*. The former enacts the requirements based on quality of service profiles (data accuracy and precision, timeliness, *etc.* ...); for instance, a requester may trust more a service that takes acceptable time to perform a given task . The latter considers mainly the service credibility, which can be measured by a Trusted Third Party.

In e-commerce, security services – such as authentication, data integrity, confidentiality *etc.* – are deployed in order to realize the reliability-based aspect of trust. Security services are usually implemented in terms of security mechanisms based on Trusted Third Party (TTP) concepts and Public Key Cryptography.

Y. Sure and J. Domingue (Eds.): ESWC 2006, LNCS 4011, pp. 697–711, 2006.
© Springer-Verlag Berlin Heidelberg 2006

There are other approaches concerned also with reliability-based trust. In some environments, it seems appropriate to calculate the trustworthiness by reasoning only on security issues. At the other extreme, pure reputation-based algorithms have been implemented especially in those fields where all involved parties can express their opinions, as the social networks.

We concentrate on aspects of trust that we claim are fundamental in the Semantic Web Service context. In the open dynamic environment where the Semantic Web Services lie, trust-based discovery and selection are crucial issues in order to avoid invocation of malicious or unreliable services.

Until now, there are no defined protocols by which Semantic Web Services may expose their trust characteristics. Web Service technology provides only syntactic statements. The interface definition language WSDL specifies only the syntactic signature for a Web Service, but does not specify any semantics or non-functional characteristics.

Adding semantic descriptions to services should allow also reliability specifications and support different notions of trust from both requester and provider perspectives.

Our first assumption is that different users have different demands on trust parameters. Moreover, we believe that in different contexts trust assumes different meanings. Essentially the trust judgement of a service requester will strictly depend on the goal she intends to achieve.

In this paper, we provide a framework that fulfils given requirements for the description of trust properties of Semantic Web Services and enables their selection based on these properties. We represent the notion of trust via an ontology, named WSTO (Web Service Trust-management Ontology), through which both requester and Web Service provider can instantiate their individual trust policies. Then, a reasoning module will activate Web Service selection taking into account trust-related properties.

We characterise trust analysis as a classification process, within which valid solutions are those Web Services that match given classification criteria. Consequently, we have found beneficial and enlightening to apply an existing classification ontology [13] to this scheme, creating constructs that adapt the framework for our specific purposes. On the other hand, we preferred to keep our model as general as possible in order to accommodate this extension to a variety of requesters' preferences and requirements for trust-related matters.

We chose WSMO [16] as underlying ontology to state the basic concepts of Semantic Web Services. One of the common principles to our ontology and WSMO is the ontological role separation of client, Web Service and goal.

Our approach implies the concept of delegation to a centralized trusted evaluator, in order to reason about the criteria expressed by the participants. We adopt IRS-III [2] as our prototypical trust-based broker. IRS-III is a framework and implemented platform, which acts as a broker mediating between the goals of a user or client and available deployed Web Services. Moreover, IRS-III uses WSMO as its basic ontology and follows the WSMO design principles.

The paper is organized as follows. First, we provide in Section 2, a rough description of trust assumptions in different contexts. Then we describe in Section 3 our approach via a brief presentation of the underlying classification ontology, and a detailed explanation of WSTO. In Section 4 we introduce the execution layer of our approach, by referring to future implementation within IRS-III. Finally, in Section 5 we conclude by summarizing WSTO benefits and proposing future work.

2 Trust Considerations

The meaning of trust is very difficult to catch. Trust is a social phenomenon inherent to human beings. In that context trust is:

- A means for understanding and adapting to the complexity of the environment;
- A means of providing robustness to independent agents;
- A useful judgement in the light of experience of the behaviour of others
- Applicable to artificial agents.

Trust in an artificial agent is a means of providing an additional tool for the consideration of other agents and the environment in which it exists. The provision of explicit trust into an agent is still rather a research subject. The current approaches to trust are more about how to assume trust (to establish a replacement for trust).

The most of the systems that are at present being designed *assume* trust, i.e., an agent entering into communication with an other agent (believes absolutely or to a certain degree) that good (promised or intended) things will happen. In this context, security is about how to ensure that bad (not intended) things do not happen.

The different existing approaches to trust are about how the trust assumption is made and its enforcement ensured. The most popular approaches are: i) Reputation-based; ii) Trusted Third Party; iii) Contract-based.

These general approaches can be refined and/or combined in order to build a concrete trust establishment solution that can be deployed in a real system.

Web-based social network models have been one of the first research fields where trust, in terms of reliability, has become a central issue. Every actor in a social network can express his opinion on another one, by means of an available vocabulary. Several algorithms for trust propagation and different metrics have been defined in this field. Some systems use discrete values, for instance "low", "medium" and "high", to express the trustworthiness, others make use of real-valued measures, usually expressed in the interval [0,1], especially in those algorithms requiring high precision. At the other extreme, some networks make use of binary rating, either 1 for trustworthy neighbours, or 0 for who are not trustworthy.

Two main trust properties, modelled in many network systems, are transitivity and asymmetry. In general, trust is not symmetric; one actor can trusts another one, belonging to same network, and the latter can no trust the former. The trust can be transitive, but many different meanings, not properly mathematical, have been associated to transitivity [7].

Many new projects based on social networks have arisen in the last few years. The most famous is perhaps Friend-Of-A-Friend (FOAF), a Semantic Web based social network with many users distributed on the Web [6]. One application of FOAF concerns the creation of a trust module is based on users' rating of each other's trustworthiness and expressed on a discrete scale between 1 and 10 [7].

In the last few years, trust has become of crucial importance within peer-to-peer networks. A peer-to-peer (P2P) computer network is a network that relies on the computing power and bandwidth of the participants in the network rather than concentrating it in a relatively few servers. In order to use P2P networks in a useful setting, it is extremely important to provide security and to prevent unwanted elements from participating. Several algorithms are available for peer trust rating; most of them are based on security considerations (e.g., public or private key cryptography) and on reputation [14, 15, 18]. The basic idea is to assign to each peer a trust rating based on its credentials, in case provided by trusted third parties, such as certification authorities, and on its performance in the overlay network and to store it at a suitable repository. The existing trust algorithms consider different aspects, most of them monitor the peer behaviour on the time; other ones emphasize the concept of cooperation. In [18], for instance, the authors present an algorithm where all peers in the network cooperate to compute and store the global trust vector. In general, in peer-to-peer systems, the information propagation and the reputation management are central issues of trust rating.

On the other hand, to evaluate the Semantic Web Services trustworthiness, several different approaches are already proposed. Existing technologies for Web Services only provide descriptions at the syntactic level, making it difficult for requesters and providers to interpret or represent nontrivial statements. Semantic descriptions of Web Services are, in fact, necessary in order to enable their automatic discovery, composition and execution across heterogeneous users and domains. In Semantic Web Service contexts, when the user expresses the goal she would like to achieve, the actual Web Service that matches the goal is dynamically discovered and selected, and so its features are not completely known *a priori*. In this environment, semantic annotation of trust features becomes a considerable parameter during the discovery phase. Most of existing approaches inherit methodologies from the peer-to-peer networks [11, 15], as Semantic Web Services provide P2P interaction between services. Several approaches rely on an external matchmaker that works as repository of service description and policies [8] and calculates the service trustworthiness according with given algorithms. Trust evaluation algorithms for Semantic Web Services consider especially security issues, such as confidentiality, authorization, authentication, as rating statements [8, 9, 10, 11]. Even W3C Web Service architecture [22] recommendations consider trust policies inside security consideration, but the way to disclose their security policies is still not clear. UDDI does not refer to security features for Web Services.

In Semantic Web Services context, some trust algorithms are more generically Quality of service based [1, 20], by making the service ability the main trust statement. Quality of service (QoS) is defined by a set of properties related to the service performance. Precision and accuracy of data, timeliness in executing a task, are the main features, but even security is a part of QoS.

We deem that the key to enable a trust based discovery for Semantic Web Services lies in a common ontological representation, where Web Service and client perform their trust requirements. Some QoS taxonomy [17] or service policy ontology [9] already exist, nevertheless an exploration of how to provide a common means for runtime monitoring the services trustworthiness is only beginning.

3 Our Approach

In this paper, we present an ontology, WSTO (Web Service Trust-management Ontology), that enables both client and Web Service to express their trust requirements in a Semantic Web Services environment. Our starting point is to identify the goal that the requester wishes to achieve, and to describe the trust requirements associated with this goal.

We have shown that in different contexts trust assumes different meanings. On the one hand a requester tends to trust a travel agency that proposes to fly by airlines deemed safe, on the other hand, a banking service is trusted as it provides confidentiality or authentication certifications that promise data privacy.

The more fruitful way to express the actual trust requirements is providing a shared and common framework that allows both requester and provider to express their policies, but even enables them to extend the framework according to their needs. Our ontology pursues this purpose.

We adopt WSMO [16] as basic vision that provides ontological specifications for the core elements of Semantic Web Services.

The primary concepts in our ontology are "web-service", "user" and "goal". The ontologically specified concept of "user" is not stated in WSMO. This specification facilitates the description of the individual policies by a service requester. The user instantiates a goal during the goal-based invocation process. The expected outcome is the selection of a class of Web Service that fits the goal and trust requirements of all transaction participants. It is worth to emphasize that, while the goal specified by the user is an instance of the class "goal" represented in WSMO, the selected Web Services are the instances of the class of Web Services that meet all policies declared by trading partners involved in the transaction. For this reason, we have characterised the analysis of trust-related properties and requirements as a classification process, within which valid solutions are those Web Services that match given criteria.

Selecting one, or a set of Web Services that match a given criterion corresponds to the task of finding the solutions in a classification problem. The solution will be the class of Web Services that fit criteria established by requester and provider. The match criteria represent the trust requirements. This vision, intentionally general, allows also natural application to other fields, not strictly related with trust. In our framework, in fact, participants (user and Web Services) can easily express any kind of policies, in particular, their trust policies.

WSTO builds on the classification library, created within the IBROW project [5, 13], then it makes use of the classification mechanisms already defined in that task. We opportunely extend and adapt it to the Semantic Web Services field, emphasizing the role of service selection as an important part of goal invocation.

In the following of this section, we expose the main features of the underlying classification task and then we describe in details WSTO.

3.1 Classification

The classification problem is an important issue in several fields [19]. For example, identifying a class of symptoms is crucial in the investigation of diseases; or, classifying goals and requirements is the starting point of a planning process. In general, reasoning about classes is simpler, especially in the presence of a large set of instances.

In order to find the proper class for a set of objects, it is necessary for an agent to reason about differences among a given set of features. For instance, we can classify living beings as separate classes *plants* and *animals* – and continue to further sub-classify the animals as *carnivores* and *herbivores* – by identifying different observable characteristics. This problem can be expressed in terms of search within a solution space, by applying a criterion over a given set of facts.

The classification ontology we extended is a 'task ontology' [3, 12, 13], which specifies the general classification problem. The classification library, as a whole, is very extensive, being composed by a huge number of classes, relations and functions; it also provides heuristic evaluations and refinement methods. We extend only a subset of the classification task, useful for our trust requirements. Figure 1 illustrates the classification framework by means of a UML Class Diagram; the large open-headed arrows relate classes in *is-a* relations, the simple arrows represent normal relations between classes.

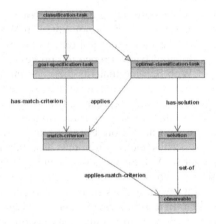

Fig. 1. The classification task ontology

The `classification-task` class is a subclass of the general `goal-specification-task`. The `optimal-classification-task` is a reasoning module, it applies match criteria in order to derive the best solutions by evaluating the facts, stored in the class `observable`. The observables are a finite set of facts represented by pairs like (f, v), where f are features and v their associated values. The solution space is defined by a set of predefined classes (solutions) under which an unknown object may fall. The `match-criterion` specifies the methods to find a solution, according to a chosen classification task.

A solution itself can be described as a finite set of feature specifications, which is a pair of the form (f, c), where f is a feature and c specifies a condition on the values that the feature can take. Then, we say that an observable (f, v) matches a feature specification (f, c) if v satisfies the condition c.

Several definitions of classification tasks can be provided. In some cases, only an admissible solution is required, in other cases optimal solutions may be requested. In Figure 1 we show only optimal-classification-task, which requires a solution to be optimal with respect to a given match criterion.

3.2 WSTO: Web Services Trust-Based Selection Ontology

WSTO is composed of two logical levels: a static layer that provides our vision of Semantic Web Services invocation scenario, and a dynamic level, composed by a reasoning module, where every requestor can specify its own trust requirements.

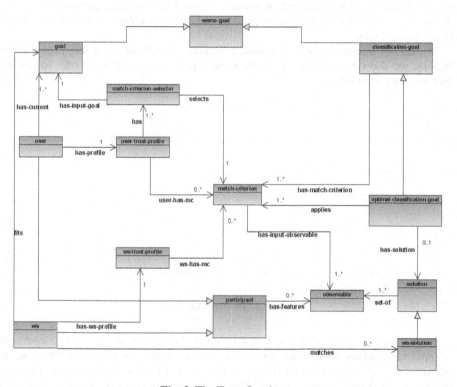

Fig. 2. The Trust Ontology

The former identifies three main components during a service invocation: user, goal, ws (Web Service); the latter describes how dynamically is established a solving method to select the Web Service according with all trust requirements.

The *user* is the client, which can be a human actor or in turn another Web Service. The class *ws* represents the Web Service. A *goal* specifies the objectives that a client may have when consulting a Web Service, describing aspects related to user desires with respect to the requested functionality and behaviour. Our goal definition can be a WSMO goal [16].

In the WSMO vision, a goal specifies the objectives that a client may have when consulting a Web Service, describing aspects related to user desires with respect to the requested functionality and behaviour. Ontologies are used as the semantically defined terminology for goal specification. Goals model the user view in the Web Service usage process and therefore are a separate top level entity in WSMO.

As shown in figure 2, *ws* and *user* are subclasses of *participant*. We include the class *participant* as superclass of *user* and *ws*, to compactly specify common relations involving both user and Web Service entities. User and Web Service should be able to express their trust requirements and publish their own guarantees. For instance, they could expose promised execution parameters or security certifications, as non-functional properties. Several certification authorities, such as the well-known Verisign [21], may provide either requester or Web Service with security certification.

We do not intend to provide technical security consideration in this paper, nevertheless, we show how easily the participants can extend WSTO in order to disclose their security guarantees.

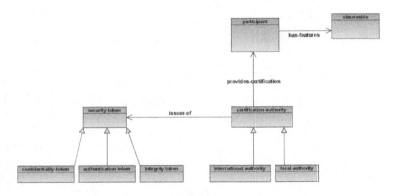

Fig. 3. Security Ontology

In the figure 3 we show a possible ontology extension. *Certification-authority* class represents an entity that provides security certification, for instance, the aforementioned Verisign. There exist different kinds of authorities, international, national, university, etc.. Usually the certificates (like the certificates exploited in the well-known SSL protocol, X509), provide different classes of security. Authentication verifies whether a potential partner in a conversation is capable of representing a person or an organization. Integrity assures that the data must be identically maintained during any operation. Confidentiality serves to keep the message secret by using encryption.

A user requesting a service on the Web usually demands authentication and encryptions services (confidentiality). Our general framework allows the participants to express their individual requirements in a flexible way.

The certification authority may provide other guarantees not mentioned in our framework (non-repudiation, legislative requirements, etc.), and, moreover, we consider explicitly the case in which security requirements could change in the future, due, for instance to legislative requirements. For this reason both actors, WS and user, are enabled to dynamically extend our ontology in accordance with their own needs. Trust preferences of a requester may also relate to Web Service execution properties. Timeliness, precision and accuracy are all judged with respect to execution data, although often represented as objective and invariant QoS properties. While security is certificated by trusted authorities, evaluation of QoS execution properties is inherently more complex. In essence, the provider usually describes its own quality of service, and the requestor selection is based on the promised parameters.

In this context, an objective third party performing selection would have to take into account the historical behaviour of the Web Service, and compare the promised QoS statements with the properties of actual executions. This mechanism will be one subject of our future work.

Security or execution parameters can be represented as *(f,v)*, pairs of features and relative values, as per *observable* in the general classification task ontology. Thus the relation has-feature, between the classes *participants* and *observable*, stores all of the considered Web Service's non-functional trust properties (see Figures 2 and 3).

A goal matches with a number of Web Service; we express the goal in terms of WSMO notion. Moreover, a classification goal specifies the general goal in the previously described classification task, and may itself be expressed as a WSMO goal.

In our scenario, the user asks for a goal and establishes its criteria to be applied in the trust-based selection. The *user-trust-profile* represents the set of criteria associated to the user requirements. All criteria are stored in the class match-criterion, derived from the classification ontology. This class is the core of the dynamic level of our framework, in the sense that a user can populate it by defining new methods according to their own particular trust requirements. A user, for instance, can state that authentication has a greater weight than confidentiality certification and she can establish furthermore the score for the type of certification authorities. Furthermore, she can designate a particular given Web Service as trusted, without relating her choice with any QoS or Security parameters; in this case, she will instantiate a new criterion in the class match-criterion.

Given a *user-profile* instance, a selector engine (*match-criterion-selector* in figure 2) will select the right criterion associated to requested goal. Only one match criterion will be executed for a given goal invocation and a given corresponding user trust profile.

On the other hand, the Web Service owns its trust policies and can decide what to disclose. The class ws-trust-profile represents trust policy of the Web Service. While the user selects both the match criterion and the goal that wishes to achieve, instead, the Web Service is associated to a goal by its capability, and it will select (or define) only the preferred criterion.

The *optimal-classification-goal* class, inherited from the general classification ontology, contains a set of problem solving methods, applied to the class *match-criterion*. Essentially, the reasoning module identifies a class of Web Services that satisfy the requested goal, according with both user and Web Service trust requirements. The solutions will essentially be a set of pairs *(f, c)*, according to the classification task, where *f* expresses the trustworthiness features and *c* the conditions established in the match criterion. For example, {*(certification-authority, verisign), (key-length,128)}* is a possible solution. In our ontology, the class $solution$ represents general solutions in the classification task, but we specialize, in ws-profile, the solutions of our interest. The relation $matches$ between ws and $ws-profile$ identifies all Web Service descriptions compatible with the solutions.

4 Execution

In this section, we provide more details about WSTO dynamic layer, that is, how actually the WSTO reasoner works. For example, we outline a scenario where the user looks for a secure loan Web Service with some security certifications. We assume that there exist several services fitting with goal and user trust needs. In turn, every loan service has its trust policies. For instance, concerning financial guarantees we may specify that the user has to have a bank account, a credit card, a permanent job, *etc.*.

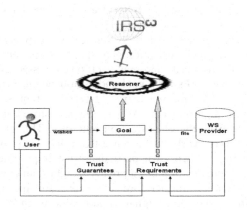

Fig. 4. The anchor to IRS-III

The user could consent to show only bank account and credit card number, but withhold information regarding his job. WSTO target is to find the class of loan Web Services conformant with both user and Web Services trust policies. Figure 4 shows the basic idea: both user and WS disclose their policies at two levels, by providing trust guarantees and requirements. The trust guarantees are stored in the observables, as discussed above; the requirements are expressed in terms of match criteria. We now turn our attention to the role of the reasoner that applies the match criteria, according to each party's trust policies, in order to find the correct set of Web Services.

Our approach implies a centralized trust-based matchmaker. WSTO has to use the services of an external broker, to carry out the reasoning. In P2P and Semantic Web Services community [15, 8], several approaches adopt this centralized matchmaker idea, especially because the delegation to a trusted third party becomes essential when more than one entity is involved while taking a decision.

We believe that the centralized approach carries many advantages. First, a broker can store information and apply reputation-based algorithms that learn from involved parties' historical behaviours. The second big advantage is the simplicity of interaction, being a one-shot access of the broker.

We plan to use IRS-III (see Figure 4), as trust-based matchmaker for WSTO. In the following subsections we provide an IRS-III overview and a sketch of a possible execution example by using IRS-III.

4.1 IRS-III Overview

IRS-III is a tool and an implemented framework with the overall aim of supporting the automated or semi-automated construction of semantically enhanced systems over the Internet. The IRS uses WSMO as its basic ontology and follows the WSMO design principles [16].

IRS-III has three main classes of features, which distinguish it from other work on Semantic Web Services: Firstly, it supports *one-click publishing* of 'standard' program code. In other words, it automatically transforms programming code (currently we support Java and Lisp environments) into a Web Service, by automatically creating an appropriate wrapper. Hence, it is very easy to make existing standalone software available on the Internet, as Web Services. Secondly, by extending the WSMO goal and Web Service concepts, clients of IRS-III can directly invoke Web Services via goals - that is IRS-III supports *capability-driven* service invocation. Finally, IRS-III services are Web Service compatible – standard Web Services can be trivially published through the IRS-III.

The main components of the IRS-III architecture are the IRS-III Server, the IRS-III Publisher and the IRS-III Client, which communicate through the SOAP protocol.

IRS-III was designed for ease of use, in fact a key feature of IRS-III is that Web Service invocation is capability driven. The IRS-III Client supports this by providing a goal-centric invocation mechanism. An IRS-III user simply asks for a goal to be solved and the IRS-III broker locates an appropriate Web Service semantic description and then invokes the underlying deployed Web Service. We plan to implement WSTO in IRS-III, in order to make the client invocation, now capability-based, further trust-based. We believe that IRS-III is particularly suitable for our purpose because it is already a broker between goal and semantically described Web Service. Moreover, the classification library, to which we refer, is already implemented in IRS-III.

4.2 Execution Example in IRS-III

We now propose the outlined scenario in the beginning of this section and detail how IRS-III manages the trust-based Web Service selection.

The client is a construction company that, through IRS-III, asks for a loan service, specifying its trust policies. In turn, various loan services disclose their trust requirements and guarantees. The only data the client intends to disclose is its bank account, but only to the services that promise given security guarantees. In particular, its constraints are that Web Service provider uses encryption algorithm type *DES*, or one based on this, and that it owns an authentication certificate released by Verisign or any American certification authority. This last requirement is a weak constraint: in the case that are no available Web Services with American authentication certificates, the client considers certification from German or Italian authorities to be acceptable, in that order of preference. IRS-III maintains a user trust profile for regular clients, which contains personal preferences; and it updates their profiles every time those clients specify new trust policies.

Several Web Services with capabilities functionally fitting the goal are semantically described in IRS-III, but only a sub class of them will match with the client's trust requirements. For instance, those loan services that need the company's credit card number as guarantee are automatically excluded, because the client discloses only its bank account.

Both Web Service and client can extend WSTO. The security extension example, shown in the section 3.1 is a typical extension that can occur in this case study. In fact, in order to disclose security guarantees, it makes sense to add to WSTO classes that store the main certification authorities, or the possible security tokens, as shown in Figure 3.

The loan services populate the class observable with their trust guarantees. We consider three different loan Web Services that instantiate the following pairs:

- WS1: *(certification-authority, verisign);*
       (country-authority, united_states);
       (encryption, AES);
       (certificate-type,X.509);
- WS2: *(certification-authority, globalsign-austria);*
       (country-authority, austria);
       (encryption, 3DES);
- WS3: *(certification-authority, tc-trustCenter);*
       (country-authority, germany);
       (encryption, DES);
       (keyType, RSA);

To simplify the case study we do not instantiate any Web Service trust requirement, and assume that all those three services accept as clients' guarantees only their bank accounts, the only data the construction company wants to disclose. The client, instead, selects an available parametric match criterion, which allows the client to establish weighs for parameters, concerning encryption algorithms and certification authorities' properties.

Our client will provide the following values:

$$
\begin{cases}
encryption \Rightarrow (value:DES, score:1) \\
authority \Rightarrow (value:veriSign, score:0.5) \\
nationality \Rightarrow \begin{pmatrix} value:american, score:0.5 \\ value:german, score:0.3 \\ value:italian, score:0.2 \end{pmatrix}
\end{cases}
$$

This criterion provides a trust value in the real interval [0,1] for every parameter. The score 0 means that there is no trust at all, the score 1 signifies absolute trust, the values between 0 and 1 represent the linear variation in trust. For values that are given no score, a score of 0 automatically applies. For instance, it is implicit that the client does not trust any English certification authority. The criterion returns the final computed trust measure as a real value between 0 and 1, by normalization of some composition of the scores for all provided values. The optimal classification task provides the class of best solutions, by reasoning on all match criteria selected or created. The solutions are a set of valid observables, those represent all features the Web Services must have. This set is stored in the class *ws-solution*. The actual Web Services correspond to the valid features are returned by the relation matches, between *ws* and *ws-solution*.

No one among the loan services considered has maximal trustworthiness, i.e. is the subject of absolute trust. In fact, the only Web Service that matches both the goal and client trust requirements is WS3. WS1 does not respect the encryption constraint; and the client does not accept the nationality of the authority that provides WS2 with security certification.

5 Conclusions

In this paper, we have presented an ontology, WSTO, that facilitates trust based invocation and selection in the Semantic Web Services environment. We have considered the trust-based selection as a classification problem. This simplifies the problem's tractability, especially in presence of a lot of instances. This is of particular relevance in our context due to the distributed and open nature of the web.
WSTO presents several important benefits that we summarize as follows:

- **Generality.** Trust has different meanings in different contexts, we differentiated trust on ability and trust reliability and even trust on reputation and trust through third parties. Often the trust evaluation depends on the perceptions of the parties involved in a communication. WSTO allows specifying any trust needs; its general nature makes it adaptable to any scenario.
- **Open.** Our aim is to make WSTO as open as possible. We intend to implement it in IRS-III, which is publicly accessible. More significantly, the constituents of WSTO are Semantic Web Services, so they can be represented a) in term of ontologies e b) in terms of components. All participants can replace the main parts of the WSTO, by instantiating new match criteria, or publishing new semantic descriptions of own trust policies.
- **Trust-based invocation.** The core purpose of our ontology is to enable trust-based invocation. We believe that this approach is useful in an open and distributed environment such as the Semantic Web Services environment.
- **Explicitness.** Policies and their evaluation mechanism are explicitly formally described.

We adopt WSMO [16] as basic vision that provides ontological specifications for the core elements of Semantic Web Services. WSMO specifies a set of and *non-functional properties* that describe information that does not affect the functionality of the element, such as title, authorship, copyrights, etc. Among them "trust" is listed as a recommended property for web service description. Nevertheless, until now, the WSMO effort has not specified any process to enable trust-based discovery and selection. We claim that our approach has a natural fit with the WSMO requirements and so propose to extend WSMO with our ontology.

Further work is underway on implementation of WSTO in IRS-III.

Acknowledgements

This work is supported by DIP (Data, Information and Process Integration with Semantic Web Services) (EU FP6 - 507483) and AKT (Advanced Knowledge Technologies) (UK EPSRC GR/N15764/01) projects.

I would like specially to thank John Domingue for his constructive guidance and feedback. I also have benefited from discussion with Barry Norton and Andreas Friesen.

References

1. Bilgin, A. S., Singh, M. P. (2004). A DAML-based repository for QoS-aware Semantic Web Service selection. In Proceedings of the IEEE International Conference on Web Services (ICWS'04), Washington, DC, USA, 2004.
2. Domingue, J., Cabral, L., Hakimpour, F., Sell, D., Motta, E. (2004). Irs-III: A platform and infrastructure for creating WSMO-based Semantic Web Services. In Proceedings of the Workshop on WSMO Implementations (WIW 2004), Frankfurt, Germany, September 2004.
3. Fensel, D., Benjamins, V. R., Motta, E. and Wielinga, B. J. (1999a). A Framework for knowledge system reuse. Proceedings of the International Joint Conference on Artificial Intelligence (IJCAI-99). Stockholm, Sweden, July 31 – August 5, 1999.
4. Fensel, D., Bussler C. (2002). *The Web Service Modeling Framework WSMF*. Electronic Commerce Research and Applications, 1(2), 2002.
5. Fensel, D., Motta, E., Benjamins, V. R., Decker, S., Gaspari, M., Groenboom, R., Grosso, W., Musen, M., Plaza E., Schreiber, G., Studer, R. and Wielinga, B. (1999b). The Unified Problem-solving Method Development Language UPML. IBROW3 Project Deliverable 1.1.
6. The Friend-Of-A-Friend (FOAF) Project. (2004). Available at http://www.foaf-project.org/.
7. Golbeck, J. and Hendler, J. (2005). Inferring trust relationships in web-based social networks. *submitted to ACM Transactions on Internet Technology*, 2005.
8. Kagal, L., Paoucci, M., Srinivasan, N., Denker G, Finin, T., Sycara K. (2004). Authorization and privacy for Semantic Web Services. In Proceeding of AAAI 2004 Spring Symposium on Semantic Web Services, Stanford University, Mar. 2004.
9. Kolovski, V., Parsia, B., Katz, Y., Hendler, J. (2005). Representing Web Service Policies in OWL-DL. in Proceedings of 4th International Semantic Web Conference (ISWC 2005), November 6-10, 2005, Galway, Ireland.
10. Mani, A., Nagarajan, A. (2002). Understanding quality of service for Web Services: Improving the performance of your Web Services -IBM-report- 2002. (Available at http://www-128.ibm.com/developerworks/library/ws-quality.html).
11. Maximilien, E. M., Singh, M. P. (2004). Toward Autonomic Web Services Trust and Selection. In Proceedings of 2nd International Conference on Service Oriented Computing (ICSOC 2004), New York, November 2004.

12. Motta E. (1999). Reusable Components for Knowledge Models: Principles and Case Studies in Parametric Design Problem Solving. IOS Press.
13. Motta, E., Lu, W. (2000). A Library of Components for Classification Problem Solving. In Proceedings of PKAW 2000 - The 2000 Pacific Rim Knowledge Acquisition, Workshop, Sydney, Australia, December 11-13, 2000.
14. Ngan, T. W., J, Wallach, D., S., Druschel, P. (2003). Enforcing Fair Sharing of Peer-to-peer Resources. 2nd International Workshop on Peer-to-Peer Systems (IPTPS) (Berkeley, California), February 2003.
15. Olmedilla, D., Lara, R., Polleres, A., Lausen, H. (2004). Trust Negotiation for Semantic Web Services. 1st International Workshop on Semantic Web Services and Web Process Composition in conjunction with the 2004 IEEE International Conference on Web Services, Jul.. 2004, San Diego, California, USA.
16. Roman, D., Lausen, H. and Keller, U. (Eds) (2005). The Web Service Modeling Ontology WSMO, final version 1.1. WSMO Final Draft D2, 2005.
17. Sabata, B., Chatterjee, S., Davis., M., Sydir, J., Lawrence, T. (1997). Taxonomy for QoS Specifications. In Proceedings of the 3rd Workshop on Object-Oriented Real-Time Dependable Systems (WORDS '97), February 1997.
18. Sependar D., K., Schlosser, M. T., Garcia-Molina, H. (2003). The EigenTrust Algorithm for Reputation Management in P2P Networks. In Proceedings of the Twelfth International World Wide Web Conference. Budapest, Hungary, 20-24 May 2003.
19. Stefik M. (1995). Introduction to Knowledge Systems. Morgan Kaufmann, San Francisco, CA.
20. Vu L., H., Hauswirth, M. and Aberer, K. (2005). QoS-based Service Selection and Ranking with Trust and Reputation Management. Technical Report IC2005029, Swiss Federal Institute of Technology at Lausanne (EPFL), Switzerland, June 2005.
21. VeriSign. (2005). Intelligent Infrastructure Services At Work. Information available at: http://www.verisign.com/.
22. W3C (2004). Web Services Architecture. W3C Working Draft 11 February 2004 (Available at http://www.w3.org/TR/ws-arch/).

Semantic Web Policies – A Discussion of Requirements and Research Issues

* P.A. Bonatti[1], C. Duma[2], N. Fuchs[3], W. Nejdl[4], D. Olmedilla[4], J. Peer[5], and N. Shahmehri[2]

[1] Università di Napoli Federico II, Napoli, Italy
bonatti@na.infn.it
[2] Linköpings universitet, Linköpings, Sweden
{cladu, nahsh}@ida.liu.se
[3] University of Zurich, Zurich, Switzerland
fuchs@ifi.unizh.ch
[4] L3S Research Center and University of Hanover, Hanover, Germany
{olmedilla, nejdl}@l3s.de
[5] St. Gallen University, St. Gallen, Switzerland
joachim.peer@unisg.ch

Abstract. Policies are pervasive in web applications. They play crucial roles in enhancing security, privacy and usability of distributed services. There has been extensive research in the area, including the Semantic Web community, but several aspects still exist that prevent policy frameworks from widespread adoption and real world application. This paper discusses important requirements and open research issues in this context, focusing on policies in general and their integration into trust management frameworks, as well as on approaches to increase system cooperation, usability and user-awareness of policy issues.

Keywords: Integrated heterogeneous policies, Cooperative policy enforcement, Lightweight trust, Trust management, Natural language interfaces, Explanation mechanisms.

1 Introduction

Policies are pervasive in web applications. They play crucial roles in enhancing security, privacy and usability of distributed services, and indeed may determine the success (or failure) of a web service. However, users will not be able to benefit from these protection mechanisms unless they understand and are able to personalize policies applied in such contexts. For web services this includes policies for access control, privacy and business rules, among others.

In this paper, we summarize research performed over the past years on semantic policies and especially aim to analyse those aspects that did not receive so much attention so far. We will focus our discussion on the following strategic goals and lines of research:

---

* In alphabetical order.

Y. Sure and J. Domingue (Eds.): ESWC 2006, LNCS 4011, pp. 712–724, 2006.

- Adoption of a *broad notion of policy*, encompassing not only access control policies, but also privacy policies, business rules, quality of service, and others. We believe that all these different kinds of policies should eventually be integrated into a single framework.
- *Strong and lightweight evidence*: Policies make decisions based on properties of the peers interacting with the system. These properties may be strongly certified by cryptographic techniques, or may be reliable to some intermediate degree with lightweight evidence gathering and validation. A flexible policy framework should try to merge these two forms of evidence to meet the efficiency and usability requirements of web applications.
- These desiderata imply that trust negotiation, reputation models, business rules, and action specification languages have to be integrated into a single framework at least to some extent. It is crucial to find the right tradeoff between generality and efficiency. *So far, no framework has tried to merge all aspects into a coherent system.*
- *Automated trust negotiation* is one of the main ingredients that can be used to make heterogeneous peers effectively interoperate. This approach relies on and actively contributes to advances in the area of *trust management*.
- *Lightweight knowledge representation and reasoning* does not only refer to computational complexity; it should also reduce the effort to specialize general frameworks to specific application domains; and the corresponding tools should be easy to learn and use for common users, with no particular training in computers or logic. We regard these properties as crucial for the success of a semantic web framework.
- The last issue cannot be tackled simply by adopting a rule language. Solutions like *controlled natural language syntax for policy rules*, to be translated by a parser into the internal logical format, will definitively ease the adoption of any policy language.
- *Cooperative policy enforcement*: A secure cooperative system should (almost) never say *no*. Web applications need to help new users in obtaining the services that the application provides, so potential customers should not be discouraged. Whenever prerequisites for accessing a service are not met, web applications should explain what is missing and help the user in obtaining the required permissions.
- As part of cooperative enforcement, advanced *explanation mechanisms* are necessary to help users in understanding policy decisions and obtaining the permission to access a desired service.

In the remainder of this paper we describe the current state of the art on these issues, expand on them and point out several interesting research directions related to them. Section 2 discusses the different types of policies which must be considered in order to address real world scenarios. The need for strong and lightweight evidence on the information that policies require is discussed in Section 3. Section 4 then highlights the importance of trust management as part of a policy framework, describing in detail negotiations and provisional actions. Section 5 describes how cooperative systems which explain their decisions to users as well as policy specification in natural language increase user awareness and understanding. We finish with conclusions and perspectives in Section 6

2   A Broad Notion of Policy

Policies are pervasive in all web-related contexts. Access control policies are needed to protect any system open to the internet. Privacy policies are needed to assist users while they are browsing the web and interacting with web services. Business rules specify which conditions apply to each customer of a web service. Other policies specify constraints related to Quality of Service (QoS). In E-government applications, visas and other documents are released according to specific eligibility policies. This list is not exhaustive and is limited only by the class of applications that can be deployed in the world wide web.

Most of these policies make their decisions based on similar pieces of information [3] – essentially, properties of the peers involved in the transaction. For example, age, nationality, customer profile, identity, and reputation may all be considered both in access control decisions, and in determining which discounts are applicable (as well as other eligibility criteria). It is appealing to integrate these kinds of policies into a coherent framework, so that (i) a common infrastructure can be used to support interoperability and decision making, and (ii) the policies themselves can be harmonized and synchronized.

In the general view depicted above, policies may also establish that some events must be logged (audit policies), that user profiles must be updated, and that when a transaction fails, the user should be told how to obtain missing permissions. In other words, policies may specify *actions* whose execution may be interleaved with the decision process. Such policies are called *provisional policies*. In this context, *policies act both as decision support systems and as declarative behavior specifications.* An effective user-friendly approach to policy specification could give common users (with no training in computer science or logic) better control on the behavior of their own system (see the discussion in Section 5).

Of course, the extent to which this goal can be achieved depends on the policy's ability to *interoperate* with legacy software and data – or more generally, with the rest of the system. Then a policy specification language should support suitable primitives for interacting with external packages and data in a flexible way.

The main challenges raised by these issues are then the following:

– Harmonizing security and privacy policies with business rules, provisional policies, and other kinds of policy is difficult because their standard formalizations are based on different derivation strategies, and even different reasoning mechanisms (cf. Section 4). Deduction, abduction, and event-condition-action rule semantics need to be integrated into a coherent framework, trying to minimize subtleties and technical intricacies (otherwise the framework would not be accessible to common users).

- Interactions between a rule-based theory and "external" software and data have been extensively investigated in the framework of logic-based mediation and logic-based agent programming [18, 17]. However, there are novel issues related to implementing high-level policy rules with low-level mechanisms such as firewalls, web server and DBMS security mechanisms, and operating system features, that are often faster and more difficult to bypass than rule interpreters [14]. A convincing realization of this approach might boost the application of the rich and flexible languages developed by the security community.

3 Strong and Lightweight Evidence

Currently two major approaches for managing trust exist: policy-based and reputation-based trust management. The two approaches have been developed within the context of different environments and target different requirements. On the one hand, policy-based trust relies on "strong security" mechanisms such as signed certificates and trusted certification authorities (CAs) in order to regulate access of users to services. Moreover, access decisions are usually based on mechanisms with well defined semantics (e.g., logic programming) providing strong verification and analysis support. The result of such a policy-based trust management approach usually consists of a binary decision according to which the requester is trusted or not, and thus the service (or resource) is allowed or denied. On the other hand, reputation-based trust relies on a "soft computational" approach to the problem of trust. In this case, trust is typically computed from local experiences together with the feedback given by other entities in the network. For instance, eBay buyers and sellers rate each other after each transaction. The ratings pertaining to a certain seller (or buyer) are aggregated by eBay's reputation system into a number reflecting seller (or buyer) trustworthiness as judged by the eBay community. The reputation-based approach has been favored for environments such as Peer-to-Peer or Semantic Web, where the existence of certifying authorities can not always be assumed but where a large pool of individual user ratings is often available.

Another approach – very common in today's applications – is based on forcing users to commit to contracts or copyrights by having users click an "accept" button on a pop-up window. This is perhaps the lightest approach to trust, that can be generalized by having users utter *declarations* (on their e-mail address, on their preferences, etc.) e.g. by filling an HTML form.

Real life scenarios often require to make decisions based on a combination of these approaches. Transaction policies must handle expenses of all magnitudes, from micropayments (e.g. a few cents for a song downloaded to your iPod) to credit card payments of a thousand euros (e.g. for a plane ticket) or even more. The cost of the traded goods or services contributes to determine the risk associated to the transaction and hence the trust measure required.

Strong evidence is generally harder to gather and verify than lightweight evidence. Sometimes, a "soft" reputation measure or a declaration in the sense outlined above is all one can obtain in a given scenario. We believe that the success of a trust management framework will be determined by the ability of *balancing trust levels and risk levels* for each particular task supported by the application, adding the following to the list of interesting research directions:

- How should different forms of trust be integrated? Some hints on modelling context aware trust, recommendation and risk with rules is given in [16] and a first proposal for a full integration in a policy framework can be found in [6]. However, new reputation models are being introduced, and there is a large number of open research issues in the reputation area (e.g., vulnerability to coalitions). Today, it is not clear which of the current approaches will be successful and how the open problems will be solved. Any proposal should therefore aim at maximal modularity in the integration of numerical and logical trust.
- How many different forms of evidence can be conceived? In principle, properties of (and statements about) an individual can be extracted from any – possibly unstructured – web resource. Supporting such a variety of information in policy decisions is a typical semantic web issue – and an intriguing one. However, such general policies are not even vaguely as close to become real as the policies based on more "traditional" forms of evidence (see the discussion in the next section).

4   Trust Management

During the past few years, some of the most innovative ideas on security policies arose in the area of *automated trust negotiation* [2, 7, 5, 9, 22, 23, 24, 25, 1]. That branch of research considers peers that are able to automatically negotiate credentials according to their own declarative, rule-based policies. Rules specify for each resource or credential request which properties should be satisfied by the subjects and objects involved. At each negotiation step, the next credential request is formulated essentially by *reasoning* with the policy, e.g. by inferring implications or computing abductions.

Since about five years frameworks exist where credential requests are formulated by exchanging *sets of rules* [7, 5]. Requests are formulated *intensionally* in order to express compactly and simultaneously all the possible ways in which a resource can be accessed — shortening negotiations and improving privacy protection because peers can choose the best option from the point of view of sensitivity. It is not appealing to request *"an ID and a credit card"* by enumerating all possible pairs of ID credentials and credit card credentials; it is much better to *define* what IDs and credit cards are and send the definition itself. Another peer may use it to check whether some subset of its own credentials fulfills the request. This boils down to gathering the relevant concept definitions in the policy (so-called *abbreviation rules*) and sending them to the other peer that reasons with those rules locally.

In [7, 5] *peers communicate by sharing their ontologies*. Interestingly, typical policies require peers to have a common a priori understanding only of the predicate representing credentials and arithmetic predicates, as any other predicate can be understood by sharing its definition. The only nontrivial knowledge to be shared is the X.509 standard credential format. In this framework, interoperability based on ontology sharing is already at reach! This is one of the aspects that make policies and automated trust negotiation a most attractive application for semantic web ideas.

Another interesting proposal of [5] is the notion of *declaration*, that has already been discussed in Section 3. This was the first step towards a more flexible and lightweight approach to policy enforcement, aiming at a better tradeoff between protection efforts and risks. According to [15], this framework was one of the most complete trust negotiation systems. The major limitation was the lack of distributed negotiations and credential discovery, which are now supported as specified in [7].

Negotiations. In response to a resource request, a web server may ask for credentials proving that the client can access the resource. However, the credentials themselves can be sensitive resources. So the two peers are in a completely symmetrical situation: the client, in turn, asks the server for credentials (e.g. proving that it participates in the Better Business Bureau program) before sending off the required credentials. Each peer decides how to react to incoming requests according to a local policy, which is typically a set of rules written in some logic programming dialect. As we pointed out, requests are formulated by selecting some rules from the policies. This basic schema has been refined along the years taking several factors into account [2, 7, 5, 9, 22, 23, 24, 25, 1].

First, policy rules may possibly inspect a *local state* (such as a legacy database) that typically is not accessible by other peers. In that case, in order to make rules intelligible to the recepient, they are partially evaluated with respect to the current state.

Second, *policies themselves are sensitive resources*, therefore not all relevant rules are shown immediately to the peer. They are first filtered according to policy release rules; the same schema may be applied to policy release rules themselves for an arbitrary but finite number of levels. As a consequence, some negotiations that might succeed, in fact fail just because the peers do not tell each other what they want. The study of methodologies and properties that guarantee negotiation success is an interesting open research issue.

Moreover, *credentials are not necessarily on the peer's host*. It may be necessary to locate them on the network [11]. As part of the automated support to *cooperative enforcement*, peers may give each other hints on where a credential can be found [26].

There are further complications related to actions (cf. Section 4). In order to tune the negotiation strategy to handle these aspects optimally, we can rely on a *metapolicy language* [7] that specifies which predicates are sensitive, which are associated to actions, which peer is responsible for each action, and where credentials can be searched for, guiding negotiation in a declarative fashion and making it more cooperative and interoperable. Moreover, the metapolicy language can be used to instantiate the framework in different application domains and link predicates to the ontologies where they are defined.

Provisional Policies. Policies may state that certain requests or decisions have to be logged, or that the system itself should search for certain credentials. In other words, policy languages should be able to specify *actions*. Event-condition-action (ECA) rules constitute one possible approach. Another approach consists in labelling some predicates as *provisional*, and associating them to actions that (if successful) make the predicate true [7]. We may also specify that an action should be executed by some other peer; this results in a request.

A cooperative peer tries to execute actions under its responsibility whenever this helps in making negotiations succeed. For example, provisional predicates may be used to encode business rules. The next rule[1] enables discounts on low-selling articles in a specific session:

$$\text{allow}(Srv) \leftarrow \ldots, \text{session}(ID),$$
$$\text{in}(X, \text{sql:query}('\text{select} * \text{from low\_selling}')),$$
$$\text{enabled}(\text{discount}(X), ID).$$

Intuitively, if $\text{enabled}(\text{discount}(X), ID)$ is not yet true but the other conditions are verified, then the negotiator may execute the action associated to **enabled** and the rule becomes applicable (if $\text{enabled}(\text{discount}(X), ID)$ is already true, no action is executed). The (application dependent) action can be defined and associated to **enabled** through the metapolicy language. With the metalanguage one can also specify when an action is to be executed.

Some actions would be more naturally expressed as ECA rules. However, it is not obvious how the natural bottom-up evaluation schema of ECA rules should be integrated with the top-down evaluation adopted by the current core policy language. The latter fits more naturally the abductive nature of negotiation steps. So integration of ECA rules is still an interesting open research issue.

Stateful vs. Stateless Negotiations. Negotiations as described above are in general stateful, because (i) they may refer to a local state – including legacy software and data – and (ii) the sequence of requests and counter requests may become more efficient if credentials and declarations are not submitted again and again, but kept in a local negotiation state. However, negotiations are not *necessarily* stateful because

– the server may refuse to answer counter-requests, or – alternatively – the credentials and declarations disclosed during the transaction may be included in every message and need not be cached locally;
– the policy does not necessarily refer to external packages.

Stateless protocols are just special cases of the frameworks introduced so far. Whether a stateless protocol is really more efficient depends on the application. Moreover, efficiency at all costs might imply less cooperative systems.

---

[1] Formulated in PROTUNE's language.

Are stateful protocols related to scalability issues? We do not think so. The web started as a stateless protocol, but soon a number of techniques were implemented to simulate stateful protocols and transactions in quite a few real world applications and systems, capable of answering a huge number of requests per time unit. We observe that if the support for stateful negotiations had been cast into http, probably many of the intrinsic vulnerabilities of simulated solutions (like cookies) might have been avoided.

New Issues. Existing approaches to trust management and trust negotiation already tackle the need for flexible, knowledge-based interoperability, and take into account the main idiosyncrasies of the web – because automated trust negotiation frameworks have been designed with exactly that scenario in mind. Today, to make a real contribution (even in the context of a policy-aware web), we should further perform research on the open issues of trust management, including at least the following topics:

- Negotiation success: how can we guarantee that negotiations succeed despite all the difficulties that may interfere: rules not disclosed because of lack of trust; credentials not found because their repository is unknown. What kind of properties of the policy protection policy and of the *hints* (see Section 4) guarantee a successful termination when the policy "theoretically" permits access to a resource?
- Optimal negotiations: which strategies optimize information disclosure during negotiation? Can reasonable preconditions prevent unnecessary information disclosure?
- In the presence of multiple ways of fulfilling a request, how should the client choose a response? We need both a language for expressing preferences, and efficient algorithms for solving the corresponding optimization problem. While this negotiation step is more or less explicitly assumed by most approaches on trust negotiation, there is no concrete proposal so far.

Additionally, integration of abductive semantics and ECA semantics is an open issue, as we have pointed out in a previous section.

5   Cooperative Policy Enforcement

Cooperative enforcement involves both machine-to-machine and human-machine aspects. The former is handled by negotiation mechanisms: published policies, provisional actions, hints, and other metalevel information (see Section 4) can be interpreted by the client to identify what information is needed to access a resource, and how to obtain that information.

Let us discuss the human-machine interaction aspect in more detail: One of the most important causes of the enormous number of computer security violations on the Internet is the users' lack of technical expertise. Users are typically not aware of the security policies applied by their system, neither of course about how those policies can be changed and how they might be improved by tailoring them to specific needs. As a consequence, most users ignore their computer's vulnerabilities and the corresponding countermeasures, so the system's protection facilities cannot be effectively exploited.

It is well known that the default, generic policies that come with system installations – often biased toward functionality rather than protection – are significantly less secure than a policy specialized to a specific context, but very few users know how to tune or replace the default policy. Moreover, users frequently do not understand what the policy really checks, and hence are unaware of the risks involved in many common operations.

Similar problems affect privacy protection. In trust negotiation, credential release policies are meant to achieve a satisfactory tradeoff between privacy and functionality – many interesting services cannot be obtained without releasing some information about the user. However, we cannot expect such techniques to be effective unless users are able to understand and possibly personalize the privacy policy enforced by their system.

A better understanding of a web service's policy makes it also easier for a first-time user to interact with the service. If denied access results simply in a *"no"* answer, the user has no clue on how he or she can possibly acquire the permission to get the desired service (e.g., by completing a registration procedure, by supplying more credentials or by filling in some form). This is why we advocate *cooperative policy enforcement*, where negative responses are enriched with suggestions and other explanations whenever such information does not violate confidentiality (sometimes, part of the policy itself is sensitive).

For these reasons, *greater user awareness and control on policies* is one of our main objectives, making policies easier to understand and formulate to the common user in the following ways:

- Adopt a *rule-based policy specification language*, because these languages are flexible and at the same time structurally similar to the way in which policies are expressed by nontechnical users.
- Make the policy specification language more friendly by e.g. developing a *controlled natural language* front-end to translate natural language text into executable rules (see next section).
- Develop *advanced explanation mechanisms* [4, 12, 13] to help the user understand what policies prescribe and control.

Inference Web (IW) [12, 13] is a toolkit that aims at providing useful explanations for the behavior of (Semantic-) Web based systems. In particular, [12] propose support for knowledge provenance information using metadata (e.g., Dublin Core information) about the distributed information systems involved in a particular reasoning task. [12] also deals with the issue of representing heterogeneous reasoning approaches, domain description languages and proof representations; the latter issue is addressed by using PML, the OWL-based Proof Markup Language [8].

Specifically applied to policies, [4] contains a requirements analysis for explanations in the context of automated trust negotiation and defines explanation mechanisms for *why, why-not, how-to,* and *what-if* queries. Several novel aspects are described:

- Adoption of a *tabled explanation structure* as opposed to more traditional approaches based on single derivations or proof trees. The tabled approach makes it possible to describe infinite failures, which is essential for *why not* queries.
- Explanations show simultaneously different possible proof attempts and allow users to see both local and global proof details at the same time. This combination of local and global (intra-proof and inter-proof) information facilitates navigation across the explanation structures.
- Introduction of suitable heuristics for focussing explanations by removing irrelevant parts of the proof attempts. A second level of explanations can recover missing details, if desired.
- Heuristics are *generic*, i.e. domain independent, they require no manual configuration.
- The combination of tabling techniques and heuristics yields a novel method for explaining failure.

Explanation mechanisms should be *lightweight* and *scalable* in the sense that (i) they do not require any major effort when the general framework is instantiated in a specific application domain, and (ii) most of the computational effort can be delegated to the clients. Queries are answered using the same policy specifications used for negotiation. Query answering is conceived for the following categories of users:

- Users who try to understand how to obtain access permissions;
- Users who monitor and verify their own privacy policy;
- Policy managers who verify and monitor their policies.

Currently, advanced queries comprise *why/why not, how-to,* and *what-if* queries. Why/why not queries can be used by security managers to understand why some specific request has been accepted or rejected, which may be useful for debugging purposes. Why-not queries may help a user to understand what needs to be done in order to obtain the required permissions, a process that in general may include a combination of automated and manual actions. Such features are absolutely essential to enforce security requirements without discouraging users that try to connect to a web service for the first time. How-to queries have a similar role, and differ from why-not queries mainly because the former do not assume a previous query as a context, while the latter do.

What-if queries are hypothetical queries that allow to predict the behavior of a policy before credentials are actually searched for and before a request is actually submitted. What-if queries are good both for validation purposes and for helping users in obtaining permissions.

Among the technical challenges related to explanations, we mention:

- Find the right tradeoff between explanation quality and the effort for instantiating the framework in new application domains. Second generation explanation systems [19, 20, 21] prescribe a sequence of expensive steps, including

722 P.A. Bonatti et al.

the creation of an independent domain knowledge base expressly for communicating with the user. This would be a serious obstacle to the applicability of the framework.

Natural Language Policies. Policies should be written by and understandable to users, to let them control behavior of their system. Otherwise the risk that users keep on adopting generic hence ineffective built-in policies, and remain unaware of which controls are actually made by the system is extremely high – and this significantly reduces the benefits of a flexible policy framework.

Most users have no specific training in programming nor in formal logics. Fortunately, they spontaneously tend to formulate policies as rules; still, logical languages may be intimidating. For this reason, the design of front ends based on graphical formalisms as well as *natural language interfaces* are crucial to the adoption of formal policy languages. We want policy rules to be formulated like: *"Academic users can download the files in folder historical_data whenever their creation date precedes 1942"*.

Clearly, the inherent ambiguity of natural language is incompatible with the precision needed by security and privacy specifications. Solutions to that can be the adoption of a *controlled* fragment of English (e.g., the ATTEMPTO system[2]) where a few simple rules determine a unique meaning for each sentence. This approach can be complemented with a suitable interface that clarifies what the machine understands.

6   Conclusions and Perspectives

Policies are really knowledge bases: a single body of declarative rules used in many possible ways, for negotiations, query answering, and other forms of system behavior control. As far as trust negotiation is concerned, we further argue that transparent interoperation based on ontology sharing can become "everyday technology" in a short time, and trust negotiation especially will become a success story for semantic web ideas and techniques.

In addition to stateless negotiation (see [10]), we need stateful negotiation as well [5]. Even the Web, which started as a stateless protocol, now implements a number of techniques to simulate stateful protocols and transactions, especially in applications for accessing data other than web pages.

Cooperative policy enforcement and trust management gives common users better understanding and control on the policies that govern their systems and the services they interact with. The closer we get to this objective, the higher the impact of our techniques and ideas will be.

Policies will have to handle decisions under a wide range of risk levels, performance requirements, and traffic patterns. It is good to know that the rule-based techniques that different research communities are currently converging to are powerful enough to effectively address such a wide spectrum of scenarios. This is the level of flexibility needed by the Semantic Web.

---

[2] http://www.ifi.unizh.ch/attempto/

Acknowledgment

This research has been partially funded by the European Commission and by the Swiss State Secretariat for Education and Research within the 6th Framework Programme project REWERSE number 506779 (cf. http://rewerse.net).

References

1. M. Y. Becker and P. Sewell. Cassandra: distributed access control policies with tunable expressiveness. In *5th IEEE International Workshop on Policies for Distributed Systems and Networks*, Yorktown Heights, June 2004.
2. M. Blaze, J. Feigenbaum, and M. Strauss. Compliance Checking in the Policy-Maker Trust Management System. In *Financial Cryptography*, British West Indies, February 1998.
3. P. A. Bonatti, N. Shahmehri, C. Duma, D. Olmedilla, W. Nejdl, M. Baldoni, C. Baroglio, A. Martelli, V. Patti, P. Coraggio, G. Antoniou, J. Peer, and N. E. Fuchs. Rule-based policy specification: State of the art and future work. Technical report, Working Group I2, EU NoE REWERSE, aug 2004. http://rewerse.net/deliverables/i2-d1.pdf.
4. P.A. Bonatti, D. Olmedilla, and J. Peer. Advanced policy queries. Technical Report I2-D4, Working Group I2, EU NoE REWERSE, Aug 2005. http://www.rewerse.net.
5. P.A. Bonatti and P. Samarati. A uniform framework for regulating service access and information release on the web. *Journal of Computer Security*, 10(3):241–272, 2002. Short version in the Proc. of the Conference on Computer and Communications Security (CCS'00), Athens, 2000.
6. Piero A. Bonatti, Claudiu Duma, Daniel Olmedilla, and Nahid Shahmehri. An integration of reputation-based and policy-based trust management. In *Semantic Web Policy Workshop in conjunction with 4th International Semantic Web Conference*, Galway, Ireland, nov 2005.
7. Piero A. Bonatti and Daniel Olmedilla. Driving and monitoring provisional trust negotiation with metapolicies. In *6th IEEE International Workshop on Policies for Distributed Systems and Networks (POLICY 2005)*, pages 14–23, Stockholm, Sweden, jun 2005. IEEE Computer Society.
8. Paulo P. da Silva, Deborah L. McGuinness, and Richard Fikes. A proof markup language for semantic web services. Technical Report KSL Tech Report KSL-04-01, January, 2004.
9. Rita Gavriloaie, Wolfgang Nejdl, Daniel Olmedilla, Kent E. Seamons, and Marianne Winslett. No registration needed: How to use declarative policies and negotiation to access sensitive resources on the semantic web. In *1st European Semantic Web Symposium (ESWS 2004)*, volume 3053 of *Lecture Notes in Computer Science*, pages 342–356, Heraklion, Crete, Greece, may 2004. Springer.
10. Vladimir Kolovski, Yarden Katz, James Hendler, Daniel Weitzner, and Tim Berners-Lee. Towards a policy-aware web. In *Semantic Web Policy Workshop in conjunction with 4th International Semantic Web Conference*, Galway, Ireland, nov 2005.
11. N. Li, W. Winsborough, and J.C. Mitchell. Distributed Credential Chain Discovery in Trust Management (Extended Abstract). In *ACM Conference on Computer and Communications Security*, Philadelphia, Pennsylvania, November 2001.

12. Deborah L. McGuinness and Paulo Pinheiro da Silva. Explaining answers from the semantic web: The inference web approach. *Journal of Web Semantics*, 1(4):397–413, 2004.

13. Deborah L. McGuinness and Paulo Pinheiro da Silva. Trusting answers from web applications. In *New Directions in Question Answering*, pages 275–286, 2004.

14. Arnon Rosenthal and Marianne Winslett. Security of shared data in large systems: State of the art and research directions. In *Proceedings of the ACM SIGMOD International Conference on Management of Data, Paris, France, June 13-18, 2004*, pages 962–964. ACM, 2004.

15. K. Seamons, M. Winslett, T. Yu, B. Smith, E. Child, J. Jacobsen, H. Mills, and L. Yu. Requirements for Policy Languages for Trust Negotiation. In *3rd International Workshop on Policies for Distributed Systems and Networks*, Monterey, CA, June 2002.

16. Steffen Staab, Bharat K. Bhargava, Leszek Lilien, Arnon Rosenthal, Marianne Winslett, Morris Sloman, Tharam S. Dillon, Elizabeth Chang, Farookh Khadeer Hussain, Wolfgang Nejdl, Daniel Olmedilla, and Vipul Kashyap. The pudding of trust. *IEEE Intelligent Systems*, 19(5):74–88, 2004.

17. V. S. Subrahmanian, Piero A. Bonatti, Jürgen Dix, Thomas Eiter, Sarit Kraus, Fatma Ozcan, and Robert Ross. *Heterogenous Active Agents*. MIT Press, 2000.

18. V.S. Subrahmanian, S. Adali, A. Brink, R. Emery, J.J. Lu, A. Rajput, T.J. Rogers, R. Ross, and C. Ward. Hermes: Heterogeneous reasoning and mediator system. http://www.cs.umd.edu/projects/publications/ abstracts/hermes. html.

19. William Swartout, Cecile Paris, and Johanna Moore. Explanations in knowledge systems: Design for explainable expert systems. *IEEE Expert: Intelligent Systems and Their Applications*, 6(3):58–64, 1991.

20. Michael C. Tanner and Anne M. Keuneke. Explanations in knowledge systems: The roles of the task structure and domain functional models. *IEEE Expert: Intelligent Systems and Their Applications*, 6(3):50–57, 1991.

21. M. R. Wick. Second generation expert system explanation. In J.-M. David, J.-P. Krivine, and R. Simmons, editors, *Second Generation Expert Systems*, pages 614–640. Springer Verlag, 1993.

22. W. Winsborough, K. Seamons, and V. Jones. Negotiating Disclosure of Sensitive Credentials. In *Second Conference on Security in Communication Networks*, Amalfi, Italy, September 1999.

23. W. Winsborough, K. Seamons, and V. Jones. Automated Trust Negotiation. In *DARPA Information Survivability Conference and Exposition*, Hilton Head Island, SC, January 2000.

24. Marianne Winslett, Ting Yu, Kent E. Seamons, Adam Hess, Jared Jacobson, Ryan Jarvis, Bryan Smith, and Lina Yu. Negotiating trust on the web. *IEEE Internet Computing*, 6(6):30–37, 2002.

25. Ting Yu, Marianne Winslett, and Kent E. Seamons. Supporting structured credentials and sensitive policies through interoperable strategies for automated trust negotiation. *ACM Trans. Inf. Syst. Secur.*, 6(1):1–42, 2003.

26. C. Zhang, P.A. Bonatti, and M. Winslett. Peeraccess: A logic for distributed authorization. In *12th ACM Conference on Computer and Communication Security (CCS 2005)*, Alexandria, VA, USA. ACM.

Author Index

Lecture Notes in Computer Science

For information about Vols. 1–3956

please contact your bookseller or Springer

Vol. 3998: T. Calamoneri, I. Finocchi, G.F. Italiano (Eds.), Algorithms and Complexity. XII, 394 pages. 2006.

Vol. 3997: W. Grieskamp, C. Weise (Eds.), Formal Approaches to Software Testing. XII, 219 pages. 2006.

Vol. 3996: A. Keller, J.-P. Martin-Flatin (Eds.), Self-Managed Networks, Systems, and Services. X, 185 pages. 2006.

Vol. 3995: G. Müller (Ed.), Emerging Trends in Information and Communication Security. XX, 524 pages. 2006.

Vol. 3994: V.N. Alexandrov, G.D. van Albada, P.M.A. Sloot, J. Dongarra (Eds.), Computational Science – ICCS 2006, Part IV. XXXV, 1096 pages. 2006.

Vol. 3993: V.N. Alexandrov, G.D. van Albada, P.M.A. Sloot, J. Dongarra (Eds.), Computational Science – ICCS 2006, Part III. XXXVI, 1136 pages. 2006.

Vol. 3992: V.N. Alexandrov, G.D. van Albada, P.M.A. Sloot, J. Dongarra (Eds.), Computational Science – ICCS 2006, Part II. XXXV, 1122 pages. 2006.

Vol. 3991: V.N. Alexandrov, G.D. van Albada, P.M.A. Sloot, J. Dongarra (Eds.), Computational Science – ICCS 2006, Part I. LXXXI, 1096 pages. 2006.

Vol. 3990: J. C. Beck, B.M. Smith (Eds.), Integration of AI and OR Techniques in Constraint Programming for Combinatorial Optimization Problems. X, 301 pages. 2006.

Vol. 3989: J. Zhou, M. Yung, F. Bao, Applied Cryptography and Network Security. XIV, 488 pages. 2006.

Vol. 3987: M. Hazas, J. Krumm, T. Strang (Eds.), Location- and Context-Awareness. X, 289 pages. 2006.

Vol. 3986: K. Stølen, W.H. Winsborough, F. Martinelli, F. Massacci (Eds.), Trust Management. XIV, 474 pages. 2006.

Vol. 3984: M. Gavrilova, O. Gervasi, V. Kumar, C.J. K. Tan, D. Taniar, A. Laganà, Y. Mun, H. Choo (Eds.), Computational Science and Its Applications - ICCSA 2006, Part V. XXV, 1045 pages. 2006.

Vol. 3983: M. Gavrilova, O. Gervasi, V. Kumar, C.J. K. Tan, D. Taniar, A. Laganà, Y. Mun, H. Choo (Eds.), Computational Science and Its Applications - ICCSA 2006, Part IV. XXVI, 1191 pages. 2006.

Vol. 3982: M. Gavrilova, O. Gervasi, V. Kumar, C.J. K. Tan, D. Taniar, A. Laganà, Y. Mun, H. Choo (Eds.), Computational Science and Its Applications - ICCSA 2006, Part III. XXV, 1243 pages. 2006.

Vol. 3981: M. Gavrilova, O. Gervasi, V. Kumar, C.J. K. Tan, D. Taniar, A. Laganà, Y. Mun, H. Choo (Eds.), Computational Science and Its Applications - ICCSA 2006, Part II. XXVI, 1255 pages. 2006.

Vol. 3980: M. Gavrilova, O. Gervasi, V. Kumar, C.J. K. Tan, D. Taniar, A. Laganà, Y. Mun, H. Choo (Eds.), Computational Science and Its Applications - ICCSA 2006, Part I. LXXV, 1199 pages. 2006.

Vol. 3979: T.S. Huang, N. Sebe, M.S. Lew, V. Pavlović, M. Kölsch, A. Galata, B. Kisačanin (Eds.), Computer Vision in Human-Computer Interaction. XII, 121 pages. 2006.

Vol. 3978: B. Hnich, M. Carlsson, F. Fages, F. Rossi (Eds.), Recent Advances in Constraints. VIII, 179 pages. 2006. (Sublibrary LNAI).

Vol. 3977: N. Fuhr, M. Lalmas, S. Malik, G. Kazai (Eds.), Advances in XML Information Retrieval and Evaluation. XII, 556 pages. 2006.

Vol. 3976: F. Boavida, T. Plagemann, B. Stiller, C. Westphal, E. Monteiro (Eds.), Networking 2006. Networking Technologies, Services, and Protocols; Performance of Computer and Communication Networks; Mobile and Wireless Communications Systems. XXVI, 1276 pages. 2006.

Vol. 3975: S. Mehrotra, D.D. Zeng, H. Chen, B.M. Thuraisingham, F.-Y. Wang (Eds.), Intelligence and Security Informatics. XXII, 772 pages. 2006.

Vol. 3973: J. Wang, Z. Yi, J.M. Zurada, B.-L. Lu, H. Yin (Eds.), Advances in Neural Networks - ISNN 2006, Part III. XXIX, 1402 pages. 2006.

Vol. 3972: J. Wang, Z. Yi, J.M. Zurada, B.-L. Lu, H. Yin (Eds.), Advances in Neural Networks - ISNN 2006, Part II. XXVII, 1444 pages. 2006.

Vol. 3971: J. Wang, Z. Yi, J.M. Zurada, B.-L. Lu, H. Yin (Eds.), Advances in Neural Networks - ISNN 2006, Part I. LXVII, 1442 pages. 2006.

Vol. 3970: T. Braun, G. Carle, S. Fahmy, Y. Koucheryavy (Eds.), Wired/Wireless Internet Communications. XIV, 350 pages. 2006.

Vol. 3969: Ø. Ytrehus (Ed.), Coding and Cryptography. XI, 443 pages. 2006.

Vol. 3968: K.P. Fishkin, B. Schiele, P. Nixon, A. Quigley (Eds.), Pervasive Computing. XV, 402 pages. 2006.

Vol. 3967: D. Grigoriev, J. Harrison, E.A. Hirsch (Eds.), Computer Science – Theory and Applications. XVI, 684 pages. 2006.

Vol. 3966: Q. Wang, D. Pfahl, D.M. Raffo, P. Wernick (Eds.), Software Process Change. XIV, 356 pages. 2006.

Vol. 3965: M. Bernardo, A. Cimatti (Eds.), Formal Methods for Hardware Verification. VII, 243 pages. 2006.

Vol. 3964: M. Ü. Uyar, A.Y. Duale, M.A. Fecko (Eds.), Testing of Communicating Systems. XI, 373 pages. 2006.

Vol. 3963: O. Dikenelli, M.-P. Gleizes, A. Ricci (Eds.), Engineering Societies in the Agents World VI. XII, 303 pages. 2006. (Sublibrary LNAI).

Vol. 3962: W. IJsselsteijn, Y. de Kort, C. Midden, B. Eggen, E. van den Hoven (Eds.), Persuasive Technology. XII, 216 pages. 2006.

Vol. 3960: R. Vieira, P. Quaresma, M.d.G.V. Nunes, N.J. Mamede, C. Oliveira, M.C. Dias (Eds.), Computational Processing of the Portuguese Language. XII, 274 pages. 2006. (Sublibrary LNAI).

Vol. 3959: J.-Y. Cai, S. B. Cooper, A. Li (Eds.), Theory and Applications of Models of Computation. XV, 794 pages. 2006.

Vol. 3958: M. Yung, Y. Dodis, A. Kiayias, T. Malkin (Eds.), Public Key Cryptography - PKC 2006. XIV, 543 pages. 2006.